HANDBOOK OF FAMILY COMMUNICATION

LEA'S COMMUNICATION SERIES

Jennings Bryant/Dolf Zillmann, General Editors

Selected Titles in Applied Communication
(Teresa L. Thompson, Advisory Editor) include:

Braithwaite/Thompson • Handbook of Communication and People With Disabilities: Research and Application

Greene/Derlega/Yep/Petranio • Privacy and Disclosure of HIV in Interpersonal Relationships: A Sourcebook for Researchers and Practitioners

Hummert/Nussbaum • Aging, Communication, and Health: Linking Research and Practice for Successful Aging

Nussbaum/Pecchioni/Robinson/Thompson • Communication and Aging, Second Edition

Socha/Diggs • Communication, Race, and Family: Exploring Communication in Black, White, and Biracial Families

Thompson/Dorsey/Miller/Parrott • Handbook of Health Communication

Williams/Nussbaum • Intergenerational Communication Across The Life Span

For a complete list of titles in LEA's Communication Series, please contact
Lawrence Erlbaum Associates, Publishers, at www.erlbaum.com.

HANDBOOK OF FAMILY COMMUNICATION

EDITED BY

ANITA L. VANGELISTI
UNIVERSITY OF TEXAS AT AUSTIN

2004

LAWRENCE ERLBAUM ASSOCIATES, PUBLISHERS
MAHWAH, NEW JERSEY   LONDON

Senior Acquisitions Editor:	Linda Bathgate
Editorial Assistant:	Karen Wittig Bates
Cover Design:	Kathryn Houghtaling Lacey
Textbook Production Manager:	Paul Smolenski
Full-Service Compositor:	TechBooks
Text and Cover Printer:	Hamilton Printing Company

This book was typeset in 10.5/12 pt. Times, Italic, Bold, Bold Italic.
The heads were typeset in Engravers Gothic, Zapf Humanist and Revival.

Lawrence Erlbaum Associates, Inc., Publishers
10 Industrial Avenue
Mahwah, New Jersey 07430
www.erlbaum.com

Library of Congress Cataloging-in-Publication Data

Handbook of family communication / edited by Anita L. Vangelisti.
    p.   cm.—(LEA's communication series)
   Includes bibliographical references and index.
   ISBN 0-8058-4130-X (casebound)—ISBN 0-8058-4131-8 (pbk.)
   1. Communication in the family.   2. Interpersonal communication.   I. Vangelisti, Anita L.   II. Series.
   HQ519 .H36   2003
   306.87—dc22

                                                                          2003015733

Books published by Lawrence Erlbaum Associates are printed on
acid-free paper, and their bindings are chosen for strength and
durability.

Printed in the United States of America
10 9 8 7 6 5 4 3 2 1

CONTENTS

PREFACE

The family is the crucible of society. In large part, this vital social entity is defined by the way its members interact. Over the past 30 years, enormous strides have been made in our understanding of how communication affects, and is affected by, family members and their relationships. Researchers have described patterns of communication that lead to dissatisfaction in marriage (Gottman & Krokoff, 1989; Heavey, Christensen, & Malamuth, 1995); they have identified links between communication behaviors in families and certain demographic variables (Conger, Ge, Elder, Lorenz, & Simmons, 1994; Conger, Rueter, & Elder, 1999); they have begun to unravel the meanings that family members associate with particular behaviors or experiences (Baxter, Braithwaite, & Nicholson, 1999; Leeds-Hurwitz, 2002); and they have demonstrated how the communication patterns of one generation influence the behaviors of the next (Cummings, Goeke-Morey, Papp, & Dukewich, 2002; Goodman, Barfoot, Frye, & Belli, 1999).

The *Handbook of Family Communication* presents an analysis and synthesis of cutting-edge research and theory on family interaction. This volume is the first to integrate the varying perspectives and issues addressed by researchers, theorists, and practitioners who study how family members communicate and relate to each other. As a consequence, it offers a unique and timely view of family interaction and family relationships.

Although a wide range of perspectives and issues are presented in the volume, three assumptions about families and family relationships tie the chapters together. The first is that families are systems (Minuchin, 1984). Family members and family relationships are interdependent (Kelley, 1983). They simultaneously influence, and are influenced by, each other. Change in one component of the system affects all other components. Because the various parts of family systems are interconnected, families are best conceived as "wholes" and should be studied with regard to the interrelationship of their parts (Reis, Collins, & Berscheid, 2000). Given this, it is important to examine individual members (e.g., infants, children, adolescents) in terms of the ways they relate to other members, to investigate the links between dyadic relationships (e.g., spouses, parents, siblings) and others in the family, and to examine the influences of sociocultural and historical variables (e.g., family work, media, technology) on family interaction.

The second assumption is that families are coherent (Sroufe & Fleeson, 1986). Family processes are patterned and structured. This is not to say that families are static or that they do not change. Rather, the supposition here is that the constant changes that occur in the context of families are, to some degree, organized and predictable. Family relationships and processes fluctuate in response to day-to-day pressures (e.g., economic stress), relational events (e.g., marriage), and the passage of time (e.g., aging), but the fluctuations experienced and enacted by family members are patterned. It is this patterning that allows researchers to study developmental trends in families, interactions that characterize different types of families, and responses that family members have to various social issues.

The third assumption that ties the chapters in this volume together is that families are constituted through social interaction (Fitzpatrick, 1988; Noller & Fitzpatrick, 1993). Communication is what creates families. When family members communicate, they do more than send messages to each other—they enact their relationships. It is through communication that family members establish roles (e.g., parent or child), maintain rules (e.g., about privacy or conflict), perform functions (e.g., provide emotional or physical support), and sustain behavioral patterns (e.g., concerning media use or health). Understanding family communication processes, thus, is fundamental to understanding family members and family relationships.

The purpose of the *Handbook of Family Communication* is to analyze, synthesize, and advance existing literature. In order to capture the breadth and depth of research on family communication and family relationships, the work of scholars from a variety of disciplines—including communication, social psychology, clinical psychology, sociology, and family studies—is highlighted. The authors are internationally known scholars. They approach family interaction from a number of different perspectives and focus on topics ranging from the influence of structural characteristics on family relationships to the importance of specific communication processes. The authors were selected as contributors for this volume because they are recognized for the contributions they have made to the study of issues associated with social interaction in family relationships.

Because the *Handbook* spotlights the work of top-notch scholars, many researchers and theorists who study family interaction and family relationships will want to have this volume in their library. The ideas presented in the pages of this book offer both researchers and theorists new perspectives on extant literature as well as important theoretical and methodological recommendations for future work. Graduate students in communication, social psychology, family studies, sociology, and clinical psychology also will want to read this volume. Advanced students who study family relationships will need to know the research findings and the theories that are articulated in this book and, in many cases, will want to apply the material to their own work. Upper-division undergraduate students comprise yet another audience. Many instructors who teach upper-division courses will see all or part of this volume as an important addition to their current assigned reading lists. Finally, practitioners who deal with families on a regular basis will be interested in the *Handbook*. Counselors and therapists will find that the theory and research presented in the volume are extremely relevant to the work they do with individuals and families.

I am indebted to many people for their invaluable contributions to this project. This book exists only because a group of excellent authors were willing to dedicate a great deal of time, effort, and thought to writing chapters. Their work made this volume possible. My Editor, Linda Bathgate, prompted this project and kept it moving forward. Her keen awareness of the literature and her enthusiasm and unwavering support for the *Handbook* made my work a pleasure. I also would like to thank the families, couples, and individuals who participated in the studies that are reported in this volume. Their willingness to devote their time to research gave all of us the opportunity to uncover information about family communication and family relationships that we never would have otherwise. Finally, I am grateful to, and for, my own family—John, Johnny, Erin, and little Ms. Abigail. I have learned my best and most important lessons about family communication from them.

REFERENCES

Baxter, L. A., Braithwaite, D. O., & Nicholson, J. H. (1999). Turning points in the development of blended families. *Journal of Social and Personal Relationships, 16*, 291–313.

Conger, R., Ge, X., Elder, G., Lorenz, F., & Simmons, R. (1994). Economic stress, coercive family process, and developmental problems of adolescents. *Child Development, 65*, 541–561.

Conger, R., Rueter, M., & Elder, G., Jr. (1999). Couple resilience to economic pressure. *Journal of Personality and Social Psychology, 76*, 54–71.

Cummings, E. M., Goeke-Morey, M. C., Papp, L. M., & Dukewich, T. L. (2002). Children's responses to mothers' and fathers' emotionality and tactics in marital conflict in the home. *Journal of Family Psychology, 16*, 478–492.

Fitzpatrick, M. A. (1988). *Between husbands and wives*. Newbury Park, CA: Sage.

Goodman, S. H., Barfoot, B., Frye, A. A., & Belli, A. M. (1999). Dimensions of marital conflict and children's social problem-solving skills. *Journal of Family Psychology, 13*, 33–45.

Gottman, J. M., & Krokoff, L. J. (1989). Marital interaction and satisfaction: A longitudinal view. *Journal of Consulting and Clinical Psychology, 57*, 47–52.

Heavey, C. L., Christensen, A., & Malamuth, N. M. (1995). The longitudinal impact of demand and withdrawal during marital conflict. *Journal of Consulting and Clinical Psychology, 63*, 797–801.

Kelley, H. H. (1983). Analyzing close relationships. In H. H. Kelley, E. Berscheid, A. Christensen, J. H. Harvey, T. L. Huston, G. Levinger, E. McClintock, L. A. Peplau, & D. R. Peterson (Eds.), *Close relationships* (pp. 20–678). New York: Freeman.

Leeds-Hurwitz, W. (2002). *Weddings as text: Communicating cultural identities trhough ritual*. Mahwah, NJ: Lawrence Erlbaum Associates.

Minuchin, S. (1984). *Family kaleidoscope*. Cambridge, MA: Harvard University Press.

Noller, P., & Fitzpatrick, M. A. (1993). *Communication and family relationships.* Englewood Cliffs, NJ: Prentice Hall.

Reis, H. T., Collins, W. A., & Berscheid, E. (2000). The relationship context of human behavior and development. *Psychological Bulletin, 126,* 844–872.

Sroufe, L. A., & Fleeson, J. (1986). Attachment and the construction of relationships. In W. W. Hartup & Z. Rubin (Eds.), *Relationships and development* (pp. 51–71). Hillsdale, NJ: Lawrence Erlbaum Associates.

INTRODUCTION

The word "family" is laden with imagery. For some, it brings to mind warm, supportive thoughts—scenes of chatty dinners, laughter-filled holidays, and comforting embraces. For others, it elicits painful memories—visions of being left alone, feeling unwanted, or being abused at the hands of a loved one. For some, the term "family" suggests a motto or a call to action—family members work hard, they stick together, or they prioritize the well-being of the group over the individual. For yet others, the word "family" embodies a set of values—values that distinguish individuals who are normal from those who are abnormal and people who are right from those who are wrong.

Although the images evoked by the term "family" vary widely, they tend to have one thing in common: They are based on, formed, and maintained through communication. Indeed, our families, and our images of families, are constituted through social interaction (Fitzpatrick, 1988; Noller & Fitzpatrick, 1993). When family members communicate, they enact their relationships. It is through communication that family members create mental models of family life and through communication that those models endure over time and across generations.

The constitutive link between communication and families is one reason that studying family communication is important. If families are created through social interaction, understanding family communication is essential to understanding family members and family relationships. This link, however, is not the only reason that scholars have focused their attention on family communication. The burgeoning literature on family interaction suggests at least three additional reasons that researchers and theorists have turned to this area as a focus of study.

First, family communication is the mechanism for most early socialization experiences. It is by observing and interacting with family members that most people learn to communicate and, perhaps more importantly, where they learn to think about communication (Bruner, 1990). From a very early age—some even argue before birth—infants engage in social interactions with their primary caregivers (Barrett, 1995). These early interactions are the basis for what later become automated communication behaviors (Cappella, 1991). They also serve as a model for future interactions (Bowlby, 1973). By communicating with close family members, infants and children quickly learn what they should (and should not) anticipate from others. They learn how relationships function and they learn how they should behave in the context of those relationships. Indeed, communication is the means by which rules about social interaction and social relationships are established and maintained (Shimanoff, 1985). Parents use communication to teach children when they should speak, to whom they should speak, and what they should say. These rules shape the way children, and later adults, coordinate meaning with others (Pearce, 1976).

Second, communication is the vehicle through which family members establish, maintain, and dissolve their intimate relationships. People form their families through social interaction. Communication enables dating partners to meet and to evaluate the status of their relationship (e.g., Berger, Gardner, Clatterbuck, & Shulman, 1976). Individuals who are dating move toward marriage based in part on their assessments of the way they interact (Surra, Arizzi, & Asmussen, 1988). Once families are formed, members continue to relate to each other through communication. Spouses employ communication strategies to maintain their marriage (Canary & Stafford, 1992). Children's relationships with their parents and stepparents are influenced by both the amount and the type of interaction that takes place in those relationships (Stafford & Bayer, 1993). The associations that adolescents have with family members mature in part because the communication patterns that characterize their relationships change (Noller, 1995). Family relationships also are terminated using communication. Divorce is associated with particular communication patterns (e.g., Gottman, 1994) and, except in rare cases, only takes place after spouses discuss ending their relationship (Riessman, 1990).

A third reason that scholars have turned their attention to studying family communication is that communication reflects the interpersonal connections among family members. As such, it offers researchers and theorists a way to predict the quality and the course of family relationships. For instance, researchers have long argued that communication is an indicator of the quality of marital relationships. Spouses who are distressed generally express more negative affect, less positive affect, and more reciprocity of negative affect than do those who are not distressed (Margolin & Wampold, 1981; Noller, 1984; Notarius & Johnson, 1982). Further, when initial levels of satisfaction are controlled, the expression of negative affect within marriage predicts declines in satisfaction over time (Gottman & Krokoff, 1989; Huston & Vangelisti, 1991; Levenson & Gottman, 1985). In addition to reflecting the quality of particular family relationships (e.g., marriage), the communication that occurs among members of one family subsystem (e.g., parents) can influence other family members (e.g., children). Studies have demonstrated that the quality of parents' communication can affect children's problem-solving skills (Goodman, Barfoot, Frye, & Belli, 1999) as well as children's ability to relate with peers (Burleson, Delia, & Applegate, 1995). Also, parents' tendency to engage in certain types of conflict is associated with distress in children (Grych & Fincham, 1990). Perhaps because family communication patterns predict the quality of family relationships, these patterns also offer an indication of how families adapt to structural changes such as the birth of a child (MacDermid, Huston, & McHale, 1990) or remarriage (Coleman, Fine, Ganong, Downs, & Pauk, 2001).

Although a case has been made here for the centrality of communication to family members and family relationships, the study of family communication is not, nor should it be, dominated only by communication researchers. Communication creates and maintains family systems—but those systems evolve through developmental stages, are composed of many parts, and are situated in particular contexts. Scholars from a number of different fields study the developmental processes that affect family members, the components of family systems, and the contexts that influence family interaction. The study of family communication, in short, is multidisciplinary.

Multidisciplinary research—research from fields including communication, social psychology, clinical psychology, sociology, and family studies—is essential to understanding family communication because families operate as systems. The systemic nature of family relationships dictates that they be studied in terms of the associations among their parts as well as of the contexts in which they are situated (Reis, Collins, & Berscheid, 2000). A clear understanding of families, thus, demands an awareness of the relationships that exist among several factors: (a) the various developmental stages of the family life course, (b) the different forms or structures of families, (c) the individuals that comprise families, (d) communication processes that take place among family members, and (e) contemporary issues and concerns that affect family relationships. The proposed volume is organized along these important conceptual dimensions.

In the first section of the book, both theoretical and methodological issues that influence current conceptions of the family are described. The definitional concerns raised in this section provide a foundation for examining family interaction because they set the baseline for the instantiation and evaluation of family members' behavior. For example, in chapter 1, Glen Stamp provides a careful analysis of the theories that have guided research in recent years. By identifying and categorizing frequently cited theories, Stamp is able to generate a model of family relationships. His model offers a reflection of current research as well as a guideline for future work. Chapter 2, authored by Patricia Noller and Judith Feeney, focuses on the various methods that researchers use to study family interaction. Noller and Feeney not only describe the way that self-report, observational, and experimental techniques are employed but also discuss the advantages and disadvantages associated with each of these methodologies. Noller and Feeney's discussion raises important issues that researchers need to consider in selecting methods to address their research questions and hypotheses.

In the second section, research and theory centering around the family life course is covered. Although the life course itself may be viewed as somewhat traditional— beginning with mate selection, progressing to marriage and parenthood, and then moving to the family relationships that characterize old age—many of the issues raised in this section challenge long-held beliefs about the ways family members interact. Chapters include material on nontraditional families and make note of the unique hurdles that individuals in these families face as they move through the life course. For instance, the influence of demographic changes on mate selection and premarital relationships becomes apparent in chapter 3. In this chapter, Catherine Surra and her colleagues offer a comprehensive synthesis of recent literature on both premarital relationships and mate selection. These authors point to important theoretical and methodological issues that scholars need to be aware of as they interpret and build on existing research. In chapter 4,

Frank Fincham examines communication in marriage. He offers an historical overview of the literature on marital communication, reviews major findings, and identifies critical gaps in the literature that scholars need to address. Ted Huston and Erin Kramer Holmes review and analyze work on the transition to parenthood in chapter 5. In addition to highlighting empirical findings, these authors make special note of the ways in which the methodological choices of researchers have affected the conclusions that have been drawn concerning the influence of parenthood on marriage. In chapter 6, Karen Fingerman, Jon Nussbaum, and Kira Birditt look at the communication patterns of adults at midlife. They describe the distinctive characteristics of midlife and the developmental goals and experiences of middle-aged adults. Fingerman and her colleagues also discuss the content of family communication during midlife and the factors that affect how middle-aged adults communicate with family members. The communication of older adults is covered by Fran Dickson, Allison Christian, and Clyde Remmo in chapter 7. Like many of the other authors in this section, Dickson and her colleagues point out how changes in the structure of families have influenced family interaction.

The third section of the volume focuses on communication that occurs in different family forms. Some of the social interactions that people experience when they are members of divorced or single-parent families, stepfamilies, or gay/lesbian families are unique. The relationships that individuals in these, and other types of families, experience include challenges and benefits that set them apart from many who see themselves as members of an intact, biological family unit. Chapters in this section, thus, describe some of the particular communication patterns that distinguish social interaction in various types of families. Ascan Koerner and Mary Anne Fitzpatrick set the stage for this section by describing the communication patterns of intact families in chapter 8. These authors provide an insightful discussion of issues associated with defining intact families, describe the theoretical "roots" of research on family communication patterns, and review studies concerning factors that influence the communication patterns of intact families. In chapter 9, Julia Lewis, Judith Wallerstein, and Linda Johnson-Reitz look at changes that occur in communication as families move through the process of divorce. They examine the characteristics of family interaction prior to divorce, review findings concerning relationships among family members after divorce, and offer an analysis of metamessages that are generated in divorced families. Marilyn Coleman, Lawrence Ganong, and Mark Fine focus on the communication of stepfamilies in chapter 10. In synthesizing the literature on the communication processes that typify these families, Coleman, Ganong, and Fine shed light on the many demands that both adults and children in stepfamilies address when they interact. In chapter 11, Letitia Anne Peplau and Kristin Beals examine the family lives of lesbians and gay men. To provide a context for their discussion, Peplau and Beals begin by looking at societal attitudes toward gay men and lesbians. The authors then review research on the relationships that lesbians and gay men have with their family of origin, on homosexual couples, and on the families that are created when gay and lesbian parents have children of their own. Rhunette Diggs and Thomas Socha address some of the complex issues associated with families and cultural diversity in chapter 12. Diggs and Socha discuss the various ways scholars have treated culture and offer important recommendations for research on communication and cultural diversity in families.

Individual family members and their relationships are the centerpiece of the fourth section. The communication skills of family members and the relational issues members must deal with vary. Infants face one set of developmental tasks; adolescents and young adults face another. Mothers and fathers adopt particular roles in the family that affect the way they communicate with their children. This section describes some of the special concerns that influence the relational lives of different family members. For example, in chapter 13, William Doherty and John Beaton review research on the parenting relationship between mothers and fathers. Their careful analysis of conceptual frameworks that have been used to examine co-parenting positions them to develop a theoretical model of the factors that influence the co-parenting relationship. In chapter 14, Van Egeren and Barratt focus on infants and the interaction that takes place between infants and their parents. These authors note the methods that have been used to quantify infants' communication and review the theoretical bases from which parent–infant interaction has been studied. Their thoughtful synthesis of the literature on parent–infant communication points to some important directions for future research. Laura Stafford reviews studies on children's communication in chapter 15. Stafford takes a systems approach to analyzing this literature and looks at interactions among children, their siblings, and their parents. The analysis that Stafford offers clearly demonstrates that childhood is a critical period for socialization concerning communication and interpersonal relationships. In chapter 16, Brett Laursen and W. Andrew Collins describe the ways in which patterns of parent–child communication change over the adolescent years. Laursen and Collins contextualize their discussion by reviewing theoretical accounts of parent–child relationships during adolescence and then go on to offer a nuanced description of research on changes in closeness and conflict between adolescents and their parents. In chapter 17, Maria Schmeeckle and Susan Sprecher take a step back from the individuals that comprise the typical nuclear family to examine the extended family and social networks. These authors note how social networks and members of the extended family can affect couple relationships, parenting, and child outcomes. They also look at how various changes in nuclear families can influence extended families and social networks.

The fifth section presents a sampling of the dynamic communication processes that take place in virtually any family. Because the communication that occurs in the family can be so varied, selecting the topics for this section was difficult. The processes that were ultimately included in the section were those that have received substantial attention from researchers and theorists—they are definitely not the only processes that have been studied but the sustained attention they have received allowed the authors who wrote chapters for this section to make some important claims about the current and future state of research on family communication. In chapter 18, John Caughlin and Sandra Petronio examine privacy and disclosure in families. These authors look at the use of communication in managing private information, the development of rules to coordinate family privacy, and the consequences of changes in privacy boundaries. Petronio's communication privacy management theory offers a clear organizing framework for the literature as well as a basis for making thoughtful recommendations concerning future research. In chapter 19, Alan Sillars, Daniel Canary, and Melissa Tafoya focus on the communication processes that occur during marital and family conflicts. Research on the association between the quality of family relationships and both the amount and the type of conflict is examined. The authors synthesize work on manifest communication patterns and subjective interpretations of communication to generate an insightful critique of the literature. Steven Wilson and Wendy Morgan look at research on persuasion in chapter 20.

Although many scholars who study persuasion have neglected the family as a context for persuasive communication, those who study families have recognized that the opportunities for research in this area abound. Wilson and Morgan explain how persuasive messages in family relationships have been conceptualized and, in reviewing the literature, offer a compelling rationale for future studies. In chapter 21, Julie Fitness and Jill Duffield integrate empirical and theoretical work on communication and emotion in families. Fitness and Duffield discuss the functions of emotions, the ways family members are socialized concerning emotions, the transmission of emotion, and the influence of emotions on family functioning. These authors argue, quite effectively, that emotions provide critical information about individuals and their family relationships. Closely linked to research on emotions is the study of social support. In chapter 22, Kelli Gardner and Carolyn Cutrona define social support and discuss the benefits of supportive interactions. They analyze research on predictors of effective support as well as barriers to support in three different family contexts: marriage, parent–child relationships, and sibling relationships. The last chapter in this section, chapter 23, concerns the roles of stories and rituals in families. In this chapter, Jane Jorgenson and Arthur Bochner argue that families are constituted, in part, by stories and that family members use narrative to "create and recreate their identities and realities" (p. 518). Stories and rituals, as such, offer an important way for researchers (and family members) to understand communication and family relationships.

The sixth section of the *Handbook* underlines the fact that family communication is embedded in social, cultural, and physical contexts. Because family interaction and family relationships are influenced by these contexts, a full understanding of the communication processes that take place in the family requires researchers to attend to the environmental factors and current issues that impinge on family life. For instance, in chapter 24, Maureen Perry-Jenkins, Courtney Pierce, and Abbie Goldberg focus on family communication and the division of household labor. As women have moved into the paid labor force, family members have been compelled to change the way they do household work and child care. By synthesizing the literatures on family work and family communication, Perry-Jenkins and her colleagues demonstrate that the symbolic meaning associated with the division of labor often mediates the effects of household labor on family relationships. In chapter 25, Barbara Wilson discusses the links between family communication and traditional mass media (i.e., television, film, radio, and print). She reviews research on how family members use the media, describes how families are portrayed in the media, and notes the effects of the media on family interaction as well as the influence of family interaction on media experiences. Wilson's discussion offers clear evidence concerning the central role of the media in family life. Nancy Jennings and Ellen Wartella then go on to analyze the effects of digital media technology (i.e., computers, the Internet, and videogames) on families in chapter 26. Using family systems theory as a framework for their analysis, Jennings and Wartella illustrate the increasing role of technology in various family relationships and put forth an important agenda for further research. In chapter 27, Beth Le Poire turns to a topic that touches many families: substance abuse. She reviews literature on the effects of drug and alcohol abuse on family members and discusses the association between communication and members' tendency to abuse substances. Le Poire employs Inconsistent Nurturing as Control theory to explain the subtle ways that family communication can sustain or deter addiction. Another sort of abuse is covered in chapter 28. In this chapter, Kristin Anderson, Debra Umberson, and Sinikka Elliott look at the link between family interaction and family violence. They use research and theory to argue that this association is bidirectional—that certain communication patterns create a context for violence and that violence undermines healthy family communication. In chapter 29, Deborah Jones, Steven Beach, and Hope Jackson discuss the influence of family interaction and family relationships on health. These authors describe how family interaction affects various aspects of the disease process and identify several mediators that likely account for some of the influence of family processes on disease. Jones and her colleagues use depression as an example to illustrate advances in treatment and, after doing so, highlight important avenues for future study.

Finally, because the current volume includes scholarship from a variety of disciplines and a number of different theoretical perspectives, the seventh section provides a commentary emphasizing themes that tie the various chapters together. In forecasting common issues that will face families, Kathleen Galvin points out the concerns that those who study, treat, and work with families likely will confront in the future.

It is important to note that the chapters in this volume do not represent a complete summary of all of the topics associated with family communication. Instead, these chapters offer a synthesis of research on issues that are key to understanding family interaction as well as an analysis of many of the theoretical and methodological choices that have been made by researchers who study family communication. It is my hope that the insightful commentaries offered in each of the chapters will advance the field—both by reframing old questions and by stimulating new ones.

REFERENCES

Barrett, M. S. (1995). Communication in infancy. In M. A. Fitzpatrick & A. L. Vangelisti (Eds.), *Explaining family interactions* (pp. 5–33). Thousand Oaks, CA: Sage.

Berger, C. R., Gardner, R. R., Clatterbuck, G. W., & Shulman, L. S. (1976). Perceptions of information sequencing in relationship development. *Human Communication Research, 3*, 34–39.

Bowlby, J. (1973). *Attachment and loss: Vol. 2. Separation: Anxiety and anger.* New York: Basic Books.

Bruner, J. (1990). *Acts of meaning.* Cambridge, MA: Harvard University Press.

Burleson, B. R., Delia, J. G., & Applegate, J. L. (1995). The socialization of person-centered communication. In M. A. Fitzpatrick & A. L. Vangelisti (Eds.), *Explaining family interactions* (pp. 34–76). Thousand Oaks, CA: Sage.

Canary, D. J., & Stafford, L. (1992). Relational maintenance strategies and equity in marriage. *Communication Monographs, 59*, 243–267.

Cappella, J. N. (1991). The biological origins of automated patterns of human interaction. *Communication Theory, 1*, 4–35.

Coleman, M., Fine, M. A., Ganong, L. H., Downs, K. J. M., & Pauk, N. (2001). When you're not the Brady Bunch: Identifying perceived conflicts and resolution strategies in stepfamilies. *Personal Relationships, 8*, 55–73.

Fitzpatrick, M. A. (1988). *Between husbands and wives.* Newbury Park, CA: Sage.

Goodman, S. H., Barfoot, B., Frye, A. A., & Belli, A. M. (1999). Dimensions of marital conflict and children's social problem-solving skills. *Journal of Family Psychology, 13*, 33–45.

Gottman, J. M. (1994). *What predicts divorce? The relationship between marital processes and martial outcomes*. Hillsdale, NJ: Lawrence Erlbaum Associates.

Gottman, J. M., & Krokoff, L. J. (1989). Marital interaction and satisfaction: A longitudinal view. *Journal of Consulting and Clinical Psychology, 57*, 47–52.

Grych, J. H., & Fincham, F. D. (1990). Marital conflict and children's adjustment: A cognitive-contextual framework. *Psychological Bulletin, 108*, 267–290.

Huston, T. L., & Vangelisti, A. L. (1991). Socioemotional behavior and satisfaction in marital relationships. *Journal of Personality and Social Psychology, 61*, 721–733.

Levenson, R. W., & Gottman, J. M. (1985). Physiological and affective predictors of change in relationship satisfaction. *Journal of Personality and Social Psychology, 49*, 85–94.

Margolin, G., & Wampold, B. (1981). Sequential analysis of conflict and accord in distressed and nondistressed marital partners. *Journal of Consulting and Clinical Psychology, 49*, 554–567.

MacDermid, S. M., Huston, T. L., & McHale, S. M. (1990). Changes in marriage associated with the transition to parenthood: Individual differences as a function of sex-role attitudes and changes in the division of household labor. *Journal of Marriage and the Family, 52*, 475–486.

Noller, P. (1984). *Nonverbal communication an marital interaction*. Oxford: Pergamon.

Noller, P. (1995). Parent-adolescent relationships. In M. A. Fitzpatrick & A. L. Vangelisti (Eds.), *Explaining family interactions* (pp. 77–111). Thousand Oaks, CA: Sage.

Noller, P., & Fitzpatrick, M. A. (1993). *Communication and family relationships*. Englewood Cliffs, NJ: Prentice Hall.

Notarius, C. I., & Johnson, J. S. (1982). Emotional expression in husbands and wives. *Journal of Marriage and the Family, 45*, 483–489.

Pearce, W. B. (1976). The coordinated management of meaning: A rules-based theory of interpersonal communication. In G. R. Miller (Ed.), *Explorations in interpersonal communication* (pp. 17–36). Beverly Hills, CA: Sage.

Reis, H. T., Collins, W. A., & Berscheid, E. (2000). The relationship context of human behavior and development. *Psychological Bulletin, 126*, 844–872.

Riessman, C. K. (1990). *Divorce talk: Woman and men make sense of personal relationships*. New Brunwick, NJ: Rutgers University Press.

Shimanoff, S. B. (1985). *Communication rules: Theory and research*. Beverly Hills, CA: Sage.

Stafford, L., & Bayer, C. L. (1993). *Interaction between parents and children*. Newbury Park, CA: Sage.

Surra, C. A., Arizzi, P., & Asmussen, L. A. (1988). The association between reasons for commitment and the development and outcome of marital relationships. *Journal of Social and Personal Relationships, 5*, 47–63.

HANDBOOK OF FAMILY COMMUNICATION

FAMILY DEFINITIONS, THEORIES, AND METHODS

1

THEORIES OF FAMILY RELATIONSHIPS AND A FAMILY RELATIONSHIPS THEORETICAL MODEL

GLEN H. STAMP

BALL STATE UNIVERSITY

The field of family studies is a complicated entity, intersecting numerous disciplines and areas of inquiry. As Stephen (2001) states, "the study of intimacy, courtship, marriage and family, parenting, and relationships between family process and individual development comprises an interdiscipline with contributions from nearly every corridor in the sciences and humanities" (p. 91). The area is so large that the pool of articles, from just communication journals over the last 40 years, as identified by Stephen (2001) in his computer-assisted textual analysis of the family literature, comprised a database of 33,000 entries.

Within such a large field, a variety of theoretical perspectives has developed over the past 200 years as the area of family study emerged as a systematic area of inquiry (Thomas & Wilcox, 1987), and metatheoretical commentary has been provided in a number of sources. For example, chapter overviews of the theoretical foundations of the area of family relationships have been included in other family handbooks (e.g., Burr, Hill, Nye, & Reiss, 1979; Doherty, 1999; Osmond, 1987; Thomas & Wilcox, 1987; Vargus, 1999), and book-length treatises on the state of family theory have been written (e.g., Burr, 1973; Cheal, 1991; Klein & White, 1996; Sprey, 1990), as well as textbooks in the family area that typically articulate a theoretical perspective (e.g., Anderson & Sabatelli, 1999; Galvin & Brommel, 1996; Knox & Schacht, 2002; Noller & Fitzpatrick, 1993; Shehan & Kammeyer, 1997; Yerby, Buerkel-Rothfuss, & Bochner, 1995). The objective of this chapter is not to replicate the type of theoretical overviews and reviews, such as the fine examples just cited, but to add a slightly different orientation and approach to the dialog regarding family theory. The objective is to systematically examine the research literature in the family area with the following four goals in mind:

(a) to identify the perspectives of inquiry guiding the major family relationships research literature;

(b) to identify the most common theories guiding family research;

(c)   to identify the most common concepts used in the family literature and to group those concepts into a category system; and

(d)   to construct a grounded theory model of family relationships from the concepts identified in (c), the third goal.

METHOD

Initial Procedures

The data set used to accomplish the previously cited goals consisted of 12 different journals covering the communication, personal relationships, and family fields. The journals examined were *Journal of Marriage and (the) Family (JMF)*, *Journal of Social and Personal Relationships (JSPR)*, *Personal Relationships (PR)*, *Journal of Family Communication (JFC)*, *Communication Monographs (CM)*, *Human Communication Research (HCR)*, *Journal of Applied Communication Research (JACR)*, *Western Journal of Communication (WJC)*, *Communication Studies (CS)*, *Communication Quarterly (CQ)*, *Southern Communication Journal (SCJ)*, and the *Journal of Communication (JC)*.

The 9 communication journals include the major national and regional journals in the communication discipline in which family communication research might be published, whereas the 2 personal relationship journals contain the major literature in the fairly new personal relationships field. Only 1 journal was included from the marriage and family area (*Journal of Marriage and the Family*); however, *JMF* is arguably the most important interdisciplinary journal of family research. In addition, because each issue of *JMF* contains some 15 to 20 research articles, over two thirds of the articles reviewed in the 12 journals were contained in *JMF*.

To obtain a large sample of recent research and theoretical trends, the 12-year time frame from 1990 to 2001 was used.[1] This provided a workable corpus of material for identifying the recent guiding theories and perspectives in the family area.

Using search engines (e.g., ERIC, Periodical Abstracts, Psychinfo), the titles and abstracts of the articles within the journals were searched for family-relevant key words.[2] The initial list was taken from Stephen (2001) and extended for this search. The list is as follows:

> Marriage or marital or marriages or married or couple or couples or couple's or divorce or divorced or family or familiar or families or brother or brothers or brother's or sister or sisters or sister's or daughter or daughters or daughter's or son or sons or son's or sibling or siblings or sibling's or mother or mothers or mother's or father or fathers or father's or infant or infants or infant's or baby or babies or parent or parents or parent's or parental or parenthood or intimate or intimates or intimate's or spouse or spouses or spouse's or spousal or husband or husbands or husband's or wife or wives or wive's or wed or wedding or blended or grandfather or grandfathers or grandfather's or grandmother or grandmothers

---

[1]The only exception was *Personal Relationships*, which was first published in 1994.

[2]The exception was *Journal of Marriage and the Family*, where it was assumed (correctly) that all articles were family related.

or grandmother's or grandparent or grandparents or grandparent's or widow or widows or widow's or remarry or remarried or adoptive or adopt or adoption or adoptions or adoption's or cohabitate or cohabitation or cohabiting or cohabit or in-law or in-laws or in-law's or stepparent or stepparents or stepparent's or stepchildren or stepchildren's or kin or kinship or child or child's or children's or children.

Once the articles were identified, they were individually examined to determine if they were indeed family research articles (not conceptual or "state-of-the-art" pieces), because the objective of this chapter was to identify the actual theories and perspectives guiding research on families. The final number of family research articles totaled 1,254. This included 272 articles (22%) from the 2 personal relationships journals (*JSPR* and *PR*), 129 articles (10%) from the 9 communication journals (*JFC, CM, HCR, JACR, WJC, CS, CQ, SCJ,* and *JC*), and 853 articles (68%) from *JMF*.

Coding and Categorization

The vast majority of journal articles were individually examined.[3] To accomplish the first goal, each article was examined for the perspective of inquiry (Bochner, 1985) guiding the research. Essentially, if an article was quantitative or experimental in nature, used surveys or behavioral coding, and/or was oriented toward prediction and control, it was coded as *empirical*. If an article was naturalistic, qualitative, ethnographic, and/or oriented toward interpretation and understanding, it was coded as *interpretive*. Finally, if an article was ideological; openly critical; reflective of existing family practices; including research practices; and/or oriented toward criticism or social change, it was coded as *critical*. Articles that seemed to overlap two areas were coded in terms of what seemed to be the more dominant category.

The second goal was to identify the actual theoretical perspectives guiding family research. To accomplish Goal 2, a working definition of "theory" was needed, because what constitutes a theory generally, and a family theory specifically, differs greatly among theorists or practitioners. Theories can be defined either as generally as "any attempt to explain or represent an experience" (Littlejohn, 1999, p. 2) or as specifically as "a set of logically interrelated propositional statements that identify how variables are covariationally related to each other" (Burr et al., 1979, p. 17). For the analysis performed here, a slightly more rigorous approach to the definition of (family) theory is used than the first example cited previously, but not as limiting as the second example. Noller and Fitzpatrick (1993) assert that:

> Theories are systematic ideas about how the world is and the way people operate. A theory attempts to explain a phenomena and involves a particular way of looking at a given set of objects or events. A theory of family communication would generally involve ideas about the ways family members relate to one another and the factors that affect those relationships. (p. 37)

---

[3]Some articles were not available to the author; most of those articles, however, were available using the full-text search engines. The abstracts, obtained via other search engines, were used for the few remaining articles (less than 10% of the total).

Because of the slightly more rigorous definition, many articles did not mention a specific theoretical perspective; rather they were oriented around areas of research (such as self-disclosure, conflict, or compliance gaining) or variables (such as satisfaction, gender, or family economics). If an article, therefore, had a guiding theory or theories, those were written down and tabulated in order to identify the theories most used in the research.

To accomplish Goal 3, the identification of the most common concepts used in the family literature, both the theories (e.g., attachment theory, systems theory) as well as the guiding terms/concepts (e.g., satisfaction, conflict) in those articles without specific theories were identified and listed for each article. After each article was individually examined, there were 2,036 terms. Once the terms were identified, they were analyzed through a method of constant comparison (Glaser & Strauss, 1967; Strauss & Corbin, 1990, 1998). The terms were repeatedly grouped together with other concepts, creating a succession of increasingly general arrangements with all terms/concepts eventually placed within 28 conceptually distinct categories.

The fourth, and final, goal was to construct a model of family relationships. This goal was accomplished using procedures consistent with the grounded theory approach. This method entails "taking apart a data set and putting the data together in a new categorical arrangement. . . . This brings the data analysis full circle with the re-creation of a coherent whole from the categorical system initially derived from disparate data points" (Stamp, 1999, p. 534).

The categories identified from the research articles were examined for possible relationships. Each of the categories was placed on index cards and tangibly moved around in order to explore how they might fit with one another. Conceptual links between the categories were explored as well as more general categories into which groups of individual categories might be placed (identified as levels) and still other higher order categories (referred to as components). During this process, notes were taken as relationships were explored. As the relationships were explored and clusters of categories were identified, a core category was also identified. The core category is the "central phenomenon around which all the other categories were related" (Strauss & Corbin, 1990, p. 116).

The final result was a theoretical model of family relationships, systematically derived from the family research literature, containing 1 core category, 4 components, 9 levels, and the 28 conceptual categories.

RESULTS

Perspectives of Inquiry

Of the 1,254 articles examined, over 90% were identified as empirical in nature. The final tally is presented in the following, with the number of articles within each category, the percentage of the total, and two representative examples from the research.

Empirical (1,152; 91.87%). The first example of the empirical perspective was the examination of the relationship between nonstandard work schedules and marital instability (Presser, 2000). A sample of 3,476 married couples supported the primary hypothesis that nonstandard work schedules increased the likelihood of marital instability, but the length of the marriage, the presence of children, and the type of work shifts were also variables affecting the relationship. A second example is offered by Alexander, Feeney, Hohaus, and Noller (2001) on the relationship between attachment style, coping resources and strategies, and appraised strain during the transition to parenthood. Attachment and coping resources were measured during pregnancy, and parenting strain and coping strategies were measured after the child was born in a sample of 92 married couples. The results indicated that the type of attachment was predictive of both coping resources and appraised strain, and that attachment, resources, and strain were predictive of coping strategies.

Interpretive (81; 6.46%).   One example of the interpretive perspective was the examination of the symbolic origins of conflict in divorce (Hopper, 2001). In this research, the author used extensive ethnographic research methods (fieldwork and interviewing over 4 years) in order to understand the personal experiences of couples who divorce, with a particular emphasis on the symbolic and cultural dimensions associated with this life change. A second example was the examination of the experience of adoptive parents (Krusiewicz & Wood, 2001). In this research, in-depth interviews were conducted with 18 adoptive parents resulting in five interactive themes pertaining to how meaning was constructed by these parents during the process of adoption.

Critical (21; 1.67%).   The essay, "Mothers, Daughters, and Female Identity Therapy in *How to Make an American Quilt*" (Golombisky, 2001), provides an example of the critical perspective. The essay was a feminist critical analysis of the film *How to Make an American Quilt* and explored the different definitions of motherhood that compete in public discourse, as well as how the film might help emancipate viewers as a type of female identity therapy. A second example of research within the critical perspective was the analysis of the maternal archetype in ecofeminist rhetoric (Stearney, 1994). In this essay, the author dismantled the notion of motherhood as an archetypal image and argued that "the use of motherhood as a unifying principle confounds womanhood with motherhood, and fails to honor the complexity of motherhood as an ideologically and socially constructed institution" (Stearney, 1994, p. 145).

Guiding Theories

There were many "theories" tabulated across the articles examined, including those oriented toward the 28 different major categories (e.g., communication, conflict, culture, etc.) identified for the third part of the analysis. The following 16 theories occurred most frequently. Each theory is listed, along with the number of times the theory appeared in different research articles, as well as a representative research example.

Attachment Theory (61).   Attachment typically refers to the close bond that forms between an infant and a caregiver (Ainsworth, Blehar, Waters, & Wall, 1978; Bowlby, 1988). Attachment is considered to be a part of human evolution, as a survival mechanism, associated with behaviors by the infant, such as crying, separation anxiety, or clinging, and developed through ongoing interactions between the infant and the caregiver (Peterson & Hand, 1999). The development of particular attachment styles (e.g., secure, avoidant, anxious) is believed to affect both the way in which adults perceive themselves (as worthy of love, for example) and their close relationships. An example from the research was a study that examined the association between mothers' attachment with their spouse and parenting during the first year (Scher & Mayseless, 1994). The researchers found that mothers who fear being abandoned by their spouses assigned more limited developmental goals to their children, and mothers who fear close and dependent relationships had higher levels of maternal separation anxiety.

Family Life Course Theory (54).   The family life course or family life cycle is a developmental approach examining broad stages through which a family might move. Cooper (1999), for example, noted that this perspective has been oriented toward both the specific stages through which an individual might pass, as part of a family (e.g., infancy, childhood, adolescence, etc.), and the more specific family transitions that occur (e.g., leaving home, parenthood, marriage, etc.). Drobnic, Blossfeld, and Rohwer (1999) examined the dynamics of women's employment patterns over the family life course in German and American women. They found that similarities and differences existed between women in the two countries as they moved into and out of employment. For example, although marriage and childbearing continued to influence exit from, and entry into, paid work in both countries, family structure played a stronger role in women's working lives in Germany than in the United States.

Family Systems Theory (50).   Sprey (1999) states that "the concepts of system and systemness are basic tools in family studies" (p. 668). As a system, a family embodies qualities such as wholeness and interdependence, hierarchy, change and adaptability, and interchange with the environment (Littlejohn, 1999), with particular emphasis on the relationships between family members (Yerby et al., 1995). An example of research within a family systems perspective was the exploration of boundary ambiguity and co-parental conflict after parental divorce (Madden-Derdich, Leonard, & Christopher, 1999). Boundaries, from a systems perspective, refer to the explicit and implicit rules guiding, and regulating, relationship interaction among family members (Minuchin, 1974). Within this research, "the failure to establish relationship boundaries that clearly define the former partner as a coparent, but not as a spouse, is a major source of coparental conflict after divorce" (Madden-Derdich et al., 1999, p. 588).[4]

Role Theory (38).   A role describes the "set of prescribed behaviors that a family member performs in relation to other family members" including how each member negotiates, with the others, their "place" within the family (Yerby et al., 1995, p. 255). The roles of mother, wife, or sister are constructed, therefore, in reference to other members (child, husband, and brother) and can evolve and change over time. Individuals can also experience conflict when enacting a role (such as parent) or between various roles (such

---

[4]While some theorists (e.g., Klein & White, 1996) distinguish between systems theory and ecological theory, ecological theory was subsumed under a systems perspective during the coding for this project because many of the core features of an ecological approach (e.g., adaptability, change, organization, interdependence, interchange with the environment) seem compatible with a more general systems perspective.

as wife and mother). Adams and Parrott (1994) examined the role performance of both pediatric nurses and mothers in relation to hospitalized children. Of particular interest was the role ambiguity associated with uncertainty regarding the rules guiding both nurse and parent behavior toward the children. When specific role expectations were communicated to parents by the nurses, the nurses had increased job satisfaction and the parents were more satisfied with the care given to the children.

Exchange Theory (34).   Thibaut and Kelley (1959) argue that interpersonal relationships, including relationships in the family, are guided by the exchange of resources (such as love, information, services, money, etc.) and the assessment of rewards and costs within the relationship, or other prospective relationships. Heaton and Albrecht (1991) used an exchange perspective in examining stable unhappy marriages. As the authors stated, "exchange theory predicts that the costs and benefits of remaining in the current marriage, the barrier to change, and the attractiveness of alternatives explain marital stability" (p. 747). From their results, they noted that such resources as age, lack of prior marital experience, commitment to marriage as an institution, low social activity, lack of control over one's life, and belief that divorce would detract from happiness were all predictive of stability in unhappy marriages.

Network Theory (28).   Family network theory involves the flow and exchange of information and/or resources both within the family (between family members) and with significant other people outside the family (Galvin & Brommel, 1996). Both internal and external family networks function to facilitate decision making, negotiate power, organize activities, provide support, and communicate information (Galvin & Brommel, 1996, pp. 100–101). One application of this perspective was the examination of the formation of new (nonkin) networks by widows and widowers (Lamme, Dykstra, & Broese van Groenou, 1996). Among the factors influencing the establishment of new networks after the death of a spouse were the availability of neighbors, the duration of widowhood, the effort in seeking new relationships, and the quality of the social network prior to widowhood.

Theory of Marital Types (24).   Fitzpatrick's (1988) theory of marital types provides a means of categorizing couples into distinct groups (traditionals, independents, separates) based on the three factors of ideology, interdependence, and conflict. Traditionals tend to be more conventional, independents tend to be more unconventional, and separates tend to be more ambivalent about their marriage (Littlejohn, 1999). Although about 60% of couples can be placed in one of the three categories, couples can also be "mixed" if the husband and wife each are a different type (e.g., husband is traditional, whereas wife is separate). An application of the theory of marital types was provided by Fitzpatrick and Ritchie (1994). In this study, the relationship between marital types and family communication patterns were explored (using the Relational Dimensions Inventory and the Revised Family Communication Patterns instrument). Those families headed by traditional, separate, and separate/traditional couples saw family interaction as high on conformity orientation, whereas those families headed by independent and traditional couples perceived family interaction as higher on conversational orientation.

Feminist Theory (18).   Feminist theory (or studies) explores the meaning of gender in interpersonal life specifically, and in society more generally. Three common assumptions of a feminist perspective are that gender is socially constructed, inequality through patriarchal and oppressive conditions is common, and that marriage and family life is often more problematic for women than for men (Glenn, 1987; Littlejohn, 1999). An example of research guided by feminist theory is offered by Blaisure and Allen (1995), who were interested in the actual practice of marriage by feminist women and their husbands. Although they found that a distinction existed between the ideology and practice of equality within marriage, a feminist orientation offered the possibility of "upgrading" the marriage for women through the establishment of more marital equality.

Social Learning Theory (18).   According to social learning theory (Bandura, 1977), behavior (and behavior change) occurs through the acquisition of information from the environment. The most common type of information involves modeling the behavior of other people. As one example, violence toward others is learned through modeling and imitating the behavior of others (including people performing violent acts on television and in the media). Within families, children may model or imitate the behaviors of their parents. Social learning theory suggests that those who are subjected to harsh discipline learn that violence can be an effective way to change the behavior of others (Simons, Lin, & Gordon, 1998). Swinford, DeMaris, Cernkovich, and Giordano (2000) used a social learning approach to examine the relationship between harsh physical discipline in childhood and subsequent violence in later intimate relationships. They found that harsh physical punishment in childhood was related to greater perpetration of violence against an intimate partner later in life. From a social learning theory orientation, the violence that is enacted toward others is learned behavior based on personal experience.

Attribution/Accounts Theory (15).   Attribution theory and the theory of accounts are cognitive and linguistic perspectives dealing with the way people assign meaning to both their own behavior and the behavior of others (Heider, 1958; Scott & Lyman, 1968). For attribution theorists, one way in which explanations for behavior can occur is through source criteria. For example, those attributions external to the source are explanations based on situational constraints, whereas those internal to the source are based on personality explanations. Accounts, on the other hand, are often seen in terms of whether a person offers an explanation, a justification, or some other way of explaining their (or another person's) behavior. An example of family research that used an attribution approach was the examination of blame placing (attribution of responsibility) by victims of domestic violence (Andrews & Brewin, 1990). Results indicated that women who were presently living with violent partners, and experiencing ongoing abuse, were more likely to engage in self-blame, whereas those no longer living with a violent partner made more attributions of blame toward the abuser. In addition, self-blame was associated with repeated physical or sexual abuse in childhood.

Narrative Theory (14).   The study of personal narratives refers to the examination of individual or collective stories about one's own lived experience (Bochner, 1994). Narratives are typically organized around some consequential event and may involve moral perspectives. The way in which an individual experiences (or constructs) reality as well as the exploration of issues related to individual or relational identity can also be functions of narratives (Riessman, 1993). An example of narrative theory, as applied to family communication, was the exploration of the marital experience of newlyweds (Orbuch, Veroff, & Holmberg, 1993) in which the researchers examined the courtship stories of newlyweds. The stories were coded according to story style, storytelling process, and story content with the findings indicating that courtship stories helped explain lived experience and meaning within the couple relationship.

Dialectical Theory (14).   The study of family relationships from a dialectical approach focuses on change (or process) in the relationship and the experience of contradictions within interpersonal life such as autonomy and connection, stability and change, and openness and closedness (Baxter, 1988). The role of rituals in the management of the dialectical tension of "old" and "new" in blended families provides an example of family research using a dialectical perspective (Braithwaite, Baxter, & Harper 1998). In their study, the researchers examined the means through which blended families develop and adapt (successful and unsuccessful) rituals. An ongoing dialectic tension between the "old family" and the "new family," which needed to be managed by the family members, was found to exist. The enactment of successful rituals allowed the blended family to embrace the new family while valuing what was important in the old family.

Social Construction Theory (10).   The social construction of reality has philosophical roots in the tradition of phenomenology. Through socialization, interaction, and language, individuals, within the contexts of social institutions such as the family, collectively construct the realities in which they live. Reality, therefore, is both objectively present and subjectively apprehended (Berger & Luckmann, 1967). The social construction of the welfare mother provides an example of research with a social construction orientation (Seccombe, James, & Walters, 1998). In their research, Seccombe et al. found that stereotypical perceptions of welfare mothers do exist in society (are objectively present) and are internalized by the welfare recipients themselves (subjectively apprehended). They found that the recipients were not only familiar with the stigma attached to welfare (e.g., lazy, unmotivated) but also constructed their own identities as a way of accounting for that stigma. As a result, welfare recipients were more likely to see themselves as victims, and in need of legitimate help through welfare, while casting aspersions on other welfare recipients. As such, they legitimized the social welfare system as a socially constructed reality.

Symbolic Interactionism (9).   According to symbolic interactionists, personal experience is derived from ongoing interaction with significant others and/or important social groups. This interaction is mediated through the use of symbols, allowing people to understand, shape, and share their experience, including their actions within the social world (Blumer, 1969). An example of symbolic interactionism theory was the study of the change in personal identity in one spouse with the loss of a significant other (the other spouse) through divorce or death (DeGarmo & Kitson, 1996). Results indicated that a process of identity reconstruction occurred as the person shifted from being part of marriage (identity of coupleness) to being single (identity of uncoupleness). In addition, widowhood was more distressing and disruptive than divorce, but regardless of the type of marital loss, the higher the identity relevance (seeing oneself as part of a couple), the higher the psychological distress after the loss.

Equity Theory (9).   Equity theory, although somewhat similar to social exchange theory, is based on the norm of "distributive justice" (Deutsch, 1985). Through the comparison of each person's outcome–input ratio, the equity in the relationship can be determined. When the ratios are equal, equity exists; when the ratios are not equal, inequity occurs. In addition, people will try to maximize their outcomes, be more rewarding to people who treat them equitably (and punishing to those that do not), and be more distressed in an inequitable relationship. An example of research that used equity theory was the study of relationship maintenance strategies and equity in marriage (Canary & Stafford, 1992). The researchers found that "equity is a salient feature in the use and perception of relational maintenance strategies" (p. 257) in marriage, and self-reported maintenance strategies correlated with the (perception of the) other person's maintenance strategies.

Interdependence Theory (9).   Interdependence theory (Kelley et al., 1983) is oriented around the elements in a relationship (thoughts, feelings, actions, emotions, etc.), the properties of those elements, and most important, causal connections between the participants in a close relationship, in terms of respective events. As Kelley et al. (1983) assert, "all investigations of dyadic relationships deal with data that derive in some way from the two causally interconnected chains. All theories and hypotheses about such relationships involve conceptual terms that refer in some way to the interdependence between the two chains" (pp. 31–32). Johnson and Huston (1998) used an interdependence approach in their investigation of changes during the transition to parenthood. The advent of parenthood involves increased coordination, because each spouse's actions are more contingent on the other spouse's actions. Their findings indicated that wives' preferences about the division of child care tasks dramatically changed during the transition to parenthood, at least in part due to the husbands' preferences for child care as a source of influence.

Family Categories

The third goal was to identify the concepts/terms within the literature and organize them into categories. The 2,036 terms were organized into 28 categories using the constant comparison approach. Each category is listed (in alphabetical order), along with a representative research example.

Bonding.   Bonding referred to the emotional connection between individuals in the family. Sample terms in this category included attachment, commitment, interdependence, closeness, trust, intimacy, and love. An example of a research article with a focus on bonding was the exploration of the strength of bonds between children and their parents (Van-Wel, 1994). Findings indicated that children in early adolescence and early adulthood had closer bonds with their parents than children in late adolescence. In addition, closeness to one parent did not decrease closeness with the other parent, and bonds with friends also did not decrease the child–parent bond.

Children. The category of children referred to those areas involving the offspring in the family. Concepts within this category included (child) development, delinquency, time usage, behaviors, disabilities, and academic achievement. An example of a research article with a focus on children was the examination of the impact of divorce on adolescent substance use (Needle, Su, & Doherty, 1990). Adolescents who experienced parental divorce were found to have greater overall drug involvement than either younger children experiencing divorce or children from continuously married families. In addition, although divorce had a more negative impact on boys than on girls, parental remarriage increased substance use among girls but not among boys.

Cognition. The category of cognition referred to the internal mental state of family members. Within this category were such concepts as attitudes, motives, dissonance, schemas, information processing, psychological states, and memories. An example of a research article was the examination of cognition during marital conflict by Sillars, Roberts, Leonard, and Dun (2000). Upon viewing a videotape of a conflict with their partner, spouses described their thoughts as having limited complexity, infrequent perspective taking, a concern for relationship issues over content issues, and a more favorable view of their own communication as opposed to their spouse's communication. In severe conflicts and dissatisfied relationships, the thoughts of the spouses were angrier, contained more blame, and were more negative than those thoughts from spouses with less severe conflicts and more satisfied relationships.

Communication. The communication category was composed of both speech and non-speech–message aspects. Examples of this category included communication problems, instrumental and emotional support, verbal confirmation, boundary management, communication patterns, speech accommodation, self-disclosure, and nonverbal communication. An example of a research article was the exploration of secrets within family relationships, including the factors influencing why some secrets are revealed and others concealed (Vangelisti & Caughlin, 1997). Although family members were more likely to recall family secrets about a taboo topic (rather than about a rule violation, for example), taboo topics did not appear to be either revealed or concealed more than other types of family secrets. Among the factors that did predict the concealment of a secret were the avoidance of a negative evaluation from others and preventing a stressful situation.

Conflict. The category of conflict was oriented toward disagreements or differences within the family. Included in this category were aggression, disagreement, violence, corporal punishment, arguments, conflict tactics, and sibling rivalry. Pecchioni and Nussbaum (2001) offered an example of conflict in the mother–adult daughter relationship, focusing specifically on discussions of caregiving prior to the mother's dependency. One of the factors that influenced the degree of daughter involvement in the discussion regarding caregiving was the control orientation of the mother during conflict; mothers with fewer control strategies had more involved daughters.

Context. Context was composed of the background, situation, or environment influencing family life. Examples of the context category were neighborhoods, social changes, modernity, environment, residential stability, context, and social context. An example of a research article was the examination of contextual factors on parental behaviors (Pinderhughes, Nix, Foster, & Jones, 2001). Findings indicated that neighborhood poverty, inadequate public services, and danger of violence and crime not only undermined positive parenting but also made it difficult for parents to be warm, nonharsh, and consistent in their parenting.

Control. The category of control was defined by power or authority within the family. Examples included control, relationship control, status, and power. An example of a research article was the investigation of control strategies in the mother–daughter relationship (Morgan & Hummert, 2000). Individuals evaluated a direct control strategy more negatively and an indirect control strategy as more nurturing when a middle-aged female was confronting either her young adult daughter or her older adult mother about a problem behavior.

Courtship. The category of courtship focused on the stage of relationship development, by a couple, leading to marriage. Concepts within this category included mate availability, mate selection, romantic development, romantic attraction, courtship, compatibility theory, and social selection. "Compatibility and the development of premarital relationships," by Houts, Robins, and Huston (1996), was an example of a research article in the courtship category. In this research, the connection between similarity and compatibility during courtship was explored. Findings indicated that couples with similar role performance preferences and similar leisure interests were more compatible with each other than were couples with dissimilar preferences and interests.

Culture. This category was defined by those areas directed toward the impact of cultural processes on the family or by examples of families from different cultural backgrounds. Examples within this category were acculturation, socialization, assimilation, ethnicity, ethnography, intercultural, and convergence. An example of a research article in the culture category was the exploration of acculturation in Mexican-American families and the impact on family relationship quality of adult grandchild–grandparent relationships (Silverstein & Chen, 1999). As a result of the socialization of young, adult Mexican-American children, the grandparent–grandchild relationship was inhibited.

Divorce. The category of divorce focused on the process leading to the divorce, or on the effects of the divorce, within the family. Concepts included divorce, marital failure, risk of divorce, divorce conflict, dissolution, and postdivorce parenting. As an example of a research article, Cooney and Uhlenberg (1990) examined the role of divorce in the relationship between divorced men and their adult children. Findings indicated that divorce had a negative effect on both the frequency of contact and the overall quality of the parent–adult child relationship.

Economic. This category was defined by the economic status of the family or issues related to money. Among the topics in this category were economic status, child support, income effects, welfare, paid leave, and relative earnings. An example of the economic category was the examination of the relationship of economic hardship and marital quality (Conger et al., 1990). Results of this research indicated subjects experiencing economic pressures tended to evaluate their marriage more negatively by facilitating more hostility, and less supportive behaviors, in marital interactions.

Emotions.   The category of emotions was composed of issues related to emotional expression within the family. Examples of this category included emotions, affection, anger, display rules, empathy, jealousy, and emotional development. One example of emotion within the family was the examination of emotional transmission in marital couples under stress (Thompson & Bolger, 1999). Findings indicated that stress experienced by one spouse impacted the emotional state of the other spouse; for example, the negative mood experienced by one spouse was related to the other spouse feeling more negative about the relationship.

Gender.   The category of gender was oriented toward issues of maleness or femaleness within the family. Concepts included gender, feminine and masculine issues, feminism, sex roles, sex differences, and gender inequality. An example of the gender category was provided by the research by Downey, Ainsworth-Darnell, and Dufur (1998) that examined the relationship between parental gender in single-parent households and the impact on the child. Their findings suggested that few, if any, differences in either child development or child well-being existed in children raised by single mothers or single fathers.

Influence.   The area of influence was composed of issues related to influence and persuasion within the family. Concepts included compliance gaining, persuasion, social learning, social influence, rhetoric, and modeling. As a research example within the influence category, Newton and Burgoon (1990) examined the influence strategies used by married couples during interpersonal disagreements. The findings indicated that both spouses experienced greater communication satisfaction when the partner who was attempting to influence used more supportive, rather than accusatory, tactics.

Intergenerational.   Issues associated with relationships between generations made up this category. Concepts included generational effects, generational differences, intergenerational transmission, intergenerational communication, and intergenerational relationships. One example within this category was the examination of the intergenerational transmission of constructive parenting (Chen & Kaplan, 2001). In a research program spanning 30 years, the link between parenting, as experienced by children, and the subsequent experiences of children, as adults, were explored. Findings indicated that good parenting experiences as a child promoted less psychological disturbance and better interpersonal relations as an adult and had significant effects on constructive parenting as an adult.

Life Course.   The life course category was oriented toward developmental issues within the family over a life span. This category included life course, life cycle, family development, relationship change, family formation, stages of relationships, and family transitions. "Sibling relationships over the life course: A panel analysis" by White (2001) provided an example of this category. Four sibling behaviors (proximity, contact, giving help, and receiving help) were examined over the life course. Findings indicated that all four aspects of the sibling relationship declined during early adulthood.

Lived Experience. The category of lived experience involved personal and family experience. Examples of this category included social construction, personal narratives, phenomenology, self-fulfilling prophesy, symbolic interaction, perception, family realities, and subjective experiences. An example of research with a lived experience approach was the social construction of "in-law" relationships, utilizing stories detailing the meaning of address practices within the family (Jorgenson, 1994). Among the factors guiding the selection of particular address forms were social conventions, loyalty, and marking the marriage as a significant transition.

Marriage. Issues related to the spousal relationship comprised this category. Some of the concepts included marital equality, marital functioning, marital ideals, marital inter-action, marital understanding, marital similarity, and marital expectations. An example of a research study with a focus on the marital relationship was the examination of similarity and understanding within the marital relationship (Acitelli, Kenny, & Weiner, 2001). Results indicated that similarity in values was correlated with relationship satisfaction, and marital discord decreased when male spouses had increased understanding of their wives.

Networks. The category of networks was composed of those people external to the family through which the family is connected. Examples of networks included social support, personal networks, friendship, peers, and cohort effects. The examination of the networks of recent widows provided an example of the network category (Morgan, Carder, & Neal, 1997). After the death of a spouse, widowed women changed their networks to include other recently widowed women; however, this seemed to be less the result of social support but due to the similarity of the experience with other women who had also lost their spouses.

Personality. This category was composed of the different personality dimensions and constructs of the individuals within the family. Examples included self-esteem, self-monitoring, identity theory, personality theory, shyness, learned helplessness, and extro-version/introversion. Huang (1999) examined the relationship between family communi-cation patterns and seven different personality characteristics. The results indicated the existence of personality differences between individuals from conversation-oriented fam-ilies and those from conformity-oriented families. Individuals from conversation-oriented families were higher in self-disclosure, desire for control, self-esteem, and sociability; in-dividuals from conformity-oriented families were higher in self-monitoring and shyness.

Process. The category of process focused on the dynamic quality of the family system.[5] Examples of this category included family systems, family functioning, family decision making, family process, family management, family consensus, and family rituals. Smith,

---

[5]Sprey (1999) discusses the historical roots of the term process and the notion of system as a substitute for process (p. 668).

Prinz, Dumas, and Laughlin (2001) examined the relationship of family processes to child outcomes in African-American families. Their assessment of family process indicated that the quality of family cohesion, family communication, type of family structure, and family belief orientation were all related to child competence, achievement, and problem behavior in African-American families.

Quality. Family quality referred to the overall quality of life within the marriage or the family. Examples of quality included adjustment, stability, satisfaction, quality, and well-being. As an example of the quality category, Johnson and Bradbury (1999) examined the marital satisfaction, measuring both the marital adjustment and the marital quality, of newlywed couples. One factor influencing marital satisfaction was the changes within marital interactions over time; for example, couples were lower in marital satisfaction when their initial interactions were characterized with behavioral parity and their later interactions were characterized by asymmetrical patterns of behavior.

Resources. Resources referred to those tangible and intangible assets that individuals bring to the family. Examples of resource areas included exchange theory, investment model, resources, social capital, and social or emotional investment. An example of the resource category was the examination of parents' socioemotional investment in children (Bradley, Whiteside-Mansell, Brisby, & Caldwell, 1997). The results indicated that parental investment was composed of four factors (acceptance of the parenting role, delight, knowledge/sensitivity, and separation anxiety), and parental investment, as a resource, was related to the quality of both the caregiving and the marital relationship, as well as maternal depression, neuroticism, parenting stress, and child difficulty.

Roles. The category of roles was composed of those roles, and behaviors associated with those roles, held by family members vis-à-vis one another. Examples included mother, father, parent, grandparent, maternal, paternal, and role theory. The examination of the role conflict between motherhood and worker provided an example of the role category. Lindberg (1996) investigated the relationship between breast-feeding and maternal employment and found not only that women were more likely to stop breast-feeding when they (re)entered employment but also that women employed part-time were more likely to breast-feed than women employed full-time.

Sex. Sex referred to the actual sexual activity by family members. Examples of the category of sex included sexual involvement, premarital sex, sexual activity, sexual infidelity, sexual intercourse, and sexual satisfaction. The investigation of the relationship between sexual satisfaction and marital well-being in the first years of marriage (Henderson-King & Veroff, 1994) provided an example of the sex category. In this longitudinal study, the researchers found that sexual satisfaction was important to both wives and husbands, affectional feelings were related to sexual satisfaction, and, for women, marital equity was related to sex.

Stress. Stress referred to strain or tensions within, or against, the family. Included in this category were coping behaviors, strain, bereavement processes, stress theory, family stress, and terminal illness. Jones, Beach, and Forehand (2001) examined stress generation within families and the relationship to depression. Women with depression experienced more stress in their marriage and with their children, and the stress exacerbated the depression. In addition, mother-reported stress created depressive symptoms in adolescent children.

Structure.   The category of structure referred to the actual arrangement or composition of the family unit. Examples of structure included family type, blended families, family adoption, family formation, homosexual families, cohabitating couples, and co-residency. As an example of research on different types of family structures, Kurdek (1998) examined and compared different relationship qualities and outcomes for heterosexual married, gay-cohabiting, and lesbian-cohabiting couples. Findings indicated that compared to married partners, gay partners had more autonomy, fewer barriers to leaving, and more frequent relationship dissolution. Lesbian partners, when compared to married partners, had more intimacy, more autonomy, more equality, fewer barriers to leaving, and more frequent relationship dissolution.

Work.   Work referred to the actual duties performed at a job or within the house by family members. Included in the work category were division of labor, employment effects, work demands, allocation of household responsibilities, child care issues, and occupational status. An example of the category of work was provided by Folk and Yi (1994), with the examination of the child care arrangements used by employed parents. They found that employed mothers frequently used multiple child care arrangements to care for preschool children, with fathers, relatives, family day care homes, and group care all commonly employed. Although single mothers obtained more total hours of care from relatives than did married mothers, there were no differences in the use of multiple care between the two groups.

Grounded Theory Model

The final objective was to create a model of family life derived from the data. The finished model was composed of the 28 categories, arranged into 9 levels, 4 components, and 1 core category (see Fig. 1.1).

Core Category.   At the center of the model is the core category, the "category that is central to the integration of the theory" (Strauss, 1987, p. 21). Since the model, and project, is oriented around family life, and all the other categories are related to this integral concept, an additional category was created, added, and deemed the core category. The core category of *family life* (number 1 on the model) is central to all other categories; indeed, the category of family life is at such a high level of abstraction that the other categories could be subsumed within it. This core category, therefore, is centrally located, both symbolically and literally, in the model, and all other categories, levels, and components relate to this category.

The other 28 categories are organized into 4 components (substance, form, space, and time) and 9 levels (personal, relationship, interaction, communication, experiential,

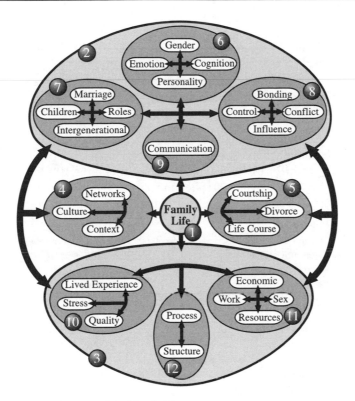

FIG. 1.1. A grounded theory model of family life.

activity, system, spacial, and temporal) (see Table 1.1). The term component is meant to imply the essential constituent parts of the whole of family life, whereas level refers to different areas or positions of family life within each component, relatively equal in importance, but different in terms of function or purpose. Each is described in the following, along with the corresponding reference number from the model.

Substance. The first component (identified as number 2 on the model) comprises the substance of family life. Substance is defined as the "essential part or element of anything" (*Webster's New World Dictionary of the American Language*, 1984, p. 1420); for the family, the essential elements or parts are the people within the family, along with their interactions, their relationships, and their communication within the family. The component of substance is composed of the personal level, relationship level, interaction level, and communication level.

The *personal level* (number 6) contains the categories of gender, personality, cognition, and emotion, all essential aspects of each person within the family. Each of these basic personal concepts impact the others at the same level (e.g., how individuals think may impact their affective state, or different personality characteristics may be gender specific). In one respect, the people, defined by their cognitions, emotions, personality, and gender, are the foundational units within the family.

TABLE 1.1

Core Category, Components, Levels, and Categories

(1) *Family Life (Core Category)*

(2) Substance (component)	(3) Form (component)
(6) Personal level	(10) Experiential level
Gender	Lived experience
Emotion	Stress
Cognition	Quality
Personality	(11) Activity level
(7) Relationship level	Economic
Marriage	Work
Children	Sex
Roles	Resources
Intergenerational	(12) System level
(8) Interaction level	Process
Bonding	Structure
Control	(5) Time (component)
Conflict	(5) Temporal level
Influence	Courtship
(9) Communication Level	Life course
Communication	Divorce
(4) Space (component)	
(4) Spacial level	
Networks	
Culture	
Context	

The *relationship level* (number 7) is made up by the categories of roles, marriage, children, and intergenerational relationships. Within this level, the various relationship possibilities between the people in the family exist, such as husband–wife, parent–child, grandparent–grandchild, etc., as well as the roles that each family member enacts within those various relationships. Each of these categories is connected to the others on this level; the quality of the marriage, for example, will change as a result of having children, or the number of children will affect the marriage (or other intergenerational relationships).

The *interaction level* is composed of the categories of control, conflict, influence, and bonding (number 8). These categories are both activities in which the family members engage (e.g., they engage in conflict) or outcomes of their activities (e.g., the strength of their bonds as a result of their interactions). Each category is also connected to the others. For example, the type of control behaviors used by one person with another might impact the interpersonal bond between the dyad, or during conflict, family members may try to influence each other to further personal or family agendas.

The *communication level* (number 9) is composed of the single category of communication. At the level of communication, each member of the family engages in communicative behavior and exchanges verbal and nonverbal messages and information with other family members. Through this communication the unique individuals of the family engage in interaction and create and maintain relationships with one another.[6]

All four levels within the substance component are related; the basic personal features of any person within the family can impact, through communication, the type of relationship or interaction with another family member. For example, a child with a particular personality feature (e.g., extrovertion) may communicate a certain way within the mother–child relationship (e.g., interruptions), which may lead to repeated conflict episodes.

Form. The second component, identified by number 3 on the model, is the form of family life. Form, according to *Webster's New World Dictionary of the American Language* (1984) is the shape, configuration, mode of existence, arrangement, pattern, or style of anything (p. 548). Form exists as the counterpart to substance, with each providing an integral perspective through which to understand family life. Without form, the substance of the family would be meaningless; without substance, the form of life would be empty. For the family, form is composed of the three levels of experience, activity, and system.

At the *experiential level* (number 10), the family and family members encounter the world, have knowledge of life (including family life), and bring meaning to their sustained existence with each other. The experiential level is composed of the categories of quality, lived experience, and stress, with each connected to the others; the satisfaction, for example, one has in the family may be influenced by stress within the family and is also part of one's lived experience of family life.

At the *activity level* (number 11), family members are engaged in behaviors such as work or sex, dealing with economic matters, such as earning a living or living on welfare, and exchanging resources with each other, such as sex, affection, time, or information. As part of the formal component, the pattern of sexual activity within the marriage, the arrangement of the division of labor, the style of living because of economic conditions, or the configuration of resource exchange all impact the life of the family. These concepts are each related to the others; sex, for example, can be a commodity exchanged within the marriage, or the work demands of one parent can impact the emotional exchange that occurs between parent and child.

The structure and process categories comprise the *system level* (number 12). The family structure (the actual arrangement or composition of the family) as well as the process (the dynamic ongoing interrelated and interdependent nature of the family) are each equally integral to the form of family life. The two concepts are connected to each other; for example, a gay couple may engage in different patterns of behavior than a heterosexual couple, or a couple with a child may experience more interdependence than a childless couple.

All three levels within the form component are related; the experience of individuals is mediated through their activities within the family system. For example, when the family structure changes through the birth of a child, one spouse's satisfaction (quality) within the

---

[6]Within the literature, interaction and communication are often used as interchangeable constructs. A distinction is being made between the two within the model. The interactional categories (control, conflict, influence, and bonding) are functions accomplished through communication; however, the type and quality of the interactional dimensions will also reciprocally influence the type and quality of the communication.

marriage may decrease and the other spouse may work more to help offset the increased expenses of having a child.

Space. The third component is space (number 4 on the model) and represents the area, both literally and figuratively, in which the family resides. This would include the external environment, social conditions, cultural effects, and people external to the family unit. The component is comprised solely of the spacial level, consisting of context, culture, and networks.

At the *spacial level*, the family resides in a context that impacts the family. The surroundings, such as the neighborhood, or the situation, such as a child starting a new school, would be examples of contextual space. The culture includes the political or social climate of life or the types of cultural practices that influence life within the family. External to the core constituency of the family are other people that can impact the family. These personal and social networks, such as friends, peers, colleagues, and other support groups, are also examples of the spacial configuration of the family.

Time. The fourth component is time (number 5 on the model) and represents the ongoing change and development of the family. The time component is composed solely of the temporal level, consisting of the categories of courtship, life course, and divorce.

At the *temporal level*, families are undergoing ongoing alterations and transformations. Courtship and divorce represent two points on a temporal continuum, with marriage in the middle. It is through courtship that two people may decide to marry (and, perhaps, in a symbolic sense, start a family); at the other end of the continuum is divorce, when two people sever their ties with each other but not necessarily with the family that has been created. The life course represents all of those changes that can occur within a family, or members of a family, over time.

Within the model, as explained previously, the concepts within each particular level can, and do, relate and impact the other concepts at that level (e.g., gender and personality within the personal level). However, the dynamic nature of the family is also represented by the numerous arrows from one level to another, indicating that there is a reciprocal connection between any two levels (e.g., interaction and relationship), or concepts from within different levels, even those contained within different components (e.g., control and stress).

CONCLUSIONS

The objective of this project was to identify the perspectives, theories, and concepts, and to develop a model, from a sample of the family relationships literature. Each objective is discussed in the following.

An examination of the perspectives of inquiry determined that almost 92% of the recent literature within the family area was empirical in nature. As such, the family research within the empirical perspective reflects such traditional scientific procedures as randomized samples, systematic data collection, objective measurement tools, and orderly theory development as a means to accurately represent family reality and discover laws of family life (Bochner, 1985). On one hand, this is a laudatory achievement and may be indicative of family studies as a legitimate area of (social) science, as well as the emergence of the received view as the dominant perspective in family theorizing and research (Thomas & Wilcox, 1987). In addition, although no paradigmatic (Kuhn, 1962) theory may exist within the social sciences, a methodological paradigm, that of the empirical perspective, may be present (A. Bochner, personal communication, Spring, 1986). This conclusion would certainly be supported by the domination of empiricist work within the family area.

On the other hand, from a pragmatist perspective (Rorty, 1982; as cited in Bochner, 1985), no perspective of inquiry is privileged over another; all have something to offer in understanding family life. If the interpretive or critical perspectives can provide different types of knowledge and insight about family life (i.e., a focus on the meanings of human actions from the perspective of the agents within the family or the enlightenment or emancipation of family members through the exposure of implicit values [Bochner, 1985]), then a call for more research within those perspectives is warranted.[7] In chapters on both qualitative research (Gilgun, 1999) and quantitative research (Acock, 1999) in the second edition of the *Handbook of Marriage and the Family*, authors argue for methodological pluralism on family research. I would echo that argument and call for more diversified research in family interaction and family relationships.

The 16 theories offer few surprises and perhaps some reassurance that the theories that are often mentioned in textbooks and other family reviews are, indeed, the ones guiding the research. For example, in the 1979 two-volume overview titled *Contemporary Theories about the Family*, published 11 years before the first article reviewed for this project, 5 general theories are offered in volume 2: exchange theory, symbolic interactionism, systems theory, conflict theory, and phenomenological theory (social construction theory). With the exception of conflict, which is a common category in the present project but deemed too general to be a theory, the other 4 theories are among the 16.

In their excellent overview of major conceptual frameworks in family research and theory in the first edition of the *Handbook of Marriage and the Family*, Thomas and Wilcox (1987) identify 12 different theoretical frameworks from 1950 to 1980. Only 5 would overlap with the 16 in the present project: symbolic interactionism, developmental (life change), systems, exchange (social exchange), and phenomenological (social construction theory). It should be noted, however, that 6 (situational, structure-function, institutional, household economic, psychoanalytic, and learning-maturational) of the other 7 (conflict being the seventh) are identified as frameworks "failing to generate sufficient research to qualify as a major framework or otherwise not very important in the study of the family" (p. 87). The present project would lend empirical support to this claim because the 6 theories were not theories sufficiently represented within the research literature from 1990 to 2001.

In terms of representative family communication textbooks, Yerby et al. (1995) discuss three major theoretical perspectives (social construction theory, systems theory, and

---

[7]One might also do a metacritical commentary on the dominance of the empiricist perspective itself. For example, since empiricist research is intended to "mirror reality," then the assumption is that what is represented is objective and ahistorical. However, if one concludes, as Gergen (1973) does, that social science is a historical enterprise and that all conclusions based on such research are only valid and meaningful from within the cultural context in which the research occurs, then the empiricist enterprise itself is interpretive in nature and can be criticized in terms of value assumptions that are not explicitly addressed.

dialectical theory) (pp. 6–10), with other full chapters on family stories (narrative theory), roles and family types (role theory and the theory of marital types), and change and growth (life course theory). In addition, attachment theory, network theory, feminist theory, symbolic interactionism (subsumed under social construction), and interdependence (subsumed under systems) are all briefly mentioned. Noller and Fitzpatrick (1993) offer four theoretical perspectives on the family (pp. 39–57): systems theory, social exchange theory, symbolic interactionism, and behaviorism (with social learning theory discussed as a particular type of behaviorism). In addition, chapters are centered on marital types and different family roles such as parent–child and sibling relationships, along with a brief mention in other chapters of attachment theory and equity theory.

From these examples, much overlap exists between what researchers are using and what synthesizers (in handbooks and textbooks) are reviewing, as the major guiding theories in family studies. Certainly, some of the theories that have been the dominant perspectives in much of the latter part of the 20th century (e.g., systems, symbolic interactionism, social exchange theory) still hold much influence within family studies at the beginning of the 21st century.

Other theories are rarely mentioned by either textbook or handbook authors. Attribution theory, for example, is mentioned in the subject index of only 2 (Pearson, 1993; Shehan & Kammeyer, 1997) of 12 representative family textbooks (Anderson & Sabatelli, 1999; Arliss, 1993; Aulette, 2002; Davidson & Moore, 1992; DeGenova & Rice, 2002; Galvin & Brommel, 1996; Janosik & Green, 1992; Knox & Schacht, 2002; Noller & Fitzpatrick, 1993; Pearson, 1993; Shehan & Kammeyer, 1997; Yerby et al., 1995). In each case only a page or two are devoted to attribution theory. Accounts are not mentioned at all. And curiously, there are more citations in various chapters in the subject index of the first *Handbook of Marriage and the Family* (1987) than the second, where only two pages are devoted to attribution theory.

Recommendations are few, based on the evidence. The 16 theories represent some of the dominant paradigms in the family area, with a variety of orientations through which the family might be understood. Perhaps theories such as attribution theory could have more space devoted in handbook chapters and family textbooks; however, one could also argue that a specific theory such as attribution theory, as opposed to more general theories such as systems theory, is not as critical in providing an encompassing understanding of family life.[8]

----

[8]There were, obviously, many more theories mentioned in the research than the 16 that dominated; the following are some of the others that were not included, because either they were identified more as perspectives for this project (e.g., conflict theory) than actual theories or did not appear in enough research articles (e.g., psychoanalytic theory): cultural theory, spillover theory, conflict theory, intergenerational theory, gender role theory, cognition theory, interpersonal construct theory, constructivism, stress theory, self-disclosure theory, structural theory, conversation analysis, coping theory, human capital theory, identity theory, communication apprehension, social control theory, ethnography, self-verification theory, play theory, affect regulatory theory, argument theory, rhetorical theory, appraisal theory, diffusion of innovations theory, humor theory, media richness theory, psychoanalytic theory, sex ratio theory, reactance theory, learned helplessness theory, relevant face concerns theory, and marianismo theory.

The 28 concepts also seem to represent most, if not all, of the relevant dimensions of family life. Because they are derived from the actual literature, this is as it should be. An examination of the table of contents in two different family handbooks verifies the relevance of many of these concepts within the family area.

In volume 1 of the 1979 edition of *Contemporary Theories about the Family*, there are 24 chapters, including chapters on networks, generations, family organization, employment, mate selection, quality and stability, power, sibling relationships, communication, process, and stress. All of these chapter topics would overlap with categories within the present book. However, there were also chapters on heterosexual permissiveness, marital timing, socialization, recreation, discipline, violence, problem solving, and deviance. Although most of these were represented within the literature, they were subsumed into more general categories through the constant comparison method. Marital timing was categorized within courtship, for example, while socialization became part of culture.

The *Handbook* you hold in your hand provides a similar perspective. Included are chapters (or partial chapters based on the titles) on courtship, marriage, family types, divorce, culture, children, networks, conflict, persuasion, emotion, and work; all are reflected in the current typology. However, there are also specific chapters on the transition to parenthood, middle adulthood, old age, step families, gay/lesbian families, infants, adolescents, self-disclosure, media, technology, drugs, violence, and mental health; most of these did appear in the literature and were subsumed within more general categories (e.g., infants and adolescents with the category of children; self-disclosure within communication).

Two points are warranted: First, the substantial overlap between chapter headings and the categories derived from the research is expected; after all, the chapters in family handbooks are authored by experts in family studies (and coordinated by an editor or editors who are also family authorities). As experts, they are knowledgeable about the research literature and are typically actively publishing in the journals as well. So, it should not be surprising that substantial overlap does exist. The second point is oriented around those categories that do not overlap. Gender, cognition, and lived experience were categories derived from the research but not represented by chapters in the two representative books. Similarly, concepts such as recreation or technology, although worthy enough for an entire chapter, were not substantially represented within the literature. Different procedures lead to different results; the categories are derived through one particular method; chapters in handbooks, through another. Either 0 or 100% correspondence would be a truly unusual exception, not the norm.

The model created from the categories, as derived from the literature, is also interesting in terms of comparison. It would be an intriguing (and less time-consuming) endeavor to create a model from the representative terms from chapter headings. If all terms were used from the two examples cited previously, as well as from the two editions of the *Handbook of Marriage and the Family*, that model would actually have more categories than the 28 ultimately utilized in this research. And, like all the comparisons above, the models would have substantial overlap but clear differences as well, because they are derived from different sources.

Speculation about other models is not as pragmatic as what the model, as developed, might offer to family scholars. Because it is derived from the research, we can see reflected in the model both research examples and research possibilities. That is, virtually any, if not all, of the categories could be, or have been, combined with other categories. For example, in the research used as examples for the various categories cited previously, Thompson and Bolger (1999) examined the relationship between emotion and stress, Sillars et al. (2000) combined conflict and cognition, whereas Downey et al. (1998) examined (parental) gender and (family) structure.

Obviously, the combinations are virtually limitless, particularly if more than two categories are combined. Examples of other possible research questions might include:

1. What is the relationship between personality and parent–child bonding?
2. How do cognitive changes in children during development affect the quality of family life?
3. Is there a relationship between family structure and resources? Does this relationship affect the quality of intergenerational (parent–child; grandparent–grandchild) relationships?
4. How do people in different cultures accomplish courtship, and is there a relationship among courtship, culture, and marital satisfaction (quality)?
5. What effects do networks have on the parental role during the transition to parenthood (life course), particularly with unmarried (family structure) women?

These questions are not necessarily atheoretical; the following theories might guide research on the previous questions: 1, attachment theory; 2, family life course theory; 3, social exchange theory; 4, social construction theory; 5, role theory.

One could also use a specific theory to guide a variety of research questions; as a result, the theory could be further developed through actual application to family issues. For example, the following research questions might be addressed from a dialectic perspective:

1. How do families at various stages of development (life course) experience the dialectical tension of autonomy connection, and is there a relationship between different stages and family stress or family quality?
2. How does the number of children (family structure) influence the communication dialectic of openness and closedness in the marital relationship, parent–child relationships, and sibling relationships?
3. How does a family maintain stability during a period of family stress resulting from change through the loss of a job by one parent (work)?
4. What are the dialectic tensions that occur in the grandparent–grandchild relationship (intergenerational), and are either the specific tensions, or the experience of those tensions, impacted by the gender of either the grandparent or the grandchild?
5. Are certain personality types more likely to exhibit particular dialectic properties (such as closedness or need for stability) during family conflict?

Certainly, research examining the previous or other questions would advance our understanding of both dialectic theory and family life.

In the final analysis, theories, categories, and models are only useful if they serve some pragmatic purpose for other theorists and researchers attempting to understand the complexity of family life; hopefully, the categories provided here, and the model developed, are a modest contribution to that endeavor and add to the ongoing dialog regarding family theory.

REFERENCES

Acitelli, L. K., Kenny, D. A., & Weiner, D. (2001). The importance of similarity and understanding of partners' marital ideals to relationship satisfaction. *Personal Relationships, 8*, 167–185.

Acock, A. C. (1999). Quantitative methodology for studying families. In M. B. Sussman, S. K. Steinmetz, & G. W. Peterson (Eds.), *Handbook of marriage and the family* (2nd ed., pp. 263–289). New York: Plenum Press.

Adams, R. J., & Parrott, R. (1994). Pediatric nurses' communication of role expectations to parents of hospitalized children. *Journal of Applied Communication Research, 22*, 36–47.

Ainsworth, M. D. S., Blehar, M. C., Waters, E., & Wall, S. (1978). *Patterns of attachment: A psychological study of the strange situation*. Hillsdale, NJ: Lawrence Erlbaum Associates.

Alexander, R., Feeney, J., Hohaus, L., & Noller, P. (2001). Attachment style and coping resources as predictors of coping strategies in the transition to parenthood. *Personal Relationships, 8*, 137–152.

Anderson, S. A., & Sabatelli, R. M. (1999). *Family interaction: A multigenerational developmental perspective* (2nd ed.). Boston: Allyn & Bacon.

Andrews, B., & Brewin, C. R. (1990). Attributions of blame for marital violence: A study of antecedents and consequences. *Journal of Marriage and the Family, 52*, 757–767.

Arliss, L. P. (1993). *Contemporary family communication: Messages and meanings*. New York: St. Martin's Press.

Aulette, J. R. (2002). *Changing American families*. Boston: Allyn & Bacon.

Bandure, A. (1977). *Social Learning Theory*. Englewood Cliffs, NJ: Prentice-Hall.

Baxter, L. A. (1988). A dialectic perspective on communication strategies in relationship development. In S. W. Duck (Ed.), *Handbook of personal relationships: Theory, research, and interventions* (pp. 257–273). Chichester: Wiley.

Berger, P. L., & Luckmann, T. (1967). *The social construction of reality*. Garden City, New York: Doubleday.

Blaisure, K. R., & Allen, K. R. (1995). Feminists and the ideology and practice of marital equality. *Journal of Marriage and the Family, 57*, 5–19.

Blumer, H. (1969). *Symbolic interactionism: Perspective and method*. Englewood Cliffs, NJ: Prentice-Hall.

Bochner, A. P. (1994). Perspectives on inquiry II: Theories and stories. In M. L. Knapp & G. R. Miller (Eds.), *Handbook of interpersonal communication* (2nd ed., pp. 21–41). Beverly Hills, CA: Sage.

Bochner, A. P. (1985). Perspectives on inquiry: Representation, conversation, and reflection. In M. L. Knapp & G. R. Miller (Eds.), *Handbook of interpersonal communication* (pp. 27–58). Beverly Hills, CA: Sage.

Bowlby, J. A. (1988). *A secure base: Parent–child attachment and healthy human development*. New York: Basic Books.

Bradley, R. H., Whiteside-Mansell, L., Brisby, J., & Caldwell, B. M. (1997). Parents' socioemotional investment in children. *Journal of Marriage and the Family, 59*, 77–90.

Braithwaite, D. O., Baxter, L. A., & Harper, A. M. (1998). The role of rituals in the management of the dialectical tension of "old" and "new" in blended families. *Communication Studies, 49*, 101–120.

Burr, W. R. (1973). *Theory construction and the sociology of the family*. New York: Wiley.

Burr, W. R., Hill, R., Nye, F. I., & Reiss, I. L. (1979). Metatheory and diagramming conventions. In W. R. Burr, R. Hill, F. I. Nye, & I. L. Reiss (Eds.), *Contemporary theories about the family: Research based theories* (Vol. 1, pp. 17–26). New York: The Free Press.

Canary, D. J., & Stafford, L. (1992). Relational maintenance strategies and equity in marriage. *Communication Monographs, 59*, 243–267.

Cheal, D. (1991). *Family and the state of theory*. Toronto: University of Toronto Press.

Chen, Z. Y., & Kaplan, H. B. (2001). Intergenerational transmission of constructive parenting. *Journal of Marriage and Family, 63*, 17–31.

Conger, R. D., Elder, G. H., Lorenz, F. O., Conger, K. J., Simons, R. L., Whitbeck, L. B., Huck, S., & Melby, J. N. (1990). Linking economic hardship to marital quality and instability. *Journal of Marriage and the Family, 52*, 643–656.

Cooney, T. M., & Uhlenberg, P. (1990). The role of divorce in men's relations with their adult children after mid-life. *Journal of Marriage and the Family, 52*, 677–688.

Cooper, S. M. (1999). Historical analysis of the family. In M. B. Sussman, S. K. Steinmetz, & G. W. Peterson (Eds.), *Handbook of Marriage and the Family* (2nd ed., pp. 13–37). New York: Plenum Press.

Davidson, J. K., & Moore, N. B. (1992). *Marriage and family*. Dubuque, IA: Brown.

DeGarmo, D. S., & Kitson, G. C. (1996). Identity relevance and disruption as predictors of psychological distress for widowed and divorced women. *Journal of Marriage and the Family, 58*, 983–997.

DeGenova, M. K., & Rice, F. P. (2002). *Intimate relationships, marriages, and families*. Boston: McGraw-Hill.

Deutsch, M. (1985). *Distributive justice: A social-psychological perspective*. New Haven, NJ: Yale University Press.

Doherty, W. J. (1999). Postmodernism and family theory. In M. B. Sussman, S. K. Steinmetz, & G. W. Peterson (Eds.), *Handbook of marriage and the family* (2nd ed., pp. 205–218). New York: Plenum Press.

Downey, D. B., Ainsworth-Darnell, J. W., & Dufur, M. J. (1998). Sex of parent and children's well-being in single-parent households. *Journal of Marriage and the Family, 60*, 878–893.

Drobnic, S., Blossfeld, H., & Rohwer, G. (1999). Dynamics of women's employment patterns over the family life course: A comparison of the United States and Germany. *Journal of Marriage and the Family, 6*, 133–146.

Fitzpatrick, M. A., & Ritchie, D. L. (1994). Communication schemata within the family: Multiple perspectives on family interaction. *Human Communication Research, 20*, 275–301.

Folk, K. F., & Yi, Y. (1994). Piecing together child care with multiple arrangements: Crazy quilt or preferred pattern for employed parents of preschool children? *Journal of Marriage and the Family, 56,* 669–680.

Galvin, K. M., & Brommel, B. J. (1996). *Family communication: Cohesion and change* (4th ed.). New York: HarperCollins.

Gergen, K. (1973). Social science as history. *Journal of Personality and Social Psychology, 26,* 309–320.

Gilgun, J. F. (1999). Methodological pluralism and qualitative family research. In M. B. Sussman, S. K. Steinmetz, & G. W. Peterson (Eds.), *Handbook of marriage and the family* (2nd ed., pp. 219–261). New York: Plenum Press.

Glaser, B. G., & Strauss, A. L. (1967). *The discovery of grounded theory: Strategies for qualitative research.* Chicago: Aldine Publishing.

Glenn, E. N. (1987). Gender and the family. In B. B. Hess & M. M. Ferree (Eds.), *Analyzing gender* (pp. 348–380). Newbury Park, CA: Sage.

Golombisky, K. (2001). Mothers, daughters, and female identity therapy in "How to Make an American Quilt." *Western Journal of Communication, 65,* 65–88.

Heaton, T. B., & Albrecht, S. L. (1991). Stable unhappy marriages. *Journal of Marriage and the Family, 53,* 747–758.

Heider, F. (1958). *The psychology of interpersonal relations.* New York: Wiley.

Henderson-King, D. H., & Veroff, J. (1994). Sexual satisfaction and marital well-being in the first years of marriage. *Journal of Social and Personal Relationships, 11,* 509–534.

Hopper, J. (2001). The symbolic origins of conflict in divorce. *Journal of Marriage and Family, 63,* 430–445.

Houts, R. M., Robins, E., & Huston, T. L. (1996). Compatibility and the development of premarital relationships. *Journal of Marriage and the Family, 58,* 7–20.

Huang, L. N. (1999). Family communication patterns and personality characteristics. *Communication Quarterly, 47,* 230–243.

Janosik, E., & Green, E. (1992). *Family life: Process and practice.* Boston: Jones and Bartlett.

Johnson, E. M., & Huston, T. L. (1998). The perils of love, or why wives adapt to husbands during the transition to parenthood. *Journal of Marriage and the Family, 60,* 195–204.

Johnson, M.. D., & Bradbury, T. N. (1999). Marital satisfaction and topographical assessment of marital interaction: A longitudinal analysis of newlywed couples. *Personal Relationships, 6,* 19–40.

Jones, D. J., Beach, S. R. H., & Forehand, R. (2001). Stress generation in intact community families: Depressive symptoms, perceived family relationship stress, and implications for adolescent adjustment. *Journal of Social and Personal Relationships, 18,* 443–462.

Jorgenson, J. (1994). Situated address and the social construction of "in-law" relationships. *Southern Communication Journal, 59,* 196–204.

Kelley, H. H., Berscheid, E., Christensen, A., Harvey, J. H., Huston, T. L., Levinger, G., et al. (1983). Analyzing close relationships. In H. H. Kelley, E. Berscheid, A. Christensen, J. H. Harvey, T. L. Huston, G. Levinger, E. McClintock, L. A. Peplau, & D. R. Peterson (Eds.), *Close relationships* (pp. 20–67). New York: Freeman.

Klein, D. M., & White, J. M. (1996). *Family theories: An introduction.* Thousand Oaks, CA: Sage.

Knox, D., & Schacht, C. (2002). *Choices in relationships: An introduction to marriage and the family* (7th ed.). Belmont, CA: Wadsworth.

Krusiewicz, E. S., & Wood, J. (2001). "He was our child from the moment we walked in that room": Entrance stories of adoptive parents. *Journal of Social and Personal Relationships, 18*, 785–803.

Kuhn, T. S. (1962). *The structure of scientific revolutions.* Chicago: University of Chicago Press.

Kurdek, L. A. (1998). Relationship outcomes and their predictors: Longitudinal evidence from heterosexual married, gay cohabiting, and lesbian cohabiting couples. *Journal of Marriage and the Family, 60*, 553–568.

Lamme, S., Dykstra, P. A., & Broese van Groenou, M. I. (1996). Rebuilding the network: New relationships in widowhood. *Personal Relationships, 3*, 337–349.

Lindberg, L. D. (1996). Women's decisions about breastfeeding and maternal employment. *Journal of Marriage and the Family, 58*, 239–251.

Littlejohn, S. W. (1999). *Theories of human communication* (6th ed.). Belmont, CA: Wadsworth.

Madden-Derdich, D. A., Leonard, S. A., & Christopher, F S. (1999). Boundary ambiguity and coparental conflict after divorce: An empirical test of a family systems model of the divorce process. *Journal of Marriage and the Family, 61*, 588–598.

Minuchin, S. (1974). *Families and family therapy.* Cambridge, MA: Harvard University Press.

Morgan, D., Carder, P., & Neal, M. (1997). Are some relationships more useful than others? The value of similar others in the networks of recent widows. *Journal of Social and Personal Relationships, 14*, 745–759.

Morgan, M., & Hummert, M. L. (2000). Perceptions of communicative control strategies in mother-daughter dyads across the life span. *Journal of Communication, 50*, 48–64.

Needle, R. H., Su, S. S., & Doherty, W. J. (1990). Divorce, remarriage, and adolescent substance use: A prospective longitudinal study. *Journal of Marriage and the Family, 52*, 157–169.

Newton, D. A., & Burgoon, J. K. (1990). The use and consequences of verbal influence strategies during interpersonal disagreements. *Human Communication Research, 16*, 477–518.

Noller, P., & Fitzpatrick, M. A. (1993). *Communication in family relationships.* Englewood Cliffs, NJ: Prentice-Hall.

Orbuch, T. L., Veroff, J., & Holmberg, D. (1993). Becoming a married couple: The emergence of meaning in the first years of marriage. *Journal of Marriage and the Family, 55*, 815–826.

Osmond, M. W. (1987). Radical critical theory. In M. B. Sussman & S. K. Steinmetz (Eds.), *Handbook of marriage and the family* (pp. 103–124). New York: Plenum Press.

Pearson, J. C. (1993). *Communication in the family* (2nd ed.). New York: HarperCollins.

Pecchioni, L. L., & Nussbaum, J. F. (2001). Mother-adult daughter discussions of caregiving prior to dependency: Exploring conflicts among European-American women. *Journal of Family Communication, 1*, 133–149.

Peterson, G. W., & Hand, D. (1999). Socializing children and parents in families. In M. B.

Sussman, S. K. Steinmetz, & G. W. Peterson (Eds.), *Handbook of marriage and the family* (2nd ed., pp. 327–370). New York: Plenum Press.

Pinderhughes, E. E., Nix, R., Foster, E. M., & Jones, D. (2001). Parenting in context: Impact of neighborhood poverty, residential stability, public services, social networks, and danger on parental behaviors. *Journal of Marriage and Family, 63*, 941–953.

Presser, H. B. (2000). Nonstandard work schedules and marital instability. *Journal of Marriage and the Family, 62*, 93–110.

Riessman, C. K. (1993). *Narrative analysis.* Newbury Park, CA: Sage.

Rorty, R. (1982). *Consequences of pragmatism* (Essays: 1972–1980). Minneapolis: University of Minnesota Press.

Scher, A., & Mayseless, O. (1994). Mothers' attachment with spouse and parenting in the first year. *Journal of Social and Personal Relationships, 11*, 601–609.

Scott, M. B., & Lyman, S. M. (1968). Accounts. *American Sociological Review, 33*, 46–62.

Seccombe, K., James, D., & Walters, K. B. (1998). "They think you ain't much of nothing": The social construction of the welfare mother. *Journal of Marriage and the Family, 60*, 849–865.

Shehan, C. L., & Kammeyer, K. C. W. (1997). *Marriages and families: Reflections of a gendered society.* Boston: Allyn & Bacon.

Sillars, A., Roberts, L. J., Leonard, K. E., & Dun, T. (2000). Cognition during marital conflict: The relationship of thought and talk. *Journal of Social and Personal Relationships, 17*, 479–502.

Silverstein, M., & Chen, X. (1999). The impact of acculturation in Mexican-American families on the quality of adult grandchild–grandparent relationships. *Journal of Marriage and the Family, 61*, 188–198.

Simons, R. L., Lin, K. H., & Gordon, L. C. (1998). Socialization in the family of origin and male dating violence: A prospectus study. *Journal of Marriage and the Family, 60*, 467–478.

Smith, E. P., Prinz, R. J., Dumas, J. E., & Laughlin, J. (2001). Latent models of family processes in African-American families: Relationships to child competence, achievement, and problem behavior. *Journal of Marriage and Family, 63*, 967–980.

Sprey, J. (1990). *Fashioning family theory: New approaches.* Newbury Park, CA: Sage

Sprey, J. (1999). Family dynamics: An essay on conflict and power. In M. B. Sussman, S. K. Steinmetz, & G. W. Peterson (Eds.), *Handbook of marriage and the family* (2nd ed., pp. 667–685). New York: Plenum Press.

Stamp, G. H. (1999). A qualitatively constructed interpersonal communication model: A grounded theory analysis. *Human Communication Research, 25*, 531–547.

Stearney, L. M. (1994). Feminism, ecofeminism, and the maternal archetype: Motherhood as a feminine universal. *Communication Quarterly, 42*, 45–59.

Stephen, T. (2001). Concept analysis of the communication literature on marriage and family. *Journal of Family Communication, 2*, 91–110.

Strauss, A. L. (1989). *Qualitative analysis for social scientists.* Cambridge: Cambridge University Press.

Strauss, A. L., & Corbin, J. M. (1990). *Basics of qualitative research.* Newbury Park, CA: Sage.

Strauss, A. L., & Corbin, J. M. (1998). *Basics of qualitative research: Techniques and procedures for developing grounded theory* (2nd ed.). Newbury Park, CA: Sage.

Swinford, S. P., DeMaris, A., Cernkovich, S. A., & Giordano, P. C. (2000). Harsh physical discipline in childhood and violence in later romantic involvements: The mediating role of problem behaviors. *Journal of Marriage and the Family, 62*, 508–519.

Thibaut, J. W., & Kelley, H. H. (1959). *The social psychology of groups.* New York: Wiley.

Thomas, D. L., & J. E. Wilcox (1987). The rise of family theory: A historical and critical analysis. In M. B. Sussman & S. K. Steinmetz (Eds.), *Handbook of marriage and the family* (pp. 81–102). New York: Plenum Press.

Thompson, A., & Bolger, N. (1999). Emotional transmission in couples under stress. *Journal of Marriage and the Family, 61*, 38–48.

Vangelisti, A. L., & Caughlin, J. P. (1997). Revealing family secrets: The influence of topic, function, and relationships. *Journal of Social and Personal Relationships, 14*, 679–705.

Van-Wel, F. (1994). "I count my parents among my best friends": Youths' bond with parents and friends in the Netherlands. *Journal of Marriage and the Family, 56*, 835–843.

Vargus, B. S. (1999). Classical social theory and family studies: The triumph of reactionary thought in contemporary family studies. In M. B. Sussman, S. K. Steinmetz, & G. W. Peterson (Eds.), *Handbook of marriage and the family* (2nd ed., pp. 179–204). New York: Plenum Press.

Webster's New World Dictionary of the American language (2nd college ed.). (1984). New York: Simon & Schuster.

White, L. (2001). Sibling relationships over the life course: A panel analysis. *Journal of Marriage and Family, 63*, 555–568.

Winch, R. F., & Spanier, G. B. (1974). Scientific method and the study of the family. In R. F. Winch & G. B. Spanier (Eds.), *Selected studies in marriage and the family*. New York: Holt, Rinehart, & Winston.

Yerby, J., Buerkel-Rothfuss, N., & Bochner, A. P. (1995). *Understanding family communication* (2nd ed.). Scottsdale, AR: Gorsuch.

2

STUDYING FAMILY COMMUNICATION: MULTIPLE METHODS AND MULTIPLE SOURCES

PATRICIA NOLLER AND JUDITH A. FEENEY

UNIVERSITY OF QUEENSLAND

Family communication can be studied using a variety of methodologies, such as self-report, observational, and experimental. In this chapter, we describe the various ways that each of these methodologies can be employed and discuss the issues related to each of them. Our overall message is that all methods have their advantages and disadvantages, and that the important issue is the appropriateness of a particular methodology for answering the research question being explored. Although we will provide examples of studies using the various methodologies, we do not claim to cover the field in any comprehensive way but rather use illustrative examples of research, including some from our own work.

Family communication can also be studied from a quantitative or a qualitative perspective, although, as we shall see, these two types of data are often collected in the same study, or series of studies. Quantitative methodologies tend to involve individuals receiving scores—for example, on a questionnaire, as a reaction time in an experiment, or as the frequency with which a particular behavior was emitted (following observational coding of an interaction). These scores can then be analyzed statistically. Although qualitative data can be analyzed using quantitative methods, these data are frequently analyzed using alternative methods. These may involve thematic analysis of intensive interviews or content analysis of diary entries, letters, utterances, or written statements. The focus of qualitative methodologies is on the experience of the participants, often as recorded in their own words. Each specific methodology, whether basically quantitative or qualitative, has advantages and disadvantages, and we will draw attention to these as we proceed.

SELF-REPORT METHODOLOGIES

Self-report methods often are used for studying family communication, either alone or in combination with other methodologies. Self-report methodologies can include questionnaires, diary methods, and other experience-sampling techniques. Interviews also involve self-report, facilitated by the interviewer.

Use of Questionnaires

Self-report questionnaires are appropriate for asking about the general or overall frequency of communication. Examples of widely used measures of family communication include the Communication Patterns Questionnaire (Christensen, 1988; Christensen & Sullaway, 1984; Noller & White, 1990), the Conflict Resolution Styles Questionnaire (Peterson, 1990; Rands, Levinger, & Mellinger, 1981), and the Primary Communication Inventory (Locke, Sabagh, & Thomes, 1956). Whereas most researchers have tended to focus on assessing conflict, Halberstadt (1986; Halberstadt, Cassidy, Stifter, Parker, & Fox, 1995) has developed a measure of family expressiveness based on the dimensions of positivity and dominance. Items include "Expressing sympathy for someone's troubles," "Going to pieces when tension builds up," "Telling a family member how hurt you are," and "Praising someone for good work."

The limitations of self-report questionnaires are well known. (In fact, the limitations of this methodology tend to be much more widely acknowledged than the limitations of other methodologies such as observation.) Problems include respondents' limited awareness of their own thoughts, feelings, and behavior; social desirability and self-serving biases (unwillingness to report undesirable behavior); and the difficulty respondents may experience in trying to mentally aggregate the occurrence of a behavior across times and situations. Huston and Robins (1982) and Metts, Sprecher, and Cupach (1991) discuss these problems in more detail.

The effects of at least some of the problems of self-report questionnaires can be minimized by using scales to assess the level of socially desirable responding. For example, Snyder (1979) included a measure of "conventionalization," or the tendency to portray one's relationship in a positive or socially desirable manner, in his Marital Satisfaction Inventory. Snyder found a correlation of .7 between this measure and the Marital Adjustment Test (Locke & Wallace, 1959). He found that controlling for social desirability tended to decrease the correlations between the various factors of his inventory and a measure of global marital satisfaction, but had little effect on the overall significance of these associations or on the rank-ordering of the scales in terms of their predictive ability.

Although the limitations of self-report questionnaires are well known, the advantages of this methodology are less well canvassed. For example, it is possible to use questionnaires to assess the frequency of a behavior across different times and situations (an application that is not possible using observational methodologies, which are generally limited to a "snapshot" taken at a single point in time and in a single context). Self-report methods are also useful for studying behavior retrospectively and for studying behaviors that are likely to occur rarely in the laboratory situation.

Questionnaires Assessing Communication Across Times and Situations. Noller and Bagi (1985) asked late adolescents and their parents about the communication in the family, using the Parent-Adolescent Communication Inventory (PACI). This measure assesses communication at the level of the topics discussed; communication on each topic is rated on evaluative dimensions such as frequency, level of self-disclosure, initiation, domination, and satisfaction. The topics of conversation included "sex roles," "interests," "politics," and "sex problems." The resulting breadth of information could not be obtained using observational methods, which tend to focus on a 5- or 10-min interaction on a relatively circumscribed topic. Similarly, Noller and Feeney (1998) employed a modification of this measure (using topics more suitable for couples) to assess the conversational patterns of their newlywed couples over 12 topics and the same 6 evaluative scales used with parents and adolescents in the earlier study. The topics included "concerns about health and fitness," "feelings about our relationship," "things that lead to anger or depression," and "plans for the future." These researchers were able to explore both the frequency with which particular topics were discussed and the quality of the communication that occurred around a particular topic.

Collecting Retrospective Data. An example of a questionnaire designed to collect retrospective data is the Parental Bonding Instrument (PBI; Parker, Tupling & Brown, 1979), which asks participants about how their parents behaved toward them when they were children. The measure assesses two dimensions: care and overprotection. Sample items include (respectively) "Spoke to me in a warm and friendly voice" and "Tried to control everything I did." A major issue with retrospective data concerns validity. That is, do responses to the items reflect what really happened "back then," or do they represent reconstructions of those events and behaviors that may be distorted by current negative or positive affect? It is important to keep in mind, however, that an individual's perception of what happened earlier in his or her life may have a greater impact on the current situation than "the objective truth." Further, there is considerable evidence that offsprings' scores on the PBI are reliably related to parents' reports of their own parenting behavior, to interview ratings of parenting, and to observers' judgments of parenting (Parker, 1983).

Studying Behaviors Unlikely To Occur in the Laboratory. Roberts (2000) discusses the advantages of self-report methods for studying behaviors such as avoidance and withdrawal. These behaviors are difficult to study observationally, because the demand characteristics in the laboratory context are such that individuals are less likely to use the more obvious forms of these behaviors. For example, participants are unlikely to get up and walk out of the laboratory and are unable to resort to such techniques as turning on the television or picking up a newspaper or magazine, even though they may use such strategies in the home.

Roberts (2000) reports on the construction of a questionnaire, the Interaction Response Patterns Questionnaire, to assess withdrawal and avoidance behaviors. Three different types of withdrawing behavior are assessed: Angry withdrawal, Intimacy avoidance, and Conflict avoidance. Participants are asked to indicate how they believe their partner would respond to certain behaviors, such as "I criticize, blame or put my partner down" (to assess angry withdrawal), " I let my partner know my deepest feelings" (to assess intimacy avoidance), and "When a problem comes up in our marriage, I try to get us to talk about it, share our feelings and work out a solution" (to assess conflict avoidance). In this way, partners' responses to situations likely to trigger withdrawal can be assessed.

Another area where self-report methods may be particularly useful for similar reasons is in the study of family violence. Violent behavior is unlikely to occur during a laboratory conversation. Hence, although laboratory paradigms can be used to compare violent and nonviolent couples in terms of arousal levels and communication patterns, the actual occurrence of violence needs to be studied using self-reports. The Conflict Tactics Scales (Straus, 1979) have been widely used and have been much criticized for being too simplistic and ignoring the context of the violent behavior. There is evidence, however, that those in abusive relationships are more likely to acknowledge the occurrence of violence in their close relationship on an anonymous questionnaire than in an interview (Szinovacz & Egley, 1995). These researchers also advocate collecting questionnaire data from both partners in a relationship in order to minimize the possibility that the occurrence of violence is underreported.

Use of Diaries

The difficulty participants may have in averaging the occurrence of a behavior across times and situations can be dealt with by using a structured diary methodology. Diaries generally require participants to complete a brief report on each conversation of a particular type (e.g., with the spouse or the child), including basic information about where and when the conversation took place, along with evaluations of the communication process. The best known versions of the diary methodology are based on the Rochester Interaction Record (Wheeler & Nezlek, 1977).

The major advantage of the diary method over other self-report methodologies is that the reports can be completed immediately, or at least soon after the event in question. The main limitation of diary methods centers on the possible reactivity of the measures. Once participants are informed of behaviors they are to record, they may change their behavior either to appear more well adjusted or to decrease the demands of the reporting task. A further problem is that participants may not complete the diary forms regularly or may complete the forms for several days at the same time. In this way, participants may miss recording important information of interest to the researcher. When this happens, diary data may become more like retrospective data.

Noller and Feeney (1998) had couples in their newlywed sample complete diaries after about 6 months of marriage. Both husbands and wives were asked to keep a record of all interactions that lasted 10 minutes or more, using a set of interaction reports based on the Rochester Interaction Record (Wheeler & Nezlek, 1977). These reports provided structural information about couple interactions (date, time, duration, who was present, and topic). Ratings of each interaction were also obtained (assessing frequency, initiation, recognition, disclosure, conflict, and satisfaction), and these were used to form measures of "quantity," "quality," and "conflict."

Other Experience-Sampling Techniques

Some researchers have collected diary-type data by using beepers to indicate when they would like the participants to complete a report. For example, Larson and Richards (1994) had family members report on their activities and affect at particular points in time.

In this way, they were able to relate family members' affect to time of day and to the activity being engaged in. In another study of this type, Huston and Vangelisti (1991) used telephone calls involving a highly structured interview protocol to obtain reports of couples' socioemotional behavior (e.g., " husband made wife laugh," "husband failed to do something wife asked," "wife approved of or complimented husband," "wife-dominated conversation"). Such methods can help ensure that data are collected regularly and soon after the occurrence of the behavior being studied.

Interviews

Another way of obtaining a participant's perspective on a situation is to use interviews. Interviews vary in terms of the level of structure imposed by the researcher. At the highest level of structure, interviews may not be very different from questionnaires as a methodology, except that the information being sought tends to be more immediate (e.g., the study of socioemotional behavior by Huston and Vangelisti [1991] reported earlier). At the lowest level of structure, the interview may be quite free-flowing and the interviewer may be free to pursue any issues that seem relevant.

Interviews have an advantage over questionnaires, in that the interviewer can use probes to elicit relevant information or ask follow-up questions to obtain more detail about topics raised by the participant. A disadvantage is that interviewers may follow their own agenda or be affected by their own biases in terms of the questions that they ask. In addition, the interviewer's nonverbal responses to the participant's answers may affect the extent to which the participant continues to be honest and truthful or produces socially desirable responses. This issue may be particularly critical when the information being sought concerns socially undesirable or even criminal behavior (e.g., see Szinovacz & Egley, 1995, as mentioned earlier).

A further disadvantage of interviews is the problem of deciding how to make sense of the data. Where the focus is on the experience of the participants (e.g., of violence, child abuse, or family life), it may be enough to describe that experience using suitable quotations from the interview transcripts. Several cautions are needed, however. For example, the researcher needs to be clear about whether the example being reported represents the modal experience of the group or is unique to that particular participant. Further, where researchers attempt thematic analyses of interview data, questions can arise about theme selection, particularly if the coder is aware of the hypotheses guiding the research. Just as biases can be problematic at the interview stage, they can also have an impact on the way the data are analyzed and reported.

Summary of Self-Report Methods

Despite the many criticisms and limitations of self-report methodologies, there is no doubt that they occupy an important place in the research arsenal of the family communication scholar. Self-report methodologies are particularly useful for collecting information about communication across times and situations, for collecting retrospective data about communication (e.g., parent–child communication at an earlier stage, or dating or premarital communication), and for collecting data about communication behaviors that occur rarely or that are unlikely to be elicited in a laboratory context (e.g., violent or withdrawing behaviors).

OBSERVATIONAL METHODS

Observational studies of family interaction generally involve having family members engage in an interaction and then rating or coding their behaviors. The behaviors of interest can be elicited in a number of different ways that vary in terms of the level of structure. Free interaction, such as that which might occur with families in a park (Sigelman & Adams, 1990) or a waiting room (Bugental, Love, & Gianetto, 1971; Noller, 1980), lies at the least structured end of the dimension, whereas experiments that involve the manipulation of the environment to observe the effect on family members' behavior lie at the most structured end.

Most observational studies of couple or family interaction involve the family or couple coming into a laboratory and engaging in an interaction that is videotaped. The topic of the interaction may be specified by the experimenter or chosen by the family. In addition, the actual content of the conversation may or may not be of interest to the researchers, because many interaction researchers are more interested in process than in what the family talks about. Videotaped conversations can be rated or coded by family members, outside coders, or both. This type of laboratory-based observational study lies somewhere between the free interaction situation and the more experimental studies involving some kind of manipulation. We discuss the latter type of study later in this chapter.

Observational methods have a number of advantages. For example, they allow the researcher to assess actual behavior rather than individuals' perceptions of their behavior. In addition, the researcher is able to focus in detail on specific types of interactions that may be of particular interest. On the other hand, there are also a number of disadvantages of observational methods. The most important one is the possible lack of ecological validity. How do we know whether the behavior observed is typical of that family's behavior in their day-to-day interactions? Further, analysis of observational data is generally based on a small sample of behavior taken at one point in time. In addition, because of the need for coding behaviors, observational research can be very time consuming and very expensive.

Choosing a Topic

Overwhelmingly, observational studies of couple interaction have focused on conflict, with little emphasis on intimate exchanges (Noller & Feeney, 2002; Roberts & Greenberg, 2002). Roberts and Greenberg make the points that what we know about the behavioral landscape of marriage is derived primarily from observations of couples in conflict and that we know much more about negative behavior between couples than about their positive behavior.

Many studies of couple interaction involve the couple being asked to talk about a current issue in their relationship (Gottman, 1994; Noller, Feeney, Bonnell, & Callan, 1994). Christensen and associates (Christensen & Heavey, 1990; Christensen & Shenk, 1991; Heavey, Layne, & Christensen, 1993) have shown, however, that behavior in a conflict interaction depends on whose issue is being discussed (that is, an issue raised by the husband or one raised by the wife), particularly in terms of demanding and withdrawing behaviors. These researchers suggest that those interested in conflict processes in couples should include two interactions: one involving a topic chosen by the wife, and one involving a topic chosen by the husband.

Despite the fact that the most commonly used strategy is to ask couples to discuss a current issue in their relationship, there is a problem associated with this methodology. Specifically, the behavioral differences found between satisfied and dissatisfied couples may be, at least partly, a function of differences in the seriousness of the problems in the two groups of couples. On the other hand, conflict topics provided by the experimenter, such as the hypothetical situations or improvisations used by Raush and his colleagues (Raush, Barry, Hertel, & Swain, 1974) may not be equally salient for all couples. Again, having couples engage in more than one interaction may help to alleviate some of these problems.

Focusing on Process

Where the focus of the researchers is on interaction processes, they may have the video-taped interaction coded by trained coders or raters ("outsiders"), or they may use the family members as informants about what was happening in the interaction.

Coding or Rating by Outside Coders. The coding or rating by outside coders may involve microcoding of each behavior, or more global ratings of the interaction. A number of coding systems are available for the microcoding of interaction, particularly couple interaction. One widely used system is the Couples' Interaction Scoring System (CISS; Gottman, Notarius, & Markman, 1976), which includes codes for content (verbal) and affect (nonverbal) behavior. Affect is coded as either positive or negative, depending on whether the unit being coded contributes to a more pleasant or more unpleasant climate. A Global Rapid Couples' Interaction Scoring Scheme (RCISS; Krokoff, Gottman, & Hass, 1989) has also been developed. This scheme involves a reduced number of coding categories and allows for coding of couple interaction in less than a quarter of the time taken for the CISS. In addition, global scores can be calculated on the dimension of positivity–negativity for both speakers and listeners. Another commonly used system is the Marital Interaction Coding System (MICS; Weiss, Hops & Patterson, 1973), which is based on operant conditioning principles. This scheme was one of the first attempts to systematize observational coding, and a number of revisions have since been undertaken.

When behavior is coded at the microlevel, the interaction is generally divided into discrete units based on either time or events (e.g., 15-second units or the talk turn), so that researchers can assess the types of behavior occurring, the frequency and/or duration of the behaviors, and even the sequence in which those behaviors occur (Roberts & Noller, 2001). Important properties of coding systems include their reliability and validity. Assessments of both interrater (level of agreement between different coders) and intrarater reliability (or the level of agreement when the same coder recodes the interaction) are needed to ensure that the behavior can be reliably coded. The validity issue concerns whether the codes used adequately reflect the interaction processes of interest (Roberts & Noller, 2001, discuss these issues in more detail than is possible here).

One problem with using outside coders lies in ensuring that the coding, as far as possible, reflects some kind of culturally shared meaning. Some researchers have tried to deal with this problem by using a "cultural informants" approach. This approach assumes that people learn the meaning and labeling of social behaviors through the process of socialization (Smith, Vivian, & O'Leary, 1990). Coders and raters using this approach are not necessarily highly trained experts; they are required to base their decisions on "an integration of all available cues, including the context, and both verbal and nonverbal channels" (Roberts & Noller, 2001, p. 388). The observers need to be demographically similar to the participants, because the approach is based on the assumption that there is a common set of culturally determined rules that are applied in, for example, couple interaction (Smith et al., 1990). Roberts and Krokoff (1990) used this approach to study hostility and withdrawal in couples.

Researchers using the cultural informants approach have often relied on outsiders making global ratings, such as those utilized in the Conflict Rating System (Christensen & Heavey, 1990; Christensen & Shenk, 1991), to assess demanding and withdrawing behavior in couple interaction. This system consists of 15 global rating scales, including "blames," "pressures for change," "avoids," and "withdraws."

Coding or Rating by Family Members. Where the family members themselves are used as the informants, a number of different strategies can be used. Callan and Noller (1986; Noller & Callan, 1988) asked family members (mothers, fathers, and adolescents) to make ratings of each family member (on different passes through the videotape), every 15 second. The ratings were made on four bipolar scales: calm–anxious, friendly–unfriendly, strong–weak, involved–uninvolved. In this way, Noller and Callan were able to compare the differing perceptions of each family member and to compare these perceptions with ratings of that family made by another family who did not know them and with those made by an outside coder.

Noller et al. (1994) had couples watch their videotaped conflict interaction and report on the strategies they had used to try to influence the course of the interaction. Participants' statements about their strategies were then coded into six categories: reason, assertion, partner support, coercion, manipulation, and avoidance. Ruzzene and Noller (1991) also had partners work through the videotape of their conflict interaction and make global ratings of their own and their partner's affect. Spouses in this study were also asked to select the three partner behaviors that had the most impact on their own feelings during the interaction and to rate the impact of these significant events. In addition, they made judgments about the partner's intention in performing that behavior; this perceived intention could be compared to the individual's actual intention, at least as self-reported. A similar strategy was used by Guthrie and Noller (1988), who had couples individually identify the "emotional moments" in their interaction. These emotional moments were then coded for the occurrence of particular nonverbal behaviors. These studies allowed the researchers not only to document patterns of interaction but also to assess their links with variables such as gender and relationship satisfaction.

Frequency Versus Sequence. Frequency data can provide information about whether one type of family member uses a particular behavior more or less often than others do. However, it may also be important to understand the links between one person's behavior and the behavior of the partner. In other words, in order to study the complexity of couple interaction, it may be necessary to examine how an action by partner A affects partner B, how B consequently acts, how partner B's actions then affect partner A, and so on (Gottman, Markman, & Notarius, 1977; Margolin, 1988). For example, subtle differences in the communication patterns of couples in violent compared to nonviolent relationships may emerge only when behaviors or emotions are analyzed in terms of their sequencing, rather than in terms of their overall levels or frequencies.

Time-series analysis can be used to investigate these issues. This method involves comparing one stream of behavior (e.g., continuous assessment of heart rate) to another stream of behavior (e.g., coding of actual behavior or emotional expression) and allows researchers to examine the strength of the associations between one data stream and the other. The z scores obtained from these analyses can then be used as the dependent variables in analyses of variance.

Roberts and Krokoff (1990) used continuous ratings by trained observers as well as time-series analysis to study the conflict interactions of married couples. Their focus, as noted earlier, was on patterns of hostility and withdrawal, specifically, whether wives became hostile in response to husbands' withdrawal or husbands' withdrawal was a response to wives' hostility. As we shall see in a later section, Noller and Roberts (2002) also used time-series analysis to explore the links among arousal, affect, and behavior in couples.

Focusing on Content

Sometimes, researchers are more interested in the content of the interaction, or what the family members actually say, than in the interaction process. In this case, researchers will generally use some method of content analysis and a more qualitative approach. There are many methods that can be used, including asking fairly global questions about the content of the interaction or using standard content analysis packages such as NUDIST or ETHNOGRAPH, which tend to focus on patterns of word usage.

Noller, Feeney, and Blakeley-Smith (2001) carried out a study of the attributions couples made about changes in their relationships. Couples were asked to discuss each of the three major relational "contradictions" (autonomy versus connectedness, openness versus closedness, and novelty versus predictability) highlighted by Baxter (1988; Baxter & Simon, 1993), with a particular focus on describing change in those areas of their relationship. These conversations were transcribed and then coded by trained coders, who were asked to study the transcripts for the answers to specific questions, such as: Did the couple report change in that area, over the course of their relationship? What was the nature of that change? To what factors did they attribute that change? By analyzing the content of these conversations, the researchers were able to gain a better understanding of how these couples experienced such changes in their relationships and how the relationships were shaped by individual, dyadic, and situational factors.

Summary of Observational Methodologies

There are a number of ways in which observational data can be used to increase our understanding of interaction processes in couples and families. Researchers can focus on the frequency of occurrence of behaviors or on the sequence in which they occur. Either the content of the interaction or the process (or both) may be of interest. The interaction can be coded or rated, and ratings may be carried out either by the family members (insiders) or by trained coders (outsiders). In addition, ratings may be either global (involving a single rating of the entire interaction) or made at regular intervals throughout the interaction.

EXPERIMENTAL STUDIES

In discussing the usefulness of experiments for studying family processes, Cummings (1995) argues that "the experimental method can make significant contributions toward explaining the bases for associations between variables, the direction of effects, and the causal relations" (p. 175). His main point is that family researchers have found many associations between family factors and child development, but that experimental methods are now needed to enable researchers to clarify patterns of cause and effect. For example, marital conflict may cause children to "act out," but children's acting out behavior may also create conflict between the parents. Cummings emphasizes that "experiments focus on immediate responses in specific contexts" (p.182) and can therefore provide valuable information about the consequences of particular behaviors in the family context. He also acknowledges that experimental methods need to be adapted to take into account the sensitive nature of family problems and the ethical issues that consequently arise. For example, it would not be appropriate for the researcher to try to elicit violent behavior in the laboratory.

Experimental studies of family communication include the analog studies pioneered by Cummings and his colleagues (Cummings & Davies, 1994); studies of responses to hypothetical situations, such as those used by Beach and his colleagues (1998); and studies using the standard content methodology (Noller, 1980, 2001). Cummings and his colleagues (Cummings, Ballard, & El-Sheikh, 1991; Cummings, Ballard, El-Sheikh, & Lake, 1991; Cummings, Simpson, & Wilson, 1993; Cummings, Vogel, Cummings, & El-Sheikh, 1989) were interested in children's responses to conflict between adults. In one study (El-Sheikh, Cummings, & Reiter, 1996), children were exposed to videotaped conflicts between a man and a woman, with the conflicts being either resolved or unresolved. Subsequently, the children's reactions to those conflicts were assessed. The children tended to be much more negative about those adults who consistently failed to resolve conflicts. In their various studies, Cummings and his colleagues have explored how children's reactions to interadult conflict are affected by such variables as parental reports of marital distress, parents' history of physical aggressiveness, whether the conflict is resolved, and whether the children have behavior problems.

Noller and her colleagues (Noller, Feeney, Peterson, & Atkin, 2000) created audiotapes of marital conflict, involving four different conflict styles: mutual negotiation, coercion, mother-demand/father withdraw, and father-demand/mother withdraw. These tapes were played to family groups consisting of mother, father, and an adolescent son or daughter. For half the tapes, the conflict was child-related; for the other half, the conflict involved only the couple. Family members' responses to the different types of interadult conflict were consistent with predictions. They saw mutual conflicts much more positively than other types of conflict and mother-demand as more typical than father-demand. The adolescents were also asked about how they would behave if the conflict occurred in their own homes, and their responses depended on whether the conflict was child-related. Overall, these data provide interesting insights into marital conflict in families with adolescents.

An example of an experimental study using hypothetical situations is that of Beach and his colleagues (Beach, Tesser, Fincham, Johnson, Jones, & Whitaker, 1998). These researchers based their study of couples on the Self-Evaluation Maintenance Model (SEM; Tesser, 1980) and asked participants to describe situations involving competition or comparison with their partner. According to the SEM model, reactions to such situations depend on relative performance (whether one outperforms or is outperformed), the closeness of the other, and the relevance of the particular activity to one's self-definition. These predictions have generally been supported by the data (e.g., Beach et al., 1998; Noller, Conway, & Blakeley-Smith, 2001). Another example of experiments using hypothetical situations is a study by Pietromonaco and Carnelley (1994), focusing on the effects of adult attachment style on evaluations of relationship partners. Respondents imagined themselves in a relationship with a hypothetical partner, whose attachment characteristics were manipulated by the researchers. In this way, Pietromonaco and Carnelley were able to assess whether respondents' own attachment style interacted with partner's attachment characteristics to influence ratings of emotion and likely conflict and tension in the imagined relationship. In short, experimental studies enable researchers to manipulate variables of interest and assess participants' reactions to those manipulations.

Noller (1980, 1984, 2001) used the standard content methodology, based on the work of Kahn (1970), to compare distressed and nondistressed couples in terms of their accuracy at decoding one another's nonverbal communication. Standard content methodology is ideal for this purpose, because it involves having participants use the same words to create messages with different meanings (by changing the nonverbal behavior accompanying those words). The validity of this methodology was supported by a study of laboratory interaction, which showed that much of the communication of these same couples was characterized by neutral words, with the emotional tenor of the messages being conveyed by nonverbal behavior (more detailed information about this methodology is provided in Noller, 2001.)

Summary of Experimental Methods

Experiments are not widely used in family research, but they are likely to be useful for helping researchers to elucidate the bases for known associations between family communication patterns and variables such as family functioning and child adjustment. Useful methodologies have been developed that need to be applied more widely in family communication research, including analog studies, descriptions of hypothetical situations, and tasks involving the standard content methodology.

STUDIES COMBINING OBSERVATIONAL AND EXPERIMENTAL METHODS

Some researchers combine observational and experimental methods by manipulating the circumstances in which an interaction takes place and then using observational methods to analyze the interaction and explore the effects of manipulated variables (e.g., comparing couples who received different information about the purpose of the interaction, or comparing mothers who were given different instructions about how to relate to their infants). For example, Stack and Arnold (1998) asked mothers to change their touch and hand gestures and then recorded the responses of the infants to these changes. Similarly,

Meltzoff and Moore (1979) reported two studies in which they instructed mothers to behave in particular ways and then assessed the ability of very young infants to imitate their mother's behavior.

Simpson, Rholes, and Nelligan (1992) induced stress in the female member of dating couples, by leading them to anticipate involvement in an unpleasant experiment. These women were then left in a waiting room with their respective partners, ostensibly while the equipment for the experiment was being prepared. The researchers then had observers rate the behavior of both partners using such adjectives as clingy/dependent, independent, anxious, friendly, reassuring, nurturant, and emotionally avoidant. Different sets of adjectives were used for males and females, because they were expected to play different roles in the interaction, with the females seeking support and the males giving support. Participants were also expected to behave differently, depending on their attachment style, which was assessed using a questionnaire. Using these methods, Simpson et al. were able to demonstrate that the effects of attachment style depended on the level of anxiety experienced by the females.

Following the work of Raush and his colleagues (Raush et al., 1974), Feeney (1998) used relationship partners as confederates, instructing one member of the couple to act distant and the other to try to reconcile. The verbal and nonverbal behaviors of the couples in each of the roles were then coded and related to attachment style. The effects of attachment style were stronger in this interaction than in a comparison condition, in which partners were primed to experience conflict over a less threatening topic (use of shared leisure time).

In a study involving parents and their sons, Jouriles and Farris (1992) manipulated the interactions of parents by having them engage in either conflictual or nonconflictual marital interactions. These researchers then examined the effects of these interactions on the parents' subsequent interactions with their sons. They were able to show that even this relatively mild and short-lived manipulation had an effect on the interactions of these nonclinical families, although the effects dissipated over time (as one would hope, given the ethical problems otherwise involved).

Summary of Research Combining Experimental and Observational Methods

Some researchers have combined observational and experimental methods, by manipulating instructions or procedures and then observing the behavior elicited. Sometimes, a member of the dyad or family group is used as a confederate and asked to behave in a particular way (e.g., act distant or change their use of nonverbal behaviors), so that researchers can study the impact of that change on behavior. This type of research may be particularly useful for studying behaviors that are unlikely to occur unsolicited in less structured types of interaction.

MULTIPLE METHODS AND SOURCES

In addition to studies combining observational and experimental methods, there are other examples of family communication research using two or more approaches to data collection. In fact, multimethod research is increasing in popularity: Nothing lends more

TABLE 2.1

Integrative Framework for Describing Different Types of Data About Communication in Relationships

Source of Information	Types of Information		
	Subjective Conditions	*Subjective Events*	*Interpersonal Events*
Insider	1. Self-reports of attitudes to, and beliefs about, the relationship	2. Reports of feelings, intentions, etc., of self and partner	3. Self-reports of behavior using video, diaries, etc.
Outsider	4. Global judgments of relationship properties, e.g., dominance, satisfaction	5. Ratings and judgments of feelings, intentions, etc.	6. Coding of behavior by trained coders or observers

Note. Reproduced from *Advances in Personal Relationships, 3,* edited by Daniel Perlman, with permission fom Jessica Kingsley Publishers. Copyright © 1991 Jessica Kingsley Publishers.

credence to a research finding than being able to state that the same results were found across samples and across methodologies, particularly when the various methodologies provide different types of information from different sources. In exploring the demand–withdraw pattern, for example, Christensen and his colleagues have obtained both self-report data (using the Communication Patterns Questionnaire) and observers' ratings of behavior, with similar patterns found using both methods. In addition, Noller and Christensen (see Feeney, Noller, Sheehan, & Peterson, 1999) have coded the actual non-verbal behavior of couples and related the frequency of particular behaviors to the ratings of demanding and withdrawing by the couples. As expected, these data showed that withdrawing behaviors, in particular, were more common when the wife's issue was being discussed.

In that series of studies, Christensen and his colleagues used both insider data (self-reports of demanding and withdrawing behavior) and outsider data (global ratings by outsiders of couples' behavior and coding of actual nonverbal behaviors by trained coders). This distinction between insider and outsider data is an important one and has been highlighted by Olson (1977) and by Noller and Guthrie (1991). Noller and Guthrie related the insider–outsider distinction to different types of data as explicated by Huston and Robins (1982) and showed how the different types of data of interest to family communication researchers (subjective conditions, subjective events, and interpersonal events) can be assessed using both insider and outsider data (see Table 2.1).

Whereas outsider data have tended to be seen as more objective and reliable than insider data, it is important to remember that outsiders cannot really know what another individual is experiencing. They may be able to describe that person's behavior very effectively, but they cannot be sure what the other person is feeling, except by making assumptions about the "true" meaning of his or her behavior. And it is a well-known fact that the more interpretation coders have to engage in, the less reliable and valid will be their conclusions.

Noller and Roberts (2002) describe a study using multiple methods to assess conflict interaction and emotional reactions in violent and nonviolent couples. This study will be

TABLE 2.2
Application of Integrative Framework to Study of Couple Violence

| Source of Information | Type of Information | | |
	Subjective Conditions	Subjective Events	Interpersonal Events
Insider	Measurement of relationship satisfaction using self-report questionnaire	Ratings of affect during interaction using hand-held dials	Reports of presence or absence of violence in the relationship (participants did not report on their own behavior during the interaction.)
Outsider	(No measure of subjective conditions by outsiders)	Physiological responding using physiograph; ratings of affective displays by coders	Ratings of behavior by trained coders using the Couple Communication scales. Both behavior and affect displays were coded.

Note. From Understanding Marriage: Developments in the Study of Couple Interaction, by P. Noller and N. D. Roberts, 2002, New York: Cambridge University Press.

discussed in some detail to highlight the advantages of the multimethod approach. Noller and Roberts drew a distinction between the *experience* and the *expression* of emotion. In their study, experience of emotion was assessed using ratings made by the individual in the situation and by physiological measures, and expression of emotion was assessed using outsiders' codings of the couples' actual behavior during the interaction. Specifically, the couples engaged in conflict interactions, and provided continuous ratings of their subjective experience of anxiety throughout the interaction, at the same time that their physiology was being monitored. They also made global ratings of their emotional reactions using hand-held dials. After the session, videotapes of the interactions were coded for behavior and affective displays by trained outside coders.

Table 2.2 shows how the various assessments used in this study fit into the categories discussed earlier. Insider data on subjective conditions were obtained using a standardized measure of relationship satisfaction. Insider data on subjective events were obtained with ratings of affect during and following the interaction, and insider data on interpersonal events were obtained using the Conflict Tactics Scales to assess the occurrence of violence in the relationship. Outsider data on subjective events were obtained using outsider coding of affective displays, and outsider data on interpersonal events were obtained using the behavioral categories of the Couple Communication Scales. (Outsider data on subjective conditions, which would involve outsiders making ratings of aspects of the relationship such as quality or level of conflict, were not obtained.)

In this study, Noller and Roberts (2002) used time-series analysis to explore the conflict interactions, by relating participants' experience of anxiety to their own and their partners' behaviors as coded by outsiders. Examining sequence may be particularly important when studying the communication patterns of couples in violent relationships, because there is evidence that the behaviors of these couples during conflict interaction show greater temporal connection than the behaviors of couples in nonviolent relationships, particularly with regard to the reciprocation of negativity (Burman, John, & Margolin, 1992; Burman, Margolin, & John, 1993; Margolin, John, & O'Brien, 1989). These findings have been interpreted as indicating either that partners in violent relationships may be more reactive to one another's immediate behavior (Margolin et al., 1989) or that they may be hypersensitive to each other's actions during conflict (Lloyd, 1990). Using time-series analysis, Noller and Roberts (2002) explored the effects of violence on the links between (a) an individual's own anxiety/arousal and his or her partner's subsequent anxiety/arousal, (b) an individual's behavior and the partner's subsequent anxiety/arousal, (c) an individual's anxiety/arousal and his or her own subsequent behavior, and (d) an individual's behavior and the partner's subsequent behavior.

The findings were further strengthened by the use of multiple measures of the extent to which one time series could be predicted from another time series. For example, three measures of the extent to which the female partner's anxiety/arousal could be predicted from the male partner's anxiety/arousal were initially created, one each for interbeat interval (a measure of heart rate), skin conductance level, and self-reported anxiety ratings. Likewise, three measures of the extent to which the male partner's anxiety/arousal could be predicted from the female partner's anxiety/arousal were created. The three measures of the predictability of female anxiety/arousal were averaged into a single measure (the "emotional linkage" score for females), as were the three measures of predictability of male anxiety/arousal (the "emotional linkage" score for males). Thus, this final variable reflects emotional linkage between partners, as measured by a combination of their self-reported anxiety and their physiological arousal (skin conductance level and interbeat interval). Of course, combining measures in this way is only meaningful when physiological and self-report data show similar patterns of association with other variables. When such convergence is demonstrated, researchers can be particularly confident in the reliability of the summary measures and in the robustness of their findings.

SUMMARY AND CONCLUSIONS

Studies employing multiple measures can be used effectively to study the complex phenomenon that is family communication. Although some excellent research has been carried out, more work is needed that takes full advantage of the range of methods available and that combines both insider and outsider data to increase our understanding of family processes. We also need to keep in mind that all methods have their advantages and their limitations and that using multiple approaches to data collection can help to offset the shortcomings of any given method. Hence, a better understanding of family communication can be achieved when we take advantage of the wide range of methods available and do not limit ourselves to one or two favorites.

AUTHOR NOTE

Correspondence regarding this chapter may be emailed to the first author: pn@psy.uq. edu.au.

REFERENCES

Baxter, L. A. (1988). A dialectical perspective on communication strategies in relationship development. In S. W. Duck (Ed.), *Handbook of personal relationships* (pp. 257–273). New York: Wiley.

Baxter, L. A., & Simon, E. P. (1993). Relationship maintenance strategies and dialectical contradiction in personal relationships. *Journal of Social and Personal Relationships, 10*, 225–242.

Beach, S. R. H., Tesser, A., Fincham, F. D., Johnson, D., Jones, D. J., & Whitaker, D. J. (1998). Pleasure and pain in doing well together: An investigation of performance-related affect in close relationships. *Journal of Personality and Social Psychology, 74*, 923–938.

Bugental, D. B., Love, L. R., & Gianetto, R. M. (1971). Perfidious feminine faces. *Journal of Personality and Social Psychology, 17,* 314–318.

Burman, B., John, R. S., & Margolin, G. (1992). Observed patterns of conflict in violent, nonviolent and nondistressed couples. *Behavioral Assessment, 14*, 15–37.

Burman, B., Margolin, G., & John, R. S. (1993). America's angriest home videos: Behavioral contingencies observed in home reenactments of marital conflict. *Journal of Consulting and Clinical Psychology, 61*, 28–39.

Callan, V. J., & Noller, P. (1986). Perception of communication in families with adolescents. *Journal of Marriage and the Family, 48*, 813–820.

Christensen, A. (1988). Dysfunctional interaction patterns in couples. In P. Noller & M. A. Fitzpatrick (Eds.), *Perspectives on marital interaction (pp. 31–52).* Clevedon & Philadelphia: Multilingual Matters.

Christensen, A., & Heavey, C. L. (1990). Gender and social structure in the demand/withdraw pattern of marital conflict. *Journal of Personality and Social Psychology, 59*, 73–81.

Christensen, A., & Shenk, J. L. (1991). Communication, conflict and psychological distance in nondistressed, clinic and divorcing couples. *Journal of Consulting and Clinical Psychology, 59*, 458–463.

Christensen, A., & Sullaway, M. (1984). Communication Patterns Questionnaire. Available from A. Christensen, Department of Psychology, UCLA, Los Angeles, CA 90024.

Cummings, E. M. (1995). Usefulness of experiments for the study of the family. *Journal of Family Psychology, 9*, 175–185.

Cummings, E. M., Ballard, M., & El-Sheikh, M. (1991). Responses of children and adults to interadult anger as a function of gender, age and mode of expression. *Merrill-Palmer Quarterly, 37*, 543–560.

Cummings, E. M., Ballard, M., El-Sheikh, M., & Lake, M. (1991). Resolution and children's responses to inter-adult anger. *Developmental Psychology, 27*, 462–470.

Cummings, E. M., & Davies, P. T. (1994). *Children and marital conflict: The impact of family dispute and resolution.* New York: Guilford Press.

Cummings, E. M., Simson, K. S., & Wilson, A. (1993). Children's responses to interadult anger as a function of information about resolution. *Developmental Psychology, 29*, 978–985.

Cummings, E. M., Vogel, D., Cummings, J. S., & El-Sheikh, M. (1989). Children's responses to different forms of expression of anger between adults. *Child Development, 60,* 1392–1404.

El-Sheikh, M., Cummings, E. M., & Reiter, S. (1996). Preschoolers' responses to ongoing interadult conflict: The role of exposure to resolved versus unresolved arguments. *Journal of Abnormal Child Psychology, 24,* 665–679.

Feeney, J. A. (1998). Adult attachment and relationship-centered anxiety: Responses to physical and emotional distancing. In W. S. Rholes & J. A. Simpson (Eds.), *Attachment theory and close relationships* (pp. 189–218). New York: Guilford Press.

Feeney, J. A., Noller, P., Sheehan, G., & Peterson, C. (1999). Conflict issues and conflict strategies as contexts for nonverbal behavior in close relationships. In P. Phillipot, R. S. Feldman, & E. J. Coats (Eds.), *The social context of nonverbal behavior* (pp. 348–371). New York: Cambridge University Press.

Gottman, J. M. (1994). *What predicts divorce: The relationship between marital processes and marital outcomes.* Hillsdale, NJ: Lawrence Erlbaum Associates.

Gottman, J. M., Markman, H., & Notarius, C. I. (1977). The topography of marital conflict: A sequential analysis of verbal and nonverbal behavior. *Journal of Marriage and the Family, 39,* 461–477.

Gottman, J. M., Notarius, C. I., & Markman, H. (1976). Couples' Interaction Scoring System (CISS). Department of Psychology, Champaign, IL.

Guthrie, D. M., & Noller, P. (1988). Spouses' perceptions of one another in emotional situations. In P. Noller & M. A. Fitzpatrick (Eds.), *Perspectives on marital interaction* (pp. 153–181). Clevedon & Philadelphia: Multilingual Matters.

Halberstadt, A. G. (1986). Family socialization of emotional expressions and nonverbal communication styles and skills. *Journal of Personality and Social Psychology, 51,* 827–836.

Halberstadt, A. G., Cassidy, J., Stifter, C. A., Parke, R. D., & Fox, N. A. (1995). Self-expressiveness within the family context: Psychometric support for a new measure. *Psychological Assessment, 7,* 93–103.

Heavey, C. l., Layne, C., & Christensen, A. (1993). Gender and conflict structure in marital interaction: A replication and extension. *Journal of Consulting and Clinical Psychology, 61,* 16–27.

Huston, T. L., & Robins, E. (1982). Conceptual and methodological issues in studying close relationships. *Journal of Marriage and the Family, 44,* 901–925.

Huston, T. L., & Vangelisti, A. L. (1991). Socioemotional behavior and satisfaction in marital relationships: A longitudinal study. *Journal of Personality and Social Psychology, 61,* 721–733.

Jouriles, E. N., & Farris, A. M. (1992). Effects of marital conflict on subsequent parent-son interactions. *Behavior Therapy, 23,* 355–374.

Kahn, M. (1970). Nonverbal communication and marital satisfaction. *Family Process, 9,* 449–456.

Krokoff, L. J., Gottman, J. M., & Hass, S. D. (1989). Validation of a Global Rapid Couples Interaction Scoring System. *Behavioral Assessment, 11,* 65–79.

Larson, R., & Richards, M. H. (1994). *Divergent realities: The emotional lives of mothers, fathers, and adolescents.* New York: Basic Books.

Locke, H. J., Sabagh, G., & Thomes, M. (1956). Correlates of primary communication and empathy. *Research Studies of the State College of Washington, 24,* 118.

Locke, H. J., & Wallace, K. M. (1959). Short marital adjustment and prediction tests: Their reliability and validity. *Marriage and Family Living, 21,* 251–255.

Lloyd, S. (1990). Conflict types and strategies in violent marriages. *Journal of Family Violence, 5,* 269–284.

Margolin, G. (1988). Marital conflict is not marital conflict is not marital conflict. In R. D. Peters & R. J. McMahon (Eds.), *Social learning and systems approaches to marriage and the family* (pp. 193–216). New York: Brunner/Mazel.

Margolin, G., John, R. S., & O'Brien, M. (1989). Sequential affective patterns as a function of marital conflict style. *Journal of Social and Clinical Psychology, 56,* 24–33.

Meltzoff, A. N., & Moore, K. M. (1979). Imitation of facial and manual gestures by human neonates: Resolving the debate about early imitation. In D. Muir & A. Slater (Eds.), *Infant development: Essential readings in developmental psychology.* Malden, MA: Blackwell.

Metts, S., Sprecher, S., & Cupach, W. R. (1991). Retrospective self-reports. In B. M. Montgomery & S. Duck (Eds), *Studying interpersonal interaction.* New York: Guilford Press.

Noller, P. (1980). Cross-gender effect in two-child families. *Developmental Psychology,16,* 159–160.

Noller, P. (1984). *Nonverbal communication and marital interaction.* Oxford: Pergamon.

Noller, P. (2001). Using standard content methodology to assess nonverbal sensitivity in dyads. In J. A. Hall & F. Bernieri (Eds.), *Interpersonal sensitivity: Theory and measurement* (pp. 243–264). Mahwah, NJ: Lawrence Erlbaum Associates.

Noller, P., & Bagi, S. (1985). Parent-adolescent communication. *Journal of Adolescence, 8,* 125–144.

Noller, P., & Callan, V. J. (1988). Understanding parent-adolescent interactions: The perceptions of family members and outsiders. *Developmental Psychology, 24,* 707–714.

Noller, P., Conway, S., & Blakeley-Smith, A. (2001, June). *Comparison and competition in young adult sibling relationships: An attachment perspective.* Paper presented at the 3rd Joint Conference of INPR & ISSPR, Prescott, Arizona.

Noller, P., & Feeney, J. A. (1998). Communication in early marriage: Responses to conflict, nonverbal accuracy and conversational patterns, In T. N. Bradbury (Ed.), *The developmental course of marital dysfunction* (pp. 11–43). New York: Cambridge University Press.

Noller, P., & Feeney, J. A. (Eds.) (2002). *Understanding marriage: Developments in the study of marital interaction.* New York: Cambridge University Press.

Noller, P., Feeney, J. A., & Blakeley-Smith, A. (2001). Handling pressures for change in marriage: Making attributions for relational dialectics. In V. Manusov & J. H. Harvey (Eds.), *Attribution, communication behavior and close relationships* (pp. 153–172). New York: Cambridge University Press.

Noller, P., Feeney, J. A., Bonnell, D., & Callan, V. J. (1994). A longitudinal study of conflict in early marriage. *Journal of Social and Personal Relationships, 11,* 233–252.

Noller, P., Feeney, J. A., Peterson, C., & Atkin, S. (2000). Marital conflict and adolescents. *Family Matters, 55,* 68–73.

Noller, P., & Guthrie, D. M. (1991). Methodological issues in studying communication in close relationships. In W. H. Jones & D. Perlman (Eds.), *Advances in personal relationships* (Vol. 3, pp. 37–73). London: Jessica Kingsley.

Noller, P., & Roberts, N. D. (2002). The communication of couples in violent and nonviolent relationships: Temporal associations with own and partners' anxiety/arousal and behavior. In P. Noller & J. A. Feeney (Eds.), *Understanding marriage: Developments in the study of couple interaction* (pp. 348–378). New York: Cambridge University Press.

Noller, P., & White, A. (1990). The validity of the Communication Patterns Questionnaire. *Psychological Assessment: A Journal of Consulting and Clinical Psychology, 2*, 478–482.

Norton, R. (1983). Measuring marital quality: A critical look at the dependent variable. *Journal of Marriage and the Family, 45*, 141–151.

Olson, D. H. (1977). Insiders' and outsiders' views of relationships: Research strategies. In G. Levinger & H. L. Raush (Eds.), *Close relationships: Perspectives on the meaning of intimacy* (pp. 115–135). Amherst, MA: University of Massachusetts Press.

Parker, G. (1983). *Parental overprotection: A risk factor in psychosocial development.* New York: Grune & Stratton.

Parker, G., Tupling, H., & Brown, L. B. (1979). A parental bonding instrument. *British Journal of Medical Psychology, 52*, 1–10.

Peterson, C. (1990). Disagreement, negotiation and conflict resolution in families with adolescents. In P. Heaven & V. J. Callan (Eds.), *Adolescence: An Australian perspective.* Sydney: Harcourt, Brace, Jovanovich.

Pietromonaco, P. R., & Carnelley, K. B. (1994). Gender and working models of attachment: Consequences for perceptions of self and romantic relationships. *Personal Relationships, 1*, 63–82.

Rands, M., Levinger, G., & Mellinger, G. (1981). Patterns of conflict resolution and marital satisfaction. *Journal of Family Issues, 2*, 297–321.

Raush, H. L., Barry, W. A., Hertel, R. K., & Swain, M. E. (1974). *Communication and conflict in marriage.* San Francisco: Jossey-Bass.

Roberts, L. J. (2000). Fire and ice in marital communication: Hostile and distancing behaviors as predictors of marital distress. *Journal of Marriage and the Family, 62*, 693–707.

Roberts, L. J., & Greenberg, D. R. (2002). Observational "Windows" to intimacy processes in marriage. In P. Noller & J. A. Feeney (Eds.), *Understanding marriage: Developments in the study of marital interaction* (pp. 118–149). New York: Cambridge University Press.

Roberts, L. J., & Krokoff, L. J. (1990). A time-series analysis of withdrawal, hostility and displeasure in satisfied and dissatisfied marriages. *Journal of Marriage and the Family, 52*, 95–105.

Ruzzene, M., & Noller, P. (1991). Communication in marriage: The influence of affect and cognition. In F. D. Fincham & G. J. O. Fletcher (Eds.), *Cognition in close relationships* (pp. 203–233). Hillsdale, NJ: Lawrence Erlbaum Associates.

Roberts, N. D., & Noller, P. (2001). The observation of marital interaction. In W. P. Robinson & H. Giles (Eds.), *Handbook of language and social psychology.* London: Wiley.

Sigelman, C. K., & Adams, R. M. (1990). Family interactions in public: Parent-child distance and touching. *Journal of Nonverbal Behavior, 14*, 63–75.

Simpson, J. A., Rholes, W. S., & Nelligan, J. S. (1992). Support-seeking and support giving among couples in an anxiety-provoking situation. *Journal of Personality and Social Psychology, 62*, 434–446.

Smith, D. A., Vivian, D., & O'Leary, K. D. (1990). Longitudinal prediction of marital discord from premarital expressions of affect. *Journal of Consulting and Clinical Psychology, 58*, 790–797.

Snyder, D. K. (1979). Multidimensional Assessment of Marital Satisfaction. *Journal of Marriage and the Family, 41*, 813–823.

Spanier, G. B. (1976). Measuring dyadic adjustment: New scales for assessing the quality of marriage and similar dyads. *Journal of Marriage and the Family, 38*, 15–28.

Stack, D. M., & Arnold, S. L. (1998). Changes in mothers' touch and hand gestures influence infant behavior during face-to-face exchanges. *Infant Behavior and Development, 21*, 451–468.

Straus, M. A. (1979). Measuring intrafamily conflict and violence: The Conflict Tactics (CT) scales. *Journal of Marriage and the Family, 41*, 75–88.

Szinovacz, M. E., & Egley, L. C. (1995). Comparing one-partner and couple data on sensitive marital behaviors: The case of marital violence. *Journal of Marriage and the Family, 57*, 995–1010.

Tesser, A. (1980). Self-esteem maintenance in family dynamics. *Journal of Personality and Social Psychology, 39*, 77–91.

Weiss, R. L., Hops, H., & Patterson, G. R. (1973). A framework for conceptualizing marital conflict, a technology for altering it, some data for evaluating it. In F. W. Clarke & L. A. Hamerlynck (Eds.), Critical issues in research and practice. *Proceedings of the Fourth Banff International Conference on Behavior Modification.*

Wheeler, L., & Nezlek, J. (1977). Sex differences in social participation. *Journal of Personality and Social Psychology, 35*, 742–754.

COMMUNICATION ACROSS THE FAMILY LIFE COURSE

3

RESEARCH ON MATE SELECTION AND PREMARITAL RELATIONSHIPS: WHAT DO WE REALLY KNOW?

CATHERINE A. SURRA, CHRISTINE R. GRAY, NATE COTTLE,
AND TYFANY M. J. BOETTCHER
THE UNIVERSITY OF TEXAS AT AUSTIN

Writing a review of literature on mate selection and premarital relationships is much more challenging now than it used to be. As recently as 1 to 2 decades ago, the literature to be included in such a review was well circumscribed. Studies were clearly aimed at understanding dating relationships, and samples usually were recruited because they fit into the premarital period of mate choice. In this era, however, when individuals believe that dating is passé, form serial unions that may or may not be marriage-like prior to their first legal marriage, and form multiple intermarital unions following one or more divorces, the behaviors that constitute mate selection are ambiguous. Researchers, too, seem to be influenced by the trend toward ambiguity, in that the phenomena of mating and dating are less well defined in the literature. As we attempted to identify the empirical papers for this chapter, it became apparent, for example, that current methodological practices, such as including cohabitors with marrieds in some studies and including them with daters in other studies, made it difficult to set the scope of the review. Ambiguity is apparent not only in the samples used to study these topics but also in the observational and statistical methods used to study them (for a fuller discussion, see Surra, Gray, Boettcher, Cottle, & Jarvis, 2002). For these reasons, we first strictly defined the purview of our search.

METHOD USED TO DEFINE THE SCOPE OF THE REVIEW

To guide our review, we defined mate selection as the study of the processes by which individuals choose their heterosexual or homosexual romantic partners and of the factors that predict whether relationships progress, maintain, or dissolve over time. Study of mate selection includes courtship, cohabitation, and other statuses and forms relevant to premarital romantic relationships. Our definition includes questions of partner choice, what makes for more or less successful or permanent choices, and, by implication, marital choice. Our definition is developmental in that it focuses attention on questions of change over time in relationships. We defined the study of dating relationships as investigation of the properties and phenomena that characterize the nature of romantic heterosexual or homosexual relationships and the factors that affect relational properties. Here, we include cognitive, affective, and behavioral characteristics, as well as other properties that are relevant to any type of relationship (e.g., conflict, communication). Both definitions include the individual, social, economic, and cultural factors that affect premarital relationships and mate selection.

Identifying Articles for Inclusion in the Review

We searched for articles in eight leading journals from the three fields that historically have published articles on these topics. The journals were: *American Sociological Review* and *American Journal of Sociology*, representing sociology; *Communication Monographs* and *Human Communication Research*, representing interpersonal communication; *The Journal of Marriage and the Family*, representing family studies; the *Journal of Personality and Social Psychology*, sections on Interpersonal Relationships and Group Processes and on Personality Processes and Individual Differences, representing psychology; and *Personal Relationships* and the *Journal of Social and Personal Relationships*, representing interdisciplinary journals that publish literature from all of the fields. We read the title and the abstract of each article published during the years 1991 to 2001, with the exception of *Personal Relationships*, which was first published in 1994. If this information indicated that the article fit our definition of dating or mate selection, we included it in our sample. If an article was about marriage or any other type of relationship, we excluded it, unless it mentioned something specific about dating and mate selection in the abstract. If an article was about a property that applies across relationships, we included it. We identified 524 articles this way, 40 of which were nonempirical.

In this chapter, we review the topics that had the most articles written about them in the last decade and that have not been the subject of other recent, major reviews. These are: marriage markets, marriage rates, and marital timing; cohabitation; evolutionary approaches to mate selection; romantic attachment; and relationship development and outcomes (for more information on topic and how it was coded, see Surra et al., 2002). When writing the review of each topic, we concentrated on the articles identified in the eight journals, although when necessary we included other important sources to round out our conclusions. Not all articles coded within a topic are included in the review. (Contact the first author for a list of references of the coded articles.)

Sampling Issues in Articles Reviewed

After identifying articles for the review, we still found it difficult to interpret how relevant the findings were to our review because of problems with the samples used. As a result, we decided to code systematically the marital status of the samples reported in each article. We coded whether the study was done on a married sample, a nonmarried sample, a combination of the two, or whether the marital status was unspecified. Cohabitors were considered nonmarried. Unspecified samples were those in which no information or insufficient information was given to ascertain whether the sample was marital. If the sample was a combination of married and nonmarried, we also coded whether the data were analyzed in a way that separated out the effects or findings by marital status (see Surra et al., 2002, for more details).

The coding revealed that 28% of the articles relied on nonmarried samples; however, an even larger percentage (36%) relied on combinations of married and nonmarried samples. Of the articles that combined marrieds and nonmarrieds in one sample, roughly half (49%) lumped them together in the analysis, and in the other half (51%), the two statuses were analyzed separately. Another 5% of the articles relied on married samples to study mate selection or premarital relationships, and in the remaining 32% of the articles, the status of the sample was unspecified. The majority of unspecified samples was college students, and we can guess that some small percentage of individuals in most of these samples was married. In some cases, authors noted that the individuals in the sample were not dating or not married, but they did not tell what relationships they were in, if any.

Thus, readers of the literature on premarital relationships and mate selection, including this review, should proceed with caution. Most research is done on mixed samples of married and nonmarried individuals or on samples in which the marital status is unreported. Researchers may be assuming that the phenomena under investigation behave the same way, regardless of the type of relationship or its developmental stage. We argue that such assumptions should be put to empirical test. In our review, we note how the conclusions drawn are likely to be affected by sampling concerns.

DEMOGRAPHIC CHANGES, MARITAL TIMING, AND MARRIAGE RATES

Mate selection has undergone major demographic changes in recent decades. First, nonmarital relationships, such as cohabitating unions, have become increasingly common and, for some individuals, have replaced marriage as the natural developmental endpoint of a lifelong relationship (Bernhardt & Goldscheider, 2001; Sassler & Schoen, 1999). Second, because rates of marriage have declined for persons age 20 to 29, families increasingly have been formed outside of marriage through nonmarital childbirth (South & Lloyd, 1992; the effect of nonmarital childbirth on the transition to first marriage has been reviewed by Seltzer, 2000). Last, and perhaps most influential to marital timing, from 1970 to 2000, the median age at first marriage increased by 3.6 years for men from 23.2 to 26.8 years and by 4.3 years for women from 20.8 to 25.1 years (U.S. Bureau of the Census, 2001). The number of individuals who will ever marry, 9 out of 10, has remained consistent with historical numbers (Goldstein & Kenney, 2001; Sassler & Schoen, 1999). Various theories suggest that the increase in age at marriage can be explained by greater prevalence and acceptance of remaining single longer, by increases in cohabitation (Sassler & Schoen, 1999), by greater selectivity in partner choice (Ahuvia & Adelman, 1992), or by decreased economic opportunities over the life course (Cooney & Hogan, 1991). Given these trends in marital timing, researchers have explored the mechanisms behind the changes.

The transition to first marriage plays out in local areas called marriage markets (Lichter, LeClere, & McLaughlin, 1991). Because these markets function at the community level, they are based on the principles of propinquity, defined as individuals' proximity in geographic space and time (Fossett & Kiecolt, 1991). Within these markets, individuals exchange economic and interpersonal assets in search of a partner. The process of mate selection is thought to occur in three stages: Individuals first seek information about potential partners, then determine the quality of match with a potential partner, and then interact more deeply with a partner to choose to form or reject a relationship (Sassler & Schoen, 1999). Marriage markets are thought to determine availability of mates. If markets provide plenty of opportunities for good matches with potential partners (e.g., homogamous social characteristics, never-married status, childlessness, and good economic opportunities), more people are likely to get married; however, if there is a shortage of potential partners of one sex, the opposite sex will experience a marriage squeeze. Research done on trends in the 1980s showed that women typically are caught in this squeeze with a scarcity of men; this is especially true of African American women (South & Lloyd, 1992).

To measure the effects of the marriage squeeze, researchers have used the sex ratio to predict mate selection outcomes, such as marriage, age at marriage, nonmarital fertility, and sexual behavior (Fossett & Kiecolt, 1991). This ratio is usually computed within each separate marriage market as the number of men divided by the number of women; however, the count of men and women within a market will vary greatly if factors such as race, age of available partners, marital status, institutionalization, and employment are considered. Most research using the sex ratio has focused on the shortage of marriageable men, especially for African American women (South & Lloyd, 1992), and the effects of men's economic opportunities as an exclusionary factor in sex ratios (Fossett & Kiecolt, 1991; Sassler & Schoen, 1999). The calculation of the ratio may differ depending on one's theoretical perspective but should exclude segments of the population who are unlikely to make the transition to first marriage, such as those who are too young, too old, or institutionalized (Fossett & Kiecolt, 1991, 1993). Although this ratio mostly measures differences in the composition of the population, it also captures individual characteristics of respondents (Oropesa, Lichter, & Anderson, 1994).

Because racial and ethnic endogamy, or the tendency to marry within a group, is thought to influence mate choice, most of the research regarding the effects of race has used sex ratios computed within racial boundaries to predict marriage rates. Historical trends show that African Americans have lower marriage rates compared to Whites, especially African American women (Bulcroft & Bulcroft, 1993; Raley, 1996). These differences remain even after correcting for undercounts caused by a lack of participation of African American men in survey research (Raley, 2002). A consistent finding of this research is that the severe marriage squeeze placed on African American women is caused to a large degree by a shortage of marriageable African American men (Bulcroft & Bulcroft, 1993; Crowder & Tolnay, 2000; Fossett & Kiecolt, 1993; South & Lloyd, 1992). Significant predictors of the scarcity of marriageable African American men and the delay in marital timing include the negative outlook for African American men's economic opportunities (Lichter et al., 1991; Lichter, McLaughlin, Kephart, & Landry, 1992; South & Lloyd, 1992), a higher percentage of African American men institutionalized in prisons (Fossett & Kiecolt, 1991), and an increasing rate of interracial marriage among African American men (Crowder & Tolnay, 2000). Even though each of these factors contributes unique variance to the prediction of marital timing, sex ratios do not completely explain the effect of race in differences in marital timing (Lichter et al., 1991; Oropesa et al., 1994). Other significant predictors of the racial differences in marriage rates include African American males' negative attitudes toward marriage (Bulcroft & Bulcroft, 1993; South, 1993), the negative effect of residential segregation in large cities (Oropesa et al., 1994), and greater amounts of time spent in cohabiting unions (Raley, 1996).

In addition to the research on the marriage squeeze for African American women, researchers have uncovered differences for other racial and ethnic groups. Sex ratios may not be as important when studying Hispanics and Whites, who generally have less of a shortage of marriageable partners compared to African Americans. Hispanics also have a different set of predictors of marital timing; the predictors are thought to be affected by different cultural values and by greater interracial marriage of Hispanics than other minority groups. They appear most similar to Whites (Oropesa et al., 1994; South, 1993). Also, due to generational and cultural heterogeneity, researchers have suggested that Hispanics should not be treated as a monolithic group (Oropesa et al., 1994). Racial differences in marital timing should continue to be researched, especially as racial barriers weaken and the number of interracial relationships continues to increase.

In addition to the effect of race, researchers have explored the impacts of men's and women's economic opportunities on their marital choices. Men's labor force participation has been shown to have a positive effect on women's marriage behavior (Cooney & Hogan, 1991; Fossett & Kiecolt, 1991; South & Lloyd, 1992). Because the magnitude of this effect is so strong, researchers have suggested that labor force participation be required of males for their inclusion in sex ratios (Fossett & Kiecolt, 1991) or that it be given more attention by itself in research rather than the focus of sex ratios (Lichter et al., 1991). A closer look at the effects of a lack of economic opportunities for men showed that under the age of 25, it reduced the likelihood of marriage, but surprisingly, it increased the likelihood of marriage for men over 26 (Cooney & Hogan, 1991). Given the magnitude of the impact of men's economic opportunities, more research is needed, especially as economic conditions or other period effects change over time.

Researchers also have explored the impact of women's economic opportunities on declines in marriage rates. Contrary to the general positive effect of men's economic opportunities, economic theories of marriage, particularly those of Becker, suggest that women's labor force participation should have a negative effect on marital timing, allowing women the freedom to buy their way out of marriage (Goldstein & Kenney, 2001). The results of several studies, however, have demonstrated that women's opportunities do not have a negative effect on their rates of marriage; in fact, they have the same positive effect as men's economic opportunities (Goldstein & Kenney, 2001; Lichter et al., 1991; McLaughlin & Lichter, 1997; Qian & Preston, 1993; Sassler & Schoen, 1999; South & Lloyd, 1992). Although economic opportunities have been shown to affect marital rates, men and women may envision economic readiness for marriage differently (Sassler & Schoen, 1999).

Similar to the effect of men's and women's economic opportunities, education has a positive influence on the likelihood of marriage for both men and women (Goldstein & Kenney, 2001; McLaughlin & Lichter, 1997; Qian & Preston, 1993). This positive effect of education on marriage rates remained despite tight marriage market conditions for women (Qian & Preston, 1993). The gains to marrying a highly educated partner have grown with the importance individuals place on economic opportunities in marital choice and are thought to increase educational homogamy (Mare, 1991). Although the effect of education on the chance of ever marrying is positive, years spent in the pursuit of education have delayed entry into marriage for women (Goldstein & Kenney, 2001). The delay in entry into marriage has also been found for men when the effect of income is controlled (Bernhardt & Goldscheider, 2001). As more and more individuals attend college and the need for a college education increases, the impact of education on the delay in marital timing should continue to be explored.

The study of marriage markets has produced robust findings as to the structural influences of mate selection. Because of its focus on the transition to marriage, this research has avoided the problem of blurring marital statuses by using statistical models, such as hazard models, that use change in status as the dependent variable. Researchers, however, have acknowledged limitations and challenges in this research. One of these limitations lies in the fact that most of the research on marital timing has been done from a sociological perspective that is mainly concerned with macrofactors. This perspective primarily explores distal, structural predictors such as sex ratios, economic opportunities, and education as the sole predictors of marriage and marital timing. Researchers have acknowledged that these variables do not account for all of the variance in marriage and marital timing. Nor do they explain the mechanisms by which mate selection decisions are made (Mastekaasa, 1992). Research has shown, for example, that low marriage rates for African Americans may be a function of a proximal predictor, such as African American men's reluctance to marry, more than they are a function of distal predictors, such as sex ratios (South, 1993).

A second related limitation of this literature is the overreliance on large data sets. Although these data sets are representative of the population, most of the research so far has used one-dimensional variables such as sex ratios, employment, or educational levels. These data sets often lack microlevel or nonstructural variables such as attitudes, perceptions, or expectations that are apt to affect marital timing. Even if these microlevel variables are collected in large survey data sets, they tend to be measured unidimensionally, which is likely to limit the reliability and validity of the data. Given the volume of the research on macroinfluences on marital timing, the focus of the literature may need to shift to the individual and couple characteristics that influence the decision to marry. Collecting both macro- and microlevel data on marital timing will become crucial given changes in mate preferences, increases in interracial marriages, and the influence of formal intermediaries, such as dating services, on marriage (Ahuvia & Adelman, 1992; Buss, Shackelford, Kirkpatrick, & Larsen, 2001; Crowder & Tolnay, 2000).

COHABITATION IN MATE SELECTION AND PREMARITAL RELATIONSHIPS

Three perspectives predominate in attempts to address the relationship between cohabitation and marriage. The first perspective is that, for all intents and purposes, cohabitation is marriage. Cohabitors merely lack the piece of paper that would identify them as married individuals, but they behave as married individuals in all other ways. The second perspective is that cohabitation is a stage in courtship that is a logical progression from dating to marriage. Cohabitors use this period of time to test their compatibility and to decide whether to progress or terminate the relationship. The third perspective is that cohabitation is similar to being single. In this view, cohabitation is similar to dating a partner without intentions to marry and cohabitors behave in ways that closely resemble singlehood (Manning, 1993).

Cohabitation as a Marriage-Like Relationship

Cohabitation has been compared conceptually to marriage by several researchers, and this view has garnered some empirical support. Individuals enter cohabiting unions at almost the same age that previous generations of individuals married (Bumpass, Sweet, & Cherlin, 1991). Cohabitors and married individuals have qualitatively similar relationships if cohabitors have plans to marry their partner (Brown & Booth, 1996). Cohabitation relationships are also similar to marriages on racial homogamy (Schoen & Weinick, 1993), frequency of disagreements (Brown & Booth, 1996), female contraceptive and sexual behavior (Seltzer, 2000), and individual partners' levels of depression (Horwitz & White, 1998).

The results of research on the idea that cohabitation is marriage-like have not been altogether supportive, however. When plans to marry the cohabitation partner were not accounted for, but several demographic variables and relationship duration were, cohabitors had poorer relationship quality than marrieds (Brown & Booth, 1996). Marital relationships were happier, had lower conflict (Brown, 2000), and were less likely to be physically aggressive (Stets, 1991) than cohabiting relationships. One study found a strong relationship between marital status and happiness in 16 of 17 nations studied, but this association did not hold for cohabitors (Stack & Eshleman, 1998). Not all comparisons show deficiencies in cohabitations compared to marriages. Compared to married persons, cohabitors reported higher rates of interaction with their partners (Brown & Booth, 1996) and divided household labor more equally (Seltzer, 2000). Marital unions were more homogamous on age and religion (Schoen & Weinick, 1993), and cohabitation unions were more homogamous on earnings outside the home (Seltzer, 2000).

Cohabitation as a Stage of Premarital Relationships

Could cohabitation be a stage in courtship that couples progress through on the path to marriage? For pregnant White women in their 20s, there is support for this idea. If cohabitation were a stage in courtship before marriage, cohabiting women who found themselves pregnant would be more likely to legitimate their pregnancies through marriage than single women, a hypothesis that was supported (Manning, 1993). Evidence has shown that 50% of those recently married cohabited first (Bumpass et al., 1991). Fifty-one percent of the population surveyed in one study agreed that cohabitation was "all right," and 35% expressed a definite desire to cohabit (DeMaris & Rao, 1992). Another study found that 77% of those surveyed agreed that cohabitation is acceptable for couples who want to make sure their future marriage will last (Hall & Zhao, 1995). Thus, for a majority of persons, cohabitation has become an acceptable, even desirable, step toward marriage.

Cohabitation as Singlehood

Cohabitation has also been compared to singlehood in recent studies. If cohabitation is comparable to being single, single and cohabiting women who became pregnant should be equally likely to legitimate the pregnancy through marriage. Support was found for this hypothesis for pregnant Black and teenage White women (Manning, 1993). Cohabitors also were more similar to single persons in fertility plans (Landale & Fennelly, 1992; Schoen & Weinick, 1993), mental health (Horwitz & White, 1998), employment (Landale & Fennelly, 1992; Schoen & Weinick, 1993), financial matters (Schoen & Weinick, 1993), per capita income (Seltzer, 2000), and home ownership (Schoen & Weinick, 1993).

Quality and Stability of Cohabitation Relationships

Two measures of relationship success, quality and stability, are often used to examine the success of cohabiting relationships. One study of a nationally representative sample evaluated the subsequent quality of marriages that originated as cohabitations and found that married persons who once cohabited had lower quality marriages than those who married directly (Thomson & Colella, 1992). Marital quality was measured by ratings of relationship happiness, frequency of disagreements over seven items (e.g., household tasks, money), and assessment of communication skills during conflict.

Another way to assess relationship quality is to compare cohabiting relationships to marriages. In a study of a nationally representative sample, cohabiting couples had significantly poorer relationship quality than marrieds, even when relationship duration and demographic characteristics were controlled (Brown & Booth, 1996). Relationship quality was measured by reports of frequency of disagreement, perceptions of fairness, ratings of overall relationship happiness, and assessment of conflict management. When the researchers examined only cohabitors who reported plans to marry or thoughts of marrying their partners, the significant difference between married and cohabiting couples on relationship quality disappeared. In fact, cohabitors reported more interaction, operationalized as frequency of time spent alone with the partner in the previous month, than married persons. The majority of cohabiting relationships, however, did not differ from marital relationships on relationship quality.

A second dimension often utilized to judge relationship success is the stability of the relationship. Cohabitating relationships themselves are relatively short-lived; within $1\frac{1}{2}$ years, half of cohabiting couples have either married or ended the relationship (Bumpass et al., 1991). Only 1 in 10 cohabiting relationships are long-term relationships that rarely result in formal marriage (Bumpass & Sweet, 1989). Due to the temporary nature of and instability of cohabiting relationships, researchers often study the longevity of subsequent marriage to assess relationship stability. In one nationally representative sample, married respondents evaluated their perceptions of marital stability by rating their likelihood of eventual separation or divorce (Thomson & Colella, 1992). Couples who had cohabited were more likely than couples who had not cohabited to perceive some chance of divorce, and persons who had cohabited longer perceived a greater chance of divorce (Thomson & Colella, 1992). Premarital cohabitation was associated with a greater risk of divorce even after controlling for several variables, including parental divorce (Hall & Zhao, 1995). Previously cohabiting with others in addition to the spouse, or serial cohabitation, was the determining factor in perceptions of marital instability in a second nationally representative sample (DeMaris & MacDonald, 1993).

Selection as an Explanation for the Instability of Cohabitating Relationships

Several explanations have been offered for why cohabitation is associated with greater instability in subsequent marriage. One is that cohabitors are a select group of individuals who are predisposed to divorce to begin with. Axinn and Thornton (1992) found evidence of this selection effect; strong disagreement with divorce decreased the likelihood of entering into a cohabitating union, whereas strong agreement with divorce increased the likelihood of cohabiting, with a difference of 144% between the groups. These data were gathered using a 7-wave longitudinal study to assess both history of union formation and attitudes toward marriage and divorce between the ages of 15 and 23.5. Cohabitors were less committed to the institution of marriage (Brown & Booth, 1996; Thomson & Colella, 1992; Wu & Balakvishnan, 1994) and were more likely than noncohabitors to perceive a greater likelihood of divorce for problematic marriages (Thomson & Colella, 1992). Persons for whom being married is less important as a life goal were more likely to enter into cohabitation, rather than into marriage, as a first union (Clarkberg, Stolzenberg, & Waite, 1995). Thus, cohabitation itself may not cause marital dissolution. Instead, the association between cohabitation and marital instability may be due, in part, to the fact that people who cohabit are less traditional in their attitudes toward marriage (DeMaris & MacDonald, 1993; DeMaris & Rao, 1992; Hall & Zhao, 1995; Thomson & Colella, 1992) and less committed before marriage to a lifelong commitment (Thomson & Colella, 1992).

Some evidence suggests that the selection effect as an explanation for the connection between cohabitation and marital instability is weakening over time. Schoen (1992) detected differences in cohabitation behavior and subsequent marital stability over several generations, accomplished by tracking birth cohorts over a period of time in a nationally representative sample of women born between 1928 and 1957. Subsequent marriages for cohabitors generally were less stable than marriages for noncohabitors. However, for later cohorts, born between 1948 and 1957, the probability of instability of marriage preceded by cohabitation decreased. The author proposed that this decrease in instability for later birth cohorts is a result of a less select group of individuals choosing to cohabit. Cohabitation in earlier birth cohorts may have reflected individual departures from societal norms more than in later cohorts, where cohabitation is more common and occurs within a more diverse population.

Additional data indicate that selection does not fully account for the association between cohabitation and marital instability. The experience of cohabitation significantly changed attitudes toward divorce in the direction of nontraditionalism, even when attitudes toward divorce prior to cohabitation were controlled (Axinn & Thornton, 1992). The attractiveness of a cohabiting lifestyle was predicted by attitudes and beliefs about family; however, these beliefs did not explain the difference in marital stability between cohabitors and noncohabitors (DeMaris & MacDonald, 1993). These data indicate that the experience of cohabitation itself may cause changes that contribute to divorce.

Experience with the termination of one relationship may make it easier to end subsequent ones. As noted previously, only persons with cohabitation experiences that included others in addition to the current marital partner perceived greater instability in intact first marriages of up to 10 years duration (DeMaris & MacDonald, 1993). The difficulties associated with ending relationships (e.g., finding separate residences), which have the power to enhance commitments (Johnson, 1991), may lose some of their impact the more prior experience individuals have with the processes of terminating relationships.

An assumption often underlying the study of cohabitation and popular beliefs about it is that marriages will be more successful when partners cohabit beforehand because cohabitation is a good opportunity to screen out bad matches and test compatibility. As just described, support is weak for the hypothesis that the experience of living with one's potential marriage partner increases the stability of subsequent marriage. Even if cohabitation does increase marital stability because it allows opportunities for information gathering, this advantage may be offset by the change in commitment to the institution of marriage (Lillard, Brien, & Waite, 1995).

Research on cohabitation has several limitations. One of the most common in this research is reliance on retrospective reports of cohabitation, problematic due to faulty recall and telescoping (Axinn & Thornton, 1992; Hall & Zhao, 1995; Thomson & Colella, 1992). At times coupled with retrospective data collection, researchers have also gathered data from only one member of a couple. Research has shown that, in one fifth of cohabiting couples, partners disagreed on whether marriage was expected (Bumpass et al., 1991). The potential for partner disagreement is a problem for researchers who want to assign cohabitors into categories determined by their future plans (Casper & Sayer, 2000). Researchers also have haphazardly massed all cohabitors together, regardless of their intentions to marry their partner, previous cohabitation experience (Horwitz & White, 1998; Stets, 1991), or length of time cohabited (Thomson & Colella, 1992). There are several studies of cohabitors' perceptions of divorce (Axinn & Thornton, 1992; Brown & Booth, 1996; Thomson & Colella, 1992), with very few longitudinal studies of premarital cohabitation and actual divorce. As with all research, care should be used to embrace diverse samples including interracial couples and other heterogamous and nontraditional samples that are not based on convenience. Contrary to the image of cohabitation as a college-student phenomenon, cohabitation compensates for decreasing marriage rates the least for college students (Bumpass et al., 1991).

Even though cohabitation frequently is treated in demographic studies as a monolithic phenomenon, the research just reviewed indicates that it encompasses a great variety of relationship experiences. For the remainder of this chapter, we examine research on the evolutionary and psychological forces that help to account for the diversity of experiences in premarital relationships.

EVOLUTIONARY APPROACHES TO MATE SELECTION

Evolutionary psychology, based on Darwin's theories of natural and sexual selection, contends that innate, psychophysiological mechanisms embedded in humans guide their mate choices (Kenrick, Groth, Trost, & Sadalla, 1993; Simpson & Gangestad, 2001). Sexual selection, defined as the access to mates in terms of either quality or quantity, is primarily concerned with mate selection, attraction, and retention (Buss, Schakelford, Choe, Buunk, & Dijkstra, 2000; Simpson, & Gangestad, 2001). Individuals who are making mate choices are thought to consider cross-sex mate preferences, the desired permanence of the relationship sought, and the presence or absence of rivals (Schmitt & Buss, 1996). Individuals are believed to select partners who possess desired traits to enable their reproductive success and to promote the survival of their offspring (Kenrick et al., 1993; Singh, 1993). Parental investment theory further suggests that because one sex, usually the female, is more involved in the rearing of offspring, men and women seek different qualities in their mates (Simpson & Gangestad, 2001). Evolutionary psychology is primarily concerned with the explanation of sex differences in mate preferences (Kenrick et al., 1993).

The first of these sex differences is the commitment to mating relationships. Because women make a greater physical investment in child rearing, they must be very prudent in choosing a mate (Booth, Carver, & Granger, 2000; Kenrick et al., 1993). When asked about factors that would influence their choice of a partner for a 1-night stand, men were much less discriminating than women, but when asked about a marital partner in which their parental investment is much higher, men's selectivity approached that of women's (Kenrick, Sundie, Nicastle, & Stone, 2001; Kenrick et al., 1993). Thus, men's selectivity in mate choice may fluctuate with level of commitment and permanence of relationships much more than women's.

The majority of the research on mate preferences focuses on partners' economic resources and status, sexual behaviors and desires, perceptions of attractiveness, and physical health. According to the evolutionary perspective, women depend on their partners to provide for their offspring and value their partners' economic status much more than men do (Ben Hamida, Mineka, & Bailey, 1998). In a study of changes in mate preferences over the last 57 years, women's preference for economic status has increased when compared to other mate preferences (Buss et al., 2001). However, the association between attraction and women's desire for economic status has been shown to be curvilinear, with a desire primarily to avoid poverty and a ceiling effect of attraction with statuses above the middle class (Kenrick et al., 2001). Although men rate their preference for economic resources lower than women, men's preference for gaining economic resources from their mates has increased sharply in the last 57 years (Buss et al., 2001).

Regarding mate preferences for sexual behavior, to increase their ability to reproduce, men are thought to possess evolutionary psychological mechanisms that promote greater permissiveness and sexual availability in short-term mating relationships (Schmitt & Buss, 1996; Simpson & Gangestad, 1991). Men also must guard against contributing their resources to another man's child. Consistent with this view, heterosexual men have the highest levels of jealousy for sexual infidelity compared to heterosexual women and homosexual women and men (Bailey, Gaulin, Agyei, & Gladue, 1994).

In an effort to find a partner who is fertile and with genetic health, men more than women have been shown to prefer the health, beauty, and youth of their partners (Ben Hamida et al., 1998; Kenrick et al., 1993). Women prefer men who appear physically large, strong, and attractive, knowing they will be able to provide for and protect their offspring. Evidence of the predicted preferences for body size has been seen in research using the waist-to-hip ratio, a quantifiable, somatic measure of weight distribution that successfully predicts perceived attractiveness and potential health of individuals (Singh, 1993, 1995). Men preferred women with hourglass figures, or those with lower waist-to-hip ratios, whereas women preferred men with higher waist-to-hip ratios, a sign of strength and status. Both men's and women's preferences for attractive mates have increased in the last 57 years, compared to other mate preferences (Buss et al., 2001).

Although evolutionary researchers have enjoyed consistent, parsimonious prediction of sex differences in mate preferences, they have also acknowledged limitations and criticisms of the theory. Earlier in the chapter we suggested that the boundaries between marital statuses within research samples have been blurred; research on evolutionary approaches to mate selection is no exception. The vast majority of evolutionary research has been conducted on college-student samples; exceptions include the research of Bailey et al. (1994), Buss and Shackelford (1997), and that of Kenrick, Keefe, Bryan, Barr, and Brown (1995). Although it is likely that a vast majority of these individuals are single, it is unlikely that all are. Evolutionary psychologists would likely ascribe to the argument that mate preferences are instinctual and, therefore, would not be affected by relationship status, and perhaps as a result, relationship or marital status is generally not reported in this research. However, we would argue that relationship or marital status may bias mate preferences such that individuals' would likely be influenced by characteristics found in their current partners.

Second, another major criticism of evolutionary research is that it is preoccupied with mate preferences but not with eventual mate choice behaviors. Evolutionary researchers have asked individuals to rank characteristics they prefer in potential mates but do little to explain how these preferences actually play out in mate selection. They have used these preferences as evidence in support of their theory without explaining how or why people eventually choose the partners they do. Thus, even though men may desire attractive partners, some men may choose women who are judged to be unattractive but possess other redeeming qualities such as kindness or dependability. Similarly, even though women may desire economic resources, they may marry a less affluent man who is attentive and helpful.

An extension of this criticism is that influences on mating decisions are not all evolutionary and that the environment and social culture in which mates interact affects their selection preferences (Buss et al., 2001; Simpson & Gangestad, 2001). Evidence that demographic, economic, and social trends may affect mate preferences has been found in changes in mate preferences over time in a 50-year study (Buss et al., 2001). A multitheoretical approach integrating social, psychological, and exchange perspectives with evolutionary theory is necessary (Kenrick et al., 1993). Most of the evolutionary research has explored sex differences or between-group variation rather than individual differences or within-group variation, even though the variance in the latter is often greater (Bailey et al., 1994; Simpson, Gangestad, Christensen, & Leck, 1999). Although some evolutionary research has explored homosexual mating preferences, the theory offers little explanation for same-sex romantic relationships (Bailey et al., 1994; Kenrick et al., 1995; for a further review of evolutionary psychology or biosocial perspectives on the family, see Simpson & Gangestad, 2001, and Booth et al., 2000, respectively).

ADULT ROMANTIC ATTACHMENT

Research on adult romantic attachment has flourished since the publication of Hazan and Shaver's (1987) seminal paper linking attachment theory to adult romantic relationships. Of the articles that we reviewed, the most articles on any one topic were done on attachment (10.1% of the sample). Concerns about romantic attachment are important to insiders of relationships as well as to researchers. Data from open-ended interviews showed that individuals spontaneously mentioned issues that are relevant to attachment (Feeney & Noller, 1991). Almost 90% of respondents referenced one of the following five attachment issues: openness, closeness, dependence, commitment, or affection.

Our review of empirical studies indicates that researchers have applied attachment theory to examine a variety of behavioral and affective phenomena in dating relationships and mate selection. Researchers have conceptualized adult attachment in slightly different ways and have designed and utilized somewhat incongruous measurement tools to examine attachment. The result of this broad application of attachment theory, varied conceptualizations, and inconsistent measurement is a body of evidence that often seems scattered and disjointed. Adding to the confusion is the problem that researchers use different terminology to describe the attachment relationship, such as styles, patterns, or models of self and others. For clarity of writing, we use the term *attachment style*. We have limited our review of the attachment research to three subtopics that are directly connected to the themes of this chapter: partner preference and choice, gender differences, and accommodation.

Conceptualizations and Measurement of Attachment

Based on a history of experiences with a primary caregiver, infants are thought to develop models of how worthy of love and care they are and of how available and dependable others are (Bowlby, 1973). Researchers have suggested that these working models of self and others are carried into adulthood and resurface in romantic relationships (Bartholomew & Horowitz, 1991; Collins & Read, 1990; Hazan & Shaver, 1987). Hazan and Shaver (1987) first developed a three-category measure that identified adult attachment styles that directly correspond to the three patterns of infant attachment: secure, anxious-resistant, and avoidant (Ainsworth, Blehar, Waters, & Wall, 1978). The measure assesses individuals' cognitions and affective responses toward getting close to others, relying on others, and having others rely or depend on them. The three adult attachment styles were similarly named secure, anxious-ambivalent, and avoidant. Secure individuals have a trusting view of others and believe that they are worthy of others' responsiveness. Anxious-ambivalent individuals lack confidence that others consistently will respond to their needs and, as a result, are vigilant about signs of partners' availability and care. Avoidant individuals are not trusting of others and believe that they must be self-reliant in relationships. Bartholomew and Horowitz (1991) argued that attachment models can be described in terms of two orthogonal dimensions, self and other, each with positive and negative poles. This results in four attachment classifications: secure (positive self-views, positive views of others), preoccupied (negative self-views, positive views of others), dismissing-avoidants (positive self-views, negative views of others), and fearful-avoidants (negative self-views, negative views of other). The latter two classifications tend to be subcategories of Hazan and Shaver's (1987) original avoidant style. Still other researchers have developed continuous measures of confidence in the availability and dependability of others (Bartholomew & Horowitz, 1991; Collins & Read, 1990). Most of the research reviewed for this chapter utilized Hazan and Shaver's (1987) measure, Bartholomew and Horowitz's (1991) measures, or variations on these measures, none of which are directly comparable.

Partner Preference and Choice

The data examining how partner preference and choice relate to own and other's attachment styles provide mixed support for three competing hypotheses: the attachment-security hypothesis, the similarity hypothesis, and the complementarity hypothesis. The attachment-security hypothesis posits that individuals are attracted to and seek out partners who provide an opportunity to form a secure attachment bond (Chappell & Davis, 1998; Davis & Chappell, 1993; Latty-Mann & Davis, 1996). This hypothesis suggests that, similar to parent–child attachment relationships, a romantic attachment figure serves three important functions: a target for maintenance of proximity, a safe haven for comfort during distress, and a secure base for exploration (Hazan, Hutt, Sturgeon, & Bricker, 1991; Hazan & Shaver, 1994). Romantic partners most capable of providing these functions are securely attached partners, followed by preoccupied partners and avoidant partners. The similarity hypothesis suggests that individuals will be most attracted to and select partners who endorse models of self and others similar to their own. According to the complementarity hypothesis, individuals should be more attracted to and more likely to select partners who complement their models of self and others.

Attachment-Security Hypothesis. Some data support the attachment-security hypothesis. Studies of married couples and of seriously dating couples have higher proportions of secure individuals than studies that do not use relationship involvement as a criterion for inclusion in the study (Kirkpatrick & Davis, 1994; Kobak & Hazan, 1991; Senchak & Leonard, 1992). This finding suggests that partners' attractiveness is related, in part, to their ability to provide security. A self-report study of students and their mothers showed that individuals, regardless of their own attachment style, rated hypothetical, secure partners as more ideal than hypothetical, insecure partners (Latty-Mann & Davis, 1996). Individuals rated the preoccupied style as more ideal in comparison to the two avoidant styles. Findings from two different experimental studies also supported the attachment-security hypothesis (Chappell & Davis, 1998; Pietromonaco & Carnelley, 1994). In one study, individuals who imagined a secure partner, compared to individuals who imagined an anxious-ambivalent partner or an avoidant partner, reported more positive and less negative feelings about the hypothetical relationship, a greater likelihood that the hypothetical relationship would result in marriage, and more liking for the partner and enjoyment of the relationship (Pietromonaco & Carnelley, 1994). The other experimental study (Chappell & Davis, 1998) examined whether findings differed when the two avoidant categories were broken down by means of the Bartholomew and Horowitz (1991) measure. Individuals reported more positive emotions when imagining a secure partner than a preoccupied partner and even fewer positive emotions when imagining a fearful or a dismissing partner, and individuals reported significantly fewer negative emotions, particularly depression, when imagining a secure partner than all other insecure partners. The data also showed that, when asked about liking for, enjoyment of, and conflict or tension with the imagined partner, individuals explicitly preferred imaginary secure partners to all other insecure partners.

Additional evidence to support this hypothesis comes from studies that investigate the transference of attachment functions from parents to peers. Researchers have articulated a model that suggests that transferring attachment-related functions from parents to peers (best friends and romantic partners) follows a specific order (Hazan et al., 1991; Hazan, &

Shaver, 1994). First, proximity maintenance is transferred; individuals come to enjoy being in the presence of and protest separations from their peers. Next, individuals use their friends and romantic partners as a safe haven, turning to them for contact and reassurance when they are distressed. Finally, individuals use their peers as a secure base from which to explore their environment. Both individuals' own attachment style and perceived security of the peer appear to facilitate the process of transfer (Fraley & Davis, 1997). Individuals who viewed their romantic partners as insecure were less likely to have transferred their attachment functions from their parent to their romantic partner than individuals who viewed their romantic partner as secure. Furthermore, individuals who rated their romantic relationships as higher in mutual trust, intimacy, mutual caring, support, and sexual desire and fascination were more likely to have transferred their attachment functions from parents to romantic partners than individuals who rated their romantic relationships as lower in these qualities. The data imply that insecure partners afford fewer opportunities for security, and, therefore, individuals are more reluctant to use them as a source of proximity, a safe haven, and a secure base.

Similarity Hypothesis. Some data support the hypothesis that individuals prefer partners who have an attachment style similar to their own. This hypothesis is consistent with self-verification theory, which suggests that individuals prefer partners who verify their self-beliefs (Swann, 1992). A study of college-student dating couples showed that secure individuals were more satisfied with their relationships and more attracted to and more likely to be dating secure partners (Frazier, Byer, Fisher, Wright, & DeBord, 1996). Although this evidence also supports the attachment-security hypothesis, researchers have argued that other data show that not all individuals prefer secure partners. For example, data from the same study showed that anxious individuals were more likely to be dating anxious partners and reported more satisfaction in relationships with anxious partners. Anxious individuals were the most attracted to the possibility of a relationship with an anxious partner and the least attracted to the possibility of a relationship with an avoidant partner (Frazier et al., 1996). Thus, a correlational study of real partners showed the similarity effect with respect to secure–secure and anxious–anxious pairings, and only an experimental study of possible partners showed a preference for avoidant–avoidant pairings.

Complementarity Hypothesis. The complementarity hypothesis is that individuals should be most attracted to and choose partners who complement their own attachment styles. One longitudinal study of college-student couples who had steady or serious dating relationships found that male and female attachment styles were nonrandomly paired such that there were no anxious–anxious or avoidant–avoidant pairs (Kirkpatrick & Davis, 1994). These data suggest that, when relationship status is a criterion for sample inclusion, couples whose partners' attachment styles are not complementary are less likely to be included in the sample. Despite low rates of satisfaction, couples with avoidant men and anxious-ambivalent women were at least as stable over a 4-year period as couples with a secure–secure pairing. However, couples in which anxious-ambivalent men were paired with avoidant women were the least likely to remain together over the course of the study. The researchers interpreted their data to mean that pairings of avoidant men with anxious-ambivalent women confirm gender stereotypes, in which women are thought to be more relationship oriented and men, more aloof and less involved with the maintenance of their romantic relationships. This also confirms the types of models avoidants and anxious-ambivalents have of themselves and others.

Gender

The data on adult romantic attachment suggest that characteristics of both partners play a role in relationship functioning and quality but that this role may have patterns that are gendered. In a self-report study of 52 heterosexual, college-age couples, both men and women's relationship functioning was associated with their own and their partners' models of attachment (Carnelley, Pietromonaco, & Jaffe, 1994; Carnelley, Pietromonaco, & Jaffe, 1996). Both women and men who reported greater fearful avoidance also reported less relationship satisfaction and fewer positive exchanges with their partners. Only men's functioning was directly associated with their partners' model of attachment; men whose female partners reported greater preoccupation reported less satisfaction with their relationships. The pattern of findings, however, pointed to the possibility of an indirect connection between men's attachment styles and women's satisfaction, through her male partners' caregiving behaviors.

Other evidence suggests that, in hypothetical situations at least, women are more attuned to the effects of having an insecure partner. In an experimental study, researchers examined the effects of subjects' own and hypothetical partners' attachment styles on perceptions of the quality of romantic relationships and found that, regardless of their own attachment style, women were more likely than men to perceive both more negative and fewer positive effects of having a hypothetical insecure partner (Pietromonaco & Carnelley, 1994). For example, although women and men both liked hypothetical secure partners more than insecure partners, men liked their hypothetical insecure partners more than women did. Furthermore, regardless of their own attachment style, women reported a stronger belief that the hypothetical relationship would result in marriage if their imagined male partner were secure than if he were avoidant or preoccupied. Avoidant men reported a stronger likelihood that the relationship would result in marriage if they imagined a preoccupied partner than an avoidant partner.

As suggested earlier, particular pairings of avoidant men and anxious or preoccupied women are as stable as, but often poorer in quality than, relationships with secure–secure pairings (Kirkpatrick & Davis, 1994). Researchers who experimentally manipulated hypothetical partners' attachment style paid close attention to the effects of pairings that confirmed stereotypic gender roles of preoccupied women paired with avoidant men (Pietromonaco & Carnelley, 1994). Data showed that both men and women reported lower social self-esteem and feeling more depressed about the imagined relationship if they were paired with hypothetical partners who confirmed and exaggerated gender-role stereotypes (i.e., avoidant males and preoccupied females).

Accommodation

Accommodation refers to individuals' reacting in a constructive manner when their partners act in a destructive manner that threatens the relationship (Rusbult, Verette, Whitney, Slovik, & Lipkus, 1991). Responses to destructive behavior fall into four categories: voice, a constructive response that involves talking to the partner about the problem; loyalty, a constructive response that involves waiting patiently for partners to act better or turning the other cheek; exit, a destructive response that involves walking away from the partner or leaving the relationship; and neglect, a destructive response that involves lacking attention to or maintenance of the relationship. Researchers have explored whether attachment style, which predisposes people to trust others more or less easily, is related to accommodation. A meta-analysis has shown that when confronted with a partner acting destructively, compared to insecure individuals, secure individuals were more likely to use voice (Gaines et al., 1997). Studies have also shown that secure attachment is positively correlated with voice and negatively correlated with exit and neglect. Scharfe and Bartholomew (1995) found, however, that the pattern of destructive and constructive results was qualified by sex differences. For men only, the higher the rating of security, the more likely they were to use voice. Although both men and women were more likely to use exit as security declined, only men were more likely to use neglect as security declined. Findings pertaining to the association between loyalty and attachment style are inconsistent.

The findings relating insecure attachment to accommodation are less clear. The evidence suggests that, in comparison to secure individuals, insecure individuals are more likely to use exit and neglect (Gaines et al., 1997). Due to differences in measurement, the evidence is still mixed as to how insecure individuals differ in their use of accommodation strategies. Studies utilizing Hazan and Shaver's (1987) three-category measure found no clear differences between individuals classified as avoidant and anxious-ambivalent in their reactions during accommodative dilemmas (Gaines et al., 1997). A study utilizing a measure derived from Bartholomew and Horowitz's (1991) four-category framework, however, found that fearfulness was positively associated with neglect for both women and men. For men only, fearfulness was positively associated with exit and negatively associated with voice (Scharfe & Bartholomew, 1995).

The association between attachment style and accommodating responses may vary with depth of involvement. A meta-analysis of four studies indicated that attachment style was more strongly related to accommodation in married than in dating samples (Gaines et al., 1997).

Several problems have yet to be resolved in the literature on adult romantic attachment. Most of what we know about this topic is from research conducted on young adults, mostly college students, and couples who do not have a long relationship history. The question remains about whether findings will hold true in random or community samples or samples of different relationship statuses (e.g., dating vs. married partners). In addition, the literature is plagued with measurement disunity. Patterns of findings differ, depending on whether a three-category, a four-category, or a continuous measure of attachment is used. Researchers in this area disagree about which measure is most appropriate for assessing adult romantic attachment and why. Because of this, findings are difficult to compare across studies.

DEVELOPMENT AND OUTCOMES OF PREMARITAL RELATIONSHIPS

In this section, we review literature aimed at describing and explaining how premarital relationships change over time. Consistent with the goal of this chapter, we focus on outcomes that concern why partners do or do not become increasingly involved and committed over time and what makes relationships last or dissolve over the long term. Research on these topics conducted during the past 10 years has been marked by strong theory and longitudinal designs. As a result, we know much more about change in these relationships over time than we did 10 years ago. Research falls into one of three camps: studies of interdependence and social exchange theories, studies of contextual models, and studies of insiders' accounts of the development of their relationships.

Social Exchange and Interdependence Theories

Studies have shown that variables derived from social exchange theory and from investment or interdependence models predict commitment, satisfaction, and stability in dating relationships, although predictability is much stronger for some outcomes than others. Typically, these models include Rusbult's investment model of commitment (Rusbult, 1980, 1983); more recently, her model of commitment as dependence on a relationship (Wieselquist, Rusbult, Agnew, & Foster, 1999), or models that are close relatives of the investment model.

Predictors of Satisfaction.   Research in this decade confirmed earlier work (Rusbult, 1980, 1983) showing that specific rewards derived from resources exchanged in heterosexual dating relationships were the strongest predictors of satisfaction in relationships and increases in satisfaction over time (Sprecher, 2001). Recent evidence has suggested, however, that the connection between rewards and satisfaction was stronger for women than for men (Sprecher, 2001). The association between rewards and satisfaction generalizes from opposite-sex to same-sex romantic relationships. For gay and lesbian partners, rewards predicted satisfaction in cross-sectional analyses (Kurdek, 1991), but linear decreases in rewards did not uniquely predict linear decreases in satisfaction over a 5-year period (Kurdek, 1992).

Variables from the investment model other than rewards relate to satisfaction as well. In cross-sectional analyses, alternatives to the relationship uniquely predicted satisfaction for both men and women (Sprecher, 2001). Neither alternatives nor investments predicted change in satisfaction over a 6-month period, however. With respect to gay and lesbian partners, linear changes in relationship satisfaction over a 4-year period were uniquely predicted by changes in the interdependence model variables of alternatives and investments (Kurdek, 1992). Earlier findings had indicated that costs were not associated with or only weakly associated with satisfaction in heterosexual relationships (Rusbult, 1980, 1983). Yet in the relationships of gay and lesbian partners, costs were associated with less satisfaction (Kurdek, 1991), and linear decreases in costs were associated with linear increases in satisfaction measured over a 4-year period (Kurdek, 1992). Costs were measured differently in the Kurdek and Rusbult studies, however. In the Kurdek studies, costs were measured using the consensus subscale of the dyadic adjustment scale, an assessment of agreement on a variety of content areas (e.g., finances). Rusbult measured costs in terms of conflict, similarity, personal qualities, and a range of other issues. Kurdek (1992) noted that some of his findings may be due to similarities in the wording of the independent and dependent variables.

Sprecher (2001) examined how well a construct derived from social exchange theory, inequity in resources, explained satisfaction. She found that satisfaction for men was best predicted by underbenefiting inequity, measured as the extent to which the partner was perceived as getting the better deal in the exchange of resources relative to the self. Some evidence suggested that the less men perceived that they were underbenefited at one point in time, the greater was the increase in their satisfaction 1 year later. In a longitudinal study of cohabiting gay, lesbian, and married couples, Kurdek (1998) found that initial perceptions of equal contributions to the relationship predicted increases in satisfaction over a 5-year period.

Predictors of Commitment. Findings that pertain to the predictors of commitment differ somewhat from findings that pertain to satisfaction and, on the whole, are less strong. In cross-sectional analyses of a heterosexual, college-student dating sample, the best predictors of commitment for both genders were alternatives and investments; rewards predicted commitment only for men, and underbenefiting inequity predicted it for women (Sprecher, 2001). Increases in commitment over a 6-month period for women were predicted by initially higher levels of investments, but none of the other predictors from the investment model predicted change in commitment over time. For men, earlier reports of underbenefiting inequity did predict increases in commitment over 1 year's time. Virtually no results were found for overbenefiting inequity. Wieselquist et al. (1999) predicted commitment in two studies from a composite measure of dependence that included items measuring satisfaction, alternatives, and investments. One study included a sample of primarily dating partners along with some married partners, and the second study included only married partners. The findings were the same for both samples: Dependence strongly predicted commitment in cross-sectional analyses but marginally predicted change over time. Investment model variables also predicted commitment in two samples of Dutch daters, American daters, and American married couples (Van Lange, Rusbult, Drigotas, Arriaga, Witcher, & Cox, 1997).

Kurdek (2000) studied how attractions to relationships and constraints that keep individuals from ending relationships predicted changes in commitment over 5 years for lesbian, gay, and heterosexual married partners. Attractions included measures of rewards, costs, match to comparison level, and alternatives, whereas constraints included investments and barriers to leaving the relationship. Changes in attractions and in constraints predicted changes in commitment for all types of partners, even when satisfaction was controlled. High average levels of own constraints predicted high average levels of commitment best under conditions where the average levels of own and partners' attractions were low.

Predictors of Stability Over Time. In a careful operationalization of the concept comparison level for alternatives, Drigotas and Rusbult (1992) measured the extent to which breakups can be explained by means of dependence on relationships for need satisfaction. The importance of and satisfaction with such needs as companionship, sex, and intimacy were assessed in college-student individuals who were in dating relationships at some point during an 8- to 9-week period. Respondents also rated whether and how much each need was being satisfied in a specific alternative relationship. Need dependence was assessed in two ways: (a) as the extent to which needs were satisfied in the current relationship relative to alternatives and (b) as the discrepancy between need satisfaction in the current and alternative relationships, weighted by the importance of the need. Need dependence consistently predicted breakups in two studies much more strongly than either need satisfaction in current relationships or need satisfaction in alternative relationships. Those who stayed in relationships had higher need dependence scores than those who were abandoned by their partners. Other evidence indicated that commitment fully mediated the association between need dependence and whether or not individuals broke up.

In a study of breakups over a 5-year period in heterosexual couples, the best unique predictor from among a set of social exchange variables, satisfaction, and commitment was women's reports of commitment (Sprecher, 2001). Another study of investment model variables found that the breakup of gay and lesbian relationships over a 4-year period was related to lower investments (Kurdek, 1998). High levels of barriers to termination, a variable derived from commitment theory, predicted dissolution for lesbian partners, whereas low levels of barriers predicted termination for married partners. It may be that over the 5 years of this study, the level of barriers changed over time to precipitate breakup.

Research on the predictors of stability over time suggests that it is harder to predict stability from social exchange and interdependence variables than it is from satisfaction or commitment. This may be due, in part, to the fact that method variance is less for stability than for either of the other variables.

The Contextual Model of Relationships

The basic premise of Bradbury and Fincham's (1991) contextual model of relationships is that both intrapersonal and dyadic factors affect satisfaction with relationships. Partners' intrapersonal characteristics, such as their personalities or beliefs about relationships, are thought to form a distal context that affects the way in which partners process information about interactions. The proximal context is the momentary thoughts and behaviors that occur during interaction. Proximal factors are thought to mediate the impact of the distal context on relationship quality.

Studies have assessed the value of the contextual model for predicting the development and outcomes of premarital relationships. Fitzpatrick and Sollie (1999) operationalized the distal context in terms of three intrapersonal attributes, the value placed on autonomy and on attachment, and unrealistic relationship beliefs or standards. The proximal context was measured based on three behaviors, self-disclosure, positive and negative socioemotional behaviors, and style of conflict resolution. For both male and female respondents, the distal factors of attachment motivation and standards for relationships had direct and indirect effects on satisfaction. Not only proximal factors, especially self-disclosure, but also positive behaviors and compromising conflict tactics were important to satisfaction. Initial reports of attachment motives, positive behaviors, and self-disclosure predicted breakup 6 months later.

In a study of the contextual model in gay and lesbian relationships, Kurdek (1991) measured the distal factors of satisfaction with social support, expressiveness, dysfunctional relational beliefs, and self-consciousness, and variables from the investment model as mediators. Proximal variables were six conflict resolution strategies for constructive problem solving. Problem solving and investment variables were directly related to satisfaction and mediated the link between contextual variables and satisfaction. Investment variables were directly related to problem solving and fully mediated the effects of the contextual variables on problem solving. Contextual variables, in turn, were directly related to investment variables. Variables from the investment model consistently explained satisfaction better than did variables from either the contextual model or the problem-solving or conflict resolution model.

Measurement Issues

At first glance, the findings just described seem to provide a fairly lucid account of how variables from social exchange, interdependence, and contextual approaches explain the development of premarital relationships. The coherence of the findings is not as strong as it appears, however. One difficulty is that variables given the same names frequently are measured quite differently in different studies. Alternatives, for example, were measured using items that assess the importance placed on activities outside of the relationship (Kurdek, 1992), items that assess the availability and quality of alternatives compared to the present partner (Sprecher, 2001), and items that assess the quality of alternatives as part of a larger dependence scale (Wieselquist et al., 1997). Differences in measurement are problematic when comparing findings across studies.

Another difficulty is that some of the covariance between and among independent and dependent variables is surely due to the fact that instruments are tapping into the same construct or a general positivity toward the relationship. In some cases, independent and dependent variables are so highly correlated that empirically, at least, they are the same variable. Kurdek (1991) found such high correlations between two dependent variables, satisfaction and commitment, that he dropped commitment from the analyses, but not all researchers report the degree of intercorrelation among independent and dependent variables. Researchers frequently report results from many different models within the same study, including tests of both univariate and multivariate models, tests of combinations of different independent variables, and tests with different orders of entry of the same variables. Because of moderate to high intercorrelations among independent variables, such tests yield conflicting results. In two of the studies just reviewed, for example, researchers found support for alternative causal orderings (Kurdek, 1991; Sprecher, 2001). Future work might employ structural equation modeling to develop more sound measurement models, to test hypothesized models, and to compare statistically the adequacy of more than one model for accounting for the observations.

Variables from the social exchange, interdependence, and contextual approaches have good power for explaining relationship outcomes regardless of the sexual orientation of the sample (gay, lesbian, heterosexual). However, how well these approaches predict outcomes for different relationship statuses (e.g., married vs. nonmarried) is unclear because of differences in the samples used across studies and in the way relationship status is analyzed within studies.

A question that remains for understanding mate selection is the developmental progression and regression of relationships as they move through time. In order to understand mate selection more fully, alternative measures of developmental change, such as progressions or regressions in global commitment or commitment to marry, increases or decreases in stage of involvement (e.g., causal vs. serious dating), and length of relationship, should be examined. How well these models predict alternative indicators of developmental change is yet to be determined.

Accounts of Changes in Involvement Over Time

Studies that examine insiders' accounts of how their relationships developed over time provide a view of variations in developmental change that is difficult to obtain with questionnaires. In addition, this research provides information about how individuals' early explanations for developmental changes relate to long-term outcomes of relationships.

Surra and colleagues (Surra & Gray, 2000; Surra & Hughes, 1997) have identified a typology of developmental changes in commitment to wed. The typology is based on two sources of data: (a) graphs of changes in commitment to marrying the partner, drawn retrospectively from the time the relationship began to the present; and (b) accounts of why each upturn or downturn in the graph occurred. Two types were identified initially in a sample of college-student daters, and the typology was replicated in a random sample of daters: relationship driven and event driven. For relationship-driven partners, changes in commitment were mostly positive in direction and moderate in rate. The reasons for changes given by relationship-driven partners more often referred to activities and time spent with the partner and positive beliefs about the relationship. They also referred more to the couple's interaction with the network and to positive beliefs about the network. Findings for event-driven partners showed that changes in commitment were more often negative in direction, and the rate of both positive and negative changes was fast. The accounts of commitment for these partners were dominated by references to conflict, negative beliefs about the relationship and about the network, and each partner's separate interaction with the network. Compared to event-driven individuals, relationship-driven individuals reported less conflict, less ambivalence about getting involved, more satisfaction initially, and greater increases in satisfaction over a 1-year period. Relationship-driven women also were more similar to their partners on preferences for leisure activities. Despite these differences, the two types did not differ on any measure of depth of involvement, love, or stability of the relationship over 1 year.

Using a random sample of couples, Surra and Gray (2000) tested hypotheses derived from commitment theory to explain why event-driven partners might stay involved in their seemingly problematic relationships. Contrary to the hypothesis that event-driven partners stayed involved because of structural constraints, event-driven women reported that they would have an easier time replacing their partners, and event-driven men reported that they would be better off economically without their partners, compared to relationship-driven men and women. Relationship-driven men reported that they desired alternative partners less than did event-driven men, but the two groups did not differ on friendship-based love or passionate love. In addition, event-driven partners were more likely to explain changes in commitment in terms of self-attributions than were relationship-driven partners, suggesting that they believe it is something about them that is responsible for problems and changes in commitment, rather than something about their relationship. Event-driven partners had greater ambivalence about serious involvement and less trust in the benevolence and in the honesty of their partners. These findings suggest that uncertainty about whether they can trust their partners might explain the rocky ups and downs in the relationships of event-driven partners. Taken together, the results suggest that, because of their uncertainty and lack of trust, event-driven partners might be hypervigilant for diagnostic information about commitment. Uncertainty may prompt them to remain involved, despite the fact they know they can do better elsewhere.

Using a similar technique with a racially diverse sample, Orbuch, Veroff, and colleagues (Orbuch, Veroff, & Holmberg, 1993; Veroff, Sutherland, Chadiha, & Ortega, 1993) had newlywed spouses jointly reconstruct from memory the progression of their courtship. They coded the accounts for their content and the collaborative process between spouses. Accounts that were dominated by a nonromantic plot predicted greater well-being after 3 years of marriage. For White, but not Black, couples, reports of not having to overcome obstacles during courtship were associated with greater well-being 3 years later. For all but Black husbands, greater conflict between spouses during story telling was related to lower marital well-being. Elsewhere, we have discussed the similarities between nonromantic plots in these studies and relationship-driven commitments (Surra, Batchelder, & Hughes, 1995).

Dialectical Approaches to Relationship Development

Dialectical approaches offer good possibilities for understanding how relationships change over time (Baxter & Erbert, 1999; Baxter & Montgomery, 1996; Montgomery, 1993). Dialectical theory assumes that relationships are in a constant state of flux due to the action of opposing forces. Opposing forces may reside within the relationship or its environments. Research by Baxter and Erbert (1999), using a turning point analysis of graphs of relationships, showed that internal dialectics were more important than were external dialectics in explaining relationship change. Autonomy–connectedness was the most central dialectic, but the dialectic of openness–closedness was also important in explaining turning points. The external dialectics of inclusion–seclusion and revelation–concealment were more central to turning points that involved interaction with the network. Because the study of dialectics is compatible with approaches that rely on descriptions of relationship stages or phases, dialectics may help researchers to distinguish between changes that sustain, redefine, or deteriorate relationships (Montgomery, 1993).

When it comes to understanding mate selection, studies of insiders' views are especially useful because they tap into the factors that individuals themselves use to explain their decisions about whether to increase or decrease involvement. Although it is assumed that, when making accounts, individuals pay attention to interaction patterns, including the exchange of resources, conflict, compatibility, and the like, we found no studies of the interactions that insiders use as sources of data about their relationships. Future studies might provide a more complete picture by examining the connections between insiders' accounts and more objective measures of interaction.

Investigations that rely on retrospective methods to obtain a continuous picture of change underscore the idea that measures of variability in change in commitment are at least as important as measures of level of commitment (see Surra, Hughes, & Jacquet, 1999). Similarly, an investigation of fluctuations in satisfaction over 10 weeks showed that individuals who ended their newly formed dating relationships within 4 months had greater variability in satisfaction ratings, even after controlling for the level of satisfaction

(Arriaga, 2001). Thus, measures of variability in level of key relationship constructs may provide a more discerning explanation of developmental change than do measures of level alone.

All of the studies in this section left unanswered one key question: Do the nature and extent of developmental change vary, depending on the depth, stage, or length of relationship involvement to begin with? Clearly, involvement at the first time of observation should have something to do with subsequent change. Yet little information typically was given about initial levels of involvement, and researchers rarely studied whether the pattern of change differed by initial level. The assumption seems to be that constructs under investigation will behave in the same way regardless of initial levels of involvement (for an exception, see Fletcher, Simpson, & Thomas, 2000). In many cases, for example, married individuals are assumed to change in the same way that dating individuals do, and the possibility of different patterns of developmental change for the two groups goes untested. Much of the change in relationships may happen at initial stages or in stages of growth that go undetected in investigations that concentrate on deterioration or breakup. In future investigations, where relationships were at the start of a study may be as important as where they ended up.

CONCLUSIONS

The beauty, and the inelegance, of research on mate selection and premarital relationships flow from the same source: the attention this research gets from many disciplines. It would be nice to say that the research is interdisciplinary, but, for the most part, it is not. Instead, we are left with a set of threads that weave together a frayed fabric. From sociology comes the study of societal trends in and structural and economic influences on mate choice. From evolutionary psychology, we have research on the backdrop of mate choice formed by gendered preferences for partners who possess certain characteristics. From developmental and social psychology and interpersonal communication, we have the study of romantic attachment style, interdependence, and other, more general processes that characterize the functioning of premarital (and other close) relationships.

The problem, of course, is that the threads, although by themselves strong and interesting to look at, do not form a fabric we can easily live with. The connections between the disciplinary threads are lacking; for example, we know little about how preferences studied by evolutionary psychologists interact with more social psychological variables that help to explain how relationships change. We know less about how social psychological constructs operate within the structure of marriage markets. Although many such connections are possible, they have yet to be explored. The upshot of the disconnection is that the topic of mate choice is separate from the topic of premarital relationships. For those of us interested in the linkages between them, the gaps leave large holes in our scholarly garb. Leave it for researchers in the next decade to repair the threads.

AUTHOR NOTE

The authors gratefully acknowledge the assistance of Anita Vangelisti and Marko Jarvis with the preparation of this chapter.

REFERENCES

Ahuvia, A. C., & Adelman, M. B. (1992). Formal intermediaries in the marriage market: A typology and review. *Journal of Marriage and the Family, 54*, 452–463.

Ainsworth, M. D. S., Blehar, M. C., Waters, E., & Wall, S. (1978). *Patterns of attachment: A psychological study of the Strange Situation.* Hillsdale, NJ: Lawrence Erlbaum Associates.

Arriaga, X. B. (2001). The ups and downs of dating: Fluctuations in satisfaction in newly formed romantic relationships. *Journal of Personality and Social Psychology, 80*, 754–765.

Axinn, W. G., & Thornton, A. (1992). The relationship between cohabitation and divorce: Selectivity or causal influence? *Demography, 29*, 357–373.

Bailey, J. M., Gaulin, S., Agyei, Y., & Gladue, B. A. (1994). Effects of gender and sexual orientation on evolutionary relevant aspects of human mating psychology. *Journal of Personality and Social Psychology, 66*, 1081–1093.

Bartholomew, K., & Horowitz, L. M. (1991). Attachment styles among young adults: A test of a four-category model. *Journal of Personality and Social Psychology, 61*, 226–244.

Baxter, L. A., & Erbert, L. A. (1999). Perceptions of dialectical contradictions in turning points of development in heterosexual romantic relationships. *Journal of Social and Personal Relationships, 16*, 547–569.

Baxter, L. A., & Montgomery, B. M. (1996). *Relating: Dialogues and dialectics.* New York: Guilford Press.

Ben Hamida, S., Mineka, S., & Bailey, J. M. (1998). Sex differences in perceived controllability of mate value: An evolutionary perspective. *Journal of Personality and Social Psychology, 75*, 953–966.

Bernhardt, E. M., & Goldscheider, F. K. (2001). Men, resources, and family living: The determinants of union and parental status in the United States and Sweden. *Journal of Marriage and Family, 63*, 793–803.

Booth, A., Carver, K., & Granger, D. (2000). Biosocial perspectives on the family. *Journal of Marriage and the Family, 62*, 1018–1034.

Bowlby, J. (1973). *Attachment and loss: Vol. 2. Separation: Anxiety and Anger.* New York: Basic Books.

Bradbury, T., & Fincham, F. (1991). A contextual model for advancing the study of marital interaction. In G. Fletcher & F. Fincham (Eds.), *Cognition in close relationships* (pp. 127–147). Hillsdale, NJ: Lawrence Erlbaum Associates.

Brown, S. L. (2000). Union transitions among cohabitors: The significance of relationship assessments and expectations. *Journal of Marriage and the Family, 62*, 833–846.

Brown, S. L., & Booth, A. (1996). Cohabitation versus marriage: A comparison of relationship quality. *Journal of Marriage and the Family, 58*, 668–678.

Bulcroft, R. A., & Bulcroft, K. A. (1993). Race differences in attitudinal and motivational factors in the decision to marry. *Journal of Marriage and the Family, 55*, 338–355.

Bumpass, L. L., & Sweet, J. A. (1989). National estimates of cohabitation. *Demography, 26*, 615–625.

Bumpass, L. L., Sweet, J. A., & Cherlin, A. (1991). The role of cohabitation in declining rates of marriage. *Journal of Marriage and the Family, 53*, 913–927.

Buss, D. M., & Shackelford, T. K. (1997). From vigilance to violence: Mate retention tactics in married couples. *Journal of Personality and Social Psychology, 72*, 346–361.

Buss, D. M., Shackelford, T. K., Choe, J., Buunk, B. P., & Dijkstra, P. (2000). Distress about mating rivals. *Personal Relationships, 7*, 235–243.

Buss, D. M., Shackelford, T. K., Kirkpatrick, L. A., & Larsen, R. J. (2001). A half century of mate preferences: The cultural evolution of values. *Journal of Marriage and Family, 63*, 491–503.

Carnelley, K. B., Pietromonaco, P. R., & Jaffe, K. (1994). Depression, working models of others, and relationship functioning. *Journal of Personality and Social Psychology, 66*, 127–140.

Carnelly, K. B., Pietromonaco, P. R., & Jaffe, K. (1996). Attachment, caregiving, and relationship functioning in couples: Effects of self and partner. *Personal Relationships, 3*, 257–278.

Casper, L. M., & Sayer, C. (2000). *Cohabitation transitions: Different attitudes and purposes, different paths.* Paper presented at the Annual Meeting of the Population Association of America, Los Angeles, March 2000.

Chappell, K. D., & Davis, K. E. (1998). Attachment, partner choice, and perception of romantic partners: An experimental test of the attachment-security hypothesis. *Personal Relationships, 5*, 327–342.

Clarkberg, M., Stolzenberg, R. M., & Waite, L. J. (1995). Attitudes, values, and entrance into cohabitational versus marital unions. *Social Forces, 74*, 609–634.

Collins, N. L., & Read, S. J. (1990). Adult attachment, working models, and relationship quality in dating couples. *Journal of Personality and Social Psychology, 58*, 644–663.

Cooney, T. M., & Hogan, D. P. (1991). Marriage as an institutionalized life course: First marriage among American men in the twentieth century. *Journal of Marriage and the Family, 53*, 178–190.

Crowder, K. D., & Tolnay, S. E. (2000). A new marriage squeeze for black women: The role of interracial marriage by black men. *Journal of Marriage and the Family, 62*, 792–807.

Davis, K. E., & Chappel, K. D. (1993, November). *Attachment theory and romantic partner choice.* Paper presented at the National Council on Family Relations, Baltimore, MD.

DeMaris, A., & MacDonald, W. (1993). Premarital cohabitation and marital instability: A test of the unconventionality hypothesis. *Journal of Marriage and the Family, 55*, 399–407.

DeMaris, A., & Rao, K. V. (1992). Premarital cohabitation and subsequent marital stability in the United States: A reassessment. *Journal of Marriage and the Family, 54*, 178–190.

Drigotas, S. M., & Rusbult, C. E. (1992). Should I stay or should I go? A dependence model of breakups. *Journal of Personality and Social Psychology, 62*, 62–87.

Feeney, J. A., & Noller, P. (1991). Attachment style and verbal descriptions of romantic partners. *Journal of Social and Personal Relationships, 8*, 187–215.

Fitzpatrick, J., & Sollie, D. L. (1999). Influence of individual and interpersonal factors on satisfaciton and stability in romantic relationships. *Personal Relationships, 6*, 337–350.

Fletcher, G. J. O., Simpson, J. A., & Thomas, G. T. (2000). Ideals, perceptions, and evaluations in early relationship development. *Journal of Personality and Social Psychology, 79*, 933–940.

Fossett, M. A., & Kiecolt, K. J. (1991). A methodological review of the sex ratio: Alternatives for comparative research. *Journal of Marriage and the Family, 53*, 941–957.

Fossett, M. A., & Kiecolt, K. J. (1993). Mate availability and family structure among African Americans in U.S. metropolitan areas. *Journal of Marriage and the Family, 55*, 288–302.

Fraley, R. C., & Davis, K. E. (1997). Attachment formation and transfer in young adults' close friendships and romantic relationships. *Personal Relationships, 4*, 131–144.

Frazier, P. A., Byer, A. L., Fisher, A. R., Wright, D. M., & DeBord, K. A. (1996). Adult attachment style and partner choice: Correlational and experimental findings. *Personal Relationships, 3*, 117–136.

Gaines, S. O., Reiss, H. T., Summers, S., Rusbult, C. E., Cox, C. L., Wexler, M. O., Marelich, W. D., & Kurkland, G. J. (1997). Impact of attachment style on reactions to accommodative dilemmas in close relationships. *Personal Relationships, 4*, 93–113.

Goldstein, J. R., & Kenney, C. T. (2001). Marriage delayed or marriage forgone? New cohort forecasts of first marriage for U.S. women. *American Sociological Review, 66*, 506–519.

Hall, D. R., & Zhao, J. Z. (1995). Cohabitation and divorce in Canada: Testing the selectivity hypothesis. *Journal of Marriage and the Family, 57*, 421–427.

Hazan, C., Hutt, M. J., Sturgeon, J., & Bricker, T. (1991, April). *The process of relinguishing parents as attachment figures.* Paper presented at the bienniel meeting of the Society for Research in Child Development, Seattle, WA.

Hazan, C., & Shaver, P. R. (1987). Romantic love conceptualized as an attachment process. *Journal of Personality and Social Psychology, 52*, 511–524.

Hazan, C., & Shaver, P. R. (1994). Attachment as an organizing framework for research on close relationships. *Psychological Inquiry, 5*, 1–22.

Horwitz, A. V., & White, H. R. (1998). The relationship of cohabitation and mental health: A study of a young adult cohort. *Journal of Marriage and the Family, 80*, 505–514.

Johnson, M. P. (1991). Commitment to personal relationships. In W. H. Jones & D. Perlman (Eds.), *Advances in personal relationships* (Vol. 3, pp. 117–143). London: Jessica Kingsley.

Kenrick, D. T., Groth, G. E., Trost, M. R., & Sadalla, E. K. (1993). Integrating evolutionary and social exchange perspectives on relationships: Effects of gender, self-appraisal, and involvement level on mate selection criteria. *Journal of Personality and Social Psychology, 64*, 951–969.

Kenrick, D. T., Keefe, R. C., Bryan, A., Barr, A., & Brown, S. (1995). Age preferences among homosexuals and heterosexuals: A case for modular psychological mechanisms. *Journal of Personality and Social Psychology, 69*, 1166–1172.

Kenrick, D. T., Sundie, J. M., Nicastle, L. D., & Stone, G. O. (2001). Can one ever be too wealthy or too chaste? Searching for nonlinearities in mate judgments. *Journal of Personality and Social Psychology, 80*, 462–471.

Kirkpatrick, L. A., & Davis, K. E. (1994). Attachment style, gender, and relationship stability: A longitudinal analysis. *Journal of Personality and Social Psychology, 66*, 502–512.

Kobak, R., & Hazan, C. (1991). Attachment in marriage: Effects of security and accuracy in working models. *Journal of Personality and Social Psychology, 60*, 681–689.

Kurdek, L. A. (1991). Correlates of relationship satisfaction in cohabiting gay and lesbian couples: Integration of contextual, investment, and problem-solving models. *Journal of Personality and Social Psychology, 61*, 910–922.

Kurdek, L. A. (1992). Relationship stability and relationship satisfaction in cohabiting gay and lesbian couples: A prospective test of the contextual and interdependence models. *Journal of Social and Personal Relationships, 9*, 125–142.

Kurdek, L. A. (1998). Relationship outcomes and their predictors: Longitudinal evidence from heterosexual married, gay cohabiting, and lesbian cohabiting couples. *Journal of Marriage and the Family, 60*, 553–568.

Kurdek, L. A. (2000). Attractions and constraints as determinants of relationship commitment: Longitudinal evidence from gay, lesbian, and heterosexual couples. *Personal Relationships, 7*, 245–262.

Landale, N. S., & Fennelly, K. (1992). Informal unions among mainland Puerto Ricans: Cohabitation or an alternative to marriage? *Journal of Marriage and the Family, 54*, 269–280.

Latty-Mann, H., & Davis, K. E. (1996). Attachment theory and partner choice: Preference and actuality. *Journal of Personality and Social Psychology, 13*, 5–23.

Lichter, D. T., LeClere, F. B., & McLaughlin, D. K. (1991). Local marriage markets and the marital behavior of black and white women. *American Journal of Sociology, 96*, 843–867.

Lichter, D. T., McLaughlin, D. K., Kephart, G., & Landry, D. J. (1992). Race and the retreat from marriage: A shortage of marriageable men. *American Sociological Review, 57*, 781–799.

Lillard, L. A., Brien, M. J., & Waite, L. J. (1995). Premarital cohabitation and subsequent marital dissolution: A matter of self-selection? *Demography, 32*, 437–457.

Manning, W. D. (1993). Marriage and cohabitation following premarital conception. *Journal of Marriage and the Family, 55*, 839–850.

Mare, R. D. (1991). Five decades of educational assortative mating. *American Sociological Review, 56*, 15–32.

Mastekaasa, A. (1992). Marriage and psychological well-being: Some evidence on selection into marriage. *Journal of Marriage and the Family, 54*, 901–911.

McLaughlin, D. K., & Lichter, D. T. (1997). Poverty and the marital behavior of young women. *Journal of Marriage and the Family, 59*, 582–594.

Montgomery, B. M. (1993). Relationship maintenance versus relationship change: A dialectical dilemma. *Journal of Social and Personal Relationships, 10*, 205–223.

Orbuch, T. L., Veroff, J., & Holmberg, D. (1993). Becoming a married couple: The emergence of meaning in the first years of marriage. *Journal of Marriage and the Family, 55*, 815–826.

Oropesa, R. S., Lichter, D. T., & Anderson, R. N. (1994). Marriage markets and the paradox of Mexican American nuptiality. *Journal of Marriage and the Family, 56*, 889–907.

Pietromonaco, P. R., & Carnelley, K. B. (1994). Gender and working models of attachment: Consequences for perceptions of self and romantic relationships. *Personal Relationships, 1*, 63–82.

Qian, Z., & Preston, S. H. (1993). Changes in American marriage 1972 to 1987: Availability and forces of attraction by age and education. *American Sociological Review, 58*, 482–495.

Raley, R. K. (1996). A shortage of marriageable men? A note on the role of cohabitation in black-white differences in marriage rates. *American Sociological Review, 61*, 973–983.

Raley, R. K. (2002). The effects of the differential undercount on survey estimates of race differences in marriage. *Journal of Marriage and Family, 64*, 774–779.

Rusbult, C. E. (1980). Commitment and satisfaction in romantic associations: A test of the investment model. *Journal of Experimental Social Psychology, 16*, 172–186.

Rusbult, C. E. (1983). A longitudinal test of the investment model: The development (and deterioration) of satisfaction and commitment in heterosexual involvements. *Journal of Personality and Social Psychology, 45*, 101–117.

Rusbult, C. E., Verette, J., Whitney, G. A., Slovik, L. F., & Lipkus, I. (1991). Accommodation processes in close relationships: Theory and preliminary evidence. *Journal of Personality and Social Psychology, 60*, 53–78.

Sassler, S., & Schoen, R. (1999). The effect of attitudes on economic activity on marriage. *Journal of Marriage and the Family, 61*, 147–159.

Scharfe, E., & Bartholomew, K. (1995). Accommodation and attachment representation in young couples. *Journal of Social and Personal Relationships, 12*, 389–401.

Schmitt, D. P., & Buss, D. M. (1996). Strategic self-promotion and competitor derogation: Sex and context effects on the perceived effectiveness of mate attraction tactics. *Journal of Personality and Social Psychology, 70*, 1185–1204.

Schoen, R. (1992). First unions and the stability of first marriages. *Journal of Marriage and the Family, 54*, 281–284.

Schoen, R., & Weinick, R. M. (1993). Partner choice in marriages and cohabitation. *Journal of Marriage and the Family, 55*, 408–414.

Seltzer, J. A. (2000). Families formed outside of marriage. *Journal of Marriage and the Family, 62*, 1247–1268.

Senchak M., & Leonard, K. (1992). Attachment styles and marital adjustment among newlywed couples. *Journal of Social and Personal Relationships, 9*, 51–64.

Simpson, J. A., & Gangestad, S. W. (1991). Individual differences in sociosexuality: Evidence for convergent and discriminant validity. *Journal of Personality and Social Psychology, 60*, 870–883.

Simpson, J. A., & Gangestad, S. W. (2001). Evolution and relationships: A call for integration. *Personal Relationships, 8*, 341–355.

Simpson, J. A., Gangestad, S. W., Christensen, P. N., & Leck, K. (1999). Fluctuating asymmetry, sociosexuality, and intrasexual competitive tactics. *Journal of Personality and Social Psychology, 76*, 159–172.

Singh, D. (1993). Adaptive significance of female physical attractiveness: Role of waist-to-hip ratio. *Journal of Personality and Social Psychology, 65*, 293–307.

Singh, D. (1995). Female judgement of male attractiveness and desirablility for relationships: Role of waist-to-hip ratio and financial status. *Journal of Personality and Social Psychology, 69*, 1089–1101.

South, S. J. (1993). Racial and ethnic differences in the desire to marry. *Journal of Marriage and the Family, 55*, 357–370.

South, S. J., & Lloyd, K. M. (1992). Marriage opportunities and family formation: Further implications of imbalanced sex ratios. *Journal of Marriage and the Family, 54*, 440–451.

Sprecher, S. (2001). Equity and social exchange in dating couples: Associations with satisfaction, commitment, and stability. *Journal of Marriage and Family, 63*, 599–613.

Stack, S., & Eshleman, J. R. (1998). Marital status and happiness: A 17-nation study. *Journal of Marriage and the Family, 60*, 527–536.

Stets, J. F. (1991). Cohabiting and marital aggression: The role of social isolation. *Journal of Marriage and the Family, 53*, 669–680.

Surra, C. A., Batchelder, M. L., & Hughes, D. K. (1995). Accounts and the demystification of courtship. In M. A. Fitzpatrick & A. L. Vangelisti (Eds.), *Explaining family interactions* (pp. 112–141). Thousand Oaks, CA: Sage.

Surra, C. A., & Gray, C. R. (2000). A typology of processes of commitment to marriage: Why do partners commit to problematic relationships. In L. J. Waite, C. Bachrach, M. Hindin, E. Thomson, & A. Thornton (Eds.), *The ties that bind: Perspectives on marriage and cohabitation* (pp. 253–280). New York: Aldine de Gruyter.

Surra, C. A., Gray, C. R., Boettcher, T. M. J., Cottle, N. R., & Jarvis, M. O. (2002, November). *Research on dating and mate selection: Where does it stand?* Paper presented at the Theory Construction and Research Methodology Workshop, National Council on Family Relations, Houston, TX.

Surra, C. A., & Hughes, D. K. (1997). Commitment processes in accounts of the development of premarital relationships. *Journal of Marriage and the Family, 59*, 5–21.

Surra, C. A., Hughes, D. K., & Jacquet, S. E. (1999). The development of commitment to marriage: A phenomenological approach. In J. M. Adams & W. H. Jones (Eds.), *Handbook of interpersonal commitment and relationship stability* (pp. 125–148). New York: Kluwer Academic/Plenum.

Swann, W. (1992). Seeking "truth," finding despair: Some unhappy consequences of a negative self-concept. *Current Directions in Psychological Science, 1*, 15–18.

Thomson, E., & Colella, U. (1992). Cohabitation and marital stability: Quality or commitment? *Journal of Marriage and the Family, 54*, 259–267.

U.S. Bureau of the Census. (2001). *America's families and living arrangements.* (Current Population Reports, Series P20, No. 537). Washington, DC: U.S. Government Printing Office.

Van Lange, P. A. M., Rusbult, C. E., Drigotas, S. M., Arriaga, X. B., Witcher, B. S., & Cox, C. L. (1997). Willingness to sacrifice in close relationships. *Journal of Personality and Social Psychology, 72*, 1373–1395.

Veroff, J., Sutherland, L., Chadiha, L., & Ortega, R. M. (1993). Newlyweds tell their stories: A narrative method for assessing marital experiences. *Journal of Social and Personal Relationships, 10*, 437–457.

Wieselquist, J., Rusbult, C. E., Agnew, C. R., & Foster, C. A. (1999). Commitment, pro-relationship behaviors, and trust in close relationships. *Journal of Personality and Social Psychology, 77*, 942–966.

Wu, Z., & Balakvishnan, T. R. (1994). Cohabitation after a marital disruption in Canada. *Journal of Marriage and the Family, 56*, 723–734.

4

COMMUNICATION IN MARRIAGE

FRANK D. FINCHAM

UNIVERSITY AT BUFFALO,
THE STATE UNIVERSITY OF NEW YORK

The most common reason for which people seek professional help is relationship problems (Veroff, Kulka, & Douvan, 1981), and poor communication is the relationship problem most frequently identified by couples (Broderick, 1981). Marital therapists also rate dysfunctional communication as the most frequent and damaging problem they confront in their work with couples (Geiss & O'Leary, 1981). Not surprisingly, a great deal of research has been conducted on communication in marriage. For example, a PsychINFO (1967–2002) search using the key words *marital* and *communication* yields 2,062 entries, whereas the same search of Sociofile (1974–2002) turns up 416 entries. Similar searches using the key words *love* and *marital* yield 501 and 213 references, respectively. Although we cannot read too much into these figures without a more detailed analysis of the content of the papers, it is probably safe to infer that the study of communication is a dominant theme in the marital literature.

The volume of work on communication in marriage presents a challenge to any writer attempting to provide an overview of the field, especially when it is noted that the work derives from several disciplines, each with its own traditions and subdisciplinary boundaries in the study of marital communication. This chapter does not therefore purport to provide a comprehensive review; rather, it highlights some major findings and identifies new avenues for research. It is divided into three sections. The first provides a brief overview of the historical context in which marital communication research evolved, paying particular attention to the disciplines of communication and psychology. This serves as a springboard in identifying themes for the second section in which major findings are highlighted. The third section identifies research directions that need to be pursued to provide a more complete understanding of marital communication.

THE EVOLUTION OF RESEARCH ON COMMUNICATION IN MARRIAGE

Although the study of marriage is an interdisciplinary endeavor, two disciplines have been at the forefront of research on marital communication. However, both of these disciplines, communication and psychology, are relative newcomers to the study of marital communication with systematic work on marital communication in these disciplines emerging only later in the 1900s. Social reform efforts to combat the deleterious effects of adverse economic and social conditions on families at the end of the 19th century had ushered in a period of "emerging" science in family studies in the early 1900s (Jacob, 1987). An important element of this emerging science was the attention devoted to relationships between spouses and family members. Indeed, Burgess (1926) defined the family in terms of its interaction, namely, as "a unity of interacting personalities" (p. 5). However, it was not until 1959 that this definition gave rise to an empirical publication, Hess and Handel's (1959) qualitative analysis of internal family dynamics. Preceding this publication, research relating to marital communication emerged from large-scale surveys conducted primarily by sociologists to identify correlates of marital satisfaction, including communication. In reviewing 50 years of this research genre, Nye (1988, p. 315) concluded "early on [1939] . . . Burgess and Cottrell . . . took every individual characteristic they could think of and correlated it with marital success, producing an R of about .50 . . . Not a bad start, but we have not progressed much beyond that point in 50 years."

Communication

Research on family communication as a specialty area in the communication discipline was inaugurated by two dissertations (Fitzpatrick, 1976; Rogers, 1972) completed in the 1970s (Whitchurch & Dickson, 1999). By 1989, it had built sufficient momentum to be established as an interest group in the National Communication Association and shortly thereafter, in 1995, became a division of the Association. Although the specialty area of interpersonal communication predated these developments, research informed by it tended to use the marital dyad as one of several contexts in which to study constructs of interest (e.g., compliance-gaining, self-disclosure). In contrast, for family communication researchers, family interaction is the central organizing construct of study, and families (and constituent dyads) are not compared to other social units. Moreover, family communication tends to be viewed in terms of systems theory, an approach that has not been dominant in the area of interpersonal communication. This general theoretical approach tends to be informed by two ways of understanding communication, the aforementioned interactionist perspective (in which relationships and meaning are constituted though interaction, Berger & Kelner, 1964) and the pragmatic perspective outlined in *Pragmatics of Human Communication* (Watzlawick, Beavin, & Jackson, 1967).

These differences between interpersonal and family communication specialties have resulted in some fragmentation in the marital literature generated by communication scholars. This work, in turn, is distinct from the literature generated by psychologists, which reflects a rather different theoretical perspective and starting point.

Psychology

Systematic research on marriage in psychology emerged largely among clinical psychologists in response to the desire to better assist couples experiencing marital distress. The investigation of conflictual interaction assumed center stage as it was widely accepted that "distress results from couples' aversive and ineffectual response to conflict" (Koerner & Jacobson 1994, p. 208). In reaction to the prior reliance on self-report, heavy emphasis was placed on the observation of couple interaction with much of the research, which first began to emerge in the 1970s, focusing almost exclusively on describing the behavior that distinguished distressed from nondistressed couples. To the extent that attention was given to theory, social exchange theories and social learning theory dominated research generated in psychology.

Despite repeated acknowledgment of the value of a systems perspective (e.g., Emery, 1992) this framework has had a minimal impact on marital communication research in psychology. With the emergence of the field of "personal," "intimate," or "close" relationships (see Fincham, 1995; for overviews of the field, see Brehm, Miller, Perlman, & Campbell, 2002; Hinde, 1997) social psychologists have also become more noticeable contributors to marital research. The dominant theoretical perspectives informing this research are social exchange theories and the interdependence framework (Kelley et al., 1983). As in communication, the contributions from psychology's subdisciplines lack integration.

One can see that the study of communication in marriage has evolved from very diverse origins both within and across disciplines. The resulting literatures therefore represent a loosely sewn together patchwork quilt rather than an evenly spun blanket. This will become more apparent as we turn to highlight some of the major findings on marital communication.

OVERVIEW OF FINDINGS ON COMMUNICATION IN MARRIAGE

The presumed role of communication skill deficits in generating marital distress has led to a substantial research literature on the topography of communication behavior during marital conflict.

Communication Behaviors

Compared to nondistressed couples, distressed couples' problem-solving communications show more interruptions (Schaap, 1984), criticisms and complaining (Fichten & Wright, 1983; Revensdorf, Hahlweg, Schindler, & Vogel, 1984), negative solutions (e.g., "Let's just forget the whole thing"; Weiss & Tolman, 1990), and fewer self-disclosures and positive suggestions (Birchler, Clopton, & Adams, 1984; Margolin, Burman, & John, 1989). In addition, distressed couples show less pinpointing and verbalize problems in a critical way (Birchler et al., 1984; Margolin & Wampold, 1981) suggesting that they have poor message production skills.

Nonverbal communication is more strongly related to relationship satisfaction than verbal communication (Gottman, Markman, & Notarius, 1977; Krokoff, 1987; Smith,

Vivian, & O'Leary, 1990), and when couples are instructed to act as if they are happy, independent observers can still reliably distinguish happy from unhappy couples on the basis of nonverbal communication (Vincent, Friedman, Nugent, & Messerly, 1979). Indeed, when one studies the interactions of happy couples, what stands out are the pleasurable emotions, the smiles, laughs, affection, and warmth. Similarly, it is the agitation, tears, distress, anger, and coldness in distressed couples that are often immediately evident. For example, Birchler, Weiss, and Vincent (1975) found that distressed couples behaved with less humor, assent, smiling, and laughter than happy couples (see also Gottman & Krokoff, 1989). Also characteristic of distressed couples are high levels of fear, anger, disgust, and sadness as well as withdrawal (e.g., maintaining silence, looking away, leaving the room), and body postures that are stiff, closed, and turned away from the partner (Weiss & Heyman 1997).

Communication Patterns

With regard to sequences of communication behavior, the "signature" of distressed couple communication is the existence of reciprocated negative behavior. Indeed, escalating, negative sequences during conflict are associated with marital distress and both frequency and sequences of negative behavior are more pronounced in couples where physical aggression is found (e.g., Burman, John, & Margolin, 1992; Gottman, 1994). In fact, one of the greatest challenges for couples locked into negative exchanges is to find an adaptive way of exiting from such cycles (Gottman, 1998). This is usually attempted through responses designed to repair the interaction (e.g., metacommunication, "You're not listening to me") that are typically delivered with negative affect (e.g., irritation, sadness). Distressed couples tend to respond to the negative affect, thereby continuing the cycle. This makes their interactions more structured and predictable. In contrast, nondistressed couples appear to be more responsive to the repair attempt and are thereby able to exit from negative exchanges early on. For example, a spouse may respond to "Please, you're not letting me finish" with "Sorry . . . please finish what you were saying." Their interaction therefore appears more random and less predicable (Gottman, 1979).

Rogers and her colleagues have used a relational control model, based on a pragmatic theoretical perspective, to study dyadic communication (e.g., Millar, Rogers, & Courtright, 1979; Millar & Rogers, 1988). The focus of their work has been on contiguous pairs of control moves (transacts). Dominance scores (number of one-up moves responded to with one-down moves by spouse) were used to compute dominance ratios (one spouse's score divided by the other's score) that were shown to predict level of understanding. That is, the clearer the dominance hierarchy, the less likely that each spouse was to know the behaviors expected of him or her by the other. The dominance ratio was also related to husbands' frequency of feeling understood by the wife and his satisfaction with several communication behaviors (e.g., the couple's ability to talk things out, the ease with which complaints and problems are discussed). Couples in relationships characterized by complementary transacts (one spouse's message asserts control, and other spouse's message accepts assertion or vice versa) are more satisfied than those in relationships where symmetrical transacts (both spouses make the same control moves) dominate (Rogers-Millar & Millar, 1979).

A third key communication pattern commonly observed in distressed couples is that one spouse pressures the other with demands, complaints, and criticisms, while the partner withdraws with defensiveness and passive inaction. This interaction pattern is commonly referred to as the demand–withdraw pattern (Christensen, 1987, 1988). Building on a series of early studies on self-reported demand–withdraw patterns (Christensen, 1987, 1988; Christensen & Shenk, 1991), Christensen and Heavey (1990) videotaped interactions of families discussing a topic chosen by each spouse. Topics were related to parenting behavior in each spouse. It was found that frequency of demands by the female partner and withdrawal by the male partner were negatively related to marital satisfaction. That female-demand and male-withdrawal behaviors are associated with low marital satisfaction is consistent with several other studies of gender differences in communication. In particular, women display more negative affect and behavior than do men (Margolin & Wampold, 1981; Notarius & Johnson, 1982; Schaap, 1982), and male partners make more statements suggestive of withdrawal, such as not responding and making irrelevant comments (Schaap, 1982; Schaap, Buunk, & Kerkstra, 1988).

However, inferring reliable gender differences in demand–withdraw patterns would be premature as who withdraws may vary according to which partner desires change (Heavey, Layne, & Christensen, 1993). To clarify this issue, Heavey, Christensen, and Malamuth (1995) explored how demand/withdraw patterns vary according to which partner's problem issue was discussed. When discussing the husband's issue, there were no systematic differences in the roles taken by each spouse. However, when discussing the wife's issue, women were much more likely to be demanding and men more likely to be withdrawing than the reverse. Similarly, Klinetob and Smith (1996) found that demand–withdraw patterns switch polarity when the topics chosen for discussion clearly focus on an issue of change for each partner. These results provide good evidence that although men and women tend to play different roles in typical dysfunctional communications, these roles are sensitive to context and are particularly sensitive to whose issue is under discussion.

Finally, conflict communication patterns seem to be relatively stable over time (e.g., Noller, Feeney, Bonnell, & Callan, 1994) and to predict changes in marital satisfaction and marital stability (see Karney & Bradbury, 1995). For example, Gottman, Coan, Carrerre, and Swanson (1998) found that active listening, anger, and negative affect reciprocity among newlyweds predicted marital satisfaction and stability 6 years later.

In summary, there is greater net negativity, reciprocity of negative behavior, more sustained negative interaction, and escalation of negative interactions among distressed couples than among nondistressed couples. Moreover, communication behavior seems to be relatively stable over time (for reviews, see Gottman & Notarius, 2000; Kelly, Fincham, & Beach, 2003; Weiss & Heyman, 1990, 1997).

Variation by Couple Type

Reflecting scholars' belief that categorization of marriages into different types will lead to better understanding of marital communication, numerous typologies of marriage have been proposed (e.g., Cuber & Haroff, 1965; Olson, 1981). Although intuitive, logical, and empirical approaches have been used to derive typologies, it is the last mentioned that have shown the most promise. Among empirically derived typologies (e.g., Gottman, 1994;

Johnson, Huston, Gaines, & Levinger, 1992) Fitzpatrick's (1988) classification stands out
as both the most thoroughly investigated and the most promising.

Based on a content analysis of extant studies, Fitzpatrick set out to assess the essential
dimensions of married life. The resulting Relational Dimensions Instrument (RDI) yielded
eight dimensions (*sharing, traditionalism, uncertainty*, assertiveness, temporal regulation,
conflict avoidance, undifferentiated space, and autonomy), four of which proved important in classifying couples (those in italics) into three types. Couples that are classified
as traditionals hold conventional values, value stability over spontaneity, are highly interdependent showing a high degree of sharing and companionship in marriage, and do not
avoid conflict. Independents differ from traditionals by holding unconventional values and
believing that marriage should not constrain their individual freedoms. Separates appear
to hold opposing ideological views simultaneously supporting the values of traditionals
and independents, but keep a psychological distance from the spouse and avoid conflict.
About 60% of couples agree as to their marital type with the remainder falling into six
possible mixed-type categories.

The couple types predict a number of communication outcomes that cannot be predicted from either spouse's type alone. Specifically, independent couples self-disclose to
their spouses more than traditionals who, in turn, self-disclose more than separates. Power
moves during conflict discussions also differ across couple types; in contrast to other
types, separates do not engage in competitive, symmetrical transacts. In addition, traditionals display more conciliatory messages and less confrontation than expected by chance
(possibly reflecting their "sweeping problems under the rug"), whereas separates are more
confrontational than expected by chance. As regards affect, the types do not differ in the
positive affect they communicate but do differ in neutral and negative affect; independents show significantly less neutral nonverbal behavior and significantly more negative
affect during conflict. Finally, separates exhibit the most compliance in their communications (see Fitzpatrick, 1988).

The Role of Social Perception

Both communication scholars (see Burleson, 1992) and psychologists (see Fincham,
Fernandes, & Humphreys, 1993) have emphasized the importance of social perception in
understanding marital communication. A growing body of research supports this view. For
example, there is increasing evidence that explanations or attributions for partner behavior are related to less effective problem-solving communication (Bradbury & Fincham,
1992), more negative communication during problem-solving and support-giving tasks
(Bradbury, Beach, Fincham, & Nelson, 1996, Miller & Bradbury, 1995), and to specific
affects (whining and anger) displayed during problem solving (Fincham & Bradbury,
1992). As regards communication patterns, wives' attributions are related to the tendency to reciprocate negative partner behavior (e.g., Bradbury & Fincham, 1992; Miller &
Bradbury, 1995). The partialling out of marital satisfaction from these relations shows that
they do not simply reflect the spouse's sentiment toward the marriage (Bradbury et al.,
1996). Finally, manipulating attributions for a negative partner behavior influenced distressed spouses' subsequent communication toward the partner (Fincham & Bradbury,
1988).

Building on an important theoretical statement by Doherty (1981a, 1981b), there is also evidence that efficacy expectations or the spouse's belief that she or he can execute the behaviors needed to negotiate a resolution of couple conflicts may determine a couple's persistence in conflict resolution discussions, the styles employed in conflict resolution, and their willingness to engage in discussion of marital problems (Fincham & Bradbury, 1987; Fincham, Bradbury, & Grych, 1990; Notarius & Vanzetti, 1983). There is also some evidence that efficacy beliefs may mediate the relation between attributions and marital outcomes (Fincham, Harold, & Gano-Phillips, 2000).

Finally, a provocative set of findings has emerged for a nonconscious process, the accessibility of partner evaluations typically assessed as the speed (in milliseconds) with which a spouse makes an evaluative judgment of the partner. Specifically, the cognitive accessibility of evaluative judgments of the spouse moderates the relation between marital satisfaction and communication behavior such that stronger associations are found for spouses with more accessible judgments (Fincham & Beach, 1999a). Such findings suggest that high accessibility should lead to more stable satisfaction over time (top-down processing occurs) relative to low accessibility (bottom-up processing occurs), an implication that is consistent with data collected over 18 months of marriage (Fincham, Beach, & Kemp-Fincham, 1997). Thus, it may be necessary to revisit many of the communication behaviors correlated with marital satisfaction to determine whether there is a differential association for spouses characterized by high and low accessibility.

Critique

What we know about marital communication is necessarily a function of how we have studied the phenomenon. This points to several factors that limit what we know about marital communication. First, and perhaps most obviously, most of our findings about marital communication are based on laboratory interactions. Do observations of communication in the artificial setting of the laboratory yield samples of typical communication behavior? This is a particularly important question in view of findings showing that couple communication varies according to contextual factors. For example, diary studies illustrate that stressful marital interactions occur more frequently in couples' homes on days of high, general life stress and at times and places associated with multiple competing demands (e.g., Halford, Gravestock, Lowe, & Scheldt, 1992). Similarly, Bolger, DeLongis, Kessler, and Wethington (1989) found that arguments at work were related to marital arguments, a finding consistent with the association observed between problem-solving communication and the occurrence of stressful life events (Cohan & Bradbury, 1997). Although couples undoubtedly bring some life stressors into the laboratory, we may be losing important information by studying communication skills outside the natural ecology of couple interaction. It is therefore noteworthy that couples themselves report that laboratory interactions are reminiscent of their typical interactions (Margolin, John, & Gleberman, 1989) and that there is some evidence to show an association between communication in the laboratory and that in the home (Kelly & Halford, 1995; Krokoff, Gottman, & Hass, 1989).

Second, in the absence of attempts to study goals in the marital literature (see Fincham & Beach, 1999b), it is difficult to distinguish communication behavior from communication skills. Communication skills refer to the ability to realize communicative goals during the course of interaction, whereas communication behavior may be thought of as verbal and nonverbal behavior occurring when a couple is interacting (Burleson & Denton, 1997). Although the problem-solving/conflict discussions that dominate research on marital communication may be a good operationalization of communicative behavior, they may not be a good measure of communication skills. Burleson and Denton persuasively argue that communicative behavior may say as much about the intent or motivation of participants as about communication skills. Hence, a failed communication may reflect an unclear communication goal just as easily as it may reflect a lack of communication skills. Moreover, Jacobson and Christensen (1996) argue that observation codes are too often based on a value judgment of what constitutes "good" and "bad" communication.

Finally, what we know about marital communication is necessarily limited by the focus on communication in conflict and problem-solving situations. McGonagle, Kessler, and Schiling (1992) collected data about the frequency of overt disagreements from an equal probability sample of 778 couples and found a modal response of once or twice a month. A subsample that kept diaries reported similar rates, and when contacted 3 years later, reported the same rate of disagreement. However, about 80% of the sample reported disagreements once a month or less. Thus, we appear to have built our knowledge of marital communication on a relatively infrequent event. Infrequent events may be consequential for relationships (e.g., a one night stand), but whether problem-solving communications are consequential (rather than reflecting existing characteristics of the marriage) is open to question as Karney and Bradbury (1995), in a meta-analysis, found very small effect sizes ($r = -.06$ to $-.25$) when using communication behavior to predict later spousal satisfaction. Whether problem-solving communication behavior is representative of communication in general remains an unanswered empirical question.

TOWARD A MORE COMPLETE UNDERSTANDING OF MARITAL COMMUNICATION

In light of the observations made thus far, it is apparent that there is a need to investigate communication in contexts other than problem-solving or conflict discussions. Accordingly the next two sections each identify potentially important contexts in which to do so. However, a more complete understanding requires consideration of the broader communication context, including factors external to the marriage. The third section therefore considers such factors.

Communication in the Contexts of Support Giving and Affectional Expression

Although support processes in marriage have been of interest for some time (e.g., Barker & Lemle, 1984; Coyne & DeLongis, 1986), only recently have methods been used that allow detailed investigation of potentially supportive transactions. For example, daily diary methods have helped clarify the operation of support in marriage; in a study of couples in which one spouse was preparing to take the bar exam, Bolger, Zuckerman, and Kessler (1998) showed that the examinees' distress did not rise as the exam drew near to the extent that the partner communicated increasing levels of support.

Observational methods for assessing the provision and receipt of supportive behaviors have also been developed (e.g., Cutrona, 1996) to code interactions where one spouse talks about a personal issue he or she would like to change and the other is asked to respond as she or he normally would. It appears that supportive spouse behavior is related to marital satisfaction and is more important than negative behavior in determining the perceived supportiveness of an interaction. Moreover, wives' supportive behavior predicts marital stress 12 months later while controlling for initial marital stress and depression (Cutrona 1996; Cutrona & Suhr, 1992, 1994; Davila, Bradbury, Cohan, & Tochluk, 1997). Importantly, in their study of newlyweds, Pasch and Bradbury (1998) showed that, although behavior exhibited during conflict and support tasks tended to covary, their shared variance was small (<20%). Wives' supportive behaviors also predicted marital deterioration 24 months later independently of either partners' conflict behaviors, and supportive behaviors moderated the association between conflict behavior and later marital deterioration with compromised conflict skills leading to greater risk of marital deterioration in the context of poor support communication (see also Carels & Baucom, 1999; Saitzyk, Floyd, & Kroll, 1997).

Research on affectional expression is similarly informative. Specifically, in the context of high levels of affectional expression between spouses, the inverse correlation between negative spouse behavior and marital satisfaction decreases significantly (Huston & Chorost, 1994). High levels of positivity in problem-solving discussions also moderate the negative effect of disengagement on marital satisfaction 30 months later (Smith, Vivian, & O'Leary, 1990). As regards communication patterns, Caughlin and Huston (2002) found that the interaction between the demand–withdraw pattern and affectional expression was a significant predictor of marital satisfaction; the demand–withdraw pattern was unrelated to marital satisfaction in the context of high affectional expression, but the two variables were inversely related in the context of average or low affectional expression.

Interestingly, research on communication in the context of support alerts us to the importance of support obtained by spouses outside the marriage for interpersonal processes within a marriage (Bryant & Conger, in press). For example, Julien, Markman, Leveille, Chartrand, and Begin (1994) found that when extramarital confidants were more supportive, wives were less distressed and closer to their husbands after the confiding interaction. However, before turning to the broader environment in which marital communication occurs, a much needed line of research is considered, communication in the context of relationship repair following a spousal transgression.

Communication in the Context of Relationship Repair Following a Spousal Transgression: Focus on Forgiveness

In marriage, we voluntarily make ourselves most vulnerable to another human being by linking the realization of our needs, aspirations, and hopes to the good will of our spouse. Rendering ourselves vulnerable is a double-edged sword. It makes possible the profound sense of well-being that can be experienced in marriage. At the same time, the imperfection of any partner means that hurt or injury is inevitable, and when it occurs, the hurt is particularly poignant precisely because we have made ourselves vulnerable. How partners deal with this inevitable hurt is critical to individual and relational well-being.

One means of meeting this challenge is through forgiveness, a concept that has received remarkably little attention in science despite its pervasiveness across cultures and major religions (Worthington & Wade, 1999). In fact, spouses themselves acknowledge that the capacity to seek and grant forgiveness is one of the most important factors contributing to marital longevity and satisfaction (Fenell, 1993).

Although forgiveness is fast becoming a topic of inquiry in marital research (e.g., Coop-Gordon, Baucom, & Snyder, 2000; Fincham, 2000; Fincham et al., 2002), understanding of its relation to communication is limited. There is evidence that for both hypothetical and actual partner transgressions a spouse's self-reported willingness to forgive is a significant predictor of the partner's psychological aggression (verbal aggression and nonverbal behaviors that are not directed at the partner's body) even after controlling for the satisfaction of both partners. In addition, there is evidence that forgiveness is multidimensional consisting of at least two dimensions: a negative dimension defined by retaliatory motivation and a positive dimension defined by benevolence motivation. Each of these two dimensions accounts for unique variance in partner reports of constructive communication independently of both spouses' marital satisfaction (Fincham & Beach, 2002, Study 2). Finally, among British couples in their third year of marriage, husbands' retaliatory motivation or unforgiveness was a significant predictor of wife-reported ineffective arguing, whereas wives' benevolence motivation or forgiveness predicted less husband-reported ineffective arguing. In longer term marriages in the United States, three forgiveness dimensions were identified: retaliation, avoidance, and benevolence. Whereas wives' benevolence again predicted ineffective arguing, only husbands' avoidance predicted wives' reports of conflict. In each sample, findings were independent of both spouses' marital satisfaction (Fincham, Beach, & Davila, in press).

A limitation of the previously cited research is that it does not examine communication specifically in the context of forgiveness. However, in a study of forgiveness narratives, many of which involved spouses, Kelly (1998) identified three forgiver strategies, direct, indirect, and conditional, by which forgiveness was mediated in a relationship. The majority were direct strategies that involved the forgiver telling the transgressor that she or he understood or saying "I forgive you." Indirect strategies, constituting 43% of responses, included use of humor, diminishing the magnitude of the transgression (e.g., saying it was "no big deal"), nonverbal displays of affection, returning to normal interaction patterns without explicit comment, and implicit understanding.

The importance of studying directly forgiveness transactions between spouses is matched only by the challenge of doing so. The temptation to identify forgiveness with a specific statement or an overt act (e.g., Baumeister, Exline, & Sommer, 1998; Hargave & Sells, 1997) is problematic. Here is why. The verb "to forgive" is not performative. So, for example, to say "I promise" is to make a promise even in the absence of any intention to do what is promised. But to say "I forgive you" does not thereby constitute forgiveness even if one fully intends to forgive the person addressed. As Horsburgh (1974) points out, the phrase "I'll try to forgive you" is sufficient evidence to support this argument as "to try" cannot be used in conjunction with any performative verb (e.g., "I'll try to promise"). By extension, a specific act does not constitute forgiveness, though it might well be the first sign that a decision to forgive has been made. This analysis uncovers something important about forgiveness—forgiveness is not achieved immediately. Rather, the decision to forgive starts a difficult process that involves conquering negative feelings and acting with good will toward someone who has done us harm. It is this process, set in motion by a decision to forgive, that makes statements like "I'm trying to forgive you" meaningful.

This creates particular challenges when a spouse offers a verbal statement of forgiveness. The transgressing spouse is likely to experience the statement as performative and be puzzled, annoyed, or angry when incompletely resolved feelings of resentment about the harm-doing intrude upon subsequent discourse or behavior in the marriage. Statements of forgiveness are also important for another reason: They can be bungled. Setting aside the strategic use of such statements, genuinely motivated attempts to tell the partner that she or he is forgiven can easily be seen as a put down, a form of retaliation, and so on if unskillfully executed. Thus, they can lead to conflict and might themselves end up being a source of hurt.

The challenge for researchers is magnified by the fact that forgiveness behavior has no specific topography as it is the respectful, interpersonal behavior expected in everyday life that, in the context of injury, assumes the mantle of forgiveness (Downie, 1971). Notwithstanding these difficulties there is a glaring need for research on forgiveness transactions in marriage as there is little doubt that forgiveness constitutes an important relationship repair mechanism that leads to reconciliation between hitherto estranged spouses. At a very minimum, it is possible to study interactions where forgiveness is an explicit part of the discourse and identify the factors associated with communicative success and failure in such contexts.

Because a more complete understanding of communication in marriage requires consideration of the broader communication context, it is considered next.

The Broader Communication Context

Two different classes of factors are examined, each of which helps shape the broader communication context: spouses' backgrounds and characteristics and the environmental influence on the marriage.

Spouses' Backgrounds and Characteristics. Evidence on the importance of communication for marital well-being leads naturally to questions about what each spouse brings to the relationship that predicts communication in the marriage. Interest in individual differences that might predict marital functioning have been subject to study since research on marriage first began. Notwithstanding the conclusion of some (e.g., Gottman, 1979; see also Gottman, 1994, p. 87), that study of individual difference variables is not particularly informative for understanding marriage and should be eschewed in favor of studying relationship variables, there is growing evidence for the importance of spouses' backgrounds and characteristics for understanding marital communication.

As regards spouse background, for example, continuing work on intergenerational processes shows that parental divorce is associated with poorer communication observed among their offspring around the time of marriage (Sanders, Halford, & Behrens, 1999) and that the association between parental divorce and offspring divorce is mediated by problematic behaviors, such as hostile, domineering, and critical behaviors, among the offspring (Amato, 1996). Along similar lines, Gotlib, Lewinsohn, and Seeley (1998) have shown that individuals with a history of depression during adolescence are more likely to marry earlier and to experience higher rates of marital problems than individuals with other diagnoses or no diagnosis. Data of this kind demonstrate that a history of psychopathology is an important antecedent of marital functioning and, together with concurrent symptomatology, cannot be overlooked in models of marital functioning (see Beach, 2001). Individual risk factors extend beyond parental divorce and psychopathology, and there is growing evidence that such personal risk factors, evident prior to marriage, increase the likelihood of conflict and communication problems in the marriage.

Particularly informative in the area of spousal characteristics and relationship functioning is research on attachment, which aims to address questions about how the experience of relationships early in life are manifest in individuals' working models of relationships and subsequent interpersonal functioning in adulthood (Bowlby, 1969; see Simpson & Rholes, 1998). Kobak and Hazan (1991), for example, have shown that securely attached husbands were less rejecting and more supportive than insecurely attached husbands during problem solving, and wives displayed more rejection during a problem-solving discussion to the extent that they described themselves as less reliant on their husband and described their husband as less psychologically available to them (also see Rholes, Simpson, & Orina, 1999). Secure and ambivalently attached individuals report more self-disclosure than avoidant individuals (Keelan, Dion, & Dion, 1998), with securely attached persons showing the greatest range of self-discourse across social situations. Feeney, Noller, and Callan (1994) found that the attachment dimension of anxiety over relationships was related to destructive patterns of communication. In a later study, they showed that the dimension, anxiety over abandonment, was related to the demand-withdraw communication pattern which served as a mediator of the association between attachment and couple violence (Roberts & Noller, 1998). Although the richness of theorizing about the role of attachment in adult relationships can sometimes exceed the data used to test key hypotheses, this area of inquiry provides strong, conceptually guided evidence for how an overarching framework can integrate individual-level variables to further understanding of marital communication.

Although study of communication across different contexts and consideration of the background and characteristics that spouses bring to the communicative context will enhance our understanding of marital communication, it is also important to consider the broader environment in which the marriage is situated.

Broader Environment Influences on the Marriage. The environment in which marriages are situated and the intersection between interior processes and external factors that impinge upon marriage are important to consider in painting a more textured picture of marital communication. In this regard, investigation of the economic and work environment comprises the largest body of research on environmental influences on marriage. Numerous self-report studies that outline links between job characteristics and marital outcomes (e.g., Hughes, Galinsky, & Morris, 1992) have been supplemented by observational or diary methods to specify the interactional processes affected by financial and work stress (see Menaghan, 1991). Using observational methods, Krokoff, Gottman, and Roy (1988) demonstrated that displays of negative affect, but not reciprocation of negative affect, were linked to occupational status in a sample of white- and blue-collar workers.

And in perhaps the most comprehensive analysis of economic stress and marital functioning to date, Conger, Rueter, and Elder (1999) found support for a model, whereby economic pressure in a sample of predominantly rural families at Time 1 predicted individual distress and observed marital conflict at Time 2, which in turn predicted marital distress at Time 3. The effect of economic pressure on emotional distress was greater in marriages poor in observed social support.

There is also a substantial body of work that addresses the impact of discrete, often traumatic events on marriage. However, there is a dearth of work in this area that focuses on communication, a deficit that clearly needs to be addressed. This is because, in the absence of external stressors, communication skills may have little impact on the marriage (Karney & Bradbury, 1995). External stressors also may influence marital processes directly. In particular, nonmarital stressors may lead to more negative patterns of communication (e.g., Repetti, 1989) and lower relationship satisfaction (e.g., Cohan & Bradbury, 1997). In addition, moderate levels of negative life events provide a context in which positive and negative partner communications can have a greater impact on the marriage (Tesser & Beach, 1998). Level of negative life events may therefore moderate the effect of communication behaviors on subsequent marital satisfaction (see Cohan & Bradbury, 1997).

Incorporation of life events assessments into examinations of marital communication is likely to enhance understanding. For example, Cohan and Bradbury (1997) propose that communication may influence the relationship between stressful events and marital satisfaction in three ways. First, they propose that communication may buffer, or moderate, the effect of stressful events on marital satisfaction (e.g., good communication may decrease the impact of stressful events whereas poor communication may magnify their effects). Second, they propose that communication may lead to enhanced marital satisfaction when stressful events occur (termed the "personal growth model of stress"). Third, they propose that communication may mediate the association of stressful events and marital satisfaction. That is, stressful events predict communication, and communication, in turn, predicts marital satisfaction. Two studies inform us of how stressful events, communication, and marital satisfaction are related. In a longitudinal study, Cohan and Bradbury (1997) administered checklists of stressful events, behavioral measures of verbal and nonverbal behavior during problem solving, and measures of marital satisfaction at two time points 18 months apart. They found evidence that problem solving moderates the effect of life events. They also found evidence of a personal growth effect: when wives expressed higher proportions of anger, reports of stressful events predicted increased marital satisfaction, suggesting that wives' anger was beneficial for personal and marital adjustment in the context of stressful life events. Perhaps anger expression (without contempt or whining) by the female partner constitutes a functional communication skill that signals high distress and engages the male partner in support and/or problem-solving behaviors.

Bradbury, Rogge, and Lawrence (2001) in considering the ecological niche of the couple—their life events, family constellation, socioeconomic standing, and stressful circumstances—argue that it may be "at least as important to examine the struggle that exists between the couple ... and the environment they inhabit as it is to examine the interpersonal struggles that are the focus of our work" (p. 76). From this perspective, couple communication processes may reflect the adequacy of couple resources—personal, interpersonal, material—to cope with the environment in which they are situated. We continue to ignore this at our own risk. There is a growing need to map out the life events that are and are not influential for different couples and for different stages of marriage, to investigate how these events influence marital communication, to clarify how individuals and marriages may inadvertently generate stressful events, and to examine how spouses take life events into account when making evaluations of their relationship (see Tesser & Beach, 1998).

CONCLUSION

The topic of marital communication has received a considerable amount of attention from researchers across different disciplines and subdisciplines. As noted, the disciplines of communication and psychology have been at the forefront of this work, and each has approached the topic from a different perspective. Diversity of perspective also occurs across subareas within each discipline resulting in several relevant literatures that are at best only loosely connected. The need for research that integrates existing lines of inquiry is clearly evident.

The material reviewed in this chapter also shows that the overwhelming majority of the studies on marital communication have focused on communication in conflict situations, a circumstance that, it turns out, is relatively infrequent in community samples (McGonagle et al., 1992). Notwithstanding the large volume of work on the topic, it is therefore perhaps not surprising that a number of important gaps remain in the literatures relevant to understanding marital communication. Some, such as communication in the context of support and affectional expression, are now receiving attention, whereas others, such as communication in the context of relationship repair, have yet to receive focused attention. However, the lacunae in the literature are not limited to specific communication contexts. A more complete understanding of marital communication also requires consideration of the broader communication context, including environmental factors that might be influencing individual spouses and/or the couple. Thus, attention to such factors is also needed if our knowledge of marital communication is to change from that resembling an undersized patchwork quilt to that of a larger, evenly spun blanket.

REFERENCES

Amato, P. R. (1996). Explaining the intergenerational transmission of divorce. *Journal of Marriage and the Family, 58*, 628–640.

Barker, C., & Lemle, R. (1984). The helping process in couples. *American Journal of Community Psychology, 12*, 321–336.

Baumeister, R. F., Exline, J. J., & Sommer, K. L. (1998). The victim role, grudge theory, and two dimensions of forgiveness. In E. L. Worthington (Ed.), *Dimensions of forgiveness: Psychological research and theological perspectives* (pp. 79–106). Philadelphia: Templeton Press.

Beach, S. R. H. (2001). *Marital and family processes in depression: A scientific foundation for clinical practice.* Washington, DC: APA Press.

Berger, P., & Kellner, H. (1964). Marriage and the construction of reality. *Diogenes, 64*, 1–24.

Birchler, G. R., Clopton, P. L., & Adams, N. L. (1984). Marital conflict resolution: Factors influencing concordance between partners and trained coders. *American Journal of Family Therapy, 12*, 15–28.

Birchler, G. R., Weiss, R. L., & Vincent, J. P. (1975). Multimethod analysis of social reinforcement exchange between maritally distressed and nondistressed spouse and stranger dyads. *Journal of Personality and Social Psychology, 31*, 349–360.

Bolger, N., DeLongis, A., Kessler, R. C., & Wethington, E. (1989). The contagion of stress across multiple roles. *Journal of Marriage and the Family, 51*, 175–183.

Bolger, N., Zuckerman, A., & Kessler, R. (1998). *Visible support, invisible support, and adjustment to stress.* Manuscript submitted for publication.

Bowlby, J. (1969*). Attachment and loss: Volume 1. Attachment.* New York: Basic Books.

Bradbury, T. B., Beach, S. R. H., Fincham, F. D., & Nelson, G. M. (1996). Attributions and behavior in functional and dysfunctional marriages. *Journal of Consulting and Clinical Psychology, 64*, 569–576.

Bradbury, T. N., & Fincham, F. D. (1992). Attributions and behavior in marital interaction. *Journal of Personality and Social Psychology, 63*, 613–628.

Bradbury, T. N., Rogge, R., & Lawrence, E. (2001). Reconsidering the role of conflict in marriage. In A. Booth, A. C. Crouter, & M. Clements (Eds.), *Couples in conflict* (pp. 59–81). Mahwah, NJ: Lawrence Erlbaum Associates.

Brehm, S. S., Miller, R., Perlman, D., & Campbell, S. (2002). *Intimate relationships* (3rd ed). New York: McGraw-Hill.

Broderick, J. E. (1981). A method for derivation of areas of assessment in marital relationships. *The American Journal of Family Therapy, 9*, 25–34.

Bryant, C. M., & Conger, R. D. (in press). Marital success and domains of social support in long-term relationships: Does the influence of network members ever end? *Journal of Marriage and Family.*

Burgess, E. W. (1926). The family as a unit of interacting personalities. *The Family, 7*, 3–9.

Burleson, B. R. (1992). Taking communication seriously. *Communication Monographs, 59*, 79–86.

Burleson, B. R., & Denton, W. H. (1997). The relationship between communication skill and marital satisfaction: Some moderating effects. *Journal of Marriage and the Family, 59*, 884–902.

Burman B., John R. S., & Margolin G. (1992). Observed patterns of conflict in violent, non-violent, and non-distressed couples. *Behavioral Assessment, 14*, 15–37.

Carels, R. A., & Baucom, D. H. (1999). Support in marriage: Factors associated with on-line perceptions of support helpfulness. *Journal of Family Psychology, 13*, 131–144.

Caughlin, J. P., & Huston, T. L. (2002). A contextual analysis of the association between demand/withdraw and marital satisfaction. *Personal Relationships, 9*, 95–119.

Christensen, A. (1987). Detection of conflict patterns in couples. In K. Hahlweg & M. J. Goldstein (Ed.), Understanding major mental disorder. *The contribution of family interaction research* (pp. 250–265). New York: Family Process Press.

Christensen, A. (1988). Dysfunctional interaction patterns in couples. In P. Noller & M. A. Fitzpatrick (Eds.), *Perspectives on marital interaction* (pp. 31–52). Clevedon, Avon, England: Multilingual Matters.

Christensen, A., & Heavey, C. L. (1990). Gender and social structure in the demand/withdraw pattern of marital conflict. *Journal of Personality and Social Psychology, 59*, 73–81.

Christensen, A., & Shenk, J. L. (1991) Communication, conflict, and psychological distance in nondistressed, clinic, and divorcing couples. *Journal of Consulting and Clinical Psychology, 59*, 458–463.

Cohan, C. L., & Bradbury, T. N. (1997). Negative life events, marital interaction, and the longitudinal course of newlywed marriage. *Journal of Personality and Social Psychology, 73*, 114–128.

Conger, R. D., Rueter, M. A., & Elder, G. H., Jr. (1999). Couple resilience to economic pressure. *Journal of Personality and Social Psychology, 76*, 54–71.

Coop-Gordon, K., Baucom, D. H., & Snyder, D. K. (2000). The use of forgiveness in marital therapy. In M. E. McCullough, K. I. Pargament, & C. E. Thoresen (Eds.), *Forgiveness: Theory, research and practice*. New York: Guilford Press.

Coyne, J. C., & DeLongis, A. (1986). Going beyond social support: The role of social relationships in adaptation. *Journal of Consulting and Clinical Psychology, 54*, 454–460.

Cuber, J. F., & Harroff, P. (1965). *The significant Americans: A study of sexual behavior among the affluent*. New York: Appleton-Century–Crofts.

Cutrona, C. (1996). *Social support in couples*. Thousand Oaks, CA: Sage.

Cutrona C. E., & Suhr, J. A. (1994). Social support communication in the context of marriage: An analysis of couples' supportive interactions. In B. B. Burleson, T. L. Albrecht, & I. G. Sarason (Eds.), *Communication of social support: Messages, relationships, and community* (pp. 113–135). Thousand Oaks, CA: Sage.

Davila, J., Bradbury, T. N., Cohan, C. L., & Tochluk, S. (1997). Marital functioning and depressive symptoms: Evidence for a stress generation model. *Journal of Personality and Social Psychology, 73*, 849–861.

Doherty, W. J. (1981a). Cognitive processes in intimate conflict: I. Extending attribution theory. *American Journal of Family Therapy, 9*, 3–13.

Doherty, W. J. (1981b). Cognitive processes in intimate conflict: II. Efficacy and learned helplessness. *American Journal of Family Therapy, 9*, 35–44.

Downie, R. S. (1971). *Roles and values*. London: Methuen.

Emery, R. E. (1992). Family conflict and its developmental implications: A conceptual analysis of deep meanings and systemic processes. In C. U. Shantz & W. W. Hartup (Eds.), *Conflict in child and adolescent development* (pp. 270–297). London: Cambridge University Press.

Feeney, J. A., Noller, P., & Callan, V. J. (1994). Attachment style, communication, and satisfaction in the early years of marriage. In K. Bartholomew & D. Perlman (Eds.), *Attachment processes in adulthood* (pp. 269–308). London: Jessica Kingsley.

Fenell, D. (1993). Characteristics of long-term first marriages. *Journal of Mental Health Counseling, 15*, 446–460.

Fichten, C. S., & Wright, J. (1983). Problem-solving skills in happy and distressed couples: Effects of videotape and verbal feedback. *Journal of Clinical Psychology, 39*, 340–352.

Fincham, F. D. (1995). From the orthogenic principle to the fish-scale model of omniscience: Advancing understanding of personal relationships. *Journal of Social and Personal Relationships, 12*, 523–527.

Fincham, F. D. (2000). The kiss of the porcupines: From attributing responsibility to forgiving. *Personal Relationships, 7*, 1–23.

Fincham, F. D., & Beach, S. R. (1999a). Marriage in the new millenium: Is there a place for social cognition in marital research? *Journal of Social and Personal Relationships, 16*, 685–704.

Fincham, F. D., & Beach, S. R. (1999b). Marital conflict: Implications for working with couples. *Annual Review of Psychology, 50*, 47–77.

Fincham, F. D., & Beach, S. R. (2002). Forgiveness in marriage: Implications for psychological aggression and constructive communication. *Personal Relationships, 9*, 239–251.

Fincham, F. D., Beach, S. R. H., & Davila, J. (in press). Forgiveness and conflict resolution in marriage. *Journal of Family Psychology.*

Fincham, F. D., Beach, S. R., & Kemp-Fincham, S. I. (1997). Marital quality: A new theoretical perspective. In R. J. Sternberg & M. Hojjat (Eds.), *Satisfaction in close relationships* (pp. 275–304). New York: Guilford Press.

Fincham, F. D., & Bradbury, T.N. (1987). Cognitive processes and conflict in close relationships: An attribution-efficacy model. *Journal of Personality and Social Psychology, 53*, 1106–1118.

Fincham, F. D., & Bradbury, T. N. (1988). The impact of attributions in marriage: An experimental analysis. *Journal of Social and Clinical Psychology, 7*, 147–162.

Fincham, F. D., & Bradbury, T. N. (1992). Assessing attributions in marriage: The Relationship Attribution Measure. *Journal of Personality and Social Psychology, 62*, 457–468.

Fincham, F. D., Bradbury, T. N., & Grych, J. (1990). Conflict in close relationships: The role of intrapersonal phenomena. In S. Graham & V. Folkes (Eds.), *Attribution theory: Applications to achievement, mental health, and interpersonal conflict* (pp. 161–184). Hillsdale, NJ: Lawrence Erlbaum Asssociates.

Fincham, F. D., Fernandes, L. O., & Humphreys, K. H. (1993). *Communicating in relationships: A guide for couples and professionals.* Champaign: Research Press.

Fincham, F. D., Harold, G., & Gano-Phillips, S. (2000). The longitudinal relation between attributions and marital satisfaction: Direction of effects and role of efficacy expectations. *Journal of Family Psychology, 14*, 267–285.

Fincham, F. D., Paleari, G., & Regalia, C. (2002). Forgiveness in marriage: The role of relationship quality, attributions and empathy. *Personal Relationships, 9*, 27–37.

Fitzpatrick, M. A. (1976). *A typological examination of communication in enduring relationships.* Unpublished doctoral dissertation, Temple University, Philadelphia.

Fitzpatrick, M. A. (1988). *Between husbands and wives.* Beverly Hills, CA: Sage.

Geiss, S. K., & O'Leary, K. D. (1981). Therapist ratings of frequency and severity of marital problems: Implications for research. *Journal of Marital and Family Therapy, 7*, 515–520.

Gotlib, I. H., Lewinsohn, P. M., & Seeley, J. R. (1998). Consequences of depression during adolescnce: Marital status and marital functioning in early adulthood. *Journal of Abnormal Psychology, 107*, 686–690.

Gottman, J. M. (1979). *Marital interaction: Experimental investigations.* New York: Academic Press.

Gottman J. M. (1994). *What predicts divorce?* Hillsdale, NJ: Lawrence Erlbaum Associates.

Gottman, J. M. (1998). Psychology and the study of marital processes. *Annual Review of Psychology, 49*, 169–197.

Gottman, J. M., Coan, J., Carrerre, S., & Swanson, C. (1998). Predicting marital happiness and stability from newlywed interactions. *Journal of Marriage and the Family, 60*, 5–22.

Gottman, J. M., & Krokoff, L. J. (1989). Marital interaction and satisfaction: A longitudinal view. *Journal of Consulting and Clinical Psychology, 57*, 47–52.

Gottman, J. M., Markman, H. J., & Notarius, C. I. (1977). The topography of marital conflict: A sequential analysis of verbal and nonverbal behavior. *Journal of Marriage and the Family, 49*, 461–477.

Gottman, J. M., & Notarius, C. I. (2000). Decade review: Observing marital interaction. *Journal of Marriage and the Family, 62*, 927–947.

Halford, W. K., Gravestock, F. M., Lowe, R., & Scheldt, S. (1992). Toward a behavioral ecology of stressful marital interactions. *Behavioral Assessment, 14*, 199–217.

Hargrave, T. D., & Sells, J. N. (1997). The development of a forgiveness scale. *Journal of Marital and Family Therapy, 23*, 41–62.

Heavey, C. L., Christensen, A., & Malamuth, N. M. (1995). The longitudinal impact of demand and withdrawal during marital conflict. *Journal of Consulting and Clinical Psychology, 63*, 797–801.

Heavey, C. L., Layne, C., & Christensen, A. (1993). Gender and conflict structure in marital interaction: A replication and extension. *Journal of Consulting and Clinical Psychology, 61*, 16–27.

Hess, R., & Handel, G. (1959). *Family worlds.* Chicago: University of Chicago Press.

Hinde, R. A. (1997). *Relationships: A dialectical perspective.* Hove: Psychology Press.

Horsburgh, H. J. (1974). Forgiveness. *Canadian Journal of Philosophy, 4*, 269–289.

Hughes, D., Galinsky, E., & Morris, A. (1992). The effects of job characteristics on marital quality: Specifying linking mechanisms. *Journal of Marriage and the Family, 54*, 31–42.

Huston, T. L., & Chorost, A. F. (1994). Behavioral buffers on the effect of negativity on marital satisfaction: A longitudinal study. *Personal Relationships, 1*, 223–239.

Jacob, T. (1987). Family interaction and psychopathology: Historical overview. In T. Jacob (Ed.), *Family interaction and psychopathology* (pp. 3–22). New York: Plenum Press.

Jacobson, N. S., & Christensen, A. (1996). *Integrative couple therapy: Promoting acceptance and change.* New York: Norton.

Johnson, M. P., Huston, T. L., Gaines, S. O., & Levinger, G. (1992). Patterns of married life among young couples. *Journal of Social and Personal Relationships, 9*, 343–364.

Julien, D., Markman, H. J., Leveille, S., Chartrand, E., & Begin, J. (1994). Networks' support and interference with regard to marriage: Disclosures of marital problems to confidants. *Journal of Family Psychology, 8,* 16–31.

Karney, B. R., & Bradbury, T. N. (1995). The longitudinal course of marital quality and stability: A review of theory, method, and research. *Psychological Bulletin, 118,* 3–34.

Keelan, J. P. R., Dion, K. K., & Dion, K. L. (1998). Attachment style and relationship satisfaction: Test of a self-disclosure explanation. *Canadian Journal of Behavioural Science, 30,* 24–35.

Kelly, D. (1998). The communication of forgiveness. *Communication Studies, 49,* 1–17.

Kelly, A., Fincham, F. D., & Beach, S. R. H. (2003). Emerging perspectives on couple communication. In J. O. Greene & B. R. Burlson (Eds.), *Handbook of communication and social interaction skills* (pp. 273–752). NJ: Lawrence Erlbaum Associates.

Kelly, A. B., & Halford, W. K. (1995). The generalization of behavioral marital therapy to behavioral, cognitive and physiological domains. *Cognitive and Behavioral Psychotherapy, 23,* 381–398.

Kelley, H. H., Berscheid, E., Christensen, A., Harvey, J. H., Huston, T. L., Levinger, G., McClintock, E., Peplau, L. A., & Peterson, D. R. (1983). Analyzing close relationships. In H. H. Kelley, E. Berscheid, A. Christensen, J. H. Harvey, T. L. Huston, G. Levinger, E. McClintock, L. A. Peplau, & D. R. Peterson (Eds.), *Close relationships* (pp. 20–67). New York: W. H. Freeman and Company.

Klinetob, N. A., & Smith, D. A. (1996). Demand-withdraw communication in marital interaction: Tests of interpersonal contingency and gender role hypotheses. *Journal of Marriage and the Family, 58,* 945–957.

Kobak, R. R., & Hazan, C. (1991). Attachment in marriage: Effects of security and accuracy in working models. *Journal of Personality and Social Psychology, 60,* 861–869.

Koerner K., & Jacobson N. J. (1994). Emotion and behavior in couple therapy. In S. M. Johnson & L. S. Greenberg (Eds.), *The heart of the matter: Perspectives on emotion in marital therapy* (pp. 207–226). New York: Brunner/Mazel.

Krokoff, L. J. (1987). The correlates of negative affect in marriage: An exploratory study of gender differences. *Journal of Family Issues, 8,* 111–135.

Krokoff, L. J., Gottman, J. M., & Hass, S. D. (1989). Validation of a global rapid couples interaction scoring system. *Behavioral Assessment, 11,* 65–79.

Krokoff, L. J., Gottman, J. M., & Roy, A. K. (1988). Blue-collar and white-collar marital interaction and communication orientation. *Journal of Social and Personal Relationships, 5,* 201–221.

Margolin, G., Burman, B., John, R. S. (1989). Home observations of married couples reenacting naturalistic conflicts. *Behavioral Assessment, 11,* 101–118.

Margolin, G., John, R. S., & Gleberman, L. (1989). Affective responses to conflictual discussion in violent and nonviolent couples. *Journal of Consulting and Clinical Psychology, 56,* 24–33.

Margolin, G., & Wampold, B. E. (1981). Sequential analysis of conflict and accord in distressed and nondistressed marital partners. *Journal of Consulting and Clinical Psychology, 49,* 554–567.

McGonagle, K. A., Kessler R. C., & Schiling, E. A. (1992). The frequency and determinants of marital disagreements in a community sample. *Journal of Social and Personal Relationships, 9*, 507–524.

Menaghan, E. G. (1991). Work experiences and family interaction processes: The long reach of the job? *Annual Review of Psychology, 17*, 419–444.

Millar, F. E., & Rogers, L. E. (1988). Power dynamics in marital relationships. In P. Noller & M. A. Fitzpatrick (Eds.), *Perspectives on marital interaction* (pp. 78–97). Philadelphia: Multilingual Matters.

Millar, F. E., Rogers, L. E., & Courtright, J. A. (1979). Relational control and dyadic understanding: An exploratory predictive regression model. In D. Nimmo (Ed.), *Communication Yearbook 3* (pp. 213–224). New Brunswick, NJ: Transaction Books.

Miller, G. E., & Bradbury, T. N. (1995). Refining the association between attributions and behavior in marital interaction. *Journal of Family Psychology, 9*, 196–208.

Noller, P., Feeney, J. A., Bonnell, D., & Callan, V. J. (1994). A longitudinal study of conflict in early marriage. *Journal of Social and Personal Relationships, 11*, 233–252.

Notarius, C. I., & Johnson, J. S. (1982). Emotional expression in husbands and wives. *Journal of Marriage and the Family, 44*, 483–489.

Notarius, C. I., & Vanzetti, N. A. (1983). The marital agendas protocol. In E. Filsinger (Ed.), *Marriage and family assessment: A sourcebook for family therapy*. Beverley Hills, CA: Sage.

Nye, F. I. (1988). Fifty years of family research, 1937–1987. *Journal of Marriage and the Family, 50*, 305–316.

Olson, D. H. (1981). Family typologies: Bridging family research and family therapy. In E. E. Filsinger & R. A. Lewis (Eds.), *Assessing marriage: New behavioral approaches* (pp. 74–89). Beverly Hills, CA: Sage.

Pasch, L. A., & Bradbury, T. N. (1998). Social support, conflict, and the development of marital dysfunction. *Journal of Consulting and Clinical Psychology, 66*, 219–230.

Repetti, R. (1989). Effects of daily workload on subsequent behavior during marital interaction: The roles of social withdrawal and spouse support. *Journal of Personality and Social Psychology, 57*, 651–659.

Revensdorf, D., Hahlweg, K., Schindler L., & Vogel, B. (1984). Interaction analysis of marital conflict. In K. Hahlweg & N. S. Jacobson (Eds.), *Marital interaction: Analysis and modification* (pp.159–181). New York: Guilford Press.

Rholes, W. S., Simpson, J. A., & Orina, M. M. (1999). Attachment and anger in an anxiety-provoking situation. *Journal of Personality and Social Psychology, 76*, 940–957.

Roberts, N., & Noller, P. (1998). The associations between adult attachment and couple violence: The role of communication patterns and relationship satisfaction. In J. A. Simpson & W. S. Rholes (Eds.), *Attachment theory and close relationships* (pp. 317–352). New York: Guilford Press.

Rogers, L. E. (1972). *Dyadic systems and transactional communication in a family context*. Unpublished doctoral dissertation, Michigan State University.

Rogers-Millar, L. E., & Millar, F. E. (1979). Domineeringness and dominance: A transactional view. *Human Communication Research, 5*, 238–246.

Saitzyk, A. R., Floyd, F. J., & Kroll, A. B. (1997). Sequential analysis of autonomy-interdependence and affiliation-disaffiliation in couples' social support interactions. *Personal Relationships, 4*, 341–360.

Sanders, M. R., Halford, W. K., & Behrens, B. C. (1999). Parental divorce and premarital couple communication. *Journal of Family Psychology, 13*, 60–74.

Schaap, C. (1982). *Communication and adjustment in marriage.* Lisse, The Netherlands: Swets & Zeitlinger.

Schaap, C. (1984). A comparison of the interaction of distressed and nondistressed married couples in a laboratory situation: Literature survey, methodological issues, and an empirical investigation. In K. Hahlweg & N. S. Jacobson (Eds.), *Marital interaction: Analysis and modification* (pp. 133–158). New York: Guilford Press.

Schaap, C., Buunk, B., & Kerkstra, A. (1988). Marital conflict resolution. In P. Noller, & M. A. Fitzpatrick (Eds.), *Perspectives on Marital interaction* (pp. 203–244). Clevedon, Avon, England: Multilingual Matters.

Simpson, J. A., & Rholes, W. S. (Eds.). (1998). *Attachment theory and close relationships.* New York: Guilford Press.

Smith, D. A., Vivian, D., & O'Leary, K. D. (1990). Longitudinal prediction of marital discord from premarital expressions of affect. *Journal of Consulting and Clinical Psychology, 58*, 790–798.

Tesser, A., & Beach, S. R. H. (1998). Life events, relationship quality, and depression: An investigation of judgment discontinuity in vivo. *Journal of Personality and Social Psychology, 74*, 36–52.

Veroff, J., Kulka, R. A., & Douvan, E. (1981). *Mental health in American patterns of help seeking from 1957–1976.* New York: Basic Books.

Vincent, J. P., Friedman, L. C., Nugent, J., & Messerly, L. (1979). Demand characteristics in observations of marital interaction. *Journal of Consulting and Clinical Psychology, 47*, 557–566.

Weiss, R. L., & Heyman, R. E. (1990). Observation of marital interaction. In F. D. Fincham & T. N. Bradbury (Eds.), *The psychology of marriage* (pp. 87–118). New York: Guilford.

Weiss, R. L., & Heyman, R. E. (1997). A clinical-research overview of couple interactions. In W. K. Halford & H. Markman (Eds.), *The clinical handbook of marriage and couples interventions* (pp. 13–41). Brisbane: Wiley.

Weiss, R. L., & Tolman, A. O. (1990). The Marital Interaction Coding System-Global (MICS-G): A global companion to the MICS. *Behavioral Assessment, 12*, 271–294.

Watzlawick, P, Beavin, J., & Jackson, D. (1967). *The pragmatics of human communication.* New York: Norton.

Whitchurch, G. G., & Dickson, F. C. (1999) Family communication. In M. B. Sussman, S. K. Steinmetz, & G. W. Peterson (Eds.), *Handbook of marriage and the family* (2nd ed., pp. 687–704). New York: Plenum Press.

Worthington, E. L. & Wade, N. G. (1999). The psychology of unforgiveness and forgiveness and implications for clinical practice. *Journal of Social and Clinical Psychology, 18*, 385–418.

CHAPTER

5

BECOMING PARENTS

TED L. HUSTON AND ERIN KRAMER HOLMES
THE UNIVERSITY OF TEXAS AT AUSTIN

There can be no doubt that parenthood produces changes in the lives of mothers and fathers. New parents become true experts on things like strollers, car seats, bottles, diapers, and late-night feedings. Not only does everyday life change for couples as they add more tasks to the seemingly full list of family chores, but having a baby also absorbs much of their time and attention—particularly for new mothers. Erdrich's (1995) compelling memoir of her own transition to parenthood captures the extent to which newborns consume a mother's energies and gives a real sense of the intensity of new motherhood:

> One reason there is not a great deal written about what it is like to be the mother of a new infant is that there is rarely a moment to think of anything else besides that infant's needs. Endless time with a small baby is spent asking, What do you want? What do you want? The sounds of her unhappiness range from mild yodeling to extended bawls. What do you want? Our baby's cries are not monotonous. They seem quite purposeful, though hard to describe.... I do what she tells me to do—feed, burp, change, amuse, distract, hold, help, look at, help to sleep, reassure—without constantly choosing to do it. I take her instructions without translating her meaning into words, but simply bypass straight to action. My brain is a white blur. I lose track of what I've been doing, where I've been, who I am. (p. 56–57)

As we read her account, we feel her pressure, her sense of urgency, and the constant monotony that are all part of life as she transitions to parenthood. Though her days seem an endless wash of baby's cries, her next telling confession demonstrates a deeper emotional connection to her child as she admits "that in deep love, I want her, I choose her. I adore the privilege of our baby's constant care" (p. 56).

New fathers also adapt, though changes in a new father's life may appear to be less dramatic for those whose wives leave the work force when their baby is born, or for those whose wives have always chosen to stay home (see Cowan, 1988). Cowan (1988) reports that fathers experience a more dramatic transition to parenthood at least 6 months after the birth of their children. Fathers expect changes in the early months following the birth of their first child. They anticipate changes in their spouses' time use and in their partners' body as it readjusts after childbirth. However, fathers' lives do not appear to bounce back as easily or as readily as once projected. This impact of parenthood on fathers takes hold more gradually than it does for mothers; thus, the likelihood they are to report stress associated with the transition is greater once the high of becoming a new parent wears off (for an excellent review of men's transitions to parenthood, see Berman & Pedersen, 1987). However, how fathers experience the transition to parenthood is still a widely unexplored area of research (Strauss & Goldberg, 1999).

Aside from changing one's focus from oneself to a new baby, couples have reported changes in their marital relationship. A participant in a recent longitudinal study complained, "Our everyday talk just isn't there any more, because suddenly all the focus is on the baby. And although that brings a lot of joy, you also start to notice those things that have dropped away" (Feeney, Hohaus, Noller, & Alexander, 2001, p. 88).

The changes to one's lifestyle, particularly the changing climate of the marital relationship, have sparked much scholarly debate. Historically, academic writing concerned with the introduction of a baby into a family emphasized its strong negative impact (although occasionally a researcher such as Russell, 1974, would come forward to propose that parenthood brings forth compensating gratifications). LeMasters' (1957) classic article declared that new fathers and mothers were unprepared for and overwhelmed by the "crisis" accompanying the arrival of a child. His thesis aroused strong public interest in this issue. Almost a dozen years later, LeMasters noted, his conclusion was continuing to be put forth in national magazines and major newspapers (LeMasters, 1970). Longitudinal studies initiated in the early 1980s, however, began to create cracks in this monolithic negative view of the impact of parenthood on marriage. Over time, as scholars examined correlates of the direction and extent of change in satisfaction following the birth of a child, they have increasingly recognized that parenthood may enhance some marriages, undermine others, and have little effect on still others (Belsky & Kelly, 1994; Cowan & Cowan, 2000; Feeney et al., 2001).

In this chapter we present a framework that researchers can use to address the adjustments and adaptations spouses make when they become parents. We consider both research design and other methodological issues that have undermined research in this area. Our central concern will be on the impact of primiparous parenting on marital well-being, but we will also discuss the process of becoming a parent, focusing on the adaptations partners make as they incorporate a child into their life together. We organize our discussion around our own longitudinal study of couples, some of whom became parents, and examine how marriages and lifestyles change when couples have their first baby. As we move from how having a baby affects various facets of married life, we place our findings in the context of the larger body of research, showing both the contribution of our own research and its limitations.

RESEARCH DESIGN AND METHODOLOGICAL CONSIDERATIONS

On Establishing Parenthood as a Causal Agent

Research on the transition to parenthood has implemented successively more sophisticated strategies for establishing the role parenthood plays in marital life. Cook and Campbell (1979) identify three hallmarks of causal explanation that can be used to characterize the evolution of work on the transition to parenthood. The first criterion for establishing causality is showing that the presumed cause (parenthood) covaries with its putative effect (marital quality). Cross-sectional studies comparing parents and nonparents meet this criterion (e.g., Figley, 1973; Miller, 1976). Cross-sectional studies that find parents less happily married than nonparents do not provide compelling support for the idea that parenthood undermines marital quality for three reasons. First, couples who become parents may differ in satisfaction independent of their parental status. The lesser satisfaction of such couples may have been present prior to parenthood. Helms-Erikson (2001) discovered that couples who entered parenthood both before marriage and shortly after they were wed reported lower marital quality prior to becoming parents than couples who had their first baby either "on time" or "delayed." The purported differences associated with parenthood may to some extent reflect differences between the couples who became parents before building a strong relationship foundation, not simply parenthood in general. Further, differences associated with parenthood may actually reflect one's values and expectations for parenthood which, as Helms-Erikson suggests, are critical aspects of timing and life-course transitions.

Second, having children encourages unhappy couples to stay married out of the belief that divorce would put their children at risk (Glenn & McLanahan, 1982; Waite, Haggstrom, & Kanouse, 1985; Waite & Lillard, 1991; White & Booth, 1985). The stability of their union is not, however, a function of their marital happiness; thus, any group of parents is likely to include more unhappy couples than a comparable group of nonparents (Shapiro, Gottman, & Carrère, 2000; Waite & Lillard, 1991; White, Booth, & Edwards, 1986).

Third, couples who become parents may differ from nonparents in other ways, including but not limited to their own attitudes and desires toward parenting, their expectations about the experience of parenthood, and their feelings of adequacy or inadequacy as a caregiver (Rholes, Simpson, Blakely, Lanigan, & Allen, 1997). Differences between nonparents and parents may well be reflected in reports of satisfaction (Menaghan, 1982). A cross-sectional comparison of married couples who are parents with those who are nonparents would include sets of couples who were married at different ages and who have been married for different lengths of time. Even with changing demographic trends suggesting that women are bearing their first children at older ages than they have in the past 40 to 50 years (Waldrop, 1994), the parent group is likely to be younger and married for a shorter length of time than the nonparent group, and these factors, rather than parenthood status alone, may account for group differences in marital satisfaction or marital stability (Huston & Vangelisti, 1995; Moore & Waite, 1981).

Cook and Campbell's (1979) second criterion for proving causal significance is establishing the temporal precedence of the putative cause. With data gathered from couples

before and after they become parents, longitudinal designs establish the temporal precedence of parenthood as the putative cause. In the most common longitudinal design, a
single group of couples in which the wives are pregnant is followed from before to after the
births of the children. These studies often (Belsky, Lang, & Rovine, 1985; Belsky, Spanier,
& Rovine, 1983; Cowan et al., 1985; Feldman & Nash, 1984; Ruble, Fleming, Hackel,
& Stangor, 1988; Tomlinson, 1987), although not invariably (Cox, Paley, Burchinal, &
Payne, 1999; Meyerowitz & Feldman, 1966; Miller & Sollie, 1980; Waldron & Routh,
1981; Wallace & Gotlib, 1990), report linear declines in marital well-being from before to
1 year after childbirth. Cowan and Cowan (1988), in one of the longer longitudinal studies,
followed couples over 2 years and reported declines in satisfaction among couples who
became parents.

Although the designs used in most longitudinal investigations provide information
that was unavailable in earlier cross-sectional studies, they have at least three limitations
(Cook & Campbell, 1979). First, couples about to become parents may, as a consequence
of their pregnancies, be temporarily happier with their marriages; thus, changes in marital
satisfaction may reflect regression toward the mean (regression effects). Second, as couples settle into marriage, their satisfaction may decline over time regardless of whether
they become parents (maturation effects). This is important because a sizable proportion
of couples become parents during the first few years of marriage, a period over which declines in satisfaction are normative (see Glenn, 1998; see also Vaillant & Vaillant, 1993).
Third, the before/after design used in the studies that investigate the impact of parenthood on marriage, coupled with the participants' awareness of the general purposes of the
investigation, may affect the data (testing effects).

The third criterion for establishing causality is the exclusion of alternative explanations for the putative cause–effect relationship (Cook & Campbell, 1979). The use of a
comparison group of couples who do not make the transition to parenthood provides one
way of eliminating alternative explanations such as maturation effects. The few studies
that have included comparison groups of couples who do not make the transition over the
same period, however, provide little support for the idea that parenthood produces a linear
decline in marital satisfaction. White and Booth (1985) in one such study assessed marital
satisfaction using a purely evaluative index in their 3-year longitudinal study. Both parents
and nonparent groups experienced declines in satisfaction over the 3 years studied: People
who became parents, however, did not differ from those who remained childless, either
before or after the former group made the transition to parenthood. This study was the first
of many that has shown that marital satisfaction among new parents does not decline more
so than among nonparents (Cowan & Cowan, 1988; Karney & Bradbury, 1997; Kurdek,
1993; MacDermid, Huston, & McHale, 1990; McHale & Huston, 1985). Crohan (1996),
however, reported a marginally greater decline among White (but not among African-
American) parents in marital satisfaction). The fact is that couples become less satisfied
with their marriages with time, particularly during the early years when many of them
have their first child.

We have uncovered two additional studies that used a comparison group that would seem
to report findings that are contrary to our general pattern, but both of them used the Locke–
Wallace (1959) Marital Adjustment Test (MAT), a scale that confounds global assessments
of satisfaction with reports of behavioral change in marriage (Ryder, 1973; Shapiro et al.,

2000) (see Fincham and Bradbury, 1987, for an airing of the interpretive problems the use of these scales presents). Because the MAT and the commonly used Dyadic Adjustment Scale (DAS) do not focus exclusively (or even primarily) on how satisfied spouses are with their marriage, we cannot conclude from studies that use these measures that change associated with parenthood reflect alterations in "marital satisfaction" rather than changes in spouses' perceptions of how they function together on a day-to-day basis.

The preponderance of the data fail to support the view that parenthood typically undermines marital satisfaction. Parenthood clearly instigates changes in marital lifestyle, largely because the dependence of a baby on the parents requires their constant attention; yet, for many, the difficulties of parenthood appear to be offset by the pleasures the new role brings to the mother and father. Because couples differ in how much they welcome the changes that parenthood brings, researchers have begun to shift their attention to examining differences in how parenthood affects marital satisfaction. Nonetheless, researchers continue to presume that changes in nonparents' satisfaction in studies that do not include a comparison group of nonparents are the result of parenthood—not recognizing that marriages ordinarily become less satisfying with time, particularly over the first few years, a time when many couples have children. Social scientific reports on the transition to parenthood continue to cite these studies uncritically, as well as those that use scales that confound spouses' evaluations of their marriage with their characterizations of their lifestyle.

Temporal Aspects of the Impact of Parenthood on Marriage

Practical considerations have led most researchers to gather data on one or two occasions within a year after childbirth from couples who have become parents. Because the processes through which parenthood affects marital well-being are poorly understood, social scientists have given little attention to the timing of marital assessments. Kelly and McGrath (1988) argue that researchers need to incorporate temporal parameters into their conceptualization of causal agents and to articulate the hypothesized temporal path created by the putative cause. They describe a variety of ways an event, X (e.g., the birth of a child) might affect an outcome, Y (e.g., marital satisfaction).

Figure 5.1a portrays a process that develops in a linear fashion over time. Figures 5.1b and 5.1c, in contrast, portray parenthood as creating an immediate effect that persists over time in the first case and fades in the second. Research that uses data gathered from parents soon after childbirth assumes parenthood has an almost immediate impact. Much of the research on the transition to parenthood, even that of a longitudinal nature, is based on reports gathered from new parents on only one or two occasions relatively soon after the birth of the first child (please note two important recent exceptions, Belsky & Hsieh, 1998, and Cox et al., 1999, discussed in further detail later in the chapter). As a consequence, studies may pick up short-term fluctuations in satisfaction but may fail to detect more slowly emerging effects of parenthood. Thus, although the literature on the transition to parenthood tends to characterize parenthood as a "crisis," it is unclear whether the crisis and its effects dissipate over time as couples reconcile differences (Fig. 5.1c) or whether the marital patterns instigated by the crisis build over time, creating long-lasting change in marital well-being (Fig. 5.1a).

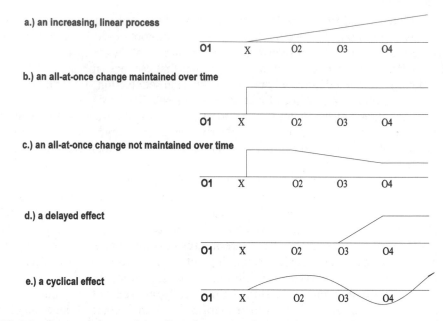

FIG. 5.1.   Temporal shapes of the effect of parenthood on marriage. *Note.* From *On Time and Method,* by J. R. Kelly and J. E. McGrath, 1988, Newbury Park, CA: Sage. Adapted with permission from Sage.

Figure 5.1d suggests another possible pattern. Here, the effect of parenthood does not surface immediately but increases gradually over time and then levels off. For example, if parenthood increases stress and conflict in marriage (Hill, 1949; LeMasters, 1957), the impact of the conflictual and negative patterns may not surface immediately but may cumulate with time and erode satisfaction. On the other hand, parenthood may bring with it a sense of elation that might be reflected in a short-lived upswing in satisfaction, followed by a decline (as shown in Fig. 5.1c) (see Miller & Sollie, 1980; Wallace & Gotlib, 1990). Figure 5.1d, in contrast, shows parenthood as having a delayed or "sleeper" impact on marriage. The influence of parenthood on marital satisfaction may surface years later, for example, as a consequence of spouses' having very different religious values or ideas about child rearing.

Finally, Fig. 5.1e shows a cyclical pattern reflecting modulations in spouses' marital satisfaction over time. Marital satisfaction contains both a relatively stable traitlike component and a statelike element that resonates to the vicissitudes of day-to-day life (Robins, 1990; Wiggins, 1979). If the cyclical pattern of spouses' satisfaction is the same from one couple to another, different conclusions might be reached about the impact of parenthood, depending on the timing of measurement. Parenthood could create highs and lows in the lives of couples, but the timing of these highs and lows may be largely idiosyncratic. If the pattern is not timed similarly across couples, the effects of parenthood are likely to be masked.

Moreover, many questions about the long-term effects of the transition to parenthood still exist. When only a few data points are considered, even in longitudinal research, our impression of the transition to parenthood may be warped by our lack of knowledge about the periods in a couple's relationship prior to the pregnancy and years after the first child is born. For example, Goldberg, Michaels, and Lamb (1985) describe one important problem when only a few data points are considered, even in longitudinal research. Due to an increase in fathers' involvement in household tasks during late pregnancy (measured at 7 to 8 months), a time when most researchers have taken their first assessment of the effects of the transition to parenthood on marriage, some researchers may overstate the shift toward traditional roles brought on by the transition to parenthood. On the other hand, Cowan and Cowan (1988) argue husbands often increase their active participation in the home during the early postpartum weeks; thus, 4-month follow-ups may underestimate the extent to which roles shift with parenthood toward traditional gendered patterns.

Links Among Parenthood, Marital Patterns, and Satisfaction

Parenthood marks a transition for couples, but that transition begins before the physical birth of the child (Cowan, 1991). Pregnancy itself can strengthen couples' feelings of togetherness (Feeney et al., 2001), increase a wife's sense of her husband's care for her (Kramer, 1998), increase a man's potential to develop generativity (Hawkins & Dollahite, 1997), or provide the couple with new leisure opportunities (e.g., buying materials for baby, planning for baby's future, choosing baby's names, and attending birthing classes together). Pregnancy can initiate the transition to parenthood for working women as they consider how their new child-care responsibilities fit in with their current career goals. These considerations suggest that parenthood "as a cause" can be viewed in a number of different ways. Following Cook and Campbell (1979), parenthood can be taken as a "macro" event that sets in motion a number of other adjustments of a macro nature (e.g., changes in spouses' labor force participation or economic well-being) that may affect marital satisfaction. According to Cook and Campbell (1979), macro events may also set in motion other, more specific, events—referred to as "micromediational" events—that affect the satisfactoriness of the marriage. Thus, for example, parenthood may be the root cause of alterations in the division of household labor, sleep deficits, increases in the amount of stress spouses experience, or decreases in the opportunity for spouses to pursue enjoyable leisure activities—any of which may undermine partners' sense of satisfaction with their marriage. It is critical to identify how parenthood affects the day-to-day lives of marital couples and to pinpoint which of these changes make differences in how spouses come to feel about each other and their marriage. Parenthood may be a "big change" for many couples, as Cowan and Cowan (2000) suggest, but whether on balance it is an unwelcome change for marriage is another matter.

THE PAIR[1] PROJECT AS A CONTEXT FOR STUDYING THE IMPACT OF PARENTHOOD ON MARRIAGE

We organize the rest of our discussion of the transition to parenthood around our longitudinal study of newlyweds, because the study has several design strengths that are unusual in research in this area. First, by gathering systematic diary data from couples, we were able

---

[1] PAIR stands for Processes of Adaptation in Intimate Relationships. The acronym captures our interest in studying how couples adapt or adjust to one another as they move through their life together. Readers interested in learning more about the results should consult the project Website: www.utexas.edu/research/pair

to explore in considerable depth the impact having a baby has on a great many aspects of married life, including the roles played by the husband and the wife, their companionship, their sexual behavior in the marriage, expressions of affection, and the degree to which they were irritable with each other. Second, we were able to compare the earlier marital patterns of couples who became parents with those of childless couples, making it possible for us to discover whether parents differ from nonparents before they have a child with regard to various features of their marriages. Third, the comparison over time of couples who became parents with those who do not have a child early in marriage make it possible to determine whether it is parenthood, rather than the passage of time, that accounts for changes in the quality of marriage. Fourth, we could examine the influence of the timing of parenthood on aspects of the marriage. We were thereby in a position to determine whether parenthood hastens the loss of romance, as others have suggested, or whether previous researchers were mistaken and that such a loss, if it occurs, is part of the ordinary waning of romance as marriage progresses. Fifth, participants were not sensitized to the nature of the study. The issue of parenthood was never identified as a focal point of the research, nor was the timing of births used to determine data collection periods.

We initially gathered data approximately 2 months after couples were wed. The second and third phases of data collection took place 14 months and 26 months into marriage. The initial sample, drawn from marriage license records in four counties in central Pennsylvania, consisted of 168 first-time married couples, 128 of whom stayed married and were followed across all three phases of the study. We differentiated three groups: (a) *first-year parents* ($N = 29$ couples)—those who had a baby during the initial year of their marriage. Couples in this category were younger than those in the other two, and the wives worked fewer hours for pay than women in the other two groups; (b) *second-year parents* ($N = 23$ couples); and (c) *nonparents* ($N = 46$ couples). This roster eliminated 10 couples to whom a child was born before they married and another 10 who divorced during the first 26 months of marriage. A few couples were also dropped because they did not complete the full complement of diary-based interviews we used.

Because we collected detailed diary data on three occasions that were spaced a year apart, beginning when couples were newlyweds, we could see how marriages unfolded and how becoming parents affected the couples' marriages and their lifestyle. It is important to note here that because "newlywed" data were gathered about 2 months into marriage, with the next two data collections occurring at 14 months and 26 months, the couples who made the transition to parenthood did so between 2 and 26 months of their wedding. Husbands and wives supplied detailed information on several evenings about their participation with regard to a comprehensive list of 26 household chores, 14 child-care tasks, and more than 50 leisure activities. They also provided regular diary information concerning each other's overt expressions of affection; about sexual intercourse; and about how often they criticized, displayed anger, or otherwise showed offense. The data concerning these interpersonal events were subsequently grouped, based on a series of factor analyses, into three types of events: (a) the expression of affection, (b) negativity, and (c) sexual interest (Huston & Vangelisti, 1991; the interested reader should consult Huston, Robins, Atkinson, & McHale, 1987, for details concerning the diary procedure).

The PAIR project study, like most of the research on parenthood, focuses largely on the changes that take place relatively soon after couples have their first baby, and for the most part, the couples are drawn from a White, largely working-class rural area. This kind of subpopulation has not been studied much when it comes to the effects of parenthood on marriage. In some sense, then, our research can be taken as providing a test of the broader generalizability of conclusions about the impact of parenthood on marriage that have been based on convenience samples of highly educated urbanites.

HOW PARENTHOOD AFFECTS MARRIED LIFE

Parenthood is generally thought to nudge marriages away from what might be regarded as "loving companionships" toward more "working partnerships" (Bernard, 1964; Cowan & Cowan, 1987). We examined division of labor, spouses' leisure and companionship, and socioemotional behavior to assess the ways in which parenthood affects the day-to-day life of couples, including whether the division of labor becomes more traditionalized, whether spouses' companionship is reduced, and whether marriages become less affectionate or more conflict ridden over time.

The Expansion of Work at Home

Figure 5.2 uses PAIR project data to illustrate alterations in couples' lifestyle that accompany parenthood (Huston & Vangelisti, 1995; MacDermid et al., 1990). Before parenthood, we see that wives do 67.2% of the chores (an average of 3.9 chores a day), leaving husbands with the remaining 32.8% of the chores (an average of 1.9 chores a day). The arrival of a child produces a sixfold increase in the number of family-related activities performed on an average day, from 5.8 tasks completed per day before parenthood to 36.2 tasks per day after parenthood. New mothers increase their household tasks to 5.3 tasks on average per day and accumulate another 22.7 child-care tasks. New fathers also increase their participation in household tasks to 2.4 per day and accrue an average of 5.9 child-care tasks. One can see the great expansion of the couples' workload in the home after they become parents, particularly as new mothers dramatically increase their involvement in child-care tasks (see also Cowan et al., 1985; Ruble et al., 1988). Fathers' responsibilities grow as they become involved in child-care tasks, but the escalation of their duties is clearly more modest than that of mothers.

The expansion of work at home is a commonly reported finding related to the transition to parenthood (Belsky & Kelly, 1994). Though inequity in the amount of work women do at home versus the amount of work men do at home still exists, empirical evidence shows that women will complete up to two thirds of household work before they feel a sense of unfairness in the division of labor (Lennon & Rosenfield, 1994). Men will complete roughly 36% of family work when they begin to sense the load landing unjustly on them (Lennon & Rosenfield, 1994). Why might such a rift exist between men's and women's sense of equity in the completion of household tasks? Does this gap continue as domestic tasks increase so drastically in the transition to parenthood? Grote, Naylor, and Clark (in press) explored women's and men's sense of fairness in family work across the transition to parenthood. They focus on what might lead mothers and fathers to view their unequal workloads as fair or unfair. Among other findings, Grote et al. (in press) reported that women's perceptions of inequity are greater the less pleasure they get out of doing

Before Parenthood

Average Number of Tasks Done Per Day = 5.8

After Parenthood

Average Number of Tasks Done Per Day = 36.2

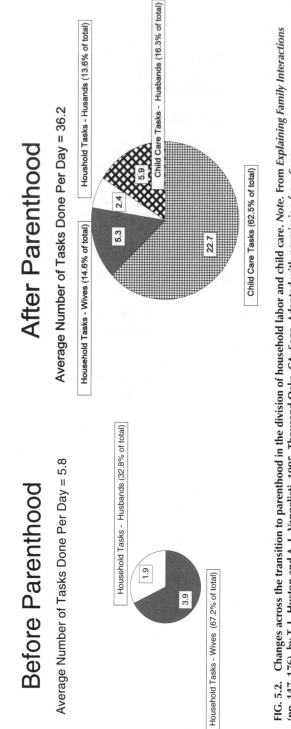

FIG. 5.2. Changes across the transition to parenthood in the division of household labor and child care. *Note.* From *Explaining Family Interactions* (pp. 147–176), by T. L. Huston and A. L. Vangelisti, 1995, Thousand Oaks, CA: Sage. Adapted with permission from Sage.

household and child-care tasks; men's enjoyment for these tasks does not consistently predict their sense of equity as reflected in their reports of satisfaction with the division of labor. Further, the most consistent predictor of a husband's sense of fairness was how competent he felt at family work and his wife's sense of his competence in performing such work. The more husbands thought their wives viewed them as competent, the more husbands contributed to both housework and child care. The sense of competence of wives, either as they perceived it or as their spouse perceived it, was unrelated to how wives felt about the division of family tasks. Finally, mothers' perceptions that fathers were good at family work were linked with reports that their husbands actually did more housework and child care. (For those interested in the impact of perceptions of fairness on marital satisfaction, please note that we will discuss these questions later in our chapter.)

Family Roles and the Division of Labor.   Most wives in the United States work outside the home—even when they are mothers of young children (U.S. Bureau of the Census, 1999), though they usually earn less money and work less consistently over the years than their husbands. In today's world, women generally prefer to work rather than to stay at home, even when their husband's income could support a relatively luxurious lifestyle (Barnett & Rivers, 1996). At the same time, working wives who become mothers continue to see themselves, and are generally identified by their husbands, as the primary caregiver. In most cases, both spouses appear to be comfortable with this understanding (McHale & Huston, 1984).

Most of the newlyweds we interviewed fashioned a lifestyle with the husband as primary breadwinner and the wife as primary caregiver. As a group, wives who became parents in our sample reduced their involvement in work for pay outside the home and increased their involvement in household work (MacDermid et al., 1990). During our data collection, we asked the husbands and wives to indicate whether they believed the mother, the father, or both parents should carry out child-care tasks, such as soothing the child, changing wet diapers, and putting the child to sleep. Spouses invariably saw mothers as the primary caregiver in that they named mothers as the appropriate caregiver for nearly all of the regular tasks. Their ideas held firm from before they became parents to after the couples had made the transition to parenthood. A few activities, specifically playing games or roughhousing with the child, however, were generally viewed as equally appropriate for mothers and fathers (see also Parke, 1996). The role of fathers as playmate is consistent with Parke's findings that a distinct aspect of father–child interaction is fathers' playful connections with their children.

Traditional views held even among couples in which both spouses worked 30 hours or more for pay (Crouter, Perry-Jenkins, Huston, & McHale, 1987). Only 12% of the spouses we interviewed thought that men should be equally responsible for chores when both spouses work outside the home, although working mothers generally wanted their husbands to be more involved with the newborn and toddler than their husbands preferred to be. We would not, however, want to leave the impression that the men and women we interviewed held fast to all facets of the idea that men and women should function primarily in "separate spheres." Like most Americans, they subscribed to some tenets more than others.

Although about half of them held to the idea that men should be given preference over women in being hired or promoted, most of them disagreed with the idea that men should be the community leaders, that fathers should have greater authority than mothers in making decisions about raising children, or that sons should be given greater encouragement to go to college than daughters.

Our initial analyses demonstrated that wives were more likely to come to support their husbands' views on child care than husbands were to move to their wives' views. An in-depth exploration of this process between spouses showed that the wives' reported love for their husbands led them to accommodate to their husbands' preferences with regard to child care. The more wives loved their husbands, the more they came to support whatever level of involvement their husband wanted regardless of whether wives wanted husbands to be more involved in child care or less involved with such activity (Johnson & Huston, 1998). The loving wives' aim was to create a harmonious family atmosphere, one that they thought encouraged the kind of fathering and parent–child interaction that they believed would benefit the child. Husbands' love, in contrast, had no significant association with the extent to which they adopted their wives' ideas about child care.

We found that women more than men on the precipice of parenthood reported that they were more skilled than their spouse in dealing with their infants (McHale & Huston, 1984). Married partners generally agreed—both before and after couples had their first child—that the mother was the more skilled of the two at child care. The comfort level of the fathers—and the mothers' comfort with them as caregivers—played into how involved the fathers became in primary care.

Women's identities as mothers appear to be an integral part of their perception of female roles and responsibilities. Josephs, Markus, and Tafarodi (1992) argue that women's self-esteem is linked to their adherence to cultural norms about gender; thus, women may be particularly responsive to societal pressure to assume the role of primary caregiver, particularly during a child's infancy. Men's skill in child care, however, is less central to the cultural definition of what it means to be a man, and as such, it is a less central aspect of their psycholgical identity. Historically, fathers' economic contributions to their children's development have been emphasized more heavily than fathers' contributions to child care and housework (Griswold, 1993). The increased participation of women in the work force coupled with the difficulty some couples have in finding affordable yet quality child care combine to encourage fathers to become more involved with their children's day-to-day care. Deutsch (1999) suggests cultural ideology continues to push parents toward more traditional roles, regardless of their desires to equitably divide family work. She interviewed couples who were overtly committed to each other, allocating the same resources to work inside and outside of the home, but even so, they often reported that they contradicted their values in practice. In spite of their ideology, they felt an internal pull to play out traditional norms regarding the division of labor and child care. When a mother hears a baby cry, she may mobilize herself quickly; the father may not immediately process that the baby needs attention. In either event, the couple may find themselves "automatically" gravitating toward traditional roles. Deutsch concluded that couples who hope to share parenting responsibilities equally are unlikely to succeed unless they are vigilant to guard against cultural habits of thought and reflex directing their behavior.

Who Actually Does What With the Child?

The actual roles of mothers and fathers in the PAIR project as caregivers are more strongly demarcated with regard to some tasks than others, as illustrated in Fig. 5.3. Fathers' and mothers' actual involvement in 14 child care activities as gleaned from our diary data can be read from the figure. The number in parentheses to the right-hand side of each specified activity indicates its ranking in terms of the frequency with which it is performed compared to the other tasks. For example, "changing wet diapers" is the most frequent activity parents performed, whereas "putting the child to sleep" is the seventh most commonly carried out task with the child. The vertical axis on the graph shows the proportion of times that tasks were carried out by the mothers in contrast to the fathers. Thus, "changing wet diapers" is done 79% of the time by the mother. "Putting the child to sleep" is done about 75% of the time by the mother.

Mothers are clearly in charge. They plan the child's activities, and they do more than 80% of the routine child-care tasks, such as changing diapers, feeding the child, soothing, and dressing it (see Eiduson, Kornfein, Zimmerman, & Weisner, 1982, for further discussion

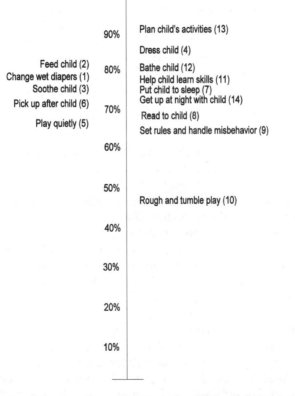

FIG. 5.3. The proportion of times mothers perform various child care activities. Numbers in parentheses indicate the frequency with which the tasks are performed, with 1 referring to the most frequent and 14 referring to the least frequent.

of mothers' and fathers' roles as caregivers for infants). The fathers help care for their children, but their role appears to be to lighten mothers' load. They play with the child, read to the child, set rules and handle misbehavior, pick up after their child, and get up at night with their child to demonstrate their desire to support and to extend a hand of responsibility. As John Burris,[2] one of the fathers we interviewed, put it: "I try to help if I can—not because I feel sorry for her [his wife, Marilyn], but because I want to. I consider playing with Joel part of my responsibility. I entertain him, amuse him, and spend time with him."

As infants and children move from infancy to toddlers, fathers become more actively involved caregivers (Parke, in press). One father we interviewed, talking about his bond with his daughter, explained: "I enjoy her now because she can do more for herself; she can walk and talk and feed herself; if you ask her to get something, she'll get it. Sometimes she's bad, but I'm glad she's more independent. She's becoming more of a person." Then, laughing at himself, he adds, "Not that she wasn't a person a year ago." The lesser role of fathers in the daily lives of young children should not be taken to imply that what they do with their children is not important. Parke and Brott (1999) point out that fathers generally allow their children more freedom to explore, they encourage independence, and they play in a more physical fashion than mothers. Father–infant play is rhythmic, filled more with peaks of excitement and quiet valleys in contrast to mother–infant play, which usually involves quiet talk, with moms often imitating or repeating their infants' sounds. Of course, the impact that any collection of fathers like those we studied have on their children depends on how well their parenting matches up with the prototype of the "good" fathers described in the studies Parke and Brott (1999) reviewed. This same observation is equally pertinent to evaluating mothers' as parents.

Work Roles and Child Care

Couples in our study sorted themselves into two groups—those in which the husband was the sole breadwinner (57%) and those in which both spouses worked for pay (43%). Couples, who subscribed to the central tenets of separate-spheres thinking were found to have married at a younger age, become parents earlier in marriage, and as new parents were more likely to set up a family pattern with the husband as the primary breadwinner and the wife as the homemaker (Huston & Geis, 1993).

In our own research, when husbands worked and their wives were the primary care-givers, fathers rarely stepped forward much to help with their child, unless they felt confident they knew what they were doing (McHale & Huston, 1984) and unless they experienced stronger than average feelings of love for their wife (Crouter et al., 1987). The tendency of any spouse—whether traditional or egalitarian—to engage in more child-care activity in part depends on their perceived skills (Maccoby & Martin, 1983; McHale & Huston, 1984). Fathers who feel skilled with regard to parenting are more involved in child-oriented activities than are those who feel unskilled (Bonney, Kelley, & Levant, 1999; Feldman, Nash, & Aschenbrenner, 1983). In addition such fathers tend to do more caregiving relative to play and leisure activities with their children. Fathers' perceived skill

---

[2]The names of the participants have been changed to protect their anonymity.

also tends to bring their families together, suggesting as Palkovitz (2002) has argued that "good fathering is good for everyone." Fathers who feel competent about performing child care are more involved in child-oriented activities with their wives. It is also interesting to note that paternal competence in infant care is mediated by men's marital satisfaction, such that the more satisfied a father is with his marriage before the transition to parenthood, the more competent he will feel as a parent after the transition (Bonney et al., 1999; Cowan & Cowan, 1987). Further, a close, confiding marriage before the transition to parenthood continues to breed men's sense of paternal skill with their infants during the first 6 months postpartum (Cox, Owen, Lewis, & Henderson, 1989).

For fathers in our sample, perceived skill in child care is a relatively stable trait. It does not significantly change when they become parents (McHale & Huston, 1984)—husbands who feel skilled at child care before becoming fathers also tend to feel skilled afterward. In an exploration of men's transition to fatherhood, Strauss and Goldberg (1999) emphasize not only the general continuity between men's early caregiving competence and later competence but also the match between their ideal roles and their actual roles. Those fathers who were more able to achieve their ideal roles felt competent and satisfied in their roles as fathers, often being more inclined to be involved in child-care tasks (McHale & Huston, 1984). In contrast, wives' feelings of competence with regard to their child-care skills are more likely to change over the transition to parenthood. Mothers who are highly involved in child-oriented activities after their babies are born come to see themselves as more competent and come to prefer being more involved in child care (McHale & Huston, 1984). Although husbands' and wives' role preferences are not related to each other before they become parents; afterward, mothers' expressivity (defined in terms of warmth in relations with others, gentleness, ability to devote self completely to others, kindness, awareness of others' feelings, etc.) and their perceived skill are inversely related to fathers' preferences for being involved in child care. The more expressive mothers are, and the more skilled they perceive themselves to be in terms of child care, the less their husbands prefer to engage in child-care activities (MacDermid et al., 1990).

Recently, scholars have become more attuned to the ways women's attitudes toward men's roles as parents (prior to the transition to parenthood and much after) influence men's involvement in child care. For example, some mothers may serve as "gatekeepers" to fathers' relationships with their children, limiting fathers' involvement with their children (Allen & Hawkins, 1999; Belsky & Volling, 1987; DeLuccie, 1995). Gatekeeping has been defined by Allen and Hawkins (1999) as "a collection of beliefs and behaviors that ultimately inhibit a collaborative effort between men and women in families by limiting men's opportunities for learning and growing through caring for home and children" (p. 200). Women's beliefs about the importance of a father's role in rearing children, high standards for household work and child care, traditional attitudes about womanhood, and seeking control over family tasks are all important aspects of gatekeeping (Allen & Hawkins, 1999; DeLuccie, 1995). Allen and Hawkins (1999) suggest that high expectations, desires to manage family tasks, and having an identity that is based on "well-groomed children" and a clean house make it difficult for women to share child care with fathers. Scholars concerned about gatekeeping behaviors and attitudes suggest that gatekeeping prevents fathers from developing their skills in child care and parenting, thus decreasing fathers' involvement in child-care tasks (Fagan & Barnett, in press).

Many women report a desire for their partners to be more involved with their children (McBride & Darragh, 1995). Some mothers, recognizing that fathers are uncertain and sometimes reluctant, actively encourage fathers to be involved in parenting. Women's ideas about the role of fathers affect father involvement, such that women who are more liberal in their gender role ideology are more likely to have husbands who have higher involvement in child care (Arendell, 1996; Barnett & Baruch, 1987). Further, in two empirical studies on father involvement during the transition to parenthood, mothers' scores on the Role of the Father Questionnaire (ROFQ) were the best predictors of father involvement when mothers, fathers, and infants were observed interacting with one another (Fagan & Barnett, in press; Palkovitz, 1984). When fathers and infants interacted alone, mothers' scores on the ROFQ were still significant predictors of fathers' involvement with their infants (Palkovitz, 1984). The ROFQ measures the extent to which one believes the fathers' role is important to child development. It includes 15 items, with a 5-point agreement scale. Higher scores reflect attitudes that fathers are capable parents and should be involved in childrearing (Palkovitz, 1984). Finally, many women report a desire for their husbands/partners to be more involved with their children and try to encourage them to do so (Erickson, 1993; McBride & Darragh, 1995).

From our own data, it appears that the changing role preferences of wives influence husbands' involvement with their children (MacDermid et al., 1990). The associations between wives' role-related characteristics and their husbands' activities are stronger than the associations between husbands' characteristics and their own activities (MacDermid et al., 1990). Although husbands who are more expressive tend to believe that they are more skilled in terms of child care, husbands' expressivity does not by itself predict their tendency to engage in child-oriented activities. Wives' role preferences (measured after they become mothers), however, covaried with husbands' involvement with their children (MacDermid et al., 1990). Wives who prefer their husbands to be involved in child care after they become parents tend to have husbands who engage in more child-oriented activities (McHale & Huston, 1984). As we will see later, however, husbands' greater involvement in child care does not always bode well for the marriage.

Many discussions of the transition to parenthood include concern that fluctuating roles and responsibilities, especially for women, are at the very root of marital crisis. There is surely a consensus among researchers that the transition to parenthood brings with it a bucket full of new responsibilities. Women tend to work less outside the home and more inside the home after becoming parents (Sanchez & Thomson, 1997; Shelton, 1992). Though we have focused our discussion on women and men who make the transition to parenthood early in adult life, it is important to keep in mind those who make the transition to parenthood later usually divide domestic labor and child care more equally (Coltrane & Ishii-Kuntz, 1992; Pittman & Blanchard, 1996).

We have found in our study that the initial comfort level new parents experience with the shift in roles depends in large measure on whether the changes coincide with their views about appropriate marital roles. Spouses who held traditional ideas and whose lifestyle shifted to reflect these ideas generally found themselves at ease with the alterations that occurred when they became parents (MacDermid et al., 1990). However, when the marriages of traditional spouses did *not* shift toward the hoped-for gender-differentiated pattern with parenthood, spouses expressed more negative feelings toward each other after becoming parents and became less satisfied with their marriage compared to nonparents. Further, their feelings of love toward each other abated to a greater extent. Mothers holding more traditional gender-role attitudes who were involved in marriages in which the division of labor was relatively equal were less in love with their husbands and behaved more negatively toward them. Fathers holding more traditional gender-role attitudes but who were, nonetheless, highly involved with child care and household tasks reported being less in love with their wives and more negative toward them (Crouter et al., 1987; see also Helms-Erikson, 2001, for an in-depth discussion of the relationship between division of labor and timing of the transition to parenthood). Traditional spouses' reactions to the failure to make the expected—even hoped for—shift toward traditional roles with parenthood eventually had become reconciled to their situation. When we returned to talk with the couples more than 10 years later, we found their marriages to be indistinguishable from those of other couples with regard to the spouses' satisfaction, their love, and how often they expressed negative feelings toward each other (Huston & Geis, in preparation).

Balancing Career and Family Life: Dual-Earner Couples

Many new parents juggle the demands of two jobs and their new baby. Forty-three percent of those we interviewed found themselves in such a situation. The total work burden was rarely equally balanced between the parents when both partners worked for pay outside the home. All told, in such situations fathers took on a fourth of the child-care and household responsibilities. By the second year of the child's life, working mothers were employed an average of 30 hr a week for pay while performing 26 household and child-care tasks. Their husbands worked 34 hr a week for pay while performing about 5 household and child-care tasks (Smith & Huston, in press). Since there was a strong correlation between the number of tasks performed and the total amount of time devoted to them, we can use the number of tasks and the time spent in tasks interchangeably. The imbalance of the household work would have been even greater had not employed mothers cut back on the number of tasks they took on compared to the mothers who did not work outside the home (Crouter et al., 1987): beds went unmade, sinks were left filled with dishes, couples grabbed fast foods, or had pizza delivered. The dual-earner couples generally chose efficiency (e.g., one parent caring for the child—mostly the mother—while the other engaged in another activity) over companionship (e.g., both parents spending time together with the child). Another adaptation parents created to manage paid work and home life involved working staggered shifts. Three fourths of the dual-earner parents we interviewed worked separate shifts. One partner usually worked the daylight hours, with the other working in the evening, or on the overnight shift.

In our research we did not ask dual-earner couples *why* they chose one form of child-care arrangement rather than another. Johnson (2000) found that couples generally leave child-care decisions up to the mother, rather than jointly considering the merits of alternative solutions. According to Johnson (2000), mothers' ideas about the importance of family care, the availability of kin to provide such care, cost considerations, and quality of care play important roles in child-care decisions.

Working mothers usually wanted their husbands to be more involved in child care than the husbands tended to be. For many reasons, working women are reluctant to push men.

Not the least of these reasons is that new mothers often gain considerable satisfaction from doing the job themselves. Hannah and Jay Belmont, both of whom worked outside the home as new parents, had a closer to equal distribution of labor than most couples in our sample. Nonetheless, Hannah, who did 57% of the housework and child care, felt that Jay should do more. At the same time, she was far from ready to give the caregiver role over to him explaining, "I don't mind doing things because I know he's had a hard day at work. If Jay knows that I'm tired or not feeling well, he will help me out, but mostly I do it. A lot of times, Jay offers to help, but I tell him not to because I would rather do it myself."

Employed mothers in our sample discovered that securing help from their employed husbands could carry significant costs (Crouter et al., 1987). When the fathers assisted them, they often did so with obvious reluctance, offering clear signs that they believed they were being exploited, saddled with chores that were not included in their job description. The more fathers in dual-earner marriages were involved with child care, the more they complained, criticized, and otherwise showed dissatisfaction toward their wives. Furthermore, fathers in dual-earner marriages who behaved more negatively tended to be less satisfied with the division of child-care tasks and also less in love with their wives. Conversely, fathers in dual-earner marriages who were less involved with their children in child-care and leisure activities were more in love with their wives. It is critical to note that for wives decreases in satisfaction with the division of household labor are not associated with declines in marital satisfaction or their love for their husbands (see also Ruble et al., 1988). Wives apparently separate their evaluation of the instrumental realm of their marriage from their overall assessment of the marital relationship.

These findings suggest on the surface that drawing reluctant husbands into household work creates dissatisfaction with the division of labor for husbands, which in turn is reflected in a reduction in men's overall satisfaction with marriage. Since men's ideas about their roles in families are changing, contemporary men may be drawn into domestic work and child care more than they have in the past (Coltrane, 1996). Moreover they may see such greater involvement as equitable and fair. As men are more involved in caring for their children, particularly if they have a son, they are more likely to participate in household work (Fish, New, & Van Cleave, 1992; Ishii- Kuntz & Coltrane, 1992; Presser, 1994). Although we do not know whether fathers care more about their children now than they did in the past, we do know that caring for one's children is now defined by researchers as not only providing economically for one's children but also being available, responsible, committed, accessible, and actively involved in raising one's children (Palkovitz, 1997). Finally, only continued research will uncover how changing cultural perceptions of fatherhood and men's work in their families will also affect the ways men and women handle the changing environment of home life after they become parents (Marsiglio, Amato, Day, & Lamb, 2001).

DOES PARENTHOOD UNDERMINE ROMANCE AND LEAD TO CONFLICT?

Does the addition of a child restrict the amount of time spouses have to be with each other as a couple? The answer is "yes." The amount of time husbands and wives pursue leisure activities together as a couple decreases dramatically once they become parents (Crawford & Huston, 1993). Prior to the child's birth, 44% of spouses' activities are done together as a couple. That percentage is cut in half after their first-born arrives. The disenchantment new parents express with the limited amount of time they now spend together reflects in part the fact that they pursue fewer activities that they both enjoy. Moreover, even when parents engage in leisure together, they often have to keep a sharp eye on the child. "We haven't been alone for any length of time since Amy was born," a frustrated Annie Gilmour told us. "I won't pull any punches with you. It is very hard to get used to. It's downright discouraging." At this point, Annie began to cry. "You gotta burp her, or pamper her, or change a diaper. Right when I'm ready to pick up a book, she starts crying. It's almost like she knows."

The extent to which mothers, in particular, spend time with their child doing leisure activity comes to rival time they spend in leisure with their husbands alone as a pair. Fathers and children pursue relatively few leisure activities together without the mother also involved. Having a baby allows mothers to spend more time doing leisure activities that they like and less leisure time in activities they dislike (Crawford & Huston, 1993), whereas the reverse is true for new fathers. New fathers' leisure time shifts from activities with friends and in solitary pursuits—things they particularly enjoy—toward less enjoyable family- and home-centered pursuits. The restrictions on men's movement are likely to make men feel hemmed in by fatherhood. The need to negotiate with their wives about stopping to have a beer or to see how a buddy's garage project is coming along discourages such detours from a homeward route.

Annie's husband, Kevin, for example, did not feel free to play softball with his co-workers after work or to attend office parties. "Annie's home all day with the baby. If I go out after work, it's just gonna drive her crazy 'cause she needs a break. My interest is in getting home at night and relieving her," he says. "I don't think I'm the ideal parent or the ideal person taking over. But I'm doing what is expected of me and more."

Kevin was in fact a particularly attentive father, according to the diary data we obtained from him. Annie agreed: "He'll come home and play with the baby, then he helps with bathing. I never really bathe her myself. He'll change her and I'll feed her, and if I'm really tired he'll burp her after I go back to sleep, and if she's fussy at night he'll take her and play around with her."

Our data indicate that the disquiet fathers feel about changes in their social life does not undermine their overall feelings of marital satisfaction (MacDermid et al., 1990) or weaken their expressed love for their wives, or conversely, their wives' love for them (Crouter et al., 1987). Nor does the reduced amount of time couples have alone together affect such feelings. This may be explained, in part, by their recognition that such changes are an inevitable part of parenthood. They may also be sustained by a feeling of pride. Their production of a child anchors them in the mainstream of the culture and is an achievement regarded as praiseworthy.

Aside from leisure pursuits, parents spend less time talking together than do nonparents (McHale & Huston, 1985). Given the centrality of communication to spouses' marital satisfaction (see Noller, 2001), this reported decrease in partners' time together would not seem to bode well for the quality of their marriage. When we examined the parents' affectionate expressions toward one another, however, we found that parenthood has little impact on such behavior. Though new parents may spend less time conversing with each other, they are no less affectionate than couples who do not yet have children (MacDermid et al., 1990). New parents say "I love you" to each other as often as nonparents; they also try to make one another laugh, hug and kiss each other, share their feelings, and do something nice for each other about as often as nonparents (MacDermid et al., 1990). In short, new parents seem to make the most of their limited time together. Furthermore, the data show that for some couples the amount of affection that husbands express toward their wives actually increases during the transition to parenthood (McHale & Huston, 1985). Parents and nonparents also were equally involved in talking about their personal needs and trying to work out their problems. Cowan and Cowan (1988) say the parents (when compared to the nonparents in their study) were able to communicate even more effectively with one another, solving problems more efficiently knowing that they had less time to interact with each other.

The diary data we gathered showed that although sexual intercourse is curtailed during the later stages of pregnancy and during the postpartum period, declines in sexual activity among new parents are otherwise no greater than the abatement of nonparents' sexual behavior. At times new parents have to be creative about sex, and even then things some- times do not go as planned. They seem to recognize these changes as part of their own decisions regarding childbearing, not just as a result of the presence of their child.

The parent and nonparent groups we studied were equally likely to bicker, argue, criticize, or turn down each other's sexual overtures—either before or after the birth of a child. Because negativity is a particularly sensitive barometer of spouses' marital satisfaction (Karney & Bradbury, 1997), this finding lends further credence to describing the arrival of a child as changing couple lifestyles rather than producing a "crisis" in their marriages. What takes place is largely a shift in lifestyle rather than diminishing affection resulting from more restricted schedules and greater tension.

PARENTHOOD AND MARITAL HAPPINESS

Cowan and Cowan (2000) maintained that their review of several careful longitudinal studies showed that "on the average, men's and women's dissatisfaction with marriage tends to increase from pregnancy into the early child-rearing years." They concluded that "parenthood puts marriage at risk" (p. 30). They reeled off an array of numbers intended to support the conclusion regarding the psychological devastation caused by the birth of a child: "Seven percent to fifteen percent will be diagnosed as clinically depressed, and thirty percent to fifty percent (some claim as high as eighty percent) will experience the 'blues'" (Cowan & Cowan, 2000, p. 29). We do not learn from them how often a matched sample of nonparents also experience the "blues," nor how such a state of mind translates into more lasting and significant outcomes.

Parenthood does not generally produce marital discontent (Karney & Bradbury, 1997; Kurdek, 1993; Ryder, 1973) or erode spouses' feelings of love (MacDermid et al., 1990). This conclusion is counter to conventional social science wisdom. Such wisdom—rooted as it has been largely in research using weak "before-after" designs and/or flawed assess- ments of marital satisfaction—does not hold up to careful scrutiny.

We found that new parents do not complain about each other's lack of affection or about each other's insensitivity any more than nonparents. Typically couples, regardless of whether or not they became parents, feel more love and are more satisfied with their marriage as newlyweds than 2 years into marriage. These changes, however, are subtle rather than dramatic. Had we asked new parents why their romance became less intense, most of them no doubt would have pointed to the baby and the increased workload. We might have been tempted to draw the same erroneous conclusion had we not been in position to compare the relationships of parents and nonparents. Three other research teams, using somewhat different samples and a design like ours, have also shown that parenthood does not, in general, lead to an erosion of marital satisfaction (Kurdek, 1993; Karney & Bradbury, 1997; Ryder, 1973).

Though as a group parents do not differ from nonparents in terms of how they evaluate the quality of their relationships, it must be appreciated that changes involved in having a baby are handled more easily by some couples than by others. Cox et al. (1999) reported that declines in couples' marital quality over the first 2 years postpartum could be explained by whether the pregnancy was "planned" (as reported by both mothers and fathers in the prenatal interview), child's gender (marital quality declined more for those with a baby girl), as well as by new parents' levels of depression.

The ease for wives appears to depend, in part, on how much their husbands express fondness and affection toward them before parenthood as well as on their husbands' awareness of relationship issues (Shapiro et al., 2000). Husbands' negativity—as reflected in such things as acting critically and showing negative affect—and their disappointment or disillusionment foreshadowed declines in their wives' "satisfaction" across the transition to parenthood (Shapiro et al., 2000; see also Crohan, 1996).

Those who hold traditional views find the baby path easier than those with less traditional views about family roles (MacDermid et al., 1990). More generally, the degree to which the spouses have consensus about marital roles also matters; thus, for example, if wives have a less traditional view than their husbands, their marital intimacy declines across the transition to parenthood (O'Brien & Peyton, 2002). Regardless of whether spouses have traditional views about household tasks, those who perceive inequity in the division of labor 6 months after their first child is born have an increased likelihood of reporting marital conflict and marital dissatisfaction when their first child is between 12 and 15 months old (Grote & Clark, 2001). Interestingly, marital conflict and marital satisfaction reports before a baby's birth seem to cause men's and women's perceptions of fairness of household labor. Thus, it appears that a person's perception of the equity of family work after the transition to parenthood is a product of the earlier feelings about the relationship, not a product of the increased child-care responsibilities of becoming a parent (Grote & Clark, 2001). Whether both spouses work for pay also plays a considerable part in how smoothly the transition to parenthood goes. Dual-earning fathers, for example, are more likely to become somewhat involved in household and child care arrangements, but often at the expense of a degree of marital amity.

Belsky and Hsieh (1998) studied families up to 5 years (60 months) postpartum. They explored husband and wife conflict and love scores as related to co-parenting processes and three specific personality traits: agreeableness, neuroticism, and extraversion. Over time, three different types of marital patterns emerged. Parents whose relationship began well and stayed the same over the 5 years studied, parents whose relationship began well and worsened over time, and parents whose relationship began poorly and worsened over the study period. Interestingly, spousal personality traits provided a stabilizing force for marriage over time; those marriages that worsened over time—regardless of how well they started—involved parents who were not in agreement about how they should parent their children. The lack of consensus resulted in such parents contravening each other in front of their children.

CONCLUSIONS AND DIRECTIONS FOR FUTURE RESEARCH

The birth of a baby clearly has an impact on marital behavior patterns. Spouses change the way they organize their instrumental tasks and leisure time. Wives' day-to-day activities become more home and family centered. Husbands engage in fewer of the leisure activities they enjoy. The responsibilities that accompany child care limit the amount of time spouses have to spend together as a couple. Accordingly, parents report spending less time in conversation together than do nonparents. Although new parents change many of their behavioral patterns, the socioemotional aspects of their interaction do not differ from those of nonparents. Because socioemotional behavior is an important predictor of spouses' relational satisfaction, the lack of difference in this domain of marriage for parents and nonparents suggests that parenthood, per se, will not lead to decreases in spouses' marital satisfaction and love. Our data support this claim.

Having noted that parents do not differ from nonparents in terms of the way they evaluate the quality of their marriages, it is important to remember that the changes that accompany parenthood are more easily managed by some than by others. Those with traditional gender role attitudes who make the transition to parenthood in the first 2 years of marriage and who tend to hold beliefs about marriage that are congruent with many of the transformations spouses experience when they become parents handle the transition more smoothly. Those with more egalitarian gender-role attitudes, in contrast, hold beliefs that clash with the changes that typically accompany parenthood. In addition, spouses' occupational status constrains the way they organize their time together. Dual-earner husbands, for instance, are slightly more involved in child care than are their single-earner counterparts. Although drawing these husbands into child care may reduce marital tension by decreasing wives' workloads, it can have negative influences on the ways dual-earner husbands evaluate their marriages.

Our efforts to trace the multiple ways parenthood affects marriage and to identify the conditions under which parenthood affects marriage fit into a new, emerging paradigm that seeks to create a richer, more balanced portrait of the transition to parenthood. Researchers are poised, we believe, to recognize that parenthood includes greater opportunities as well as problems and that the overall effect of parenthood on marriage reflects the operation of a number of causal dynamics. It is important to keep in mind, moreover, that our more optimistic portrait of couples undergoing the transition to parenthood may reflect our having drawn our sample from a rural, largely working-class area and that our focus was on couples who underwent the transition to parenthood relatively early in marriage; most researchers have studied relatively educated middle-class couples, many of whom were married for longer periods prior to becoming parents.

In addition to studying the potential differences between working-class and middle-class couples, researchers need to expand work on the transition to parenthood to include unwed mothers and fathers because first-time parenthood increasingly takes place outside of marriage. One third of unwed mothers and fathers are teenagers (Luker, 1996). Scholars are beginning to examine how the relational world of unmarried parents changes, in both the short run and the long run (Furstenberg, 1976; Furstenberg, 1995; Furstenberg, Brooks-Gunn, & Morgan, 1987; Peters, Peterson, Steinmetz, & Day, 2000). Increasing research on the larger sociocultural context of the transition to parenthood, including particularly race and ethnicity, will help us better understand the larger meaning of the transition to parenthood and its effects on parents and their relationships.

AUTHOR NOTE

This research was supported by grants from the National Science Foundation (SBR-9311846) and National Institute of Mental Health (MH-33938), Ted L. Huston, principal investigator.

REFERENCES

Allen, S. M., & Hawkins, A. J. (1999). Maternal gatekeeping: Mothers' beliefs and behaviors that inhibit greater father involvement in family work. *Journal of Marriage and the Family, 61*, 199–212.

Arendell, T. (1996). *Co-parenting: A review of the literature.* Philadelphia, PA: National Center on Fathers and Families.

Barnett, R. C., & Baruch, G. K. (1987). Determinants of fathers' participation in family work. *Journal of Marriage and the Family, 49*, 29–40.

Barnett, R. C., & Rivers, C. (1996). *She works/he works: How two-income families are happier, healthier, and better-off* New York: HarperCollins.

Belsky, J. (1985). Exploring individual differences in marital change across the transition to parenthood: The role of violated expectations. *Journal of Marriage and the Family, 47*, 1037–1044.

Belsky, J., & Hsieh, K.-H. (1998). Patterns of marital change during the early childhood years: Parent personality, coparenting, and division-of-labor correlates. *Journal of Family Psychology, 12*, 511–528

Belsky, J., & Kelly, J. (1994). *The transition to parenthood: How a first child changes a marriage.* London: Vermilion.

Belsky, J., Lang, M. E., & Rovine, M. (1985). Stability and change in marriage across the transition to parenthood: A second study. *Journal of Marriage and the Family, 47*, 855–865.

Belsky, J., Spanier, G., & Rovine, M. (1983). Stability and change across the transition to parenthood: A second study. *Journal of Marriage and the Family, 47*, 855–865.

Belksy, J., & Volling, B. (1987). Mothering, fathering, and marital interaction in the family triad during infancy: Exploring family system's processes. In P. W. Berman & F. A. Pedersen (Eds.), *Men's transitions to parenthood: Longitudinal studies of early family experience* (pp. 37–63). Hillsdale, NJ: Lawrence Erlbaum Associates.

Berman, P. W., & Pedersen, F. A. (1987). *Men's transitions to parenthood: Longitudinal studies of early family experience.* Hillsdale, NJ: Lawrence Erlbaum Associates.

Bernard, J. (1964). The adjustments of married mates. In H. T. Christensen (Ed.), *Handbook of marriage and the family* (pp. 675–739). Chicago, IL: Rand McNally.

Bonney, J. F., Kelley, M. L., & Levant, R. F. (1999). A model of fathers' behavioral involvement in child care in dual-earner families. *Journal of Family Psychology, 13*, 401–415.

Coltrane, S. M. (1996). *Family man: Parenthood, housework, and gender equity.* New York: Oxford University Press.

Coltrane, S., & Ishii-Kuntz, M. (1992). Men's housework: A life-course perspective. *Journal of Marriage and the Family, 54*, 43–57.

Cook, T., & Campbell, D. T. (1979). *Quasi-experimentation: Design and analysis issues for field settings.* Chicago: Rand McNally,

Cowan, P. A. (1988). Becoming a father: A time of change, an opportunity for development. In P. Bronstein & C. P. Cowan (Eds.), *Fatherhood today: Men's changing role in the family* (pp. 13–35). New York: Wiley.

Cowan, P. A. (1991). Individual and family life transitions: A proposal for a new definition. In P. A. Cowan, & M. Hetherington (Eds.), *Family transitions* (pp. 3–30). Hillsdale, NJ: Lawrence Erlbaum Associates.

Cowan, C. P., & Cowan, P. A. (1987). Men's involvement in parenthood: Identifying the antecedents and understanding the barriers. In P.W. Berman & F. A. Pedersen (Eds.), *Men's transitions to parenthood: Longitudinal studies of early family experience* (pp. 145–171). Hillsdale, NJ: Lawrence Erlbaum Associates.

Cowan, P. A., & Cowan, C. P. (1988). Changes in marriage during the transition to parenthood: Must we blame the baby? In G. Michaels & W. Goldberg (Eds.), *The transition to parenthood: Current theory and research* (pp. 114–154). Cambridge: Cambridge University Press.

Cowan, C. P., & Cowan, P. A. (2000). *When partners become parents: The big life change for couples.* Mahwah, NJ: Lawrence Erlbaum Associates.

Cowan, C. P., Cowan, P. A., Heming, G., Heming, G., Garrett, E., Coysh, W. S., Curtis-Boles, H., & Boles, A. J. (1985). Transitions to parenthood: His, hers, and theirs. *Journal of Family Issues, 6*, 451–481.

Cox, M. J., Owen, M., Lewis, J., & Henderson, V. K. (1989). Marriage, adult adjustment, and early parenting. *Child Development, 60*, 1015–1024.

Cox, M. J., Paley, B., Burchinal, M., & Payne, C. C. (1999). Marital perceptions and interactions across the transition to parenthood. *Journal of Marriage and the Family, 61*, 611–625.

Crawford, D. W., & Huston, T. L. (1993). The impact of the transition to parenthood on marital leisure. *Personality and Social Psychology Bulletin, 19*, 39–46.

Crohan, S. (1996). Marital quality and conflict across the transition to parenthood in African American and White couples. *Journal of Marriage and the Family, 58*, 933–944.

Crouter, A. C., Perry-Jenkins, M., Huston, T. L., & McHale, S. M. (1987). Processes underlying father involvement in dual-earner and single-earner families. *Developmental Psychology, 23*, 431–440.

DeLuccie, M. F. (1995). Mothers as gatekeepers: A model of maternal mediators of father involvement. *The Journal of Genetic Psychology, 156*, 115–131.

Deutsch, F. (1999). *Halving it all: How equally shared parenting works.* Cambridge, MA: Harvard University Press.

Eiduson, B. T., Kornfein, M., Zimmerman, I. L., & Weisner, T. S. (1982). Comparative socialization practices in traditional and alternative families. In M. E. Lamb (Ed.), *Nontraditional family forms: Parenting and child development.* Hillsdale, NJ: Lawrence Erlbaum Associates.

Erdrich, L. (1995). *The blue jay's dance: A birth year.* New York: HarperCollins.

Erickson, R. J. (1993). Reconceptualizing family work: The effect of emotion work on perceptions of marital quality. *Journal of Marriage and the Family, 55,* 888–900.

Fagan, J., & Barnett, M. (in press). The relationship between maternal gatekeeping, paternal competence, mothers' attitudes about the father role, and father involvement. *Journal of Family Issues.*

Feeney, J. A., Hohaus, L., Noller, P., & Alexander, R. P. (2001). *Becoming parents: Exploring the bonds between mothers, fathers, and their infants.* Cambridge: Cambridge University Press.

Feldman, S. S., & Nash, S. C. (1984). The transition from expectancy to parenthood: Impact of the firstborn child on men and women. *Sex Roles, 11,* 61–78.

Feldman, S. S., Nash, S. C., & Aschenbrenner, B. G. (1983). Antecedents of fathering. *Child Development, 54,* 1628–1636.

Figley, C. R. (1973). Child density and the marital relationship. *Journal of Marriage and the Family, 35,* 272–282.

Fincham, F. D., & Bradbury, T. N. (1987). The assessment of marital quality: A reevaluation. *Journal of Marriage and the Family, 49,* 797–809.

Fish, L. S., New, R. S., & Van Cleave, N. J. (1992). Shared parenting in dual-income families. *American Journal of Orthopsychiatry, 62,* 83–92.

Fitzpatrick, M. A., Vangelisti, A. L., & Firman, S. M. (1994). Perceptions of marital interaction and change during pregnancy: A typological approach. *Personal Relationships, 1,* 101–122.

Furstenberg, F. F., Jr. (1976). *Unplanned parenthood: The social consequence of teenage childbearing.* New York: Free Press.

Furstenberg, F. F., Jr. (1995). Fathering in the inner city: Paternal participation and public policy. In W. Marsiglio (Ed.), *Fatherhood: Contemporary theory, research, and social policy* (pp. 119–147). Thousand Oaks, CA: Sage.

Furstenberg, F. F., Brooks-Gunn, J., & Morgan, S. P. (1987). *Adolescent mothers in later life.* Cambridge: Cambridge University Press.

Glenn, N. D. (1998). The course of marital success and failure in five American 10-year marriage cohorts. *Journal of Marriage and the Family, 60,* 569–576.

Glenn, N. D., & McLanahan, S. (1982). Children and marital happiness: A further specification of the relationship. *Journal of Marriage and the Family, 44,* 63–72.

Goldberg, W. A., Michaels, G. Y., & Lamb, M. E. (1985). Husbands' and wives' adjustment to pregnancy and first parenthood. *Family Issues, 6,* 485–503.

Griswold, R. L. (1993). *Fatherhood in America: A history.* New York, NY: Basic Books.

Grote, N. K., & Clark, M. S. (2001). Perceiving unfairness in the family: Cause or consequence of marital distress? *Journal of Personality and Social Psychology, 80,* 281–293.

Grote, N. K., Naylor, K., & Clark, M. S. (in press). Perceiving the division of family work to be unfair: Do social comparisons, enjoyment and competence matter? *Journal of Family Issues.*

Hawkins, A. J., & Dollahite, D. C. (Eds.). (1997). *Generative fathering.* Thousand Oaks, CA: Sage.

Helms-Erikson, H. (2001). Marital quality ten years after the transition to parenthood: Implications of the timing of parenthood and the division of housework. *Journal of Marriage and Family, 63,* 1099–1110.

Hill, R. (1949). *Families under stress: Adjustment to the crises of war and separation and reunion.* New York: Harper.

Huston, T. L., & Geis, G. (1993). In what ways do gender-related attributes and beliefs affect marriage? *Journal of Social Issues, 49,* 87–106.

Huston, T. L., & Geis, G. (in preparation). *When the honeymoon is over: Why some marriages succeed and others fail.* Manuscript in preparation.

Huston, T. L., Robins, E., Atkinson, J., & McHale, S. (1987). Surveying the landscape of marital behavior: A behavioral self-report approach to studying marriage. In S. Oskamp (Ed.) *Family processes and problems: Social psychological aspects* (pp. 45–72). Newbury Park, CA: Sage.

Huston, T. L., & Vangelisti, A. L. (1991). Socioemotional behavior and satisfaction in marital relationships: A longitudinal study. *Journal of Personality and Social Psychology, 61,* 721–733.

Huston, T. L., & Vangelisti, A. L. (1995). How parenthood affects marriage. In M. A. Fitzpatrick & A. L. Vangelisti (Eds.), *Explaining family interactions* (pp. 147–176). Thousand Oaks, CA: Sage.

Ishii-Kuntz, M., & Coltrane, S. (1992). Predicting the sharing of household labor: Are parenting and housework distinct? *Sociological Perspectives, 35,* 629–647.

Johnson, E M. (2000). *The child care and employment decision-making process of expecting parents.* Unpublished doctoral dissertation, The University of Texas at Austin.

Johnson, E. M., & Huston, T. L. (1998). The perils of love, or why wives adapt to husbands during the transition to parenthood. *Journal of Marriage and the Family, 60,* 195–204.

Johnson, M., Huston, T. L., Gaines, S. O., & Levinger, G. (1992). Patterns of married life among young couples. *Journal of Social and Personal Relationships, 9,* 343–364.

Josephs, R. A., Markus, H. R., & Tafarodi, R. W. (1992). Gender and self-esteem. *Journal of Personality and Social Psychology, 63,* 391–402.

Karney, B. R., & Bradbury, T. N. (1995). The longitudinal course of marital quality and stability: A review of theory, method, and research. *Psychological Bulletin, 118,* 3–34.

Karney, B. R., & Bradbury, T. N. (1997). Neuroticism, marital interaction, and the trajectory of marital satisfaction. *Journal of Personality and Social Psychology, 72,* 1075–1092.

Kelly, J. R., & McGrath, J. E. (1988). *On time and method.* Newbury Park, CA: Sage.

Kramer, E. (1998). *Uniting men's work as husbands and fathers: Another look at generative care.* Unpublished honors thesis, Brigham Young University Provo, UT.

Kurdek, L. (1993). Nature and prediction of changes in marital quality for first-time parent and nonparent husbands and wives. *Journal of Family Psychology, 6,* 255–265.

LaRossa, R., & LaRossa, M. M. (1981). *Transition to parenthood.* Beverly Hills, CA: Sage.

LeMasters, E. E. (1957). Parenthood as crisis. *Marriage and Family Living, 19,* 352–355.

LeMasters, E. E. (1970). *Parents in modern society: A sociological analysis.* Homewood, IL: Dorsey.

Lennon, M. C., & Rosenfield, S. (1994). Relative fairness and the division of housework: The importance of options. *American Journal of Sociology, 100*, 506–531.

Locke, H. J., & Wallace, K. M. (1959). Short marital-adjustment and prediction tests: Their reliability and validity. *Marriage and Family Living, 21*, 251–255.

Luker, K. (1996). *Dubious conceptions: The politics of teenage pregnancy.* Cambridge, MA: Harvard University Press.

Maccoby, E., E., & Martin, J. A. (1983). Socialization in the context of the family: Parent-child interaction. In P. H. Mussen & E. M. Hetherington (Eds.), *Handbook of child psychology, vol. 4: Socialization, personality, and social development* (4th ed., pp. 1–101). New York: Wiley.

MacDermid, S. M., Huston, T. L., & McHale, S. M. (1990). Changes in marriage associated with the transition to parenthood: Individual differences as a function of sex-role attitudes and changes in the division of household labor. *Journal of Marriage and the Family, 52*, 475–486.

Markman, H. J. (1981). Prediction of marital distress: A 5-year follow-up. *Journal of Consulting and Clinical Psychology, 49*, 760–762.

Marsiglio, W., Amato, P., Day, R. D., & Lamb, M. E. (2001). Scholarship on fatherhood in the 1990s and beyond. *Journal of Marriage and Family, 60*, 1173–1191.

McBride, B. A., & Darragh, J. (1995). Interpreting the data on father involvement: Implications for parenting programs for men. *Families in Society: The Journal of Contemporary Human Services, 76*, 490–497.

McHale, S. M., & Huston, T. L. (1984). Men and women as parents: Sex role orientations, employment, and parental roles with infants. *Child Development, 55*, 1349–1361.

McHale, S. M., & Huston, T. L. (1985). The effect of the transition to parenthood on the marriage relationship: A longitudinal study. *Journal of Family Issues, 6*, 409–433.

Menaghan, E. (1982). Assessing the impact of family transitions on marital experience. In H. I. McCubbin, A. E. Cauble, & J. M. Patterson (Eds.), *Family stress, coping, and social support* (pp. 90–108). Springfield, IL: Thomas.

Meyerowitz, J. H., & Feldman, H. (1966). Transition to parenthood. *Psychiatric Research Reports, 20*, 78–84.

Miller, B. C. (1976). A multivariate developmental model of marital satisfaction. *Journal of Marriage and the Family, 38*, 643–657.

Miller, B. C., & Sollie, D. L. (1980). Normal stresses during the transition to parenthood. *Family Relations, 29*, 459–465.

Moore, K. A., & Waite, L. J. (1981). Marital dissolution, early motherhood and early marriage. *Social Forces, 60*, 20–40.

Noller, P. (2001). *Personal relationships across the lifespan.* Philadelphia, PA: Psychology Press.

Noller, P., & Fitzpatrick, M. A. (1990). Marital communication in the eighties. *Journal of Marriage and the Family, 52*, 832–843.

O'Brien, M., & Peyton, V. (2002). Parenting attitudes and marital intimacy: A longitudinal analysis. *Journal of Family Psychology, 16*, 118–127.

Palkovitz, R. (1984). Parental attitudes and fathers' interaction with their 5-month-old infants. *Developmental Psychology, 20*, 1054–1060.

Palkovitz, R. (1997). Reconstructing "involvement:" Expanding conceptualizations of men's caring in contemporary families. In A. J. Hawkins & D. C. Dollahite (Eds.), *Generative fathering: Beyond deficit perspectives* (pp. 200–216). Thousand Oaks, CA: Sage.

Palkovitz, R. (2002). *Involved fathering and men's adult development: Provisional balances*. Hillsdale, NJ: Lawrence Erlbaum Associates.

Parke, R. D. (1996). *Fatherhood*. Cambridge, MA: Harvard University Press.

Parke, R. D. (in press). Fathers and families. In M. Bornstein (Ed.), *Handbook of parenting*. Hillsdale, NJ: Lawrence Erlbaum Associates.

Parke, R. D., & Brott, A. A. (1999). *Throwaway dads: The myths and barriers that keep men from being the fathers they want to be.* Boston: Houghton Mifflin.

Peters, H. E., Peterson, G. W., Steinmetz, S. K., & Day, R. D. (Eds.) (2000). *Fatherhood: Research, interventions, and policies.* Binghamton, New York: Haworth.

Pittman, J. F., & Blanchard, D. (1996). The effects of work history and timing of marriage on the division of household labor: A life-course perspective. *Journal of Marriage and the Family, 58,* 78–90.

Presser, H. B. (1994). Employment schedules among dual-earner spouses and the division of household labor by gender. *American Sociological Review, 59,* 348–364.

Rholes, W. S., Simpson, J. A., Blakely, B. S., Lanigan, L., & Allen, E. A. (1997). Adult attachment styles, the desire to have children, and working models of parenthood. *Journal of Personality, 65,* 357–385.

Robins, E. (1990). The study of interdependence in marriage. In F. D. Fincham & T. Bradbury (Eds.), *The psychology of marriage: Basic issues and applications* (pp. 59–86). New York: Guilford Press.

Ruble, D. N., Fleming, A. S., Hackel, L. S., & Stangor, C. (1988). Changes in the marital relationship during the transition to first time motherhood: Effects of violated expectations concerning the division of labor. *Journal of Personality and Social Psychology, 55,* 78–87.

Russell, C. S. (1974). Transition to parenthood: Problems and gratifications. *Journal of Marriage and the Family, 36,* 294–302.

Ryder, R. G. (1973). Longitudinal data relating marriage satisfaction and having a child. *Journal of Marriage and the Family, 35,* 604–606.

Sanchez, L., & Thomson, E. (1997). Becoming mothers and fathers: Parenthood, gender, and the division of labor. *Gender and Society, 11,* 747–772.

Shapiro, A. F., Gottman, J. M., & Carrère, S. (2000). The baby and marriage: Identifying factors that buffer against decline in marital satisfaction after the first baby arrives. *Journal of Family Psychology, 14,* 59–70.

Shelton, B. A. (1992). *Women, men and time: Gender differences in paid work, housework and leisure* (Contributions in Women's Studies 127). New York: Greenwood Press.

Smith, S. E., & Huston, T. L. (in press). How and why marriages change over time: Shifting patterns of companionship and partnership. In R. Conger (Ed.), *Continuity and change: Family structure and family process.* Mahwah, NJ: Lawrence Erlbaum Associates.

Spanier, G. B. (1976). Measuring dyadic adjustment: New scales for assessing the quality of marriage and similar dyads. *Journal of Marriage and the Family, 38,* 15–28.

Strauss, R., & Goldberg, W. A. (1999). Self and possible selves during the transition to fatherhood. *Journal of Family Psychology, 13,* 244–259.

Thornton, A., & Young-DeMarco, L. (2001). Four decades of trends in attitudes toward family issues in the United States: The 1960s through the 1990s. *Journal of Marriage and Family, 63*, 1009–1937.

Tomlinson, P. S. (1987). Spousal differences in marital satisfaction during the transition to parenthood. *Nursing Research, 36*, 239–243.

U.S. Bureau of the Census. (1999). *Statistical abstract of the United State*s (119th ed.). Washington, DC: U.S. Government Printing Office.

Vaillant, C. O., & Vaillant, G. E. (1993). Is the U-curve of marital satisfaction an illusion? A 40-year study of marriage. *Journal of Marriage and the Family, 55*, 230–239.

Waite, L., J., Haggstrom, G. W., & Kanouse, D. E. (1985). The consequences of parenthood for the marital stability of young adults. *American Sociological Review, 50*, 850–857.

Waite, L. J., & Lillard, L. A. (1991). Children and marital disruption. *American Journal of Sociology, 96*, 930–953.

Waldron, H., & Routh, D. K. (1981). The effect of the first child on the marital relationship. *Journal of Marriage and the Family, 43*, 785–788.

Waldrop, J. (1994). What do working women want? *American Demographics, 16*, 36–37.

Wallace, P. M., & Gotlib, I. H. (1990). Marital adjustment during the transition to parenthood: Stability and predictors of change. *Journal of Marriage and the Family, 52*, 21–29.

White, L. K., & Booth, A. (1985). The transition to parenthood and marital quality. *Journal of Family Issues, 6*, 435–449.

White, L. K., Booth, A., & Edwards, J. N. (1986). Children and marital happiness: Why the negative correlation? *Journal of Family Issues, 7*, 131–147.

Wiggins, J. (1979). Dynamic theories of social relationship and resulting research strategies. In R. L. Burgess & T. L. Huston (Eds.), *Social exchange in developing relationships* (pp. 381–407). New York: Academic Press.

CHAPTER

6

KEEPING ALL FIVE BALLS IN THE AIR: JUGGLING FAMILY COMMUNICATION AT MIDLIFE

KAREN L. FINGERMAN
PURDUE UNIVERSITY

JON NUSSBAUM AND KIRA S. BIRDITT
PENNSYLVANIA STATE UNIVERSITY

Adulthood, like a good story, has a beginning, a middle, and an end. Like many stories, however, the beginning and the end of adulthood are more clearly explicated than the middle. Although the start of adulthood in most Western societies does not involve a formal ceremony, there are definable indicators of this period of life. As a matter of course, in general, young adults complete schooling, enter the work world, find mates, and start new families. Likewise, late adulthood includes physical and social markers such as retirement, an intensification of ties to family, chronic disease, and physical decline. But, what are the characteristics of midlife?

Until recently, the middle years of adulthood received little scholarly attention (see Willis & Reid, 1999, for a discussion) and definitions of this period remain nebulous. For example, the MacArthur Foundation study of Midlife Development in the United States, a comprehensive national survey of middle-aged adults, included individuals aged 25 to 74. The survey was intended to capture transitions into and out of midlife as well as the period of midlife, but participants' subjective definitions of "middle age" varied considerably. Adults in their 20s often reported that midlife begins at 30, whereas some healthy and active adults in their 70s claimed to be middle-aged themselves (Lachman, 2001). Rather than attempt to deal with the parameters of midlife in this chapter, we propose a comparative approach. We ask, what occurs in the middle years of adult family life that differentiates it from the beginning and the end?

More specifically, this chapter examines the ways in which family communication patterns are distinct at midlife. Other chapters in this volume address relationships that pepper middle-aged adults' lives—middle-aged adults communicate with romantic partners, children, and extended family. They engage in conflict resolution, attend reunions, build new relationships, and maintain friendships. In this chapter, however, we consider specific characteristics of middle adulthood that may contribute to family communication.

As an overarching theme, we argue that a lifespan model of family communication must consider three issues: (a) sociological structures that influence family communication among individuals of different ages, (b) psychological processes, and (c) the characteristics and responses of other family members. In this regard, communication processes reflect the social roles individuals occupy and the concurrent demands they face. At the same time, middle-aged adults bring perspectives to their relationships based on their prior experiences and their current developmental goals. Finally, families are systems with dynamic processes; middle-aged adults respond to interactions with other family members in their communications (Fingerman & Bermann, 2000).

To address these issues, we first describe aspects of middle-aged adults' family life and the roles they occupy as well as their developmental goals and experiences. Then, we address two questions about family communication in midlife: (a) What is the content of family communication for middle-aged individuals? (b) What factors determine how middle-aged individuals communicate with family members? Finally, we devote considerable attention to topics in this area ripe for future research. As the population grows older, the middle years of adulthood become increasingly discreet and increasingly important for family functioning. Scholarly work in this area has only begun to investigate what is happening to individuals within families at midlife.

CHARACTERISTICS OF MIDLIFE

Individual differences in life experiences and family roles are rampant at midlife. Middle-aged adults manifest variation on nearly every issue of interest to family scholars: marital status, presence and age of children, physical health, career development, grandparenting roles, ties to family of origin and their own aging parents, leisure time, and personal style of communication. Indeed, treatises on midlife development commonly begin with disclaimers about the vast diversity evident at this period of life (e.g., Lachman, 2000; Willis & Reid, 1998). Add to these considerations macrolevel differences with regard to gender, socioeconomic status, and ethnicity, and the question arises, should we even attempt to describe commonalities of midlife communication?

In fact, convergent experiences exist at midlife, just as they exist at other stages of life (infancy, adolescence, old age). People communicate in different ways based on their accumulated life experiences, who they are communicating with, their available time and energy, and the roles or social positions they occupy; these factors vary systematically by age (Nussbaum, Pecchioni, Robinson, & Thompson, 2000). In the following, we first describe the social contexts in which middle-aged adults function and then consider psychological goals that middle-aged adults share. Family communication reflects these two aspects of midlife development.

Social Contexts of Midlife Communication

The popular culture often describes midlife as a period of increasing demands from others, as "life in the middle" with regard to social and work pressures. Yet, little systemic information is available with regard to whether middle-aged adults do, in fact, face greater demands than do younger or older adults.

To assess the challenges middle-aged adults deal with we pulled together national data regarding the roles and demands middle-aged adults confront in their daily lives in comparison to younger and older adults. Table 6.1 provides a summary of this information (see table footnotes for citations). This table is intended as a heuristic rather than as precise information about the activities of middle-aged adults. For example, published reports of the percentages of adults who have children over the age of 18 and who have living parents include data from the 1980s (e.g., Rossi & Rossi, 1990; Sweet, Bumpass, & Vaugn, 1988). Instead, we used unpublished data from the more recent National Survey of Midlife Development (MIDUS) study to estimate these probabilities. For some activities, we could not obtain precise information for all age categories. When data were available for a wider age range than used in the table, we repeated numbers across columns (e.g., physical disability rates for individuals aged 20 to 34 and 35 to 44 in the table reflect reported disability rates for individuals aged 20 to 44). In this section, we describe three general aspects of this table: (a) the family relationships middle-aged adults have, (b) the other social roles in which they are embedded, and (c) the task demands in which family communication takes place.

Family Ties at Midlife.   The term "midlife" is highly descriptive with regard to family ties—it is literally a period in the middle of the family. A study of individuals aged 13 to 99 revealed that middle-aged adults had more living family members than did younger or older adults (Fingerman & Birditt, in press). Middle-aged adults have ties to family members in generations above them (e.g., parents), generations below them (e.g., children and grandchildren), and their own generation (e.g., partner, siblings, and cousins). Younger adults have ties to their family of origin, but are generally in the process of finding mates and having children. By contrast, at the end of life, older adults have often lost their parents and may have outlived their spouses, siblings, and even some of their children.

Obviously, there is considerable diversity in middle-aged adults' family ties. For example, although a majority of middle-aged adults are in romantic liaisons, high divorce rates, alternative lifestyles, and decisions from early adulthood leave a high proportion of adults unpartnered at midlife (U.S. Bureau of the Census, 2000). The presence and ages of children also varies. Some individuals who had children early in life are showing pictures of grandchildren to co-workers at midlife, whereas other individuals who had children in their 30s or 40s are organizing play dates for their toddlers, and still other individuals enjoy evenings out on the town in the absence of ties to children. Nonetheless, midlife tends to be the period when individuals of all backgrounds have the greatest number of close family ties (Antonucci & Akiyama, 1987; Lang, in press).

Middle-aged adults not only *have* more family members, they are more engaged with these family members than are younger or older adults. Young adults are interested in fostering new ties to people outside the family (Carstensen, 1995) and are unlikely to take on the work involved in family demands. At the same time, however, young adults turn to their middle-aged parents for advice about their careers, schooling, and even love affairs, generating family work for this generation (Fingerman, 2000). Likewise, by late life, many older adults have lost members of their own generation and turn to middle-aged children,

TABLE 6.1

Competing Demands at Midlife: Proportions of Individuals Fitting Each Category by Age Group

	Aged 20 to 34	Aged 35 to 44	Aged 45 to 54	Aged 55 to 64	Aged 65 to 74	Aged 75+
Health status						
Has a physical disability[a]	.134	.134	.226	.357	.457	.656
Limitation in activity[b]	.069	.069	.131	.211	.275	.456
4+ health care appointments past year[c]	.152	.152	.192	.221	.272	.309
Had major depression in past year[d]	.032	.032	.021	.021	.009	.009
Social engagement						
Working for pay[e]	.769	.816	.798	.584	.436	.052
Enrolled in school[f]	.235	.036	.021	.006	.002	.002
Community activity 2+ hours a week[g]	.616	.642	.564	.512	.466	.324
Uses the internet[h]	.423	.398	.387	.144	.144	.144
Exercises at least 3 times a week[i]	.238	.238	.247	.247	.278	.287
Family roles						
Married[j]	.613	.661	.661	.672	.635	.404
Widowed[j]	.002	.009	.023	.074	.205	.394
Children in home under 18[j]	.292	.335	.176	.036	.006	.002
Children ages 18 to 24 in home[j]	.001	.021	.103	.042	.008	.001
Children over 18[k]	.004	.260	.620	.771	.743	.743
Has grandchildren[l]	.028	.334	.334	.787	.814	.814
Grandmother regularly helps w/ grandchildren[m]	—	—	.536	.451	.285	—
Has a living mother[k]	.708	.688	.548	.297	.089	—
Has a living father[k]	.612	.508	.314	.101	.012	—
Providing care for spouse[n]	.009	.026	.046	.046	.065	.067
Providing care for aging parent[n]	.047	.098	.107	.107	.055	.008
Total U.S. Population in year 2001 in 1,000s	55,934	44,390	38,341	24,203	17,757	15,092

[a]U.S. Bureau of the Census. (2001). *Statistical Abstracts of the United States*. Retrieved March 1, 2002, from http://www.census.gov/ prod/2002pubs/ 01statab/ health.pdf

[b]National Center for Health Statistics. (2001). *Health, United States*. Retrieved March 1, 2002, from http://www.cdc.gov/nchs/products/pubs/pubd/hus/tables/2001/01hus057.pdf

[c]National Center for Health Statistics. (2001). *Health, United States*. Retrieved March 1, 2002, from http://www.cdc.gov/nchs/products/pubs/pubd/hus/tables/2001/01hus072.pdf

[d]Weissman, M. M., Leaf, P. J., Tischler, G. L., & Blazer, D. G. (1988). Affective disorders in five United States communities. *Psychological Medicine, 18*, 141–153.

[e]Bureau of Labor Statistics. (2001). *Labor Force Statistics from the Current Population Survey*. Retrieved March 1, 2002, from http://www.bls.gov/cps/home.html

[f]U. S. Bureau of the Census. (October, 2000). *School enrollment—Social and economic characteristics of students*. Retrieved February 26, 2002, from http://www.census.gov/population/www/socdemo/school/pp1-148.html

[g]Gallup Organization. (1990). *Giving and volunteering in the United States: Findings from a National Survey*. Washington DC: Independent Sector.

nieces, or nephews for assistance or comfort (Connidis & Davies, 1990). Middle-aged adults talk with members of generations above and below them. They assist young adult offspring, take pride in nieces, nephews, and care for grandchildren. With older family members, they discuss their own careers, children, grandchildren, the older adult's health and daily happenings, and long-time family friends and traditions. They are likely to be in communication with their siblings and cousins.

Middle-aged adults are sometimes colloquially labeled "the sandwich generation" in reference to finding themselves "sandwiched" between generations. This term has a negative connotation with regard to caregiving demands. Twenty years ago, Brody (1981) warned that a significant percentage of middle-aged women would find themselves "sandwiched" in the overwhelming role of managing multiple family responsibilities that would cause harmful individual and family outcomes. It is important to keep in mind, however, that social scientists do not find evidence for such "sandwiching" when they study families at midlife (Putney & Bengtson, 2001; Williams & Nussbaum, 2001). For the most part, the nearly impossible task of simultaneously caring for an older parent and a misbehaving teen in the same house is quite rare.

However, the fact that multiple individuals across generations do indeed depend upon the middle generation for emotional, physical, and financial support at various times and in various crisis situations is a reality. As can be seen in the table, over a third of middle-aged adults have children in their homes, and a third have grandchildren. Of those middle-aged adults who have grandchildren, the majority of these grandparents provide at least some care for them. Further, although information is not available concerning the age distribution of grandparents who are raising their grandchildren full-time, data from a national study indicated that their mean age is 59 (Fuller-Thomson, Minkler, & Driver, 1997). As such, a sizable group of middle-aged adults serve as surrogate parents for their grandchildren.

In short, the family context of midlife reflects a vast accumulation of ties from prior stages of life. Middle-aged adults retain ties to their families of origin, their spouse or romantic partner, their family of procreation, and often reap the benefits of grown children's ventures to create their own families. Middle-aged adults also have the stamina to foster new ties and build on existing relationships. The resulting family network provides multiple

←───────────────────────────────

[h]National Telecommunications and Information Administration. (1998). *A Nation online: How Americans are expanding their use of the Internet*. Retrieved February 21, 2002, from http://www.ntia.doc.gov

[i]U.S. Bureau of the Census. (2001). *Statistical Abstracts of the United States*. Retrieved March 1, 2002, from http://www.census.gov/ prod/2002pubs/ 01statab/ health.pdf

[j]U.S. Bureau of the Census. (March, 2000). America's families and living arrangements. Retrieved March 1, 2002, from http://www.census.gov/population/www/socdemo/hh-fam /p20-537_00.html

[k]*Midlife in the United States Survey*. (1995–1996) [Data file.]. John D. and Catherine T. MacArthur Foundation Network on Successful Midlife.

[l]Szinovacz, M. E. (1998). Grandparents today: A demographic profile. *The Gerontologist, 38*, 37–52.

[m]Baydar, N., & Brooks-Gunn, J. (1998). Profiles of grandmothers who help care for their grandchildren in the United States. *Family Relations, 47*, 385–393.

[n]Marks, N. F. (1996). Caregiving across the lifespan. National prevalence and predictors. *Family Relations*, 45, 27–36.

venues for communication. Middle-aged adults also often feel torn in many directions as they attempt to meet the needs of multiple family members.

Nonfamilial Demands at Midlife.   Although they deal with multiple family roles, middle-aged adults also confront multiple demands outside the family. Some demands may impede the processes of family communication (by drawing middle-aged adults away from family) and may also generate the substance of that communication. Middle-aged adults are likely to talk about extrafamilial issues, such as work and civic activities, with family members.

For example, at the individual level, functional ability contributes to the nature of family communication. As can be seen in Table 6.1, most middle-aged adults are in good health and confront few physical difficulties getting around or communicating with loved ones. At the same time, limitations in daily activities increase around age 45, as do visits to doctors. By age 55, this shift is even more dramatic. As such, middle-aged adults must devote time and energy to their own health care in ways that younger adults (who rebound quickly from life's physical demands and a night of partying) do not. From this perspective, the capacity to communicate remains intact at midlife, but the content of communication may become more health focused.

Midlife is also a period of relative emotional stability. Rates of clinical depression appear to be lowest in late life, but in fact, middle-aged adults have the lowest rates of depressive symptomatology (Gatz & Zarit, 1999). Furthermore, emotional well-being appears to be quite high in midlife (Ryff, 1995). In this regard, middle-aged adults may find that other family members rely on them during periods of distress.

Yet, as can be seen in Table 6.1, family communication at midlife occurs in concurrence with demands from work and leisure activities. Research examining American's use of time indicates that parents of small children face the greatest demands on their use of time (Robinson & Godbey, 1999). For middle-aged adults who have small children, family communication must take place in the harried context of children's demands and schedules. Many middle-aged adults have passed this stage of hands-on childrearing, however, and have greater latitude in the use of their time on a day-to-day basis. Yet, middle-aged adults commonly confront increasing task demands at work and from multiple generations of family members who turn to them in periods of crisis. As will be discussed, middle-aged adults also often take on tasks associated with maintaining ties to a variety of family members, such as holiday celebrations and special occasions. As such, we liken family communication at midlife to a juggling act: Middle-aged adults must keep a hand out to keep many interactive balls in the air simultaneously.

Experiences and Goals at Midlife

Discussion thus far has centered on how the social context contributes to the nature of family communication at midlife. In addition to finding themselves in different roles and relationships than younger or older adults, middle-aged adults bring different points of view to these family ties. Three issues tend to characterize individuals' psychological lives in middle adulthood (Fingerman, 1997). First, midlife is a period during which relationships with others tend to become salient and responsibilities for other individuals increase (Erikson, 1963). Second, it is a time when individuals' conceptions of the self gain increasing complexity (Labouvie-Vief, Chiodo, Goguen, Diehl, & Orwoll, 1995). Finally, individuals become more aware of time remaining, of continuities with the past, and discontinuities into the future (Neugarten, 1968). These developmental issues provide a foundation for communication at midlife.

Indeed, the interface between social structural variables and psychological functioning is at the core of understanding family ties throughout life (Bronfenbrenner & Morris, 1998; Fingerman & Bermann, 2000). Yet, most research and theoretical discussion of midlife has focused on managing multiple roles and role transitions. Psychological reactions to these transitions have been studied in the context of research examining psychological distress with loss of roles (for a discussion see Moen & Wethington, 1999), but the goals and experiences individuals bring to their relationships at midlife have not been clearly articulated. In the next section, we describe how social roles and psychological features of midlife may contribute to family communication.

CONTENT OF COMMUNICATION WITH FAMILY MEMBERS AT MIDLIFE

Communication research often focuses on the expression of information rather than on the content of information. From a developmental perspective, what people talk about is important. Midlife is a time of numerous familial roles such as spouse, parent, child, sibling, and possibly grandchild and grandparent. At the same time, individuals encounter new responsibilities in their careers and civic lives. Individuals find themselves engaged in the most diverse set of communicative encounters of their lives, ranging from appropriate curfew times for the children, to bathroom wallpaper decisions with a spouse, to organizing the family reunion, to decisions about parental health care. At no time in life is the content of communication more diverse and thus more challenging for the individuals involved.

The content of family communication is likely to reflect the developmental position of the focal individuals and the needs and demands of the family members with whom they communicate. Again, social contexts and psychological processes may direct the content of family communication.

Social Contexts and the Content of Family Communication at Midlife

As mentioned previously, family communication at midlife partially reflects the complicated social situations in which middle-aged adults are embedded and the multiple roles they juggle. The question arises—how does the diverse content of these interactive lives relate to the construction and management of specific familial roles? At midlife, individuals are faced with maintaining several different, and at times contradictory, relational roles. For instance, they are simultaneously a parent who must raise children and a child who must manage an ever-changing power dynamic with a parent. The middle-aged adult must exhibit appropriate controlling and dominant behavior with adolescent children while indicating respect and submission with parents. The children may observe this submissive behavior and attempt to take advantage. At the same time, the middle-aged adults' parents may view the controlling behavior toward their grandchildren and attempt to interject their opinions on child rearing. The middle-aged adult must respond with appropriate communication across parties—juggling multiple roles simultaneously.

An additional challenge that adults face at midlife concerns the choice as to whether particular topics should or should not be communicated to a specific individual, to numerous individuals, or to no family members. Unlike at other points in the life span where context or developmental determinants limit the number of possible family partners, midlife presents the individual with an overwhelming number of conversation options. The richness of possible partners presents a dilemma as to with whom it is appropriate discuss certain topics. It is not unreasonable to imagine that certain familial relationships are appropriate for certain conversations, whereas other relationships would be threatened if not destroyed by a similar conversation. For example, a divorced, middle-aged woman might talk with her teenage daughter about the daughter's desire to date a young man in her class at school, to her mother about the loneliness of being unpartnered in widowhood, but to neither party about her own sexual behavior. Similarly, a husband and wife might discuss financial problems with one another, but seek to hide these problems from grown children and aging parents who have their own problems to worry about.

There is little doubt that middle-aged adults are aware of their conversational choices and the effects that these choices have upon the family members with whom they interact. The juggling act of maintaining appropriate conversational boundaries adds to the complexities of family ties at midlife. Middle-aged adults not only find themselves in multiple family roles but also must possess an understanding of the parameters of those roles that help determine what and with whom they communicate if their communication is to be successful.

Content Reflecting Middle-Aged Adults' Psychological Development

Features of psychological development may also contribute to what middle-aged adults talk about with family members. Middle-aged adults tend to demonstrate greater cognitive complexity, ego strength, and more mature coping styles than do younger or older adults (Labouvie-Vief, Hakim-Larson, & Hobart, 1987). These features of individual development contribute to a more sophisticated pattern of communication and to greater control over the content of that communication. For example, observational studies of middle-aged women talking with their adolescent children and with their mothers reveals that the middle-aged adult does most of the talking, regardless of the family partner (Lefkowitz & Fingerman, under review; Lefkowitz et al., 1996). Further, the content of those communiqués tends to involve the middle-aged adult's efforts to guide other family members, to provide advice or input into their behaviors (Fingerman, 2000).

The emotional qualities of relationships at midlife also tend to be complex. Carstensen and her colleagues have argued that individuals focus on emotional goals in relationships as they approach the end of life. In other words, older adults select relationships that are most rewarding and describe their relationships in more positive terms than do younger adults (Carstensen, 1995; Carstensen, Charles, & Isaacowitz, 1999). Yet, middle-aged adults tend to view their relationships in more complicated emotional terms than do older or younger adults. For example, middle-aged adults are both more positive and more negative about their parents and their children than are younger or older adults; they may see nuances of the strengths and weaknesses of these family members in any given encounter (Fingerman,

2000; Fingerman & Hay, in press). By contrast, younger adults tend to think in black-and-white terms, viewing people and encounters as wholly good or bad (Labouvie-Vief, 1994). By late life, individuals are able to focus primarily on the positive emotional qualities of their family relationships, because the demands from family members may lessen.

Middle-aged adults may also talk more about the "other" rather than the "self" in family communication based on both social contexts and psychological processes that encourage others to think outwards at midlife. From a theoretical perspective, Erikson (1950) initially argued that midlife is a period of generativity, a time during which individuals increasingly derive rewards from assisting and guiding younger people. Subsequent research suggests middle-aged adults are also likely to nurture individuals in their own generation and generations above them (Stewart & Vandewater, 1998). For example, in one study, middle-aged women were asked to describe what they enjoy about their aging mothers and their grown daughters. Middle-aged women reported that conversations about everyday events were a source of pleasure in both relationships. The women enjoyed conversations about the daughter's decisions at school, romantic ties, and her children (if she had them). With their mothers, they talked about daily events, friends, or the larger family network in which both women were invested (Fingerman, 2000).

As an extension of generativity, middle-aged adults may engage in conversations aimed at protecting other family members. Neugarten (1968) initially argued that in midlife, individuals become increasingly aware of time remaining. In a family context, this awareness may shift to heightened concerns about family members' health and safety as well. Studies suggest middle-aged offspring worry about their parents' future health needs long before the parents incur any actual needs for care (Cicirelli, 1988; Fingerman, 1997). Further, middle-aged grandparents worry about their grandchildren's home environments more than do older grandparents (though older grandparents worry more about their grandchildren overall) (Fingerman, 1998). Middle-aged adults are likely to communicate these concerns to other family members in their efforts to nurture them or to contribute to their growth.

Finally, by midlife, gender differences in family communication notable in the early years of adulthood may become muted (Huyck, 1999). Men and women alike may feel increasing value for their relationships, and the content of communication may focus increasingly on efforts to connect to family members. Gerontologists have argued that an older woman in the family often serves as the "kinkeeper" who rallies family members to celebrations and reunions (Troll, 1988). Yet, it is middle-aged adults who are the "kinkeepees," the individuals who respond to the kinkeeper's efforts by attending such festivities and bringing along their spouses, children, and other relatives (Fingerman, 2001). As grown children leave home and return to visit, men and women alike may become invested in fortifying ties, organizing family structure, and bridging relationships. In sum, from both a theoretical and a practical perspective, the content of middle-aged adults' family conversations may focus on the details of keeping the family going.

COMMUNICATION STYLES AT MIDLIFE

In addition to considering *what* middle-aged adults communicate within families, we might ask, *how* do they communicate it? Williams and Nussbaum (2001) argued that middle-aged adults must develop a complex set of communicative behaviors to simultaneously meet the disparate needs of multiple generations of family members. Family communication is often difficult under the most perfect of conditions. Numerous studies (see Williams & Nussbaum, 2001, for a review) have shown middle-aged adults face distinct challenges, however, as they interact with family and nonfamily members of differing ages. The general issues surrounding competent family communication encompass use of language, cognitive processing ability, stereotypes that may result in misjudged accommodations to the conversational partner, and general skills that are required to send and receive messages. Yet, middle-aged adults face particular demands in these processes. Middle-aged adults must develop sophisticated approaches to communication given their need to interact with multiple partners of different ages. These partners have specific familial roles, a wide range of cognitive abilities, differing interactive styles, and may or may not possess the necessary skills to manage an effective conversation at times. Furthermore, middle-aged adults must adjust their communication styles to facilitate family unity.

Middle-aged adults' communication styles may reflect their social contexts and their psychological development. From a contextual perspective, they must simultaneously serve as listeners and communicators in their family relationships, while processing what is taking place. To illustrate this point, a young child wishes to communicate her desire to go to the park to her parents. Appropriate to her age, she is not concerned with her parents' desires, whether going to the park conflicts with her older brother's desire for help with his homework, or drawing the larger family together (e.g., her mother's need to telephone the child's grandmother). Middle-aged adults possess the capacity to consider others' needs. At times, their own needs may dominate their concerns, but middle-aged adults often turn outward to balance the needs of other family members.

As a result, middle-aged adults must "analyze the audience" as they juggle; they must determine what each family member wants and understands. This task requires specific skills to communicate with an appropriate style and intensity for each family member. Furthermore, middle-aged adults not only are concerned with communication in each of their multiple relationships (e.g., with spouse, parent, child) but also are concerned *across* these ties. Midlife communication styles may reflect a desire to unify the family or at least to handle multiple relationships.

Middle-aged adults' positions in the family may also diminish their likelihood of confronting other family members in an aggressive manner. Rook (1995) argued that certain family ties, such as long-term marriage, parenting, and caring for an aging parent, entail enduring responsibilities. Such responsibilities may curtail negative behaviors and even negative feelings. Individuals who have responsibilities to others are forced to combat feelings of sadness or fatigue because they are required to carry out duties to others, regardless of their own feelings at the time (Rook, 1995).

At the same time, psychological processes such as the ability to regulate emotions may contribute to individuals' ways of dealing with interpersonal problems (Birditt, Fingerman, & Almeida, in preparation). Birditt and Fingerman (2001) asked individuals how they handled problems they experienced in their close and problematic relationships. They found that people in their 40s and 60s were more likely to listen to other people or try to solve the problems with family members than were adolescents and young adults (who used confrontational means of handling problems more often). Furthermore, Bergstrom and Nussbaum (1996) reasoned that younger and middle-aged adults might differ in their strategies for dealing with interpersonal conflict in general. Results from their investigation point toward more cooperative conflict management as individuals grow older. For the most part, in their study, younger adults were found to be more aggressive and competitive in their style of conflict, whereas older adults were more conciliatory in working out a solution that benefited both family members.

Of course, some middle-aged adults are confrontational and have difficulties in their dealings with family members. A developmental perspective on family communication must consider such individual differences as well as mean differences across age groups. Therefore, it would be overstating the case to suggest that all middle-aged adults communicate in constructive ways across family contexts. Rather, within families, the person who is most likely to behave in conciliatory ways when problems come up and in ways that unify the family is likely to be middle aged. Middle-aged adults possess the psychological capacities to deal with complex communication tasks, and they often find themselves in roles and social contexts that evoke such behaviors.

In sum, as middle-aged adults find themselves in positions of increasing responsibility and authority, they may be more likely to take charge of family communication. In this regard, middle-aged adults may attempt to direct conversation, ask questions, include multiple family members' perspectives, and adjust their conversational style to the needs of the other family members. Of course, such communication may be more an ideal than a reality. Research suggests middle-aged spouses may still engage in overt confrontation when they are upset with one another (Carstensen, Levenson, & Gottman, 1993), and middle-aged parents may still engage in conflict with their adolescent children (Laursen & Collins, 1994; Laursen, Coy, & Collins, 1998). Furthermore, middle-aged adults may be forced to focus so much on other people, they feel cast into a role of listener or director rather than that of communicator. Their ability to communicate their own needs may become stifled. Nonetheless, most middle-aged adults rise to the occasion and deal with family communication issues successfully.

SUGGESTIONS FOR FUTURE RESEARCH

We have described family communication in midlife in this chapter. As is the case with regard to other issues in midlife, however, basic questions remain to be investigated. For example, in comparison to assessments of family ties in childhood and young adulthood, researchers have relied on a limited set of methodologies to examine communication between middle-aged adults and their family members. In this section, we describe the next steps family scholars might take to examine family communication at midlife.

Questions To Examine

Scientific methodology by definition involves addressing unanswered questions, but we know considerably more about family communication at some periods of life than at others. Future studies might seek to ascertain information about basic questions such as: (a) With whom do middle-aged adults communicate most frequently in the family? (b) What contexts require communication with different family members? (c) What is the content of communication? With regard to the first question, we might look at the primacy of different social partners. For example, who do middle-aged adults communicate with most often on a daily basis? Given the demands involved with growing children and adolescents, certain middle-aged adults may have the majority of their interactions with their children. Other middle-aged adults may have a much broader and more multigenerational family interaction pattern. For still other middle-aged adults, the oft-cited increase in martial satisfaction when children leave the nest (White & Edwards, 1990) may reflect the fact that they have more time to communicate with one another and are also now communicating with a more diverse network of family members.

Certain contexts, of course, also require contact with a wide array of family members. When an aging parent incurs health problems, middle-aged offspring may turn to siblings for discussion of the ongoing crisis (Connidis, 1992). Alternately, one of the middle-aged daughters may take over primary care of the parents, talking primarily to her spouse about the stress incurred (Connidis, Rosenthal, & McMullin, 1996). These stressful contexts for communication often occur with little time for planning or preparation. The siblings may have communication skills or relationship patterns that allow them to work together to assist the aging parent, or they may experience discord and conflict. Research addressing caregivers should consider the ramifications of different approaches to family communication about this topic.

Other contexts of midlife communication are much more positive. Family celebrations that surround activities such as first holy communions, bar mitzvahs, graduations, and marriages bring families together to celebrate. These life events offer ample opportunities for family members to contact one another, share experiences, and to maintain high levels of family solidarity. Within these positive contexts, the multiple communicative roles of midlife adults may emerge as numerous generations of family members interact in a pleasant atmosphere.

Further, the content of family communication is an excellent, empirical indicator of what issues are most important to the family and which family members are involved in managing these issues. The persistence of certain communicative content within the family can also indicate how well the middle-aged adults are managing various family issues. If family communication consistently focuses on stressful interactions, does this indicate that the family may be dysfunctional? Do topics of family discussion change across middle adulthood? We know little about normal changes in the content of communication across a typical day, a week, a year, or across the entirety of midlife.

Scant evidence suggests young adults talk about themselves, their goals, and their dreams, and expect family members to be interested in these topics (Fingerman, 2000). It seems less likely that middle-aged adults are so intrigued with their own development or that family members would indulge them in talking about it. Middle-aged adults are the workers who keep the family running. As a result, are middle-aged adults confined to talking with family members about tasks that must be accomplished in daily life? Further, given the demands on middle-aged adults' time, few individuals have time for the deep friendships characteristic of younger adulthood. How do middle-aged adults nurture their sense of art, creativity, and leisure within the family?

Expanded Use of Methodologies

In addition to these questions, future research should use diverse methodologies to tap the complexities of family communication at midlife. The questions above prioritize the study of verbal communication. Yet, effective family communication involves the sending and the interpretation of nonverbal communication as well. The interpretation of messages depends upon such factors as the intensity, passion, timing, gestures, eye behavior, touch, and paralanguage of communication. Observational studies of middle-aged adults that have incorporated analysis of nonverbal behavior are notably sparse. Prior observational studies have focused on how middle-aged parents communicate with their adolescent children (Flannery, Montemayor, & Eberly, 1994; Grotevant & Cooper, 1985; Lefkowitz, Kahlbaugh, & Sigman, 1996; Smetana, Yua, Restrepo, & Braeges, 1991). Indeed, most observational studies of marital couples focus on newlyweds (e.g., Cobb, Davila, & Bradbury, 2001; Hawkins, Carrere, & Gottman, 2001). Few studies have focused on communication with other family members at midlife such as parents or spouse (for exceptions see Carstensen, Levenson & Gottmann, 1993; Lefkowitz & Fingerman, 2001).

Researchers will also be well served to go beyond the traditional quantitative or qualitative survey methodologies typically employed to capture family interaction. The juggling of multigenerational familial roles and responsibilities by middle-aged adults must be documented. Survey methods, experiments, observational methodologies, and various forms of interpretive procedures including discourse analysis and ethnomethodology can be useful in an attempt to understand the complexities of middle-aged adults' families. Furthermore, combinations of methodologies such as videotaping ongoing family interactions, collecting family members' perceptions of communication, and diaries might be useful tools of investigation.

Finally, few studies have attempted to capture changes in family communication across midlife. Families clearly undergo shifts in structure in midlife, as individuals focus increasingly on their own descendants rather than on their family of origin (Connidis, 1992). Over time, individuals transition from seeking advice from others in young adulthood, to providing advice in midlife, to eventually needing care at the very end of life. There is little understanding of how family communication changes across these stages. Numerous methodological innovations would permit researchers to capture significant behavioral change within traditional longitudinal designs as well as different permutations of cross-sectional designs (Rudinger & Rietz, 2001; Schaie & Hofer, 2001).

Micro- and Macrolevel Variables

Communication scholars must consider macrolevel and microlevel influences on family communication involving middle-aged adults. Ecological theories suggest that basic changes in the structure of society funnel into family processes at different stages of life (Bronfenbrenner & Morris, 1997). For example, the current cohort of middle-aged adults, the Baby Boomers, have molded, and been molded by, larger societal influences around them.

Further, we know something about gender differences in communication but little about how socioeconomic status or ethnic differences may contribute to family processes at midlife. Research examining Mexican, Chinese, Filipino, and European American adolescents suggests that ethnicity may play subtle roles in ties between middle-aged parents and teenage offspring (Fuligni, 1998). Yet, there is not a theoretical consensus as to whether such variation in family communication reflects parenting practices, economic class, midlife issues, values for autonomy, or a combination of factors. Additional work should attempt to disentangle these issues at a theoretical level.

Investigators might also consider how changes in family structures over the past 50 years have altered family communication. For example, what demands do single parents, parents in blended families, and parents in dual career families confront communicating with and about their children? Further, middle-aged adults must communicate not only with family members but also with outside parties *about* family members. Parents in some contexts may have greater ease in communicating with their children's teachers, peers, or after-school providers than parents in other contexts (Bronfenbrenner & Morris, 1998).

The increasing older population can serve as either a source of support or a drain on middle-aged adults' resources, depending on the family members involved. The next chapter in this volume describes particularities of older adults' communication with family members, but we note here that an expanding older population is also a shifting context for middle-aged adults' family communication.

Finally, increasing outside pressures (work, commute, geographic moves) pull people away from family ties at midlife. Technological advances over the past 50 years have rendered communication by phone or email everyday occurrences within families, regardless of distance. Likewise, car and air travel have become easier and less expensive over the past 50 years (long waits, traffic delays, and detours notwithstanding). Yet, such advances have also increased demands on middle-aged adults' time (Adams & Stevenson, in press; Fingerman, in press; Gergen, 2000). Family no longer holds the center stage on the social world that it might have in foregone eras. And middle-aged adults may find themselves reaping the benefits and weathering the communication demands of life in the middle.

In summary, scholars have only begun to examine how middle-aged adults communicate with family members. It is clear that families are strengthened by the work of middle-aged adults in bridging members of many generations. It is also clear that middle-aged adults respond to family members by juggling multiple demands and needs. Future research must focus on understanding how this act is accomplished with such apparent ease for an audience of so many.

AUTHOR NOTE

Karen Fingerman was supported by Grant AG17916-01A from the National Institute on Aging, "Problems between Parents and Offspring in Adulthood," and by a grant from the Brookdale Foundation, "Sensory Impairments and Family Ties in Late Life." We are grateful to Kelly Cichy for assistance with this chapter.

REFERENCES

Adams, R., G., & Stevenson, M. (in press). A lifetime of relationships mediated by technology. In F. Lang & K. L. Fingerman (Eds.), *Growing together: Personal relationships across the lifespan.* New York: Cambridge University Press.

Antonucci, T. C., & Akiyama, H. (1987). Social networks in adult life and a preliminary examination of the convoy model. *Journal of Gerontology, 42,* 519–527.

Baydar, N., & Brooks-Gunn, J. (1998). Profiles of grandmothers who help care for their grandchildren in the United States. *Family Relations, 47,* 385–393.

Bergstrom, M. J., & Nussbaum, J. F. (1996). Cohort differences in interpersonal conflict: Implications for older patient–younger care provider interaction. *Health Communication, 8,* 233–245.

Birditt, K. S., Fingerman, K. L., & Almeida, D. (in preparation). *Age and gender differences in reactions to daily interpersonal stressors.* Manuscript in Preparation.

Blieszner, R., & Roberto, K. A. (in press). Friendship across the lifespan: Reciprocity in individual and relationship development. In F. Lang & K. L. Fingerman (Eds.), *Growing together: Personal relationships across the lifespan.* New York: Cambridge University Press.

Brody, E. M. (1981). Women in the middle and family help to older people. *The Gerontologist, 21,* 471–451.

Bronfenbrenner, U., & Morris, P. A. (1997). The ecology of developmental processes. In W. Damon (Ed.), *Handbook of child psychology* (5th ed., pp. 993–1028). New York: Wiley.

Bureau of Labor Statistics. (2001). *Labor Force Statistics from the Current Population Survey.* Retrieved March 1, 2002, from http://www.bls.gov/cps/home.html

Carstensen, L. L., Gottman, J. M., & Levenson, R. W. (1993). Emotional behavior in long-term marriage. *Psychology and Aging, 8,* 301–313.

Carstensen, L. L., Isaacowitz, D., & Charles, S. T. (1999). Taking time seriously: A theory of socioemotional selectivity. *American Psychologist, 54,* 165–181.

Cicirelli, V. G. (1988). A measure of filial anxiety regarding anticipated care of elderly parents. *The Gerontologist, 28,* 478–482.

Cobb, R. J., Davila, J., & Bradbury, T. N. (2001). Attachment security and marital satisfaction: The role of positive perceptions and social support. *Personality and Social Psychology Bulletin, 27,* 1131–1143.

Connidis, I. A. (1992). Life transitions and the adult sibling tie: A qualitative study. *Journal of Marriage and the Family, 54,* 972–982.

Connidis, I. A., & Davies, L. (1990). Confidants and companions in later life: The place of family and friends. *Journal of Gerontology: Social Sciences, 45,* S141–149.

Connidis, I. A., Rosenthal, C. J., & McMullin, J. A. (1996). The impact of family composition on providing help to older parents: A study of employed adults. *Research on Aging, 18,* 402–429.

Durkheim, E. (1951). *Suicide: A study in sociology* (J. Spaulding & G. Simpson, Trans.). New York: The Free Press. (Original work published 1897)

Erikson, E. H. (1950). *Childhood and society.* New York: Norton.

Erikson, E. H. (1963). *Childhood and society* (2nd ed.). New York: Norton.

Fingerman, K. L. (1997). Being more than a daughter: Middle-aged women's conceptions of their mothers. *Journal of Women and Aging, 9,* 55–72.

Fingerman, K. L. (1998). Tight lips: Aging mothers' and their adult daughters' responses to interpersonal tensions in their relationship. *Personal Relationships, 5,* 121–138.

Fingerman, K. L. (2000). "We had a nice little chat": Age and generational differences in mothers' and daughters' descriptions of enjoyable visits. *Journals of Gerontology: Psychological Sciences, 55,* 95–106.

Fingerman, K. L. (2001). *Aging mothers and their adult daughters: A study in mixed emotions.* New York: Springer.

Fingerman, K. L. (in press). The consequential stranger: Peripheral ties across the lifespan. In F. Lang & K. L. Fingerman (Eds.), *Growing together: Personal relationships across the lifespan*. New York: Cambridge University Press.

Fingerman, K. L., & Bermann, E. (2000). Applications of family systems theory to the state of adulthood. *International Journal of Aging and Human Development, 51*(1), 5–29.

Fingerman, K. L., & Birditt, K. S. (in press). Do age differences in close and problematic family networks reflect the pool of available relatives? *Journals of Gerontology: Psychological Sciences.*

Fingerman, K. L., & Hay, E. L. (in press). Intergenerational ambivalence in the context of the larger social network. K. Luescher & K. Pillemer (Eds.), *Intergenerational ambivalence*. Belgium: Elsevier/JAI Press.

Flannery, D. J., Montemayor, R., & Eberly, M. B. (1994). The influence of parent negative emotional expression on adolescents' perceptions of their relationship with their parents. *Personal Relationships, 1*, 259–274.

Fuligni, A. (1998). Authority, autonomy, and parent-adolescent conflict and cohesion: A study of adolescents from Mexican, Chinese, Filipino, and European backgrounds. *Developmental Psychology, 34*, 782–792.

Fuller-Thomson, E., Minkler, M., & Driver, D. (1997). A profile of grandparents raising grandchildren in the United States. *The Gerontologist, 37*, 406–411.

Gallup Organization. (1990). *Giving and volunteering in the United States: Findings from a National Survey*. Washington DC: Independent Sector.

Gatz, M., & Zarit, S. H. (1999). A good old age: Paradox or possibility. In V. L. Bengtson & K. W. Schaie (Eds.), *Handbook of theories of aging* (pp. 396–416). New York: Springer.

Gergen, K. J. (2000). *The saturated self: Dilemmas of identity in contemporary life* (2nd ed.). New York: Basic Books.

Grotevant, H. D., & Cooper, C. R. (1985). Patterns of interaction in family relationships and the development of identity exploration in adolescence. *Child Development, 56*, 415–428.

Hawkins, M. W., Carrere, S., & Gottman, J. M. (2002). Marital sentiment override: Does it influence couples' perceptions? *Journal of Marriage and Family, 64*, 193–201.

Huyck, M. H. (1999). Gender roles and gender identity in midlife. In S. L. Willis & J. D. Reid (Eds.), *Life in the middle: Psychological and social development in midlife* (pp. 209–232). San Diego, CA: Academic Press.

Labouvie-Vief, G. (1994). *Psyche and Eros: Mind and gender in the life course* (pp. 182–192 and 199–202). Cambridge, England: Cambridge University Press.

Labouvie-Vief, G., Chiodo, L. M., Goguen, L. A., Diehl, M., & Orwoll, L. (1995). Representations of self across the lifespan. *Psychology and Aging, 10*, 404–415.

Labouvie-Vief, G., Hakim-Larson, J., & Hobart, C. J. (1987). Age, ego level, and the lifespan development of coping and defense processes. *Psychology and Aging, 2*, 286–293.

Lachman, M. E. (Ed.). (2001). *Handbook of midlife development*. New York: Wiley.

Lang, F. R. (in press). Regulating personal relationships across the lifespan: Individuals as proactive producers of their social world. F. Lang & K. L. Fingerman (Eds.), *Growing together: Personal relationships across the lifespan*. New York: Cambridge University Press.

Laursen, B., & Collins, W. A. (1994). Interpersonal conflict during adolescence. *Psychological Bulletin, 115*, 197–209.

Laursen, B., Coy, K. C., & Collins, A. (1998). Reconsidering changes in parent-child conflict across adolescence: A meta-analysis. *Child Development, 69*, 817–832.

Lefkowitz, E. S., & Fingerman, K. L. (in press). Positive and negative emotional feelings and behaviors in the aging mother and adult daughter relationship. *Journal of Family Psychology*.

Lefkowitz, E. S., Kahlbaugh, P., & Sigman, M. D. (1996). Turn-taking in mother-adolescent conversations about sexuality and conflict. *Journal of Youth and Adolescence, 25*, 307–321.

Marks, N. F. (1996). Caregiving across the lifespan. National prevalence and predictors. *Family Relations, 45*, 27–36.

Moen, P., & Wethington, E. (1999). Midlife development in a life course context. In S. L. Willis & J. D. Reid (Eds.), *Life in the middle: Psychological and social development in midlife* (pp. 3–24). San Diego, CA: Academic Press.

National Center for Health Statistics. (2001). *Health, United States*. Retrieved March 1, 2002, from http://www.cdc.gov/nchs/products/pubs/pubd/hus/tables/2001/01hus057.pdf

National Center for Health Statistics. (2001). *Health, United States*. Retrieved March 1, 2002, from http://www.cdc.gov/nchs/products/pubs/pubd/hus/tables/2001/01hus072.pdf

National Telecommunications and Information Administration. (1998). *A Nation Online: How Americans are expanding their use of the Internet*. Retrieved February 21, 2002, from http://www.ntia.doc.gov

Neugarten, B. L. (1968). The awareness of middle-age. In B. L. Neugarten (Ed.), *Middle age and aging* (pp. 93–98). Chicago, IL: The University of Chicago Press.

Nussbaum, J. F., Pecchioni, L. L., Robinson, J. D., & Thompson, T. L. (2000). *Communication and aging* (2nd ed.). Mahwah, NJ: Lawrence Erlbaum Associates.

Putney, N. M., & Bengtson, V. L. (2001). Families, intergenerational relationships, and kinkeeping in midlife. In M. E. Lachman (Ed.), *Handbook of midlife development* (pp. 528–570). New York: Wiley.

Robinson, J. P., & Godbey, G. (1999). *Time for life: The surprising ways Americans use their time*. University Park, PA: Pennsylvania State University Press.

Rook, K. S. (1995). Support, companionship, and control in older adults' social networks: Implications for well-being. In J. F. Nussbaum & J. Coupland (Eds.), *Handbook of communication and aging research* (pp. 437–464). Mahwah, NJ: Lawrence Erlbaum Associates.

Rossi, A. S., & Rossi, P. H. (1990). *Of human bonding: Parent-child relations across the life course*. New York: Aldine de Gruyter.

Rudinger, G., & Rietz, C. (2001). Structural equation modeling in longitudinal research of aging. In J. E. Birren & K. W. Schaie (Eds.), *Handbook of the psychology of aging* (pp. 29–52). San Diego, CA: Academic Press.

Ryff, C. D. (1995). Psychological well-being in adult life. *Current Directions in Psychological Science, 4*, 99–104.

Ryff, C. D., Lee, Y. H., Essex, M. J., & Schmutte, P. S. (1994). My children and me: Midlife evaluations of grown children and of self. *Psychology and Aging, 9*, 195–205.

Schaie, K. W., & Hofer, S. M. (2001). Longitudinal studies in aging research. In J. E. Birren & K. W. Schaie (Eds.), *Handbook of the psychology of aging* (pp. 53–77). San Diego, CA: Academic Press.

Smetana, J. G., Yua, J., Restrepo, A., & Braeges, J. L. (1991). Adolescent-parent conflict in married and divorced families. *Developmental Psychology, 1991*, 1000–1010.

Stewart, A. J., & Vandewater, E. (1998). The course of generativity. In D. P. McAdams & E. de St. Aubin (Eds.), *Generativity and adult development: Psychosocial perspective on caring for and contributing to the next generation* (pp. 75–100). Washington, DC: American Psychological Association Press.

Sweet, J., Bumpass, L., & Vaughn, C. (1988). *The design and content of the National Survey of Families and Households* (Working Paper No. 1). Center for Demography and Ecology: University of Wisconsin.

Szinovacz, M. E. (1998). Grandparents today: A demographic profile. *The Gerontologist, 38*, 37–52.

Troll, L. E. (1988). New thoughts on old families. *Gerontologist, 28*, 586–591.

U.S. Bureau of the Census. (2001). *Statistical Abstracts of the United States*. Retrieved March 1, 2002, from http://www.census.gov/ prod/2002pubs/ 01statab/ health.pdf

Weissman, M. M., Leaf, P. J., Tischler, G. L., & Blazer, D. G. (1988). Affective disorders in five United States communities. *Psychological Medicine, 18*, 141–153.

White, L., & Edwards, J. N. (1990). Emptying the nest and parental well-being: An analysis of national panel data. *American Sociological Review, 55*, 235–242.

Williams, A., & Nussbaum, J. F. (2001). Intergenerational communication across the lifespan. Mahwah, NJ: Lawrence Erlbaum Associates.

Willis, S. L., & Reid, J. D. (Eds.). (1999). *Life in the middle: Psychological and social development in midlife*. San Diego, CA: Academic Press.

An Exploration of the Marital and Family Issues of the Later-Life Adult

Fran C. Dickson, Allison Christian, and Clyde J. Remmo
University of Denver

We are a population that is aging. Presently, more than 25% of our population is older than 65 years of age. In addition, our aging members are no longer characterized as the "frail elderly." Our senior population is far more educated, healthier, and more financially stable than previous generations of the elderly. Therefore, significant new issues face our society regarding the role and place of the senior citizen in our families and in our culture.

This chapter examines how these issues are played out in the marriage and extended family of the later-life adult. Specific attention is focused on the marital couple and the marital couple in their role as grandparents. Initially, we examine issues and challenges that confront later-life couples. We specifically examine marriage, divorce, widowhood, and remarriage among later-life couples. We then examine how couples function in the family system in settings such as being grandparents.

THEORETICAL PERSPECTIVES ON LATER-LIFE RELATIONSHIPS

To better understand later-life adults, we need to situate them within the context of the family and other social relationships. The following theoretical perspectives increase our understanding of how later-life adults interact with their world. Among the numerous perspectives for understanding communication and relationships with later-life adults, this chapter focuses on four: family solidarity (Bengtson & Roberts, 1991), the convoy of relationships (Antonucci & Akiyama,1995), relational competencies in later life (Hansson & Carpenter, 1994), and the socioemotional approach to later-life relationships (Carstensen, 1992).

Family Solidarity

This theoretical perspective, posited by Bengtson and Roberts (1991), focuses on the behaviors that families utilize to foster and maintain a sense of cohesion after the children in the family reach adulthood. To achieve intergenerational family solidarity, a number of communicative elements must be present. For example, families need to have contact or interpersonal association; affection needs to be displayed; consensus or agreement must be reached regarding certain aspects of family life; the family must function as a source of instrumental support for all members (not just the elderly family members); and the family needs to create the opportunity for family interaction. This perspective focuses on the quality of intergenerational interactions that occur within the family unit. As a result of these interactions and connections, family members form social support systems for each other. This perspective is particularly relevant to aging families because the elderly in the family often play more significant roles than they did in the past. For example, with the increased rate of divorce, grandparents have become more central figures in their grandchildren's lives, providing day care, financial support, and even housing support.

The family solidarity perspective presents an ideal that healthy families attempt to achieve. Although the behaviors that represent solidarity may not be present as everyday occurrences, the awareness and spirit of solidarity are the foundations for the family unit with later-life adults. Families who experience solidarity may more easily adjust to and be supportive of the remarriage of the later-life adult in the family.

Convoy of Relationships

Whereas family solidarity focuses on the entire family unit, the convoy of relationships focuses on the later-life adult (Antonucci & Akiyama, 1995). This theoretical perspective emphasizes how interpersonal relationships change over the life course. Antonucci (1990) suggests that individuals (not just later-life adults) have a collection of supporters and, as they age, the collection of supporters changes. This is particularly relevant for later-life adults, because their networks tend to shrink due to illnesses, death, retirement, and re-location. Connection with new supporters also becomes more difficult for the later-life adult. Later-life adults prefer consistency in their social networks and are more appre-hensive about starting new relationships so late in life (Antonucci, 1990). Although such connections do happen, such as in remarriage or when one relocates to a new residential community, they are difficult to establish.

The family thus becomes more central to later-life adults because other interpersonal connections have drifted away. The family also becomes more central because it is familiar to the later-life adult. Families may observe a closeness between members of later-life couples that was not present in earlier years. This closeness could result from the shrinking social network and the need to have a connection with others. Some individuals may not be aware of the changing social needs of their later-life family members and may be surprised at the expectations and demands that may be made by these family members. These expectations and demands are likely to be even greater when one member of the couple dies.

Relational Competencies in Later Life

Hansson and Carpenter (1994) have highlighted the interpersonal skills necessary to have satisfying social relationships in later life. Their contention that those with greater in-terpersonal skills tend to have more successful interpersonal relationships challenges Antonucci's (1990) convoy approach to social relationships in later life, which claims that social networks may shrink due to a decline in social skills. Hansson and Carpenter stress that greater interpersonal skill leads to more successful interpersonal relationships, therefore decreasing the likelihood of social isolation. By contrast Antonucci stresses that a lack of interpersonal skill in the later years may lead to fewer interpersonal relationships and an increase in the likelihood of social isolation.

Hansson and Carpenter's (1994) work is interesting in that it describes physiological changes that may hinder later-life adults' abilities to interpret interpersonal cues. For example, those who lose their hearing may not hear the rising tone of a family member's voice at the end of a question and thus may not respond. Those who have difficulty with their sight may not see cues that help them regulate interpersonal conversation. These physiological changes may contribute to lowering the confidence level of later-life adults when they are in social situations, thereby contributing to more social isolation.

This perspective also supports the notion that married later-life adults may place more focus on their spouses due to their familiarity with each other. Physiological changes may not be as apparent in the interactions of the later-life couples. However, other family members' or friends' interactions with later-life adults may become more frustrating and negative, again contributing to an increase in social isolation.

Socioemotional Approach to Later-Life Relationships

Carstensen (1992) examined the adaptive strategies later-life adults use to reduce the number of members in their social network. Her perspective states that although later-life adults reduce the size of their social network, they increase the emotional closeness experienced with those that remain in their social network. In other words, as later-life adults age, they prefer fewer friends and supporters, and, of those who remain, they prefer to have closer, more intense relationships. This perspective also helps to explain the closeness and dependency that emerges in the later-life marriage and small social circles.

Summary

These four theoretical perspectives highlight how later-life adults negotiate social relation-ships, while helping us to understand the communication dynamics that occur in marriage, families, and remarriage for later-life adults. We suggest that a constellation of these per-spectives best explains the interpersonal dynamics among families with later-life adults. The next section of this chapter reviews later-life marriage, later-life divorce, and later-life remarriage. We suggest that the four perspectives just presented are embedded in the findings discussed next. The research cited explains what happens in intimate later-life re-lationships, and these theoretical perspectives explain why these communication dynamics occur.

LATER-LIFE COUPLES

Marriage in Later Life

Our increased longevity is having a significant impact on marital dynamics today. One might imagine that as we live longer, we would also stay married longer. This is not necessarily the case—the divorce rate has increased, and the number of couples celebrating their 50th wedding anniversaries has declined. Only 20% of later-life married couples celebrate their 50th wedding anniversaries (Cavanuagh & Parks, 1993). The other 80% are either divorced, remarried, or widowed. Our society holds onto the stereotype of the long-term happily married couple. However, although some couples do embody this stereotype, a number of older couples struggle in their marriages and in their lives.

Unique issues and challenges face later-life married couples that are not present for younger couples. Understanding these issues is critical to understanding the communication and relational dynamics of later-life couples. Specifically, family members' awareness of these issues can contextualize the experiences of the later-life couple. Instead of assuming that the older couple "is as they always have been," positive involvement of family members has the potential both to reduce the stress associated with the challenges of aging and to increase the quality of life for later-life family members. Those who do not have family support are at most risk for the negative effects of these challenges.

Arp and Arp (1996) note seven challenges that later-life couples struggle with during the later stages of their lives together. First and foremost, later-life couples struggle with redefining their marital relationship after one member of the dyad has retired. This is likely the most researched, recognized, and discussed problem associated with later-life couples. For example, findings have indicated that it is not uncommon for the wife and husband to struggle over their domestic roles once the husband retires (Keating & Cole, 1980; Mancini, 1984). Increased conflict arises around daily tasks (Harper, Schaalje, & Sandberg, 2000), and wives' marital satisfaction decreases after their husbands have retired (Tamir & Antonucci, 1981). The processes associated with retirement issues directly relate to how the couple negotiates their new relational definition and retirement, and such negotiations can propel later-life couples into conflict.

Second, later-life couples struggle with the need to create a partner-focused (rather than a child-focused) marriage (Arp & Arp, 1996). Many people assume that after the children are launched from the nest, the marriage changes from a child-focused marriage to a partner-focused marriage, but this is not necessarily the case. Generally, many parental tasks still dominate the couple's attention, such as paying for college, paying for weddings of their children, and attending to the needs of grandchildren. Research has indicated that it is actually retirement that forces the couple to become more partner focused. This can be very difficult for spouses who have dedicated their lives to career and child care.

Third, later-life couples struggle with letting go of past marital disappointment (Arp & Arp, 1996). At the end of a marriage, it is common to reflect on the past. Both husbands and wives need to come to terms with disappointments that have occurred over their years together. When they were younger, they may have dealt with these disappointments through feeling and expressing resentment. In their later years, however, the expression of negative affect seems to occur less frequently than it did in the earlier years (Dickson, Hughes, Manning, Walker, Bollis-Pecci, & Gratson, 2001; Levenson, Carstensen, & Gottman 1993; Carstensen, Gottman, & Levenson, 1995). Therefore, couples find themselves attempting to make peace with previous life events in their relationships.

Fourth, later-life couples need to adjust to their changing roles and integrate health-related problems into their marital relationship (Arp & Arp, 1996). Aging creates multiple stressors that later-life couples need to incorporate into their adult lives. For example, physical activities can become more difficult, vision and hearing problems may decrease the ability to decode messages, the partners may be more susceptible to illness, and the onset of chronic or life-threatening illnesses can occur. These stressors and others can have negative impacts on marital satisfaction and life satisfaction.

Health concerns are a major issue among later-life couples. Illness can impact the expression and experience of intimacy in the marriage. A number of studies have documented the decline in marital satisfaction as a result of health problems of one or both later-life couple members (Adamson, Feinauer, Lund, & Caserta, 1992; Booth & Johnson, 1994; Levenson et al., 1993; Turk, Wach, & Derns, 1985; Wright, 1991). In addition, older spouses who are caretakers assume a nursing role and typically forego their role as intimate partner. Marital caretakers are also at risk for depression, physical illness, and isolation (Gagnon, Hersen, Kabacoff, & Van Hasselt, 1999).

Fifth, later-life couples struggle with renewing romance and sustaining a pleasurable sexual relationship (Arp & Arp, 1996). This too can create stress in the marriage. Later-life couples may have difficulty in sexual situations due to health issues. They may also feel awkward engaging in romantic activities that have been absent in their recent past relationship. Although rekindling romantic activities may feel awkward at first, many self-help books can help the later-life couple create a satisfying sexual and romantic relationship (e.g., *Love and Sex after 60*, by Butler & Lewis, 1993).

Sixth, later-life couples need to adjust to their changing roles with their adult children (Arp & Arp, 1996). The parental later-life couple moves from a position of authority in the family to a secondary advisory role. Adult children often opt not to turn to their parents for advice; they may even consider themselves to be in the expert role with their older parents. It is common for adult children to believe that they know best where their parents should live, how they should invest their money, and how they should handle health-related issues. This self-assigned authority of the adult children can create role confusion and serious tension in the parent/adult–child relationship. Although adult children believe that they know what is best for their later-life parents, they also turn to their parents, typically the mother/grandmother, to become the caretaker of the grandchildren in times of economic difficulties, divorce, or health crises. This situation creates a rational paradox for the later-life couple. They are placed in a position of authority over the grandchildren, while they also are in a situation where their authority over their own life is questioned. This complex dynamic can contribute to role confusion in the family.

Finally, later-life couples need to cope with end-of-life stresses (Arp & Arp, 1996). The fear of death, terminal illness, and being alone are major stressors that face the later-life couple. Some couples discuss these issues in detail and prepare for what they believe is the inevitable, whereas others do not overtly face the issue of death of one spouse in the marriage. The denial of this process can place stress on the spouses and the extended families.

In spite of these, and other, challenges, later-life couples often experience shared intimacy with their partners. After the children leave home, they have the opportunity to travel, share leisure activities, spend more time together, and redevelop their relationship (Brubaker, 1990). Researchers continually report that the later-life marriage is a happy, positive relationship. For example, Guilford and Bengtson (1979) reported that it is typical for negative sentiments to decrease with age and that the older marriage benefits from this change in the emotions of the couple members. Other researchers believe that the increase in activities and time together contributes to high marital satisfaction (Sporakowski & Hughston, 1978; Vinick & Ekerdt, 1990). Carstensen (1992) claims that the narrowing social networks experienced by later-life adults place the primary focus on the marriage and promote greater marital intimacy. Overall, the literature stresses the positive nature of the later-life marriage, although it presents varying perspectives on why this is so.

The issue facing researchers today involves why later-life couples are viewed as happy and content in their marital relationships. One possibility is that the later-life population consists of those who did not divorce or desert their families; therefore, that population must be happy (Gagnon et al., 1999). In other words, in earlier life stages, those who were unhappy divorced; therefore, those who did not divorce must have been happily married, a state that has then endured in the later years. With this perspective, a significant sample bias exists in many studies that explore later-life marriages.

Another explanation is that the interpersonal disposition of the later-life adult has grown more congenial and less adversarial with time. Dickson et al. (2001) found that later-life couples report they no longer feel the need to battle over issues as they did in their earlier years of marriage. This change may also contribute to the positive experience of the later-life couple. In another study, Dickson and Walker (2001) reported that men became more affiliative and emotionally expressive in their senior years. This could contribute to the positive nature of the marriage, in which the husbands are more connected to their wives emotionally than they were in the early years of the marriage.

Overall, later-life couples report less conflict and more positive and shared activities with their spouses than do younger or middle-aged couples. Older couples report greater satisfaction in discussing children or grandchildren, sharing activities together, taking vacations together, and dreaming together than do middle-aged couples (Levenson, Carstensen, & Gottman, 1993). Many of these pleasures result from the continuity of interaction time and the sharing of a family history (Brubaker, 1985).

Remarriage in Later Life

Remarriage in later life is a rare occurrence. When it occurs, however, it is a significant event for the new spouses as well as for their families. Presently, little research exists on later-life remarriages and the challenges that couples in these marriages face. Of the existing research on this topic, most has focused on remarriage among later-life widowed adults. This may be due to the fact that it is more likely for a widowed later-life adult to remarry than a divorced later-life adult (Bowers & Bahr, 1989). There is a higher incidence of men remarrying younger women than later-life women remarrying at all (Bowers & Bahr, 1989; Grurak & Dean, 1979). In addition, remarriage rates for widowed men are significantly higher than those for widowed women (Smith, Zick, & Duncan, 1991; Wilson & Clarke, 1992). Finally, it is most common for widowed individuals to marry other widowed individuals and least likely for divorced individuals to marry widowed persons (Wilson & Clarke, 1992).

Older remarried couples tend to be at less risk for divorce and tend to be happier in their marriages than their younger counterparts. Remarriage in later life typically occurs for two different reasons: to alleviate loneliness and to satisfy the need for companionship (Bowers, & Bahr, 1989). Therefore, later-life remarriages tend to be very stable and satisfying for the couple members.

When remarriage occurs in later life, it is a complicated matter. The couple members are merging not only their social circles but also their extended families and previous family histories. Many researchers view the later-life widowed remarriage as a triad, with the deceased spouse present in the marital dyad (e.g., Moss & Moss, 1996). This can create a situation in which the marital partners may find it difficult to share their past without comparing their present spouse to their past spouse. However, Moss and Moss (1996) reported that only 5% of new wives felt jealousy toward the deceased wife, and 8% of new husbands felt jealousy toward the deceased husband. Therefore, it appears that the majority of widowed, later-life remarried couples are comfortable with the presence of the deceased spouse in their marriage.

The stereotypical belief that adult children of later-life couple members oppose the remarriage of one of their parents is not supported in the research. Findings have shown that adult children are most supportive of the remarriage when the remarriage has been discussed openly with them prior to the wedding (Bowers & Bahr, 1989). Interestingly, friends of the later-life adult have more difficulty and are more negative about the remarriage of their friend. It appears that they are fearful that the new marriage will negatively impact their friendship (Bowers & Bahr, 1989).

Men tend to be happier in the later-life remarriage than women (Bowers & Bahr, 1989; Glenn, 1981). One of the reasons behind this is that later-life men have a wider range of potential spouses than later-life women (Norton & Moorman, 1987; Spanier & Furstenberg, 1987; Thornton, 1979). Society looks more kindly on a later-life man marrying a younger woman then it does on a later-life woman marrying a younger man. In addition, women tend to live longer than men, so men have a larger pool of later-life women from which they can select a mate.

The process of remarriage in later life is very complicated. Couples need to consider financial and familial issues that can seriously impact the marriage. In addition, many later-life women fear that they may become a caretaker for their aging spouse. As a consequence, it is common for the later-life remarriage to be entered into with great deliberation and concern for the implications.

Divorce in Later Life

Few studies have examined the relationship between aging and divorce (Birchler & Fals-Stewart, 1998). However, the average American will live some 25 years after raising children to adulthood (Goldberg, 1992), creating more of a need to deal with the "two greatest threats to older couples"—health problems and financial insecurity (Askham, 1994; Condie, 1989; Hess & Markson, 1986; Quirouette & Gold, 1992). The prominence of such stresses on the later-life couple creates a concern that divorce rates for elderly couples may be increasing (Birchler & Fals-Stewart, 1998). In a study of 9,041 respondents, Solomou, Richards, Huppart, Brayne, and Morgan (1998) reported that approximately 9% of adults age 65 years and older had been divorced, with 66% of those remarrying. Hammond and Muller (1992) reported an increase of divorce in elderly populations, with the proportion of divorced women outnumbering that of divorced men. This section outlines possible causes for divorce in later life and addresses the resulting outcomes on the family system and individuals involved.

Research that attempts an in-depth examination of the causes for divorce has identified a number of factors that contribute to divorce in later life. For example, Lester (1999) found unemployment, population size, homicide rates, percentage of elderly within a population, birth rates, death rates, and crime rates to be positively correlated with divorce rates. Findings such as these allow for little indication of where and how to identify the roots of divorce in elderly populations. In fact, most research attributes the increase of divorce in later-life populations to increases in divorce overall (Cooney & Dunne, 2001).

Yet other research points to such elements as the increase in life expectancy (Treas, 1995), increases in educational attainment for both men and women (Spain & Bianchi, 1996), and heightened emphasis on individualism (Buchmann, 1989) as possible factors that may contribute to higher divorce rates among elderly populations. Whatever the causes may be, it is clear that divorce has a great impact on later-life couples, including economic setbacks, changes in family support, negative psychological and emotional effects, and changes in family support (Cooney & Dunne, 2001).

The economic impact of divorce on later-life adults is severe. For example, Stroup and Pollock (1999) found a significant difference in reported incomes between married and nonmarried individuals, and marital status was found to be the most significant predictor of income among the elderly population. At first glance, this statistic does not seem exceptionally noteworthy. But Gander (1991) more specifically reported a 61% decline in income among divorced men and a 66% loss among divorced women, providing a better understanding of the possible financial impact of divorce on the elderly population.

Although the impact of divorce on the parent–child relationship in younger and middle-aged families is well documented, the impact of divorce on later-life family relationships may be just as great. Pezzin and Schone (1999) found that the quality and quantity of communication between elderly parents and adult children were negatively affected by divorce, especially for later-life fathers. Additionally, research showed that remarriage negatively affected exchanges between parent and child even further, such that the elderly parent–adult child relationships may never recover from divorce. Dykstra (1997) found similar results, citing that divorced older adults were less likely to have supportive exchanges with their adult children than nondivorced individuals. Bulcroft and Bulcroft's (1991) work directly supports evidence that "divorce has a negative effect on interaction with adult children, though more so for men than women" (p. 241). Finally, Cicerelli (1984) found that divorce was indirectly associated with lowered future help by adult children to their later-life parents.

Divorce has a serious impact on the psychological and emotional well-being of later-life couple members. Fengler, Danigelis, and Grams, (1982) found life satisfaction among the elderly to be significantly related to marital status, differences in family support, and living arrangements. A divorced person, living alone, with little or no family support (as research cited previously indicates), has less chance of being satisfied with life. Additionally, divorced later-life women report less satisfaction with family life and life in general than married later-life women, and divorced later-life men report less satisfaction with their friendships, family, and life in general than married later-life men (Hyman, 1983).

Widowhood in Later Life

Although the increase of divorce among later-life couples is a fairly new trend in our society, the challenges and issues presented to widows and widowers have been evident for some time. Even so, the effects of this experience of widowhood, which many later-life individuals face, need continued research (Cooney & Dunne, 2001). This section outlines important research involving the following consequences of widowhood: economic changes, changes in social and emotional support, health concerns, and psychological adjustment. All of these issues have implications for the quality of the relationship between the surviving spouse and the extended family.

Similar to the economic challenges a person faces after divorce, newly widowed individuals face a large economic strain. Research has shown that both men and women must deal with economic loss after the death of a spouse (Cooney & Dunne, 2001). However, the particular challenges may differ according to gender. For instance, Smith and Zick (1986) reported that women often lose their main source of income, whereas men face challenges due to a lack of planning for the possibility of their wives' deaths.

As reported by Cooney and Dunne (2001), many older couples spend more money on life insurance for the husband than for the wife, creating a situation that could prove particularly difficult for men who lose their wives. However, women tend to face greater economic risk than men due to differences in the lengths of widowship (Burkhauser, Butler, & Holden, 1991). Whatever the case, it is clear that the economic challenges brought about by the death of a spouse can be particularly difficult. These economic challenges can place stress on members of the extended family, who feel that they need to provide financially for the widowed parent. The most common situation is an adult son who feels the need to provide financially for his widowed mother. This feeling of obligation can create stress on his own marriage and family. The negotiation of these kinds of agreements is also very complicated and has great potential to create conflict among the adult children of the widowed parent.

The emotional support that an older person receives may play an important role in adjustment after the death of a spouse. Not surprisingly, widowed individuals have been found to report considerably lower levels of well-being (Thuen, Reime, & Skrautvoll, 1997). However, research has demonstrated a relationship between social support received by the widowed spouse and that individual's morale (Matthews, 1991). In fact, some research has shown a "buffering" effect of social support on an individual's psychological well-being following a spouse's death (Thuen et al., 1997).

Unfortunately, research has also demonstrated a decline in social participation following a spouse's death, especially for widowed men (Bennett, 1998; Matthews, 1991; Thuen et al., 1997). In addition, widowed men who do not belong to a religious organization have reported some of the highest levels of depression among the elderly (Siegel & Kuykendall, 1990), providing even more justification for the importance of social support to widowed individuals. In terms of living arrangements, men, in general, are more likely than women to live alone following the loss of their spouse (Bowling & Windsor, 1995). The research indicates that widowed men are far more isolated than widowed women.

Ethnicity may also play a part in the level of social participation among widowed later-life adults. For example, Choi (1991) found that, overall, non-White individuals were less likely to live alone than were White individuals in the same circumstances.

However, Himes (1992) reported that of any group, elderly African American women are most likely to live alone. Research indicates variations across different ethnic groups, which demonstrates a further need to study cultural differences in social support and living arrangements following the loss of a spouse.

A large amount of research has examined the negative physical and psychological effects that surviving partners experience following the death of a spouse (Arbuckle & deVries, 1995; Bennett, 1998; Bernardo, 1970; Bowling & Windsor, 1995; Burkhauser et al., 1991; Burks, Lund, Gregg, & Bluhm, 1988; Byrne & Raphael, 1997; Carey, 1979; Cooney & Dunne, 2001; Gentry & Shulman, 1988; Gibbs, 1985; Heinemann, 1983; Hong & Duff, 1994; Lee, Willetts, & Seccombe, 1998; Lund, Caserta, Dimond, & Shaffer, 1989; Miller, Smerglia, Gaudet, & Kitson, 1998; Moss & Moss, 1985; Murrel, Himmelfarb, & Phifer, 1995; Nieboer, Lindenberg, & Ormel, 1999; O'Bryant & Hansson, 1995; Siegel & Kuykendall, 1990; Thuen et al., 1997; Umberson, Wortman, & Kessler, 1992). Bowling and Windsor (1995) analyzed the mortality rates of a national random sample of 503 recently widowed elderly people and found that 62% of the sample died within 3 years of their spouse's death.

Perhaps the most striking research examines the differences between men and women in how they react physically and psychologically to widowhood. Siegel and Kuykendall (1990) found that spousal loss was significantly related to higher levels of depression in men, but not in women. Byrne and Raphael (1997) found later-life widowers to have higher levels of anxiety, general psychological distress, sleep disturbance, and thoughts of death and suicide. Bennett (1998) found that men's mental health and morale are greatly affected by widowhood. In addition, Lee et al. (1998) reported that widowhood has a stronger effect on depression for men than it does for women. Yet, in another study by Bennett (1998), widowed women reported declines in mental and physical health when compared to nonwidowed women; however, the widowed women still had significantly fewer mental and physical health problems than widowed men.

Although the majority of research does tend to indicate larger declines in mental health for men and smaller declines in physical health for women experiencing the loss of a spouse, much of the gender difference remains unexplained (Lee et al., 1998). Although a great deal of research has examined the physical and psychological correlates of widowhood, little research focuses on the communicative processes present when one loses a lifetime mate.

GRANDPARENTING IN TODAY'S SOCIETY: AN OVERVIEW OF CURRENT TRENDS

The previous section discussed later-life marriage, divorce, widowhood, and remarriage. Whereas later-life adults may face any one or more of these experiences, the most common experience for later-life adults who have children is grandparenthood. The role of a grandparent is complex and central in the family, and a better understanding of the processes involved in grandparenting can increase our understanding of the later-life adult in general.

Like many family roles, the role of grandparent is much different today from what it was in the past due to changes in our society. For example, today, more grandparents are raising their grandchildren, helping with child care, or have their adult children and their families living with them. In addition, significantly more members of the "sandwich generation" are caring for aging parents while also raising a family. This section outlines some current demographic trends and their impact on the grandparent role and discusses some of the factors that affect the grandparent role and the grandparent–grandchild relationship.

Demographic Trends

Many trends in our society have shaped the current status of grandparents. Advances in medicine have resulted in a declining mortality rate, which means the length of time that grandparents occupy that role is increasing. As Silverstein and Marenco (2001) have stated, "Grandparents today might expect to live almost half their lives in that role" (p. 494). More than 90% of all older adults with children are now living long enough to have grandchildren (Mills, Wakeman, & Fea, 2001). This, of course, means that more children today will know their grandparents for longer periods of time than in the past. "Today, it is more likely that 20-year-olds will have a grandmother still living (91%) than 20-year-olds alive in 1900 had a mother still living (83%)" (Uhlenberg, 1996).

Family Structure

In addition to the grandparent–grandchild relationship experiencing increased longevity, the relationship has also become more complex due to changing trends in family structure. Bengtson (2001) argued, "because the increase in marital instability and divorce over the last several decades has weakened the ability of nuclear families to provide the socialization, nurturance, and support needed by family members . . . kin across several generations will be increasingly called upon to provide these essential family functions in 21st-century society" (p. 4). In short, changes in family structure have created different roles, opportunities, and stresses for today's grandparents than for grandparents of the past. First, among the structural changes that have influenced grandparents' roles, is the trend toward smaller family size. Women are less likely today than in the past to have young children at the same time their older children are starting families (Wiscott & Kopera-Frye, 2000). This means that grandparents today are likely to have fewer children than in the past, and they can thus focus more of their energy on the grandparent role. This can result not only in closer relationships but also in added pressure for the grandparent.

Second, an adult child's divorce also has an impact on the grandparent role. Having divorced parents can result in a grandchild relying more heavily on the grandparent for emotional support, whereas the adult child often relies on the grandparent for financial and child care support. The impact of divorce on the grandparent–grandchild relationship generally depends on the custody outcome. "Divorce generally weakens grandparent–grandchild relations on the noncustodial (usually paternal) side of the family but strengthens those relations on the custodial (usually maternal) side of the family" (Silverstein, Giarrusso, & Bengtson, 1998, p. 152).

Third, grandparent roles are changing due to remarriage of adult children. These remarriages create new issues for the grandparent, some positive and some stressful. On the one hand, an adult child's remarriage means a decrease in expectations of the grandparent to assume custodial or financial responsibility for the grandchild (Kivett, 1998). On the other hand, the possible entrance of stepgrandchildren into the grandparent's life can create increased ambiguity about the grandparent's role. "A 'new' grandchild can be an infant, juvenile, adult, or even a retiree" (Mills et al., 2001, p. 428).

Despite the increased complexity of the grandparent role in blended family life, Kennedy and Kennedy (1993) found that a blended family often increases the bond between the grandparent and the grandchild. Given the increasing likelihood for longer and more complex grandparent–grandchild relationships, it is helpful to gain an understanding of the factors that create these circumstances. It is also, then, increasingly important to examine the factors that affect these relationships and the impact they have on grandparents and grandchildren.

The Grandparent–Grandchild Relationship

Grandparents provide many roles and functions for their grandchildren, including listening, socialization, mentoring, transmitting cultural backgrounds, financial and emotional support, surrogate parenting or babysitting, or just "being there" (Bengtson, 2001; Silverstein et al., 1998; Silverstein & Marenco, 2001; Tomlin, 1998; Wiscott & Kopera-Frye, 2000). There is little question of the importance of a grandparent in a grandchild's life. A grandchild's experience with a grandparent is likely to influence her or his perceptions of and relationships with all older adults (Harwood, & Lin, 2000). In addition, King, Russell, and Elder, (1998) found that children with closer relationships with grandparents are more likely to succeed "socially and psychologically, and in making the transition to adult roles" (p. 57). The degree to which the grandparent is able to influence the grandchild in these ways, however, is mitigated by many factors, such as parental divorce and custody arrangements, geographical distance, the grandparent's relationship with the parents, socioeconomic status, health of the grandparent, time spent together, and life stages of both grandparent and grandchild (Harwood & Lin, 2000; King et al., 1998; Peterson, 1999; Silverstein et al., 1998; Tomlin, 1998). Despite these myriad factors that may impact this relationship, the grandparent is clearly an important figure in a grandchild's life.

If the grandparent–grandchild relationship is important to grandchildren, it is even more vital to grandparents. However, there are factors that may cause stress for some grandparents. One of the most common stressors associated with being a grandparent is not being able to see the grandchild often enough (Silverstein et al., 1998). Grandmothers are more likely to name "not having enough contact with grandchildren as the 'worst thing' about grandparenthood" (Peterson, 1999, p. 72). A lack of contact with grandchildren can result in increased emotional stress and declining health of the grandparent.

Other factors contribute to the stress of grandparenting as well. For example, King et al. (1998) found that those who become grandparents "off-time," (i.e., at an early age) are more likely to be resentful of being placed into the grandparent role. Further, scholars have found significant evidence that suggests being placed in a caregiver role results in enormous stress for a grandparent (Edwards, 2001; Sands & Goldberg-Glen, 2000; Wiscott & Kopera-Frye, 2000). These situations are generally fraught with other complications, such as lack of social support, lack of financial support, lack of emotional support from the grandchild, and conflict with the parents, who are often drug addicts or young mothers.

Research strongly supports the notion that, even though some stressors are associated with grandparenting, the positive benefits of being a grandparent far outweigh any negatives. Harwood and Lin (2000) found that grandparents consistently expressed affiliations with grandchildren as contributing to a feeling of being "privileged" or "blessed" to have the relationship in their life (p. 36). These feelings were enhanced when grandchildren initiated contact or shared a fairly intimate aspect of their personal life with grandparents. In addition, Harwood and Lin found that grandparents valued being able to take pride in their grandchildren. This pride often manifested in descriptions about grandchildren's accomplishments or personality characteristics. Peterson (1999) found "the pleasures associated with contact and companionship as among the most important satisfactions of grandparenthood" (p. 70).

Possibly the most interesting finding about the benefits of being a grandparent is the likelihood that grandparents deal better with the negative aspects of aging than older adults who are not grandparents. One might think the age difference between a grandparent and grandchild could entail some negative feelings for the grandparent, such as feeling older and unappreciated. Harwood and Lin (2000) discovered quite the opposite. Grandparents reported feeling proud of the fact that grandchildren listened to their advice because it came from experience. In addition, grandparents reported gaining a "youthful feeling" from interactions with their grandchildren and relished the grandchild's assistance with "keeping up with today's world" (Harwood & Lin, 2000, p. 40). In other words, grandparents seem to look to their grandchildren to provide them with a link to "today's world" and, perhaps, their own former youth.

Despite the possible help in dealing with the aging process, some differences in life stages can, nonetheless, impact the grandparent–grandchild relationship. The age difference means grandparents and grandchildren are always experiencing different life stages. These divergent life stages may contribute to feelings of being misunderstood by either the grandparent or the grandchild. Further, as in all family relationships, the grandparent–grandchild relationship changes over time, depending on the individuals' life stages. For example, Silverstein et al. (1998) reported that the grandparent–grandchild relationship weakens as grandchildren age and thus become less involved with grandparents. In addition, they found in general that "grandparents report a greater degree of closeness in the relationship than do grandchildren" (p. 145). However, they also report that, despite a less interactive relationship over time, grandchildren report a consistently close feeling to grandparents based on close relations throughout childhood. Bengtson (2001) asserts that the average solidarity scores among grandparents and grandchildren are not only high, they are "remarkably stable over 26 years of measurement" (p. 8). Mills et al. (2001) found that "most adult grandchildren perceived that their relationships with their grandparents were close and enduring" (p. 429). Therefore, research supports the notion that, despite changes in life stages, the grandparent–grandchild relationship remains strong and valuable to both parties.

Summary

Today's changing demographics, such as longer life expectancies, smaller families, higher divorce rates, and remarriage, are key components in the ever-increasing complexity of the grandparent role. These factors can contribute both positively and negatively to the grandparent–grandchild relationship. However, evidence overwhelmingly supports the positive impact this relationship has for both grandchildren and grandparents. The major benefit of this relationship is its strong, long-lasting intergenerational solidarity. As our society and its families continue to change, grandparents will no doubt make an increasingly important contribution to the support of the family.

FUTURE RESEARCH

Future research needs to examine the impact of the challenges that face later-life individuals and couples. Much of what we know about these challenges has emerged from the therapeutic literature that only examines the existence of the issues facing later-life adults, not the impact of these challenges on the adults and their entire family system. Studies in this area will have implications for the therapeutic context as well as for research and theory.

Little is also known about later-life remarriage. The majority of the existing research that examines later-life remarriage focuses on the widowed partner member. Focus needs to include the divorced later-life remarriage. As our longevity increases, the configuration of marriage and remarriage in later life changes. In addition, more emphasis needs to be placed on the family members of the remarried later-life couple and how they negotiate the new relational status of their aged parents, as well as how they deal with having a new stepfamily. Future research needs to examine the processes involved in merging two family histories and family networks. These are complex processes that can create a great deal of stress and strain for later-life adults.

Due to the continuing increases in diversity in later-life populations, future research involving widowhood, divorce, or other aspects of later life will demand recognition of ethnic and racial groups. In addition, the multitude of relationship experiences that has resulted from longer lives, increased educational opportunities, and increased independence among individuals should be taken into account when studying later-life experiences. Specifically, as we move toward a better understanding of all these issues, family clinicians and scholars alike must work together to set up programs that might help to alleviate the potential difficulties that face the later-life population. Additionally, more research is needed to delineate between how gender plays a part in experiencing widowhood and later-life divorce.

Research examining possible causes for divorce in later life has led us down many avenues. Additional research in this area could prove beneficial to the counseling profession as well as to scholarly pursuits. If we had more tangible evidence of the various causes for divorce, we might be able to identify and begin a dialogue about ways to counteract the phenomenon of increased rates of divorce in older populations. Also, a clinical approach is needed that addresses parent–child relationships following divorce in older populations. Last, because divorce is a phenomenon that is beginning to transcend life stage, more emphasis should be put on finding ways in which to help alleviate the negative psychological and emotional effects that are apparent in older individuals who experience divorce.

There is a great deal of literature that examines various aspects of the grandparent role as well as the grandparent–grandchild relationship. However, research is still needed to further our understanding of these processes and relationships and their impact on the family system. There are three main areas in which future research could yield interesting findings. Future research should focus on grandparents in blended families, grandparents as caregivers, and grandparents and increasing diversity.

There can be little doubt that blended families are increasing in number every day. Some research has examined the grandparents' roles in blended families; however, more is needed. Future research should delineate between families in which becoming a 'stepgrandparent' is a result of the remarriage of the grandparent or of the divorce and remarriage of the adult child. The difference in the origin of the stepgrandparent role could have significant effects on the stepgrandparent–stepgrandchild relationship. These avenues should be examined from the perspectives of the grandparents as well as of the grandchildren. Additionally, since it is more common for later-life adults to remarry today, future research needs to examine the overall effects of the remarriage of grandparents on the family system as a whole. There is a large body of literature that focuses on the grandparent's role as family historian or source of culture. An interesting avenue of research with regard to grandparents would be to examine how their role as family historian changes or adapts to a new blended family. Scholars should examine the perceptions of the stepgrandparent as well as those of the stepgrandchild in giving and receiving such important family knowledge.

Some research has examined the effects of grandparents being the sole caregiver of grandchildren on the perceptions of grandparents and grandchildren. The majority of this body of research indicates the negative impacts this situation can have on grandparents and grandchildren. Future research should focus on discovering the factors that can affect these situations, both positively and negatively, so that scholars and clinicians alike can work to create more successful outcomes for these "grandfamilies." Some studies have examined caregiver grandparents' use of support groups and social services in these situations. However, later-life individuals tend to depend more on community networks (i.e., friends, community centers, etc.) for support. Future research could investigate whether access to these important social networks has an impact on grandparenting, especially for grandparents who act as the primary caregiver.

There has been an increase in the call for diversity in many areas of research. The grandparenting body of literature is no different. Although some research has examined differences among minority grandparent–grandchild relationships, little research has focused on diversity in family forms. With the increase in number of gay and lesbian parents adopting children, it would be a worthwhile pursuit to facilitate an understanding of the grandparent role as well as of the grandparent–grandchild relationship in these families. Also, with an increase in diverse family forms comes diversity in the life stages at which someone may become a grandparent. As many grandparents now step into this role at various ages, studies should focus on differences in transitioning into the grandparent role at different life stages. Research should also examine whether the way in which the new grandparent handles this transition affects the overall family system and intergenerational solidarity. Finally, increased diversity in today's society and all its family forms demands that we move away from studying traditional avenues of the grandparent role. Grandparents increasingly enact different roles in the family system today, and they do so at various life stages in various types of family systems. Future research should branch out to create an understanding of all the possibilities open to grandparents today.

In conclusion, scholars need to rethink the role of the later-life individual and couple in family systems. Family members need to understand and empathize with the complexity of grandparenting, later-life marriage, and remarriage. Later-life individuals and couples are an enormous asset and resource in family systems. Instead of viewing the later-life family member as a burden to the family, acknowledging and utilizing their experience, knowledge, and support can enhance and enrich a family system.

REFERENCES

Adams, R. G., & Blieszner, R. (1994a). An integrative conceptual framework for friendship research. *Journal of Social and Personal Relationships, 11*, 163–184.

Adams, R. G., & Blieszner, R. (1994b). Resources for friendship intervention. *Journal of Sociology and Social Welfare, 20*, 159–175.

Adams, R. G., & Blieszner, R. (1995). Aging well with friends and family. *American Behavioral Scientist, 39*, 209–224.

Adamson, D., Feinauer, L., Lund, D., & Caserta, M. (1992). Factors affecting marital happiness of caregivers of the elderly in multigenerational families. *The American Journal of Family Therapy, 20*, 62–70.

Antonucci, T. C. (1990). Social support and social relationships. In R. H. Binstock & E. Shanas (Eds.), *Handbook of aging and the social sciences* (2nd ed., pp. 205–227). New York: Van Nostrand Reinhold.

Antonucci, T. C., & Akiyama, H. (1995). Convoys of social relations: Family and friendships within a life span context. In R. Blieszner & V. H. Bedford (Eds.), *The handbook of family and aging* (pp. 355–371). Westport, CT: Greenwood.

Arbuckle, N. W., & deVries, B. (1995). The long-term effects of later life spousal and parental bereavement on personal functioning. *The Gerontologist, 35*, 637–647.

Arp, D., & Arp, C. (1996). *The second half of marriage.* New York: Zondervan.

Askham, J. (1994). Marriage relationships of older people. *Reviews in Clinical Gerontology, 4*, 261–268.

Bee, H. L. (2000). *The journey of adulthood.* Englewood Cliffs, NJ: Prentice-Hall.

Bengtson, V. L. (2001). Beyond the nuclear family: The increasing importance of multigenerational bonds. *Journal of Marriage and Family, 63*, 1–16.

Bengtson, V. L., & Roberts, R. E. L. (1991). Intergenerational solidarity in aging families: An example of formal theory construction. *Journal of Marriage and the Family, 53*, 856–870.

Bengtson, V., Rosenthal, C., & Burton, L. (1996). Paradoxes of families and aging. In R. H. Binstock & L. K. George (Eds.), *Handbook of aging and the social sciences.* (4th ed., pp. 263–287). San Diego: Academic Press.

Bennett, K. M. (1998). Longitudinal changes in mental and physical health among elderly, recently widowed men. *Mortality, 3*, 265–273.

Bernardo, F. (1970). Survivorship and social isolation: The case of the aged widower. *Family Coordinator, 19*, 11–15.

Birchler, G. R. & Fals-Stewart, W. (1998). Marriage and divorce. In Hersen, M. & Hasselt, V. B. (Eds.), *Handbook of Clinical Geropsychology: The Plenum Series in adult development and aging* (pp. 449–467). New York: Plenum Press.

Booth, A., & Johnson, D. R. (1994). Declining health and marital quality. *Journal of Marriage and the Family, 56*, 218–223.

Bowers, S. P. (1999). Gender role identity and the caregiving experience of widowed men. *Sex Roles, 41*, 645–655.

Bowers, I. C., & Bahr, S. J. (1989). Remarriage of widowed persons. In S. Bahr & E. Peterson (Eds.), *Aging and the family* (pp. 83–95). Lexington, MA: Lexington.

Bowling, A., & Windsor, J. (1995). Death after widow(er)hood: An analysis of mortality rates up to 13 years after bereavement. *Omega: Journal of Death and Dying, 31*, 35–49.

Bradbury, T. N., Fincham, F. D., & Beach, S. R. (2000). Research on the nature and determinants of marital satisfaction: A decade in review. *Journal of Marriage and the Family, 62*, 964–980.

Brubaker, T. H. (1985). *Later life families.* Beverly Hills, CA: Sage.

Brubaker, T. H. (1990). Families in later-life: A burgeoning research area. *Journal of Marriage & the family, 52*, 959–981.

Buchmann, M. (1989). *The script of life in modern society.* Chicago: University of Chicago Press.

Bulcroft, K. A., & Bulcroft, R. A. (1991). The timing of divorce: Effects on parent-child relationships in later-life. *Research on Aging, 13*, 226–243.

Burkhauser, R. V., Butler, J. S., & Holden, K. C. (1991). How the death of the spouse affects economic well-being after retirement: A hazard model approach. *Social Science Quarterly, 72*, 504–519.

Burks, V., Lund, D. A., Gregg, C. H., & Bluhm, H. P. (1988). Bereavement and remarriage for older adults. *Death Studies, 12*, 51–60.

Butler, R. N., & Lewis, M. I. (1993). *Love and sex after 60.* New York: Ballantine.

Byrne, G. J. A., & Raphael, B. (1997). The psychological symptoms of conjugal bereavement in elderly men over the first 13 months. *International Journal of Geriatric Psychiatry, 12*, 241–251.

Carey, R. G. (1979). Weathering widowhood: Problems and adjustment of the widowed during the first year. *Omega: The Journal of Death and Dying, 10*, 140–149.

Carstensen, L. L. (1992). Social and emotional patterns in adulthood: Support for socio-emotional selectivity theory. *Psychology and Aging, 7*, 331–338.

Carstensen, L. L., Gottman, J. M., & Levensen, R. W. (1995). Emotional behavior in long-term marriage. *Psychology and Aging, 10*, 140–149.

Carstensen, L. L., Isaacowitz, D. M., & Charles, S. T. (1999). Taking time seriously: A theory of socioemotional selectivity. *American Psychologist, 54*, 165–181.

Carter, H., & Glick, P. C. (1976). *Marriage and divorce: A social and economic study.* Cambridge, MA: Harvard University Press.

Cavanaugh, J. C., & Parks, D. C. (1993). Vitality for life: Psychological research for productive aging. *APS Observer, 2* [Special issue, Report 2] (pp. 1–2). Washington, DC: American Psychological Association.

Choi, N. G. (1991). Racial differences in the determinants of living arrangements of widowed and divorced elderly women. *Gerontologist, 31*, 496–504.

Cicerelli, V. G. (1984). Adult children's helping behavior to elderly parents: The influence of divorce. *Journal of Family Issues, 5*, 419–440.

Clements, R., & Swensen, C. H. (1999). Development of a marriage problems scale for use with older couples. *Clinical Gerontologist, 20*, 35–46.

Clements, R., & Swensen, C. H. (2000). Commitment to one's spouse as a predictor of marital quality among older couples. *Current Psychology: Developmental, Learning, Personality, Social, 19*, 110–119.

Cole, C. L. (1995). Marital quality in later life. In J. F. Nussbaum & J. Coupland (Eds.), *Handbook of communication and aging research* (pp. 73–90). Mahwah, NJ: Lawrence Erlbaum Associates.

Condie, S. J. (1989). Older married couples. In S. J. Bahr & E. T. Peterson (Eds.), *Aging and the family* (pp. 143–158). Lexington, MA: Lexington.

Cooney, T. M., & Dunne, K. (2001). Intimate relationships in later life. *Journal of Family Issues, 22*, 838–858.

Dickson, F. C., Hughes, P. C., Manning, L. D., Walker, K. L., Bollis-Pecci, T., & Gratson, S. D. (2001). An analysis of conflict in long-term, later-life, married couples. *Southern Communication Journal, 67*, 110–121.

Dickson, F. C., & Walker, K. L. (2001). The expression of emotion in married, later-life men. *Qualitative Research Reports, 2*, 66–71.

Dykstra, P. A. (1997). The effects of divorce on intergenerational exchanges in families. *Netherlands' Journal of Social Sciences, 33*, 77–93.

Edwards, O. W. (2001). Grandparents raising grandchildren. In M. J. Fine & S. W. Lee (Eds.), *Handbook of diversity in parent education: The changing faces of parenting and parent education* (pp. 199–211). San Diego: Academic Press.

Fengler, A. P., Danigelis, N. L., & Grams, A. (1982). Marital status and life satisfaction among the elderly. *International Journal of Sociology of the Family, 12*, 63–76.

Gagnon, M. D., Hersen, M., Kabacoff, R. I., & Van Hasselt, V. B. (1999). Interpersonal and psychological correlates of martial dissatisfaction in later life: A review. *Clinical Psychological Review, 19*, 359–378.

Gander, A. M. (1991). Economics and well-being of older divorced persons. *Journal of Women and Aging, 3*, 37–57.

Gentry, M., & Shulman, A. D. (1988). Remarriage as a coping response for widowhood. *Psychology and Aging, 3*, 191–196.

Gibbs, J. (1985). Family relations of the older widow: Their location and importance for her social life. In W. Peterson & J. Quadagno (Eds.), *Social bonds in later life* (pp. 91–114). Beverly Hills, CA: Sage.

Glenn, N. D. (1981). The well-being of persons remarried after divorce. *Journal of Family Issues, 2*, 61–75.

Goldberg, J. R. (1992). The new frontier: Marriage and family therapy with aging families. *Family Therapy News, 23*, 1–12.

Grurak, D. T., & Dean, G. (1979). The remarriage market: Factors influencing the selection of second husband. *Journal of Divorce, 3*, 161–171.

Guilford, R., & Bengtson, V. (1979). Measuring marital satisfaction in three generations: Positive and negative dimension. *Journal of Marriage and the Family, 41*, 387–398.

Hammond, R. J., & Muller, G. O. (1992). The late-life divorced: Another look. *Journal of Divorce and Remarriage, 17*, 135–150.

Hansson, R. O., & Carpenter, B. N. (1994). *Relationships in old age.* New York: Guilford.

Hansson, R. O., Jones, W. H., & Fletcher, W. L (1990). Troubled relationships in later life: Implications for support. *Journal of Social and personal relationships, 7*, 451–463.

Harper, J. M., Schaalje, B. G., & Sandberg, J. G. (2000). Daily hassles, intimacy, and marital quality in later life marriages. *The American Journal of Family Therapy, 28,* 1–18.

Harwood, J., & Lin, M. (2000). Affiliation, pride, exchange, and distance in grandparents' accounts of relationships with their college-aged grandchildren. *Journal of Communication, 50,* 31–47.

Heinemann, G. D. (1983). Family involvement and support for widowed persons. In T. H. Brubaker (Ed.), *Family relationships in late life* (pp. 127–148). Beverly Hills, CA: Sage.

Hess, B. B., & Markson, E. W. (1986). *Growing old in America* (3rd ed.). New Brunswick, NJ: Transition Books.

Himes, C. L. (1992). Social demography of contemporary families and aging. *Generations, 16,* 13–16.

Hong, L. K., & Duff, R. W. (1994). Widows in retirement communities: The social context of subjective well-being. *The Gerontologist, 34,* 347–352.

Hyman, H. H. (1983). *Of time and widowhood.* Durham, NC: Duke University Press.

Keating, N., & Cole, P. (1980). What do I do with him 25 hours a day? Changes in the housewife role after retirement. *Gerontologist, 20,* 84–89.

Kennedy, G. E., & Kennedy, C. E. (1993). Grandparents: A special resource for children in stepfamilies. *Journal of Divorce and Remarriage, 19,* 45–68.

King, V., Russell, S. T., & Elder, G. H., Jr. (1998). Grandparenting in family systems: An ecological perspective. In M. E. Szinovacz (Ed.), *Handbook on grandparenthood* (pp. 53–69). Westport, CT: Greenwood.

Kivett, V. R. (1998). Transitions in grandparents' lives: Effects on the grandparent role. In M. E. Szinovacz (Ed.), *Handbook on grandparenthood* (pp. 131–143). Westport, CT: Greenwood.

Lawrence, R. H., Bennett, J. M., & Markides, K. S. (1992). Perceived intergenerational solidarity and psychological distress among older Mexican Americans. *Journal of Gerontology: Social Sciences, 47,* S55–S65.

Lee, G. R., Willetts, M. C., & Seccombe, K. (1998). Widowhood and depression: Gender differences. *Research on Aging, 20,* 611–630.

Lester, D. (1999). Regional differences in divorce rates: A preliminary study. *Journal of Divorce and Remarriage, 30,* 121–124.

Levensen, R. W., Carstensen, L. L., & Gottman, J. M. (1993). Long-term marriage: Age gender, and satisfaction. *Psychology and Aging, 8,* 301–313.

Luescher, K., & Pillemer, K. (1998). Intergenerational ambivalence: A new approach to the study of parent-child relations in later life. *Journal of Marriage and the Family, 60,* 413–425.

Lund, D. A. Caserta, M. S., Dimond, M. F., & Shaffer, S. K. (1989). Competencies, tasks of daily living, and adjustments to spousal bereavement in later life. In D. Lund (Ed.), *Older bereaved spouses: Research with practical applications* (pp. 135–152). New York: Hemisphere.

Mancini, J. (1984). Research in family life in old age: Exploring the frontiers. In W. H. Quinn & G. A. Hughston (Eds.), *Independent aging* (pp. 265–284). Rockville, MD: Aspen.

Matthews, A. M. (1991). The relationship between social support and morale: Comparisons of the widowed and never married in life. *Canadian Journal of Community Mental Health, 10*, 47–63.

Miller, N. B. Smerglia, V. L., Gaudet, D. S., & Kitson, G. C. (1998). Stressful life events, social support, and the distress of widowed and divorced women. *Journal of Family Issues, 19*, 181–203.

Mills, T. L., Wakeman, M. A., & Fea, C. B. (2001). Adult grandchildren's perceptions of emotional closeness and consensus with their maternal and paternal grandparents. *Journal of Family Issues, 22*, 427–455.

Moss, M. S., & Moss, S. Z. (1985). Some aspects of the elderly widow(er)'s persistent tie with the deceased spouse. *Omega, 15*, 195–206.

Moss, M. S., & Moss, S. Z. (1996). Remarriage of widowed persons: A triadic relationship. In D. Klass, P. R. Silverman, & S. L. Nickman (Eds.), *Continuing bonds: New understandings of grief* (pp. 163–178). Washington, DC: Taylor and Frances.

Murrell, S. A., Himmelfarb, S., & Phifer, J. F. (1995). Effects of bereavement/loss and pre-event status on subsequent physical health in older adults. In J. Hendricks (Ed.), *Health and health care utilization in later life* (pp. 159–177). Amityville, NY: Baywood.

Nieboer, A. P., Lindenberg, S. M., & Ormel, J. (1999). Conjugal bereavement and well-being of elderly men and women: A preliminary study. *Omega: Journal of Death and Dying, 38*, 113–141.

Norton, A. J., & Glick, P. C. (1979). Marital instability in America: Past, present, and future. In G. Levinger and O. C. Moles (Eds.), *Divorce and separation: Context, causes, and consequences* (pp. 161–167). New York: Basic Books.

Norton, A. J., & Moorman, J. E. (1987). Current trends in marriage and divorce among American women. *Journal of Marriage and the Family, 49*, 3–14.

Nussbaum, J. F., Hummert, M. L., Williams, A., & Harwood, J. (1996). Communication and older adults, In B. R. Burleson (Ed.), *Communication Yearbook 19* (pp. 1–48). Thousand Oaks, CA: Sage.

O'Bryant, S., & Hansson, R. (1995). Widowhood. In R. Blieszner & V. H. Bedford (Eds.), *Handbook of aging and the family* (pp. 440–458). Westport, CT: Greenwood.

Parrott, T. M., & Bengtson, V. L. (1999). The effects of earlier intergenerational affection, normative expectations, and family conflict on contemporary exchanges of help and support. *Research on Aging, 21*, 73–105.

Peterson, C. C. (1999). Grandfathers' and grandmothers' satisfaction with the grandparenting role: Seeking new answers to old questions. *International Journal of Aging and Human Development, 49*, 61–78.

Pezzin, L. E., & Schone, B. S. (1999). Parental marital disruption and intergenerational transfers: An analysis of lone elderly parents and their children. *Demography, 36*, 287–297.

Quirouette, C., & Gold, D. P. (1992). Spousal characteristics as predictors of well-being in older couples. *International Journal of Aging and Human Development, 34*, 257–269.

Sands, R. G., & Goldberg-Glen, R. S. (2000). Grandparent caregivers' perception of the stress of surrogate parenting. *Journal of Social Science Research, 26*, 77–95.

Siegel, J. M., & Kuykendall, D. H. (1990). Loss, widowhood, and psychological distress among the elderly. *Journal of Consulting and Clinical Psychology, 58,* 519–524.

Silverstein, M., Giarrusso, R., & Bengtson, V. L. (1998). Intergenerational solidarity and the grandparent role. In M. E. Szinovacz (Ed.), *Handbook on grandparenthood* (pp. 144–158). Westport, CT: Greenwood.

Silverstein, M., & Marenco, A. (2001). How Americans enact the grandparent role across the family life course. *Journal of Family Issues, 22,* 493–522.

Smith, K. R., & Zick, C. D. (1986). The incidence of poverty among the recently widowed: Mediating factors in the life course. *Journal of Marriage and the Family, 48,* 619–630.

Smith, K. R., Zick, C. D., & Duncan, G. J. (1991). Remarriage patterns among recent widows and widowers. *Demography, 28,* 361–374.

Solomou, W., Richards, M., Huppart, F. A., Brayne, C., & Morgan, K. (1998). Divorce, current marital status and well-being in and elderly population. *International Journal of Law, Policy and the Family, 12,* 323–344.

Spain, D., & Bianchi, S. M. (1996). *Balancing Act.* New York: Russell Sage.

Spanier, G. B., & Furstenberg, F. F., Jr. (1987). Remarriage and reconstituted families. In M. B. Sussman & S. K. Steinmetz (Eds.), *Handbook of marriage and the family.* New York: Plenum Press.

Sporakowski, M. J., & Hughston, G. A. (1978). Prescriptions for a happy marriage: Adjustment and satisfaction of couples married for 50 or more years. *The Family Coordinator, 27,* 321–327.

Stroup, A. L., & Pollock, G. E. (1999). Economic well-being among white elderly divorced. *Journal of Divorce and Remarriage, 31,* 53–68.

Tamir, L., & Antonucci, T. (1981). Self-perception, motivation, and social support through the family life cycle. *Journal of Marriage and the Family, 43,* 151–160.

Thornton, A. (1979). Decomposing the remarriage process. *Population Studies, 31,* 383–392.

Thuen, F., Reime, M. H., & Skrautvoll, K. (1997). The effect of widowhood on psychological well being and social support in the oldest group of the elderly. *Journal of Mental Health, 6,* 265–274.

Tomlin, A. M. (1998). Grandparents' influences on grandchildren. In M. E. Szinovacz (Ed.), *Handbook on grandparenthood* (pp. 159–170). Westport, CT: Greenwood.

Treas, J. (1995). Older Americans in the 1990's and beyond. *Population Bulletin, 50,* 1–47.

Turk, C., Wach, J., & Derns, R. (1985). An empirical examination of the "pain behavior" construct. *Journal of Geriatric Psychiatry, 24,* 23–40.

Uhlenberg, P. (1996). Mutual attraction: Demography and life-course analysis. *Gerontologist, 36,* 226–229.

Uhlenberg, P., & Kirby. J. B. (1998). Grandparenthood over time: Historical and demographic trends. In. M. E. Szinovacz (Ed.), *Handbook on grandparenthood* (pp. 23–39). Westport, CT: Greenwood.

Umberson, D., Wortman, C. B., & Kessler, R. C. (1992). Widowhood and depression: Explaining long-term gender differences in vulnerability. *Journal of Health and Social Behavior, 33,* 10–24.

Vinick, B. H., & Ekerdt, D. J. (1990). Retirement: What happens to husband-wife relationship? *Journal of Geriatric Psychiatry, 24*, 23–40.

Wilson, B. F., & Clarke, S. C. (1992). Remarriage: A demographic profile. *Journal of Social Issues, 13*, 123–141.

Wiscott, R., & Kopera-Frye, K. (2000). Sharing of culture: Adult grandchildren's perceptions of intergenerational relations. *International Journal of Aging and Human Development, 51*, 199–215.

Wright, L. K. (1991). The impact of Alzheimer's Disease on the marital relationship. *The Gerontologist, 31*, 224–237.

COMMUNICATION IN VARIOUS FAMILY FORMS

8

COMMUNICATION IN INTACT FAMILIES

ASCAN F. KOERNER
UNIVERSITY OF MINNESOTA–TWIN CITIES

MARY ANNE FITZPATRICK
UNIVERSITY OF WISCONSIN-MADISON

The communication of intact families can be best understood by looking at their family communication patterns. Family communication patterns emerge from the processes by which families create a shared social reality and broadly define four different family types. Each type is characterized by distinct communication behaviors that allow each type to function well in general, although each type has particular strengths and weaknesses in different areas of family life, such as conflict resolution or decision making. Because the parental relationship is particularly strong in intact families, parents in these families have a relatively greater influence on family communication through their marriage type and parenting style than parents in nonintact families.

DEFINING INTACT FAMILIES

Historically, there have been three distinct perspectives from which to define family (Wamboldt & Reiss, 1991). *Structural* definitions are based on the presence or absence of certain family members such as parents and children and allow for distinctions between, for example, families of origin, families of procreation, and extended families. *Psychosocial task* definitions are based on whether groups of people accomplish certain tasks together, such as maintaining a household, educating children, and providing emotional and material support to one another. Finally, *transactional* definitions are based on whether groups of intimates through their behavior generate a sense of family identity with emotional ties and an experience of a history and a future (for detailed discussions, see Fitzpatrick & Ritchie, 1993).

Defining a family as intact, then, makes sense only from a structural perspective, which focuses on who is part of a family and where intactness depends on whether a family has all the members ascribed to them, for example, parents and children in a family of procreation. The other two perspectives, in contrast, focus on what families do and how they do it, meaning that it makes little sense from these perspectives to define families as intact. From these perspectives, a family can be any group of people that fulfills the respective functions of a family, regardless of the structure of that group. In addition, intactness is a categorical attribute, whereas function exists along a continuum. That is, intactness is binominal (intact vs. nonintact), whereas functioning can assume an infinite number of values ranging from completely dysfunctional to perfectly functioning. As the title of this chapter suggests, in this chapter we adopt a structural definition of family.

This statement is of more than technical importance, because when researchers and laypersons alike think and write about families, the three distinct theoretical perspectives are often conflated (Fitzpatrick & Caughlin, 2002). That is, few people would argue that any definition based upon only one of the three perspectives adequately captures the entire theoretical concept "family." For example, a family consisting of two parents and their biological children might meet a structural definition, but if the parents do not talk to their children regularly and, as a consequence, the family does not develop a shared identity nor accomplishes much as a group, they lack some fundamental attributes of a family. Similarly, two single-parent neighbors who raise their children together also lack some of the attributes of a family, even though they meet the requirements of a psychosocial task or a transactional definition. In other words, although it is theoretically possible to define family from only one perspective, in practice families are usually defined from all three perspectives simultaneously. As a consequence, at least in the context of family communication, "intact" usually implies "well functioning," and "well functioning" often implies "intact."

Equating being intact with functioning well, however, can be problematic for family communication scholars, especially if the connections between structure and functioning are only implied and not made explicitly. As discussed earlier, neither the psychosocial task definition of family nor the transactional definition require structural intactness, they require that groups fulfill certain functions. At the same time, structural definitions are based on group membership and do not require any functioning. Thus, at least theoretically, structurally defined families do not need to function well, and functionally defined families do not need to be structurally intact. Assuming that intact structures means that families function well can obfuscate important causal factors for family functioning, especially in cases when structure is used as an indicator of the quality of functioning, as in studies that compare intact families with divorced families or with families of runaway teens.

The reverse, however, is equally problematic. To assume that structure and function are unrelated just because structural and functional definitions of families are independent may also lead researchers to miss important causal factors for family functioning. In fact, there are many reasons that suggest that structurally intact families often do function better than structurally nonintact families. In intact families, the bond between parents and children is often stronger and more intimate because it is more enduring and not interrupted by events such as parental divorce or death (Noller & Fitzpatrick, 1993). Intact families generally experience less conflict and stress than families where the parents are divorced, separated, or widowed (Gano-Phillips & Fincham, 1995). Furthermore, intact families usually have more economic and social resources available to them (Gringlas &

Weinraub, 1995; Kissman & Allen, 1993). Although none of these factors is deterministic in regard to family functioning, combined they give intact families significant advantages over nonintact families and make it much more probable that intact families function well.

"Intact" usually implies "well functioning" in the mind of many researchers and readers because the theoretical construct family is defined simultaneously based on competing and independent approaches that stress either structure or functioning, respectively. In addition, through a number of mediating variables, intactness and functioning correlate empirically. Although this empirical correlation between intactness and functioning seems to suggest that little real harm is done by equating one with the other, from a theoretical perspective it is important to recognize their definitional independence and to focus on those mediating variables that causally connect structure and functioning.

In addition to being more functional, another important aspect of intact families that differentiates them from nonintact families is the stability of the parental (i.e., usually marital) relationship. Because in normal circumstances children cannot and do not leave their parents, it is the stability of the parents' relationship that determines whether a family is intact. This seemingly innocuous fact has important implications for family communication, particularly in regard to the relative power of parents and children in families.

An enduring parental relationship suggests that parents in intact families have more satisfying intimate relationships than adults in nonintact families,[1] which should have a generally positive effect for their own satisfaction and, by extension, for their relationships with their children as well (Gano-Phillips & Fincham, 1995; Noller & Fitzpatrick, 1993). In addition, these couples have an intimate and fulfilling relationship that has a history and a future independent from their children. Also, individuals in these couples are able to form coalitions with their spouses in conflict situations with their children and to support each other in stressful or challenging situations. As a consequence, parents in intact families can rely on each other for emotional support. In contrast, parents in nonintact families often lack this supportive relationship with another adult, and if they have it, they often perceive it to be less important than their relationships with their children (Burrell, 1995). Consequently, these parents often are emotionally more dependent on their children, which makes them less powerful in their relationship with their children than parents in intact families. In other words, the power dynamics between parents and children often are vastly different between intact and nonintact families. Parents in intact families are relatively more powerful and influential on family communication behaviors compared to parents in nonintact families.

To summarize, even though labeling a family as intact is initially a statement about the structure of a family, for both theoretical and empirical reasons, it also often implies a well-functioning family. In addition, intact families are different from nonintact families in that usually the parents have a more powerful position within the family as compared

---

[1]Of course, not all parents that stay married are in satisfying relationships. A great number of parents in dissatisfying relationships stay together for numerous reasons, including economic, religious, and for the sake of the children. At the same time, some divorced and single parents have very satisfying intimate relationships with a partner they are not married to. Nonetheless, married couples as a whole are more satisfied with their intimate relationships than either divorced or single parents.

to parents in nonintact families and therefore have relatively more influence on family communication behaviors than parents in nonintact families.

Intact Families in American Society

Although an increasing number of children in the United States are growing up in nontraditional family arrangements, according to the last census, the vast majority of children (71%) are still living in families headed by two heterosexual adults. Of children in these families, 78% live with both their biological parents, 19% live in families with a stepparent, and 3% live in families headed by two unmarried adults (Fields, 2001). Thus, the intact family headed by two adults is still the predominant form of family in American society, and understanding the communication in the intact family is therefore of great importance for scholars and lay persons alike interested in family communication.

Although intact families are often regarded as the most natural or most normative way to raise children and researchers pay much attention to investigations of families that are nonintact (see chapters 10–13, this volume), family communication in intact families is neither unproblematic nor uninteresting. Quite the opposite! Far from being a homogenous group exhibiting similar behaviors that lead to only positive outcomes for families, individual family members, and society at large, intact families exhibit a wide range of communication behaviors that are associated with both positive and negative outcomes for families and their members. In addition, there is no single pattern of family communication that is functional for all families. In fact, as our own research on family types over the last decade has shown, different types of families function quite well employing very different communication patterns. At the same time, the different family communication patterns do not result uniformly in the best possible outcomes in all areas. Each family communication pattern has distinct strengths and weaknesses for families and individual family members.

Thus, there is no easy way to describe family communication in intact families. Rather, understanding of communication of intact families requires a consideration of different types of intact families, each with their own communication patterns and with an appreciation of the particular strengths and weaknesses of each pattern. To this end, we will first discuss the roots of family communication patterns and how communication patterns define different types of families. Then, we will show the profound effects that family communication patterns have on various outcomes for families and conclude with a review of factors that influence family communication patterns.

FAMILY COMMUNICATION PATTERNS IN INTACT FAMILIES

The Roots of Family Communication Patterns

Family communication patterns describe families' tendencies to develop fairly stable and thus predictable ways of communicating with one another. These communication patterns not only allow researchers to distinguish between different types of families, but, as the following review will show, they also are predictive of a number of important family processes and psychosocial outcomes for families and individual family members.

Family communication patterns are neither accidental, nor do they constitute an end in and of themselves. Rather, family communication patterns emerge from the process by which families create and share their social realities. That is, they are inextricably linked to the most basic social functioning of the family. Specifically, family communication patterns result from the process of coorientation without which human interaction in general, and family communication in particular, would not be possible. The process of coorientation and its role in creating social reality was described in detail by McLeod and Chaffee and their colleagues (1972, 1973; Kim, 1981). Because it is crucial for an understanding of family communication patters, however, we will review the main argument here.

The Process of Coorientation.   The concept of coorientation is one of the basic concepts of social cognition and was popularized by, among others, Newcomb (1953) and Heider (1946, 1958). Coorientation refers to two or more persons focusing on, and evaluating, the same object in their social or material environment and being aware of their shared focus. In dyads and larger groups, the process of coorientation results in two distinct cognitions for each person involved. The first cognition is an attitude about the observed object, and the second cognition is the perception of the other person's attitude about the object. These distinct cognitions determine three attributes of the cooriented group: agreement, accuracy, and congruence. *Agreement* refers to similarity between the persons' attitudes about the object. *Accuracy* refers to the similarity between one person's perception of another person's attitude and the other person's actual attitude. Finally, *congruence* refers to the similarity between one person's own attitude about the object and the person's perception of another person's attitude about the object. These three attributes of the group are linearly dependent on one another. That is, the state of any two determines the state of the third. For example, agreement and congruence mean that there is accuracy $(+ * + = +)$, congruence and inaccuracy mean there is disagreement $(+ * - =)$, and inaccuracy and disagreement mean that there is congruence $(- * - = +)$.

Coorientation and Shared Social Reality.   Families and similar social groups that are cooriented do not necessarily share a social reality. Social reality is shared only when the family system has agreement, accuracy, and congruence (McLeod & Chaffee, 1972). There are psychological and pragmatic factors, however, that favor congruence and accuracy, respectively, and, because of the linear dependency among congruence, accuracy, and agreement described earlier, also agreement. As we will explain in the following, because of these factors, coorientation in families usually leads to a shared social reality.

The psychological factor favoring congruence is described in Heider's (1946, 1958) Balance Theory. Balance Theory is based on the general assumption that people strive for consistency among their cognitions, including their attitudes about objects in their environment and their attitudes about other people. For example, if person "A" has a positive attitude about person "B" and a positive attitude about object "X," person "A's" cognition would be balanced if person "A" perceives person "B" to also have a positive attitude about object "X." If, on the other hand, person "A" perceives person "B" to have a negative attitude about "X," person "A's" cognition would be unbalanced. That is, in cases where persons have positive attitudes about others they have relationships with (e.g., family members), cognitive balance is achieved when the persons have congruence, whereas in cases of negative interpersonal relationships, cognitive balance is achieved when the persons have dissimilar attitudes about objects in their environment. In other words, positive interpersonal relationships favor congruence.

The reason that accuracy is favored among family members is purely pragmatic. To sustain themselves as functioning social systems, families have to coordinate many of their activities and behaviors. This requires them to make reasonably accurate predictions about each other in regard to how they behave and communicate (Fitzpatrick & Ritchie, 1993; Koerner & Fitzpatrick, 2002b). Without family members' ability to predict others' behaviors and their reactions to one's own behavior, families simply could not function. Thus, the need to coordinate behavior leads to accuracy.

To summarize, in close interpersonal relationships such as family relationships, the psychological need for consistent cognitions (congruence) and the pragmatic need to correctly predict other's behaviors (accuracy) create a social situation that also leads to agreement. High congruence, high accuracy, and high agreement, however, are characteristics of a social group that shares a social reality. In other words, psychological and pragmatic reasons cause families to share a social reality. The processes of coorientation that establish that shared social reality, however, are communication processes that determine family communication patterns.

Coorientation Strategies in Families

Essentially, family members can achieve a shared social reality in two distinct ways. One way is for individuals to discern another family member's attitude about an object and to adopt that attitude. In other words, they can conform to other family members. Because this process emphasizes the relationships between family members over their relationships to the concept, McLeod and Chaffee (1972) called this process *socioorientation*. The other way to achieve a shared social reality is for families to discuss the object of coorientation and its role in the family's social reality and thus arrive at a shared perception of the object. Because this process emphasizes how family members conceptualize the objects over their interpersonal relationships, McLeod and Chaffee called this process *concept orientation*.

Concept orientation and socioorientation, however, are not only important because they describe the processes by which families arrive at a shared social reality. Rather, they are important because they determine the communication behavior and practices in families and therefore are associated with a large number of important outcomes for families that ostensibly have nothing to do with sharing social reality. Concept orientation and socioorientation have this impact on family communication and functioning, because the process of creating a shared social reality for families is usually not a process that families are aware of or that they conduct purposefully. Rather, although the process of creating a shared social reality is continuous and pervasive, it is an unintentional but necessary by-product of family interaction that family members engage in ostensibly for other reasons. That is, much in the same way as social groups develop and maintain a language's grammar, syntax, and vocabulary every time they use that language, family members develop and maintain their shared social reality every time they say or do anything within the context of the family. Every family interaction contributes to how a family constructs its reality, even though individual family members engage in these interactions for entirely different reasons.

That families are constantly in the process of creating a shared social reality in itself has important implications for our understanding of family communication. For example, one can expect that the amount of misunderstandings in families and the problems that result from misunderstandings are a direct consequence of how well families share their social reality (Koerner & Fitzpatrick, 2002b). Similarly, to the extent that families share a social reality that is very different from the social reality of other persons in these families' social environments, families can experience sociopathologies or contribute to psychopathologies of individual members (Reiss, 1981). More importantly for the study of normally functioning families, however, is the fact that families develop preferences for how they achieve a shared social reality. That is, some families prefer socioorientation to concept orientation, whereas other families prefer concept orientation over socioorientation. Yet other families make ample use of both strategies, and finally some families seem to use neither strategy particularly frequently.

Family Communication Patterns

Although the two processes of coorientation ultimately take place in the minds of individual family members, they do have important effects on the behavior of family members. Recognizing that families' preferences for different strategies to achieve a shared social reality has important implications for their communicative behaviors, Fitzpatrick and Ritchie (1994; Ritchie, 1991, 1997; Ritchie & Fitzpatrick, 1990) refined and reconceptualized McLeod and Chaffee's (1972, 1973) socio- and concept orientation by placing a greater emphasis on the communication behaviors typical of the two orientations. Thus, they reconceptualized socioorientation as conformity orientation because the communication behavior typical of socioorientation is one that emphasizes conformity within families. Similarly, concept orientation was reconceptualized as conversation orientation, because the communication behavior typical of concept orientation is one that emphasizes family discussions.

In addition to the greater emphasis on communication behaviors, the resulting Revised Family Communication Patterns (RFCP) instrument also produced more reliable measurements of the two orientations (Ritchie & Fitzpatrick, 1990). Finally, Fitzpatrick and her colleagues have continued to refine the theory of family communication patterns. In its most recent formulation, the theory of family communication patterns states that the two dimensions of conformity and conversation orientation are part of families' basic belief structures about family communication behaviors that constitute family communication schemas (Koerner & Fitzpatrick, 2002a). Recent work by Fitzpatrick and her colleagues demonstrated the influence of family communication patterns on various outcomes for families, including conflict and conflict resolution (Koerner & Fitzpatrick, 1997), resiliency of children (Fitzpatrick & Koerner, 1996), children's future romantic relationships (Koerner & Fitzpatrick, 2002c), children's communication apprehension (Elwood & Schrader, 1998), utilization of social self-restraint and social withdrawal behaviors (Fitzpatrick, Marshall, Leutwiler, & Krcmar, 1996), the enactment of family rituals

(Baxter & Clark, 1996), and effects of parents' work environments on family communication (Ritchie, 1997).

Conversation Orientation. The first dimension of family communication, conversation orientation, is defined as the degree to which families create a climate where all family members are encouraged to participate in unrestrained interaction about a wide array of topics. In families on the high end of this dimension, family members freely, frequently, and spontaneously interact with each other without many limitations in regard to time spent in interaction and topics discussed. These families spend a lot of time interacting with each other, and family members share their individual activities, thoughts, and feelings with each other. In these families, actions or activities that the family plans to engage in as a unit are discussed within the family, as are family decisions. Conversely, in families at the low end of the conversation orientation dimension, members interact less frequently with each other and there are only a few topics that are openly discussed with all family members. There is less exchange of private thoughts, feelings, and activities. In these families, activities that family members engage in as a unit are not usually discussed in great detail, nor is everybody's input sought after for family decisions.

Associated with high conversation orientation is the belief that open and frequent communication is essential to an enjoyable and rewarding family life. Families holding this view value the exchange of ideas, and parents holding this belief see frequent communication with their children as the main means to educate and to socialize them. Conversely, families low in conversation orientation believe that open and frequent exchanges of ideas, opinion, and values are not necessary for the function of the family in general and for the children's education and socialization in particular.

Conformity Orientation. The other dimension of family communication is conformity orientation. Conformity orientation refers to the degree to which family communication stresses a climate of homogeneity of attitudes, values, and beliefs. Families on the high end of this dimension are characterized by interactions that emphasize a uniformity of beliefs and attitudes. Their interactions typically focus on harmony, conflict avoidance, and the interdependence of family members. In intergenerational exchanges, communication in these families reflects obedience to both parents and other adults. Families on the low end of the conformity orientation dimension are characterized by interactions that focus on heterogeneous attitudes and beliefs as well as on the individuality of family members and their independence from their families. In intergenerational exchanges, communication reflects the equality of all family members; for example, children are usually involved in decision making.

Associated with high-conformity orientation is the belief in what might be called a traditional family structure. In this view, families are cohesive and hierarchical. That is, family members favor their family relationships over relationships external to the family and they expect that resources such as space and money are to be shared among family members. Families high in conformity orientation believe that individual schedules should be coordinated among family members to maximize family time, and they expect family members to subordinate personal interests to those of the family. Parents are expected to make the decisions for the family, and the children are expected to act according to their parents' wishes. Conversely, families low in conformity orientation do not believe in a traditional family structure. Instead, they believe in less cohesive and hierarchically organized families. Families on the low end of the conformity dimension believe that relationships outside the family are equally important as family relationships and that families should encourage the personal growth of individual family members, even if that leads to a weakening of the family structure. They believe in the independence of family members, they value personal space, and they subordinate family interests to personal interests.

The effects that these two core dimensions of communication in families have on actual family communication are often dependent on one another. That is, rather than having simple main effects on family communication, these two dimensions often interact with one another, such that the impact of conversation orientation on family outcomes is moderated by the degree of conformity orientation of the family and vice versa. Therefore, to predict the influence of family communication patterns on family outcomes, it is rarely sufficient to investigate only one dimension without assessing the other dimension as well (Koerner & Fitzpatrick, 2002b). Because the two dimensions of conformity orientation and conversation orientation interact consistently with one another, in effect they create four family types that differ from each other in qualitative ways. To distinguish these types is therefore of theoretical significance and not just a convenient way of describing four family types that are created by crossing these two dimensions.

Family Types and Communication

Consensual Families. Families high in both conversation and conformity orientation are labeled *consensual*. Their communication is characterized by a tension between pressure to agree and to preserve the existing hierarchy within the family, on the one hand, and an interest in open communication and in exploring new ideas, on the other. That is, parents in these families are very interested in their children and what the children have to say but at the same time also believe that they, as the parents, should make decisions for the family and for the children. They resolve this tension by listening to their children and by spending time and energy in explaining their decisions to their children in the hope that their children will understand the reasoning, beliefs, and values behind the parents' decisions. Children in these families usually learn to value family conversations and tend to adopt their parents' values and beliefs. In these families, conflict is generally regarded as negative and harmful to the family, but because unresolved conflict is perceived as potentially threatening to the relationships within the family, these families also value and engage in conflict resolution (Koerner & Fitzpatrick, 1997).

Pluralistic Families. Families high in conversation orientation but low in conformity orientation are labeled *pluralistic*. Communication in pluralistic families is characterized by open, unconstrained discussions that involve all family members. Parents in these families do not feel the need to be in control of their children or to make all their decisions for them. This parental attitude leads to family discussions where opinions are evaluated based on the merit of arguments rather than on which family members supports them. That is, parents are willing to accept their children's opinions and to let them participate equally in family decision making. Because of their emphasis on the free exchange of ideas and the absence of overt pressure to conform or to obey, these families openly address their conflicts with one another, are low in conflict avoidance, engage in positive conflict resolution strategies, and most often resolve their conflicts. Children of these families learn to value family conversations and, at the same time, learn to be independent and autonomous, which fosters their communication competence and their confidence in their ability to make their own decisions.

Protective Families.   Families low on conversation orientation but high on conformity orientation are labeled *protective*. Communication in protective families is characterized by an emphasis on obedience to parental authority and by little concern for conceptual matters or for open communication within the family. Parents in these families believe that they should be making the decisions for their families and their children, and they see little value in explaining their reasoning to their children. Conflict in protective families is perceived negatively because these families place great emphasis on conformity and little value on open communication (Koerner & Fitzpatrick, 1997). Family members are expected not to have any conflicts with one another and to behave according to the interests and norms of the family. Because communication skills are not valued and not practiced much, these families often lack the necessary skills to engage productively in conflict resolution. Children in protective families learn that there is little value in family conversations and to distrust their own decision-making ability.

Laissez-Faire Families.   Families low in both conversation orientation and conformity orientation are labeled *laissez-faire*. Their communication is characterized by few and usually uninvolving interactions among family members that are limited to a small number of topics. Parents in laissez-faire families do believe that all family members should be able to make their own decisions, but unlike parents in pluralistic families, they have little interest in their children's decisions, nor do they value communicating with them. Most members of laissez-faire families are emotionally divorced from their families. Laissez-faire families value neither conformity nor communication very much. As a result, they do not experience their families as constraining their individual interests and incidents of colliding interests; thus, conflicts are rare (Koerner & Fitzpatrick, 1997). These families do not engage much in conversation with one another and therefore tend to avoid conflict. Children of these families learn that there is little value in family conversation and that they have to make their own decisions. Because they do not receive much support from their parents, however, they come to question their decision-making ability.

Family Communication Patterns and Other Family Typologies

The family typology resulting from family communication patterns is different from other family typologies in a number of important ways. First, unlike most other typologies, it is not based on a distinction between high- and low-functioning families. That is, this typology recognizes that families can be functioning well based on very different types of behavior. What is functional in the context of one family type might be dysfunctional in the context of another family type and vice versa. Thus, there is no ideal type of family and no ideal way of communicating within families. Second, the typology is not just a convenient way to describe different types of observable behaviors, but it is based on a sound theoretical model explaining how families create social reality. Thus, it provides a satisfactory answer to the question of the etiology of the different family types rather than just having to refer back to itself as a means of verifying its existence. Finally, the typology, unlike many others, is associated with a strong and reliable measurement, the Revised Family Communication Patterns instrument (RFCP) (Ritchie & Fitzpatrick, 1990).

Most family typologies were developed by scholars interested in the question: What distinguishes well-functioning families from poorly functioning families? Thus, it is no surprise then that they usually distinguish between well- and poorly functioning families. For example, Kantor and Lehr (1975) distinguished among open, closed, and random families based both on their communication behavior and on how well these families function in regard to distance organization. Open families employ the most functional behaviors, closed families are moderately functional, and random families are the least functional families in this typology. Similarly, Olson's (Olson, Sprenkle, & Russell, 1979; Olson, Russell, & Sprenkle, 1983) Circumplex Model of family functioning, which in addition to communication behaviors is based on families' cohesion and adaptability, distinguishes between family types that function well (balanced families), moderately (midrange families), and poorly (extreme families).

Unlike these typologies, the typology based on family communication patterns does not assume that just because families communicate differently they also function differently well. Rather, similarly to Fitzpatrick's (1988) marital typology and Gottman's (1994) typology of conflict styles, this typology recognizes that different families function well by employing different types of behaviors. In this model, certain behaviors contribute or distract from family functioning not because they are inherently functional or dysfunctional, but because of the way they interact with the different communication contexts created by the family types. Thus, this typology directs researchers to focus on how behaviors interact with specific communication environments to explain the effects they have on family functioning.

The typology based on family communication patterns also has the advantage over other typologies, because it is based on a well-established model explaining how families create a shared social reality through the process of coorientation. As a result, it is not only based on observable differences of the behavior of the different family types but also explains the source of these differences. Other typologies that are solely based on observable differences in the behavior of different types they describe can justly be criticized, because they essentially reify themselves with the arguments that families are different because they behave differently and that they behave differently because they are different. Obviously, a typology that is based on a less tautological claim is theoretically stronger.

A final strength of the family typology based communication patterns is that it is associated with a strong empirical measure of the underlying dimensions and the resulting family types (Koerner & Fitzpatrick, 2002b). The 26-item RFCP is an easily administered questionnaire with robust psychometric properties. It and its predecessor, McLeod and Chaffee's (1972) FCP, have been used in countless studies and proven to be both reliable and valid. Thus, the RFCP offers researchers interested in family communication a convenient and powerful measure of family communication behaviors.

FACTORS AFFECTING FAMILY COMMUNICATION PATTERNS OF INTACT FAMILIES

Family Communication Patterns and Marriage Types

Families' shared beliefs about family communication, however, are not the only beliefs that influence how families communicate. In intact families in particular, the relationship between the parents is very important, because it usually precedes the relationships between parents and children and among siblings. In addition, children usually model their behavior after that of their parents. Thus, the beliefs parents have about their own marital relationship and how they communicate with one another have a great influence on how a family as a whole communicates. Furthermore, parents take an active role in socializing their children in regard to communication behaviors, rewarding them for some behaviors and punishing them for others. Consequently, there should be a positive correlation between marital and family schemas and, by extension, between marital and family communication. Investigating this connection, Fitzpatrick and Ritchie (1994) have linked the RFCP family typology to Fitzpatrick's (1988) typology of marriages.

Based on theoretical and empirical research of people's marital beliefs and behaviors, Fitzpatrick (1988) identified three distinct types of married people, which she labeled as *traditional*, *independent*, and *separate*. These three marriage types are defined by three dimensions of marital relationships measured with the relational dimension inventory (RDI): ideology (conventional versus nonconventional), interdependence (interdependent versus independent), and communication (avoidance vs. engagement of conflict). Although these three dimensions yield eight theoretical marital types ($2 * 2 * 2 = 8$), in her research Fitzpatrick (1988) showed that most persons fall into only the three marital types, which she labeled traditionals, independents, and separates. Fitzpatrick's research further showed that in about two thirds of all marriages both partners are of the same married type, resulting in marriages of pure types. In about one third of marriages, however, partners are of dissimilar marital types, resulting in mixed-type marriages. Among mixed-type marriages, the type combining a separate husband with a traditional wife is the most frequent one (Fitzpatrick, 1988).

Traditional couples hold conventional ideological values about marital relationships (e.g., the wife adopts the husband's last name; infidelity is unacceptable), are interdependent (e.g., share time, space, and companionship), and describe their communication as nonassertive but engage in, rather than avoid, marital conflicts about important issues. *Independent* couples hold nonconventional values about marital relationships (e.g., marriage should not constrain individual achievement; wives keep their own last name), exhibit a high degree of sharing and companionship while maintaining separate time schedules and physical space (e.g., spouses have their own individual bathrooms and offices), and also tend to engage in, rather than avoid, marital conflict. *Separate* couples hold conventional values about relationships and families, but at the same time value individual freedom over relational maintenance, have significantly less companionship and sharing, and describe their communication as persuasive and assertive, yet avoid rather than engage in open marital conflict.

Recognizing the similarities between marital beliefs and the beliefs associated with family communication patterns, Fitzpatrick and Ritchie (1994) investigated the relationships between marital types and family types in intact families. Based on questionnaires completed by 169 family triads (father, mother, one child) that contained the RFCP for all family members and Fitzpatrick's RDI for the parents, Fitzpatrick and Ritchie were able to establish links between the marital types and the family types. In regard to the underlying dimensions, members of families headed by traditional or separate parents described their families as high in conformity orientation and members of families headed by traditional and independent parents described their families as high in conversation orientation. In other words, consensual families are most likely to be headed by parents that fall into Fitzpatrick's traditional category. Parents heading pluralistic families are likely to be of Fitzpatrick's independent type. Protective families are likely to be headed by parents of Fitzpatrick's separate type, and parents heading laissez-faire families are likely to be separate/independent or of another mixed type of Fitzpatrick's typology. Spouses in mixed couples define their marriages very differently, which makes it difficult for them to agree even on fundamental values and beliefs associated with their families and to form cohesive family units.

Family Communication Patterns and Parenting Styles

As already mentioned previously, parents have great influence on how families communicate not only because children model their behavior after that of their parents but also because they socialize their children by actively teaching them how to communicate. Burleson, Delia, and Applegate (1995) discussed the socializing influence of parents on their children's communication styles and identified two contrasting communication strategies that parents use to regulate children's behavior: a person-centered or position-centered approach. In the *person-centered* approach, parents communicate discipline and comforting rationalizations to their children with an emphasis on the other people that are affected by the child's behavior. Conversely, the *position-centered* approach emphasizes rules and norms that apply regardless of whether or how others are affected by the behavior. In other words, the person-centered approach encourages children to develop communication skills that enhance their ability to be empathetic and to take the other person's perspective on their own behavior. In contrast, the position-centered approach encourages children to develop communication skills that enhance their ability to identify pertinent rules and norms but that do not require them to take the other person's perspective into consideration.

Findings in the family context suggest that family conformity orientation is associated with a greater use of position-centered strategies. Ritchie (1991) found that parental power to enforce conformity was reflected by the parent's ability to convince children to accept decisions and information with little or no need for explanations. That is, in high-conformity families, children were socialized to follow rules rather than to engage in perspective taking as a means of regulating their behaviors. Similarly, Baxter and Clark (1996) found a positive correlation between a family's conformity orientation and adherence to normative guidelines. Finally, Koerner and Cvancara (2002) found that conformity orientation is associated with less empathy in family communication. Combined, these studies suggest that a position-centered parenting style is associated with the family's conformity orientation, whereas a person-centered parenting style is associated with a family's conversation orientation.

Thus far, we have discussed four different types of families based on their communication patterns that ultimately result from their differences in conformity and conversation
orientation. We have also discussed how these distinct family types are associated with
significant differences not only in their communication patterns but also in how family
communication patterns relate to marital types and parenting styles. During this discussion, we have treated family communication patterns as a temporally stable variable that
varies between families, but not within, and that is largely determined by the parents. As
we argue in the following sections, these assumptions should be treated with some caution.

Children's Influence on Family Communication Patterns

Although the parents' marriage type has a large influence on family communication patterns, especially in intact families, we are not trying to suggest that family communication
patterns are exclusively determined by parents. Certainly, children also have influence
on family communication patters, although probably less so in intact families where a
stronger relationship between the parents exist than in nonintact families, where single
parents often are more dependent on their children. Children influence parental communication from an early age. Even infants have been shown to have a large influence on how
adults communicate with them, and parents adapt their behavior to that of their children. As
children grow older, their influence increases. In regard to family communication patterns,
Saphir and Chaffee (2002) found in a longitudinal study of the influence of civic lessons
at school on adolescents' initiated family discussion of politics that adolescents indeed
exerted influence on family communication patterns. This influence declined somewhat
over time, but persisted even after 6 months in the evaluations of family communication
patterns by both parents and their children.

Other variables associated with the children that thus far have not been empirically
investigated should have similar effects on family communication patterns. Generally,
we would expect children who are extroverted, trusting, and feel close to their parents
and siblings to be more likely to seek conversations with their parents and siblings and
thereby contribute to a greater conversation orientation of families. By contrast, we would
expect children who are introverted, less trusting, and more distant from their parents and
siblings to avoid family conversations and contribute to a lower conversation orientation of
their families. Similarly, children that are confident, have high self-esteem, and experience
themselves as competent in their dealings outside the family (e.g., school, peers) should be
more likely to reject parental pressures to conform and contribute to a lower conformity
orientation in families. Conversely, children with low self-esteem and confidence who
experience themselves as less competent in their dealings outside the family should be
more likely to conform with their families and contribute to greater conformity orientation
in families.

Divergent Perceptions of Family Communication Patterns by Family Members

Given that even in very close families individual family members have individual histories
and experiences that they do not share with each other, it is plausible that family members should have different perceptions of their families and their families' communicative

behaviors. Indeed, there is compelling empirical evidence that persons' perceptions of their families depend at least in part on their own family role (Ritchie & Fitzpatrick, 1990). Ritchie and Fitzpatrick reported data from a random sample of 169 families that indicated, for example, that mothers report their families to be more conversation oriented than other family members and that sons report their families to be higher in conformity orientation than other family members. A possible explanation for these findings is that mothers are more concerned about communicating with other family members and value communication among family members more. As a result, both their individual communication behaviors as well as their individual standards for family communication bias their perception. Similarly, sons more than daughters are concerned about becoming independent from their families and therefore subjectively experience a greater pressure to conformity in their families than other family members. In addition, they are more likely to challenge parental authority and thus are more likely to experience parental efforts to obtain their conformity than other family members.

In addition to these role-specific biases in how members perceive and experience their families, Ritchie and Fitzpatrick (1990) also discovered divergent perceptions among family members that were not related to their family roles. That is, even though family members' perceptions of conformity orientation and conversation orientation were positively correlated with one another, these correlations were not extremely large (correlations corrected for attenuation were between .38 and .43 for conformity orientation, and between .30 and .50 for conversation orientation). In other words, there was some variance within families in how individual family members perceived their family communication patterns.

Some of that variance can be explained by the age of the children. In their study, Ritchie and Fitzpatrick (1990) compared parents' conformity and conversation orientations to those of their children in grades 7, 9, and 11. They found that whereas 7th-graders' perception of their families' conversation orientation was more closely related to that of their mothers than to that of their fathers, by grade 11 that pattern had reversed and children's perceptions were more closely related to that of their fathers than to that of their mothers. With regard to conformity orientation, this pattern was reversed. Younger children agreed more with their fathers' perception and older children agreed more with their mothers' perceptions. Although the exact reasons for these interesting changes in agreement between fathers and children and mothers and children are unclear, they suggest that the parents at different times are more or less attuned to their children's perception of how their families communicate. Because conformity orientation is highlighted whenever there is conflict, these findings suggest that younger children experience more conflict with their fathers, whereas older children experience more conflict with their mothers. Similarly, because conversation orientation is highlighted whenever parents communicate with their children, these results suggest that mothers communicated more with their younger children, whereas older children are communicating more with their fathers.

Another source of the variance in how family members perceive their family's communication patterns is associated with the family communication patterns themselves. Although a large part of beliefs and behaviors that constitute family communication schemas are implicit, that is, they are enacted rather than talked about, some of the beliefs and behaviors are also the topic of family conversations. As a result, families high in conversation orientation, which value and encourage such discussions, are more likely to agree on their family communication norms than are families low in conversation orientation. In the Ritchie and Fitzpatrick (1990) study, for example, families high in conversation orientation (i.e., consensual and pluralistic) were twice as likely to be unanimous in their perception of family type than were families low in conversation orientation (i.e., protective and laissez-faire). Interestingly, this pattern was largely due to fathers' greater agreement with both their wives and children in high-conversation families. For mothers, the degree of conversation orientation did not seem to affect their agreement with other family members regarding their families' communication patterns. A possible explanation for this gender difference among parents is that mothers communicate frequently with all family regardless of the family's conversation orientation, whereas fathers communicate frequently with their children only in high-conversation orientation families. As a result, only fathers' experiences of their families' communication are affected by conversation orientation, whereas mothers' experiences are unaffected by conversation orientation.

CONCLUSION

Intact families deserve the continued attention of family researchers for at least two reasons. First, they are still by far the most frequent type of family in American society, and the vast majority of American children grow up in intact families. Second, family communication behaviors of intact families vary considerably between families, as do the consequences that family communication behaviors have for families and individual family members. Although the label "intact" often seems to imply that these families are highly functional, normative, and uninteresting, in reality the communication of intact families is varied, often surprising, and quite interesting.

Despite good reasons to believe that intact families are also better functioning than nonintact families and empirical evidence that buttresses this assumption, one has to be careful not to equate being intact with being highly functional. As we argued earlier, these terms stem from different theoretical approaches for defining families and are therefore theoretically independent from one another. Rather, researchers should focus on those variables that are different between intact and nonintact families and that ultimately are responsible for family functioning, such as the quality of the relationship between parents, the ability of children to attach to both parents, and the power dynamics between parents and children, to name a few.

The theoretical approach we favor for research of family communication is one that focuses on family communication patterns. Family communication patterns result from the basic psychological processes by which family members coorient themselves and, through their communication behavior, create a shared social reality. As such, family communication patterns not only are grounded in a sound theoretical model but also have empirical validity. Furthermore, family communication patterns are likely to have a greater ecological validity than family typologies that essentially only distinguish between well- and poorly functioning families, because they take into consideration that behaviors are never inherently just positive or just negative. Rather, the same behavior can have different outcomes depending on the communication context in which it occurs. Finally, family communication patterns are based on two continuous dimensions but also create a fairly parsimonious family typology with four distinct types that are intuitively appealing. Thus, the approach is flexible enough to accommodate a wide variety of research methods, from simple comparisons of group means to causal modeling. Because family communication patterns involve both outright communication behaviors and cognitive processes, they also allow researchers to use them to investigate a wide range of interesting questions involving both psychological and behavioral phenomena.

Although based on the cognitive processes of individuals, family communication patterns and the family communication schemata associated with them are ultimately social processes. Thus, they are subject to influence from all family members, although parents in intact families have a greater influence on family communication patterns than parents in nonintact families. Consequently, the type of marriage parents have and their parenting styles have great influence on family communication patterns of intact families. Family communication patterns, however, also are influenced by other factors, such as children's personalities, their dyadic relationships with the parents and their siblings, their ages, and even how they respond to minor external influences, such as civic lessons. That is, although family communication patterns in intact families are fairly stable over time because they are based on an enduring parental relationship, they can also change fairly rapidly and become quite dynamic in response to changing circumstances.

This dynamism does not make family communication patterns less useful for researchers, however. Rather, because much of this dynamism is systematic and predictable rather than random, it actually increases the explanatory power of family communication patterns. For example, knowing that different family members have different conformity and conversation orientations allows predictions about how family communication patterns change when certain family members are absent from a family conversation. Thus, in families where the father is more conformity oriented than the mother, family interactions that involve the children and only the father should be more conformity oriented, whereas interactions that involve the children and only the mother should be more conversation oriented. Similarly, families in which parents attend parenting classes that stress person-centered parenting should become more conversation orientated, and families whose children have experiences (e.g., at school) that lower their self-esteem should become more conformity orientated.

In this chapter, we have described only the groundwork of what already is a substantial body of research of family communication based on the theoretical model of family communication patterns. That research based on family communication patterns is still thriving more than 30 years after McLeod and Chaffee (1972, 1973) first introduced the model and more than 10 years after Fitzpatrick and Ritchie (1993, 1994) reconceptualized it as a more behavioral based theory is evidence of the continuous ability of the model to produce powerful explanations of family behavior. We are looking forward to building on the theory and refining it in the process and hope that other researchers will find the model as useful and as informative as we do.

AUTHOR NOTE

Ascan F. Koerner (PhD, University of Wisconsin-Madison, 1998) is an Assistant Professor of Speech Communication at the University of Minnesota. Mary Anne Fitzpatrick (PhD, Temple University, 1976) is the Kellett WARF Professor of Communication Arts and the Deputy Dean in the College of Letters and Science, University of Wisconsin-Madison.

Correspondence regarding this paper may be addressed to the first author: Department of Speech Communication, Ford Hall, 224 Church St. S.E., Minneapolis, MN 55455. Send email to koern011@tc.umn.edu.

REFERENCES

Baxter, L. A., & Clark, C. L. (1996). Perceptions of family communication patterns and the enactment of family rituals. *Western Journal of Communication, 60*, 254–268.

Burleson, B. R., Delia, J. G., & Applegate, J. L. (1995). The socialization of person-centered communication: Parents' contributions to their children's social-cognitive and communication skills. In M. A. Fitzpatrick & A. Vangelisti (Eds.), *Explaining family interactions* (pp. 34–76). Thousand Oaks, CA: Sage.

Burrell, N. A. (1995). Communication patterns in step families. In M. A. Fitzpatrick & A. Vangelisti (Eds.), *Explaining family interactions* (pp. 290–309). Thousand Oaks, CA: Sage.

Elwood, T. D., & Schrader, D. C. (1998). Family communication patterns and communication apprehension. *Journal of Social Behavior and Personality, 13*, 493–502.

Fields, J. (2001). *Living arrangements of children: Fall 1996.* Washington, DC: U.S. Census Bureau.

Fitzpatrick, M. A. (1988). *Between husbands and wives: Communication in marriage.* Newbury Park, CA: Sage.

Fitzpatrick, M. A., & Caughlin, J. P. (2002). Interpersonal communication in family relationships. In M. L. Knapp & J. A. Daly (Eds.), *Handbook if interpersonal communication* (3rd ed., pp. 726–777). Thousand Oaks, CA: Sage.

Fitzpatrick, M. A., & Koerner, A. F. (1996, July). *Family communication schemata and social functions of communication.* Paper presented at the International Research Colloquium on Communication Research, Moscow, Russia.

Fitzpatrick, M. A., Marshall, L. J., Leutwiler, T. J., & Krcmar, M. (1996). The effect of family communication environments on children's social behavior during middle childhood. *Communication Research, 23*, 379–406.

Fitzpatrick, M. A., & Ritchie, L. D. (1993). Communication theory and the family. In P. G. Boss, W. J. Doherty, W. R. Schumm, & S. K. Steinmetz (Eds.), *Sourcebook of family theories and methods: A contextual approach* (pp. 565–585). New York: Plenum Press.

Fitzpatrick, M. A., & Ritchie, L. D. (1994). Communication schemata within the family: Multiple perspectives on family interaction. *Human Communication Research, 20*, 275–301.

Gano-Phillips, S., & Fincham, F. D. (1995). Family conflict, divorce, and children's adjustment. In M. A. Fitzpatrick & A. Vangelisti (Eds.), *Explaining family interactions* (pp. 206–231). Thousand Oaks, CA: Sage.

Gottman, J. (1994). *Why marriages succeed of fail... and how you can make yours last.* New York: Simon & Schuster.

Gringlas M., & Weinraub, M. (1995). The more things change: Single parenting revisited. *Journal of Family Issues, 16*, 29–52.

Heider, F. (1946). Attitudes and cognitive organization. *Journal of Psychology, 21*, 107–112.

Heider, F. (1958). *The psychology of interpersonal relations.* New York: Wiley.

Kantor, D., & Lehr, W. (1975). *Inside the family.* San Francisco: Jossey-Bass.

Kim, H. S. (1981). Coorientation and communication. In B. Dervin & M. J. Voigt (Eds.), *Progress in communication sciences* (Vol. 7, pp. 31–54). Norwood, NJ: Ablex.

Kissman, K., & Allen, J. A. (1993). *Single parent families.* Newbury Park, CA: Sage.

Koerner, A. F., & Cvancara, K. E. (2002). The influence of conformity orientation on communication patterns in family conversations. *The Journal of Family Communication, 2*, 132–152.

Koerner, A. F., & Fitzpatrick, M. A. (1997). Family type and conflict: The impact of conversation orientation and conformity orientation on conflict in the family. *Communication Studies, 48*, 59–75.

Koerner, A. F., & Fitzpatrick, M. A. (2002a). Toward a theory of family communication. *Communication Theory, 12*, 70–91.

Koerner, A. F., & Fitzpatrick, M. A. (2002b). Understanding family communication patterns and family functioning: The roles of conversation orientation and conformity orientation. *Communication Yearbook, 26*, 37–69.

Koerner, A. F., & Fitzpatrick, M. A. (2002c). You never leave your family in a fight: The impact of families of origins on conflict-behavior in romantic relationships. *Communication Studies, 53*, 234–251.

McLeod, J. M., & Chaffee, S. H. (1972). The construction of social reality. In J. Tedeschi (Ed.), *The social influence process* (pp. 50–59). Chicago, IL: Aldine-Atherton.

McLeod, J. M., & Chaffee, S. H. (1973). Interpersonal approaches to communication research. *American Behavioral Scientist, 16*, 469–499.

Newcomb, T. M. (1953). An approach to the study of communicative acts. *Psychological Review, 60*, 393–404.

Noller, P., & Fitzpatrick, M. A. (1993). *Communication in family relationships.* Englewood Cliffs, NJ: Prentice-Hall.

Olson, D. H., Russell, C. S., & Sprenkle, D. H. (1983). Circumplex model of marital and family systems, VI: Theoretical update. *Family Process, 22*, 69–83.

Olson, D. H., Sprenkle, D. H., & Russell, C. S. (1979). Circumplex model of marital and family systems I: Cohesion and adaptability dimensions, family types, and clinical applications. *Family Process, 18*, 3–28.

Reiss, D. (1981). *The family's construction of reality.* Cambridge, MA: Harvard University Press.

Ritchie, D. L. (1991). Family communication patterns: An epistemic analysis and conceptual reinterpretation. *Communication Research, 18*, 548–565.

Ritchie, D. L. (1997). Parents' workplace experiences and family communication patterns. *Communication Research, 24*, 175–187.

Ritchie, L. D., & Fitzpatrick, M. A. (1990). Family communication patterns: Measuring interpersonal perceptions of interpersonal relationships. *Communication Research, 17*, 523–544.

Saphir, M. N., & Chaffee, S. H. (2002). Adolescents' contributions to family communication patterns. *Human Communication Research, 28*, 86–108.

Wamboldt, F., & Reiss, D. (1991). Task performance and the social construction of meaning: Juxtaposing normality with contemporary family research. In D. Offer & M. Sabshin (Eds.), *The diversity of normal behavior: Further contributions to normatology* (pp. 164–206). New York: Basic Books.

9

Communication in Divorced and Single-Parent Families

Julia M. Lewis and Linda Johnson-Reitz
California State University, San Francisco

Judith S. Wallerstein
Senior Lecturer Emerita, University of California at Berkeley

Communication patterns are a reflection of relationship dynamics, and changes in intra-familial relationships are a central dynamic in the divorce process. Communication per se has not been a primary focus in divorce research, although certain aspects of communication, such as parental conflict, have been intensively studied mostly for their impact on offspring adjustment. In examining the literature with communication as the lens, the yield can be narrow if only those variables that are directly related to expression of communication, such as degree of conflict, quality of affect, and frequency of interaction, are considered. The yield is considerably higher if variables that are more broadly reflective of relationship dynamics are included, as we did for this chapter. Most divorce research has as its aim the elucidation of how parental divorce and its host of related factors affect the adjustment of offspring in the short and, more recently, in the long term. For the purpose of this endeavor, we shift the focus to highlighting changes in communication patterns and relevant relationship dynamics as families go through the divorce process and include the association with outcomes only secondarily.

Defined broadly, communication includes not only verbal, paraverbal, and nonverbal messages exchanged when people are interacting but also the metacommnication over time of themes, attitudes, and values. In families, metacommunication from parents to children involves information imparted from the accumulation of parent–child interactions as they are repeated and evolve over time and information absorbed by children observing and witnessing parental interactions and behavior, again over time. Within the family, metacommunication establishes a shared, internalized sense of family including history, relationships, roles, worldviews, loyalty issues, and orientation to others and to the future

(Laing, 1971). In addition to patterns and styles of direct, interpersonal communication that have been observed or reported between members of divorced families, we also discuss the nature of metamessages, particularly those that may be communicated to offspring as a consequence of divorce.

The predominant method of study in divorce research has been through self-report measures in which one or more family members either fill out paper and pencil questionnaires consisting of rating scales and symptom checklists or respond to highly structured scaled items during a short face-to-face or telephone interview. This method is especially useful in large-scale demographic research (Booth, Johnson, White, & Edwards, 1991; Chase-Lansdale, Cherlin, & Kiernan, 1995; Furstenberg, Nord, Peterson, & Zill, 1983). The use of observational methodology in which family members interact together so that the communication between them can be directly observed is rare. Hetherington's early work (Hetherington, Cox, & Cox, 1979, 1982) and more recent research by Gottman and associates (Gottman, 1993; Gottman & Katz, 1989; Gottman & Levenson, 2000; Katz & Gottman, 1993) are exceptional instances. Our own method utilizes individual, face-to-face, semistructured clinical interviews with all available family members. Often lasting for hours, these interviews are conducted by highly trained professionals who encourage the participants to explain in detail their feelings, perceptions, attitudes, behaviors, and expectations about targeted areas of their lives (Lewis & Wallerstein, 1987; Wallerstein, Corbin, & Lewis, 1988). These different methodologies result in very different ways of operationalizing and measuring dimensions of human behavior, such as marital conflict. Although being labeled similar names, such as conflict or discord, the actual slices of human behavior each study includes in its designation are often quite dissimilar. Mitigating this apparent confusion is the fact that results from all longitudinal studies of divorce over 10 years show a remarkable convergence in their main findings despite different sample sizes and different approaches to studying the same, critical arenas of divorce-related behavior. In this chapter, we focus on the commonalities in the findings across studies and highlight the different methodologies as they inform and illuminate the discussion.

PREDIVORCE COMMUNICATION CHARACTERISTICS

Recent investigation has included a focus on family characteristics that existed prior to divorce, sometimes shown to have predated the divorce by many years. Although it is common sense to assume that there were problems in a marriage prior to the decision to divorce, and that these problems were likely causal in bringing about the divorce, these recent reports have helped elucidate differences in family patterns and the nature of interactions between families who have problems but who continue to stay intact versus families who split up. This line of investigation has also led to intriguing insights regarding the relative influence of family process (communication style) and family structure (divorce) on long-term offspring attitudes and behavior in commitment and marriage.

Frequency of marital conflict has been the most intensively studied process variable in divorce research and has been the main focus of investigations into predivorce family characteristics. Prospective longitudinal studies have found higher levels of marital discord reported in families who later divorced as long as 12 years prior to the decision to separate

(Amato, Loomis, & Booth, 1995; Cherlin et al., 1991; Furstenberg & Teitler, 1994). The presence of high amounts of negative affect, including criticism, defensiveness, contempt and "stonewalling," a form of withdrawal, predicted couples who were more likely to divorce within the first 7 years, whereas it was the absence of more positive affect that was the best predictor of later divorces (Gottman & Levenson, 2000).

Poorer and more dysfunctional patterns of parenting have been associated with higher levels of marital discord along with a decrease in quality of parent–child relationships. These factors have been repeatedly shown to affect children's adjustment (Amato & Booth, 1996; Block, Block, & Gjerde, 1986; Cherlin et al., 1991; Emery, 1982). For example, parents in families that later divorced showed more rejection and less involvement with their sons (Shaw, Emery, & Tuer, 1993). In their research on processes linking marital interaction and its impact on child behavior, Gottman and Katz (Gottman & Katz, 1989; Katz & Gottman, 1993) found maritally distressed couples to show parenting styles which were associated with anger and noncompliance in their children, that were cold, unresponsive, angry, and low in limit setting and structuring. Furthermore, different patterns of marital discord were predictive of different types of child behavior as mutual spousal hostility was predictive of some forms of externalizing behavior, whereas marital strategies containing anger and distancing tended to produce offspring with internalizing problems.

Conflict that directly involves the children is universally regarded as most harmful to children's well-being and is the most detrimental to parent–child relationships (Amato, 1986; Johnston, Kline, & Tschann, 1989; Wallerstein & Kelly, 1980). This includes involving children in physical violence or directly exposing children to parental violence, fighting about the children, and making the child a player, such as enlisting them in loyalty conflicts or bitter alliances or as conduits of negative communication (Buchanan, Maccoby, & Dornbusch, 1992; Davies & Cummings, 1994; Maccoby, Buchanan, Mnookin, Dornbusch, 1993; Maccoby & Mnookin, 1992). A critical distinction may be drawn between those families in which parental conflict is kept within boundaries that protect the children from witnessing, being the focus of, or being involved with the conflict as participants. In some families parents are unhappy and discordant but manage to keep a firm boundary between their marital difficulties and exposing the children in any way to these problems. Both parents have the psychological capability to control and direct their negative feelings to venues away from the children as well as the mutual motivation to keep their parenting functioning well. Their children have a dim sense that conflict happens behind closed doors, but their functioning is not compromised (Wallerstein, Lewis, & Blakeslee, 2000). An intermediate atmosphere exists when children are not directly involved, but marital conflict takes its toll in diminished parenting as parents are more irritable and have less energy and motivation to support and monitor their children's activities (Hetherington, Bridges, & Isabella, 1998).

A critical question currently being discussed is whether children in families where there is toxic conflict that chronically and directly involves the children are better off if their parents divorce. There is little argument that marital conflict and poorer parenting lead to difficulties for children regardless of whether the family later divorces (Hetherington & Stanley-Hagan, 1999). In fact, in a survey of research done throughout the 1980s, children from high-conflict families where the parents did not divorce showed the most adjustment problems followed by children from divorced families (Amato & Keith, 1991a, 1991b). In his meta-analysis of studies done in the 1990s Amato again found relatively better long-term outcomes in offspring from families with chronic, intense, high levels of conflict when the parents did divorce as compared to those who remained in nondivorced chronically high-conflict families (Amato, 2001).

Various explanations and challenges have been raised regarding this issue. Amato, Booth, and colleagues have hypothesized that divorce removes children from highly stressful and destructive family relationships, and the assumed less stressful postdivorce environment mitigates other divorce-related losses such as decline in living standards and less frequent parental contact (Amato et al., 1995). They speculate that having lived through and then escaping a high conflict, difficult family confers a type of resiliency on the offspring, which then helps them in adult relationships (Booth, 1999).

An unaddressed issue that is difficult to research concerns the nature of the high levels of conflict in families who later divorce and in those who remain married. Do families that later divorce have the highest levels and the most destructive types of conflict? Alternatively, do high-conflict families who stay married develop even more toxic destructive cycles of interaction that involve the children? Our own recent research confirms that highly dysfunctional marriages containing violence and involvement of the children in all sorts of unhealthy interactions not only endure over the long term but also can be mutually satisfying to both adults. The only distinguishing feature from these and our group of high-conflict families who divorced was that one of the adults became unhappy and disillusioned and eventually found a way to get out (Wallerstein et al., 2000).

Central to the argument that divorce leads to a decrease in stress for offspring from high-conflict families is the assumption that conflict declines after divorce. In fact, the overwhelming evidence points to the contrary—that conflict is exacerbated by the demands and circumstances of divorce, particularly in the months and years immediately following separation (Hetherington, 1993; Wallerstein & Kelly, 1980). Enduring high levels of acrimony and bitterness was found in over half of our sample of divorced parents 10 years later (Wallerstein & Blakeslee, 1989). A related assumption is that unhealthy, abusive patterns of behavior between spouses and between parents and children will be stopped by divorce. Although less extensively studied, the existing evidence points to a more pessimistic outcome in which patterns of dysfunction and abuse continue despite the divorce, both between former spouses and in new, postdivorce relationships and remarriages (Fitzgerald, 1986; Nelson, 1989; Wallerstein & Blakeslee, 1989).

Thus far, we have been considering the impact of high levels of marital conflict on family functioning and its role in the divorce process. But not all families who later divorce can be characterized as high conflict. In our sample, less than 30% reported high, chronic levels of conflict in the predivorce years. Although large-scale survey studies found more predivorce conflict in parents who later divorced, recent statistics indicate that higher levels of enduring conflict do not precede the majority of more recent divorces (Amato, 2001).

There is some evidence that outcomes for offspring in the long term are more compromised when parents divorce following a relatively low-conflict marriage (Amato et al., 1995; Booth, 1999). One of the explanations offered is in low-conflict marriages the children do not anticipate divorce because there have been no overt warning signs, such as open discord. The actuality of the divorce is an unwelcome shock with no preparation. Because the offspring have not been negatively impacted or stressed by ongoing conflict and involvement in dysfunctional interactions, the changes in the postdivorce environment cause a net increase in stress with no positive consequences. The distress of the children in such families may be further exacerbated because of the well-documented rise in conflict around the time of parental separation. This conflict not only may be a new and unwelcome style of parental interaction but also may be the type of conflict regarding custody, child support, visitation, and time sharing—all issues that are likely to involve the children (Booth & Amato, 2001).

Low levels of conflict should not be equated with low levels of marital problems. Conflict is an easily observed, measured, and recordable aspect of communication and certainly is a signal for distress and unhappiness in a relationship. But the presence of conflict is not the only marker of trouble in marriage. Although beyond the scope of this chapter, there are forces outside the immediate structure of a marriage that can drastically affect its functioning and course. In our sample, events such as the loss of employment, the death of a parent, the influence of cultural and political movements, and the birth of a child had profound psychological effects on a spouse, which then altered the marital dynamics and precipitated divorce. Other marriages absorbed similar events and remained intact. Some marriages characterized by low levels of overt conflict functioned well enough until an extramarital affair caused disruption.

A commonality between high-conflict marriages that dissolve and apparent low-conflict marriages that end in divorce may be a deficiency in relationship skills and dynamics. One or both spouses has trouble psychologically as well as with communicating, getting their own needs recognized and met, and being able to empathize with and satisfy the needs of the other. This is not a new concept and there are many studies, both recent and over the years, that shed light on the nature of these deficiencies. The underlying assumption is that people who later divorce have psychological attributes that are manifested in communication that are dysfunctional to maintaining interpersonal relationships. Some of these styles of communication result in escalating conflict. These include difficulty in solving problems constructively, in controlling anger and resolving tension along with the tendency to respond to criticism defensively, in being overtly critical, in expressing more negative and less positive emotion, and in experiencing more feelings of moodiness and jealousy. Some interactional styles are dysfunctional in that they culminate in withdrawal and involve suppressing not only conflict but also any constructive exchange of feelings and ideas. People with these characteristics tend to be less articulate and clear in their verbal communication, self-disclose less frequently, avoid or withdraw from conflict and problem solving, maintain stable, negative attributions regarding their spouses' behavior while having difficulty taking in their spouses' communication, and utilize contempt, denial, and withdrawal (Bradbury & Fincham, 1990; Fincham, Bradbury, & Scott, 1990; Gottman, 1993, 1994; Leonard & Roberts, 1998; Matthews, Wickrama, & Conger, 1996; Olsen, 1990). In studies on marital satisfaction over time, levels of disagreement and exchange of anger, commonly viewed as markers of marital discord and dissatisfaction, did not predict long-term deterioration or divorce in families where the marriage had lasted longer than 7 years. Other communication characteristics including defensiveness, stubbornness, and withdrawal as well as the absence of positive valence in affect were better predictors (Gottman, 1993; Gottman & Krokoff, 1989). Communication characteristics highly predictive of marital failure seen even early on in newlyweds as well as in more established couples with young children are indicative of underlying cognitive deficits and learned patterns of perceiving and reacting to others. These deficits and patterns set the stage for nonconstructive communication and in effect predispose the relationship to more negative, less rewarding interaction (Buehlman, Gottman, & Katz, 1992; Carrere, Buehlman, Gottman, Coan, & Ruckstuhl, 2000).

RELATIONSHIP BETWEEN PREDIVORCE AND POSTDIVORCE PATTERNS OF INTERACTION

Divorce profoundly alters not only the structure of the family but also the essential nature of family interactions and relationships. Early on, divorce researchers found little correlation between pre- and postdivorce behavior in families. Fathers who had previously been distant became more engaged and connected, whereas very involved fathers drifted away following divorce (Wallerstein & Kelly, 1980). Mothers radically altered the nature of their caregiving, and children experienced dramatic and unsettling changes in household routine and management, which could not be predicted by predivorce patterns of parenting (Hetherington, Cox, & Cox, 1979). Adults who were apparently stable and mature in their marriages experienced wildly fluctuating emotions and displayed chaotic and risky behaviors after the marriage ended, and some who had been fragile and insecure showed unexpected strength and fortitude after their divorce (Hetherington & Kelly, 2002; Wallerstein & Blakeslee, 1989).

Although conflict is widely regarded as a harbinger of divorce, recent findings show that predivorce conflict is not a good predictor of postdivorce conflict (Booth & Amato, 2001). Conflict increases after divorce in most families regardless of how much or little conflict was present before. In some families conflict remains high for years, even decades following divorce; in others conflict subsides after the initial period of adjustment.

In contrast, one of the most stable characteristics measured is style of communication between spouses. Partners' communication style has been shown to be consistent over type of interaction (situations involving high vs. low conflict during marriage) and, by inference, across pre- and postdivorce years (Gottman & Levenson, 1999.) The manner in which spouses communicate, including the dysfunctional patterns that promoted dissatisfaction and divorce within the marriage, continues into the postdivorce years. There is no indication that physical separation and the legal event of divorce have power, in themselves, to change deeply ingrained patterns of human behavior. The stress of divorce can exacerbate these modes of interaction so that couples whose marriages were typified by high negativity, much strife, and high involvement would only continue this style as they struggle to confront contentious postdivorce issues. Conversely, couples that tended to avoid conflict and meaningful ongoing engagement in their marriages are forced to engage, with little background or skill, in constructive problem solving after they divorce.

There is general agreement that higher postdivorce parental conflict has negative consequences for children and may be one of the most influential factors affecting children's adjustment, especially in the short term (Amato et al., 1995; Guidabaldi, Cleminshaw, Perry, Nastasi, & Lightel, 1986; Johnston et al., 1989; Linker, Stolberg, & Green, 1999; Shaw et al., 1993). Research delving into nature or type of conflict suggests that postdivorce conflict is more likely to involve the children and to be enacted in the children's presence as much parental contact revolves around child-related issues such as time-sharing and child support. In addition to higher conflict, postdivorce communication styles reflect those reported in families before the divorce. These involve more controlling and demands, more expression of negative affect, less expression of positive emotion, and difficulties in solving problems constructively (Amato & Keith, 1991a; Hetherington et al., 1998; Simons, 1996). Suggesting again that it is the more subtle concomitants related to conflict rather than just conflict in general that make the most difference to offspring, a few studies have shown that factors such as conflict resolution style and degree of cooperation (Camara & Resnick, 1988) and interparent hostility (Linker et al., 1999) are more influential in children's postdivorce adjustment.

COMMUNICATION STYLES BETWEEN FORMER SPOUSES AFTER DIVORCE

Research on what happens to the level of communication between ex-spouses indicates that most couples do not discontinue interacting following finalization of the divorce, but that over time the level of intensity and intimacy in interactions subsides. The most significant decline was present in nonparental couples, where for many contact eventually almost entirely disappears (Metts & Cupach, 1995). In addition to frequency, the content of communication also shifts as time passes after divorce. Topics of communication became less personal and less focused on past and present relationship issues. If communication persists at all it tends to revolve around "safe" areas of mutual concern, such as children (if any) or family or "new experiences" (Metts & Cupach, 1995).

A variety of different patterns of communication have been described between ex-spouses following divorce. "Mutual constructive communication" (Christensen & Shank, 1991) and "cooperative colleagues" (Emery, 1994) is generally designated as the healthiest, most functional postdivorce interactive pattern that is relatively impersonal and involves constructive problem solving and avoidance of conflict. "Demand/withdraw communication" (Christensen & Shank, 1991) and "the pursuer and the pursued" (Emery, 1994) involves a pattern where one partner pursues more closeness and contact, although this may take the form of demands and criticism, while the other partner desires more distance and responds by withdrawing and avoiding. Wives typically have been shown to be the "demanders"; and husbands, the "withdrawers," although recent studies, which include nonconflict interactions that precede these patterns, implicate both spouses (Gottman & Levenson, 1999). A third communication style, referred to as "mutual avoidance" (Christensen & Shank, 1991) and "dissolved duos" (Ahrons & Rodgers, 1987), is typified by both partners avoiding communicating as much as possible or altogether. Another style characterized by positive interactions is "Perfect Pals" (Ahrons & Rodgers, 1987), although the greater level of intimacy it entails may border on enmeshment (Emery, 1994). "Angry Associates" and "Fiery Foes" are different variations of postdivorce relationships that utilize negative communication styles (Ahrons & Rodgers, 1987).

"Distressed" couples seeking counseling for marital problems showed the same types and levels of poorer communicational styles as divorced couples, both being significantly more avoidant and engaging in more demand/withdraw communication (Christensen & Shank, 1991). Communication styles containing more negative affect, hostility, and angry withdrawing characterized marital interactions in couples who were more likely to later divorce (Gottman, 1993).

COMMUNICATION AND POSTDIVORCE PARENTING

"Partners who are also parents can never fully divorce" (Emery, 1994). Because parental responsibilities of former spouses do not end, they must instead undergo transformations and adaptations in an attempt to accommodate to their new roles as parents to their mutual children in their respective postdivorce family contexts. It is expected that separated and divorced parents must be willing to interact, communicate, and cooperate with each other regarding child-related issues despite any feelings of rejection, remorse, bitterness, or anger that they may harbor. Optimally, this mode of cooperative communication should be sustained, at least until the children enter adulthood (Metts & Cupach, 1995). Unfortunately, the majority of former spouses never attain the cooperative level of communication needed to maintain effective mutual parenting. Instead, the majority engage in "parallel" parenting where their relationship is disengaged with little or no communication or cooperation between them. A substantial minority maintain highly conflictual relationships in which the children are often actively involved (Ahrons & Wallisch, 1987; Hetherington & Stanley-Hagan, 1999; Maccoby et al., 1993; Maccoby & Mnookin, 1992; Wallerstein et al., 2000).

Parenting is harder after divorce. The often unexpected and overwhelming demands in postdivorce life for single parents temporarily and sometimes permanently derail their energy and ability to parent effectively. Increased external demands, increased stress, the loss of resources, the addition of other adults and responsibilities all take their toll on time, energy, motivation, and emotional availability. For example, at 1 year postdivorce custodial mothers showed less affection, communicated less often, punished more harshly, and showed more inconsistent discipline (Hetherington et al., 1982). Custodial fathers had fewer problems with discipline and control, but they also communicated less, self-disclosed less, and monitored their children's activities less competently (Buchanan, Maccoby, & Dornbusch, 1991). Noncustodial fathers became less parental and authoritative and they interacted in a more peer-related manner with their children (Hetherington & Stanley-Hagan, 1999).

In addition to these increased pressures on single parenting, newly divorced single parents face the enormously complex task of learning to be a co-parent with their ex-spouse. Co-parenting is a qualitatively different form of parenting and one for which few have any experience or skills. Over the years there has been a growing body of knowledge regarding the set of skills and interactive styles that facilitate optimal co-parenting. Co-parents should work together to avoid conflict, share resources, and respect and support each other's parenting. Both parents should maintain authoritative parenting styles in which there is warmth, support, effective monitoring of activities, firm, consistent discipline and control, positive discussion, and responsiveness to children's growing needs and development. Furthermore, co-parents need to communicate often and effectively so that rules, discipline, and parenting styles remain consistent in the two households. The ideal co-parenting arrangement results in the parents maintaining the same level of mutual investment and involvement in parenting their children as they did predivorce and children experiencing the same framework of dual parental focus (Ahrons & Wallisch, 1987; Emery, 1994; Hetherington et al., 1982; Maccoby et al., 1993; Wallerstein & Kelly, 1980).

The ability of divorced parents to co-parent together, to communicate about their children, to cooperate to set limits, to problem solve effectively, and to provide consistent, positive affective messages has been shown to be one of the strongest influences on how well children adjust after divorce (Emery, 1982; Linker et al., 1999; Nelson, 1989). Underlying these skills is the basic task of redefining boundaries and roles in order to separate the former spousal relationship from the new co-parent relationship (Emery, 1994). This renegotiation of relationship dynamics is critical in order for divorced parents to give up or encapsulate old patterns of communication and behavior associated with the marital relationship and move on to create new methods of communication that facilitate co-parenting. Maintaining old roles and patterns of communication in the more ambiguous, acrimonious and stressful post divorce environment serves to exacerbate dysfunctional interactions so that conflict escalates or the likelihood of distancing and withdrawal increases (Serovich, Price, Chapman, & Wright, 1982).

The endurance of conflict and hostility is not only detrimental to the children but its presence in the post divorce family serves to block and break down the communication necessary for co-parenting activities (Linker et al., 1999). For many divorced parents the greater acccss to children as is present in many time-sharing arrangements promotes more frequent parental contact, which then leads to higher levels of hostile communication including open conflict (Nelson, 1989). The presence of ongoing hostility and conflict can ultimately result in less contact as parents, particularly noncustodial fathers, are driven away (Furstenberg & Nord, 1985; Healy, Malley, & Stewart, 1990; Seltzer, 1991). There is some evidence that custodial mothers control access between fathers and children through the degree of hostility and resentment directed at father, who avoids contact and involvement when negativity is high (Ahrons, 1983; Seltzer & Brandreth, 1994). Frequent and ongoing contact with both parents is promoted as beneficial to children; however, more detailed research indicates contact in the context of high conflict is more detrimental to children's well-being, especially if the conflict occurs in their presence (Amato & Rezac, 1994; Johnston et al., 1989).

Although families who maintain actively high hostility and high conflict are most visible and take up a huge share of professional attention, again, they do not characterize how most divorced parents interact. Over time, the majority settle into patterns of "parallel parenting" where they operate as independent parents, consulting and communicating with the other parent as infrequently as possible, if at all (Furstenberg, 1988). This mode keeps the level of active conflict down but creates two distinct family worlds that may have very different rules, norms, and values for the children to shuttle between (Johnson, 1988). The adjustment to living in parallel worlds that often have little relationship to each other and no access between them compromises psychological development and often imposes economic hardship (Furstenberg, 1990; Wallerstein et al., 2000).

This compromised capacity to parent is thrown into bold relief as children grow into adolescence where the natural volatility and need for monitoring and compassionate limit setting tax the resources of even the most competent parents. Communication quality and the level of constructive communication have been repeatedly shown to be poorest in divorced families of adolescents. Although all parents disengage some as children move into adolescence, communication patterns in families of divorce show higher levels of disengagement in both parents and adolescents, less and less effective parental monitoring, less parental involvement, and high negativity and conflict, particularly between mothers and daughters (Hetherington, 1993). More adolescents from divorced families leave home or spend little time at home, avoid communication and interaction with family members, and are more likely to be involved in high-risk behaviors such as early sex, alcohol, and drugs (Hetherington, 1998; Wallerstein et al., 2000).

Postdivorce Parent–Child Relationships

Divorce usually results in less contact between children and their noncustodial parent (Amato et al., 1995; Furstenberg & Nord, 1985), although in some cases contact with the nonresidential parent becomes closer following divorce (Hetherington et al., 1982; Wallerstein & Kelly, 1980). Both the quantity and the quality of noncustodial father–child relationship decrease over time (Amato & Booth, 1996). Noncustodial fathers maintain more contact and more involvement when conflict and hostility are low with their ex-wives and when they are actively involved in decision making regarding their children (Braver, Wolchik, Sandler, Sheets, Fogas, & Bay, 1993; Cosbie-Burnett & Ahrons, 1985; Seltzer, 1990). Fathers have been more likely to maintain involvement with their sons following divorce (Zill & Rogers, 1988), and father–son involvement has been found to be especially important in the development of sons (Amato & Keith, 1991a).

Divorce results in a lowering of the quality of the child's relationship with the mother as well as with the father (Amato & Keith, 1991a). Although fathers find it hardest to maintain relationships with their daughters in terms of frequency of contact, more overt strain and difficulty have been noted in postdivorce mother–son relationships (Booth & Amato, 1994). In the years immediately following divorce, boys did least well in single-mother households than in other family structures including high-conflict intact families. Girls did as well in mother-headed households when conflict was low as in low-conflict intact families (Hetherington & Stanley-Hagan, 1999). Girls in mother-headed households often took on the role of helpmate and confidant to their overburdened mothers, which aided in their adjustment in the short-term but, if maintained, negatively affected their adult relationships with men (Wallerstein et al., 2000).

Difficulties persist in parent–child relationships as children from divorced families grow into adulthood. Research suggests that the relationship with the less involved, noncustodial parent was particularly compromised. Earlier feelings of loyalty and yearning for more involvement and contact evolved into counterrejection, lack of respect, and feelings of contempt and pity when children reached adulthood (Wallerstein et al., 2000). Custodial parents who had sacrificed and worked hard to maintain the household during difficult postdivorce years earned respect and admiration, although their adult children felt less closeness and warmth than those for the same parent in nondivorced families. Particularly notable were differences in father–adult son relationships in divorced versus relatively harmonious intact families. We saw a marked increase in closeness and camaraderie as sons grew up and fathers had more time in nondivorced families, whereas sons increased their negative feelings and attributions for their divorced fathers and emotionally disengaged as they grew into adulthood (Wallerstein, Lewis, & Blakeslee, 2000).

Adult children are less likely to spend time with and, importantly as parents become older, less willing to offer financial assistance and feel less responsible for arranging care for their divorced parents, especially for those parents who had been inconsistent, uninvolved, and peripheral in their children's lives (Amato & Booth, 1996). On a more positive note, we found a resurgence in contact and positive communication in some families as the children of divorced parents had their own children. Even parents who had been distant and uninvolved as well as those who had kept in closer contact were drawn in to more rewarding interactions and renewed relationships with their children after they became grandparents (Wallerstein et al., 2000).

Transmission Over Time: Metamessages in Divorced Families

What is the long-term impact of growing up within the communicational and relational context of a divorced family? What dynamics have been shown to be important influences in adult offspring adjustment? What has been transmitted through the years and how does it show up in how adult children conduct their lives and relationships? Both adults from divorced families and adults from conflicted but intact families report more problems in relationships including marriage and show poorer communication skills in dating and in marital interactions (Amato & DeBoer, 2001; Wallerstein et al., 2000).

From their participant–observer perch through countless interactions with and between their parents, it is no surprise that children absorb and then display communicational styles similar to those of their parents. Longitudinal studies demonstrate that adult offspring from both divorced and married but discordant parents showed dysfunctional interactional styles that were negatively affecting the offspring's relationships including their marriages. The content of these interpersonal difficulties sounds very similar to that reported in the marital interactions of the parents: difficulty controlling anger, engagement in more negative, escalating exchanges, more belligerence, criticism and contempt, more denial, and less problem-solving ability (Amato, 1996; Hetherington, 1988; Wallerstein et al., 2000).

Although adults from discordant parental marriages showed similar levels and styles of interactive difficulties as adults from divorced families, these relational difficulties did not lead to higher levels of divorce in their marriages. Although reporting that they had thoughts about divorce, adults from discordant but intact parental marriages were more likely to stay in their marriages, much as their parents had remained in their own troubled marriages (Amato & DeBoer, 2001). Only adults from divorced families showed higher levels of divorce in their own marriages. This higher risk for divorce was present whether or not their parents had high-conflict marriages prior to divorcing (Amato & DeBoer, 2001). Over and above interpersonal interactive problems, what is it that children from divorced families bring to marriage that causes them to leave rather than stay?

Amato and DeBoer (2001) speculate that the additional element is that children of divorce actually experience divorce—they have witnessed and lived through not only their parents' marital difficulties but also one (or both) parents' voluntary decision to end the marriage, the wrenching and highly painful process of separation, and the years of postdivorce readjustment. This actual life experience communicates to children from divorced families a different view of marriage—that difficulties should not be endured and relationship problems are not worked out. Our own intensive interviews with adult children 25 years after their parents' divorce enable us to derive a fuller picture of the metamessages communicated from observing and living through parental divorce.

Experiencing parental separation and the dissolution of the family leaves an indelible impression. Years later adults who were old enough to remember had clear and vivid memories of scenes and images that happened at the time that their parents separated. It is clear that the divorce experience is traumatic for most children and that traumatic events make a profound and lasting psychological and physiological impression. Many children of divorce spend years reacting to this experience—longing for the family to be together, wondering how life would have been different, wishing for more contact and involvement with one or both parents. We found little or no indication that children of divorce have a positive or even a casual attitude toward divorce. Their firsthand experience resulted in a great desire not to repeat what happened to their parents together with an underlying fear that relationships were not to be trusted.

It was striking what was and was not communicated about why parents divorced. At most, the great majority of children received a terse description largely involving who was moving where shortly before the parents separated. In the face of parental pain and reluctance to dredge up traumatic feelings, few children were able to engage in a meaningful dialog with their parents regarding what happened to the parents' marriage and why it failed as the children were growing up. Most were left with explanations largely of their own construction—that their parents had been simply unsuited to one another, that they never should have married in the first place, that one parent had betrayed the other, that their parents had fallen out of love. These children grew into adulthood with no real understanding of what went wrong and certainly with no grasp of the depth and complexity of how two people in a marriage can come to the point of divorce. This lack of a meaningful understanding of marital dynamics that can lead to divorce together with the little they had been told and what they had witnessed left the adult children with a great deal of anxiety regarding relationships. It was hard to trust that love and promises and happiness would really last. Their parents' experience showed otherwise, and they lacked an internal roadmap of how to avoid it happening in their own relationships.

Children of divorce also lacked firsthand experience of how to make a marriage work. They had internalized relational dynamics and methods of communication from their parents that were not facilitative in maintaining a satisfying long-term relationship. They had not developed attitudes, skills, reactions, and expectations that would help them create a successful marriage. Most, having lived through their parents' unsuccessful marriage and divorce as well as subsequent parental relationships and remarriages, had never witnessed two people interacting in a satisfying, lasting relationship.

Tension and conflict were particularly problematic as metamessages that had been absorbed from their families of origin linked relational difficulties with traumatic images of separation and divorce. As adults in their own marriages, they emotionally equated normal stresses inherent in any relationship with the wrenching difficulties, such as betrayal and abandonment, associated with a relationship in trouble and ultimately ending. What had never been communicated was the sense of difficulties being worked through, the expectation that relationships went through high and low periods, and the idea that constructive resolution of conflict and tension could lead to greater intimacy.

What was communicated to children growing up in divorced families were images and skills about how to make it on their own. From watching single parents manage jobs, households, children, and relationships, and from their own experience either living with a single parent who had limited time and availability or living between two parallel parental households, they acquired characteristics that they were proud of as adults. They learned that it was possible to work through difficulty and hardship alone. They learned the value of working hard and what it takes to run a household. They learned self-reliance, independence, and to make their own judgments and decisions. Many learned to be good negotiators and mediators from years of balancing and going between their divorced parents—skills that served them well in the workplace but that were not particularly useful in their own relationships. Although most wished to share their lives with a partner, unlike adults from ever married families, adults from divorced parents had actual life experience being divorced and living in a postdivorce family. All of these metamessages made divorce more painful but more probable for children of divorced families.

CONCLUSIONS

The state of the research on communication in divorced and single-parent families presents a complex and provocative picture. Most research has been conducted using self-report measures on a small number of process variables; a smaller number of studies have conducted more in-depth clinical examination across a wider arena of intrafamilial variables, and only a few investigations have directly observed family members interacting together. The same label, such as marital conflict, has been used to describe very different slices of human experience depending on the method of investigation employed. Marital conflict, as rated on a 5-point scale by one of the marriage partners in a short, anonymous telephone interview is probably a different variable from marital conflict assessed by a trained clinican after intensively interviewing both spouses individually, and both of these are different phenomena from the marital conflict observed as marital partners interact together discussing a stressful situation. The time frame of divorce research also spans across an impressive range. A handful of studies have data spanning over 20 years; most examine divorce in the months to 2 or 3 years following parental separation; and a very few prospectively predict divorce from interactions in the first months of a new marriage or even before marriage. Yet, in the past few years, longitudinal studies have reported long-term findings, and there have been meta-analyses integrating decades of individual studies, both of which have contributed to a consolidation and convergence of findings and a clearer perspective on what happens when families divorce.

Nonfacilitative and disruptive communication patterns between spouses have been repeatedly noted both before and after divorce and in marriages that endured but were troubled. These have been linked to less adequate parental behavior, which in turn results in poorer outcomes in offspring. There is evidence to suggest that these maladaptive parental patterns are learned by offspring who then exhibit them in their own adult intimate relationships that are also seen as more troubled. When spouses divorce, additional metamessages about handling stress and conflict, about leaving rather than staying, about surviving after separation, and about forming new relationships after divorce are also communicated to offspring, who then incorporate them into their own tendency to divorce. It seems clear that certain critical points in family life need further, more intensive study and intervention, as they are pivotal in whether communication patterns that are more likely to lead to divorce are maintained and passed on. One point for more study and intervention is in late adolescence and early adulthood as patterns learned from the family of origin begin to emerge in intimate relationships. Related time periods are just before and after marriage when communication systems and patterns begin to be consolidated between the committed couple. Another critical period is at the time of divorce when the stress of divorce exacerbates existing problems and creates new ones. The enormous task of learning new ways to effectively co-parent after divorce, which clearly contributes to better outcomes for the children, is a third arena where more understanding of the processes that derail and facilitate co-parenting would then lead to the development of more informed policies and more focused, effective intervention.

REFERENCES

Ahrons, C. R. (1983). Predictors of paternal involvement postdivorce: Mothers' and fathers' perceptions. *Journal of Divorce, 6*, 55–69.

Ahrons, C. R., & Rogers, R. H. (1987). *Divorced families: A multidisciplinary, developmental view.* New York: Norton.

Ahrons, C. R., & Wallisch, L. S. (1987). The relationship between former souses. In D. Perlman & S. Duck (Eds.), *Intimate relationships: Development, dynamics, and deterioration* (pp. 269–295). Newbury Park, CA: Sage.

Amato, P. R. (1986). Marital conflict, the parent-child relationship, and child self-esteem. *Family Relations, 35*, 403–410.

Amato, P. R. (1996). Explaining the intergenerational transmission of divorce. *Journal of Marriage and the Family, 58*, 628–640.

Amato, P. R. (2001). Children of divorce in the 1990's: An update of the Amato and Keith (1991) meta-analysis. *Journal of Family Psychology, 15*, 355–370.

Amato, P. R., & Booth, A. (1996). A prospective study of divorce and parent-child relationships. *Journal of Marriage and the Family, 58*, 356–365.

Amato, P. R., & DeBoer, D. D. (2001). The transmission of marital instability across generation: Relationship skills or commitment to marriage? *Journal of Marriage and Family, 63*, 1038–1051.

Amato, P. R., & Keith, B. (1991a). Parental divorce and adult well-being: A meta-analysis. *Journal of Marriage and the Family, 53*, 43–58.

Amato, P. R., & Keith, B. (1991b). Parental divorce and the well-being of children: A meta-analysis. *Psychological Bulletin, 110*, 26–46.

Amato, P. R., Loomis, L. S., & Booth, A. (1995). Parental divorce, marital conflict, and off-spring well-being during early adulthood. *Social Forces, 73*, 895–915.

Amato P. R., & Rezac, S. J. (1994). Contact with nonresident parents, interparental conflict, and children's behavior. *Journal of Family Issues, 15*, 191–207.

Block, J. H., Block, J., & Gjerde, P. F. (1986). The personality of children prior to divorce: A prospective study. *Child Development, 57*, 827–840.

Booth, A. (1999). Causes and consequences of divorce: Reflections on recent research. In R. A. Thompson & P. R. Amato (Eds.), *The postdivorce family: Children, parenting and society* (pp. 3–28). Thousand Oaks, CA: Sage.

Booth, A., & Amato, P. R. (2001). Parental predivorce relations and offspring postdivorce well-being. *Journal of Marriage and Family, 63*, 197–212.

Booth, A., & Amato, P. R. (1994). Parental marital quality, divorce, and relations with offspring in young adulthood. *Journal of Marriage and the Family, 56*, 21–34.

Booth, A., Johnson, D. R., White, L., & Edwards, J. N. (1991). *Marital instability over the life course: Methodology report and code book for three wave panel study.* Lincoln, NE: Bureau of Sociological Research.

Bradbury, T. N., & Fincham, F. D. (1990). Attributions in marriage: Review and critique. *Psychological Bulletin, 107*, 3–33.

Braver, S. L., Wolchik, S. A., Sandler, I. N., Sheets, V. L., Fogas, B., & Bay, R. C. (1993). A longitudinal study of noncustodial parents: Parents without children. *Journal of Family Psychology, 7*, 1–16.

Buchanan, C. M., Maccoby, M. M., & Dornbusch, S. M. (1991). Caught between parents: Adolescents' experience in divorced homes. *Child Development, 62*, 1008–1029.

Buehlman, K. T., Gottman, J. M., & Katz, L. F. (1992). How a couple views their past predicts their future: Predicting divorce from an oral history interview. *Journal of Family Psychology, 5*, 295–318.

Camara, K. A., & Resnick, G. (1988). Interparental conflict and cooperation: Factors moderating children's post-divorce adjustment. In E. M. Hetherington & J. D. Arasteh (Eds.), *Impact of divorce, single parenting and stepparenting on children* (pp. 169–195). Hillsdale, NJ: Lawrence Erlbaum Associates.

Carrere, S., Buehlman, K. T., Gottman, J. M., Coan, J. A., & Ruckstuhl, L. R. (2000). Predicting marital stability and divorce in newlywed couples. *Journal of Family Psychology, 14*, 42–58.

Chase-Lansdale, P. L., Cherlin, A. J., & Kiernan, K. E. (1995). The long-term effects of parental divorce on the mental health of young adults: A developmental perspective. *Child Development, 66*, 1614–1634.

Cherlin, A. J., Furstenberg, F. F., Chase-Lansdale, L. P., Kiernan, K. E., Robbins, P. K., Morrison, D. R., & Teitler, J. O. (1991). Longitudinal studies of effects of divorce on children in Great Britain and the United States. *Science, 252*, 1386–1389.

Christensen, A., & Shank, J. (1991). Communication, conflict and psychological distance in nondistressed, clinic and divorcing couples. *Journal of Consulting and Clinical Psychology, 59*, 458–463.

Cosbie-Burnett, M., & Ahrons, C. (1985). From divorce to remarriage: Implications for therapy for families in transition. *Journal of Psychotherapy and the Family, 1*, 121–137.

Davies, P. T., & Cummings, E. M. (1994). Marital conflict and child adjustment: An emotional security hypothesis. *Psychological Bulletin, 116*, 387–411.

Emery, R. E. (1982). Interparental conflict and the children of discord and divorce. *Psychological Bulletin, 92*, 310–330.

Emery, R. E. (1994). *Renegotiating family relationships: Divorce, child custody, and mediation.* New York: Guilford.

Fincham, F. D., Bradbury, T. M., & Scott, C. K. (1990). Cognition in marriage. In F. D. Fincham & T. N. Bradbury (Eds.), *The psychology of marriage* (pp. 118–149). New York: Guilford Press.

Fitzgerald, R. V. (1986). When parents divorce. *Medical Aspects of Human Sexuality, 20*, 86–92.

Furstenberg, F. F. (1988). Child care after divorce and remarriage. In E. M. Hetherington & J. D. Arasteh (Eds.), *Impact of divorce, single parenting and stepparenting on children* (pp. 245–261). Hillsdale, NJ: Lawrence Erlbaum Associates.

Furstenberg, F. F. (1990). Divorce and the American family. *Annual Review of Sociology, 16*, 379–403.

Furstenberg, F. F., & Nord, C. W. (1985). Parenting apart: Patterns of childrearing after marital disruption. *Journal of Marriage and the Family, 47*, 893–904.

Furstenberg, F. F., & Teitler, J. O. (1994). Reconsidering the effects of marital disruption: What happens to children of divorce in early adulthood. *Journal of Family Issues, 15*, 173–190.

Furstenberg, F. F., Nord, C. W., Peterson, J. L., & Zill, N. (1983). The life-course of children of divorce: Marital disruption and parental contact. *American Sociological Review, 48*, 656–667.

Gottman, J. M. (1993). A theory of marital dissolution and stability. *Journal of Family Psychology, 7*, 57–75.

Gottman, J. M. (1994). *What predicts divorce? The relationship between marital processes and marital outcomes.* Hillsdale, NJ: Lawrence Erlbaum Associates.

Gottman, J. M., & Katz, L. F. (1989). Effects of marital discord on young children's peer interaction and health. *Developmental Psychology, 25*, 373–381.

Gottman, J. M., & Krokoff, L. J. (1989). Marital interaction and satisfaction: A longitudinal view. *Journal of Consulting and Clinical Psychology, 57*, 47–52.

Gottman, J. M., & Levenson, R. W. (1999). Dysfunctional marital conflict: Women are being unfairly blamed. *Journal of Divorce and Remarriage, 31*, 1–17.

Gottman, J. M., & Levenson, R. W. (2000). The timing of divorce: Predicting when a couple will divorce over a 14-year period. *Journal of Marriage and the Family, 62*, 737–745.

Guidubaldi, J., Cleminshaw, H. K., Perry, J. D., Nastasi, B. D., & Lightel, J. (1986). The role of selected family environment factors in children's post-divorce adjustment. *Family Relations, 35*, 141–151.

Healy, J. M., Malley, J. E., & Stewart, A. J. (1990). Children and their fathers after separation. *American Journal of Orthopsychiatry, 60*, 531–543.

Hetherington, E. M. (1993). An overview of the Virginia Longitudinal Study of Divorce and Remarriage with a focus on early adolescence. *Journal of Family Psychology, 7*, 39–56.

Hetherington, E. M. (1998) Social capitol and the development of youth from nondivorced, divorced and remarried families. In A. Collins & R. Laursen (Eds.), *Relationships as developmental contexts. Minnesota symposium of child development, 30*, 177–210.

Hetherington, E. M., Bridges, M., & Isabella, G. M. (1998). What matters, what doesn't. Five perspectives on the association between divorce and remarriage and children's adjustment. *American Psychologist, 53*, 167–183.

Hetherington, E. M., Cox, M., & Cox, R. (1979). Family interaction and the social, emotional and cognitive development of children following divorce. In V. Vaughn & T. Brazelton (Eds.), *The family: Setting priorities* (pp. 89–128). New York: Science and Medicine.

Hetherington, E. M., Cox, M., & Cox, R. (1982). Effects of divorce on parents and children.

In M. Lamb (Ed.), *Nontraditional families: Parenting and child development* (pp. 233–288). Hillsdale, NJ: Lawrence Erlbaum Associates.

Hetherington, E. M., & Kelly, J. (2002). *For better or for worse: Divorce reconsidered.* New York: Norton.

Hetherington, E. M., & Stanley-Hagan, M. M. (1999). The adjustment of children with divorced parents: A risk and resiliency perspective. *Journal of Child Psychology and Psychiatry, 40,* 129–140.

Johnson, C. L. (1988). *ExFamilia.* New Brunswick, NJ: Rutgers University Press.

Johnston, J. R., Kline, M., & Tschann, J. M. (1989). Ongoing post-divorce conflict: Effects on children of joint custody and frequent access. *American Journal of Orthopsychiatry, 59,* 576–592.

Katz, L. F., & Gottman, J. M. (1993). Patterns of marital conflict predict children's internalizing and externalizing behaviors. *Developmental Psychology, 29,* 940–950.

Laing, R. D. (1971). *The politics of the family and other essays.* New York: Vintage Books.

Leonard, K. E., & Roberts, L. J. (1998). Marital aggression, quality and stability in the first year of marriage: Findings from the Buffalo Newlywed Study. In T. N. Bradbury (Ed.), *The developmental course of marital dysfunction* (pp. 44–73). New York: Cambridge University Press.

Lewis, J. M., & Wallerstein, J. S. (1987). Family profile variables and long-term outcome in divorce research: Issues at a ten-year follow-up. In J. P. Vincent (Ed.), *Advances in family intervention, assessment and theory: A research annual* (pp. 121–142). Greenwich, CT: JAI.

Linker, J., Stolberg, A., & Green, R. (1999). Family communication as a mediator of child adjustment to divorce. *Journal of Divorce and Remarriage, 30,* 83–97.

Maccoby, M. M., Buchanan, C. M., Mnookin, R. H., & Dornbusch, S. M. (1993). Post-divorce roles of mothers and fathers in the lives of their children. *Journal of Family Psychology, 7,* 24–38.

Maccoby, E. E., & Mnookin, R. H. (1992). *Dividing the child: Social and legal dilemmas of custody.* Cambridge, MA: Harvard University Press.

Matthews, L. S., Wickrama, K. A., & Conger, R. D. (1996). Predicting marital instability from spouse and observer reports of marital interaction. *Journal of Marriage and the Family, 58,* 641–655.

Metts, S., & Cupach, W. R. (1995). Postdivorce relations. In M. A. Fitzpatrick & A. L. Vangelisti (Eds.), *Explaining family interactions* (pp. 232–251). Thousand Oaks, CA: Sage.

Nelson, R. (1989). Parental hostility, conflict and communication in joint and sole custody families. *Journal of Divorce, 13,* 145–157.

Olsen, D. H. (1990). Marriage in perspective. In F. D. Fincham & T. N. Bradbury (Eds.), *The psychology of marriage* (pp. 402–419). New York: Guilford Press.

Seltzer, J. A. (1990). Legal and physical custody arrangements in recent divorces. *Social Science Quarterly, 71,* 250–266.

Seltzer, J. A. (1991). Relationships between fathers and children who live apart: The father's role after separation. *Journal of Marriage and the Family, 53,* 79–102.

Seltzer, J. A., & Brandreth, Y. (1994). What fathers say about involvement with children after separation. *Journal of Family Issues, 15,* 49–77.

Serovich, J., Price, S., Chapman, S., & Wright, D. (1982). Attachment between former spouses: Impact on co-parental communication and parental involvement. *Journal of Divorce and Remarriage, 17*, 109–119.

Shaw, D., Emery, R., & Tuer, M. (1993). Parental functioning and children's adjustment in families of divorce: A prospective study. *Journal of Abnormal Child Psychology, 21*, 119–134.

Simons, R. L. (1996). The effect of divorce on adult and child adjustment. In R. L. Simons & Associates (Eds.), *Understanding differences between divorced and intact families: Stress, interaction and child outcome.* Thousand Oaks, CA: Sage.

Wallerstein, J. W., & Blakeslee, S. (1989). *Second chances: Men, women and children a decade after divorce.* New York: Ticknor and Fields.

Wallerstein, J. W., Corbin, S. B., & Lewis, J. M. (1988). Children of divorce: A ten year study. In E. M. Hetherington & J. D. Arasteh (Eds.), *Impact of divorce, single parenting and stepparenting on children* (pp. 114–123). Hillsdale, NJ: Lawrence Erlbaum Associates.

Wallerstein, J. W., & Kelly, J. B. (1980). *Surviving the breakup: How children and parents cope with divorce.* New York: Basic Books.

Wallerstein, J. W., Lewis, J. M., & Blakeslee, S. (2000). *The unexpected legacy of divorce: A 25 Year landmark study.* New York: Hyperion.

Zill, N., & Rogers, C. C. (1988). Recent trends in the well-being of children in the United States and their implications for public policy. In A. J. Cherlin (Ed.), *The changing American family and public policy* (pp. 31–115). Washington, DC: Urban Institute Press.

10

COMMUNICATION IN STEPFAMILIES

MARILYN COLEMAN, LAWRENCE GANONG, AND MARK FINE
UNIVERSITY OF MISSOURI—COLUMBIA

The merging of individuals from prior families is a complex process, and stepfamily development and maintenance present many communication challenges to parents, stepparents, and stepchildren. In this chapter we review research on communication processes among the adults in stepfamilies (former partners, current partners, etc.) and among adults and children (parent–child, stepparent–stepchild communication). We do not limit the focus of this review to intrahousehold communication—stepfamily members often reside in two or more households. We also examine stepfamily communication across the life course. Gaps in the body of knowledge regarding stepfamily communication are identified and suggestions for future research are offered.

Stepfamilies, formed when an adult with a child or children enters a new union, are common in Western societies, although the precursor is now primarily divorce or unmarried motherhood rather than death (Cherlin, 1992). The number of legally formed stepfamilies has recently dropped slightly, a phenomenon often attributed to an increase in cohabitation (Bumpass, Raley, & Sweet, 1995). In 1996, seventeen percent of children under age 18 in the United States lived in a stepparent household (Fields, 2001), and an unknown number of children lived with a single parent and spent part of the time residing with a stepparent. An estimated 30% of children in the United States will spend at least some time living in a stepparent household before they become adults (Bumpass et al., 1995). Although the percentages are lower, stepfamilies also have become increasingly common in other industrialized nations (Allan, Hawker, & Crow, 2001; Wu, 1994).

Stepfamilies are not created only when children are young. In fact, about half a million people over the age of 65 in the United States remarry each year (United States Bureau of the Census, 1995). The number of older people who remarry and cohabit is likely to grow, given extensions in the life span, improvements in the quality of later life, and the growing numbers of adults who have experienced earlier marital transitions (Cornman & Kingson, 1996). Consequently, intergenerational stepfamilies are common—an estimated 40% of White and Hispanic American families and 55% of African American families contain stepgrandparents (Szinovacz, 1998).

PRE-STEPFAMILY COMMUNICATION

When writing about communication in stepfamilies, it is difficult to know where to start. Someone has made the analogy between joining a stepfamily and beginning a novel in the middle of the book. You aren't sure what transpired previously, and you don't always know all the characters or their relationships with the characters you do know—you are missing the history. Similarly, when studying stepfamily communication, it is difficult to identify and understand the current communication patterns if you don't know the family history. How did they get to this place?

We have chosen to start the stepfamily communication cycle during the single-parent household phase, and, more specifically, the mother/children single-parent household stage. At the same time, we are keeping in mind that children are never the product of a single parent. Even parents they never see or who are deceased continue to influence children in ways we often are slow to understand. We argue that communication processes occurring before the remarriage or cohabitation play a critical role in stepfamily interaction and subsequent development. From the earliest moments when the two adults who will ultimately remarry meet and begin to develop their relationship, and particularly when either or both of their children become involved in family activities with the new partner, communication is setting the stage for later interaction patterns and for how well the stepfamily will function.

Although shared physical custody is increasing, mothers are far more likely than fathers to have physical custody of their children (Bumpass et al., 1995). As a result, the mother–child relationship often becomes very close, sometimes to the point of enmeshment. Comments such as these from an 18-year-old girl discussing the beginning of her relationship with her stepfather are quite typical: "I didn't like him at all. Hated him. Because it was always me and my mom my whole life practically. I hated any guy that she dated. So—I really hated him for some reason. I don't know why" (Weaver & Coleman, in review).

She may not know why she "hated him," but it is easy to speculate about it. Children often become quite comfortable in a single-parent household, and they are reluctant to face still more family changes. Therefore, a potential stepparent is seen as a threat. Some speculate that it is better for parents to remarry quickly before the single-parent household establishes comfortable rules and routines (Rodgers, 1986)—before it is "always me and my mom my whole life practically . . . ." Others express concern about how rapidly parents remarry, question whether adequate thought has been given to their remarriage, or if they (primarily women) are remarrying for financial stability. Either route—quick remarriage/cohabitation or a long period as a single parent—has consequences for communication patterns in the stepfamily.

COMMUNICATION IN THE EARLY YEARS OF STEPFAMILY DEVELOPMENT

Because of the large number of issues that need to be addressed and managed in newly formed stepfamilies, communication is perhaps never more important than it is in the early years of the stepfamily. Among the critical issues that need to be managed are boundary management (Who is and is not a member of the family? How much privacy will family members have? Which subsystems or alliances in the family will be formed?), conflict resolution (How are conflicts resolved—actively and deliberately? Passively?), power (Who has the greatest influence over family decision making? Which subsystems have more control over family interaction?), and the negotiation of roles (What will the role of the stepparent be? How will the parent balance the roles of parent and new spouse?).

The fact that people cohabit and remarry quickly following divorce (i.e., most remarried couples live together before they marry, and the average time between divorce and remarriage is less than 4 years; Wilson & Clarke, 1992) is a factor in the communication patterns that develop in many stepfamilies. During the divorce process, one parent usually is ahead of the other in disengaging from the relationship; it is rare for two people to mutually decide that it is time to divorce. The last family members to absorb the reality of the dissolution are usually the children. This means that the parents (or at least one of the parents) have typically moved far beyond the children in cognitively and emotionally processing the divorce, and they are often thinking about new romantic relationships when the children have barely begun to realize that their family of origin has radically changed. Additionally, many children feel that family changes and transitions are not explained, which confuses them (Dunn, Davies, O'Connor, & Sturgess, 2001). "There is often a gulf between what an adult thinks has been communicated to a child and a child's need to process the information in repeated conversations through time" (p. 283). Therefore, when the children's parents enter quickly into new relationships, and they inadequately communicate about these changes, they may find that their children are resentful. This may play out as a refusal to talk to the parent's new romantic partner or it can lead to hostile communication.

The typically brief courtships prior to living together suggest that there is relatively little time for stepfamily members to discuss potentially important issues, to build relationships, and to prepare for stepfamily life (Ganong & Coleman, 1989). In contrast, couples in first marriages generally have the opportunity to work issues out slowly over time and establish some patterns of relating before having children. In stepfamilies these issues need to be dealt with quickly and sometimes without time for careful deliberation and negotiation. Stepfamilies also must deal with new members who likely will alter established household patterns and routines.

A stepfamily characteristic that may make communication awkward in newly formed units is the fact that some members (i.e., parent–child) have long-term relationships, whereas others (i.e., stepparent–stepchild, stepsiblings) are in new relationships. In addition, adults are usually highly motivated to communicate with their new partners, to self-disclose, and to learn as much as they can about their partner. Similar motivation to communicate and to develop a relationship may or may not be present among stepparents and stepchildren. Consequently, in newly formed stepfamilies there are relationships with well-established patterns of communication and familiar "dictionaries" of relational partners' nonverbal cues, communication skills, and habits, coexisting with relationships in which the communication dynamics are tentative, partner habits are unknown, and motivation to develop bonds may vary.

Clinicians have written extensively about how stepfamily members should communicate with each other when developing new relationships (e.g., Visher & Visher, 1996). Not surprisingly, clinicians also have focused more on desirable outcomes (e.g., clear roles, effective conflict management) than on the communicative processes that might lead to these outcomes. For example, Visher and Visher have suggested that it is important for the marital couple to be a particularly strong unit in thwarting possibly disruptive influences from stepchildren and nonresidential parents. However, we know little about how remarried couples can strengthen their bond and function as a united front in their relations with the children (see Cissna, Cox, & Bochner, 1990, for an exception).

Papernow (1993), also a clinician whose work draws on Gestalt and family systems theory, describes the importance of "middle ground" for stepfamilies. Middle ground is the area of shared values and experiences that makes being together easier. Shared middle ground brings stability to stepfamilies, but it is not easy to acquire. Stepfamilies who communicate early in the relationship formation process and share realistic assumptions about the tasks that must be accomplished develop middle ground much sooner than those who do not. As newly formed stepfamilies communicate about rules (e.g., mealtimes, curfews) and rituals (e.g., holiday celebrations, birthdays), they build middle ground that reduces the intensity of effort it takes to accomplish understanding and stability. However, as family transitions occur (e.g., babies born, children moving in and out of the household), stepfamilies who do not communicate with renewed vigor may get stuck, which decreases satisfaction and stifles positive and nurturing interaction. The six styles that Papernow proposes in her Stepfamily Cycle can take anywhere from 4 to 12 years to negotiate. Good communication skills, including empathic listening and support via validation of feelings and understanding of painful feelings, are essential to negotiating the stages of the cycle. Papernow noted particularly that those families who became "stuck" were those containing stepparents who had not talked with anyone who understood their experience.

To what extent have researchers shed light on communication processes in stepfamilies and on how stepfamily members interact with each other to achieve positive outcomes? Perhaps surprisingly, relatively little empirical work has specifically focused on communication as it unfolds in newly formed stepfamilies.

Bray and Kelly (1998) found that the first 2 years of stepfamily life were particularly stressful and tense, a phenomenon that they attributed to unrealistic expectations held by stepfamily members. The unrealistic expectations could be subsumed under one general core belief that the stepfamily can and should function like a nuclear family. Stemming from this core unrealistic belief were a series of more specific unrealistic expectations, including the belief that stepkin can expect to instantly care for and love one another and that the creation of the stepfamily will help heal wounds stemming from the previous family units (e.g., emotional pain related to divorce).

Although it is not clear how these unrealistic beliefs influence communication processes, it is clear that they have a negative impact on family functioning and typically lead to frustration. Our sense is that the belief that one's stepfamily should function like a nuclear family plays itself out in subtle ways that might be easy for an outsider to miss. For example, a stepmother may become angry with her stepchildren when they do not appreciate her attempts to nurture them; the spouses do not talk about how they are going to make their new stepfamily function well because they believe that they should follow the template for how a "regular family" functions; or a parent criticizes his or her spouse when the new spouse does not show the "right" amount of interest in the child's life. These sorts of communication efforts, or a lack of them, can take their toll because they fly in the face of the realities and experiences of most stepfamilies. Interestingly, Bray and Kelly (1998) reported that these unrealistic expectations were nearly universal across different types of stepfamilies.

Hetherington and Clingempeel (1992), in their multimethod, multi-informant longitudinal study of newly formed stepfather households with young adolescents, also found considerable turmoil in these early stages of stepfamily life, with little improvement over time in some areas (e.g., the quality of stepfather–stepchild relationships). As they described, ". . . the disruptions in family functioning were found to be pervasive and to extend beyond parent-child relationships to nonsupportive or even antagonistic sibling relationships" (p. 200). Hetherington and Clingempeel's work highlights the particularly difficult period in stepfamilies when at least one of the children in the home reaches adolescence. Presumably, the increasing self-focus, growing autonomy, and, for some, rebellious characteristics of adolescence exacerbate difficulties in stepfamily relationships and functioning. Stepfathers reported making attempts to bond with stepchildren but were rebuffed by the young adolescent stepchildren. Given the lack of available research, we can only speculate about some of the communications occurring in such stepfamilies (e.g., "Why don't you go out for football? I really loved football when I was in high school, and I think you would enjoy it too." "You can't tell me what to do. You're not my father!").

Papernow (1993), whose qualitative methods differed substantially from those described by Bray and Kelly (1998) and Hetherington and Clingempeel (1992), also described somewhat tumultuous early stages of becoming a stepfamily. Rather than labeling the predominant cognitions at this stage as unrealistic expectations, Papernow refers to them as "fantasies." In the fantasy stage (the first stage in stepfamily development), for example, stepparents may have positive fantasies of loving their stepchildren and being loved by them, of joining an already established family, and of filling the gap left by the absence of the nonresidential parent. However, later, looking back, these fantasies are often recalled with disappointment and frustration, partly because children have very different fantasies (e.g., the desire for their parents to reunite).

Ganong, Coleman, Fine, and Martin (1999) studied the process of how stepparents attempt to elicit liking (affinity) from their stepchildren and, once it is established, maintain it. Although the families in their study were, on average, not in the early years of stepfamily life (mean duration was approximately 5 years), stepfamily members reported on their perceptions of the early years of their stepfamily and, indeed, even before the remarriage. Ganong et al. identified three distinct types of stepparent affinity seeking: (a) those who made consistent and regular attempts to elicit liking from their stepchildren, both before and after the remarriage (*continuous affinity-seeking*); (b) those who initially made attempts to elicit affinity from their stepchildren, but who made relatively few attempts after the remarriage (*early affinity-seeking*); and (c) those who made relatively few attempts at any time to generate affinity from their stepchildren (*non-affinity-seeking*). Not surprisingly, the first group of stepparents had the most cohesive relationships with their stepchildren, an impression shared by both the stepparents and the stepchildren. These successful stepparents were far more likely than stepparents in the other groups to engage in activities in which the child wanted to participate, as opposed to activities of interest to the stepparent only. Moreover, dyadic interactions were more effective at developing affinity than activities that involved the whole household. Although we do not know all of the communication strategies used by this group of successful stepparents, these findings suggest that this group of stepparents is more likely to communicate empathy and an understanding of the child's needs and interests than are the other stepparents. Certainly, the stepparents that continued to seek affinity either asked their stepchildren what they liked to do or they observed their stepchildren carefully enough to know what activities to suggest. These stepparents attempted to communicate warmth and an interest in becoming friends with their stepchildren. Non-affinity-seeking stepparents either communicated little with stepchildren or they conveyed little of the interest and affection normally associated with making friends. The early affinity seekers discontinued such efforts after they moved in with their stepchildren, assuming the role of parent, which they apparently saw as incompatible with getting their stepchildren to like them.

Coleman, Fine, Ganong, Downs, and Pauk (2001) examined communication issues pertaining to conflict in their intensive study of stepfamilies. Based on interviews with stepparents, parents, and children in these families, they found four distinct types of conflict, all of which revolved around boundary issues: (a) disagreements over resources; (b) loyalty conflicts; (c) individuals holding a "guard and protect" ideology, particularly with respect to their biological kin; and (d) conflict with extended family members. In addition, they identified several conflict management strategies, some of which were more successful than others. Although Cissna et al. (1990) identified two primary approaches (i.e., showing a united front to the children and establishing the stepparent's authority) that couples used to manage conflicts in their newly formed stepfamilies, they did not identify the specific communication mechanisms that were used to address conflict when it occurred. Coleman et al., not surprisingly, found that in stepfather family households, mothers and stepfathers engaged in more deliberate efforts to resolve conflicts than did stepchildren. The most common communication strategies used were compromising on rules and discipline, presenting a united parental front with respect to rules/discipline, speaking directly with the person one is having conflict with, reframing the problem as less serious or making a joke of it, or avoiding conflict through withdrawal. In fewer cases, professional counseling, having family meetings, and spending leisure time together were used as strategies to manage conflict.

Another recent study examined the development of closeness not just in the stepparent–stepchild dyad but also in stepfamilies as a whole. Baxter, Braithwaite, and Nicholson (1999) explored some of the communication processes that occurred in the early years of stepfamily life and, based on stepparents' and stepchildren's retrospective descriptions of family "turning points" and levels of "feeling like a family" over a 4-year period, identified five trajectories for stepfamilies. They found considerable diversity in these pathways, with some families starting at low levels of feeling like a family and rapidly increasing their sense of cohesiveness (*accelerated*), some starting at low levels and only gradually increasing (*prolonged*), some beginning at high levels and declining to near zero levels by the end of the period (*declining*), some starting and ending at low levels (*stagnating*), and some experiencing both rapid increases and decreases in levels of feeling like a family (*high-amplitude turbulent*).

In a follow-up to Baxter et al. (1999), Braithwaite, Olson, Golish, Soukup, and Turman (2001) explored some of the communication processes that occurred in the early years of stepfamily life. Stepfamily members in the accelerated trajectory in the first year attempted to create their stepfamilies as nuclear families. They created new or modified rituals and routines that helped them identify themselves as a family, and although some stepparents reported feeling unsure about their roles, they were generally able to work through these challenges and reported that their families became more cohesive. Members of prolonged stepfamilies reported initial discomfort and awkwardness, and often wanted to return to the routines of their former families. These family members did not think of their stepfamilies as nuclear families and accepted that they needed to slowly get to know each other. The amount of communication increased as family members gained familiarity with each other. The small number of declining trajectory stepfamilies began with high, perhaps unrealistic, expectations that were not met because of loyalty conflicts and boundary issues. Conflicts became severe, boundaries became more rigid, and subgroup alliances led to some family members having little contact and interaction with each other. Stagnating trajectory stepfamilies initially felt thrown together, and many family members felt significant tensions and conflicts relating to boundary and loyalty issues. These conflicts and problems continued with little improvement. Finally, in the high-amplitude turbulent stepfamilies, many members initially had unrealistic expectations that they could immediately foster a well-functioning family. These unrealistic expectations led to frustration when it became clear that instant intimacy could not be achieved. Nevertheless, many family members felt positively about their new stepfamily relationships. By the second year, however, there was greater turmoil and instability, leading to more conflict. Braithwaite et al. noted that a key pattern in these families was that the adult couple did not exhibit a united front for children; instead, they competed for the children's approval. The results of these two studies highlight the diversity in how stepfamilies develop over time; however, they did not shed light on the specific communicative processes that characterized the stepfamilies developing in these different ways.

COMMUNICATION IN ESTABLISHED STEPFAMILIES

There are fewer studies of established stepfamilies than there are of stepfamilies in the early, formative phases. In part this is because most stepfamily research has been cross sectional rather than longitudinal. Occasionally, researchers conducting cross-sectional studies have examined how long the stepfamily has been together or how many years the steprelationship has existed, but this sheds little light on communication behaviors in established stepfamilies.

However, a number of relatively recent longitudinal studies have revealed some stepfamily dynamics beyond the early years (e.g., Booth & Amato, 2001; Bray & Kelly, 1998; Dunn et al., 2001; Hetherington & Clingempeel; 1992; Kurdek, 1999). National panel studies (e.g., National Study of Families and Households (NSFH), National Child Development Study (NCDS), New York Longitudinal Study (NYLS)) also have allowed researchers to look at stepfamily changes over time, so the body of research on established stepfamilies is growing.

What Is an Established Stepfamily?

When does a stepfamily cease to be in the early stages of development? When does it become, as clinicians say, *integrated*? Although clinicians have suggested that stepfamily integration occurs after 2, 3, or 5 or more years (e.g., Mills, 1984; Visher & Visher, 1996), few researchers have addressed this issue. Bray and Papernow, two scholars who have approached stepfamilies developmentally, have come the closest to an answer. Bray asserted that the stepfather households he studied "did not start to think and act like a family until the end of the second or third year" (Bray & Kelly, 1998, p. 11). At that point, stepfamilies consolidate gains in family identity and "unify further" (p. 181). In Papernow's (1993) Gestalt Stepfamily Life Cycle, maturity is defined less by years than by actions. Stepfamilies move past the early stages only after family members abandon fantasies, sort out their feelings and communicate them to other family members, and replace unrealistic expectations with more matter-of-fact viewpoints. Papernow contends that some stepfamilies never achieve these tasks and therefore never reach maturity, whereas others move quickly into what she calls *mobilization* and *action* phases, periods in which stepfamily members negotiate differences and begin the processes of establishing rituals, customs, and codes of conduct for family members. Only after successfully accomplishing these tasks can stepfamily members communicate intimately and feel a sense of cohesion. The conflict-ridden mobilization period could be considered the beginning of the established stepfamily.

Patterns of Communication

Stepfamilies are complex structurally. Some stepfamily households contain children from prior unions of one or both partners most of the time, in some households children from previous unions of one or both partners are occasional residents, some have half-sibling relationships while others have siblings or stepsiblings only, and still others have step-, half- and full siblings. Stepfamilies do not form a monolithic group interpersonally, so discussing communication processes in established stepfamilies is complicated.

One solution to this complexity by researchers has been to create typologies of stepfamilies based on how family members think about their families and how family members interact (e.g., Bray & Kelly, 1998; Burgoyne & Clark, 1984; Gross, 1986). These typologies provide a framework for examining communication in established stepfamilies.

Brady Bunch Stepfamilies. Nearly every typology identifies a sizable proportion of stepfamilies that attempt to reconstitute themselves as first-marriage families (Berger, 1995; Braithwaite et al., 2001; Bray & Kelly, 1998; Burgoyne & Clark, 1984; Erera-Weatherly, 1996). Members of these stepfamilies think of themselves and interact as if they were a first-marriage family. Prior family members, such as the nonresidential or deceased parents of children, are not mentioned, stepparents relate to stepchildren as if they were their parents, and role performances and relationships are expected to be identical to first-marriage families. Think of the Brady Bunch, and you understand how these families interact and communicate. For years, clinicians have described these families as unrealistic, unprepared, and in denial (e.g., Visher & Visher, 1996).

There is some research to support this clinical view. In several studies, some stepfamilies that attempted to recreate nuclear families were not able to do so successfully (Baxter et al., 1999; Bray & Kelly, 1998; Burgoyne & Clark, 1984). Instead, feelings of betrayal and disloyalty to the absent parent among children, such as discomfort at having to pretend feelings that did not exist, anger at not being able to talk about pasts that existed prior to the stepfamily, and ineffective problem solving when situational demands for negotiation and communication did not fit with the Brady Bunch identity, led to dissatisfaction. Some researchers have argued that structural complexity prevents stepfamilies from adapting in the same manner as first-marriage families (Banker & Gaertner, 1996).

However, despite the frequent failures at trying to recreate a nuclear family, other step-families have made this work (Berger, 1995; Braithwaite et al., 2001; Burgoyne & Clark, 1984; Erera-Weatherly, 1996). Researchers have not identified why some stepfamilies are successful at establishing this model of stepfamily life, although it may be assumed that they achieve a fairly high level of agreement among adults and children to act as if they were a nuclear family. This may be more easily achieved when children are young when the stepfamily begins, when nonresidential parents are perceived to have abandoned the children, or when there has been violence or emotional abuse in prior families. The factors that contribute to some stepfamilies being successful at recreating a nuclear family model clearly need to be addressed in future research.

It may be that all well-functioning stepfamilies, over time, function more and more like first-marriage families do (Menaghan, Kowaleski-Jones, & Mott, 1997; O'Connor, Hawkins, Dunn, Thorpe, & Golding, 1998; Waldren, Bell, Peek, & Sorell, 1990). For example, stepfather families with adolescent stepsons problem-solve more like nuclear families over time (Vuchinich, Vuchinich, & Wood, 1993) with stepparents and parents often shar-ing the discipline of children (Giles-Sims, 1987). It seems to us that a gradual movement toward some similarity to first-marriage families is not surprising—after all, households with children face similar household maintenance tasks—doing chores, getting groceries, giving children rides to activities, teaching children manners, seeing that schoolwork is completed, earning money, and making decisions that affect individual family members and the entire unit. Although there are many ways to accomplish these household tasks, it would not be unexpected for many stepfamily members to gradually employ what they know from their first-marriage family experiences. Again, the issue of how stepfamilies change in everyday interactions and communications has not been studied adequately.

A final reason that acting like a first-marriage family may be workable for some step-families is because outsiders have more favorable impressions of stepfamilies who present themselves to others as first-marriage families (Ganong, Coleman, & Kennedy, 1990). This impression management strategy could reduce stress for stepfamily members (Dainton, 1993), in part because an implicit assumption held by many people, both within step-families and outside, is that they should be similar to first-marriage families (Coleman & Ganong, 1990). Matching the expectations of others may be easier for stepfamilies than creating new ways to function. It should be noted that about 35% of all adopted children in the United States who live with two parents were adopted by a stepparent (Fields, 2001). These families may be extreme examples of impression management because stepparent adoption legally changes the stepfamily into a nuclear family. The success of this tactic is difficult to determine because the families are no longer identified as stepfamilies, so they are invisible to researchers.

Stepfamilies with Detached Stepparents/Engaged Parents. In some established stepfamily households, the stepparent, usually a stepfather, is less involved with the stepchildren than is the parent (Berger, 1995; Bray & Kelly, 1998; Erera-Weatherly,

1996). Some stepfathers show little affect toward stepchildren, are less involved with children, engage in relatively little supervision and control of stepchildren, and may even be disengaged from the stepchild (Cooksey & Fondell, 1996; Erera-Weatherly, 1996; Fine, Voydanoff, & Donnelly, 1993; Hetherington & Clingempeel, 1992; Kurdek & Fine, 1995). In some cases, stepfathers disengage from their stepchildren at the direction of the children's mothers (Weaver & Coleman, in review). Because mothers may be extremely close to their children as a result of experiences when they were in single-mother house-holds, they may consequently be unwilling to let their new spouses get too close to their children. For example, in a recent study mothers in stepfamilies used analogies such as "I felt like a grizzly bear protecting my cubs" and " I had to circle the wagons to protect my daughter" to describe their responses to situations in which they thought the stepfathers were unfair (Weaver & Coleman, in review). One mother described wanting to remain a single parent yet have a partner for herself.

In these families, communication between the adults focuses on couple issues; parenting is left mostly to the mother, and she alone makes discipline and child-rearing decisions. Interaction between stepfathers and stepchildren may be minimal and perfunctory, whereas communication between mothers and children is frequent, intense, and important to both generations. In many ways, the stepfather is added to the mother–child unit without blending or integrating into that unit. Stepfathers are detached-as-stepparents-but-involved-as-partners, sometimes because they choose to be (Berger, 1995), sometimes because they have withdrawn after attempts to become closer were rebuffed by stepchildren (Hetherington & Clingempeel, 1992), and sometimes because parents have served as gatekeepers because they want to be the primary influences on their children (Bray & Kelly, 1998). It is likely that these different pathways lead to different family communication patterns and to diverse outcomes for children and adults; this awaits further investigation.

Couple-Focused Stepfamilies.   Some stepfamilies are formed primarily to fulfill the adults' needs for a partner. Obviously the desire for a satisfying romantic relationship is present to some degree in all stepfamilies, but some are distinguished by a strong emphasis placed on the adult union (Bray & Kelly, 1998; Burgoyne & Clark, 1984). Usually the stepparent is relatively disengaged from parent-related activities on purpose, rather than in reaction to children's behavior toward them, and both of the adults focus energies on enhancing their relationship. Although the research literature is not clear on why some stepfamilies are so focused on the romantic relationship, it seems to us that older stepfamilies (those in which the children were grown or nearly grown at the start of the stepfamily) would choose this pattern of interacting more often than stepfamilies with young children (Vinick, 1998). Also, nonresidential stepfamily households, those in which the children reside elsewhere all or most of the time, would seem to be more likely to be couple focused, particularly if the couples do not reproduce.

Progressive Stepfamilies.   For a variety of reasons, most of which have not been investigated, some established stepfamilies develop communication and interaction patterns that are creatively adaptive to the structural and interpersonal complexity characteristic of many stepfamilies (Braithwaite et al., 2001; Bray & Kelly, 1998). Weaver and Coleman (in review) found that mothers in stepfamilies who were most satisfied were those who interpreted stepfathers to stepchildren and vice versa, a communication technique that seemed to resolve issues created by their lack of mutual history. For lack of a better label, we will refer to them as progressive stepfamilies, a term used by Burgoyne and Clark (1984) in their in-depth study of British stepfamilies. In their study, progressive stepfamilies had resolved any conflicts with former spouses and they approached stepfamily living with a sense of "the positive value of differentness" (p. 193). "Their imagery of family life is pluralistic; they are aware of a diversity of patterns in family and domestic life and depict themselves as making choices . . ." (p. 193). These stepfamily members were good communicators and problem solvers, both within the household and with other households with which they may share children.

It is this model of stepfamily functioning that Papernow (1993), a family therapist, describes in her study of stepfamily development. In her view, established stepfamilies are those that deal with the realities of stepfamily life, including the feelings and relationships that may not seem normal or familylike, and go on to create ways of interacting that reflect new approaches to being a family. Using family systems models, clinicians have long advocated for the progressive mode of stepfamily life, one that has flexible external boundaries, that shares decision making for children across households, that defines nonparental relationships for stepparents (e.g., such as friend), and that communicates about issues that first-marriage families take for granted, such as how birthdays will be observed and meal-time deportment (Visher & Visher, 1996). Progressive stepfamilies accept that parent–child relationships may be closer than those in first-marriage families (e.g., Anderson & White, 1986), that stepparent–stepchild relationships are less close than those in parent–child bonds (e.g., Kurdek & Fine, 1995), and that stepfamily members may see their families as composed of two combined groups (Banker & Gaertner, 1996). Such differences from first-marriage families are not seen as deficits or as goals to be achieved by progressive stepfamilies.

Although some researchers have reported that a substantial proportion of stepfamilies fit this mode, little is known about how and why they become established as functional stepfamilies. It is likely that some of the reasons that Erera-Weatherly found for stepparents' and biological parents' choice of stepparent roles apply (Erera-Weatherly, 1996). That is, established stepfamilies develop communication patterns and family identities based on stepparents' views of appropriate roles for themselves, stepchildren's acceptance of the stepparent, whether the stepparents think that stepchildren are well behaved, ages of the stepchildren, nonresidential parents' involvement and the quality of their relationships with children, and how residential parents mediate the relationships between stepparents and stepchildren.

COMMUNICATION IN LATER-LIFE STEPFAMILIES

The research on older stepfamilies, those that have survived until the stepchildren have become adults or those that form when the remarried adults are well past the age of reproduction, is very limited. As of yet, there are no systematic, longitudinal studies of stepfamilies that take us much past initial family formation. Stepfamily samples in cross-sectional studies may contain such families, but the length of time in the stepfamily is typically a control variable rather than one of the primary variables of interest. Often, as is the case with much of the research reported here, samples of older remarried couples include those who married when stepchildren were still in the home as well as those who remarried long after the children were grown and gone. It is doubtful that these two groups have a great deal in common, but this is speculation and not based on empirical evidence.

To offset the lack of longitudinal work on stepfamilies, Burchardt (1989) examined life-story interviews of elderly British people who grew up in stepfamilies. Although the study was not designed to elucidate family relationships, some questions were asked about family relationships. Keeping in mind that these were elderly people's retrospective views of their stepfamily experiences as children, the information provides some insight into the changes in stepfamily perceptions over time. Burchardt reported "childhood experiences in stepfamilies had remained vivid, but often time had softened their judgments, adding new dimensions of understanding, not only of parents but also of stepparents; and sometimes also forgiveness" (p. 314). Many were aware that their temperament had played an important part in their communication with their stepparents as well as in their recollections of stepfamily life. It is also noteworthy that mutual children (children born to the remarried couple) nearly all had positive recollections of their family compared to only about half of those with stepparents. The most successful stepfamilies, according to these recollections, were those in which the stepparents brought either emotional or material resources that the family would not have otherwise had. Additionally, the families that functioned best were those with strong parental bonds and firmly established parental authority, either by the remarried couple or by the parent.

In one of the few U.S. studies of long-term stepfamily relationships, Vinick and Lanspery (2000) examined older (ages ranged from 60s to 80s) stepmothers' perceptions of their relationships with their adult stepchildren whom they had first met when the children were ages 3 to 37. Similar to the British study, these were retrospective accounts obtained primarily from interviews. Nearly all of the women viewed the stepmother–stepdaughter relationship as "stable positive" or as "positive movement" with some residue of previous issues remaining. In the broader study of couples who had been remarried an average of 20 years, Vinick (1998) found that most stepfathers and stepmothers acknowledged one or more current or past problematic issues. The ex-spouse was often targeted as the cause of these problems, although both stepmothers and stepfathers expressed feeling unaccepted by one or more stepchildren, as the most prevalent problem, past and present. Women were more likely than men to see improvement in stepfamily relationships over time, and they were also more likely than men to attempt to repair damaged stepfamily relations. Vinick referred to stepmothers as *carpenters* because of their efforts to reestablish communication and rebuild their husband's relationships with his children. Men appeared to give up if their initial efforts to develop a relationship with their children or stepchildren did not work, a phenomenon, in the case of stepfathers, also found by Hetherington and Clingempeel (1992).

Additionally, men seemed to sing the old song, "If you can't be with the one you love, love the one you're with." The men in the study willingly provided services and support for their stepchildren and did not resent the children's biological fathers for not supporting them, yet few of them had close relationships or communicated often with their own biological children who typically lived elsewhere. In the least successful stepfamilies, mothers continued their heavy emotional investment in their children to the detriment of investments in their marital relationships. These long-term stepfamilies worked best when the partners had similar perceptions of the wife's children and presented a united front, a conclusion that is consistent with findings from the Burchardt (1989) study.

There is a growing but still small body of literature on remarriage among older adults, and communication is a variable in some of these studies. For example, Bograd and Spilka (1996) compared people who had remarried at midlife (ages 30–45) and late life (ages 60–75), and although they found that marital satisfaction was greatest in late-life remarriages, primarily due to the high level of male satisfaction in that group, there was a positive association between marital satisfaction and self-disclosure in both groups. However, rather than the amount of self-disclosure, it was the intentionality, positiveness, depth, and honesty of disclosure that was communicated that correlated with marital satisfaction. Pasley and Ihinger-Tallman (1990) also found communication in the form of conflict-resolution strategies to be important among the relatively recently remarried men and women aged 55 and older that they surveyed. The use of neutral conflict-resolution strategies such as silence, ignoring or dropping an issue, and few disruptive interchanges (high consensus on issues) were likely to result in greater family satisfaction.

Using both waves of NSFH data, White and Wang (2001) examined the effect of parents' remarriage on their adult child's contact and global relationship quality and found it depended on the relationship between the adult child and the new stepparent. When the relationship was poor, more often true for stepmothers than for stepfathers, parental remarriage was associated with reduced contact and relationship quality. However, the low quality of relationships with new stepmothers was largely explained by the lower quality of the relationships adult children had with their fathers prior to the remarriage. The end result appeared to be that remarriage of older parents likely strengthens an already strong parent–adult child relationship and weakens an already weak one, so it is the communication patterns prior to older adult remarriage that are the key to the current parent/child relationship.

The study of communication in older stepfamilies, whether they are long-term stepfamilies or stepfamilies formed by older adults marrying, is exceptionally complex. Following stepfamilies over a period of decades is expensive and has not been accomplished to date. There is some indication that communication patterns begin to resemble first-married families over time, but no studies have yet focused on communication patterns over time. When older adults remarry, issues of inheritance may create intergenerational communication problems, although there is little systematic study of these later-life remarriage issues.

FUTURE RESEARCH DIRECTIONS

In general, most of what we know about communication in stepfamilies comes from studies that were not specifically designed to investigate communication patterns. Conversational analyses of stepfamilies have not yet been attempted. Observational studies designed for the express purpose of examining communication patterns in stepfamilies have yet to be conducted as well. Greater attention to communication patterns in longitudinal studies could provide insight, and grounded theory studies, case studies, and other qualitative methods could provide helpful guides to better understand the ways in which various styles of communication promote or detract from the effectiveness of stepfamily functioning.

In particular, we believe that longitudinal studies that focus on communication patterns across the life course are needed. Studies that begin with marriage, then follow families through divorce and into remarriage would give us invaluable information on the effects of communication on the well-being of family members during transitions as well as during times of stability. We need to investigate how experiences and interactions of stepfamily members change over time and how these changes affect communication within and outside the stepfamily. Such studies would be incredibly expensive, but there is virtually no other way to generate the kind of data that are necessary to draw important conclusions about the effects of communication on the interpersonal relationships and well-being of stepfamily members.

We know far too little about how gender relations in stepfamilies affect stepfamily communication patterns. If women in remarriage report having more power in their family than they did in their first-marriage family (Pyke, 1994), is this power then reflected in communication patterns that differ from those in first-married families? We need to know as well if communication patterns differ between stepfather households, stepmother households, and those households that contain children belonging to both adults. Further, does the addition of a mutual child change communication patterns in stepfamily households?

It would also be important to know more about the communication patterns between or across households (i.e., what Ahrons & Wallisch, 1987, refer to as the binuclear family). For example, if communication is frequent and positive, frequent and negative, or nearly nonexistent between the two households, then how are the children affected? In addition to studies between households, we need studies examining the bidirectional effects of communication within households (i.e., how stepchildren's communication affects their (step)parents and how their (step)parents' communication affects them). Studies of bidirectional communication effects between children and nonresidential parents and nonresidential stepparents and vice versa could yield important information on relationships that are often considered to be problematic.

CONCLUSIONS

Despite the obvious importance of communication processes in stepfamilies, a theme throughout this chapter is that unfortunately, we have very little empirically generated information on these processes. The study of communication in stepfamilies is, thus, fertile ground for the efforts of the many researchers who are interested in interpersonal relationships. Further, our sense is that this work will be most effectively accomplished by interdisciplinary teams of researchers, involving scholars not only from communication studies but also from family studies, psychology, sociology, and other related disciplines. Not only can such research shed light on important processes occurring in stepfamilies, but also the unique characteristics of stepfamilies may yield new insights into our understanding of communication patterns and dynamics in families.

REFERENCES

Allan, G., Hawker, S., & Crow, G. (2001). Family diversity and change in Britain and Western Europe. *Journal of Family Issues, 22*, 819–837.

Ahrons, C. R., & Wallisch, L. (1987). Parenting in the binuclear family: Relationships between biological and sepparents. In K. Pasley & M. Ihinger-Tallman (Eds.), *Remarriage and stepparenting: Current research and theory* (pp. 225–256). New York: Guilford Press.

Anderson, J., & White, G. (1986). An empirical investigation of interactive and relationship patterns in functional and dysfunctional nuclear families and stepfamilies. *Family Process, 25*, 407–422.

Banker, B. S., & Gaertner, S. L. (1998). Achieving stepfamily harmony: An intergroup-relations approach. *Journal of Family Psychology, 12*, 310–325.

Baxter, L., Braithwaite, D. O., & Nicholson, J. (1999). Turning points in the development of blended family relationships. *Journal of Social and Personal Relationships, 16*, 291–313.

Berger, R. (1995). Three types of stepfamilies. *Journal of Divorce and Remarriage, 24*(1/2), 35–50.

Bograd, R., & Spilka, B. (1996). Self-disclosure and marital satisfaction in mid-life and late-life remarriages. *International Journal of Aging and Human Development, 42*(3), 161–172.

Booth, A., & Amato, P. R. (2001). Parental predivorce relations and offspring postdivorce well-being. *Journal of Marriage and Family, 63*, 197–212.

Braithwaite, D. O., Olson, L. N., Golish, T. D., Soukup, C., & Turman, P. (2001). "Becoming a family": Developmental processes represented in blended family discourse. *Journal of Applied Communication Research, 29*, 221–247.

Bray, J. H., & Kelly, J. (1998). *Stepfamilies: Love, marriage, and parenting in the first decade.* New York: Broadway.

Bumpass, L. L., Raley, R.K., & Sweet, J. (1995). The changing character of stepfamilies: Implications of cohabitation and nonmarital childbearing. *Demography, 32*, 425–436.

Burchardt, N. (1989). Structure and relationships in stepfamilies in early twentieth-century Britain. *Continuity and Change, 4*(2), 293–322.

Burgoyne, J., & Clark, D. (1984). *Making a go of it: A study of stepfamilies in Sheffield.* Boston: Routledge & Kegan.

Cherlin, A. (1978). Remarriage as an incomplete institution. *American Journal of Sociology, 84*, 634–650.

Cherlin, A. (1992). *Marriage, divorce, and remarriage: Social Trends in the United States.* Cambridge, MA: Harvard University Press.

Cissna, K. N., Cox, D. E., & Bochner, A. P. (1990). The dialectic of marital and parental relationships within the blended family. *Communication Monographs, 37*,44–61.

Coleman, M. A., Fine, M. A., Ganong, L. G., Downs, K. M., & Pauk, N. (2001). When you're not the Brady Bunch: Identifying perceived conflicts and resolution strategies in stepfamilies. *Personal Relationships, 8*, 55–73.

Coleman, M., & Ganong, L. (1990). Remarriage and stepfamily research in the '80s: New interest in an old family form. *Journal of Marriage and the Family, 52*, 925–940.

Cooksey, E. C., & Fondell, M. M. (1996). Spending time with his kids: Effects of family structure on fathers' and children's lives. *Journal of Marriage and the Family, 58*, 693–707.

Cornman, J. M., & Kingson, E. R. (1996). Trends, issues, perspectives, and values for the aging of the baby boom cohorts. *The Gerontologist, 36*, 15–26.

Dainton, M. (1993). The myths and misconceptions of the stepmother identity: Descriptions and prescriptions for identity management. *Family Relations, 42*, 93–98.

Dunn, J., Davies, L. C., O'Connor, T. G., & Sturgess, W. (2001). Family lives and friendships: The perspectives of children in step-, single-parent, and nonstep families. *Journal of Family Psychology, 15*, 272–287.

Erera-Weatherly, P. I. (1996). On becoming a stepparent: Factors associated with the adoption of alternative stepparenting styles. *Journal of Divorce and Remarriage, 25*(3/4), 155–174.

Fields, J. (April, 2001). *Living arrangements of children: Household economic studies* (Current Population Reports, P70–74). Washington, DC: U.S. Census Bureau.

Fine, M. A., Voydanoff, P., & Donnelly, B. W. (1993). Relations between parental control and warmth and child well-being in stepfamilies. *Journal of Family Psychology, 7*, 222–232.

Ganong, L., & Coleman, M. (1989). Preparing for remarriage: Anticipating the issues, seeking solutions. *Family Relations, 38*, 28–33.

Ganong, L. H., Coleman, M., Fine, M. A., & Martin, P. (1999). Stepparents' affinity-seeking and affinity-maintaining strategies in stepfamilies. *Journal of Family Issues, 20*, 299–327.

Ganong, L., Coleman, M., Fine, M. A., & McDaniel, A. K. (1998). Issues considered in stepparent adoption. *Family Relations, 47*, 63–72.

Ganong, L., Coleman, M., & Kennedy, G. (1990). The effects of using alternate labels in denoting stepparent or stepfamily status. *Journal of Social Behavior and Personality, 5*, 453–463.

Giles-Sims, J. (1987). Parental role sharing between remarrieds and ex-spouses. *Youth and Society, 19*, 134–150.

Gross, P. E. (1986). Defining post-divorce remarriage families: A typology based on the subjective perceptions of children. *Journal of Divorce, 10*(1–2), 205–217.

Henry, C. S., & Lovelace, S. G. (1995). Family resources and adolescent family life satisfaction in remarried family households. *Journal of Family Issues, 16*, 765–786.

Hetherington, E. M., & Clingempeel, W. G. (1992). Coping with marital transitions: A family systems perspective. *Monographs of the Society for Research in Child Development, 57* (2–3, Serial No. 227).

Kurdek, L. (1999). The nature and predictors of the trajectory of change of marital quality for husbands and wives over the first 10 years of marriage. *Developmental Psychology, 35*, 1283–1296.

Kurdek, L. A., & Fine, M. A. (1995). Mothers, fathers, stepfathers, and siblings as providers of supervision, acceptance, and autonomy to young adolescents. *Journal of Family Psychology, 9*, 95–99.

Menaghan, E. G., Kowaleski-Jones, L., & Mott, F. L. (1997). The intergenerational costs of parental social stressors: Academic and social difficulties in early adolescence for children of young mothers. *Journal of Health and Social Behavior, 38,* 72–86.

Mills, D. (1984). A model for stepfamily development. *Family Relations, 33,* 365–372.

Montgomery, M. J., Anderson, E. R., Hetherington, E. M., & Clingempeel, W. G. (1992). Patterns of courtship for remarriage: Implications for child adjustment and parent-child relationships. *Journal of Marriage and the Family, 54,* 686–698.

O'Connor, T. G., Dunn, J., Jenkins, J. M., Pickering, K., & Rasbash, J. (2001). Family settings and children's adjustment: Differential adjustment within and across families. *British Journal of Psychiatry, 179,* 110–115.

O'Connor, T. G., Hawkins, N., Dunn, J., Thorpe, K., & Golding, J. (1998). Family type and depression in pregnancy: Factors mediating risk in a community sample. *Journal of Marriage and the Family, 60,* 757–770.

Papernow, P. L. (1993). *Becoming a stepfamily: Patterns of development in remarried families.* San Francisco: Jossey-Bass.

Pasley, K., & Ihinger-Tallman, M. (1990). Remarriage in later adulthood: Correlates of perceptions of family adjustment. *Family Perspective, 24*(3), 263–274.

Pyke, K. (1994). Women's employment as a gift or burden? Marital power across marriage, divorce, and remarriage. *Gender and Society, 8*(1), 73–91.

Rodgers, R. H. (1986). Postmarital family reorganization: A propositional theory. In S. Duck & D. Perlman (eds.), *Close relationships: Development, dynamics, and deterioration* (pp. 239–268). Beverly Hills, CA: Sage.

Skopin, A. R., Newman, B. M., & McKenry, P. (1993). Influences on the quality of stepfather-adolescent relationships: View of both family members. *Journal of Divorce and Remarriage, 19,* 181–196.

Szinovacz, M. E. (1998). Grandparents today: A demographic profile. *The Gerontologist, 38,* 37–52.

United States Bureau of the Census. (1995). *Statistical Abstract of the United States: 1995* (115th ed.). Washington, DC: Author.

Vinick, B. H. (1998). *Older stepfamilies: Views from the parental generation.* Report to the AARP—Andrus Foundation.

Vinick, B. H., & Lanspery, S. (2000). Cinderalla's sequel: Stepmothers' long-term relationships with adult stepchildren. *Journal of Comparative Family Studies, 31*(3), 377–384.

Visher, E. B., & Visher, J. S. (1996). *Therapy with stepfamilies.* New York: Brunner/Mazel.

Vuchinich, S., Vuchinich, R., & Wood, B. (1993). The interparental relationship and family problem-solving with preadolescent males. *Child Development, 64,* 1389–1400.

Waldren, T., Bell, N. J., Peek, C. W., & Sorell, G. (1990). Cohesion and adaptability in post-divorce remarried and first-married families: Relationships with family stress and coping styles. *Journal of Divorce and Remarriage, 14*(1), 13–28.

Weaver, S.E., & Coleman, M. (in review). *A grounded theory study of women's role construction in stepfamilies.* Manuscript in review.

White, L., & Wang, H. (2001, October). *Acquiring stepparents in adulthood: Effect on child's relationships with parents.* Paper presented at the annual conference of the National Council on Family Relations, Rochester, NY.

Wilson, B., & Clarke, S. (1992). Remarriages: A demographic profile. *Journal of Family Issues, 13*, 123–141.

Wu, Z. (1994). Remarriage in Canada: A social exchange perspective. *Journal of Divorce and Remarriage, 21*, 191–224.

11

The Family Lives of Lesbians and Gay Men

Letitia Anne Peplau and Kristin P. Beals

University of California, Los Angeles

Most lesbians and gay men today grew up in a family headed by heterosexual parents. As adults, lesbians and gay men often establish committed partner relationships. Increasing numbers of lesbians and gay men are becoming parents and raising children. Research about these different aspects of the family lives of lesbians and gay men—as children, as romantic partners, and as parents—is relatively new. Of the 1,521 articles published in the *Journal of Marriage and the Family* and the *Journal of Social and Personal Relationships* from 1980 to 1993, only 5 focused on some aspect of sexual orientation (Allen & Demo, 1995). In the past decade, however, there has been a noticeable increase in research on gays and lesbians in families.

This chapter reviews empirical research about the family lives of lesbians and gay men. We focus on four main topics: societal attitudes about gay men and lesbians, the relations of lesbians and gay men to their family of origin, the nature of gay and lesbian couples, and the experiences of homosexual parents and their children. Throughout, we highlight areas where additional research is needed.

THE SOCIAL CLIMATE: PUBLIC ATTITUDES ABOUT LESBIANS, GAY MEN, AND FAMILIES

The family relationships of lesbians and gay men cannot be understood without recognizing the social climate of sexual prejudice in U.S. society (Herek, 2000). Representative national surveys conducted during the past 30 years show that Americans' attitudes about homosexuality have become more tolerant (see review by Loftus, 2001). Lesbians and gay men are aware of this change. In an important new survey, the Kaiser Foundation (2001) conducted telephone interviews with 405 randomly selected, self-identified gay, lesbian, and bisexual adults from 15 major U.S. cities. In this survey, 76% of respondents said they believed there was more acceptance of homosexuals today than in the past. Nonetheless, 74% also reported that they had experienced some form of prejudice or discrimination because of their sexual orientation, and 32% had been the target of violence against themselves or their property.

Today, a strong majority of Americans (often 75% or more) approves of laws to protect the civil rights of lesbians and gay men in such areas as employment and housing (Loftus, 2001). However, public attitudes about morality and family issues are more strongly divided. In a recent national survey (Kaiser Foundation, 2001), about half of Americans agreed that "homosexual behavior is morally wrong," opposed legally sanctioned gay and lesbian marriages, and indicated that "allowing gays and lesbians to legally marry would undermine the traditional American family." There was somewhat less opposition (42%) to legally sanctioned gay and lesbian unions other than marriage. Approximately half of those surveyed (56%) agreed that "gay and lesbian couples can be as good parents as heterosexual couples," and 46% approved of permitting gay and lesbian couples to legally adopt children. In short, the general public is fairly evenly divided in their views about the morality of homosexuality and the wisdom of same-sex unions and gay adoptions.

RELATIONSHIPS OF GAY MEN AND LESBIANS WITH THEIR PARENTS AND FAMILY OF ORIGIN

Lesbians and gay men are usually raised by heterosexual parents who assume that their children will be heterosexual. The revelation that a child is gay or lesbian often precipitates a family crisis. Perhaps because of the turmoil associated with this event, available research has focused on the individual's initial disclosure of his or her sexual orientation ("coming out") and the parents' reactions to this disclosure.

Disclosing a Minority Sexual Orientation

Many lesbians and gay men anguish about the decision whether or not to disclose their sexual identity to family members. Some individuals who anticipate a negative response and want to preserve family bonds never reveal their sexual orientation. In other cases, family members learn about the person's sexual orientation indirectly, perhaps by overhearing a conversation, or they may suspect a person is gay or lesbian based on the person's choice of friends, hairstyle, or dress. In most cases, however, gays and lesbians intentionally share this important information with at least some family members.

Recent surveys provide information about disclosure to parents and relatives (e.g., Morris, Waldo, & Rothblum, 2001). In a study of nearly 2,300 gay, lesbian, and bisexual adults from northern California (Herek, Gillis, & Cogan, 1996), 79% of respondents said that their mother knew about their sexual orientation, and 65% had talked directly with her about the topic. Siblings were the next most likely to know: 74% of respondents indicated that one or more sisters knew, and 69% reported that one or more brothers knew. Gay men, lesbians, and bisexuals were somewhat less likely to disclose to their father: 62% said that their father knew, but only 39% had talked with him about their sexual orientation. In a national telephone survey (Kaiser Foundation, 2001), 84% of lesbians and gay men said that they were generally open about their sexual orientation with family members. These rates of disclosure are higher than those reported in earlier studies (e.g., Bell & Weinberg, 1978), suggesting that an increasing percentage of gay men and lesbians are coming out to their families.

Studies of adolescents and younger adults show generally similar findings. Based on their review of existing studies, Savin-Williams and Esterberg (2000) estimated that 40 to 75% of young gay men and lesbians have disclosed to their mother and 30 to 55% to their father. These researchers also suggested that "with each passing year, a greater percentage of youths are disclosing to their parents" (p. 201).

In summary, three general findings emerge. First, although most lesbians and gay men are open with their family, a substantial minority conceals this important aspect of their identity from parents or other family members. Second, mothers are more likely than fathers to know about their child's sexual orientation and to have discussed it with the child. Third, the proportion of gays and lesbians who disclose their sexual orientation to parents and relatives appears to be increasing over time.

Research is needed to map systematically the patterns of disclosure in families from diverse backgrounds. First, it appears that a greater proportion of lesbians and gay men are disclosing to their families today than in the past and are doing so at a younger age. Studies systematically examining disclosure among different age cohorts would be valuable. Second, researchers have speculated about the reasons why gay men and lesbians may disclose to some family members before others, but empirical support for these hypotheses is largely lacking. For instance, do individuals tend to come out first to their mother because they have a closer relationship with her and expect a less negative reaction? Do some individuals disclose first to siblings to "test how the family will react" as Crosbie-Burnett, Foster, Murray, and Bowen (1996, p. 400) suggested? Studies examining the transmission of disclosure information among siblings and other family members would also be informative. Third, little is known about the experiences of lesbians and gay men from diverse ethnic, cultural, or religious groups. Some have suggested that lesbians and gay men from traditional ethnic backgrounds may be especially reluctant to disclose their sexual orientation to family members for fear of losing a vital source of social support and connection to their ethnic community (Savin-Williams, 1996). In some cases, ethnic minority lesbians and gay men may also fear that revealing their sexual orientation will bring embarrassment or shame to their family. Finally, prior research has tended to view disclosure as a single, one-time event. In reality, individuals often engage in a continuing process of sharing greater information about their sexual orientation with family members over time. We know little about temporal patterns of disclosure.

FAMILY REACTIONS TO A GAY OR LESBIAN CHILD

Initially, family members' reactions to learning that a son is gay or a daughter is lesbian are often negative (see review by Savin-Williams & Esterberg, 2000). Common reactions include such feelings as shock, disbelief, guilt, and anger (see review by Savin-Williams & Dube, 1998). In a recent survey, 50% of lesbians and 32% of gay men reported that their "family or a family member" had refused to accept them because of their sexual orientation (Kaiser Foundation, 2001).

Many factors contribute to this negativity. Family members may view homosexuality as immoral or a sign of mental illness. They may believe myths about the lives of gays and lesbians, fearing, for example, that their child is doomed to a life of loneliness. Families may also worry about the dangers of sexual prejudice or have concerns about an increased risk of HIV infection. They may fear that they have contributed to their child's being gay or lesbian through their inadequacy as parents. Further, since the lives of parents and children are interdependent in important ways, parents may have concerns about their own future, wondering if they will have grandchildren or if their child's "secret" will affect connections among their extended family and community.

Over time, many families recover from the initial turmoil of disclosure, and relations with the gay or lesbian child improve. We know little about the processes that enable families to restore positive relations, although the quality of predisclosure family relations appears to be important (Patterson, 2000). Popular writers and parent support groups have suggested that parents' reactions follow predictable stages of denial, anger, bargaining, depression, and acceptance. Researchers such as Savin-Williams and Dube (1998) are skeptical of this stage model and note that empirical confirmation of a normative sequence of parental reactions is lacking.

It would be valuable to know more about the ways families cope with having a gay or lesbian child. After the initial disclosure, some parents strive to learn more about their child's personal experiences and about homosexuality in general, perhaps by participating in groups such as Parents and Friends of Lesbians and Gays (PFLAG) that provide support, education, and advocacy opportunities. In contrast, other parents seek to avoid continued discussion and treat the topic of homosexuality as a dark family secret. Research is needed to identify characteristics of the gay or lesbian individual, of the family, and of their social environment that are associated with differing family reactions to disclosure, both immediately and over time. To date, studies of parents' reactions have typically recruited participants from organizations such as PFLAG. As Savin-Williams (2001) has noted, research based on these parents may "distort the reality of how typical parents react to having a sexual-minority child" (p. 249). Investigations of parents who do not join support groups are needed to understand the full range of parental reactions. Another limitation of existing studies is that they describe how families respond to disclosure from only one perspective, either that of a parent or that of the gay/lesbian individual. It is possible, however, that the gay or lesbian person and the family perceive events quite differently. Consequently, studies that include multiple family members would be useful. Finally, the study of disclosure patterns among family members will benefit from the development of more adequate conceptual frameworks and more comprehensive measures (see Beals & Peplau, 2002, for one example).

GAY AND LESBIAN COUPLES

This section provides an overview of research about gay and lesbian couples. We begin with basic information about couples and then consider the initiation of relationships, satisfaction and commitment, the division of labor and power, and needed research on gay and lesbian couples. For more detailed reviews, see Patterson (2000), Patterson, Ciabattari, and Schwartz (1999), Peplau and Beals (2001), and Peplau and Spalding (2000).

Basic Facts About Couples

Many lesbians and gay men want to have a committed love relationship. In a recent national survey (Kaiser Foundation, 2001), 74% of lesbians and gay men said that if they could legally marry someone of the same sex, they would like to do so some day. Most (68%)

lesbians and gay men said that legal marriage rights were very important to them. Many studies find that a majority of gays and lesbians are currently in a romantic relationship (see review in Peplau & Spalding, 2000). For example, in a large-scale survey of lesbians, 65% of women reported currently being in a same-sex primary relationship (Morris et al., 2001). Information about the percentage of gay and lesbian adults who live together with a same-sex partner has recently become available from the 2000 U.S. Census and other national surveys (e.g., Black, Gates, Sanders, & Taylor, 2000; Human Rights Campaign, 2001; Kaiser Foundation, 2001). The best estimate is that about 25 to 30% of gay men and lesbians live with a same-sex partner. A recent survey of more than 2600 African American lesbians and gay men found that 41% of women and 20% of men were in a committed relationship (Battle, Cohen, Warren, Fergerson, & Audam, 2002).

The experiences of gay and lesbian couples are colored by the social climate of sexual prejudice. Simply being seen together as a couple can increase the risk of hate crimes and violence against gay men and lesbians. Laws against same-sex marriage deprive gay and lesbian couples of legal benefits in such areas as taxation, health insurance, social welfare, pensions, inheritance, and immigration (Savin-Williams & Esterberg, 2000). In an extreme example of sexual prejudice that took place in 2002, Carla Grayson, her partner Adrianne, and their 22-month old son barely escaped with their lives when an arson fire destroyed their home in Missoula, Montana. A psychology professor at the University of Montana, Carla had been active in efforts to extend the university's insurance benefits to same-sex partners of employees.

Same-sex couples are also vulnerable to daily hassles, inconveniences that are a constant reminder of the stigma of homosexuality. Studies have found that hotels are significantly less likely to make a room reservation for a same-sex couple than for a cross-sex couple (Jones, 1996). In shopping malls, same-sex couples may receive slower service by store clerks and experience more incidents of staring and rude treatment (Walters & Curran, 1996). Taken together, realistic fears about sexual prejudice and chronic daily stressors associated with being gay or lesbian may increase an individual's feelings of psychological distress and adversely affect physical health (Lewis, Derlega, Berndt, Morris, & Rose, 2001). Research is needed to assess how often gay and lesbian couples experience discrimination, the strategies that couples use to cope with these experiences, and the impact of these events on same-sex relationships.

Initiating a Relationship

Lesbians and gay men report that they are most likely to meet potential dates through friends, at work, at a bar, or at a social event (Bryant & Demian, 1994). We know very little about how gay men and lesbians identify potential partners or how they communicate romantic and sexual interest verbally or nonverbally. Opportunities to meet potential partners may be more abundant in urban areas with visible gay and lesbian communities. The Internet has rapidly become a new way for gay men and lesbians to meet each other, and research about the use of this technology would be particularly valuable.

Many studies have compared the attributes that lesbians, gay men, and heterosexuals seek in romantic partners (see review by Peplau & Spalding, 2000). Regardless of sexual orientation, most individuals emphasize affection, dependability, and similarity in interests and religious beliefs. Male–female differences have also been found. For example, gay and heterosexual men are more likely to emphasize a partner's physical attractiveness; lesbian and heterosexual women give greater emphasis to desirable personality characteristics.

When gay men and lesbians go on dates, they may rely on fairly conventional scripts that depict a predictable sequence of dating events. One study analyzed gay mens' and lesbians' accounts of typical and actual first dates (Klinkenberg & Rose, 1994). Many common events were listed by both gay men and lesbians, such as discussing plans, getting to know each other, going to an activity like a concert or movie, having a meal, and initiating physical contact. However, gay men were more likely than lesbians to include sexual activity as part of a first date, and lesbians were more likely to evaluate their feelings about the date.

In addition to understanding same-sex dating, it may also be important to understand how same-sex friendships can be transformed into romantic relationships. Rose, Zand, and Cini (1993) found that many lesbian romantic relationships began as friendships, then developed into love relationships, and later became sexual. Some women reported difficulties with this pattern of relationship development, such as problems in knowing if a relationship was shifting from friendship to romance and problems gauging the friend's possible sexual interest.

Relationship Satisfaction and Commitment

Stereotypes depict gay and lesbian relationships as unhappy. In one study, heterosexual college students described gay and lesbian relationships as less satisfying, more prone to discord, and "less in love" than heterosexual relationships (Testa, Kinder, & Ironson, 1987). In reality, comparative research finds striking similarities in the reports of love and satisfaction among contemporary lesbian, gay, and heterosexual couples (see review by Kurdek, 1995a). For example, Kurdek (1998) compared married heterosexual and cohabiting gay and lesbian couples, controlling for age, education, income, and years cohabiting. The three types of couples did not differ in relationship satisfaction at initial testing. Over a 5-year period, all couples tended to decrease in relationship satisfaction, but no differences were found among gay, lesbian, and heterosexual couples in the rate of change in satisfaction.

Like their heterosexual counterparts, gay and lesbian couples benefit from similarity between partners. Further, consistent with social exchange theory, happiness tends to be high when partners perceive many rewards and few costs from their relationship (e.g., Beals, Impett, & Peplau, 2002). Several studies show that satisfaction is higher when same-sex partners believe they share relatively equally in power and decision making (Peplau & Spalding, 2000). For lesbian couples, greater satisfaction has also been linked to perceptions of greater equity or fairness in the relationship.

Research has begun to investigate factors that affect partners' psychological commitment to each other and the longevity of their relationship (see review by Peplau & Spalding, 2000). Of obvious importance are positive attraction forces such as love and satisfaction that make partners want to stay together. The availability of alternative partners is also important: the lack of desirable alternatives is an obstacle to ending a relationship. Finally, barriers that make it difficult for a person to leave a relationship also matter (Kurdek, 2000).

Barriers include things that increase the psychological, emotional, or financial costs of ending a relationship. Heterosexual marriage can create many barriers such as the cost of divorce, investments in joint property, concerns about children, and the wife's financial dependence on her husband. These obstacles may encourage married couples to work toward improving a declining relationship, rather than ending it. In contrast, systematic comparisons find that gay men and lesbians experience significantly fewer barriers to ending their relationships than do married heterosexuals, and for all couples, barriers are a significant predictor of relationship stability (Kurdek, 1998). A recent path analysis of data from 301 lesbian couples provided support for the idea that attractions, barriers, and alternatives each significantly predicts psychological commitment that, in turn, predicts relationship stability over time (Beals et al., 2002).

Conflict can also detract from the happiness and stability of same-sex couples, depending on how successfully partners manage their disagreements. Available research documents many common sources of conflict. For example, Kurdek (1994) found that gay male, lesbian, and heterosexual couples had similar ratings of the topics they most often fought about, with intimacy and power issues ranked at the top.

The Division of Labor and Power

A common stereotype is that same-sex couples adopt husband–wife roles as a model for their intimate relationships. Traditional heterosexual marriage has two core characteristics: a division of labor based on gender and a norm of greater male status and power. Most lesbians and gay men today reject both of these ideas.

Several studies have examined the division of labor in same-sex couples (see review by Peplau & Spalding, 2000). Most lesbians and gay men are in dual-earner relationships, so that neither partner is the exclusive breadwinner and each partner has some degree of economic independence. The most common division of labor at home involves flexibility, with partners sharing domestic activities or dividing tasks according to personal preferences or time constraints. In an illustrative study, Kurdek (1993) compared the allocation of household labor (e.g., cooking, shopping, cleaning) in cohabiting gay and lesbian couples and heterosexual married couples. None of the couples had children. Among heterosexual couples, wives typically did most of the housework. In contrast, gay and lesbian couples were likely to split tasks so that each partner performed an equal number of different activities. Gay male partners tended to arrive at equality by each partner specializing in certain tasks; lesbian partners were more likely to share tasks.

Many lesbians and gay men seek power equality in their relationships. In an early study, 92% of gay men and 97% of lesbians defined the ideal balance of power as one in which both partners were "exactly equal" (Peplau & Cochran, 1980). In a more recent study (Kurdek, 1995b), partners in gay and lesbian couples responded to multi-item measures assessing various facets of equality in an ideal relationship. On average, both lesbians and gay men rated equality as quite important, although lesbians scored significantly higher on the value of equality than did gay men. Not all couples who strive for equality achieve this ideal. Social exchange theory predicts that greater power accrues to the partner who has relatively greater personal resources, such as education, money, or social standing. Several studies have provided empirical support for this hypothesis among gay men. In their large-scale couples study, Blumstein and Schwartz (1983) concluded that "in gay male couples, income is an extremely important force in determining which partner will be dominant" (p. 59). In contrast, there is some evidence that lesbians strive to avoid letting financial resources affect power in their relationships.

Needed Research on Gay and Lesbian Couples

One useful approach to studying gay and lesbian couples has been comparative. Studies comparing lesbian, gay, and heterosexual relationships can dispel harmful myths about gay and lesbian couples by documenting the many commonalities across all couples regardless of sexual orientation. Comparative research can also test the generalizability of theories originally developed with heterosexuals. Most comparative research has assessed individual levels of love and satisfaction or such structural characteristics of relationships as the balance of power or the division of labor. Consequently, little is currently known about the patterns of interaction in gay and lesbian couples—the specifics of how gay and lesbian partners talk to each other and seek to resolve the conflicts of interest that inevitably arise in close relationships. These topics of investigation are of interest in their own right but also hold the promise of illuminating ways in which gender influences close relationships. Several interactional topics warrant further examination, including conversational patterns (e.g., Kollock, Blumstein, & Schwartz, 1985), influence tactics (e.g., Falbo & Peplau, 1980), styles of problem solving (e.g., Kurdek, 1998), intimate communication (e.g., Mackey, Diemer, & O'Brien, 2000), and relationship maintenance behaviors (e.g., Gaines & Henderson, 2002). Research might also fruitfully investigate such topics as self-disclosure between partners, the provision and receipt of help and social support, and efforts to resolve conflicts.

Another timely research direction concerns unique issues facing gay and lesbian couples. For example, how do same-sex partners cope with problems created by sexual prejudice both at work and in their social lives? In a recent review, Oswald (2002) outlined some of the strategies that gay men and lesbians use to legitimize and support their relationships, including the creation of "family" networks that combine kin and friends, and the use of rituals such as commitment ceremonies to strengthen relationships. Further, how do partners negotiate issues about concealing versus disclosing their own sexual identity and the nature of their couple relationship to other people (e.g., Beals & Peplau, 2001)? To what extent do couples incorporate elements of gay or lesbian culture into their couple activities, for example, in the social events they attend; the holidays they celebrate; their choice of residence, dress, or friends? How do individuals and couples integrate being gay or lesbian into other important aspects of the lives including religion and ethnicity? How has the AIDS epidemic affected gay and lesbian dating and relationships (e.g., Haas, 2002)?

GAY AND LESBIAN PARENTS AND THEIR CHILDREN

In 2002, gay and lesbian parenting took center stage in the U.S. media when popular television talk show host Rosie O'Donnell revealed on national TV that she is a lesbian mom. O'Donnell and her partner, Kelli Carpenter, went public in part to lend support to a gay couple in Florida who are challenging the state's ban on gay adoption. In the past, most gays and lesbians became parents while in a heterosexual relationship. Today, however, many gay men and lesbians, like Rosie O'Donnell, are deciding to have children either alone or in a same-sex partner relationship. Gay men and lesbians who want to become parents use a variety of approaches including adoption, which is legal in most states, artificial insemination for lesbians, and surrogate mothers for gay men (see review by Buell, 2001). It appears that a growing percentage of gay men and lesbians are considering parenthood. In a recent national poll, 49% of gays and lesbians who were not parents said they would like to have or adopt children of their own (Kaiser Foundation, 2001). Given the obstacles to parenthood faced by self-identified gay men and lesbians, there is a high likelihood that their children are strongly desired and planned.

The best information about the frequency of lesbians and gay men raising children comes from analyses of U.S. census data and other national polls. Black, Gates, Sanders, and Taylor (2000) recently estimated that 22% of partnered lesbians and 5% of partnered gay men currently have children present in the home. A large-scale survey of African American lesbians and gay men found very similar results: 25% of women and 4% of men said they lived with children (Battle et al., 2002). These percentages compare to 59% of married heterosexuals and 36% of partnered heterosexuals who have children at home (Black et al., 2000).

In this section, we review the small body of research about the family lives of gay and lesbian parents, focusing first on the parenting couple, then on their children, and last on special concerns of gay and lesbian parents.

Gay and Lesbian Couples With Children

How does the transition to parenthood affect gay and lesbian couples? For married heterosexuals, parenthood often creates a less balanced division of domestic work, with mothers providing the bulk of child care and household labor. Does parenthood alter the ideology of equality that often characterizes lesbian and gay relationships? Although limited, available research indicates that parenthood does not change this general pattern of shared family responsibilities (see review on lesbian parenthood by Parks, 1998). For example, Chan, Brooks, Raboy, and Patterson (1998) compared 30 lesbian couples and 16 heterosexual couples, all of whom became parents using anonymous donor insemination and had at least 1 child in elementary school. In this highly educated sample, both lesbian and heterosexual couples reported a relatively equal division of paid employment, housework, and decision making. However, lesbian couples reported sharing child-care tasks more equally than did heterosexual parents.

Very little is known about gay male couples with children (see Bigner & Bozett, 1990, for a general review of research on gay fathers). One study found a more even division of child care and housework among gay male parenting couples than among heterosexual couples (McPherson, 1993, cited in Savin-Williams & Esterberg, 2000). Additional studies of gay couples who become parents by choice would provide a unique perspective on fathering. Gay couples who adopt or use surrogate mothers are highly motivated to parent and know that there will not be a woman in the home to provide child care. How do these men perceive the father role and how do they handle their parental responsibilities?

Many questions about the family lives of gay and lesbian parents remain. Available descriptions of gay and lesbian parents tend to be based on relatively older, well-educated, financially secure couples with young children. Lesbian mothers in these studies are likely to have liberal and feminist attitudes. Research is needed with larger, more representative samples. One question concerns the impact of children on the parents' relationship satisfaction. Among heterosexuals, the transition to parenting is often accompanied by a decline in marital satisfaction, sometimes attributed to the uneven division of labor in the couple and the stress of parenting. Does this occur among same-sex couples, or does a pattern of more equal sharing of family work counteract this effect (see, for example, Koepke, Hare & Moran, 1992)? Longitudinal studies of the transition to parenthood among gay and lesbian couples would be particularly valuable.

Another question relevant to some same-sex couples is whether the biological and nonbiological parent are equally involved in child care and paid work. To date, studies on this topic have examined lesbian mothers only, and the results have been inconsistent. Studies of gay male couples with a biological and nonbiological parent would be informative. Finally, it appears that lesbians and gay men who adopt children often parent children from different cultural and racial backgrounds. What impact does this have on their family life?

Children of Gay and Lesbian Parents

A top priority for researchers studying the children of lesbian and gay parents has been to debunk stereotypes that homosexuals are unfit parents whose children are at risk for a variety of psychosocial problems. Several studies have been conducted, most involving children of lesbian mothers (see reviews by Parks, 1998; Patterson, 2000; Stacey & Biblarz, 2001).

There is no evidence that the children of gay and lesbian parents differ systematically from children of heterosexual parents on standard measures of psychological functioning. No significant differences have been found in psychological well-being, self-esteem, behavioral problems, intelligence, cognitive abilities, or peer relations. A recent report by the American Academy of Pediatrics concluded that "no data have pointed to any risk to children as a result of growing up in a family with 1 or more gay parents" (Perrin, 2002, p. 343).

A related research question has been the possible impact of gay and lesbian parents on a child's gender identity and gender-typed behavior (see review by Stacey & Biblarz, 2001). There is no evidence that the children of gay and lesbian parents are confused or uncertain about their gender identity, that is, their self-knowledge that they are male or female (Patterson, 2000). Stacey and Biblarz (2001) suggested that these children may be somewhat more flexible or nontraditional in their views about a range of gender-typed behaviors including clothing, play activities, school activities, and occupational aspiration. Currently, support for this plausible hypothesis is extremely limited. In one study, for example, 53% of the daughters of lesbians aspired to professional careers such as doctor, lawyer, or astronaut compared to 21% of the daughters of heterosexuals (Green, Mandel, Hotvedt, Gray, & Smith, 1986). Additional research on children's gender-typed interests and behaviors would be useful.

A final research question concerns the sexual behavior and sexual orientation of children raised by gay and lesbian parents. For gay rights advocates, this research has the potential to counter the argument that children of lesbian moms and gay dads are at "increased risk" of becoming gay or lesbian themselves. Of course, in a completely accepting society, this would not be a fear, but in our climate of sexual prejudice, this argument has been used in court cases and legislative decisions to limit gay parenting. This research also provides important information about the influence of parents' sexual orientation on child outcomes. Unfortunately, as noted by Patterson (2000), Stacey and Biblarz (2001), and by others, available studies are limited in scope and methodology. Specifically, current research is largely based on small, nonrepresentative samples of White, middle-class, well-educated gay men and lesbians. Most studies rely on self-report questionnaires or interviews collected at one time point. Studies using longitudinal designs or observational methods are not available.

Despite these limitations, two patterns emerge. First, the great majority of children of gay and lesbian parents grow up to identify as heterosexual (Patterson, 2000). Whether the percentage of gay and lesbian offspring differs depending on the parents' sexual orientation is open to debate, and a final conclusion must await more extensive research. Second, children of lesbian parents appear to be more open to same-sex sexual experiences (Stacey & Biblarz, 2001). For example, in the only relevant longitudinal study, Golombok and Tasker (1996) studied 25 lesbian and 21 heterosexual mothers and their children. At the start of the study, the children were on average 10 years old and they were followed into young adulthood. No significant differences were found in the percentage of children identifying as gay or lesbian. However, compared to the children of heterosexual mothers, a greater percentage of children raised by lesbian mothers had had a same-sex sexual relationship or were open to this possibility in the future. Comparable scientific research on the children of gay fathers is not available.

There is a clear need for additional research on the experiences of children of gay and lesbian parents. A promising research direction concerns the resilience of children raised by parents from this socially stigmatized group. Despite teasing and other problems that children of gay and lesbian parents encounter, their psychological adjustment is comparable to that of other children. What processes make this possible? Further, are there compensating benefits of having gay and lesbian parents? For example, are gay and lesbian parents more likely to teach values of tolerance? Stacey and Biblarz (2001) argued that because children of lesbian and gay parents "contend with the burdens of vicarious social stigma" they may "display more empathy for social diversity" (p. 177). As another example, does the lesser concern of gay and lesbian parents about conformity to traditional gender roles provide their children with greater freedom to explore their own individual interests and preferences?

Special Concerns of Gay and Lesbian Parents

The diversity among gay and lesbian parents makes it impossible to characterize a "typical" family. Nonetheless, several issues common to gay and lesbian parenting can be identified (Dundas & Kaufman, 2000; Gartrell et al., 1996). Legal issues are often a major source of worry. Many lesbian and gay parents live in fear that their children can be taken away from them because of their sexual orientation, and some parents engage in lengthy legal battles with a former spouse or family member who disputes their fitness to parent. For gays and lesbians in a couple relationship, there are issues surrounding the legal status of the second parent. Only a few states allow a second same-sex parent to have legal rights and corresponding parental obligations.

Second, gay and lesbian parents have many concerns about the possible impact of sexual prejudice on the experiences of their children at school, in the neighborhood, with friends, with healthcare providers, and so on. Researchers have not yet examined the strategies that gay and lesbian parents use to shelter their children from negative experiences, to help children cope with instances of prejudice, to build resilience in their children, and to create supportive social networks.

Third, gay and lesbian parents, like single heterosexual parents, may have concerns about the availability of other-sex adults to provide role models for their children (e.g., Dundas & Kaufman, 2000). In some cases, siblings, other family members, and friends may fill this role. Gay and lesbian parents may face special problems not experienced by heterosexuals. For example, single heterosexual mothers may encourage their sons to participate in the Boy Scouts as a way to provide models of male leadership, but the anti-gay policies of the Boy Scouts might be discouraging to lesbian mothers.

Fourth, gay and lesbian parents must communicate with their children about potentially sensitive topics, such as the parent's sexual orientation or, in the case of artificial insemination or surrogate motherhood, how the child was conceived (e.g., Barrett, 1997; West & Turner, 1995). Research will need to examine the different aspects of disclosure to children and the consequences of these decisions.

Finally, the experiences of lesbian and gay parents challenge many popular beliefs about "normal" human development. Conceptual analyses of these issues would be beneficial. For example, models of identity development have often emphasized the role that parents play in socializing their children. Yet most gay and lesbian parents avoid socializing their children to conform to the parents' own sexual orientation. In a qualitative interview study, both lesbian and gay parents thought it most likely that their children would be heterosexual (Costello, 1997). All parents emphasized that they would accept their child's sexual orientation, whatever it might be. Parents often taught the value of accepting people in all their diversity. Asked how she thought her sexual orientation would influence her daughter, one lesbian mother replied, "I hope it helps her realize that we need to be true to ourselves, no matter who we are" (cited in Costello, 1997, p. 79).

AUTHOR NOTE

Preparation of this chapter was supported in part by a UCLA Academic Senate grant to Anne Peplau and by National Research Service Award 1F31 MH 12836-01A1 from the National Institute of Mental Health to Kristin Beals. Cynthia Carrion provided valuable library assistance. We appreciate the thoughtful comments on an earlier draft by Anita Vangelisti, Adam Fingerhut, and Linda Garnets. Correspondence regarding this chapter may be addressed to the first author: Psychology Department, UCLA, Los Angeles, CA 90095-1563. Send email to LAPEPLAU@UCLA.EDU.

REFERENCES

Allen, K. R., & Demo, D. H. (1995). The families of lesbians and gay men: A new frontier in family research. *Journal of Marriage and the Family, 57,* 111–127.

Barrett, S. E. (1997). Children of lesbian parents: The what, when and how of talking about donor identity. *Women and Therapy, 20,* 43–55.

Battle, J., Cohen, C. J., Warren, D., Fergerson, G., & Audam, S. (2002). *Say it loud, I'm Black and I'm proud: Black Pride Survey 2000.* New York: The Policy Institute of the National Gay and Lesbian Task Force. www.ngltf.org

Beals, K. P., Impett, E. A., & Peplau, L. A. (2002). Lesbians in love: Why some relationships endure and others end. *Journal of Lesbian Studies, 6,* 53–64.

Beals, K. P., & Peplau, L. A. (2001). Social involvement, disclosure of sexual orientation, and the quality of lesbian relationships. *Psychology of Women Quarterly, 25,* 10–19.

Beals, K. P., & Peplau, L. A. (2002, July). *Conceptualizing and measuring the disclosure of sexual orientation.* Poster presented at the International Conference on Personal Relationships, Halifax, Nova Scotia.

Bell, A. P., & Weinberg, M. S. (1978). *Homosexualities: A study of diversity among men and women.* New York: Simon and Schuster.

Bigner, J. J., & Bozett, F. W. (1990). Parenting by gay fathers. In F. W. Bozett & M. B. Sussman (Eds.), *Homosexuality and the family* (pp. 155–176). New York: Haworth.

Black, D., Gates, G., Sanders, S., & Taylor, L. (2000). Demographics of the gay and lesbian population in the United States. *Demography, 37,* 139–154.

Blumstein, P., & Schwartz, P. (1983). *American couples.* New York: Morrow.

Bryant, A. S., & Demian (1994). Relationship characteristics of American gay and lesbian couples: Findings from a national survey. In L. A. Kurdek (Ed.), *Social services for gay and lesbian couples* (pp. 101–117). New York: Haworth.

Buell, C. (2001). Legal issues affecting alternative families. *Journal of Gay and Lesbian Psychotherapy, 4,* 75–90.

Chan, R. W., Brooks, R. C., Raboy, B., & Patterson, C. J. (1998). Division of labor among lesbian and heterosexual parents. *Journal of Family Psychology, 12,* 402–419.

Costello, C. Y. (1997). Conceiving identity: Bisexual, lesbian and gay parents consider their children's sexual orientations. *Journal of Sociology and Social Welfare, XXIV,* 63–89.

Crosbie-Burnett, M., Foster, T. L., Murray, C. I., & Bowen, G. L. (1996). Gays' and lesbians' families-of-origin: A social-cognitive-behavioral model of adjustment. *Family Relations, 45,* 397–403.

Dundas, S., & Kaufman, M. (2000). The Toronto lesbian family study. *Journal of Homosexuality, 40,* 65–79.

Falbo, T., & Peplau, L. A. (1980). Power strategies in intimate relationships. *Journal of Personality and Social Psychology, 38,* 618–628.

Gaines, S. O., & Henderson, M. C. (2002). Impact of attachment style on responses to accommodative dilemmas among same-sex couples. *Personal Relationships, 9,* 89–94.

Gartrell, N., Hamilton, J., Banks, A., Mosbacher, D., Reed, N., Sparks, C., & Bishop, H. (1996). The national lesbian family study: Interviews with prospective mothers. *American Journal of Orthopsychiatry, 66,* 272–281.

Golombok, S., & Tasker, F. (1996). Do parents influence the sexual orientation of their children? Findings from a longitudinal study of lesbian families. *Developmental Psychology, 32*, 3–11.

Green, R., Mandel, J. B., Hotvedt, M. E., Gray, J., & Smith, L. (1986). Lesbian mothers and their children: A comparison with solo parent heterosexual mothers and their children. *Archives of Sexual Behavior, 15*, 167–184.

Haas, S. M. (2002). Social support as relationship maintenance in gay male couples coping with HIV or AIDS. *Journal of Social and Personal Relationships, 19*, 87–111.

Herek, G. M. (2000). The psychology of sexual prejudice. *Current Directions in Psychological Science, 9*, 19–22.

Herek, G. M., Gillis, J. R., & Cogan, J. C. (1996, August). *Hate crimes against gay men, lesbians, and bisexuals: Psychological consequences.* American Psychological Association, Toronto.

Human Rights Campaign. (2001, August 22). *Gay and lesbian families in the United States.* Washington, DC: Human Rights Campaign.

Jones, D. A. (1996). Discrimination against same-sex couples in hotel reservation policies. *Journal of Homosexuality, 31*, 153–159.

Kaiser Foundation. (2001, November). *Inside-out: A report on the experiences of lesbians, gays and bisexuals in America and the public's view on issues and policies related to sexual orientation.* Mento Park, CA.

Klinkenberg, D., & Rose, S. (1994). Dating scripts of gay men and lesbians. *Journal of Homosexuality, 26*, 23–35.

Koepke, L., Hare, J., & Moran, P. B. (1992). Relationship quality in a sample of lesbian couples with children and child-free lesbian couples. *Family Relations, 41*, 224–229.

Kollock, P., Blumstein, P., & Schwartz, P. (1985). Sex and power in interaction: Conversational privileges and duties. *American Sociological Review, 50*, 34–46.

Kurdek, L. A. (1993). The allocation of household labor in gay, lesbian, and heterosexual married couples. *Journal of Social Issues, 49* (3), 127–139.

Kurdek, L. A. (1994). Areas of conflict for gay, lesbian, and heterosexual couples. *Journal of Marriage and the Family, 56*, 923–934.

Kurdek, L. A. (1995a). Lesbian and gay couples. In A. R. D'Augelli & C. J. Patterson (Eds.), *Lesbian, gay, and bisexual identities over the lifespan* (pp. 243–261). New York: Oxford.

Kurdek, L. A. (1995b). Developmental changes in relationship quality in gay and lesbian cohabiting couples. *Developmental Psychology, 31*, 86–94.

Kurdek, L. A. (1998). Relationship outcomes and their predictors: Longitudinal evidence from heterosexual married, gay cohabiting, and lesbian cohabiting couples. *Journal of Marriage and the Family, 60*, 553–568.

Kurdek, L. A. (2000). Attractions and constraints as determinants of relationship commitment: Longitudinal evidence from gay, lesbian, and heterosexual couples. *Personal Relationships, 7*, 245–262.

Lewis, R. J., Derlega, V. J., Berndt, A., Morris, L. M., & Rose, S. (2001). An empirical analysis of stressors for gay men and lesbians. *Journal of Homosexuality, 42*, 63–88.

Loftus, J. (2001). America's liberalization in attitudes toward homosexuality, 1973–1998. *American Sociological Review, 66*, 762–782.

Mackey, R. A., Diemer, M. A., & O'Brien, B. A. (2000). Psychological intimacy in the lasting relationships of heterosexual and same-gender couples. *Sex Roles, 43,* 201–227.

McPherson, D. (1993). *Gay parenting couples.* Unpublished doctoral dissertation, Pacific Graduate School of Psychology, Palo Alto, CA.

Morris, J. F., Waldo, C. R., & Rothblum, E. D. (2001). A model of predictors and outcomes of outness among lesbian and bisexual women. *American Journal of Orthopsychiatry, 71,* 61–71.

Oswald, R. F. (2002). Resilience within the family networks of lesbians and gay men: Intentionality and redefinition. *Journal of Marriage and Family, 64,* 374–383.

Parks, C. A. (1998). Lesbian parenthood: A review of the literature. *American Journal of Orthopsychiatry, 68,* 376–389.

Patterson, C. J. (2000). Family relationships of lesbians and gay men. *Journal of Marriage and the Family, 62,* 1052–1069.

Patterson, D. G., Ciabattari, T., & Schwartz, P. (1999). The constraints of innovation: Commitment and stability among same-sex couples. In J. M. Adams & W. H. Jones (Eds.), *Handbook of interpersonal commitment and relationship stability* (pp. 339–359). New York: Kluwer.

Peplau, L. A., & Beals, K. P. (2001). Lesbians, gay men, and bisexuals in relationships. In J. Worell (Ed.), *Encyclopedia of women and gender* (Vol. 2, pp. 657–666). San Diego: Academic Press.

Peplau, L. A., & Cochran, S. D. (1980, September). *Sex differences in values concerning love relationships.* Paper presented at the annual meeting of the American Psychological Association, Montreal, Canada.

Peplau, L. A., & Spalding, L. R. (2000). The close relationships of lesbians, gay men and bisexuals. In C. Hendrick & S. S. Hendrick (Eds.), *Close relationships: A sourcebook* (pp. 111–124). Thousand Oaks, CA: Sage.

Perrin, E. C. (2002). Technical report: Coparent or second-parent adoption by same-sex parents. *Pediatrics, 109,* 341–344.

Rose, S., Zand, D., & Cini, M. (1993). Lesbian courtship scripts. In E. D. Rothblum & K. A. Brehony (Eds.), *Boston marriages: Romantic but asexual relationships among contemporary lesbians* (pp. 70–85). Amherst: University of Massachusetts Press.

Savin-Williams, R. C. (1996). Ethnic-minority and sexual-minority youth. In R. C. Savin-Williams & K. M. Cohen (Eds.), *The lives of lesbians, gays and bisexuals* (pp. 152–165). New York: Harcourt Brace College Publishers.

Savin-Williams, R. C. (1998). Lesbian, gay, and bisexual youths' relationships with their parents. In C. J. Patterson & A. R. D'Augelli (Eds.), *Lesbian, gay, and bisexual identities in families* (pp. 75–98). New York: Oxford University Press.

Savin-Williams, R. C. (2001). *Mom. Dad. I'm gay. How families negotiate coming out.* Washington, DC: American Psychological Association.

Savin-Williams, R. C., & Dube, E. M. (1998). Parental reactions to their child's disclosure of a gay/lesbian identity. *Family Relations, 47,* 7–13.

Savin-Williams, R. C., & Esterberg, K. G. (2000). Lesbian, gay, and bisexual families. In D. H. Demo, K. R. Allen, & M. Fine (Eds.), *Handbook of family diversity* (pp. 197–214). New York: Oxford University Press.

Stacey, J., & Biblarz, T. J. (2001). (How) does the sexual orientation of parents matter? *American Sociological Review, 66*, 159–183.

Testa, R. J., Kinder, B. N., & Ironson, G. (1987). Heterosexual bias in the perception of loving relationships of gay males and lesbians. *Journal of Sex Research, 23*, 163–172.

Walters, A. S., & Curran, M. (1996). "Excuse me, sir? May I help you and your boyfriend?": Salespersons' differential treatment of homosexual and straight customers. *Journal of Homosexuality, 31*(1/2), 135–152.

West, R., & Turner, L. H. (1995). Communication in lesbian and gay families. In T. J. Socha & G. H. Stamp (Eds), *Parents, children and communication* (pp. 147–169). Mahwah, NJ: Lawrence Erlbaum Associates.

12

COMMUNICATION, FAMILIES, AND EXPLORING THE BOUNDARIES OF CULTURAL DIVERSITY

RHUNETTE C. DIGGS
DENISON UNIVERSITY

THOMAS SOCHA
OLD DOMINION UNIVERSITY

Satellites, television, tourism, computer communications, cheap oil, cheap transport—these have brought images, foods, clothing, entertainment from various corners of the world into one place, collapsing distance, eliding space, compressing time, and glossing over cultural difference.

—Weiner (1997, p. 110)

Socha and Diggs (1999), Gudykunst and Lee (2001), and others developed a preliminary rationale for the study of family communication framed by ethnic culture. This chapter adds to that work in three ways by: (a) increasing understanding of the role of culture (ethnic and otherwise) in framing how family communication scholars conceptualize and study communication in family units and relationships, (b) reviewing recent family communication studies and communication studies from allied fields with an eye to how this work might illuminate and challenge current understandings of family communication, and (c) utilizing insights gained from these sources to offer future directions for scholarship.

Before addressing these aims, we discuss some of the complexities of the terminology to be used, specifically culture and cultural diversity, and the particular ideologies[1] on which this chapter is built. We begin by considering the term "cultural diversity" at some

---

[1] The term ideology is taken to mean that which we accept unconsciously, without reflection. It is defined by Palermo (1997) as "not recognized; the world naturally as the normal state of affairs of the taken for granted" (p. 4). The goal of critical and qualitative research is to reveal participants' ideologies; however, as researchers, we often overlook our own invisible ideologies or taken-for-granted assumptions that impact on our work unbeknownst to us.

length, because of the recent popular and public debates about this concept, especially in the context of communication and family.

CULTURE AND DIVERSITY

Prevailing ideas and definitions about communication, family, and diversity are connected explicitly and implicitly to scholars' attitudes, teachings, and the way they position culture in their research. For example, researchers' worldviews and traditions operate, perhaps unconsciously *and* strategically, to perpetuate cultural homogeneity rather than cultural diversity in scholarship and teaching. Scholarly references often are familiar or "known" (here to be interpreted as similar in ideology, theory, and race or ethnicity) as opposed to unfamiliar and "unknown" (here to be interpreted as different ideology, theory, and race or ethnicity) (see Socha & Diggs, 1999). The quote by Weiner (1997) that opens the present chapter situates well the current emphasis on globalization in the field of communication studies (e.g., Braman & Sreberny-Mohammadi, 1996; Chen & Starosta, 2000; Collier, 2000; Mowlana, 1996). However, the extent to which current trends of globalization have seeped into family communication studies is not clear. That is, the acknowledgment of cultural differences has been common in the theory and research on family communication, but the depth of their representation is debatable. Mowlana (1996) frames this problem in broad terms:

> ... lack of conceptual clarity, epistemological and disciplinary rigidities, insufficient amounts of skill in language and cultural studies, a high level of ethnocentrism and parochialism, and ideological biases. Consequently, our knowledge of communication, cultural and social systems, is provincial rather than universal. (p. 200)

Historically, family communication textbooks and conceptualizations have mentioned family "cultures" (e.g., Fitzpatrick & Ritchie, 1993; Galvin & Brommel, 1996; Whitchurch & Dickson, 1999), and more recently family communication scholars have been challenged to go beyond their "cultural habits" (characterized by ethnocentricism) to include other worldviews and approaches in their theoretical research perspectives (e.g., Gudykunst & Lee, 2001; Socha & Diggs, 1999). However, even one's allegiance to a particular perspective on diversity is potential for adherence to a certain view of families, families' roles in society, and thus the directions that research on family communication should take.

To understand cultural diversity in the contexts of domestic life, we begin with the term "culture." Definitional treatments of this term can range from a stable, unchanging characteristic to something that is unstable and fluid. The definitions correspondingly fit within epistemological[2] frameworks that consider knowledge in a variety of

---

[2]The term epistemology is defined as the basis of knowledge. For example, in Western philosophy and science, the realm of ideas was separated from that of matter which created a dualism between theory and practice (Mowlana, 1996, p. 208); "knowledge is validated through a combination of objectivity and scientific method" (Harris, 1998, p. 19). Mowlana believes that we currently have an ethnocentric epistemological approach operating, which is a barrier to cultural understanding. Harris (1998) indicated that "Afrocentric epistemology validates knowledge through a combination of historical understanding and intuition; what is known is a harmonization of the individual consciousness with the best traditions of the African past" (p. 18).

ways ranging from knowledge as given and universal (objective reality) to knowledge as contextual and constructed (social construction). These epistemological and ideological perspectives undergird public and scholarly conversations about cultural diversity as well.

Matthew Arnold's (1971) contribution to early debates about the value of culture (or high culture) in England during the 1860s offers a start to a brief tour of the historical lineage of culture. Arnold notes:

> Culture seeks to do away with classes; to make the best that has been thought and known in the world current everywhere; to make all men [sic] live in an atmosphere of sweetness and light, where they may use ideas, as it uses them itself, freely, —nourished, and not bound by them. This is the *social idea;* and the men [sic] of culture are the true apostles of equality. The great men [sic] of culture are those who have had a passion for diffusing, for making prevail, for carrying from one end of society to the other, the best knowledge, the best ideas of their time; who have laboured to divest knowledge of all that was harsh, uncouth, difficult, abstract, professional, exclusive; to humanise it, to make it efficient outside the clique of the cultivated and learned, yet still remaining the best knowledge and thought of the time, and a true source, therefore of sweetness and light. (p. 56)

This modern sense of culture is still evident in our contemporary society.

In contrast to Arnold's (1971) description of culture, the anthropological understanding of culture as the study of the human species has evolved from primarily examining how different ("remote" or "isolated") groups subsisted and sustained, physically and socially. Eventually, anthropologists and others came to see that "all peoples have unique histories" (Singer, 1987, p. 6). For example, Hecht, Collier, and Ribeau (1993) offered a socially constructed perspective in their definition of culture: "... whether national, ethnic, professional, organizational, or gender based, as a social organization. By this we mean that a culture is the common pattern of interaction and perception shared by a group of people" (p. 15).

Other conceptions of culture include the following characteristics: shared language or code that manifests the perceptions, attitudes, values, beliefs, and disbelief systems of the group; change; a way of life of a people; patterns of behavior (e.g., see Asante, 1988; Gudykunst & Kim, 1997; Kim & Gudykunst, 1996; Myers, 1998; Singer, 1987). It is these latter perspectives that can best serve the study of family communication because they speak to concepts at the foundation of family interaction including communication in service of socializing the young. Common to all of these definitions is that culture is a set of shared meanings or understandings about a group or organization and its problems, goals, and practices.

However, wholesale use of the term "culture" is not unproblematic. As implicated by the study of different groups with different values, beliefs, and language, critical perspectives have argued for particular ways of approaching the study of culture and communication. Critical scholars in a range of disciplines (e.g., anthropology, communication, ethnic studies, sociology, and psychology) have cautioned against cultural imperialism and cultural consumption (Asante, 1988; Bodley, 1976; Braman, 1996; Myers, 1998). These critical perspectives suggest that different family meanings, family values, and family work and leisure are inextricably tied to larger societal and mainstream cultural conceptual systems.

Also these perspectives alert us to the terrain facing scholars who explicitly choose to intersect family, communication, and cultural diversity.

In spite of the challenges that face researchers who study cultural diversity and family interactions, it is generally accepted that culture is important to communication because of its impact on language, behavior, perception, and interpretation. Cognizant of our words and endeavors, we have chosen to use the terms race and ethnicity interchangeably. We have chosen to use the term "co-culture" rather than "minority" to refer to groups that are deemed other than the "majority" within their society (see Orbe, 1998, for a complete commentary on this choice).

Scholars' treatments of culture have impacted on present hopes, fears, anxieties, and conversations about cultural "diversity." Based on public debates and existing scholarship on diversity, the current chapter organizes the meanings of cultural diversity into four categories, that is, culture as: Aspiration, Dilemma, Fear, and Opportunity. These four categories attempt to convey general themes rather than mutually exclusive categories. In brief, cultural-diversity-as-aspiration suggests an ideal positive rhetoric that implies cultural diversity will improve people's personal, private, and public lives. This perspective views any tensions experienced as potential positive by-products of difference (e.g., Freedman, 2002; Makau, 1997; Orbe, 1998; Socha & Diggs, 1999). Cultural-diversity-as-dilemma reflects the anxiety or discomfort experienced and felt about difference (e.g., Benhabib, 1999; Chen & Starosta, 2000). Cultural-diversity-as-fear emphasizes what is lost or the fear of threat to self and civil society (e.g., Wuthnow, 1999). Finally, cultural-diversity-as-opportunity is offered as an extension of the somewhat polarized perspectives (aspiration and fear) to acknowledge real struggles (optimistic orientation vs. anxiety orientation) within the contexts of cultural differences (e.g., Clark & Diggs, 2002; Diggs & Clark, 2002).

Cultural Diversity as Aspiration

Mowlana's (1996) summary and critique of the efforts of the International Communication Division of the Association for Education in Journalism and Mass Communication (AEJMC) to examine globalization seem instructive in terms of building an understanding of the term culture and how it fits with the study of family communication. He explains:

> The birth of nations from the 1950s through the 1990s, and the upheavals and changes occurring in the old nations, are not simply the result of drastic changes in demographic or economic sectors. They also indicate an important development on the intellectual level. Advances in communication technologies and transportation, for example, have helped to lessen cultural isolationism and to increase the cultural awareness of minorities by making them more conscious of the distinctions between themselves and other groups. (pp. 95–96)

This statement implies that people (including families) take notice of their environments, near and far, to determine their moves. When individuals observe their life experiences, events in the world (i.e., 911 or September 11, 2001, "Attack on America"), and local and transnational events, then they begin to move globally. That is, families are aware of their local communication environments but also are aware that other families in other parts of the world communicate differently. In a recent lecture, Socha (2002) modified the 1960s' environmental movement slogan to capture this idea: Families need to think globally, but communicate locally.

Makau (1997) wants to "celebrate" differences and believes that "problems commonly attributed to diversity are actually problems of communication ethics" (p. 49). She used varied scholarship to recount the history of the "construction" of diversity in the United States. She argued that this construction was influenced by discourses around changing demographics, the myth of changing demographics rather than the reality of economic shift, cultural standpoints and locations, and "context specific conceptions of identity," with essentialization of groups (pp. 49–53). Makau advocates a healthy dose of tension around the topic of diversity. Such a perspective, she believes, allows the individual and group culture to simultaneously manifest in each communicative encounter.

Freedman (2002), believes that "it is persons least like ourselves who teach us the most about ourselves" (p. 32). This ideal is pointed especially at the young college student to promote campus diversity. This promotion of diversity seems to fit the concept of high culture whose aim is to generate leaders and the elite. Freedman points out that it is our obligation to seek diversity, "as it always has been for positions of national leadership" (p. 32). At the same time that this clearly is an aspiration, a focus on cultural diversity as a commodity (something to be bought and sold) creates a dilemma, especially for those who become the "objects" blamed for the cultural diversity "problems."

Cultural Diversity as a Dilemma

Contained within this perspective is a tension between "essential" and "constructed" identities. Benhabib (1999) addressed this tension in her analysis of nationalist groups:

> Whereas identity claims are said to be fundamental, essential, nonnegotiable, and clearly distinguishable from the claims of competitors, in the process of social and political mobilization and cultural articulation, identity claims are "created" that are negotiable, contestable, and open to political redefinition and redescription. . . . All identity/difference movements struggle for the distribution of resources as well—be these land, power, representation, cultural space, or linguistic access—although the political grammar . . . is dominated by the vocabulary of recognition rather than redistribution. (pp. 295 and 307)

Benhabib seems to present this perspective as a dilemma in that there are real and serious struggles that exist within and between those who identify themselves as part of a collective that provokes some discomfort. Although the existence of struggles over identity issues should be acknowledged, the essential versus constructed identity can be viewed as an acknowledgment of the Afrocentric principle that "all things work together" (not necessarily in opposition). There is not simply one way to think of oneself; potentially developmental or cyclical, essential and constructed identities both are operative in how people think of themselves and their families. Benhabib's concern for citizenship challenges researchers to theoretically account for this (i.e., offer a theory that explains how this fundamental and negotiable/created identity works). How are identity claims communicated in different kinds of families? To what extent do these identity claims create obstacles to dialog between different kinds of families?

Chen and Starosta (2000) also raised the dilemma about what the "dialectic tension between cultural identity and cultural diversity poses for the future global society" (p. 5). How do people maintain a balance between their sense of identity and their understanding and acceptance of *other* as different? The authors are interested in how communication scholars might address (via research) the cultural competence that is needed in a global society that assumes "as the world becomes more interdependent and interconnected, the nation-state becomes more culturally heterogeneous" (p. 1).

Philosopher, Çinar (2002), reviewed Parekh's "pro-multiculturalism" book which addressed strengths and weaknesses in thinking about multiculturalism. In the review, he asserts that a problem or weakness is the conceptualization of culture. For Çinar, the view of culture as stable or unchanging without internal differences reflects passive and not active people, who can be overtaken by the powerful economic and political structures; this is cause for anxiety.

Cultural Diversity as Fear

Underlying many of the popular discussions about diversity is the "fear factor." Wuthnow (1999) asserts that:

> Questions have arisen about the extent to which the nation is being fragmented by tensions separating racial, ethnic, and religious groups, and about Americans' willingness to shoulder the difficult tasks of working together for the common good.... Many interpreters sense that Americans are neither maintaining their traditional values nor responding well to social diversity. (p. 19)

In this statement, "Americans" are assumed to be "White" Americans who are suddenly sensing "tensions" and "fear." These emotions, however, have been a staple of the Black experience in America. In Withnow's terms, diversity involves questions about how White people overcome their fear that Black people and other persons of ethnic difference are entering space on a somewhat equal footing.

Wuthnow's (1999) sociological analysis questions these fear-based assumptions. For example, "Much of the recent anxiety about the condition of civil society points directly or indirectly to diversity as a major source of America's current problems" (p. 23). The civil rights movement is indirectly blamed as part of the problem when people point to "African Americans, Hispanics, women, and gays and lesbians as sources of a perceived retreat from common values and responsibilities" (p. 23). Wuthnow concludes that diversity "challenges the social order" but is unjustly blamed for the potential demise of civil society and societal discontent. Rather it is the "loosening of social bonds or porousness compared to tightly bounded institutions" and their fragility that prompt Americans' worry (p. 28). In addition, there are examples of what we term as the commodification of diversity: The diversity slogan is used as a means to gain votes or to buy or sell things.

Cultural Diversity as an Opportunity

Critics in varied disciplines (e.g., Asante, 1988, in African and African American Studies and Intercultural Communication; Lather, 1991, in Cultural Education; West, 1989, in Philosophy and Religion) have argued that now that people of color, women, and others of different groups are impacting academia and gaining equality, there is a broadening of ideas and some resistance to those perspectives that they bring. From a family communication perspective, these conversations about culture, whether stable or changing, can be viewed as opportunities. The conversations and debates are a prime opportunity for family communication scholars to ask themselves personal questions about culture and to inspect how they enter into the discussion with co-cultures within the United States and with families beyond the United States (e.g., Diggs & Clark, 2002, autoethnography of interracial talk). For certain, family communication research has embraced a perspective on culture as noted earlier, but scholars need to question the fruitfulness of the perspective in enabling them to see their own ethnic thinking and its impact on who they study, what they study, and how they study various phenomena.

Implications for Researchers

Ethnicity is defined as "givens (objective perspective), such as blood, customs, language, ritual, religion, social values" (Mindel, Habenstein, & Wright, Jr., 1998, p. 6). The problems associated with entering into the discussion of culture as synonymous with ethnicity (as we have) abound, as it obscures the diversity contained within particular ethnicities or races. These problems, however, are unavoidable. To place culture as synonymous with ethnicity places a boundary on the term "culture." In this sense culture is defined as a focus on different races or ethnic peoples. This categorization should not be limiting for prospective researchers as they can pick and choose or argue for the interdependence of many aspects of the ethnic person. Rather than take rigid positions in the debate over pluralism, cultural diversity, or multiculturalism, family communication scholars would do well to continue to openly examine their assumptions and pursue both respect for their research on participant families and sensitivity to the myriad of cultural ways of knowing.

Fitzpatrick's and Ritchie's (1993) assertion that, "our variable field focuses attention across many levels of analysis to study" can be viewed as a strength of the vision to intersect communication, family, and culture. Whitchurch and Dickson (1999) more specifically described a communication approach to the study of family relationships that emphasized the meaning of family as grounded in verbal and nonverbal communication. Certainly this perspective accommodates family diversity, in that the suggestion is that researchers can understand different families by examining their communication. It is important to note, however, that such conceptualizations about family will not necessarily ensure that diversity makes it into our studies. For example, Nicholson (2001) argued that the family communication literature has focused its attention primarily on the parental and marital subsystems. His study on sibling relationships reflects how researchers can attempt to go deeper inside the family to pursue a particular level of analysis (i.e., subsystems). However, such a pursuit also may keep researchers inside only one kind of family culture rather than encourage them to venture outside into the cultural world to examine the communication and creation of different racial and ethnic families. Gudykunst, Ting-Toomey, and Nishida (1996) indicate that interpersonal communication researchers "ignore the relationships between culture and communication and study communication in a cultural vacuum" (p. 3).

Conceptualizations of family communication and family relationships have always accommodated the examination of diverse families, yet, it is researchers' worldviews, theoretical orientations, and habits that are, perhaps, their greatest challenges (and obstacles) to the study of communication of different families. What cultural standpoint do researchers begin from? Have they examined their worldviews and ethnocentrism? What ideological values are implied by their studies? By examining published studies in the family communication literature and in allied fields, scholars can draw conclusions and advance an agenda about the current state of communication and the boundaries of diversity in research and pedagogy.

DIVERSITY IN FAMILY COMMUNICATION STUDIES

Although the goal of this chapter, ultimately, is to expand the scope of our understanding of family communication in diverse families, it is important to first acknowledge the progress researchers have made in their back yard (see Amason's, 2002, review of family communication textbooks; Socha & Diggs, 1999). To accomplish this latter goal, a review of recent studies of family communication, culture, and diversity was conducted. Empirical studies that focused on different culture samples and family communication as independent or dependent variables and those studies that simply described the ethnic makeup of the sample were examined.

A number of studies reported "diverse" demographics or identified the sample by race but did not conceptualize culture as a relevant or substantive variable (see Aune & Comstock, 2002; Koesten, Miller, & Hummert, 2002; Pecchioni & Nussbaum, 2002; Segrin & Flora, 2001). Studies that addressed family context (culture), communication characteristics, and ethnicity or race also were examined (see Day & Remigy, 1999; Diggs, 2001; Duneier, 1992; Durrheim & Dixon, 2001; Fisherkeller, 1997; Georgas et al., 2001; Jenkins, 1991; Julian, McKenry, & McKelvy, 1994; Kane, 2000; Mosby, Rawls, Meehan, Mays, & Pettinari, 1999; Schönpflug, 2001; Socha & Diggs, 1999; Socha & Stamp, 1995; Xu & Burleson, 2001). In these studies culture was conceptualized as a specific, concrete, objective ethnic category (by virtue of the distinctive labeling) and as socially constructed by virtue of the discourse and social influences that shape family meanings, values, and family identities. Even though we cannot draw specific conclusions about who benefits from the culture conceptualizations of the studies, we can say that knowledge of these ethnic families is enhanced when descriptions of contexts, communication and behavior patterns, and interpretations of particular family members and families communication are provided.

If scholars remain aware of the varied metatheoretical, epistemological, and methodological assumptions and purposes underlying scholarly work about families, then the literature about families and domestic life outside the United States has something important to offer. It can provide researchers with information about families from cultures beyond the borders of the United States and it can be used to study those cultures.

TABLE 12.1

A Preliminary Primer of Selected Books About Families and Familial Relationships in Countries
Outside the United States

Country	Author	Synopsis
Africa South Africa	Mathabane (1994)	An ethnography of three generations of women (the author's grandmother, mother, and sister) spanning the time of apartheid in South Africa, to their flight, and adjusting to life in the United States.
Africa Middle East	Fernea (1985)	An edited volume that includes six chapters pertaining to women and family life in the Middle East (featuring Saudi Arabia and Egypt).
Asia China	Baker (1979)	A study of traditional Chinese family composition, lineage, worship, and kinship patterns. The book includes sections about terms of address for kin and non-kin as kin.
Asia Korea	Lee & Kim (1979)	A sociological study that focuses on values and family practices concerning children in South Korea. A volume in a series of studies about the value of children conducted in China, Japan, Philippines, Thailand, and U.S. (Hawaii).
Asia Vietnam	Van Bich (1999)	A sociological dissertation from Sweden that examined traditional Vietnamese family life, historical changes, husband–wife relationships, and the influence of Confucianism and Marxism on family living patterns.
India	Ramu (1977)	A sociological dissertation from the University of Illinois that reports an in-depth case study of the daily life of a family living in urban south India with particular attention to the role of India's caste system in family life.
India	Khatri (1983)	A sociological study of familial relationships that uses content analysis of Indian fictional novels to examine familial relationships including: courtship, marriage, parent–child, siblings, and in-laws.
North America Mexico	Lewis (1959) Lewis (1961)	A University of Illinois anthropologist writes extensively about families living in poverty in Mexico. These two volumes represent case studies of five families (Lewis, 1959) and one poor family in Mexico city (Lewis, 1961). These are classic works of extensive "thick" description.

Table 12.1 offers a limited preliminary primer of readings that can begin to add to the picture of family communication as a global activity. The table includes books that display countries not often appearing in family communication studies, as well as works that provide a flavor for the different kinds of research that have been conducted. Some of the books are considered "classic" studies. These include the work of anthropologist Oscar Lewis, who examined five families living in poverty in Mexico (Lewis, 1959) and a family living in Mexico City (Lewis, 1961). The methods typically used to study different

family cultures include detailed, in-depth chronicles of day-to-day family lives, sociological portraits, and content analysis.

EXPLORING THE BOUNDARIES OF DIVERSITY IN FAMILY COMMUNICATION STUDIES

In addition to providing a summary of the literature on cultural diversity and family communication, this review offers an opportunity to reflect on some of the factors that have yet to be systematically examined by those who study family interaction.

For Richer or Poorer

In communication studies, some scholars have examined "the poor" or those in poverty (e.g., Daniel, 1970), but those experiencing economic prosperity have not received attention, nor have these studies examined domestic poverty–prosperity and communication in domestic contexts. Studies in allied fields, in particular those of sociologist Lillian Rubin (1976, 1994), stand out in providing insight into blue-collar family life (e.g., especially see Rubin, 1994, chapter 4—"Mother Goes to Work"). This work focuses on the development and interconnections of macroeconomic policies and their effects on the microlevel of everyday family life. It seems that economic poverty–prosperity can exert a tremendous force on how families communicate (e.g., research in mass communication about Internet use shows differences so large between rich and poor as to create a "digital divide"), and conversely how families communicate can affect their relative levels of poverty–prosperity. But, research on family communication to date has not systematically considered the role of economic diversity in explaining family communication processes and outcomes. This would seem to be an important and fruitful area for future study. For example, does the relative importance of communication in family and family relationships change with a family's socioeconomic status? How do qualities of communication in families and family relationships change with high or low, rising or falling income levels? Also, what commitments and conceptions of culture exist in rich, working-class, and poor families (e.g., Duneier, 1992)?

In Sickness and in Health

Family members and their systems confront a wide array of physical and mental illnesses over the life span, and, at any given point families can vary widely in wellness–illness. That is, some families have members who struggle with chronic illness and debilitation, whereas others experience years of wellness. The family communication literature and textbooks have attempted to consider issues associated with "wellness–illness." For example, many textbooks cite the therapeutic literature extensively (individual psychological as well as family systems) and seek to develop models of family communication that incorporate concepts of wellness (e.g., satisfaction, optimal family functioning). Communication scholars have also examined "illness" as a communication act (Chesebro, 1982). However, to date there have not been systematic research efforts to examine the array of communication that occurs in families along the wellness–illness continuum. It would seem that wellness–illness would have great potential to affect family communication processes and outcomes and that family communication in turn can affect managing illness (e.g., Henry, 1973).

Religion

A search for studies that examine participation in organized religion (i.e., Baptist, Buddhist, Catholic, Hindu, Jewish) and family communication revealed that this, too, is uncharted territory on the landscape of diversity. In contrast, a search of nonacademic literature yielded a variety of publications from a wide array of religions that seek to have a say in everyday family life. For example, texts of homilies given in the early 1700s show that early colonial pastors were preaching about ways to achieve "the well-ordered family" (Wadsworth, 1712). Families vary not only in terms of religious participation but also in terms of the extent to which a chosen faith tradition is lived or practiced. Similar to ethnic culture, there is much diversity of adherence to and identification with religious beliefs and prescriptions that also needs to be considered. Theological approaches and families of various religious traditions, rather than being ignored, potentially, could be sources for culturally diverse interrogation of family communication (e.g., Barton, 1996; Furrow, 1998; Hughes & Dickson, 2001).

Urban-Rural

Sociologist Richard Sennett (1970), among others, has examined the effects of urban environments (as well as rural ones) on family life in the United States. Studies in family communication, however, have been less concerned with diversity of family space. This might be due in part not only to the overuse of convenience samples and the difficulties in recruiting and gathering diverse samples (e.g., due to lack of funding) but also to the relative homogenization of life in the United States. Stepping outside the United States, one finds the contrast of the lives of those who live in the cities and those who live in rural, often remote environments to be quite stark. For example, during a visit to South Africa, the second author viewed (albeit briefly) the radically different worlds of living in beehive huts in rural Kwazulu-Natal near the Shlu-Shluwe game reserve (home to white rhino and others of the "big seven") to living in modern condos in Cape Town; from living in tin-roofed shanty houses of Soweto Township to living in a mansion in a suburb of Johannesburg. Diversity of place seems to matter a great deal in setting the context for communication in families and familial relationships and seems worthy of future study (also see Al-Oofy & McDaniel, 1992; Durrheim & Dixon, 2001).

CONCLUSION: FUTURE DIRECTIONS

At this stage in the history of family communication studies, there is a need to keep at the forefront the goal of creating a portrait of family communication that is diverse, complex, and inclusive. As family communication textbooks suggest, efforts to show openness toward diversity by including pictures of diverse families (see Amason, 2002) have sketched an orientation toward embracing diverse families, but the image is inadequate nationally and does not go far enough globally. As research moves forward, scholars need to look for ethnically and racially diverse samples (substantive to research questions, of course), to ask questions that reveal similarities as well as differences in our diversity, and to understand differences in family communication.

Mowlana (1996) stated, "the decline of nationalism and secular national ideologies patterned on European and Western schools of thought and the concurrent discourse and revival of notions of community along sociocultural lines open an entirely new area of inquiry and research that needs to be studied by those interested in societal change and evolution" (p. 92). Collier (2002) stated that "scholars, teachers, and practitioners construct and produce what nation and culture are known to be in historically situated sites and moments of time" (p. xi). How do these statements affect scholars interested in family communication? First, these statements suggest that researchers need to include families in their studies that substantively (as cultural variables) bring the diversity of interest to the research situation. Next, these statements suggest that scholars and professionals need to critique themselves in their apolitical and noncommittal stance toward diversity in their scholarship. Perhaps our most evident expressions of studying family communication and diversity suggest that scholars are bound to all of the ideologies about cultures, particularly culture as fear and culture as dilemma. Personal narratives and empirical data on researchers' culture-based fears and dilemmas could reveal how these ideologies influence theorizing, research decisions, and outcomes. Cultures as opportunity and aspiration are more apparent when we see special calls for diversity in research and convention programs that generate works in progress toward publication. The question now is, "What direction should we take to promote diversity in future family communication research and pedagogy?"

Who Do We Study?

Studies of varied family subsystems and communication contexts (i.e., parent–child communication, sibling communication, gay and lesbian families) offer the opportunity to describe the family culture that members create and the kind of communication that constructs and impacts personal, social, and cultural or ethnic identities within a changing social context. The challenges of a global society (e.g., not meeting face to face; children communicating via email) urge family communication scholars to study varied national and international families. For example, a model for studying families globally is reflected in collaborative studies that take advantage of technology and the international contacts that such technology affords. Georgas and 17 other researchers (2001) situated in various countries studied a 16-country sample. Although multiple researcher studies offer a model for collaboration, researchers still are tied to the single, two-, or three-co-author model that is most likely attached to existing Western tenure and promotion practices.

A commitment to diversity in sampling with substantive questions of culture will require openness to creativity and ways of knowing, inclusive of objective, qualitative, rhetorical, and critical paradigms. For example, Diggs' (2001) qualitative study asked diverse Black and White participants to talk about their experiences with racial profiling in a public library setting. In reflection, Diggs speculated that the discussion of racial profiling was viewed as a "threatening and fearful" topic to most non-Black library patrons, due to mediated information rather than to personal experiences with racial profiling and the very real current events surrounding the topic. Therefore, the study generated more Black participants than White ones. In this context, age, sex, and location differences within the predominantly same-race sample were deemed important.

What Do We Study?

A conceptualization of family communication and culture that recognizes the larger social influence on family communication as evidenced in media and other institutional messages prompts us to move beyond the private-home site to the public as well. For example, Diggs' (2001) study that examined family and community racial profiling discourse used a family member's spontaneous response to a media message about racial profiling to frame family and community experiences with racial profiling. Media (TV/film, visual, and print) continue to be a prime source of subject matter for family communication research as traditional family meanings and family values are being contested in the public arena (e.g., MTV reality TV shows such as *Real World* and more recently, *The Osbourne's*).

Gudykunst and Lee (2001), Collier (2000, 2001), and McAdoo (2001) are among communication and family researchers who emphasize caution in treating ethnic or racial groups monolithically. For example, theoretical models from cross-cultural and intercultural communication research grounded in sensitivity to intragroup difference are offered by the first two sets of authors. Gudykunst and Lee offer concepts of strength and content, and Collier (2000) offers co-construction, salience, and overlapping identities as concepts to help researchers attend to differences within ethnic or racial groups. These conceptualizations direct researchers to consider how family communication varies by virtue of cultural valuing of ethnic and cultural identity, how members are affected by family discourse, and how the family discourse creates family cultures (or patterns) and distinctiveness.

Comparisons of family meanings within ethnic families and cross-culturally will be able to reveal those differences that seem to make a difference. For example, Day and Remigy's (1999) study of Mexican and French preschool to school-age children revealed that those children who were from two-parent, traditional families typically viewed "family" to mean the presence of both parents in the physical setting, whereas those children from single-parent homes were less likely to reference the presence of both parents to mean "family."

How Do We Study?

Closely related to what we study is how we conduct our studies. Scholars (e.g., Stephen, 2001; Turner & West, 2002) have called for greater diversity in the methods used by researchers. Some researchers have begun to respond to this call. For example, Alexander (2001) examined the concept of a self-defined family. This study is undergirded by a constructivist view of culture (or culture as constituted through communication); that is, one can create a family through language and interaction. In this ethnographic study, Alexander examined a self-defined family at a local bar (no characterization of race or ethnicity). The importance of future studies of this kind is explicated in this statement concerning the study's findings: "as our society becomes increasingly global and fast-paced and hectic, individuals are likely to become progressively more stressed . . . . and more inclined to look towards a self-defined family for kinship" (p. 25).

What Is Our Responsibility?

We are preparing ourselves, our community, and society for a world that is postcolonial (e.g., Collier, 2000; Cooks, 2001) and open to all. Even though this openness is acknowledged in our civil rights laws and national commitment, many people of co-cultures are still navigating spaces where this is fiction. As scholars who study family communication and family relationships, we are in a unique position to teach, to learn, and to study cultural diversity from a variety of vantage points. As we engage in all of these tasks, we need to continually seek "an earnestness and good faith that in the end will create a far better climate for the achievement of true equality" (Freedman, 2002, p. 33).

REFERENCES

Al-Oofy, A., & McDaniel, D. (1992). Home VCR viewing among adolescents in rural Saudi Arabia. *Journal of Broadcasting and Electronic Media, 36,* 217–223.

Alexander, A. L. (2001). *Regulars at the Hole in the Wall: An ethnographic study of a self-defined family at a local bar.* Paper presented at the National Communication Association Conference, Atlanta, GA.

Amason, P. (2002). Choosing an undergraduate text from a limited range of options: A review essay of family communication textbooks. *Journal of Family Communication, 2,* 41–56.

Arnold, M. (1971). *Culture and anarchy: An essay in political and social criticism.* New York: The Bobbs-Merrill Company.

Asante, M. K. (1988). *Afrocentricity* (Rev. ed.). Trenton, NJ: Africa World Press.

Aune, K. S., & Comstock, J. (2002). An exploratory investigation of jealousy in the family. *Journal of Family Communication, 2,* 28–39.

Baker, H. D. R. (1979). *Chinese family and kinship.* London: Macmillan.

Barton, S. C. (1996). Biblical hermeneutics and the family. In S. C. Barton (Ed.), *The family in theological perspective* (pp. 3–23). Edinburg: T & T Clark.

Benhabib, S. (1999). Civil society and the politics of identity and difference in a global context. In N. J. Smelser & J. C. Alexander (Eds.), *Diversity and its discontents: Cultural conflict and common ground in contemporary American society* (pp. 293–312). Princeton, NJ: Princeton University Press.

Bodley, J. H. (1976). *Anthropology and contemporary human problems.* Menlo, CA: Cummings.

Braman, S. (1996). Interpenetrated globalization: Scaling, power, and the public sphere. In S. Braman & A. Sreberny-Mohammadi (Eds.), *Globalization, communication and transnational civil society* (pp. 21–36). Cresskill, NJ: Hampton Press.

Braman, S., & Sreberny-Mohammadi, A. (Eds.). (1996). *Globalization, communication and transnational civil society.* Cresskill, NJ: Hampton Press.

Chen, G. M., & Starosta, W. J. (2000). Communication and global society: An introduction.

In G. M. Chen & W. J. Starosta (Eds.), *Communication and global society* (pp 1–6). New York: Peter Lang.

Chesebro, J. W. (1982). Illness as a rhetorical act: A cross-cultural perspective. *Communication Quarterly, 30*, 321–331.

Çignar, D. (2002). Cultural diversity and dialogue: On Bhikhu Parekh: Rethinking multiculturalism. Cultural diversity and political talk. Review section of polylog. *Forum for Intercultural Philosophizing 2*, 1–11. Retrieved March 12, 2002, from http://www.polylog.org.org/lit/2/rvw1-en.htm

Clark, K., & Diggs, R. C. (2002). Connected or separated?: Towards a dialectical view of interethnic relationships. In T. A. McDonald, M. Orbe, & T. Ford-Ahmed (Eds.), *Building diverse communities: Applications of communication research* (pp. 3–25). Creskill, NJ: Hampton Press.

Collier, M. J. (2000). Reconstructing cultural diversity in global relationships: Negotiating the borderlands. In G. M. Chen & W. J. Starosta (Eds.), *Communication and global society* (pp. 215–236). New York: Peter Lang.

Collier, M. J. (2001). Constituting cultural difference through discourse: Current research themes of politics, perspectives. In M. J. Collier (Ed.), *Constituting cultural difference through discourse* (pp. 1–25). Thousand Oaks, CA: Sage.

Collier, M. J. (Ed.). (2002). Introduction. *Transforming communication about culture: Critical new directions* (pp. ix–xix). Thousand Oaks, CA: Sage.

Collier, M. J., Hedge, R. S., Lee, W., Nakayama, T. K., & Yep, G. A. (2002). Dialogue on the edges: Ferment in communication and culture. In M. J. Collier (Ed.), *Transforming communication about culture: Critical new directions* (pp. 219–277). Thousand Oaks, CA: Sage.

Cooks, L. (2001). From distance and uncertainty to research and pedagogy in the borderlands: Implications for the future of intercultural communication *Communication Theory 11*, 339–351.

Daniel, J. (1970). The poor: Aliens in an affluent society. *Today's Speech, 18*, 5–21.

Day, E. D., & Remigy, M. J. (1999). Mexican and French children's conceptions about family: A developmental approach. *Journal of Comparative Family Studies, 30*(3), 95–112.

Diggs, R. C. (2001). Optimizing family/community places and spaces for racial profiling discourse [Special Issue]. *The Journal of Intergroup Relations, 28*(3), 42–58.

Diggs, R. C., & Clark, K. D. (2002). It's a struggle but worth it: Identifying and managing identities in an interracial friendship [Special issue]. *Communication Quarterly, 50*, 368–390.

Duneier, M. (1992). *Slim's table: Race, respectability, and masculinity*. Chicago: The University of Chicago Press.

Durrheim, K., & Dixon, J. (2001). The role of place and metaphor in racial exclusion: South Africa's beaches as sites of shifting racialization. *Ethnic and Racial Studies, 24*, 433–450.

Fernea, E. W. (Ed.). (1985). *Women and the family in the Middle East*. Austin, TX: University of Texas Press.

Fisherkeller, J. (1997). Everyday learning about identities among young adolescents in television culture. *Anthropology and Education Quarterly, 28*, 467–492.

Fitzpatrick, M. A., & Ritchie, L. D. (1993). Communication theory and the family. In P. G. Boss, W. J. Doherty, R. LaRossa, W. R. Schumm, & S. K. Steinmetz (Eds.), *Sourcebook of family theories and methods: A contextual approach* (pp. 565–589). New York: Plenum Press.

Freedman, J. O. (2002). Dealing with difference: Why it's important to attend a college that's racially, culturally, and ethnically diverse. *Private Colleges and Universities*, 32–33.

Furrow, J. L. (1998). The ideal father: Religious narratives and the role of fatherhood. *The Journal of Men's Studies, 7*, 17–32.

Galvin, K. M., & Brommel, B. (1996). *Family communication cohesion and change* (4th ed.). New York: HarperCollins.

Georgas, J., Mylonas, K., Bafiti, T., Poortinga, Y. H., Christakopoulou, S., Kagitcibasi, C., et al. (2001). Functional relationships in the nuclear and extended family: A 16-culture study. *International Journal of Psychology, 36*, 289–300.

Gudykunst, W. B., & Kim, Y. Y. (1997). *Communicating with strangers* (3rd ed.). New York: McGraw-Hill.

Gudykunst, W. B., & Lee, C. M. (2001). An agenda for studying ethnicity and family communication. *Journal of Family Communication, 1*, 75–85.

Gudykunst W. B., Ting-Toomey, S., & Nishida, T. (Eds.). (1996). *Communication in personal relationships across cultures*. Thousand Oaks: CA: Sage.

Harris, N. (1998). The philosophical basis for an Afrocentric orientation. In J. D. Hamlet (Ed.), *Afrocentric visions: Studies in culture and communication* (pp. 15–25). Thousand Oaks, CA: Sage.

Hecht, M. L., Collier, M. J., & Ribeau, S. A. (1993). *African American communication*. Thousand Oaks, CA: Sage.

Henry, J. (1973). *Pathways to madness*. New York: Random House.

Hughes, P. C., & Dickson, F. C. (2001). *Keeping the faith(s): Religion, communication, and marital satisfaction in interfaith marriages.* Paper presented at the National Communication Association, Atlanta, GA.

Jenkins, K. W. (1991). Inside the family's culture: A communicative-oriented analysis of culture within the family unit. *Dissertation Abstracts International, 51*(12), 4288A. (UMI No. 9112814).

Julian, T. W., McKenry, P. C., & McKelvey, M. W. (1994). Cultural variations in parenting: Perceptions of caucasian, African-American, Hispanic, and Asian-American parents. *Family Relations, 43*, 30–37.

Kane, C. M. (2000). African American family dynamics as perceived by family members. *Journal of Black Studies, 30*, 691–702.

Khatri, A. A. (1983). *Marriage and family: Relations through literature: A study of Indian fiction*. Bayside, NY: General Hall.

Kim, Y. Y., & Gudykunst, W. B. (Eds.). (1996). *Theories in intercultural communication* (pp. 299–321). Newbury Park, CA: Sage.

Koesten, J., Miller, K. I., & Hummert, M. L. (2002). Family communication, self-efficacy, and White female adolescents. *Journal of Family Communication 2*, 7–27.

Lather, P. (1991). *Feminist research in education: Within/against*. Geelong, Victoria: Deakin University Press.

Lee, S. J., & Kim, J. O. (1979). *The value of children—A cross national study: Korea.* Honolulu, HA: East-West Population Institute.

Lewis, O. (1959). *Five families: Mexican case studies in the culture of poverty.* New York: Basic Books.

Lewis, O. (1961). *The children of Sanchez: Autobiography of a Mexican family.* New York: Random House.

Makau, J. (1997). Embracing diversity in the classroom. In J. M. Makau & R. C. Arnett (Eds.), *Communicating ethics in an age of diversity* (pp. 48–67). Urbana: University of Illinois Press.

Mathabane, M. (1994). *African women: Three generations.* New York: HarperCollins.

McAdoo, H. P. (2001). Point of view: Ethnicity and family dialogue. *Journal of Family Communication, 1,* 87–90.

Mindel, C. H., Habenstein, R. W., & Wright, R., Jr. (Eds.). (1988). *Ethnic families in America: Patterns and variations.* New York: Elsevier.

Mosby, L., Rawls, A. W., Meehan, A. J., Mays, E., & Pettinari, C. J. (1999). Troubles in interracial talk about discipline: An examination of African child rearing narratives. *Journal of Comparative Family Studies, 30,* 89–521.

Mowlana, H. (1996). *Global communication in transition: The end of diversity?* Thousand Oaks, CA: Sage.

Myers, L. J. (1998). The deep structure of culture: Relevance of traditional African culture in contemporary life. In J. D. Hamlet (Ed.), *Afrocentric visions: Studies in culture and communication* (pp. 3–14). Thousand Oaks, CA: Sage

Nicholson, J. H. (2001, November). *Relational effects of sibling alliances.* Paper presented at the National Communication Association, Atlanta, GA.

Orbe, M. P. (1998). *Constructing co-cultural theory: An explication of culture, power, and communication.* Thousand Oaks, CA: Sage.

Palermo, J. (1997). Reading Asante's myth of *Afrocentricity:* An ideological critique. Retrieved April 1, 2002, *http://www.ed.uiuc.edu/EPS/PES-Yearbook/97_docs/palermo.html*

Pecchioni, L. L., & Nussbaum, J. F. (2002). Mother-adult daughter discussions of caregiving prior to dependency: Exploring conflict styles of European-American women. *Journal of Family communication, 1,* 133–150.

Ramu, G. N. (1977). *Family and caste in urban India: A case study.* New Delhi, India: Vikas Publishing House.

Rubin, L. B. (1976). *World's of pain: Life in the working-class family.* New York: Basic Books.

Rubin, L. B. (1994). *Families on the fault line: America's working class speaks about the family, the economy, race, and ethnicity.* New York: HarperCollins.

Schönpflug, U. (2001). Intergenerational transmission of values: The role of transmission belts. *Journal of Cross-Cultural Psychology, 32,* 174–85.

Segrin, C., & Flora, J. (2001). Perceptions of relational histories, marital quality, and loneliness when communication is limited: An examination of married prison inmates. *Journal of Family Communication, 3,* 151–173.

Sennett, R. (1970). *Families against the city: Middle class homes in industrial Chicago.* Cambridge, MA: Harvard Press.

Singer, M. R. (1987). *Intercultural communication: A perceptual approach.* Englewood Cliffs, NJ: Prentice-Hall.

Socha, T. J. (2002, April). *Diversity and family communication.* A lecture given at the Family Communication and Stress Forum, University of Nebraska-Lincoln, Lincoln, NE.

Socha, T. J., & Diggs, R. C. (1999). *Communication, race, and family: Exploring communication in Black, White, and Biracial families.* Mahwah, NJ: Lawrence Erlbaum Associates.

Socha, T. J., & Stamp, G. H. (Eds.). (1995). *Parents, children and communication: Frontiers of theory and research.* Mahwah, NJ: Lawrence Erlbaum Associates.

Stephen, T. (2001). Concept analysis of the communication literature on marriage and family. *The Journal of Family Communication, 1,* 91–110.

Turner, L. H., & West, R. (2002). Call for papers: Communication with diversity in contemporary families [Special issue]. *Journal of Family Communication, 2,* 57–58.

Van Bich, P. (1999). *The Vietnamese family in change: The case of the Red River delta.* Surry, UK: Curzon.

Wadsworth, B. (1712). *The well-ordered-family: Relative duties—Early American Reprints.* Boston and New York: Readux Microprint [No. 1591].

Weiner, A. B. (1997). The false assumptions of traditional values. In S. Dreman (Ed.), T*he family on the threshold of the 21st century: Trends and implications* (pp. 103–112). Mahwah, NJ: Lawrence Erlbaum Associates.

West, C. (1989). *The American evasion of philosophy: A genealogy of pragmatism.* Madison, WI: The University of Wisconsin Press.

Whitchurch, G. G., & Dickson, F. C. (1999). Family communication. In M. B. Sussman, S. K. Steinmetz, & G. W. Peterson (Eds.), *Handbook of marriage and the family* (pp. 687–704). New York: Plenum Press.

Wuthnow, R. (1999). Democratic liberalism and the challenge of diversity in late-twentieth century America. In N. J. Smelser & J. C. Alexander (Eds.), *Diversity and its discontents: Cultural conflict and common ground in contemporary American society* (pp. 19–35). Princeton, NJ: Princeton University Press.

Xu, Y., & Burleson, B. R. (2001). Effects of sex, culture, and support type on perceptions of spousal social support. An assessment of the "support-gap" hypothesis in early marriage. *Human Communication Research, 27,* 535–566.

IV

The Relational Communication of Family Members

13

MOTHERS AND FATHERS
PARENTING TOGETHER

WILLIAM J. DOHERTY
UNIVERSITY OF MINNESOTA

JOHN M. BEATON
UNIVERSITY OF GUELPH

Coparenting may be the most daunting yet significant experience that two adults share. It is through this relationship that parents negotiate their respective roles, responsibilities, and contributions to their children. . . . Parents either support or undermine one another's parenting efforts. When parents divorce, the coparenting relationship often is the only arena in which the parents continue to relate.

—Margolin, Godris, and John (2001, p. 3)

The parenting relationship between mothers and fathers is so obviously a central feature of family life that its neglect by scholars and researchers, at least until the mid-1990s, calls for explanation. Indeed, until recently the construct of "co-parenting" was usually synonymous with postdivorce co-parenting and confined to the study of conflict and cooperation across households. When intact families were studied, early research treated parenting as equivalent to mothering. After fathering research emerged in the 1980s (see Lamb, 1987), researchers studied father–child relationships and mother–child relationships separately, looking for similarities, differences, and unique contributions, while generally ignoring the interaction between mothers and fathers. This gap is especially striking in light of the outpouring of research on marital communication during the 1970s and 1980s (e.g., Fitzpatrick, 1988; Gottman, 1979).

One explanation for the neglect of co-parenting (at least outside of divorced families) is that the field had not yet absorbed the systems theories that were prominent in family therapy. Whereas psychology and interpersonal communication were invested in dyadic formulations of family relationships—husband–wife, parent–child—family therapists had long focused on triadic interaction, claiming that the triad is the minimal unit needed for understanding family communication (Bowen, 1976; Minuchin, 1974). Triads allowed for examining the influence of one relationship, such as the mother–father relationship, on a third member of the family, such as a child. A triadic analysis also illuminates how one relationship affects another relationship, such as how the marital relationship affects the father–child relationship.

Why did triadic, family systems models become appealing to family researchers only during the 1990s? We note that this was the decade of powerful research findings on the negative impact of marital and co-parental conflict on parent–child relations and children's well-being in intact families (see review by Erel & Burman, 1995) and of parallel findings in studies of postdivorce families. Beyond the empirical findings, we believe that scholars became disenchanted with the oversimplifications of dyadic models of family communication and decided to take the plunge into family systems theory by trying to operationalize heuristically interesting ideas that family therapists had observed but never measured. Jay Belsky (1981) and Patricia Minuchin (1985) were early leaders in this integration of developmental and family systems theories.

Since the mid-1990s, there has been an explosion of research on co-parenting relationships in families, especially in intact families. Theoretical work, however, has lagged. The outline of this chapter follows its purposes: to summarize contemporary research on co-parenting, to delineate conceptual frameworks that can be fruitful for understanding the co-parenting relationship, to offer a preliminary theoretical model of factors influencing co-parenting, and to suggest fruitful areas for further research.

REVIEW OF CO-PARENTING RESEARCH

Although Belsky did not explicitly focus on co-parenting in the early 1980s, he was among the first scholars to propose that parenting was influenced by multiple systems: parent, marital, and child subsystems. Belsky (1981) proposed that the marital relationship was the most important support system for parents. That is, in order to understand the influence of parenting on child development, consideration must be given to the marital relationship. Belsky (1979, 1984) developed a pioneering conceptual model to study how parenting was multidetermined by parents' developmental histories, personalities, marital relations, employment characteristics, social networks, and by individual child characteristics. This conceptual model set the stage for future research that focused on both dyadic and triadic relationships.

Lewis, Owen, and Cox (1988) were among the first researchers to study both dyadic and triadic relationships: the marital relationship, mother–child relationship, the father–child relationship, and the mother–father–child relationship. They argued that it was insufficient to only focus on the marital dyad and the mother–child dyad. Using a triadic interactional competence scale to code videotapes of interactions among mothers, fathers, and children, they discovered that the parents' positive marital quality prenatally predicted higher levels of parental investment at 3 months and 1 year following birth. Although Lewis et al. (1988) did not focus specifically on the co-parenting relationship, their research was the beginning of many other studies that would investigate how marital relationships influence parental involvement (see Erel & Burman, 1995).

Philip and Carolyn Cowan (1999) were among the first researchers to investigate how marital relationships impact co-parenting over time. In a 10-year longitudinal intervention study, the Cowans followed couples expecting their first child (Cowan & Cowan, 1999). They found that declining marital satisfaction measured at three time periods—pregnancy and when the child was 1.5 and 3.5 years old—was associated with low warmth in mother–child and father–child interactions at age 3.5 (Cowan, Cowan, Schulz, & Heming, 1994). Recently, the Cowans (2003) have developed a model that shows how multiple domains of family life (including the quality of the relationship between the parents) influence child development. Other domains in their model are individual parental well-being, the quality of relationships between parents and their parents, the quality of relationships between each parent and child, the quality of sibling relationships, the balance of life stress, and social supports for parents.

An important distinction that has emerged in the field is between the co-parenting relationship and the marital relationship. Numerous studies have shown how supportive co-parenting has positive outcomes for child development beyond the quality of the marital relationship. McHale (1997) was one of the first researchers to study co-parenting distinct from marital and parent–child relationships. Previous research primarily focused on co-parenting within the marital relationship, and measures were comprised of marital satisfaction items as opposed to triadic co-parenting items. McHale developed a self-report co-parenting scale to measure parents' perceptions about how they engaged in co-parenting activities and promoted a sense of family. The items were divided into two groups: behavior in the family triad (e.g., physical affection to partner, physical affection to child) and behavior when alone with child (e.g., affirming the absent parent, criticizing the absent parent). McHale focused his analyses of co-parenting on the dimensions of hostility/competition versus harmony and on balance in involvement. In assessing triadic interactions, he found that increased marital distress leads to more hostile–competitive parenting and imbalances of mother and father involvement. Moreover, the interplay between the quality of the marital relationship and a child's gender affected parental involvement. In the face of marital distress, boys were more likely to encounter hostile–competitive co-parenting, whereas girls were more likely to encounter larger discrepancies in co-parental involvement.

McHale's (1997) research specifically on the co-parental relationship set the foundation for further research in this area. Belsky, Crnic, and Gable (1995), with a sample of mothers, fathers, and their toddler boys, discovered that parents with similar individual psychological attributes had more positive co-parenting relationships. The more mothers and fathers differed on characteristics of introversion and extraversion, the more likely they were to engage in unsupportive co-parenting behaviors. Furthermore, Belsky et al. discovered that co-parenting dynamics and whole-family dynamics played distinctive roles in the development of behavioral inhibition in children, beyond the child's temperament, individual parenting, individual parent well-being, and marital quality.

In the next study from McHale's project, McHale and Rasmussen (1998) found that family warmth during infancy was associated with men's positive co-parenting practices (self-reported) when the child was age 3, which in turn were linked to fewer internalizing and aggressive behaviors in preschool. The authors used the construct "promoting family integrity" to describe what the fathers' self-report measure captured. It included items such as showing love to wife when family is together and talking positively about mother with the children in her absence. For mothers, just one item—disparagement of her co-parent—was related to child aggression and internalizing behaviors.

In a breakthrough study, McHale, Lauretti, Kuersten-Hogan, and Rasmussen (2000) did observational assessments of both dyadic (parent–child) and triadic (mother–father–child) interactions. This was one of the first studies to investigate potential differences in how parents behave in these two contexts. The authors discovered that maternal and paternal behaviors within parent–child dyadic observations are very different from maternal and paternal behaviors within whole-family dynamics. Parents' limit-setting behaviors with their children during the whole-family interaction were unrelated to their individual limit-setting behaviors in the parent–child dyadic interactions. Additionally, fathers' family integrity scores (positive parental engagement during family interaction) and mothers' conflict scores (interpersonal disputes in front of child) and reprimand scores (setting limits with child or inviting the partner to set limits) were able to distinguish three family group patterns of co-parenting—oppositional, cohesive, and nonrestrictive co-parenting.

As assessed in this study, oppositional families were low on warmth and cooperation and had high levels of interparental antagonism; mothers' conflict scores in particular were linked to higher interparental antagonism. Cohesive families were high on warmth and cooperation and were child centered. These families were characterized by fathers who scored high on family integrity. Nonrestrictive families were low on structure and did little limit setting with children; mothers' higher reprimand scores in particular were associated with inadequate toddler management. Although these specific findings require replication using different samples and assessment tools, this study was a landmark in co-parenting research.

As momentum on co-parenting research increased, new researchers were drawn to the area, and theoretical discussions increased. Margolin, Godris, and John (2001) proposed a model of co-parenting based on three dimensions: conflict between parents, cooperation between parents, and triangulation (a condition that occurs when a parent forms a coalition with a child that undermines the other parent). They designed a 14-item co-parenting scale to assess parents' perceptions of one another. Mothers' co-parenting scores were taken from fathers' questionnaires and vice versa. Thus, mothers' scores assessed their perceptions about father involvement and fathers' scores tapped their perceptions about mother involvement. Examples: "My spouse tells me lots of things about this child." "My spouse supports my discipline decisions." Margolin et al. found that co-parenting dynamics were a function of a child's age, parents' gender, and a child's gender. Parents tended to cooperate more with preschool children than they did with preadolescent children. Wives tended to cooperate with children of all ages more than their husbands did. Wives rated the parenting alliance less positively than did husbands. There was higher triangulation with mothers with sons, suggesting that fathers believed that mothers tended to draw sons into interparental conflict. Margolin et al. also observed marital conflict discussions concerning a child-related topic for preadolescents. They divided couples along the categories of hostility/defensiveness and agreeableness/problem solving. Couples who were more agreeable and displayed more problem-solving skills scored higher on total co-parenting.

Finally, in a follow-up study of their longitudinal sample, Cowan and Cowan (2003) have begun to focus more explicitly on co-parenting. Using an observational coding system, they studied parents' interaction style in the presence of a child. They coded for parental warmth, coldness, anger, and competition. The results indicated that when parents showed displeasure with one another in the form of anger and disagreement, children showed higher levels of externalizing and internalizing behaviors in first grade.

In summary, an emerging body of research is demonstrating the importance of co-parenting relationships in families and the value of a triadic approach to studying families. Prominent conceptualizations of the co-parenting relationship focus on the dimensions of conflict, cooperation, and triangulation with a child. Evidence is mounting that the co-parenting dynamics have effects on child development and adjustment beyond the effects of individual parenting practices and that parents behave differently in and out of the presence of the other parent.

CONCEPTUAL FRAMEWORKS

Co-parenting research has been more descriptive than theory driven, with the literature concentrating on characterizing co-parenting patterns, developing assessment tools, and examining influences on children's adjustment. Here we briefly discuss four conceptual frameworks to shed light on the co-parental relationship, and in the next section we present a model to guide research on factors that influence the co-parental relationship.

Social constructionism seems an ideal fit for understanding the co-parental relationship. As developed by Berger and Luckmann (1966) and a variety of symbolic-interactionist scholars (Blumer, 1986; La Rossa & Reitzes, 1993), social constructionism emphasizes the shared construction of a social reality by the participants in a relationship. From this perspective, social roles are created through ongoing interaction and through the negotiation of mutual expectations in the context of broader cultural norms. A social constructionist view of co-parenting would stress how the creation of a couple's co-parental relationship begins from the first time they discuss children and parenting. The negotiation process becomes more intense when they are expecting their first child together, and a negotiated co-parenting relationship is set in motion quickly after the baby is born. Some aspects of co-parenting may be openly negotiated—such as who will work more for pay and who will stay home more with the child—whereas other aspects are decided implicitly—as when both assume the mother's preeminence as a child care expert and the father's auxiliary role. From a social constructionist standpoint, when researchers observe a couple interacting with their child in the laboratory, they are witnessing the public demonstration of a relationship that has been worked out over thousands of interactions and will continue to be worked out over time.

This framework can offer researchers access to the inner worlds of the partners—how they see their own behavior and that of their partner, how close what they see is to their expectations, how they see their co-parenting in light of broader family and cultural norms they are aware of, and even how the developing child participates in the social construction of his or her parents' relationship. ("I want Mommy to put me to bed!" is a statement that offers a way to define the co-parenting relationship.) Social constructionism lends itself best to in-depth qualitative research on this inner world of co-parenting. This type of research can probe deeply into underlying beliefs, expectations, and values that motivate parents' behavior alone and with their partners.

Family systems theories have served as a principle framework for much of he co-parenting research. As articulated by Bowen (1976), Minuchin (1974), and others, family systems theory focuses on multiple simultaneous interactions in the family, with particular reference here to the triangular relationship consisting of the parents and a child. As mentioned earlier, family systems theory allows the researcher to focus on triadic interactions, not just the dyadic interactions that are the forte of social constructionism. It can also illuminate the ways in which parents develop complementary or competitive relationships with each other. The work of Bowen also points to the influence of each parent's family of origin on current co-parental dynamics.

Family development theories are important for understanding co-parenting over time. As articulated by Aldous (1978), Hill and Mattessich (1979), and Rodgers and White (1993), family development theories emphasize the changing structures and roles in the family as members grow older and the family undergoes important transitions. From this perspective, the developmental tasks of co-parenting differ considerably depending on the family's life stage, from co-parenting an infant to co-parenting an adult child. And of course, children in the family might be at considerably different developmental stages, requiring complex coordination of co-parenting roles, with, say, one parent being more central to the younger child and the other parent being more central to the older child. Researchers have barely begun to tap into the complexities of co-parenting from a family life cycle perspective.

Human ecology theories focus on the interdependent web of personal, familial, and community influences on human development and functioning (Bateson, 1972; Bronfenbrenner, 1979; Bubolz & Sontag, 1993). Whereas the other three theories mentioned previously emphasize intrafamilial dynamics, ecological theories concentrate on the niches within which children and families function, from the family system to the surrounding community systems to the broader societal and even environmental systems. From this perspective, co-parenting plays out in a complex ecology of social and economic influences. Using an ecological framework, Doherty, Kouneski, and Erickson (1998) summarized research showing that fathering is influenced more strongly by ecological factors than mothering is. Co-parenting researchers have looked at the influence of the marital relationship and childhood factors on the co-parenting relationship but have only begun to examine the influence of broader ecological factors (for an exception, see Conger & Conger, 2002).

A CONCEPTUAL MODEL OF INFLUENCES ON THE CO-PARENTAL RELATIONSHIP

Based on the four frameworks discussed previously, Fig. 13.1 depicts a model of influences on co-parenting. The focal point of the model is the triadic mother–father–child relationship, with the lines connecting the three participants representing how they mutually construct the co-parenting relationship through ongoing systemic interaction and negotiation of roles. Because the marital status of the parents is such an important context for co-parenting, we include this variable within the triangle itself, indicated by slashes rather than by a straight line because obviously not all mothers and fathers are married to each other. The straight lines indicate the co-parenting relationship, which in turn is influenced by whether or not the parents are married. For simplicity's sake, we omit

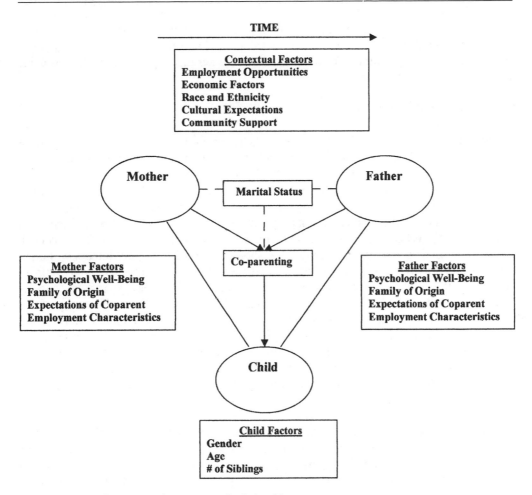

FIG. 13.1.   Influences on the co-parental relationship.

cohabitating relationships, which vary considerably in commitment from a permanent, marriagelike relationship to a transitory relationship of convenience. However, to the extent that cohabiting parents define their couple relationship as permanently committed and independent of their co-parenting relationship, they would be functionally "married" in this model.

Outside the triangle are depicted several categories of influences on the co-parental relationship: individual factors in the mother and father, child factors, mother–father relationship factors, and broader ecological factors. The top line in the model depicts the arrow of time, which stands for the developmental process of the individuals involved, the family system, and the changing nature of the ecological influences. In this model, we are trying to capture key elements of the four conceptual frameworks outlined previously: social constructionism, family systems theories, family developmental theories, and human ecological theories as they help us understand the dynamics of co-parenting relationships. We offer the model for heuristic purposes as a guide to further research. For some domains of the model, there is considerable research evidence for the influence of the variables (e.g., mothers' expectations about fathering), whereas for other domains there is relatively little at this time.

The Impact of Marital Status

Marital status is such an obviously important factor in co-parenting that researchers have developed nonoverlapping conceptual models for married and nonmarried parents and have generally studied one group or the other but not both together. There is little overlap between the work of researchers who study postdivorce co-parenting (e.g., Ahrons & Miller (1993) and the work of those who study intact family co-parenting (McHale, 1997). But in any conceptual model of influences on co-parenting, marital status must be included as a central variable, because it sets the context for nearly every other variable. As Doherty et al. (1998) note in their review of research on responsible fathering, many fathers withdraw from their children over time after a divorce, and even more never-married fathers exit from the lives of their children. Even optimistic researchers on postdivorce co-parenting, such as Ahrons and Miller (1993), find that only a minority of ex-spouses have close, cooperative co-parenting relationships. As Furstenberg and Cherlin (1991) have maintained, for many men, fatherhood and marriage are "a package deal." Not marrying the mother or divorcing the mother signals to these men that active fathering and co-parenting are optional.

Many studies of postdivorce co-parenting are concerned with the influence of paternal involvement on children, and recent findings suggest that father involvement must be seen as a triadic variable, not just as a dyadic one. When nonresidential fathers exercise authoritative parenting and cooperate with the mother, child well-being is positively affected (Amato & Gilbreth, 1999; Marsiglio, Amato, Day, & Lamb, 2000). Both of these factors must be in place: positive individual parenting and positive co-parenting in the form of payment of child support and cooperative child rearing. In other words, both dyadic and triadic functioning, both parenting and co-parenting need to be present for the well-being of children.

In sum, the presence or absence of a marital relationship (legally or functionally married as noted previously) is the most powerful influence on the co-parenting relationship. Cooperative co-parenting is possible outside of an intact couple relationship, and such co-parenting relationships aid children's development. But the severing of the intimate couple bond strikes a blow to the co-parental relationship that only a minority of couples overcome well enough to have co-parenting relationships characterized in McHale (1997) and Margolin et al.'s (2001) research as high in harmony and cooperation and as low in competition, hostility, and triangulation.

Inside married couple families, the quality of the marital relationship itself is the best documented influence on co-parenting. In the presence of serious marital conflict, fathers tend to withdraw from their children and from co-parenting, whereas mothers do not show the same level of withdrawal (Cummings & O'Reilly, 1997; Doherty et al., 1998). On the other side of the equation, studies indicate that a loving and supportive marriage during the infant and toddler years, with its positive influence on co-parenting, can predict infant attachment security (see Belsky, 1999) and has other positive outcomes for children. In general, though, research indicates that it is the absence of marital conflict, especially conflict that involves the children, that is protective of children's well-being, perhaps because it helps to preserve the co-parenting relationship (Erel & Burman, 1995; Grych & Fincham, 1990).

Contextual Factors

With the exception of Conger and Conger's (2002) work, little attention has been paid to the influence of factors outside of the family on co-parenting. However, there is considerable indirect research from the literature on work/family balance and from the fathering literature. In making use of the fathering literature, we are working from the assumption that factors that influence fathers' involvement with their children have at least indirect effects on the co-parenting relationship.

We begin with Conger and Conger's (2002) contextual model, based on their longitudinal study of farm families in the Midwest facing economic hardship. The authors propose, and offer supportive evidence for, a model demonstrating how economic hardship leads to economic pressure, which impacts co-parenting through two sources: increased parent emotional distress and increased interparental conflict–withdrawal patterns. Both of these factors lead in turn to disrupted parenting and then to poorer child and adolescent adjustment. Of special importance is the replication of this contextual model of influences of economic hardship on parenting and co-parenting in a study of over 400 two-parent African American families (Conger et al., 2002).

One area of research associated with contextual factors in co-parenting relates to employment. Parents face increasing challenges in balancing work, parenting, and family time (see Daly, 1996, 2001, Fraenkel, 2003). Recent decades have witnessed an increase in dual-earning families and in jobs requiring shift work, combined with a dramatic increase of employment opportunities for women (see Bianchi, 2000). The U.S Bureau of Labor Statistics (2001) indicates that the majority of married couples (67%) are dual earners. A positive side to the increased work responsibilities of parents has been an increase in the amount of time fathers spend with their children, especially when mothers work different shifts from fathers (Bianchi, 2000). The 1990s saw a dramatic increase in the number of temporary jobs with few benefits (Seccombe, 2000). The increase in temporary jobs has the potential to put more emotional strain on parents, and as Conger and Conger (2002) have found, makes it harder for mothers and fathers to co-parent effectively. Furthermore, co-parental strain can be the result of the total number of work hours per family increasing (Perry-Jenkins, Repetti, & Crouter, 2000), specifically in the managerial, professional, and technical occupations (Daly, 2001). In dual-earning couples the average number of work hours per person per week in the late 1990s was 46 hr (Bond, Galinsky, & Swanberg, 1998).

These employment-related factors present challenges for contemporary parents to negotiate their co-parenting roles when both parents are breadwinners at the same time that traditional cultural norms call for mothers to work a "second shift" when they come home (Hothschild, 1989). This is an important area for co-parenting researchers to explore.

Other literature bearing on contextual influences on co-parenting comes from the extensive body of work on father involvement. As noted earlier, this research can be examined through a "co-parenting lens" to show how shifts in father involvement have an impact on co-parenting. When fathers are less involved with their children because of contextual forces, there is less balance in the co-parental relationship, and there may be more conflict and triangulation. The research reviewed by Doherty et al. (1998) is quite clear: Father involvement is influenced by a variety of contextual factors, especially employment opportunities and other economic factors, and this influence is stronger for fathers than for mothers. Fathers who do not have viable opportunities to provide for their families feel less successful in the external work environment and tend to withdraw from their children (Jones, 1991). Doherty et al. (1998) explain this phenomenon by suggesting that cultural norms are stricter about the centrality and the endurance of the mother–child dyad, no matter what is taking place outside the relationship. Father–child relationships, on the other hand, are seen as requiring men's success as breadwinners and protectors in the public sphere and therefore may require a greater level of support from external contexts. Given this, fathers may withdraw from responsible fathering and co-parenting as a result of contextual factors unless their own individual level of devotion to fathering is strong and resilient.

Unfortunately, there has been little research investigating how race and ethnicity influence co-parenting dynamics. One study conducted by Brody, Flor, and Neubaum (1998) with African American families showed that harmonious interactions between parents who shared responsibilities for child rearing had positive outcomes for children. Much like research with White families (e.g., McHale, Lauretti, Talbot, & Pouquette, 2002) supportive interactions between co-parents were important in positive child development. Brody et al. argue that the definition of co-parenting as including a biological father and a biological mother needs to be expanded for different ethnic groups. African American families tend to establish extended family kin networks that may play significant child-rearing roles. For example, Allen and Connor (1997) found that role flexibility in the African American community provided men with opportunities to be surrogate fathers to children who did not have everyday contact with their biological fathers. Extended kin networks are also very common with Latino, American Indian, and Asian American families (see Parke & Buriel, 1998). Clearly there is a need for more research about how various ethnic groups co-parent their children, keeping in mind that this may involve members of extended kin networks and "fictive" kin.

Another contextual factor in the model, broad cultural expectations, can influence how parents are involved with their children and how they co-parent. Pleck and Pleck (1997) describe the emerging ideal of fatherhood in the late 20th century as father as equal co-parent. In his historical studies, LaRossa (1997) has documented how cultural norms wax and wane over time for how fathers should be involved with their children and, implicitly, how fathers and mothers should co-parent. The emergence in the 1970s of the expectation for cooperative labor and delivery of babies, with fathers actively participating in the process, is an example of how cultural norms influence co-parenting practices. More research on cultural influences on co-parenting needs to be done. These influences probably show themselves in the form of community support for co-parenting, as in the previous example when hospitals provide vehicles for fathers and mothers to work together on bringing their children into the world. Community influences can go another way too, as when recent norms about scheduling of children in extracurricular activities threaten to turn parents into individual chauffeurs driving their children in different directions (Doherty & Carlson, 2002).

Mother Factors

Numerous studies have shown that mothers' expectations about father involvement have a direct influence on how fathers are involved with their children, and thus, indirectly, on the kind of co-parenting relationship mothers have with the father (Cowan, Cowan, Heming, Garrett, Coysh, Curtis-Boles, & Boles 1985; McBride & Rane, 1997; Maurer, Pleck, & Rane, 2001; Pasley, Futris, & Skinner, 2002). In general, mothers' expectations for fathers' behavior are more influential than fathers' own expectations for their own behavior. For example, McBride and Rane (1997) used self-report and interview data to study role identity, role investments, and parental involvement with couples. The study was designed to measure how participants perceive their own investments in four adult roles (spouse, parent, worker, and social roles). The parent role was the most important for both mothers and fathers. Findings indicated that mothers' perceptions of their partners' investments in parent, spouse, and worker roles were the best predictors of total father involvement.

Mother's work experience is also a contributor to co-parenting, beyond ways we discussed earlier. Women seem to be happier at home and work when they have flexible workplace options, they are supported in their jobs by their partners, and they can afford high-quality daycare (Arendell, 2000). Mothers tend to experience more work/family tension than fathers, since mothers are more likely to be interrupted at work about a family issue than are fathers (Perry-Jenkins et al., 2000). Interestingly, Galinsky's (1999) interviews with children indicate that it is not women entering the workforce that has negative effects on children, but the degree of work stress experienced by both mothers and fathers that affects children's well-being. This body of research has implications for the study of co-parenting, because mothers' experiences of work/home stress might influence their expectations about father involvement and the co-parenting relationship, and because fathers' cooperation or lack of cooperation with mothers' expectations might be an important source of co-parental conflict.

Father Factors

As with other areas in our model, the research on father factors in family involvement with children can be looked at through the lens of co-parenting: More involved fathers are more active coparents. On the other hand, direct research needs to be conducted to examine the possible offsetting influences on co-parenting, such as increased conflict between parents when fathers are more active parents.

Studies clearly demonstrate a positive association between fathers' psychological well-being and their involvement with their children (Pleck, 1997). Fathers who feel competent about themselves as parents are more involved with their children and adolescents (Bogenschneider, Small, & Tsay, 1997; Lamb, Pleck, Charnov, & Levine, 1985; Pleck, 1997). For example, Blair, Wenk, and Hardesty, (1994) found that positive father involvement was associated with fathers' higher self-esteem and fewer symptoms of depression.

A father's psychological well-being may also be connected to his family of origin experiences. Studies based on fathers' retrospective reports of childhood have shown how secure attachments for fathers are associated with securely attached infants (e.g., Cowan &

Cowan, 1999; Steele, Steele, & Fongay, 1996). For example, Steele and colleagues (1996), with a sample of married couples and their 18-month-old children, found that both mothers' and fathers' secure attachments in adulthood predicted infants' secure attachment. By contrast, studies have also shown that some men who experienced little affection from their own fathers compensate for this negative family of origin experience by being highly affectionate with their own children. For example, Floyd and Morman (2000) with a sample of men and their adolescent sons found that men were the most affectionate with their sons when their own fathers were either highly affectionate or highly unaffectionate. Snarey (1993), in a 35-year longitudinal study, showed how men who experienced distant fathers during their childhood were more involved with the social–emotional development of their adolescent children. Therefore, for fathers, both negative and positive family-of-origin experiences can lead to fathers being more involved with their children and being more active co-parents.

Less research has been conducted on fathers' expectations about motherhood. Maurer, Pleck, and Rane (2001) designed a questionnaire to study both maternal and paternal identities. They studied parental identity for both mothers and fathers in relationship to caregiving and breadwinning identities and reflected appraisals. Caregiving tasks referred to direct involvement with a child, for example, playing with the child or making a doctor's appointment. Breadwinning identity refers to items about providing financially for a child; for example, how important is it to work in order to provide for a child. Reflected appraisals refer to perceptions about how you think your partner wants you to parent. Results indicated that mothers were more likely to be involved in caregiving tasks and fathers were more likely to be involved in caregiving and breadwinning tasks if they believed these tasks were supported by their partners. Clearly more research is needed that investigates fathers' expectations of maternal involvement in co-parenting, especially as it relates to mothers' participation in the paid labor force.

As mentioned before, father's employment characteristics play a significant role in father involvement. Fathers who lose their job generally struggle emotionally, and this adversely affects their involvement with their children (Jones, 1991). In addition, greater work flextime and profamily policies are associated with more father involvement (Pleck, 1997). Furthermore, research indicates that mothers' work schedules have more effect on father involvement than fathers' work schedules, because fathers are more involved with their children when mothers enter the paid workforce (Bianchi, 2000; Pleck, 1997). Researchers can examine how fathers' employment situations influence their everyday co-parenting practices with mothers.

Child Factors

Researchers are in the early stages of discovering child factors that influence co-parenting, but clearly this is an important area of work. We suggest three areas that might be especially fruitful: gender, age, and number of siblings. With regard to gender, in a study reviewed earlier, McHale (1995) examined how the interplay between the quality of the marital relationship and a child's gender can affect parental involvement. He found that when the parents are in marital distress boys are more likely to encounter hostile competitive co-parenting, whereas girls are more likely to encounter larger discrepancies in co-parental involvement. This is not to suggest that fathers are not just as enamored with their girls as with their boys, but that during marital conflict men may draw closer to sons in a triangle with their wives (Albow, 1997; McHale et al., 2002).

A child's gender seems to influence father involvement, but not mother involvement. Fathers tend to be more involved with their sons, especially when their sons get older, perhaps because fathers identify more easily with their older sons (Blair, Wenk, & Hardesty, 1994; Marsiglio, 1991; Pleck, 1997). These gender patterns may have especially important implications for co-parenting dynamics in families with adolescents.

Finally, we suggest that age of the child and number of children bear attention as influences on co-parenting. Co-parenting young children may require more physical labor from parents, and more "tag-team" co-parenting, whereas older children may require more difficult decision making by co-parents. The number of siblings, and the need to divide parenting attention among them, may also be an important influence on co-parenting practices. Coalitions between children might influence co-parenting just as a coalition between a parent and a child does.

Future Directions in Co-Parenting Research

Here we summarize some of the gaps in the current research on co-parenting, and go on to propose new areas of investigation. First, the majority of research related to co-parenting focuses on the infant and toddler years and particularly neglects co-parenting relationships during adolescence and young adulthood. This gap is especially important to close because, as Margolin et al. (2001) note, co-parenting may become harder as children get older, because parents tend to cooperate more when children are young and disagree more about parenting when children become adolescents.

Second, little attention has been paid to how children participate in socially constructing the co-parenting relationship. The bidirectional nature of parent–child relationships has long been a focus of child development literature, with children seen as playing an active role in shaping dyadic parent–child interactions. The same case can be made for triadic interactions. For example, Fivaz-Depeursinge and colleagues (1994) have shown how cues from infants have a direct impact on triadic interactions as well as on mothers' and fathers' responses to infants. Further research is needed that looks at how children influence co-parental interactions.

Third, as noted earlier, there has been little research that focuses on co-parenting among various racial groups. The rise in interracial marriages and parenting also presents an opportunity to expand our understanding of the roles of race and ethnicity in co-parenting, both at the nuclear family level and at the extended family and community levels.

Fourth, the limited empirical evidence for several domains in our ecological model suggests areas for future research, especially in contextual factors such as employment and child factors such as age and gender. For example, in our increasingly busy world, more research is needed that studies how both mothers' and fathers' work schedules affect parental involvement. Furthermore, more research is needed on why fathers seem to place more importance on their relationships with their sons.

Beyond these straightforward next steps in co-parenting research, we offer ideas for bolder steps. With so many children now spending substantial time in stepfamilies, there is a need for expanding co-parenting research to this challenging family form. Bray and Kelly (1998) have documented how a particular co-parenting style—one in which the biological parent plays the lead and the stepparent plays backup—is associated with successful stepfamily adjustment. Indeed co-parenting research could be enriched by comparing findings across biological, stepfamily, never-married, and postdivorce family structure in order to tease out what is core to successful co-parenting across contexts and what is dependent on family structure.

In addition, the field should move beyond process models of co-parenting, which focus on cooperation and conflict as interpersonal processes, to also include constructs that capture the *content* of co-parenting—for example, who is doing what kind and amount of nurturing and limit setting and physical care; what is the balance between the parents' involvement in these areas; and what are the parents' expectations of their co-parenting relationship. In other words, process variables focus only on how the parents communicate, leaving out what they are communicating about. Staying only with process variables could limit the usefulness of co-parenting research and could lead to a theoretical dead end in which little advance is made beyond the generalization that effective co-parenting involves high levels of positive cooperation and low levels of conflict. For example, studies have demonstrated that what mothers expect of fathers is a strong predictor of what fathers actually do in the co-parenting relationship; process models alone will not capture this aspect of co-parenting.

Another area ripe for research is co-parenting practices as they occur outside of the presence of the children. Much co-parenting occurs in dyadic conversation between parents about their child-rearing decisions and strategies. Examining these conversations could provide a glimpse into the world of co-parental decision making, which may not show itself in current research designs that focus on direct parent–child interaction. For example, co-parental consensus could be a central predictor of co-parental cooperation. Consensus itself could be categorized into agreement about the content of child rearing (say, policies on limit setting) and agreement about the process of child rearing (e.g., how to interact with a child when administering a limit). We offer these ideas to suggest the scale of the untapped potential in co-parenting research.

The emergence of research on co-parenting has opened up a new vista for the study of family communication. The application of rigorous assessment tools to family systems ideas that have proved themselves clinically useful for over 40 years represents a long-awaited rapprochement between family therapy and academic family researchers that bodes well for the future of the field and for our ability to understand families in their fascinating complexity.

REFERENCES

Ahrons, C. R., & Miller, R. B. (1993). The effect of the post-divorce relationship on paternal involvement: A longitudinal analysis: *American Journal of Orthopsychiatry, 63*, 441–450.

Albow, J. (1997). *Marital conflict across family contexts: Does the presence of children make a difference?* Paper presented at the Society for Research in Child Development, Washington, DC.

Aldous, J. (1978). *Family careers: Developmental change in families.* New York: Wiley.

Allen, W. D., & Connor, M. (1997). An African American perspective on generative fathering. In A. J. Hawkins & D. C. Dollahite (Eds.), *Generative fathering: Beyond deficit perspectives* (pp. 52–70). Newbury Park, CA: Sage.

Amato, P. R., & Gilbreth, J. G. (1999). Nonresident fathers and children's well-being: A meta-analysis. *Journal of Marriage and the Family, 61*, 557–573.

Arendell. T. (2000). Conceiving and investigating motherhood: The decade's scholarship. *Journal of Marriage and the Family, 62*, 1192–1207.

Bateson, G. (1972). *Steps to an ecology of mind.* New York: Ballantine.

Belsky, J. (1979). The interrelation of parental and spousal behavior during infancy in traditional nuclear families: An exploratory analysis. *Journal of Marriage and the Family, 41*, 62–68.

Belsky, J. (1981). Early human experience: A family perspective. *Developmental Psychology, 17*, 3–23.

Belsky, J. (1984). The determinants of parenting: A process model. *Child Development, 55*, 83–96.

Belsky, J. (1999). Interactional and contextual determinants of attachment security. In J. Cassidy & P. R. Shaver (Eds.), *Handbook of attachment: Theory, research, and clinical applications* (pp. 249–263). New York: Guilford Press.

Belsky, J., Crnic, K., & Gable, S. (1995). The determinants of co-parenting in families with toddler boys: Spousal differences and daily hassles. *Child Development, 66*, 629–642.

Berger, P. L., & Luckmann, T. (1966). *The social construction of reality: A treatise in the sociology of knowledge.* New York: Doubleday.

Bianchi, S. M. (2000). Maternal employment and time with children: Dramatic change or surprising continuity. *Demography, 37*, 401–414.

Blair, S. L., & Hardesty, C. (1994). Parental involvement and the well-being of fathers and mothers of young children. *Journal of Men's Studies, 3*, 49–68.

Blair, S. L., Wenk, D., & Hardesty, C. (1994). Marital quality and paternal involvement: Interconnections of men's spousal and parental roles. *Journal of Men's Studies, 2*, 221–237.

Blumer, H. (1986). *Symbolic-interactionism: Perspectives and method.* Berkeley, CA: University of California Press.

Bogenschneider, K., Small, S. A., & Tsay, J. C. (1997). Child, parent, and contextual influences on perceived parenting competence among parents of adolescents. *Journal of Marriage and the Family, 59*, 345–362.

Bond, J. T., Galinsky, E., & Swanberg, J. E. (1998). *The 1997 national study of the changing workforce.* New York: Families and Work Institute.

Bowen, M. (1976). Theory in the practice of psychotherapy. In P. Guerin (Ed.), *Family Therapy.* New York: Gardner.

Bray, J. H., & Kelly, J. (1998). *Stepfamilies: Love, marriage, and parenting in the first decade.* New York: Broadway Books.

Brody, G. H., Flor, D. L., & Neubaum, E. (1998). Co-parenting processes and child competence among rural African-American families. In M. Lewis & C. Feiring (Eds.), *Families, risk, and competence* (pp. 227–244). Mahwah, NJ: Lawrence Erlbaum Associates.

Bronfenbrenner, U. (1979). *The ecology of human development: Experiments by nature and design.* Cambridge, MA: Harvard University Press.

Bubolz, M. M., & Sontag, M. S. (1993). Human ecology theory. In P. G. Boss, W. J. Doherty, R. LaRossa, W. R. Schumm, & S. K. Steinmetz (Eds.), *Sourcebook of family theories and methods* (pp. 419–450). New York: Plenum Press.

Conger, R. D., & Conger, K. J. (2002). Resilience in midwestern families: Selected findings from the first decade of a prospective, longitudinal study. *Journal of Marriage and Family, 64,* 361–373.

Conger, R. D., Wallace, L. E., Sun, Y., Simons, R. L., McLoyd, V. C., & Brody, G. H. (2002). Economic pressure in African American families: A replication and extension of the Family Stress Model. *Developmental Psychology, 38,* 179–193.

Cowan, P. A., & Cowan, C. P. (1999). *When partners become parents: The big life change.* Mahwah, NJ: Lawrence Erlbaum Associates.

Cowan, P. A., & Cowan, C. P. (2003). Normative family transitions, normal family processes, and healthy child development. In F. Walsh (Ed.), *Normal family processes* (3rd ed., pp. 424–459). New York: Guilford Press.

Cowan, C. P., Cowan, P. A., Heming, G., Garrett, E., Coysh, W. S., Curtis-Boles, H., & Boles, A. J. (1985). Transitions to parenthood: His, hers, and theirs. *Journal of Family Issues, 6,* 451–481.

Cowan, P. A., Cowan, C. P., Schulz, M. S., & Heming, G. (1994). Prebirth to preschool family factors in children's adaptation to kindergarten. In R. D. Parke & S. G. Kellam (Eds.), *Exploring family relationships with other social contexts. Family research consortium: Advances in family research* (Vol. 4, pp. 75–114). Hillsdale, NJ: Lawrence Erlbaum Associates.

Cummings, E. M., & O'Reilly, A. W. (1997). Fathers in family context: Effects of marital quality on child adjustment. In. M. E. Lamb (Ed.), *The role of the father in child development* (pp. 49–65). New York: Wiley.

Daly, K. J. (1996). *Families and time: Keeping pace in a hurried culture.* Thousand Oaks, CA: Sage.

Daly, K. J. (2001). Deconstructing family time: From ideology to lived experience. *Journal of Marriage and Family, 63,* 283–295.

Doherty, W. J., & Carlson, B. Z. (2002). *Putting family first.* New York: Henry Holt.

Doherty, W. J., Kouneski, E. F., & Erickson, M. F. (1998). Responsible fathering: An overview and conceptual framework. *Journal of Marriage and the Family, 60,* 277–292.

Erel, O., & Burman, B. (1995). Interrelatedness of marital relations and parent-child relations: A meta-analytic review. *Psychological Bulletin, 118,* 108–132.

Fitzpatrick, M. A. (1988). *Between husbands and wives.* Newbury Park, CA: Sage.

Fivaz-Depeursinge, E., Burgin, D., Corboz-Warney, A., Lebovci, S., Stern, D., Byng-Hall, J., & Lamour, M. (1994). The dynamics of interfaces: Seven authors in search of encounters across levels of description of an event involving a mother, father, and baby. *Infant Mental Health Journal, 15,* 69–89.

Floyd, K., & Morman, M. T. (2000). Affection received from fathers as a predictor of men's affection with their own sons: Tests of the modeling and compensation hypotheses. *Communication Monographs, 67,* 347–361.

Fraenkel, P. (2003). Contemporary two-parent families: Navigating work and family challenges. In F. Walsh (Ed.), *Normal family processes* (3rd ed., pp. 61–95). New York: Guilford Press.

Furstenberg, F. F., & Cherlin, A. J. (1991). *Divided families: What happens to children when parents part.* Cambridge, MA: Harvard University Press.

Galinsky, E. (1999). *Ask the children: What America's children really think about working parents.* New York: William Morrow.

Gottman, J. M. (1979). *Marital interaction: Experimental investigations.* New York: Academic Press.

Grych, J. H., & Fincham, F. D. (1990). Marital conflict and children's adjustment: A cognitive-contextual framework. *Psychological Bulletin, 108,* 267–290.

Hill, R., & Mattessich, P. (1979). Family development theory and life span development. In P. Baltes & O. Brim (Eds.), *Life span development and behavior* (Vol. 2, pp. 161–204). New York: Academic Press.

Hothschild, A. R. (1989). *The second shift: Working parents and the revolution at home.* New York: Viking.

Jones, L. (1991). Unemployed fathers and their children: Implications for policy and practice. *Child and Adolescent Social Work Journal, 8,* 101–116.

Lamb, M. E. (1987). Introduction: The emergent American father. In M. E. Lamb (Ed.), *The father's role: Cross-cultural perspectives.* Hillsdale, NJ: Lawrence Erlbaum Associates.

Lamb, M. E., Pleck, J., Charnov, E. L., & Levine, J. A. (1985). Paternal behavior in humans. *American Zoologist, 25,* 883–894.

LaRossa, R. (1997). *The modernization of fatherhood: A social and political history.* Chicago: University of Chicago Press.

LaRossa, R., & Reitzes, D. C. (1993). Symbolic interactionism and family studies. In P. G. Boss, W. J. Doherty, R. LaRossa, W. R. Schumm, & S. K. Steinmetz (Eds.), *Sourcebook of family theories and methods* (pp. 135–163). New York: Plenum Press.

Lewis, J. M., Owen, M. T., & Cox, M. J. (1988). The transition to parenthood: III. Incorporation of the child into the family. *Family Process, 27,* 411–421.

Margolin, G., Gordis, E. B., & John, R. S. (2001). Co-parenting: A link between marital conflict and parenting in two-parent families. *Journal of Family Psychology, 15,* 3–21.

Marsiglio, W. (1991). Paternal engagement activities with minor children. *Journal of Marriage and the Family, 53,* 973–986.

Marsiglio, W., Amato, P., Day, R. D., & Lamb, M.E. (2000). Scholarship on fatherhood in the 1990's and beyond. *Journal of Marriage and the Family, 62,* 1173–1191.

Maurer, T. W., Pleck, J. H., & Rane, T. R. (2001). Parental identity and behavior: A contextual model. *Journal of Marriage and Family, 63,* 394–403.

McBride, B. A, & Rane, T. R. (1997). Role identity, role investments, and paternal involvement: Implications for parenting programs for men. *Early Childhood Research Quarterly, 12,* 173–197.

McHale, J. P. (1995). Coparenting and triadic interactions during infancy: The roles of marital distress and child gender. *Developmental Psychology, 31,* 985–996.

McHale, J. P. (1997). Overt and covert co-parenting processes in the family. *Family Process, 36,* 183–201.

McHale, J. P., & Rasmussen, J. L. (1998). Coparental and family group-level dynamics during infancy: Early family precursors of child and family functioning during preschool. *Development and Psychopathology, 10*, 39–59.

McHale, J. P., Lauretti, A. Kuersten-Hogan, R., & Rasmussen, J. L. (2000). Parental reports of co-parenting and observed co-parenting behavior during the toddler period. *Journal of Family Psychology, 14*, 220–236.

McHale, J. P., Lauretti, A., Talbot, J., & Pouquette, C. (2002). Retrospect and prospect in the psychological study of co-parenting and family group process. In J. P. McHale & W. S. Grolick (Eds.), *Retrospect and prospect in the psychological study of families.* (pp. 127–166). Mahwah, NJ: Lawrence Erlbaum Associates.

Minuchin, S. (1974). *Families and family therapy.* Cambridge, MA: Harvard University Press.

Minuchin, P. (1985). Families and individual development: Provocations from the field of family therapy. *Child Development, 56,* 289–302.

Parke, R. D., & Buriel, R. (1998). Socialization in the family: Ethnic and ecological perspectives. In W. Damon (Ed.), *Handbook of child psychology* (pp. 463–552). New York: Wiley.

Pasley, K., Futris, T. G., & Skinner. M. L. (2002). Effects of commitment and psychological centrality on fathering. *Journal of Marriage and Family, 64,* 130–138.

Perry-Jenkins, M., Repetti, R. L., & Crouter, A. C. (2000). Work and family in the 1990s. *Journal of Marriage and the Family, 62,* 981–1017.

Pleck, E. H., & Pleck, J. H. (1997). Fatherhood ideals in the United States: Historical dimensions. In M. E. Lamb (Ed.), *The role of the father in child development* (3rd ed., pp. 38–48). New York: Wiley.

Pleck, J. H. (1997). Paternal involvement: Levels, sources, and consequences. In M. L. Lamb (Ed.), *The role of the father in child development* (pp. 66–104). New York: Wiley.

Rodgers, R. H., & White, J. M. (1993). Family development theory. In P. G. Boss, W. J. Doherty, R. LaRossa, W. R. Schumm, & S. K. Steinmetz (Eds.), *Sourcebook of family theories and methods* (pp. 225–254). New York: Plenum Press.

Seccombe, K. (2000). Families in poverty in the 1990's: Trends, causes, consequences, and lessons learned. *Journal of Marriage and the Family, 62,* 1094–1113.

Snarey, J. (1993). *How fathers care for the next generation: A four-decade study.* Cambridge, MA: Harvard University Press.

Steele, H., Steele, M., & Fongay, P. (1996). Associations among attachment classifications of mothers, fathers, and their infants. *Child Development, 67,* 541–555.

U.S. Bureau of Labor Statistics. (2001). *Employment characteristics of families in 2000.* [Available on-line: http://stats.bls.gov/newsrels.htm]

14

THE DEVELOPMENTAL ORIGINS OF COMMUNICATION: INTERACTIONAL SYSTEMS IN INFANCY

LAURIE A. VAN EGEREN AND MARGUERITE S. BARRATT

MICHIGAN STATE UNIVERSITY

The birth of an infant is both a landmark moment in family development and the initiation of a remarkable responsibility. Born with an immature nervous system that will take years to become fully integrated, the infant has a limited capacity to express even basic needs in a way that adults can understand. Infants must rely completely on caregivers to understand their needs for nourishment and physical comfort. For their part, adults must use overt signs of the infant's state, such as crying, calm, or sleep, to determine when to intervene and when to let well enough alone.

Yet meeting physical needs is only one part of the family's responsibility for an infant. From the moment the newborn is placed in a parent's arms, early interactions provide the critical foundation for emotional, cognitive, and social development. Although mastery of language has been cited as the cornerstone of these fundamental developmental dimensions (Shonkoff & Phillips, 2000), prelinguistic communicative interactions underlie subsequent linguistic–cognitive processes (Coates & Lewis, 1984; Feldman, Greenbaum, Yirmiya, & Mayes, 1996; Tamis-LeMonda, Bornstein, Baumwell, & Damast, 1996) as well as self-regulation (Feldman, Greenbaum, & Yirmiya, 1999; Malatesta, Grigoryev, Lamb, Albin, & Culver, 1986), competence (Clarke Stewart, 1973; Kochanska, Forman, & Coy, 1999), relationship formation (NICHD Early Child Care Research Network, 1997; Voelker, Keller, Lohaus, Cappenberg, & Chasiotis, 1999), and socialization into the rules of one's culture of origin (Richman, Miller, & LeVine, 1992; Rogoff, 1990; Schulze, Harwood, & Schoelmerich, 2001). The communicative system that emerges from those infant–caregiver interactions will in large part lay the foundation for the child's ability to function as an effective communicator in subsequent settings, tasks, and relationships.

QUANTIFYING INFANT COMMUNICATION

Three primary methods of quantifying observations of communication in infancy have emerged in the literature. At the most general level, ratings of caregiver sensitivity provide an overall index of the degree of responsiveness to infant cues and didactic stimulation of the infant (e.g., Caldwell & Bradley, 1978; Lohaus, Keller, Ball, Elben, & Voelker, 2001; Nicholls & Kirkland, 1996). Although these assessments often require substantial training to achieve interrater reliability, they are comparatively efficient and have produced an extensive literature on caregiver interactions in relation to child outcomes (Bradley, 1994). However, the global nature of such assessments precludes their use in identifying dynamic change and development within the infant–caregiver subsystem and they do not focus on moment-by-moment processes.

A second method is the construction of content-based behavioral composites according to preestablished contingency relations that denote positive, neutral, or negative exchanges (Isabella, Belsky, & von Eye, 1989; Tronick, Als, & Brazelton, 1980); or symmetrical, asymmetrical, or unilateral dyadic communication (Hsu & Fogel, 2001). Composites, which require highly detailed inspection of video observations, have informed our understanding of the frequency and correlates of particular types of exchanges as well as furthered theoretical discourse regarding the nature of dyadic communication; however, investigations are constrained to the definitions of composites designated by the researchers. For example, responses in the visual, tactile, and auditory modalities may be collapsed under a particular coding system and considered essentially equivalent, although they may have different pathways of development and be associated with different patterns of individual differences in later communication (Heimann, 1989).

Third, microanalytic approaches have been used for many years. They provide the most specific information because they allow analysis of moment-by-moment interactional processes across several modalities. Microanalytic approaches have been used to describe processes underlying infant cries and caregiver speech patterns (Papousek & Papousek, 1991), postural adjustments in dyads (Fogel, Messinger, Dickson, & Hsu, 1999) and triads (Fivaz Depeursinge & Corboz Warnery, 1999), gaze patterns (Fogel et al., 1999), tactile stimulation (Stack & Arnold, 1998; Weiss, Wilson, Hertenstein, & Campos, 2000), affect dynamics, and contingent patterns among all these behaviors (Fogel, Toda, & Kawai, 1988; Van Egeren, Barratt, & Roach, 2001; Weinberg & Tronick, 1994). Most of these approaches pinpoint behaviors at increments of less than a second and result in a descriptive stream of moment-by-moment behavior of, for example, mother and infant that can be analyzed to identify patterns of temporal and event-related contingencies. Microanalytic approaches require intensive coder training to achieve reliability and are more time intensive; for example, in our work (e.g., Van Egeren et al., 2001), videotapes of mothers and infants were coded in four separate passes, with coders attending to different behaviors in each pass to maximize reliability by minimizing the number of behaviors coded at one time. Lavelli and Fogel (2002) conducted frame analysis, in which tapes were played in slow motion and coded for one set of frames, or commonly occurring dyadic communication patterns, in the first pass and a set of subframes in a second pass. Nonetheless, the information gleaned from microanalytic methods provides a unique perspective on dynamic processes that characterize the early dyadic communication system.

THEORETICAL BASES FOR INFANT–CAREGIVER COMMUNICATION

Theories applicable to communication in infancy have tended to focus on the adult's, specifically the mother's, role in raising a competent, socially skilled, and emotionally attuned child. For example, from a social learning perspective, adults provide models for infant behaviors, which then contribute to emotional awareness and appropriate social communication (e.g., Malatesta et al., 1986). Operant conditioning principles attribute the development of self-efficacy, behavioral adjustment, and focused attention to infant learning that occurs when adults respond contingently to infant signals (Gewirtz & Pelaez Nogueras, 2000; Watson, 1977). Psychodynamic theories discuss the contribution of maternal sensitivity to object relations development (Brody & Axelrad, 1978). From an ethological-attachment perspective, prompt and appropriate caregiver responses to infant cues provide infants with a critical sense of security and a secure base from which to encounter challenging situations (Ainsworth, Blehar, Waters, & Wall, 1978).

These theoretical perspectives of early infant–caregiver interaction consistently identify adult responsiveness (contingency, sensitivity) to infant cues as the core process in optimal child development. They also share the viewpoint that early dyadic interaction relies on the skill of the caregiver to communicate to the infant, who is perceived to be a generally passive receiver. However, infants have emerged as playing an important role in the *mutual* regulation of communicative interaction (Bell & Harper, 1977; Sameroff, 1993). Increasingly sophisticated analyses that focus on microprocesses of dyadic interaction and feedback loops have allowed more detailed examination of mutual influences, identifying patterns of co-regulated adaptation in infant–caregiver communicative development (Fogel, 1993; Papousek & Papousek, 1984; Tronick et al., 1980).

Dynamic Systems Theory

The dynamic systems perspective (Fogel, 1993; Thelen & Fogel, 1989) is a broad-based approach to identifying and quantifying patterns of complex systems in areas as diverse as biology, engineering, and meteorology. Dynamic systems models are also well suited for describing the intricate interactions that emerge within infant–caregiver communication. Basically, the system emerges from constraints of the participating entities. Infants and caregivers can be characterized as two distinct systems, with their own biological constraints and psychological motivations. However, from a dynamic systems perspective, the infant and the caregiver systems merge into a single unique system within which each partner's behavior is necessarily influenced by the behavior of the other partner.

Research thus far has tended to focus on behavioral changes in the adult that occur during infant–parent interaction (e.g., Lohaus et al., 2001; Smith, Landry, & Swank, 2000). However, multiple adaptations that infants make in response to adult cues, and subsequent adult responses to those adaptations, have also been identified (e.g., Kaye & Fogel, 1980). Thus, characteristics of and changes within a single partner are inadequate to describe characteristics of and changes within the system as a whole. These emergent dynamic patterns of interaction must be described through the collective characteristics of the dyadic system, and in recent years researchers have begun to attend to and model bidirectional effects between infant and adult behaviors (Hsu & Fogel, 2001; Lavelli & Fogel, 2002).

In a typically developing infant–caregiver dyad, the characteristics, or parameters, of the infant and adult that set the boundaries of their communicative system change relatively little within any defined developmental period. Adaptations of each partner's behaviors to the behaviors of the other are continual but relatively minor, because the characteristics that define the quality of the exchanges (e.g., the infant's ability to vocalize or move; the adult's tendency to respond to ambiguous vocalizations or only to identifiable words; the amount of time the infant and adult spend together as a function of parental employment or infant sleep patterns) remain fairly stable. Moreover, a limited number of manifest systems or processes are available out of the possible combinations of behaviors. The patterns of communication into which systems most often tend to organize are termed *attractor states*; examples of attractor states defined by the degree of participation in the interaction might include mutually engaged communication, communication emphasizing the engagement of one partner rather than of another, or communication in which neither partner is engaged (Hsu & Fogel, 2001). Other characteristics of attractor states might be based on the quality of the emotion expressed within the interaction or the ways in which partners respond to one another. Thus, the dyad is in an ongoing process of homeostasis; individuals consistently regulate one another within a particular attractor state, resulting in patterns of behavior that are flexible within a certain range but do not represent a marked change from the previous attractor state.

However, from a dynamic systems perspective, when one or more of the constraining parameters shifts past a certain point, the stable system grows unstable. Over this transition period, new adaptations on the part of each partner enable new attractor states to emerge and become stable until the cycle begins again. This reorganization can result in linear, quantitative change (e.g., the infant vocalizes more) or nonlinear, qualitative change (e.g., the infant produces different kinds of vocalizations) that can be captured as a "stage change." Overall, two types of dynamic interaction occur in the developing communication system: one that enables ongoing, moment-by-moment, synergistic communication to develop within any particular interaction between infant and adult and one that enables new forms of communication to arise as the infant, the adult, and the context of the interaction change due to physiological maturity or life circumstances.

The remainder of this chapter examines the literature on early infant–caregiver communication systems, placing it within the context of dynamic systems theory. We focus on two critical factors in trying to identify processes of developmental change in early communication: What parameters constrain the communication system into a particular set of patterns, and what causes those parameters to shift and create new forms of communicative organization?

EXPERTS AND NOVICES: WHAT DO PARTNERS BRING TO THE INTERACTION?

When interacting with infants, adults are indisputably the experts at communication (Papousek & Papousek, 1984). Relative to infants, adults are linguistically and expressively sophisticated, are able to integrate sensory information about social systems, and are experienced in the contextual nuances that constrain communicative interpretation. In contrast, newborns are novices. Expression through language is many months away, and integrating sensations, perceptions, and social input into meaningful streams of information remains a task to be accomplished. This disparity in skill levels has led to an emphasis on adult communication directed toward the infant.

However, communication is bounded by the perceptual capacities of the partner to whom the message is directed. The success of a communicative attempt by one individual depends not on "the intention of the acting partner, but on processes of the recipient's attention, perception, comprehension, and responsiveness" (Papousek & Papousek, 1991, p. 301). When communication is framed in these terms, infants' and adults' levels of mutual influence are more equalized. The success of communicative efforts directed from caregiver to infant can be as difficult to interpret as that from infant to caregiver, resulting in early communicative systems characterized by attempts, errors, adaptations, and repairs. To determine the parameters that define the boundaries of early communication, the basic capacities that infants and adults bring to the interaction must first be examined.

Infants: Prepared to Attend

One of the major parameters that defines the possibilities for the development of the early communication system is the capacity of the infant to engage in communication at all. Infants' initial experiences are not the "buzzing, blooming confusion" (James, 1890) presumed in the past. Although physically and neurologically immature, infants emerge from the womb with sensory abilities that, though in some sense rudimentary, prepare them to immediately assimilate into the communicative system. Most importantly, infants appear to be attracted to characteristics that define the human species (Mondloch et al., 1999; Valenza, Simion, Cassia, & Umilta, 1996). At birth, infants' visual abilities are poor overall. However, their acuity is best for objects within a foot or two—the distance to the caregiver's face when the infant is cradled (Haynes, White, & Held, 1965). Contrasting light and dark patterns and movement are preferred by infants (Slater, Earle, Morison, & Rose, 1985), and human faces, particularly when interacting with a baby, are marked by shifts in contrasts (e.g., open mouth with teeth, eyes) (Slater & Johnson, 1998). Newborns can recognize such stimuli even when presented only a few times (Barrile, Armstrong, & Bower, 1999), so it is unsurprising that infants quickly learn to prefer their own mother's face.

Other sensory channels also facilitate infant–caregiver communication. At birth, infants are nearly as sensitive to odors as they will be in adulthood, although their limited capacity for intersensory integration constrains the associations they can make to smell (Schaal, 1988). Breastfeeding seems to accelerate infant recognition of maternal odors, as breast-fed (Porter, Makin, Davis, & Christensen, 1992), but not bottle-fed (Cernoch & Porter, 1985) infants prefer their mother's smell, perhaps because of its chemical similarity to amniotic fluid (Porter & Winberg, 1999). Notably, infants do not recognize fathers by smell (Cernoch & Porter, 1985).

It has been suggested that infants have a particular proclivity to notice the sounds of human speech (Jusczyk & Bertoncini, 1988). For months prior to birth, the fetus is able to sense auditory stimuli and is exposed to low-frequency maternal speech. Even newborns have remarkable abilities to discriminate sounds, particularly the low-frequency sounds with which they are familiar (Spence & Freeman, 1996). Further, infants distinguish between speech sounds and nonspeech sounds (Jusczyk, 1997), between male and female voices (Miller, 1983), and between the voices of parents and strangers (Ockleford, Vince, Layton, & Reader, 1988). They prefer the sound of human voices over other sounds (Jusczyk, 1997) and their mother's voice over the voice of a female stranger (DeCasper & Fifer, 1980). Newborn infants also have the capacity to distinguish small differences, such as phonetic structures, between particular speech sounds, improving consistently over the subsequent few months (Jusczyk, 1997; Shi, Werker, & Morgan, 1999), and are sensitive to the rising and falling pitches that provide salient information about affect and security (Papousek, Bornstein, Nuzzo, Papousek, & Symmes, 1990).

Infants have several different modes of behavior that potentially comprise signals in dyadic interaction, including nondistressed and distressed vocalizations, gaze, motor movements, and smiling. This chapter will concentrate on the two modes of behavior most described in the literature: vocalizations and gaze. Two broad categories of infant vocalization can be identified, distinguished by acoustic properties, affective meaning, responses elicited by adult caregivers, and developmental trajectories: distress and nondistress.

Nondistress Vocalizations.   Within the infant–adult communicative system, vocalizations are the most frequent signal and response produced by both partners (Van Egeren et al., 2001). Initially, infants have little control over their vocalizations, but within 6 to 8 weeks begin to control their vocal apparatus and respirations, producing syllabic sounds that approximate vowel sounds (Lieberman, 1984). By 2 to 3 months of age, infants begin to make cooing sounds that draw adult interest. Around the middle of the first year, infants begin to babble—repeat strings of vowel–consonant combinations such as "ba ba ba"—and expand their repertoires of sounds, marking a turning point in co-regulated communication (Oller, 1986). In fact, children begin to emit the phrase "mama" during crying bouts on average around 2 months (Goldman, 2001). Although this production of "mama" is an artifact of crying and is not associated with any particular object or person, it nonetheless appears to be a powerful attention-getter for English-speaking parents.

The infant's nondistress *vocalizations* comprise the foundation of the toddler's *verbalizations*. As the vocal system becomes increasingly mature, infants engage in intentional vocalizations that represent relatively specific affective states (Keller & Schoelmerich, 1987). And in the presence of adults, solo vocal play, such as squeals, grunts, and yelling, designed to exercise newfound vocal control, gives way to vocalizations that are more consistent with adult speech. For example, during interaction with adults, infants vocalize more frequently than when alone (Masataka, 1993) and the syllabic nature of the vocalizations becomes more apparent (Stark, 1981). And when adults respond in a contingent way to the infant vocalizations, the frequency of syllabic vocalizations increases further still (Legerstee, 1991). By 4 months of age, precursors to components of the language system, most notably phonology and syntax, are already evident (Kuhl & Meltzoff, 1996; Papousek, 1989).

Interactions characterized by nondistress vocalizations provide practice for infant–adult dyads as the partners learn to adapt to one another's interaction styles. Within this interactional context, each dyad develops a number of distinctive communicative patterns, forming the foundation of the infant's communication skills. In a longitudinal study of infant–mother dyads from ages 4 to 24 weeks, Hsu and Fogel (2001) identified three frequent early dyadic attractor states: symmetrical (mutual engagement by partners), asymmetrical (engaged adult and interested but inactive infant), and unilateral (engaged adult and disengaged, disinterested infant). Disruptive (interfering adult and unresponsive infant) and unengaged (no engagement between partners at all) communication was less common.

In addition, Hsu and Fogel (2001) found that developmental patterns of speechlike syllabic vocalizations varied for each attractor state. For symmetrical communication, rates of syllabic vocalizations showed a curvilinear pattern, peaking at around 14 weeks and then decreasing. For unilateral communication, syllabic vocalizations showed a linear increase. The authors suggest that one factor contributing to the change in syllabic production might be the interest that infants begin to demonstrate in objects beginning around age 4 months. Although they are not mutually engaged in the infant–mother dyad, infants are engaged in an infant–mother–object triad; it may be that syllabic vocalizations previously directed to the mother are now focused upon the object.

Distress Vocalizations. The most intense and frequent crying occurs in the first 4 to 5 months, although crying decreases after 2 months (Stark, Rose, & McLagen, 1975). Within individuals, crying patterns are quite stable through the first year (Keller, Lohaus, Voelker, Cappenberg, & Chasiotis, 1998). Distress vocalizations, especially full-blown crying, are highly potent and arousing signals for caregivers—and perhaps the most overt and adaptive communicative expression possessed by very young infants. All individuals, whether male or female, adult or child, or parent or nonparent, are able to interpret the affective meaning behind infant crying (Papousek, 1989). However, mothers, especially mothers who have more than one child, are better than fathers (and presumably also better than everyone else) at distinguishing between distress cries that denote hunger versus pain (Gustafson & Harris, 1990; Stallings, Fleming, Corter, Worthman, & Steiner, 2001). Mothers, although aroused by the cries of any infant (Stallings et al., 2001), quickly become attuned to the cries of their own child (Cismaresco & Montagner, 1990).

Across cultures, parents respond to distress vocalizations in similar ways. When the infant is in close proximity, parents soothe the infant through holding, vestibular stimulation such as rocking or bouncing, singing, or talking to the infant with melodic contours that fall at the end of the statement (Keller et al., 1996; Papousek & Papousek, 1991). When the infant is out of reach, parents resort to high-pitched, rapid verbalizations in which the pitch falls by the end of the phrase—an action apparently designed to override crying (Papousek, Papousek, & Bornstein, 1985). Parents are sensitive to even small signs of discomfort in infants and intervene to prevent crying before it occurs (Papousek & Papousek, 1990). For example, distressed infants have difficultly maintaining eye contact. Concomitantly, mothers who are confronted with distressed infants intensify their soothing efforts and attempt to reestablish eye contact by increasing their use of touches, smiles, and social play (Beebe & Stern, 1977).

Gaze and Joint Attention. Eye contact is a potent form of communication between prelinguistic infants and their caregivers. Across cultures, infants produce more frequent positive vocalizations during periods of mutual gaze (Keller, Schoelmerich, & Eibl Eibesfeldt, 1988). Simultaneously, vocal responsiveness of both partners, but particularly that of parents, increases during mutual gaze (Stevenson, Ver Hoeve, Roach, & Leavitt,

1986). When infants are attending to an object the mother is showing rather than looking directly into her eyes, however, the responsiveness of both infant and mother decreases (Van Egeren et al., 2001). Within the context of object exploration, the dyad may be less vocally responsive, but more responsive through nonverbal means such as object-related demonstrating and pointing.

Research on joint attention between infant and parent has suggested that those infants using relatively high frequencies of gestures may acquire language more rapidly. At around 3 months, infants gain sufficient control to point their index fingers, although not intentionally toward a particular target. By 10 or 11 months, infants use gestures to indicate desires, interests, and the need for assistance (Blake & Dolgoy, 1993). By 12 months, infants' attention can be redirected to a different object by the pointing gesture of a caregiver, even to targets behind the infant when the pointing is sufficiently exaggerated (Deak, Flom, & Pick, 2000). Successful nonverbal communication of interests and needs results in adults and infants attending to the same object, and more importantly, attending to the object to which the *infant* is motivated to attend. A context is therefore created that is ripe for communicative interaction to take place.

Indeed, as early as 3 months of age, infant pointing is accompanied by a larger proportion of syllabic speechlike sounds than indistinct vocalic sounds (Masataka, 1995), and children who begin pointing relatively early subsequently use more gestures and have better speech comprehension than children who begin pointing at a later age (Butterworth & Morissette, 1996). In one study, Goldfield (1990) found that those children who were "referential," using nouns frequently, also showed a greater frequency of pointing, and, concomitantly, their mothers introduced more talk about objects. In conjunction with parental responsiveness, maintenance of joint attention appears to be an important mediator of the relations between dyadic interaction and language development (Tomasello & Farrar, 1986).

Few strategies for screening incoming stimuli are available to infants. Therefore, when overwhelmed, one of an infant's few options is to look away. Even at 6 months of age, gaze aversion and distress vocalizations are common reactions to unexpected stimuli, such as an encounter with a stranger. However, by entry into the second year, infants become better able to use self-soothing and other distraction strategies (Mangelsdorf, Shapiro, & Marzolf, 1995). Subtle cues from infants can indicate overstimulation, which can be denoted not only by distress but also by joy (Kopp, 1989; Stifter & Moyer, 1991). Infant reactions to stimulation show a curvilinear pattern in which both low amounts and high amounts of stimulation are met with more gaze aversion. In addition, infant heart rate accelerates just prior to an infant looking away and then decelerates during the gaze aversion period, providing support for the use of gaze aversion in regulating affective arousal (Field, 1981).

Interestingly, infants who are better imitators of their mother's actions at 2 to 3 days old show less gaze aversion at 3 months of age (Heimann, 1989). Early imitation may reflect more mature levels of brain organization in these newborns that is reflected by better integration of stimuli at 3 months. Alternatively, infants who imitate well as newborns may have mothers who are better able to adapt to infant behaviors and can somehow both elicit imitative behaviors from their infants and modulate the degree of stimulation they provide for the infant. And, early imitation may reflect better organization early on, which may itself elicit more effective maternal responsiveness, resulting in a co-regulated process that emerges across the first months.

Adults: Prepared To Teach

Just as infants are born with the predisposition to attend to adults and to emit communicative vocal and nonverbal behavior, adults enter parenthood intuitively prepared to communicate directly with infants. To encourage the continuous contact that comprises the infant's social world, evolutionary processes appear to have promoted adults to be innately attracted to babies—most adults like to talk to infants and gravitate toward even unfamiliar infants (Rheingold & Adams, 1980).

Biological systems and hormones may play a part in adults' understanding of how to talk to infants, particularly in encouraging behaviors that regulate infant–caregiver contact. New mothers are physiologically aroused by infant cries, suggesting that the neuroendocrine system may facilitate maternal sensitivity to infant cues (Stallings et al., 2001). Although both mothers and fathers react to full-out crying, only mothers' biostress systems are activated when infants fuss mildly (Stallings et al., 1997). Mothers interpret infant sounds, associating whining and fussing as an indication of physical need, laughing as a lack of physical need and a mark of positive affect, and gazing as attention–curiosity (Baird, Peterson, & Reilly, 1995; Keller & Schoelmerich, 1987). Within a couple of days after birth, mothers are able to identify their own infant by scent (Fleming, Corter, Surbey, Franks, & Steiner, 1995; Porter, Cernoch, & Perry, 1983). However, just as infants cannot identify their father's smell (Cernoch & Porter, 1985), fathers are less successful at identifying their infant's smell (Russell, Mendelson, & Peeke, 1983). Early contact appears to encourage mothers and infants to be exceptionally sensitive to the presence of the other, even more so than fathers and infants.

Adults are not only physiologically but also emotionally sensitive to infant signals. In a series of studies with American, German, and Chinese 2-month-old infant–mother pairs, regardless of culture, parents were able to distinguish between infant distress and nondistress vocalizations based solely on a brief single vocalization, and mothers responded as befit their interpretation with concern or smiling. Acoustic analyses linked to infant movements confirmed that different types of vocalizations had specific patterns of accompanying infant physiological arousal that supported the mothers' interpretations. Interestingly, the most difficult sounds to distinguish were between high levels of distress and squeals of joy, which were only assessed correctly by mothers and fathers who had had previous children; acoustical analysis found that distress and joy had similar levels of acoustical intensity and pitch, explaining why adults often must check other cues to determine whether an infant is excited or upset.

Few parents frame talking to an infant as a teaching interaction, but teaching forms the context of most caregiver behaviors. Teaching behaviors range from the explicit (e.g., "say 'Mama'! Come on: 'Mama'!") to the indirect (e.g., reducing "conversation" with infants to rudimentary components of speaking and pausing). Parents make frequent adjustments and modifications in reaction to infant behaviors in order to maintain the didactic function of the interaction. These dynamic adjustments appear to be intuitive (Papousek, Papousek, & Haekel, 1987). By scaffolding the communicative interaction in what Vygotsky (1978) termed the *zone of proximal development*, parents help the infant progress to increasingly sophisticated levels of communication.

The Foundation of Early Communication: Infant-Directed Speech.   Communication requires that one partner receive a message, and to receive a message, one must be aware that a message was sent. Thus, the parents' first task in the developing communicative system is to engage the infant's attention. Unconsciously, parents modify their language in such a way that it explicitly courts the infant's notice (Brousseau, Malcuit, Pomerleau, & Feider, 1996). Once termed "motherese," the distinctive speech patterns used with infants are now more accurately labeled "infant-directed speech," reflecting the propensity for not only mothers but also fathers, children, and strangers to modify their speech in specific ways when addressing infants and young children.

Infant-directed speech has similar characteristics regardless of culture and the language used (Papousek, Papousek, & Symmes, 1991). Compared to adult-directed speech, voice pitch is substantially higher, more intense, and replete with short, emphatic words, exclamations, noises, and gasps (Cooper & Aslin, 1989; Fernald, 1985). The characteristic musicality and rhythmicity of infant-directed speech is created by melodic boundaries around pauses (Ochs & Schieffelin, 1984). These markers assist in maintaining the infant's attention and mark word and phrase separations that denote segments of speech (Fernald, Taeschner, Dunn, Papousek, et al., 1989). Infants appear to be particularly sensitive to markers of speech chunks (Jusczyk & Bertoncini, 1988) and are, in fact, more attracted to infant-directed speech with pauses between sentence clauses than to adult-directed speech in any form or to infant-directed speech with pauses inserted within sentence clauses (Kemler Nelson, Hirsh Pasek, Jusczyk, & Cassidy, 1989). This separation of the stream of sounds that very young infants experience is likely to form the first steps toward the learning of words and syntactic structure.

Infant-directed communication is not limited to speech. Deaf adults sign to their deaf infants in a gestural version of motherese, using slow, exaggerated, repetitive motions, and are better able to retain the infant's attention than when using signing similar to that directed to adults (Masataka, 1996). Infant-directed communication has also been shown to be manifest in what has been called "multimodal motherese" (Gogate, Walker Andrews, & Bahrick, 2001). The words adults speak are often also supported by simultaneous words, gestures, touches, or actions. This temporal synchrony of both auditory and visual or tactile information has been suggested to reinforce infant comprehension by facilitating intersensory integration (Gogate et al., 2001).

Regardless of the language used, babies attend better when infant-directed speech is used, even in societies with very different pitch structures, such as Chinese tonal languages (Werker, Pegg, & McLeod, 1994). Infants' preferences for infant-directed vocalizations appear to be hard-wired; hearing newborns (2 days old) of deaf parents prefer infant-directed singing to adult-directed singing (Masataka, 1999). In particular, high-frequency pitches are a primary factor in infants' attraction to infant-directed speech (Cooper & Aslin, 1994). Although we might presume that this would bias infant attention toward women's voices, the little literature on infant preferences for parental voice indicates that infants are just as attracted to infant-directed speech produced by men. Exaggerated modulation may be an adaptive behavior constituting the best means to gaining the infant's attention. Recent research (Trainor, Austin, & Desjardins, 2000) has suggested that the special properties of infant-directed speech are a function of high levels of emotional expressiveness when adults speak to infants, as similar acoustical structures are present in both typical infant-directed speech and affectively laden adult-directed speech.

HOW DOES PARENT–INFANT COMMUNICATION DEVELOP?

The match between the preparedness of both the infant and the caregiver to immediately initiate communication, even in the first hours after birth, is a remarkable example of evolutionary adaptation. The infant is uniquely prepared, despite its immaturity, to notice exactly those signals that parents use; parents are intuitively expert at providing infants with the signals that will capture their attention. However, the surrounding conditions in which the interaction is taking place, including the noise level, density of visual stimuli, and number of people attempting to engage the infant, constitute another parameter that constrains the quality of the communication (Roe, Roe, Drivas, & Bronstein, 1990). The infant's ability to screen sensory information interacts with the context in which the communication occurs, thereby contributing to the likelihood that the message will be received.

Newborns, in particular, require optimal conditions in order to receive information intentionally addressed to them (Papousek & Papousek, 1991). Early on, infants are best prepared to interact when alert and responsive, few distractions exist, and the adult is responsive and producing messages that are repetitive, distinct, and comprised of characteristics that take advantage of the infant's perceptual abilities and interests. Notably, most research investigates infant communication when contextual conditions are maximized by, for example, using controlled laboratory settings and/or placing the infant in a seat directly facing the adult (e.g., Tronick & Cohn, 1989; Zlochower & Cohn, 1996). This suggests that available information on early infant–adult communication should be considered to tap the *maximum* capacities of the infant–adult communication system.

Very subtle changes in the contexts of interaction also play a role in the way that communication is conducted between infants and adults. Microcontexts that emerge as an ongoing process within the exchange between partners include holding the infant, posture, and the presence of an object. Each of these microcontexts is linked to changes in the nature of communication from a previous state. When infants are held, even when facing the caregiver, both they and the adults are visually and vocally less responsive to one another (Lavelli & Fogel, 2002; Van Egeren et al., 2001). When infants are held upright, they are more likely to focus on their environments than on the adult compared to when they are lying down (Fogel, Dedo, & McEwen, 1992; Fogel et al., 1999). When the infant is engaged in exploring an object, both are highly attuned (Leyendecker, Lamb, & Scholmerich, 1997), but both partners respond less vocally to one another (Van Egeren et al., 2001).

Contingent Responsiveness and Early "Conversations"

At the core of the communicative system formed from the infant, adult, and interactional context is the notion of contingent responsiveness (Bornstein & Tamis LeMonda, 1989; Martin, 1989; Skinner, 1986). Contingently responsive mothers produce immediate, qualitatively appropriate responses to the infant's cues. Mothers are initially more sensitive to infant cues than infants are to maternal cues (Fogel, 1982a; Van Egeren et al., 2001). Nonetheless, infants are also contingently responsive to mothers by at least 4 months (Stevenson et al., 1986; Van Egeren et al., 2001).

Caregivers tend to infer meaningfulness from their infant's actions and vocalizations, providing an additional frame for early communication (Keller & Schoelmerich, 1987). Moreover, caregivers overestimate their infant's communicative abilities, assuming that the messages are perceived by the infant as the caregiver intended (Miller, 1988). Thus, the mothers' cognitions interplay with the infant's behavior to determine her proclivity to treat the child as an active communicative partner. In doing so, they are anticipating linguistic capabilities that have not yet actually emerged.

Treating interaction with the infant as a context for meaningful communication despite the inability of infants to speak, adults introduce the rhythms of conversation into the interaction using both nonverbal and verbal means (Bloom, Russell, & Wassenberg, 1987; Kaye & Fogel, 1980). For example, Kaye (1982) discussed how the mothers' rhythmic jiggling of the nipple encourages infant feeding, and the games and songs that are a fundamental part of adult–infant interaction are inherently rhythmical (Ratner & Bruner, 1978).

The most common process through which conversational give-and-take is embedded into early dyadic communication is through pauses. Regardless of culture, both mothers and infants pause between vocalizations, giving an opportunity for the partner to respond and resulting in "communicative chains" that progressively lengthen as infants mature (Keller et al., 1988; Stevenson et al., 1986). Thus, very early on, a pattern of communication is developed in which turn taking is the norm. The implication that these turn-taking events are imbued with meaning drives parents to treat interactions with the child as conversational events. Turn-taking and conversation-like interactions are pragmatic components of communication that provide a prototype of mature conversational rules for the infant.

Mutual Regulation

The parameters of infant maturation, adult skill and motivation in responsiveness, and interactional context set the bounds for the emerging patterns of communication. Among dyads with young infants, research suggests that communication processes are initiated by the infant rather than by the adult. In fact, in many studies of infant–mother interaction, attempts to quantify the amount of time mothers spend *not* attending to the child are useless because the mothers are virtually always looking at or holding the infant (Hsu & Fogel, 2001; Van Egeren et al., 2001). That is, mothers tend to watch until the infant makes eye contact, which appears to activate the mother's vocalizing, smiling, and touching behaviors (Stern, 1974). If the infant responds in some way, the chain of communication is continued and intensified until the infant breaks the cycle. The partner whose behavior can best be predicted by the other person is thus subject to the "dominance" of the other person (Gottman & Ringland, 1981). From this perspective, early mother–infant interactions are dominated by the infant, because it is particularly when the infant signals that mother responses are activated (Fogel, 1982a; Van Egeren et al., 2001).

Concurrently, the infant must depend on the parent's responsiveness to provide a model for the rules of give-and-take communication. Parents adjust their behavior to the existing capacities of the infant, making subtle, intuitive adaptations to maintain the interaction until terminated by the infant (Papousek & Papousek, 1991). When adults become unresponsive, as, for example, when they close their eyes or are instructed to remain impassive, infants react by becoming more animated and attempting to establish contact; if bids to communicate fail, infants' efforts subside or they display distress (Papousek et al., 1987). Yet as Hsu and Fogel (2001) note, responsiveness on the part of the adult is not sufficient for communication; rather, when the infant is also engaged and behaves in such a way that the adult has opportunities to respond, the creative process of co-regulation is able to emerge and allow new forms of dyadic engagement to develop.

The interplay between adults' use of infant-directed speech and infant engagement in communication is a prime example of mutually regulated interaction. The switch to infant-directed speech when interacting with infants appears to be a universal adjustment to the sensory capacities of the infant (Papousek & Papousek, 1991). Parents are not aware of the extent of their use of infant-directed speech (Miller, 1988), but it can be elicited by a single infant sound. In one study, when played a tape of an isolated infant vocalization, mothers produced typical infant-directed content such as greetings, imitations, reassurances, and encouragements (Papousek, 1992). Adults particularly prefer infants who vocalize with sounds similar to speech and are especially likely to attribute conversational meaning to the sounds and social favorableness to these infants (Beaumont & Bloom, 1993; Bloom & Lo, 1990). In response, 3-month-old infants are more likely to produce syllabic sounds during turn taking than during interactions in which adults respond randomly (Bloom et al., 1987; Masataka, 1995). Thus, mutual regulatory processes emerge in which caregivers respond more intensely to infant syllabic vocalizations, reinforcing infants' production of speechlike sounds.

THE DYNAMICS OF EARLY COMMUNICATION

From the dynamic systems perspective (Fogel, 1993; Thelen & Fogel, 1989), the ability of the infant to attend to and engage with the adult and the skill and motivation of the adult to engage with the infant represent two of the universal parameters that begin to define the characteristics of the communicative system; the context of interaction is the third. However, infancy marks one of the most extreme periods of rapid physical, cognitive, and social change in human life. Change deriving from infant development results in the systemic reorganization of the communication system several times across the first year of life. Parameter changes that may initiate changes in communication systems include the maturation of muscular structures and neurological pathways that underlie infant vocal expression, limb control, sensory functioning, and attentional capacities. Among typically developing infants, we can identify developmental "stages" that can be linked to the reorganization of the dyadic communication system. And, of course, within the dynamic systems perspective, systemic instabilities initiated by maturational changes on the part of the infant influence and are influenced by mutual adaptations on the part of the adult.

To illustrate, a newborn may be less attentive and able to engage when hungry. The attentive adult adapts accordingly, attempting to interact with the infant more if the infant is full and willing and less if hungry and fussy. Despite these and other relatively minor adaptations to changes in the infant's state over the course of an hour or a day, the general pattern of interaction remains stable. At times, however, one or more of the constraining parameters may change to a sufficient degree that the system enters a period of instability. For example, between the middle and the end of the second month, infants undergo physiological maturation that produces what has been called the biobehavioral shift (Emde & Buchsbaum, 1989). This shift is marked by a qualitatively observable improvement in the integration of neural systems as indexed by social smiling (Fogel, 1982b; Sroufe & Waters, 1976), longer periods of sleep, and the beginnings of adult-like cortisol rhythms (Ponirakis, 1999). Infants become more alert, are better able to incorporate sensory information, and have greater muscular control (Hopkins et al., 1990), all adding up to an infant with a greater capacity to engage in interaction.

In short, the biobehavioral shift produces changes in the way the infant behaves. Infant visual acuity improves, enabling more direct and purposive eye contact. Vocalizations begin to match adult structures as infants gain control of their air flow and vocal mechanisms (Rosenblith, 1992) and initiate greetings of their own (Kaye & Fogel, 1980). Small and large muscle movements become more coordinated with other expressive systems so that, for example, unmistakable expressions of joy are identifiable as infants break into big smiles, kick their legs, and flap their arms. These new infant capacities tip the dyadic system into instability. Subsequently, the system is reorganized into new patterns of functioning marked by increasing attunement in the interactional patterns between mothers and infants (Tronick & Cohn, 1989).

In an application of a dynamic systems approach to change in early communication systems, Lavelli and Fogel (2002) conducted a longitudinal study of infant–mother dyads followed weekly from ages 1 to 14 weeks. They found that face-to-face communication increased significantly during the period between 4 and 9 weeks, with individual differences among infants in the point at which the transition to more face-to-face communication occurred. The authors noted changes not only in the amount of infant–mother communication but also in the quality of the exchanges. Through about 4 weeks of age, infants simply gazed at mothers during face-to-face interaction, but then they began to incorporate facial expressions, smiles, and gestures into their communicative repertoires. Mothers reacted to the increased intensity of infant engagement by smiling, vocalizing, and using pauses to mark turn taking that for the first time appeared to have real expectations of give-and-take interaction by both partners.

In addition, individual differences in the patterns of interaction emerged during this transition period. All dyads displayed increasing face-to-face communicative exchanges over time; however, one subgroup eventually peaked and decreased, whereas another peaked and stabilized at higher levels of communication. Although not addressed in this chapter, Lavelli and Fogel's (2002) study also illustrates the dynamic systems principle that transitional periods of instability are also the points at which individual differences are most likely to emerge and subsequently be reinforced in new patterns of system organization.

FUTURE DIRECTIONS

Dynamic systems approaches provide a unique window into the nonlinear pathways of infant communication. However, apart from the work of Fogel and colleagues (Fogel, 1990; Fogel et al., 1988, 1999, 1992; Hsu & Fogel, 2001; Lavelli & Fogel, 2002), relatively little research has addressed early communication development from a longitudinal dynamic systems perspective. In addition to the biobehavioral shift, other major transition points in infant development include the interest in objects that arises around age 4 months, mobility—crawling, then cruising, then walking—that begins around age 6 months and language acquisition, occurring around age 12 months. The centrality and rapidity of these transitions make the period of infancy a prime field for dynamic systems applications, both to shed light on the development of the first communicative processes and to refine and experiment with dynamic systems methodology.

Studies of infant–adult communication would also benefit from expanding use of naturalistic contexts rather than from relying on laboratory settings. Much of the literature on early communication is based on studies occurring in the laboratory in which the infant is placed in an infant seat directly facing the adult. As discussed previously, this paradigm—few distractions, not held, face-to-face interaction—maximizes the frequency and quality of communication. We suggest research that looks explicitly at subtle contextual characteristics inherent in different settings that may tilt interpretation of findings. This includes not only laboratory and home but also child-care settings, contexts that include multiple children, and interaction with fathers or extended family. Virtually all the studies reviewed in this chapter assessed infant–*mother* interaction; yet infants also have extensive contact with others. For example, there are suggestions that communication systems of infant–father dyads may develop along their own course (Bridges & Connell, 1991; Kokkinaki & Kugiumutzakis, 2000).

A final area for future study is the effect of individual differences in constraining parameters of the communication system on system development, as well as the development of individual differences in infant communication itself. As stated earlier, transitions from one attractor state to another attractor state result in a limited number of outcomes—systems tend to organize in a few general ways. Thus, there are many pathways to similar outcomes. At the same time, similar sets of processes can result in different outcomes. The dyadic system is only one subsystem within a set of systems, all of which are interdependent, and changes in another level of the system can initiate considerable reorganization within the dyad. Maturational changes of the infant that enable increased vocal and motor control provide an example of a lower level system that impels change in the dyadic system. A higher order change that might impel reorganization of dyadic communication is a mother's return to work, potentially represented by different amounts of time spent in dyadic interaction, an additional caregiver in the form of a child-care provider, and a reduced degree of unimpeded focus on the infant as the mother juggles more responsibilities simultaneously. The upshot is that specific outcomes of dynamic systems cannot be easily predicted due to the number of variables that can influence the system and the fact that the point at which a particular variable tips the system into instability also differs. Nonetheless, variations in the constraining parameters—the influence of individual differences in infant, adult, and context—have been studied, although for the most part from a descriptive rather than from a process-oriented perspective.

Links have been demonstrated between the developing communication system and the variations among infants, such as temperament (Feldman, Greenbaum, Mayes, & Erlich, 1997; Hann, 1989; van den Boom, 1994); among adults, such as age (Barratt & Roach, 1995), perceptions of social support (Burchinal, Follmer, & Bryant, 1996), and depression

(Bettes, 1988; NICHD Early Child Care Research Network, 1999); and among contexts, such as socioeconomic status (Richman et al., 1992) and culture (Fogel et al., 1988; Leyendecker, Lamb, Schoelmerich, & Fracasso, 1995). However, most of the variables studied thus far constitute general markers of individual differences in the communication system, useful for identifying risk factors but inadequate for delineating underlying processes that characterize the communication system. *What* happens between an irritable infant and a mother to elicit negative or lower frequencies of maternal communication bids? *Why* does social support apparently make it easier for a mother to respond to her child? And *how* do the ways that adults across cultures construe the social context around them play out in their interactions with young infants? Applications of dynamic systems perspectives to these problems are likely to assist in illuminating the processes through which infants emerge from the dyad to be skilled communicators in a larger social world.

REFERENCES

Ainsworth, M. S., Blehar, M. C., Waters, E., & Wall, S. (1978). *Patterns of attachment: A psychological study of the strange situation.* Hillsdale, NJ: Lawrence Erlbaum Associates.

Baird, S. M., Peterson, J., & Reilly, A. (1995). Patterns of specific infant behavior interpretation. *Infant-Toddler Intervention, 5*, 255–275.

Barratt, M. S., & Roach, M. A. (1995). Early interactive processes: Parenting by adolescent and adult single mothers. *Infant Behavior and Development, 18*, 97–109.

Barrile, M., Armstrong, E. S., & Bower, T. G. R. (1999). Novelty and frequency as determinants of newborn preference. *Developmental Science, 2*, 47–52.

Beaumont, S. L., & Bloom, K. (1993). Adults' attributions of intentionality to vocalizing infants. *First Language, 13*, 235–247.

Beebe, B., & Stern, D. N. (1977). Engagement-disengagement and early object experiences. In N. Freedman & S. Granel (Eds.), *Communicative structures and psychic structures* (pp. 35–55). New York: Plenum Press.

Bell, R. Q., & Harper, L. V. (1977). *Child effects on adults.* New York: Wiley.

Bettes, B. A. (1988). Maternal depression and motherese: Temporal and intonational features. *Child Development, 59*, 1089–1096.

Blake, J., & Dolgoy, S. J. (1993). Gestural development and its relation to cognition during the transition to language. *Journal of Nonverbal Behavior, 17*, 87–102.

Bloom, K., & Lo, E. (1990). Adult perceptions of vocalizing infants. *Infant Behavior and Development, 13*, 209–219.

Bloom, K., Russell, A., & Wassenberg, K. (1987). Turn taking affects the quality of infant vocalizations. *Journal of Child Language, 14*, 211–227.

Bornstein, M. H., & Tamis LeMonda, C. S. (1989). Maternal responsiveness and cognitive development in children. *New Directions for Child Development*, 49–61.

Bradley, R. H. (1994). The HOME Inventory: Review and reflections. In H. W. Reese (Ed.), *Advances in child development and behavior* (Vol. 25, pp. 241–288). San Diego: Academic Press.

Bridges, L. J., & Connell, J. P. (1991). Consistency and inconsistency in infant emotional and social interactive behavior across contexts and caregivers. *Infant Behavior and Development, 14*, 471–487.

Brody, S., & Axelrad, S. (1978). *Mothers, fathers, and children: Explorations in the formation of character in the first seven years.* New York: International Universities Press.

Brousseau, L., Malcuit, G., Pomerleau, A., & Feider, H. (1996). Relations between lexical-temporal features in mothers' speech and infants' interactive behaviours. *First Language, 16*, 41–59.

Burchinal, M. R., Follmer, A., & Bryant, D. M. (1996). The relations of maternal social support and family structure with maternal responsiveness and child outcomes among African American families. *Developmental Psychology, 32*, 1073–1083.

Butterworth, G., & Morissette, P. (1996). Onset of pointing and the acquisition of language in infancy. *Journal of Reproductive and Infant Psychology, 14*, 219–231.

Caldwell, B., & Bradley, R. (1978). *Manual for the home observation for measurement of the environment.* Little Rock: University of Arkansas.

Cernoch, J. M., & Porter, R. H. (1985). Recognition of maternal axillary odors by infants. *Child Development, 56*, 1593–1598.

Cismaresco, A. S., & Montagner, H. (1990). Mothers' discrimination of their neonates' cry in relation to cry acoustics: The first week of life. *Early Child Development and Care, 65*, 3–11.

Clarke Stewart, K. A. (1973). Interactions between mothers and their young children: Characteristics and consequences. *Monographs of the Society for Research in Child Development, 38*, 1–108.

Coates, D. L., & Lewis, M. (1984). Early mother-infant interaction and infant cognitive status as predictors of school performance and cognitive behavior in six-year-olds. *Child Development, 55*, 1219–1230.

Cooper, R. P., & Aslin, R. N. (1989). The language environment of the young infant: Implications for early perceptual development. *Canadian Journal of Psychology, 43*, 247–265.

Cooper, R. P., & Aslin, R. N. (1994). Developmental differences in infant attention to the spectral properties of infant-directed speech. *Child Development, 65*, 1663–1677.

Deak, G. O., Flom, R. A., & Pick, A. D. (2000). Effects of gesture and target on 12- and 18-month-olds' joint visual attention to objects in front of or behind them. *Developmental Psychology, 36*, 511–523.

DeCasper, A. J., & Fifer, W. P. (1980). Of human bonding: Newborns prefer their mothers' voices. *Science, 208*, 1174–1176.

Emde, R. N., & Buchsbaum, H. K. (1989). Toward a psychoanalytic theory of affect: II. Emotional development and signaling in infancy. In S. I. Greenspan & G. H. Pollack (Eds.), *The course of life, Vol. 1: Infancy* (pp. 193–227). Madison, CT: International Universities Press.

Feldman, R., Greenbaum, C. W., Mayes, L. C., & Erlich, S. H. (1997). Change in mother-infant interactive behavior: Relations to change in the mother, the infant, and the social context. *Infant Behavior and Development, 20*, 151–163.

Feldman, R., Greenbaum, C. W., & Yirmiya, N. (1999). Mother-infant affect synchrony as an antecedent of the emergence of self-control. *Developmental Psychology, 35,* 223–231.

Feldman, R., Greenbaum, C. W., Yirmiya, N., & Mayes, L. C. (1996). Relations between cyclicity and regulation in mother-infant interaction at 3 and 9 months and cognition at 2 years. *Journal of Applied Developmental Psychology, 17,* 347–365.

Fernald, A. (1985). Four-month-old infants prefer to listen to motherese. *Infant Behavior and Development, 8,* 181–195.

Fernald, A., Taeschner, T., Dunn, J., Papousek, M., et al. (1989). A cross-language study of prosodic modifications in mothers' and fathers' speech to preverbal infants. *Journal of Child Language, 16,* 477–501.

Field, T. M. (1981). Infant gaze aversion and heart rate during face-to-face interactions. *Infant Behavior and Development, 4,* 307–315.

Fivaz Depeursinge, E., & Corboz Warnery, A. (1999). *The primary triangle: A developmental systems view of mothers, fathers, and infants.* New York: Basic Books.

Fleming, A., Corter, C., Surbey, M., Franks, P., & Steiner, M. (1995). Postpartum factors related to mother's recognition of newborn infant odours. *Journal of Reproductive and Infant Psychology, 13,* 197–210.

Fogel, A. (1982a). Early adult-infant interaction: Expectable sequences of behavior. *Journal of Pediatric Psychology, 7,* 1–22.

Fogel, A. (1982b). Social play, positive affect, and coping skills in the first 6 months of life. *Topics in Early Childhood Special Education, 2,* 53–65.

Fogel, A. (1990). The process of developmental change in infant communicative action: Using dynamic systems theory to study individual ontogenies. In J. Colombo & J. Fagen (Eds.), *Individual differences in infancy: Reliability, stability, and prediction* (pp. 341–358). Hillsdale, NJ: Lawrence Erlbaum Associates.

Fogel, A. (1993). *Developing through relationships: Origins of communication, self, and culture.* Chicago: University of Chicago Press.

Fogel, A., Dedo, J. Y., & McEwen, I. (1992). Effect of postural position and reaching on gaze during mother-infant face-to-face interaction. *Infant Behavior and Development, 15,* 231–244.

Fogel, A., Messinger, D. S., Dickson, K. L., & Hsu, H. C. (1999). Posture and gaze in early mother-infant communication: Synchronization of developmental trajectories. *Developmental Science, 2,* 325–332.

Fogel, A., Toda, S., & Kawai, M. (1988). Mother-infant face-to-face interaction in Japan and the United States: A laboratory comparison using 3-month-old infants. *Developmental Psychology, 24,* 398–406.

Gewirtz, J. L., & Pelaez Nogueras, M. (2000). Infant emotions under the positive-reinforcer control of caregiver attention and touch. In J. C. Leslie & D. Blackman (Eds.), *Experimental and applied analysis of human behavior* (pp. 271–291). Reno, NV: Context Press.

Gogate, L. J., Walker Andrews, A. S., & Bahrick, L. E. (2001). The intersensory origins of word comprehension: An ecological-dynamic systems view. *Developmental Science, 4,* 1–18.

Goldfield, B. A. (1990). Pointing, naming, and talk about objects: Referential behaviour in children and mothers. *First Language, 10*, 231–242.

Goldman, H. I. (2001). Parental reports of 'MAMA' sounds in infants: An exploratory study. *Journal of Child Language, 28*, 497–506.

Gottman, J. M., & Ringland, J. T. (1981). The analysis of dominance and bidirectionality in social development. *Child Development, 52*, 393–412.

Gustafson, G. E., & Harris, K. L. (1990). Women's responses to young infants' cries. *Developmental Psychology, 26*, 144–152.

Hann, D. M. (1989). A systems conceptualization of the quality of mother-infant interaction. *Infant Behavior and Development, 12*, 251–263.

Haynes, H., White, B. L., & Held, R. (1965). Visual accommodation in human infants. *Science, 148*, 528–530.

Heimann, M. (1989). Neonatal imitation, gaze aversion, and mother-infant interaction. *Infant Behavior and Development, 12*, 495–505.

Hopkins, B., Lcms, Y. L., Van Wulfften Palthe, T., Hoeksma, J., et al. (1990). Development of head position preference during early infancy: A longitudinal study in the daily life situation. *Developmental Psychobiology, 23*, 39–53.

Hsu, H. C., & Fogel, A. (2001). Infant vocal development in a dynamic mother-infant communication system. *Infancy, 2*, 87–109.

Isabella, R. A., Belsky, J., & von Eye, A. (1989). Origins of infant-mother attachment: An examination of interactional synchrony during the infant's first year. *Developmental Psychology, 25*, 12–21.

James, W. (1890). *The principles of psychology.* (1981 ed.). Cambridge, MA: Harvard University Press.

Jusczyk, P. W. (1997). *The discovery of spoken language.* Cambridge, MA: MIT Press.

Jusczyk, P. W., & Bertoncini, J. (1988). Viewing the development of speech perception as an innately guided learning process. *Language and Speech, 31*, 217–238.

Kaye, K. (1982). *The mental and social life of babies: How parents create persons.* Chicago: University of Chicago Press.

Kaye, K., & Fogel, A. (1980). The temporal structure of face-to-face communication between mothers and infants. *Developmental Psychology, 16*, 454–464.

Keller, H., Chasiotis, A., Risau Peters, J., Voelker, S., Zach, U., & Restemeier, R. (1996). Psychobiological aspects of infant crying. *Early Development and Parenting, 5*, 1–13.

Keller, H., Lohaus, A., Voelker, S., Cappenberg, M., & Chasiotis, A. (1998). Relationship between infant crying, birth complications, and maternal variables. *Child: Care, Health and Development, 24*, 377–394.

Keller, H., & Schoelmerich, A. (1987). Infant vocalizations and parental reactions during the first 4 months of life. *Developmental Psychology, 23*, 62–67.

Keller, H., Schoelmerich, A., & Eibl Eibesfeldt, I. (1988). Communication patterns in adult infant interactions in Western and non-Western cultures. *Journal of Cross Cultural Psychology, 19*, 427–445.

Kemler Nelson, D. G., Hirsh Pasek, K., Jusczyk, P. W., & Cassidy, K. W. (1989). How the prosodic cues in motherese might assist language learning. *Journal of Child Language, 16*, 55–68.

Kochanska, G., Forman, D. R., & Coy, K. C. (1999). Implications of the mother-child relationship in infancy socialization in the second year of life. *Infant Behavior and Development, 22*, 249–265.

Kokkinaki, T., & Kugiumutzakis, G. (2000). Basic aspects of vocal imitation in infant-parent interaction during the first 6 months. *Journal of Reproductive and Infant Psychology, 18*, 173–187.

Kopp, C. B. (1989). Regulation of distress and negative emotions: A developmental view. *Developmental Psychology, 25*, 343–354.

Kuhl, P. K., & Meltzoff, A. N. (1996). Infant vocalizations in response to speech: Vocal imitation and developmental change. *Journal of the Acoustical Society of America, 100*, 2425–2438.

Lavelli, M., & Fogel, A. (2002). Developmental changes in mother-infant face-to-face communication: Birth to 3 months. *Developmental Psychology, 38*, 288–305.

Legerstee, M. (1991). Changes in the quality of infant sounds as a function of social and nonsocial stimulation. *First Language, 11*, 327–343.

Leyendecker, B., Lamb, M. E., Schoelmerich, A., & Fracasso, M. P. (1995). The social worlds of 8- and 12-month-old infants: Early experiences in two subcultural contexts. *Social Development, 4*, 194–208.

Leyendecker, B., Lamb, M. E., & Scholmerich, A. (1997). Studying mother-infant interaction: The effects of context and length of observation in two subcultural groups. *Infant Behavior and Development, 20*, 325–337.

Lieberman, P. (1984). *The biology and evolution of language.* Cambridge, MA: Harvard University Press.

Lohaus, A., Keller, H., Ball, J., Elben, C., & Voelker, S. (2001). Maternal sensitivity: Components and relations to warmth and contingency. *Parenting: Science and Practice, 1*, 267–284.

Malatesta, C. Z., Grigoryev, P., Lamb, C., Albin, M., & Culver, C. (1986). Emotion socialization and expressive development in preterm and full-term infants. *Child Development, 57*, 316–330.

Mangelsdorf, S. C., Shapiro, J. R., & Marzolf, D. (1995). Developmental and temperamental differences in emotional regulation in infancy. *Child Development, 66*, 1817–1828.

Martin, J. A. (1989). Personal and interpersonal components of responsiveness. *New Directions for Child Development*, 5–14.

Masataka, N. (1993). Effects of contingent and noncontingent maternal stimulation on the vocal behaviour of three- to four-month-old Japanese infants. *Journal of Child Language, 20*, 303–312.

Masataka, N. (1995). The relation between index-finger extension and the acoustic quality of cooing in three-month-old infants. *Journal of Child Language, 22*, 247–257.

Masataka, N. (1996). Perception of motherese in a signed language by 6-month-old deaf infants. *Developmental Psychology, 32*, 874–879.

Masataka, N. (1999). Preference for infant-directed singing in 2-day-old hearing infants of deaf parents. *Developmental Psychology, 35*, 1001–1005.

Miller, C. L. (1983). Developmental changes in male/female voice classification by infants. *Infant Behavior and Development, 6*, 313–330.

Miller, C. L. (1988). Parents' perceptions and attributions of infant vocal behaviour and development. *First Language, 8*, 125–141.

Mondloch, C. J., Lewis, T. L., Budreau, D. R., Maurer, D., Dannemiller, J. L., Stephens, B. R., & Kleiner-Gathercoal, K. A. (1999). Face perception during early infancy. *Psychological Science, 10*, 419–422.

NICHD Early Child Care Research Network (1997). The effects of infant child care on infant-mother attachment security: Results of the NICHD study of early child care. *Child Development, 68*, 860–879.

NICHD Early Child Care Research Network (1999). Chronicity of maternal depressive symptoms, maternal sensitivity, and child functioning at 36 months. *Developmental Psychology, 35*, 1297–1310.

Nicholls, A., & Kirkland, J. (1996). Maternal sensitivity: A review of attachment literature definitions. *Early Child Development and Care, 120*, 55–65.

Ochs, E., & Schieffelin, B. B. (1984). Language acquisition and socialization: Three developmental stories and their implications. In R. Schweder & R. A. LeVine (Ed.), *Culture theory: Essays on minds, self, and emotion* (pp. 276–332). New York: Cambridge University Press.

Ockleford, E. M., Vince, M. A., Layton, C., & Reader, M. R. (1988). Responses of neonates to parents' and others' voices. *Early Human Development, 18*, 27–36.

Oller, D. K. (1986). Metaphonology and infant vocalizations. In R. Z. B. Lindblom (Ed.), *Precursors of early speech* (pp. 21–35). New York: Stockton.

Papousek, M. (1989). Determinants of responsiveness to infant vocal expression of emotional state. *Infant Behavior and Development, 12*, 507–524.

Papousek, M. (1992). Early ontogeny of vocal communication in parent-infant interactions. In H. Papousek & U. Juergens (Eds.), *Nonverbal vocal communication: Comparative and developmental approaches. Studies in emotion and social interaction* (pp. 230–261). New York: Cambridge University Press.

Papousek, M., Bornstein, M. H., Nuzzo, C., Papousek, H., & Symmes, D. (1990). Infant responses to prototypical melodic contours in parental speech. *Infant Behavior and Development, 13*, 539–545.

Papousek, H., & Papousek, M. (1984). Learning and cognition in the everyday life of human infants. In J. Rosenblatt (Ed.), *Advances in the study of behavior* (Vol. 14, pp. 127–163). New York: Academic Press.

Papousek, M., & Papousek, H. (1990). Excessive infant crying and intuitive parental care: Buffering support and its failures in parent-infant interaction. *Early Child Development and Care, 65*, 117–126.

Papousek, M., & Papousek, H. (1991). Early verbalizations as precursors of language development. In M. E. Lamb & H. Keller (Eds.), *Infant development: Perspectives from German speaking countries* (pp. 299–328). Hillsdale, NJ: Lawrence Erlbaum Associates.

Papousek, M., Papousek, H., & Bornstein, M. H. (1985). The naturalistic vocal environment of young infants: On the significance of homogeneity and variability in parent speech. In T. Field & N. Fox (Eds.), *Social perception in infants* (pp. 269–297). Norwood, NJ: Ablex.

Papousek, M., Papousek, H., & Haekel, M. (1987). Didactic adjustments in fathers' and mothers' speech to their 3-month-old infants. *Journal of Psycholinguistic Research, 16*, 491–516.

Papousek, M., Papousek, H., & Symmes, D. (1991). The meanings of melodies in motherese in tone and stress languages. *Infant Behavior and Development, 14*, 415–440.

Ponirakis, A. (1999). *Biobehavioral aspects of temperament and externalizing behavior problems in children of young mothers.* Unpublished dissertation, Penn State University, College Park. PA.

Porter, R. H., Cernoch, J. M., & Perry, S. (1983). The importance of odors in mother-infant interactions. *Maternal Child Nursing Journal, 12*, 147–154.

Porter, R. H., Makin, J. W., Davis, L. B., & Christensen, K. M. (1992). Breast-fed infants respond to olfactory cues from their own mother and unfamiliar lactating females. *Infant Behavior and Development, 15*, 85–93.

Porter, R. H., & Winberg, J. (1999). Unique salience of maternal breast odors for newborn infants. *Neuroscience and Biobehavioral Reviews, 23*, 439–449.

Ratner, N., & Bruner, J. (1978). Games, social exchange and the acquisition of language. *Journal of Child Language, 5*, 391–401.

Rheingold, H. L., & Adams, J. L. (1980). The significance of speech to newborns. *Developmental Psychology, 16*, 397–403.

Richman, A. L., Miller, P. M., & LeVine, R. A. (1992). Cultural and educational variations in maternal responsiveness. *Developmental Psychology, 28*, 614–621.

Roe, K. V., Roe, A., Drivas, A., & Bronstein, R. (1990). A curvilinear relationship between maternal vocal stimulation and three-month-olds' cognitive processing: A cross-cultural phenomenon. *Infant Mental Health Journal, 11*, 175–189.

Rogoff, B. (1990). *Apprenticeship in thinking.* New York: Oxford University Press.

Rosenblith, J. F. (1992). *In the beginning: Development from conception to age two* (2nd ed.). Thousand Oaks, CA: Sage.

Russell, M. J., Mendelson, T., & Peeke, H. V. (1983). Mothers' identification of their infant's odors. *Ethology and Sociobiology, 4*, 29–31.

Sameroff, A. J. (1993). *Handbook of infant mental health.* New York: Guilford Press.

Schaal, B. (1988). Olfaction in infants and children: Developmental and functional perspectives. *Chemical Senses, 13*, 145–190.

Schulze, P. A., Harwood, R. L., & Schoelmerich, A. (2001). Feeding practices and expectations among middle-class Anglo and Puerto Rican mothers of 12-month-old infants. *Journal of Cross Cultural Psychology, 32*, 397–406.

Shi, R., Werker, J. F., & Morgan, J. L. (1999). Newborn infants' sensitivity to perceptual cues to lexical and grammatical words. *Cognition, 72*, B11–B21.

Shonkoff, J. P., & Phillips, D. A. (2000). *From neurons to neighborhoods: The science of early childhood development.* Washington, DC: National Academy Press.

Skinner, E. A. (1986). The origins of young children's perceived control: Mother contingent and sensitive behavior. *International Journal of Behavioral Development, 9*, 359–382.

Slater, A., Earle, D. C., Morison, V., & Rose, D. (1985). Pattern preferences at birth and their interaction with habituation-induced novelty preferences. *Journal of Experimental Child Psychology, 39*, 37–54.

Slater, A., & Johnson, S. P. (1998). Visual sensory and perceptual abilities of the newborn: Beyond the blooming, buzzing confusion. In F. Simion & G. Butterworth (Eds.), *The development of sensory, motor and cognitive capacities in early infancy: From perception to cognition* (pp. 121–141). Hove, England: Psychology Press/ Lawrence Erlbaum Associates (UK) Taylor & Francis.

Smith, K. E., Landry, S. H., & Swank, P. R. (2000). The influence of early patterns of positive parenting on children's preschool outcomes. *Early Education and Development, 11*, 147–169.

Spence, M. J., & Freeman, M. S. (1996). Newborn infants prefer the maternal low-pass filtered voice, but not the maternal whispered voice. *Infant Behavior and Development, 19*, 199–212.

Sroufe, L. A., & Waters, E. (1976). The ontogenesis of smiling and laughter: A perspective on the organization of development in infancy. *Psychological Review, 83*, 173–189.

Stack, D. M., & Arnold, S. L. (1998). Changes in mothers' touch and hand gestures influence infant behavior during face-to-face interchanges. *Infant Behavior and Development, 21*, 451–468.

Stallings, J., Fleming, A. S., Corter, C., Worthman, C., & Steiner, M. (2001). The effects of infant cries and odors on sympathy, cortisol, and autonomic responses in new mothers and nonpostpartum women. *Parenting: Science and Practice, 1*, 71–100.

Stallings, J. F., Fleming, A. S., Worthman, C. M., Steiner, M., Corter, C., & Coote, M. (1997). Mother/father differences in response to infant crying. *American Journal of Physical Anthropology, 24*, 217.

Stark, R. E. (1981). Infant vocalization: A comprehensive view. *Infant Mental Health Journal, 2*, 118–128.

Stark, R. E., Rose, S. N., & McLagen, M. (1975). Features of infant sounds: The first eight weeks of life. *Journal of Child Language, 2*, 205–221.

Stern, D. N. (1974). The goal and structure of mother-infant play. *Journal of the American Academy of Child Psychiatry, 13*, 402–421.

Stevenson, M. B., Ver Hoeve, J. N., Roach, M. A., & Leavitt, L. A. (1986). The beginning of conversation: Early patterns of mother-infant vocal responsiveness. *Infant Behavior and Development, 9*, 423–440.

Stifter, C. A., & Moyer, D. (1991). The regulation of positive affect: Gaze aversion activity during mother-infant interaction. *Infant Behavior and Development, 14*, 111–123.

Tamis-LeMonda, C. S., Bornstein, M. H., Baumwell, L., & Damast, A. M. (1996). Responsive parenting in the second year: Specific influences on children's language and play. *Early Development and Parenting, 5*, 173–183.

Thelen, E., & Fogel, A. (1989). Toward an action-based theory of infant development. In J. J. Lockman & N. L. Hazen (Eds.), *Action in social context: Perspectives on early development. Perspectives in developmental psychology* (pp. 23–63). New York: Plenum Press.

Tomasello, M., & Farrar, M. J. (1986). Joint attention and early language. *Child Development, 57*, 1454–1463.

Trainor, L. J., Austin, C. M., & Desjardins, R. N. (2000). Is infant-directed speech prosody a result of the vocal expression of emotion? *Psychological Science, 11*, 188–195.

Tronick, E., Als, H., & Brazelton, T. B. (1980). Monadic phases: A structural descriptive analysis of infant-mother face to face interaction. *Merrill Palmer Quarterly, 26*, 3–24.

Tronick, E. Z., & Cohn, J. F. (1989). Infant-mother face-to-face interaction: Age and gender differences in coordination and the occurrence of miscoordination. *Child Development, 60*, 85–92.

Valenza, E., Simion, F., Cassia, V. M., & Umilta, C. (1996). Face preference at birth. *Journal of Experimental Psychology: Human Perception and Performance, 22*, 892–903.

van den Boom, D. C. (1994). The influence of temperament and mothering on attachment and exploration: An experimental manipulation of sensitive responsiveness among lower-class mothers with irritable infants. *Child Development, 65*, 1457–1477.

Van Egeren, L. A., Barratt, M. S., & Roach, M. A. (2001). Mother-infant responsiveness: Timing, mutual regulation, and interactional context. *Developmental Psychology, 37*, 684–697.

Voelker, S., Keller, H., Lohaus, A., Cappenberg, M., & Chasiotis, A. (1999). Maternal interactive behaviour in early infancy and later attachment. *International Journal of Behavioral Development, 23*, 921–936.

Vygotsky, L. (1978). *Mind in society: The development of higher psychological processes.* Cambridge: Harvard University Press.

Watson, J. S. (1977). Perception of contingency as a determinant of social responsiveness (pp. 33–64). New York.

Weinberg, M. K., & Tronick, E. Z. (1994). Beyond the face: An empirical study of infant affective configurations of facial, vocal, gestural, and regulatory behaviors. *Child Development, 65*, 1503–1515.

Weiss, S. J., Wilson, P., Hertenstein, M. J., & Campos, R. (2000). The tactile context of a mother's caregiving: Implications for attachment of low birth weight infants. *Infant Behavior and Development, 23*, 91–111.

Werker, J. F., Pegg, J. E., & McLeod, P. J. (1994). A cross-language investigation of infant preference for infant-directed communication. *Infant Behavior and Development, 17*, 323–333.

Zlochower, A. J., & Cohn, J. F. (1996). Vocal timing in face-to-face interaction of clinically depressed and nondepressed mothers and their 4-month-old infants. *Infant Behavior and Development, 19*, 371–374.

15

Communication Competencies and Sociocultural Priorities of Middle Childhood

Laura Stafford

The Ohio State University

Little children disturb your sleep, big ones your life.
—Yiddish Proverb

Middle childhood has been characterized as a time of innocence. It might even be considered a time of relative calm for many parents. We are past the physical demands of the sleepless nights of infancy and not yet enduring the emotional demands of parenting an adolescent. This is not to imply this period is any less filled with change, including the continuing development of communication competencies in multifaceted domains and relationships.

The purpose of this chapter is to provide an overview of communication competencies during middle childhood. A brief discussion of socialization, selected communication competencies, and a condensed historical account of the construction of childhood is offered. Three specific communication competencies, caring behaviors, argumentation or conflict management, and emotional display rules are discussed, as these are particularly relevant to two cultural priorities of middle childhood: school performance and successful peer relationships. The competencies are then explored in terms of their individual development as well as of their association with sibling interactions. Finally, Olson's (2000) Circumplex model is offered as a promising framework for future research on communication development during the elementary school years.

Unfortunately, although there has been much work on infants' development of language and communication competencies and adolescents' interaction skills, less research has been conducted on the middle childhood years, in terms of both communicative competencies (Moore, Evans, Brooks-Gunn, & Roth, 2001) and family interactions (Fitzpatrick & Caughlin, 2002).

Yet, attention has been turning, somewhat, to communication competencies of middle childhood. Such competencies may include a variety of languages or code switching within the same language and nonliteral uses of language such as irony, humor, and fantasy. Children learn what roles are appropriate in which communication contexts, how to plan and strategize, how to decontextualize language, how to tell stories, and even how to engage in multiple genres. They become able to discern teasing from threats and facts from fiction. Children even realize that more than one "truth" may exist, and they understand what is appropriate to talk about to whom, as well as which topics might be taboo. Rules of who has the right to speak, how to request and take the floor, and the like, are acquired along with norms for roles and relationships (Snow & Blum-Kulka, 2002). "Compared to language during the preschool years, language during the school years requires an increased variety of language functions, greater variety of discourse styles, and organization, more abstract vocabulary, more complex syntax, and the ability to reflect on these aspects of language" (Westby, 1998a, p. 311).

This list is not intended to be comprehensive or representative of a particular taxonomic scheme. Yet such a listing illustrates several points. First, the development of communication involves an enormous array of interlinked interactive discourse skills involving multiple parties. Second, children must know not only what to say but also the rules for saying it. Finally, in order to participate in the "adult world," children must become active creators of social knowledge, not merely recipients of it.

From an anthropological point of view, language acquisition and communication development are part and parcel of socialization (Blum-Kulka & Snow, 2002). Children do not simply acquire language, or communication; children discover "sensitivities and flexibilities" in discourse through multiparty family interactions that are valuable in negotiating the larger culture. In other words, children learn language and communication practices "holistically" in "achieving cultural membership" (Blum-Kulka & Snow, 2002, p. 3).

This emphasis on becoming members of society is consistent with much research in family and communication studies. Socialization of children is generally considered the foremost task among families. Whereas family researchers may be concerned with marital satisfaction and parental satisfaction, child satisfaction or happiness is generally not considered; rather, child socialization is (Fitzpatrick & Caughlin, 2002). Despite numerous family constellations: whether one parent or two, biological or not; whether the parent is a grandparent or stepparent or other primary caregiver, if a family has children; society accords the family the responsibility of socializing children (Lerner & Spainer 1978).

In U.S. culture today, socialization is primarily considered to be social competence (Peterson & Hann, 1999). This necessarily brings us to the consideration of what social communication competencies are valued, and thus are formed or extended, during middle childhood.

SOCIAL COMMUNICATION COMPETENCE AND THE SOCIAL CONSTRUCTION OF CHILDHOOD

Definitions of social competence for children vary greatly. Still, the term is frequently invoked as if general agreement exists (Rose-Krasnor, 1997). Rose-Krasnor notes that the lack of consensus as to what constitutes socially competent behaviors, coupled with the propensity for researchers to write as if meanings were shared, is problematic. For most family and communication researchers, the notion that children develop competencies is a given. However, attention to defining and explicating communication competence is rare. Rather, researchers are interested in how this assumed competence is expressed and influenced in children's relationships.

In such a view, the search is often for universal childhood competencies that either unfold with other areas of maturation or are optimally facilitated through maternal interaction. James (1998) offers an alternative. She proposes a need for awareness of the variety of ways competencies can be construed in society and the intertwined nature of assumptions of childhood and presumed competencies. She challenges the taken-for-granted linear progression of the child from socially incompetent to socially competent.

In James' (1998) view, childhood is a social construction; it varies historically and cross-culturally. Indeed, "childhood" was invented relatively recently in history. A person was considered an adult by the age of 7 in the medieval period (Ariès, 1962). Not until the 17th century did the idea that childhood might be a separate stage between infancy and adulthood have much prominence, and even then, childhood was seen as a time of preparation for adult life and was accorded little importance as a period in its own right. Although Locke (1693/1964) argued for a unique nature for children, his writings were not particularly influential at the time. Rousseau (1762/1911) delineated stages of childhood: infancy, childhood, preadolescence, and adolescence. His view was gradually accepted. Today we have childhood, and a separate period of adolescence, by sociohistorical convention. Parents and children behave as generally expected by society. Consequently, what are considered appropriate accomplishments for a child at different ages and the practices of age-dependent competent parenting are contingent on cultural considerations of childhood.

Even in the last century we have seen the emphasis of optimal child attributes shift from compliance, obedience, and internalization of parental values to those of independence and "thinking for one's self" (Smith, 1999). Though both independence and interdependence are considered necessary for healthy relationship functioning, U.S. society today values and fosters independence and individualism over interdependence (Raeff, 1997). Bronfenbrenner (2001) has proposed that the United States has gone too far in valuing independence, and this valuation has led to chaos in the home and in the society. In addition, focus has moved from the child as an economic asset to an economic liability, a "sacred" privilege, and a responsibility (Ambert, 2001; Zelizer, 1985). In short, the competencies required of today's child and today's parent are quite subjective, historically and culturally.

Current conceptualizations of social competence include communication or social skills (Hart, Olsen, Robinson, & Mandleco, 1997; Peterson & Hann, 1999). Merrell and Gimpel (1998) offer a myriad of definitions of social skills, one of which is social validity, which defines social skills as behaviors that are associated with valued social outcomes (Gersham, 1986). This view of social skills is adopted here; social competence skills are those that help the individual achieve culturally desirable social outcomes.

SOCIALLY DESIRABLE OUTCOMES

"Middle childhood is the stage during which children begin to adapt to life outside the family, especially to the multifaceted demands of school and relationships with peers" (Defries, Plomin, & Fulker, 1994, p. 1). Accordingly, the socially desirable accomplishments for middle childhood are considered successful peer relationships and school adjustment (Evangelista, 2001). Each of these two areas will be reviewed briefly, followed by selected competencies considered to contribute to success or failure in these two realms.

Peer Competence

The area of socialization that has received the majority of attention for middle school children is that of child–peer competence (see *Journal of Social and Personal Relationships*, 1991). Popularity with peers has frequently been considered a measure social competence (Rose-Krasnor, 1997). Peer acceptance is somewhat reciprocally defined as socialization. If one is accepted by one's peers, one is socialized; if one is competently socialized, one is accepted by one's peers. Generally children's difficulties with peers reflect either internalizing or externalizing behaviors (Hart, Olsen, Robinson, & Mandleco, 1997). Internalizing behaviors are manifested as withdrawal, shyness, inhibition, or solitary or immature play. Externalizing behaviors are characterized by aggression (both proactive and reactive). Sociable behaviors are those contributing to healthy psychosocial outcomes, especially positive peer relationships. Hart et al.'s review summarizes these behaviors as conforming and friendly interactions, impulse control, leadership, cooperative play, and other prosocial behaviors such as helping, sharing, and comforting.

A great deal of support exists for the contention that peer rejection is correlated with a host of later problems, including poor academic performance. However, the evidence is less clear that popularity is associated with subsequent achievements. Besides, the skills that are necessary to gain access to a peer group are not necessarily those that serve to maintain a peer group. Confusion between lack of acceptance (or popularity) and lack of friends also is problematic (Parker & Asher, 1993). Popularity and friendship are not the same. Friendships may be more strongly associated with positive characteristics than popularity or peer status (Vandell & Hembree, 1994). The skills involved in forming and managing friendships are likely a better index of social competence than general group acceptance. Furthermore, friendships contribute to the continued development of social competencies (Burleson, Delia, & Applegate, 1995). Friends provide children with support, information, instrumental aid, affection, self-validation, companionship, and opportunities for learning conflict resolution in a supportive environment (Rose-Krasnor, 1997).

Future studies aimed at associating selected communication competencies with peer relationships must distinguish among friendship, quality of friendship, and popularity. Popularity is especially problematic as children may be popular; however, they may be popular with the "wrong" peer group. Research indicates that popularity with high-risk, socially deviant groups is related to subsequent social and academic difficulties (Cairns & Cairns, 1994). Yet, for some children, most of their peers, and those with whom they seek to be popular, are those that society at large might consider high risk.

School Readiness and Academic Performance

In addition to having successful peer relationships, a major task at this age is simply learning to do school (Westby, 1998a). School readiness typically means "the developmental maturation of linguistic, cognitive, and social skills that allow children to take advantage of a formal educational curriculum" (Durlak, 2001, p. 564). As children continue through school, more and more emphasis is placed on academic achievement. Substantial literature validates the significance of social and personal competencies for successful achievement in elementary school (Evanglista, 2002).

Learning historically has been considered the responsibility of the family. Children who enter school with the expected capabilities have greater peer adjustment and greater achievement, especially in terms of retention and graduation rates (Kagan & Cohen, 1995). Children who fare well in school have fewer behavioral and social problems, better peer relations, less drug use and delinquency, and heightened psychological well-being (self-esteem, self-efficacy, and life satisfaction). Conversely, poor academic performance is a major risk factor for many "behavior and social problems, such as acting out, delinquency, drug use, poor peer relations, teenage pregnancy, depression, and dropping out of school" (Durlak, 2001, p. 562).

To thrive in a classroom, answers must not only be academically correct in terms of content but also socially correct (Erikson, 1963; Westby, 1998a). Learning to participate in the classroom necessitates acquiring new rules of discourse. How "new" the rules are is dependent on the similarity of the valued communication practices of an individual child's home and those of that child's particular school (Snow & Blum-Kulka, 2002). Classrooms with culturally and linguistically varied children present greater challenges, and perhaps greater opportunities, for teachers as well as for children, to adapt to culturally valued communication systems. Unfortunately, it is the child who generally must conform to the demands of "mainstream" culture put forth by their teachers and by their schools. This puts many children at risk before they enter the school building.

These two aspects of socialization, peer relationships and academic achievement, are not isomorphic, as peer acceptance influences academic performance and vice versa (Rose-Krasnor, 1997). Yet, these domains can serve as guidelines for the selection of particular communication competencies. Those reviewed herein are not meant to be comprehensive, but rather illustrative of competencies that are related and interrelated to both peer acceptance and school sucess.

COMMUNICATION COMPETENCIES

On a very general level we might relate all interaction to what Haslett and Samter (1997) have termed conversational competence. These researchers contend that after recognizing that communication is interpersonal in nature, children use it to create effects. This is the primary use of communication in children from the fourth month to the third year of life. From ages 3 to 5 children begin to exhibit conversational competence. The beginning of the final stage of developing communication skills starts around 5 years of age when children acquire skills in monitoring their own and others' communication. Of course the appropriate use and continued advancement of all of these skills is contingent on a host of developmental factors beyond the scope of the current chapter. Rather, three areas of conversational competencies with strong ties to both peer relationships and academic performance are reviewed here. These are caring behaviors, argumentation skills, and emotional/affective display rules.

Caring Behaviors, Emotional Support, and Comforting

The provision of emotional support becomes increasingly important for children as they turn more and more to peers for emotional support and less to parents and families. The "capacity to provide emotional support is a central component of the child's social competence" (Burleson & Kunkel, 2002, p.81).

Though caring behaviors might include a broader domain, Burleson and Kunkel (1996) consider emotional support and comforting to be virtually synonymous. Emotional support or comforting focuses "on the support efforts directed at overcoming sadness, anxiety, fear, anger, and other negative emotions" (p. 111). Burleson and Kunkel outline three general skills a child must master in order to capably provide emotional support. First is the ability to acquire knowledge about the psychological state and feelings of the others— thus including social perception skills such as recognizing and interpreting emotional cues, integrating information, and taking the others' perspective. In addition, children must have a battery of nonverbal, linguistic, and rhetorical resources to enact supportive intentions. Finally, children, as support providers, must be motivated to offer support.

Additional pro-social behaviors include caring, helping, and sharing, and are also de-pendent on the ability to take another's perspective (Eisenberg, 1992). The ability for empathy does not truly emerge until "the cognitive abilities to discriminate affective cues in others, more mature cognitive skills assuming the perspective and role of another per-son, and emotional responsiveness" have adequately developed (Fessbach, 1987, p. 273). This occurs sometime in early middle childhood (Chase-Lansdale, Wakschlag, & Brooks-Gunn, 1995).

Burleson and Kunkel (2002) review considerable evidence that the ability to provide emotional support has been linked to peer acceptance. By mid elementary school, children define friends as people who support and help each other (Merrell & Gimpel, 1998). Evidence suggests that children with such sensitivities also fare better academically, as offering caring behaviors has been related to children's feelings of resourcefulness and willingness to take on difficult tasks and challenges (Lamborn, Mounts, Steinberg, & Dornbusch, 1991; Chase-Lansdale, Wakschag, & Brooks-Gunn, 1995).

Argumentation and Conflict Management

Another competence needed by middle school is the ability to employ persuasive argumen-tation skills (Moffett, 1968). Effective conflict resolution, which often involves persuasion and argumentation, predicts academic success (Westby, 1998a), friendship relationships (Dunn, 1993), and popularity (Erwin, 1993).

Skillful argumentation and conflict management are dependent on recognition of mul-tiple goals in discourse (achieve an instrumental end, maintain a relationship, exert power and dominance, etc.), emotional maturity, and capacity for perspective taking (Stein & Albro, 2001). Conflict management often involves finding mutually acceptable solutions; thus, "adaptive conflict resolution involves an integration of self and other perspectives" (Rose-Krasnor, 1997, p. 121).

Children begin with requests for objects, invitations to play or participate in an activity, or requests for a supportive action (e.g., asking a parent to do or get something for the child)

(Brunner, 1983). Around age 4 children begin to offer reasons for requests and attempt to persuade adults with the grounds adults have used to grant or refuse previous requests (e.g., "I'll eat all my dinner if I can have a popsicle now") (Westby, 1998b, p. 183). Preschoolers are able to "express their desires and views with assertions, actions, and requests, and express opposition to other's acts with challenges, contradictions, denials, insults, and threats" (Kline, 1998, p. 368). Between the ages of 4 and 8 children become more adept at using politeness rules and become more sensitive to others. By 8 years of age, children begin to understand and offer "hints" as a means of requesting (Haslett & Samter, 1997).

Of course what defines a good argument varies considerably. Yet in summarizing their program of research, Stein and Albro (2001) maintain that most individuals, from preschool to adulthood, offer the central features of a good argument (i.e., claim, evidence, warrant, backing, counterargument, and qualifier, Toulmin, 1958). As children move through preschool and elementary school years they offer more reasons, find more holes in their opponents' arguments, and offer longer arguments. Kline (1998) similarly reports that by preschool, most children demonstrate the basic knowledge of discourse needed to participate in argumentation and that by age 5, most children have developed some capabilities in conflict resolution. During middle childhood these skills continue to expand; children are able to construct situation-specific arguments, adapt more to the views of others, and utilize politeness (Kline, 1998). Kline and Clinton (1998) found that from second to sixth grade children's persuasive abilities matured; children were better able to motivate others, act as advocates for proposals, and achieve a consensus to resolve problems. Even with these many early abilities, children have difficulty analyzing the reasoning of others until adolescence (Kline & Oseroff-Varnell, 1993).

Laursen, Finkelstein, and Betts (2001) conducted a series of meta-analyses to examine developmental trends in managing conflict. They found that negotiation among peers, from preschool to college age, increases and coercion declines. This trend apparently starts young: preschoolers used more coercion than middle school children, and middle school children used more negotiation and disengagement. Laursen et al. conclude these findings reveal a developmental increase in negotiation strategies.

Emotional Expression, Display Rules, Self Monitoring

Display rules refer to the appropriate suppression or expression of emotions. Such rules are significant, as children are increasingly concerned with self-presentation through elementary school (Merrell & Gimpel, 1998). Peers tend to ostracize children who fail to put up required emotional fronts (von Salisch, 2001). Most notably, children unable to express anger in socially acceptable ways, which often means masking or hiding anger, have difficulty with peers and with academics (Debaryshe & Fryxell, 1998). Children who successfully project appropriate emotions are seen as more competent by their teachers as well (McDowell & Parke, 2000).

Rules concerning the display of affect are culturally defined, and a part of communication competence is the ability to express particular kinds of emotions in particular contexts as well as to read the emotional expressions of others. Knowing which situations warrant concealment of feelings is considered a necessity for "appropriate socialization" (Talwar & Lee, 2002).

Although much research has been conducted on display rules in adults and across cultures, beginning with Ekman and Freisen (1975), much less work has been conducted on display rules during childhood, despite their strong link to perceived social competence (however, see Guerrero, Andersen, & Trost, 1998). Nevertheless, the extant literature does suggest that somewhere in early elementary school children realize that the emotions they should present to others do not necessarily correspond to the way they actually feel (von Salisch, 2001).

Display rules occupy a unique place in childhood, as they are related to the ability to self-monitor. In their review of children's developing communication skills, Haslett and Samter (1997) conclude that it is around the age of 5 that children begin to monitor their own communication; children start to evaluate their own messages and become more adept at sending socially appropriate messages. Yet some research has suggested that children as young as 3 years old understand rudimentary politeness norms and can mask disappointment (Cole, 1986).

Display rules are differentially invoked, not only in accordance with age but also with emotion and audience. Rules include the inhibition of felt emotions as well as the projection of unfelt ones. These abilities develop between the ages of 5 and 12 (Saarni, Mumme, & Campos, 1998; von Salisch, 2001). Hiding emotions generally has self-protective motivations (McDowell & Parke, 2000). With peers, children learn to hide fear, pain, or sadness, to stay calm, and not to show anger (Zeman & Garber, 1996). As children mature, they learn they may need to mask "positive" emotions, such as happiness at another child losing, along with negative ones (McDowell & Parke, 2000). While simultaneously learning to dampen certain emotional displays, children are also becoming practiced at portraying emotions they are "supposed" to feel, such as happiness or gratitude in accordance with culturally prescribed politeness rules, which even extends to telling "white lies" along with the nonverbal display of happiness (Talwar & Lee, 2002).

Children come to understand different rules are in effect for differing audiences. As children progress from third to seventh grade, they increase their masking of facial expressions of anger with teachers much more than with peers (Underwood, Coie, & Herbsman, 1992). They mask some emotions, such as fear and hurt, with peers, but not with parents (Zeman & Garber, 1996).

Across communication competencies, children must be able to make inferences about others' inner states and have an understanding of social contexts, social rules, and social conventions (Dimitracopoulou, 1990). In addition, a vast difference exists between knowledge of communication skills and the motivation to use those skills. Children move from copying behaviors they have seen rewarded in others, without real understanding or empathy, to invoking competencies due to an understanding of the social or moral reasons behind the communicative rule (Evangelista, 2002). Communication skills, per se, then are contingent on a number of other factors and make up only a small part of social competence.

COMMUNICATION COMPETENCIES AND THE FAMILY

But how are children socialized? From whom do children learn competencies to form peer relationships and to achieve success in school settings? The primary agent of this socialization is considered to be the family, and more specifically, U.S. cultural emphasis is on the parents, or more precisely the mother, to the exclusion of most other potential sources of influence (Fitzpatrick & Caughlin, 2002). Within the family, communication has long been considered the most instrumental agent of socialization (Berger & Luckmann, 1967, Streeck, 2002).

Parental Influence on Children's Communication Skills

Many U.S. mothers are subjected to a fantasy world with mythical deterministic and immutable powers over their children's lifetime outcomes (Ambert, 2001; Kagan, 1984; McGoldrick, Heiman, & Carter, 1993). Although this unidirectional emphasis on direct effects from mother to child has given way to more bidirectional and systemic multiparty interrelationships, the primary emphasis remains on the mother–child interaction.

Teti and Candelaria (2002) offer an intriguing definition of "competent parenting." Competent parenting can only be considered in light of the socialization desired. Thus, parents' actions and attitudes that facilitate desired child "outcomes" are considered competent, and those that inhibit the development of the desired social competencies are considered "incompetent." Though much space could be used to delineate what these unidirectional parenting practices are generally thought to be, Sillars (1995) offers a concise summary: "The cultural ideal for adult-child communication in Western, middle-class society is suggested by Baumrind's [1967] concept of 'authoritative' parenting (see Maccoby & Martin, 1983)" (p. 388). Sillars points out authoritative parenting is quite similar to the construct of "person-centered" messages, which is thought to be conducive of social competence (Burelson et al., 1995). Yet, considerations of optimal parenting vary culturally along with visions of child competencies. As Sillars points out, authoritative parenting or person-centered messages would likely be unrelated to social competence in some societies, due to differing cultural constructions of appropriate social skills. Traditional theories that focus on the relatively limited set of endorsed parenting practices have come into question recently. Though the importance of parents is not diminished, scholars are beginning to urge examination and understanding of the characteristics of a particular child in a particular set of circumstances and offer consideration to a wider array of parenting behaviors than those typically endorsed as the cultural ideal (Grusec, Goodnow, & Kuczynski, 2000).

Given the abundance of literature on the topic of mother–infant interaction and the relative dearth of literature on middle childhood (Fitzpatrick & Caughlin, 2002; Teti & Candelaria, 2002) as well as a societal emphasis on "mothering," space will be devoted to another relationship that is, arguably as, if not more, influential than the mother–child relationship in the child's development of the aforementioned competencies, the sibling relationship.

Siblings

Siblings increase time spent with each other and decrease time spent with their mother from 2 to 5 years old (Dunn & Creps, 1996). This continues through middle childhood (Dunn, 1993). They engage in more creative and symbolic play and role taking with each other than with anyone else (Dunn & Dale, 1984). They also have intense and frequent conflict (Katz,

Kramer, & Gottman, 1992). Thus, the sibling environment provides ample opportunity for caring behaviors, argumentation or conflict management, and self-monitoring of emotional displays.

Children's peer relationships may be facilitated though the enactment of social skills acquired in interaction with siblings (McCoy, Brody, & Stoneman, 2002). Siblings afford opportunities for practices such as teasing, comforting, reasoning, and managing conflict (Haslett & Sameter, 1997). Siblings also may promote empathy and role-taking abilities (Perner, Ruffman, & Leekam, 1994). In effect, siblings serve as a training ground for peer competencies (Parke & Buriel, 1998).

This interpretation of siblings as a training ground for later peer interaction is buttressed by the findings that children with younger siblings have better peer relationships than children without siblings (Bayder, Greek, & Brooks-Gunn, 1997), and children with siblings have been found to have higher level of perspective-taking skills than only children (Perner et al., 1994).

Older siblings are often enlisted by parents to help in the caregiving of younger siblings, and socialization may occur during this activity (Cicirelli, 1994). Teti, Gibbs, and Bond (1989) found that younger siblings benefited from such interactions with older siblings. On the other hand, benefits for older siblings maybe curvilinear. Moderate amounts of interaction seemed to facilitate older children's achievement, but when caregiving responsibilities for the older sibling children become too much, academic achievement is lowered (Cicirelli, 1994).

Kitzmann, Cohen, and Lockwood (2002) directly examined the question of whether only children are at a disadvantage in social skills with peers. They found that only-children fared worse than a sibling in that they were less popular; they found no differences among only-children, children with older siblings, and children with younger siblings in terms of the *quality* of mutual friendships. They note the complexity in measuring peer acceptance and rejection. Sibling relationships may facilitate some aspects of peer-related social competence, but not others. Moreover, they found the quality of the relationship among middle-school-age siblings to be more critical in predicting the quality of a child's friendship with peers than simply the presence or absence of a sibling. Though older sibs seldom consciously intend to "teach" younger siblings, younger siblings nonetheless learn much from their older siblings, both directly and indirectly, about social norms and rules of interaction (Cicirelli, 1994).

Although the primary assumption is that positive sibling relationships are associated with positive peer relationships and aid later peer competencies (McCoy et al., 2002), not all sibling interactions or relationships are positive. Antisocial interactions and negative relationships among siblings are associated with antisocial interactions with peers (Hinde, Tamplin, Barett, 1993). Siblings can help shape aggressive behavior in each other (Patterson, 1986). Lewin, Hops, Davis, and Dishion (1993) found peer ratings of negative behaviors at school were highly correlated with negative behaviors among same-sex sibling pairs. Bank, Patterson, and Reid (1996) propose that coercive or aggressive behaviors may be a dyadic trait of a sibling pair; if one child is aggressive or antisocial, so are other siblings. Also we cannot simply assume younger siblings learn positive norms from their older ones. Older siblings' use of alcohol, drugs, engagement in sexual activities and delinquent behaviors, and poor school performance in adolescence appear to trickle down to younger children's earlier engagement in similar behaviors (Rowe & Gulley, 1992).

Compensatory models have also been reported in that *negative* sibling relationships have been linked to the development of positive skills with which children form friendships and vice versa (Stocker, 1994). Thus, the role of sibling relationships in promoting or inhibiting social competencies or prompting socially desirable behaviors is complex, and the quality of sibling relationships must be considered, not simply the presence or absence of a sibling. Yet, even the quality may not be static. During middle childhood and into adolescence, the same sibling relationship may be characterized at any given moment by "closeness, rivalry, or indifference" (Cicirelli, 1996, p. 67).

The Siblings and the Family

Bank, Patterson, and Reid (1996) argue that coercive family environments are shared by siblings and parents alike. Aggressive children are more likely to be antisocial to peers, parents, and other siblings. Behaviors such as temper outbursts, arguing, and hitting are often inadvertently rewarded by parents and siblings. Parents and other siblings reinforce antisocial behavior by giving in to the aggressive child. Patterson (1982) conjectures a combination of an aggressive nature in the child, marginal parenting skills, and reinforcement by siblings through deference are ideal fodder for aggression. In other words, siblings act as "amplifiers and trainers" for aggression. Some studies have found some support for this model (e.g., Brody & Stoneman, 1996). In families where children are treated with varying levels of parental partiality, siblings are more likely to have conflictual relationships with each other (Dunn, 1993). In theory then, this should spill over to antisocial relationships with peers.

It is doubtful that a general conclusion that siblings have either a positive or a negative effect on one another's communication competencies can be offered. Evidence for a positive role of siblings in socialization is far from conclusive, though the general consensus is that siblings promote each other's communication competencies. Yet, as noted, negative behaviors may be amplified by siblings, and negative interactions among siblings may spill over into peer relationships. The older sibling may serve as a role model and socialization agent for undesired behaviors in younger siblings. In addition the age, birth order, spacing, parental treatment, sex, and number of siblings may play vital roles.

Little is known about the role of stepsiblings (residential, nonresidential, or partly residential), half-siblings, or foster siblings. Moreover, studies of siblings in the family seldom extend beyond two children or across more than one household (except in the cases of separated twins). When asked to draw family maps, some children include stepbrothers and stepsisters; others do not. Some children include stepfathers and birth fathers; others include only one or the other; some include neither. The same is likely true for mothers. Some children's families extend beyond one household (Brannen, Heptinstall, & Bhopal, 2000). The quality of the relationship with whomever one considers to be a sibling is more likely to play a role in the development of social competencies than any other single sibling factor.

Bidirectionality: From Child to Parent

Ideally, bidirectionality involves mutual reciprocity. Although numerous reconceptualizations have advanced work in bidirectionality, Lollis and Kuczynski (1997) point out three in particular: changes in conceptions of causality, viewing the child as agent, and concepts of power balances. For example, Pettit and Lollis (1997) examined research on reciprocity in parent–child relationships and found that many relationship proprieties are accomplished through mutual adjustment and accommodation on the part of both the child and the parent. Also, Lollis and Kuczynski, building on Hinde (1979), contend that parent–child interactions are intertwined with parent–child relationships. Central to such a view is that both child and parent contribute to their interactions and parent–child relationships themselves have dyadic interaction patterns (Patterson, DeBaryshe, & Ramsey, 1989).

Most work, however, does not examine mutual causality, agency, or negotiations of power balance. Rather the majority of the research on bidirectionally has examined the child's effect on the parent. Though such research on mutual reciprocity during middle childhood is increasing (see, e.g., Bugental & Goodnow, 1998; Petitt & Lollis, 1997), most attention has been granted to child temperament in infancy and its reported links to increased parental stress and depression and decreased parental responsiveness and involvement (e.g., Clark, Kochanska, & Ready, 2000; Lerner, Castellino, Terry, Villarruel, & McKinney, 1995; McBride, Schoppe, & Rane, 2002; Rothbart & Bates, 1998). Studies are beginning to examine the influence of temperament in a more systemic manner. For example, difficult temperaments may be amplified by parenting or family interactions setting recursive coercive patterns in the parent–child interaction, which in turn may contribute to peer rejection (Lytton, 2000; Patterson, 1982).

Although it is recognized that children must socialize adults, socialization of parents during middle childhood is relatively unstudied (Peterson & Hann, 1999). Children serve as socialization agents of their parents simply by their existence. As children move through school, their parents are often exposed to more external influences. Parents' activities and schedules change as children become more involved in sports, lessons, scouts, and so forth (Adler & Adler, 1998). As the child ages, parents are more likely to attend church (Nock, 1998) and tend to be more involved in the community (Ambert, 2001). As a result, children indirectly socialize parents by exposing them to broader and more divergent networks and activities.

Children also affect parents differentially based upon the children's age, as parents hold beliefs about age-appropriate behavior. When parents think the child is already old enough to know and understand expectations, parents become more harsh in their parenting, as opposed to granting the benefit of the doubt to the younger child, who might not have understood (Petersen & Hann, 1999). For example, as children grow from ages 4 to 12, parents tend to become more authoritarian in response to violations of expected age-appropriate behaviors (Dix, Ruble, & Zambrano, 1989). Similarly, Mills and Rubin (1992) found that as children matured from ages 4 to 6, parents attributed aggression less to immaturity and more to the internal disposition of the child, and consequently reacted with increased authoritarian parenting.

Examinations of temperament, mere presence, and changing parental beliefs according to the child's age, although offering promise in terms of bidirectional perspectives, still refer to the child in nonagentic terms. Fortunately, "Increasingly, children are being seen as competent social agents in their own right" (Hutchby & Moran-Ellis, 1998, p. 1). Researchers are beginning to recognize that children actively resist control by their parents, negotiate conflict with them (Kuczynski & Kochanska, 1995), and evaluate their parents' behavior (Grusec & Goodnow, 1994). Despite such progress, we still have comparatively little knowledge about how children actively participate in their own, parental, and overall family socialization.

Communication competence is not only historically and culturally contingent but also transactional and context dependent. It is performance relative to specific goals (Rose-Krasnor, 1997). Although U.S. culture emphasizes self-oriented priorities over other-oriented ones, competent social interaction may require high levels of both. As children mature, they are better able to consider other-oriented concerns as well as balance their own concerns with them. Social competence is not something simply handed over to children, nor does it naturally unfold. From the perspective of children, the socialization process involves the selection, evaluation, and incorporation of "input" from many significant others (Broderick, 1993). Consequently, children are accorded agency.

OLSON'S CIRCUMPLEX MODEL OF FAMILY FUNCTIONING

Olson's model offers one way for researchers and theorists to foreground children's agency in their own, and the family's, socialization. Although it may seem an odd frame through which to consider the development of communication skills, the model incorporates agency, negotiation, and changing power balances, all of which we have been recognized as key factors in the development of communication competencies.

The model has three basic components: cohesion, adaptability, and communication (Olson, 2000). Cohesion is defined as the emotional bonding that family members have toward one another. It can be seen in the use of boundaries, coalitions, decision-making practices, and the like. The emphasis is on how the family system manages separateness and togetherness. The second dimension is flexibility, which refers to the amount of change in the family's leadership, role relationships, and relationship rules. Flexibility in family systems is concerned with the juxtaposition of stability and change. The third dimension is communication. This is the mechanism which facilitates movement in the other two dimensions.

This model allows the integration of systems theory with family development theory, (Hill, 1970; Olson, 2000). The Circumplex model implicitly incorporates both Bronfenbrenner's (1979, 1986) ecological systems perspective and Hinde's (1979; Hinde & Stevenson-Hinde, 1988) interpersonal relationships perspective. The ultimate purpose of Bronfenbrenner's ecological perspective is understanding individual development within larger frameworks. The individual grows and adapts through interactions with the immediate ecosystem (the family) and more distant environments such as school (Bronfenbrenner, 1979). Thus, children's maturation takes place within an interactional context. For Hinde, a child must be considered as "a social being, formed by and forming part of a social network" (Hinde & Stevenson-Hinde, 1988, p. 2). Both Hinde and Bronfenbrenner concur that the most important considerations for the development of children are the relational interactions and systems of relationships that exist for children or within larger sociocultural contexts.

The Circumplex model is congruent with Hinde's model because it includes the importance of relationships among individual family members to the overall health of the family system. Further, Olson's model has been extended to explicit consideration of family ecosystems so that interconnections among individuals and relationships as well as work and school environments are included (see Gorall & Olson, 1995), thus echoing Bronfenbrenner's perspective.

The paradigm put forth by Olson is also consistent with symbolic interactionist views. Olson's early work assumed that a healthy family was one that was "balanced" on both cohesion and adaptability. He acknowledges that in his first formulations he took little account of various cultures or family forms (Gorall & Olson, 1995). In later work, he recognized that what was healthy for one family may not be for another family. Though there is little research on shared realities of family members, Hess and Handel (1959) suggested that each family "constitutes its own world" (p. 14). This is now recognized: "Each family must be viewed as a unique system and treated with regard to its unique conditions and relationships" (Gorall & Olson, 1995, p. 231). Particular families and cultures have different norms for "healthy" cohesion and adaptability; hence, this model is consistent with a symbolic interactionist perspective.

Thus, Olson's model of family functioning provides an ideal framework for the examination of children's developing communication competencies within a particular family ecosystem. The explicit emphasis on systemic flexibility (adaptation) necessitates consideration of multiple causalities, agency of the child (and other family members), and negotiations of power. Olson's emphasis on managing cohesion implicitly recognizes the dialectic of autonomy and interdependence. As such, his model has the potential to capture the features of family interaction we have identified as relevant for children's growing communication competencies within a particular cultural–historical family context.

Olson's dimension of "family communication" is the mechanism through which change in the other two dimensions occurs. It is the "facilitating dimension." The communication dimension has not received as much research attention as the other two dimensions (Gorall & Olson, 1995). Although the role of communication as facilitator of the other two dimensions is sound, the emphasis on "good communication skills" (e.g., listening skills, self-disclosure, and the like) is in need of conceptual refinement. This view of communication skills is a bit out of step with Olson's otherwise culturally sensitive model. Olson's model did, however, grow out of the numerous family theories that emphasize warmth and affect (see Olson, 2000). Nonetheless, he has articulated specific communication practices as valued over others, and as a result, has limited the application of the model. This may account in part for Peterson and Hann's (1999) conclusion that cumulative evidence on the Circumplex model has been inconclusive.

Yet the spirit of Olson's model allows one to infer that "good communication" may vary among families, just as optimal cohesion may vary among families. Given his overall premise that "positive communication skills" are those that facilitate appropriate levels of cohesion and adaptability and poor communication impedes such movement (Olson, 2000) his view of what exactly comprises good and poor communication maybe susceptible to some interpretation, and that liberty is taken here.

The fundamental premise of the Circumplex model is in that in order for families to cope with stress and developmental changes across the individual and family life cycle, families will change (Olson, 2000). The growth and development of every individual within the family system and how other family members adapt to that change are the bases of this framework. The family system is also the basis of sociocommunication development. Communication skills do not develop in isolation; they develop in conjunction with cognitive, social, and biological maturation. They also grow within a system of caregivers and siblings who are developing and changing themselves. The family is both adhering to broader sociocultural environments and creating its own unique family culture. If we were to examine communication patterns more holistically within the Circumplex model, as opposed to examining culturally prescribed communication practices, insights into the movement of family and individual communication practices in accordance with cohesion and adaptability could aid understanding of the development of communication competence.

Moreover, given that a healthy family is an adaptable one, the child who is socialized within such a family may further contribute to family health. In theory, the ability to negotiate separateness and connectedness and the ability to adapt to changing circumstances may facilitate sensitivities to differing communication practices in various contexts, consequently aiding communication competencies in multiple domains.

CONCLUSION

I have concentrated here only on the family, and only on a small part of the family at that. Despite the previously proffered claims, we must remain open to the possibility that, even by middle childhood, the family may not be the primary agent of socialization. It is likely that much socialization takes place out of the home, prior to school years. In 2001, sixty-one percent of children from birth through age 6 (and not yet in kindergarten) received child care on a regular basis from nonparents. From ages 3 to 6, care was most likely to be non-home-based with a nonrelative, and approximately 50% of children in kindergarten to grade 8 received before or after school care on a regular basis (Federal Interagency Forum on Child and Family Statistics, 2002).

Children are socialized by the media, their peers, siblings, multiple parenting figures, teachers, and by other societal members. We actually know very little about which potential influences carry more weight than others at given points of development, or even if more weight should be accorded to nurture than to nature. Thus, although the focus of this chapter, and that of this book, is on family communication, continued attention to the entire family system, the family ecosystem, and to the overall environment in the socialization of children must be explored in conjunction with biological factors. An examination of the family communication patterns that facilitate movement on Olson's dimensions of cohesion and adaptability in relationship to children's developing communication competencies is particularly ripe for study.

REFERENCES

Adler, P. A., & Adler, P. (1998). *Peer power: Preadolescent culture and identity.* New Brunswick, NJ: Rutgers University Press.

Ambert, A. M. (2001). *The effect of children on parents* (2nd ed.). Binghamton, New York: Haworth.

Ariès, P. (1962). *Centuries of childhood: A social history of family life.* In R. Baldick (Trans.). New York: Knopf.

Bank, L., Patterson, G. R., & Reid, J. B. (1996). Negative sibling interaction patterns as predictors of later adjustment problems in adolescent and young adult males. In G. H. Brody (Ed.), *Sibling relationships: Their causes and consequences* (pp. 196–230). Norwood NJ: Ablex.

Baumrind, D. (1967). Child care practices anteceding three patterns of preschool behavior. *Genetic Psychology Monographs, 75,* 43–83.

Bayder, N., Greek, A., & Brooks-Gunn, J. (1997). A longitudinal study of the effects of birth of a sibling during the first 6 years of life. *Journal of Marriage and the Family, 59,* 939–956.

Berger, P., & Luckmann, T. (1967). *The social construction of reality: A treatise in the sociology of knowledge.* Garden City, NY: Doubleday.

Blum-Kulka, S., & Snow, C. E. (2002). Editors introduction. In S. Blum-Kalka & C. E. Snow (Eds.), *Talking to adults: The contribution of multiparty discourse to language acquisition* (pp. 1–12). Mahwah, NJ: Lawrence Erlbaum Associates.

Brannen, J., Heptinstall, E., & Bhopal, K. (2000). *Connecting children: Care and family life in later childhood.* London: Routledge Falmer.

Broderick, C. B. (1993). *Understanding family process: Basics of family systems theory.* Newbury Park, CA: Sage.

Brody, G., & Stoneman, Z. (1996). A risk-amelioration model of sibling relationships: Conceptual underpinnings and preliminary findings. In G. H. Brody (Ed.), *Sibling relationships: Their causes and consequences* (pp. 231–248). Norwood NJ: Ablex.

Bronfenbrenner, U. (1979). *The ecology of human development. Experiments by nature and by design.* Cambridge, MA: Harvard University Press.

Bronfenbrenner, U. (1986). Ecology of the family as a context for human development: Research perspectives. *Developmental Psychology 22,* 723–742.

Bronfenbrenner, U. (2001). Growing chaos in the lives of children, youth and families: How can we turn it around? In J. C. Westman (Ed.), *Parenthood in America: Under-valued, underpaid, under siege* (pp. 197–210). Madison, WI: University of Wisconsin Press.

Brunner, J. (1983). *Child's talk: Learning to use language.* New York: Norton.

Bugental, D. B., & Goodnow, J. J. (1998). Socialization processes. In W. Damon (Series Ed.) & N. Eisenberg (Vol. Ed.), *Handbook of child psychology, Vol. 3. Social, emotional, and personality development* (pp. 389–462). New York: Wiley.

Burleson, B. R., Delia, J. G., & Applegate, J. L. (1995). The socialization of person-centered communication: Parents' contributions to their children's social-cognitive and communication skills. In M. A. Fitzpatrick & A. L. Vangelisti (Eds.), *Explaining family interactions* (pp. 34–76). Thousand Oaks, CA: Sage.

Burleson, B. R., & Kunkel, A. W. (1996). The socialization of emotional support skills in childhood. In B. R. Pierce, B. R. Sarason, & I. G. Sarason (Eds.), *Handbook of social support and the family* (pp. 105–140). New York: Plenum Press.

Burleson, B. R., & Kunkel, A. W. (2002). Parental and peer contributions to the emotional support skills of the child: From whom do children learn to express support? *Journal of Family Communication, 2*, 79–98.

Cairns, R. B., & Cairns, B. D. (1994). *Lifelines and risks: Pathways of youth in our time.* New York: Cambridge University Press.

Chase-Lansdale, P. L., Wakschlag, L. S., & Brooks-Gunn, J. (1995). A psychological perspective on the development of caring in children and youth: The role of the family. *Journal of Adolescence, 18*, 515–556.

Cicirelli, V. G. (1994). Sibling relationships in cross-cultural perspectives. *Journal of Marriage and the Family, 56*, 7–20.

Cicirelli, V. G. (1996). Sibling relationships in middle and old age. In G. Brody (Ed.), *Sibling relationships: Their causes and consequences* (pp. 47–73), Norwood, NJ: Ablex.

Clark, L. A., Kochanska, G., & Ready, R. (2000). Mothers' personality and its interaction with child temperament as predictors of parenting. *Journal of Personality and Social Psychology, 79*, 274–285.

Cole, P. M. (1986). Children's spontaneous control of facial expression. *Child Development, 57*, 1309–1321.

Debaryshe, B. D., & Fryxell, D. (1998). A developmental perspective on anger: Family and peer contexts. *Psychology in the Schools, 34*, 205–216.

DeFries, J. C., Plomin, R., & Fulker, D. W. (1994). Nature and nurture in middle childhood. In J. C. DeFries, R. Polmin, & D. W. Fulker (Eds.), *Nature and nurture during middle childhood* (pp. 1–8). Cambridge, MA: Blackwell.

Dimitracopoulou, I. (1990). *Conversational competence and social development.* New York: Cambridge University Press.

Dix, T., Ruble, D. N., & Zambrano, R. J. (1989). Mothers' implicit theories of discipline: Child effects, parent effects, and the attribution process. *Child Development, 60*, 1373–1391.

Dunn, J. (1993). *Young children's close relationships.* Newbury Park, CA: Sage.

Dunn J., & Creps, C. (1996). Children's family relationships between two and five: Developmental changes and individual differences. *Social Development, 5*, 230–250.

Dunn, J., & Dale, N. (1984). I a daddy: 2-year-olds' collaboration in joint pretend play with sibling and mother. In I. Bretherton (Ed.), *Symbolic play* (pp. 131–158). New York: Academic Press.

Dunn, J., Slomkowski, C., & Beardsall, L. (1994). Sibling relationships from the preschool period through middle childhood and early adolescence. *Developmental Psychology, 30*, 315–324.

Durlak, J. A. (2001). School problems of children. In C. Walker & M. C. Roberts (Eds.), *Handbook of clinical child psychology* (3rd ed., pp. 561–575). New York: Wiley.

Ekman, P., & Freisen, W. W. (1975). *Unmasking the face: A guide to recognizing emotions from facial clues.* New Jersey: Prentice-Hall.

Eisenberg, N. (1992). *The caring child.* Cambridge, MA: Harvard University Press.

Erikson, E. (1963). *Childhood and society* (2nd ed.). New York: Norton.

Erwin, P. (1993). *Friendship and peer relations in children*. Chichester, England: Wiley.

Evangelista, N. J. (2001). Understanding the social and personal needs of the early school-aged child. In J. F. Carlson & B. B. Waterman (Eds.), *Social and personality assessment of school-aged children: Developing interventions for educational and clinical use* (pp. 207–228). Boston: Allyn & Bacon.

Federal Interagency Forum on Child and Family Statistics. (2002). *America's children: Key national indicators of well-being. Part 1: Population and family characteristics.* National Institute of Child Health and Human Population. Washington, DC: Government Printing Office.

Fessbach, N. D. (1987). Parental empathy and child adjustment/maladjustment. In N. Eisenberg & J. Strayer (Eds.), *Empathy and its development* (pp. 271–289). New York: Cambridge University Press.

Fitzpatrick, M. A., & Caughlin, J. P. (2002). Interpersonal communication in family relationships. In M. L. Knapp & J. A. Daly (Eds.), *The handbook of interpersonal communication* (3rd ed., pp. 726–777). Thousand Oaks, CA: Sage.

Gersham, F. M. (1986). Conceptual issues in the assessment of social competence in children. In P. S. Streain, M. J. Guralnick, & H. M. Walker (Eds.), *Children's societal behavior: Development, assessment and modification* (pp. 143–179). New York: Academic Press.

Gorall, D. M., & Olson, D. H. (1995) Circumplex Model of Family Systems: Integrating ethnic diversity and other social systems. In R. H. Mikesell, D. D. Lusterman, & S. H. McDaniel (Eds.), *Integrating family therapy: Handbook of family psychology* (pp. 217–233). Washington, DC: American Psychological Association.

Grusec, J. E., & Goodnow, J. J. (1994). Impact of parental discipline methods on the child's internalization of values: A reconceptualization of current points of view. *Developmental Psychology, 30*, 4–19.

Grusec, J. E., Goodnow, J. J., & Kuczynski, L. (2000). New directions in analysis of parenting contributions to children's acquisitions of values. *Child Development, 71*, 205–211.

Guerrero, L. K, Andersen, P. A., & Trost, M. (1998). Communication and emotion: Basic concepts and approaches. In P. A. Andersen & L. W. Guerrero (Eds.), *Handbook of communication and emotion: Research, theory, applications, and contexts* (pp. 3–28). San Diego: Academic Press.

Hart, C. H., Olsen, S. F., Robinson, C. C., & Mandleco, B. L. (1997). The development of social and communicative competence in childhood: Review and a model of personal, familial, and extrafamilial processes. In B. R. Burleson (Ed.), *Communication yearbook: Vol. 20* (pp. 305–373). Thousand Oaks, CA: Sage.

Haslett, B. B., & Samter, W. (1997). *Children communicating: The first five years.* Mahwah, NJ: Lawrence Erlbaum Associates.

Hess, R. D., & Handel, G. (1959). *Family worlds: A psychosocial approach to family life.* Chicago: University of Chicago Press.

Hill, R. (1970). *Family development in three generations*. Cambridge, MA: Schenkman.

Hinde, R. A. (1979) *Towards understanding relationships*. London: Academic Press.

Hinde, R. A., & Stevenson-Hinde, J. (Eds.). (1988). *Relationships within families: Mutual influences.* New York: Oxford University Press.

Hinde, R. A., Tamplin, A., & Barett, J. (1993). A comparative study of relationship structure. *British Journal of Social Psychology, 32*, 191–207.

Hutchby, I., & Moran-Ellis, J. (1998). Situating children's social competence. In I. Hutchby & J. Moran-Ellis (Eds.), *Children and social competence* (pp. 7–26). London: Falmer Press.

James, A. (1998). Forward. In I. Hutchby & J. Moran-Ellis (Eds.), *Children and social competence* (pp. vii–x). London: Falmer Press.

Kagan, J. (1984). *The nature of the child.* New York: Basic Books.

Kagan, S. L., & Cohen, N. E. (1995). *Solving the quality problem: A vision for America's early care and education system. A final report of the Quality 2000 initiative.* New Haven, CT: Yale University Press.

Katz, L. F., Kramer, L., & Gottman, J. M. (1992). Conflict and emotions in martial, sibling, and peer relationships. In C. U. Shantz & W. W. Hartup (Eds.), *Conflict in child and adolescent development* (pp. 122–149). New York: Cambridge University Press.

Kitzmann, K. M., Cohen, R., & Lockwood, R. L. (2002). Are only children missing out? Comparison of the peer-related social competence of only children and siblings. *Journal of Social and Personal Relationships, 19*, 299–316.

Kline, S. L. (1998). Influence opportunities and the development of argumentation competencies in childhood. *Argumentation, 12*, 367–385.

Kline, S. L., & Clinton, B. L. (1998). Developments in children's persuasive message practices. *Communication Education, 47*, 120–136.

Kline, S. L., & Oseroff-Varnell, D. (1993). The development of argument analysis skill in children. *Argumentation and Advocacy, 30*, 1–16.

Kuczynski, L., & Kochanska, L. (1995). Function and content of maternal demands: Developmental significance of early demands for competent action. *Child Development, 66*, 616–628.

Ladd, G. W. (Ed.). (1991). Family-peer relationships [Special issue]. *Journal of Social and Personal Relationships, 8*(3).

Lamborn, D. D., Mounts, N. S., Steinberg, L., & Dornbusch, S. M. (1991). Patterns of competence and adjustment among adolescents from authoritative, authoritarian, indulgent, and neglectful families. *Child Development, 62*, 1049–1065.

Laursen, B., Finkelstein, B. D., & Betts, N. T. (2001). A developmental meta-analysis of peer conflict resolution. *Developmental Review, 21*, 423–429.

Lerner, R. Castellino, D., Terry, P., Villarruel, F., & McKinney, M. (1995). Developmental contextual perspective on parenting. In M. Bornstein (Ed.), *Handbook of parenting. Vol. 4. Biology and ecology of parenting* (pp. 285–309). Mahwah, NJ: Lawrence Erlbaum Associates.

Lerner, R., & Spainer, G. L. (Eds.). (1978). *Child influences on marital interaction: A life-span perspective.* New York: Academic Press.

Lewin, L. M., Hops, H. Davis, B., & Dishion, T. J. (1993). Mulitmethod comparison of similarity in school adjustment of siblings and unrelated children. *Developmental Psychology, 29*, 963–969.

Locke, J. (1964). *Some thoughts concerning education.* In F. W. Garforth (Trans.). Woodbury, NY: Barrons. (Original work published 1693)

Lollis, S., & Kuczynski, L. (1997). Beyond one hand clapping: Seeing bidirectionality in parent-child relations. *Journal of Social and Personal Relationships, 14*, 441–461.

Lytton, H. (2000). Toward a model of family-environmental and child-biological influences on development. *Developmental Review, 20*, 150–179.

Maccoby, E. E., & Martin, J. A. (1983). Socialization in the context of the family: Parent-child interaction. In E. M. Heaterington (Ed.), *Handbook of child psychology: Vol. 4. Socialization, personality, and social development* (pp. 1–101). New York: Wiley.

McBride, B. A., Schoppe, S. J., & Rane, T. R. (2002). Child characteristics, parenting stress, and parental involvement: Fathers versus mothers. *Journal of Marriage and the Family, 64*, 988–1011.

McCoy, J. L., Brody, G. H., & Stoneman, Z. (1994). A longitudinal analysis of sibling relationships as mediators of the link between family processes and youths' best friendships. *Family Relations, 43*, 400–408.

McCoy, J. K., Brody, G. H., & Stoneman, Z. (2002). Temperament and the quality of best friendships: Effect of same-sex sibling relationships. *Family Relations, 51*, 245–255.

McDowell, D. J., & Parke, R. D. (2000). Differential knowledge of display rules for positive and negative emotions: Influences from parents, influences on peers. *Social Development, 9*, 415–432.

McGoldrick, M., Heiman, M., & Carter, B. (1993). The changing family life cycle: A perspective on normalcy (pp. 405–443). In F. Walsh (Ed.), *Normal family processes* (2nd ed.). New York: Guilford Press.

Merrell, K. W., & Gimpel, G. A. (1998). *Social skills of children and adolescents: Conceptualization, assessment, treatment.* Mahwah, NJ: Lawrence Erlbaum Associates.

Mills, R. S., & Rubin, K. H. (1990). Parental believes about problematic social behaviors in early childhood. *Child Development, 61*, 138–151.

Moffett, J. (1968). *The universe of discourse.* Boston: Houghton Mifflin.

Moore, K., Evans, J., Brooks-Gunn, J., & Roth, J. (2001). What are good child outcomes. In A. Thornton (Ed.), *The well-being of children and families: Research and data* needs (pp. 59–84). Ann Arbor: University of Michigan Press.

Nock, S. L. (1998). *Marriage in men's lives.* New York: Oxford University Press.

Olson, D. H. (2000). Circumplex model of marital and family systems. *Journal of Family Therapy, 22*, 144–167.

Parke, R. D., & Buriel, R. (1998). Socialization in the family: Ethnic and ecological perspectives. In W. Damon (Series Ed.) & N. Eisenberg (Vol. Ed.*), Handbook of child psychology: Vol. 3: Social emotional and personality developmen*t (5th ed., pp. 463–552). New York: Asher.

Parker, J. G., & Asher, S. R. (1993). Friendship and friendship quality in middle childhood: Links with peer group acceptance and feelings of loneliness and social dissatisfaction. *Developmental Psychology, 29*, 611–621.

Patterson, G. R. (1982). *Coercive family processes.* Eugene, OR: Castillia.

Patterson, G. R. (1986). The contribution of siblings to training for fighting: A microsocial analysis. In D. Olweus, J. Block, & M. Radke-Yarrow (Eds.), *Development of anti-social and prosocial behavior* (pp. 235–261). New York: Academic Press.

Patterson, G. R., DeBaryshe, B. D., & Ramsey, E. (1989). A developmental perspective on anti-social behavior. *American Psychologist, 44*, 329–335.

Perner, J., Ruffman, T., & Leekam, S. R. (1994). Theory of mind is contagious: You catch it from your sibs. *Child Development, 65*, 1228–1238.

Peterson, G. W., & Hann, D. (1999). Socializing children and parents in families. In M. B. Sussman, S. K. Steinmetz, & G. W. Peterson (Eds.), *Handbook of marriage and the family* (2nd ed., pp. 327–370). New York: Plenum Press.

Pettit, G. S., & Lollis, S. (1997). Introduction to special issue: Reciprocity and bidirectionality in parent-child relationships: New approaches to the study of enduring relationships. *Journal of Social and Personal Relationships, 14*, 435–461.

Raeff, C. (1997). Individuals in relationships: Culture values, children's social interactions, and the development of an American individualistic self. *Developmental Review, 17*, 205–238.

Rose-Krasnor, L. (1997). The nature of social competence: A theoretical review. *Social Development, 6*, 111–135.

Rothbart, M. K., & Bates, J. E. (1988). Temperament. In W. Damon (Series Ed.) & N. Eisenberg (Vol. Ed.), *Handbook of child psychology, Vol. 3: Social, emotional and personality development* (5th ed., pp. 105–176). New York: Wiley.

Rousseau, J. J. (1911). *Emile, or on education.* In B. Foxley (Trans.). London: Dent. (Original work published 1762)

Rowe, D., & Gulley, B. L. (1992). Sibling effects on substance use and delinquency. *Criminology 30*, 217–233

Saarni, C., Mumme, D., & Campos, J. (1998). Emotional development: Action, communication, and understanding. In W. Damon (Series Ed.) & N. Eisenberg (Vol. Ed), *Handbook of child psychology: Vol. 3. Social, emotional and personality development* (5th ed., pp. 237–309). New York: Wiley.

Sillars, A. L. (1995). Communication and family culture. In M. A. Fitzpatrick & A. L. Vangelisti, (Eds.), *Explaining family interactions* (pp. 375–399). Thousand Oaks, CA: Sage.

Smith, T. W. (1999). *The emerging 21st century American family* (GSS Social Change Report No. 42). University of Chicago, National Opinion Research Center.

Snow, C. E., & Blum-Kulka, S. (2002). From home to school: School-age children talking with adults. In S. Blum-Kalka & C. E. Snow (Eds.), *Talking to adults: The contribution of multiparty discourse to language acquisition* (pp. 327–341). Mahwah, NJ: Lawrence Erlbaum Associates.

Stein, N. L., & Albro, E. R. (2001). The origins and nature of arguments: Studies in conflict understanding, emotion, and negotiation. *Discourse Processes, 32*, 113–133.

Stocker, C. (1994). Children's perceptions of relationships with siblings, friends and mothers: Compensatory processes and links with adjustment. *Journal of Child Psychology and Psychiatry, 35*, 1447–1459.

Streeck, J. (2002). Culture, meaning, and interpersonal communication. In M. L. Knapp & J. A. Daly (Eds.), *The handbook of interpersonal communication* (3rd ed., pp. 300–336). Thousand Oaks, CA: Sage.

Talwar V., & Lee, K. (2002). Emergence of white-lie telling in children between 3 and 7 years of age. *Merrill Palmer Quarterly, 48*, 160–181.

Teti, D. M., & Candelaria, M. A. (2002). Parenting competence. In M. H. Bornstein (Ed.), *Handbook of parenting: Vol. 4. Social conditions and applied parenting* (2nd ed., pp. 149–180). Mahwah, NJ: Lawrence Erlbaum Associates.

Teti, D. M., Gibbs, E. D., & Bond L. A. (1989). Sibling interaction, birth spacing, and intellectual/linguistic development. In P. G. Zukow (Ed.), *Sibling interaction across cultures: Theoretical and methodological issues* (pp. 117–139). New York: Springer-Verlag.

Toulmin, S. E. (1958). *The uses of argument*. Cambridge, England: Cambridge University Press.

Underwood, M. K., Coie, J. D., & Herbsman, C. R. (1992). Display rules for anger and aggression in school-age children. *Child Development, 63*, 366–380.

Vandell, D. L., & Hembree, S. E. (1994). Peer social-status and friendship: Independent contributors to children's' social and academic adjustment. *Merrill Palmer Quarterly, 40*, 461–477.

von Salisch, M. (2001). Children's emotional development: Challenges in their relationships to parents, peers, and friends. *International Journal of Behavioral Development, 25*, 310–319.

Westby, C. E. (1998a). Communicative refinement in school age and adolescence. In W. O. Haynes & B. B. Shulman (Eds.), *Communication development* (pp. 311–360). Baltimore: New Waverly Press.

Westby, C. E. (1998b). Social-emotional basis of communication development. In W. O. Haynes & B. B. Shulman (Eds.), *Communication development* (pp. 165–204). Baltimore: New Waverly Press.

Zelizer, V. A. R. (1985). *Pricing the priceless child: The changing social value of children.* New York: Basic Books.

Zeman, J., & Garber, J. (1996). Display rules for anger, sadness, and pain: It depends on who is watching. *Child Development, 67*, 957–973.

16

PARENT–CHILD COMMUNICATION
DURING ADOLESCENCE

BRETT LAURSEN
FLORIDA ATLANTIC UNIVERSITY

W. ANDREW COLLINS
UNIVERSITY OF MINNESOTA

Conventional wisdom regards parent–adolescent communication as an oxymoron. As is often the case with adolescence, however, conventional wisdom can be misleading. Although it is certainly true that communication during the adolescent years is a significant challenge for parents and children, this challenge stems primarily from the changing nature of the relationship, not from an inherent inability of adolescents and parents to engage in meaningful conversation (Collins, Gleason, & Sesma, 1997). As families navigate the transition from childhood into adulthood, the frequency and content of their interactions change. Increasing adolescent autonomy inevitably alters patterns of self-disclosure, commonly shared experiences, and perceptions of privacy and responsibilities. Yet even in the face of these significant alterations, familial emotional bonds are noteworthy for their resilience and continuity.

To the extent that there is a generation gap, it is as much a product of incongruent perceptions and expectations as it is of inadequate or insufficient conversation (Steinberg, 2001). Parents and adolescents (relationship insiders) do not necessarily share the same view of the relationship and their ability to communicate, nor are their perspectives typically congruent with those of observers (relationship outsiders). Parents and adolescents pursue different implicit goals and timetables regarding the adolescent's autonomy, which may give rise to communication difficulties (Collins & Luebker, 1994). But communication problems are not preordained. Families differ widely in the extent to which autonomy has a corrosive effect on parent–child interactions. For some it is a difficult passage, but most families are well equipped to navigate the developmental challenges of adolescence.

This chapter describes how patterns of parent–child communication are transformed across the adolescent years in terms of changes in the nature and functions of relationships.

Because of space limitations, we focus on salient aspects of parent–adolescent relationships that best illustrate alterations in patterns of communication. The chapter is divided into four sections. The first section provides an overview of theoretical accounts of parent–child relationships during adolescence. Most models of development assume perturbations in family relationships during the adolescent years, although there is little agreement as to the implications for family communication. The second section describes continuity and change in manifestations of parent–adolescent closeness. For most families, closeness and interdependence decline across adolescence, but the falloff in constructive communication appears to be especially pronounced for those in troubled relationships. The third section describes continuity and change in manifestations of parent–adolescent conflict. Expressions of anger and coercion may increase during the transition from childhood to adolescence, particularly among families with prior communication difficulties, but strife is not a normative feature of this age period. The concluding remarks place changing patterns of parent–adolescent communication in the larger context of relationship transformations from childhood to adulthood.

THEORETICAL ACCOUNTS OF CONTINUITY AND CHANGE IN PARENT–ADOLESCENT RELATIONSHIPS

Conceptual models of parent–adolescent relationships may be distinguished according to whether their primary focus is on the adolescent or on the relationship. Those that focus on the individual tend to emphasize the child's biological and/or cognitive maturation as the impetus for changes in the parent–adolescent relationship. Long the prevalent theoretical perspective, these models hold that the manner in which family relationships are transformed and the ensuing consequences for family communication depend on the nature and processes of individual maturation. In contrast, conceptual models that focus on the relationship tend to emphasize continuity and the enduring nature of bonds forged between parents and children. These models hold that because the relationship is inherently stable, functional properties of family communication remain constant despite adolescent development and alterations in the content and form of interactions.

Models of Individual Change and Their Implications for Parent–Adolescent Communication

Both Sigmund Freud (1921/1949) and Anna Freud (1958) assumed that hormonal changes at puberty give rise to unwelcome Oedipal urges that foster impulse control problems and anxiety, as well as rebelliousness and distance from the family. More recent psychoanalytic formulations (Blos, 1979; Erikson, 1968) also implicate puberty in the drive toward individuation from parents, through a process that emphasizes adolescent autonomy striving and ego identity development rather than impulse control. These models agree that deidealization (an awareness of parental fallibility) and psychic emancipation drive a wedge between parents and children; inner turmoil produced by adolescent hormonal fluctuations exacerbates these relationship difficulties. Family communication is expected to deteriorate as heightened parent–child conflict and diminished closeness follow pubertal maturation. Once pubertal maturation and individuation are complete, typically by late adolescence, conflict should abate and efforts may be undertaken to reestablish relationship closeness. The end result is permanent changes in the parent–child relationship that permit the adolescent to participate in family communication as an adult.

Evolutionary views of adolescent development also emphasize the role of puberty in transforming relationships and communication (Hill, 1988; Steinberg, 1989). The origins of this process, however, lie not with impulses related to puberty, but rather with evolutionary pressures on the child to move away from the family to find a sexual partner. This model suggests that cognitive advances foster autonomy striving and individuation, which heighten conflict with and diminish closeness to parents. Increased independence may even help to promote pubertal development such that autonomy and individuation create distance between the adolescent and the family, which fosters physical maturation and encourages children to look elsewhere for mates. Increased conflict and diminished closeness are presumed to be an integral part of the move toward adolescent independence. Conflict should eventually subside, but there is no provision for the reestablishment of parent–child closeness. Although relationship transformations inevitably impede family communication, greater parental investment in offspring, as indicated by a prior history of responsive parenting, is thought to provide a foundation of warmth and respect that may enable both parties to transcend the difficulties of adolescence.

A related group of maturational models hold that cognitive development is the impetus for change in parent–adolescent relationships. Predicated on the principle that changes in cognitive capabilities mediate interpersonal behavior (Kohlberg, 1969), the various models all start from the premise that global advances in adolescent logical thought capacities promote abstract and complex reasoning (Piaget, 1932/1965), which foster a nuanced appreciation of interpersonal distinctions and an increasingly reciprocal view of parent–child relationships. As a result, adolescents come to view parents in egalitarian terms, similar to friends; parental reluctance to conform with this view by transforming their vertical affiliation into a horizontal one creates conflict and curtails closeness until family roles are renegotiated (Selman, 1980; Youniss, 1980). Cognitive advances may also prompt adolescents to perceive as personal decisions issues that were previously considered to be under parental jurisdiction. In this view, parental insistence on a conventional perspective that emphasizes adult authority over adolescent autonomy heightens conflict until family roles and responsibilities are revised (Smetana, 1988).

These models imply that because parents and adolescents necessarily go through a period in which they experience the same interactions differently, communication between parents and adolescents may be impaired as a consequence of relationship change. After relationship roles have been successfully renegotiated, conflict should subside and parents and children may reestablish closeness and develop a more sophisticated framework for constructive communication (Collins & Luebker, 1994). Given that perceptions mediate relationship experiences, reports of change in parent–adolescent communication are expected to vary across participants, and one or both of these insider perspectives are likely to be at odds with independent outsider perspectives.

Models of Relationship Change and Their Implications for Parent–Adolescent Communication

Alternative models of parent–adolescent relationships focus on forces for stability and change within the dyad rather than on the impact of individual change on the dyad.

Attachment, the most common relational perspective, argues that parent–child relationships are inherently stable over time in terms of the quality of their functioning. Bowlby's (1969) theory focused primarily on infant–caregiver relationships; others (e.g., Ainsworth, 1989) have charted pathways of parent–child relationships through adolescence and beyond. According to this perspective, one person's behavior with another is guided by a set of cognitive representations derived from a history of interactions in relationships. Once established, representations of attachment relationships are presumed to be relatively stable. As a mutually regulated system, parents and children jointly work to maintain the relationship in a manner consistent with their cognitive representations. Specific interactions may vary from one age to the next, depending on the developmental challenges of the period, but the functional significance of interactions and their meaning to the partners are expected to vary little over time (Sroufe & Fleeson, 1988). Applied to adolescence, this suggests that although maturational changes in the child stimulate greater autonomy striving that transforms patterns of communication with parents, perceptions of the quality of the relationship should remain fairly stable (Collins, 1995). Separation and individuation may precipitate conflict and diminished feelings of closeness for a time, but the magnitude of these changes and their impact on the relationship should reflect the prior history of the relationship (Allen & Land, 1999). Adolescents and parents with a history of sensitive, responsive interactions and strong emotional bonds may experience only temporary communication difficulties, whereas those in poorer quality relationships are more likely to sustain disruption and unresolved issues.

Social relations or interdependence models also emphasize the inherent stability of parent–child relationships. In an interdependent relationship, partners engage in mutually influential exchanges and share the perception that their connections are reciprocal and enduring (Reis, Collins, & Berscheid, 2000). According to this view, interdependence is a hallmark of all close relationships and is manifested in frequent, strong, and diverse interconnections maintained over an extended time (Kelley et al., 1983). These enduring interconnections are internalized by participants and organized into mental schemas that shape expectations concerning future interactions. The obligatory nature of parent–child relationships fosters expectations of interdependence, and participants come to expect behaviors of each other that maintain the connections between them (Collins & Repinski, 1994). Patterns of communication established during childhood are likely to be carried forward into adolescence by both partners, but cognitive advances provide adolescents with a realization that the rules of reciprocity and social exchange that govern interactions with friends are not similarly applied to interactions with parents (Youniss, 1980). Greater autonomy offers adolescents the opportunity to influence interconnections with parents on the basis of perceived relationship costs and benefits (Laursen & Bukowski, 1997). The amount of change should vary, depending on the degree to which the relationship is perceived to be inequitable. Poor-quality relationships may experience an upsurge in conflict and a concomitant decline in closeness as adolescents express a growing dissatisfaction with unequal treatment and unfavorable outcomes. High-quality relationships, however, may change little, or even may improve, as participants build on mutually beneficent patterns of exchange and attempt to adjust for past inequities.

Both the individual and the relational perspectives on parent–adolescent relationships emphasize two key features of communication: closeness, which functions as a potential attractor that helps to maintain connections between family members despite changes in the individuals, and conflict, which functions as a potential repellent that creates psychological and physical distance between family members. The remaining sections of our chapter focus on these two relationship features, with particular attention to their implications for communication in the family.

CONTINUITY AND CHANGE IN PARENT–ADOLESCENT CLOSENESS

Closeness refers to the degree to which individuals affect and are affected by each other. Commonly invoked indicators of closeness include affection, cohesion, companionship, interdependence, intimacy, and trust (Collins & Repinski, 1994). There is considerable continuity between positive features of relationships during adolescence and those earlier in life, despite the altered patterns of interaction, emotion, and cognition. Surveys of families in Europe and North America repeatedly indicate that parents and adolescents perceive relationships with one another as warm and pleasant (Collins, 1995). Two comprehensive studies encapsulate these findings. In the first, an epidemiological study of all 14-year-olds on the Isle of Wight (United Kingdom), both parents and adolescents reported a high incidence of positive interactions and a very low incidence of relationship problems such as physical withdrawal and communication difficulties (Rutter, Graham, Chadwick, & Yule, 1976). In the second, a longitudinal study of a representative birth cohort in Stockholm (Sweden), more than 75% of youth in each adolescent age period described "good" relationships with mothers and fathers, whereas fewer than 10% reported a "bad" relationship (Stattin & Klackenberg, 1992).

Developmental Trends

Continuities in parent–child relationships coexist with significant changes in the amount, content, and perceived meaning of interactions, in expressions of positive and negative affect and in interpersonal perceptions of participants (Collins & Russell, 1991). Connectedness during adolescence is manifest in forms that differ from those in earlier life. Parent–child intimacy, as expressed by cuddling and extensive joint interactions, declines as children mature, but conversations in which information is conveyed and feelings are expressed increase (Hartup & Laursen, 1991). These adaptations are appropriate responses to the maturity level and changing needs of the adolescent. Parents remain the most influential of all adolescent relationships, shaping most of the important decisions confronting children, even as their authority over mundane details such as attire wanes (Collins, Maccoby, Steinberg, Hetherington, & Bornstein, 2000). Stability in parental authority appears to be predicated on flexibility in parent–child communication.

Developmental changes in parent–child closeness are well documented. Subjective rankings of closeness and objective measures of interdependence similarly decrease across the adolescent years (Laursen & Williams, 1997). The amount of time parents and adolescents spend together declines in a linear fashion from preadolescence to late adolescence (Larson, Richards, Moneta, Holmbeck, & Duckett, 1996). Relative to preadolescents, adolescents perceive less companionship and intimacy with parents (Buhrmester & Furman, 1987) and report lower feelings of acceptance by parents and satisfaction with family life (Hill, 1988). Although perceptions of relationships remain generally warm and supportive, both adolescents and parents report less frequent expressions of positive emotions and

more frequent expressions of negative emotions when compared to parents and preadolescent children (Steinberg & Silk, 2002). Not all trends are negative: Friendliness and
positive affect typically rebound to preadolescent levels sometime during mid to late
adolescence (Larson et al., 1996). Thus, measured in absolute terms, most indices of
closeness in parent–child relationships decline across early adolescence; warmth may increase somewhat during the latter part of adolescence, but interdependence continues to
decline.

Reports of age-related diminished closeness tell but part of the story of relationship
change during adolescence. Such depictions may overstate the significance of changes
in parent–adolescent relationships because they focus exclusively on change at the level
of the group without considering change at the level of the family. When closeness is
examined in terms of the rank order of a single family on a particular dimension relative
to other families on the same dimension, a picture of relationship cohesion emerges.
For instance, longitudinal data from the Pittsburgh Youth Study revealed moderate to
high levels of stability in parent and child reports of positive and negative relationship
qualities (Loeber, Drinkwater, Yin, Anderson, Schmidt, & Crawford, 2000). Indeed, across
childhood and adolescence the relative ordering of families on various dimensions of
closeness remained fairly constant from one year to the next, even though the mean
level of each variable fell. Put in somewhat different terms, despite decreases across the
adolescent years, parents remain second only to friends or romantic partners in closeness,
support, and interdependence (Furman & Buhrmester, 1987; Laursen & Williams, 1997).
These findings suggest a complex dynamic of relationship continuity and change that belie
the conventional view of an abrupt descent into distance and alienation.

Reporter Perspectives

Parent and adolescent views of the family are notable for their divergence, particularly
during early adolescence. Perceptions of family functioning and the treatment of individual
family members vary considerably (Paikoff, 1991). In general, children and parents tend
to see the family in quite different terms. There is considerable overlap between maternal
and paternal reports of their own relationship with an adolescent child and in their reports
of a spouse's relationship with a child (Cook & Goldstein, 1993). Parents seem to agree on
the distinctiveness of their relationships with children. In contrast, adolescents perceive
fewer distinctions between mother–child and father–child relationships. Parents, especially
mothers, tend to hold a more optimistic view of the family than adolescents; mothers
routinely report more warmth and affection among family members than do children, which
may be an attempt to ward off the decline in maternal life satisfaction that accompanies
adolescent detachment (Noller & Callan, 1988; Silverberg & Steinberg, 1990). To recap,
where mothers and fathers see unique relationships, adolescents see a monolithic one, and
where parents see closeness, adolescents see something less.

Emerging evidence points to developmental differences in discrepant views of parent–
child relationship closeness. Consistent with findings that perceptions of self and others
increasingly converge with parents' perceptions during the transition to adolescence
(Allesandri & Wozniak, 1987), adolescent and parent views of positive and negative features of their relationship appear to grow more convergent over time. Mismatches in

developmental expectations are highest at the outset of adolescence, with views gradually converging over time (Collins, Laursen, Mortensen, Luebker, & Ferreira, 1997). This point was illustrated in a longitudinal study of German family relationships in which large initial discrepancies in reports of cohesion, expressiveness, and support declined across adolescence, at the same time that reports indicated diminished closeness on each dimension (Seiffge-Krenke, 1999).

Individual Differences

Closeness varies from one adolescent to another and from one parent–adolescent pair to another. There are pronounced differences between mother–adolescent and father–adolescent relationships. Adolescents tend to be a good deal closer to their mothers than to their fathers; they spend more time with their mothers and are more apt to share feelings with their mothers (Steinberg & Silk, 2002). In contrast, adolescents view fathers as somewhat distant authority figures to be consulted primarily for information and material support. Sons and daughters have similarly warm relationships with mothers, but sons are typically much closer to fathers than daughters. Differences also emerge as a function of child gender. Parents are better informed about the lives of daughters than about the lives of sons: Parents solicit more information from girls than boys, and girls freely volunteer more information than boys (Stattin & Kerr, 2000). All of these trends tend to accelerate across the adolescent years; pubertal maturation has been linked to diminished relationship closeness, particularly for fathers and daughters (Hill, 1988), and to declines in the amount of time sons spend with mothers and fathers (Larson et al., 1996). Yet it appears that gender differences also have roots in earlier phases of the relationship. One longitudinal study showed that although parent involvement during childhood predicted parent–adolescent closeness for sons and daughters, links between early father involvement and subsequent closeness to father were stronger for girls than for boys (Flouri & Buchanan, 2002).

Little is known about variations in closeness among adolescents and parents of different socioeconomic statuses or ethnic minority groups. One issue in comparing across diverse groups is how to equate the degree of closeness associated with different norms and cultural forms of relating. The suggestion that closeness be operationalized as interdependence may provide a partial solution to this quandary by allowing for members of cultural groups to specify and report on the frequency, duration, diversity, and salience of activities that denote closeness in their respective contexts (Reis et al., 2000). More is known about variation associated with family structure. Warmth and intimacy appear to be higher in divorced, single-parent families relative to intact, two-parent families, but this closeness is sorely tested when the parent remarries (Hetherington & Clingempeel, 1992).

Implications for Family Communication

Communication is a core element of both interdependence between family members and their subjective feelings of closeness. Disruptions of established patterns of interaction inevitably mean that parent–adolescent communication will differ in frequency, content, and tenor from that of earlier age periods (Collins, 1995). Families differ in the degree to which they are affected by individual and relationship changes. Most are able to capitalize on greater adolescent maturity by fostering patterns of sustained communication that promote a psychological closeness that is less dependent on frequent interaction. They do so by adapting prior interconnections to meet new demands for adolescent autonomy (Steinberg & Silk, 2002). Families with a history of communication problems, however, are missing the adaptive interconnections that form the foundation for new forms of closeness during this period of detachment and, thus, may be unable to surmount the barriers to effective communication that arise during adolescence. These families are at risk for distress and disorder.

CONTINUITY AND CHANGE IN PARENT–ADOLESCENT CONFLICT

Conflict is ubiquitous in all close relationships, but it is especially prominent between family members. Surveys of adolescents indicate that disagreements are most common with mothers, followed by siblings, friends, and romantic partners, and finally fathers; angry disputes arise more frequently with family members than with close peers (Laursen & Collins, 1994). Some scholars view conflict as shorthand for all manner of interpersonal unpleasantness, but this broad definition fosters confusion. In this chapter, conflict is defined in terms of disagreement and overt behavioral opposition (Shantz, 1987) in order to distinguish it from other negative interactions.

Developmental Trends

Disagreements are composed of discrete components with a sequential structure that may be likened to a play or novel (Laursen & Collins, 1994). Typically, there is a protagonist and an antagonist (the conflict participants), a theme (the topic), a complication (the initiation), rising action and crisis (the resolution), and a denouement (the outcome). Most parent–adolescent disagreements concern mundane topics, famously tagged by Hill (1988) as "garbage and galoshes" disputes. Regardless of the topic, the majority of disagreements between parents and adolescents are resolved through submission or disengagement; compromise is relatively rare (Laursen, 1993). Most conflicts between parents and children do not have a negative impact on the relationship, although chronic fighting has been linked to adolescent maladjustment (Smetana, 1996). Disagreements further resemble plots because they unfold according to a prescribed sequence. Parent–adolescent conflicts usually adhere to a coercive script: Relative to those with friends, disagreements with parents more often involve a combination of mundane topics, power-assertive resolutions, neutral or angry affect, and win–lose outcomes (Adams & Laursen, 2001).

Until recently, conflict with parents was thought to follow an inverted U-shaped function that peaked during mid-adolescence. But meta-analytic methods revealed that this presumed trend was an artifact of the failure to distinguish quantity from affective tenor (Laursen, Coy, & Collins, 1998). The evidence indicates a decline in the frequency of conflict with parents from early adolescence to mid-adolescence and again from mid-adolescence to late adolescence. However, anger in these conflicts increases from early adolescence to mid-adolescence, with little change thereafter. No reliable age differences have been found in topics or outcomes of parent–adolescent conflict, but there is some indication that resolutions may change across the adolescent years, with rates of submission declining and rates of disengagement increasing (Smetana & Gaines, 1999).

Given the amount of detail available on parent–child conflict during adolescence, it is remarkable how little we know about changes in parent–child conflict from childhood to adolescence and from adolescence to adulthood. As best we can tell, evidence is limited to a single cross-sectional survey indicating that conflict with mothers and fathers is perceived to be more prevalent during adolescence than during childhood or young adulthood (Furman & Buhrmester, 1992). Resisting speculation without sufficient evidence, we tentatively offer two additional propositions concerning long-term developmental trends in parent–child conflict: (a) The level of negative affect in parent–child conflict is probably higher during adolescence than it is during any other age period except toddlerhood. (b) The prevalence of coercion in parent–child conflict probably declines across successive age periods from toddlerhood to adulthood.

Reporter Perspectives

Parents and adolescents are known to experience their relationships in dramatically different terms (Larson & Richards, 1994). Less well known, however, is the fact that adolescents appear to have a more accurate (or more honest) view than parents of unpleasant aspects of the relationship. When it comes to describing family conflict, reports from independent observers frequently match those of adolescent children, but neither observer nor adolescent reports accord with parent reports of the same events (Gonzales, Caucé, & Mason, 1996). Although fathers are stereotyped as the family member most likely to be out of touch, accumulating evidence suggests that it is mothers who tend to underestimate the incidence of parent–adolescent conflict and overestimate its severity (Steinberg, 2001). Not coincidentally, mothers also report the most negative repercussions from conflict with adolescent children (Silverberg & Steinberg, 1990). Several explanations have been offered. Chief among them is that (a) conflict represents a personal failure for mothers, because it is an indictment of their ability to serve as family conciliators and peacemakers (Vuchinich, 1987); and (b) conflict is the primary vehicle through which adolescents renegotiate their role in the family, which inevitably diminishes maternal (but not necessarily paternal) authority (Steinberg, 1981). The fact that parent and child reports of conflict appear to converge during late adolescence suggests that disagreements, however unpleasant they may be, play an important role in aligning expectations and facilitating communication among family members (Collins et al., 1997).

Individual Differences

Parent–child conflict behavior and patterns of developmental change may be moderated by characteristics of individual participants. We focus here on two important individual level variables: gender and puberty. Accumulating evidence shows that rates of conflict and levels of negative affect are higher in mother–daughter relationships than in other parent–child relationships (Laursen & Collins, 1994). Results from a meta–analysis indicate that conflict rates decline more across adolescence in mother-child relationships than in father–child relationships (Laursen et al., 1998). Few studies have considered conflict affect, but those that have generally agree that gender does not moderate developmental trends. Conflict resolutions vary as a function of parent and adolescent gender. Compromise is more common with mothers than with fathers, and disengagement is more typical of conflict with sons than of conflict with daughters (Smetana, Yau, & Hanson, 1991; Vuchinich, 1987). Again, there is no reliable evidence that gender moderates patterns of developmental change.

Variation attributed to puberty may be parsed into two sources: pubertal status and pubertal timing. Pubertal status refers to the child's absolute level of physical maturation. Meta-analytic comparisons yield a small positive linear association between pubertal status and parent–adolescent conflict affect, such that greater maturity is linked to greater negative affect (Laursen et al., 1998). No similar association was found for pubertal status and conflict frequency. Observational studies shed light on how family communication patterns may be reorganized in response to conflict at puberty (Hill, 1988; Steinberg, 1981). During the course of a disagreement, fathers interrupt children more at the apex of puberty than during other developmental periods, successfully maintaining their dominant role in family decision making. Mothers and children also interrupt each other more during this period, as the latter challenge the authority of the former. Inevitably, mothers gradually lose influence over decision making to sons and, to a lesser extent, daughters. Pubertal timing refers to the child's relative level of physical maturation. Early maturing sons and daughters appear to experience more frequent and more intense parent–child conflict than adolescents maturing on time (Steinberg, 1989). Several explanations for these findings have been offered, most suggesting that parents do not agree with children that physical precocity is a sufficient basis for enhanced autonomy. In general, the effects of pubertal timing on parent–adolescent conflict are larger and more robust than those for pubertal status (Laursen & Collins, 1994).

Conflict behavior may also be moderated by characteristics of the dyad. Although families vary considerably in terms of their discordant experiences, storm and stress are not normative. Studies suggest that turmoil characterizes a small minority of families with adolescent children (Rutter et al., 1976). Relationship difficulties in these households usually have more to do with dysfunctional family systems or individual mental health problems than with the challenges posed by adolescent development (Offer & Offer, 1975). Setting these troubled families aside, it is still the case that different families have different experiences with parent–adolescent conflict. Cluster analyses based on the rate and severity of parent–adolescent conflict yield three types of families (Smetana, 1996): placid, squabbling, and tumultuous. Placid families reported few conflicts of moderate intensity. Squabbling families reported frequent conflict of low intensity. Tumultuous families reported frequent conflict of high intensity. Of these groups, only the tumultuous appear to experience serious interpersonal strife: Relative to other families, tumultuous families were least likely to successfully resolve conflicts. Conflict outcomes also vary across dyads, such that the significance of a disagreement depends on qualities of connectedness in the relationship (Cooper, 1988). Positive connectedness promotes constructive resolutions to disagreement that foster growth and insight; in less supportive relationships, conflict is considered a hostile attack that may have negative repercussions (Hauser, Powers, Noam, Jacobson, Weiss, & Follansbee, 1984).

Implications for Family Communication

Almost 40 years ago, Bandura (1964) argued against the notion of adolescent turmoil, in general, and against the impression that adolescence brought about a precipitous upsurge in parent–child conflict, in particular: "The behavioral characteristics exhibited by children during the so-called adolescent stage are lawfully related to, and consistent with, pre-adolescent social behavior" (p. 231). Subsequent longitudinal evidence corroborates this view (Rutter et al., 1976; Stattin & Klackenberg, 1992): Family contentiousness during adolescence is best forecast by family contentiousness during childhood and preadolescence. This means that although many families experience a modest uptick in conflict at the outset of adolescence, disagreement is not a threat to these relationships. It is our view that conflict during adolescence actually strengthens the parent–child relationship by providing a much-needed vehicle for communication (Laursen & Collins, 1994). Disagreements, more than any other form of social interaction, offer parents and adolescents a forum for revising expectations and renegotiating roles and responsibilities in a manner commensurate with the autonomy typically accorded to youth in a particular culture (Collins, 1995). Most families successfully meet this challenge because they are able to draw on healthy patterns of communication established in response to the challenges of earlier age periods. Some families, however, are not so fortunate. Those who do not learn to communicate effectively when children are young are at risk for dysfunctional discord during adolescence because these families may be incapable of constructively addressing the developmental challenges of autonomy and the transformations in parent–child relationships that accompany it.

CONCLUSIONS

This brief, selective review underscores several principles of parent–child communication during adolescence and points the way to areas of inquiry requiring greater attention. We begin with a look forward. Future scholars of family communication would be well advised to consider adolescence as part of a larger developmental transition from childhood to adulthood. Although studies are increasingly exploring family communication across the transition from childhood into adolescence, little is known about the period from adolescence into adulthood. Given that transformations during adolescence purportedly presage adult relationships, it is surprising to discover that we do not know the extent to which parent–child conflict and closeness continue to be transformed through to young adulthood. The broad outlines of change in family communication from one age period to the next have begun to be documented, but specific processes of relationship transformation have yet to be elaborated.

Of additional concern is the relative absence of studies that identify context-specific features of communication. Parent–adolescent relationships are known to differ as a function of characteristics of the family and the environment, including culture and ethnicity, household structure, and socioeconomic status (see Collins & Laursen, in press, for a review). Some contextual variables, such as differences in family communication related to parental divorce and remarriage, are beginning to come into focus (Hetherington & Stanley-Hagan, 2002). Unfortunately, this is the exception rather than the rule. The influence of other critical variables, such as ethnicity (García Coll & Pachter, 2002) and social class (Hoff, Laursen, & Tardiff, 2002), remain poorly understood. A better understanding of individual and group differences is essential, because differences among families that result from circumstances of economic disadvantage and experiences as members of minority groups almost certainly affect responses to the changes and prospects of adolescence.

Greater attention to contextual process is imperative, because it may very well be the case that normative adolescent development encompasses several different pathways of parent–child relationship transformation that vary as a function of environmental demands (Collins et al., 2000). We anticipate this research will reveal differences across settings in typical patterns of communication and control but similarities in pathways of influence, such that families emphasizing mutuality, respect for the child's opinions, and training for maturity will be most effective in helping adolescents develop attitudes and behaviors appropriate to their society.

Three principles of family communication stand out from our review. First, the vagaries of communication are deeply embedded in qualities of the parent–adolescent relationship. Some differences between communication during adolescence and communication during childhood reflect physical and cognitive development, as well as normative psychosocial changes in peer involvement and autonomy striving. Other differences, however, reflect the ability of the family to cope with the developmental demands of adolescence. As families adapt long-standing expectations and patterns of interaction to maturational changes in the child, communication typically falters for a time and then recovers much of its accustomed fluency, albeit in more adult forms. Second, despite significant changes in communication during the adolescent years, most families experience a reassuring continuity in their emotional bonds. Moreover, relative to families with a history of communication difficulties, those families that enter adolescence with a history of positive, responsive relations appear to experience fewer disruptions in communication and cope more constructively with those that inevitably do occur. In this manner, families that build upon prior successful developmental transitions handle the demands of adolescence by revising communication patterns in a manner appropriate for incipiently adult offspring. Third, parent–adolescent conflict not only is normative but also fosters communication that is integral to necessary realignments of relationship roles. This constructive process is most likely to occur when conflicts are neither extreme nor persistent and when they arise in a relationship characterized by warmth and closeness. The successful ability of most parents and adolescents to balance conflict and closeness during this period of relationship transformation reaffirms the integral role of communication in human functioning.

AUTHOR NOTE

Correspondence concerning this chapter may be addressed to the first author: Department of Psychology, Florida Atlantic University, 2912 College Avenue, Fort Lauderdale, Florida 33314. Send email to either laursen@fau.edu or wcollins@tc.umn.edu.

REFERENCES

Adams, R., & Laursen, B. (2001). The organization and dynamics of adolescent conflict with parents and friends. *Journal of Marriage and Family, 63*, 97–110.

Ainsworth, M. D. S. (1989). Attachments beyond infancy. *American Psychologist, 44*, 709–716.

Allen, J. P., & Land, D. (1999). Attachment in adolescence. In J. Cassidy & P. Shaver (Eds.), *Handbook of attachment* (pp. 319–335). New York: Guilford Press.

Alessandri, S. M., & Wozniak, R. H. (1987). The child's awareness of parental beliefs concerning the child: A developmental study. *Child Development, 58,* 316–323.

Bandura, A. (1964). The stormy decade: Fact or fiction? *Psychology in the Schools, 1,* 244–231.

Blos, P. (1979). *The adolescent passage.* New York: International Universities Press.

Bowlby, J. (1969). *Attachment and loss. Vol. 1: Attachment.* New York: Basic Books.

Buhrmester, D., & Furman, W. (1987). The development of companionship and intimacy. *Child Development, 58,* 1101–1113.

Collins, W. A. (1995). Relationships and development: Family adaptation to individual change. In S. Shulman (Ed.), *Close relationships and sociemotional development* (pp. 128–154). New York: Ablex.

Collins, W. A., Gleason, T., & Sesma, A., Jr. (1997). Internalization, autonomy, and relationships: Development during adolescence. In J. E. Grusec & L. Kuczynski (Eds.), *Parenting and children's internalization of values: A handbook of contemporary theory* (pp. 78–99). New York: Wiley.

Collins, W. A., & Laursen, B. (in press). Parent–adolescent relationships and influences. In R. Lerner & L. Steinberg (Eds.), *Handbook of adolescent psychology.* New York: Wiley.

Collins, W. A., Laursen, B., Mortensen, N., Luebker, C., & Ferreira, M. (1997). Conflict processes and transitions in parent and peer relationships: Implications for autonomy and regulation. *Journal of Adolescence, 12,* 178–198.

Collins, W. A., & Luebker, C. (1994). Parent and adolescent expectancies: Individual and relationship significance. In J. G. Smetana (Ed.), *Beliefs about parenting: Origins and developmental implications. New Directions for Child Development* (No. 66, pp. 65–80). San Francisco: Jossey-Bass.

Collins, W. A., Maccoby, E., Steinberg, L., Hetherington, E. M., & Bornstein, M. (2000). Contemporary research on parenting: The case for nature *and* nurture. *American Psychologist, 55,* 218–232.

Collins, W. A., & Repinski, D. J. (1994). Relationships during adolescence: Continuity and change in interpersonal perspective. In R. Montemayor, G. Adams, & T. Gullotta (Eds.), *Personal relationships during adolescence* (pp. 7–36). Thousand Oaks, CA: Sage.

Collins, W. A., & Russell, G. (1991). Mother–child and father–child relationships in middle childhood and adolescence: A developmental analysis. *Developmental Review, 11,* 99–136.

Cook, W. L., & Goldstein, M. J. (1993). Multiple perspectives on family relationships: A latent variables model. *Child Development, 64,* 1377–1388.

Cooper, C. R. (1988). Commentary: The role of conflict in adolescent–parent relationships. In M. R. Gunnar & W. A. Collins (Eds.), *The Minnesota Symposia on Child Psychology: Vol. 21. Development during the transition to adolescence* (pp. 181–187). Hillsdale, NJ: Lawrence Erlbaum Associates.

Erikson, E. H. (1968). *Identity: Youth and crisis.* New York: Norton.

Flouri, E., & Buchanan, A. (2002). What predicts good relationships with parents in adolescence and partners in adult life: Findings from the 1958 British birth cohort. *Journal of Family Psychology, 16,* 186–198.

Freud, A. (1958). Adolescence. *Psychoanalytic Study of the Child, 13,* 255–278.

Freud, S. (1949). *Group psychology and the analysis of the ego.* New York: Bantam. (Original work published 1921)

Furman, W., & Buhrmester, D. (1992). Age and sex differences in perceptions of networks of personal relationships. *Child Development, 63,* 103–115.

García Coll, C., & Pachter, L. M. (2002). Ethnic and minority parenting. In M. Bornstein (Ed.), *Handbook of parenting* (Vol. 4, pp. 1–20). Mahwah, NJ: Lawrence Erlbaum Associates.

Gonzales, N. A., Caucé, A. M., & Mason, C. A. (1996). Interobserver agreement in the assessment of parental behavior and parent–adolescent conflict: African American mothers, daughters, and independent observers. *Child Development, 67,* 1483–1498.

Hartup, W. W., & Laursen, B. (1991). Relationships as developmental contexts. In R. Cohen & A. W. Siegel (Eds.), *Context and development* (pp. 253–279). Hillsdale, NJ: Lawrence Erlbaum Associates.

Hauser, S. T., Powers, S. I., Noam, G. G., Jacobson, A. M., Weiss, B., & Follansbee, D. J. (1984). Familial contexts of adolescent ego development. *Child Development, 55,* 195–213.

Hetherington, E. M., & Clingempeel, W. (Eds.). (1992). *Coping with marital transitions: A family systems perspective. Monographs of the Society for Research in Child Development, 57* (Serial No. 227).

Hetherington, E. M., & Stanley-Hagan, M. (2002). Parenting in divorced and remarried families. In M. Bornstein (Ed.), *Handbook of parenting* (Vol. 3, pp. 287–315). Mahwah, NJ: Lawrence Erlbaum Associates.

Hill, J. P. (1988). Adapting to menarche: Familial control and conflict. In M. R. Gunnar & W. A. Collins (Eds.), *The Minnesota Symposia on Child Psychology: Vol. 21. Development during the transition to adolescence* (pp. 43–77). Hillsdale, NJ: Lawrence Erlbaum Associates.

Hoff, E., Laursen, B., & Tardiff, T. (2002). Socioeconomic status and parenting. In M. Bornstein (Ed.), *Handbook of parenting* (Vol. 2, pp. 231–252). Mahwah, NJ: Lawrence Erlbaum Associates.

Kelley, H. H., Berscheid, E., Christiansen, A., Harvey, J. H., Huston, T. L., Levinger, G., McClintock, E., Peplau, L. A., & Peterson, D. R. (1983). *Close relationships.* New York: Freeman.

Kohlberg, L. (1969). Stage and sequence: The cognitive-developmental approach to socialization. In D. A. Goslin (Ed.), *Handbook of socialization theory and research* (pp. 347–480). Skokie, IL: Rand-McNally.

Larson, R., & Richards, M. H. (1994). *Divergent realities: The emotional lives of mothers, fathers, and adolescents.* New York: Basic Books.

Larson, R. W., Richards, M. H., Moneta, G., Holmbeck, G., & Duckett, E. (1996). Changes in adolescents' daily interactions with their families from ages 10 to 18: Disengagement and transformation. *Developmental Psychology, 32,* 744–754.

Laursen, B. (1993). Conflict management among close peers. In B. Laursen (Ed.), *Close friendships in adolescence. New Directions for Child Development* (No. 60, pp. 39–54). San Francisco: Jossey-Bass.

Laursen, B., & Bukowski, W. M. (1997). A developmental guide to the organisation of close relationships. *International Journal of Behavioral Development, 21*, 747–770.

Laursen, B., & Collins, W. A. (1994). Interpersonal conflict during adolescence. *Psychological Bulletin, 115*, 197–209.

Laursen, B., Coy, K. C., & Collins, W. A. (1998). Reconsidering changes in parent–child conflict across adolescence: A meta-analysis. *Child Development, 69*, 817–832.

Laursen, B., & Williams, V. (1997). Perceptions of interdependence and closeness in family and peer relationships among adolescents with and without romantic partners. In S. Shulman & W. A. Collins (Eds.), *Romantic relationships in adolescence: Developmental perspectives. New Directions for Child Development* (No. 78, pp. 3–20). San Francisco: Jossey-Bass.

Loeber, R., Drinkwater, M., Yin, Y., Anderson, S. J., Schmidt, L. C., & Crawford, A. (2000). Stability of family interaction from ages 6 to 18. *Journal of Abnormal Child Psychology, 28*, 353–369.

Noller, P., & Callan, V. J. (1988). Understanding parent–adolescent interactions: Perceptions of family members and outsiders. *Developmental Psychology, 24*, 707–714.

Offer, D., & Offer, J. B. (1975). *From teenage to young manhood: A psychological study.* New York: Basic Books.

Paikoff, R. (Ed.). (1991). *Shared views in the family during adolescence. New Directions for Child Development* (No. 51). San Francisco: Jossey-Bass.

Piaget, J. (1965). *The moral judgment of the child.* New York: Free Press. (Original work published 1932)

Reis, H. T., Collins, W. A., & Berscheid, E. (2000). The relationship context of human behavior and development. *Psychological Bulletin, 126*, 844–872.

Rutter, M., Graham, P., Chadwick, O., & Yule, W. (1976). Adolescent turmoil: Fact or fiction? *Journal of Child Psychology and Psychiatry, 17*, 35–56.

Seiffge-Krenke, I. (1999). Families with daughters, families with sons: Different challenges for family relationships and marital satisfaction? *Journal of Youth and Adolescence, 28*, 325–342.

Selman, R. L. (1980). *The growth of interpersonal understanding: Developmental and clinical analyses.* New York: Academic Press.

Shantz, C. U. (1987). Conflict between children. *Child Development, 58*, 283–305.

Silverberg, S. B., & Steinberg, L. (1990). Psychological well-being of parents with early adolescent children. *Developmental Psychology, 26*, 658–666.

Smetana, J. G. (1988). Concepts of self and social convention: Adolescents' and parents' reasoning about hypothetical and actual family conflicts. In M. R. Gunnar & W. A. Collins (Eds.), *The Minnesota Symposia on Child Psychology: Vol. 21. Development during the transition to adolescence* (pp. 79–122). Hillsdale, NJ: Lawrence Erlbaum Associates.

Smetana, J. G. (1996). Adolescent–parent conflict: Implications for adaptive and maladaptive development. In D. Cicchetti & S. L. Toth (Eds.), *Rochester Symposium on Developmental Psychopathology: Vol. 7. Adolescence: Opportunities and challenges* (pp. 1–46). Rochester: University of Rochester.

Smetana, J., & Gaines, C. (1999). Adolescent–parent conflict in middle-class African American families. *Child Development, 70*, 1447–1463.

Smetana, J., Yau, J., & Hanson, S. (1991). Conflict resolution in families with adolescents. *Journal of Research on Adolescence, 1*, 189–206.

Sroufe, L. A., & Fleeson, J. (1988). The coherence of family relationships. In R. A. Hinde & J. Stevenson-Hinde (Eds.), *Relationships within families: Mutual influences* (pp. 27–47). New York: Oxford.

Stattin, H., & Kerr, M. (2000). Parental monitoring: A reinterpretation. *Child Development, 71*, 1072–1085.

Stattin, H., & Klackenberg, G. (1992). Discordant family relations in intact families: Developmental tendencies over 18 years. *Journal of Marriage and the Family, 54*, 940–956.

Steinberg, L. (1981). Transformations in family relations at puberty. *Developmental Psychology, 17*, 833–840.

Steinberg, L. (1989). Pubertal maturation and parent–adolescent distance: An evolutionary perspective. In G. Adams, R. Montemayor, & T. Gullota (Eds.), *Biology of adolescent behavior and development* (pp. 82–114). Newbury Park, CA: Sage.

Steinberg, L. (2001). We know some things: Adolescent–parent relationships in retrospect and prospect. *Journal of Research on Adolescence, 11*, 1–19.

Steinberg, L., & Silk, J. S. (2002). Parenting adolescents. In M. H. Bornstein (Ed.), *Handbook of parenting*. Mahwah, NJ: Lawrence Erlbaum Associates.

Vuchinich, S. (1987). Starting and stopping spontaneous family conflicts. *Journal of Marriage and the Family, 49*, 591–601.

Youniss, J. (1980). *Parents and peers in social development: A Sullivan-Piaget perspective.* Chicago: University of Chicago Press.

CHAPTER

17

EXTENDED FAMILY AND SOCIAL NETWORKS

MARIA SCHMEECKLE AND SUSAN SPRECHER
ILLINOIS STATE UNIVERSITY

The purpose of this chapter is to review research and concepts that connect our knowledge about primary partnerships and immediate families with our knowledge about extended family and social networks. We look at reciprocal influences between social networks (which include extended family) and immediate family interactions. Throughout this chapter, we will refer to *primary partnerships* and *committed couples* as a way of acknowledging that couplehood today is not limited to married couples, but includes cohabiting heterosexual and same-sex partners. When we write about the "immediate family," we mean "parenting adult(s) and dependent children." This allows for variation in types of parents, be they grandparents raising grandchildren, a remarried couple raising biological and stepchildren, or a heterosexual nuclear family.

We begin the chapter by defining *extended family* and discussing how size and involvement with extended families differ across time, life course, and social groups. We then define *social network* and related concepts and discuss how these also differ across time, life course, and social groups. Next, we explore how social networks (including extended family) affect primary partnerships, as well as parenting and child outcomes. We then look the other way, exploring how transitions in primary partnerships and immediate families affect extended family and social networks. To conclude, we offer suggestions for future directions in these areas of research.

EXTENDED FAMILY

Most people belong to a kinship group beyond the immediate family that can be referred to as extended family. In this section, we begin by presenting definitions of extended family. We then explore variation in the size and composition of extended family experiences across multiple dimensions.

349

Definition of Extended Family

Extended family relationships in America today occur in diverse, voluntary, and flexible contexts (Johnson, 1988; Riley & Riley, 1993; Stacey, 1991), making membership changeable and somewhat nebulous. Extended family relationships include those of cousins, cohabiting partners of adult children, godparents, ex-stepparents, "fictive kin" (those perceived as extended family members, though they are not related by blood or law), and in-laws. As a starting point for a definition of extended family, we draw from Johnson's (2000) definition, which she uses as synonymous with the concept of *kinship*. Johnson defines extended family/kinship as "social relationships among those related by blood, marriage, or self-ascribed association that extend beyond the marital dyad, the nuclear family of parents and dependent children, or one-parent households" (2000, p. 625).

Although this definition provides a useful baseline, it is important to note that in today's society, some who would typically be defined as extended family members act as immediate family members for dependent children. An example of this is grandparents raising grandchildren. Other groups that do not easily fit into immediate or extended family definitions are stepparents and cohabiting partners of parents/children. Subjective perceptions about family membership among these types of relationships vary widely (Schmeeckle, 2001), making it difficult to construct a definition that would apply to all relationships. Thus, we place an added emphasis on the "self-ascribed" aspect of Johnson's definition and, for the purposes of this chapter, define extended family as "social relationships among those related by blood, law, or self-ascribed association that extend beyond the marriage *or committed partner couple* and *the immediate family of parenting adult(s) and dependent children*" (adapted from Johnson, 2000; our changes are in italics).

Historical Change, Life Course, and Social Group Differences

Historical Change.   Historical shifts have occurred that make the size and composition of extended families different from what they were decades ago. These include demographic shifts in family structure and changes in technology. In terms of demographic shifts, developed countries such as the United States have experienced decreases in fertility and increases in life expectancy across the past century. This has led to a decline in the number of biological family members within each generation, but to an increase in the number of family generations living at the same time (Kinsella, 1995). Thus, there is a greater opportunity for more meaningful and long-lasting extended family relationships with grandparents and even great-grandparents (Bengtson, 2001).

In recent decades, Western societies have also seen a decrease in the proportion of marriages that last a lifetime. People are more likely to marry later, have children outside of marriage, cohabit outside of marriage, divorce, belong to step- and blended families, live in nonfamily households, and are less likely to remarry after divorce than they were a few decades ago (Stacey, 1996; Teachman, Tedrow, & Crowder, 2000; Tucker & Mitchell-Kernan, 1995). In addition, same sex partnerships have become more visible, and gay couples are beginning to gain rights to be legally recognized and receive benefits (Stacey, 1996). These changes have contributed to the formation of extended family networks that are complex, diverse, and influenced by personal choice (Johnson, 1988; Riley & Riley, 1993; Stacey, 1991; Weston, 1991).

Technological change is another historical shift affecting extended families. A long-range historical view reveals the growth in airplane travel and the use of telephones (Sprecher, Felmlee, Orbuch, & Willetts, 2002), facilitating active ties with relatives who are geographically dispersed. More recently, email and other forms of computer-assisted communication have added to the modes of interaction available to individuals in modern societies. These developments also facilitate interaction with extended family members who are not geographically close (Boneva, Kraut, & Frohlich, 2001; Franzen, 2000). Another issue concerns the impact of reproductive technology, which facilitates children coming into the world with a variety of potential biological and social extended family connections. Sometimes it takes years for an individual to activate some of these ties.

Life Course. Differences in extended family experiences may also be seen across the life course. For instance, young children do not have full autonomy over the extended family members they see and interact with, as parenting adults may limit or facilitate this interaction as they see fit. Young adults may branch out in ways they choose, given the autonomy of adulthood. Extended family membership changes as one ages; according to our definition, parents become extended family members to their children once they are no longer dependent. In later life when time in life is perceived as limited, older people tend to interact mostly with others they know well—close family members and long-term friends (Carstensen, Isaacowitz, & Charles, 1999).

Cross-Cultural Differences. Many differences in extended family patterns are observable across the world. In many agricultural societies, extended family ties are central to ongoing activities and institutional organization. The kinship tie affects inheritance, property ownership, economic division of labor, local governance, and religious rituals. Although extended families in industrialized nations provide affection, support, housing, and inheritance to some extent, they are not as central to everyday life when compared to agricultural societies (Adams, 1999).

Even among industrialized countries, differences in extended family patterns are apparent. For example, Hollinger and Haller (1990) found differences in contact with extended family members across several European countries, the United States, and Australia, and argued that these differences were related to differing levels of technological infrastructure (such as availability of telephones) and sociocultural factors (such as preference for certain types of housing). Geographic mobility and size of the country were also considered important factors. Geographic moves, common in countries like the United States and Australia, resulted in greater geographic distances and fewer face-to-face contacts with extended family members than moves within European countries.

Race. Many differences have been identified in the area of immediate family structure across different racial groups in the United States (Teachman et al., 2000; Tucker & Mitchell-Kernan, 1995). It seems likely that there would be differences in extended family experiences as well. For instance, contrary to the stereotype of close-knit extended family relations in minority families, several studies have found that Anglo Americans see more of their extended family members and exchange more assistance with them than African Americans do (Johnson, 2000; Roschelle, 1997). This may be due to fewer resources that African Americans have to share, due to disadvantages by social class (Johnson, 2000).

African Americans are notable for their participation in *fictive kin* networks—supportive relationships with others who are treated as relatives but are not related by blood or law (Chatters, Taylor, & Jayakody, 1994). This type of relationship fits under the "self-ascribed association" part of our definition of extended family. Fictive kin relationships have been observed among those of African descent since before the time of slavery, but they were likely enhanced by the constraints of slavery. These relationships are particularly likely for women, younger, and more highly educated people (Chatters et al., 1994). In Puerto Rican families, fictive kin are particularly important in building support networks around children through the role of godparents (Chatters et al., 1994). Relationships with fictive kin appear to be less prominent for Anglo Americans than they are for other groups.

Another important issue is the extent to which extended family relationships cross racial boundaries. Recent estimates based on national data show that about 1% of U.S. adults marry someone from a different racial group and that 20% have members of other racial groups within their extended families (Goldstein, 1999). Racial groups differ in their experience of multiracial extended family networks as well. One in seven Whites, 1 in 3 Blacks, 4 out of 5 Asian Americans, and over 19 of 20 American Indians experience multiracial extended family networks according to conservative estimates (Goldstein, 1999).

Social Class.   Class privilege appears to bring with it advantages related to extended family membership. U.S. adults who are highly educated and highly paid are more likely to belong to diverse, far-reaching extended family networks than less educated and lower paid U.S. adults (Goldstein & Warren, 2000). High socioeconomic status appears to facilitate participation in social support networks and access to support, including from extended family members, in times of need (Goldstein & Warren, 2000; Roschelle, 1997). Some studies suggest more mixed results on the topic of social class and extended family networks, however. For example, geographic dispersion that accompanies high education levels may contribute to social and emotional distance from extended family members (Johnson, 2000).

Gender.   Women appear to put more energy into and be more incorporated in extended family relationships than are men. This is likely in part because women are apt to engage in activities of "kinkeeping" (di Leonardo, 1992; Hagestad, 1986; Johnson, 1988, 2000; Rosenthal, 1985; Salmon, 1999). Kinkeeping behaviors include arranging the details of visits, initiating contact, facilitating others' inclusion in extended family gatherings, remembering birthday and holiday greetings and gifts, discussing emotional and personal life, giving affection and nurture, and providing various types of support. The work of kinkeeping is most often done by middle-aged women who keep extended family members in touch with each other for many years. Men are also involved in kinkeeping, but not nearly to the same degree (Rosenthal, 1985).

Although kinship terminology in America reflects bilateral characteristics (an equal emphasis on mothers' and fathers' extended families) (Adams, 1999), extended family relations tend to exhibit a matrilateral focus (Johnson, 1988; Schmeeckle, 2001). This means that extended family interaction is often nurtured more on the women's side of the family than on the men's. An example of this is that husbands tend to interact more frequently with their wives' parents than with their own (Rosenthal, 1985). In addition, grandfathers are found to be active with grandchildren only when their wives are (Johnson, 1988).

Sexual Orientation. The political and social climate has been softening in recent years toward gay, lesbian, and bisexual individuals and their intimate relationships. Yet people with these identities continue to face intense discrimination with regard to basic rights (like marriage and adoption) that heterosexuals take for granted (Stacey, 1996). Intolerance causes homosexuals to experience extended family relationships in unique ways. Because acceptance from biological relatives is not a given, gays and lesbians often create extended family ties with friends and ex-lovers. In claiming family ties with *chosen kin*, they build significant extended family relationships that would fit with the "fictive kin" notion discussed previously (Weston, 1991). Chosen kin of homosexuals may differ from fictive kin in ethnic minority networks, however. Fictive kin relationships for ethnic minorities tend to be well integrated with biolegal extended families, an integration that cannot be assumed for gay and lesbian individuals (Oswald, 2002).

SOCIAL NETWORKS

Primary partnerships and immediate families are embedded not only in extended families but also in social networks. In addition, extended family members are embedded in social networks. Hence, social networks is the more-encompassing concept. In this section, we present definitions and types of social networks and highlight a few additional variations based on historical change, life course, and social group membership. We also introduce characteristics applicable to the interconnections of the social networks (including extended family) of two primary partners.

Definitions, Types, and Properties of Social Networks

In most social network theory and research, the focus is on individuals' (and not romantic couples' or the family's) social networks. Individuals' social networks have been defined and measured in a variety of ways (e.g., Felmlee, 2003). Most generally, an individual's social network consists of a collection of individuals known by him or her. Social networks consist of both kin (e.g., grandparents, cousins, aunts and uncles, and in-laws) and nonkin (e.g., friends, neighbors, co-workers, organizational affiliates).

Social networks can also be defined and operationalized in a variety of more specific ways. For example, one distinction is between the *psychological network*, which consists of people defined to be important or significant, and the *interactive network*, which consists of people with whom one interacts on a frequent basis (Surra & Milardo, 1991). Research indicates that there is little overlap between these two types of networks (Milardo, 1989). Another distinction is between a network of *active ties* and a network of *passive ties*.

Active ties are network members with whom individuals have "ongoing social exchanges," whereas passive ties are "purely emotional or obligatory in nature without any ongoing social exchanges between individuals" (Marsiglio & Scanzoni, 1995, p. 27).

There are also several properties of social networks, including size, composition, and density. *Size* refers to the number of people in the particular network or network sector. *Composition* refers to the breakdown of the social network on any number of dimensions, for example, by type of relationship (proportion of kin to nonkin, proportion of emotionally close others to peripheral members), by age (proportion of age similar to age-discrepant network members), or by race (proportion of network members of one's own race vs. another race). The *density* of a person's network refers to the degree that network members are interconnected.

Variation in Social Networks

Just as size, composition, and other attributes of extended family networks vary as a function of historical change, life course, and social group differences, as discussed previously, there is also variation in attributes of social networks based on the same factors. Here, we focus specifically on variation in the proportion of nonkin to kin in the social network and variation in the overall size of the friendship sector of the network.

Size and composition of social networks have probably changed over *historical time*. As noted earlier, it is reasonable to speculate that due to increased travel, geographic dispersion from one's family of origin, mobility, and computer technology (internet), people have larger and more diverse social networks than they did at an earlier historical time. In addition, compared to previous times, children's social networks may contain a greater number of emotionally close adults who are not parents (such as child-care providers, teachers, and friends of parents) and a smaller proportion of kin to nonkin (Marsiglio & Scanzoni, 1995).

Carstensen's (e.g., 1991, 1993) socioemotional selectivity theory has implications for predicting and explaining changes in the size and composition of social networks across the *life course*. This theory predicts that individuals who are older and/or perceive they have limited time left will emphasize emotional goals and want to associate with a small number of individuals who best satisfy their emotional needs. In support of this theory, in both longitudinal and cross-sectional research, Carstensen and her colleagues (e.g., Carstensen, 1992; Lang & Carstensen, 1994) have found that later life is associated with a decrease in the size of the total network but that aging individuals continue to maintain relationships with close friends and relatives (see, also, Antonucci & Akiyama, 1987). Thus, with increasing age, a greater proportion of one's network is emotionally close.

Although generally no differences are found between men and women in overall network size or in number of friends (e.g., Julien, Chartrand, & Begin, 1999), women report having more kin in their network than do men (e.g., Antonucci & Akiyama, 1987; Julien et al., 1999) and usually report having more emotionally close friends (e.g., Sapadin, 1988). Compared to women, men report more coworkers in their networks and tend to have more diverse networks (Moore, 1990), which has been attributed to their greater structural opportunities (e.g., employment). More generally, being female, non-White, poor, and noneducated are all factors associated with having less diverse and smaller networks, and especially fewer friends (Fischer, 1982; Moore, 1990).

Network Attributes Associated with the Primary Partnership

Network concepts also have been developed to refer to the characteristics or the interconnections of the social networks of two relational partners. The most common such concept is *network overlap*. Network overlap refers to the degree to which the two partners have social network members in common, or "the proportion of network members shared by two members in a close relationship" (Milardo & Helms-Erikson, 2000, p. 35). Research has found that two people who form a romantic relationship are likely to have friends in common even before they meet (Parks & Eggert, 1991). In addition, as a couple develops interdependence and advances in commitment and possibly to marriage, the partners' network overlap increases further (Kalmijn & Bernasco, 2001).

Milardo and Helms-Erikson (2000) noted that there are two ways to calculate network overlap. At the individual level of analysis, it is the proportion of network members one shares with the partner relative to the total number of members in one's network. At the level of the couple, network overlap is calculated as the proportion of network members shared between the two people relative to the number of members in their combined network (e.g., Julien et al., 1999). Degree of network overlap is greater when calculated at the individual level than at the couple level (Milardo & Helms-Erikson, 2000).

In addition, research suggests that there is more likely to be overlap in kin network members than in friend network members (e.g., Stein, Bush, Ross, & Ward, 1992). That is, partners are more likely to include each other's extended family members than each other's friends in their own social networks. One exception is for gay and lesbian couples, who have been found to have a smaller proportion of kin to nonkin in their mutual networks than do heterosexual couples (Julien et al., 1999).

Other network concepts are related to but distinct from network overlap. One such concept is *cross-network contact*, which refers to "the degree to which each partner knows and communicates with members of the other's network" (Parks, 2000, p. 61). Some researchers (e.g., Parks, 2000; Sprecher & Felmlee, 2000) also refer to *attraction (or repulsion) to the partner's network members* and have indicated that balance theory (e.g., Heider, 1946) would predict that liking for network members would lead to more stable relationships with the partner. Another structural attribute of networks at the dyadic level is *cross-network density*, which refers to "the extent to which members of each partner's network knows and communicates with members of the other partner's network" (Parks, 2000, p. 61).

Although the previously cited network concepts have most frequently been applied to the study of *adult dyads* (e.g., husband and wife), these concepts also have applications to parent–child relationships and could even be expanded to the family level. For example, network overlap at the family level would likely consist of a high proportion of extended kin. The network of a child is likely to be a subset of the network of the child's parents, at least until school age.

THE INFLUENCE OF SOCIAL NETWORKS ON MARRIAGE AND OTHER PRIMARY PARTNERSHIPS

Social networks influence the process of mate selection, or the likelihood that two people become partners and develop their relationship. The literature on that topic will not be discussed in this chapter, but see Sprecher et al. (2002) and Felmlee (2003) for reviews. In this section, we discuss how social networks (including extended family members) continue to affect primary partnerships after the relationships have made the transition to marriage or other similar commitment. We first discuss the various theoretical processes by which social networks influence the couple. Second, we review the empirical literature that has examined the influences of various network attributes on the internal dynamics of the partnership, including relationship satisfaction and stability.

Processes of Network Influence

One of the major ways in which social networks can influence the primary partnership is through *messages of support*, or conversely, *messages of interference*, for the couple's relationship. For example, when trying to be supportive, friends and relatives can comment about what a great couple the two make and invite the two as a pair to social events. According to a symbolic interactionist perspective, these positive reactions enhance the partners' identity as a couple (Lewis, 1973, 1975). Conversely, network members can make negative comments about the couple and encourage them to end their relationship (e.g., Bryant & Conger, 1999). The social network and extended family also can provide the couple with *general personal support* or assistance. For example, friends and extended family members may offer to babysit so that the couple can have time alone, offer financial assistance, and provide general emotional support. Another process by which social networks influence primary partnerships is through the *information* provided about one partner to the other, which may be positive or negative. The information obtained from the network can serve to reduce uncertainty about the partner. According to uncertainty reduction theory (e.g., Berger, 1988), relationships develop and are maintained when uncertainty is reduced.

Social networks also provide *opportunities* for alternative romances. According to social exchange theory (e.g., Rusbult, Johnson, & Morrow, 1986), people consider the possible benefits from an alternative partner and compare them to the benefits provided by the current partner in deciding whether to stay or leave the relationship. Alternatives often either come from the larger social network or are friends or acquaintances of one's network members. In addition, social networks provide sources of *social comparison* for one's relationship. Based on classic social comparison theory (e.g., Festinger, 1954), it can be inferred that people judge the quality of their relationships based on perceptions of others' relationships in their social network. Research indicates that most individuals perceive their own dating or marital relationship to be superior (or to have fewer negative aspects) than others' relationships (e.g., Van Lange & Rusbult, 1995). One explanation given for these findings (e.g., Van Lange & Rusbult, 1995) is that people engage in downward social comparison, selecting for comparison those couples in their network who have problematic relationships.

Finally, another way that social networks can influence the couple is by serving as *substitute* sources of companionship, social support, and intimate exchange. However, the perceived availability of substitute relationships for meeting important intimacy needs may be either good or bad for the primary partnership, depending on a number of other factors, including beliefs about the primacy of the marriage or partnership. Research (Harrison, 1998; Oliker, 1989; Rubin, 1985) suggests that married women are more likely than married men to seek emotional support and intimacy from friends and often do so to a greater degree than they do with their spouses (partners). In addition, intimacy and support sought from friends can sometimes make it possible for women to remain in a less than satisfactory relationship. Based on in-depth interviews conducted with middle-aged married individuals, Rubin (1985) wrote (as quoted in Milardo & Helms-Erikson, 2000): "Woman after woman told of the ways in which friends fill the gaps the marriage relationship leaves, allowing the wife to appreciate those things the husband can give rather than to focus on those he can't" (p. 141).

In sum, there are several types of processes by which networks affect the primary partnership. In addition, these processes are likely to be linked to various social network attributes, including size, composition, density, and network overlap between two relational partners. In the next subsection, we consider the specific network attributes and processes that have been studied in the network literature.

The Empirical Literature on Network Influences on the Primary Partnership

Relationship scholars interested in identifying the predictors of relationship satisfaction and stability have often focused on individual attributes and relationship qualities and generally ignored the social environment of the relationship. This has been referred to as a "conceptual blindness" (Ridley & Avery, 1979). Although relationship scholars continue to be chastised for not giving enough attention to the social environment of the relationship (e.g., Berscheid, 1999), findings have accumulated concerning the effects on relationships of the following: (*a*) network density, (*b*) network overlap, (*c*) size of the network and/or degree of involvement with the network, and (*d*) social reactions to the relationship.

Network Density.   Bott's (1955) in-depth, interview study of 20 London families is usually credited as the first study that examined how the structure of the social network affects internal processes of the marital relationship. Bott hypothesized and found that couples who had close-knit networks (now referred to as dense networks) were more likely to have role segregation (e.g., division of labor by sex, leisure activities) in their marriage than couples who had less dense networks. Her argument was that highly interdependent and well-coordinated networks are likely to have similar (traditional) beliefs about husband and wife roles and thus can provide more influence on the couple. Another argument in Bott's work, as summarized by Milardo and Allan (1996), is that dense (close-knit) networks are likely to provide assistance to a couple, and as a result, the spouses will have less need for help from each other and therefore will develop more segregated roles. A major criticism of Bott's work, as noted by Milardo and Allan, is that she did not explain why the network would be more likely to encourage sex-role segregation than another role behavior for the marital relationship. Milardo and Allan summarized 14 studies that were conducted since Bott's classic study and reported that only 5 were generally supportive of her hypotheses.

   Network Overlap.   Network overlap between primary partners, or the degree to which the partners share friends and are involved with each other's extended family members, has been examined as a predictor of relationship satisfaction and stability. One of the first studies to demonstrate that network overlap may have a positive effect on marriage was conducted by Ackerman (1963), an anthropologist who examined data collected in 62 societies. He found that divorce rates were higher in societies in which husbands and wives maintained separate social networks than in societies in which husbands and wives had overlapping social networks.

   More recent research on this topic has focused on interview or survey data collected from one or both partners of couples about their shared networks and their marital satisfaction and/or success. In one such study, conducted with Australian married couples, Cotton, Cunningham, and Antill (1993) found that wives experienced greater marital satisfaction when they were friends with their husbands' network members. Husbands reported greater marital satisfaction when more of their wives' network members were related to their own network members and when they considered more of their wives' network members to be their own friends. The researchers concluded that marital relationships "were more likely to flourish when the couple is embedded in a close network of mutual friends and extended family" (p. 180). A positive association between network overlap and marital satisfaction was also found by Julien and Markman (1991), in a study of 87 couples.

   Stein et al. (1992) interviewed a sample of 49 working and middle-class married couples and classified these couples, based on information obtained from both members, into different types of conjoint networks. The couples who had the highest marital satisfaction were those who were identified as sharing family ties. The researchers speculated that, "Shared family ties are thought to provide a consistent set of norms about the marital relationship . . . and reinforce the identity of partners as a couple" (pp. 380–381). The partners in the couples included in this particular network type, however, also tended to have separate friends, which the authors speculated enhanced the marriage because of the additional emotional gratification and assistance that was provided by these friends.

   Other research, however, suggests that shared friendship networks may not be a strong predictor of marital satisfaction. Bryant and Conger (1999) analyzed data collected from rural, middle-aged, Midwestern couples at two different times. Although network overlap was not measured, the researchers assessed the degree to which the husbands and wives liked their partner's closest friends (i.e., affective overlap). In analyses conducted at each of the waves, measures of affective overlap were only weakly and inconsistently correlated with indicators of marital success, which included satisfaction, commitment, and stability. The researchers speculated that affective overlap may not be an important predictor of marital success for couples who are beyond the early years of marriage and hence have probably already merged their social worlds. Julien et al. (1999) came to the same conclusion when they found no association between overlap in the partners' social networks and relationship adjustment among married and cohabiting couples.

   However, couples who *spend time together* with mutual friends are likely to experience greater interdependence in their relationship, which is likely to increase satisfaction and commitment (Milardo, 1986). In addition, spending time together with mutual friends may create enjoyable and fun experiences. This was demonstrated by Larson and Bradney (1988), who used the Experience Sampling Method, in which respondents are paged at random times and asked to report on their activities and feelings. They found that spouses reported the most favorable feelings toward their partner when they were in the company of mutual friends. The authors argued that the company of mutual friends allows the spouses to focus on the playful and unique qualities of their partner rather than on the routine and ordinary business of the family.

Size of Network and/or Involvement With the Network.

Some research has examined how social network size or involvement with networks is associated with satisfaction in the primary partnership. It appears that the overall size of a couple's network is generally unrelated to relationship quality (e.g., Burger & Milardo, 1995). However, measures of size of or involvement with specific sectors of the network have been found to be associated with relationship quality, although the results vary based on gender and the specific sector of the network (e.g., extended family vs. friends). For example, Burger and Milardo's (1995) study conducted with a small sample of married couples illustrates the complexity of linking network size or interaction with marital quality. Although size of overall network and size of the friendship network were unrelated to marital quality, size of the kinship network was associated with various measures of relationship quality. The greater the size of the wife's extended family network, the greater the conflict in the marriage, as reported by both the husband and wife. Size of the husband's extended family network was associated with his greater love for his wife. Frequency of interaction with extended family and friends was also found to be associated with marital quality, although in complex ways. For wives, greater contact with extended family was associated with their greater love for their spouse and lower levels of conflict (even though, as reported above, size of the kinship network was associated with greater conflict). Similarly, for husbands, greater contact with extended family was associated with lower levels of marital conflict.

Other research has also demonstrated that involvement with extended family members generally has a positive effect on the quality of the marriage. For example, Cotton and her colleagues found that greater involvement with relatives, especially by husbands, was associated with relationship satisfaction (Cotton et al., 1993). In addition, the number of relatives defined to be potentially supportive in times of need has been found to be positively associated with relationship satisfaction (Veroff, Douvan, & Hatchett, 1995). However, Kearns and Leonard (2001) reported that wives had an increase in their marital quality over their first year of marriage when their husband decreased the amount of interaction with his friends and family.

Social Reactions to the Relationship.

Research shows that individuals who perceive support for their developing romantic relationships are more likely to stay together and advance to greater commitment than individuals who perceive their relationship is not supported by their network (e.g., Lewis, 1973; Sprecher & Felmlee, 1992, 2000). However, only limited research has examined the effect of network approval or disapproval on relationship quality in long-term relationships, perhaps because it is assumed that extended family members and friends approve of long-term relationships and are unlikely to try to end them. However, in a study of long-term relationships, Bryant and Conger (1999) found that a measure of relationship-specific support was strongly associated with marital success (satisfaction, commitment, and stability) for both wives and husbands.

In sum, several studies have demonstrated that network attributes are associated with the internal dynamics of marriage and of other similar, committed couples.

THE INFLUENCE OF SOCIAL NETWORKS ON PARENTING AND CHILD OUTCOMES

Social networks influence not only the primary adult partnership in the family but also the parent-child relationship and the child's development. In particular, parents' integration within a larger social network can influence their success at raising children who are academically and socially well-adjusted and who are launched successfully into adulthood.

As discussed many years ago in a classic paper by Cochran and Brassard (1979) and more recently by Cochran (1990), a distinction can be made between direct and indirect influences of parents' networks on the development of the child. Parents' social networks can provide direct influences on children by providing other sources of interactions, experiences, and resources for children in addition to that which can be provided by parents. For example, parents' adult friends and relatives may provide child care, alternative role models, gifts, and additional social stimulation and opportunities. Social networks influence the development of the child indirectly by affecting the ability of parents to perform parental roles. For example, social networks can provide parents with support and advice about parenting behaviors, role models for parenting behavior, and emotional and instrumental support which contribute to the parents' adult development (e.g., Cochran, 1990).

Although the direct and indirect influences of having available friends and extended family members are likely to be generally positive for raising children, negative effects are possible as well. For example, network members can place demands upon parents, which can reduce the amount of time they have for parenting. In addition, some network members may be poor role models, give bad parenting advice, or provide harmful experiences for others' children.

Of all network members, grandparents (the parents' parents) are likely to be the most helpful in the assistance of raising children. Bengston (2001) and others (e.g., Szinovacz, 1998; Uhlenberg, 1996) have argued that because of demographic changes, including decreased mortality rates and the increase in the divorce rate, grandparents are becoming more important than ever as sources of nuturance, socialization, economic resources, role models, and other types of support for children raised in various family forms. Indeed, some grandparents take on the parenting role, either part-time or full-time, as mentioned earlier.

Other relatives (e.g., aunts and uncles to the children), but particularly close adult friends, may also play important roles in the development of children. Research (Burchinal, Follmer, & Bryant, 1996; Cochran, 1990; Nitz, Ketterlinus, & Brandt, 1995; Uhlendorff, 2000; Voight, Hans, & Bernstein, 1996), has found that the number of close and reliable friends is associated with a number of positive outcomes for the parenting process, including mother's satisfaction with parenting, mother's responsiveness to the child, positive mother-child interaction, and the social and academic adjustment of the child. (Most studies examining network influences on child development focus on mothers, and often those disadvantaged in some way [e.g., adolescent mothers; single mothers]).

An illustrative study on parental social network influences on child development that included data from both mothers and fathers was conducted by Homel, Burns, and Goodnow (1987). They interviewed the mother, the father, and the child (aged 9 to 11 years of age) in 305 families from Australia. Information (including frequency of interaction and dependability) was obtained from the parents about three network sectors: friends, extended family members, and neighbors. In addition, the parents were asked about their involvement in community organizations. The researchers examined the possible associations of these network measures with several child outcomes, including happiness, school adjustment, friendship networks, and social skills. The parents' identification of dependable friends (defined as "someone you see regularly and whom you could turn to in a crisis") and ties to organizations were both strong predictors of several positive outcomes for the children. Conversely, variables associated with relatives and neighbors were less consistently and less strongly associated with the child outcomes.

Large, diverse, and loosely knit social networks may be especially useful at the time a family is launching an adolescent. This is because having a range of diverse social ties increases the likelihood that there will be social ties (called "weak ties" by Granovetter, 1973) that can connect the family to other persons previously unknown to them but who might be able to provide educational or work opportunities (Granovetter, 1982) as well as romantic opportunities (Sprecher et al., 2002).

THE INFLUENCE OF THE PRIMARY PARTNERSHIP AND FAMILY ON THE EXTENDED FAMILY AND SOCIAL NETWORK

Although most of the theory and research linking the extended family and social networks to the primary partnership and the immediate family has focused on the effects of the former on the latter, the primary partnership and immediate family also have effects on extended family and social networks. In this section, we focus on the effects of various transitions in the primary partnership (and immediate family) on the partners' social networks.

Transition to Marriage or Other Committed Union

Many years ago, the hypothesis of *dyadic withdrawal* was proposed (e.g., Johnson & Leslie, 1982; Slater, 1963). This hypothesis predicts that as a couple progresses toward marriage, both partners withdraw from their respective social networks. One explanation for this phenomenon involves constraints due to time and social energy. As partners invest more time and emotion in each other, they have less to give their friends and relatives. Another explanation offered is that withdrawal from others may occur as part of a couple's attempt to develop their identity as a unit separate from others (Krain, 1977; Lewis, 1973). As evidence for the dyadic withdrawal hypothesis, cross-sectional research has indicated that network size and amount of interaction with the network (especially friends) decrease as couples advance from casually dating to marriage (e.g., Johnson & Leslie, 1982; Milardo, Johnson, & Huston, 1983). In addition, Huston, Surra, Fitzgerald, and Cate (1981) found that married couples reported engaging in fewer leisure activities with network members after marriage than during the premarital stage of their relationship. In a longitudinal study of over 400 newlywed couples, assessed at the time of marriage and again a year later, Kearns and Leonard (2001) reported that, for both husbands and wives, there was a decrease in number of friends in the network, and for wives only, there was a decrease in the amount of time spent socializing with friends. Milardo (1987) also reported that social withdrawal continues for women but not for men into the early years of marriage.

Although the transition to marriage (or to a similar bond) may result in the partners withdrawing from some of their network members, another task often accomplished during this transition is the blending of the partners' social networks. Over time, the partners develop mutual friends and incorporate each other's relatives and prior friends into their networks. Hence, network overlap typically increases during the transition to marriage (e.g., Kim & Stiff, 1991; Milardo, 1982; Milardo et al., 1983). Parks, Stan, and Eggert (1983) suggested that *dyadic realignment* may be a more appropriate description than dyadic withdrawal for what occurs to couples as they progress in involvement.

Transition to a public commitment is also sometimes associated with the geographic relocation of one or both partners, which can impact the couple's social networks. After a move, there may be a period of social isolation in which the size of each partner's interactive network is reduced drastically. However, although new friends can be developed in a new location, relatives cannot be replaced. In general, geographical moves, especially if they are long distance, result in greater distance from kin (Rogerson, Weng, & Lin, 1993). Thus, geographic mobility that occurs in the process of a couple establishing a joint life in a new location is likely to change the composition of partners' interactive networks. In particular, the proportion of kin to nonkin included in the interactive social network is likely to be reduced for one or both partners. However, ties to extended family can remain significant and important despite geographical moves, whereas specific friendships formed in previous geographical locations tend to be less durable (e.g., Magdol, 2000).

Transition to Parenthood

Research on how childbearing affects social networks confirms the importance of this major transition for parents' networks. Several longitudinal studies have traced network changes for new parents from prebirth to 9–24 months after the birth (Belsky & Rovine, 1984; Bost, Cox, Burchinal, & Payne, 2002; McCannell, 1988). Interactive social networks, including the number of extended family members, tend to become smaller after the birth of a child (Bost et al., 2002; McCannell, 1988). Although the overall size of interactive networks becomes smaller, contact with those remaining in the network tends to increase. Contact especially increases with new parents' parents and with friends who are also parents. Despite these changes, there is also evidence of network continuity across time. Couples with considerable contact with family and friends before having children tend to continue this after the birth of a child (Belsky & Rovine, 1984; Bost et al, 2002; McCannell, 1988).

Cross-sectional findings about parents with a wide age range of children suggest changes in network patterns across many years of childrearing. Munch, McPherson, and Smith-Lovin (1997) found that mothers' interactive networks were largest when children were infants, smallest when children reached age 3, and larger again when children were older.

Fathers' interactive networks remained the same size over the childrearing years, but the composition of these networks shifted toward women and family ties during the early years of childrearing. For both women and men, interactive networks tended to be primarily composed of extended family members during their children's first few years of life.

Children and parents are also likely to influence each other's networks. For instance, studies have revealed significant positive relationships between the size of parents' and children's friendship networks (Uhlendorff, 2000). This can be explained in part by the broadening of children's social competencies that comes about with exposure to their parents' friends. Although parents' networks are usually thought of as affecting children's networks, children have also been found to increase parents' ties with neighbors and organization members (Moore, 1990).

Transition to Divorce or Dissolution

Most research demonstrating how social networks have changed after divorce are based on perceptions provided by divorced respondents after the dissolution. A sample of divorced respondents may be asked to report specifically on how they believe their networks have changed from before to after divorce (e.g., Albrecht, 1980). Alternatively, participants may be asked to provide retrospective data, assessed with more objective measures, about the size and composition of their network prior to the divorce and currently, and these measures are compared (e.g., Rands, 1988). Almost no research has been longitudinal in which predivorce social network contact is compared to the postdivorce social network contact, and what research exists was not designed specifically to examine how social networks change (e.g., Hetherington, Cox, & Cox, 1977).

Regardless of how pre- and postdivorce networks are assessed, the research suggests that social networks change after dissolution of a partnership. Each partner's social network is usually reduced in size. Individuals often sharply reduce interaction with their partner's relatives, friends, and associates. Divorced women, to a greater degree than divorced men, appear to have fewer friends in their social network. However, divorced women are more likely than divorced men to retain ties to their kin (for a review, see Milardo, 1987).

Other network attributes are also likely to change after a divorce. Most obviously, network overlap between partners is reduced, as each partner withdraws from his or her partner's extended family and friends. In addition, network density (degree to which network members have connections with each other) has been found to be lower in postdivorce networks than in predivorce networks. The composition of networks also is likely to change, including an increase in the proportion of unmarried friends to married friends in the postdivorce network (e.g., Milardo, 1987; Rands, 1988).

Not only do structural aspects of social networks change after a couple's dissolution, but also the well-being of other couples and families in the larger social network can be affected. During the process of a relationship dissolution, each member of the couple is likely to seek support for the breakup from his or her close friends and relatives. For example, according to Duck's (1982) stage model of the breakup process, one step of the breakup is the *social phase* in which members of the social network are confided in. An individual who is in the process of initiating a breakup may gossip and make negative statements to friends and relatives about his or her partner, which can elicit sympathy and support (e.g., Baxter, 1984). Occasionally, a network member may be asked to be an arbitrator who can help repair the relationship (e.g, Duck, 1986).

When a couple breaks up, other couples and families in the social network are likely to experience disruption in their social networks and social worlds. This has been referred to as the "social limbo" that occurs after divorce (Goode, 1956). It can be difficult for others to remain close to both ex-partners, and social network members may be forced to take sides. Couple friends may also become uncomfortable including a single friend in their social activities (e.g., Bohannan, 1970).

There is also a ripple effect of divorce, in that other couples in the network can become more susceptible to dissolution. In part, this occurs because having a friend or relative experience a divorce makes it seem more acceptable to an individual, already considering divorce, to also take this step (Berscheid & Campbell, 1981). For example, according to Levinger's (1976) theory about relationship stability, when barrier forces, including social barriers, are high, the couple is more likely to remain in the relationship. However, social barriers to divorce are reduced as members in one's social network divorce. In addition, the ripple effect of divorce occurs because two additional people become potentially available as relationship partners to others in the network (Berscheid & Campbell, 1981). As evidence that this occurs, South and Lloyd (1995) found that divorce rates in various communities are related to the local supply of potential alternative partners.

Another network effect of a couple divorcing or dissolving occurs when a child or children are involved. Grandparents and aunts and uncles from both sides of the couple have a relationship with the child. If one partner receives sole or primary custody, the other partner's family may experience a reduction in the amount of time spent with the child (e.g., Johnson & Barer, 1987).

Transition to Remarriage

Remarriage can also shift the focus of interaction within a social network. With remarriage, a complex collection of new immediate and extended stepfamily relationships can be considered. The handling of special occasions and how they evolve across time after remarriage can reveal how a given stepfamily defines its network boundaries (Whiteside, 1989). Children of divorce may live part time in the households of both biological parents, creating what has been called the *binuclear family* (Ahrons & Rodgers, 1987) The divorces and remarriages of multiple parents and stepparents can create very complicated interconnected binuclear households and necessitate complex decisions about inclusion and exclusion related to extended family gatherings (Whiteside, 1989).

With all this complexity, change and choice become key factors in remarriage-extended family networks. Kinship systems may become larger and more complex over time (Johnson, 1988), and some of the possible relationships may remain latent with the possibility of becoming activated later (Riley & Riley, 1993). Inclusive or exclusive behaviors can occur from all sides—there may not be consensus about who is in the extended family system. For example, some grandmothers whose adult sons divorce and remarry may embrace their sons' new wives into the extended family system, but also maintain relationships with their sons' ex-wives, through whom they have access to their grandchildren.

Other grandmothers may cut off relationships with their ex-daughters-in-law, giving primacy to their sons and their sons' current partners (Johnson & Barer, 1987). Of course, ex-daughters-in-law may be the ones to decide to discontinue relationships with their former mothers-in-law. Children too make inclusion decisions after remarriage. Co-residence with a parent's new spouse affects the extent to which children consider stepparents to be members of the family, and the probability of ties with a whole new branch of extended family and social contacts (Schmeeckle, 2001).

Transitions Related to Death

Anticipation of death has been shown to affect social interaction in some predictable ways. As noted earlier, Carstensen's (1993) socioemotional selectivity theory predicts that as people face death, they will become more selective about their social interactions. Thus, we may expect to see a shrinking of active social networks in later life as death approaches. Research has shown that older adults as well as younger adults facing a terminal illness prefer to interact with a small group of close friends and family members (Carstensen, 1993; Carstensen et al., 1999)

Death of a family member is a powerful impetus as well for changing relationships in the broader social network. One particularly salient death is that of a "kinkeeper"—one who was highly involved in maintaining ties with the extended family and social network. Death of an elderly kinkeeper can fragment or weaken the extended family network, as the labor involved in maintaining the network may be left undone (Adams, 1999; di Leonardo, 1992). It is common for middle-aged women to take on the work of kinkeeping after the death of a parent (Rosenthal, 1985).

Another salient consequence of death affecting the broader social network is that of widowhood. The loss of a spouse can weaken certain relationships in the social network, such as those with in-laws and couple-oriented friendships (Lamme, Dykstra, & Broese Van Groenou, 1996). Often widowed persons spend a period of time grieving, calling upon extended family and friends who are comfortable nurturing the intense feelings of the bereaved (Heinemann & Evans, 1990). Daughters, daughters-in-law, and elderly mothers often provide much needed support (Heinemann & Evans, 1990). Widows (and widowers) do seek out new friendships even in later life. They often develop new relationships with neighbors (Lamme et al., 1996), support group members, coworkers, and organizational affiliates (Heinemann & Evans, 1990).

CONCLUSIONS AND FUTURE RESEARCH DIRECTIONS

In this chapter, we have reviewed research connecting extended family and social networks with primary partnerships and immediate families. The literature we reviewed shows that immediate families and social networks affect each other in many different ways. Shifts into and out of primary partnerships are common; shifts in social networks are also common, and these shifts are often interrelated. Where are the gaps and weaknesses in the literatures we have discussed? What kinds of future directions would be beneficial? We start with comments that relate to the whole chapter, follow with additional observations, then discuss methodological, interdisciplinary, and practical concerns.

In this chapter, we drew from two literatures that were largely separate from one another: the literature on extended family and that on social networks. These literatures would benefit from being linked more; that was one of our goals for this chapter. Although extended family is technically a subset of the larger social network, there is abundant research on extended family relationships that does not draw upon concepts in the social networks literature. This may be because research on extended family relationships often focuses on a specific type of relationship (e.g., parents of adult children, grandparents, stepfamily relationships) and therefore neglects the fact that these relationships are taking place within a larger extended family and social network.

On the other hand, research on social networks often lumps large groups of people together, ignoring the fact that many network sectors are internally complex and diverse. For instance, "kin" are often assumed to be a largely uncomplicated category in the social network literature, yet the review here reveals that many kin relationships are negotiated and voluntary, similar to friendships. Another example is research on network aspects of primary partnerships that does not take the stage of the relationship into account. The mutual networks of couples in long-term marriages are likely to be very different from those of newly married couples. Network researchers should take care when combining sectors of the network and groups at different relationship stages in order to avoid lumping very different groups together.

Another suggestion we have for researchers in this area is to pay more attention to the impact of historical change. We believe that more research should be conducted on the impact of cohabitation, divorce, remarriage, reproductive technology, and computer-assisted technology on extended family and social network ties, including on the changing ways in which social networks affect primary partnerships. For example, a wide array of relationships have been made possible by demographic and technological changes, increasing the number of steprelatives, pseudo-steprelatives, ex-relatives, cyber-friends, and other diversely connected associates. Although these ties may be weaker than traditional kin ties, they create the possibility of close connection, ongoing interaction, and support through life (Wachter, 1997).

We also believe that research on extended families and social networks is too focused on the closest of ties. How much do we really know about weaker ties, intermittent contacts, and relationships that persist despite years of being passive or inactive? We have seen some work on the importance of weak ties (Granovetter, 1982), but believe that more on this topic could be very illuminating. When do passive ties become active again? What is the impact of attending school reunions, or occasionally visiting extended relatives? When can contact with those in the network who are rarely seen still have a major impact on the experience of a couple or immediate family?

Another area of research that we believe is neglected is that of the psychological network. We have discussed already how psychological and interactive networks are often not made up of the same people (Milardo, 1989). Who are the individuals in the psychological network, and what are the characteristics of these relationships? The research we have reviewed seems to overwhelmingly focus on interactive networks, but it may be missing some important insights about social life by neglecting psychological networks.

In addition, more should be done to connect the breadth of social network ideas to marriage and other primary partnerships. The processes of network influence that we discussed (messages of support/interference, general personal support, information, opportunities, social comparisons, substitutability) come from varied literatures and have not been fully integrated into network research. Most of the empirical network literature is focused on messages of support/interference and general personal support. It would be fruitful to develop our knowledge about the other processes and how they work in conjunction with other network attributes. For example, the idea of substitutability has not been explored much. We do not know under what conditions individuals benefit from having emotional needs met by those other than the partner (as evidenced by the women interviewed by Rubin, 1985) and when or under what conditions substitutability of emotional needs becomes a threat to the primary relationship. Furthermore, geographic moves may cause changes in the interactive network and raise issues of substitutability that were not present earlier. Some primary relationships may suffer after a move because others (friends, etc.) who are no longer around are unable to supplement the needs being filled by the primary partnership.

We have methodological concerns as well. Most of the research on social networks tends to focus on only one or two network attributes or processes at a time. In keeping with our previous suggestion, larger scale research that incorporates multiple network concepts would be beneficial. Also, causal directions tend to be ambiguous in cross-sectional research. For example, if positive associations are found between social reactions to the relationship and relationship satisfaction, how do we know that social reactions lead to relationship satisfaction? Perhaps those couples who are happy elicit positive social reactions from others. Similarly, if there are positive associations between network overlap and happiness in the primary partnership, we cannot necessarily assume that network overlap contributes to happiness. Being happy in a relationship may lead one to want to get to know the partner's friends and relatives and incorporate them into one's own network. To address these concerns, we recommend more longitudinal research to unravel these causal directions.

Another methodological concern we have is that much of the research seems to conceive of causal relationships in a linear way. It is possible, however, that some network variables have curvilinear associations with outcome variables for the primary partnership and immediate family. For example, perhaps interaction with the network is positively associated with relational satisfaction only up to a certain point of interaction, beyond which greater interaction has no additional effect or is even negatively associated with satisfaction. As another example, perhaps number of friends is associated with good parenting (and good outcomes for children) only up to a certain point. Having a very large number of friends could become detrimental to parenting.

A final methodological comment has to do with how what we know about the effects of networks on primary partnerships is generally based on the perception of the partner members only. It would be beneficial to also obtain the perspectives of the network members. The picture of network effects may look very different from the network's perspective. For a recent research example attempting to do this, in the area of romantic relationships, see Agnew, Loving, and Drigotas (2001).

The literature on extended families and social networks comes from different disciplines (sociology, communication, family studies, psychology). The diversity of disciplines represented makes findings sometimes hard to compare, but also introduces a variety of ideas about causal mechanisms and partnership/family outcomes. Although multiple disciplines have insights to offer this area of inquiry, the research conducted has rarely been truly interdisciplinary, combining approaches and concepts from different disciplines within the same study. Researchers can benefit from considering simultaneously psychological factors such as personality influences, communication factors such as interaction routines, and sociological factors such as gender and culture. Considering a variety of influences at a variety of levels (micro to macro) allows us to interpret social network processes more powerfully. For example, we might ask to what degree are network effects on the primary partnership (e.g., greater involvement with network associated with more stable relationships) simply due to personality differences? That is, is the type of person who is involved with many friends and relatives (has a large network) also the type of person who has the skills to maintain an intimate relationship? If so, the association found between network variables and relationship outcomes may be spurious. Another example demonstrating the value of an interdisciplinary perspective was raised by Cochran (1990), who discussed social network effects on child outcomes. Research suggests that being involved in larger networks and organizations is associated with good parenting and good outcomes for children, and thus it is concluded that the former affects the latter. However, it is possible that both are affected by one's placement in the larger social structure. That is, adults in the middle to higher social classes are likely to both have the resources to develop and maintain friendships and have the resources to successfully parent.

The communication discipline also offers some insights related to extended families and social networks that are worth blending into an interdisciplinary project. A focus on interaction routines and interaction rituals (Burleson, Metts, & Kirch, 2000) could be effectively related to extended families and social networks. For example, networks of friends (and extended families) may have repetitive interactions or rituals that serve important functions linking individuals, primary partnerships, and immediate families with larger groups. A focus on norms and rules that are developed as partners' networks overlap could also be illuminating (Burleson, et al., 2000). These norms and rules may need to be periodically negotiated, as couples deal with different levels of openness and preferences for contact.

We would also like to discuss the practical implications of the findings reviewed in this chapter. For example, the literature suggests that it is beneficial for couples to develop mutual friends and spend time together with them and to interact with extended family members. In addition, children's academic and social competencies can be enhanced when parents involve friends and extended family members in the parenting process. Practitioners should be aware that social network resources tend not to be as available to those of lower socioeconomic status, so extensive network support should not be assumed for lower income families. Therapeutic and policy interventions should also respond to historical shifts in how people form and maintain relationships. Internet dating, commuter marriages, and a social context of serial monogamy are relatively new phenomena that are part of today's context of primary partnerships.

In summary, in this concluding section, we have made a number of suggestions that we feel would strengthen this research area. There is much to be done in this field, and it is clear that extended families and social networks have important effects on primary partnerships and immediate families. It is also clear that transitions involving partnerships and children have important effects on extended family and social network interaction. We hope this chapter will provide a stepping stone for more research in this complex yet fascinating area of study.

AUTHOR NOTE

The authors have contributed equally to the writing of this chapter. Correspondence regarding this chapter may be addressed to the authors: Department of Sociology & Anthropology, Illinois State University, Normal, IL 61790-4660. Send email to mhschme@ilstu.edu or sprecher@ilstu.edu.

REFERENCES

Adams, B. N. (1999). Cross-cultural and U.S. kinship. In M. B. Sussman, S. K. Steinmetz, & G. W. Peterson (Eds.), *Handbook of marriage and the family* (2nd ed., pp. 77–92). New York: Plenum Press.

Ackerman, C. (1963). Affiliations: Structural determination of differential divorce rates. *American Journal of Sociology, 69*, 13–20.

Agnew, C. R., Loving, T. J., & Drigotas, S. M. (2001). Substituting the forest for the trees: Social networks and the prediction of romantic relationship state and fate. *Journal of Personality and Social Psychology, 81*, 1042–1057.

Ahrons, C. R., & Rodgers, R. H. (1987). *Divorced families: Meeting the challenge of divorce and remarriage.* New York: Norton.

Albrecht, S. (1980). Reactions and adjustments to divorce: Differences in the experiences of males and females. *Family Relations, 29*, 59–68.

Antonucci, T. C., & Akiyama, H. (1987). Social networks in adult life and a preliminary examination of the convoy model. *Journal of Gerontology, 42*, 519–527.

Baxter, L. A. (1984). Trajectories of relationship disengagement. *Journal of Social and Personal Relationships, 1*, 29–48.

Belsky, J., & Rovine, M. (1984). Social-network contact, family support, and the transition to parenthood. *Journal of Marriage and the Family, 46*, 455–462.

Bengtson, V. L. (2001). Beyond the nuclear family: The increasing importance of multi-generational bonds. *Journal of Marriage and Family, 63*, 1–16.

Berger, C. R. (1988). Uncertainty and information exchange in developing relationships. In S. Duck (Ed.), *Handbook of personal relationships: Theory, research, and interventions* (pp. 239–256). Chichester: Wiley.

Berscheid, E. (1999). The greening of relationship science. *American Psychologist, 54*, 260–266.

Berscheid, E., & Campbell, B. (1981). The changing longevity of heterosexual close relationships: A commentary and forecast. In M. J. Lerner & S. C. Lerner (Eds.), *The justice motive in social behavior* (pp. 209–234). New York: Plenum Press.

Bohannan, P. (1970). The six stations of divorce. In P. Bohannan (Ed.), *Divorce and after* (pp. 33–62). New York: Anchor Books.

Boneva, B., Kraut, R., & Frohlich, D. (2001). Using e-mail for personal relationships: The difference gender makes. *American Behavioral Scientist, 45*, 530–549.

Bost, K. K., Cox, M. J., Burchinal, M. R., & Payne, C. (2002). Structural and supportive changes in couple's family and friendship networks across the transition to parenthood. *Journal of Marriage and Family, 64*, 517–531.

Bott, E. (1955). Urban families: Conjugal roles and social networks. *Human Relations, 8*, 345–384.

Bryant, C. M., & Conger, R. D. (1999). Marital success and domains of social support in long-term relationships: Does the influence of network members ever end? *Journal of Marriage and the Family, 61*, 437–450.

Burchinal, M., Follmer, A., & Bryant, D. (1996). The relations of maternal social support and family structure with maternal responsiveness and child outcomes among African American families. *Developmental Psychology, 32*, 1073–1083.

Burger, E., & Milardo, R. M. (1995). Marital interdependence and social networks. *Journal of Social and Personal Relationships, 12*, 403–415.

Burleson, B. R., Metts, S., & Kirch, M. W. (2000). Communication in close relationships. In C. Hendrick & S. S. Hendrick (Eds.), *Close relationships: A sourcebook* (pp. 245–258). Thousand Oaks, CA: Sage.

Carstensen, L. L. (1991). Selectivity theory: Social activity in life-span context. *Annual Review of Gerontology and Geriatrics, 11*, 195–217.

Carstensen, L. L. (1992). Social and emotional patterns in adulthood: Support for socio-emotional selectivity theory. *Psychology and Aging, 7*, 331–338.

Carstensen, L. L. (1993). Motivation for social contact across the life span: A theory of socioemotional selectivity. *Nebraska Symposium on Motivation, 40*, 209–254.

Carstensen, L. L., Isaacowitz, D. M., & Charles, S. T. (1999). Taking time seriously: A theory of socioemotional selectivity. *American Psychologist, 54*, 165–181.

Chatters, L. M., Taylor, R. J., & Jayakody, R. (1994). Fictive kin relations in black extended families. *Journal of Comparative Family Studies, 25*, 297–312.

Cochran, M. (1990). Personal networks in the ecology of human development. In M. Cochran, M. Larner, D. Riley, L. Gunnarsson, & C. R. Henderson, Jr. (Eds.), *Extending families: The social networks of parents and children* (pp. 3–33). Cambridge, UK: Cambridge University Press.

Cochran, M. M., & Brassard, J. A. (1979). Child development and personal social networks. *Child Development, 50*, 601–616.

Cotton, S., Cunningham, J. D., & Antill, J. K. (1993). Network structure, network support and marital satisfaction of husbands and wives. *Australian Journal of Psychology, 45*, 176–181.

di Leonardo, M. (1992). The female world of cards and holidays: Women, families and the work of kinship. In B. Thorne & M. Yalom (Eds.), *Rethinking the family: Some feminist questions*. (Rev. ed., pp. 246–261). Boston, MA: Northeastern University Press.

Duck, S. W. (1982). A topography of relationship disengagement and dissolution. In S. W. Duck (Ed.), *Personal relationships 4: Dissolving personal relationships* (pp. 1–30). London and New York: Academic Press.

Duck, S. W. (1986). *Human relations: An introduction to social psychology.* London: Sage.

Felmlee, D. H. (2003). Interaction in social networks. In J. DeLamater (Ed.), *Handbook of social psychology* (pp. 389–409). New York: Kluwer-Plenum.

Festinger, L. (1954). A theory of social comparison processes. *Human Relations, 7,* 117–140.

Fischer, C. (1982). *To dwell among friends: Personal networks in town and city.* Chicago: University of Chicago Press.

Fischer, C., & Oliker, S. (1983). A research note on friendship, gender, and the life cycle. *Social Forces, 62,* 124–132.

Franzen, A. (2000). Does the internet make us lonely? *European Sociological Review, 16,* 427–438.

Goldstein, J. R. (1999). Kinship networks that cross racial lines: The exception or the rule? *Demography, 36,* 399–407.

Goldstein, J. R., & Warren, J. R. (2000). Socioeconomic research and heterogeneity in the extended family: Contours and consequences. *Social Science Research, 29,* 382–404.

Goode, W. (1956). *Women in divorce.* New York: The Free Press.

Granovetter, M. (1973). The strength of weak ties. *American Journal of Sociology, 78,* 1360–1380.

Granovetter, M. (1982). The strength of weak ties: A network theory revisited. In P. V. Marsden & N. Lin (Eds.), *Social structure and network analysis* (pp. 105–130). London: Sage.

Hagestad, G. O. (1986). The family: Women and grandparents as kin-keepers. In A. Pifer, & L. Bronte (Eds.), *Our aging society: Paradox and promise.* New York: Norton.

Harrison, K. (1998). Rich friendships, affluent friends: Middle-class practices of friendship. In R. G. Adams & G. Allan (Eds.), *Placing friendship in context* (pp. 92–116). New York: Cambridge University Press.

Heider, F. (1946). Attitudes and cognitive organization. *Psychology, 21,* 107–122.

Heinemann, G. D., & Evans, P. L. (1990). Widowhood: Loss, change, and adaptation. In T. H. Brubaker (Ed.), *Family relationships in later life* (2nd ed., pp. 142–168). Newbury Park, CA: Sage.

Hetherington, E. M., Cox, M., & Cox. R. (1977). The aftermath of divorce. In J. H. Stevens & M. Mathews (Eds.), *Mother-child, father-child relationships* (pp. 95–135). Washington, DC: National Association for the Education of Young Children.

Hollinger, F., & Haller, M. (1990). Kinship and social networks in modern societies: A cross-cultural comparison among seven nations. *European Sociological Review, 6,* 103–124.

Homel, R., Burns, A., & Goodnow, J. (1987). Parental social networks and child development. *Journal of Social and Personal Relationships, 4,* 159–177.

Huston, T. L., Surra, C., Fitzgerald, N., & Cate, R. (1981). From courtship to marriage: Mate selection as an interpersonal process. In S. Duck & R. Gilmour (Eds.), *Personal relationships* (Vol. 2, pp. 53–88). London: Academic Press.

Johnson, C. L. (1988). *Ex familia.* New Brunswick, NJ: Rutgers University Press.

Johnson, C. L. (2000). Perspectives on American kinship in the later 1990s. *Journal of Marriage and the Family, 62,* 623–639.

Johnson, C. L., & Barer, B. M. (1987). Marital instability and the changing kinship networks of grandparents. *The Gerontologist, 27,* 330–335.

Johnson, M. P., & Leslie, L. (1982). Couple involvement and network structure: A test of the dyadic withdrawal hypothesis. *Social Psychology Quarterly, 45,* 34–43.

Julien, D., Chartrand, E., & Begin, J. (1999). Social networks, structural interdependence, and conjugal adjustment in heterosexual, gay, and lesbian couples. *Journal of Marriage and the Family, 61*, 516–530.

Julien, D., & Markman, H. J. (1991). Social support and social networks as determinants of individual and marital outcomes. *Journal of Social and Personal Relationships, 8*, 549–568.

Kalmijn, M., & Bernasco, W. (2001). Joint and separated lifestyles in couple relationships. *Journal of Marriage and Family, 63*, 639–654.

Kearns, J. N., & Leonard, K. E. (August 2001). *Social network involvement and marital quality over the marital transition*. Paper presented at the Annual Convention of the American Psychological Association, San Francisco, CA.

Kim, H. J., & Stiff, J. B. (1991). Social networks and the development of close relationships. *Human Communication Research, 18*, 70–91.

Kinsella, K. (1995). Aging and the family: Present and future demographic issues. In R. Blieszner & V. Hilkevitch Bedford (Eds.), *Handbook of aging and the family* (pp. 32–56). Westport, CT: Greenwood Press.

Krain, M. (1977). A definition of dyadic boundaries and an empirical study of boundary establishment in courtship. *International Journal of the Family, 7*, 107–123.

Lamme, S., Dykstra, P. A., & Broese Van Groenou, M. I. (1996). Rebuilding the network: New relationships in widowhood. *Personal Relationships, 3*, 337–349.

Lang, F. R., & Carstensen, L. L. (1994). Close emotional relationships in late life: Further support for proactive aging in the social domain. *Psychology and Aging, 9*, 315–324.

Larson, R. W., & Bradney, N. (1988). Precious moments with family members and friends. In R. M. Milardo (Ed.), *Families and social networks* (pp. 107–126). Newbury Park, CA: Sage.

Levinger, G. A. (1976). A social psychological perspective on marital dissolution. *Journal of Social Issues, 3*, 21–47.

Lewis, R. A. (1973). Social reactions and the formation of dyads: An interactionist approach to mate selection. *Sociometry, 36*, 409–418.

Lewis, R. A. (1975). Social influences on marital choice. In S. E. Dragastin & G. H. Elder, Jr. (Eds.), *Adolescence in the life cycle* (pp. 211–225). New York: Hemisphere.

Magdol, L. (2000). The people you know: The impact of residential mobility on mothers' social network ties. *Journal of Social and Personal Relationships, 17*, 183–204.

Marsiglio, W., & Scanzoni, J. (1995). *Families and friendships: Applying the sociological imagination*. New York: HarperCollins.

McCannell, K. (1988). Social networks and the transition to motherhood. In R. M. Milardo (Ed.), *Families and social networks* (pp. 83–106). Newbury Park, CA: Sage.

Milardo, R. M. (1982). Friendship networks in developing relationships: Converging and diverging social environments. *Social Psychology Quarterly, 45*, 162–172.

Milardo, R. M. (1986). Personal choice and social constraint in close relationships: Applications of network analysis. In V. J. Derlega & B. A. Winstead (Eds.), *Friendship and social interaction* (pp. 145–166). New York: Springer-Verlag.

Milardo, R. M. (1987). Changes in social networks of men and women following divorce. *Journal of Family Issues, 8*, 78–96.

Milardo, R. M. (1989). Theoretical and methodological issues in identifying the social networks of spouses. *Journal of Marriage and the Family, 51*, 165–174.

Milardo, R. M., & Allan, G. (1996). Social networks and marital relationships. In S. Duck, K. Dindia, W. Ickes, R. Milardo, R. Mills, & B. Saranson (Eds.), *Handbook of personal relationships* (pp. 505–522). London: Wiley.

Milardo, R. M., & Helms-Erikson, H. (2000). Network overlap and third-party influence in close relationships. In C. Hendrick & S. S. Hendrick (Eds.), *Close relationships: A sourcebook* (pp. 33–45). Thousand Oaks, CA: Sage.

Milardo, R. M., Johnson, M. P., & Huston, T. L. (1983). Developing close relationship: Changing patterns of interactions between pair members and social networks. *Journal of Personality and Social Psychology, 44*, 964–976.

Moore, G. (1990). Structural determinants of men's and women's personal networks. *American Sociological Review, 55*, 726–735.

Munch, A., McPherson, J. M., & Smith-Lovin, L. (1997). Gender, children and social contact: The effects of childrearing for men and women. *American Sociological Review, 62*, 509–520.

Nitz, K., Ketterlinus, R., & Brandt, L. (1995). The role of stress, social support, and family environment in adolescent mothers' parenting. *Journal of Adolescent Research, 10*, 358–382.

Oliker, S. J. (1989). *Best friends and marriage.* Berkeley: University of California Press.

Oswald, R. F. (2002). Resilience within the family networks of lesbians and gay men: Intentionality and redefinition. *Journal of Marriage and Family, 64*, 374–383.

Parks, M. R. (2000). Communication networks and relationship life cycles. In K. Dindia & S. Duck (Eds.), *Communication and personal relationships* (pp. 56–75). New York: Wiley.

Parks, M. R., & Eggert, L. (1991). The role of social context in the dynamics of personal relationships. In W. H. Jones & D. Perlman (Eds.), *Advances in personal relationships* (Vol. 2, pp. 1–34). London: Jessica Kinglsey.

Parks, M. R., Stan, C., & Eggert, L. (1983). Romantic involvement and social network involvement. *Social Psychology Quarterly, 46*, 116–130.

Rands, M. (1988). Changes in social networks following marital separation and divorce. In R. Milardo (Ed.), *Families and social networks* (pp. 127–146). Newbury Park, CA: Sage.

Riley, M. W., & Riley, J. W. (1993). Connections: Kin and cohort. In V. L. Bengtson & W. A. Achenbaum (Eds.), *The changing contract across generations* (pp. 169–189). New York: Aldine De Gruyter.

Ridley, C. A., & Avery, A. W. (1979). Social network influence on the dyadic relationship. In R. Burgess & T. Huston (Eds.), *Social exchange in developing relationships* (pp. 223–246). New York: Academic Press.

Rogerson, P. A., Weng, R. H., & Lin, G. (1993). The spatial separation of parents and their adult children. *Annals of the Association of American Geographers, 83*, 656–671.

Roschelle, A. (1997). *No more kin: Exploring race, class, and gender in family networks.* Thousand Oaks, CA: Sage.

Rosenthal, C. J. (1985). Kinkeeping in the familial division of labor. *Journal of Marriage and the Family, 47*, 965–974.

Rubin, L. B. (1985). *Just friends.* New York: Harper & Row.

Rusbult, C. E., Johnson, D. J., & Morrow, G. D. (1986). Predicting satisfaction and commitment in adult romantic involvements: An assessment of the generalizability of the investment model. *Social Psychology Quarterly, 49,* 81–89.

Salmon, C. A. (1999). On the impact of sex and birth order on contact with kin. *Human Nature, 10,* 183–197.

Sapadin, L. A. (1988). Friendship and gender: Perspectives of professional men and women. *Journal of Social and Personal Relationships, 5,* 387–403.

Schmeeckle, M. (2001). *Rethinking the ties that bind: Adult children's perceptions of step, ex-step, and biological parents.* Unpublished dissertation, University of Southern California.

Slater, P. E. (1963). On social regression. *American Sociological Review, 28,* 339–358.

South, S. J., & Lloyd, K. M. (1995). Spousal alternatives and marital dissolution. *American Sociological Review, 60,* 21–35.

Sprecher, S., & Felmlee, D. (1992). The influence of parents and friends on the quality and stability of romantic relationships: A three-wave longitudinal investigation. *Journal of Marriage and the Family, 54,* 888–900.

Sprecher, S., & Felmlee, D. (2000). Romantic partners' perceptions of social network attributes with the passage of time and relationship transitions. *Personal Relationships, 7,* 325–340.

Sprecher, S., Felmlee, D., Orbuch, D. L., & Willetts, M. C. (2002). Social networks and change in personal relationships. In A. Vangelisti, H. Reis, & M. A. Fitzpatrick (Eds.), *Stability and change in relationships* (pp. 257–284). Cambridge, UK: Cambridge University Press.

Stacey, J. (1991). *Brave new families: Stories of domestic upheaval in late twentieth century America.* New York: Basic Books.

Stacey, J. (1996). *In the name of the family: Rethinking values in the postmodern age.* Boston, MA: Beacon Press.

Stein, C. H., Bush, E. G., Ross, R. R., & Ward, M. (1992). Mine, yours and ours: A configural analysis of the networks of married couples in relation to marital satisfaction and individual well-being. *Journal of Social and Personal Relationships, 9,* 365–383.

Surra, C., & Milardo, R. (1991). The social psychological context of developing relationships: Psychological and interactive networks. In D. Perlman & W. Jones (Eds.), *Advances in personal relationships* (Vol., 3, pp. 1–36). London: Jessica Kingsley.

Szinovacz, M. (1998). *Handbook on grandparenthood.* Westport, CT: Greenwood Press.

Teachman, J. D., Tedrow, L. M., & Crowder, K. D. (2000). The changing demography of America's families. *Journal of Marriage and the Family, 62,* 1234–1246.

Tucker, M. B., & Mitchell-Kernan, C. (1995). *The decline in marriage among African Americans: Causes, consequences and policy implications.* New York: Russell Sage.

Uhlenberg, P. (1996). Mutual attraction: Demography and life-course analysis. *Gerontologist, 36,* 226–229.

Uhlendorff, H. (2000). Parents' and children's friendship networks. *Journal of Family Issues, 21,* 191–204.

Van Lange, P. A. M., & Rusbult, C. E. (1995). My relationship is better than—and not as bad as—yours is: The perception of superiority in close relationships. *Personality and Social Psychology Bulletin, 21,* 32–44.

Veroff, J., Douvan, E., & Hatchett, S. L. (1995). *Marital instability: A social and behavioral study of the early years.* Westport, CT: Praeger.

Voight, J., Hans, S., & Bernstein, V. (1996). Support networks of adolescent mothers: Effects of parenting experience and behavior. *Infant Mental Health Journal, 17,* 58–73.

Wachter, K. W. (1997). Kinship resources for the elderly. *Philosophical transactions of the Royal Society of London, 352,* 1811–1817.

Weston, K. (1991). *Families we choose: Lesbians, gays, kinship.* New York: Columbia University Press.

Whiteside, M. F. (1989). Family rituals as a key to kinship connections in remarried families. *Family Relations, 38,* 34–39.

FAMILY COMMUNICATION PROCESSES

PRIVACY IN FAMILIES

JOHN P. CAUGHLIN
UNIVERSITY OF ILLINOIS AT URBANA-CHAMPAIGN

SANDRA PETRONIO
INDIANA UNIVERSITY–PURDUE UNIVERSITY INDIANAPOLIS

DEAR ABBY: I have worn a hairpiece for about 15 years and have been at my present job for the past five. My toupee was expensive and it's not obvious. I have never told anyone at work that my full head of hair isn't natural. Last weekend at a work-related social function, my wife astonished me by mentioning to a group of my co-workers over cocktails that I wear a hairpiece. After we left for the party, I became angry with her for making this revelation, but she refused to accept why I was so upset.[1]

Much of the advice about private information in families has focused on the dangers of family members keeping "dark secrets" (Bradshaw, 1995, p. 27) or on "...the emotional fallout that often occurs when families keep secrets" (Webster, 1991, p. xi). Other advice cautions that many family members reveal private information too frequently or at inappropriate times (e.g., Hunt & Paine-Gernée, 1994; Imber-Black, 1998). Clearly, both of these positions have some merit. Many families conspire to keep dangerous secrets like wife battering (Kaufman, 1993), child abuse (Melzak, 1992; Smith, 1992), or intentions to hurt other people (Imber-Black, 1998). Such secrets certainly are associated with "emotional fallout," and family members wishing to end such destructive practices may be best served by divulging the secret to someone outside the family (e.g., an appropriate authority figure). However, family members also may conceal private information for prosocial reasons. For example, a wife may protect her husband from embarrassment by refraining from mentioning his secret toupee to others. When family members collaborate to keep such information private, it can contribute to their sense of bonding and trust with each

---

[1] As seen in DEAR ABBY by Abigail Van Buren a.k.a. Jeanne Phillips and founded by her mother Pauline Phillips. © 2002 Universal Press Syndicate. Reprinted with permission. All rights reserved.

other (Goffman, 1959; Petronio, Jones, & Morr, 2003; Vangelisti, 1994). In contrast, as demonstrated by the example from Dear Abby, revealing private information about another family member can be viewed as a betrayal (Simmel, 1950).

At first glance, such examples may suggest that deciding whether to reveal or conceal private information about the family is easy; for example, one might have a simple rule forbidding disclosures that are harmful to family members. However, privacy issues are far more complicated for three reasons. First, revealing and concealing both are necessary for family functioning. Family members need to be connected to each other through shared confidences, but they also need to keep some information from others to build or maintain their own distinct identities. Hence, disclosure and privacy work in conjunction to provide a level of attachment with other family members while also allowing for needed independence. Second, because both revealing and concealing are beneficial to family members, people must manage the way they make choices about disclosing and retaining their privacy. Although some choices may be easy (e.g., if the decision about a certain family privacy issue has become routinized), many choices are not. When such choices are not easy, the dialectic between wanting to reveal and wanting to conceal becomes salient; that is, people experience a sense of conflict over how to manage their needs to be both connected and autonomous in families.[2] For example, even in some cases of domestic violence, family members feel two simultaneous needs: one to protect the solidarity of the family by limiting disclosure and another to alleviate the harmful effects of the violence by disclosing to outsiders (Fitzpatrick, 2002). Third, many family privacy issues involve information that some family members keep from others within the same family. In such instances, bonding with one family member by sharing private information with that individual may simultaneously betray another family member (Petronio, 2002). In short, the privacy issues among and between family members are myriad and have important implications for the success of the family and its members.

The current chapter examines such issues by selectively reviewing research on family privacy, secrecy, topic avoidance, and disclosure. This review is intended to illustrate the main foci of this literature rather than offer a comprehensive summary. In addition, the chapter is framed by Petronio's (1991, 2000a, 2002) communication privacy management (CPM) theory, which uses a boundary metaphor to illustrate the way people manage their privacy. The theory argues that people want to control private information because they feel they own it (and therefore have the right to control it) and because revealing the information has the potential to make them vulnerable. For CPM theory, control is achieved through the use of privacy rules that individuals develop for making decisions about how to regulate boundary permeability (i.e., degree of access to private information), linkages (i.e., connections formed by allowing others into a privacy boundary), and ownership (i.e., which individual or individuals are privy to the private information). In groups such as families, people typically own both personally private information and co-own information with

---

[2]The term "dialectic" has a number of distinct meanings. The theoretical framework of the current chapter, communication privacy management (CPM) theory, subscribes to a particular set of dialectical assumptions (Petronio, 2002). CPM theory, moves beyond recognizing a dialectic between revealing and concealing by offering a framework for understanding and investigating how individuals (and groups of individuals) manage the conflict between revealing and concealing.

other family members. When family members are co-owners of private information, they are expected to coordinate the kind of privacy rules used to disclose. Using the theoretical structure of CPM, the chapter is divided into four main sections, which examine (a) how private information is managed in families, (b) how rules are developed to coordinate family privacy boundaries, (c) consequences of changes in permeability for family privacy boundaries, and (d) some suggestions for future research on privacy within families.

MANAGING PRIVATE DISCLOSURES IN THE FAMILY

Two main concepts from CPM theory are particularly useful for understanding how family members manage private information: family privacy boundaries and boundary coordination among family members.

Family Privacy Boundaries

CPM theory posits that family members create and manage privacy boundaries by granting or denying access to private information.[3] Privacy boundaries are metaphorical markers of who controls, regulates, and shares ownership of private information. Information is considered private when individuals perceive it as belonging to them, giving them the right to regulate access to it (Petronio, 2002). The concept of private information is similar to, but broader than, the content of self-disclosures. Whereas self-disclosures primarily concern information about the person doing the disclosing, private information is any information that people believe they have the right to control personally. According to CPM theory, people not only claim ownership of information about themselves, but they also are often co-owners of private information that is shared by others (Petronio, 2002). That is, private information need not be directly about the person controlling access to it. This notion is particularly important when studying privacy in groups like families because much of what individuals consider private concerns family members other than themselves. For example, a brother with knowledge that his sister violated parental rules (e.g., by drinking while underage) may cooperate with his sister to keep that information from the parents (Vangelisti, 1994). In such an instance, controlling the access to this information would create a privacy boundary that separates the two siblings from their parents.

A boundary between parents and children is only one example of family privacy boundaries. Given the complex sets of relationships found in families, there are numerous interrelated boundaries operating simultaneously. These family privacy boundaries fall into two types of boundary systems (Petronio, 2002). First, families have exterior privacy boundaries around information that is managed by and belongs to all family members (Karpel,

---

[3]It is important to recognize that the CPM theory focus on private information excludes some issues that can be described as privacy issues within families. For example, the term "privacy" sometimes refers to family members' rights to make decisions without being influenced by the larger community or government (Alderman & Kennedy, 1995; Frey, 2000; Gerber, 2000). A pregnant woman's decision regarding whether she should have an abortion, for instance, can be discussed as a type of privacy issue. Such "decisional privacy" issues are beyond the scope of the current chapter.

1980; Vangelisti, 1994). For example, some people might say, "in my family, we never tell outsiders about family finances." Because all family members co-own such information, they typically coordinate to regulate this information in a unified manner, meaning that each member works to manage the private information according to a set of privacy rules that all members have adopted or agreed to use (Petronio, 2002).

In addition to an exterior privacy boundary, families form internal privacy cells around information that belongs to a smaller number of family members (Petronio, 2002). Families generally have several interior cells that represent privacy boundaries; for example, some private information may be owned and managed by a father and son, other information may belong to two siblings, and yet other information may be owned by a husband and wife. The information within each interior privacy boundary is restricted to only those family members allowed within the boundary. However, someone in the boundary may become a "privacy spanner," linking others into the boundary by telling them the private information (Petronio, 2002). For instance, a mother may decide to tell her husband information that was shared by their daughter, even if the daughter stipulated that her father should not be told.

Privacy Coordination Among Family Members

When family members participate in collective privacy boundaries, they coordinate rules used to manage the private information. Coordinating privacy boundaries involves negotiating to make decisions about how to regulate linkages (i.e., connections that allow someone into a privacy boundary), boundary permeability (i.e., the extent to which access is granted to private information), and ownership (i.e., which individuals share the mutual responsibilities of co-ownership).

Linkage. As mentioned previously, families manage both interior and exterior privacy boundaries around information. Interior linkages typically are established when one family member (or one group of family members) discloses personal or collectively held private information to another family member (or family members). The formation of such linkages depends on rules that people use to make judgments about who should be privy to the information (Petronio, 2002). For instance, one common "linkage rule" within families is evident in the tendency of children to tell their mother more private information than they tell their father (e.g., Denholm-Carey & Chabassol, 1987).

Permeability. Privacy boundaries vary in permeability, meaning that there are gradations in the extent to which access is granted to private information (Petronio, 2000a, 2002). The notion of permeability is important because simply acknowledging that a privacy boundary exists may not be particularly informative. For example, as evidenced by reports that almost all families keep some secrets from outsiders (Vangelisti & Caughlin, 1997), the existence of a privacy boundary around family members is likely ubiquitous. Thus, rather than only considering whether a privacy boundary exists, it is also important to consider the level of permeability.

A factor that influences family members' decisions about the permeability of a privacy boundary is the perceived risk involved in revealing the information. Generally, stating relatively banal self-disclosures such as "I am enjoying my breakfast" (Stiles, 1995, p. 74) is considered low risk, which minimizes the likelihood that an individual would create an impermeable boundary around the information. Thus, most family members would be willing to talk about this information. In contrast, disclosing that one had an incestuous relationship generally would be viewed as high risk (Norton, Feldman, & Tafoya, 1974); therefore, family members who had participated in incestuous relationships likely would create a relatively impermeable boundary around that information.

There are a number of ways for family members to make privacy boundaries more or less permeable. For example, family members can limit the degree of accessibility to private information by keeping a secret, which involves intentionally concealing the information from others (Bok, 1983). The effort involved in restricting access to secrets indicates that secrets are a form of private information that is viewed as particularly risky to reveal (Petronio, 2002).[4] Another way family members decrease the permeability of privacy boundaries is avoiding topics (Afifi & Burgoon, 1998; Afifi & Guerrero, 1998; Guerrero & Afifi, 1995a). Finally, family members can increase the permeability of a privacy boundary by granting greater access to private information across personal and collective boundaries (Waterman, 1979).[5]

Co-ownership. Although disclosing, avoiding topics, and keeping secrets may seem to be actions individuals engage in alone, Petronio (2002; Petronio et al., 2003) argues that collective boundaries can be constructed through the linkages that are created when individuals divulge personal private information to others. Once information is shared by an individual, the information is said to be co-owned because the individual can no longer unilaterally control how the information is (or is not) disseminated further. Co-owners of private information must collectively negotiate decisions about potential future revelations. With families, there are a number of possible collective privacy boundaries, including ones involving dyads, larger groups, or even the whole family.

---

[4]Several scholars (e.g., Bellman, 1981; Imber-Black, 1998; Kelly, 2002; Szajnberg, 1988) have attempted to distinguish between privacy and secrecy. One suggested distinction is that secrecy involves keeping information from people who have a legitimate claim to the information (e.g., the information affects them directly), whereas privacy involves information that the others have no right to know (Bellman, 1981; Kelly, 2002). Although this distinction may be useful in some contexts, it does not seem applicable to many instances that are commonly labeled family secrets. Karpel (1980), for example, notes that a whole family may pledge to keep a daughter's premarital pregnancy a secret from all outsiders. Although it is difficult to argue that this information directly affects the outsiders, family members often consider such information to be secret (Vangelisti, 1994; Vangelisti & Caughlin, 1997). Our view is consistent with that of Bok (1983), who views secrecy as the special case of privacy in which information is intentionally concealed.

[5]Although disclosing private information typically is a means of creating a relatively permeable boundary (and keeping secrets or avoiding topics are typically means of creating relatively impermeable boundaries), it is important to recognize that such associations are not absolute. As Cooper (1994) pointed out in her study of a Soviet spy, disclosing private information about oneself can be done selectively to create a false impression, even if the disclosures are true. For example, one can create the impression of being an open person by disclosing about one's attitudes or personal life. In the case of the Soviet spy, the openness about some issues functioned to prevent other individuals from questioning whether the spy might be hiding something; thus, disclosing information actually helped the spy create a very impermeable boundary with respect to some private information.

The extant literature contains numerous examples of how ownership or co-ownership of information is associated with various privacy boundaries within or around families. For example, when children reach adolescence, they often decrease the extent to which they share private information with their parent or parents (Guerrero & Afifi, 1995b; Noller, 1995; Petronio, 1994; Rothenberg, 1995), reflecting an interior boundary between parent and child. Also, siblings often cooperate to keep secrets from their parents (Caughlin et al., 2000; Grolnick, 1983), creating a collective privacy boundary around the siblings. Individuals in blended families frequently co-own information with other members of their original family, keeping the same information from stepfamily members (Banker & Gaertner, 1998; Caughlin et al., 2000; Peek, Bell, Waldren, & Sorell, 1988). Most families keep at least one secret that all family members co-own, which forms a privacy boundary around those members (Karpel, 1980; Morr, 2002; Petronio, 2002; Vangelisti, 1994; Vangelisti & Caughlin, 1997). Family members can also co-own private information with somebody outside the family and keep it from others in their family; for example, Tardy, Hosman, and Bradac (1981) reported that college students had more frequent and intimate disclosure with friends than with parents. If such information pertains to the family, it becomes a family privacy issue, as in cases in which a family member confides feelings about other family members with a therapist but not with other family members (Brendel & Nelson, 1999; Grolnick, 1983).

Additionally, privacy boundaries within a family must be negotiated, and coordination is difficult in many instances. CPM theory refers to such cases as boundary turbulence (Petronio, 2000a, 2002). There are many possible causes of boundary turbulence. For example, one family member may attempt to create greater linkages with another, as in the case of parents who are perceived as invading their child's privacy (Petronio, 1994) or in a case when one family member's standard for the ideal amount of disclosure differs from that of another family member (Caughlin, 2003). In addition, confidants sometimes may wish that they were not linked to certain boundaries (i.e., that they did not know private information pertaining to another family member). Regardless of the specific cause of boundary turbulence, its occurrence likely will stimulate attempts by family members to negotiate a more successfully coordinated boundary. However, even if such attempts are successful, they are not permanent. That is, there are various times when privacy boundaries need to be renegotiated.

DEVELOPING RULES TO COORDINATE FAMILY PRIVACY BOUNDARIES

Numerous rules are used to manage privacy boundaries on both personal and collective levels (Petronio, 2002). Although there probably are an infinite number of specific rules regarding the management of privacy boundaries, Petronio (2002) argues that the rules are developed based on five criteria: culture, gender, motivations, context, and perceived risk–benefit ratio. These criteria interact to shape specific decisions about whether to reveal private information, which confidant(s) should receive the information, when the information should be divulged, and how it should be framed to manage an impression. For example, Petronio, Reeder, Hecht, and Mon't Ros-Mendoza (1996) suggested that even if abused children have decided that the potential benefits of disclosing outweigh the risks, they are still careful to pick a particular set of circumstances and a particular target before disclosing. Much of the research on privacy in families has examined factors that influence family members' decisions to conceal or reveal private information. Such research allows one to infer individuals' rules for protecting privacy and rules for revealing private information.

Privacy Protection Rules for Family Members

Why do family members sometimes make rules leading them to heighten privacy by keeping secrets or avoiding topics? As suggested previously, culture, gender, and motivations are among the important factors, and these are examined in more detail in the following.

Culture. Cultures differ in terms of the information they consider private and in the extent to which individuals are socialized to protect private information (Spiro, 1971). Parents teach their children privacy rules such as what sorts of affectional expressions are appropriate in public (Margolis, 1966) and the types of information that should only be shared within the family (Avery, 1982). Moreover, a given culture changes over time with respect to family privacy issues. Families in the United States now keep much more information private from the larger community than did families in Colonial America (Gadlin, 1974; Nock, 1998).

There have also been great changes in North American culture with respect to rules about privacy within families. For example, whereas adoption frequently was kept secret from children in the past, most adopted children today are told that are adopted. In fact, 90% of a Canadian sample believed that children should be told if they were adopted (Miall, 1998). Moreover, clinicians recommend and report increased disclosure of information such as the background of the child (Hartman, 1993; Imber-Black, 1998).

Gender. Privacy protection rules in families also are influenced by gender and sex. Certain types of private information, such as abortion or premarital pregnancy, can pertain directly to women but not to men. Other information, like instances of severe and repeated spousal battering, are typically perpetrated by husbands on wives (Johnson, 1995; Johnson & Ferraro, 2000; Kaufman, 1993). Of course, family members of both sexes may co-own such information, but their reasons for doing so will likely be very different based on their experiences with the information. In addition, even when information could pertain to either men or women, privacy rules often are gendered. For instance, women historically have been encouraged to avoid discussing issues related to sexuality both inside and outside their family (Laird, 1993). Although such strictures on women's discussion of sexuality have loosened since the 1960s, they are still more stringent than those applied to men (Laird, 1993).

Individuals also have privacy rules regarding the gender of people from whom they keep information. As noted previously, children tend to share more private information with their mothers than with their fathers (e.g., Denholm-Carey & Chabassol, 1987). Similarly, adolescents and young adults avoid topics more with fathers than they do with mothers (Golish & Caughlin, 2002; Guerrero & Afifi, 1995b).

Despite the clear evidence that gender influences privacy protection rules in a variety of ways, it is important to recognize that there are also similarities between men and women with respect to privacy boundaries. Although not pertaining directly to families, Rosenfeld's (1979) study of 360 undergraduate students suggested that men and women frequently have similar motivations for avoiding disclosure. For instance, both men and women often reported keeping information private to avoid projecting an unwanted image of themselves. Of course, even this similarity between men and women may be gendered because men and women often wish to project different images.

Motivations. The extant literature suggests that individuals have many motivations for protecting privacy boundaries in families. Vangelisti (1994; Vangelisti & Caughlin, 1997) conducted a series of studies in which undergraduate students were asked to report why they kept secrets from other members of their family and from outsiders. Vangelisti labeled the family members' responses "functions," but these functions can also be thought of as motivations for keeping secrets. These motivations centered around six general categories. The first was *bonding*, which involves keeping a secret because it promotes cohesiveness and identification among the family members who keep the secret. That is, co-owning a secret can make family members feel they have a special bond because the ownership of the secret marks who belongs and who does not belong to the group (Goffman, 1959; Petronio, Ellemers, Giles, & Gallois, 1998).

Family members also keep secrets to avoid negative *evaluation* (Vangelisti, 1994). In many instances, a family member may see the secret as a source of shame that others would view negatively (Mason, 1993). Even when such feelings are completely unjustified, family members may believe that they will be blamed or rejected by others if they were to reveal the secret. Concerns about negative evaluations are common among sexual abuse victims (see Paine & Hansen, 2002, for a review) and among gay and lesbian sons and daughters contemplating coming out to their parents (Ben-Ari, 1995).

Family members may also keep secrets for *maintenance* reasons (Vangelisti, 1994). This involves preventing disruptions to the family closeness and preventing stress to family members. Sometimes a family member chooses not to disclose private information so that another family member will not worry (Brown-Smith, 1998; Papp, 1993). For example, parents with HIV may not disclose this to a child who is thought to be too young to understand or too likely to suffer from excessive worrying (Schrimshaw & Siegel, 2002).

Some individuals also report keeping family secrets to maintain *privacy*; that is, they believe the information is not relevant to others (Vangelisti, 1994). Another reason for keeping secrets is *defense*. People sometimes people keep secrets because they fear others would use the information against them in some way. The last reason for keeping secrets Vangelisti reported was labeled *communication*; for example, some people kept secrets because they believed those involved would not have the knowledge or skill to talk about the information.

A related set of motivations for protecting privacy boundaries is implied by Afifi and Guerrero's (2000; Guerrero & Afifi, 1995a, 1995b) research on the reasons why family members avoid topics. In summarizing their work on topic avoidance, Afifi and Guerrero (2000) argued that the reasons for topic avoidance center around (a) relationship-based motivations (e.g., protecting close bonds, preventing relational harm, and preventing conflicts), (b) individual-based motivations (e.g., managing an impression, avoiding embarrassment, maintaining personal privacy, and being social appropriate), and (c) information-based motivations (e.g., thinking the other person would be unresponsive or incapable of providing useful support).

Afifi and Guerrero's (2000) taxonomy is a useful way to classify motivations for privacy protection rules. However, in some cases it may be important to make distinctions within Afifi and Guerrero's three classes of motivations. In fact, Caughlin and Golish (2002b) found that college students and their parents often make such distinctions. For example, a confirmatory factor analysis suggested that the general category of relationship-based motivations contained at least two empirically distinct reasons for avoiding. The first was *relationship protection,* or avoiding a topic because it could undermine the relationship (Baxter & Wilmot, 1985), and the second was *preventing conflict,* which may help foster more satisfying relationships under some conditions but may undermine the relationship in other cases (Roloff & Ifert, 2000).

Privacy Access Rules for Family Members

Culture. Although privacy access rules are distinct from privacy protection rules, they are based on similar criteria (Petronio, 2002; Petronio et al., 1996). For instance, culture influences individuals' rules for revealing information. Americans tend to value open disclosure in intimate relationships (Bochner, 1982; Derlega, Metts, Petronio, & Margulis, 1993; Parks, 1982). This premium placed on openness certainly influences decisions about revealing information, but it does not necessarily translate into frequent disclosures. People sometimes may perceive that they are quite open, even if they do not disclose much in any objective sense (Bochner, 1982; Dindia, 1994).

Gender. Privacy access rules are also influenced by gender. There is a small, but statistically significant, tendency for women to disclose more to their spouse and to their parents than do men (Dindia & Allen, 1992), suggesting slightly different rules for revelation depending on gender. Although even small gender differences are important, gender is only one of a number of factors influencing privacy revelation processes. Thus, gender is probably salient for some disclosure decisions but not others. Serovich and Greene (1993), for instance, found that married women were more likely than married men to think it is appropriate to disclose HIV testing information to members of their nuclear and extended families; however, Serovich and Greene found no gender differences regarding disclosures to nuclear and extended families among dating individuals. Moreover, although female family members generally may disclose somewhat more than do male family members, there is evidence that men's and women's motivations for disclosing (when they do disclose) are similar. In one study of 189 married couples, both husbands and wives cited the same four reasons as the most common motivations for disclosing to each other: unburdening—catharsis, increasing spouse's understanding, seeking solutions or advice, and valuing discussion of experiences and problems (Burke, Weir, & Harrison, 1976).

Motivations. In addition to research on husbands' and wives' motivations for disclosure (Burke et al., 1976), the extant literature suggests a number of motivations for revealing private information in families. Vangelisti, Caughlin, and Timmerman (2001) identified nine criteria that individuals commonly use when deciding whether to reveal a secret that their family had previously kept from outsiders. Consistent with the CPM notion that individuals engage in a complex mental calculus when determining whether to reveal private information, the nine criteria interacted in theoretically interesting ways to predict whether an individual would reveal a secret. For example, one criterion was *relational security* (i.e., feelings of closeness and trust with the potential confidant). Although scholars have long recognized that the tendency to reveal secrets is associated with emotional closeness (e.g., Margolis, 1974), relational security by itself was not a good indicator that a person would reveal a secret. Instead, relational security seemed to be a minimum precursor before considering other criteria for whether the person should be told the secret.

Another interesting criterion reported by Vangelisti et al. (2001) was *important reason*. Generally, individuals were likely to reveal a family secret if they thought somebody had an important reason to know the information (e.g., that person was having a crisis that could be alleviated by knowing the information). This criterion seemed to supercede other criteria in that individuals reported that they would be likely to tell a family secret if they had an important reason—even if they would not normally tell based on other criteria (e.g., they did not feel particularly close to the other person). Again, such findings support the CPM theory claim that decision rules regarding revealing private information can be quite complex. Even when generalizations can be made (e.g., family members have a general rule about relational security), such generalizations are likely contingent on other criteria.

In addition to the criteria for revealing secrets already mentioned, the extant literature contains a number of other criteria that influence family members' decisions regarding revealing private information. For example, family members sometimes may feel an urgent need to talk to somebody about private information (Vangelisti et al., 2001). According to Stiles' (1987; Stiles, Shuster, & Harrigan, 1992) fever model, individuals' need to talk with someone can be so great that they experience psychological distress. To relieve this burden, they may feel compelled to disclose. This fever model is consistent with a number of findings; for instance, Kimberly, Serovich, and Greene (1995) found that desire for catharsis was a primary motivation for women with HIV to disclose their status.

Decisions to reveal private information also are influenced by beliefs about whether the confidant will still approve of and accept the family member if the private information is revealed (Vangelisti et al., 2001). For instance, gay sons and lesbian daughters are more likely to come out to a parent if they believe the parent will be accepting rather than rejecting (Ben-Ari, 1995). Along similar lines, some family members wait for implicit or explicit permission before revealing private information. Permission can involve tacit permission from the confidant that revealing the information is acceptable (Petronio et al., 1996), or it can involve wanting to receive consent from other family members before revealing collectively owned private information to somebody outside the family (Vangelisti et al., 2001).

From a CPM perspective, permission is an example of how decisions to reveal private information often are complicated by information being co-owned (e.g., by a whole family) rather than owned by a single family member. In some cases, the mutual responsibility implied by co-ownership is so salient that individual family members report that they would not reveal certain private information unless the potential confidant became a member of the family (Vangelisti et al., 2001). This suggests that an exterior privacy boundary around their family can be very salient to some individuals; for example, some people with a stigmatized disease only disclose this information to others in their family (Greene, 2000; Greene & Serovich, 1996).

In addition, family members often are motivated to use the revelation of private information as a means of controlling their social identity (Derlega & Grzelak, 1979). That is, individuals are selective about which information to disclose and how to present it when they do so. Using disclosure like this reflects the development of rules motivated by impression management goals (Jones & Pittman, 1982; Petronio, 2002).

Context.   As noted previously, contextual factors are also important to family members' privacy access rules. For example, if a family member believes that another person will inevitably find out about some private information, that family member may reveal the information regardless of other factors (Vangelisti et al., 2001). Indeed, people with a secret tend to reveal it when they think the other person can guess the secret without being told (Vrij, Nunkoosing, Paterson, Oosterwegel, & Soukara, 2002).

In addition, even when family members are relatively certain that they want to reveal private information, they often carefully select a particular context before divulging private information (Derlega & Chaiken, 1977; Petronio, 2002). Sometimes, individuals will wait for a chance to have a reciprocal intimate exchange with a potential confidant, or they will wait until the conversational topic is appropriate for divulging the private information (Berg & Archer, 1982; Dindia, 1982; Vangelisti et al., 2001). In other instances, individuals will seek circumstances that are otherwise mundane; for example, Petronio et al. (1996) found that some abused children seek to reveal this crime while doing common activities (e.g., watching television or washing the dishes).

Summary.   Given the varied factors that influence privacy protection and privacy access rules, individuals' decisions about revealing private information can be complex. As family therapists (e.g., Imber-Black, 1993) point out, revealing some private information creates the potential for growth or healing, but revealing private information can also have serious risks. Consequently, in instances such as a woman who decides to reveal that her husband abuses her, "disclosure is always ambivalent" (Dieckmann, 2000, p. 279). Moreover, decisions about revealing private information are complicated by uncertainty. Individuals may be unsure of what the various risks and benefits are, or they may be unsure of how likely the potential rewarding or harmful outcomes are. Alternatively, individuals may be certain that some risk (or benefit) would occur, but their certainty does not mean that it actually would occur (see Brashers, 2001).

CONSEQUENCES OF CHANGES IN PERMEABILITY FOR FAMILY PRIVACY BOUNDARIES

Although it will never be possible to accurately forecast all the ramifications of disclosing private information pertaining to families, it is important to examine what actually occurs when such information is concealed or revealed. In addition to a theoretical importance, an understanding of the consequences of revealing and concealing may assist family members in making more informed decisions regarding how they coordinate the permeability of family privacy boundaries.

Consequences of Families Concealing Private Information

A number of outcomes can occur when family members are able to successfully coordinate privacy rules so that they conceal information within interior and exterior privacy boundaries. Such coordination means that the family has been able to synchronize the development of privacy rules and the coordinated implementation of the rules. This synchronization may indicate that a family is functioning well; however, in some instances coordination can also have negative consequences for the family and its members. Thus, successfully coordinating the concealment of information can have both positive and negative implications simultaneously. Three consequences for concealing private information that are mentioned frequently in the family privacy literature are bonding, creating and maintaining boundaries, and experiencing stress when keeping secrets.

Bonding. Perhaps the most often cited potential benefit of concealing private information is the bonding that can occur among those who are linked within a collective privacy boundary. Individuals who share private information can feel marked as insiders, leading to a sense of loyalty and cohesiveness (Bok, 1983; Rigney, 1979). Being linked into a collective privacy boundary can also lead to increased attraction and liking. For instance, Wegner, Lane, and Dimitri (1994) conducted a study that demonstrated an association between co-owning private information and attraction. Specifically, Wegner et al. gave mixed-sex dyads one of three sets of instructions: (a) keep their feet in contact during a card game and not tell the other dyad in the room, (b) make contact and tell the other dyad about it, and (c) make no contact. Individuals who played "footsie" and kept it a secret reported being more attracted to their partner than did those who told the others about the contact and those who made no contact.

Sharing a bond can also lead individual family members to keep the group's secrets. Vangelisti and Caughlin (1997) found that individuals who were relatively satisfied with their family were comparatively unlikely to reveal a family secret to an outsider. Although such findings are consistent with the notion that keeping private information can be associated with bonding, there is a potential risk of such bonding. Sometimes, family members feel so connected and loyal that they will not reveal a family secret, despite high personal costs, such as when a child develops symptoms of a psychotic disorder rather than revealing a family secret (Saffer, Sansone, & Gentry, 1979).

Creating and Maintaining Boundaries. In addition to bonding with those who share privacy linkages, privacy boundaries can help families with the general task of creating and maintaining functional family boundaries. There is a long history within the family therapy literature emphasizing the need for boundaries to separate certain family subsystems (e.g., Minuchin, 1974). For example, it is often considered problematic for families to have boundaries that rigidly cut across generations, as in cases when a boundary around a parent and a child excludes another parent (Minuchin, 1974; Papp, 1993). Instead, it generally is considered healthier for boundaries to be relatively impermeable between generations and for the strongest alliances to exist within generations (Grolnick, 1983; Papp, 1993; Roman & Blackburn, 1979).

Although the notion of functional family boundaries has been useful in therapeutic settings, Klein and White (1996) argue that the concept of boundaries, in general, is too broad and imprecisely defined for research purposes. CPM theory offers a more concrete conceptualization of one important means of establishing boundaries; in particular, the coordination of private information is one way to establish appropriate boundaries within families (Caughlin et al., 2000; Petronio et al., 2003). When a less permeable boundary is needed, for example, family members can respond by creating and maintaining an interior privacy cell that includes the appropriate family members.

Such internal privacy boundaries can be beneficial at various levels within the family. At the individual level, Welter-Enderlin (1993) suggested that some married couples believe so strongly in the value of openness that they believe they have no right to keep some private information from their partner. This can lead to an overemphasis on the connections between the individuals, a loss of a sense of self, and even a backlash such as engaging in unsanctioned behaviors like a clandestine extramarital affair (Welter-Enderlin, 1993). Along similar lines, Adams (1993) described the family of an adolescent who was experiencing depression, problems in school, and excessive conflict with his adoptive stepfather. After a series of inquiries, the therapist discovered that the teen reported having absolutely no secrets that he kept from his parents. After encouraging the adolescent to keep some innocuous secrets, his problematic depression and behaviors improved (Adams, 1993).

Beyond the individual level, privacy regulation can aid families in maintaining functional collective boundaries such as the aforementioned boundaries between generations. Failure to protect privacy between generations can influence family members negatively; for example, daughters sometimes become anorexic if a parent engages in overly zealous information seeking regarding the daughter (Dalzell, 2000). Another potentially functional collective privacy boundary occurs in blended families when members of one's original family keep some private information from new stepfamily members. Given that many children and adolescents brought into blended families feel pressured to immediately form close bonds (Bray & Kelly, 1999; Visher & Visher, 1993), keeping some information from stepfamily members may be a normal and even functional reaction to entering a new family (Caughlin et al., 2000).

Although managing appropriate privacy boundaries is important in families, CPM theory suggests that privacy boundaries can become too impermeable (Petronio, 2002). For example, if family members are very successful at negotiating extremely restrictive privacy boundaries around the family, the relatively impermeable boundary that results may have negative consequences for the family or its members. Indeed, family members' perceptions of how many secrets their family keeps are inversely associated with their family satisfaction (Vangelisti & Caughlin, 1997). Similarly, college students' family satisfaction is inversely associated with the extent to which they avoid topics with their parents, and their parents' satisfaction is inversely associated with the extent to which they perceive their child avoids topics (Caughlin & Golish, 2002a).

Moreover, family therapists suggest that overly impermeable privacy boundaries can affect family members who do not even know about the private information. Selvini (1997), for example, reported "hundreds of families" (p. 318) in which a family member who is not told a family secret develops problematic symptoms like depression, drug use, or suicide attempts. Selvini described a number of reasons why this may occur, including the possibility that those who do not know a family secret can become confused when those who do know exhibit anxiety associated with the secret yet deny the existence of anything secret.

Experiencing Stress From Keeping Secrets. There are a number of reasons why keeping a secret can cause tension or anxiety that could be noticed by family members who do not know the secret. Parents who decide to keep an extramarital affair secret to protect the children, for example, would likely exhibit residual tension, even after the affair had ended and the couple had decided to stay together. Secrets also can harm those who keep them. Keeping secrets is associated with individuals' level of tension, loneliness, behavioral impulsiveness, and even stress-related physical health problems (Kelly, 2002).

Of course, it is difficult to untangle the causal links between such problems and keeping secrets because it is often not clear whether the negative outcomes are due to keeping the secret or to the negative impact of the secret itself. This is especially true of research on family secrets because researchers cannot experimentally manipulate many of the types of information that family members keep secret. Nevertheless, some laboratory studies using relatively innocuous manipulations of secret information suggest that the mere act of keeping a secret (regardless of the content of the secret) can cause stress and anxiety. For example, Lane and Wegner (1995; Wegner & Lane, 1995) conducted a series of studies in support of their preoccupation model of secrecy. This model suggests that trying to keep a secret typically involves a cognitive cycle in which (a) the individual attempts to suppress thoughts about the secret, (b) the attempts to suppress thoughts actually lead to more thoughts about the secret, and (c) these intrusive thoughts lead to renewed cognitive efforts to suppress the secret (Wegner & Lane, 1995).

Although much of the research on the preoccupation model of secrecy involves types of information that may not readily generalize to privacy in families, there is evidence that preoccupation with secrets can be costly in families. Major and Gramzow (1999) conducted a study of 442 women who had abortions. Shortly before the abortion and again 2 years later, the women provided information about whether they kept the abortion secret from family and friends, whether they attempted to suppress thoughts about the abortion, and whether they experienced intrusive thoughts. Consistent with Lane and Wegners's (1995) preoccupation model, secrecy predicted attempted thought suppression, which in turn predicted intrusive thoughts (Major & Gramzow, 1999). Both thought suppression and intrusive thoughts were associated positively with psychological distress.

Summary. As this discussion illustrates, concealing private information in families has a number of possible positive and negative outcomes. The linkages created when family members share a secret can help those family members form a more cohesive and emotionally bonded unit. This benefit can be offset, however, if the cohesiveness becomes so strong that a family member will not reveal a dangerous secret because of loyalty to the family. The management of private information also can aid the family in constructing useful boundaries between generations, or it can create boundaries that are so impermeable that family members are adversely affected. Keeping a secret can also lead an individual to experience intrusive thoughts and psychological distress.

Although the aforementioned list of potential consequences may make it seem like individuals ought to be able to balance the relative risks and costs when deciding whether they should conceal information, the impact of these risks and costs likely depend on numerous factors such as culture, gender, motivations, and context. For example, although perceiving other family members as avoiding topics is generally associated with dissatisfaction, Caughlin and Golish (2002b) found that this association is moderated by perceived motivations (e.g., thinking the other person is avoiding to protect the relationship). Also, deciding whether to conceal private information in families is often complicated by the interdependence of family members. Indeed, individual family members may need to weigh their own risks and benefits with those of other family members. For example, even if a family member incurs a psychological cost from concealing private information (Lane & Wegner, 1995), that cost might be offset if concealing the information enhances family relationships by preventing conflict (Roloff & Ifert, 2000).

Consequences of Families Revealing Private Information

Kelly and McKillop (1996) suggested that one benefit of revealing personal information is that one can avoid the problems associated with keeping information private. That is, some of the consequences of revealing private information can be inferred by the consequences of concealing private information. For example, revealing a secret may alleviate the problems associated with intrusive thoughts about secret information (Lane & Wegner, 1995). However, the revelation of private information also has consequences that are not easily inferred by research examining the effects of concealing private information. Such consequences are discussed in the following.

Self-Disclosure and Marital Satisfaction.   Numerous studies have demonstrated a connection between revealing private information and liking (see Collins & Miller, 1994, for a review). Within families, a primary research issue has been whether the association between spouses' self-disclosure and their marital satisfaction is linear and positive or curvilinear. Although there have been theoretical arguments for a curvilinear association (Gilbert, 1976), empirical findings seem to support a linear association (Burke et al., 1976; Jorgensen & Gaudy, 1980).

This general conclusion requires at least one caveat: The content of the self-disclosure matters (Derlega, Metts, Petronio, & Margulis, 1993).[6] In particular, self-disclosures involving negative information about the partner probably diminish rather than increase marital satisfaction. Schumm, Barnes, Bollman, Jurich, and Bugaighis (1986) reported an interaction between the amount of self-disclosure and whether the self-disclosure showed positive or negative regard for the partner. Self-disclosures that conveyed positive feelings toward the spouse were associated with higher satisfaction, but greater negative self-disclosures did not seem to contribute to marital satisfaction. The least satisfying combination was a small amount of self-disclosure coupled with "low-quality" disclosure (i.e., negative disclosures directed toward the partner).

It is also important to note that not all disclosures with negative affect are inversely associated with marital satisfaction. Shimanoff's (1987) study of compliance gaining messages with various types of emotional disclosures suggested that disclosing negative emotions sometimes can enhance marital relationships. Specifically, when individuals' marital partner disclosed negative emotional information about an absent other (e.g., hostile feelings toward a third party), the partner was viewed more favorably than when the partner made

---

[6]Derlega et al. (1993) provide a more extensive discussion of caveats to the general tendency for self-disclosure to enhance liking.

no emotional disclosures or made negative emotional disclosures about his or her spouse. Shimanoff's work suggests that, much like sharing a secret, revealing negative emotions about a third party can be seen as a privacy linkage, enhancing the sense of solidarity or liking in a relationship.

Revealing Private Information and Family Members' Well-Being.

There is abundant evidence that disclosing about traumatic experiences can have both mental and physical health benefits (for reviews, see Kelly, 2002; Smyth & Pennebaker, 2001). Although it may seem like this benefit of revealing private information provides a strong reason for such revelations, it is important to recognize that many of the benefits of revealing can also be obtained by writing about the same events (Pennebaker, 1993, 1997). For example, Pennebaker and Beall (1986) found that individuals who spent four sessions writing about their thoughts and feeling concerning a traumatic experience had significantly fewer visits to medical care providers over the subsequent 6 months than did individuals who wrote about a more mundane topic. Writing about such experiences tends to be particularly helpful if the writing is directed toward increasing the individuals' understanding of the event (Kelly & Carter, 2001; Kelly, Klusas, von Weiss, & Kenny, 2001; Pennebaker, 1993). Given that writing about traumatic experiences can be an effective way to deal with such information, the relative benefits of revealing this information to another person can be diminished.

It is also important to recognize that there are probably limits to the effectiveness of disclosing about traumatic events. In two longitudinal studies of individuals whose spouses had recently died, Stroebe, Stroebe, Schut, Zech, and van den Bout (2002) found no evidence that emotional disclosures or writing about the event helped spouses recover from bereavement. Stroebe et al. suggested that most individuals' well-being improves with time, and heightened disclosures or a writing procedure may only be needed if the bereavement is particularly problematic.

Moreover, disclosing about traumatic events can risk family members' well-being. Even revelations that eventually lead to greater mental health can be disturbing in the short term (Frawley, 1990). In addition, disclosures about traumatic events can negatively influence the confidant's emotions (Pennebaker, 1995, 1997; Perrine, 1993), and potential confidants can be unsupportive (Petrie, Booth, & Davison, 1995). In cases in which the potential confidant is another family member, any benefit of revealing might need to be balanced against the maintenance needs of the family, including the desire to prevent undue stress for family members (Papp, 1993; Vangelisti, 1994).

Considering the effects on the confidants is also important when the confidant is not a family member. For example, Pennebaker (1997) described an instance in which a married couple's grief over the death of their child was compounded by the loss of most of their social network because others found talking about the traumatic event to be discomforting. The possibility of being abandoned by individuals in one's social network can pose a particularly challenging dilemma for those who wish to disclose, because some benefits of revealing private information may be accrued best by confiding to somebody outside the family. Jahn (1995), for example, found that families who frequently discuss their family secrets within the family are more emotionally distressed than families who discuss secrets less. This suggests that family members can share a preoccupation with private information

(Lane & Wegner, 1995; Wegner & Lane, 1995), leading the discussions among members to foster stress rather than provide the catharsis and insights that might be achieved if the information were revealed to outsiders.

Revealing Private Information and Social Support. Despite the risk that family members might not be supportive when another family member divulges private information, disclosing private information is a primary way to solicit social support from family members (Derlega et al., 1993). Parents living with AIDS, for example, may find it necessary to discuss their symptoms and prognosis with extended family members to secure instrumental assistance in caring for their children (Gewirtz & Gossart-Walker, 2000). Also, disclosing one's HIV status to members of one's family of origin is positively associated with perceptions of receiving social support from the family (Kadushin, 2000).

Reactions to Revealing Private Information to Family Members. As noted earlier, family members considering whether they should reveal private information attempt to anticipate the reactions of potential confidants; for example, individuals may keep secrets from other family members to avoid negative evaluation (Vangelisti, 1994). However, such anticipated responses are not necessarily indicative of family members' actual responses to revelations of private information. One limitation in the extant literature is that most of the research has focused on the perceptions of individuals who reveal information (Petronio, 2000b); thus, not enough is known about actual reactions of family members when they are told another family member's private information.

Despite this limitation, there is evidence that reactions by family members can be very complex. Consider, for example, Serovich, Kimberly, and Greene's (1998) study of HIV-positive women who disclosed their health status to family members. The women in this study reported 31 different types of reactions, and many family members' reactions were multifaceted. One mother, for example, was described as having 5 distinct reactions immediately after the initial disclosure, including (a) shock, (b) intellectual questions about how her daughter acquired the virus, (c) comforting, (d) questioning why the daughter did not trust her sooner with the information, and (e) hope that they would find a cure.

Reactions by family members are also complicated by the fact that families often have multiple potential confidants. Obviously, different individuals within a family can have different reactions. In addition, the relationships among the various family members—even those to whom the information does not directly apply—likely will influence reactions to the disclosure of private information. Serovich et al. (1998) reported that when individuals are first told about a family member's HIV-positive status, they sometimes question the closeness of the relationship because they had not been told sooner. Such reactions would certainly be exacerbated if the family member found out that all the other family members had been told much sooner. Conversely, the special position of being the first family member told some private information could lead to a more sympathetic response than would have otherwise occurred.

Along similar lines, there is evidence that family members' reactions depend on whether they are told private information separately or in larger groups. Ben-Ari (1995) found that mothers whose gay son or lesbian daughter "came out" to them without other family members present were more accepting than were mothers who were told with the father present. In contrast, fathers reacted more favorably when they were told in the presence of the mother than when they were alone with the son or daughter. Although it is not entirely clear why fathers prefer to be told in the presence of the mother (e.g., perhaps they perceive being told individually as an indication that others were told first, or perhaps the mother's presences provides supports for the father), Ben-Ari's findings clearly demonstrate that the connections among various potential confidants within families influence reactions to learning about private information.

FUTURE DIRECTIONS IN FAMILY PRIVACY RESEARCH

The review in this chapter suggests several additional research foci. We will overview four that are particularly important, including the need for greater attention to (a) managing multiple privacy boundaries within families, (b) the recipients of private disclosures about families, (c) the impact of new technologies on family privacy, and (d) privacy issues surrounding family members' health.

Managing Multiple Privacy Boundaries Within Families

CPM theory emphasizes the importance of examining how family members coordinate with each other to maintain collective privacy boundaries. As co-owners of jointly held information, family members must negotiate rules for regulating access to their private information. However, because most of the research on families has focused primarily on individual family members, our knowledge about how families, as a whole, deal with privacy is limited. Addressing this significant gap in our understanding involves numerous interrelated questions. For example, when a family forms an exterior privacy boundary around private information, how do all the family members know that the information is supposed to be protected?

As CPM theory argues, private information is marked as such by those who own it. Presumably, there are many specific means for negotiating rules regulating when, how, and if private information is reveal or concealed. Some families may reach an agreement about protecting private information through easy and implicit negotiations that are not even noticed. The rules for boundary management in these cases likely are derived from family members' previous experiences with similar situations or with similar types of private information. In other cases, members must explicitly negotiate privacy rules, especially in situations where the privacy needs are new or different than those families have experienced before. Additionally, those family members wanting to protect private information from outsiders may need to make threats of sanctions against members who do not readily comply with the desire to conceal.

One factor that influences families' negotiations of collective privacy boundaries is the extent to which they concretize privacy rules in the form of privacy orientations (Petronio, 2002). Privacy orientations, which represent family members' beliefs and values about what information is (and should be) co-owned by the entire family, influence families' decisions about how they treat information that they define as private matters for the whole family. Morr (2002) found three types of privacy orientations for the exterior privacy boundary in families. Specifically, families had high, moderate, or low privacy boundary permeability orientations that matched the amount of information accessible to those outside the family.

Even with a relatively unified family privacy orientation, the complexity of families means that the joint negotiation of privacy rules and privacy boundaries may not always happen smoothly. Boundary turbulence erupts when family members are unable to reach agreement about how to handle the information or when someone makes a mistake (Petronio, 2002). For example, family members may fail to understand a larger family agreement that they should not tell their grandmother about Gloria's pregnancy because their grandmother is ill and may find Gloria's situation stressful. When Rob reveals Gloria's pregnancy to his grandmother, he has initiated boundary turbulence because he has not complied with the family rules for keeping grandmother out of the interior family boundary cell of those who know. By telling, Rob may have brought shame to Gloria and embarrassment or stress to his grandmother. As suggested by this example, violating expected rules for privacy management within families can have important practical implications; thus, understanding boundary coordination and turbulence in families is a very useful enterprise.

Considering the Recipient

Along with a greater emphasis on privacy coordination, more research is needed about confidants within families. Currently, we know more about persons revealing or concealing information than we do about recipients of private information (Petronio, 2000b, 2002). This is problematic because one cannot truly understand how privacy boundaries are coordinated by two or more family members without considering the confidant. Family members who function as recipients often are challenged to maintain a relationship with the discloser, even if they are not prepared to cope with the information that is revealed (Petronio et al., 2003). For example, consider a recent study of children whose mothers had HIV or AIDS (Kirshenbaum & Nevid, 2002). This study reported that 57% of the children were told that their mothers had HIV or AIDS and that 64% were given details about their mothers' condition including prognosis of death. At least some of these children probably were not ready to deal with such an important disclosure; however, if their mothers told them, they faired better than if someone else told them. Kirshenbaum and Nevid (2002) also found that children asked to conceal information about their mothers were more likely to have behavior problems than were those who were allowed to talk to others.

Of course, the effect on recipients is not always negative. Indeed, being a recipient may be a positive experience (Petronio, 2002). For example, Dolgin and Berndt (1997) found that college-aged children often reported that their mothers disclosed to seek advice and for emotional reasons. Children perceiving that their mothers are seeking advice, for example, might view the experience as reinforcing their worth and their standing in the family. Consequently, functioning as a confidant for children in these circumstances may have a positive effect on the parent–child relationship.

Considering the confidant underscores the need to recognize that disclosure, privacy, and secrecy involve both a person who reveals or conceals and a potential recipient. This point is particularly evident in families because families are systemic, which implies that each individual's actions can influence the other family members. Methodologically, it is often easiest to examine the way one member treats another at one point in time. However, a more complete picture of family communication would involve focusing on the interplay of family members functioning as a group. Such group-level analyses are particularly important for understanding and investigating boundary coordination and turbulence within families (Petronio et al., 2003). Thus, at a minimum, considering recipients in conjunction with those revealing and concealing is the first step in coming to a more complete understanding of family privacy.

New Technologies and Privacy in Families

A number of new and emerging technologies have the potential to greatly influence privacy issues within families (e.g., Baran & Pannor, 1993; Rothstein, 1997). The new media, genetics, and reproductive technologies are obvious examples of such technologies (Andrews, 1997; Bryant & Bryant, 2001; Robinson & Stewart, 1996).

Family privacy issues surrounding mass media have received enormous scholarly attention (Bryant & Bryant, 2001). Although parents often try to regulate the privacy boundary around the family by monitoring the influence of mass media, it is now generally accepted that media frequently influence the nature of family interaction (Bryant & Bryant, 2001). The information that family members are exposed to through the media often affects role expectations, the content of family conversations, and the context of family interaction (Alexander, 2001).

Less is known, however, about newer media that, in addition to providing information to families, can also be used to gather information about family members. For instance, one cannot assume that viewing information on the Internet is anonymous (Agre & Rotenberg, 1998). Given the ready accessibility of personal information, the question of ownership rights to this information is a looming issue for families. Children using the Internet may reveal information about family income or the household's telephone numbers. These actions may compromise parents' privacy, yet be seen by the children as innocent actions (Branscomb, 1994). Families often have to develop new rules for regulating privacy at a level the whole family wishes to maintain. Computer technology is becoming essential to many families' everyday existence, but it is not immediately clear how families can manage their privacy while still benefiting from the advantages of the technological advances. Through CPM theory, we can understand the manner in which families cope with integrating media technologies into their day-to-day actions.

Another set of new technologies that has enormous implications for family privacy are emerging health technologies (Committee on Maintaining Privacy and Security, 1997; Rothstein, 1997). For instance, the advent of genetic testing has a number of family privacy implications. Generally, individuals assume that their healthcare providers will keep medical information confidential, and, in fact, physicians have legal and ethical obligations to provide some confidentiality to patients (Byers, MacDonald, Severin, & Fishbach, 1999; Hakimian, 2000). This frequently creates a collective privacy boundary around the provider and patient.

Confidentiality obligations are not absolute, however, and sometimes must be weighed against the harm that could be done to another family member if the information is not revealed (Boetzkes, 1999; Deftos, 1998; Hakimian, 2000). When one family member has tested positive for some genetic predisposition for a disease, it might create strong reasons for a health provider to disclose this information to other family members, perhaps even over the original patient's objections (Wai-Ching, 2000). From an ethical standpoint, Deftos (1998) argued that the reasons to divulge such information become more compelling if others would be harmed and if that harm could be prevented by revealing the information early enough. For example, if a brother's test result implied that his sister would likely develop a serious disease, and if knowing about the prognosis would allow the sister to obtain effective preventative treatment, Deftos would argue that it may make sense for a physician to tell the sister about the test results—even if it means violating the confidentiality obligations to the brother. Regardless of whether patients would endorse such logic, the fact that such arguments are being considered by healthcare providers suggests that what was once considered a relatively impermeable privacy boundary around the provider–patient dyad may become more permeable due to certain new technologies.

Even when a physician does not become involved directly, issues surrounding genetic testing have the potential to influence family privacy boundaries. With some conditions, parents may feel guilt about being carriers or may not even understand the nature of the disease (Fanos & Johnson, 1995). Such attitudes and beliefs about genetic diagnoses can lead parents and grandparents to conceal information about diseases, as in the case of grandparents who know Huntington's Disease exists in the family but purposely conceal the information from subsequent generations (Sobel & Cowan, 2000).

Although such intrafamily secrets may seem extreme, it is important to recognize that disclosing such information can entail large risks to family members. Sobel and Cowan (2000), for example, reported an instance in which a husband divorced his wife after he learned of her positive test for the gene causing Huntington's disease. Given such high stakes, hiding the family history of such diseases could be viewed as protecting a family member from the risks involved with testing.

In addition, some family members may not want to know the results of genetic tests on another family member. The results of such tests often have implications for individuals' own health risks (Andrews, 1997), but individuals may not want to know such information because they fear being stigmatized, they worry that the information might be misused by a third party (e.g., an insurance company), or they would rather not feel pressured to be tested themselves because they are anxious about the testing procedure (Decruyenaere, Evers-Kiebooms, & Van den Berghe, 1993). If the family member who was tested desires to reveal the results (e.g., to share the good news or seek social support for bad news), desires by other family members to not know the information could easily create boundary turbulence within families. Given the potential importance of dealing with such issues, examining how families coordinate privacy issues regarding genetic testing promises to be an extremely important avenue for future endeavors.

Along with genetic testing, new technologies have been developed to help people who are unable to become pregnant. Reproductive technologies include a wide spectrum of privacy and disclosure concerns for families (Robinson & Stewart, 1996). For example, some argue that practices of anonymity for donor insemination have led to complex problems for family members (Landau, 1998). The impermeable boundaries around this private information, though perhaps helpful for the parents, make it difficult for the children to contact their biological father. Thus, the children often are not able to obtain needed health information (Daniels & Lewis, 1996).

Boundary cells around various types of reproductive donors, whether they donate eggs, sperm, or gametes (embryos), are developed through linkages based on the need to know. Access to such information often is restricted due to fears that revealing it might discourage donations, may discourage families dealing with infertility from seeking a donor, or may make coping more difficult for those who receive a donation. Consequently, families often try to keep the children born from such procedures outside of the privacy boundary, but physicians often play the role of privacy spanner (Petronio, 2002). Thus, the physicians frequently must help negotiate the level of privacy permeability among the donor, the recipient, other family members, and the offspring (Daniels, 1998).

As this discussion on new technologies illustrates, the complexity of managing privacy boundaries for families promises to increase. This observation underscores the synergistic relationship between new technologies and privacy, particularly when considering the impact on family interactions. Many of the issues for new technological advances center on medical concerns for family members, and the future holds significant changes in the way that families and healthcare professionals interact.

Family Health and Privacy

There are many ways to think about the intersection of families and healthcare. Obviously, as discussed earlier, new technologies influence health and privacy for families. However, there are other circumstances where privacy interacts with family health. For example, there is a growing concern that when patients visit their physicians, they use impression management to regulate disclosure about their health needs (Parrott, Duncan, & Duggan, 2000). Given our aging population, it is becoming more common for older adults to have a family member accompany them on healthcare visits to serve as an advocate and to help them interpret medical diagnoses and instructions for medications. Having another family member present may complicate the impression management goals individuals have when interacting with physicians. Such complications may prove either helpful or problematic. A recent study found that family advocates may contradict the patient or reveal more information than the patient wishes to disclose to a physician (Petronio et al., 2001). The patient and family advocate frequently do not negotiate boundary rules prior to making clinical visits. Consequently, the advocate may enact behavior that violates privacy rules used to convey impressions that the patient wishes to create with the physician.

The boundary turbulence that erupts as a result can cause conflicts for the whole family. For example, consider an adult daughter functioning as an advocate for her father who has severe heart disease. During a clinical visit, the physician asks the father whether he quit smoking. The father says adamantly that he has quit, but the daughter interrupts and states that the father has not stopped smoking and that she is angry with him. The father is upset that his daughter's disclosure has revealed that he lied to the physician. The daughter is upset that the father did not confess his smoking. The physician is caught in a family conflict. Because the father and daughter did not negotiate privacy rules for managing the boundary with the physician, the daughter breached her father's privacy boundary rules, which embarrassed the father and perplexed the physician. The daughter further violated the father's privacy boundary by telling her siblings about the lie.

Family members also might function as caregivers for spouses, partners, or parents with Alzheimer's disease, cancer, or strokes. Doing so is often very stressful, and the healthcare profession is not easily accessible to relieve the burden (Kerr & Smith, 2001). Consequently, to reduce the pressure of coping with these situations, family members often turn to friends outside the family. Although the social support available outside the family may be a good resource, members within the family may not want the experiences revealed outside the family privacy boundary. Some families may have low permeable privacy orientations that limit the options for seeking outside help (Morr, 2002; Petronio, 2002). Such restrictive privacy rules can be problematic because it is helpful, and sometimes even essential, for caregivers to disclose their frustrations, disappointments, and even anger to others (Miller et al., 2001; Pennebaker, 1997). When a family's privacy orientation advocates a relatively impermeable privacy boundary, the caregiver's options for seeking support are limited to other family members. When only family members are available to provide support, it can lead to support fatigue for the family members and may leave few resources available for the caregiver (Miller et al., 2001).

In addition to the more general issues associated with care giving for a family member, recent trends suggest that more adult children are caring for aging parents with dementia (Sherrell, Buckwalter, & Morhardt, 2001). During this process, adult children cope with a reversal of role responsibilities. To effectively care for a parent with dementia, the adult child must ask the parent for private information that once was taboo. Accordingly, privacy rules long established to manage the interior family cell between parent and child must be redesigned to meet the needs of the situation. CPM theory maintains that when the context of the situation changes, privacy rules, at times, do not function effectively to regulate boundaries around certain private information (Petronio, 2002). As is the case for adult children with parents who have dementia, the privacy rules need to be adjusted so that parents, to the best of their ability, disclose previously restricted and protected information (e.g., personal habits, financial issues, and bodily needs). Older adults often are willing to change their privacy rules as a trade off for security (Petronio & Kovach, 1997). Thus, parents with dementia who are cognizant enough to make such a decision are likely to willingly open previously impermeable privacy boundaries to their children.

No discussion of family health and privacy would be complete without turning briefly to two additional issues: privacy issues associated with child sexual abuse and privacy issues associated with a family member having HIV or AIDS. Child sexual abuse is a crime shrouded in secrecy and has an enormous impact on the health and well-being of the family. The privacy issues surrounding this crime are complicated by the fact that most perpetrators are members of the family (Schultz, 2000). Understanding privacy rules that abused children might use is critical in learning how to help children out of a web of secrecy (Petronio et al, 1996).

Although disclosure of the abuse is considered helpful, when the abuse is particularly severe and the perpetrator is a member of the family, the victim is less able to talk about the experience (Arata, 1998). Consequently, the child develops impermeable privacy boundaries around the information and rules that limit accessibility to others. The restricted access to this information assists perpetrators in their desire to keep the abuse secret and contributes to greater psychological distress for the child (Arata, 1998).

Understanding children's attempts to disclose might aid them in opening up the privacy boundary and making a full disclosure. Research suggests that there is a certain logic to privacy rules among children who have been abused (Petronio et al., 1996). For example, children may incrementally disclose, first hinting to see if the confidant takes the revelation seriously and then making a full disclosure if the confidant reacts according to the child's expectations. In this way, the child slowly takes steps giving co-ownership to a confidant, but a level of trustworthiness must be exhibited by the confidant before the child will share control over the information. A positive reaction to these kinds of disclosure patterns by family members helps aid in recovery of the child (Gries et al., 2000).

Managing privacy issues surrounding HIV status is another issue important to families' health that needs further investigation. From all accounts, disclosure of HIV status by a family member has a significant impact on the members, in terms of both relationships and need for social support (e.g., Greene, Derlega, Yep, & Petronio, 2003; Sachperoglou & Bor, 2001). Obviously, there are many issues that families face when one of its members becomes HIV positive. Of the most problematic is the struggle that mothers who are HIV positive have in coming to terms with telling their children (Muphy, Steers, & Dello Stritto, 2001). Revealing HIV status means implicitly requesting that children share in the responsibility for co-owning the information (Petronio, 2002).

Depending on the age of the children, this revelation may seem a burden for them. However, research suggests that even most young children benefit from being included in the privacy boundary around their mother's health status (Murphy et al., 2001). For example, young children whose mother tells them that she is HIV positive are less likely to become aggressive (Murphy et al., 2001), have negative self-esteem (Murphy et al., 2001), or experience depression (Mellins et al., 2002) than are children whose mother has HIV but are not told of the diagnosis. Apparently, when children are not linked into the privacy boundary around HIV status, they may feel afraid and confused by what is happening to their mother. Although telling children about the mother's HIV status implicitly asks them to share in the control over the information, the issue of having some control over what is happening in their family may be one of the ways they are able to cope with the illness.

Although revealing to the children appears helpful to them, the decision to change privacy rules regarding the permeability of boundaries around HIV status often depends on how advanced the disease is and how obvious the physical symptoms are (Armistead, Tannenbaum, Forehand, Morse, & Morse, 2001). As this discussion shows, HIV status is often a family problem requiring that "within-family privacy rules" be altered to accommodate the changes in a family member's health status. More research is needed into the way privacy rules change and how parents who are HIV positive make those decisions.

Throughout this section on family health and privacy, there are several trends that need further exploration. For example, although scholars recognize that there are privacy issues for families coping with the care of an older family member, there are many related concerns that need to be addressed. This is also true for the difficult problems of child sexual abuse and families grappling with members who have HIV or AIDS.

CONCLUSION

We had two main goals for this chapter: selectively reviewing the existing research on privacy in families and suggesting areas for future research. By using CPM theory to frame the chapter, we discussed how family members collectively manage privacy boundaries. Because there are multiple relationships within families, family privacy issues are often complex. For instance, unlike most traditional self-disclosure scholarship, research into family privacy must recognize that much of what is considered private information is co-owned or shared among members within internal family privacy cells. This has numerous implications, including the need for family members to negotiate with each other when creating and maintaining collective rules for coordinating family privacy boundaries. Although we discussed the existing literature on how family members develop privacy rules, we also noted that more work needs to be done before we have an adequate understanding of how such rules are negotiated among family members.

This chapter also summarized a number of consequences for revealing or concealing private information pertaining to families. One theme that ran through this discussion is that consequences are often simultaneously positive and negative. When a family collaborates to keep a secret, for example, that may lead the family members to bond in a satisfying way. That same bonding, however, may make it difficult for a family member to break family privacy rules when it would be better to do so (e.g., if one knows that a child in the family is being abused). In short, the consequences of revealing or concealing private information are typically complex, which makes simple prescriptions about revealing or concealing private information foolhardy.

Finally, based on the existing literature and trends in society, we suggested four corridors for future research on family privacy. From a theoretical standpoint, CPM theory points to a greater need for scholars to examine how family members simultaneously manage multiple privacy boundaries. There is also a need to balance the voluminous research on individuals who reveal or conceal information with more research on the potential confidants of that information. From a practical standpoint, technological innovations and the intersection between healthcare and families provide important and interesting questions for scholars interested in family privacy. In each of these areas, there are many more research questions than there are answers.

REFERENCES

Adams, J. F. (1993). The utilization of family secrets as constructive resources in strategic therapy. *Journal of Family Psychotherapy, 4*, 19–33.

Afifi, W. A., & Burgoon, J. K. (1998). "We never talk about that:" A comparison of cross-sex friendships and dating relationships on uncertainty and topic avoidance. *Personal Relationships, 5*, 255–272.

Afifi, W. A., & Guerrero, L. K. (1998). Some things are better left unsaid II: Topic avoidance in friendships. *Communication Quarterly, 36*, 231–249.

Afifi, W. A., & Guerrero, L. K. (2000). Motivations underlying topic avoidance in close relationships. In S. Petronio (Ed.), *Balancing the secrets of private disclosures* (pp. 165–180). Mahwah, NJ: Lawrence Erlbaum Associates.

Agre, P. E., & Rotenberg, M. (Eds.). (1998). *Technology and privacy: The new landscape*. Cambridge, MA: MIT Press.

Alderman, E., & Kennedy, C. (1995). *The right to privacy*. New York: Knopf.

Alexander, A. (2001). The meaning of television in the American family. In J. Bryant & J. A. Bryant (Eds.), *Television and the American family* (2nd ed., pp. 273–287). Mahwah, NJ: Lawrence Erlbaum Associates.

Andrews, L. B. (1997). Gen-etiquette: Genetic information, family relationships, and adoption. In M. A. Rothstein (Ed.), *Genetic secrets: Protecting privacy and confidentiality in the genetic era* (pp. 255–280). New Haven, CT: Yale University Press.

Arata, C. M. (1998). To tell or not to tell: Current functioning of child sexual abuse survivors who disclosed their victimization. *Child Maltreatment: Journal of the American Professional Society on the Abuse of Children, 3*, 63–71.

Armistead, L., Tannenbaum, L., Forehand, R., Morse, E., & Morse, P. (2001). Disclosing HIV status: Are mothers telling their children? *Journal of Pediatric Psychology, 26*, 11–20.

Avery, N. C. (1982). Family secrets. *Psychoanalytic Review, 69*, 471–486.

Banker, B. S., & Gaertner, S. L. (1998). Achieving stepfamily harmony: An intergroup-relations approach. *Journal of Family Psychology, 12*, 310–325.

Baran, A., & Pannor, R. (1993). *Lethal secrets: The psychology of donor insemination*. New York: Amistad.

Baxter, L. A., & Wilmot, W. W. (1985). Taboo topics in close relationships. *Journal of Social and Personal Relationships, 2*, 253–269.

Bellman, B. L. (1981). The paradox of secrecy. *Human Studies, 4*, 1–24.

Ben-Ari, A. (1995). Coming out: A dialectic of intimacy and privacy. *Families in Society, 76*, 306–314.

Berg, J.H., & Archer, R.L. (1982). Responses to self-disclosure and interaction goals. *Journal of Experimental Psychology, 18*, 501–512.

Bochner, A. P. (1982). On the efficacy of openness in close relationships. In M. Burgoon (Ed.), *Communication yearbook 6* (pp. 109–123). Beverly Hills, CA: Sage.

Boetzkes, E. (1999). Genetic knowledge and third-party interests. *Cambridge Quarterly of Healthcare Ethics, 8*, 386–392.

Bok, S. (1983). *Secrets: On the ethics of concealment and revelation*. New York: Vintage Books.

Bradshaw, J. (1995). *Family secrets: What you don't know can hurt you*. New York: Bantam Books.

Branscomb, A. W. (1994). *Who owns information? From privacy to public access*. New York: Basic Books.

Brashers, D. E. (2001). Communication and uncertainty management. *Journal of Communication, 51*, 477–497.

Bray, J. H., & Kelly, J. (1999). *Stepfamilies: Love, marriage, and parenting in the first decade*. New York: Broadway Books.

Brendel, J. M., & Nelson, K. W. (1999). The stream of family secrets: Navigating the islands of confidentiality and triangulation involving family therapists. *Family Journal: Counseling and Therapy for Couples and Families, 7*, 112–117.

Brown-Smith, N. (1998). Family secrets. *Journal of Family Issues, 19,* 20–42.

Bryant, J., & Bryant, J. A. (Eds.). (2001). *Television and the American family* (2nd ed.). Mahwah, NJ: Lawrence Erlbaum Associates.

Burke, R. J., Weir, T., & Harrison, D. (1976). Disclosure problems and tensions experienced by marital partners. *Psychological Reports, 38,* 531–542.

Byers T., MacDonald, D. J., Severin, M. J., & Fishbach, A. A. (1999). Cancer genetic counseling: Need for confidentiality versus responsibility to notify. *Cancer Practice, 7,* 93–95.

Caughlin, J. P. (2003). Family communication standards: What counts as excellent family communication and how are such standards associated with family satisfaction? *Human Communication Research, 29,* 5–40

Caughlin, J. P., & Golish, T. D. (2002a). An analysis of the association between topic avoidance and dissatisfaction: Comparing perceptual and interpersonal explanations. *Communication Monographs, 69,* 275–295.

Caughlin, J. P., & Golish, T. D. (2002b, November). *When is topic avoidance unsatisfying?: Toward a more complete understanding of the links between topic avoidance and dissatisfaction in parent-child and dating relationships.* Paper presented at the annual convention of the National Communication Association, New Orleans.

Caughlin, J. P., Golish, T. D., Olson, L. N., Sargent, J. E., Cook, J. S., & Petronio, S. (2000). Intrafamily secrets in various family configurations: A communication boundary management perspective. *Communication Studies, 51,* 116–134.

Collins, N. L., & Miller, L. C. (1994). Self-disclosure and liking: A meta-analytic review. *Psychological Bulletin, 116,* 457–475.

Committee on Maintaining Privacy and Security in Health Care Applications of National Information Infrastructure. (1997). *For the record: Protecting electronic health information.* Washington, DC: National Academy Press.

Cooper, V. W. (1994). The disguise of self-disclosure: The relationship ruse of a Soviet spy. *Journal of Applied Communication Research, 22,* 338–347.

Dalzell, H. J. (2000). Whispers: The role of family secrets in eating disorders. *Eating Disorders, 8,* 43–61.

Daniels, K. R. (1998). The social responsibility of gamete providers. *Journal of Community and Applied Social Psychology, 8,* 261–271.

Daniels, K., & Lewis, G. M. (1996). Openness of information in use of donor gametes: Developments in New Zealand. *Journal of Reproductive and Infant Psychology, 14,* 57–68.

Decruyenaere, M., Evers-Kiebooms, G., & Van den Berghe, H. (1993). Perception of predictive testing for Huntington's disease by young women: Preferring uncertainty to certainty. *Journal of Medical Genetics, 30,* 557–561.

Deftos, L. J. (1998). The evolving duty to disclose the presence of genetic disease to relatives. *Academic Medicine, 73,* 962–968.

Denholm-Carey, J., & Chabassol, D. J. (1987). Adolescents' self-disclosure of potentially embarrassing events. *Psychological Reports, 60,* 45–46.

Derlega, V. J., & Chaikin, A. L. (1977). Privacy and self-disclosure in social relationships. *Journal of Social Issues, 33,* 102–115.

Derlega, V. J., & Grzelak, J. (1979). Appropriateness of self-disclosure. In G. Chelune (Ed.), *Self-disclosure: Origins, patterns, and implications of openness in interpersonal relationships* (pp. 151–176). San Francisco: Jossey-Bass.

Derlega, V. J., Metts, S., Petronio, S., & Margulis, S. T. (1993). *Self-disclosure.* Newbury Park, CA: Sage.

Dieckmann, L. E. (2000). Private secrets and public disclosures: The case of battered women. In S. Petronio (Ed.), *Balancing the secrets of private disclosures* (pp. 275–286). Mahwah, NJ: Lawrence Erlbaum Associates.

Dindia, K. (1994). The intrapersonal-interpersonal dialectical process of self-disclosure. In S. Duck (Ed.), *Dynamics of relationships* (pp. 27–57). Thousand Oaks, CA: Sage.

Dindia, K., & Allen, M. (1992). Sex differences in self-disclosure: A meta-analysis. *Psychological Bulletin, 112,* 106–124.

Dolgin, K., & Berndt, N. (1997). Adolescents' perceptions of their parents' disclosure to them. *Journal of Adolescence, 20,* 431–441.

Fanos, J. H., & Johnson, J. P. (1995). Barriers to carrier testing for adult cystic fibrosis sibs: The importance of not knowing. *American Journal of Medical Genetics, 59,* 85–91.

Fitzpatrick, M. A. (2002). Policing family violence. In H. Giles (Ed.), *Law enforcement, communication and community* (pp. 129–153). Amsterdam: Benjamins.

Frawley, M. G. (1990). From secrecy to self-disclosure: Healing the scars of incest. In G. Stricker & M. Fisher (Eds.), *Self-disclosure in the therapeutic relationship* (pp. 247–259). New York: Plenum Press.

Frey, R. G. (2000). Privacy, control, and talk of rights. In E. F. Paul, F. D. Miller, Jr., & J. Paul (Eds.), *The right to privacy* (pp. 45–67). New York: Cambridge University Press.

Gadlin, H. (1974). Private lives and public order: A critical view of the history of intimate relations in the United States. In G. Levinger & H. Rausch (Eds.), *Close relationships: Perspectives on the meaning of intimacy* (pp. 33–72). Amherst: University of Massachusetts Press.

Gerber, S. D. (2000). Privacy and constitutional theory. In E. F. Paul, F. D. Miller, Jr., & J. Paul (Eds.), *The right to privacy* (pp. 165–185). New York: Cambridge University Press.

Gewirtz, A., & Gossart-Walker, S. (2000). Home-based treatment for children and families affected by HIV and AIDS: Dealing with stigma, secrecy, disclosure, and loss. *Child and Adolescent Psychiatric Clinics of North America, 9,* 313–330.

Gilbert, S. J. (1976). Self-disclosure, intimacy and communication in families. *The Family Coordinator, 25,* 221–231.

Goffman, E. (1959). *The presentation of self in everyday life.* Garden City, NY: Doubleday.

Golish, T. D., & Caughlin, J. P. (2002). "I'd rather not talk about it." Adolescents' and young adults' use of topic avoidance in stepfamilies. *Journal of Applied Communication Research, 30,* 78–106.

Greene, K. L. (2000). Disclosure of chronic illness varies by topic and target: The role of stigma and boundaries in willingness to disclose. In S. Petronio (Ed.), *Balancing the secrets of private disclosures* (pp. 123–135). Mahwah, NJ: Lawrence Erlbaum Associates.

Greene, K. L, Derlega, V., Yep, G. A., & Petronio, S. (2003). *Privacy and disclosure of HIV in interpersonal relationships: A sourcebook for researchers and practitioners.* Mahwah, NJ: Lawrence Erlbaum Associates.

Greene, K. L., & Serovich, J. M. (1996). Appropriateness of disclosure of HIV-testing information: The perspective of PLWAs. *Journal of Applied Communication Research, 24,* 50–65.

Gries, L., Goh, D. S., Andrews, M. B., Gilbert, J., Praver, F., & Stelzer, D. N. (2000). Positive reaction to disclosure and recovery from child sexual abuse. *Journal of Child Sexual Abuse, 9,* 29–51.

Grolnick, L. (1983). Ibsen's truth, family secrets, and family therapy. *Family Process, 22,* 275–288.

Guerrero, L. K., & Afifi, W. A. (1995a). Some things are better left unsaid: Topic avoidance in family relationships. *Communication Quarterly, 43,* 276–296.

Guerrero, L., K., & Afifi, W. A. (1995b). What parents don't know: Topic avoidance in parent-child relationships. In T. Socha & G. Stamp (Eds.), *Parents, children, and communication: Frontiers of theory and research* (pp. 219–246). Mahwah, NJ: Lawrence Erlbaum Associates.

Hakimian, R. (2000). Disclosure of Huntington's disease to family members: The dilemma of known but unknowing parties. *Genetic Testing, 4,* 359–364.

Hartman, A. (1993). Secrecy in adoption. In E. Imber-Black (Ed.), *Secrets in families and family therapy* (pp. 86–105). New York: Norton.

Hoyt, M. F. (1978). Secrets in psychotherapy: Theoretical and practical considerations. *The International Review of PsychoAnalysis, 5,* 231–241.

Hunt, T., & Paine-Gernée, K. (1994). *Secrets to tell, secrets to keep.* New York: Warner Books.

Imber-Black, E. (1993). Secrets in families and family therapy: An overview. In E. Imber-Black (Ed.), *Secrets in families and family therapy* (pp. 3–28). New York: Norton.

Imber-Black, E. (1998). *The secret life of families.* New York: Bantam Books.

Jahn, M. (1995). Family secrets and family environment: Their relation to later adult functioning. *Alcoholism Treatment Quarterly, 13,* 71–80.

Johnson, M. P. (1995). Patriarchal terrorism and common couple violence: Two forms of violence against women. *Journal of Marriage and the Family, 57,* 283–294.

Johnson, M. P., & Ferraro, K. J. (2000). Research on domestic violence in the 1990s: Making distinctions. *Journal of Marriage and the Family, 62,* 948–963.

Jones, E. E., & Pittman, T. S. (1982). Toward a general theory of strategic self-presentation. In J. Suls (Ed.), *Psychological perspectives on the self* (Vol. 1, pp. 231–262). Hillsdale, NJ: Lawrence Erlbaum Associates.

Jorgensen, S. R., & Gaudy, J. C. (1980). Self-disclosure and satisfaction in marriage: The relation examined. *Family Relations, 29,* 281–287.

Kadushin, G. (2000). Family secrets: Disclosure of HIV status among gay men with HIV/AIDS to the family of origin. *Social Work in Health Care, 30*(3), 1–17.

Karpel, M. A. (1980). Family Secrets: I. Conceptual and ethical issues in the relational context, II. Ethical and practical considerations in therapeutic management. *Family Processes, 19,* 295–306.

Kaufman, G., Jr. (1993). The mysterious disappearance of battered women in family therapists' offices: Male privilege colluding with male violence. In E. Imber-Black (Ed.), *Secrets in families and family therapy* (pp. 196–212). New York: Norton.

Kelly, A. E. (2002). *The psychology of secrets.* New York: Kluwer Academic/ Plenum.

Kelly, A. E., & Carter, J. E. (2001). Dealing with secrets. In C. R. Snyder (Ed.), *Coping with stress: Effective people and processes* (pp. 196–221). New York: Oxford University Press.

Kelly, A. E., Klusas, J. A., von Weiss, R. T., & Kenny, C. (2001). What is it about revealing secrets that is beneficial? *Personality and Social Psychology Bulletin, 27,* 651–665.

Kelly, A. E., & McKillop, K. J. (1996). Consequences of revealing personal secrets. *Psychological Bulletin, 120,* 450–465.

Kerr, S. M., & Smith, L. N. (2001). Stroke: An exploration of the experience of informal caregiving. *Clinical Rehabilitation, 15,* 428–436.

Kimberly, J. A., Serovich, J. M., & Greene, K. (1995). Disclosure of HIV-positive status: Five women's stories. *Family Relations, 44,* 316–322.

Klein, D. M., & White, J. M. (1996). *Family theories: An introduction.* Thousand Oaks, CA: Sage.

Kirshenbaum, S. B., & Nevid, J. S. (2002). The specificity of maternal disclosure of HIV/AIDS in relationship to children's adjustment. *AIDS Education and Prevention, 14,* 1–16.

Laird, J. (1993). Women's secrets—Women's silences. In E. Imber-Black (Ed.), *Secrets in families and family therapy* (pp. 243–267). New York: Norton.

Landau, R. (1998). Secrecy, anonymity, and deception in donor insemination: A genetic, psycho-social and ethical critique. *Social Work in Health Care, 28,* 75–89.

Lane, J. D., & Wegner, D. M. (1995). The cognitive consequences of secrecy. *Journal of Personality and Social Psychology, 69,* 237–253.

Major, B., & Gramzow, R. H. (1999). Abortion as stigma: Cognitive and emotional implications of concealment. *Journal of Personality and Social Psychology, 77,* 735–745.

Margolis, G. J. (1966). Secrecy and identity. *The International Journal of Psycho-Analysis, 47,* 517–522.

Margolis, G. J. (1974). The psychology of keeping secrets. *The International Review of Psycho-Analysis, 1,* 291–296.

Mason, M. (1993). Shame: Reservoir for family secrets. In E. Imber-Black (Ed.), *Secrets in families and family therapy* (pp. 29–43). New York: Norton.

Mellins, C. A., Brackis-Cott, E., Dolezal, C., Richards, A., Nicholas, S. W., & Abrams, E. J. (2002). Patterns of status disclosure to perinatally HIV-infected children and subsequent mental health outcomes. *Clinical Child Psychology and Psychiatry, 7,* 101–114.

Melzak, S. (1992). The secret life of children who have experienced physical aggression and violence. In V. P. Varma (Ed.), *The secret life of vulnerable children* (pp. 101–129). New York: Routledge.

Miall, C. E. (1998). Community assessments of adoption issues: Open adoption, birth reunions, and the disclosure of confidential information. *Journal of Family Issues, 19,* 556–577.

Miller, B., Townsend, A., Carpenter, E., Montgomery, R. V. J., Stull, D., & Young, R. F. (2001). Social support and caregiver distress: A replication analysis. *Journals of Gerontology: Series B: Psychological Sciences and Social Sciences, 56B,* S249–S256.

Minuchin, S. (1974). *Families and family therapy*. Cambridge, MA: Harvard University Press.

Morr, M. C. (2002). Private disclosure in a family membership transition: In-laws' disclosures to newlyweds. (Doctoral dissertation, Arizona State University, 2002), *Dissertation Abstracts International, 63,* 1627.

Murphy, D. A., Steers, W. N., & Dello Stritto, M. E. (2001). Maternal disclosure of mothers' HIV serostatus to their young children. *Journal of Family Psychology, 15,* 441–450.

Nock, S. L. (1998). Too much privacy? *Journal of Family Issues, 19,* 101–118.

Noller, P. (1995). Parent-adolescent relationships. In M. A. Fitzpatrick & A. L. Vangelisti (Eds.), *Explaining family interaction* (pp. 77–111). Thousand Oaks, CA: Sage.

Norton, R., Feldman, C., & Tafoya, D. (1974). Risk parameters across types of secrets. *Journal of Consulting Psychology, 21,* 450–454.

Paine, M. L., & Hansen, D. J. (2002). Factors influencing children to self-disclose sexual abuse. *Clinical Psychology Review, 22,* 271–295.

Papp, P. (1993). The worm in the bud: Secrets between parents and children. In E. Imber-Black (Ed.), *Secrets in families and family therapy* (pp. 66–85). New York: Norton.

Parks, M. R. (1982). Ideology in interpersonal communication: Off the couch and into the world. In M. Burgoon (Ed.), *Communication yearbook 6* (pp. 79–107). Beverly Hills, CA: Sage.

Parrott, R., Duncan, V., & Duggan, A. (2000). Promoting patients' full and honest disclosure during conversations with health caregivers. In S. Petronio (Ed.), *Balancing the secrets of private disclosures* (pp. 137–148). Mahwah, NJ: Lawrence Erlbaum Associates.

Peek, C. W., Bell, N. J., Waldren, T., & Sorell, G. T. (1988). Patterns of functioning in families of remarried and first-married couples. *Journal of Marriage and the Family, 50,* 699–708.

Pennebaker, J. W. (1993). Putting stress into words: Health, linguistic, and therapeutic implications. *Behaviour Research and Therapy, 31,* 539–548.

Pennebaker, J. W. (1995). Emotion, disclosure, and health: An overview. In J. W. Pennebaker (Ed.), *Emotion, disclosure, and health* (pp. 3–10). Washington, DC: American Psychological Association.

Pennebaker, J. W. (1997). *Opening up: The healing power of expressing emotions* (Rev. ed.). New York: Guilford Press.

Pennebaker, J. W., & Beall, S. K. (1986). Confronting a traumatic event: Toward an understanding of inhibition and disease. *Journal of Abnormal Psychology, 95,* 274–281.

Perrine, R. M. (1993). On being supportive: The emotional consequences of listening to another's distress. *Journal of Social and Personal Relationships, 10,* 371–384.

Petrie, K. J., Booth, R. J., & Davison, K. P. (1995). Repression disclosure, and immune function: Recent findings and methodological issues. In J. W. Pennebaker (Ed.), *Emotion, disclosure, and health* (pp. 223–240). Washington, DC: American Psychological Association.

Petronio, S. (1991). Communication boundary management: A theoretical model of managing disclosure of private information between marital couples. *Communication Theory, 1,* 311–335.

Petronio, S. (1994). Privacy binds in family interactions: The case of parental privacy invasion. In W. R. Cupach & B. H. Spitzberg (Eds.), *The dark side of interpersonal communication* (pp. 241–257). Mahwah, NJ: Lawrence Erlbaum Associates.

Petronio, S. (2000a). The boundaries of privacy: Praxis of everyday life. In S. Petronio (Ed.), *Balancing the secrets of private disclosures* (pp. 37–49). Mahwah, NJ: Lawrence Erlbaum Associates.

Petronio, S. (2000b). The ramifications of a reluctant confidant. In A. C. Richards & T. Schumrum (Eds.), *Invitations to dialogue: The legacy of Sidney Jourard* (pp. 113–132). Dubuque, IA: Kendall/Hunt Publishers.

Petronio, S. (2002). *Boundaries of privacy: Dialectics of disclosure.* Albany, NY: SUNY Press.

Petronio, S., Ellemers, N., Giles, H., & Gallois, C. (1998). (Mis)communicating across boundaries: Interpersonal and intergroup considerations. *Communication Research, 25,* 571–595.

Petronio, S., Jones, S., & Morr, M. C. (2003). Family privacy dilemmas: Managing communication boundaries with family groups. In L. Frey (Ed.), Group communication in context: Studies of bonafide groups (pp. 23–56). Mahwah, NJ: Lawrence Erlbaum Associates.

Petronio, S., & Kovach, S. (1997). Managing privacy boundaries: Health providers' perceptions of resident care in Scottish nursing homes. *Journal of Applied Communication Research, 25,* 115–131.

Petronio, S., Reeder, H. M., Hecht, M. L., & Mon't Ros-Mendoza, T. (1996). Disclosure of sexual abuse by children and adolescents. *Journal of Applied Communication Research, 24,* 181–199.

Petronio, S., Sargent, J., Cichocki, D., Andea, L., Reganis, P., & Speike-Stuckey, H. (2001, May). *Family and friends as health advocates: Demands of confidentiality and privacy.* Paper presented at the International Communication Association Convention, Washington, DC.

Rigney, D. (1979). Secrecy and social cohesion. *Cohesion, 52–55.*

Robinson, G. E., & Stewart, D. E. (1996). The psychological impact of infertility and new reproductive technologies. *Harvard Review of Psychiatry, 4,* 168–172.

Roloff, M. E., & Ifert, D. E. (2000). Conflict management through avoidance: Withholding complaints, suppressing arguments, and declaring topics taboo. In S. Petronio (Ed.), *Balancing the secrets of private disclosures* (pp. 151–179). Mahwah, NJ: Lawrence Erlbaum Associates.

Roman, M., & Blackburn, S. (1979). *Family secrets: The experience of emotional crisis.* New York: Times Books.

Rosenfeld, L. B. (1979). Self-disclosure avoidance: Why am I afraid to tell you who I am. *Communication Monographs, 46,* 63–74.

Rothenberg, K. (Ed.) (1995). *Disclosure processes in children and adolescents.* Cambridge, UK: Cambridge University Press.

Rothstein, M. A. (Ed.) (1997). *Genetic secrets: Protecting privacy and confidentiality in the genetic era.* New Haven, CT: Yale University Press.

Sachperoglou, E., & Bor, R. (2001). Disclosure of HIV seropositivity and social support: General patterns in Greece. *European Journal of Psychotherapy, Counselling and Health, 4,* 103–122.

Saffer, J. B., Sansone, P., & Gentry, J. (1979). The awesome burden upon the child who must keep a family secret. *Child Psychiatry and Human Development, 10,* 35–40.

Schrimshaw, E. W., & Siegel, K. (2002). HIV-infected mothers' disclosure to their uninfected children: Rates, reasons, and reactions. *Journal of Social and Personal Relationships, 19,* 19–43.

Schultz, P. D. (2000). Sex offender community notification policies: Balancing privacy and disclosure. In S. Petronio (Ed.), *Balancing the secrets of private disclosures* (pp. 263–274). Mahwah, NJ: Lawrence Erlbaum Associates.

Schumm, W. R., Barnes, H. L., Bollman, S. R., Jurich, A. P., & Bugaighis, M. A. (1986). Self-disclosure and marital satisfaction revisited. *Family Relations, 34,* 241–247.

Selvini, M. (1997). Family secrets: The case of the patient kept in the dark. *Contemporary Family Therapy, 19,* 315–335.

Serovich, J. M., & Greene, K. (1993). Perceptions of family boundaries: The case of disclosure of HIV testing information. *Family Relations, 42,* 193–97.

Serovich, J. M., Kimberly, J. A., & Greene, K. (1998). Perceived family member reaction to women's disclosure of HIV-positive information. *Family Relations, 47,* 15–22.

Sherrell, K., Buckwalter, K. C., & Morhardt, D. (2001). Negotiating family relationships: Dementia care as a midlife developmental task. *Families in Society, 82,* 383–392.

Shimanoff, S. B. (1987). Types of emotional disclosures and request compliance between spouses. *Communication Monographs, 54,* 86–100.

Simmel, G. (1950). *The sociology of Georg Simmel* (trans. Kurt H. Wolff). Glencoe, IL: Free Press.

Smith, G. (1992). The unbearable traumatic past: Child sexual abuse. In V. P. Varma (Ed.), *The secret life of vulnerable children* (pp. 130–156). New York: Routledge.

Smyth, J. M., & Pennebaker, J. W. (2001). What are the health effects of disclosure? In A. Baum, T. A. Revenson, & J. E. Singer (Eds.), *Handbook of health psychology* (pp. 339–348). Mahwah, NJ: Lawrence Erlbaum Associates.

Sobel, S. K., & Cowan, D. B. (2000). Impact of genetic testing for Huntington disease on the family system. *American Journal of Medical Genetics, 90,* 49–59.

Spiro, H. (1971). Privacy in comparative perspectives. In J. R. Pennock & J. W. Chapman (Eds.), *Privacy* (pp. 121–148). New York: Atherton Press.

Stiles, W. B. (1987). "I have to talk to somebody:" A fever model of disclosure. In V. Derlega & J. Berg (Eds.), *Self-disclosure: Theory, research, and therapy* (pp. 257–282). New York: Plenum Press.

Stiles, W. B. (1995). Disclosure as a speech act: Is it psychotherapeutic to disclose? In J. W. Pennebaker (Ed.), *Emotion, disclosure, and health* (pp. 71–91). Washington, DC: American Psychological Association.

Stiles, W. B., Shuster, P. L., & Harrigan, J. A. (1992). Disclosure and anxiety: A test of the fever model. *Journal of Personality and Social Psychology, 63,* 980–988.

Stroebe, M., Stroebe, W., Schut, H., Zech, E., & van den Bout, J. (2002). Does disclosure of emotions facilitate recovery from bereavement? Evidence from two prospective studies. *Journal of Consulting and Clinical Psychology, 70,* 169–178.

Szajnberg, N. (1988). The developmental continuum from secrecy to privacy in a psychodynamic milieu. *Residential Treatment for Children and Youth, 6*(2), 9–28.

Tardy, C. H., Hosman, L. A., & Bradac, J. J. (1981). Disclosing self to friends and family: A reexamination of initial questions. *Communication Quarterly, 29,* 263–268.

Vangelisti, A. L. (1994). Family secrets: Forms, functions, and correlates. *Journal of Social and Personal Relationships, 11,* 113–135.

Vangelisti, A. L., & Caughlin J. P. (1997). Revealing family secrets: The influence of topic, function, and relationships. *Journal of Social and Personal Relationships, 14,* 679–705.

Vangelisti, A. L., Caughlin, J. P., & Timmerman, L. M. (2001). Criteria for revealing family secrets. *Communication Monographs, 68,* 1–27.

Visher, E. B., & Visher, J. S. (1993). Remarriage families and stepparenting. In F. Walsh (Ed.), *Normal family processes* (2nd ed., pp. 235–253). New York: Guilford Press.

Vrij, A., Nunkoosing, K., Paterson, B., Oosterwegel, A., & Soukara, S. (2002). Characteristics of secrets and the frequency, reasons and effects of secret keeping and disclosure. *Journal of Community and Applied Social Psychology, 12,* 56–70.

Wai-Ching, L. (2000). Results of genetic testing: When confidentiality conflicts with a duty to warn relatives: Case study. *British Medical Journal, 321,* 1464–1465.

Waterman, J. (1979). Family patterns of self-disclosure. In G. J. Chelune and Associates (Eds.), *Self-disclosure: Origins, patterns, and implications of openness in interpersonal relationships* (pp. 225–242). San Francisco: Jossey-Bass.

Webster, H. (1991). *Family secrets: How telling and not telling affects our children, our relationships, and our lives.* Reading, MA: Addison-Wesley.

Wegner, D. M., & Lane, J. D. (1995). From secrecy to psychopathology. In J. W. Pennebaker (Ed.), *Emotion, disclosure, and health* (pp. 25–46). Washington, DC: American Psychological Association.

Wegner, D. M., Lane, J. D., & Dimitri, S. (1994). The allure of secret relationships. *Journal of Personality and Social Psychology, 66,* 287–300.

Welter-Enderlin, R. (1993). Secrets of couples and couples' therapy. In E. Imber-Black (Ed.), *Secrets in families and family therapy* (pp. 47–65). New York: Norton.

19

Communication, Conflict, and the Quality of Family Relationships

Alan Sillars

University of Montana

Daniel J. Canary and Melissa Tafoya

Arizona State University

Conflict is one of the most (if not *the* most) studied and discussed subjects in the area of family communication. In fact, some authors suggest that conflict has been emphasized to such an extent that it has eclipsed positive aspects of marital and family interaction (Bradbury, Rogge, & Lawrence, 2001; Roberts & Greenberg, in press). Why do scholars show so much interest in communication and family conflict?

First, and perhaps obviously, many families face difficult struggles that are often quite volatile and troubling. Conflict theories emphasize that conflicts are ubiquitous and inherent (Deutsch, 1973; Simmel, 1955), especially given the interdependence and emotional involvement of close relationships (Braiker & Kelley, 1979), and of families in particular (Shantz & Hobart, 1989). These points are so familiar and thoroughly accepted that, in some respects, we may have overdramatized the prominence of conflict in family life (Beach, 2001; Bradbury et al., 2001). Nonetheless, conflict represents the side of family interaction that family members themselves find difficult, unsettling, and perplexing.

Research on communication in family conflict is further motivated by a practical interest in improving family relationships. Much of the research tries to isolate constructive versus problematic aspects of communication, with the hope that communication processes may then be appropriately modeled, suppressed, or otherwise changed. Although communication patterns are not easily manipulated, more potential exists to control and change communication patterns than many other factors that contribute to family conflict, such as personality traits; basic differences in individual values, goals, or expectations; social and economic conditions; and other structural factors.

Finally, how individuals manage conflict affects their personal development. The process of managing interpersonal conflict helps children to learn about various rules that guide behavior, to take into account how other people think and feel, to monitor their own expression of thoughts and feelings, to adopt strategies for obtaining valued goals, and to learn about alternative relational models (Dunn & Slomkowski, 1992; Laursen Finkelstein, & Betts, 2001). Family interaction provides an important context for individual development during the management of conflict, insofar as families have the most conflict of all social groups (Shantz & Hobart, 1989). Thus, there is considerable interest in what children learn from family conflict, how they are impacted by exposure to negative conflict, and how relational models learned from family conflict may carry over into other relationships.

In this chapter, we review communication processes in marital and family conflict, with the central focus being the influence that communication has on the quality of family relationships. Relationship quality, broadly conceived, constitutes the overriding concern of most research on family conflict. By the usual account, communication is the means by which quality relationships are achieved (i.e., communication has a *causal* influence on relationship quality); or even, communication *is* the relationship (or its observable manifestation), so relationship quality is necessarily defined by the nature of communication (Montgomery, 1988). In addition, the focus of research is almost exclusively on the "relational dimension" of communication, that is, *how* families communicate about conflict and what this suggests about their relationship (Gottman, 1994; Watzlawick, Beavin, & Jackson, 1967), not what they disagree about, what they do about it, or even how well conflicts are resolved. With some exceptions (e.g., Erbert, 2000; Kirchler, Rodler, Holzl, & Meier, 2001, Kluwer, Heesink, & Van de Vliert, 2000), researchers tend to treat the content of conflict as peripheral or unimportant, perhaps because underlying relationship issues are so often transparent and surface content issues mundane in family conflicts (Wilmot & Hocker, 2001).

In reviewing this literature, we followed researcher efforts in the recent past. Accordingly, we emphasize studies of marital conflict, followed by parent–child and sibling conflict. We examine in turn, how the quality of family relationships relates to the amount and type of conflict, manifest communication patterns, and subjective interpretations of communication. Later, we offer an assessment and critique of research trends, focusing on what we see as the two primary limitations: (a) the dominant practice of dichotomizing between well-adjusted and poorly adjusted couples or families (and, by extension, good/bad communication) and (b) the treatment of communication as objective behavior with fixed meaning.

The first issue that arises is how to define the extent or range of conflict that might be considered normative. That is, are all families engaged in continual or frequent conflict, or is conflict episodic, reflecting issues at particular points in family development that are typically resolved or put aside over time? Do all families experience similar conflict and only differ in the way conflict is handled, or is the amount and type of conflict indicative of different types of relationships and relationship quality? We now turn to these questions.

NORMATIVE FAMILY CONFLICT

Most authors in the family literature have followed the lead of classic conflict theorists who emphasized the inevitability of social conflict (e.g., Deutsch, 1973; Simmel, 1955). From this perspective, all families are assumed to experience frequent conflict. Further, the occurrence of conflict is neither good nor bad; rather, the response to conflict is what determines the long-term vitality and resilience of relationships. Charny (1980) exemplifies this spirit by declaring that: "... what really becomes important in family life is not the ability to stay out of trouble but to get out of trouble, that is the ability to process conflicts and dilemmas and unfairness constructively" (p. 43).

Research provides a mixed assessment regarding the pervasiveness of family conflict. On the one hand, conflict appears to be more frequent and intense within families than in other social contexts. Both adolescents and adults report greater conflict and negativity within family relationships by comparison to friend or coworker relationships (Adams & Laursen, 2001; Buzzanell & Burrell, 1997; Infante, Myers, & Buerkel, 1994). On the other hand, the amount of identified conflict varies a great deal with the nature of specific relationships.

In contrast to the prevailing view that people are bathed in conflict, Bradbury et al. (2001) suggest that marital conflict is really a low base rate event. Bradbury et al. cite McGonagle, Kessler, and Schilling (1992), who analyzed self-reported conflicts in a large, equal-probability sample of married couples. Individuals were asked, "How often do you and your spouse have an unpleasant disagreement?" Although very few said "never," 80% reported that they had unpleasant marital disagreements no more than once per month. Only 6% reported one or more disagreement per week. Aside from minor discrepancies, the validity of these global self-reports was supported by daily diaries completed by a subgroup within the sample over a 6-week period.

Likewise, Kirchler et al. (2001) reported a study in which 40 Austrian married couples kept daily diaries of their conversations over the course of 1 year and reported in detail on discussions that involved disagreements. Individuals reported an average of three to four conversations per day, with less than 3% of these involving disagreement. Extrapolating from figures reported by Kirchler et al. (p. 136), individuals reported an average of two to three disagreements per month, which is close to the estimates from the McGonagle et al. research. Both studies suggest that overt conflict is not a daily or even a weekly occurrence for most couples.

In terms of parent–adolescent interactions, Montemayor (1986) reported about two significant conflicts per week, whereas Laursen (1993) reported high school students had 7.4 conflicts on average per day, with parents included as one of three relationships that endured these sorts of conflict.

Estimates of sibling conflict are more dramatic. One study found that conflict with two preschool-age siblings occurs an average of seven times an hour (Perlman & Ross, 1997, p. 464). Similarly, Lollis, Ross, and Leroux (1996) estimated that conflicts with siblings occurred more than six times an hour, regardless of age. Sibling relationships are a significant source of conflict for most children and adolescents (Raffaelli, 1997), and they have heightened significance because children cannot put an end to their sibling relationships. By contrast, children's relationships with peers tend to end before conflicts reach the same level of intensity reached in sibling conflicts (Bedford, Volling, & Avioli, 2000, p. 57). Further, conflict with siblings tends to increase with the amount of contact. Raffaelli (1997) found that spending time together predicted the frequency of sibling conflict more than age, sex, family size, and other variables. On the other hand, Jensen-Campbell and Graziano (2000) found that adolescents rated conflicts with siblings as being less important than conflicts with friends.

The previous picture suggests that conflict is most prevalent in sibling relationships, followed by parent–adolescent and marital relationships. However, these comparisons are tenuous, partly because they mask variation within specific relationship types and also because of the different methods used to quantify conflict. For one thing, observational studies (e.g., Lollis et al., 1996; Perlman & Ross, 1997; Vuchinich, 1984) find much more frequent conflicts than studies that utilize diaries or global self-reports (Kirchler et al., 2001; McGonagle et al., 1992). This suggests that researchers may use more inclusive criteria for identifying conflict than family members do. Further, in some observational studies, conflict is defined as a string of successive opposing behaviors. Accordingly, "conflict" does not reference an episode of disagreement that includes any number of exchanges; rather, each exchange counts as a conflict. For example, in examining tape-recorded conversations during dinner, Vuchinich (1984) found that families engaged in approximately 18 disputes per meal, though most of these were short-lived and concluded in stand-offs (i.e., the final disagreement lingered without response). In a study of mother–toddler interactions, Eisenberg (1992) found an average of 1.4 conflicts every 5 minutes. Eisenberg did indicate that most of these conflicts were very brief (average turn = 3 moves) and mild.

There are clear indications that the amount of reported or observed conflict reflects the quality of family relationships. For example, Vincent, Weiss, and Birchler (1975) found that distressed spouses reported approximately a conflict per day, whereas nondistressed spouses reported a conflict per week, on average. These findings no doubt reflect perceptual and interpretive processes as well as overt negativity or disagreement, as dissatisfied partners are especially vigilant toward conflict, whereas satisfied partners discount behaviors that could be construed negatively (see Noller, Beach, & Osgarby, 1997). In any event, the research dispels the notion that couples experience conflict to a similar extent but simply handle it differently.

The amount or intensity of conflict may be more significant than the topic of conflict, at least in marriage. Birchler (1979) found great similarity in the types of behavioral changes that distressed and nondistressed spouses wanted from their partners (e.g., express emotions more clearly, express appreciation, initiate having sex); distressed spouses just wanted more drastic changes. In addition, relationship quality may be impacted by the way individuals frame conflict issues. As Braiker and Kelley (1979) have observed, the same action may be framed as a behavioral complaint (e.g., not cleaning the dishes) or a personality problem (e.g., not cleaning the dishes indicates an irresponsible attitude). Braiker and Kelley concluded that framing issues as personality problems escalates conflict and may contribute to relationship distress. This conclusion was supported by Alberts (1988), who found that poorly adjusted married couples were more likely than well-adjusted couples to direct complaints at broad personal characteristics of the partner.

While relationship quality seems to reflect the overall amount of conflict and the way issues are framed, it is difficult to say what amount of conflict exceeds the critical threshold for typically happy or well-adjusted relationships, because conflict base rates vary a great deal according to stages and events in family relationships. In parent–adolescent relationships, some researchers have reported a curvilinear trend for conflict, wherein conflict increases in early adolescence, peaks in mid-adolescence, and subsides in late adolescence (Montemayor, 1983; Selman, 1980). Other researchers found a linear decline in conflict from early to late adolescence (Laursen, Coy, & Collins, 1998). Although each of these trends suggests a decrease in conflict during late adolescence, families may follow different trajectories. More precisely, Rueter and Conger (1995) found support for the idea that, over time, conflict increases in hostile families but decreases in supportive families.

Other research suggests that conflict between siblings typically decreases over time. For instance, the positive association between time spent together and the frequency of conflict during childhood and adolescence transforms to a negative association during adulthood. In other words, increased interaction with a sibling is positively associated with perceptions of warmth, whereas decreased contact is linked to perceptions of conflict (Stocker, Lanthier, & Furman, 1997). Presumably, once siblings are not forced to live together, their relationships become more like voluntary friendships.

Considerable research has examined conflict and satisfaction at different stages of marriage, with most studies suggesting that conflicts and problem-solving interactions usually increase during the adjustment to marriage and parenthood (e.g., Crohan, 1996) and then decline at some point thereafter. Thus, longer married couples tend to report fewer disagreements (Johnson, White, Edwards, & Booth, 1986; McGonagle et al., 1992) and engage in less explicit negotiation of conflicts, less negativity, and more avoidance or deference by comparison to young couples (Carstensen, Gottman, & Levenson, 1995; Kirchler et al., 2001; VanLear, 1992; Zietlow & Sillars, 1988; Zietlow & VanLear, 1991). We cannot be certain about the reasons behind these trends, because most studies are cross sectional, and it is often difficult to say whether older and younger couples differ because of generational cohort, mutual accommodation over time, divorce that occurs among incompatible couples in early marriage, or other factors (Bedford & Blieszner, 1997; Mares, 1995). Even longitudinal studies have a number of ambiguities (Huston & Vangelisti, 1995). Further, couples have diverse reactions to family life stages, such that some relationships are enhanced and others become more contentious by virtue of life stage events and the passage of time (Bedford & Blieszner, 1997; Dickson, 1997; Huston & Vangelisti, 1995).

Nonetheless, the pressures associated with transition points in the family life cycle may account for some aggregate trends in marital conflict. Transitions occur throughout the life cycle; however, they tend be more compacted in early marriage, so this is often a period of continual relational negotiation that may place a premium on explicit and direct conflict management (Sillars & Wilmot, 1989). In contrast, stable older couples might accomplish relationship adjustments more gradually and implicitly. Most research supports the view that marital conflicts tend to subside in later stages of marriage (Sillars & Wilmot, 1989). Again, however, there are exceptions that reflect relationship quality. Longitudinal data from the National Survey of Families and Households indicated a decline in marital disagreements following the wife's retirement and increased engagement in calm discussion upon the husband's retirement, but only among strongly attached couples (Szinovacz & Schaffer, 2000). Couples who were low in attachment reported less calm discussion after the husband's retirement, presumably because greater time spent together sharpened existing conflicts. Similarly, a small number of the retired, elderly couples observed by Zietlow and Sillars (1988) reported deep dissatisfaction and engaged in mutual bickering during a conflict discussion, in sharp contrast to the pleasant and placid conversations of most elderly couples in this research. Dickson (1995) identified a subgroup of long married couples, called "dysfunctional separates," whose joint story-telling interviews revealed a cold and distant manner of speaking to one another, frequent contradictions, and sadness or anger when discussing the marriage. These couples maintained unhappy marriages for over 50 years, largely due to a sense that divorce was never an option, especially among wives.

The aforementioned studies suggest that the amount of conflict in families reflects both the state and the stage of family relationships. There are three further implications for communication and relationship quality, which we suggest as working hypotheses. First, how family members discuss or otherwise address conflicts partly reflects the pressures associated with particular stages; for example, we can expect families to engage in more confrontational and emotional communication during volatile and stressful periods. Second, problem-solving communication probably has the greatest impact on relationship quality in turbulent versus stable periods. During stable periods, the significance of conflict management may recede relative to other facets of relationships (e.g., companionship and "survivorship" in later marriage). Third, expectations for conflict may be calibrated against experiences that seem typical at a given stage. For example a family with early-adolescent children or a newly formed blended family might anticipate and, therefore, tolerate greater conflict during these stages. It is notable in this regard, that both parent–child and marital studies document aggregate trends in the amount of conflict experienced over time, but also find exceptions among unhappy couples and families. These exceptions involve alternate trajectories characterized by continued or increased conflict in later stages of relationships. Thus, it is apparently not the experience of intense conflict at particular stages that is most symptomatic of relationship trouble but rather the tendency to maintain or increase conflict over time. This supports Charny's (1980) observation, quoted earlier, about the relative significance of getting out of versus staying out of trouble.

We now turn to research that considers the association between communication patterns and relationship quality in families. We refer here to "manifest communication patterns" to distinguish between the overt manifestations of communication (or communication "behavior") versus the subjective interpretation of these overt signals and patterns.

MANIFEST COMMUNICATION PATTERNS

One way to conceptualize how family members manage conflict is to consider how communication varies along two continua: directness versus indirectness and degree of cooperation versus competition (or valence, or positive/negative affect). For instance, van de Vliert and Euwema (1994) separated conflict acts based on dimensions of "not active" versus active behaviors (i.e., directness) and agreeableness versus disagreeableness (i.e., affect). Accordingly, they derived four general conflict management approaches: *negotiation* (cooperative/active), *nonconfrontation* (cooperative/not active), *direct fighting* (competitive/active), and *indirect fighting* (competitive/not active) (p. 684). Using van de Vliert and Euwmena's categories, we synthesized communicative acts that are reported in several of the most popular coding schemes used in observational research on couple conflict (see Table 19.1). As Table 19.1 indicates, most codes can be readily subsumed under van de Vliert and Euwmena's categories. However, as Table 19.1 also indicates, what comprises cooperative versus competitive acts (or positive versus negative acts) varies from coding manual to coding manual, so the generalizations made gloss over the precise communication codes that were examined in each study.

TABLE 19.1

Conflict Strategies in Marital Observational Research

Negotiation: Direct and Cooperative

Agreement (Gottman, 1979)

Agreement involves direct agreement, acceptance of responsibility, compliance, assent, and change of opinion.

Appealing acts (Raush et al., 1974)

Appeals to fairness; appeals to other's motives; offering something else to win one's goal; appealing to other's love; pleading or coaxing.

Analytic remarks (Sillars, 1986)

Descriptive statements—Nonevaluative statements about observable events related to conflict.

Disclosive statements—Nonevaluative statements about events related to conflict that the partner cannot observe, such as thoughts, feelings, intentions, etc.

Qualifying statements—Statements that explicitly qualify the nature and extent of the conflict.

Soliciting disclosure—Nonhostile questions about events related to conflict that cannot be observed.

Soliciting criticism—Nonhostile questions soliciting criticism of self.

Cognitive acts (Raush et al., 1974)

Conventional remarks; opening the issue/probe; seeking information; giving information; withholding information; suggesting course of action; agreeing with other; giving reasons for course of action; exploring consequences for course of action; denying validity of other's arguments.

Communication talk (Gottman, 1979)

Concerns communication about communication as well as statements directing the discussion to the task or seeking clarification

Conciliatory remarks (Sillars, 1986)

Supportive remarks—Statements that refer to understanding, acceptance, support, etc., for the partner and shared interests.

Concessions—Statements that express a willingness to change, show flexibility, make concessions, or consider mutually acceptable solutions to conflicts.

Acceptance of responsibility—Attributions of responsibility to self or both parties.

Description (Weiss, 1993)

Problem description external—A statement describing a problem as external to both parties.

Problem description internal—Describing a problem as internal to both parties.

Expressing feelings about a problem (Gottman, 1979)

Talking about a general personal issue or the relationship in particular.

Mindreading/positive (Gottman, 1979)

Beliefs about the partner's internal states—Beliefs, emotions, attitudes, and the like—as well as explaining or predicting behaviors. Said with positive or neutral affect.

Problem solving/information exchange (Gottman, 1979)

Instances where one offers some kind of specific or nonspecific solution, or one provides information about one's beliefs or relational activities.

Propose change (Weiss, 1993)

Compromise—A negotiation of a mutual exchange of behavior.

Negative solution—Proposal for termination or decrease of some behavior.

Positive solution—Proposal for initiation or increase of some behavior.

(continued)

TABLE 19.1
(*Continued*)

Reconciling acts (Raush et al., 1974)

  Avoiding blame or responsibility; accepting blame or responsibility; showing concern for other's feelings; seeking reassurance; attempting to makeup; offering help or reassurance.

Summarizing self (Gottman, 1979)

  Statements about one's expressed opinions.

Summarizing other (Gottman, 1979)

  Includes summaries of the partner or both parties' behavior.

Validation (Weiss, 1993)

  Agree—Statement of agreement with partner's opinion.

  Approve—Statement that favors couple's or partner's attributions, actions, or statements.

  Accept responsibility—Statement that conveys that "I" or "we" are responsible for the problem.

  Compliance–Fulfills command within 10 seconds.

Direct Fighting: Direct and Competitive

Blame (Weiss, 1993)

  Criticize—Hostile statement of unambiguous dislike or disapproval of a specific behavior of the spouse. Nonneutral voice tone.

  Mindread negative—Statement of fact that assumes a negative mindset or motivation of the partner.

  Put down—Verbal or nonverbal behavior that demeans or mocks the partner.

  Threat—A verbal or nonverbal threat of physical or emotional harm.

  Voice tone (indicates hostile or negative voice tone).

Coercive acts/personal attacks (Raush et al., 1974).

  Using an external power to induce compliance; commanding; demanding compensation; inducing guilt or attacking other's motives; disparaging the other; threatening the other.

Confrontative remarks (Sillars, 1986)

  Personal criticism—Remarks that directly criticize the personal characteristics or behaviors of the partner.

  Rejection—Statements in response to the partner's previous statements that imply personal antagonism as well as disagreement toward the partner.

  Hostile imperatives—Requests, demands, arguments, threats, or other prescriptive statements that implicitly blame the partner and seek change in the partner's behavior.

  Hostile jokes—Joking, teasing, or sarcasm at the expense of the partner.

  Hostile questions—Directive or leading questions that fault the partner.

  Presumptive remarks—Statements that attribute thoughts, feelings, etc. to the partner that the partner does not acknowledge.

  Denial of responsibility—Statements that minimize or deny personal responsibility for the conflict.

Disagreement (Gottman, 1979)

  Disagreement can be explicit, involve "yes-but" answers (i.e., initial agreement stating why one disagrees), be offered with a rationale, or be stated in the form of a command or explicit noncompliance.

Invalidation (Weiss, 1993)

  Disagree—Statement or nonverbal gesture that indicates disagreement with spouse's opinion.

  Deny responsibility—Statement that "I" or "we" are not responsible for the problem.

  Excuse—Denial of personal responsibility, based on implausible or weak rationale.

TABLE 19.1

(Continued)

Interrupt—Partner breaks in or attempts to break in while other is speaking.
Noncompliance—Failure to fulfill command within 10 seconds.
Turn off—Nonverbal gestures that indicate displeasure, disgust, disapproval.
Withdrawal—Verbal and nonverbal behavior that implies that a partner is pulling back from the
  interaction.
Mindreading/negative (Gottman, 1979)
  Beliefs about the partner's internal states—Beliefs, emotions, attitudes, and the like—as well as
    explaining or predicting behaviors. Said with negative affect.
Rejecting Acts (Raush et al., 1974)
  Giving up or leaving the field; recognizing other's motive as a strategy or calling the other's bluff;
    rejection (of the partner).

Nonconfrontation: Indirect and Cooperative

Facilitation (Weiss, 1993)
  Assent—Listener states "yeah," nods head to facilitate conversation.
  Disengage—A statement expressing the desire not to talk about a specific issue at that time.
  Excuse other—Excusing partner's behavior or statement by providing a reason for that behavior
    or statement.
  Humor—Lighthearted humor; not sarcasm.
  Metacommunication—Statement that attempts to direct the flow of conversation.
  Positive mindread—Statement that implies favorable qualities of the other.
  Question—Any interrogative statement, including rhetorical questions.
  Positive physical contact—Any affectionate touch, hug, kiss, etc.
  Paraphrase/reflection—Statement that restates a preceding statement by the partner.
  Smile/laugh—(smile or laughter).
Irreverent remarks (Sillars, 1986)
  Friendly joking—Whenever there is friendly joking or laughter that is not at the expense of the other
    person.
Noncommittal remarks (Sillars, 1986)
  Noncommittal statements—Statements that neither affirm nor deny the presence of conflict and
    which are not evasive replies or topic shifts.
  Noncommittal questions—Include unfocused questions, rephrasing the question given by the
    researcher, and conflict-irrelevant information.
  Abstract remarks—Abstract principles, generalizations, or hypothetical statements.
  Procedural remarks—Procedural statements that supplant discussion of conflict.
Resolving acts (Raush et al., 1974)
  Changing the subject; using humor; accepting the other's plans, ideas, feelings; diversion to increase
    one's gain; Introduce compromise; offer to collaborate in planning.
Topic management (Sillars, 1986)
  Topic shifts—Statements that terminate discussion of a conflict issue before each person has fully
    expressed an opinion or before the discussion has reached a sense of completion.
  Topic avoidance—Statements that explicitly terminate discussion of a conflict issue before it has
    been fully discussed.

(continued)

TABLE 19.1

(*Continued*)

Indirect Fighting: Indirect and Competitive

Denial and equivocation (Sillars, 1986)

　　Direct denial—Statements that deny a conflict is present.

　　Implicit denial—Statements that imply denial by providing a rationale for a denial statement, although the denial is not explicit.

　　Evasive remarks—Failure to acknowledge or deny the presence of a conflict following a statement or inquiry about the conflict by the partner.

Dysphoric affect (Weiss, 1993)

　　Dysphoric affect—Affect communicating depression or sadness, any self-complaint or whiny voice tone.

Withdrawal (Weiss, 1993)

　　Off topic—Comments irrelevant to the topic of discussion, including statements directed toward the experimenter, about the experimenter, or about the physical environment during the experiment.

　　Withdrawal—Verbal and nonverbal behavior that implies that a partner is pulling back from the interaction.

Directness of Communication

What are the findings regarding relational quality in terms of these communication codes? With respect to the directness dimension, research suggests that the impacts of communication are quite variable, depending on a number of factors. Some researchers hold that indirect (versus direct) communication is associated with perceptions of agreeableness (van de Vliert & Euwema, 1994) and politeness (Goldsmith, 1992), whereas other studies suggest that direct communication is more functional (e.g., Gottman & Krokoff, 1989; Kurdek, 1994). The inconsistency in findings regarding (in)directness stems in part from not separating indirect acts into their cooperative versus competitive forms. In addition, indirectness can be functional in some relationships and contexts but not in others (Fitzpatrick, Fallis, & Vance, 1982; Raush, Barry, Hertel, & Swain, 1974; Roberts, 2000)— an issue we elaborate in the following. Preferences for directness can also be a function of culture (Gilani, 1999; Haar & Krahe, 1999; Kim & Leung, 2000), although cultural norms regarding indirectness in family settings are complex and do not always mirror cultural preferences for indirectness in public settings (see Sillars, 1995). Finally, age probably affects the functionality of directness, insofar as adults often use indirectness with better results than do children and adolescents (Laursen et al., 2001).

　　In one of the most original and thoughtful statements about indirectness in conflict, Raush et al. (1974) found that the harmonious couples they observed were evenly split between those who were comfortable and adept at expressing conflict and those who avoided it. Both subgroups expressed satisfaction in the marriage, dealt with conflict efficiently, and interacted in a benign and positive manner. Raush et al. noted that the spouses who avoided confrontation often colluded by supporting one another's denial and externalization of conflict. They further observed that this collusion had different consequences depending on the purpose of avoidance:

> The conjoint defensive contract... usually fails when avoidance is used for coping with an existent conflict. That is, when each partner denies any interpersonal implications of his own or his partner's behavior, yet by his actions implies fault in the other, the interpersonal tension mounts. And since the underlying interpersonal issue is avoided, there can be no genuine mutually satisfactory resolution. (pp. 79–80)

On the other hand, when avoidance occurs in a context of clearly differentiated roles, a mutual bond of affection, and congruous intrapsychic styles (e.g., a deemphasis of feeling and introspection), then avoidance may foster a stable, compatible, and comfortable marriage, although, Raush et al. (1974) add that "an observer might well find it dull" (p. 73).

Gottman (1994) shows similar ambivalence about the impact of conflict avoidance. Based on longitudinal research with Krokoff (Gottman & Krokoff, 1989), Gottman suggests that some marital interaction patterns are associated with concurrent marital satisfaction but lead to deterioration of satisfaction over time. In this research, the wife's agreement and compliance predicted concurrent satisfaction but also predicted deterioration in satisfaction at a later point. Conversely, negative conflict engagement predicted concurrent dissatisfaction but improvement in wife marital satisfaction over time. While the methods and interpretation of this study have proven controversial (see Bradbury & Karney, 1993), Gottman (1994, p. 133) concluded that confrontation of disagreement is important to marital satisfaction over time, whereas avoidance of conflict is generally dysfunctional. On the other hand, Gottman also distinguished the impacts of avoidance based on the type of couple. Specifically, Gottman identified one type of happily married couple, called "conflict minimizers," who minimized the importance of disagreements and engaged in little verbal give and take. Like Raush et al. (1974), Gottman observed that these happy but conflict-avoiding couples were nonintrospective and they combined avoidance with positive affection, particularly on the part of the listener.

Thus, one way of making sense out of inconsistent findings regarding indirectness is that avoidance of conflict has a different meaning and consequence when it occurs in the context of a generally positive and affectionate relationship, as opposed to a context in which avoidance masks latent hostility that leaks out in various ways (e.g., through paradoxical messages or "hit-and-run" tactics; Sillars & Weisberg, 1987; Watzlawick et al., 1967). Two additional studies support this picture. Smith, Vivian, and O'Leary (1990) found that disengagement during problem-solving interactions predicted increased satisfaction over a 30-month period but only when disengagement was coupled with positivity. Otherwise, disengagement was associated with decreased satisfaction over time. Caughlin and Huston (2002) found an overall, inverse association between satisfaction and spousal withdrawal in response to partner demands; however, this association was much weaker when there was also a high rate of affectionate behavior in the marriage.

Other studies reveal several differences in avoidance and engagement tactics based on Fitzpatrick's couple typology, which categorizes couples according to beliefs and values about relationships or "relational schema" (Fitzpatrick, 1988; Koerner & Fitzpatrick,

2002). The couples distinguished by Fitzpatrick respond to conflict in ways that are consistent with their particular construction of intimate relationships. "Traditional" couples interact in a manner that reflects their conventionality and emphasis on openness balanced with social restraint; for example, these couples tend to use positive tactics, make reference to relationship expectations, and enact "validation" and "contract" sequences (e.g., husband offers information, wife agrees) during couple interactions. "Independent" couples stress the importance of verbal negotiation; thus, they tend to confront one another, share information, and provide justifications for the spouse's compliance. Wanting to remain autonomous, "separate" partners tend to use indirect messages and avoid solving each other's problems, but they confront each other when one partner complains (Fitzpatrick, 1988).

Apart from having different baserates for avoidance and engagement tactics, Sillars, Pike, Jones, and Redmon (1983) found a different association between communication and satisfaction within different couple types. Whereas conflict engagement predicted marital satisfaction among independent couples, virtually the opposite was true among separate couples. The satisfied, separate couples engaged in a great deal of avoidance during conflict discussions, including verbal denial of conflict and topic shifts, and they rarely spoke with a negative tone of voice, maintaining instead, consistently neutral, nonverbal affect. Thus, satisfaction may be predicted either by engagement or by avoidance, depending on how the pattern of communication fits with the couple's preferred pattern of relating (i.e., interdependence achieved through discussion versus autonomy maintained through conversational restraint and strategic disengagement).

Cooperation and Competition

In terms of the cooperation–competition dimension, studies largely confirm the ubiquitous presence of negative and competitive communication in unhappy, maladjusted relationships and greater incidence of cooperative and supportive messages in well-adjusted relationships (see Canary, Cupach, & Messman, 1995; Gottman, 1994). There are also several refinements on this theme. First, the reciprocation of negative affect, complaints, and other competitive acts has been linked to marital distress, independent of negative base rates, across a number of studies (e.g., Alberts, 1988; Billings, 1979, Gottman, 1979, 1994; Margolin & Wampold, 1981; Pike & Sillars, 1985; Ting-Toomey, 1983). Thus, unhappy couples may contain conflict for a time, but once there is a felt provocation from one partner, they tend to construct extended chains of negative and competitive messages, such that negativity becomes an "absorbing state" (Gottman, 1994). As this picture implies, dissatisfied couples tend to become proportionately more negative as their conversations progress (Billings, 1979; Gottman, 1994). That is, dissatisfied couples often begin their conversations with polite behaviors but tend to lapse into patterns of increasing hostility. The balance between cooperative and competitive messages may be important as well (e.g., Gottman & Levenson, 1992). Gottman (1994) reported a positive/negative behavior ratio of 5:1 for stable couples and a ratio of less than 1:1 for unstable couples.

Longitudinal studies offer some support for the ability of both positive and negative communication to predict marital dissatisfaction and dissolution over time (see Karney & Bradbury, 1995). For example, Noller, Feeney, Bonnell, and Callan (1994) found that communication predicted both concurrent and longitudinal satisfaction during the initial years of marriage; further, initial satisfaction also predicted later communication. Spouses high in satisfaction after 2 years were less likely to manipulate the partner, to avoid dealing with conflict, to behave coercively, or to enact demand–withdraw patterns. Likewise, Pasch and Bradbury (1998) found that wife supportiveness during a problem-solving task was positively linked to marital quality 2 years later, whereas husband expression of anger was negatively linked to subsequent marital quality. Huston and Chorost (1994) found that husbands' negativity early in marriage predicted a decline wives' satisfaction 1 and 2 years later. However, wives were buffered from this effect when husbands were also highly affectionate. Gottman and Levenson (2000) found that negative conflict interaction predicted divorce early in the marriage (i.e., the first 7 years) but not later in marriage (i.e., 7–14 years). They also found that a lack of positive messages during a discussion about events of the day predicted later, but not earlier, divorce.

Although longitudinal studies are generally supportive of a link between earlier communication and later satisfaction and stability in marriage, Bradbury et al. (2001) suggest that the effect sizes in longitudinal studies are not impressive. Further, these authors note troubling inconsistencies; for example, studies variously suggest that expression of anger early in marriage predicts decreased satisfaction (Johnson, 1999), predicts increased satisfaction (Gottman & Krokoff, 1989; Karney & Bradbury, 1997), or is unrelated to satisfaction at a later time (Gottman, Coan, Carrere, & Swanson, 1998).

Demand–Withdrawal

We have alluded to the manner in which a certain sequential pattern of conflict (i.e., negative reciprocity) is linked to relational quality. A number of additional sequential patterns are discussed in other sources (e.g., Gottman, 1994; Messman & Canary, 1998; Schaap, Buunk, & Kerkstra, 1988). In this chapter, we discuss one type of conflict sequence that lately has received considerable attention.

The *demand–withdraw* sequence refers to instances wherein one person approaches the partner on an issue and the partner attempts to avoid discussion of the issue (e.g., Caughlin & Vangelisti, 1999; 2000; Christensen & Heavey, 1990; Heavey, Christensen, & Malamuth, 1995; Heavey, Layne, & Christensen, 1993). This sequence typically occurs when a dissatisfied person seeks change from the partner on a particular issue, and then the partner who wants to sustain the status quo withdraws or seeks to minimize the discussion (Klinetob & Smith, 1996; Kluwer, de Dreu, & Buunk, 1998). This research also indicates that women are more likely to demand change (and men are more likely to withdraw), due to the inequity women face in maintaining marriage (e.g., Heavey et al., 1993). However, some recent evidence suggests that the demand–withdraw pattern may not be entirely asymmetrical. That is, both partners might reciprocate each other's demands and/or withdrawals. For instance, wife dissatisfaction with husband execution of household chores is associated with the *husband* demanding change in how the wife cleans the house, in addition to the wife demanding change in how the husband cleans the house (Caughlin & Vangelisti, 1999, 2000; Kluwer, Heensink, & Van de Vliert, 1997). Further, the "demand" and "withdrawal" roles may shift, depending on the conflict issue. Whereas women tend to demand and men withdraw when the wife seeks change, this sequence is reversed when discussing an issue in which the husband seeks change (Klinetob & Smith, 1996). Regardless of whether the pattern is symmetrical or asymmetrical, the demand–withdraw pattern occurs more in dissatisfied relationships (Heavey et al., 1993, 1995). Further, even though the "demand" portion of demand–withdraw is another reflection of competitive interaction and overall negativity, the demand–withdraw pattern predicts marital satisfaction above and beyond overall negativity in marriage (Caughlin & Huston, 2002).

Effects of Conflict on Children

Another way to assess the relationship between manifest conflict and relationship quality is in terms of the impact of family conflict on the well-being of children. There is a voluminous and still-expanding literature on the impact of marital conflict on children. This research indicates that children are affected by parental conflict both immediately (in terms of emotional response) and over time (in terms of psychological adjustment and development).

Consistently, research has found that intense, negative marital conflict may threaten a child's sense of security and safety in the home and in the outside world (Gordis, Margolin, & John, 2001). For example, Cummings and colleagues (e.g., Cummings, Iannotti, & Zahn-Waxler, 1985; for a review, see Cummings, Goeke-Morey, & Papp, 2001) have found that young children respond to adult anger with various negative emotions, such as distress, fear, sadness, and anger, which are often manifested in nonverbal signals, such as changes in body movement and facial distortion.

Other research shows that children who observe their parents' competitive conflict may experience developmental problems (Cummings et al., 2001). First, children learn how to manage conflict indirectly by watching their parents and modeling their behavioral style. For example, Jenkins (2000) found that children in high-conflict homes showed higher levels of anger and aggression as rated by their peers, teachers, and mothers, and that children who observe angry conflict between their parents showed more frequent anger expressions and more deviant anger behaviors than did their counterparts. Also, conflict styles that parents use with each other and with their children tend to be mirrored in sibling relationships (Boer, Goedhart, & Teffers, 1992; Noller, Feeney, Peterson, & Sheehan, 1995; Reese-Weber, 2000). Moreover, conflict patterns from the family of origin may carry over into adult intimate relationships (Andrews, Foster, Capaldi, & Hops, 2000).

Children who witness competitive parental conflict tend to have more adjustment problems than children not exposed to such conflict. Such problems include internalizing emotions, acting out, behaving in socially incompetent ways, and performing poorly in school (Cummings et al., 2001). Competitive parental conflict appears to be such a powerful predictor of children maladjustment that it overrides the effects of divorce. That is, if couples decide to remain married for the "sake of the children" but they engage in competitive conflict that the children witness, the tendency is for children to be hurt psychologically and behaviorally more so than if the couple separated, divorced, and demonstrated more cooperative behaviors toward one another (Amato & Keith, 1991). Parental conflict also has more powerful effects than other forms of parental interaction (e.g., showing affection, Cummings et al., 2001). In brief, severe parental conflict appears to have a substantial effect on children's immediate emotional reactions and on their long-term psychological and behavioral adjustment.

Nevertheless, children differ in the way they react to parental conflict and they demonstrate different degrees of resilience, even in the face of extreme conflict. Grych, Jouriles, Swank, McDonald, and Norwood (2000) identified five distinct patterns of adjustment among children living in shelters for battered women, and nearly a third of the children showed no evidence of adjustment problems of any sort. Presumably, less extreme forms of parental conflict have even more variable effects on individual children. Further, although children often model parental conflict, they may also reject the model provided by their parents. In evaluating the intergenerational transmission of family conflict styles, VanLear (1992) found that young couples appeared to model some aspects of their parents' marriages and rebel against others. For example, conflict avoidance reported by young husbands was negatively associated with conflict avoidance reported by their fathers, especially when the father's own marriage was an unhappy one.

This section has examined manifest communication patterns that show some connection to relational quality. The results suggest that there are a few well-replicated findings but also considerable variation in the apparent impacts of communication. In the following section, we consider communication and conflict from a different angle, namely, the subjective interpretation of communication by family members. We have labeled this section "communication infidelity" to suggest that family conflicts are frequently characterized by problematic episodes in which different and incompatible interpretations are assigned to the same manifest signals.

COMMUNICATION INFIDELITY

One of the most compelling and confounding features of intimate conflict is the tendency for individuals to construct profoundly different interpretations of the same interactions. Differences in perception are a basic, even defining feature of conflict (Wilmot & Hocker, 2001). Moreover, differences in perception seem to increase as conflicts intensify. Thus, a number of studies of marital conflict find that unhappy spouses often hold sharply incongruent images of conflict (Fincham & Bradbury, 1991) and provide different interpretations for communication, including the emotional meaning assigned to messages (Guthrie & Noller, 1988); perceptions of self- and partner-conflict behaviors (Acitelli, Douvan, and Veroff, 1993; Sillars, Roberts, Leonard & Dun, 2000); and thoughts, feelings, and intentions attributed to the partner during communication (Ickes & Simpson, 1997; Noller & Ruzzene, 1991). There appears to be a reciprocal relationship between incongruent perception and conflict escalation/deescalation. As conflicts escalate, perceptions and interpretations may become more selective, idiosyncratic, and extreme. This, in turn, influences subsequent communication in such a way as to drive further escalation and entrenchment of conflict (Bradbury & Fincham, 1991).

Information Versus Bias

The extent to which family members coordinate perspectives and understand one another during conflict partly depends on the characteristics of manifest communication we have been discussing. Naturally, we would expect greater understanding among family members who communicate about conflict more directly and cooperatively, as some research confirms (Knudson, Sommers, & Golding, 1980). Although this much is intuitively obvious, the manifest features of communication do not fully account for the extent of shared meaning and mutual understanding among family members. Cognitive factors, especially theory-driven processing of messages (e.g., Noller & Ruzzene, 1991; Thomas & Fletcher, 1997), sometimes foster interpretations that are dramatically at odds with conventional meanings for explicit information (i.e., the linguistic code and obvious nonverbal signals). Thus, several studies of marital conflict have found a weak or null relationship between the amount of information directly disclosed during communication and mutual understanding between spouses (see Sillars, 1998; Thomas & Fletcher, 1997).

Sillars and others identify two general factors that encourage theory-driven processing of communication during family conflicts. First, the intense familiarity of family relationships increases the temptation to view potential sources of information selectively, to monitor interactions less actively for new sources of information, to make new inferences conform to existing relationship theories, and to attach a high degree of certainty to inferences, regardless of their actual diagnostic value (Sillars, 1998; Thomas & Fletcher, 1997). Second, the cognitive demands and constraints associated with communication, particularly during angry, stressful interactions, increase selective attention to information that serves persuasive and defensive goals within the interaction and limits consideration of alternative positions, inferences, and perspectives (Sillars et al., 2000).

Other authors emphasize the extent to which selective attention to and interpretation of messages depends on mood state and the emotional climate in the relationship (e.g., Forgas, 2001). Bradbury and Fincham (1991) suggest that the observed negativity of distressed couples is linked to selective attention to and recall of negative relationship events. Distressed spouses tend to see their partner's negative behavior as highly meaningful and relevant to self; thus, they process it more fully, leading to elaborate, negative representations of the partner that are easily evoked by interaction. In contrast, happy spouses are more likely to discount the partner's negative communication, because it does not evoke elaborate, well-rehearsed, negative memories.

Watzlawick et al. (1967) discuss the consequences of incongruent perceptions of communication in their landmark work on relational communication. Watzlawick et al. suggest that repetitive conflicts may be perpetuated by an "inability to metacommunicate," a condition characterized by incongruent interpretations of messages at a relational level (e.g., a husband believes he is being helpful, his wife sees his message as arrogant and condescending). This condition is "binding" in the sense that efforts to talk about the conflict rely on the same patterns of communication and interpretation that are the source of difficulty. Thus, talking about the conflict may exacerbate it (e.g., the husband's self-explanations may be taken as further evidence of arrogance).

Encoding–Decoding of Emotional Communication

The "inability to metacommunicate" phenomena described by Watzlawick et al. (1967) is quite parallel to the misunderstanding of emotional communication found among distressed married couples. This trend is documented by a series of studies by Noller, Gottman, and others. Research in this tradition indicates that unhappy couples often construct incongruent interpretations of emotional messages.

Noller's (1980) research used a highly structured and carefully controlled procedure (adapted from Kahn, 1970) in which one spouse expressed various messages in a manner that was meant to suggest positive, neutral, or negative meanings. The literal content of messages was ambiguous (e.g., "What are you doing?" "You really surprised me this time."), so the meaning had to be inferred from nonverbal cues. The partner judged the intended meaning and outside raters also judged the message to determine whether the intended meaning was conveyed clearly. High-adjustment couples had greater encoding–decoding accuracy than did low-adjustment couples, primarily because the low-adjustment husbands fared poorly in both encoding and decoding roles. As senders, these husbands had fewer messages deemed "good communication"; as receivers, they supplied inaccurate interpretations of their wives' messages, even when these were considered clearly encoded. The receiving deficit of dissatisfied husbands was apparently specific to the relationship and not a general trait, as the same men were more accurate when decoding married women who were not their own wives (Noller, 1981). Gottman and Porterfield (1981), using a variant of the same encoding–decoding procedure, also found that marital satisfaction was negatively correlated with the decoding accuracy of husbands. Most dissatisfied wives were understood better by married men who were strangers than by their own husbands, whereas most satisfied wives were understood better by their husbands.

The association between marital adjustment and encoding–decoding accuracy has been replicated several times (Gottman, et al., 1976; Guthrie & Noller, 1988; Noller & Venardos, 1988; Kahn, 1970). Gottman, et al. (1976) utilized "talk table" procedures in which couples talked to one another about a problem in their marriage, at the same time electronically rating the intent of each message sent and the impact of those received on 5-point scales. Although the happy and unhappy couples did not differ in the rated intent of messages, the rated effect was more negative in unhappy marriages. Notarius, Benson, Sloane, Vanzetti, and Hornyak (1989) also utilized the talk table procedure and found evidence of "negative sentiment override" among distressed spouses (i.e., allowing negative sentiment to color behavioral interpretation) and "positive sentiment override" among nondistressed spouses (Weiss, 1980). Distressed wives frequently attributed negative intent to their husbands' messages when these messages were seen as neutral by observers, whereas nondistressed wives often rated messages as neutral or positive when they were seen as negative by observers. Using procedures similar to Noller (1980), Noller and Venardos (1986) found a relationship between marital adjustment and decoding accuracy for wives. Further, spouses rated their confidence that they had decoded messages accurately. Spouses high in marital adjustment were more confident when messages were decoded accurately; thus, their self-assessment was realistic. Spouses low in adjustment were just as confident regardless of whether the message was decoded accurately or not.

In Vivo Thoughts and Feelings

Another series of studies has relied on video-assisted recall methods to elicit specific thoughts and feelings that accompany communication during family conflict. In this research, couples or families first discussed issues that represented points of contention. Afterwards, each family member viewed a videotape of the discussion (in most cases, separately), reporting their thoughts, feelings, and perceptions, usually with the goal of reconstructing thought processes that occurred during the interaction (see Halford & Sanders, 1988). In some cases, the researchers also assessed whether an individual could guess what another person reported thinking or feeling during the interaction, using a variant of Ickes' protocol for assessing empathic accuracy (see Ickes & Tooke, 1988). Studies of family conflict utilizing video-assisted recall have emerged from a variety of research programs and do not constitute an integrated research literature. Still, these studies provide the most realistic simulation to date of *in vivo* thought processes accompanying conflict and they suggest several important characteristics of inferences made during the heat of the moment.

In a study that confirmed the thrust of encoding–decoding studies, Noller and Ruzzene (1991) had spouses discuss a long-standing problem, then watch a videotape of the discussion and provide reports about intentions, affective states, and the impact of messages. Distressed spouses were less accurate than nondistressed spouses at judging the partner's intent, the affect associated with partner intentions, and the affective impact of their own behaviors on the partner. Distressed spouses also made more negative inferences, which is a trend born out in other studies as well (e.g., Sillars et al., 2000; Vangelisti, Corbin, Lucchetti, & Sprague, 1999).

Although individuals report widely ranging thoughts and feelings during conflict (Fletcher & Fitness, 1990; Sillars et al., 2000), many of the conscious inferences reported by spouses involve interpretation of specific communicative acts and pragmatic intentions, for example, whether the partner is presumed to be listening, empathizing, criticizing, or evading a point (Manusov & Koenig, 2001; Sillars et al., 2000). Spouses often differ in their interpretation of specific and even seemingly objective communication "behaviors" (e.g., topic shifts or interruptions). Indeed, their thoughts may reflect a completely different focus of attention and framing of the communication episode.

Sillars et al. (2000) had spouses watch a videotape of their discussion, reporting out loud the thoughts and feelings they remembered having while the discussion was in progress. Inductive coding of these reports revealed that spouses often constructed different interpretations of the immediate interaction, with the partner generally seen as being less cooperative and more confrontational than self. Further, there was less correspondence between these spontaneous attributions about communication and observer-assigned codes for the interactions in more intense conflicts, suggesting that insider perceptions of communication were more subjective when there was greater conflict. Typically, husbands thought about literal content issues more than wives, and they showed other indications of being less attuned to the partner and relationship. However, these gender differences may partly reflect the sample of couples, which was fairly sex-stereotypic. Vangelisti et al. (1999), using an analogous procedure that employed computer-mediated communication, did not find gender differences in relationship-oriented thoughts during communication with a romantic partner.

There is a well-replicated tendency for adolescents to perceive more negativity during family interactions than parents do, prompting speculation about whether parent or adolescent reports are more realistic (see Noller, 1995). However, research suggests that there are biases in both directions. In a study by Noller and Callan (1988), fathers, mothers, and adolescent children rated one another's behavior during video recall of a family problem-solving discussion. The ratings that family members provided for one another were either uncorrelated or negatively correlated with ratings provided by observers (members of other families who were strangers) and with a trained rater. A further study utilizing video recall identified specific biases in parent and adolescent perceptions of communication during a discussion of family conflicts (Sillars, Smith, Koerner, & Fitzpatrick, 2003). In this research, parents overattributed negative thoughts and underattributed agreement thoughts to their adolescent children, relative to the thoughts that the adolescents reported having. On the other hand, adolescents overattributed controlling thoughts to their parents, relative to the thoughts that parents reported having. Thus, it appeared that both parents and adolescents overgeneralized from conflicts at this family stage, perceiving a greater underlying tone of resistance, negativity, and control associated with messages than that reflected in the reported thoughts of the sender.

A few studies have directly considered how cognition during interaction can either reinforce or mitigate negative reciprocity in communication. First, Gaelick, Bodenhausen, and Wyer (1985) considered how overattribution of negative versus positive sentiment may contribute to negative reciprocity. Several studies have found that negative messages and sentiments were more accurately judged (by comparison to either partner or observer reports) than positive messages and sentiments (Fletcher & Fitness, 1990; Noller, 1980; Noller & Venardos, 1986; Sillars et al., 1984; for exceptions, see Noller & Ruzzene, 1991; Thomas & Fletcher, 1997). Gaelick et al. (1985) note an ironic consequence of the greater accuracy sometimes associated with negative affect. The spouses in their research watched videotaped segments of their own interactions and identified feelings of hostility or love that they or their partner intended to convey. According to these reports, spouses attempted to reciprocate the emotion that the partner was perceived to intend; however, only hostility was perceived accurately, so they reciprocated intended hostility and not love.

On a somewhat more optimistic note, Bissonnette, Rusbult, and Kilpatrick (1997) suggest that spouses may suppress and transform an initial urge to reciprocate negative messages or provocations based on commitment, concern for the relationship, and understanding of the other's thoughts and feelings. Bissonette et al. found some evidence supporting this reasoning in a longitudinal study of newlywed couples who completed an interaction and video-recall task modeled after Ickes' empathic accuracy paradigm. Spouses who had higher commitment and empathic accuracy reported more accommodation during conflict (i.e., "voice" and "loyalty" versus "exit" and "neglect" strategies in response to the partner's bad behavior). However, these effects were observed only during the first data collection and not a subsequent session 12 to 16 months later. The authors speculated that empathic accuracy declines in importance over the course of a relationship, as active analysis of conflict is supplanted by motives and habits that operate automatically.

The research on subjective interpretations of communication is helpful in making sense out of the most problematic cases of family conflict, in which individuals enact recurring episodes of negative reciprocity and other toxic patterns. In these cases, individuals may adopt dramatically different interpretive frameworks for interaction; thus, they attend to different aspects of the immediate interaction and background knowledge and they interpret communication in an incongruous manner. In this sense, relationship conflicts may become one-sided affairs, in which the parties neither participate in the same issues nor observe the same sequence of events.

ASSESSMENT AND CRITIQUE

One cannot help but be impressed by the scale and sophistication of research brought on by the explosion of interest in family conflict over the past 2 decades. It is a challenge to stay abreast of this area, given the pace of activity. Further, many recent interaction studies are far more ambitious than earlier efforts, as reflected, for example, in the growing number of multiyear longitudinal designs. Moreover, the research has important implications. The many studies documenting correlates of chronic, negative family conflict are sobering, with the impacts of conflict on children being especially poignant. Gottman (1994, p. 45) acknowledges hearing criticism to the effect that the connection between negativity and marital dissatisfaction is obvious and uninteresting. In response, Gottman (pp. 64–65) argues that the results are not trivial when one examines specific codes and code sequences associated with dissatisfaction. In addition, Weiss and Heyman (1997), among others, point out important practical and clinical implications of this research.

Although we do not regard research on negativity in family conflict as trivial, one is struck by how much of the research on family communication can be subsumed under the general investigation of negativity in its various disguises. In part, this reflects the influence of social learning theory and the tendency to conceptualize family communication patterns in terms of rewarding and punishing behavior (see Caughlin & Huston, 2002). However, the focus on positivity/negativity would likely emerge even without a strong theoretical push, as this is arguably the most pervasive dimension of human experience and also the surest route to achieving statistical significance in one's research.

The view of communication as rewarding and punishing behavior is useful in the context of a certain clinical perspective that has stimulated much research (i.e., behavioral marriage therapy). However, this view also carries certain liabilities when applied too widely to family communication. We now suggest what a few of these liabilities might be.

Clinical Comparisons and Their Limitations

The most common strategy for investigating family conflict is to compare the communication patterns of couples or families who are experiencing an explicit form of family distress (e.g., they express dissatisfaction, seek counseling, separate or file for divorce) with others who lack the same unkind symptoms. Generally, this research is conducted under the assumption that whatever discriminates families in distress from other families also helps to explain their distress and ways to alleviate it (Beach, 2001; Bradbury et al., 2001; Huston & Vangelisti, 1991).

Research that compares distressed and nondistressed families has the obvious advantage that it is easily translated into clinical practice (Cordova, 2001). Further, by focusing on families in distress, certain processes that characterize normal family conflict are magnified and can be seen with greater clarity (Belsky, 2001).

On the other hand, comparisons to distressed and maladjusted families also have the potential to mislead, especially when such comparisons come to represent the default strategy for studying conflict in diverse family settings. First, when communication is consistently viewed in clinical terms, one can easily confuse normal variations in family interaction with analogous extremes associated with family disturbance. Some 2 decades ago, scholars discussed the need to study normal family interactions in their own right, and not just as a counterpoint to disturbed families (Walsh, 1982). Although these arguments increased attention to structural and cultural diversity within families, normalcy in communication still tends to be equated with an ideal family type or statistical average (Stafford & Dainton, 1994). What tends to be lacking in either case is attention to the range of conflict styles and communication patterns found among families who could be considered "adequately functioning."

A second disadvantage of dichotomizing between distressed and nondistressed or adjusted versus maladjusted families is that the mean interaction characteristics discriminating these groups may also come to be dichotomized as bad/good communication (Erbert & Duck, 1997). Arguing from a dialectical perspective, Erbert and Duck (1997) note that ostensibly "positive" communication behaviors can serve negative functions and vice versa, as when positive behaviors reproduce unnecessary and damaging patterns of accommodation. Although a number of authors make much the same point (e.g., Charny, 1980; Gottman & Krokoff, 1989; Wilmot & Hocker, 2001), there still exists an overriding instinct to search for ideal patterns of communication, with the implicit assumption that the goal of communication is to increase closeness and bonding (Erbert & Duck, 1997). In contrast, dialectical theorists emphasize that relationships naturally cycle between states of closeness/distance, as well as of satisfaction/dissatisfaction (Erbert, 2000). Outside of distressed, disturbed, or violent relationships, where reduction of negativity is a matter of relational (and individual) survival, cycles involving negative as well as positive behavior constitute both normal and functional adaptation to relational polarities and contradictions, such as the simultaneous need for connection and autonomy (Erbert & Duck, 1997).

Sillars and Weisberg (1987) make a similar argument about the variable impacts of communication, albeit on different grounds than do Erbert and Duck. Sillars and Weisberg argue that the literature on intimate conflict reflects an overly simplistic "skill" metaphor for communication. In this metaphor, communication is seen as a straightforward set of behavioral skills (i.e., the ability to be clear, consistent, direct, supportive, focused, and reciprocal) that operate in roughly the same manner across relationships, independent of various contextual factors, such as the source and depth of conflict, the degree of informal consensus within relationships, and individual or cultural preferences regarding communication. Sillars and Weisberg further suggest that there is a qualitatively different context for communication in distressed versus nondistressed relationships, because the conflict issues found in distressed relationships involve core relationship issues that are more profound, diffuse, ambiguous, and difficult to resolve than the relatively concrete and focused conflicts that may characterize generally harmonious couples and families. Thus, the communication "skills" demonstrated by compatible individuals are not necessarily illuminating, because the process of communication is naturally more orderly and transparent when individuals have generally congruent perceptions and expectations. Conversely, the communicative incompetency shown by other couples and families may relate, at least in part, to the disorderly and ambiguous properties of communication within serious relationship conflict.

A third tradeoff of clinical comparisons is that they direct attention (quite intentionally) to those aspects of communication that successfully discriminate distressed and nondistressed families, thus directing attention away from other aspects of communication that are either characteristic of all families (distressed along with nondistressed) or characteristic of only certain families within either distressed or nondistressed categories. Subtlety is inevitably lost when one searches for aspects of communication that discriminate distressed couples or families, as a group, from nondistressed couples or families, as a group. Both categories are obviously heterogeneous, and the "nondistressed" (or "happy," "nonviolent," "well-adjusted," "stable," "nonalcoholic," etc.) category is apt to be especially diverse. The effect of averaging across diverse couples or families is to highlight elements that are the greatest common denominator (primarily, negativity of communication) and to gloss over other dynamics that might have important functions within individual families or family subtypes.

As we have seen, chronic negativity, manifested variably in either verbal and/or nonverbal behavior, is the most consistent factor discriminating distressed and nondistressed family relationships, probably because negative communication has an intrinsic connection to relationship unhappiness. Other characteristics of communication (e.g., humor, indirectness, involvement by informal third parties) are more likely to function in a manner that reflects family identity, tradition, preferred mode of expression, and other characteristics of individual families. By attempting to isolate those elements of communication that best discriminate distressed and nondistressed families, researchers may instinctively focus on negativity to the exclusion of other important aspects of communication. For example, only a few studies we are aware of have looked at something as basic as having a sense of humor about conflict (Alberts, 1990; Jacobs, 1985; Krokoff, 1991). Even here, one of the primary conclusions boils down to negativity; that is, biting humor is related to relationship distress, whereas well-adjusted couples use more positive and benign humor (Alberts, 1990; Jacobs, 1985).

Communication as "Behavior"

The organization of our review according to manifest versus subjective communication processes reflects the conventional distinction in psychology between behavioral and cognitive traditions. The line between these traditions is not tightly drawn in the literature on family conflict, as many of the authors who pioneered observational approaches to interaction (e.g., Gottman, Raush, Weiss) also focused on cognitive processes during communication. Still, the analytic separation of cognition and behavior in this literature contributes to a misleading sense that communication refers to behavior, not inference. Indeed, the terms "communication" and "behavior" occur together so often that they appear redundant.

This emphasis contrasts with contemporary theories of communication and meaning that stress the inherent ambiguity of messages (Hopper, 1981; Ritchie, 1991; Sperber & Wilson, 1986). That is, even simple examples of referential communication require an inferential leap based on nonlinguistic and noncoded contextual information. The explicitly coded signals are even less complete with respect to the types of pragmatic and affective meanings that family researchers routinely regard as objective behavior (e.g., "criticism," "withdrawal," "disgust," "assent," "problem solving," "validation"). Given the variability and indeterminancy of signals that may constitute any of these acts, it is not surprising that family members themselves often interpret the sequence of communication in an idiosyncratic fashion (e.g., Sillars et al., 2000), reflecting their goals, mood states, salient memories, and other factors discussed earlier in this review.

To be sure, there are ways of objectifying (i.e., standardizing) observer perceptions, and these data are useful insofar as we remain cognizant of what they represent. Observer perceptions represent meanings assigned by a relatively uninvolved and uninitiated onlooker, either in the general sense of naive observers who rely on conventional meanings or in the restricted sense of a coder trained to apply a particular interpretive system (Poole, Folger, & Hewes, 1986). Nonetheless, the neutral observers used in family interaction research (who are mostly other people's spouses or undergraduate students), as well as trained coders (who are mostly psychology or communication graduate students), are still people with a certain perspective and the meanings they assign to ambiguous communicative signals do not literally constitute "actual behavior."

The inherent ambiguity of communication has direct consequences for some of the issues we have been discussing. First, as we have seen, there are relatively few well-replicated connections between manifest patterns of communication and relationship quality. This fact may be largely attributable to differences in the ways that particular individuals, couples, or whole families interpret the meaning of manifest communication.

We have noted one well-replicated communication pattern, specifically, the demand–withdraw sequence in marriage, which is related to marital dissatisfaction independent of overall negativity and negative reciprocity. Given the asymmetric nature of this pattern, it may reflect a more abstract, underlying phenomena that Morton, Alexander, and Altman (1976) referred to as a "lack of mutuality in relationship definition." Morton et al. made a persuasive case that all crises in relationships entail a lack of mutuality, which, in the case of demand–withdrawal, might mean a lack of consensus about the decision to confront or disengage. Aside from the demand–withdraw pattern, other manifest communication patterns that show a consistent association with relationship satisfaction or distress are mostly variants of general negativity and escalatory processes (e.g., negative reciprocity, cross-complaining). Further, although the effects of negativity are reasonably robust, we noted exceptions and inconsistencies even in this domain. Among other things, the effects of negativity probably depend on the way in which manifest signals are interpreted within a given relationship culture.

Although the meaning of nonverbal affect displays is widely considered to be less culturally specific than other communicative phenomena, there is still great variation across cultural groups (e.g., Planalp, 1999), including the extent to which blunt expression of negative affect is considered normal and acceptable within particular families and family subsystems (Sillars, 1995). Further, some studies have tested the cross-cultural generalizability of negativity in marriage. These studies find that the association between (observer-coded) negativity and marital dissatisfaction is attenuated within cultural groups that express negative emotions more freely, relative to cultures in which the expression of negative emotion is a less common, everyday phenomenon (Halford, Hahlweg, & Dunne, 1990; Krokoff, Gottman, & Roy, 1988; Winkler, & Doherty, 1983). This suggests to us that the signals or patterns that trained coders recognize as anger or hostility may symbolize something different to the family members themselves. Further, if this conclusion applies to general negativity, it should apply that much more to other aspects of communication that are even more variable across family cultures (e.g., indirectness and humor).

A second consequence of communicative ambiguity is that the "accurate" interpretation of a message is always a matter of conjecture. Terms like "accuracy" and "understanding" in communication are often taken to mean that the receiver correctly deciphers the actual meaning or intention behind communication, either by reference to the sender's stated intention or by observer-assigned meaning. In fact, these concepts can only reference the degree of shared interpretation. This point applies particularly to the research on communication infidelity, reviewed earlier. For example, the usual interpretation of encoding–decoding studies is that happy spouses are more accurate at decoding the actual intent of messages, whereas unhappy spouses tend to assign negative meaning where none was intended. Further, some of the research seems to single out husbands as the prime culprit in the misunderstandings of distressed couples (Gottman & Porterfield, 1981; Noller, 1980). While this gender difference has not held up consistently in subsequent studies (e.g., Noller & Venardos, 1986; Notarius et al., 1989), the tendency to localize responsibility for misunderstanding is problematic in other ways. For one, the sender's account of message intent should not be taken too literally. Apart from the obvious impact of social desirability on these reports, the act of reporting communicative intent requires interpretation of complex, multiple, and mostly nonreflective communicative goals that may not be easily verbalized in the simple terms required by the experiment (e.g. "positive" versus "negative").

Neither should the observer's perspective be construed as a final account of actual behavior or meaning. Whereas the participants' perspective is biased by direct involvement in the interaction, observers lack access to context that may affect the interpretation of a message from the sender or receiver's perspective. For example, if the wife outwardly feigns positive emotion while suppressing latent hostility, she is likely to be seen as positive by observers, but not necessarily by the husband, who has access to unobserved relational context (e.g., memories of past arguments on the same topic and observations of the wife's typical manner of expression). This example is not too far-fetched; in fact, a study by Noller (1982), conducted as a follow-up to her encoding–decoding research, found that wives were more emotionally expressive than husbands but that they also created more mixed messages across multiple channels (e.g., smiling while saying something negative). This is not to suggest that wives were actually at fault for the marital miscommunication seen in encoding–decoding studies but rather that inaccuracy and misunderstanding are inherently relational. That is, both genders contribute to misunderstanding, although they may potentially contribute based on contrasting styles and tendencies (e.g., female ambivalence versus male inexpressivity or inattentiveness).

Finally, there is a need to take into account more context when evaluating the impacts of communication on relationship quality. Of course, we are not the first to call attention to the importance of context in family or relationship research, and this argument can easily become a red herring. All research selects some elements of context to focus on and excludes others, so the real issue is whether we are focusing on context in quite the right way. Duck (2002) argues that the essential elements of context that guide interpretation of messages are all tied to "history": history in the sense of the historical and cultural time and place, the history of a relationship, and the sequence of events that comprise the history of a particular interaction. While Duck critiques the general literature on interpersonal communication for having an ahistorical outlook, this same criticism could apply, oddly enough, to research on family communication, where relational history is a given. That is, few studies have investigated such things as the history of conflict involving particular issues—how certain acts come to represent significant emotional triggers or conciliatory gestures; how specific conflicts are diffused, resolved, or maintained over time—or cycles of engagement/withdrawal, either during the course of a typical week or over the duration of critical transitions and stages. While it can be presumptuous to say what other researchers should or should not attend to, irrespective of their research goals, the aforementioned aspects of context would seem to have more potential news value in the immediate future than would further documentation of aggregate differences in manifest communication associated with relationship distress.

REFERENCES

Acitelli, L. K., Douvan, E., & Veroff, J. (1993). Perceptions of conflict in the first year of marriage: How important are similarity and understanding? *Journal of Social and Personal Relationships, 10*, 5–19.

Adams, R., & Laursen, B. (2001). The organization and dynamics of adolescent conflict with parents and friends. *Journal of Marriage and Family, 63*, 97–110.

Alberts, J. K. (1988). An analysis of couples' conversational complaints. *Communication Monographs, 55*, 184–197.

Alberts, J. K. (1990). The use of humor in managing couples' conflict interactions. In D. D. Cahn (Ed.), *Intimates in conflict: A communication perspective* (pp. 105–120). Hillsdale, NJ: Lawrence Erlbaum Associates.

Amato, P. R., & Keith, B. (1991). Parental divorce and the well-being of children: A meta-analysis. *Psychological Bulletin, 110*, 26–46.

Amato, P. R., Loomis, L. S., & Booth, A. (1995). Parental divorce, marital conflict, and offspring well-being during early adulthood. *Social Forces, 73*, 895–915.

Andrews, J. A., Foster, S. L., Capaldi, D., & Hops, H. (2000). Adoleescent and family predictors of physical aggression, communication, and satisfaction in young adult couples: A prospective analysis. *Journal of Consulting and Clinical Psychology, 68*, 195–208.

Beach, S. R. H. (2001). Expanding the study of dyadic conflict: The potential role of self-evaluation maintenance processes. In A. Booth, A. C. Crouter, & M. Clements (Eds.), *Couples in conflict* (pp. 83–94). Hillsdale, NJ: Lawrence Erlbaum Associates.

Bedford, V. H., & Blieszner, R. (1997). Personal relationships in later-life families. In S. Duck (Ed.), *Handbook of personal relationships* (2nd ed., pp. 523–539). New York: Wiley.

Bedford, V. H., Volling, B. L., & Avioli, P. S. (2000). Positive consequences of sibling conflict in childhood and adulthood. *International Journal of Aging and Human Development, 51*, 53–69.

Belsky, J. (2001). Marital violence in evolutionary perspective. In A. Booth, A. C. Crouter, & M. Clements (Eds.), *Couples in conflict* (pp. 27–35). Hillsdale, NJ: Lawrence Erlbaum Associates.

Billings, A. (1979). Conflict resolution in distressed and nondistressed married couples. *Journal of Consulting and Clinical Psychology, 47*, 368–376.

Birchler, G. R. (1979). Communication skills in married couples. In A. S. Bellack & M. Hersen, *Research and practice in social skills training.* New York: Plenum Press.

Bissonnette, V. L., Rusbult, C. E., & Kilpatrick, S. D. (1997). Empathic accuracy and marital conflict resolution. In W. Ickes (Ed.), *Empathic accuracy* (pp. 251–279). New York: Guilford Press.

Boer, F., Goedhart, A. W., & Treffers, P. D. A. (1992). Siblings and their parents. In F. Boer, & J. Dunn, (Eds.), *Children's sibling relationships: Developmental and clinical issues* (pp. 41–54). Hillsdale, NJ: Lawrence Erlbaum Associates.

Bradbury, T. N., & Fincham, F. D. (1991). A contextual model for advancing the study of marriage. In G. J. O. Fletcher & F. D. Fincham (Eds.), *Cognition in close relationships,* (pp. 127–147). Hillsdale, NJ: Lawrence Erlbaum Associates.

Bradbury, T. N., & Karney, B. R. (1993). Longitudinal study of marital interaction and dysfunction: Review and analysis. *Clinical Psychology. Review, 13,* 15–27.

Bradbury, T., Rogge, R., & Lawrence, E. (2001). Reconsidering the role of conflict in marriage. In A. Booth, A. C. Crouter, & M. Clements (Eds.), *Couples in conflict* (pp. 59–81). Hillsdale, NJ: Lawrence Erlbaum Associates.

Braiker, H. B., & Kelley, H. H. (1979). Conflict in the development of close relationships. In R. L. Burgess & T. L. Huston (Eds.), *Social exchange in developing relationships* (pp. 135–168). New York: Academic Press.

Buzzanell, P. M., & Burrell, N. A. (1997). Examining metaphorical conflict schemas and expressions across contexts and sex. *Human Communication Research, 24,* 109–146.

Canary, D. J., Cupach, W. R., & Messman, S. J. (1995). *Relationship conflict.* Thousand Oaks, CA: Sage.

Carstensen, L. L., Gottman, J. M., & Levenson, R. W. (1995). *Psychology and Aging, 10,* 140–149.

Caughlin, J. P., & Huston, T. L. (2002). A contextual analysis of the association between demand/withdraw and marital satisfaction. *Personal Relationships, 9,* 95–119.

Caughlin, J. P., & Vangelisti, A. L. (1999). Desire for change in one's partner as a predictor of the demand/withdraw pattern of martial communication. *Communication Monographs, 66,* 66–89.

Caughlin, J. P., & Vangelisti, A. L. (2000). An individual difference explanation of why married couples engage in demand/withdraw pattern of conflict. *Journal of Social and Personal Relationships, 17,* 523–551.

Charny, I. W. (1980). Why are so many (if not really all) people and families disturbed? *Journal of Marital and Family Therapy, 6,* 37–45.

Christensen, A., & Heavey, C. L. (1990). Gender and social structure in the demand/ withdrawal pattern of marital conflict. *Journal of Personality and Social Psychology, 59,* 73–81.

Cordova, J. V. (2001). Broadening the scope of couples research: Pragmatics and prevention. In A. Booth, A. C. Crouter, & M. Clements (Eds.), *Couples in conflict* (pp. 105–114). Hillsdale, NJ: Lawrence Erlbaum Associates.

Crohan, S. E. (1996). Marital quality and conflict across the transition to parenthood in African American and White couples. *Journal of Marriage and the Family, 58,* 933–944.

Cummings, E. M., Goeke-Morey, M. C., & Papp, L. M. (2001). Couple conflict, children, and families: It's not just you and me, babe. In A. Booth, A. C. Crouter, & M. Clements (Eds.), *Couples in conflict* (pp. 117–148). Mahwah, NJ: Lawrence Erlbaum Associates.

Cummings, E. M., Iannotti, R. J., & Zahn-Waxler, C. (1985). The influence of conflict between adults on the emotion and aggression of young children. *Developmental Psychology, 21*, 495–507.

Deutsch, M. (1973). *The resolution of conflict: Constructive and destructive processes.* New Haven, CT: Yale University Press.

Dickson, F. C. (1995). The best is yet to be: Research on long-lasting relationships. In J. T. Wood & S. Duck (Eds.), *Understanding relationship processes: Off the beaten track* (pp. 22–50). Beverly Hills, CA: Sage.

Dickson, F. C. (1997). Aging and marriage: Understanding the long-term, later-life marriage. In W. K. Halford & H. J. Markman (Eds.), *Clinical handbook of marriage and couples interventions* (pp. 255–269). New York: Wiley.

Duck, S. (2002). Hypertext in the key of G: Three types of "history" as influences on conversational structure and flow. *Communication Theory, 12*, 41–62.

Dunn, J., & Slomkowski, C. (1992). Conflict and the development of social understanding. In C. U. Shantz & W. W. Hartup (Eds.), *Conflict in child and adolescent development* (pp. 70–92). New York: Cambridge University Press.

Durodoye, B. A. (1997). Factors of marital satisfaction among African American couples and Nigerian male/African American female couples. *Journal of Cross-Cultural Psychology, 28*, 71–80.

Eisenberg, A. R. (1992). Conflicts between mothers and their young children. *Merrill-Palmer Quarterly, 38*, 21–43.

Erbert, L. A. (2000). Conflict and dialectics: Perceptions of dialectical contradictions in marital conflict. *Journal of Social and Personal Relationships, 17*, 638–659.

Erbert, L. A., & Duck, S. W. (1997). Rethinking satisfaction in personal relationships from a dialectical perspective. In R. J. Sternberg & M. Hojjat (Eds.), *Satisfaction in close relationships* (pp. 190–216). New York: Guilford Press.

Feldman, C. M., & Ridley, C. A. (2000). The role of conflict-based communication responses and outcomes in male violence toward female partners. *Journal of Social and Personal Relationships, 17*, 552–573.

Fincham, F. D., & Bradbury, T. N. (1991). Cognition in marriage: A program of research on attributions. In W. H. Jones & D. Perlman (Eds.), *Advances in personal relationships* (Vol. 2, pp. 159–203). London: Kingsley.

Fitzpatrick, M. A. (1988). *Between husbands and wives: Communication in marriage.* Newbury Park, CA: Sage.

Fitzpatrick, M. A., Fallis, S., & Vance, L. (1982). Multifunctional coding of conflict resolution strategies in marital dyads. *Family Relations, 31*, 61–70.

Fletcher, G. J. O., & Fitness, J. (1990). Concurrent social cognition in close relationship interaction: The role of proximal and distal variables. *Journal of Personality and Social Psychology, 59*, 464–474.

Fletcher, G. J. O., & Kininmonth, L. (1991). Interaction in close relationships and social cognition. In G. J. O. Fletcher & F. Fincham (Eds.), *Cognition in close relationships* (pp. 235–255). Hillsdale, NJ: Lawrence Erlbaum Associates.

Forgas, J. P. (2001). Affective influences on communication and attribution in relationships. In V. Manusov & J. H. Harvey (Eds.), *Attribution, communication behavior, and close relationships* (pp. 3–20). New York: Cambridge University Press.

Gable, S. L., & Reis, H. T. (2001). Appetitive and aversive social interaction. In J. Harvey & A. Wenzel (Eds.), *Close romantic relationships: Maintenance and enhancement* (pp. 169–194). Mahwah, NJ: Lawrence Erlbaum Associates.

Gaelick, L., Bodenhausen, G. V., & Wyer, R. S. (1985). Emotional communication in close relationships. *Journal of Personality and Social Psychology, 49,* 1246–1265.

Gilani, N. P. (1999). Conflict management of mothers and daughters belonging to individualistic and collectivitic cultural backgrounds: A comparative study. *Journal of Adolescence, 22,* 853–865.

Goldsmith, D. (1992). Managing conflicting goals in supportive interaction: An integrative theoretical framework. *Communication Research, 19,* 264–286.

Gordis, E. B., Margolin, G., & John, R. S. (2001). Parents' hostility in dyadic marital and triadic family settings and children's behavior problems. *Journal of Consulting and Clinical Psychology, 69,* 727–734.

Gottman, J. M. (1979). *Marital interactions: Experimental investigations.* New York: Academic Press.

Gottman, J. M. (1994). *What predicts divorce? The relationship between marital processes and marital outcomes.* Hillsdale, NJ: Lawrence Erlbaum Associates.

Gottman, J. M., Coan, J., Carrere, S., & Swanson, C. (1998). Predicting marital happiness and stability from newlywed interactions. *Journal of Marriage and the Family, 60,* 5–22.

Gottman, J. M., & Krokoff, L. J. (1989). Marital interaction and satisfaction: A longitudinal view. *Journal of Counseling and Clincial Psychology, 57,* 47–52.

Gottman, J. M., & Levenson, R. W. (1992). Marital processes predictive of later dissolution: Behavior, physiology, and health. *Journal of Personality and Social Psychology, 63,* 221–233.

Gottman, J. M., & Levenson, R. W. (2000). The timing of divorce: Predicting when a couple will divorce over a 14-year period. *Journal of Marriage and the Family, 62,* 737–745.

Gottman, J. M., Notarius, C., Markman, H., Banks, S., Yoppi, B., & Rubin, M. E. (1976). Behavior exchange theory and marital decision making. *Journal of Personality and Social Psychology, 34,* 14–23.

Gottman, J. M., & Porterfield, A. L. (1981). Communicative competence in the nonverbal behavior of marrid couples. *Journal of Marriage and the Family, 4,* 817–824.

Grych, J. H., Jouriles, E. N., Swank., P. R., McDonald, R., & Norwood, W. D. (2000). Patterns of adjustment among children of battered women. *Journal of Consulting and Clinical Psychology, 68,* 84–94.

Guerrero, L. K. (1994). "I'm so mad I could scream": The effects of anger expression on relational satisfaction and communication competence. *The Southern Communication Journal, 59,* 125–141.

Guthrie, D. M., & Noller, P. (1988). Married couples' perceptions of one another in emotional situations. In P. Noller & M. A. Fitzpatrick (Eds.), *Perspectives on marital interaction* (pp. 153–181). Cleveland & Philadelphia: Multilingual Matters.

Haar, B. F., & Krahe, B. (1999). Strategies for resolving interpersonal conflicts in adolescence: A German-Indonesian comparison. *Journal of Cross Cultural Psychology, 30,* 667–683.

Halford, W. K., Hahlweg, K., & Dunne, M. (1990). The cross-cultural consistency of marital communication associated with marital distress. *Journal of Marriage and the Family, 52*, 487–500.

Halford, W. K., & Sanders, M. R. (1988). Assessment of cognitive self–statements during marital problem-solving: A comparison of two methods. *Cognitive Therapy and Research, 12*, 515–530.

Heavey, C. L., Christensen, A., & Malamuth, N. M. (1995). The longitudinal impact of demand and withdrawal during marital conflict. *Journal of Consulting and Clinical Psychology, 61*, 16–27.

Heavey, C. L., Layne, C., & Christensen, A. (1993). Gender and conflict structure in marital interaction: A replication and extension. *Journal of Consulting and Clinical Psychology, 61*, 16–27.

Hopper, R. (1981). The taken-for-granted. *Human Communication Research, 7*, 195–211.

Huston, T. L., & Chorost, A. (1994). Behavioral buffers on the effect of negativity on marital satisfaction: A longitudinal study. *Personal Relationships, 1*, 223–239.

Huston, T. L., & Vangelisti, A. L. (1991). Socioemotional behavior and satisfaction in marital relationships: A longitudinal study. *Journal of Personality and Social Psychology, 61*, 721–733.

Huston, T. L., & Vangelisti, A. L. (1995). How parenthood affects marriage. In M. A. Fitzpatrick & A. L. Vangelisti (Eds.), *Perspectives on family communication* (pp. 147–176). Thousand Oaks, CA: Sage.

Ickes, W., & Simpson, J. A. (1997). Managing empathic accuracy in close relationships. In W. Ickes (Ed.), *Empathic accuracy* (pp. 218–250). New York: Guilford Press.

Ickes, W., & Tooke, W. (1988). The observational method: Studying the interaction of minds and bodies. In S. Duck (Ed.), *Handbook of personal relationships: Theory, research, and interventions* (pp. 79–97). Chichester, England: Wiley.

Infante, D. A., Myers, S. A., & Buerkel, R. A. (1994). Argument and verbal aggression in constructive and destructive family and organizational disagreements. *Western Journal of Communication, 58*, 73–84.

Jacobs, E. C. (1985). *The functions of humor in marital adjustment.* Unpublished doctoral dissertation, The New School for Social Research, New York.

Jenkins, J. (2000). Marital conflict and children's emotions: The development of an anger organization. *Journal of Marriage and the Family, 62*, 723–736.

Jensen-Campbell, L. A., & Graziano, W. G. (2000). Beyond the school yard: Relationships as moderators of daily interpersonal conflict. *Personality and Social Psychology Bulletin, 26*, 923–935.

Johnson, M. D. (1999). *Behavioral antecedents of marital dysfunction.* Unpublished doctoral dissertation, University of California, Los Angeles.

Johnson, D. R., White, L. K., Edwards, J. N., & Booth, A. (1986). Dimensions of marital quality. *Journal of Family Issues, 7*, 31–49.

Kahn, M. (1970). Nonverbal communication and marital satisfaction. *Family Process, 9*, 449–456.

Karney, B. R., & Bradbury, T. N. (1995). The longitudinal course of marital quality and stability: A review of theory, method, and research. *Psychological Bulletin, 118*, 3–34.

Karney, B. R., & Bradbury, T. N. (1997). Neuroticism, marital interaction, and the trajectory of marital satisfaction. *Journal of Personality and Social Psychology, 72*, 1075–1092.

Kim, M-S., & Leung, T. (2000). A multicultural view of conflict management styles: Review and critical synthesis. In M. E. Roloff (Ed.), *Communication yearbook 23* (pp. 227–269). Thousand Oaks, CA: Sage.

Kirchler, E., Rodler, C., Holzl, E., & Meier, K. (2001). *Conflict and decision making in close relationships: Love, money, and daily routines.* East Sussex: Psychology Press.

Klinetob, N. A., & Smith, D. A. (1996). Demand-withdraw communication in marital interaction: Tests of interpersonal contingency and gender role hypotheses. *Journal of Marriage and the Family, 58*, 945–957.

Kluwer, E. S., de Dreu, C. K. W., & Buunk, B. P. (1998). Conflict in intimate vs. non-intimate relationships: When gender role stereotyping overrides biased self-other judgment. *Journal of Social and Personal Relationships, 15*, 637–650.

Kluwer, E. S., Heesink, J. A. M., & Van de Vliert, E. (1997). The marital dynamics of conflict over the division of labor. *Journal of Marriage and the Family, 59*, 635–653.

Kluwer, E. S., Heesink, J. A. M., & Van de Vliert, E. (2000). The division of labor in close relationships: An asymmetrical conflict issue. *Personal Relationships, 7*, 263–282.

Knudson, R. M., Sommers, A. A., & Golding, S. L. (1980). Interpersonal perception and mode of resolution in marital conflict. *Journal of Personality and Social Psychology, 38*, 751–763.

Koerner, A. F., & Fitzpatrick, M. A. (2002). Toward a theory of family communication. *Communication Theory, 12*, 70–91.

Krokoff, L. J. (1991). Job distress is no laugding matter in marriage, or is it? *Journal of Social and Personal Relationships, 8*, 5–25.

Krokoff, L. J., Gottman, J. M., & Roy, A. K. (1988). Blue-collar and white-collar marital interaction and communication orientation. *Journal of Social and Personal Relationships, 5*, 201–221.

Kurdek, L. A. (1994). Conflict resolution styles in gay, lesbian, heterosexual nonparent, and heterosexual parent couples. *Journal of Marriage and the Family, 56*, 705–722.

Laursen, B. (1993). The perceived impact of conflict on adolescent relationships. *Merrill-Palmer Quarterly, 39*, 535–550.

Laursen, B., Coy, K. C., & Collins, W. A. (1998). Reconsidering changes in parent-child conflict across adolescence: A meta-analysis. *Child Development, 69*, 817–832.

Laursen, B., Finkelstein, B. D., & Betts, N. T. (2001). A developmental meta-analysis of peer conflict resolution. *Developmental Review, 21*, 423–449.

Lollis, S., Ross, H., & Leroux, L. (1996). An observational study of parents' socialization of moral orientation during sibling conflicts. *Merrill Palmer Quarterly, 42*, 475–494.

Manusov, V., & Koenig, J. (2001). The content of attributions in couple communication. In V. Manusov & J. H. Harvey (Eds.), *Attribution, communication behavior, and close relationships* (pp. 134–152). New York: Cambridge University Press.

Mares, M. (1995). The aging family. In M. A. Fitzpatrick & A. L. Vangelisti (Eds.), *Perspectives on family communication* (pp. 344–374). Thousand Oaks, CA: Sage.

Margolin, G., & Wampold, B. E. (1981). Sequential analysis of conflict and accord in distressed and nondistressed marital partners. *Journal of Consulting and Clinical Psychology, 49*, 554–567.

Marshall, L. L., Weston, R., & Honeycutt, T. C. (2000). Relational quality among low income women: Does men's positivity mediate their abuse? *Journal of Social and Personal Relationships*, *17*, 660–675.

McGonagle, K. A., Kessler, R. C., & Schilling, E. A. (1992). The frequency and determinants of marital disagreements in a community sample. *Journal of Social and Personal Relationships*, *9*, 507–524.

Messman, S. J., & Canary, D. J. (1998). Conflict patterns. In W. R. Cupach & B. H. Spitzberg (Eds.), *The darkside of interpersonal relationships* (pp. 121–152). Mahwah, NJ: Lawrence Erlbaum Associates.

Montemayor, R. (1983). Parents and adolescents in conflict. All forms some of the time and some forms most of the time. *Journal of Early Adolescence*, *3*, 83–103.

Montemayor, R. (1986). Family variation in parent-adolescent storm and stress. *Journal of Adolescent Research*, *1*, 15–31.

Montgomery, B. M. (1988). Quality communication in personal relationships. In S. W. Duck (Ed.), *Handbook of personal relationships* (pp. 343–359). New York: Wiley.

Morton, T. L., Alexander, J. F., & Altman, I. (1976). Communication and relationship definition. In G. R. Miller (Ed.), *Explorations in interpersonal communication* (pp. 105–125). Beverly Hills, CA: Sage.

Noller, P. (1980). Misunderstandings in marital communication: A study of couples' nonverbal communication. *Journal of Personality and Social Psychology*, *39*, 1135–1148.

Noller, P. (1981). Gender and marital adjustment level differences in decoding messages from spouses and strangers. *Journal of Personality and Social Psychology*, *41*, 272–278.

Noller, P. (1982). Channel consistency and inconsistency in the communications of married couples. *Journal of Personality and Social Psychology*, *43*, 732–741.

Noller, P. (1995). Parent-adolescent relationships. In M. A. Fitzpatrick & A. L. Vangelisti (Eds.), *Perspectives on family communication* (pp. 77–111). Thousand Oaks, CA: Sage.

Noller, P., Beach, S., & Osgarby, S. (1997). Cognitive and affective processes in marriage. In W. K. Halford & H. J. Markman (Eds.), *Clinical handbook of marriage and couples interventions.* New York: Wiley.

Noller, P., & Callan, V. J. (1988). Understanding parent-adolescent interactions: Perceptions of family members and outsiders. *Developmental Psychology*, *24*, 707–714.

Noller, P., Feeney, J. A., Bonnell, D., & Callan, V. (1994). A longitudinal study of conflict in early marriage. *Journal of Social and Personal Relationships*, *11*, 233–252.

Noller, P., Feeney, J. A., Peterson, C. C., & Sheehan, G. (1995). Learning conflict patterns in the family: Links between marital, parental, and sibling relationships. In T. J. Socha, & G. H. Stamp. (Eds.), *Parents, children, and communication: Frontiers of theory and research* (pp. 273–298). Mahwah, NJ: Lawrence Erlbaum Associates.

Noller, P., & Ruzzene, M. (1991). Communication in marriage: The influence of affect and cognition. In G. J. O. Fletcher & F. Fincham (Eds.), *Cognition in close relationships* (pp. 203–233). Hillsdale, NJ: Lawrence Erlbaum Associates.

Noller, P., & Venardos, C. (1988). Communication awareness in married couples. *Journal of Social and Personal Relationships*, *3*, 31–42.

Notarius, C. I., Benson, P. R., Sloane, D., Vanzetti, N. A., & Hornyak, L. M. (1989). Exploring the interface between perception and behavior: An analysis of marital interactions in distressed and nondistressed couples. *Behavioral Assessment*, *11*, 39–64.

Pasch, L. A., & Bradbury, T. N. (1998). Social support, conflict, and the development of marital dysfunction. *Journal of Consulting and Clinical Psychology, 66,* 219–230.

Patterson, J. M. (2002). Integrating family resilience and family stress theory, *Journal of Marriage and Family, 64,* 298–322.

Perlman, M., & Ross, H. S. (1997). Who's the boss? Parents' failed attempts to influence the outcomes of conflicts between their children. *Journal of Social and Personal Relationships, 14,* 463–480.

Pike, G. R., & Sillars, A. L. (1985). Reciprocity of marital communication. *Journal of Social and Personal Relationships, 2,* 303–324.

Planalp, S. (1999). *Communicating emotion: Social, moral, and cultural processes.* New York: Cambridge University Press.

Poole, M. S., Folger, J. P., & Hewes, D. E. (1987). Analyzing interpersonal interaction. In M. E. Roloff & G. R. Miller (Eds.), *Interpersonal processes: New directions in communication research* (pp. 220–256). Newbury Park, CA: Sage.

Raffaelli, M. (1997). Young adolescents' conflicts with siblings and friends. *Journal of Youth and Adolescence, 26,* 539–558.

Raush, H. L., Barry, W. A., Hertel, R. K., & Swain, M. A. (1974). *Communication, conflict, and marriage.* San Francisco: Jossey-Bass.

Reese-Weber, M. (2000). Middle and late adolescents' conflict resolution skills and siblings: Associations with interparental and parent-adolescent conflict resolution. *Journal of Youth and Adolescences, 29,* 697–711.

Ritchie, L. D. (1991). *Information.* Newbury Park, CA: Sage.

Roberts, L. J. (2000). Fire and ice in marital communication: Hostile and distancing behaviors as predictors of marital distress. *Journal of Marriage and the Family, 62,* 693–707.

Roberts, L. J., & Greenberg, D. R. (2002). Observational "windows" to intimacy processes in marriage. In P. Noller & J. Feeney (Eds.), *Understanding marriage: Developments in the study of couple interaction* (pp 118–149). Cambridge, UK: Cambridge University Press.

Rueter, M. A., & Conger, R. D. (1995). Interaction style, problem-solving behavior, and family problem-solving effectiveness. *Child Development, 66,* 98–115.

Rusbult, C. E., Drigotas, S.M., & Verette, J. (1994). The investment model: An interdependence analysis of commitment processes and relationship maintenance. In D. J. Canary & L. Stafford (Eds.), *Communication and relational maintenance* (pp. 115–139). San Diego, CA: Academic Press.

Schaap, C., Buunk, B., & Kerkstra, A. (1988). In P. Noller & M. A. Fitzpatrick (Eds.), *Perspectives on marital interaction* (pp. 203–244). Cleveland and Philadelphia: Multilingual Matters.

Shantz, C. U., & Hobart, C. J. (1989). Social conflict and development: Peers and siblings. In T. J. Berndt & G. W. Ladd (Eds.), *Peer relationships in child development* (pp. 71–94). New York: Wiley.

Selman, R. L. (1980). *The growth of interpersonal understanding: Developmental and clinical analyses.* New York: Academic Press.

Sillars, A. L. (1986). *Procedures for coding interpersonal conflict.* Department of Communication Studies, University of Montana, Missoula, MT.

Sillars, A. L. (1995). Communication and family culture. In M. A. Fitzpatrick & A. L. Vangelisti (Eds.), *Perspectives on family communication* (pp. 375–399). Thousand Oaks, CA: Sage.

Sillars, A. L. (1998). (Mis)understanding. In B. H. Spitzberg & W. R. Cupach (Eds.), *The dark side of relationships* (pp. 73–102). Mahwah, NJ: Lawrence Erlbaum Associates.

Sillars, A. L., Pike, G. R., Jones, T. S., & Murphy, M. A. (1984). Communication and understanding in marriage. *Human Communication Research, 10*, 317–350.

Sillars, A. L., Pike, G. R., Jones, T. S., & Redmon, K. (1983). Communication and conflict in marriage. In R. Bostrom (Ed.), *Communication yearbook 7* (pp. 414–429). Beverly Hills, CA: Sage.

Sillars, A., Roberts, L. J., Leonard, K. E., & Dun, T. (2000). Cognition during marital conflict: The relationship of thought and talk. *Journal of Social and Personal Relationships, 17*, 479–502.

Sillars, A., Smith, T., Koerner, A., & Fitzpatrick, M. A. (2003). *Areas of misunderstanding in parent-adolescent communication revealed by video-assisted recall of conversation.* Unpublished manuscript, Department of Communication Studies, University of Montana, Missoula, MT.

Sillars, A. L., & Weisberg, J. (1987). Conflict as a social skill. In M. E. Roloff & G. R. Miller (Eds.), *Interpersonal processes: New directions in communication research* (pp. 140–171). Newbury Park, CA: Sage.

Sillars, A. L., & Wilmot, W. W. (1989). Marital communication across the life span. In J. F. Nussbaum (Ed.), *Life-span communication: Normative issues* (pp. 225–253). Hillsdale, NJ: Lawrence Erlbaum Associates.

Simmel, G. (1955). *Conflict.* New York: The Free Press.

Smith, D. A., Vivian, D., & O'Leary, D. (1990). Longitudinal prediction of marital discord from premarital expressions of affect. *Journal of Consulting and Clinical Psychology, 58*, 790–798.

Sperber, D., & Wilson, D. (1986). *Relevance: Communication and cognition* (2nd ed.). Cambridge, MA: Blackwell.

Stafford, L., & Dainton, M. (1994). The dark side of normal "family" interaction. In W. R. Cupach & B. H. Spitzberg (Eds.), *The dark side of interpersonal communication* (p. 259–280). Hillsdale, NJ: Lawence Erlbaum Associates.

Stocker, C. M., Lanthier, R. P., & Furman, W. (1997). Sibling relationships in early adulthood. *Journal of Family Psychology, 11*, 210–221.

Szinovacz, M. E., & Schaffer, A. M. (2000). Effects of retirement on marital conflict tactics. *Journal of Family Issues, 21*, 367–389.

Thomas, G., & Fletcher, G. J. O. (1997). Empathic accuracy in close relationships. In W. Ickes (Ed.), *Empathic accuracy* (pp. 194–217). New York: Guilford Press.

Ting-Toomey, S. (1983). An analysis of verbal communication in high and low marital adjustment groups. *Human Communication Research, 9*, 306–319.

Ting-Toomey, S. (1983). Coding conversation between intimates: A validation study of the Intimate Negotiation Coding System (INCS). *Communication Quarterly, 31*, 68–77.

van de Vliert, E., & Euwema, M. C. (1994). Agreeableness and activeness as components of conflict behaviors. *Journal of Personality and Social Psychology, 66*, 674–687.

Vangelisti, A. L., Corbin, S. D., Lucchetti, A. E., & Sprague, R. J. (1999). Couples' concurrent cognitions: The influence of relational satisfaction on the thoughts couples have as they converse. *Human Communication Research, 25,* 370–398.

VanLear, C. A. (1992). Marital communication across the generations: Learning and rebellion, continuity and change. *Journal of Social and Personal Relationships, 9,* 103–123.

Vincent, J. P., Weiss, R. L., & Birchler, G. R. (1975). A behavioral analysis of problem-solving in married and stranger dyads. *Behavior Therapy, 6,* 475–487.

Vuchinich, S. (1984). Sequencing and social structure in family conflict. *Social Psychology Quarterly, 47,* 217–234.

Walsh, F. (1982). *Normal family processes.* New York: Guilford Press.

Watzlawick, P., Beavin, J., & Jackson, D. D. (1967). *Pragmatics of human communication: A study of interactional patterns, pathologies, and paradoxes.* New York: Norton.

Weiss, R. L. (1980). Strategic behavioral and marital therapy: Toward a model for assessment and intervention. In J. P. Vincent (Ed.), *Advances in family intervention, assessment and theory* (Vol. 1, pp. 229–271). Grenwich, CT: JAI Press.

Weiss, R. L. (1993). *Marital Interaction Coding System-IV (MICS-IV).* Unpublished coding manual. University of Oregon, Eugene.

Weiss, R. L., & Heyman, R. E. (1997). A clinical-research overview of couples interactions. In W. K. Halford & H. J. Markman (Eds.), *Clinical handbook of marriage and couples interventions* (p. 41). New York: Wiley.

Wilmot, W. W., & Hocker, J. L. (2001). *Interpersonal conflict* (6th ed.). New York: McGraw-Hill.

Winkler, I., & Doherty, W. J. (1983). Communication style and marital satisfaction in Israeli and American couples. *Family Process, 22,* 221–228.

Zietlow, P. H., & Sillars, A. L. (1988). Life stage differences in communication during marital conflicts. *Journal of Social and Personal Relationships, 5,* 223–245.

Zietlow, P. H., & VanLear, C. A. (1991). Marriage duration and relational control: A study of developmental patterns. *Journal of Marriage and the Family, 53,*773–785.

20

Persuasion and Families

Steven R. Wilson and Wendy M. Morgan
Purdue University

The persuasion literature has deep roots in the humanities and social sciences, including a rhetorical tradition that dates back to the ancient Greeks (see Cooper & Nothstine, 1997) and an attitude-change tradition that dates back to the first half of the 20th century (see Dillard & Pfau, 2002). Both traditions typically have focused on persuasion in public and mass communication contexts. Rhetorical scholars, for instance, have analyzed social movements (e.g., Stewart, Smith, & Denton, 2001), whereas attitude-change scholars have provided insights regarding health communication campaigns (e.g., Perloff, 2001).

Persuasion involves an intentional attempt by a speaker (message source), via reason giving, to influence the attitudes, beliefs, and/or behaviors of others (message targets) who in turn have some measure of choice about how to respond (O'Keefe, 2002). Attempts to persuade are intentional in the sense that a message source wants to shape, strengthen, or modify the targets' beliefs or behaviors (Miller, 1980), but sources may not consciously plan nor even be highly mindful of their goals during persuasive interactions (Kellermann, 1992). The "reasons" that a message source provides for why targets should alter their beliefs or behaviors may include appeals to core values, linkages with important social groups, or explanations of tangible consequences to be gained if targets do what the source advocates (Kelman, 1958; Wheeless, Barraclough, & Stewart, 1983). The boundary between persuasion and coercion is fuzzy: Sources often include reasoning and coercion in the same appeal (Wilson, Whipple, & Grau, 1996), and targets often feel obliged to comply with the source's wishes, especially when they know the source well (Roloff, Janiszewski, McGrath, Burns, & Manrai, 1988).

Given the predominant focus of the persuasion literature, finding a chapter on the topic in the *Handbook of Family Communication* may seem odd. Yet we are exposed to persuasive appeals not just while watching TV, surfing the net, or listening to public presentations but also when interacting with our families (Baxter & Bylund, in press; Miller & Boster,

1988). Two studies illustrate just how common persuasion is within families. In the first, 60 college students kept diaries of whom they tried to influence during a 12-week period (Cody, Canary, & Smith, 1994). Students described the participants, topics, and outcomes of each episode. By the end, the 60 students recorded over 3,000 diary entries describing persuasive episodes. Parents were the third most frequent type of target for the college students' persuasive attempts (14% of all episodes), even though many students no longer lived in their parent(s)' household. Common reasons for attempting to persuade a parent included seeking assistance (47% of episodes), advocating a shared activity (16%), and offering the parent advice (14%).

Focusing earlier in the life span, Oldershaw, Walters, and Hall (1989) analyzed persuasive episodes as 43 mothers from a nonclinical sample each interacted with one of their children (*M* child age = 3.8 years). Mother–child dyads in this second study engaged in mealtime, free-play, and clean-up activities. During these interactions, mothers made an average of 75 requests of their children per hour, or more than 1 request per minute. Their children in turn did not comply with 35% of these requests—a rate of child noncompliance typical for nonclinical samples at this age (see Chamberlain & Patterson, 1996). Mothers used a variety of strategies when attempting to seek their child's compliance, such as explaining the consequences of the child's actions, expressing disapproval of perceived misbehavior, offering positive consequences if the child complied, and modeling desired behavior.

In addition to its sheer frequency, persuasion offers a lens for investigating important qualities of family relationships. Indeed, Kelley et al. (1983) advocate defining "close" relationships as those in which participants influence one another frequently across a range of topics. Studying persuasion also is important in exploring how children internalize family and community values (Grusec & Goodnow, 1994; Hoffman, 1994).

Despite the importance of persuasion in families, many persuasion texts ignore interpersonal contexts altogether (e.g., O'Keefe, 2002) or include only a single chapter on the topic (e.g., Stiff & Mongeau, 2002). To our knowledge, no single chapter has focused specifically on persuasion and families. Our goals in doing so are to clarify how persuasive messages have been conceptualized in both parent–child and marital relationships; review what currently is known regarding a limited number of questions about persuasion and families; and suggest avenues for integrating theory and research on persuasion, parenting, and marriage.

The persuasion literature typically has posed questions about *message effects*, such as whether audience members are likely to shift their attitudes toward the position advocated by a speaker after being exposed to fear appeals (see O'Keefe, 2002; Stiff & Mongeau, 2002). Although our review includes such studies, we also cover research on *message choices* to explore why family members say what they do when attempting to persuade each other (Miller & Boster, 1988; Wilson, 2002). We draw from the voluminous literatures on seeking and resisting compliance when such studies focus specifically on family relationships or when they raise issues important to the study of persuasion and families. Keeping these parameters in mind, we turn to persuasion in parent–child relationships.

PERSUASION IN PARENT–CHILD RELATIONSHIPS

Conceptualizing Persuasive Messages and Interactions

Styles of Parental Discipline. Parents' persuasive attempts have been studied most often under the label of discipline styles and strategies. Studies of parenting style have a long history (Maccoby & Martin, 1983). Perhaps the two most influential typologies that have emerged are Hoffman's (1980) forms of discipline and Baumrind's (1973) taxonomy of parenting styles.

Hoffman (1980) explores the effects on parental discipline on children's internationalization of values. Discipline episodes often arise when children face conflicts between their own desires and prevailing moral standards. According to Hoffman, parents who repeatedly use particular forms of discipline help their child develop the inner resources (e.g., empathy) needed to balance the child's own and others' desires and thus to behave morally. Along these lines, Hoffman (1980, pp. 321–322) distinguishes three forms of discipline:

1. Power assertion—in which the parent attempts to alter perceived child misbehavior by the use or threat of physical force, control over the child's material resources, or other punitive sanctions.

2. Love withdrawal—in which the parent attempts to alter perceived child misbehavior through direct but nonphysical expressions of anger or disapproval of the child, such as by ignoring the child, isolating the child, or threatening to leave the child.

3. Induction—in which the parent attempts to alter perceived child misbehavior by providing reasons why the child must behave differently. Reasons may include appeals to the child's pride, desire to be grown up, or concern for others.

Inductive discipline, defined broadly, includes any appeal in which a parent offers reasons why the child needs to change his or her behavior. "Reasoning," however, has been treated as a catch-all category that may include messages ranging from "normative statements, discussion of consequences, discussion of the feelings of others ... to non-informative and superfluous verbalizations" (Grusec & Goodnow, 1994, p. 7). Within this broad category, Hoffman (1980) argues that other-oriented induction, in which the parent points out implications of the child's actions for others, is especially important in promoting the internalization of values.

Many studies of parental discipline develop nominal-level lists of strategies organized loosely around Hoffman's forms of discipline (e.g., Dopke & Milner, 2000; Kochanska & Aksan, 1995; Oldershaw et al., 1986, 1989). As one example, Oldershaw et al. (1986) analyzed maternal control strategies during free-play, mealtime, and clean-up activities. A control sequence began each time that a mother issued a request or command and continued until either her child complied or she gave up seeking compliance. For each sequence, the authors assessed whether the mother's initial and follow-up commands were accompanied by control strategies, which in turn were coded using a 12-category system

TABLE 20.1

Oldershaw et al.'s Categories of Maternal Control Strategies

Strategy	Definition/Example
	Positively oriented control strategies
Reasoning	Verbal statements offering a specific reason why a given behavior should or should not occur (e.g., "If you throw that it might break").
Bargaining	Mother offers specific positive consequences contingent upon the child performing a behavior (e.g., "If you clean up the toys, I'll give you a candy").
Cooperation	Mother requests child to work with her by offering assistance to accomplish some task (e.g., "You stand here and I'll give you things to put on the shelf").
Modeling	Mother shows the child, by example, how to perform a specific behavior and attempts to get the child to imitate the demonstrated behavior (e.g., "Watch me put the rings on the peg. Now you try").
Approval	Must be contingent on child behavior and signify positive acceptance of that behavior. This may involve personal attribution (e.g., "You're a good boy"), social approval (e.g., "That was a nice thing to do"), or acknowledgment (e.g., "Thank you").
Physical (Pos)	Must be initiated by mother and includes such behaviors as hug, pat, kiss.
Laugh	Must be part of the parent–child interaction and be contingent on the child's behavior.
	Power-assertive control strategies
Threat	Statement followed by impending negative consequences (e.g., "If you don't clean up, you won't get any dinner tonight").
Physical (Neg)	Includes not only physical contact (e.g., hitting, grabbing an arm) but also the threat of physical contact (e.g., other raises hand as if to slap child).
Humiliation	Attempt to belittle the child on a personal level by making fun, shaming, or embarrassing the child (e.g., "Can't you do anything right?").
Disapproval	Condemnation of child's behavior rather than the child that can be expressed both verbally (e.g., I don't like the way you're behaving") and gesturally (e.g., mother shakes her finger at the child when milk is spilled).
Demand (Neg)	Mother issues a command in a strongly insistent manner (e.g., "PICK IT UP NOW").

Note. From "Control strategies and noncompliance in abusive mother–child dyads: An observational study," by L. Oldershaw, G. C. Walters, and D. K. Hall, 1986, *Child Development, 57,* p. 726. Copyright 1986. Reprinted with permission of the Society for Research in Child Development.

(see Table 20.1). Oldershaw et al. label strategies such as reasoning, bargaining, and approval as "positively oriented," because these strategies "mainly involve dealing with the child on an intellectual level and engaging in rational discussion that excludes any implied or real threat of punishment" (p. 725). Positively oriented strategies correspond with Hoffman's broad usage of inductive discipline. In contrast, Oldershaw et al.'s "power-assertive" control strategies, such as threats to punish or humiliation, "reflect the [author-itarian] role a parent assumes over a child" (p. 725). These strategies clearly correspond with Hoffman's power-assertive discipline, though some (e.g., disapproval) also could entail love withdrawal depending on how they were enacted.

In a related line of research, Applegate and colleagues have developed an ordinal-level system to capture the varying shades of gray between induction and power assertion

TABLE 20.2

Applegate et al.'s Hierarchical Scheme for Coding Degree of Reflection–Enhancement

Strategy	Definition/Example
Level 1	Strategies that explicitly discourage reflection by the child: simple commands, threats, physical punishment, nonphysical punishment (e.g., sending the child to his or her room without explanation).
Level 2	Strategies that implicitly discourage reflection by the child: stating rules without rationale (e.g., "we don't run in the house"), asking the child to review the rules.
Level 3	Strategies that implicitly encourage reflection by the child, by explaining physical consequences of misbehavior (e.g., "that could break if you touch it") or by explaining tangible benefits of a request (e.g., "it works better this way").
Level 4	Strategies that implicitly encourage reflection by the child, by giving the child behavioral choices with associated consequences or by making promises or offering bargains to gain the child's compliance.
Level 5	Strategies that explicitly encourage reflection by the child, by explaining the psychological consequences of the child's behavior for others or by suggesting alternative behaviors for handling the situation.
Level 6	Strategies that explicitly encourage reflection by the child, by asking the child to describe the psychological consequences of his or her misbehavior for others or by asking the child to generate alternative behaviors for handling the situation (e.g., "rather than calling him names, what else could you have done?").

Note. From "Regulative communication strategies within mother–child interactions: Implications for the study of reflection-enhancing parental communication," by S. R. Wilson, K. Cameron, and E. E. Whipple, 1997, *Research on Language and Social Interaction, 30*, p. 78. Copyright 1997 by Lawrence Erlbaum Associations, Inc. Reprinted with permission.

(e.g., Applegate, Burke, Burleson, Delia, & Kline, 1985; Burleson, Delia, & Applegate, 1995). Applegate et al. propose a six-level hierarchical scheme for analyzing the degree of "reflection enhancement" in parents' disciplinary responses (see Table 20.2). Reflection enhancement increases as parents give or elicit reasons to justify changing a child's behavior, provide the child choices and autonomy rather than use force, emphasize psychological consequences rather than assume or cite rules, and focus on the child's unique feelings rather than assume that all children are alike. Messages at the highest levels of the scheme are similar to Hoffman's other-oriented induction, whereas those at the lowest levels are similar to power assertion. Applegate's scheme also includes intermediate levels between these two extremes, such as when parents reference social roles, explain physical consequences, or offer bargains. Levels three and four represent alternative forms of induction aside from other-oriented induction.

Aside from Hoffman's forms of disciplinary responses, Baumrind's (1973) taxonomy of parenting styles also has been employed to describe parents' use of persuasion. Baumrind adopts an inductive approach to develop the taxonomy. She initially identified three groups of children rated as high in vitality, self-reliance, approach tendency, and self-control (Pattern I); low in peer affiliation and vitality as well as in approach tendency (Pattern II); or low on self-reliance, self-control, and approach tendency (Pattern III). Based on videotaped mother–child interactions as well as on home observations, Baumrind then compared parents of these three groups of children along four behavioral dimensions: (a) *control*, which refers to parental attempts to shape the child's goals, modify the child's behavior, and promote internalization of moral standards in a strict but not necessarily punitive fashion; (b) *maturity demands*, which refers to parental pressure for the child to perform up to his/her ability intellectually and socially; (c) *clarity of parent–child communication*, which refers to the extent to which parents use overt rather than manipulative control strategies and give reasons to obtain child compliance; and (d) *nurturance*, which refers to parental acts that express warmth and involvement. Parents of these three groups of children then were labeled authoritative, authoritarian, or permissive based on where they fell along these four dimensions.

Baumrind labeled parents of Pattern I children *authoritative*. Authoritative parents display high levels of control and maturity demands combined with high levels of nurturance. These parents rely more on positive than negative sanctions to gain their child's compliance and encourage their child to express him/herself when the child disagrees. However, authoritative parents also are likely to persist until their child complies, using power assertion if necessary.

Parents of Pattern II children are labeled *authoritarian*. Authoritarian parents display high levels of control along with low levels of clarity and nurturance. They are less likely than authoritative parents to provide reasons when attempting to alter their child's behavior, and discourage expressions of disagreement by the child. Authoritarian parents primarily rely on power-assertive forms of discipline and express less child approval than the other two groups.

Baumrind labels parents of Pattern III children *permissive*. Permissive parents display low levels of control and maturity demands combined with higher levels of nurturance. Permissive parents are less likely than authoritative parents to enforce rules or structure their child's activities, but they use love withdrawal (e.g., ridicule) more often when seeking their child's compliance.

Building on a review by Maccoby and Martin (1983), Baumrind (1996) now argues that these three parenting styles vary along two dimensions. *Responsiveness* "refers to the extent to which parents initially foster individuality and self-assertion by being attuned, supportive, and acquiescent to the child's needs and demands" (p. 410). *Demandingness* "refers to the claims that parents make on children to become integrated into the family and community by their maturity expressions, supervision, disciplinary efforts, and willingness to confront a disputative child" (p. 411). Moving beyond whether parents provide reasons or express approval, these dimensions assess the consistency and "fit" of parents' persuasive attempts. Authoritative parents display high levels of responsiveness and demandingness, whereas the other two types are distinguished by either low levels of responsiveness (authoritarian) or demandingness (permissive). Many other researchers have analyzed parental styles using Baumrind's taxonomy (e.g., Bayer & Cegala, 1992; Querido, Warner, & Eyberg, 2002).

A simplified reading of Hoffman or Baumrind's work might suggest that parents can be neatly divided into groups based on their reliance on a single form of discipline, such as "parents who reason with their children" versus "parents who are power assertive." Yet Hoffman maintains that most disciplinary responses, including those involving induction, also include elements of power assertion and love withdrawal (1980, p. 320; 1994, p. 27). Baumrind's authoritative style also depicts parents who frequently mix induction with power assertion (1973, p. 8; 1996, p. 412). Consistent with these more complex views, empirical studies reveal that parents often mix different forms of discipline both within and across conversational turns from the same control episode (Wilson, Cameron, & Whipple, 1997). In addition, parents use different types and combinations of induction and power assertion depending on how their child has misbehaved, such as other-oriented induction when their child refuses to share a new toy with a friend but alternative types of induction (e.g., bargains, choices, and consequences) when their child throws a temper tantrum at the grocery store (Wilson et al., 1996). Thus, the effects of induction depend on how a parent mixes and sequences it with other forms of discipline as well as whether the parent's reasoning fits the nature of the misdeed and their child's age (Grusec & Goodnow, 1994; Larzelere, Sather, Schneider, Larson, & Pike, 1998).

Children's Responses to Parents' Persuasive Attempts.   Children are active participants during persuasive episodes, and their behavior affects parental responses at the same time at which it is influenced by them (Wilson et al., 1997). The most common way in which children's reactions to their parents' requests have been assessed is with measures of child compliance. Compliance has been defined as instances in which "the child obeyed immediately after a parental request or after a short delay" (Chamberlain & Patterson, 1996, p. 206). Rates of child compliance typically are defined as the number of instances of child compliance divided by the total number of child responses (compliance plus non-compliance) during an interaction. Aside from assessing the compliance/noncompliance dichotomy, a smaller number of studies investigate how children comply or fail to comply with parental requests.

Kochanska and Aksan (1995; Kochanska, Aksan, & Koenig, 1995) distinguish two forms of child compliance with parental requests. Children at times display *committed compliance* when they comply wholeheartedly, "fully endorsing and 'embracing' the maternal agenda as their own" (p. 237). At other times children display *situational compliance* when they are "essentially cooperative with the parent and nonoppositional . . . [but] at the same time lack sincere commitment. Such compliance would appear to be mostly . . . maintained by the parent's sustained control" (p. 237). The authors argue that committed (but not situational) compliance reflects the degree to which the child is internalizing family norms and values. To assess the importance of this distinction, the authors videotaped 102 mothers engaged in playtime and clean-up interactions with one of their children at two points in time: when the child was a toddler (26–41 months) and when the child was a preschooler (43–56 months). As both toddlers and preschoolers, children's rates of committed compliance were inversely associated with their rates of situational compliance. Rates of committed compliance by the child, but not situational compliance, were positively associated with displays of mutual positive affect between the mother and the child. Rates of committed compliance, but not situational compliance, also were positively associated with mothers' use of induction and inversely associated with mothers' use of power assertion.

Regarding noncompliance, McQuillen, Higginbotham, and Cummings (1984) assess developmental changes in children's strategies for resisting compliance. These authors interviewed children in 1st ($n = 36$), 4th ($n = 40$), and 10th grades ($n = 41$) individually about how they would go about refusing a request from their mother, a friend, and a younger sibling. Whether the request was accompanied by an incentive or an altruistic appeal also was manipulated. Children's responses to each request were coded into one of four categories adapted from McLaughlin, Cody, and Robey's (1980) typology of compliance–resistance strategies: (a) *nonnegotiation*, where the child firmly refuses to comply with the source's request without apology or explanation; (b) *identity management*, where the child indirectly manipulates the image of one or both parties, in a positive or negative light, to avoid complying; (c) *justification*, where the child offers reasons for refusing based on the projected outcomes of compliance or noncompliance for one or both parties; and (d) *negotiation*, where the child proposes alternatives to the request action and engages in a mutual give and take with the source. Over half of the responses from 1st-graders across situations were nonnegotiation, whereas only one third of the responses from 10th-graders fell into this category. In addition, 4th- and 10th-graders were more likely than 1st-graders to vary their own compliance–resisting strategies depending on the source of the request (e.g., mother versus younger sibling) and the persuasive strategy included with the request (e.g., incentives versus altruism).

Representative Findings

Having clarified how persuasion has been conceptualized in parent–child relationships, we now turn to what is known about two specific questions about persuasion and parenting.

Physically Abusive Versus Nonmaltreating Parents. Child physical abuse is an immense, persistent social problem (Peddle & Wang, 2001). Although the etiology of child abuse is complex, reflecting the interplay of individual, family, community, and cultural factors (Belsky, 1993), parent–child interactions regarding discipline are the immediate antecedent to most episodes of child physical abuse; and physically abusive parents often seek their child's compliance in ways that heighten the risk of child maltreatment (Wilson, 2002).

A growing body of research compares interactions between physically abusive parents and children versus interactions between nonmaltreating parents and children from sociodemographically similar families (see Wilson, 2002). Oldershaw et al.'s (1986) study of maternal control strategies (see Table 20.1) is representative of this work. The authors compared 10 physically abusive mothers participating in a treatment program with 10 mothers matched in terms of education and income who had no history of child maltreatment. Mothers interacted with one of their children (*M* child age = 3.0 years) while completing multiple activities. Abusive mothers differed from comparison mothers in how they initiated control episodes. Specifically, abusive mothers (a) issued a larger number of initial commands, (b) issued more initial commands in an affectively neutral rather than positive tone of voice, (c) issued more initial commands with no accompanying control strategy, and (d) used every power-assertive strategy in Table 20.1 more often and several positively oriented strategies less often when they did include a control strategy with an initial command. Rates of child noncompliance with initial commands were much higher for abused (53%) than for nonmaltreated children (22%).

Following child noncompliance, abusive mothers again differed from control mothers in that the former group issued more repeat commands with no accompanying control strategy or with a power-assertive strategy, and also more repeat commands in a negative or neutral rather than positive tone. The two groups also reacted differently when their child actually did comply. Specifically, abusive mothers (a) were equally likely to criticize as praise their child in the conversational turn immediately after the child complied, whereas the control mothers always praised child compliance; and (b) were more likely than comparison mothers to continue seeking their child's compliance in the conversational turn after the child complied, apparently because they did not notice that the child had complied. By failing to notice or consistently praise child compliance, abusive mothers inadvertently may encourage noncompliance by their children.

Many of Oldershaw et al.'s (1986) findings have been replicated by other studies using both self-report and observational methods. Compared with nonmaltreating parents, physically abusive parents as well as parents at high risk for abuse (a) rely on power-assertive discipline more frequently (Dopke & Milner, 2000), (b) vary their disciplinary responses less depending on how their child has misbehaved (Trickett & Kuczynski, 1986), (c) display nonreinforcing responses to positive child behavior (Cerezo, D'Ocon, & Dolz, 1996), and (d) engage in longer episodes of seeking unsuccessfully their child's compliance, with increasingly intense reciprocated aversive behavior (e.g., yelling, humiliation) between parent and child (Reid, 1986).

Scholars have suggested that attributional biases may underlie physically abusive parents' discipline practices (Milner, 2000). For example, physically abusive parents are more likely than nonabusive parents to attribute frustrating child behavior such as noncompliance to internal, stable qualities of their child (Larrance & Twentyman, 1983) and to view such behavior as an intentional attempt by their child to upset them (Bauer & Twentyman, 1985). Relative to nonmaltreating parents, abusive parents also feel that they have less control and their children have greater control over unpleasant interactions (Bugental, Blue, & Cruzcosa, 1989). Attributional differences help explain why abusive parents experience greater anger and disgust than comparison parents when their children misbehave (Reid, 1986) and why they rely more heavily on power-assertive forms of discipline across many types of child misbehavior (Wilson & Whipple, 2001). In light of such findings, some child abuse interventions include an "attributional reframing" component in which parents are encouraged to refrain from automatically attributing noncompliance to negative child qualities, search for alternative explanations or mitigating information, as well as notice and provide their child credit for positive behavior (Azar, 1997). One goal of such programs is to empower parents so that they do not resort to intense types of power assertion as a means of trying to regain control.

African American Versus European American Families. Despite the fact that participants in most studies reviewed so far come from European American families, scholars often assume that research findings apply across culture. So when Baumrind (1972) concluded that African American parents, who by European American standards would be considered authoritarian, were raising self-assertive and independent daughters, her findings drew attention. Other investigators have concluded that physical discipline as practiced by African American mothers does not result in the same types of negative child outcomes as when practiced by European American mothers (e.g., Deater-Deckard, Dodge, Bates, & Pettit, 1996; McLeod, Kruttschnitt, & Dornfeld, 1994). Physical discipline among African Americans may be an adaptive response to the relatively more perilous communities in which these families often reside. Unfortunately, prior studies often fail to disentangle racial or ethnic background from socioeconomic status (SES). Because African Americans families on average fall at lower levels of SES compared to European Americans families (U.S. Census Bureau, 2001), it is uncertain how much these findings may be attributable to SES as opposed to race.

One finding common across racial groups is that the effects of physical discipline depend on the quality of the parent–child relationship in which such practices are embedded. McLoyd and Smith (2002) assessed 401 Hispanic, 550 African American, and 1,039 European American children and their mothers at four points in time over a 6-year period. Both self-report and observational measures assessed the frequency with which mothers spanked their children. Maternal emotional support was assessed through home observation, whereas children's behavior problems (internalizing and externalizing) were measured via ratings by their mother. For all three groups, spanking and maternal emotional support interacted in their effects on changes in rates of child behavior problems over time. For mothers who provided only low levels of emotional support, overall rates of spanking were positively associated with increased rates of reported child behavior problems over the 6-year period. Spanking was not associated with increases in child behavior problems in the context of high maternal emotional support. Other studies of African American families have shown that a combination of strict discipline and parental warmth produces positive child outcomes such as social skill and lower aggression (Kilgore, Snyder, & Lentz, 2000; McCabe, Clark, & Barnett, 1999).

These findings highlight the importance of attending to the meanings or messages conveyed by power-assertive forms of discipline (McLoyd & Smith, 2002). It is possible that the meaning of spanking itself may be adapted in response to risky environments. Narratives of African American community elders reveal that the women interviewed see physical discipline as essential but condemn harsh language because the latter undermines the parent–child relationship (Mosby, Rawls, Meehan, Mays, & Pettinari, 1999). If both parent and child accept spanking as an expression of necessary strict discipline, then its meaning may not be the same for low-income African Americans as for middle-class European Americans. Future research needs to disentangle how race and SES affect the meanings attributed to both power assertion and induction. More information is needed about the range of behaviors that African American and low-income communities accept as legitimate expressions of strict discipline, as well as whether community standards influence children's interpretations and outcomes.

Having summarized literature about two specific questions pertaining to persuasion and parenting, we turn to how persuasion has been conceptualized in research on marriage.

PERSUASION IN MARITAL RELATIONSHIPS

Conceptualizing Persuasive Messages and Interactions

Persuasion in marriage has been studied most frequently under the rubric of power strategies and tactics. Power is one of the most important and contested concepts in the social sciences (Sprey, 1999). Although theorized in many ways, two assumptions underlie most views. First, power is reflected in the ability of those who wield it to impact others' behaviors, beliefs, and emotions. Decision-making scholars assess spouses' perceptions of the degree to which they and/or their partner shape the couple's agreements about important issues (e.g., finances; Berger 1994), whereas critical scholars analyze how specific views of marriage come to be seen as the only natural, rational, or sensible ways of living together (Mumby, 2001). Second, power is a relational concept. Social exchange theories emphasize that power is a function of a target's dependence on the source for achieving desired outcomes (Roloff, 1981). Relational control theorists distinguish domineeringness (i.e., frequent attempts by one party to exert control over another) from dominance (i.e., attempts to control met with yielding by the other), with only the latter being indicative of power (Millar & Rogers, 1987). To analyze power as a relational concept, we must explore a spouse's ability to resist his/her partner's influence.

Because spouses test the limits of their relative power via influence attempts, scholars have turned attention to how power actually is expressed in marriage. Although many typologies of power strategies in marriage have been proposed (e.g., Howard, Blumstein, & Schwartz, 1986; Newton & Burgoon, 1990; Noller, Feeney, Bonnell, & Callan, 1994; Sagrestano, Christensen, & Heavey, 1998; Zvonkovic, Schmeige, & Hall, 1994), the two most widely used are those of Falbo and Peplau (1980) and Fitzpatrick (1988).

To develop a typology, Falbo and Peplau (1980) conducted a two-phase study. During phase one, 50 college-age lesbians, 50 gay men, 50 heterosexual women, and 50 heterosexual men wrote an open-ended essay on "how I get (my romantic partner) to do what I want" (p. 620). Based on prior typologies of power bases as well as on themes in the data, Falbo and Peplau proposed a typology of 13 power strategies (for strategy definitions and examples, see Table 20.3). During phase two, nine experts rated the similarity of these strategies, and multidimensional scaling was used to interpret these ratings. Falbo and Peplau concluded that two dimensions captured experts' ratings. *Directness* refers to the degree to which sources say what they want and attempt to alter their partner's behavior in an overt manner. Strategies such as asking, telling, stating the importance, and talking anchor the "direct" end of this dimension, whereas suggesting (hinting), withdrawal, and positive and negative affect anchor the "indirect" end. *Interactivity* refers to the degree to which sources engage their partner in an attempt to reach agreement about how to proceed. Persuasion, bargaining, reasoning, and positive affect anchor the "bilateral" end of this dimension, whereas laissez faire, withdrawal, telling, and negative affect anchor the "unilateral" end.

Although Falbo and Peplau's (1980) participants described power strategies in dating relationships, several studies have used their typology to describe influence attempts in marriage (e.g., Belk et al., 1988; Butterfield & Lewis, 2002). Rather than analyzing the 13 strategies separately, researchers generally create composite scores assessing the degree to which sources rely on direct (versus indirect) as well as on bilateral (versus unilateral) strategies. Researchers have correlated self-reported scores for the directness and interactivity of power strategies with a variety of predictor and outcome variables, including gender (wives vs. husbands), culture, perceived distribution of relational power, and marital satisfaction. In general, U.S. American couples who report higher levels of relational satisfaction also report more frequent use of direct (e.g., asking, telling) as opposed to indirect (e.g., hinting, withdrawal) power strategies (Aida & Falbo, 1991), although there

TABLE 20.3

Falbo and Peplau's Typology of Power Strategies in Intimate Relationships

Strategy	Definition/Example
Asking	Source makes a simple request (e.g., "I ask him to do what I want").
Bargaining	Source does something for target if target will reciprocate (e.g., "We usually negotiate something agreeable to both of us. We compromise").
Laissez faire	Source takes independent action; does what she/he wants on her/his own (e.g., "We do our own thing. I just do it by myself").
Negative affect	Source expresses negative feelings (e.g., "I pout or cry if I don't get my way").
Persistence	Source continues trying to influence (e.g., "I repeatedly remind him of what I want until he gives in").
Persuasion	Source literally reports using persuasion (e.g., I try to persuade him my way is right").
Positive affect	Source expresses positive affect (e.g., "I smile a lot. I am especially affectionate").
Reasoning	Source uses reason or logical arguments (e.g., "I reason with her. I argue my point logically").
Stating importance	Source tells target how important the request is (e.g., "I tell him how important it is to me").
Suggesting	Source makes suggestions or hints (e.g., "I drop hints. I mage suggestions").
Talking	Source literally reports talking or having a discussion with partner (e.g., "We talk about it. We discuss our differences and needs").
Telling	Source makes a direct statement of desired outcome (e.g., "I tell her what I want. I state my needs").
Withdrawal	Source withdraws affection, grows silent, becomes cold and distant (e.g., "I clam up. I become silent").

Note. From "Power strategies in intimate relationships," by T. Falbo and L. A. Peplau, *Journal of Personality and Social Psychology, 38*, p. 621. Copyright 1980 by the American Psychological Association. Reprinted with permission.

are reasons to be cautious about whether this association would generalize to couples in other cultures (Belk et al., 1988; also see Kim & Wilson, 1994).

Fitzpatrick and her colleagues (Dillard & Fitzpatrick, 1985; Fitzpatrick, 1988) have developed a second nominal-level typology of influence strategies in marriage called the Verbal Interaction Compliance–Gaining Scheme (VICS). The authors initially derived the VICS from a literature review by Wheeless et al. (1983), who had argued that to encourage compliance a message source might (a) preview expectancies or consequences, by asserting what will occur if the target does (does not) perform a desired action; (b) invoke relationships or identification, by activating the target's desire for acceptance, connection, or knowledge; or (c) summon values or obligations, by appealing to the target's internal values or sense of duty.

Starting with this framework, Dillard and Fitzpatrick (1985) videotaped 51 married couples as they completed two role-plays discussing areas of relational conflict (e.g., arguments about sharing time together or spending money). Before each role-play, either the husband or the wife was assigned the role of "message source" depending on which

TABLE 20.4

Fitzpatrick's Verbal Interaction Compliance-Gaining Scheme

Strategy	Definition/Example

Strategies that appeal to values/obligations

1. Me: Force to comply comes from within the source (e.g., "I really do want to." "I think I deserve it").
2. You: Force to comply comes from within the target (e.g., "I'd wish that you'd be more understanding." "Knowing your attitude is going to take the fun out of getting ready").
3. External: Force to comply comes from a specific (enabling or disabling) agent outside of the participants or their relationship (e.g., "The young couple would be disappointed if we cancelled." "My boss wants this report tomorrow").

Strategies that invoke identification/relationship

4. Us: Force to comply comes from the relationship between the interactants (e.g., "When we got married we promised to help one another." "We usually don't turn each other down when we want attention").
5. Direct: Nonevaluative statement or question expresses past, current, or future activity or activities (excluding behavioral regularities of the Me, You, or Us strategies; "I really want you to do it." "Please give in on this one").
6. Search: Information search in the form of a question. Questions are evaluatively neutral (e.g., "What would you like to do?" "What do you think we should do?").

Strategies that reference expectancies/consequences

7. Activity: Force to comply comes from the nature of the specific activity, the importance of the activity, or the outcome of the activity (e.g., "It would be fun." "A bond is an investment in the future").
8. Power: Focus is on the exertion of control in the relationship. Control may be manifested in attempts to constrain either party's behavior or internal states (e.g., "I could lose all my interest in a relationship with you." "I refuse to compromise").

Note. From "Compliance-gaining in marital interaction," by J. P. Dillard and M. A. Fitzpatrick, *Personality and Social Psychology Bulletin, 11*, p. 422. Copyright © 1985 by Sage Publications. Reprinted by permission of Sage Publication.

person actually desired change on that issue. Spouses in the "source" role were instructed to try to gain compliance from their husband or wife with regard to what they wanted. Interactions were broken into thought units. Since not every unit functioned to seek compliance, units initially were classified into five categories: compliance–gaining, refuting, discounting refutation, agreeing, and other.

After examining thought units that sought compliance, Dillard and Fitzpatrick (1985) created the eight-category VICS typology organized around three types of power (see Table 20.4). According to the authors, the Me, You, and External strategies all draw attention to values or obligations by referencing characteristics of the source, target, or demands from the larger world. The strategies of Us, Direct, and Search make reference to the relationship either directly or indirectly by presuming that the relationship itself provides a basis for issuing requests or questions. Finally, the Activity and Power strategies both highlight the expected consequences of the target complying or refusing to comply.

Researchers have analyzed frequency-of-use data for the eight individual strategies, but interpretations typically focus on the degree to which couples rely on strategies enacting the three types of power. During role-plays, spouses use the Direct and Me strategies most often (Dillard & Fitzpatrick, 1985), though it is difficult to know if this accurately reflects both sexes, because the proportion of husbands and wives who enacted the compliance-seeking role may have differed. Spouses also reciprocated each other's use of most strategies; indeed, correlations ranged from $r = .26$ to $r = .39$ between wives' and husbands' total use for six of the eight strategies.

Representative Findings

Having clarified how persuasion has been conceptualized in marital relationships, we now turn to what is known about two specific questions regarding persuasion and marriage.

Couple Types. Given that married couples can negotiate their interdependence in various ways, it would not be surprising if the frequency and form of persuasion within marriage also varied across couple types. Fitzpatrick (1988) and Gottman (1993) have explored this question.

Based on spouses' self-reports to the Relational Dimensions Instrument (RDI), Fitzpatrick (1988) identifies three implicit theories of marriage. Traditional spouses hold conventional values that emphasize stability as opposed to spontaneity, display physical and psychological interdependence, and tend not to avoid conflict. Independent spouses hold nonconventional values regarding marriage and gender, maintain psychological but less physical interdependence, and display assertiveness during conflict. Separate spouses hold ambivalent views about martial relationships (e.g., desiring tradition and freedom from constraint), display the lowest levels of physical and psychological interdependence, and tend to avoid overt conflict. Because wives and husbands may hold the same or different theories of marriage, couples are classified as traditional, independent, separate, or mixed.

To explore how married couples differ in terms of persuasion, Witteman and Fitzpatrick (1986) reexamined data from an earlier study (Dillard & Fitzpatrick, 1985) after dividing the sample of 51 couples into types based on their RDI scores. Witteman and Fitzpatrick examined both the percentage of overall talk during two role-plays that involved seeking compliance and the specific strategies that were used during compliance-gaining attempts.

Witteman and Fitzpatrick (1986) report numerous differences between couple types in terms of persuasion. Unexpectedly, separate couples did not make fewer total attempts to seek their partner's compliance relative to other couples, perhaps because the researchers instructed everyone to seek their partner's compliance. However, independent couples did have more talk that fell into the "refuting" and "discounting" categories, leading the authors to conclude that independents engaged in more intense debate relative to other couples during the role-plays.

Regarding use of specific compliance-gaining strategies, traditional couples used several strategies from the "relationship/identification" category more than would be expected by chance, whereas separate couples relied less than was expected on all three strategies from the "relationship/identification" category (see Table 20.4). In contrast, separate couples relied on most strategies from the "values/obligation" category more than would be expected by chance, whereas traditional couples relied less than was expected on all three strategies from this same category. When referring to expectancies, traditional couples tended to discuss the benefits of the proposed change (Activity), whereas separate couples tended to threaten negative reactions (Power). Finally, independent couples used the most complex set of strategies in terms of power bases, relying on some (but not all) of the strategies that enacted each type of power.

Relying on behavioral rather than on self-report data to classify couples, Gottman (1993; Gottman & Levenson, 1992) proposed a second typology of married couples with implications for persuasion. In the initial stage of a longitudinal study, 79 couples discussed a persistent topic of disagreement in their marriage. Four years later, at least 1 spouse from 73 of the original couples completed measures of marital stability including questions about separation, divorce, and serious consideration of divorce. To identify couple types, videotaped interactions were coded using the Rapid Couples Interaction Scoring System (Krokoff, Gottman, & Hass, 1989). Based on these codes, Gottman (1993) identified three types of "stable" couples, that is, couples who had neither separated/divorced nor reported having seriously considered divorce during the course of the study. All three stable couple types displayed approximately a ratio of 5:1 in terms of the relative frequency of positive versus negative speaker codes, but they differed in terms of overall amount of positive and negative behavior. *Volatile* couples displayed the highest amount of positive speaker and listener codes (e.g., laughing) but also the highest amount of negative codes (e.g., defensiveness). *Avoiding* couples displayed the lowest amount of positive and negative speaker codes combined with the highest rates of listener withdrawal, whereas *validating* couples displayed intermediate levels of positive and negative behavior.

To assess differences in persuasion, Gottman (1993) broke each couple's interaction into three phases, labeled the agenda building, arguing, and compromising phases. Using a different coding scheme, persuasive attempts were operationalized as the total number of disagreement and criticizing statements, which Gottman acknowledges to be only a "crude" measure (p. 7). Despite this, couple types displayed clear differences across the three phases of interaction. Validating couples engaged in little persuasion during the agenda phase, substantially more persuasion during the arguing phase, and less persuasion during the compromising phase. In contrast, volatile couples engaged in persuasion right from the start. Although their rates of persuasion dropped slightly during the middle and final phases, they enacted more attempts than the other two couple types during all three phases. Their intense pattern of debate mirrors Witteman and Fitzpatrick's (1986) independent couples. Finally, avoiding couples engaged in very few persuasive attempts during any phase, enacting the lowest levels across phases.

In summary, different types of couples engage in different amounts of persuasion and employ different power strategies, yet many couples from each type display predominately positive affect and remain relatively happy and stable. These findings suggest caution in drawing broad generalizations about marital stability and dimensions of power strategies.

Demand–Withdraw Patterns. Viewing power as a relational concept implies that studies of persuasion need to explore how couples seek *and* resist compliance. Research on demand–withdraw in marriage takes just this tack, by exploring a specific type of episode:

> during which one partner attempts to engage the other in discussing an issue by criticizing, complaining, or suggesting change while the other partner attempts to end the discussion or avoid the topic by changing the subject, remaining silent, or even leaving the room. (Klinetob & Smith, 1996, p. 946)

Researchers often use both self-report and observational measures to assess this pattern (e.g., Caughlin & Vangelisti, 1999, Heavey, Layne, & Christensen, 1993; Holtzworth-Munroe, Smutlzer, & Stuart, 1998). Spouses provide self-reports via the Communication Patterns Questionnaire (CPQ, Christensen, 1988; Christensen & Heavey, 1990). The CPQ assesses each spouse's perceptions of the likelihood that the couple will enact several patterns when discussing relational problems, including wife demand/husband withdraw as well as husband demand/wife withdraw. To obtain observational measures, couples have been taped while discussing one or more issues in which one spouse (e.g., the wife) wants change in the partner's behavior or their relationship, and then discussing one or more issues where the other spouse (e.g., the husband) desires change. Observers typically make global ratings of the degree to which each spouse engages in demand (e.g., blaming, pressuring for change) and withdraw (e.g., topic avoidance, silence) behavior over the entire course of each interaction. An index of wife demand/husband withdraw is computed by summing ratings for these two forms of behavior, and the same is done for husband demand/wife withdraw. Importantly, studies using self-report and observational measures have obtained similar findings regarding the precursors and effects of demand–withdraw communication (e.g., Caughlin & Vangelisti, 1999; Heavey et al., 1993).

Researchers have explored associations between demand–withdraw and marital satisfaction. When couples discuss multiple issues, wife demand/husband withdraw is more common that husband demand/wife withdraw (Caughlin & Vangelisti, 1999; Heavey et al., 1993; Holtzworth et al., 1998), but both forms of demand–withdraw are inversely associated with spouses' martial satisfaction (e.g., Caughlin & Huston, 2002; Sagrestano, Heavey, & Christensen, 1999). The picture is more complicated when demand–withdraw communication and satisfaction are assessed over time and/or within a larger relational context. For example, Caughlin and Huston (2002) show that the negative effects of demand–withdraw communication on martial satisfaction are mitigated when couples also engage in high levels of affectional expression. Prospective research indicates that current dissatisfaction appears to predict future demand–withdraw communication as much as the opposite (Noller et al., 1994). In addition, Heavey et al. (1993) found that wife demand/husband withdraw predicted a decline in wives' marital satisfaction from 1 year to the next, but husband demand/wife withdraw actually predicted an *increase* in wives' marital satisfaction over the same time period. Heavey et al. speculate that wives may interpret demanding behavior by their husbands as a sign of the man's commitment to their marriage, which may lead to more positive outcomes over time. The plausibility of this suggestion also may depend on the larger relational context, because husband demand/wife withdraw appears to function differently for couples who are (versus are not) experiencing husband-to-wife violence (Holtzworth-Munroe et al., 1998). Similar to our discussion of parental discipline and warmth, these findings highlight the importance of attending to the meaning that women and men ascribe to both demand and withdraw behavior over time and within the larger context of their marriage.

Aside from investigating associations with marital satisfaction, researchers have assessed explanations for why couples engage in demand–withdraw communication. Two major theories have been tested, both of which appear to tell part of the story. The gender/individual differences explanation asserts that women in general have greater needs for connection, whereas men have greater needs for autonomy and/or are more reactive to physiological stress; thus, men withdraw more frequently in the face of persuasive attempts (Caughlin & Vangelisti, 2000). The social–structural explanation suggests that the spouse who wants change demands, whereas the spouse who does not withdraws. Because women bear the brunt of domestic labor even when both spouses work, women are more likely to demand change (Klinetob & Smith, 1996).

In support of the social–structural explanation, several studies report an interaction between topic and type of demand–withdraw: When couples discuss an issue salient to the wife but not her husband, the predominate pattern is wife demand/husband withdraw, whereas when couples discuss an issue salient primarily to the husband, husband demand/wife withdraw is as common or even more common than the opposite pattern (Christensen & Heavey, 1990; Heavey et al., 1993; Holtzworth et al., 1998; Klinetob & Smith, 1996). For issues salient to both spouses, as the joint level of issue importance increases, so does both wife demand/husband withdraw as well as husband demand/wife withdraw (Caughlin & Vangelisti, 1999). In support of the gender differences theory, the desire for closeness and argumentativeness has been found to be positively associated with greater levels of demandingness and negatively associated with withdrawal, and neurotic spouses or those who have an external conflict locus of control tend to have relationships characterized by demand–withdrawal (Caughlin & Vangelisti, 2000).

The social–structural and gender differences explanation may not be competing positions. Rather, they may share a bidirectional relationship: Societal power differences may cause wives in general to desire more change than husbands do, but societal power differences also may be anchored, in part, by women's greater sensitivity to relational issues. An adequate explanation for demand–withdraw communication must account for the complex interplay of individual differences and the social distribution of power in marriage.

FUTURE DIRECTIONS

The traditional persuasion literature has paid limited attention to family relationships. In this chapter, we assess how persuasion has been conceptualized in the family, focusing on parent–child and marital relationships. Although scholars studying parental discipline styles rarely cite research on power strategies in marriage (or vice versa), our review reveals a number of similar findings. Several dimensions of persuasive appeals have been recognized as important in both contexts. For example, both parents (Oldershaw et al., 1986) and spouses (Dillard & Fitzpatrick, 1985) commonly make simple requests without providing explicit reasoning. When seeking change, both parents (Baumrind, 1973) and spouses (Falbo & Peplau, 1980) vary the degree to which their requests and persuasive strategies are direct/overt versus indirect/covert. Both parents (Applegate et al., 1985; Hoffman, 1980) and spouses (Witteman & Fitzpatrick, 1986) differ in whether they tend to make appeals that stress the consequences of a proposed action versus punitive sanctions, though the mixing of persuasion and coercion is common in both contexts. Scholars also have recognized the importance of investigating resistance to persuasion in the forms of both child noncompliance with parental requests (Chamberlain & Patterson, 1996) and demand–withdraw patterns in marriage (Christensen & Heavey, 1990). Message dimensions such as directness, elaboration, and coerciveness hold implications for feelings of efficacy and affection in both parent–child and marital relationships.

Aside from identifying similar message features, scholars in both contexts have recognized that power and intimacy shape family members' choices, interpretations, and responses to persuasive strategies. Family members who feel powerless at times employ aggressive forms of influence in an attempt to regain power, whether they are physically abusive parents (Bugental et al., 1989) or spouses embroiled in demand–withdraw patterns (Sagrestano et al., 1999). Intimacy shapes family members' interpretations of what others might perceive as aggressive forms of communication, such that the effects of parental power assertion on child misbehavior are mitigated by parental emotional support (McLoyd & Smith, 2002) and the effects of demand–withdraw communication on marital dissatisfaction are mitigated by affectional expression (Caughlin & Huston, 2002).

We see a need for theories that can account for regularities in persuasion across parent–child and marital relationships and provide insights about message choices and effects. Although not the only option, Brown and Levinson's (1987) politeness theory offers one promising framework because politeness both reflects *and* defines relational power and intimacy. Briefly, the theory assumes that speakers in all cultures desire to maintain face, which is subdivided into two basic wants: *positive face*, or the desire to have one's attributes and actions approved by significant others; and *negative face*, or the desire to be autonomous and free from unnecessary constraint. Although relational interdependence creates motives for supporting others' face during interaction, many speech acts threaten face. According to Brown and Levinson, persuasive appeals inherently threaten the target's negative face. Because persuasive appeals implicitly project a definition of situation, including presumed identities for both parties, they also can threaten both parties' positive face (Sanders & Fitch, 2001; Wilson, Aleman, & Leatham, 1998).

Although persuasive appeals implicate face, not all appeals threaten face equally. Brown and Levinson (1987) argue that power and intimacy influence the "weightiness" of a face-threatening act (FTA) in any culture, such that the "same" act is more face threatening as a target's power relative to a message source increases and/or as social distance between the source and target increases. Message sources often manage face threats arising from their persuasive appeals by using politeness or language that attends to the target's face. Politeness theory assumes that speakers exploit two linguistic forms to minimize FTAs. *Indirectness* occurs when a source says something that, given the circumstances, implies a different or additional meaning. *Mitigation* includes redressive actions such as accounts, apologies, or compliments. Politeness theory assumes that as the weightiness of an FTA increases, so will the degree to which sources include indirectness and redressive actions in their persuasive appeals.

It is important to recognize that power and distance are subjective perceptions; thus, two family members might well perceive the "same" persuasive appeal as differentially face threatening if they perceive different levels of power or closeness in their relationship. In addition, the relationship between politeness strategies and power or distance is reciprocal. For example, spouses who perceive that they have less power than their partner commonly use indirect forms of influence to mitigate threats to the partner's face; but spouses who believe they deserve more power in their marriage may use direct forms of influence in an intentional attempt to renegotiate relative levels of power (Brown & Levinson, 1987, pp. 228–229).

As is apparent, politeness theory offers one explanation for many similarities in persuasion in parent–child and marital relationships. Whether family members make requests indirectly, provide reasons, or avoid coercive pressure, all impact the perceived politeness of persuasive appeals. Sources may interpret resistance as a sign that targets view their desires as unimportant or lack respect for their authority, and thus use aggressive forms of influence to regain face. Relational closeness reduces the degree of FTA communicated by demands or power assertion; hence, parental warmth or spousal affection can alter interpretations and negative effects of aggressive forms of influence. Couples who enact high levels of psychological interdependence (independent or volatile) would be expected to engage in more frequent and intense persuasive exchanges, because they would view such actions as less face threatening than couples who enact lower levels of interdependence (separate or avoiding).

It might seem ironic that politeness theory offers a useful framework for studying persuasion in families, because a good deal of the research we review indicates that family members often are not polite to each other. Politeness theory, however, does not assume that message sources always will be polite but rather that sources vary their degree of politeness (vs. impoliteness) depending on the amount of perceived threat to the target's face. "Face" also might seem less relevant in family relationships, because we might hope that individuals could "just be themselves" with their families. As Cupach and Metts (1994) have argued, however,

> the complexity of managing face is increased for partners in close relationships...part of the reason a couple defines itself as intimate is that the need to "perform"...is considered unnecessary; yet in this very act of dropping pretense arises the probability of threatening each other's face and, ultimately, sense of social competence. (p. 2)

Thus, the way that a parent influences his/her child allows the child to have more or less "face" within their relationship, in the sense of validating the child's competence, worth, and autonomy. The same holds true in terms of whether spouses are responsive to each other's influence.

Politeness theory has much to offer the study of persuasion in families, including a rationale for analyzing specific features of persuasive appeals, predictions about message choices and effects, and a lens on cultural similarities and differences in the meanings of influence attempts (Baxter & Bylund, in press). Of course, analyses of persuasion based on politeness theory must be integrated with detailed analyses of family forms and structures (Wilson, 2002). Relevant questions include: What attributes do husbands and wives, mothers and fathers, sons and daughters, stepparents and stepchildren, grandmothers and grandfathers, and so forth desire to be seen as possessing in the eyes of other family members? What rights and obligations do these roles entail in various cultures? How do family members negotiate levels of power and distance in their family, and in what ways do persuasive appeals both reflect and reinforce/challenge existing levels? The literatures on persuasion in parent–child and marital relationships already offer important insights about persuasion in families. By conducting future research inspired by theories that transcend specific relationships, we may develop a more integrated understanding of persuasion and families. Politeness theory is one—though by no means the only—perspective that might guide such efforts.

AUTHORS' NOTE

Steven R. Wilson is Professor and Director of Graduate Studies, and Wendy M. Morgan is a doctoral candidate, in the Department of Communication at Purdue University. Correspondence regarding this chapter should be addressed to the first author: Department of Communication, 1366 BRNG 2114, W. Lafayette, IN 47907-1366. Send email to swilson@sla.purdue.edu.

REFERENCES

Aida, Y., & Falbo, T. (1991). Relationships between marital satisfaction, resources, and power strategies. *Sex Roles, 24,* 43–56.

Applegate, J. L., Burke, J. A., Burleson, B. R., Delia, J. G., & Kline, S. L. (1985). Reflection-enhancing parental communication. In I. E. Sigel (Ed.), *Parental belief systems: The psychological consequences for children* (pp. 107–142). Hillsdale, NJ: Lawrence Erlbaum Associates.

Azar, S T. (1997). A cognitive behavioral approach to understanding and treating parents who physically abuse their children. In D. A. Wolfe, R. J. McMahon, & R. DeV. Peters (Eds.), *Child abuse: New directions in prevention and treatment across the lifespan* (pp. 79–101). Thousand Oaks, CA: Sage.

Bauer, W. D., & Twentyman, C. T. (1985). Abusing, neglectful, and comparison mothers' responses to child-related and non-child-related stressors. *Journal of Consulting and Clinical Psychology, 53,* 335–343.

Baumrind, D. (1972). An exploratory study of the socialization effects on Black children: Some Black-White comparisons. *Child Development, 43,* 261–267.

Baumrind, D. (1973). The development of instrumental competence through socialization. In A. D. Pick (Ed.), *Minnesota symposium on child psychology* (Vol. 7, pp. 3–46). Minneapolis: University of Minnesota Press.

Baumrind, D. (1996). The discipline controversy revisited. *Family Relations, 45,* 405–411.

Baxter, L. A., & Bylund, C. L. (in press). Social influence in close relationships. In J. S. Seiter & H. Gass (Eds.), *Readings in persuasion, social influence, and compliance gaining.* Boston: Allyn & Bacon.

Bayer, C. L., & Cegala, D. (1992). Trait verbal aggressiveness and argumentativeness: Relations with parenting style. *Western Journal of Communication, 56,* 301–310.

Belk, S. S., Snell, W. E., Garcia-Falconi, R. Hernandez-Sanchez, J. E., Hargrove, L., & Holtzman, W. H. (1988). Power strategy use in the intimate relationships of women and men from Mexico and the United States. *Personality and Social Psychology Bulletin, 14,* 439–447.

Belsky, J. (1993). Etiology of child maltreatment: A developmental-ecological analysis. *Psychological Bulletin, 114*, 413–434.

Berger, C. R. (1994). Power, dominance, and social interaction. In M. Knapp & G. Miller (Eds.), *Handbook of interpersonal communication* (pp. 450–506). Thousand Oaks, CA: Sage.

Brown, P., & Levinson, S. C. (1987). *Politeness: Some universals in language usage.* Cambridge: Cambridge University Press.

Bugental, D. B., Blue, J., Cruzcosa, M. (1989). Perceived control over caregiving outcomes: Implications for child abuse. *Developmental Psychology, 25*, 532–539.

Burleson, B. R., Delia, J. G., & Applegate, J. L. (1995). The socialization of person-centered communication: Parents' contributions to their children's social-cognitive and communication skills. In M. A. Fitzpatrick & A. L. Vangelisti (Eds.), *Explaining family interactions* (pp. 34–76). Thousand Oaks, CA: Sage.

Butterfield, R. M., & Lewis, M. A. (2002). Health-related social influence: A social ecological perspective on tactic use. *Journal of Social and Personal Relationships, 19*, 505–526.

Caughlin, J. P., & Huston, T. L. (2002). A contextual analysis of the association between demand/withdraw and marital satisfaction. *Personal Relationships, 9*, 95–119.

Caughlin, J. P., & Vangelisti, A. L. (1999). Desire for change in one's partner as a predictor of the demand/withdraw pattern of marital communication. *Communication Monographs, 66*, 66–89.

Caughlin, J. P., & Vangelisti, A. L. (2000). An individual difference explanation of why married couples engage in the demand/withdraw pattern of conflict. *Journal of Social and Personal Relationships, 17*, 523–551.

Cerezo, M. A., D'Ocon, A., & Dolz, L. (1996). Mother-child interactive patterns in abusive families versus nonabusive families: An observational study. *Child Abuse and Neglect, 20*, 573–584.

Chamberlain, P., & Patterson, G. R. (1996). Discipline and child compliance in parenting. In M. Bornstein (Ed.), *Handbook of parenting, Volume 4, Applied and practical parenting* (pp. 205–225). Mahwah, NJ: Lawrence Erlbaum Associates.

Christensen, A. (1988). Dysfunctional interaction patterns in couples. In P. Noller & M. A. Fitzpatrick (Eds.), *Perspectives on marital interaction* (pp. 31–54). Clevedon, Avon, England: Multilingual Matters Ltd.

Christensen, A., & Heavey, C. L. (1990). Gender and social structure in the demand/withdraw pattern of marital conflict. *Journal of Personality and Social Psychology, 39*, 73–81.

Cody, M. J., Canary, D. J., & Smith, S. W. (1994). Compliance-gaining goals: An inductive analysis of actors' goal types, strategies, and successes. In J. A. Daly & J. M. Wiemann (Eds.), Strategic Interpersonal Communication (pp. 33–90). Mahwah, NJ: Lawrence Erlbaum Associates.

Cooper, M., D., & Nothstine, W. L. (1997). *Power persuasion: Moving an ancient art into the media age* (2nd ed.). Greenwood, IN: Educational Video Group.

Cupach, W. R., & Metts, S. (1994). *Facework.* Thousand Oaks, CA: Sage.

Deater-Deckard, K., Dodge, K. A., Bates, J. E., & Pettit, G. S. (1996). Physical discipline among African American and European American mothers: Links to children's externalizing behaviors. *Developmental Psychology, 32*, 1065–1072.

Dillard, J. P., & Fitzpatrick, M. A. (1985). Compliance-gaining in marital interaction. *Personality and Social Psychology Bulletin, 11,* 419–433.

Dillard, J. P., & Pfau, M. (Eds.). (2002). *The persuasion handbook: Developments in theory and practice.* Thousand Oaks, CA: Sage.

Dopke, C. A., & Milner, J. S. (2000). Impact of child noncompliance on stress appraisals, attributions, and disciplinary choices of mothers at high and low risk for child physical abuse. *Child Abuse and Neglect, 24,* 493–504.

Falbo, T., & Peplau, L. A. (1980). Power strategies in intimate relationships. *Journal of Personality and Social Psychology, 38,* 618–628.

Fitzpatrick, M. A. (1988). *Between husbands and wives: Communication in marriage.* Newbury Park, CA: Sage.

Gottman, J. M. (1993). The roles of conflict engagement, escalation, and avoidance in marital interaction: A longitudinal view of five couple types. *Journal of Consulting and Clinical Psychology, 61,* 6–15.

Gottman, J. M., & Levenson, R. W. (1992). Toward a typology of marriage based on affective behavior: Preliminary differences in behavior, physiology, health, and risk for dissolution. *Journal of Personality and Social Psychology, 63,* 221–233.

Grusec, J. E., & Goodnow, J. J. (1994). Impact of parental discipline methods on the child's internalization of values: A reconceptualization of current points of view. *Developmental Psychology, 30,* 4–19.

Heavey, C. L., Layne, C., & Christensen, A. (1993). Gender and conflict structure in marital interaction: A replication and extension. *Journal of Consulting and Clinical Psychology, 61,* 16–27.

Hoffman, M. L. (1980). Moral development in adolescence. In J. Adleson (Ed.), *Handbook of adolescent psychology* (pp. 295–343). New York: Wiley.

Hoffman, M. L. (1994). Discipline and internalization. *Developmental Psychology, 30,* 26–28.

Holtzworth-Munroe, A., Smutlzer, N., & Stuart, G. L. (1998). Demand and withdraw communication among couples experiencing husband violence. *Journal of Consulting and Clinical Psychology, 66,* 731–743.

Howard, J. A., Blumstein, P., & Schwartz, P. (1986). Sex, power, and influence tactics in intimate relationships. *Journal of Personality and Social Psychology, 51,* 102–109.

Kellermann, K. (1992). Communication: Inherently strategic and primarily automatic. *Communication Monographs, 59,* 288–300.

Kelley, H. H., Berscheid, E., Christensen, A., Harvey, J. H., Huston, T. L., Levinger, NG. et al. (1983). Analyzing close relationships. In H. H. Kelley, E. Berscheid, A. Christensen, J. H. Harvey, T. L. Huston, G. Levinger, et al. (Eds.), *Close relationships* (pp. 20–67). New York: Freeman.

Kelman, H. C. (1958). Compliance, identification, and internalization: Three processes of attitude change. *Journal of Conflict Resolution, 2,* 51–60.

Kilgore, K., Snyder, J., & Lentz, C. (2000). The contribution of parental discipline, parental monitoring, and school risk to early-onset conduct problems in African American boys and girls. *Developmental Psychology, 36,* 835–845.

Kim, M. S., & Wilson, S. R. (1994). A cross-cultural comparison of implicit theories of requesting. *Communication Monographs, 61*, 210–235.

Klinetob, N. A., & Smith, D. A. (1996). Demand–withdraw communication in marital interaction: Tests of interspousal contingency and gender role hypotheses. *Journal of Marriage and the Family, 58*, 945–957.

Kochanska, G., & Aksan, N. (1995). Mother–child mutually positive affect, the quality of child compliance to requests and prohibitions, and maternal control as correlates of early internalization. *Child Development, 66*, 236–254.

Kochanska, G., Aksan, N., & Koenig, A. L. (1995). A longitudinal study of the roots of preschoolers' conscience: Committed compliance and emerging internalization. *Child Development, 66*, 1752–1769.

Krokoff, L. J., Gottman, J. M., & Hass, S. D. (1989). Validation of a global rapid couples interaction scoring system. *Behavioral Assessment, 11*, 65–79.

Larrance, D. T., & Twentyman, C. T. (1983). Maternal attributions and child abuse. *Journal of Abnormal Psychology, 92*, 449–457.

Larzelere, R. E., Sather, P. R., Schneider, W. N., Larson, D. B., & Pike, P. L. (1998). Punishment enhances reasoning's effectiveness as a disciplinary response to toddlers. *Journal of Marriage and the Family, 60*, 388–403.

Maccoby, E. E., & Martin, J. A. (1983). Socialization in the context of the family: Parent–child interaction. In E. M. Hetherington (Ed.), *Handbook of child psychology, Vol. 4. Socialization, personality, and social development* (pp. 1–101). New York: Wiley.

McCabe, K. M., Clark, R., & Barnett, D. (1999). Family protective factors among urban African American youth. *Journal of Clinical Child Psychology, 28*, 137–150.

McLaughlin, M. L., Cody, M. J., & Robey, C. S. (1980). Situational influences on the selection of strategies to resist compliance-gaining attempts. *Human Communication Research, 7*, 14–36.

McLeod, J., Kruttschnitt, C., & Dornfeld, M. (1994). Does parenting explain the effects of structural conditions on children's antisocial behavior? A comparison of Blacks and Whites. *Social Forces, 73*, 575–604.

McLoyd, V. C., & Smith, J. (2002). Physical discipline and behavior problems in African American, European American, and Hispanic children: Emotional support as a moderator. *Journal of Marriage and Family, 64*, 40–53.

McQuillen, J. S., Higginbotham, D. C., & Cummings, M. C. (1984). Compliance-resisting behaviors: The effects of age, agent, and types of request. In R. N. Bostrom (Ed.), *Communication yearbook 8* (pp. 747–762). Beverly Hills, CA: Sage.

Millar, F. E., & Rogers, L. E. (1987). Relational dimensions of interpersonal dynamics. In M. E. Roloff & G. R. Miller (Eds.), *Interpersonal processes: New directions in communication research* (pp. 117–138). Newbury Park, CA: Sage.

Miller, G. R. (1980). On being persuaded: Some basic distinctions. In M. E. Roloff & G. R. Miller (Eds.), *Persuasion: New directions in theory and research* (pp. 105–122). Beverly Hills, CA: Sage.

Miller, G. R., & Boster, F. (1988). Persuasion in personal relationships. In S. W. Duck (Ed.), *Handbook of personal relationships* (pp. 275–288). New York: Wiley.

Milner, J. S. (2000). Social information processing and child physical abuse: Theory and research. In D. J. Hersen (Ed.), *Nebraska symposium on motivation: Vol. 45.*

Motivation and child maltreatment (pp. 39–84). Lincoln, NE: University of Nebraska Press.

Mosby, L., Rawls, A. W., Meehan, A. J., Mays, E., & Pettinari, C. J. (1999). Troubles in interracial talk about discipline: An examination of African American child rearing narratives. *Journal of Comparative Family Studies, 30*, 489–521.

Mumby, D. (2001). Power and politics. In F. M. Jablin & L. L. Putnam (Eds.), *The new handbook of organizational communication: Advances in theory, research, and methods* (pp. 585–623). Thousand Oaks, CA: Sage.

Newton, D. A., & Burgoon, J. K. (1990). The use and consequences of verbal influence strategies during interpersonal disagreements. *Human Communication Research, 16*, 477–518.

Noller, P., Feeney, J. A., Bonnell, D., & Callan, V. J. (1994). A longitudinal study of conflict in early marriage. *Journal of Social and Personal Relationship, 11*, 233–252.

O'Keefe, D. J. (2002). *Persuasion: Theory and research* (2nd ed.). Thousand Oaks, CA: Sage.

Oldershaw, L., Walters, G. C., & Hall, D. K. (1986). Control strategies and noncompliance in abusive mother–child dyads: An observational study. *Child Development, 57*, 722–732.

Oldershaw, L., Walters, G. C., & Hall, D. K. (1989). A behavioral approach to the classification of different types of physically abusive mother–child dyads. *Merrill-Palmer Quarterly, 35*, 255–279.

Peddle, N., & Wang, C. T. (2001). Current trends in child abuse prevention, reporting, and fatalities: The 1999 fifty states survey. Retrieved August 19, 2002, from http://www.preventchildabuse.org/learn_more/research_docs/1999_50_survey.pdf

Perloff, R. M. (2001). *Persuading people to have safer sex: Applications of social science to the AIDS crisis.* Mahwah, NJ: Lawrence Erlbaum Associates.

Querido, J. G., Warner, T. D., & Eyberg, S. M. (2002). Parenting styles and child behavior in African American families of preschool children. *Journal of Clinical Child and Adolescent Psychology, 31*, 272–277.

Reid, J. B. (1986). Social-interactional patterns in families of abused and nonabused children. In C. Zahn-Waxler, E. M. Cummings, & R. Iannotti (Eds.), *Altruism and aggression: Biological and social origins* (pp. 238–255). New York: Cambridge University Press.

Roloff, M. E. (1981). *Interpersonal communication: The social exchange approach.* Beverly Hills, CA: Sage.

Roloff, M. E., Janiszewski, C. A., McGrath, M. A., Burns, C. S., & Manrai, L.A. (1988). Acquiring resources from intimates: When obligation substitutes for persuasion. *Human Communication Research, 14*, 364–396.

Sagrestano, L. M., Christensen, A., & Heavey, C. L. (1998). Social influence techniques during marital conflict. *Personal Relationships, 5*, 75–89.

Sagrestano, L. M., Heavey, C. L., & Christensen, A. (1999). Perceived power and physical violence in marital conflict. *Journal of Social Issues, 55*, 65–79.

Sanders, R. E., & Fitch, K. L. (2001). The actual practice of compliance-seeking. *Communication Theory, 11*, 263–289.

Sprey, J. (1999). Family dynamics: An essay on conflict and power. In M. Sussman, S. K. Steinmetz, & G. W. Peterson (Eds.), *Handbook of marriage and the family* (2nd ed., pp. 667–685). New York: Plenum Press.

Stewart, C. J., Smith, C. A., & Denton, R. E. Jr. (2001). *Persuasion and social movements* (4th ed.). Prospect Heights, IL: Waveland Press.

Stiff, J. B., & Mongeau, P. (2002). *Persuasive communication* (2nd ed). New York: Guilford Press.

Trickett, P. K., & Kuczynski, L. (1986). Children's misbehaviors and parental discipline strategies in abusive and non-abusive families. *Developmental Psychology, 22,* 115–123.

U.S. Census Bureau. (2001). Median income of families by selected characteristics, race, and Hispanic origin of householder. Retrieved September 28, 2002, from http://www.census.gov/hhes/income/income01/inctab4.html.

Wheeless, L. R., Barraclough, R., & Stewart, R. (1983). Compliance-gaining and power in persuasion. In R. N. Bostrom & B. H. Westley (Eds.), *Communication yearbook 7* (pp. 105–145). Beverly Hills, CA: Sage.

Wilson, S. R. (2002). *Seeking and resisting compliance: Why people say what they do when trying to influence others.* Thousand Oaks, CA: Sage.

Wilson, S. R., Aleman, C. G., & Leatham, G. B. (1998). Identity implications of influence goals: A revised analysis of face-threatening acts and application to seeking compliance with same-sex friends. *Human Communication Research, 25,* 64–96.

Wilson, S. R., Cameron, K. A., & Whipple, E. E. (1997). Regulative communication strategies within mother–child interactions: Implications for the study of reflection-enhancing parental communication. *Research on Language and Social Interaction, 30,* 73–92.

Wilson, S. R., & Whipple, E. E. (2001). Attributions and regulative communication by parents participating in a child abuse prevention program. In V. Manusov & J. H. Harvey (Eds.), *Attributions, communication behavior, and close relationships* (pp. 227–247). New York: Cambridge University Press.

Wilson, S. R., Whipple, E. E., & Grau, J. (1996). Reflection-enhancing regulative communication: How do parents vary across misbehavior types and child resistance? *Journal of Social and Personal Relationships, 13,* 553–569.

Witteman, H., & Fitzpatrick, M. A. (1986). Compliance-gaining in marital interaction: Power bases, processes, and outcomes. *Communication Monographs, 53,* 130–143.

Zvonkovic, A. M., Schmeige, C. J., & Hall, L. D. (1994). Influence strategies used when couples make work-family decisions and their importance for marital satisfaction. *Family Relations, 43,* 182–188.

EMOTION AND COMMUNICATION IN FAMILIES

JULIE FITNESS
MACQUARIE UNIVERSITY

JILL DUFFIELD
THE UNIVERSITY OF THE WEST OF ENGLAND

> *... interpersonal communication is truly "a reciprocation of emotions—a dance of emotions."*
> —Zajonc, (1998, p. 593).

Family life is a dynamic, intricately patterned kaleidoscope of feelings and emotions, ranging from the most intense hues of anger, hate, and love to the mildest shades of irritation, hurt, and affection. There are times when the family provides an emotional refuge, a "haven in a heartless world." At other times, the family is a crucible of dark emotions that may fracture and destroy family relationships. The emotional life of the family is rich and extraordinarily complex: a complexity that derives, in part, from the sheer number of the relationships it may comprise, from adult partners/spouses to parents and children, siblings, and extended/blended family members, including aunts, uncles, grandparents, stepparents, and beyond. Every family member is a potentially powerful source of emotion for every other family member, and every family member's expression of emotion has a more or less powerful impact on other family members. Emotions, then, can be thought of as the currency of family relationships, imbuing them with meaning and importance.

In recent years, research on emotion has flourished. However, theoretical and empirical work on emotional communication in relational contexts such as the family has been relatively sparse and scattered throughout different literatures (e.g., sociology, social, developmental and clinical psychology, and communication studies). Our aim in this chapter, then, is to provide an integrative account of what we know, and do not know, about some of the most interesting and important aspects of emotion communication in families. We begin with a discussion of the functions of emotions, followed by a review of emotion in marital and sibling relationships. We then examine emotion socialization practices within the family, followed by a discussion of emotional transmission and the creation of emotion climates in the family. Finally, we discuss the role of emotion communication in adaptive family functioning and propose an agenda for future research.

THE FUNCTIONS OF EMOTION COMMUNICATION

In 1872 Darwin published a wonderfully insightful account of the origins and functions of human emotional expressions. His general thesis was that many human facial and bodily behaviors, such as smiling, snarling, and crying, are innate and universal and serve vital communicative functions. Recently, a number of emotion theorists have adopted and elaborated Darwin's functionalist perspective, arguing that we are born with several "hard-wired" emotion systems that serve crucial functions in relation to our survival and well-being (e.g., see Andersen & Guerrero, 1998a; Oatley & Jenkins, 1996). According to this perspective, the primary function of emotion is informational: Specifically, emotions inform us about the status of our needs and goals. As Tomkins (1979) noted, if we did not suffer pain when we injured ourselves, or hunger when we needed food, we would soon bleed or starve to death. In the same way, emotions ensure that we will care about our own well-being and survival and that we will be motivated to act when the need arises. Thus, anger lets us know that a goal has been thwarted and mobilizes us to deal with the obstacle; fear stops us in our tracks, alerts us to danger, and motivates us to escape; romantic love tells us that our needs are being well met and urges us on to bond with, and commit to, the source of such rewards (Gonzaga, Keltner, Londahl, & Smith, 2001).

Critically, emotions also inform *others* about what matters to us. Babies, for example, are completely dependent on caregivers to meet their needs and must communicate those needs in ways that will motivate their caregivers to respond to them. Emotional expressions serve this vital function. In particular, researchers have found that babies spontaneously produce expressions of happiness, sadness, and anger within the first few days of life, and that caregivers differentially respond to these expressions (Scharfe, 2000). A baby's cry of distress is aversive and motivates the baby's mother to attend to its needs. In turn, the comforted baby's smile rewards its mother and helps to ensure she will continue to respond to its needs. Similarly, throughout life, expressions of anger communicate goal-frustration and a desire for others to put things right; expressions of fear communicate helplessness and a desire for protection; expressions of joy communicate that one is not currently needy but rather has resources (including positive feelings) to share. This, in turn, reinforces and strengthens social bonds.

Evolutionary psychologists have noted that humans are generally much more inclined to meet the needs of close family and friends than those of acquaintances and strangers. Similarly, humans are much more likely to express their needs and vulnerabilities to kin than to strangers (Buss, 1999). This suggests that emotions are more likely to be expressed within close, communal relationships than in more business-like, exchange relationships, where people feel no particular responsibility for each other's welfare. This hypothesis has been confirmed in a program of research conducted by Margaret Clark and her colleagues (see Clark, Fitness, & Brissette, 2001, for a review). Specifically, they have found that the expression of emotion is an integral feature of communal relationships such as the family, where people feel responsible for others' needs and, in turn, expect that others will be responsive to their own needs.

Another important feature of family life that makes it such a potentially emotional context derives from the complex patterns of behavioral interdependencies that develop among family members over time (Berscheid, 1983; Berscheid & Ammazzalorzo, 2001). Many of these interdependencies are explicit (e.g., son relies on mother to drive him to school; wife relies on husband to fix the car). However, many are implicit and involve expectations that family members will follow certain "rules" (e.g., Buck, 1989; Burgoon, 1993). For example, spouses expect one another to be supportive in times of trouble; parents expect children to love and respect them; and children expect parents to treat them fairly. To the extent that family members follow the rules and meet each other's needs and expectations, life runs smoothly. However, when explicit or implicit expectations are "interrupted" (Mandler, 1975) or violated (e.g., husband ignores wife's upset; child is rude to parent; parent favors one child over another), the scene is set for negative emotion—and often, strong negative emotion, given that we expect so much from those who are close to us. On the other hand, it is also possible for family members to exceed our expectations, as, for example, when a normally forgetful husband remembers his wife's birthday, or a child behaves well when his grandmother visits. These kinds of expectancy violations may also generate emotions; only they may be positive (e.g., joy or relief) rather than negative (e.g., anger or jealousy).

It is possible to predict which kinds of emotions an "interrupted" family member is most likely to experience if we know how he or she is cognitively appraising, or interpreting, a violated expectation with respect to its importance, cause, controllability, and so forth (see Lazarus, 1991, and Roseman, 1991, for detailed cognitive appraisal-emotion models). In their study of marital emotions, for example, Fitness and Fletcher (1993) found that both anger and hate were associated with violated expectations about how spouses should treat one another (i.e., with love and respect). However, whereas spouses' anger in response to a marital transgression was associated primarily with cognitive appraisals of partner-blame, unfairness, and predictability, spouses' hate was associated with appraisals of relative powerlessness and a perceived lack of control over the situation.

Different emotions are also associated with different motivations, or action tendencies (Frijda, 1986), with profound implications for what people actually do in emotional encounters. In Fitness and Fletcher's (1993) study, for example, episodes of marital anger were associated with urges to confront the partner and seek redress for an apparent injustice, whereas marital hate was associated with urges to escape from, or reject, the partner. On the other hand, spouses' self-reported feelings of love were associated with urges to be physically close to their partners and to express their feelings to them.

In summary, emotional expressions communicate our needs and desires to others, and family members are expected to care more than anyone else about meeting those needs and desires. Thus, more emotions are expressed in the context of the family than perhaps any other relational context. Moreover, the complex networks of interdependencies that exist within families mean that family members' expectations of one another are likely to be frequently violated. A variety of positive or negative emotional consequences may follow, depending on how family members cognitively appraise the meaning and significance of the violation. In the next section of the chapter, we discuss emotion communication within one of the best studied of all familial relationships: marriage.

EMOTION COMMUNICATION IN THE MARITAL RELATIONSHIP

Given that emotional expressions communicate information about needs and provide close others with the opportunity to meet those needs, it is not surprising that marital interaction researchers have found positive associations between marital happiness and spouses' abilities to both clearly express their own emotions and accurately identify their partners' emotions (e.g., Fletcher & Thomas, 1999; Gottman, 1994; Noller & Ruzzene, 1991). In fact, there are a number of ways in which emotional miscommunication can lead to marital distress, principally because spouses' perceptions of how well they communicate their emotions are not necessarily related to how well they *actually* communicate, especially with respect to accurately encoding, or expressing, emotions (Koerner & Fitzpatrick, 2002; see also Thomas, Fletcher, & Lange, 1997). For example, a spouse may believe she is communicating anxiety and a need for support from her partner, but her facial expression, tone of voice, and gestures may actually be sending an angry, rather than an anxious, message. Moreover, because spouses tend to reciprocate the emotions they perceive, accurately or otherwise, are being expressed to them (see Gaelick, Bodenhausen, & Wyer, 1985), her partner is likely to respond to her apparently angry message with anger, rather than with support. Or a spouse may communicate an objectively clear message of anxiety, but her partner may misinterpret her emotional expression as anger and again respond with anger. In both cases the most likely outcome is an escalating spiral of reciprocated hurt and hostility and increasing marital distress (Gottman, 1994).

Researchers have identified several factors that affect emotional communication processes and outcomes in marriage (Bradbury & Fincham, 1987; Fitness, 1996). For example, researchers have found that people in good moods tend to generously attribute the causes of conflict in their intimate relationships to relatively transient, external factors, whereas people in sad moods tend to see the conflict as a function of stable, global factors, such as the partner's personality flaws (Forgas, 1994). Chronic emotional dispositions such as depression and negative affectivity, or the tendency to experience frequent episodes of anxiety, anger, and sadness, cast a similarly gloomy pall over people's habitual ways of interpreting and responding to their spouses' behaviors (Beach & Fincham, 1994; Segrin, 1998). Ironically, depressed spouses' negative expectations and perceptions may elicit the kinds of defensive partner responses that only serve to confirm their pessimistic outlooks. Marital happiness, too, plays a major role in coloring spouses' expectations and perceptions of each other's behaviors, with distressed spouses tending to interpret their partners' behaviors in much the same way as do sad spouses (Fitness, Fletcher, & Overall, in press; Fletcher & Fincham, 1991).

Another important factor that affects emotional communication in marriage derives from spouses' relationship histories and, in particular, their early attachment relationships with caregivers. According to attachment theorists (e.g., see Bowlby, 1969; Shaver, Collins, & Clark, 1996), individuals develop schemas, or mental "working models" about what to expect from intimate relationships, based on the security of their attachment relationships in childhood. Infants develop a secure attachment style when they feel safe, loved, and accepted. This results from sensitive caregiving in which the infant's emotional signals are accurately decoded and responded to. Avoidant attachment, on the other hand, results from perceptions that the caregiver is habitually unavailable and unresponsive. Infants learn that expressing needs does not bring the comfort they desire and that they must rely on themselves in times of trouble. Finally, anxious/ambivalent attachment develops when caregivers respond inconsistently to their infants' needs. Sometimes expressing distress brings comfort; sometimes it brings punishment or no response at all. Accordingly, infants tend to become preoccupied with the caregiver and to express intense anger and anxiety when they have unmet needs in order to maximize the chances of obtaining attention and care.

Within adult romantic and marital relationships, individuals' attachment schemas influence both their own emotion communication styles and their responses to their partners' needs and expressions of emotion. Individuals with secure attachment styles, for example, are comfortable with the expression of a range of emotions and are appropriately responsive to their partners' emotional expressions (e.g., Feeney, 1999). Avoidant individuals, however, tend to discount their partners' needs or react with anger to them and to distance themselves from their partners when experiencing stress themselves (Simpson, Rholes, & Nelligan, 1992). Anxious–ambivalent individuals respond inconsistently to their partners' needs and are vigilant for signs of rejection. They also express negative emotions such as anger and jealousy more intensely and more often than secure individuals (Shaver et al., 1996).

Finally, several reliable gender differences in marital emotion communication have been identified, with women generally better than men at both accurately encoding and decoding emotions (see Noller & Ruzzene, 1991). Furthermore, women tend to express emotions like sadness and fear more frequently than men, whereas men tend to express emotions like anger and contempt more frequently than women (see Brody, 1999). In her theoretical analysis of gender and emotion, Brody claimed that men are less likely than women to express sadness and fear because such emotions signal vulnerability and a need for support. Men's roles, however, are typically associated with the exercise of power and control; thus, men who display "vulnerable" emotions tend to be evaluated more negatively and are less likely to be comforted by others. Men may react to feelings of vulnerability, then, with expressions of anger, an energizing emotion that intimidates others and may provide a feeling of control, at least in the short term (see also Clark, Pataki, & Carver, 1996; Fitness, 2001b).

Expressing contempt serves a similar function. Contempt signals superiority and serves to humiliate and shame its target (see Tomkins, 1979). The destructive nature of this emotion has been demonstrated by findings that contempt expressions in marital interactions are one of most reliable predictors of eventual marital breakdown (see Gottman, 1994). Frequently in such interactions the problem is not so much what is said but rather how it is said. For example, a spouse's sneer, or sarcastic, mocking remarks, may trigger feelings of shame in the partner, who retaliates with anger or rage (Noller & Roberts, in press; Retzinger, 1991; Scheff, 1995; Tangney, 1995). As noted previously, these kinds of escalating spirals of negative emotional expressions tend to characterize unhappy marriages, even in partnerships that span decades (Carstensen, Gottman, & Levenson, 1995).

In summary, accurate encoding and decoding of emotional expressions is a crucial feature of marital happiness. In addition, mood, relationship satisfaction, attachment style, and gender have all been identified as important influences on spouses' expressions and interpretations of emotions in the marital context. We now briefly discuss emotion and emotion communication in another important familial context: sibling relationships.

EMOTION IN SIBLING RELATIONSHIPS

Sibling relationships have been described as quintessentially emotional (Bedford & Avioli, 1996). Evolutionary theorists have noted that siblings are major social allies by virtue of their relatedness (i.e., they share genes with one another); however, they are also major competitors for crucial parental resources, including time, love, and attention (Daly, Salmon, & Wilson, 1997). Sibling relationships, then, involve both cooperation and competition and may be characterized (especially in childhood) by the relatively frequent experience and expression of highly ambivalent emotions including love, resentment, and hostility (Gold, 1989; Klagsbrun, 1992).

Of all the emotions experienced by siblings, jealousy and envy tend to be regarded as prototypical (Dunn, 1988; Volling, McElwain, & Miller, 2002). Historically, however, this has not always been the case. In the 19th century, for example, jealousy-related emotions were associated with adult sexual relationships rather than with childhood ones (Stearns, 1988). In part, this was because families were typically so much larger in that era, and older children were expected to take responsibility for younger children's welfare. Today, however, families tend to be smaller and parental resources do not have to stretch as far as they once did. Children's expectations of parents, then, may be considerably higher, with constant monitoring among siblings for signs of parental favoritism. Furthermore, research suggests that a sizable majority of siblings perceive such signs of preferential treatment. One study, for example, found that 84% of 272 U.S. respondents perceived there had been parental favoritism in the family (Klagsbrun, 1992).[1]

With the birth of a second child, first-borns inevitably experience decreasing amounts of attention and other resources from their parents. In response to their perceptions that the exclusive relationship they have enjoyed with their parents is under threat, first-borns may experience intense jealousy, accompanied by urges to protect their resources, grieve for what they have lost, and/or destroy their rival. These mixed emotions may be expressed in anxious, clingy behavior, depression and withdrawal, and/or outbursts of rage and hostility toward the unfortunate later-born (Dunn, 1988; Sulloway, 1996). Later-borns, on the other hand, may experience feelings of envy and resentment in relation to their older sibling(s) if they perceive they are being unjustly treated with respect to parental love and privileges (Smith, 1991). Such feelings may find their expression in behaviors intended to hurt older siblings, such as destroying their possessions and resources, including their reputations.

Sibling jealousy and envy, then, are partly an inevitable function of birth order and the redistribution of parental resources and partly an outcome of perceived parental favoritism and differential treatment. This latter factor may not be a deliberately divisive strategy by parents. In particular, the emotional disruption experienced by maritally distressed spouses

---

[1]Interestingly, just under half of these respondents regarded themselves, rather than their sibling, as the favorite. They also reported feeling considerable guilt over their favored status.

may mean they become less vigilant about treating children equally (Brody, 1998). However, the effects of differential treatment have been shown to impact negatively on the disfavored child's sense of competence and self-worth (Dunn, Stocker, & Plomin, 1990) and on his or her attachment security and psychological adjustment (Sheehan & Noller, 2002).

Even so, the picture is not altogether bleak. As noted previously, siblings are as much allies as competitors, and sibling relationships may be a source of support and emotional warmth throughout life. Researchers have found, for example, that when exposed to marital conflict, some older siblings increase protective, care-giving behaviors toward younger siblings (Cummings & Smith, 1989). Similarly, Wilson and Weiss (1993) found that preschoolers who watched a suspenseful TV program with an older sibling were less frightened and liked the program more than did those who viewed alone. Warm sibling relationships have also been identified as powerful contexts for the development of trust, self-disclosure skills, and socioemotional understanding (Howe, Aquan-Assee, Bukowski, Lehoux, & Rinaldi, 2001). There is still much to learn, however, about how and when different emotions are experienced and expressed within sibling relationships, for example, the conditions in which a younger child might admire, rather than envy, his or her older sibling. We also know little about how emotions and emotional expressions might differ depending on the age, birth order, and gender composition of the sibling (and frequently today, stepsibling) relationship.

In summary, sibling relationships are characterized, in part, by the expression of negative emotions such as jealousy and envy as a function of their intrinsically competitive nature. However, siblings may also form strong attachment bonds and experience highly positive emotions toward one another. In the next section, we consider an important facet of emotional communication between parents and children: the socialization of emotion.

SOCIALIZING EMOTION: LEARNING EMOTION RULES IN THE FAMILY

Babies' abilities to express and recognize certain basic emotion expressions appear to be innate and play an essential role in their survival (Oatley & Jenkins, 1996). Similarly, parents appear to be generally well equipped to understand and respond appropriately to their baby's communications (e.g., Izard, 1991; Scharfe, 2000). However, as infants grow and develop motor and language skills, parents spend an increasing amount of time teaching their children the rules of emotional expression, according to the norms of their own family backgrounds and of the wider culture (Buck, 1989).

As might be expected, given the vagaries of parents' own emotional histories, parents display different orientations toward feeling, managing, and talking about emotions with their children (Planalp, 1999). Two general orientations, in particular, have been identified (though there are sure to be others): emotion coaching and dismissing (Gottman, Katz, & Hooven, 1996). The emotion coaching orientation is associated with a parental "meta-emotion philosophy" that endorses family members' feelings as valid and important. Parents holding this philosophy actively teach children about the causes, features, and consequences of emotions and help them to regulate and deal constructively with difficult emotions such as anger, fear, and sadness. The dismissing orientation, on the other hand, is associated with a meta-emotion philosophy that regards emotions like anger, fear, and sadness as dangerous and/or unimportant, to be changed (or even punished) by parents as quickly as possible.[2]

Of course, emotion socialization is a reciprocal process. Thus, although some children have calm, agreeable temperaments and may be easily coached, others may have more difficult temperaments; they may be shy, anxious, irritable, or emotionally labile (Kagan, 1984; Lytton, 1990). These children may pose difficulties for parents who have different temperaments or emotion orientations and who cannot understand, appreciate, or meet their children's (or indeed, stepchildren's) emotional needs. Furthermore, parents within the same family do not necessarily hold the same meta-emotion philosophy. One parent, for example, may favor an accepting, empathic approach to the expression of emotions, whereas the other disapproves of the expression of any emotion other than resolute cheerfulness. These conflicting orientations may only become apparent (or problematic) after their first child is born. Conflict may also arise when two families with different meta-emotion philosophies are blended as a result of parental remarriage, although little is known about the manifestation and/or outcomes of these kinds of conflicts.

There is, however, a wealth of evidence confirming the beneficial effects of parental emotion coaching on children's emotion understanding, regulation, and socioemotional competence. Harris (2000), for example, noted that conversations about emotions help children to make sense of their feelings and understand the implications of emotional events (see also Dunn, Brown, & Maguire, 1995). Parents' meta-emotion philosophies are also important in the development of parent–child attachment relationships (Denham, 1998). In a secure attachment relationship, children learn that expressing their emotions elicits parental attention to their needs. Thus, securely attached children tend to be emotionally expressive and are able to both understand and regulate their own and others' emotions (Feeney & Noller, 1996; Scharfe, 2000). These skills are valued and promoted by parents with an emotion coaching philosophy. Conversely, parents with insecure attachment styles tend to endorse emotion socialization practices in line with their own experiences and expectations of attachment relationships. Thus, for example, Magai (1999) found that parents with fearful attachment styles were more likely than other kinds of parents to physically punish and shame their children for expressing their needs, just as they were themselves shamed as children. Parents with an avoidant style, on the other hand, may discourage or dismiss children's emotional expressions altogether.

Gender, too, has an important impact on emotion socialization practices. The results of one longitudinal study found that mothers talked more about emotions, and about a greater variety of emotions, to their daughters than to their sons. By the age of 5 years, the girls talked more than the boys about a variety of emotions and initiated more emotion-related discussions (Kuebli, Butler, & Fivush, 1995). Similarly, Dunn, Bretherton, and Munn (1987) found that mothers used fewer emotion words when interacting with their 18- to 24-month-old sons than with their same-aged daughters. No doubt this kind of emotion coaching is at least partly responsible for women's abilities to accurately express and identify emotions in their adult relationships (Noller & Ruzzene, 1991).

Our prior observation that men express more anger and contempt in marital interactions than do women, who express more sadness and fear, may also derive from early

---

[2] See also Tomkins' (1979) insightful discussion of humanistic versus normative parental emotion ideologies.

socialization practices. Brody (1999) noted that boys are typically socialized to behave more aggressively than girls and to control, rather than do express, their feelings. Anger, however, is the exception, with its expression attended to in boys, but ignored or punished in girls. Boys are also rewarded for behaviors that denote dominance (including expressions of contempt), and more aggressive boys are rated as more likable by teachers and peers. Girls, on the other hand, are encouraged to express more nurturing, sensitive emotions such as empathy and cheerfulness, in preparation, presumably, for their future roles as caregivers.

Even so, there are some interesting differences between the socialization practices of mothers and fathers that warrant closer investigation. For example, Parke and McDowell (1998) argued that whereas emotional understanding may be learned in mother–child conversations, father–child exchanges may teach children how to regulate levels of arousal in the context of physical play. Importantly, Brody (1999) reported that when fathers are more involved in child care, their daughters express relatively less emotional vulnerability and become more competent and aggressive in comparison to other daughters. Conversely, their sons express relatively more vulnerability and become less competitive and aggressive in comparison to other sons. This research underscores the important and largely unexplored role for fathers in developing children's socioemotional competence.

It is also important to consider the wider cultural context when exploring emotion socialization practices. Much of the research discussed in this chapter has been conducted with middle-class American families. However, different subcultures (e.g., separated by neighborhoods, ethnicities, or socioeconomic factors) may have different emotion rules and orientations. Miller and Sperry (1987), for example, found that mothers in a tough, working-class neighborhood valued anger in their daughters and encouraged rather than suppressed it because it supported goals of self-protection and motivated them to defend themselves.

Different cultures, too, have different emotion rules depending on the relative importance they place on the self versus the group (e.g., Planalp & Fitness, 1999; Triandis, 1994). In so-called collectivist cultures (e.g., Japan, China, and Korea) family harmony is prized and individual needs are subordinated to the needs of others. Accordingly, the open expression of anger is discouraged because it disrupts social relationships and puts individual needs ahead of group needs. Conversely, in so-called individualist cultures (e.g., North America), independence and individual achievement are prized and the expression of anger is encouraged in the pursuit of individual needs and goals. These cultural differences were demonstrated in a study that found U.S. children showed much more anger and aggression in symbolic play than did Japanese children (Zahn-Waxler et al., 1996). In addition, U.S. mothers encouraged their children's open expression of emotions, whereas Japanese mothers fostered sensitivity to other children's emotional needs (see also Eisenberg, Liew, & Pidada's, 2001, study of emotional expressiveness in Indonesian families and Yang & Rosenblatt's, 2001, analysis of the role of shame in Korean families).

In summary, some parents actively coach their children about emotions and help them develop sophisticated understandings of their own and others' emotional lives, whereas other parents discourage or even punish the expression of emotions. Clearly, there is still much to learn about other styles and philosophies of emotion within the family and about the content and function of emotion rules according to gender, family history, and cultural differences. In the next section, we discuss the dynamics of emotion communication within the family and the creation of emotional family climates.

THE DYNAMICS OF EMOTION COMMUNICATION WITHIN THE FAMILY

Families are dynamic systems comprising complex patterns of interdependencies and expectations. Every family member, then, is affected by what happens to every other member. This has important implications for emotion communication within the family. For example, highly interdependent relationship contexts provide opportunities for participants to experience the same emotions at the same time ("emotional co-incidence"), such as when parents are jointly thrilled over a child's success (Planalp, 1999). In such circumstances, family members' needs and goals are aligned, expectations are exceeded, and shared positive emotions create feelings of group cohesion and closeness. However, emotion sharing is not always a positive experience. For example, when one spouse is depressed, the degree to which the couple is emotionally close is a risk factor for the other spouse also becoming depressed (Tower & Kasl, 1995). In close relationships, people feel responsible for meeting each other's needs; however, the partner of a depressed spouse may well become disheartened by his/her inability to relieve his/her spouse's chronic neediness. The potency and contagiousness of negative emotions were also demonstrated by Thompson and Bolger (1999), who found that depression in one partner reduces happiness in the other, rather than the other way around (see also Baumeister, Bratslavsky, Finkenauer, & Vohs, 2001).

Parental depression also has a variety of negative effects on children (Segrin, 1998; Zahn-Waxler, 2000). Depressed parents tend to be less affectionate toward their children, feel more guilt and resentment toward them, and experience more difficulty in communicating with them (Brody, 1998). Not surprisingly, such children tend to exhibit behavioral problems that may then aggravate their parents' depression. Even transient negative moods may be passed onto children, only to rebound on parents. For example, parents in bad moods may pay selective attention to their children's undesirable behaviors and interpret them in ways that aggravate the situation ("he is doing this deliberately to annoy me"; Jouriles & O'Leary, 1990). Children are thus more likely to be punished, with their angry reactions exacerbating parental negativity.

Parental anger has a particularly negative impact on children, with the results of several studies suggesting that children exposed to overt and intense displays of parental anger are at risk for behavioral problems such as aggression, anxiety, and depression (Grych & Fincham, 1990; Jenkins & Smith, 1991). These and other researchers have suggested that parental anger and children's emotional dysregulation may be linked, in part, because angry parents model dysfunctional ways of behaving and impart a hostile attributional style to their children. Boyum and Parke (1995), for example, observed parental emotional expressions during a family dinner and found that negative emotional exchanges between parents were associated with teacher ratings of children's verbal aggression. In effect, these children appeared to be acquiring anger scripts comprising such beliefs as "if I feel threatened, I should attack"; "if something bad happens, someone else is always to blame" (see also Fehr & Baldwin, 1996; Fitness, 1996).

Emotions, then, may cascade through families and create emotional atmospheres, or climates, that affect the day-to-day feelings and functioning of family members. Belsky,

Youngblade, Rovine, and Volling (1991), for example, reported that as men became more unhappy in their marriages, they became more negative in their interactions with their children. Their children, in turn, reciprocated the negative emotions that were being expressed to them, which exacerbated their fathers' dissatisfaction with parenting and the marital relationship. Thus, fathers withdrew further from their wives and children, which exacerbated their wives' and children's distress. Given that in such circumstances siblings may be more likely to fight with one another, which further upsets their parents (Brody, 1998), it is not difficult to imagine how a whole family may become immersed in a climate of hostility and unhappiness.

There are many other kinds of emotional family climates, though few have been well studied. One kind that has been extensively investigated is the so-called high "EE" (expressed emotion) family climate, characterized by high levels of negative emotional expression, including criticism, hostility, and intrusiveness (Blechman, 1990). This kind of volatile, aggressive emotional climate is especially detrimental to mentally ill (particularly schizophrenic) patients, who tend to relapse quickly after returning home (see Kavanagh et al., 1997). In contrast, other families are distinguished by a climate of coldness and emotional disengagement; others again may be dominated by a highly controlling family member who terrorizes the rest of the family, effectively creating a climate of fear (e.g., see Dutton, 1998). On the other hand, Blechman (1990) has documented the existence of very positive emotional family climates characterized by high levels of mutual trust, affection, and warmth. Such nurturing family climates have been found to promote children's empathy for others, including their siblings (Brody, 1998; Zahn-Waxler, 2000).

One interesting aspect of positive family climates concerns the role of women in creating and maintaining them. Some researchers have argued that women still do the bulk of nurturing "emotion work" in the family by supporting and meeting the emotional needs of their spouses and children (DeVault, 1999; Hochschild, 1979). Studies of emotional transmission in the family have demonstrated the existence of an emotional hierarchy, with men's emotions having the most impact on family members overall (Larson & Richards, 1994). This implies that, although the family is a communal context in which family members feel mutually responsible for meeting each other's needs, it is women who feel most responsible for meeting the needs of their spouses and children (see also Brody, 1999). Thus, women's emotional expressions tend to revolve around empathic responding to others' needs, whereas men's emotional expressions tend to be associated with asserting their dominance in the family (Roberts & Krokoff, 1990).

Other research supporting this interpretation comes from studies of women's mediational roles in the family. Seery and Crowley (2000), for example, noted that women are frequently responsible for nurturing the relationship between fathers and children. This involves offering suggestions for father–child activities, praising fathers for engaging with their children, and maintaining positive images of fathers to their children. Women may also initiate peace-keeping strategies when fathers and children are unhappy with one another and encourage reconciliation. However, it is important to note that family structures, norms, and gender/power relations are undergoing accelerated change, with expanding roles for men as family "emotion workers" in their own right. In particular, Rohner and Veneziano (2001) noted that despite the widespread assumption that fathers express less affection toward children than do mothers, there is a growing body of literature showing that father love is as important as mother love in child outcomes, although the expression of such love (e.g., in shared activities) may not fit the traditional feminine model (see Baumeister & Sommer, 1997). Amato (1994) also found that perceived closeness to fathers for both sons and daughters made a unique contribution, over and above perceived closeness to mother, to adults' happiness and psychological well-being.

In summary, family emotion communication patterns are dynamically interwoven. Both positive and negative emotions are transmitted among family members in ways that affect the wellbeing of all. Families also develop distinctive emotional climates, although there is much to be learned about their origins and features. We now move on to discuss the role of emotion communication in adaptive family functioning.

EMOTION COMMUNICATION AND ADAPTIVE FAMILY FUNCTIONING

According to Blechman (1990), adaptive family functioning is characterized by the open exchange of information about feelings and emotions, the frequent expression of positive emotions, and the ability to monitor and regulate the expression of emotions. There is a growing amount of evidence to support each of these assertions. For example, researchers have found that spouses generally regard emotional expressiveness as both positive and desirable in marriage, and that more emotionally expressive spouses tend to have happier partners (Feeney, 1999; Huston & Houts, 1998). However, it is the ratio of positive to negative emotional expression that counts, with spouses in long-term, happy marriages expressing negative emotions like anger and sadness to one another much less frequently than they express affection and good humor (Carstensen et al., 1995).

Open exchange of information about feelings and emotions between parents and children has also been implicated in children's health and happiness. Berenbaum and James (1994) found that people who reported having grown up in families where the open expression of emotions was discouraged showed higher levels of alexithymia, a term describing an inability to identify and talk about one's emotions. This, in turn, has been associated with health and adjustment problems in adulthood. Again, however, it is the frequent expression of positive emotions that is most crucial factor for adaptive functioning. As Cummings and Davies (1996) noted, it is not just the absence of fear and anger in children's lives that leads to optimal development, but the presence of love, joy, and contentment that allows children to feel emotionally secure (see also Halberstadt, Crisp, & Eaton, 1999).

Finally, there is a growing body of research attesting to the importance of emotion regulation in adaptive family functioning. In particular, happy spouses have been found to be more likely to inhibit their impulses to react destructively when their partners express anger and to try to respond instead in a conciliatory manner (e.g., Carstensen et al., 1995; Rusbult, Bissonnette, Arriaga, & Cox, 1998). Similarly, Fitness and Fletcher (1993) found spouses reported making efforts to control the expression of anger in the interests of marital harmony (see also Fehr & Baldwin, 1996). Children, too, who are taught by their parents how to effectively regulate their emotions display greater socioemotional competence and have more positive relationships with parents, siblings, and peers (Denham, 1998; Planalp, 1999).

This emphasis on the role of open, positive emotion expression and emotion regulation in adaptive family functioning is echoed in the growing literatures on emotional competence (e.g., Eisenberg, Cumberland, & Spinrad, 1998; Saarni, 2001) and emotional intelligence (e.g., Fitness, 2001b). Typical definitions of these closely related constructs include such features as the ability to accurately encode and decode emotions, the ability to understand the meanings of emotions and to be able to respond appropriately to them, and the ability to effectively manage and regulate both one's own and others' emotions. This raises the question of whether there might be such an entity as the emotionally intelligent family and what kinds of behaviors it might exhibit.

The work of marital and family researchers provides some clues. For example, Gottman (1998) reported that marriages become distressed when spouses become too busy to respond fully or appropriately to one another's needs. In the process of turning away from one another, they also neglect to listen to one another, fail to make "cognitive room" for each other, rarely soothe and comfort one another, and are more likely to express anger and contempt rather than spontaneous admiration and affection, in their interactions with one another (see also Huston, Caughlin, Houts, Smith, & George, 2001). This suggests that one distinctive feature of the emotionally intelligent family might be what Gottman and Levenson (2002) referred to as a culture of appreciation, whereby family members regard one another with fondness and respect; accept and respond to the emotional expression of one another's needs; and cultivate interpersonal warmth, compassion, and emotional connectedness with one another (see also Andersen & Guerrero, 1998b).

It is important to note, however, that positive emotions are not generated automatically in the absence of negative emotions. As Berscheid (1983) noted, relationships in which people are well meshed and meeting each other's needs on a day-to-day basis tend to be emotionally tranquil and may even be perceived as boring. It is not until an interruption to the well-meshed routine occurs that individuals pay attention and the scene is set for emotion. Generating positive emotions in the family, then, requires making active efforts to exceed each other's expectations; planning and delivering pleasant surprises, facilitating each other's hopes and plans, and helping each other to deal with life's problems. There is also an important role for positive emotions like interest and excitement to play in enhancing family functioning (e.g., Aron, Normans, Aron, McKenna, & Heyman, 2000; Gonzaga et al., 2001). Sharing novel and exciting activities generates feelings of cohesion and mutual pleasure and strengthens social bonds. In this sense, families that play together may well stay together.

In summary, adaptive family functioning involves the open exchange of emotions, the frequent expression of positive emotions, and the ability to effectively regulate and manage emotions. Emotionally intelligent families may be those in which family members feel validated and embraced within a culture of mutual regard. In the final section, we revisit some earlier themes and suggest further avenues for future research.

AGENDA FOR FUTURE RESEARCH

As noted in the introduction, the study of emotion communication in families has been relatively sparse. There are still large gaps in our understanding of how different kinds of emotions are communicated and miscommunicated in families, for what purposes, and with what outcomes. In addition, much of the research conducted so far has focused on dyads (i.e., spouses, or parents and children, or siblings), rather than on the family system as a whole (Duck, 1992). In researchers' defense, it should be noted that although the "family as a system" metaphor is a powerful one (Reis, Collins, & Berscheid, 2000), the scientific study of such complex patterns of interdependent relationships poses some extraordinary methodological (and ethical) challenges. It is important to acknowledge, though, that the emotional functioning of the family overall is not a simple function of the sum of its parts.

Another distinctive feature of much of the research on this topic to date has been its relatively atheoretical stance, particularly with respect to the dynamic and functional features of emotion within the family context. Certainly, interdependence theory provides a powerful framework for understanding the conditions under which emotions may arise within familial interactions. However, this theory takes us only part of the way. In particular, it does not tell us what family members' expectations of one another are, how different kinds of emotions (e.g., anger versus contempt) are generated, or what is the impact of individual differences and contextual factors on familial emotion rules and orientations.

Social–cognitive researchers have made some progress in mapping the structural features of laypeople's understandings of the causes and consequences of interpersonal emotions such as love, anger, hate, and jealousy (Fitness, 1996). They have found, for example, that individuals hold beliefs about the typical causes of angry marital interactions (e.g., unfair partner behaviors) and the typical motivations (e.g., the urge to yell) and behaviors (e.g., retaliatory insults and/or apologies) that are likely to occur as the drama of what has been described as the "anger script" unfolds over time (Fitness, 2001a; see also Fehr, Baldwin, Collins, Patterson, & Benditt, 1999). Whether accurate or not, these understandings about the whys and wherefores of emotions are important in that they are held to drive people's expectations, perceptions, and memories of emotional interactions. We still know little, however, about people's theories of the causes and consequences of specific emotions in the context of different family relationships, such as those between siblings, and of the ways in which such understandings impact on people's cognitions, motivations, and behaviors over time.

Another fascinating area about which we still know little concerns the ways in which people use their emotion knowledge strategically within the context of the family to achieve their goals. Clark et al. (1996), for example, reviewed a body of evidence showing that individuals may deliberately express sadness in order to obtain sympathy and support, feign anger in order to intimidate others and procure obedience, and suppress anger and/or feign happiness in order to appear more likable or ingratiate themselves to others. Similarly, people may feign or exaggerate hurt feelings in order to make another feel guilty, an emotional state that tends to motivate compliance with the hurt person's wishes (Vangelisti & Sprague, 1998). These kinds of strategic emotion expressions are doubtless an important aspect of emotional interactions in the family, ranging from mild, everyday manipulations to garner sympathy or persuade children to do their homework, to full-scale "emotional blackmail," such as when a parent manipulates a grown child through hurt and guilt to put the parent's interests first, regardless of the cost.

Finally, there is much we do not know about the dynamics of emotional communication with respect to family members' ongoing feelings and motivations. Again, there is a need for strong theory to help us ask the right questions about these complex processes. One sociological approach with the potential to help illuminate such dynamics is Kemper's power/status model of emotions in social interactions (e.g., Kemper, 1984). According to this model, there are two, basic dimensions underlying every human interaction: power (feelings of control, dominance) and status (feelings of worthiness, esteem, holding resources). Every relational exchange takes place along these two dimensions, with emotions signaling shifts in power/status dynamics.

To illustrate, a perceived loss of power (e.g., when a father punishes his son) triggers fear and anxiety; gaining power (e.g., when a daughter wins an argument with her mother) triggers feelings of pleasure and triumph. Gaining status (e.g., when a boy invites his younger brother to the movies) elicits the happiness that comes from feeling that one belongs and is a valued relationship partner. However, losing status (e.g., when a child must present a bad report card to his parents) elicits emotions such as shame (if the child holds himself to blame), depression (if the child feels helpless to change the situation), or even anger (if the child blames the teacher or his squabbling parents). Furthermore, within the family, as in other kinds of relational contexts, individuals' power and status are frequently signaled by others, as when a parent's praise confers status and triggers warm feelings of pride, or when a parent's contemptuous remark depletes a child's status and triggers feelings of shame (Tomkins, 1979).

One of the strengths of this theory is that it accounts for a range of subtle feeling states that often escape attention in the emotion literature, for example, the warm feelings that a child's smile may elicit (signaling a gain in status); the heart-sinking feeling that a parent's cold glance may elicit (signaling loss of status); the tense, stomach-tied-in-knots feeling that an older brother's teasing may elicit (signaling loss of power); the pleasant rush of blood to the head when one's older brother is punished for his behavior (signaling a gain of power). It is within these shifting patterns of give and take, power and status, that feelings and emotions are experienced and exchanged among family members.

It also seems likely that these feeling states are fundamental, in the sense of being hard-wired and having an evolutionary history. It is critical for humans, who are so socially interdependent, to be constantly monitoring their social environments for information about how they are doing, relative to others (i.e., how much power/control do they have, how much do others appear to care about whether they live or die). Feelings of being (figuratively speaking) "one-up" or "one-down," resource rich or resource poor, provide such information and motivate people to take particular kinds of action (e.g., retaliation, ingratiation, escape, etc). Accordingly, we believe that exploring family members' ongoing feelings about their power and status, relative to each other, may provide some fascinating insights into the complex dynamics of both spontaneous and strategically motivated emotion communication within the family context.

Of course, although it is relatively easy to identify interesting and unexplored research topics in this field, choosing appropriate methodologies is more difficult and requires considerable ingenuity and resourcefulness. No doubt, laboratory-based observational studies will continue to be important, as will more naturalistic observations in different kinds of familial contexts. The use of diaries, interviews, surveys, and experimental work also have valuable contributions to make. The most important point, however, is that the choice of method is theoretically driven so that with each piece of the puzzle we uncover, we obtain a richer, more coherent, and more integrated picture of emotion communication processes and functions within family life.

CONCLUSION

Families are profoundly emotional contexts. When we express our emotions within the family, we expose our deepest needs and vulnerabilities. In turn, the response of family members to the expression of our emotions colors our perceptions and beliefs about ourselves and others and helps form the template from which we, in turn, respond to others' needs. Throughout this chapter, we have stressed the potentially adaptive nature of emotions and the functions they serve in informing ourselves and others about our needs. Certainly, emotions can run amok and motivate dysfunctional or destructive behaviors. Nevertheless, emotions always tell us something important about who we are and what we care about, and nowhere is this informational function more important than in the context of the family.

Clearly, there is still much to discover about the processes involved in the communication of family emotion. However, given the rapidly growing scholarly interest in this topic, we are optimistic about the progress that will be achieved, particularly if researchers take a theoretically informed and integrative approach to their empirical work. Above all, it is our belief that understanding, supporting, and encouraging emotionally adaptive family functioning will ultimately be to the benefit of us all.

REFERENCES

Amato, P. R. (1994). Father-child relations, mother-child relations, and offspring psychological well-being in adulthood. *Journal of Marriage and the Family, 56*, 1031–1042.

Andersen, P., & Guerrero, L. K. (1998a). Principles of communication and emotion in social interaction. In P. Andersen & L. Guerrero (Eds.), *Handbook of communication and emotion* (pp. 49–96). New York: Academic Press.

Andersen, P., & Guerrero, L. K. (1998b). The bright side of relational communication: Interpersonal warmth as a social emotion. In P. Andersen & L. K. Guerrero (Eds.), *Handbook of communication and emotion* (pp. 303–329). New York: Academic Press.

Aron, A., Norman, C., Aron, E., McKenna, C., & Heyman R. (2000). Couples' shared participation in novel and arousing activities and experienced relationship quality. *Journal of Personality and Social Psychology, 78*, 273–284.

Baumeister, R., Bratslavsky, E., Finkenauer, C., & Vohs, K. (2001). Bad is stronger than good. *Review of General Psychology, 5*, 323–370.

Baumeister, R., & Sommer, K. (1997). What do men want? Gender differences and two spheres of belongingness. *Psychological Bulletin, 122*, 38–44.

Beach, S., & Fincham, F. (1994). Toward an integrated model of negative affectivity in marriage. In S. Johnson & L. Greenberg (Eds.), *The heart of the matter: Perspectives on emotion in marital therapy* (pp. 227–255). New York: Brunner/Mazel.

Bedford, V. H., & Avioli, P. S. (1996). Affect and sibling relationships in adulthood. In C. Magai & S. McFadden (Eds.), *Handbook of emotion, adult development, and aging* (pp. 207–225). New York: Academic Press.

Belsky, J., Youngblade, L., Rovine, M., & Volling, B. (1991). Patterns of marital change and parent-child interaction. *Journal of Marriage and the Family, 53*, 487–498.

Berenbaum, H., & James, T. (1994). Correlates and retrospectively reported antecedents of alexithymia. *Psychosomatic Medicine, 56*, 353–359.

Berscheid, E. (1983). Emotion. In H. H. Kelley, E. Berscheid, A. Christensen, J. H. Harvey, T. L. Huston, G. Levinger, E. McClintock, L. A. Peplau, & D. R. Peterson (Eds.), *Close relationships* (pp. 110–168). New York: Freeman.

Berscheid, E., & Ammazzalorso, H. (2001). Emotional experience in close relationships. In G. J. O. Fletcher & M. S. Clark (Eds.), *Blackwell handbook of social psychology: Interpersonal processes* (pp. 308–330). Malden, MA: Blackwell.

Blechman, E. A. (1990). A new look at emotions and the family: A model of effective family communication. In E. Blechman (Ed.), *Emotions and the family* (pp. 201–224). Hillsdale, NJ: Lawrence Erlbaum Associates.

Bowlby, J. (1969). *Attachment and loss.* New York: Basic Books.

Boyum, L. A., & Parke, R. D. (1995). The role of family emotional expressiveness in the development of children's social competence. *Journal of Marriage and the Family, 57,* 593–608.

Bradbury, T. N., & Fincham, F. D. (1987). Affect and cognition in close relationships: Toward an integrative model. *Cognition and Emotion, 1,* 59–87.

Brody, G. H. (1998). Sibling relationship quality: Its causes and consequences. *Annual Review of Psychology, 49,* 1–24.

Brody, L. (1999). *Gender, emotion, and the family.* MA: Harvard University Press.

Buck, R. (1989). Emotional communication in personal relationships. In C. Hendrick (Ed.), *Review of personality and social psychology, Vol. 10: Close relationships* (pp. 144–163). Newbury Park. CA: Sage.

Burgoon, J. (1993). Interpersonal expectations, expectancy violations, and emotional communication. *Journal of Language and Social Psychology, 12,* 30–48.

Buss, D. (1999). *Evolutionary psychology: The new science of the mind.* Boston, MA: Allyn & Bacon.

Carstensen, L. L., Gottman, J. M., & Levenson, R. W. (1995). Emotional behavior in long-term marriage. *Psychology and Aging, 10,* 140–149.

Clark, M. S., Fitness, J., & Brissette, I. (2001). Understanding people's perceptions of relationships is crucial to understanding their emotional lives. In G. J. O. Fletcher & M. S. Clark (Eds.), *Blackwell handbook of social psychology: Interpersonal processes* (pp. 253–278). Malden, MA: Blackwell.

Clark, M. S., Pataki, S. P., & Carver, V. H. (1996). Some thoughts and findings on self-presentation of emotions in relationships. In G. J. O. Fletcher & J. Fitness (Eds.), *Knowledge structures in close relationships: A social psychological approach* (pp. 247–274). Mahwah, NJ: Lawrence Erlbaum Associates.

Cummings, E. M., & Davies, P. T. (1996). Emotional security as a regulatory process in normal development and the development of psychopathology. *Development and Psychopathology, 8,* 123–139.

Cummings, E. M., & Smith, D. (1989). The impact of anger between adults on siblings' emotions and social behavior. *Journal of Child Psychology and Psychiatry, 25,* 63–74.

Daly, M., Salmon, C., & Wilson, M. (1997). Kinship: The conceptual hole in psychological studies of social cognition and close relationships. In J. Simpson & D. Kenrick (Eds.), *Evolutionary social psychology* (pp. 265–296). Mahwah, NJ: Lawrence Erlbaum Associates.

Darwin, C. (1872/1965). *The expression of the emotions in man and animals.* Chicago: University of Chicago Press.

Denham, S. A. (1998). *Emotional development in young children*. New York: Guilford Press.

DeVault, M. (1999). Comfort and struggle: Emotion work in family life. *Annals of the American Academy of Political and Social Science, 561*, 52–63.

Duck, S. (1992). *Human relationships*. Newbury Park, CA: Sage.

Dunn, J. (1988). *The beginnings of social understanding*. MA: Harvard University Press.

Dunn, J., Bretherton, I., & Munn, P. (1987). Conversations about feeling states between mothers and their young children. *Developmental Psychology, 11*, 107–123.

Dunn, J., Brown, J. R., & Maguire, M. (1995). The development of children's moral sensibility: Individual differences and emotion understanding. *Developmental Psychology, 31*, 649–659.

Dunn, J., Stocker, C., & Plomin, R. (1990). Nonshared experiences within the family: Correlates of behavioral problems in middle childhood. *Development and Psychopathology, 2*, 113–126.

Dutton, D. G. (1998). *The abusive personality*. New York: Guilford Press.

Eisenberg, N., Cumberland, A., & Spinrad, T. (1998). Parental socialization of emotions. *Psychological Inquiry, 9*, 241–273.

Eisenberg, N., Liew, J., & Pidada, S. (2001). The relations of parental emotional expressivity with quality of Indonesian children's social functioning. *Emotion, 1*, 116–136.

Feeney, J. (1999). Adult attachment, emotional control, and marital satisfaction. *Personal Relationships, 6*, 169–185.

Feeney, J., & Noller, P. (1996). *Adult attachment*. Thousand Oaks, CA: Sage.

Fehr, B., & Baldwin, M. (1996). Prototype and script analyses of laypeople's knowledge of anger. In G. J. O. Fletcher & J. Fitness (Eds.), *Knowledge structures in close relationships: A social psychological approach* (pp. 219–245). Mahwah, NJ: Lawrence Erlbaum Associates.

Fehr, B., Baldwin, M., Collins, L., Patterson, S., & Benditt, R. (1999). Anger in close relationships: An interpersonal script analysis. *Personality and Social Psychology Bulletin, 25*, 299–312.

Fitness, J. (1996). Emotion knowledge structures in close relationships. In G. J. O. Fletcher & J. Fitness (Eds.), *Knowledge structures in close relationships: A social psychological approach* (pp. 195–217). Mahwah, NJ: Lawrence Erlbaum Associates.

Fitness, J. (2001a). Betrayal, rejection, revenge, and forgiveness: An interpersonal script approach. In M. Leary (Ed.), *Interpersonal rejection* (pp. 73–103). New York: Oxford University Press.

Fitness, J. (2001b). Emotional intelligence in intimate relationships. In J. Ciarrochi, J. Forgas, & J. Mayer (Eds.), *Emotional intelligence in everyday life: A scientific inquiry* (pp. 98–112). Philadelphia, PA: Psychology Press.

Fitness, J., & Fletcher, G. J. O. (1993). Love, hate, anger and jealousy in close relationships: A prototype and cognitive appraisal analysis. *Journal of Personality and Social Psychology, 65*, 942–958.

Fitness, J., Fletcher, G. J. O., & Overall, N. (in press). Attraction and intimate relationships. In J. Cooper & M. Hogg (Eds.), *Handbook of social psychology*. Thousand Oaks, CA: Sage.

Fletcher, G. J. O., & Fincham, F. D. (1991). Attribution processes in close relationships. In

G. J. O. Fletcher & F. D. Fincham (Eds.), *Cognition in close relationships* (pp. 7–35). Hillsdale, NJ: Lawrence Erlbaum Associates.

Fletcher, G. J. O., & Thomas, G. (1999). Behavior and on-line cognition in marital interaction. *Personal Relationships, 7,* 111–130.

Forgas, J. P. (1994). Sad and guilty? Affective influences on the explanation of conflict episodes. *Journal of Personality and Social Psychology, 66,* 56–68.

Frijda, N. (1986). *The emotions.* New York: Cambridge University Press.

Gaelick, L., Bodenhausen, G., & Wyer, R. S. (1985). Emotional communication in close relationships. *Journal of Personality and Social Psychology, 49,* 1246–1265.

Gold, D. T. (1989). Sibling relationships in old age: A typology. *International Journal of Aging and Human Development, 28,* 37–51.

Gonzaga, G. C., Keltner, D., Londahl, E. A., & Smith, M. D. (2001). Love and the commitment problem in romantic relations and friendship. *Journal of Personality and Social Psychology, 81,* 247–262.

Gottman, J. M. (1994). *What predicts divorce? The relationship between marital processes and marital outcomes.* Hillsdale, NJ: Erlbaum.

Gottman, M. (1998). Psychology and the study of marital processes. *Annual Review of Psychology, 49,* 169–197.

Gottman, J. M., Katz, L. F., & Hooven, C. (1996). Parental meta-emotion philosophy and the emotional life of families: Theoretical models and preliminary data. *Journal of Family Psychology, 10,* 243–268.

Gottman, J. M., & Levenson, R. W. (2002). A two-factor model for predicting when a couple will divorce: Exploratory analyses using 14-year longitudinal data. *Family Process, 41,* 83–110.

Grych, J. H., & Fincham, F. D. (1990). Marital conflict and children's adjustment: A cognitive-contextual framework. *Psychological Bulletin, 108,* 267–290.

Halberstadt, A. G., Crisp, V. W., & Eaton, K. L. (1999). Family expressiveness: A retrospective and new directions for research. In P. Philippot, R. S. Feldman, & E. Coats (Eds.), *The social context of nonverbal behavior* (pp. 109–155). New York: Cambridge University Press.

Harris, P. (2000). Understanding emotion. In M. Lewis & J. Haviland-Jones (Eds.), *Handbook of emotions* (2nd ed., pp. 281–292). New York: Guilford Press.

Hochschild, A. (1979). Emotion work, feeling rules, and social structure. *American Journal of Sociology, 85,* 551–575.

Howe, N., Aquan-Assee, J., Bukowski, W., Lehoux, P., & Rinaldi, C. (2001). Siblings as confidants: Emotional understanding, relationship warmth, and sibling self-disclosure. *Social Development, 10,* 439–454.

Huston, T. L., Caughlin, J. P., Houts, R. M., Smith, S. E., & George, L. J. (2001). The connubial crucible: Newlywed years as predictors of marital delight, distress, and divorce. *Journal of Personality and Social Psychology, 80,* 237–252.

Huston, T., & Houts, R. (1998). The psychological infrastructure of courtship and marriage: The role of personality and compatibility in romantic relationships. In T. Bradbury (Ed.), *The developmental course of marital dysfunction* (pp. 114–151). New York: Cambridge University Press.

Izard, C. (1991). *The psychology of emotion.* New York: Plenum Press.

Jenkins, J., & Smith, M. A. (1991). Marital disharmony and children's behavior problems: Aspects of a poor marriage which affect children adversely. *Journal of Child Psychology and Psychiatry, 32*, 793–810.

Jouriles, E. N., & O'Leary, K. D. (1990). Influences of parental mood on parent behavior. In E. Blechman (Ed.), *Emotions and the family* (pp. 181–199). Hillsdale, NJ: Lawrence Erlbaum Associates.

Kagan, J. (1984). *The nature of the child*. New York: Basic Books.

Kavanagh, D., O'Halloran, P., Manicavasagar, V., Clark, D., Piatkowska, O., Tennant, C., & Rosen, A. (1997). The family attitude scale: Reliability and validity of a new scale for measuring the emotional climate of families. *Psychiatry Research, 70*, 185–195.

Kemper, T. D. (1984). Power, status, and emotions: A sociological contribution to a psychophysiological domain. In K. Scherer & P. Ekman (Eds.), *Approaches to emotion* (pp. 369–383). Hillsdale, NJ: Lawrence Erlbaum Associates.

Klagsbrun, F. (1992). *Mixed feelings: Love, hate, rivalry, and reconciliation among brothers and sisters*. New York: Bantam Books.

Koerner, A., & Fitzpatrick, M. (2002). Nonverbal communication and marital adjustment and satisfaction: The role of decoding relationship-relevant and relationship-irrelevant affect. *Communication Monographs, 69*, 33–51.

Kuebli, J., Butler, S., & Fivush, R. (1995). Mother-child talk about past emotions: Relations of maternal language and child gender over time. *Cognition and Emotion, 9*, 265–283.

Larson, R., & Richards, M. (1994). *Divergent realities: The emotional lives of mothers, fathers, and adolescents*. New York: Basic Books.

Lazarus, R. (1991). *Emotion and adaptation*. New York: Oxford University Press.

Lytton, H. (1990). Child and parent effects in boys' conduct disorder: A reinterpretation. *Developmental Psychology, 26*, 683–704.

Magai, C. (1999). Affect, imagery, and attachment: Working models of interpersonal affect and the socialization of emotion. In J. Cassidy & P. R. Shaver (Eds.), *Handbook of attachment* (pp. 787–802). New York: Guilford Press.

Mandler, G. (1975). *Mind and emotion*. New York: Wiley.

Miller, P., & Sperry, L. L. (1987). The socialization of anger and aggression. *Merrill-Palmer Quarterly, 33*, 1–31.

Noller, P., & Roberts, N. (2002). The communication of couples in violent and nonviolent relationships: Temporal associations with own and partners' anxiety/arousal and behavior. In P. Noller & J. Feeney (Eds.),*Understanding marriage: Developments in the study of couple interaction*. New York: Cambridge University Press.

Noller, P., & Ruzzene, M. (1991). The effects of cognition and affect on marital communication. In G. J. O. Fletcher & F. D. Fincham (Eds.), *Cognition in close relationships* (pp. 203–233). Hillsdale, NJ: Lawrence Erlbaum Associates.

Oatley, K., & Jenkins, J. M. (1996). *Understanding emotions*. MA: Blackwell.

Parke, R., & McDowell, D. J. (1998). Toward an expanded model of emotion socialization: New people, new pathways. *Psychological Inquiry, 9*, 303–307.

Planalp, S. (1999). *Communicating emotion: Social, moral, and cultural processes*. New York: Cambridge University Press.

Planalp, S., & Fitness, J. (1999). Thinking/feeling about social and personal relationships. *Journal of Social and Personal Relationships, 16*, 731–750.

Reis, H. T., Collins, W. A., & Berscheid, E. (2000). The relationship context of human behavior and development. *Psychological Bulletin, 126*, 844–872.

Retzinger, S. M. (1991). *Violent emotions: Shame and rage in marital quarrels.* Newbury Park, CA: Sage.

Roberts, L. J., & Krokoff, L. J. (1990). A time-series analysis of withdrawal, hostility, and displeasure in satisfied and dissatisfied marriages. *Journal of Marriage and the Family, 52*, 95–105.

Rohner, R., & Veneziano, R. (2001). The importance of father love: History and contemporary evidence. *Review of General Psychology, 5*, 382–405.

Roseman, I. (1991). Appraisal determinants of discrete emotions. *Cognition and Emotion, 5*, 161–200.

Rusbult, C. E., Bissonnette, V., & Arriaga, X. B., & Cox, C. (1998). Accommodation processes during the early years of marriage. In T. Bradbury (Ed.), *The developmental course of marital dysfunction* (pp. 74–113). New York: Cambridge University Press.

Saarni, C. (2001). Epilogue: Emotion communication and relationship context. *International Journal of Behavioral Development, 25*, 354–356.

Scharfe, E. (2000). Development of emotional expression, understanding, and regulation in infants and young children. In R. Bar-On & D. Parker (Eds.), *Handbook of emotional intelligence* (pp. 244–262). San Francisco: Jossey-Bass.

Scheff, T. (1995). Conflict in family systems: The role of shame. In J. P. Tangney & K. W. Fischer (Eds.), *Self-conscious emotions: The psychology of shame, guilt, embarrassment, and pride* (pp. 393–442). New York: Guilford Press.

Seery, B., & Crowley. M. S. (2000). Women's emotion work in the family. *Journal of Family Issues, 21*, 100–127.

Segrin, C. (1998). Interpersonal communication problems associated with depression and loneliness. In P. Andersen & L. Guerrero (Eds.), *Handbook of communication and emotion* (pp. 215–242). New York: Academic Press.

Shaver, P. R., Collins, N., & Clark, C. (1996). Attachment styles and internal working models of self and relationship partners. In G. J. O. Fletcher & J. Fitness (Eds.), *Knowledge structures in close relationships: A social psychological approach* (pp. 25–61). Mahwah, NJ: Lawrence Erlbaum Associates.

Sheehan, G., & Noller, P. (2002). Adolescents' perception of differential parenting: Links with attachment style and adolescent adjustment. *Personal Relationships, 9*, 173–190.

Simpson, J. A., Rholes, W. S., & Nelligan, J. S. (1992). Support-seeking and support-giving within couples in an anxiety-provoking situation: The role of attachment styles. *Journal of Personality and Social Psychology, 62*, 434–446.

Smith, R. (1991). Envy and the sense of injustice. In P. Salovey (Ed.), *The psychology of jealousy and envy* (pp. 79–102). New York: Guilford Press.

Stearns, P. (1988). The rise of sibling jealousy in the twentieth century. In C. Z. Stearns & P. Stearns (Eds.), *Emotion and social change* (pp. 193–222). New York: Holmes & Meier.

Sulloway, F. J. (1996). *Born to rebel: Birth order, family dynamics, and creative lives.* UK: Little, Brown & Company.

Tangney, J. P. (1995). Shame and guilt in interpersonal relationships. In J. P. Tangney (Ed.), *Self-conscious emotions* (pp. 114–140). New York: Guilford Press.

Thomas, G., Fletcher, G. J. O., & Lange, C. (1997). On-line empathic accuracy in marital interaction. *Journal of Personality and Social Psychology, 76,* 72–89.

Thompson, A., & Bolger, N. (1999). Emotional transmission in couples under stress. *Journal of Marriage and the Family, 61,* 38–48.

Tomkins, S. (1979). Script theory: Differential magnification of affects. In H. E. Howe & R.A. Dienstbier (Eds.), *Nebraska symposium on motivation, 1978* (pp. 201–236). Lincoln, NE: University of Nebraska Press.

Tower, R. B., & Kasl, S. V. (1995). Depressive symptoms across older spouses and the moderating effect of marital closeness. *Psychology and Aging, 10,* 625–638.

Triandis, H. (1994). *Culture and social behavior.* New York: McGraw-Hill.

Vangelisti, A., & Sprague, R. J. (1998). Guilt and hurt: Similarities, distinctions, and conversational strategies. In P. Andersen & L. Guerrero (Eds.), *Handbook of communication and emotion* (pp. 124–154). New York: Academic Press.

Volling, B., McElwain, N. L., & Miller, A. (2002). Emotion regulation in context: The jealousy complex between young siblings and its relations with child and family characteristics. *Child Development, 73,* 581–600.

Wilson, B. J., & Weiss, A. J. (1993). The effects of co-viewing with a sibling on preschoolers' reactions to a suspenseful movie scene. *Communication Research, 20,* 214–248.

Yang, S., & Rosenblatt, P. (2001). Shame in Korean families. *Journal of Comparative Family Studies, 32,* 361–375.

Zahn-Waxler, C. (2000). The development of empathy, guilt, and internalization of distress. In R. J. Davidson (Ed.), *Anxiety, depression, and emotion* (pp. 222–265). New York: Oxford University Press.

Zahn-Waxler, C., Friedman, R. J., Cole, P. M., Mizuta, I., & Hiruma, N. (1996). Japanese and U.S. preschool children's responses to conflict and distress. *Child Development, 67,* 2462–2477.

Zajonc, R. B. (1998). Emotions. In D. Gilbert, S. Fiske, & G. Lindzey (Eds.), *The handbook of social psychology* (4th ed., pp. 591–632). New York: Oxford University Press.

22

SOCIAL SUPPORT COMMUNICATION IN FAMILIES

KELLI A. GARDNER AND CAROLYN E. CUTRONA

IOWA STATE UNIVERSITY

Of the many functions served by families, social support is among the most important. In this chapter, a selective review will be provided of social support in three kinds of family relationships: marital, parent–child, and sibling. Marital support and sibling support differ somewhat from parent–child support in that the former involves transactions between peers; whereas the latter involves transactions between individuals with definite differences in power, resources, and ability. Thus, support in marital and sibling relationships is more bidirectional than that between parent and child, although children can serve support functions for their parents, especially as they enter adolescence. Hundreds of articles have been written about spousal support. Fewer have been written about parent–child support, and especially few have been written about support between siblings. We will highlight three themes in our discussion of support within each of the three kinds of family relationships. First, we will examine the benefits that are associated with support. Next, we will discuss determinants of effective support and barriers that prevent support exchanges. Finally, we will offer recommendations for future research on social support in families. In line with the theme of this book, links to communication will be made wherever possible.

WHAT IS SOCIAL SUPPORT?

For some theorists, social support is the ongoing fulfillment by others of basic interpersonal needs (Kaplan, Cassel, & Gore, 1977; Lin, 1986). For others, social support is the fulfillment of more specific time-limited needs that arise as the result of adverse life events or circumstances (House, 1981; Rook, 1984). Regardless of the extent to which adversity is a precondition for social support to occur, theorists generally agree on the kinds of acts or "functions" that constitute support. In this paper, social support is defined as verbal communication or behavior that is responsive to another's needs and serves the functions of comfort, encouragement, reassurance of caring, and/or the promotion of effective problem solving through information or tangible assistance.

MARITAL SUPPORT

Among married adults, the spouse is most frequently named as the primary source of social support (Beach, Martin, Blum, & Roman, 1993; Lanza, Cameron, & Revenson, 1995). Spouses provide a wider range of support types than other sources (Wong & Kwok, 1997), and social support from the spouse is associated more strongly and with a wider range of positive outcomes than support from other sources (Schuster, Kessler, & Aseltine, 1990; Wan, Jaccard, & Ramey, 1996; Wong & Kwok, 1997). Social support from other sources cannot compensate for the lack of a supportive relationship with the spouse (Brown & Harris, 1978; Pistrang & Barker, 1995).

Benefits of Marital Support

Relationship Benefits

One of the most robust findings in the marital literature is that individuals with supportive spouses are more satisfied with their marriages than are individuals who lack support from their spouse (e.g. Acitelli, 1996; Cobb & Davila, 2001; Matthews, Conger, & Wickrama, 1996; Perrone & Worthington, 2001). Couples who support each other also report that their marriages are less conflict-ridden (Conger, Rueter, & Elder, 1999; Gallo & Smith, 2001). In a diary study, couples kept track of how often they fought over a 2-week period and couples with high levels of support reported significantly fewer arguments (McGonagle, Kessler, & Schilling, 1992).

It is well documented that severe or chronic negative life events are associated with declines in marital quality (Bradbury, Fincham, & Beach, 2000; Cohan & Bradbury, 1997; Umberson, 1995). Another benefit of marital support is that it protects marriages from stress-related deterioration. Support acts as a buffer (Cohen & Wills, 1985), protecting the relationship from decreased closeness and increased conflict, which follow acute and chronic negative life events. For example, couples with highly supportive marriages show better marital adjustment after cancer diagnosis (Lichtman, Taylor, & Wood, 1987), economic setbacks (Lorenz, Conger, Montague, & Wickrama, 1993), and the death of a child (Broman, Riba, & Trahan, 1996).

Individual Benefits

Mental Health. Another well-replicated finding is that individuals with supportive spouses are less depressed than those without a supportive spouse (e.g., Dehle, Larsen, & Landers, 2001; Horwitz, McLaughlin, & White, 1997). Spousal support protects against depressive reactions to stressful life events. For example, couples high in spousal support are less likely to become depressed due to financial problems (Lorenz, Conger, Montague, & Wickrama, 1993). Marital support also preserves mental health during times of illness. Studies have shown that high marital support is associated with lower depression among patients with rheumatoid arthritis (Manne & Zautra, 1989), cancer (Pistrang & Barker, 1995), and patients recovering from heart surgery (Waltz, Badura, Pfaff, & Schott, 1988). In a sample of couples in which the wife had breast cancer, emotional support provided by husbands predicted wives' depression immediately after and 1 year after surgery (Hoskins, 1995).

Individuals who perceive high levels of support from their spouse report lower levels of perceived stress (Dehle et al., 2001; Rideout et al., 1990), including stress specifically related to parenting problems, work issues, and money troubles (Jackson, 1992). Those with a supportive spouse are also more likely to be satisfied with their jobs (Adams, King, & King, 1996) and with their lives more generally (Walen & Lachman, 2000). Among dual-career couples, spousal social support predicts greater life-style satisfaction (Perrone & Worthington, 2001) and lower role strain (Aryee, Luk, Leung, & Lo, 1999).

One mechanism through which spousal support reduces depression and perceived stress is by promoting more benign interpretations of negative life events (Carlson & Perrewe, 1999). In a sample of elderly couples, spousal support increased life satisfaction through the mediation of "cognitive reframing," which involves reinterpreting problems as challenges or opportunities (Ducharme, 1994). Carlson and Perrewe (1999) found that spousal support was only effective in preventing depression when it was associated with reframing events as less severe. Once events were perceived as severe, social support was not associated with lower depression.

Physical Health. The association between marital support and physical health outcomes is inconclusive. For example, little or no association was found between support and physical health among women with breast cancer (Bolger, Foster, Vinokur, & Ng, 1996), coronary bypass patients (Kulik & Mahler, 1993), and men with coronary heart disease (Helgeson, 1993). However, marital support was significantly linked to physical health in another study of cancer patients (Hagedoorn et al., 2000), and among coronary bypass patients, less time was spent in the hospital after surgery if spousal support was high (Kulik & Mahler, 1989). Marital social support was significantly associated with measures of physical health, including number of health complaints in two studies (Rosenbaum & Cohen, 1999; Wyke & Ford, 1992).

Although direct links between marital support and physical health outcomes are inconsistent, marital support clearly influences health indirectly through promoting healthy behavior. Couples with support from their partners show greater compliance with medical regimens (Kulik & Mahler, 1993), are more successful when trying to quit smoking (Mermelstein, Cohen, Lichenstein, Baer, & Kamarck, 1986; Horwitz, Hindi-Alexander, & Wagner, 1985), and are more successful when trying to combat alcoholism (Sobell, Sobell, Toneatto, & Leo, 1993). Although perhaps not directly tied to physiological functioning, marital support has an indirect effect on health, encouraging healthy decisions and behaviors that, in turn, promote good health outcomes.

Factors That Influence Marital Support Effectiveness

Not all support transactions are successful (Lehman et al., 1986). Some attempts at support actually make the recipient feel worse. It is important to understand what makes people feel supported by their partners and what makes them feel unsupported and leaves them vulnerable to the ravages of stress. Some factors that influence the effectiveness of support are described next.

Knowledge

Knowledge of effective support techniques can influence the success of support attempts. Johnson, Hobfoll, and Zalcberg-Linetzy (1993) tested social support knowledge by having couples read hypothetical situations and indicate how they would support their partner in each situation. Partners who responded with high-quality support reactions had more intimate marital relationships. Intimacy, in turn, predicted satisfaction with support in the marriage. When partners know how to be supportive (and which behaviors to avoid when trying to give support), their supportive communications foster feelings of closeness and contribute to positive evaluations of the relationship.

A basic requirement for effective support is accurate awareness of the other person's problems. An aware partner knows when to provide support and what kinds of support to provide during stressful times. For example, pregnant women who experienced hassles during pregnancy were more depressed if their husbands, when queried, were unaware of the hassles (Chapman, Hobfoll, & Ritter, 1997). Interestingly, husbands who were unaware of their wives' hassles provided just as much support as husbands who were aware of their wives' hassles. Husbands' knowledge of the difficult times their wives had experienced correlated positively with wives' mental health, independent of support provision. Presumably, husbands who were aware of the sources of their wives' distress provided support that was more sensitive to their needs. In addition, perceptions of their husband's accurate empathy may have contributed to feelings of security and closeness among wives.

Invisible Support

There is evidence that "invisible support" can be more beneficial than "visible support" for married couples. Invisible support occurs when one partner performs a supportive act for his or spouse, but the recipient does not label the act as "support." Bolger, Zuckerman, and Kessler (2000) studied a sample of married couples in which one partner was preparing to take the bar exam. Every day for a month, the test taker recorded how anxious and depressed he or she felt, and both partners reported how much support the spouse had provided the test taker. As the exam approached, depression and anxiety increased for the test takers. On days when the supporter reported giving support but the test taker did not report receiving support, anxiety showed its lowest increases and depression actually decreased. According to the investigators, accepting support erodes one's self-esteem. Receiving support can draw attention to the fact that one is in need of help. In a study of women with osteoarthritis, support from husbands sometimes made patients feel incompetent and powerless, especially when they wanted to be independent and do things for themselves (Martire, Parris Stephens, Druley, & Wojno, 2002). Maximally helpful support is provided in a sensitive manner that does not exacerbate the problem by decreasing the receiver's feelings of self-worth or efficacy.

Barriers to Effective Marital Support

Stressful circumstances impede the ability of couples to support each other. When under stress, both spouses are less able to provide support and more likely to need support. It can be difficult for individuals to reach out to their partner when their own psychological resources are depleted. For example, in a sample of couples with fertility problems, Abbey, Andrews, and Halman (1995) found that highly stressed couples reported providing each other less support than those who reported lower stress. In a prospective longitudinal study, married individuals who experienced the death of a parent received less support from their spouse after their parent died than before the death occurred (Umberson, 1995). Among parents of children with Down syndrome, Roach, Orsmond, and Barratt (1999) found that the higher the partner's perceived stress, the less support he or she received from the spouse.

A key mechanism through which stressful life events erode support is through their effect on communication. Stressful life events erode warmth and increase hostility, criticism, and negativity during marital interactions (Conger et al., 1990; Vinokur, Price, & Caplan, 1996). Couples who can maintain high-quality communication in times of stress experience less depression and erosion of marital quality (Lorenz et al., 1993).

Even when partners are trying to support each other, stylistic differences in coping can lead to problems. Men and women often have different preferred approaches to coping with adversity. In Gottlieb and Wagner's (1991) study of parents of seriously ill children, husbands were disdainful of their wives' emotional reactions to problems and preferred to bury themselves in work as a coping mechanism. By contrast, women criticized their husbands' avoidance of emotionality and lack of involvement in day-to-day health crises. Differences in coping styles added to the burden experienced by both husbands and wives. Fostering the other's preferred coping style meant sacrificing the coping approach that was maximally beneficial to oneself.

Wives and husbands tend to evaluate support communications from their partners differently. Women are more attentive to the specific content of support-intended messages from their spouse, whereas husbands' evaluations of support communications are more heavily biased by their general satisfaction with the relationship (Carels & Baucom, 1999; Cutrona, 1996; Pasch, Bradbury, & Sullivan, 1997). Women are more critical of their husband's support communications. Men are less critical, but also less positively affected by support communications from their wife if they are unhappy with the relationship. This difference in attentiveness and responsiveness to the content of specific communications may lead to misunderstanding and confusion. Husbands may be bewildered by their wife's dissatisfaction with their support attempts. Wives may be frustrated with their inability to soothe a disgruntled husband with supportive words.

PARENTAL SUPPORT

Parents are the primary support providers for their children. In a sample of fifth- and sixth-graders, Furman and Buhrmester (1985) asked children to report who provided them with various types of support. Parents were listed as the primary source of affection, reassurance of the child's worth, physical and material assistance, intimacy, and as someone who would always be there when needed by the child. For companionship needs, friends were listed as the primary support source, but parents were second after friends. In another study, children drew diagrams to indicate their closeness with people in their social network. Immediate family members were always placed closest to the child on the diagrams, and children of all ages reported more support from close family members than from all other sources (Levitt, Guacci-Franco, & Levitt, 1993). The centrality of parents as support sources for their children is clear.

Benefits of Parental Support

Children of supportive parents have numerous advantages. Supportive parenting is associated with better mental health and adaptation to stress among children. When adapting to the birth of a new sibling, daughters with supportive parents displayed less withdrawal, hostility, insecurity, and dependency (Gottlieb & Mendelson, 1990). In this sample of 2- to 5-year-old girls, support from fathers was most helpful for mildly distressed girls; support from mothers was effective in reducing all girls' distress both before and after the birth of the new baby (Gottlieb & Mendelson, 1990). Varni, Wilcox, and Hansen (1988) found that family support accounted for 22% of the variance in depression and anxiety in a sample of children with juvenile arthritis. Among high school students, Garnefski and Diekstra (1996) found the relative risk of having emotional problems was much higher if the students lacked support from their families. Students without supportive families were approximately four times more likely to have behavior or emotional problems and eight times more likely to have both emotional and behavioral problems than those with supportive families. The effects of low school or peer support were smaller and less general. Lack of peer support was related only to emotional problems and lack of school support was related only to behavioral problems. Helsen, Vollebergh, and Meeus (2000) found that parental support was negatively related to depression, poor well-being, unhappiness, and suicidal thoughts among adolescents. The relationship was significant for adolescents in all age groups, although it was weaker for older adolescents. The effects were stronger for girls than for boys, and the risk for depression increased twofold if students lacked support from both parents and friends. Support from family was associated with lower anxiety among inner-city youth. In a sample of African American sixth- and seventh-graders from an urban area, more than 75% of the adolescents had heard gunshots and witnessed drug deals and physical altercations in the streets (White, Bruce, Farrell, & Kliewer, 1988). Family support was related to lower levels of anxiety among girls in this stressful environment. Among children of both genders who began the study with relatively low levels of anxiety, low family support predicted an increase in anxiety during the subsequent 6-month period.

Children with supportive parents have higher self-esteem and belief in their own competence. Parental support has been linked to self-esteem in both fifth-graders (Franco & Levitt, 1998) and older adolescents (Barrera, Chassin, & Rogosch, 1993). Van Aken and Riksen-Walraven (1992) observed the support mothers showed when completing a puzzle task with their children and found that, for both boys and girls, children with supportive mothers were more ego-resilient than children whose mothers demonstrated less support.

Children of supportive parents are physically healthier than those with nonsupportive parents. Wickrama, Lorenz, and Conger (1997) examined the relationship between physical health and parental support in a sample of rural adolescents. These adolescents were videotaped interacting with their parents, and support communications during the interaction were evaluated. Observed parental warmth was a significant predictor of changes in the child's physical health complaints over a period of 3 months, with lower warmth predicting an increase in health complaints. The health complaints included headache, cough, sore throat, muscle aches, allergies, and acne.

Children with supportive parents have fewer behavior problems and lower rates of delinquency. Teachers of fourth- and fifth-grade children reported fewer conduct problems among those children with supportive parents than among those with less supportive parents (Quamma & Greenberg, 1994). Family support's effects were magnified when children were experiencing high stress. Scholte, van Lieshout, and van Aken (2001) found that students with low parental support were more likely to be bullies at school and experience conflict at home than students with high parental support. Many of these children had high levels of social support from their friends, but friend support did not prevent this negative pattern. Among male college undergraduates, parental support was negatively correlated with aggression. Men who were satisfied with the amount of support from both their mothers and fathers engaged in fewer aggressive thoughts and behaviors than men who felt support was lacking from their parents (Rodney, Tachia, & Rodney, 1997).

Adolescents with supportive parents are less likely to use alcohol and drugs. Barnes and Farrell (1992) found that support from mothers was negatively linked to adolescent drinking. This effect retained significance when controlling for age, gender, race, family history of substance use, single-parent status, amount of parental monitoring, and use of substances by peers. Wills and Cleary (1996) found a classic buffering effect of parental support among junior high school students. The relationship between negative life events and multiple indicators of substance use was weaker at high levels of parental support than at low levels of parental support. Support from parents shields some children who have experienced negative life events from turning to substances for relief from stress.

Marshal and Chassin (2000) found gender differences in their study of adolescents and parental social support. Parental support had a stronger effect preventing substance use in daughters than in sons. Maternal support weakened the link between affiliation with substance-using peers and substance use among girls. However, the reverse was found for boys. Boys with high support from their mothers were more susceptible to the influence of substance-using peers than those with low support from mothers. Paternal support showed a similar pattern, reducing the effect of affiliation with substance-using peers on substance use for daughters, but not for sons. The authors suggest that sons may interpret support from their parents as a threat to their autonomy and to their male gender role. They may react to this perceived threat by rebelling and using substances more. Because girls are socialized to be more dependent than boys, the authors speculate that parental support is consistent with their feminine gender role and that girls may interpret support as nurturant rather than as threatening.

Children of supportive parents also perform better in school. When children have supportive parents, family support prevents negative life events from affecting their grades (Cauce, Hannan, & Sargeant, 1992). University students with supportive parents earn better grades when controlling for intellectual ability and family achievement orientation (Cutrona, Cole, Colangelo, Assouline, & Russell, 1994). Cutrona and colleagues (1994) speculated that parental support fosters security and self-efficacy, which promote sustained effort and persistence in the face of frustration in academic pursuits.

Parental support is associated with high-quality peer relationships. Among fifth-graders, parental support was positively related to every measured dimension of friendship quality, including validation and caring, conflict resolution, betrayal, help and guidance, recreation, and intimacy (Franco & Levitt, 1998). In a study of mothers, their teenage daughters, and the daughters' best friends, the best friends were more satisfied with the emotional support in their friendship with daughters when the mothers and daughters had a supportive relationship (Gavin & Furman, 1996). When parents are supportive, their children have role models for how to be supportive to others. Children of supportive parents learn interpersonal skills that make them better friends to their peers. In addition, supportive parenting is probably associated with the development of a secure attachment style, which endows children with the ability to trust and be close to others (Pierce, Lakey, Sarason, Sarason, & Joseph, 1997).

Parental social support can buffer the effects of conflict in the parent–child relationship. Among pregnant or parenting adolescent females, when support from the adolescents' fathers was high, the negative effects of conflict between the father and the daughter were reduced or eliminated (Davis, Rhodes, & Hamilton-Leaks, 1997). Father–daughter pairs who engaged in conflict but in which the father provided high levels of support had relationships that were comparable to fathers and daughters without conflict.

Factors That Influence Parental Support Effectiveness

Parent and Child Gender

The gender of both the parent and child can affect how much support a child receives. Many studies suggest that mothers are more supportive than fathers. In a sample of adolescents hospitalized for depression, mothers received higher support ratings than fathers (Barrera & Garrison-Jones, 1992). Another study found that mothers were the most frequent providers of social support that their pregnant daughters deemed "helpful" (Rhodes & Woods, 1995). In other research, the negative effects of a nonsupportive father on a child's self-worth could only be alleviated if the child's mother was very supportive (Van Aken & Aspendorf, 1997). Evidence exists that mothers are the most important and first line of defense in supporting their children.

Other studies suggest that mother–daughter and father–son pairs are more supportive than cross-gender pairs. For example, in a sample of 12- to 16-year-old adolescents, daughters said they spent more time with and were closer to their mothers than to their fathers. Sons said the same things about their fathers relative to their mothers (Young, Miller, Norton, & Hill, 1995). Other research found that in two-parent families, girls' risk of depression was increased if either parent was nonsupportive, but the risk was greater for daughters of nonsupportive mothers than of nonsupportive fathers. For boys, however, there was no difference in depression risk as a function of which parent was nonsupportive (Patten et al., 1997).

Barriers to Effective Parental Support

With increasing age, interactions between children and their parents become more conflict-ridden and less warm (Paikoff & Brooks-Gunn, 1991). Children spend less time with their parents after puberty and begin telling parents less about their problems (Paikoff & Brooks-Gunn, 1991). This withholding of confidences makes it more difficult for parents to know what is bothering their child and to provide support when needed. Peers become a more important source of support during the teenage years. As children age, parental support decreases and peer support increases (Levitt et al., 1993). If adolescents choose to disclose their problems to their peers and not to their parents, parents' support opportunities are eliminated. The support role that in childhood was filled primarily by parents is divided between parents and friends in adolescence.

SIBLING SUPPORT

Sibling social support has not been investigated as thoroughly as marital and parental social support. However, sibling support can be important in the lives of children. Among 11th-graders who said they had a close relationship with an older sibling, the sibling relationship contributed significantly to the child's emotional and school adjustment above and beyond acceptance from mother, father, and peers (Seginer, 1998).

Benefits of Sibling Support

Children with supportive siblings are less likely to be depressed. Among elementary school children from single-parent families, support from a sibling was negatively correlated with depression (Huntley & Phelps, 1990). This link retained significance after controlling for the amount of parental support received. Among socially isolated sixth-graders, high support from the favorite sibling was related to fewer adjustment problems (East & Rook, 1992).

Sibling support also contributes to self-esteem. Among adolescents, sibling support was significantly correlated with children's self-esteem (Barrera et al., 1993). Although this correlation was smaller in magnitude than the correlations between parental support and self-esteem, it was statistically significant. Sibling support has also been linked to self-esteem in college-aged samples (Caya & Liem, 1998).

Supportive sibling relationships can foster positive social development. Sibling support was related to skillful conflict management and a sense of companionship in the peer relationships of a sample of fifth-graders (Franco & Levitt, 1998). Sibling support was significantly related to social competence in college students (Caya & Liem, 1998). According to Amato (1989), learning how to cooperate, manage conflict, and be supportive to one's sibling makes adolescents better friends later in life.

Factors That Influence Sibling Support Effectiveness

Age and gender can affect the amount of support that siblings share. In a study of fifth- and sixth-graders and their siblings, more affection and reassurance of worth were exchanged when siblings were further apart in age (Furman & Buhrmester, 1985). Younger members of sibling pairs were more willing to provide tangible assistance than were older siblings. Younger and same-sex siblings provided better companionship, and younger siblings and same sex siblings who were close in age reported the most intimacy. In a sample of adult siblings where one member of the pair had recently been released from a psychiatric hospital, female siblings provided more support than male siblings (Horwitz, Tessler, Fisher, & Gamache, 1992). Among elderly siblings, sister–sister relationships were closer and more intimate than were other sibling relationships (Wilson, Calsyn, & Orlofsky, 1994).

Siblings tend to provide less support if other resources are available, but fill in when needed. Among adolescents, Tucker, McHale, and Crouter (2001) found that in small families, siblings provided more support than they did in large families, where support responsibility was dispersed among family members. Siblings of severely mentally ill adults provided less support if their ill brother or sister had other support sources, such as parents or other siblings (Horwitz et al., 1992). It has also been observed that adults tend to receive more support from their siblings if they do not have adult children (White & Riedman, 1992), or if they are single, divorced, or widowed (Connidis, 1994).

The impact of an older sibling's support varies as a function of the older sibling's personal characteristics and behavior. Tucker et al. (2001) found that older siblings who were well adjusted, both academically and socially, provided more support to their younger sibling than those who were poorly adjusted. Older siblings with adjustment problems were less able to reach out and provide assistance. Widmer and Weiss (2000) found that support from an older sibling was only beneficial when the child had a positive image of that sibling. If children had a negative image of their sibling, support from that sibling was related to higher depression and delinquency and lower resourcefulness and school performance (Widmer & Weiss, 2000). In a study by Slomkowski, Rende, Conger, Simons, and Conger (2001), the correlation between delinquency in older and younger sibling pairs differed as a function of gender and the supportiveness of the sibling relationship. For girls, the correlation between older and younger sibling delinquency was lower if the older sibling was supportive toward her younger sister. Among high-delinquency older sisters, support may have included advice on how to avoid problem behavior. For boys, the correlation between older and younger sibling delinquency was stronger if the older sibling was supportive toward his younger brother. Among high-delinquency older brothers, support may have involved inclusion of the younger brother in delinquent activities.

FUTURE RESEARCH DIRECTIONS

Social support is associated with a wide range of positive outcomes in marital, parent–child, and sibling relationships. However, questions remain regarding the mechanisms through which social support influences well-being, the ways in which support processes differ across types of family relationships, the best methods to use in studying family support, and how to prevent support failures, unintended negative effects, and erosion of support. Research needs in each of these areas will be considered.

The mechanisms through which social support enhances well-being have been most thoroughly studied among married couples. Marital support appears to promote more benign assessments of stressors and to facilitate adherence to positive health behaviors. Social support also appears to suppress conflict and enhance marital satisfaction. The role of spousal support in maintaining marital quality merits further investigation. Cutrona (1996) proposed that over the course of marital relationships, social support behaviors promote the development of trust. Holmes (2002) argued that trust, defined as the expectation that one's partner will be responsive to one's needs, is the most important dimension of marital adjustment. When trust is high, negative partner behaviors are assigned less importance and are attributed to temporary pressures, outside of the partner's control (Rempel, Ross, & Holmes, 2001). In addition, high-trust partners are less evaluative of their partner and less vigilant in finding fault (Holmes, 2002). This may explain the lower frequency of conflict in high-support couples. Conflict and negative behaviors are strongly negatively linked to marital satisfaction and well-being (e.g., Schuster et al., 1990). Prevention of conflict may be an important mechanism through which social support affects well-being. The role of social support in the development of trust and other positive relationship characteristics requires further empirical investigation.

Mechanisms through which social support enhances well-being in parent–child and sibling relationships have not been thoroughly investigated. It is likely that consistent parental support contributes to the development of a secure attachment style. Parental support contributes to the child's development along a number of dimensions, which should be explored. The extent to which early parent–child experiences that discourage secure attachment can be detoxified by parental support in later childhood is a question that merits further investigation. A second question conerns the extent to which parental responsibilities for socializing and disciplining their children influence the kinds of support they give them. Although advice is the least valued form of social support (Cutrona & Suhr, 1992), parents may provide their children advice rather than emotional or esteem-building support out of the belief that they must provide guidance. Similarly, when a child makes a painful mistake in some aspect of his or her life, parents may reprimand the child rather than empathize with the child's feelings of distress. Research is needed on how parents can best fulfill their dual roles as socializing agents and sources of comfort.

Turning to the mechanisms through which sibling support promotes well-being, research is needed on the extent to which sibling rivalry interferes with support transactions. It may be that siblings who believe that they must compete for parental approval and resources are unable to provide support to one another. Ways to maximize the supportiveness of sibling relationships merit investigation. In addition, it would be interesting to compare the characteristics of support from siblings to those of friends at different stages across the life span. Although friend support may be more reliable and important during childhood and adolescence, sibling support increases in quality and importance during adulthood.

Most research on social support has relied on self-report measurement. In the last 12 years, observational studies of marital support transactions have emerged. However, observational studies of support transactions between parents and children and between siblings are rare. Observational studies, daily diary studies, and studies that solicit the perspectives of multiple family members on support transactions are needed to improve our understanding of family social support.

Support attempts often fail, and sometimes support is not available from family members when it is needed. Research is needed on how to maximize the effectiveness of family support. Specialized training on effective support communication would be a welcome addition to skill-building programs. Research is needed on how to prevent the erosion of support that often follows stressful life events. There is some evidence that partner distress or depression is the stimulus for support erosion, rather than the actual occurrence of stressful events (e.g., Abbey et al., 1995; Roach et al., 1999). Preventive marital interventions should advise couples of the erosive effects of depression and educate them about the importance of receiving appropriate professional help for depressive symptoms.

Support from family members is a valuable resource. Its presence can reduce stress and promote fulfillment and security. Its absence can magnify the damage sustained by adverse life conditions and limit the joy of intimacy with others.

REFERENCES

Abbey, A., Andrews, F. M., & Halman, L. J. (1995). Provision and receipt of social support and disregard: What is their impact on the marital life quality of fertile and infertile couples? *Journal of Personality and Social Psychology, 68*, 455–469.

Acitelli, L. K. (1996). The neglected links between marital support and marital satisfaction. In G. R. Pierce, B. R. Sarason, & I. G. Sarason (Eds.), *Handbook of social support and the family* (pp. 83–104). New York: Plenum Press.

Adams, G. A., King, L. A., & King, D. W. (1996). Relationships of job and family involvement, family social support, and work-family conflict with job and life satisfaction. *Journal of Applied Psychology, 81*, 411–420.

Amato, P. R. (1989). Family processes and the competence of adolescents and primary school children. *Journal of Youth and Adolescence, 18*, 39–53.

Aryee, S., Luk, V., Leung, A., & Lo, S. (1999). Role stressors, interrole conflict, and well-being: The moderating influence of spousal support and coping behaviors among employed parents in Hong-Kong. *Journal of Vocational Behavior, 54*, 259–278.

Barnes, G. M., & Farrell, M. P. (1992). Parental support and control as predictors of adolescent drinking, delinquency, and related problem behaviors. *Journal of Marriage and the Family, 54*, 763–776.

Barrera, M., Chassin, L., & Rogosch, F. (1993). Effects of social support and conflict on adolescent children of alcoholic and nonalcoholic fathers. *Journal of Personality and Social Psychology, 64*, 602–612.

Barrera, M., & Garrison-Jones, C. (1992). Family and peer social support as specific correlates of adolescent depressive symptoms. *Journal of Abnormal Child Psychology, 20*, 1–16.

Beach, S. R. H., Martin, J. K., Blum, T. C., & Roman, P. M. (1993). Effects of marital and co-worker relationships on negative affect: Testing the central role of marriage. *The American Journal of Family Therapy, 21*, 313–324.

Bolger, N., Foster, M., Vinokur, A. D., & Ng, R. (1996). Close relationships and adjustment to a life crisis: The case of breast cancer. *Journal of Personality and Social Psychology, 70*, 283–294.

Bolger, N., Zuckerman, A., & Kessler, R. C. (2000). Invisible support and adjustment to stress. *Journal of Personality and Social Psychology, 79*, 953–961.

Bradbury, T. N., Fincham, F. D., & Beach, S. R. H. (2000). Research on the nature and determinants of marital satisfaction: A decade in review. *Journal of Marriage and the Family, 62*, 964–980.

Broman, C. L., Riba, M. L., & Trahan, M. R. (1996). Traumatic events and marital well-being. *Journal of Marriage and the Family, 58*, 908–916.

Brown, G. W., & Harris, T. O. (1978). *Social origins of depression: A study of psychiatric disorder in women.* New York: The Free Press.

Carels, R. A., & Baucom, D. H. (1999). Support in marriage: Factors associated with on-line perceptions of support helpfulness. *Journal of Family Psychology, 13*, 131–144.

Carlson, D. S., & Perrewe, P. L. (1999). The role of social support in the stressor-strain relationship: An examination of work-family conflict. *Journal of Management, 25*, 513–540.

Cauce, A. M., Hannan, K., & Sargeant, M. (1992). Life stress, social support, and locus of control during early adolescence: Interactive effects. *American Journal of Community Psychology, 20*, 787–798.

Caya, M. L., & Liem, J. H. (1998). The role of sibling support in high-conflict families. *American Journal of Orthopsychiatry, 68*, 327–333.

Chapman, H. A., Hobfoll, S. E., & Ritter, C. (1997). Partner's stress underestimations lead to women's distress: A study of pregnant inner-city women. *Journal of Personality and Social Psychology, 73*, 418–425.

Cobb, R. J., & Davila, J. (2001). Attachment security and marital satisfaction: The role of positive perceptions and social support. *Personality and Social Psychology Bulletin, 27*, 1131–1143.

Cohan, C. L., & Bradbury, T. N. (1997). Negative life events, marital interaction, and the longitudinal course of newlywed marriage. *Journal of Personality and Social Psychology, 73*, 114–128.

Cohen, S., & Wills, T. A. (1985). Stress, social support, and the buffering hypothesis. *Psychological Bulletin, 98*, 310–357.

Conger, R. D., Elder Jr., G. H., Lorenz, F. O., Conger, K. J., Simons, R. L., Whitbeck, L. B., Huck, S., & Melby, J. N. (1990). Linking economic hardship to marital quality and instability. *Journal of Marriage and the Family, 52*, 643–656.

Conger, R. D., Rueter, M. A., & Elder, G. H. (1999). Couple resilience to economic pressure. *Journal of Personality and Social Psychology, 76*, 54–71.

Connidis, I. A. (1994). Sibling support in older age. *Journal of Gerontology, 49*, 309–317.

Cutrona, C. E. (1996). Social support as a determinant of marital quality: The interplay of negative and supportive behaviors. In G. R. Pierce, B. R. Sarason, & I. G. Sarason (Eds.), *Handbook of social support and the family* (pp. 173–194). New York: Plenum Press.

Cutrona, C. E., Cole, V., Colangelo, N., Assouline, S. G., & Russell, D. W. (1994). Perceived parental social support and academic achievement: An attachment theory perspective. *Journal of Personality and Social Psychology, 66*, 369–378.

Cutrona, C. E., & Suhr, J. A. (1992). Controllability of stressful events and satisfaction with spouse support behaviors. *Communication Research, 19*, 154–174.

Davis, A. A., Rhodes, J. E., & Hamilton-Leaks, J. (1997). When both parents may be a source of both support and problems: An analysis of pregnant and parenting female African American adolescents' relationships with their mothers and fathers. *Journal of Research on Adolescence, 7*, 331–348.

Dehle, C., Larsen, D., & Landers, J. E. (2001). Social support in marriage. *American Journal of Family Therapy, 29*, 307–324.

Ducharme, F. (1994). Conjugal support, coping behaviors, and psychological well-being of the elderly spouse. *Research on Aging, 16*, 167–190.

East, P. L., & Rook, K. S. (1992). Compensatory patterns of support among children's peer relationships: A test using school friends, nonschool friends, and siblings. *Developmental Psychology, 28*, 163–172.

Franco, N., & Levitt, M. J. (1998). The social ecology of middle childhood: Family support, friendship quality, and self-esteem. *Family Relations, 47*, 315–321.

Furman, W., & Buhrmester, D. (1985). Children's perceptions of the personal relationships in their social networks. *Developmental Psychology, 21*, 1016–1024.

Gallo, L. C., & Smith, T. W. (2001). Attachment style in marriage: Adjustment and responses to interaction. *Journal of Social and Personal Relationships, 18*, 263–289.

Garnefski, N., & Diekstra, R. F. W. (1996). Perceived social support from family, friends, school, and peers: Relationship with emotional and behavioral problems among adolescents. *Journal of the American Academy of Child and Adolescent Psychiatry, 35*, 1657–1664.

Gavin, L. A., & Furman, W. (1996). Adolescent girls' relationships with mothers and best friends. *Child Development, 67*, 375–386.

Gottlieb, L. N., & Mendelson, M. J. (1990). Parental support and firstborn girls' adaptation to the birth of a sibling. *Journal of Applied Developmental Psychology, 11*, 29–48.

Gottlieb, B. H., & Wagner, F. (1991). Stress and support process in close relationships. In J. Eckenrode (Ed.), *The social context of coping* (pp. 165–188). New York: Plenum Press.

Hagedoorn, M., Kuijer, R. G., Buunk, B. P., DeJong, G. M., Wobbes, T., & Sanderman, R. (2000). Martial satisfaction in patients with cancer: Does support from intimate partners benefit those who need it the most? *Health Psychology, 19*, 274–282.

Helgeson, V. S. (1993). The onset of chronic illness: Its effect on the patient-spouse relationship. *Journal of Social and Clinical Psychology, 12*, 406–428.

Helsen, M., Vollebergh, W., & Meeus, W. (2000). Social support from parents and friends and emotional problems in adolescence. *Journal of Youth and Adolescence, 29*, 319–335.

Holmes, J. G. (2002). Interpersonal expectations as the building blocks of social cognition: An interdependence theory perspective. *Personal Relationships, 9*, 1–26.

Horwitz, A. V., McLaughlin, J., & White, H. R. (1997). How the negative and positive aspects of partner relationships affect the mental health of young married people. *Journal of Health and Social Behavior, 39*, 124–136.

Horwitz, M. B., Hindi-Alexander, M., & Wagner, T. J. (1985). Psychosocial mediators of abstinence, relapse, and continued smoking: A one-year follow-up of a minimal intervention. *Addictive Behaviors, 10*, 29–39.

Horwitz, A. V., Tessler, R. C., Fisher, G. A., & Gamache, G. M. (1992). The role of adult siblings in providing social support to the severely mentally ill. *Journal of Marriage and the Family, 54*, 233–241.

Hoskins, C. N. (1995). Patterns of adjustment among women with breast cancer and their partners. *Psychological Reports, 77*, 1017–1018.

House, J. S. (1981). *Work stress and social support.* Reading, MA: Addison-Wesley.

Huntley, D. K., & Phelps, R. E. (1990). Depression and social contacts of children from one-parent families. *Journal of Community Psychology, 18*, 66–72.

Jackson, P. B. (1992). Specifying the buffering hypothesis: Support, strain, and depression. *Social Psychology Quarterly, 55*, 363–378.

Johnson, R., Hobfoll, S. E., & Zalcberg-Linetzy, A. (1993). Social support knowledge and behavior and relational intimacy: A dyadic study. *Journal of Family Psychology, 6*, 266–277.

Kaplan, B. H., Cassel, J. C., & Gore, S. (1977). Social support and health. *Medical Care, 15*, 47–58.

Kulik, J. A., & Mahler, H. I. M. (1989). Social support and recovery from surgery. *Health Psychology, 8*, 221–238.

Kulik, J. A., & Mahler, H. I. M. (1993). Emotional support as a moderator of adjustment and compliance after coronary artery bypass surgery: A longitudinal study. *Journal of Behavioral Medicine, 16*, 45–63.

Lanza, A. F., Cameron, A. E., & Revenson, T. A. (1995). Perceptions of helpful and unhelpful support among married individuals with rheumatic diseases. *Psychology and Health, 10*, 449 462.

Lehman, D. R., Ellard, J. H., & Wortman, C. B. (1986). Social support for the bereaved: Recipients' and providers' perspectives on what is helpful. *Journal of Consulting and Clinical Psychology, 54*, 438–446.

Levitt, M. J., Guacci-Franco, N., & Levitt, J. L. (1993). Convoys of social support in childhood and early adolescence: Structure and function. *Developmental Psychology, 29*, 811–818.

Lichtman, R. R., Taylor, S. E., & Wood, J. V. (1987). Social support and marital adjustment after breast cancer. *Journal of Psychosocial Oncology, 5*, 47–74.

Lin, N. (1986). Conceptualizing social support. In N. Lin, A. Dean, & W. Ensel (Eds.), *Social support life events, and depression* (pp. 17–48). Orlando, FL: Academic Press.

Lorenz, F. O., Conger, R. D., Montague, R. B., & Wickrama, K. A. S. (1993). Economic conditions, spouse support, and psychological distress of rural husbands and wives. *Rural Sociology, 58*, 247–268.

Manne, S. L., & Zautra, A. J. (1989). Spouse criticism and support: Their association with coping and psychological adjustment among women with rheumatoid arthritis. *Journal of Personality and Social Psychology, 56*, 608–617.

Marshal, M. P., & Chassin, L. (2000). Peer influence on adolescent alcohol use: The moderating role of parental support and discipline. *Applied Developmental Science, 4*, 80–88.

Martire, L. M., Parris Stephens, M. A., Druley, J. A., & Wogno, W. C. (2002). Negative reactions to received spousal care: Predictors and consequences of miscarried support. *Health Psychology, 21*, 167–176.

Matthews, L. S., Conger, R. D., & Wickrama, K. A. S. (1996). Work-family conflict and marital quality: Mediating processes. *Social Psychology Quarterly, 59*, 62–79.

McGonagle, K. A., Kessler, R. C., & Schilling, E. A. (1992). The frequency and determinants of marital disagreements in a community sample. *Journal of Social and Personal Relationships, 9*, 507–524.

Mermelstein, R., Cohen, S., Lichenstein, E., Baer, J. S., & Kamarck, T. (1986). Social support and smoking cessation and maintenance. *Journal of Consulting and Clinical Psychology, 54*, 447–453.

Paikoff, R. L., & Brooks-Gunn, J. (1991). Do parent-child relationships change during puberty? *Psychological Bulletin, 110*, 47–66.

Pasch, L. A., & Bradbury, T. N. (1998). Social support, conflict, and the development of marital dysfunction. *Journal of Consulting and Clinical Psychology, 66*, 219–230.

Pasch, L. A., Bradbury, T. N., & Sullivan, K. T. (1997). Social support in marriage: An analysis of intraindividual and interpersonal components. In G. R. Pierce & B. Lakey (Eds.), *Sourcebook of social support and personality* (pp. 229–256). New York: Plenum Press.

Patten, C. A., Gillin, J. C., Farkas, A. J., Gilpin, E. A., Berry, C. C., & Pierce, J. P. (1997). Depressive symptoms in California adolescents: Family structure and parental support. *Journal of Adolescent Health, 20*, 271–278.

Perrone, K. M., & Worthington, E. L., Jr. (2001). Factors influencing ratings of marital quality by individuals within dual-career marriages: A conceptual model. *Journal of Counseling Psychology, 48*, 3–9.

Pierce, G. R., Lakey, B., Sarason, I. G., Sarason, B. R., & Joseph, H. J. (1997). Personality and social support processes: A conceptual overview. In G. R. Pierce, B. Lakey, I. G. Sarason, & B. R. Sarason (Eds.), *Sourcebook of social support and personality* (pp. 3–18). New York: Plenum Press.

Pistrang, N., & Barker, C. (1995). The partner relationship in psychological response to breast cancer. *Social Science and Medicine, 40*, 789–799.

Quamma, J. P., & Greenberg, M. T. (1994). Children's experience of life stress: The role of family social support and social problem-solving skills as protective factors. *Journal of Clinical Child Psychology, 23*, 295–305.

Rempel, J. K., Ross, M., & Holmes, J. C. (2001). Trust and communicated attributions in close relationships. *Journal of Personality and Social Psychology, 81*, 57–64.

Rhodes, J. E., & Woods, M. (1995). Comfort and conflict in the relationships of pregnant, minority adolescents: Social support as a moderator of social strain. *Journal of Community Psychology, 23*, 74–84.

Rideout, E. M., Rodin, G. M., & Littlefield, C. H. (1990). Stress, social support, and symptoms of depression in spouses of the medically ill. *International Journal of Psychiatry in Medicine, 20*, 37–48.

Roach, M. A., Orsmond, G. I., & Barratt, M. S. (1999). Mothers and fathers of children with Down syndrome: Parental stress and involvement with child care. *American Journal on Mental Retardation, 104*, 422–436.

Rodney, H. E., Tachia, H. R., & Rodney, L. W. (1997). The effect of family and social support on feelings and past acts of violence among African Amercian college men. *Journal of American College Health, 46*, 103–108.

Rook, K. S. (1984). Research on social support, loneliness, and social isolation: Toward an integration. *Review of Personality and Social Psychology, 5*, 239–264.

Rosenbaum, M., & Cohen, E. (1999). Equalitarian marriages, spousal support, resourcefulness, and psychological distress among Israeli working women. *Journal of Vocational Behavior, 54*, 102–113.

Scholte, R. H. J., van Lieshout, C. F. M., & van Aken, M. A. G. (2001). Perceived relational support in adolescence: Dimensions, configurations, and adolescent adjustment. *Journal of Research on Adolescence, 11*, 71–94.

Schuster, T. L., Kessler, R. C., & Aseltine, Jr., R. H. (1990). Supportive interactions, negative interactions, and depressed mood. *American Journal of Community Psychology, 18*, 423–438.

Seginer, R. (1998). Adolescents' perceptions of relationships with older sibling in the context of other close relationships. *Journal of Research on Adolescence, 8*, 287–308.

Slomkowski, C., Rende, R., Conger, K. J., Simons, R. L., & Conger, R. D. (2001). Sisters, brothers and delinquency: Evaluating social influence during early and middle adolescence. *Child Development, 72*, 271–283.

Sobell, L. C., Sobell, M. B., Toneatto, T., & Leo, G. I. (1993). What triggers the resolution of alcohol problems without treatment? *Alcoholism: Clinical and Experimental Research, 17*, 217–224.

Tucker, C. J., McHale, S. M., & Crouter, A. C. (2001). Conditions of sibling support in adolescence. *Journal of Family Psychology, 15*, 254–271.

Umberson, D. (1995). Marriage as support or strain? Martial quality following the death of a parent. *Journal of Marriage and the Family, 57*, 709–723.

Van Aken, M. A. G., & Aspendorf, J. B. (1997). Support by parents, classmates, friends and siblings in preadolescence: Covariation and compensation across relationships. *Journal of Social and Personal Relationships, 14*, 79–93.

Van Aken, M. A. G., & Riksen-Walraven, J. M. (1992). Parental support and the development of competence in children. *International Journal of Behavioral Development, 15*, 101–123.

Varni, J. W., Wilcox, K. T., & Hanson, V. (1988). Mediating effects of family social support on child psychological adjustment in juvenile rheumatoid arthritis. *Health Psychology, 7*, 421–431.

Vinokur, A. D., Price, R. H., & Caplan, R. D. (1996). Hard times and hurtful partners: How financial strain affects depression and relationship satisfaction of unemployed persons and their spouses. *Journal of Personality and Social Psychology, 71*, 166–179.

Walen, H. R., & Lachman, M. E. (2000). Social support and strain from partner, family and friends: Costs and benefits for men and women in adulthood. *Journal of Social and Personal Relationships, 17*, 5–30.

Waltz, M., Badura, B., Pfaff, H., & Schott, T. (1988). Marriage and the psychosocial consequences of a heart attack: A longitudinal study of adaptation to chronic illness after three years. *Social Science and Medicine, 27*, 149–158.

Wan, C. K., Jaccard, J., & Ramey, S. L. (1996). The relationship between social support and life satisfaction as a function of family structure. *Journal of Marriage and the Family, 58*, 502–513.

White, K. S., Bruce, S. E., Farrell, A. D., & Kliewer, W. (1998). Impact of exposure to community violence on anxiety: A longitudinal study of family social support as a protective factor for urban children. *Journal of Child and Family Studies, 7*, 187–203.

White, L. K., & Riedman, A. (1992). Ties among adult siblings. *Social Forces, 71*, 85–102.

Wickrama, K. A. S., Lorenz, F. O., & Conger, R. D. (1997). Parental support and adolescent physical health status: A latent growth-curve analysis. *Journal of Health and Social Behavior, 38*, 149–163.

Widmer, E. D., & Weiss, C. C. (2000). Do older siblings make a difference? The effects of older sibling support and older sibling adjustment on the adjustment of socially disadvantaged adolescents. *Journal of Research on Adolescence, 10*, 1–27.

Wills, T. A., & Cleary, S. D. (1996). How are social support effects mediated? A test with parental support and adolescent substance abuse. *Journal of Personality and Social Psychology, 71*, 937–952.

Wilson, J. G., Calsyn, R. J., & Orlofsky, J. L. (1994). Impact of sibling relationships on social support and morale in the elderly. *Journal of Gerontological Social Work, 22*, 157–170.

Wong, D. K. F., & Kwok, S. Y. C. (1997). Difficulties and patterns of social support of mature college students in Hong Kong: Implications for student guidance and counseling services. *British Journal of Guidance and Counseling, 25*, 377–387.

Wyke, S., & Ford, G. (1992). Competing explanations for associations between marital status and health. *Social Science & Medicine, 34*, 523–532.

Young, M. H., Miller, B. C., Norton, M. C., & Hill, E. J. (1995). The effect of parental supportive behaviors on life satisfaction of adolescent offspring. *Journal of Marriage and the Family, 57*, 813–822.

23

Imagining Families Through Stories and Rituals

Jane Jorgenson and Arthur P. Bochner
University of South Florida

Family is an idea constituted in and through the images produced by family researchers, by families themselves, and by canonical narratives of family circulating through culture. As family researchers, we are preoccupied with imagining families. In the research we conduct, as well as in our personal lives, we make and shape family experience. All of us tell stories *about* families; we represent, dramatize, emplot, moralize, idealize, and formularize according to accepted conventions of academic storytelling. The texts, charts, tables, graphs, and statistical inferences that we produce represent the families we study, but they are not the families themselves. Usually, they are hard-boiled images of families, a genre of family narrative produced and governed by ritualized practices of social science research traditions.

The narratives that participants share with us give meaning and intelligibility to their family experiences. When we conduct research, we collaborate with our participants in a process of sense making. Whether we ask our participants to complete questionnaires or surveys, invite them to converse with us about their experiences, or directly observe them in their home environment, the result is a collaborative product in which participants interpret and give meaning to their experience and researchers represent those meanings in graphs, tables, anecdotes, or stories (see e.g., Steier, 1991). Participants transform or reform their experiences by making marks on interval scales, telling stories, or imagining and communicating what they would do when faced with hypothetical scenarios. Then, we transform their marks, their stories, or their anecdotes into texts that represent them as well and as accurately as we can. Data become words. We make language sit in for life. Whether we speak for our participants or allow them to speak for themselves, we embed their meanings and interpretations in a different context of understanding—the research monograph or scholarly book. Without exception, we recontextualize and thus transform what they have said, or marked, or meant. Usually, we give our interpretations of their interpretations, expressing their meanings in a different form or medium, remaking or reframing what has been said or meant.

When we write about family communication, we are immersed in a language game. We cannot extricate ourselves from language. The families we seek to describe or represent do not exist in the form of the sentences we write when we depict them (Rorty, 1989). Moreover, try as we may (and should) to report or represent accurately, our own family experiences, emotions, and subjectivity may intrude as we engage in the process of giving our interpretations of their interpretations in words. We cannot help but read something into what is there, because we are there with it. What we come to say about families involves the indistinguishable provocations of the families we observe, the mediations of language by which we make claims about them, and the images of family we have internalized and project, some of which may be outside our awareness.

Sometimes we forget that our representations are transformations—images of the experiences we are trying to understand and/or predict. Then we need to be reminded, as R. D. Laing (1971) observed, that though we may speak as if we know what families are, the more we observe and study families the more unclear they may become to us. According to Laing (1971), we should not necessarily trust what people tell us about their families not so much because they want to mislead us but because "we can *never assume* that the people in the situation know what the situation is" (p. 33).

THE FAMILY IMAGINARY

Laing was one of the first theorists to call attention to the family imaginary. "The family may be imagined as a web, a flower, a tomb, a prison, a castle," he wrote (Laing, 1971, p. 6). "Self may be more aware of an image of the family than of the family itself, and map the images onto the family itself" (p. 6). Laing (1971) believed that much of the confusion over family dynamics stemmed from a failure to grasp the subjective and interior qualities of family experience, the ways in which what the family *means* are mapped, internalized, projected, and transferred.

The process of subjectifying and transferring a family's meanings begins early in life. As Laing (1971) wrote, "The child is born into a family which is the product of the operations of human beings already in this world" (p. 11). Thus, it is both necessary and useful, according to Laing, to distinguish the observable family from the internalized family, which he referred to as 'family.' One's family can be seen as an observable or objective structure, in Laing's terms, a *we* set against or compared to *them* outside the family. But each of us also internalizes and subjectifies a particular 'family' that "entails a type of relationship between family members of a different order from the relationships of those who do not share that 'family' inside each other" (Laing, 1971, p. 5).

Although Laing emphasized that the first years of life were the crucial period in which one's 'family' meanings are inscribed onto one's body, feelings, and perceptions, he also observed that the patterns of relationship represented and inscribed by these meanings can span several generations and that meanings are subject to change and transformation over time. In other words, 'family' as a representation of internalized meanings is an historical product in flux. *The subjectified 'family' is an interactional and cultural product, a particularized, dynamic and indeterminant system of personal meanings resulting from complex connections and encounters with significant others as well as with canonical narratives of family circulating through culture.*

From the perspective of family communication, a focus on meanings revolves around the question of how family meanings are produced, inscribed, and/or changed. This question draws attention to the connections and disconnections between our experiences, which often seem fragmented and ambiguous, and the meanings we attach to them, which reflect our need to interpret and explain our experiences and ourselves to others as well as to ourselves. As Bruner (1990) concludes, by the age of 3 many children already feel the "push" to narrativize experience (p. 77). This push to get things right, to make sense, and to recount experiences, however, is not just child's play. In many respects, who we think we are and what we think we can become is constituted in and by our narrativizing activities across the seasons of our lives. Our identities hinge largely on the stories we tell about ourselves and the stories we hear and internalize that others tell about us. Thus, a person's identity, as Schechtmann (1996) observes "is constituted by the content of the self-narrative" (p. 94). Stories are not only the ways in which we describe and explain ourselves, they are, as Frank (1995) observes "the self's medium of being" (p. 53). To believe in the importance of family communication is to heed the call of stories.

We consider family life, as we do life as a whole, to be a continuous struggle to create, maintain, and/or restore narrative coherence in the face of unexpected contingencies of lived experiences. In family life, there are bound to be bumps on the road, twists of fate, unanticipated losses, shifts in the plot line. The perceived coherence of one's life may at any moment dissolve into chaos when one confronts an unexpected catastrophe such as a chronic or acute illness, a geographical dislocation, the loss of a job, or a relational betrayal. Suddenly, a family must reappraise where they have been and where they are going as a family, who they are to one another, and how they will manage. Experiences such as these challenge families to create intelligible accounts of their lives that are accessible to others, yet feel true to their experience. On a smaller scale, of course, a family continuously exerts effort to create an artful "composition" of their lives in the context of the ordinary ebb and flow of family experience (Bateson, 1990). Work–family conflicts, puberty, menopause, and the adoption or birth of a child can trigger vulnerabilities that motivate the search for continuities. Successful coping with all kinds of stressful turning points—predictable transitions as well as epiphanies—may be dependent on a family's ability to construct meanings by situating these experiences within an intelligible frame (Bochner, Ellis, & Tillman-Healey, 1997; Bruner, 1990; Crites, 1971, 1986).

No matter how serious the disruption, family members usually feel a normative pressure to narrativize a continuous life of experience (Crites, 1986). Carr (1986) observes that "Coherence seems to be a need imposed upon us whether we seek it or not" (p. 97). We exist in the present, we remember the past, and we anticipate the future. Thus, our lived experiences are constituted by a temporal flow contextualized by birth and death. Childhood, adolescence, midlife—whatever stages we have passed through up to *now*— are always with us. Though we may feel as if we move through the life cycle one stage at a time, completing the tasks normatively assigned to each stage, we also feel a need to make sense of life *as a whole*. As Carr says "the whole of life is always there, and concern with its wholeness is an underlying and recurring concern" (p. 96). The events and experiences that mark each "stage" of a life are fixed and familiar, yet each is accessible to new discoveries, reinterpretations, and narrative inventions in the face of the pressure we feel to construct a continuous and unified life of experience. The stories we tell are remembrances of the past situated in connection to the present moment in which they are recollected and projected toward an anticipated but uncertain future. "The present of things past and the present of things future," writes Crites (1971, p. 302), "are the tension of every moment of experience, both united in that present and qualitatively differentiated by it." As life progresses, we tell and retell, to ourselves and to others, the story of who we are, what we have become and how we got there, making and remaking a story of ourselves that links birth to life to death as a continuous stream of experience flowing across the temporal coordinates of our lives.

THE TEMPORAL FLOW OF FAMILY LIFE

Family life is lived within the tensions constituted by memories of the past and anticipations of the future. This sense of before and after operates as a powerful emotional and subjective dimension of our daily family lives. Every family has its own pace—the speed at which it moves to get things done. Jules Henry (1973) reminds us of the occasions on which one rushes to get home "on time," so as not to keep the kids waiting for their dinner, or make one's spouse worry because he or she can't imagine what's taking so long. Henry (1973) connects time to mood insofar as each person "must learn that his movements in time are connected with other people's feelings" (p. 11). As Henry keenly observes, "time is saturated with love, rage, and anxiety from the beginning" (p. 11). When we talk about being able "to get away," of "being tied down," of "cutting our conversation short" or of "beating it home" so as not to keep the family waiting, we recognize how powerfully time shapes language (Henry, 1973, p. 11). As we pass through early language learning, each of us is exposed to lessons on timing—"not now," "later," "after while," "not yet," "before," and so on. We learn there is a time and order to action and events—a time schedule by which we are personally and culturally bound.

From a cultural perspective, metaphors of time have evolved as the defining image of a longitudinal and process model of family life. Both academically and personally, we view (and experience) the family as a dynamic system that changes and adapts through time. The idea of family as a temporal unit defined by progressive, developmental change is pervasive in everyday discourse as well as in scholarly publications across the myriad of disciplines that focus on family process (see, e.g., Aldous, 1978; Carter & McGoldrick, 1999; Falicov, 1988; Liddle, 1983; Slater, 1995; Winnicott, 1965).

We are referring here to the life-cycle model of human development that depicts family experience as a series of passages (or seasons) along a temporal path, with progress marked by an unfolding series of age statuses and identities (Kotre & Hall, 1997). Courtship and marriage evolve into parenting—of infants, toddlers, preschoolers and young children, then of adolescents—flowing on into midlife crises, the empty nest, retirement, and old age. Popular culture saturates us with images of these milestones; a child's first steps, high-school and college graduations, weddings and golden anniversaries, each a recognizable and celebrated rite of passage. Each promotes an idealized image of life defined by passages and timetables. Each presupposes a homogeneous family: intact, heterosexual, and child centered. Though we may resist the assumptions of the "monolithic family" (Langellier & Peterson, 1993) privileged in life-cycle metaphors of "seasons" and "passages," still we find it difficult to step outside these taken-for-granted frameworks, to question the essentializing chronological construction of family as a "career" defined by processes of growth and maturation over time.

We tend to forget that passages, seasons, and stages—midlife crises and empty nests— are metaphors that signify how we are bound to contingencies of time and order. Gillis (2000) points out that the temporal vocabulary of "life span" and "stages" is a relatively recent invention, an expression of a "virtual family" that came into existence after the Industrial Revolution. Until the mid-19th century, family was assumed to be a communal unit and working household that included kin and strangers laboring side by side to produce the goods on which they all depended (Demos, 1979). Defined by spatial rather than by temporal coordinates, family life was lived *in the present*. Few people celebrated anniversaries or showed interest in ancestral origins. The "family tree," writes Gillis (2000), "had no roots."

But with industrialization, family was wrenched apart from household and became a site of memory, no longer constituted by place, but through time. Individuals were increasingly subjected to rigid expectations regarding the timing of marriage and parenthood. As families acquired a sense of past, photographs and the albums in which they were placed became "momentos" for reviving memories, and symbolic objects such as wedding rings and mourning brooches became cherished artifacts (Pleck, 2000). Ritualized celebrations of family life blossomed, for example, birthdays and anniversaries, that had been given little recognition prior to the 20th century. Together, these changes signified the beginnings of a symbolically self-contained family, one that was now responsible for producing its own meaningful representations to mark the passage of time and order the course of everyday existence.

No longer anchored in face-to-face interchange based on shared work and leisure, the virtual family of today faces the narrative challenge of keeping itself alive and coherent across the press of time. Each family must imagine, create and/or sustain symbolic images that draw past and future into the present. Ironically, this obsession with remembering the past and anticipating the future makes it increasingly difficult for families to live and be in the moment. As Daly (1996) says, "The past and the future maintain the dream of family time, but the present is the site of our disillusionment" (p. 205).

CONSTRUCTING CONTINUITY THROUGH FAMILY STORIES AND RITUALS

Stories and rituals are two forms of symbolic production that have been vital to this "chronologizing" (Kohli, 1986, cited in Gillis, 1996) of family experience, shaping the perception of life events in terms of "origins" and "outcomes" in historical succession, thus fostering a sense of temporal flow. As symbolic resources for reading the past, for preserving a sense of the past in the present, and for expressing an awareness of differences between past and future, stories and rituals are resources through which family members create shared realities of family life (Baxter & Braithwaite, 2002; Bochner, Ellis, & Tillman-Healy, 1997; Bossard & Boll, 1950; Fiese, Sameroff, & Grotevant, 1999; Imber-Black, Roberts, & Whiting, 1988; Mandelbaum, 1987; Orbuch, Veroff, & Holmberg,

1993; Reiss, 1989; Stone, 1988; Wolin & Bennet, 1984; Yerby, 1995). More than trivial embellishments, stories and rituals are dual forms of family conversational work often closely intertwined with each other. Birthdays, wedding receptions, and other family-centered holiday celebrations become the means for staging continuity and implicitly sanctioning tradition; memories of these ritual occasions themselves become the subject matter for particular storied episodes of family history, for example, the honeymoon trip to the hospital emergency room or the Christmas dinner that bombed. Together, stories and rituals serve the practical function of organizing and structuring the indefinite flow of family experiences into meaningful coherence; they are vehicles for fashioning a world that is plausible and intelligible, the means by which we "do family" (Langellier & Peterson, 1993; McLain & Weigert, 1979).

Our aim in this chapter is to explore varieties of narrative performance through which families create and recreate their identities and realities. In elaborating this approach, we draw out and highlight the interplay between the observable, "practicing family" defined by its current interactional processes, and the subjectified family, constituted through a repertoire of fantasies, images, and abstractions (Reiss, 1989). Stories and rituals are symbolic links to the past, performed in the present. Thus, they may be regarded as a means for understanding family communication as an oral tradition. Viewed from this perspective, family members are performers who assume the interactive roles of speaker and interpreter, taking part in co-productions that can beguile, irritate, or induce a "here-we-go-again" feeling if the storylines are highly predictable. Dinner table-talk creates an atmosphere of warmth and mutuality, for example, when parents' anecdotes center on a child's clever remarks or precocious behavior; at other times, however, stories embarrass, antagonize, and rupture consensus. As a guiding metaphor, the perspective of narrative performance shows how family relationships, like other kinds of working agreements between people, are established not so much through "rational discourse but through complex and subtle expressive maneuvers" involving voice, gesture, and action that work together to evoke an imaginative reality (Schieffelin, 1998, p. 195; see also Bauman, 1986).

The implications of this perspective are methodological as well as conceptual. Stories and rituals call for methods of inquiry that bridge the divides between interpretive and empiricist orientations to inquiry, encouraging a unification of literature and social science and a respect for the particular, specific, and concrete. Many of us are drawn to the study of family communication because of a desire to understand the particular in family life, to reach deeper, more fully contextualized representations of lived relationships. To grasp the significance of a story or ritual is to understand something of the local culture in terms of the specific symbols used, the relationships involved, the feelings and memories evoked. Family stories encourage us to "climb under the skin" of others, projecting ourselves imaginatively into their lives, and in the process coming into contact with memories and emotions related to experiences in and memories of our own families (Reiss, 1989; see also Ellis & Bochner, 1996).

In emphasizing the evocative, and often celebratory, side of family experience, stories and rituals open a wide domain for the exploration of how families actively construct their realities. By offering close access to the human experience of time, order, and change, they focus our attention on the subjective, emotional, and complex qualities of family meanings. In this chapter we draw from social science research and ethnography, as well as from autobiographical and fictional works that exemplify the ways in which symbolic productions do the work of temporalizing and chronologizing the family. Our analysis and interpretation of these examples are organized around several basic questions, including: How do symbolic productions operate reflexively to shape family experience? Beyond merely embellishing family conversation, what constitutive role do stories and rituals play in constructing and reconstructing family ties? And more specifically, how do they operate as emotionally laden, family metalanguages? In their positive functions, stories and rituals appear to affirm solidarity. Yet the possibility also exists for symbolic expressions to embody relationship tensions, ambivalence, and disaffection (Nydegger & Mitteness, 1988).

From our point of view, stories and rituals carry the potential to defeat their own purposes insofar as they embody fantasies, projections, and ideological constructions that make actual family life appear to be flawed in comparison to ideals. As Gillis (1996) observes, in the very moments of ritualized performance, when people are supposed to act like "family," the contradictions built into modern domesticity are most likely to surface. Stories and rituals reflect and respond to culturally canonical versions of family life, reinforcing, and sometimes challenging, dominant understandings of "family" as a privatized and gendered institution (Langellier & Peterson, 1996; Yerby, 1995). Thus, we think it important to investigate the inventive ways families find to resist the canonical, creating stories and rituals that counter oppressive narratives and open new possibilities for meaningful family experience.

PERFORMING AND TRANSFORMING IDENTITIES IN FAMILY RITUAL

One way to begin to understand the role of ritual expression in the creation of family meanings is through personal narratives that convey ritual experiences from the standpoint of speaking subjects. The interpretive analysis carried out by Grimes (1995, 2000), for example, draws on a wide spectrum of "passage narratives" from bar mitzvahs and confirmations to Hindu and Christian marriage ceremonies as well as of his own autobiographical materials. His work emphasizes the ambiguities and dilemmas of ritual experiences revealed by first-person accounts, which tend to show the narrator as a "crisis-driven self" who is off balance and "grasping for symbolic and spiritual resources" (p. 5). Ritual narratives also speak directly to the chronological construction of family experience because ritual practices are ultimately "about time" (Myerhoff, 1995). Rites of passage and cyclical family celebrations carry messages of continuity through the formal elements of repetition (from generation to generation or year to year) and through their internally ordered symbolic actions (Werner & Baxter, 1994), while also marking changes along the family's developmental path. The psychological depth of ritual narratives flows, at least in part, from the narrator's temporal perceptions, including the sense of dislocation that sometimes comes from reexperiencing the past in the present.

In a series of three autobiographical vignettes, for example, the essayist Sylvia Rothchild (1989) captures the flow of thoughts and feelings triggered by the periodic reunions of older parents and their children at Passover. Collectively, Rothchild's essays and stories focus on the varieties of adjustments and transformations experienced by Jewish American families over several decades. Her Passover narratives shed light on general characteristics of family rituals but also capture their emotional resonance. In particular, she tries to understand how occasions that promise an experience of connection and continuity can be less than unifying for the participants.

Passover, a holiday marking the Exodus of Jews from Egypt, is centered around a family dinner. However, the Passover Seder, with its precise ordering of scriptural readings, songs, and special foods, is far more elaborate than any ordinary domestic occasion. In "Home for Pesach . . . and Back Again," the first of Rothchild's (1989) vignettes, she recalls one of the regular Passover reunions that took place every year at her elderly parents' Brooklyn apartment. On its surface, the emotional tone of the remembered occasion is one of consistency and predictability. Three generations of Rothchild's family are gathering for the first night's celebration. Her mother's preparations, cleaning and beautifying the apartment, begin days in advance. The beet soup, potato pies, and roast chicken are reassuringly familiar.

Many of the customary components of ritual identified by Myerhoff (1977) are present in Rothchild's (1989) account, including its setting as a solemn occasion marked by repetitive and stylized words and gestures. The foods on the seder plate are universal symbols linking the participants to a larger religious collectivity: "the celery that symbolizes bitter herbs" (and the bitterness of slavery) and "the chicken bone that is supposed to be the paschal lamb" (Rothchild, 1989, p. 135). Rothchild recalls her father making the blessing over the wine: "My youngest nephew begins to ask the four questions that begin the ceremony. He stumbles. His father glares at him and the boy bursts into tears. He runs away from the table with his mother after him" (p. 135). Family tensions simmer below the surface as the meal continues. The grandfather, doggedly reading, is oblivious to the grandchildren kicking each other under the table, and the monotonously intoned blessings over the food remind Rothchild of his "rigidity and stubbornness," of the "lost battles" of her childhood.

In a second story, "After the Revolution: An American Passover" (Rothchild, 1989), the author develops the theme of reunions as stressful occasions that expose the limits and disappointments of the parent–child bond. Ten years have passed and Rothchild is waiting tensely in her own home, just as her mother did, for the return of her college-age children for the holiday. She prepares by polishing the silver and making the traditional "knaidlakh" or matzoh balls. Intent on maintaining long-standing family traditions, she is alert to signs of change. When the children (her "darling children") finally arrive with several college friends, she finds they have become resentful strangers, the warmth of renewed closeness overshadowed by the young people's indifference. They seemed "in disguise as if it were Halloween or Purim rather than Pesach. It was not the beards . . . It was not the jeans . . . or the boots marking my polished floor. But something made me feel not at home in my own house that Passover night. My children avoided my eyes. I felt a fence of brambles sprouting between us and didn't know how to stop it" (p. 175). At dinner, her children and their guests are bored by the proceedings, while her husband, in the role of the priestly authority, focuses on the prayers and readings, paying no attention. Later a pungent smell draws her to the basement. She finds a young visitor smoking marijuana. Another has borrowed her sewing machine to make a banner for a demonstration the following day: "Don't get hysterical," her son tells her. Her daughter complains "I can't confide in you," and, worst of all, "I'm a citizen of the world. I don't want to be Jewish." The children and guests make an early departure, leaving her with a mountain of dishes. What came to be remembered in the family folklore as "the mad seder of 1971" was a disaster from beginning to end.

"After the Revolution" contains a third vignette showing the ties to be further eroded. Nine more years have passed and Rothchild and her husband now represent a family of later life. Passover has become a bitter reminder that they are, in effect, "childless" and alone. Since their 20-something children no longer care to come home, the couple copes by collecting Russian and Israeli immigrants and non-Jewish friends to simulate a family for the holiday. At the last minute, however, a daughter telephones, asking her mother's permission to bring several coworkers to the family seder. They arrive with flowers, chocolates, and kosher wine, and then a son shows up unexpectedly, wearing a jacket and tie, his beard neatly trimmed. This time the dinner table conversation is polite and cordial (though the children sidestep personal discussion of their private lives.) The daughter, Susie, throws herself exuberantly into the seder, singing *Dayenu* and "swaying as if she 'were really into it'" (p. 177). In the context of the previous estrangement, this seder has "a dreamlike quality"; it is extraordinary in its ordinariness. The evening ends with promises from everyone to return the next year.

In addition to evoking the emotional ambivalence and strain of intergenerational relationships over time, Rothchild's stories illustrate several important features of family rituals. One of the most salient characteristics is the function of ritual as a frame that defines a reality set apart from the flow of everyday life (Durkheim, 1915; Myerhoff, 1995). By distinguishing a time and space outside the boundaries of everyday interaction, collective celebrations attempt to intensify experience, creating a profound feeling of interrelatedness and mutual understanding, termed "communitas" (Turner, 1967). Through the physicality of its symbols and sensory stimuli, the ceremony brings about a sense of transformation that demonstrates, even if only fleetingly, that the participants have something essential in common (Moore & Myerhoff, 1977). In its form, the Seder ritual includes open and closed, or fixed and variable elements, so that even though it is shaped to a large degree according to the prescriptions of Jewish religious observance, it also bears the family's unique imprint. Thus, according to Rothchild family tradition, the foods are homemade, not store bought, prepared the same way every year. In the second vignette, readings from the traditional "Haggadah" are combined with those from Arthur Waskow's (1970) "Freedom Seder," a secular version. Through the interplay of fixed and fluid parts, the formally prescribed elements are "enlivened" and made relevant to the immediate situation so that the event becomes invested with the family's idiosyncratic meanings (Moore & Myerhoff, 1977; Roberts, 1988).

By drawing from different logical orders, family rituals carry multiple and sometimes unintended meanings. These narratives speak to a basic point made by Grimes (2000), that ritual dramas often emerge somewhere in the relationship between the formal enactments and ordinary, backstage family life. An underlying theme of Rothchild's stories is the experience of developmental crisis and the difficulty for aging parents and their children to accommodate themselves to the realities of later life—a crisis thrown into relief by the ritual practices carried over faithfully from year to year. This Passover reunion, like the holiday get-togethers of many families, evokes powerful dialectical tensions around themes of autonomy/connection, attachment/loss, and wanting/fearing (Bochner, 1994; Moss & Moss, 1988; Werner & Baxter, 1994). Adult children may look forward to the annual holiday reunion in order to renew their ties with the nurturing family of childhood, but they also fear engulfment. Rothchild's children resist opening their lives to their parents. The empty discourse and ritualized conversation that often characterizes gatherings of parents and children in later life can be a smokescreen for hiding ambivalence and avoiding emotional issues that threaten relationship continuity (Nydegger & Mitteness, 1988).

The term, "family ritual" carries many shades of meaning, ranging from the celebratory and special, to the obligatory and empty (Goffman, 1967). The dilemma embodied in rituals such as the seder is that the rich and impressive image of family life conveyed in the ceremonial occasion often turns out to be "hollow," that is, a "mere ritual" (Pleck, 2000; Wolin & Bennett, 1984). Though families may seem to function as uniquely stimulating environments for the emergence and reinforcement of communitas, given their shared history and biological and cultural cohesiveness (Wolin & Bennett, 1984), the ritual's outcome is unpredictable; the hoped-for solidarity sometimes fails to materialize.

In accounts such as Rothchild's, we also see how family rituals reiterate traditional cultural assumptions about what constitutes the "ideal." There is an assumed moral obligation to be with one's family for Passover and other major holidays, and the attempt to substitute friends and emigrees for family only underscores the absence of the real thing. Recently, commentators have criticized the Norman Rockwell image of the family celebration as one that naturalizes traditional gender roles that assume women will carry the burden of planning and preparing (Pleck, 2000, p. 35; see also Laird, 1988). They also note that traditional imagery is out of sync with recent demographic changes such as rising rates of divorce and cohabitation (Gillis, 1996; Pleck, 2000; Stacey, 1990). The ritual experience of many individuals is complicated by the occurrence of multiple celebrations to accomodate their multiple "families" made up of parents, stepparents (or significant others), siblings and stepsiblings (Sutton, 1998). Obliged to take part in multiple Christmases or Thanksgivings on the same day, some people are beginning to question these arrangements, which seem to represent an effort to counteract the vulnerabilities and discontinuities of modern family life—to shore up one institution "when all the others have collapsed around it" (Sutton, 1998).

Reconstructing Family Rituals

Although family celebrations can become hollow expressions of developmental impasse, emerging research and several autobiographical accounts suggest that family rituals also present "naturally-occurring therapeutic opportunities" (Davis, 2000). Here we see how some families have creatively seized the symbolic resources of rituals to negotiate difficult developmental turning points. Davis's (1988) ethnographic study of families planning the bar mitzvahs of their children drew attention to delicate symbolic strategies used by one divorced couple—strategies such as the wording of the invitations to read "The family of Micah Lerner Steinberg invites you to . . ." rather than the specific naming of parents and stepparents, to set a tone of cooperation and family unity.

Intercultural weddings represent another, increasingly common, challenge to the canonical family story. According to Leeds-Hurwitz (2002), the emotional context of intercultural and interracial weddings is often marked by intense family opposition. In these circumstances, some couples decide not to get married; others find creative ways to negotiate their cultural conflicts. Leeds-Hurwitz (2002) conducted detailed case studies in order to examine the ways that couples of different, often complex, racial and ethnic backgrounds crafted ceremonial occasions that combined their disparate traditions into a single ceremony acceptable to both sides. In many cases, the traditional "white wedding" was carefully reworked, blending, in one case, a Catholic church marriage with the traditional Chinese elements of the pig roast and tea ceremony. By "multiplying meanings" (Leeds-Hurwitz, 2002, p. 219)—modifying traditional symbols and, when necessary, inventing new ones—the participants created ceremonial forms that retained deep emotional significance for themselves and for their families.

In addition to major life-cycle ceremonies such as the wedding and the bar mitzvah, cyclical holiday celebrations can be a locus of creative reframing when made to mark distinctions between the family past, present, and future. In a story called, "Passing the Torch," Laura Randolph (1998) describes the first time she cooked Thanksgiving dinner after her mother inexplicably announced that she would no longer be preparing the annual feast. Randolph came to realize that her mother was indirectly sending the message "that the time had come to pass on the family legacy." Randolph's cooking of Thanksgiving dinner became an initiation rite, metaphorically signifying entry into the adult role of "gathering the family together and holding it close." This story speaks to the larger question of how rituals repeated from year to year can nevertheless be "living events" (Werner & Baxter, 1994) whose reinterpretation can enable family members to embrace changing circumstances. The events of the past do not change, but the present in which they are remembered does, making it possible, even likely, that the meanings of the past are under continual revision over the course of a life.

Ronald Grimes (1995, 2000), whose recent work focuses on the psychological and social effects of rituals, is chiefly concerned with the conditions under which rituals "fail" or "succeed." His ritual autobiography is an account of his efforts to reinvigorate in his own life, ways of birthing, wedding, and dying. Grimes proposes innovative rites for many important events such as beginning school, same-sex commitment ceremonies, abortion, serious illness, divorce, and retirement. He combines poetry and dreams in an evocative genre of writing that bridges social and literary forms of academic expression.

Grimes' own wedding script (for his third wedding) reflects his concern with having a wedding that will "wed," that will effect a true and lasting realignment of relationships. The script, which was mailed as an invitation to the guests, includes many sections, including a history of the bride and groom from childhood (to be read by two friends as stand-ins), other readings of Zen parables and Biblical scriptures, poetry, plus instructions for the guests/participants about how to perform their parts in the ceremony, and explanations of how the parts of ritual were devised. There are some traditional elements such as the exchange of rings, an offering, the pronouncement, and the kiss. The following passage from the "offering" section gives insight into the way in which the script communicates directly to the guests to clarify their role as authenticators of the marriage:

> Your offering like ours will be symbolic. The point is to give us something you suspect we will need along the way. We invite you to give it in a miniature, concrete form. We do not need blenders. How about balloons for days we're deflated? We already have plenty of matching towel sets, but we could stand a little more flexibility; a bunch of rubber bands would do. . . . (Grimes, 1995, p. 93)

Grimes' wedding implicitly rejects the idea that life-cycle ceremonies must be opulent or even "elevated" occasions; the script is a patchwork, a "motley assemblage" reflecting his view that effective ritual is playful and that it approximates (and reinforces) the couple's everyday relational dynamics. In Grimes' script, we see the marrying couple "'talk[ing] back' to their own traditions" (Leeds-Hurwitz, 2002, p. 233) in order to achieve a more worthwhile and meaningful ritual practice.

FAMILY STORIES

"The primary mechanism for attaching meaning to experience," writes Brody, "is to tell stories about them" (1987, p. 5). When we remember events that happened to us in our families, usually we recall and tell about the events in the form of stories—who did what to whom, where, when, and why. We describe our experiences in the language of stories (Bruner, 1990). Although we may talk of "sharing our experiences" with other people, it is more accurate to say that we share *stories* of our experiences. The stories we tell are accounts of experience, what Bruner calls "acts of meaning" (Bruner, 1990). When an individual narrates her experience, she selects certain details of the events to include and emphasize, and ignores or omits details of the events that she may have forgotten or considered less important.

Family stories construct, coordinate, interpret, and solidify the meanings individuals attach to family experience (see, for example, Vangelisti, Crumley, & Baker, 1999). As Stone (1988) concluded in her seminal work on family stories, "our meanings are almost always inseparable from stories, in all realms of life" (p. 244). Family life as lived experience may thus be viewed as a process of interpretation through stories. The "stuff" of family stories—what is being transmitted and interpreted—is beliefs, values, desires, and aspirations. The content of stories is not nearly as important as the convictions that these narratives promote. Usually stories have a moral point. They encourage commitment to ways of acting, thinking, feeling, and living (Bochner, 2002). Most families—at least the ones that stay together—develop a corpus of stories that define their history, depict what makes them unique "as a family," establish the principles and values to which they are devoted, and characterize the identities of each family member. Many of these stories are told and retold, again and again, until they sink in. We hear some of them early in childhood "when we're as blank and unresisting as we're ever going to be" (Stone, 1988, p. 10). To a large extent, we "receive" these formative stories passively; they become "our own story," though they are passed on to us by others, usually significant others; often we grow into the stories until they fit as tight and are as unnoticeable as a layer of skin. Eventually, these received stories wield considerable power over us (Parry, 1991), shaping our values and our ways of perceiving—making us who we seem to be. Stone refers to these stories as our "first language" and our most private one. For Laing (1971), they are the means by which one's 'family' is internalized, mapped onto one's body, perceptions, and imagination, the source of one's future projections and meanings.

Langellier and Peterson (1993) appropriately point out, however, that "family stories are not merely 'under our skin' as Stone suggests, they are out there in the world as discursive practices and ways of doing family" (p. 73). Langellier and Peterson's emphasis on the *performative* qualities of family storytelling draws attention to the cultural interests represented by family stories, what Bochner, Ellis, and Tillmann-Healy (1997) discuss under the rubric of *canonical* stories (Bruner, 1990; Yerby, Bochner, & Berkel-Rothfuss, 1995). Family storytelling as narrative performance is subject to the evaluation of others—its audience—and thus must draw on situated narrative conventions and cultural typifications to achieve intelligibility. Narrative conventions endemic to one's culture constrain both how we tell our family stories and what stories we can tell. In particular, narratives that become culturally normative function to legitimate dominant forms of understanding and organizing reality and subsequently operate as a form of social control. Although they compliment Stone for the ways in which her analysis of stories exposes the family as a site of contradictions and social control, Langellier and Peterson believe her analysis overstates agreement on the meaning of family stories, assuming "the monolithic, neo-bourgeois, homogeneous, and privatized family as its norm" (p. 60), while ignoring nonnormative, alternative family forms such as same-sex partners, single-parent structures, and communal arrangements. For Langellier and Peterson, the family is largely a cultural product and the ways in which family stories oppose, oppress, dominate, and control should be a central objective in the analysis of family storytelling. Of course, Stone (1988) was not unaware of the ideological functions of family stories. She recognized that families have a special interest in promoting canonical tales: "The fact is that the family, any family, has a major stake in perpetuating itself, and in order to do so it must unrelentingly push the institutions that preserve it—the institution of marriage especially, but also the institution of heterosexual romantic love, which, if all goes the way the family would have it go, culminates in marriage, children, and enhanced family stability" (p. 50).

CANONICAL STORIES

Canonical stories express the boundaries of acceptable relationship and family practices against which alternative forms and practices are judged. When a person's actions deviate from the canonical story, the person may feel a strong need to explain, justify, excuse, or legitimize these actions (Scott & Lyman, 1968). For example, Riessman (1990) observes that individuals whose marriages end in divorce go to great lengths to explain why they are divorced; the canonical story sets the expectation, after all, that married persons will live "happily ever after," together until death. As Riessmann (1990) notes, however, the divorced person typically feels the need to convince other people that she was right to leave the marriage, because in American culture it is taken for granted that marriage is "a desired and honored state; one cannot walk away from it lightly" (p. 78). On such painful occasions, the work of narrative accounts is not only to provide a meaningful defense and justification of one's actions but also to provide a means for surviving separation and loss (Harvey, Flannery, & Morgan, 1986; Weber, Harvey, & Stanley, 1987; Weiss, 1975). Thus, one's account, told in the *present,* must justify *past* actions in such a way as to meet the challenge of going on to a better and more hopeful *future.* In this sense, family storytellers often struggle to move their lives forward in acts of self-creation that reform and reshape the meaning of the past. These struggles reveal how a family's images and dreams of the future, and thus the future itself, can precede, as much as they follow, the stories of the past they tell. The accounts families formulate, nevertheless, respond to the canonical stories against which they often are measured. Narratives of gay and lesbian families, interracial marriages, single-parent families, families with adopted children, and childless couples, to name a few notable cases, are recognizable examples of family stories lived out against a background of "official" canonical stories that silence, closet, or otherwise marginalize these forms of lived family life (Tillmann-Healy, 2001).

Which family stories typify the ways in which canonical family forms are promoted and reinforced? Stone identifies three genres of stories that appeared repeatedly in the interviews she conducted. The first genre is *the courtship story*. The courtship story reinforces and promotes heterosexual love, romance, and marriage. A story commonly told to children by their parents, the courtship story functions as a creation myth about the origins or roots of one's particular family. According to Stone (1988), it is a love story that details the adventures and perils of romance leading to marriage, often replete with images of a fateful and irrational bond of "love at first sight"; a strong sexual attraction; some opposition, usually familial, to the marriage; and/or some hesitancy on the woman's part that implies a need to be "won over" by her eventual partner. The courtship story functions as the creation myth for a particular family's collective memory. In Stone's depiction, it is a memory passed down to children who were not yet born when it happened, often embracing love's responsiveness to a calling higher than rationality and control, sometimes exaggerating a man's voracious sexual appetite, and suggesting a woman's greater loyalty to family bonds rather than to sexual impulses. For the children, the work of courtship stories is to narrate the meanings of love for men and women, how to know it when you feel it, as well as how to react to it. Overall, courtship stories are uncomplicated versions of the complexities involved in communicating love, for as Henry (1973) keenly observes: "If a man says 'I love you' to a woman, she may wonder whether he means it, whether he loves only her, how much he loves her, whether he will love her next week or next year, or whether this love only means that he wants her to love him. She may even wonder whether his love includes respect and care, or whether his love is merely physical. 'I love you' is surely an ambiguous message" (p. 191).

A second genre of canonical family stories is *the birth story*. These are the family's tales about each child's birth. They often include details about the context of the child's conception, the mother's pregnancy and labor experiences, and the first few weeks or months of a child's life. Long after the events take place, children are told how difficult or easy they were to conceive or deliver, and the events surrounding the birth that made it special. In recent years, families have begun videotaping the birth of their children, memorializing and concretizing the event itself. Often birth stories carve a place for the family's newest addition, defining how a particular child fits into the family's sense of itself and establishing some of the family's hopes and dreams for the child. They also tacitly promote and commemorate childbirth itself. Children become curious about their birth stories as they grow up and, in the absence of such a story, they may begin to wonder how much they were loved or wanted (Yerby, Bochner, & Buerkle-Rothfuss, 1995). Adopted kids, for example, may feel robbed of a birth story and thus search tirelessly for their origins.

A third genre of canonical family stories is *survival stories*. These are socializing stories that prepare children to survive in the world by making them aware of how and where they fit. As Stone (1988) says, "it is the first job of the family, through its stories, to explain to its members where they are positioned socially" (p. 145). Survival stories teach children how to cope in a world that can be dangerous, hostile, and unpredictable. To assimilate and gain some advantage in the world, individuals need to be on alert and circumspect. Survival stories locate the family in a world divided into "haves" and "have-nots" or those who "dish it out" and "those who must take it" (Stone, 1988). Thus, a family's collection of survival stories often center on distinguishing friends from enemies and preparing children emotionally and psychologically to cope with difficult and menacing circumstances. These stories also function to define the family's position in relation to other racial, ethnic, and religious groups. Regrettably, survival stories often keep racial and ethnic bigotry alive by dividing the world into "us" and "them," implicitly reinforcing racial and ethnic stereotypes that promote hatred between groups and allow prejudice to simmer beneath a veneer of friendly relations. Some of our culture's legacy of cherished clichés, such as keeping a stiff upper lip or not crying over spilt milk, are subtly advanced and reinforced in family stories that emphasize toughness, pride, and stamina. Survival stories also teach children the importance of certain values such as integrity, dignity, and self-respect in a world that often is unpredictable and potentially demeaning. Many families repeatedly tell inspirational stories of how they overcame hard times, deprivation, and suffering until the values, tactics, and coping strategies characterized in these stories begin to be taken for granted as the natural course of the world—the way things are meant to be.

Many family stories circulating through culture emphasize personal troubles, life crises, and existential dilemmas (Denzin, 1989). We try to make sense of epiphanies we experience, what Denzin (1993) refers to as "existential turning points," which may include personal traumas such as incest, child abuse, addiction, family violence, teenage pregnancy, abortion, adultery, chronic illness, and unexpected death by telling stories about them to ourselves and to others. Tales about such crises emphasize both the crisis and the recovery. Denzin's perspective, which is similar in emphasis to the critical-cultural orientation of Langellier and Peterson (1993), highlights the ways in which stories of family trauma are embedded in systems of meaning made available or forced upon us by our culture and its textual representations. Drawn from popular forms of communication such as music, television, and film, these personal stories shape the meanings and values we attach not only to family epiphanies but also to the quotidian experiences of romance, love, intimacy, and sexuality.

Portraying humans as voyeurs adrift in a sea of visual and aural symbols, Denzin (1993, 1995) argues that the images and meanings flowing through cinema, television, and music teach us ways of seeing, feeling, talking, and thinking. Thus, we live in a secondhand world of consciousness (Mills, 1963), mediated, commodified, and dispatched by mass communications. Accordingly, stories transmitted by popular culture are received passively and eventually become part of what we take for granted in performing or doing family. On this account, many of the meanings we think we make and live ourselves may actually be chosen for us, not by us. Our dreams and crises are screened for us by the cinematic world through which our consciousness is mediated. In Denzin's terms (1993), "we become storied versions of somebody else's version of who we should be" (p. 5).

But human beings are not as passive as the critical/cultural perspectives of Denzin (1993) and Langellier and Peterson (1993) may unwittingly imply. We are not condemned entirely to live out the stories passed on through cultural productions and family traditions. Often we seek to define ourselves by stories of our own making, stories that conflict with or deviate from the expected, normative, or conventional. Indeed, much of the work of personal narrative and family storytelling involves mitigating the constraints of canonical and cultural conventions. As Bruner (1990) indicates, the power of narrative rests on an ability not only to understand what is culturally canonical but also "to account for deviations that can be incorporated in narrative" (p. 68). Many personal narratives attempt to authorize and/or legitimate marginalized or exceptional experiences. These narratives function as oppositional stories that seek to reform or transform canonical ones. Family development across time is facilitated not by strict compliance of stories to conventions but by the tensions and conflicts between them (Rosenwald, 1992). If our family stories never thwarted or contested received and canonical stories, we would have no expectation of change, no account for conflict, no reason for diversity, no real demand to account for our actions, no sense of agency. We would be locked forever within the walls of normative stories. But we are not.

The cultural production thesis, as important as it is as a model for social justice and civic action, rests too squarely on the assumption of cultural determinism. But stories are underdetermined by narrative conventions. We continually remake and recreate the meanings of our social world despite, or perhaps because of, the power culture brandishes against us. It is precisely the workings of these meaning-centered negotiations between people and cultural productions that is overlooked by an insistence on the imperial control of culture (Sherwood, Smith, & Alexander, 1993). When we examine closely how people articulate and use personal narratives, we see that cultural forces are not sovereign in the realm of human subjectivity (Rosenwald, 1992). Culture may establish the parameters of experience, but it does not fill in the details or permutations. Human beings have a dazzling capacity to conceive optional ways of reforming or reframing the meaning of their actions. As Rosenwald (1992) points out, there is an uncomfortable tension between restless desire and stabilizing conventions. Culture's grip is not unbreakable. Surely, we reap certain rewards by abiding by rules and conventions, but just as surely we may recognize, however momentarily, the potential tyranny and numbing effect of blindly succumbing to them. Regarding family stories, Stone (1988) acknowledges that often we learn that they are ". . . not at all what we wanted, but a burden we either live with uncomfortably or struggle later on to get rid of" (p. 195).

STORIES ON THE MARGINS

Social science research consists of thousands of studies of attraction, courtship, love, marriage, parenting, and family life. Collectively, these studies advance canonical storylines, whether intentionally or not, about the "natural" course of personal relationships. They provide a discourse on personal relationships that may, however unwittingly, pass on the logic of the culture, both the culture of causal social scientists (Shotter, 1987) and the larger interests of the society in which social science is embedded (Gergen, 1982; Lannamann, 1991). In short, social science is itself a kind of canonical discourse on family life that promotes ways of thinking and talking about families and may discourage or ignore alternative depictions and narrative forms.

In recent years, writers committed to encouraging diversity, promoting alternatives, and resisting the domination of canonical stories that may marginalize, silence, and/or suppress alternative ways and forms for doing family have turned to personal narratives of family experience as a vehicle for better understanding and reducing the marginalization and stigma of noncanonical or unconventional forms of family experience (Bochner & Ellis, 1996, 2002; Yerby, 1995; Yerby & Gourd, 1994). The focus on personal narratives includes a wide range of perspectives on narrative inquiry spanning, for example, the critical cultural perspective of writers such as Rosenwald and Ochberg (1992) and Langellier and Peterson (1993) and the autoethnographic and family memoir perspective of Bochner and Ellis (2002; Ellis, 2003; Ellis & Bochner, 1996, 2000). The experiences represented by and/or expressed in these personal narratives, whether analyzed for themes and plotlines or used to evoke empathic identification from readers or audience members, typically focus on family experiences shrouded in secrecy.

Among the abundant examples of stories on the margin are Reissman's (1992) analysis of the personal narrative of Tessa, a 23-year-old white woman who justifies her decision to divorce her husband on the grounds of marital rape; Walkover's (1992) discussion of the interviews she conducted with 15 couples who had been unable to conceive; Ellis and Bochner's (1992) co-constructed narrative of their own struggle to make a decision about an unexpected pregnancy, and the pain, confusion, and uncertainty they felt as they exercised their freedom to choose; Fox's (1996) subversive reading of child sex abuse in which she interjects her own voice as a child sex-abuse survivor and researcher between the accounts of an offender and a survivor in order to complexify the canonical version of sex abuse that typically denies the possibility of children's agency and sexuality; Ronai's (1996) layered account of what it felt like to grow up as a child of a mentally retarded mother, showing the oppressions of pathologizing discourses and using the resources of memory and story to sort through her lingering ambivalence between a desire to love a stigmatized mother and the anger and frustration characteristic of the patterns that connect them; Tillmann-Healy's (2001) reflexive narrative ethnography of the connections between a community of gay men and her own relationship with her husband, in which she explores the complexities of deep friendships between gays and straights, problematizing definitions of what it means to be "family," and questioning norms of relationship research that inhibit friendships between researchers and participants; Jago's (1996) *reconstructed narrative* in which she actively revises the story she had inherited about "a family that does not exist," 30 years after her father disappeared one day when she was 8 years old, in order to begin to trust the choices she makes in her own relationships; Swado's *memoir* of a talented family driven apart by an incapacity to cope with personal tragedy, in which her perspective on the meanings of the past shifts as she looks at events from the point of view of each member of the family; Kiesinger's (2002) *therapeutic narrative* in which she revises the meanings of her father's abusive behavior, transforming and healing her relationship to her father by situating his rage in the broader context of the story of *his* life; and Pelias'(2002) ethnodrama of the emotional complexities and lived memories between a father and a son, an ongoing story of attachment and loss with no catharsis, no resolution, no curtain call.

These stories on the margins call our attention to family experiences that, on the whole, have not received the attention they deserve—marital rape, childlessness, unexpected pregnancies; childhood agency and sexuality; pathologizing family discourses; women who grow up in families without fathers; a family's capacity to absorb tragedy without unraveling; the self-hatred produced in survivors of family violence; the consequences of isolation and connection between gay and straight families; the search for connection to parents in later life; and our obsession for resolution and catharsis in the face of patterns that are difficult to break. These are not experiences that are easily accessible. Clearly, they do not fit comfortably within the realm of predictable human events. On the contrary, many of these stories open our eyes to an infinite unpredictability in lived family experience. They urge us, if we listen to them, to make room for variance, competing moral claims, difficult decisions, blows of fate, perverse realities, and human differences. They challenge us continually to question our assumptions about what is normal , natural, and functional, and they teach us that what is out of sight is not necessarily out of (everyone's) mind. They also show that no matter how hidden they are from view by our compulsion to concentrate on the predictable and canonical, families routinely breach conventions and expectations, cope with exceptional and transformative crises, invent new ways of acting and speaking when old or traditional ways fail them, and are stunningly adept at making the absurd sensible and the disastrous manageable.

EVOCATIVE FAMILY STORIES

Many of the stories on the margins to which we referred in the previous section fall under the rubric of what Ellis and Bochner (2000) call *evocative narratives*. These stories, often written by family and relationship researchers, break away from the traditional forms of social science reporting. Denzin (1997) refers to evocative narratives as a form of "ethnographic poetics." He emphasizes the need to set off this form of research storytelling from traditional empiricist approaches to the analysis of narratives. Following Trinh (1992, p. 141), Denzin opposes the inclination to turn a story told into a story analyzed because, in effect, the meaning of the story is sacrificed at the altar of methodological rigor, and what is lost is what makes the story a story. "They only hear and read the story from within a set of predetermined structural categories. They do not hear the story as it was told" (Denzin, p. 249).

Evocative narratives breach many of the norms of writing and research associated with orthodox social science. They do not seek to predict and control but rather to activate the subjectivity of readers and compel their emotional responses. They are stories that long to be used rather than analyzed; told and retold rather than theorized and settled; carry conversation about family experience further rather than claiming unrivaled truths. As an intimate form of communication that focuses on personal and emotional details of family interaction, evocative stories encourage family researchers to expand their sense of what they want their research to do, the forms available to them for expressing family experience, and the divisions social scientists conventionally accept and enforce that separate literature from social science.

To give a better sense of the kind of stories we have in mind, we have chosen one exemplar of evocative family storytelling to consider in greater detail, Linda Gray Sexton's (1994) family story, *Searching for Mercy Street,* in which she tells the riveting story of her troubled relationship with her mother, the poet Anne Sexton, who committed suicide in 1974 at the age of 45. Linda begins with the event that defined both her childhood and Anne's motherhood—being sent away for 2 years to live in the home of relatives while her mother recuperated from a psychotic episode. Expressing complex feelings of abandonment and confusion, isolation and yearning, and disgust and admiration, Linda describes her lifelong struggle to free herself from the grip of her powerful, dependent mother without relinquishing the love and empathy she felt for her. She recounts details of her mother's extramarital affairs with women and with men, her sexual abuse of her children, her cruelty toward her husband, and her disturbed reversal of the mother–child bond. Accounting for her mother's destructive behavior as "the price and reward of madness . . . and . . . genius" (p. 276), Linda refuses to demonize her mother as a monster or exempt her as a victim; nor is she willing to oversimplify her complicated feelings of love and rage:

> I loved my mother when she was alive; I love her still—despite anger, despite her mental illness and the things it allowed her to do. I never wanted her to seem like "a monster" to anyone. She was loving and kind, but she was also sick and destructive. She tried to be "a good mother," but in truth, she was not. Mother was simply human, subject to all sorts of frailties and problems. (Sexton, 1994, p. 281)

Linda Sexton challenges her readers to question the usefulness of applying simplistic labels such as "abused child" or "vengeful daughter" to summarize terribly complicated family relationships. Her narrative is a graceful exposition of the concrete lived circumstances within which a person struggles to deal with the dialectics of attachment/loss, separation/integration, vulnerability/cruelty, and expression/protection. Moreover, *Searching for Mercy Street* is uniquely self-reflexive. The text bends back on itself and its author puts words to her memories in order to mourn her losses and to better understand the meaning of a rich and agitated bond between daughter and mother. As her mother once said, "I write to master experience," so Linda writes to "take control of the demons inside and let them know who was boss"—to earn "the reward of a mind clearer for the effort, a soul cleansed and released" (p. 296). Inevitably her insistence on telling the whole painful truth as she remembers it leads her to confront not only the demons of a disturbed relationship but also the taboos that silence writing from the heart:

> Though I am no longer a child, to write of these things feels forbidden, to give voice to memories such as these, taboo. Family matters: dark and secret. I remember the snake who comes in the dark, the taste of fear sour in my mouth, the blackness of a bedroom not my own, and worst of all the voice whispering: If you tell they will not love you anymore. If you tell they will send you away again. (Sexton, 1994, p. 21)

Searching For Mercy Street is an exemplar of the kind of narrative inquiry that fuses social science and literature, in which the language of science merges with the aesthetics of art (Benson, 1993, p. xi). The products of what Ivan Brady (1991) called "artful science" are narratives that simulate reality, applying the imaginative power of literary, dramatic, and poetic forms to create the effect of reality, a convincing likeness to life as it is sensed, felt, and lived.

We highlight five distinguishing features of this type of inquiry, that is, evocative family storytelling. First, the author usually writes in the first person, making herself or himself the object of research (Tedlock, 1991), thus transgressing the conventional separation of researcher and subject (Jackson, 1989). Second, the narrative breaches the traditional focus on generalization across cases by focusing on generalization within a single case extended over time (Geertz, 1973). Third, the text is presented as a story replete with a narrator, characterization, and plot line, akin to forms of writing associated with the novel or biography, thus fracturing the boundaries that traditionally separate social science from literature. Fourth, the story discloses hidden details of private life and highlights emotional experience, thus challenging the rational actor model of social performance that dominates social science. And fifth, the ebb and flow of relationship experience are depicted in an episodic form that dramatizes the motion of connected lives across the curve of time (Weinstein, 1988), thus resisting the standard practice of portraying a relationship as a snapshot (Ellis, 1993).

Each of these features is present in Sexton's *Searching For Mercy Street*. Linda Sexton writes her story as a first-person account in which she is both the narrator and the main character. She observes and interprets the meanings of her own actions as well as those of her mother and other family members. Thus, she acts as both a researcher *and* a subject.

Second, Linda's story covers events that took place in her family over a period of nearly 40 years. She does not try to extend the meanings and conclusions she draws about her family to other families, though readers certainly can locate some of their own experience within that of the Sextons. Rather she focuses on the patterns of interaction that recurred over time within the case of her particular family (across the span of 3 generations). In the process, she shows how reality was constituted in this family culture, within this time frame, and at this place.

Third, Linda presents her family history as a story. She uses many of the storytelling techniques associated with fiction to animate the drama of her experience and to heighten interest in the story. But she relies on a core of empirical "facts" that give her story credibility as a "true" account. As a reader, you are aware that Linda Sexton is negotiating the meaning of these events as she goes along, using what Bruner (1990) calls the "shadowy epistemology of the story" (p. 54) to try on different interpretations. She keeps you open to the multiple and uncertain meanings of a good story. Thus, her narrative falls *between* fiction and fact, *between* the imaginary and the real. As John Berger (1983) observes that "life outstrips our vocabulary" (p. 77), so Linda Sexton (1994) recognizes the complex connection between words and reality: "Words can capture truth or promulgate lies. Words can clarify or disguise . . . what I seek is only the truth of how I *felt,* a truth far more revelatory *about me* than any exact history" (p. 39).

Fourth, by articulating her feelings within the intelligible frame of family relationships, one that centers on painful, hidden family secrets, Linda openly confronts the moral predicament of what constitutes a good life *for her*. She has to come to grips with what really matters—her children, her husband, her career as a writer—and what she gives to and takes from other people. Thus, by making sense of her past she clears a path for her future.

Finally, the story of life in the Sexton family is revealed in concrete episodes of inter-action. Linda recreates scenes from her history in which the members of her family enact the patterns that bind them. Readers witness family members interacting with each other, feel their moods, and sense their entrapment. These scenes include both the common-place of everyday life—cooking, cleaning, transporting, and celebrating holidays—and the exceptional events that characterized the family's particularity—sexual abuse, family violence, corruption of normal family roles. We learn that the Sextons are like most families much of the time, but they also endure extreme episodes of deviance and disturbance. If we witnessed only one or two of these episodes, our capacity to grasp the larger configuration of imbalance between ordinary and extraordinary events would be greatly inhibited.

EPILOGUE

As narrative performances, rituals and stories show us families in the process of producing meanings and values. Ordinarily, families feel a pressure to sustain continuity, promote shared meanings and values, and keep memories alive over time. Insofar as rituals and stories are responsive to these functional requirements of family life, they may be seen as a primary medium through which family culture is conserved. Imbued with imagination and feeling, stories and rituals nevertheless play a regulative role, teaching moral lessons, reinforcing political, religious, and ethnic identifications, giving a sense of history, and building expectations for the future. As visible symbolic productions, they give us a glimpse of who we imagine ourselves to be and what we think we can become.

But stories and rituals are not exclusively conservative. They can also function as protean narratives that resist, innovate, and/or alter family traditions. As products of the human imagination, stories and rituals are continually subject to resistance, revision, and change. By focusing on the process of story making and ritual creation, scholars of communication in the family can gain access to reality in the process of creation and to the crucial role communication plays in the process. We are only beginning to understand how families not only conserve but also transform themselves, how they set boundaries but also facilitate change and growth, how they not only narrow possibilities for experience but also open opportunities for expanded meaning. Much like the experience of change in families over time, communication research on families undoubtedly needs to conserve a respect for the history and traditions of our past while encouraging and promoting adventurous and risky inquiry that may change the face of how we understand the work to which we are committed.

REFERENCES

Aldous, J. (1978). *Family careers: Developmental change in the family.* New York: Wiley.

Bateson, M. C. (1990). *Composing a life.* New York: Plume.

Bauman, R. (1986). *Story, performance, event.* Cambridge: Cambridge University Press.

Baxter, L., & Braithwaite, D. (2002). Performing marriage: Marriage renewal rituals as cultural performance. *Southern Communication Journal, 67,* 2, 94–109.

Benson, P. (Ed.). (1993). *Anthropology and literature.* Urbana: University of Illinois Press.

Berger, J. (1983). *Once in Europa.* New York: Pantheon.

Bochner, A. P. (1994). Perspectives on inquiry II: Theories and stories. In M. L. Knapp & G. R. Miller (Eds.), *Handbook of interpersonal communication* (2nd ed. pp. 21–41). Thousand Oaks, CA: Sage.

Bochner, A. P. (2000). Criteria against ourselves. *Qualitative Inquiry, 6*, 266–272

Bochner, A. P. (2002). Perspectives on inquiry. III: The moral of stories. In M. Knapp & J. Daly (Eds.), *Handbook of interpersonal communication* (3rd ed., pp. 73–101). Thousand Oaks, CA: Sage.

Bochner, A. P. & Ellis, C. (1996). Talking over ethnography. In C. Ellis & A. P. Bochner (Eds.), *Composing ethnography: Alternative forms of qualitative writing* (pp. 13–45). Walnut Creek, CA: AltaMira Press.

Bochner, A. P., & Ellis, C. (2002). *Ethnographically speaking. Autoethnography, literature, and aesthetics.* Walnut Creek, CA: AltaMira Press.

Bochner, A. P., Ellis, C., & Tillmann-Healy, L. (1997). Relationships as stories. In S. Duck (Ed.), *Handbook of personal relationships: Theory, research and interventions* (2nd ed., pp. 307–324). New York: John Wiley.

Bossard, J., & Boll, E. (1950). *Ritual in family living.* Philadelphia: University of Pennsylvania Press.

Brady, I. (Ed.). (1991). *Anthropological poetics.* Savage, MD: Rowman & Littlefield.

Brody, H. (1987). *Stories of sickness.* New Haven: Yale University Press.

Bruner, J. (1990). *Acts of meaning.* Cambridge, MA: Harvard University Press.

Carr, D. (1986). *Time, narrative and history.* Bloomington: Indiana University Press.

Carter, B., & McGoldrick, M. (Eds.). (1999). *The expanded family life cycle: Individual family and social perspectives.* Boston: Allyn & Bacon.

Crites, S. (1971). The narrative quality of experience. *Journal of the American Academy of Religion, 39*, 291–311.

Crites, S. (1986). Storytime: Recollecting the past and projecting the future. In T. Sarbin (Ed.), *Narrative psychology: The storied nature of human conduct* (pp. 152–173). New York: Praeger.

Daly, K. (1996). *Families and time: Keeping pace in a hurried culture.* Thousand Oaks, CA: Sage.

Davis, J. (1988). Mazel Tov: The Bar Mitzvah as a multigenerational ritual of change and continuity. In E. Imber-Black, J. Roberts, & R. Whiting (Eds.), *Rituals in families and family therapy* (pp. 177–210). New York: Norton.

Davis, J. (2000). Ritual as therapy, therapy as ritual. *Journal of Feminist Family Therapy, 11*, (4), 115–130.

Demos, J. (1979). Images of the American family, then and now. In V. Tufte & B. Myerhoff (Eds.), *Changing images of the family* (pp. 43–60). New Haven, CT: Yale University Press.

Denzin, N. K. (1989). *Interpretive biography.* Newbury Park, CA: Sage.

Denzin, N. K. (1993). *Narrative's phenomena.* Paper presented at Midwest Sociological Society, Chicago.

Denzin, N. K. (1995). *The cinematic society: The voyeur's gaze.* London: Sage.

Durkheim, E. (1915). *The elementary forms of religious life.* New York: The Free Press.

Ellis, C. (in press). *The ethnographic I: An autoethnographic novel.* Walnut Creek, CA.

Ellis, C., & Bochner, A. P. (1992). Telling and performing personal stories: The constraints of choice in abortion. In C. Ellis & M. Flaherty (Eds.), *Investigating subjectivity* (pp. 79–101). Thousand Oaks, CA: Sage.

Ellis, C., & Bochner, A. P. (1996). *Composing ethnography.* Walnut Creek, CA: AltaMira Press.

Ellis, C., & Bochner, A. P. (2000). Autoethnography, personal narrative, reflexivity: Researcher as subject. In N. K. Denzin & Y. Lincoln (Eds.), *The handbook of qualitative research* (pp. 733–768). Thousand Oaks, CA: Sage.

Falicov, C. (1988). Family transitions: *Continuity and change over the life cycle.* New York: Guilford Press.

Fiese, B., Sameroff, A., & Grotevant, H. (1999). *The stories that families tell: Narrative coherence, narrative interaction, and relationship beliefs.* Maldon, MA: Blackwell.

Fox, K. (1996). Silent voices: A subversive reading of child sex abuse. In C. Ellis & A. Bochner (Eds.), *Composing ethnography: Alternative forms of qualitative writing* (pp. 330–356). Walnut Creek, CA: AltaMira Press.

Frank, A. (1995). *The wounded storyteller: Body, illness, and ethics.* Chicago: University of Chicago Press.

Geertz, C. (1973). *The interpretation of cultures.* New York: Basic Books.

Gergen, K. (1982). *Towards transformation in social knowledge.* New York: Springer-Verlag.

Gillis, J. (1996). *A world of their own making: Myth, ritual and the quest for family values.* Cambridge, MA: Harvard University Press.

Gillis, J. (2000). Our virtual families: Toward a cultural understanding of modern family life (Working Paper 002-00). The Emory Center for Myth and Ritual in American Life. http://www.emory.edu/COLLEGE/MARIAL/research/index.html

Goffman, I. (1967). *Interaction ritual: Essays on face-to-face behavior.* New York: Doubleday.

Grimes, R. (1995). *Marrying and burying: Rites of passage in a man's life.* Boulder, CO: Westview Press.

Grimes, R. (2000). *Deeply into the bone: Reinventing rites of passage.* Berkeley: University of California Press.

Harvey, J. H., Flannery, R., & Morgan, M. (1986). Vivid memories of vivid loves gone by. *Journal of Social and Personal Relationships, 3*, 359–373.

Henry, J. (1973). *Pathways to madness.* Vintage Books: New York.

Imber-Black, E., Roberts, J., & Whiting, R. (1988). *Rituals in families and family therapy.* New York: Norton.

Jackson, M. (1989). *Paths toward a clearing: Radical empiricism and ethnographic inquiry.* Bloomington: Indiana University Press.

Jago, B. (1996). Postcards, ghosts, and fathers: Revising family stories. *Qualitative Inquiry, 2*, 495–516.

Kiesinger, C. E. (2002). My father's shoes: The therapeutic value of narrative reframing. In A. P. Bochner & C. Ellis (Eds.), *Ethnographically speaking: Autoethnography, literature, and aesthetics* (pp. 95–114). Walnut Creek, CA: AltaMira Press.

Kohli, M. (1986). The world we forgot: A historical review of the life course. In V. Marshall (Ed.), *Later life: The social psychology of aging* (pp. 271–303). Beverly Hills, CA: Sage.

Kotre, J., & Hall, E. (1997). *The seasons of life: The dramatic journey from birth to death.* Ann Arbor: The University of Michigan Press.

Laing, R. (1971). *The politics of the family.* New York: Vintage Books.

Laird, J. (1988). Women and ritual in therapy. In E. Imber-Black, J. Roberts, & R. Whiting (Eds.), *Rituals in families and family therapy* (pp. 331–362). New York: Norton.

Langellier, K. M., & Peterson, E. (1993). Family storytelling as a strategy of social control. In D. Mumby (Ed.), *Narrative and social control: Critical perspectives* (pp. 49–76). Newbury Park, CA: Saga.

Lannamann, J. (1991). Interpersonal communication research as ideological practice. *Communication Theory, 1*, 179–203.

Leeds-Hurwitz, W. (2002). *Wedding as text: Communicating cultural identities through ritual.* Mahwah, NJ: Lawrence Erlbaum Associates.

Liddle, H. (Ed.). (1983). *Clinical implications of the family life cycle.* Rockville: Aspen Systems.

Mandelbaum, J. (1987). Couples sharing stories. *Communication Quarterly, 35*, 144–170.

McLain, R. & Weigert, A. (1979). Toward a phenomenological sociology of family: A programmatic essay. In W. R. Burr, R. Hill, F. I. Nye & I. Reiss (Eds.), *Contemporary theories about the family, vol. II.* (pp. 160–205). New York: The Free Press.

Mills, C. (1963). *Power, politics and people: The collected essays of C. Wright Mills.* I. Horowitz (Ed.), New York: Ballantine.

Moore, S. & Myerhoff, B. (1977). (Eds.) *Secular ritual.* Assen, The Netherlands: Royal Van Gorcum Press.

Moss, M. S. & Moss, S. (1988). Reunion between elderly parents and their distant children. *American Behavioral Scientist, 31*, pp. 654–668.

Myerhoff, B. (1977). We don't wrap herring in a printed page: Fusion, fictions and continuity in secular ritual. In S. F. Moore & B. G. Myerhoff (Eds.), *Secular ritual* (pp. 199–224). Assen and Amsterdam: Van Gorcum.

Myerhoff, B. (1978). *Number our days.* New York: Simon & Schuster.

Myerhoff, B. (1995). A death in due time: conviction, order and continuity in ritual drama. In B. Myerhoff (Ed.), *Remembered lives: The work of ritual, storytelling and growing older* (pp. 159–190). Ann Arbor: University of Michigan Press.

Myerhoff, B. & Tufte, V. (1979). Introduction. In V. Tufte & B. Myerhoff (Eds.), *Changing images of the family* (pp. 1–25). New Haven, CT: Yale University Press.

Nydegger, C., & Mitteness, L. (1988). Etiquette and ritual in family conversation. *American Behavioral Scientist, 31*, 702–716.

Orbuch, T., Veroff, J., & Holmberg, D. (1993). Becoming a married couple: The emergence of meaning in the first years of marriage. *Journal of Marriage and the Family, 45*, 141–151.

Parry, A. (1991). *A universe of stories. Family Process, 30*, 37–54.

Pelias, R. (2002). For father and son: An ethnodrama with no catharsis. In A.P. Bochner & C. Ellis (Eds.)., *Ethnographically speaking: Autoethnography, literature and aesthetics* (pp. 35–43). Walnut Creek, CA: AltaMira Press.

Pleck, E. (2000). *Celebrating the family: Ethnicity, consumer culture and family rituals.* Cambridge, MA: Harvard University Press.

Randolph, L. (1998). The torch. *Ebony, 54*, 1, 30.

Reiss, D. (1989). The represented and practicing family: Contrasting visions of family continuity. In A. Sameroff & R. Emde (Eds.), *Relationship disturbances in early childhood: A developmental approach* (pp. 191–220). New York: Basic Books.

Riessman, C. (1990). *Divorce talk: Women and men make sense of personal relationships.* New Brunswick, NJ: Rutgers University Press.

Riessman, C. K. (1992). Making sense of marital violence: One woman's narrative. In G. Rosenwald & R. Ochberg (Eds.), *Storied lives: The cultural politics of self-understanding* (pp. 231–249). New Haven, CT: Yale University Press.

Roberts, J. (1988). Setting the frame: Definition, functions, and typology of rituals. In. E. Imber-Black (Ed.), *Rituals in families and family therapy* (pp. 3–46). New York: W. W. Norton.

Ronai, C. R. (1996). My mother is mentally retarded. In C. Ellis & A. P. Bochner (Eds.), *Composing ethnography: Alternative forms of qualitative writing* (pp. 109–31). Walnut Creek, CA: AltaMira Press.

Rorty, R. (1989). *Contingency, irony, solidarity.* Cambridge: Cambridge University Press.

Rosenwald, G. (1992). Conclusion: Reflections on narrative understanding. In G. Rosenwald & R. Ochberg (Eds.), *Storied Lives: The cultural politics of self-understanding* (pp. 265–289). New Haven, CT: Yale University Press.

Rosenwald, G. C., & Ochberg, R. L. (Eds.). (1992). *Storied lives: The cultural politics of self-understanding.* New Haven, CT: Yale University Press.

Rothchild, S. *Family stories for every generation.* (1989). Detroit: Wayne State University Press.

Schechtman, M. (1996). *The constitution of selves.* Ithaca: Cornell University Press.

Schieffelin, E. (1998). Problematizing performance. In F. Hughes-Freeland (Ed.), *Ritual, performance, media* (pp. 194–207). London: Routledge.

Scott, M., & Lyman, S. (1968). Accounts. *American Sociological Review, 33,* 46–62.

Sexton, L. G. (1994). *Searching for Mercy Street: My journey back to my mother, Anne Sexton.* Boston: Little, Brown and Company.

Sherwood, S., Smith, P., & Alexander, J. (1993). The British are coming . . . again! The hidden agenda of "cultural studies." *Cultural Studies, 22,* 370–375.

Shotter, J. (1987). The social construction of an "us": Problems of accountability and narratology. In R. Burnett, P. McGee, & D. Clarke (Eds.), *Accounting for relationships: Explanation, representation, and knowledge* (pp. 225–247). London: Metheun.

Slater, S. (1995). *The lesbian family life cycle.* New York: The Free Press.

Stacey, J. (1990). *Brave new families: Stories of domestic upheaval in late twentieth century America.* New York: Basic Books.

Steier, F. (1991). Introduction: Research as self-reflexivity, self-reflexivity as social process. In F. Steier (Ed.), *Research and reflexivity* (pp. 1–11). London: Sage.

Stone, E. (1988). *Black sheep and kissing cousins: How our family stories shape us.* New York: Penguin Books.

Sutton, H. (1998). A dysfunctional family feast. *New Statesman, 127*(4416), 47–48.

Swados, E. (1991). *The four of us: A family memoir.* New York: Farrar, Straus & Giroux.

Tedlock, B. (1991). From participant observation to the observation of participation: The emergence of narrative ethnography. *Journal of Anthropological Research, 41,* 69–94.

Tillmann-Healy, L. (2001). *Between gay and straight: Understanding friendship across sexual orientation.* Walnut Creek, CA: AltaMira.

Trinh, T. M. (1992). *Framer framed.* New York: Routledge.

Turner, V. (1967). *The forest of symbols: Aspects of Ndembu ritual.* Ithaca: Cornell University Press.

Vangelisti, A., Crumley, L., & Baker, J. (1999). Family portraits: Stories as standards for family relationships. *Journal of Social and Personal Relationships, 16,* 335–368.

Walkover, B. C. (1992). The family as an overwrought object of desire. In G. C. Rosenwald & R. L. Ochberg (Eds.), *Storied lives: The cultural politics of self-understanding* (pp. 178–191). New Haven, CT: Yale University Press.

Waskow, A. (1970). *The new freedom seder: A new Haggadah for Passover.* New York: Henry Holt.

Weber, A. L., Harvey, J. H., & Stanley, M. (1987). The nature and motivations of accounts for failed relationships. In R. Burnett, P. McGhee, and D. Clarke (Eds.), *Accounting for relationships* (pp. 114–135). London: Methuen.

Weinstein, A. (1988). *The fiction of relationship.* Princeton, NJ: Princeton University Press.

Weiss, R. (1975). *Marital separation.* New York: Basic Books.

Werner, C. M., & Baxter, L. (1994). Temporal qualities of relationships: Organismic, transactional and dialectical views. In M. Knapp & G. R. Miller (Eds.), *Handbook of interpersonal communication* (2nd ed., pp. 323–379). Newbury Park, CA: Sage.

Winnicott, D. W. (1965). *The family and individual development.* London: Tavistock.

Wolin, S., & Bennett, L. (1984). Family rituals. *Family Process, 23,* 401–420.

Yerby, J. (1995). Family systems theory reconsidered: Integrating social construction theory and dialectical process. *Communication Theory, 5,* 339–365.

Yerby, J., Buerkel-Rothfuss, N., & Bochner, A. (1995). *Understanding family communication,* 2nd ed. Scottsdale, AZ: Gorsuch Scarisbrick.

Yerby, J., & Gourd, W. (1994). *Our marriage/their marriage: Performing reflexive fieldwork.* Paper presented at the annual Gregory P. and Gladys Stone Society for the Study of Symbolic Interaction Symposium at the University of Illinois, Urbana-Champaign.

VI

COMMUNICATION AND CONTEMPORARY
FAMILY ISSUES

24

Discourses on Diapers and Dirty Laundry: Family Communication About Child Care and Housework

Maureen Perry-Jenkins, Courtney P. Pierce,
and Abbie E. Goldberg
The University of Massachusetts-Amherst

The goal of this chapter is to merge two important substantive areas in the scholarship on families, namely, the literature on the division of family work and the literature on family communication. Although these topics have been the subject of considerable theorizing and research in their own right, few attempts have been made to explore the intersection of these two fields of inquiry. In light of the dramatic demographic shifts that have occurred over the past few decades, namely, the increase in women's employment and the concomitant rise in dual-earner families (Perry-Jenkins, Repetti, & Crouter, 2000), the ways in which family members divide up and negotiate family work have become hotly contested terrain in families. Thus, the question of how family members confer and create their new roles and responsibilities has taken on new importance for family scholars. One aim of this chapter is to examine key areas of overlap between the communication and family work literatures with the purpose of demonstrating how the combined expertise from these two areas can further our understanding of how families cope with work–family challenges. We also propose some new directions for future inquiry into how families communicate about family work as well as discuss the potential implications of this process for marital and parent–child relations.

Perhaps an example best exemplifies the complex nature of how family communication styles and the division of family work are played out almost daily in families' lives. In our research with couples who have just experienced the transition to parenthood followed soon thereafter with an early return to full-time employment, communication, or lack thereof, about household and child care chores continually arises as a salient issue for couples. Consider the case of Tina and Scott Meyer, a young couple who have just had their first child, Jacob. Tina took a 12-week unpaid family leave after Jacob's birth and then resumed her full-time job working in a candle-making factory. Her husband, Scott, also works full time as an auto mechanic. Tina's aunt and mother share the child care responsibilities for Jacob, while Tina and Scott work. Tina and Scott both report that Tina performs the majority of child care and household tasks. In an interview, Tina explains that Scott knows she is angry about the division of labor: "We fight about it frequently, but eventually you get tired of fighting and just do it yourself. He talks a good story but doesn't follow through." Tina indicates that in many other ways Scott is a great husband and father, but nonetheless she is frustrated and angry about his lack of participation in family work.

Tina and Scott's story is not unique. Much research documents the inequity in family work based on gender; however, far less research explores how couples communicate about and negotiate family chores. As Tina indicates, she and her husband do talk about the issue; however, Scott doesn't seem to follow through. Important questions arise as to what factors influence the ways in which couples negotiate and decide on the division of family tasks. How do couples' communication and negotiation styles vary as a function of the topic being discussed? For instance, if one partner is less invested in the outcomes surrounding the division of household work, how is the communication process affected? Moreover, how is the negotiation of family work affected by other factors, such as spouses' relative resources (e.g., income, education), their gender ideology, or their race/ethnicity?

Marital communication is one of the most contentious and frequently complained about issues in distressed marriages (Walsh, Baucom, Tyler, & Sayers, 1993). The division of household labor ranks third among topics most argued about in marital relationships (Davidson & Moore, 1992). Thus, it follows that the interaction between these two key aspects of marital life would hold important implications for relationship quality. Furthermore, looking beyond the marital dyad, what roles do children play in the negotiation and performance of household chores? The literature on parent–child communication also highlights the importance of effective communication for the quality of parent–child relations, although the question of how children's involvement in household labor affects or is shaped by these communication patterns is a topic ripe for investigation. This chapter first reviews key themes and issues in the current research on household labor and in the areas of marital and parent–child communication. Second, we explore important substantive and methodological issues that arise when examining linkages between family communication and household labor. In addition, the importance of applying an ecological perspective to the topic of family work and communication is highlighted. Race, ethnicity, social class, gender, and family structure are important factors that not only give rise to different meanings regarding communication and household labor but may also moderate the ways these two areas are related to each other. Finally, a life course perspective challenges us to consider these issues in their historical and social context as well as attend to family and individual time and life stages as they influence the importance of family work and communication

MARRIAGE AND MARITAL INTERACTION

The Division of Household Labor

The maintenance of family life through the chores of daily living, such as making meals, providing shelter, caring for children, and clothing family members is an activity at the core of family existence. Nevertheless, the importance and value of household labor has consistently been viewed as a less serious and worthy area of inquiry than the topic of paid work in the formal economy. In Coltrane's (2000) decade review of the research on household labor, he contends that, "housework can not be understood without realizing how it is related to gender, household structure, family interaction, and the operation of both formal and informal market economies" (p. 1209). For the purposes of this discussion, attention to the key terms of gender, family interaction, and housework will be critical, especially with regard to how gender and communication patterns shape not only how family chores are distributed but also the meaning and value given to the division of family work. Although an exhaustive review of the literature on household labor is beyond the purview of this chapter, those interested in a more thorough analysis should consult Coltrane's (2000) decade review on household labor as well as more classic works by Bernard (1972), Blood and Wolfe (1960), and Oakley (1974). In addition, a number of important works present critical analyses of the housework literature (Osmond & Thorne, 1993; Thompson & Walker, 1989).

In general, household labor has most often been conceptualized as unpaid work performed within the home to maintain family functioning (Coltrane, 2000; Shelton & John, 1996). A number of scholars, however, have critiqued this definition as overlooking the less visible types of family work such as household management and emotional labor (Feree, 1990, Seery & Crowley, 2000, Thomspon & Walker, 1989). There have also been inconsistencies with regard to what tasks are included in definitions of household labor. For example, oftentimes distinctions between household chores and child care tasks are not made and these activities are subsumed under the rubric of "family work," despite research that suggests the meaning and value given to child-focused chores vary markedly from household tasks (Kessler & McRae, 1982; Steil, 1997). Many studies distinguish between tasks that need to be completed on a regular basis and are thus viewed as less optional, such as cleaning, shopping, preparing meals, washing dishes, and laundry, versus those chores that are less repetitive such as household repairs, yard work, and paying bills. Despite the variability in labels and categories, a consistent finding in the household work literature is that the most significant predictor of the distribution of household chores is gender: "the average married woman does about three times as much routine housework as the average married man (32 vs. 10 hours per week)" (Coltrane, 2000, p. 1210). It should be noted that there has been a change in men's and women's *relative contribution* to household labor, especially for employed women. Specifically, Robinson and Godbey (1997) found that women are doing less housework than they used to and men are doing somewhat more; thus, the proportion of chores performed by men has increased.

The distinction between amount of chores performed by partners and the relative proportion of chores performed between partners is an important one and has been linked differentially to mental health and marital outcomes. Glass and Fujimoto (1994) found that, for both husbands and wives, the more time they spent in housework, the more depressed they were, with actual hours of housework having stronger effects than proportionate measures. Other studies have found that more important than the actual number of hours that wives spend on housework is their proportional contribution to household chores. For example, Bird (1999) found that inequity in the division of household labor had a greater impact on wives' psychological distress than did the amount of household labor.

Finally, research also indicates that it is not just how much housework husbands perform that matters, in terms of women's mental health, but the actual type of help that she is receiving. For example, several studies have indicated that women are more likely to be looking for assistance from their husbands with traditionally "female" rather than "male" tasks (Benin & Agostinelli, 1988; Blair & Johnson, 1992; Dempsey, 1997). Other studies have found that performing larger amounts of traditionally "female" tasks is associated with more depression in women, and sometimes in men (Barnett & Shen, 1997; Glass & Fujimoto, 1994; Golding, 1990).

One of the most baffling but consistent findings in the division of labor literature is that although dual-earner wives perform two to three times more household labor than their husbands, less than one third of these women report the allocation of tasks to be unfair (Blair & Johnson, 1992; Demo & Acock, 1993; Hawkins, Marshall, & Allen, 1998; Thompson, 1991). In fact, a number of scholars have argued that the lack of success in adequately predicting the division of family work using traditional economic, exchange, or role theories is due to the lack of attention that had been paid to the meaning and symbolic value men and women give to their household chores (Coltrane, 2000; Sanchez & Kane, 1996; Thompson, 1991). It is at this juncture that the linkage between family work and family communication becomes most critical. We propose that the meaning and value that men and women assign to their household chores heavily influences the ways in which they negotiate and interact around these topics. Returning to Tina and Scott, the couple introduced at the beginning of this chapter, Tina places far more importance on the upkeep of the house and the care of Jacob than does Scott, most likely because of the societal proscriptions that "require" mothers to value these things. Likewise, if these chores do not get completed it reflects far more on her abilities as a "good wife and mother" than on Scott's abilities as husband/father. In short, Tina has much more to lose in this scenario and thus enters any negotiation with more at stake.

Gender is not the only factor that influences the symbolic meaning of these tasks; race, ethnicity, social class, and social and historical time all play roles in development of meaning as well as in the family interactions and negotiations that occur around these topics. Prior to delving more deeply into the intersection of family communication patterns as they relate to family work, a brief overview of the literature on both marital and parent–child communication is in order.

Marital Communication

Much of the empirical research on marital communication focuses on aspects of couples' patterns of interaction as they relate to relationship satisfaction and stability. Such studies might have partners assess communication behaviors through self-report questionnaires that measure how frequently each uses certain styles of communication during conflictual situations. In others studies, interaction style is assessed via observation techniques where couples actually engage in a discussion around a conflictual topic and a researcher codes their interaction based on how often each partner exhibits a predetermined set of communication behaviors. Communication behaviors are typically characterized as positive, such as speaking for oneself, expressing feelings, staying on topic, paraphrasing the partner's point of view, and problem solving; or negative, such as criticism, justification, avoidance, and withdrawal. Once a "typology" is determined for an individual or dyad, based on either or both of the aforementioned techniques, the quality of partners' communication can be linked to concurrent or prospective relationship quality.

The general consensus in the literature in this area is that negative couple communication habits contribute to less effective discussions, marital dissatisfaction, and instability; whereas positive communication behaviors forecast marital happiness and stability. Negative communication behaviors have been linked to marital dissatisfaction across different cultures (Bodenmann, Kaiser, Hahlweg, & Fehm-Wolfsdorf, 1998) and among a variety of populations. For example, Rogge and Bradbury (1999) demonstrated that newlyweds' positive communication (e.g., mutual discussion, mutual expression, mutual negotiation) and problem-solving behaviors, assessed via self-report and observation techniques, were concurrently and positively related to marital satisfaction and that initial measures of the quality of communication predicted subsequent marital satisfaction. Other studies on newlyweds have demonstrated that hostile interactional styles foreshadow marital disruption (Gottman, Coan, Carrere, & Swanson, 1998; Matthews, Wickrama, & Conger, 1996). A pattern of conflict in which one partner communicates in demanding ways while the other withdraws from discussion (demand/withdraw pattern) has been identified as a destructive form of communication that has been linked to marital dissatisfaction and dissolution (e.g., Noller, Feeney, Bonnell, & Callan, 1994).

Whereas many investigations of the relationship between communication and marital quality are based upon engaged or newlywed couples, others examine this relationship for dual-earner couples or parents. Perrone and Worthington (2001) tested a model of marital quality among dual-career, middle- and upper-class spouses and revealed that couples who communicated well (e.g., felt understood and could easily share feelings with partner) also reported higher levels of marital satisfaction. In their study looking at the transition to parenthood, Cox, Paley, Burchinal, and Payne (1994) found that couples with better prenatal problem-solving abilities (assessed via videotaped interactions) reported higher marital quality (based on multiple self-report inventories) initially and experienced less of a decline in marital satisfaction following the birth of their first child.

The primary aim of current methods of conceptualizing communication skills has been to assess how often individuals and couples use positive and negative communication behaviors and patterns, implicitly assuming that these patterns are stable across topic and time. Thus, the neglect of researchers to explore communication about the topic of family work may very well be a function of the ways we have come to conceptualize communication styles and patterns of interaction. Referring back to our couple, Scott and Tina, both may use different communication styles depending on their level of investment in the issue, the degree of risk involved, or how immediately change needs to take place. Scott may distance himself from the discussion if he has little interest in how the house appears, yet he may become highly engaged if his parents are visiting that evening or if his wife is threatening to end their marriage. It may be too presumptuous to give Scott a rating scale regarding his communication styles and assume that he would respond consistently across all discussions.

Styles of Communicating Versus Topic of Communication

In their chapter on the role of conflict in marriage, Bradbury, Rogge, and Lawrence (2001) point out that the studies on marital conflict greatly outnumber those on marital communication. Despite the plethora of empirical papers and book chapters that turn up on marital conflict, few specifically address how couples communicate or resolve conflicts around issues of household and child work. Many observational studies examining couples' communication and problem-solving behaviors allow spouses to select their own issue to discuss rather than assigning one; it is likely that some spouses choose to discuss the division of labor in their household, particularly if one spouse is hopeful that the other will change his or her behavior in some way. However, studies in which couples are asked to problem solve around a highly conflictual issue do not typically include the chosen topic of discussion in their analyses, perhaps because the researchers assume communication styles are consistent across topic areas.

The few exceptions to this approach are studies that directly examined linkages between relationship conflict and the specific content areas of conflict. Storaasli and Markman (1990) explored intensity of conflict in 10 problem areas (money, communication, relatives, sex, religion, recreation, friends, alcohol/drugs, children, and jealousy) among newly married couples without children. It is interesting to note that household chores were not even listed as a possible problem area. Both spouses reported that communication issues and sex were the most conflictual areas in their relationship.

In another study, Vangelisti and Huston (1994) linked spouses' relationship satisfaction with eight domains of marriage (communication, decision making, sex, leisure activities, division of household tasks, time together, time with friends, and finances). These couples were studied in their first 2 years of marriage, and about half of the couples had children. To summarize the key findings, for both husbands' and wives' dissatisfaction with communication and decision making was linked to marital dissatisfaction. Finally, Kurdek (1994) examined areas of conflict for gay, lesbian, and heterosexual couples who did not reside with children. In a factor analysis of the 20 conflict items that individuals were asked to rate, the topic of the division of labor loaded with what Kurdek referred to as the "power" factor. Items in this factor reflected a theme of "one partner lording over the other partner" (p. 927). The power dimension was related to concurrent relationship satisfaction, such that those reporting dissatisfaction with power differentials reported less satisfaction.

In each of these studies, communication is raised as a critical area in relation to couple satisfaction; however, an interesting question becomes: communication about what? In addition, the literature suggests that the division of household labor becomes a heated topic of debate under two conditions: (a) when young children live in the household and (b) when both parents are employed outside of the home. To date, the studies that have focused on topics of marital conflict as they relate to relationship satisfaction have paid less attention to how structural family characteristics may moderate this relationship.

There is evidence that couples exhibit certain communication behaviors depending on whose issue is being discussed and whether one spouse desires change in his or her partner. In particular, this research has a strong focus on the demand/withdraw pattern of communication (Caughlin & Vangelisti, 1999; Heavey, Layne, & Christensen, 1993).

Until recently, literature in this area has consistently documented that in situations where one spouse desires change in the other, the one who desires change is more likely to be demanding, nagging, and criticizing, whereas the other is likely to withdraw, change topics, or avoid conversation (Heavey et al., 1993; Klinetob & Smith, 1996; Noller et al., 1994). In the situation of family work, where women continue to shoulder a disproportionate amount of the responsibilities, one might suspect that women are also more likely to hope for change (such that husbands chip in more equally around the house), which suggests that they too are more likely to be demanding and the husbands are more likely to withdraw. Indeed, researchers have demonstrated that when it comes to conflict over the division of labor, wives more often than husbands desire a change in their spouse's contribution and, when this is the case, spouses reported more wife-demand/husband-withdraw than husband-demand/wife-withdraw interactions (Kluwer, Heesink, & Van de Vliert, 2000). The research evidence on this topic is not consistent, however. Caughlin and Vangelisti (1999) demonstrated that individuals' desire for change in their partner was positively related to the use of the demand/withdraw pattern, regardless of which partner demands and which withdraws. This result suggests that the spouse who desires change is not necessarily the one enacting demanding and nagging behaviors. These authors argue that there is inconsistent evidence regarding desire for change and the demand/withdraw pattern of interaction. Future research should highlight the distinction between desire for change, topic salience, and communication patterns, a focus that is particularly needed around the complex negotiations that occur with regard to the division of family work.

Marital Communication and Family Work

In their chapter on communication and relational maintenance, Burleson and Samter (1994) call for an increased study of everyday relational behaviors and daily routines performed by couples to illuminate how even mundane events serve to stabilize and sustain relationships. Very few daily routines can be considered as mundane as scooping the litter box, watering plants, folding clothes, changing diapers, and making lunches, all activities that comprise the rubric of family work. Researchers have not ignored the important effects that household and child care issues have on marital quality. For example, Stafford and Canary (1991) found that couples who share tasks exhibit more mutual control, like each other more, and are more committed to and satisfied with their relationship. In a more recent study on the transition to parenthood, Grote and Clark (2001) demonstrated that perceived unfairness of the division of labor at one point predicts later marital conflict and marital dissatisfaction for wives. However, Wilkie, Ferree, and Ratcliff (1998) point out that what is considered "fair" for wives is typically at odds with what their husbands perceive as "fair." What we don't know from this line of research is how much spouses discuss with one another their ideas about fairness, how these conversations takes place, and if or when spouses make changes to balance out issues of fairness around the division of labor.

What we generally know about communication, family work, and relationship quality has been described and is depicted with solid lines in Fig. 24.1, and future areas of inquiry are depicted with dotted lines.

As we have discussed, a missing link in our research is the bridge between communication and family work. Illuminating how these issues interact with one another, and how

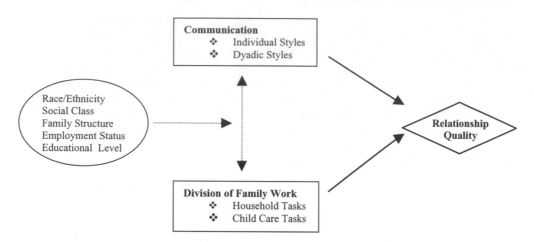

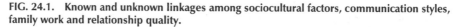

FIG. 24.1.   Known and unknown linkages among sociocultural factors, communication styles, family work and relationship quality.

this interaction subsequently influences broader outcomes such as relationship quality, is an important direction for future research. By connecting this schism, we would begin to examine how partners negotiate who will perform the daily, mundane activities that are clearly so important in maintaining a satisfying relationship. If spouses have different ideas about who should be doing what and what is considered "fair," what can we learn about how they communicate and negotiate their divergent perspectives with one another? It is likely that the quality of couples' communication moderates the relationship between the division of family work and marital outcomes. That researchers have not yet empirically explored these links speaks to the difficulty in disentangling the issue of communication about family work from the work itself. This challenge becomes more complex when recognizing that aspects of the social environment (e.g., race, class, family structure, employment status) are likely to play an instrumental role in the quality and style of family communication, in how tasks within the family are allocated, and in how communication about family work proceeds.

In her ethnographic account of equally shared parenting, Francine Deutsch (1999) points to the many sacrifices and compromises couples make to negotiate the division of work. Deutsh notes that couples vary in the amount of time they spend discussing family work issues. For some couples the patterns of work are well established and require little investment of time to negotiate issues, whereas for others discussion and negotiation about chores and equality seem to be required on a daily basis, clearly a time-consuming proposition.

Aside from the commitment of time needed to negotiate family work, Deutsch (1999) illustrates the different approaches couples take to communicating about household work, approaches that range from direct confrontation to indirect "strikes." She writes about one couple who described a "communication conflict" arising out of incompatible expectations. In this case, the husband was under the impression that his wife and he took turns on a nightly basis with child care tasks. His wife, however, assumed that if she had more employment responsibilities on a given night, then her husband would assume more of the home responsibilities, even if it was not his "official night on." Later, the husband noted, "I didn't communicate my expectations and she didn't communicate hers" (p. 20). From their conflict arising out of the wife's assumption, the couple learned to address their expectations verbally, making it clear who was going to take what responsibility and when. Other couples communicated their needs in fundamentally different ways. One woman explained that equality in family work was reached through her use of nonverbal "strikes." This woman described returning home from work to find a "mess from lunch" and deciding to simply leave it, giving the unspoken message to her husband that he was to clean up after himself. Although this couple eventually engaged in "hard negotiations" and "straight talks," they seem to have been instigated by the wife "insisting" that something change.

This raises yet another key issue; namely, who broaches the topic for discussion. Even for couples who openly negotiate the division of family work, it appears that the onus for initiating these conversations falls disproportionately on the shoulders of women. Dempsey (2000), using notions of interpersonal power to explain negotiations around the division of housework, points out that men are likely to use their superior power to resist as much change as possible to a traditional division of labor and that women face many risks when attempting to exercise power by getting their husbands to change. Specifically, a woman seeking change risks confrontations with a resistant husband, jeopardizes access to the economic resources her partner provides, and faces "a powerful tradition and a contemporary set of norms that say the tasks belong ultimately to her" (p. 23). Despite these risks, Dempsey found that working- and middle-class employed women, alike, try to persuade their husbands to share household responsibilities and report that they intend to press for further changes in the division of housework in the future.

These scenarios highlight at least three factors that come into play with regard to communication about family work: (a) how frequently couples must negotiate issues of the division of work, (b) whether negotiations occur through direct discussion or indirect acts, and (c) whose responsibility it is to initiate a discussion. Returning to Fig. 24.1, it will also be important to consider how the importance of these issues varies within different social ecological niches.

Variation in the three factors just highlighted may be a function of what women and men see as fair and equitable in a relationship. In light of the dramatic increase in dual-earner households over the past 40 years, more women feel entitled to equality when it comes to the household division of labor. In households where both spouses strive toward greater equity around household work, however, new relationship challenges and problems may arise as daily work patterns must be continually negotiated and renegotiated. Some of the depictions in Deutsch's book, for example, demonstrate that having to "fight" for equality sometimes leaves women threatening to leave their husbands. Similarly, Arlie Hochschild (1989) writes about the added strain that is experienced by women who shoulder all or most of the responsibilities of the "second shift" and the frustration of repeatedly negotiating "fair" arrangements.

Another problem arises when women fight for equality without necessarily forgoing some of the power inherent in the household manager and child care provider roles (Perry-Jenkins & Crouter, 1990). For example, in one husband's attempt to share child care responsibilities, he found his wife continually correcting him, for example, by adjusting the tapes on the diapers after he had fastened them (Deutsch, 1999). The idea that some wives are the "gatekeepers" of the household, defining when and how husbands can get involved, constitutes a new perspective on how power issues may shape the negotiation of family work (Allen & Hawkins, 1999). Many husbands are likely to perceive their wives' corrections as implicit messages that they are incapable of properly changing a diaper; fewer may be willing and prepared to speak up about how they feel about such an interchange. Thus, a challenge to researchers in this area is to explore the compatibility between what men and women preach regarding the family division of labor, versus what they actually practice, and how to capture the long-term nature of the negotiations that occur around these issues.

Although it seems that communication is critical for couples attempting to negotiate the divisions of household and child care tasks, the challenge of delineating the link between communication and family work is not an easy one. One mother commented, "If you are clear about what you want, you get it" (p. 65). It seems, however, that "being clear" could be construed in multiple ways ranging from verbally addressing an issue to physically acting in ways that get your point across (e.g., leaving out the dirty dishes until it is clear that you are not going to clean them). It also seems that the very nature of the negotiation may take on different value if it is the woman who constantly raises the topic and men who resist it. In addition, what some women are able to clearly dictate sometimes falls in opposition to their actions (e.g., saying that her husband should do the dishes but then rewashing them after he is done). In sum, it appears that there are many variables that need to be considered that extend beyond what our current investigations of communication include.

PARENT–CHILD RELATIONSHIPS AND INTERACTIONS

Although research on the association between marital communication and marital quality has flourished over the past 2 decades, the area of parent–child communication and relationship quality remains relatively uncharted. This is somewhat puzzling, given that parent–child communication plays a central role in family functioning and has been linked to the well-being of individual family members. Furthermore, parent–child communication has far-reaching implications, as what children learn from their communications with their parents necessarily informs their concurrent and future communications with individuals outside of the family (Socha & Stamp, 1995). Similar to the marital communication literature, we know little about the interactions that parents and children have around the chores of daily living, although it makes sense to argue that these processes provide a unique lens into how children and parents negotiate responsibilities.

Parent–Child Communication and Interaction

Dixson (1995) posited that "relationship work is accomplished through daily interaction" (p. 45). Such routine interaction consists of ordinary, everyday conversation about topics such as housework, homework, and what family members did that day. In her review of research on parent–child communication, Dixson describes research findings that illustrate the relationship between such routine communication and relationship outcomes. In a study of communication between mothers and their elementary-age sons, Dixson (1991) found it was the quality, and not the quantity of everyday communication, that mattered for relationship satisfaction. Specifically, mothers' reports of relationship satisfaction were significantly correlated with mothers' perceived level of understanding, listening, and conflict in the relationship; whereas amount of time spent together, measured by conversation length and average time together per day, was not. Likewise, she found that positive routine interaction served to foster a positive image of the parent–child relationship. Parent–child communication is not only associated with the parent–child relationship, as we might expect, but has also been linked to more positive routine interactions between parents and children and has been found to foster a positive self-image in children (Satir, 1988, in Dixson, 1995).

Adolescents' views of positive communication with their parents have also been linked to positive feelings of self-worth, enhanced well-being, and more positive coping behaviors (Buri, Kirchner, & Walsh, 1987; Jackson, Bijstra, Oostra, & Bosma,1998; Lanz, Iafrate, Rosnati, & Scabini, 1999). Challenging statements, and supportive versus discouraging remarks, appear to exert significant influence on adolescents' self-representations (Hauser, Power, & Noam, 1991). Effective communication with children has also been identified as a potential "buffer" to adverse effects, such as those that result from parental divorce or separation. For example, Linker, Stolberg, and Green (1999) found that separated parents' ability to communicate both affective and limit-setting messages to their children was associated with fewer behavioral problems and more positive adjustment, which is consistent with other research (Nelson, 1989).

A number of conceptual and methodological issues arise when studying parent–child communication. First, similar to the marital communication literature, there is an assumption that parents and children develop a particular style of communicating that remains stable across topic areas, be they discussions about curfew, chores, clothing, or homework. It remains an empirical question, however, as to the stability of communication style across topics. Researchers have noted that communication patterns and topics of communication do vary as a function of the child's development, and interesting questions arise as to how the intensity and frequency of communication, particularly around household chores, change as children grow up.

Another issue deserving attention regarding parent–child communication concerns the issue of the informant: Who is reporting on the quality and quantity of the communication? Some research uses parents' reports (e.g., Dixson, 1991), some uses the children's or adolescents' reports (e.g., Jackson et al., 1998), and some uses both (e.g., White, 1996). Generational (parent–child) differences in the perception of family communication have been found to exist (Barnes & Olson, 1985). For example, White (1996) found that parents' estimates of "hours spent with the family" as well a mothers' estimates of "hours spent talking with their adolescents" were higher than adolescents' estimates. White also found that both male and female adolescents viewed their family communication less positively than their parents did. Thus, parents' and children's perceptions of both the quality and the quantity of communication may differ, suggesting that it is important to obtain perspectives from multiple generations.

Another challenge in this area concerns the question of how research in related areas, such as parent–child interaction and parenting style, can and should be integrated and reconciled with the research on parent–child communication. Indeed, the lines between these domains are not always clear-cut. Often, parental strategies or styles (i.e., parental responsiveness) are examined in relation to some child outcome (i.e., child compliance) (Osborne & Fincham, 1994). If we were to look at this reciprocal pattern over time, with attention to verbal and nonverbal aspects of the exchange, most would agree we are studying some aspect of communication. Likewise, studying parenting style in relation to child outcomes can be viewed as incomplete if we fail to attend to what the child brings to a necessarily reciprocal interaction.

Parent–Child Communication and the Division of Labor

In the past decade, household labor studies have begun to include children more frequently (Coltrane, 2000). For example, Blair (1992), reporting on data from National Survey of Families and Households (NSFH), showed that in families with school-aged children about 13% of the weekly household chores were performed by children, with an average of 5.9 hours of housework being performed by (all) children. Coltrane (2000) notes that children do housework because their parents are trying to socialize them and/or because their parents need their help. The research on children's household labor participation generally finds that as children get older, they take on more tasks (e.g., Antill, Goodnow, Russell, & Cotton, 1996; Goodnow, Bowes, Warton, Dawes, & Taylor, 1991), and what they do becomes more typed by gender (e.g., McHale, Bartko, Crouter, & Perry-Jenkins, 1990). Some research has begun to explore the outcomes associated with children's performance of housework: For example, boys from dual-earner families who do more housework are more satisfied, less stressed, and have better relationships with their parents, whereas boys from single-earner households who do more household labor report less satisfaction, greater stress, and worse relationships with their parents (Crouter, McHale, & Bartko, 1993). It is possible that the communication patterns, or styles, that play out in these different family forms may be partially responsible (i.e., may function as a moderator) for the different outcomes we see. Likewise, there are a number of ways in which understanding how parents and children communicate about the division of labor could be instrumental in helping us to better understand relationship quality and individual parent and child outcomes. For example, Coltrane (2000) reports on research that shows parents and stepparents who provide more encouragement to their children are more likely to have sons who share more of the housework. How does this happen? How do parents approach and negotiate the division of chores? How are parent–child relationships affected by, and implicated in, this ongoing conversation? Likewise, how does gender of child and parent moderate these conversations?

Although no studies to date have formally examined the process of, and outcomes associated with, parent–child communication about the division of labor, the research on parent–child communication, in general, provides some clues as to how to approach this endeavor. Several points should be considered. First, research suggests that communication may vary according to family role and sex (Jackson et al., 1998). For example, adolescents report that they talk more with mothers than with fathers, and most adolescents, especially girls, see their mothers as more understanding and accepting than their fathers. Fathers are more often regarded as imposing authority and judgments during interactions, as well as being less willing to discuss emotional and personal issues (Youniss & Smoller, 1985).

Additionally, the issue of developmental status is of importance. As Jackson (1998) points out, surprisingly little is known about the ways in which parent–child communication changes as children develop. However, an interesting series of studies by Smetana (Smetana, 1988a, 1998b; Smetana & Asquity, 1994) has explored how parental authority over various areas of behavior changes throughout adolescence. For example, parents continue to see their children's activities with friends and cleaning their room as areas that fall under parental control, but at the same time they are prepared to yield some of their authority over these issues as their adolescents get older. It seems very likely that the tools, strategies, and styles that parents draw upon in communicating with their children about household chores will change as their children enter and progress through adolescence. The division of household chores is likely to emerge, increasingly, as a topic of potentially conflictual communication among adolescents and their parents (Larson & Richards, 1994). Indeed, there is research suggesting that older adolescents, more so than younger adolescents, report less open and less positive communication, in general, with their mothers and fathers (Jackson et al., 1998).

Thus, it appears that many of the same conceptual and methodological challenges exist when exploring the intersection of family communication patterns and household work, whether we are examining adult, intimate relationships or parent–child relationships. In the next section we propose new directions for research and highlight what we see as fruitful topics of inquiry for scholars interested in how family members negotiate and communicate about the daily activities of life.

RECOMMENDATIONS FOR FUTURE RESEARCH

To recap the key points thus far, it is clear that family work, including both household and child care tasks, is a routine, necessary, and "almost so obvious as to be taken for granted," aspect of family life. This topic has been spotlighted over the past few decades, as women's movement into the paid labor force has forced many couples to reassess paid and unpaid work arrangements in their homes. The dramatic increase in the family work literature indicates that beyond the number of chores completed and the relative proportion of tasks men and women perform, a key mediator of the effects of the division of household labor on family relationship quality is the symbolic meaning individuals attach to their family work. Another popular line of research that has run parallel to the scholarship on family work is research on both marital and parent–child communication. Central themes of these literatures point to the importance of constructive, positive interactions for high-quality relationships as well as to the recognition that it is the routine, mundane interactions of daily life that sustain family relationships. To date, few attempts have been made to examine the intersection of these lines of inquiry. The importance of understanding the independent effects of family communication and the division of family work on adults' and children's mental health and relationships is clearly recognized in our current research base, but much is yet to be learned from exploring the intersection of these domains of scholarship.

Communication About Family Work: Or What We Need To Know About the Art of Negotiation

A number of conceptual and methodological issues arise when considering the interconnections between communication styles and the division of household labor. First, future research must empirically examine whether variation exists in communication patterns around different topics. For example, do couples discuss household chores, money, and/or their sex lives in similar manners? The communication literature suggests that the partner most intent on creating change may be the one with the least power in an interchange; however, the topic of conversation may also bring with it unique issues and styles of communication. Research by Walsh et al. (1993) offers some insight into the importance of the topic of discussion and its "valence," whether positive, negative, or neutral, in shaping communications. These researchers found that depending on the focus of the conversation (what we refer to as topic) couples were more or less likely to engage in negative interchanges. They propose that specific topics of conversation may produce an expectancy of attack or criticism that invokes negative interaction patterns. Although these researchers did not look specifically at the division of labor as a focus topic, it is not hard to imagine that discussions about who should empty the trash or do the laundry might bring with them negatively loaded connotations.

Of course with a new conceptualization, which includes studying communication around specific topics, comes the question of how one actually measures such a phenomenon. This raises a second important issue. We propose that asking couples to discuss their household division of labor in a laboratory setting yields quite different types of information than tapping into spontaneous interactions around some given household or child care task; and both types of information could be useful. The laboratory interactions might tune the researcher into the more global issues that couples share around household chores, as well as the valence of these discussions. In contrast, more spontaneous interactions occurring at home that are tapped through observational or diary methodologies may capture how multiple stressors in the environment may shape the quality of interaction. Specifically, if when a wife and husband return home from work and the wife begins preparing dinner, the phone rings and the baby is crying, her request for "help" from her spouse may have a very different quality from that of her communication about this issue during a taped laboratory discussion. We propose that an innovative approach to tapping into those more spontaneous communications around specific tasks would be to use telephone diary techniques. Huston's (2000) phone diary methodology that taps into families' daily interaction patterns holds great promise in this arena. During daily telephone interviews, respondents could report on the household and child care tasks they completed that day, whether there was any discussion or negotiation about the chore, the valence of that negotiation, and the final outcome (i.e., who did the chore). This technique would accurately pinpoint how often issues related to household chores and child care tasks are discussed, who raises the issue, and how the issue is negotiated and resolved. A second advantage of this diary approach, especially if it is a component of a larger, longitudinal study such as Huston's, is the ability to study these phenomena over time. Based on her discussions with several equally sharing couples, Deutsch (1999) found that "the division of labor is never settled once and for all, but must be continually recreated (p. 13)." Communicating about family work is not a one-time negotiation; thus, our methodologies must be sensitive to the long-term nature of these processes. Moreover, the demands for household work and child care tasks wax and wane as a function of a families' life stage. Young couples with children face a daily task load very different from that of an empty nest couple. Our research must become more sensitive to life-course issues when examining these phenomena.

Negotiation of household chores may happen at a number of levels. For example, on a day-to-day basis family members may need to negotiate who makes dinner or picks up the children. At a broader level, couples actively negotiate lifestyles, including job choices, living arrangements, work hours and the like in an effort to establish a workable work-family arrangement (Deutsch, 1999). For example, some parents might split work based on specific tasks so that diapering, feeding, and dishes go to Mom, and changing, bathing, and cooking go to Dad. Others might split the work based on days or times, so that each parent does certain days of the week or one does the morning routine and one takes the after-school and night routine. In many equally sharing households, both parents work outside of the home but are creative in how they set up their schedules, whether it is equal jobs at equal pay, some combination of part- and full-time work, or some other arrangement. Perhaps one or both parents, using Becker and Moen's (1999) term, "scale back" their career aspirations in order to balance work and family responsibilities. In others, one parent may entirely forego a career outside of the home and create equally shared labor by placing equal weight on parents' "first shift," preventing one parent from shouldering the responsibilities of the "second shift" alone (Hochschild, 1989). Research in this area is very limited, and we know little about how much couples proactively structure their work lives to accommodate their family needs, or whether these arrangements emerge over time in response to work and family demands. Interesting questions arise as to how capable parents feel to recreate their work situations to accommodate family needs and how that opportunity varies by gender, social class, and race/ethnicity.

A third critically important issue to keep at the forefront of these discussions is the topic of the social context of family communication and the division of labor (Bronfenbrenner & Morris, 1997; Huston, 2000). The question of how race/ethnicity, social class, and sexual orientation moderate the ways in which family members communicate about family work is uncharted terrain. Past research offers some clues as to important issues that might arise in different contexts. For example, a number of studies indicate that African American men do a higher percentage of household chores than their European American counterparts; however, African American women still do almost twice as much housework as African American men (Bergen, 1991, Broman, 1991, Sanchez & Thompson, 1997). Although these findings have been documented numerous times, few have empirically examined why this is the case. Are there different negotiation processes that occur; are there different views about equality? Research results regarding Latino families are far less conclusive with some finding that Euro-American couples share more than Latino couples (Mirande, 1997), with some suggesting Latino couples share chores more (Golding, 1990), and with others finding no differences across groups. These findings, however, tell us nothing about how couples actually negotiate the division of labor and whether those negotiation processes differ by culture, race, and ethnicity.

The literature on lesbian and gay families also offers insight into how family work is negotiated in the absence of gender as a key variable in the negotiations. For example,

Kurdek (1993) found that, compared to heterosexual married couples, gay and lesbian couples were more likely to split tasks such that each partner performed an equal number of different tasks. Additionally, scholars in this area have noted that lesbian couples appear to be particularly flexible around issues of dividing up paid and unpaid work. For example, during the early childrearing years, couples will often take turns with regard to who is the primary caretaker and who is the primary breadwinner, "swapping places" based on what makes the most sense at a given time. This research allows us to directly explore how the communication processes around the division of labor are shaped by the gender constellation of the couple. Again, an understanding of how couples negotiate these arrangements is yet to be determined.

Finally a number of studies indicate that social class may moderate relationships between how chores are divided up and how the fairness of chores is perceived. Specifically, in some of our own research we found that although unequal divisions of family work occur in working-class and middle-class households alike, working-class women are more likely than middle-class women to report that this division of labor is fair (Perry-Jenkins & Folk, 1994). These findings raise interesting questions about how resources like income, education, and job prestige might affect the power arrangement and, in turn, the communication styles of couples.

A goal of future research is to delineate the various pathways that undoubtedly exist between communication and family work, to examine the potential moderators of these pathways, and to link these factors to relationship quality. "The successful maintenance of any given relationship depends, in part, on the skillfulness individuals exhibit in the communicative activities that enable them to achieve important relational functions" (Burleson & Samter, 1994, p. 68). As families continue to change in both their structure and their function, new roles, rules, and relationships will need to be negotiated among family members, providing researchers and practitioners fertile ground from which to better understand how we all communicate, plan, negotiate, and renegotiate the activities of daily life.

AUTHOR NOTE

This research is supported by a grant from the National Institute of Mental Health (R29-MH56777).

REFERENCES

Allen, S. M., & Hawkins, A. J. (1999). Maternal gatekeeping: Mother's beliefs and behaviors that inhibit greater father involvement in family work. *Journal of Marriage and the Family, 61*, 199–212.

Antill, J. K., Goodnow, J.J., Russell, G., & Cotton, S. (1996). The influence of parents and family context on children's involvement in household tasks. *Sex Roles: A Journal of Research, 34*, 215–236.

Barnes, H. L., & Olson, D. H. (1985). Parent-adolescent communication and the circumplex model. *Child Development, 56*, 438–447.

Barnett, R.C., & Shen, Y.C. (1997). Gender, high- and low-schedule-control housework tasks and psychological distress: A study of dual-earner couples. *Journal of Family Issues, 18*, 403–428.

Becker, P. E., & Moen, P. (1999). Dual-earner couples' work-family strategies. *Journal of Marriage and the Family, 61*, 995–1007.

Benin, M. H., & Agostinelli, J. (1988). Husbands' and wives' satisfaction with the division of labor. *Journal of Marriage and the Family 50*, 349–361.

Bergen, E. (1991). The economic context of labor allocation: Implications for gender stratification. *Journal of Family Issues, 12*, 140–157.

Bernard, J. (1972). *The future of marriage.* New York: World.

Bird, C. E. (1999) . Gender, household labor, and psychological distress: The impact of the amount and division of housework. *Journal of Health and Social Behavior, 40*, 32–45.

Blair, S. L. (1992). Children's participation in household labor: Child socialization versus the need for household labor. *Journal of Youth and Adolescence, 21*, 241–258.

Blair, S. L., & Johnson, M. P. (1992). Wives' perceptions of fairness of the division of household labor: The intersection of housework and ideology. *Journal of Marriage and the Family, 54*, 570–581.

Blood, R. O., & Wolfe, D. M. (1960). *Husbands and wives.* New York: The Free Press.

Bodenmann, G., Kaiser, A., Hahlweg, K., & Fehm-Wolfsdorf, G. (1998). Communication patterns during marital conflict: A cross-cultural replication. *Personal Relationships, 5*, 343–356.

Bradbury, T., Rogge, R., & Lawrence, E. (2001). Reconsidering the role of conflict in marriage. In A. Booth, A.C. Crouter, & M. Clements (Eds.), *Couples in conflict.* Mahwah, NJ: Lawrence Erlbaum Associates.

Broman, L.L. (1991). Gender, work , family roles and psychological well-being of Blacks. *Journal of Marriage and the Family, 53*, 509–520.

Bronfenbrenner, U., & Morris, P. A. (1997). The ecology of developmental processes. In W. Damon (Ed.), *Handbook of child psychology* (5th ed., pp. 993–1028). New York: Wiley.

Buri, J. R., Kirchner P. A., Walsh, J. M. (1987). Familial correlates of self-esteem in young American adults. *Journal of Social Psychology 127*, 583–588.

Burleson, B. R., & Samter, W. (1994). A social skills approach to relationship maintenance: How individual differences in communication skills affect the achievement of relationship functions. In D. J. Canary & L. Stafford (Eds.), *Communication and relational maintenance.* San Diego, CA: Academic Press.

Caughlin, J. P., & Vangelisti, A. L. (1999). Desire for change in one's partner as a predictor of the demand/withdraw pattern of marital communication. *Communication Monographs, 66*, 66–89.

Coltrane, S. (2000). Research on household labor: Modeling and measuring social embeddedness of routine family work. *Journal of Marriage and the Family, 62*, 1208–1233.

Cox, M. J., Paley, B., Burchinal, M., & Payne, C.C. (1999). Marital perceptions and interactions across the transition to parenthood. *Journal of Marriage and the Family, 61*, 611–625.

Crouter, A. C., McHale, S. M., & Bartko, W. T. (1993). Gender as an organizing feature in parent-child relationships. *Journal of Social Issues*, 161–174.

Darling, N., & Steinberg, L. (1993). Parenting style as context: An integrative model. *Psychological Bulletin, 113*, 487–496.

Davidson, J. K., Sr., & Moore, N. (1992). *Marriage and family*. Dubuque, IA: Brown.

Demo, D. H., & Acock, A.C. (1993). Family diversity and the division of domestic labor: How much have things really changed? *Family Relations, 42*, 323–331.

Dempsey, K. C. (1997). Trying to get husbands to do more work at home. *Australian & New Zealand Journal of Sociology, 33*, 216–225.

Dempsey, K. C. (2000). Men and women's power relationships and the persisting inequitable division of housework. *Journal of Family Studies, 6*, 7–24.

Deutsch, F. (1999). *Halving it all*. Cambridge, MA:Harvard University Press.

Dixson, M. (1991). *Mothers and their sons: Everyday communication as an indicator and correlate of relationship satisfaction.* Paper presented at the Meeting of the International Communication Society, Chicago.

Dixson, M. (1995). Models and perspectives of parent-child communication. In T. J. Socha & G. H. Stamp (Eds.), *Parents, children, and communication: Frontiers of theory and research* (pp. 43–61). Hillsdale, NJ: Lawrence Erlbaum Associates.

Ferree, M. M. (1990). Beyond separate spheres: Feminism and family research. *Journal of Marriage and the Family, 52*, 866–884.

Glass, J., & Fujimoto, T. (1994). Housework, paid work, and depression among husbands and wives. *Journal of Health and Social Behavior, 35*, 179–191.

Golding, J. M. (1990). Division of household labor, strain, and depressive symptoms among Mexican Americans and non-Hispanic White. *Psychology of Women Quarterly, 14*, 103–117.

Goodnow, J. J., Bowes, J. M., Warton, P. M., Dawes, L. J., & Taylor, A. J. (1991). Would you ask someone else to do this task? Parents' and children's ideas about household work requests. *Developmental Psychology, 27*, 817–828.

Gottman, J. M., Coan, J., Carrere, S., & Swanson, C. (1998). Predicting marital happiness and stability from newlywed interactions. *Journal of Marriage and the Family, 60*, 5–22.

Grote, N. K., & Clark, M. S. (2001). Perceiving unfairness in the family: Cause or consequence of marital distress? *Journal of Personality and Social Psychology*, 80, 281–293.

Hauser, S. T., Powers, S. I., & Noam, G. G. (1991). *Adolescents and their families*. New York: The Free Press.

Hawkins, A. J., Marshall, C. M., & Allen, S. M. (1998). The orientation toward domestic labor questionnaire: Exploring dual-earner wives sense of fairness about family work. *Journal of Family Psychology, 12*, 244–258.

Heavey, C., Layne, C., & Christensen, A. (1993). Gender and conflict structure in marital interaction: A replication and extension. *Journal of Consulting and Clinical Psychology, 61*, 16–27.

Hochschild, A. (1989). *The second shift*. New York: Avon Books

Honess, T. M., Charman, E. A., Zani, B., Cicognani, E., Xerri, M. L, Jackson, A. E., & Bosma, H. A. (1997). Conflict between parents and adolescents: Variations by family constitution. *British Journal of Developmental Psychology, 15*, 367–385.

Huston, T. L. (2000). The social ecology of marriage and other intimate unions. *Journal of Marriage and the Family, 62*, 298–320,

Jackson, S., Bijstra, J., Oostra, L., & Bosma, H. (1998). Adolescents' perceptions of communications with parents relative to specific aspects of relationships with parents and personal development. *Journal of Adolescence 21*, 305–322.

Kessler, R. C., & McRae, J. A. (1982). The effect of wives' employment on the mental health of married men and women. *American Sociological Review, 47*, 216–227.

Klinetob, N., & Smith, D. (1996). Demand withdraw communication in marital interaction: Tests of interpersonal contingency and gender role hypotheses. *Journal of Marriage and the Family, 58*, 945–958.

Kluwer, E. S., Heesink, J. A., & van de Vliert, E. (2000). The division of labor in close relationships: An asymmetrical conflict issue. *Personal Relationships, 7*, 263–282.

Kluwer, E.S., Heesink, J. A. M., & van de Vliert, E. (2000). The division of labor across the transition to parenthood: A justice perspective. *Journal of Marriage and the Family, 64*, 930–943.

Kurdek, L. A. (1993). The allocation of household labor in gay, lesbian, and heterosexual married couples. *Journal of Social Issues 49*, 127–139.

Kurdek, L. A. (1994). Areas of conflict for gay, lesbian and heterosexual couples: What couples argue about influences relationship satisfaction. *Journal of Marriage and the Family, 56*, 923–934.

Lanz, M., Iafrate, R., Rosnati, R., & Scabini, E. (1999). Parent-child communication and adolescent self-esteem in separated, intercountry adoptive and intact non-adoptive families. *Journal of Adolescence 22*, 785–794.

Larson, R., & Richards, M. H. (1994). *Divergent realities: The emotional lives of mothers, fathers, and adolescents.* New York: BasicBooks.

Linker, J. S., Stolberg, A. L., & Green, R. G. (1999). Family communication as a mediator of child adjustment to divorce. *Journal of Divorce and Remarriage 30*, 83–97.

Matthews, L. S., Wickrama, K. A. S., & Conger, R. (1996). Predicting marital instability from spouse and observer reports of marital interaction. *Journal of Marriage and the Family, 58*, 641–655.

McHale, S. M., Bartko, W. T., Crouter, A. C., & Perry-Jenkins, M. (1990). Children's housework and psychosocial functioning: The mediating role of parents' sex-role behaviors and attitudes. *Child Development 61*, 1413–1426.

Mirande, A. (1997). *Hombres et machos: Masculinity and Latino culture.* Boulder, CO: Westview.

Nelson, R. (1989). Parental hostility, conflict and communication in joint and sole cutody families. *Journal of Divorce 13*, 145–157.

Noller, P., Feeney, J., Bonnell, D., & Callan, V. (1994). A longitudinal study of conflict in early marriage. *Journal of Social and Personal Relationships, 11*, 233–252

Oakley, A. (1974). *The sociology of housework.* New York: Pantheon.

Oakley, A. (1974). *The sociology of housework.* New York, NY: Pantheon Books

Osborne, L. N., & Fincham, F. D. (1994). Conflict between parents and their children. In D. D. Cahn (Ed.), *Conflict in personal relationships* (pp. 117–141). Hillsdale, NJ: Lawrence Erlbaum Associates.

Osmond, M. W., & Thorne, B. (1993). Feminist theories: The social construction of gender in families and society. In P. G. Boss, W. J. Doherty, R. LaRossa, W. R. Shumm, & S. K. Steinmetz (Eds.), *Sourcebook of family theories and methods.* (pp. 591–623). New York: Plenum Press.

Perrone, K. M., & Worthington, E. L. (2001). Factors influencing ratings of marital quality by individuals within dual-career marriages: A conceptual model. *Journal of Counseling Psychology, 48,* 3–9.

Perry-Jenkins, M., & Crouter, A. C. (1990). Men's provider-role attitudes: Implications for household work and marital satisfaction. *Journal of Family Issues, 11,* 136–156.

Perry-Jenkins, M., & Folk, K. (1994). Class, couples, and conflict. Effects of the division of labor on assessments of marriage in dual-earner families. *Journal of Marriage and the Family, 56,* 165–180.

Perry-Jenkins, M., & Repetti, R., & Crouter, A.C. (2000). Work and family: A decade review. *Journal of Marriage and the Family, 62,* 981–998.

Robinson, J., & Godbey, G. (1997). *Time for life.* University Park, PA: Pennsylvania State University Press.

Rogge, R. D., & Bradbury, T. N. (1999). Till violence do us part: The differing roles of communication and aggression in predicting adverse marital outcomes. *Journal of Consulting and Clinical Psychology, 67,* 340–351.

Sanchez, L., & Kane, E. W. (1996). Women's and men's constructions of perceptions of housework fairness. *Journal of Family Issues, 17,* 358–387.

Sanchez, L., & Thompson, E. (1997). Becoming mothers and fathers: Parenthood, gender, and the division of labor. *Gender and Society, 11,* 747–772.

Satir, V. (1988). The new peoplemaking. Palo Alto, CA: Science & Behavior Books.

Seery, B. L., & Crowley, M.S. (2000). Women's emotion work in the family: Relationship management and the process of building father-child relationships. *Journal of Family Issues, 21,* 100–127.

Shelton, B. A., & John, D. (1996). The division of household labor. *Annual Review of Sociology, 22,* 299–322.

Smetana, J. G. (1988a). Adolescents' and parents' conception of parental authority. *Child Development 59,* 321–335.

Smetana, J. G. (1988b). Concepts of self and social convention: Adolescents' and parents' reasoning about hypothetical and actual family conflict. In M. R. Gunnar & W. A. Collins (Eds.), 21st *Minnesota Symposium on Child Psychology: Development during the transition to adolescence(pp. 79–122).* Hillsdale, NJ: Lawrence Erlbaum Associates.

Smetana, J. G., & Asquity, P. (1994). Adolescents' and parent' conceptions of parental authority and personal autonomy. *Child Development 65,* 1147–1162.

Socha, T. J., & Stamp, G. H. (1995). Expanding the conceptual frontier: Parents, children, and communication. In T. J. Socha & G. H. Stamp (Eds.), *Parents, children, and communication: Frontiers of theory and research* (pp. ix–xiv). Mahwah, NJ: Lawrence Erlbaum Associates.

Stafford, L., & Canary, D. (1991). Maintenance strategies and romantic relationship type, gender, and relational characteristics. *Journal of Social and Personal Relationships, 8,* 217–242.

Steil, M. (1997). *Marital equality: Its relationship to the well-being of husbands and wives.* Thousand Oaks, CA: Sage.

Storaasli, R. D., & Markman, H. J. (1990). Relationship problems in early stages of marriage: A longitudinal investigation. *Journal of Family Psychology, 4,* 80–98.

Thompson, L. (1991). Family work: Women's sense of fairness. *Journal of Family Issues, 12,* 181–196.

Thompson, L., & Walker, A. J. (1989). Gender in families: Women and men in marriage, work, and parenthood *Journal of Marriage and the Family, 51,* 845–871.

Vangelisti, A. L., & Huston, T. L. (1994). Maintaining marital satisfaction and love. In D. J. Canary & L. Stafford (Eds.), *Communication and relational maintenance* (pp. 165–186). New York: Academic Press.

Walsh, V.L., Baucom, D.H., Tyler, S., & Sayers, S.L. (1993). Impact of message valence, focus, expressive style, and gender on communication patterns among maritally distressed couples. *Journal of Family Psychology, 7,* 163–175.

White, F. A. (1996). Parent-adolescent communication and adolescent decision-making. *Journal of Family Studies, 2,* 41–56.

Wilkie, J. R., Feree, M. M., & Ratcliff, K.S. (1998). Gender and fairness: Marital satisfaction in two-earner couples. *Journal of Marriage and the Family, 60,* 577–594.

Youniss, J., & Smoller, J. (1985). *Adolescent relations with mothers, fathers, and friends.* Chicago: University of Chicago Press.

25

THE MASS MEDIA AND FAMILY COMMUNICATION

BARBARA J. WILSON

UNIVERSITY OF ILLINOIS AT URBANA-CHAMPAIGN

Mass communication technologies permeate the homes of American families today. The average child in this country lives in a household with three television sets, three tape players, three radios, two VCRs, two CD players, one video game player, and one computer (Roberts, Foehr, Rideout, & Brodie, 1999). Moreover, children spend almost $6^1/_2$ hr each day using these media (Woodard & Gridina, 2000). In many American homes, the television occupies a central space in the main gathering area, often accompanied by a surround-sound system and other technologies to heighten the quality and realism of the viewing experience.

Given their prominence, the media are clearly an integral part of the daily routines of family life. Families eat meals around the television set, parents read the newspaper comics to young children, and siblings gather together to watch a rented movie on DVD or videocassette. But mass media can be used to avoid family interactions as well. The purpose of this chapter is to explore the relationship between the media and family communication. To illustrate how multifaceted this relationship is, consider the following example of a 6-year-old girl entering her parents' bedroom one morning before school.

"Mom, what happened to her face?" the girl asked, looking at a close-up on the television screen of a woman being interviewed on *The Today Show*.

"She got burned, honey. She got too close to a fire and it burned her body. That's why we always tell you to be careful because fire is dangerous," her mother replied.

"But Mom, why is she crying?"

"Well, she's sad because she was in the hospital a long time and she's also happy because she survived. Now, that's enough, this is the news and it's not really a kid's show," her mother said as she turned the TV off.

At dinner that evening, the 6-year-old returned to the topic even though the TV was not on at the time: "Mom, Dad, I know what you're supposed to do if you are ever in a fire. You're supposed to STOP... DROP... and ROLL," she proclaimed as she fell on the floor, demonstrating the moves. "Right?"

Obviously, the media triggered this parent–child interaction, which evolved into a larger discussion of fire safety, emotional responses to tragedy, and even coping. But the example also illustrates how families influence individual media experiences. In this case, the mother curtailed her child's exposure to the story by turning the TV off and by holding back the fact that the injured woman had been inside the World Trade Center on September 11th. The mother also used this instance to establish control over the medium and to help define news as a particular genre of programming. The fact that the conversation continued later that day illustrates the widespread influence of the media beyond particular moments of exposure.

This chapter will explore how the mass media are intricately connected to the family, serving as a stimulant, a backdrop, and a negotiated space for the dynamics of daily interaction. To set the stage, the first section of the chapter describes how families use the media. Families differ in how much time they spend with different technologies and where media are placed within the household. The second section discusses how family life is portrayed in the media. Family sitcoms have been very popular on television, providing viewers with a rich source of fictional representations of parent–child relationships, sibling interactions, and even marital communication. The third section explores the impact of mass media on family communication. In addition to shaping our expectations about family roles and relationships, the media can directly stimulate family interaction, as in the previous example. It is also possible for the media to hinder family interaction and to cause family conflict.

The fourth section of the chapter turns the relationship around and explores the ways in which family communication can moderate and influence media experiences. Families differ in their communication styles, which can affect media habits. Also some parents actively engage in mediation strategies to enhance children's learning from the media and to prevent harmful effects of exposure to certain types of content. The chapter concludes with a brief discussion of the role of the mass media within the family system and with suggestions for future research.

A point about scope is in order here. Chapter 26 of this volume deals specifically with the use of interactive media in the family, so the present chapter concentrates on more traditional media, such as television, film, radio, and print. Admittedly, this distinction is somewhat artificial as all of these technologies are rapidly converging. Instead of going to a theater, families can now order a movie on demand using their home digital cable system. Or they can use their computer to watch online movie clips and even TV programs. The development of digital media is producing a high degree of interactivity and integration across different forms of media (Wartella, O'Keefe, & Scantlin, 2000).

FAMILY USE OF MASS MEDIA

Ownership

Nearly all households (98%) in the United States have a television set (Nielsen Media Research, 2000) and almost every household with children (97%) has a videocassette recorder (Woodard & Gridina, 2000). Cable television is also becoming commonplace, with 76% of households subscribing to some type of extra service (Nielsen Media Research, 2000). In fact, almost half (46%) of American families own four technologies that are now being described as "media staples" in the home: a television set, a VCR, video game equipment, and a personal computer (Woodard & Gridina, 2000).

Though most children grow up today in multimedia households, ownership of certain technologies still varies by family income. Higher income families are more likely to own a computer, have internet access, and pay for newspaper subscriptions (Woodard & Gridina, 2000). For example, 9 out of 10 families with household incomes over $75,000 have a computer, whereas only 4 out of 10 households making under $30,000 own a computer (Woodard & Gridina, 2000).

One consequence of the proliferation of newer technologies is the migration of older equipment to children's bedrooms. Indeed, over half (53%) of American children between the ages of 2 and 18 have a television set in their bedroom and nearly 30% have a VCR (Roberts et al., 1999). In addition, almost 25% of children have cable access in their rooms. As might be expected, media availability increases with age, such that a full 65% of children over the age of 8 have a TV set in their room. Somewhat surprisingly, income does not necessarily provide children with greater private access to the media. In fact, children in higher income homes are *less* likely to have a TV in their room than are children in lower income families (Roberts et al., 1999). Parental education is also negatively related to placing a TV in a child's bedroom.

Obviously, children who are experiencing the media in the privacy of their bedrooms are less likely to be supervised by their parents. In addition, as children spend time alone watching movies, listening to music, and in many cases surfing the Web, they have fewer opportunities to engage in social interaction and family activities. This issue is discussed later in the section on TV centrality.

Time Spent With Media

Given all this technology, how much actual time do families devote to using the media? The average child in this country spends over 6 hours each day with some form of mediated communication (Woodard & Gridina, 2000). Nearly $2\frac{1}{2}$ hours of this time is devoted to watching television, which continues to monopolize children's media profiles. But children are not the only members of the family who watch a lot of TV. Recent estimates suggest that the television set is turned on $7\frac{1}{2}$ hours a day in the average U.S. household (Nielsen Media Research, 2000). It is not surprising, then, that television is often referred to as another member of the family (Gunter & Svennevig, 1987).

In contrast, children spend only a half hour each day with computers (Woodard & Gridina, 2000), though this figure is likely to rise as family access increases. Still, computer use does not seem to displace television viewing among children or adults (Coffey & Stipp, 1997; Robinson, Kestnbaum, & Kohut, 2000). Thus, despite all the newer technologies, television still dominates most families' media experiences. In accord, much of the research on media and families has focused on television over other technologies, as we shall see throughout this chapter. The next two sections explore how central television is in some homes and what else families do when watching TV.

TV Centrality in the Household

When television was first introduced in the 1950s, families organized their homes around this new medium (Andreasen, 2001). The television set was considered a decorative piece of furniture that occupied a regal space in the living room. In the 1960s and 1970s, television moved to the family room but was still considered the center of household activity. As the technology improved, families purchased additional sets which migrated to other rooms in the household. Today, roughly 75% of American households have multiple TV sets (Nielsen Media Research, 1999), allowing for private and semiprivate viewing spaces in bedrooms, offices, and even basements. The consequence is that children often watch television alone or with siblings and friends (Roberts et al., 1999).

However, the trend toward privatization has been curtailed somewhat by recent architectural changes in the home. Beginning in the 1990s, new housing has tended to feature more open floor plans with cathedral ceilings and a "great room" for joint activities. Compared to those who live in traditional homes, families in these newer living spaces are more likely to watch television together, treating the set like a "magnet" rather than like a "retreat" (Pardun & Krugman, 1994). The advent of the home theater system supports this trend, allowing families to recreate the "electronic hearth" (Andreasen, 2001), this time with large-screen TVs, digital images, DVD equipment, and surround-sound systems.

But not all families orient themselves around the media. Comstock and Paik (1991) coined the term "household centrality" to refer to how central or pervasive television is in the home. According to these scholars, high centrality refers to families that watch a great deal of television and have very few rules governing the use of TV by children. In a recent national study of over 3,000 children, 42% reported that TV is turned on "most of the time" in their house, even if no one is watching it (Roberts et al., 1999). Moreover, almost 60% said television is usually on during mealtimes. Thus, for many families television is a constant backdrop to most activities.

As it turns out, centrality of television is strongly related to socioeconomic status. Parents with less income and less education are more likely themselves to watch TV, less likely to have rules about television, and more likely to allow children to have a TV in their bedroom (Desmond, Singer, Singer, Calam, & Colimore, 1985; Roberts et al., 1999; Woodard & Gridina, 2000). Television is also more central in African American families than in Caucasian families, even when controlling for socioeconomic status (Brown, Childers, Bauman, & Koch, 1990; Roberts et al., 1999). For example, African American children live in households with more TV sets, spend more time watching TV, are more likely to have a television set in their bedroom, and are more likely to eat meals with the TV on.

Centrality of television also varies by family composition. Compared to two-parent families, children in single-parent homes spend more time watching TV, are more likely to eat meals with the TV on, are more likely to have a TV in the bedroom, and are less likely to have rules in the home regarding television use (Brown et al., 1990; Roberts et al., 1999; Woodard & Gridina, 2000). These patterns suggest that in homes with less parental assistance, television gets used more for babysitting and for companionship (Woodard & Gridina, 2000).

Media Use and Other Activities

Children as well as adults rarely pay full attention to the television set when it is on (Schmitt, Anderson, & Collins, 1999). Viewers get distracted, engage in conversation, and even multitask. In one recent study, video cameras were installed in the homes of 106 families to observe viewing behaviors over a 10-day period (Schmitt, Woolf, & Anderson, 2003). The researchers found that 46% of all viewing time was spent engaged in some additional activity. Social interaction was the most common concurrent activity for all ages, dispelling the myth that television prevents families from having conversation. Children most often talked with other children in the family, though when they conversed with an adult it was more often the mother than the father. Among children, playing and eating were the next most common activities. For adults, reading and doing chores were the next most common, with women more likely than men to do household duties while viewing. The researchers also observed a fair amount of cuddling while viewing, especially between parents and young children. They concluded that "television use [in families] is quite social" (p. 276).

Nevertheless, TV can hamper conversation during particular times, especially during meals. Martini (1996) videotaped 59 Japanese American and Caucasian families while they ate dinner. Nearly half of the Japanese American families regularly had the TV set turned on during the evening meal. When the TV was on, family members often sat facing the set rather than each other, and they also moved about the room quite often during the meal. Furthermore, these families generally conversed less often than did Caucasian families, most of whom did not have the TV on during dinner. The nature of the talk differed too. Japanese American families talked more about television and about activities they were doing while they ate, whereas Caucasian families talked more about events that had occurred during the day, emotions they were experiencing, and abstract topics involving the physical and social world.

Having the television on during meal times not only constrains talk but also has health implications. A recent study found that children in households in which TV is on during meal times eat fewer fruits and vegetables and more pizza, snack foods, and sodas than do those in homes in which TV is not viewed during meals (Coon, Goldberg, Rogers, & Tucker, 2001). These relationships held up even after controlling for socioeconomic status and parents' nutritional knowledge.

Clearly, American families today spend a great deal of time with the mass media, especially television. Adults and children negotiate how central television will be in daily life, where to locate the technology in the home, and how to integrate television and other media with household activities like eating meals. Terms such as "electronic hearth" and "electronic babysitter" reveal just how pivotal television is in family life. The next section explores the types of fictional families that parents and children encounter when they spend time with the media.

PORTRAYALS OF FAMILIES IN THE MEDIA

The family situation comedy has long been a staple of television programming. *I Love Lucy* and *Father Knows Best* in the 1950s gave way to *The Dick Van Dyke Show* in the 1960s and *The Partridge Family* in the 1970s. Family sitcoms such as *The Cosby Show*,

Who's the Boss, and *Full House* dominated television in the 1980s and early 1990s. In 1981 alone, between 40 and 50 different families appeared on prime-time and Saturday morning TV each week (Pearl, Bouthilet, & Lazar, 1982).

Recently, critics have charged that family programming is being replaced by shows that concentrate on the sexual escapades of teens and young adults (Cerone, 1995; Mitchard, 1996; Salamon, 2001). But the popularity of current hits like *Malcolm in the Middle* and *Everybody Loves Raymond* suggests that family shows will survive even in the face of efforts to attract increasingly younger audiences (Gabler, 2001). As one TV executive put it, "As long as families are important, you'll see that reflected on television, but how it's reflected depends on what audience is being catered to" (Jones, as cited in Salamon, 2001).

Televised families can be construed as barometers of changing lifestyles and values in a culture (Cantor, 1991). But they also have the potential to socialize viewers about family roles and expectations. According to Bandura's (1986, 1994) social cognitive theory, children can learn attitudes and behaviors from observing televised models, particularly those who are attractive and rewarding. As it turns out, children find family programming to be very appealing (Selnow & Bettinghaus, 1982; Weiss & Wilson, 1998). In 1992, seven of the top 10 shows among 2- to 12-year-olds were family sitcoms (Nielsen, 1992). Four years later, 5 of the top 10 shows among children were still family oriented (*TV Guide*, 1996). Even today when family shows are less prevalent, *Malcolm in the Middle* and *The Simpsons* consistently rate among children's top 10 programs (Strasburger & Wilson, 2002, p. 81).

Consistent with these high ratings, children report liking the characters featured in family shows a great deal (Hoffner, 1996). Children also perceive family sitcoms to be highly realistic in nature (Dorr, Kovaric, & Doubleday, 1990; Weiss & Wilson, 1998). When asked to judge how typical TV families are, the majority of elementary schoolers rate the events and particularly the feelings in family sitcoms as very similar to those experienced by real-life families (Weiss & Wilson, 1993). These two factors, strong identification with characters and perceived realism, increase the likelihood that children will learn from such televised portrayals (Feshbach, 1972; Tannenbaum & Gaer, 1965).

How are families portrayed on television? A recent content analysis indicates that the image of the family has changed over time. Robinson and Skill (2001) assessed a total of 630 prime-time family shows that aired between 1950 and 1995. The researchers found that married couples without children were more common in the early days of TV than in recent years. In fact, the average TV family has grown from 1.8 children in the 1950s to 2.45 children by the 1990s. Over time, most families on TV have been headed by both parents, though single-parent homes have become more common since the 1980s. Single parents in early television were often widowed, whereas increasingly today they are divorced. Nevertheless, single-parent households on TV are typically headed by fathers, in marked contrast to real life. For instance, 23% of TV families were headed by single dads between 1990 and 1995, yet census figures for 1995 reveal that less than 4% of U.S. households were headed by a single father. Robinson and Skill (2001) concluded that in spite of some changes over time, "television has been and remains clearly out of sync with the structural characteristics of real-world families" (p. 161).

Perhaps more important than the form that TV families take is what families actually do when they are on the screen. Several content analyses have looked specifically at parenting behaviors on television. One early study examined 44 episodes of family-oriented prime-time shows airing in 1982 (Dail & Way, 1985). The researchers found that TV mothers were more likely to be expressive with children, including giving support, nurturing, and providing security, whereas TV fathers were more likely to exhibit instrumental behaviors such as making decisions, disciplining children, and being directive. Both parents, however, used more flexible, open-communication styles in rearing children than more authoritarian styles. Recent research indicates that some of these sex differences in parenting still persist on television (Olson & Douglas, 1997).

Other studies have looked more directly at interaction patterns in family TV shows. Two content analyses of programs airing in the 1970s found that most of the interactions in TV families were affiliative or positive in nature (Greenberg, Buerkel-Rothfuss, Neuendorf, & Atkin, 1980; Greenberg, Hines, Buerkel-Rothfuss, & Atkin,1980). However, one third of these positive interactions involved offering information rather than actually giving support. In addition, most of the talk occurred between husbands and wives in these shows. When parents did talk with a child, they were likely to interact more with a same-sex than with an opposite-sex offspring.

More recent analyses of TV families suggest that interactions in these programs are still overwhelmingly affiliative (Douglas, 1996; Heintz, 1992) and that when problems occur, they are solved relatively easily (Douglas, 1996; Weiss & Wilson, 1996). TV parents still seem to talk more with each other than with their children, and still seem to prefer same-sex children in their interactions with a younger family member (Heintz, 1992). Yet there also is a trend toward depicting more conflict in TV families than was the case in the past (Douglas & Olson, 1996; Heintz, 1992). This inclination toward harsher communication is particularly evident in family interactions involving children (Douglas, 1996; Douglas & Olson, 1996). In one historical analysis of sibling interaction on television (Larson, 2001), two 1990s programs were singled out for substantial examples of hostile sibling communication: *Married With Children* and *Roseanne*. Yet the majority of sibling talk in shows spanning from the 1950s to the 1990s was still categorized as affiliative in nature.

Even when family conflict occurs, it may not be very realistic. One recent study looked at work–family issues in a sample of 150 episodes of family programming (Heintz-Knowles, 2001). Only 15% of the episodes depicted any occurrences of conflict between work and family, and rarely was this conflict the central story line. In other words, family and work are treated as separate spheres on television. This contrasts markedly with real life, where dual-earner families are on the rise and report experiencing tremendous stress in trying to balance work with home (Jacobs & Gerson, 2001). One reason that television may overlook this issue is that only one third of the mothers in family programs are employed (Heintz-Knowles, 2001). Yet in 2000, sixty-nine percent of women with children in this country were employed outside the home (U.S. Bureau of Labor Statistics, 2001).

Television also provides a fairly limited view of families of color. African American families are featured more often now than they were in the early days of television, but they are still relatively rare (Robinson & Skill, 2001). Compared to White families, Black families on TV are more likely to be headed by a single parent (Greenberg & Neuendorf, 1980). Some studies have found more conflict in African American TV families than in

White TV families (Greenberg & Neuendorf, 1980), but others have found no differences (Merritt & Stroman, 1993). Unfortunately, with so few series featuring Black families, single episodes and programs can alter the findings from study to study. Despite the gradual increase in representations of African American families, Latino, Asian American, and Native American families are almost nonexistent on television (Dates & Stroman, 2001).

To summarize, television's portrayal of the American family is fairly idealized. Many TV families are headed by two parents, only one of whom is employed outside the home. Single-parent households do exist on TV but they are typically headed by men and rarely experience financial difficulties. Interactions in TV families are characterized primarily by mutual affection and cooperation, and problems get solved easily. Still, there are critics who argue that the quality of family life on television is declining (Zoglin, 1990). In support of this idea, current TV families do experience more conflict than those of the past. And there are some television families today that seem to almost celebrate dysfunctional relationships. Nevertheless, a recent content analysis by Bryant, Bryant, Aust, and Venugopalan (2001) suggests that mean-spirited clans are still anomalies in the television landscape. Using clinical criteria, the researchers analyzed 86 family series from the 1990s and found that modern families on television are highly cohesive, democratic and flexible in their decision making, and strong in their communication skills. The next section explores what impact these idealized images have on viewers.

THE IMPACT OF MASS MEDIA ON FAMILY COMMUNICATION

The sheer amount of time families spend with television means that the medium itself shapes and defines the context in which much of family interaction occurs. Based on his ethnographic research in family homes, Lull (1988) argued that, "Television viewing and talk about television are extensions of nearly all forms of interpersonal communication that take place between family members" (p. 246). This section will explore how the mass media contextualize and influence patterns of family interaction as well as power within the family system (Alexander, 2001).

Expectations About Family Life

Family members certainly learn about families from their own experiences, but they can also develop ideas from the media, particularly from television. According to cultivation theory (Gerbner & Gross, 1976; Gerbner, Gross, Morgan, & Signorielli, 1994), television is a centralized cultural storyteller that conveys a consistent set of images and representations of the world. These ritualized messages steadily and repeatedly shower viewers with a socially constructed view of reality (Signorielli & Morgan, 2001). In support of the theory, there is a great deal of research indicating that compared to light viewers of television, heavy viewers believe there is more violence in the world and are more frightened of being victims of that violence (see Morgan & Shanahan, 1996).

Likewise, television can cultivate ideas about family life (Signorielli & Morgan, 2001). In one study, 648 fourth, sixth, and eighth graders were surveyed about their TV habits as well as about their beliefs about families (Buerkel-Rothfuss, Greenberg, Atkin, &

Neuendorf, 1982). Children who frequently viewed family shows were more likely to believe that real-life families are supportive and compliant than were children who seldom watched these programs. These relationships held up even after controlling for grade level, sex, race, SES, number of siblings, and total amount of TV viewing. Moreover, the relationships were strongest among children who perceived television as realistic and who reported that they learned about families from TV. Notably, exposure to family shows was not related to beliefs about how much real-life families ignore one another or yell at each other, which is consistent with the overall affiliative nature of such programming.

In another study, Heintz (1992) surveyed 381 children between the ages of 7 and 13 about television and about their views of families. Roughly 50% of the children reported learning "most of the things I know" about how kids interact with parents as well as how siblings act toward each other from TV. Consistent with this social learning, Heintz (1992) found a high degree of similarity between children's descriptions of real-life families and their descriptions of TV families. Most families were characterized as happy, helpful, nice, and cohesive, though TV families were seen as funnier than real-life families. Heintz (1992) also found that children from single-parent homes gave more negative descriptions of both real and TV fathers than did children from two-parent homes. This finding supports the idea that people form generalized mental impressions or schemas that are derived from exemplars in real life as well as in the media (Shrum, 1996). Once these schemas are developed, the sources of these exemplars (real life vs. TV) often get blurred when making social reality judgments (Mares, 1996).

The correlational patterns described previously are bolstered by one experimental study of children's reactions to family sitcoms. Weiss and Wilson (1998) exposed elementary schoolers to an episode of *Full House* in which a child character experienced a negative emotional event in the family (e.g., a bicycle accident with an uncle). Among children who perceived the sitcom as realistic, exposure to the episode altered their perceptions of comparable emotional events in real life. In other words, a single family show had an impact on children's judgments about family events in the real world.

Adolescents too show evidence of cultivation from media exposure. In a national survey of over 3,000 high schoolers, heavy viewers of TV were more likely than light viewers to say that they wanted to get married, that they would stay married to the same person for life, and that they would have children (Signorielli, 1991). In another study, adolescents who frequently watched soap operas expressed fairly unrealistic views about single mothers (Larson, 1996). Compared to nonviewers, viewers were more likely to believe that single mothers have good jobs and are well-educated, do not live in poverty, and have babies who are as healthy as most babies. Young people who frequently view soap operas also are more likely to believe that marriages are fragile, that a greater proportion of people are divorced, and that a higher proportion of married people have illegitimate children and extramarital affairs (Buerkel-Rothfuss & Mayes 1981). And teens who are avid readers of romance novels are more likely to endorse idealistic notions about relationships, such as the belief in love at first sight (Kemen, 1992).

Overall, then, there is consistent evidence that heavy exposure to the media is associated with particular and often unrealistic views of marriage and family. This type of cultivation effect is strongest among those who perceive the media as realistic and among those who have less real-world experience. Yet despite the use of multiple controls, most of the evidence to date is correlational so it is difficult to assert causality. The most likely scenario is that particularly for youth, the media together with personal experiences contribute to the development of schemas about the family. Once established, those schemas affect how individuals interpret and respond to subsequent encounters with fictional families in the media (Heintz, 1992; Newcomb & Collins, 1979). These schemas also are likely to affect how individuals respond to their own families in real life. As an example, several married adults in one focus group study reported paying close attention to relationships on television and comparing those fictional examples to their own marriages (Gantz, 2001). They also reported having tried conflict resolution strategies they had seen on television in their own relationships. Likewise, in a survey of 142 married and divorced adults, nearly one fourth of the respondents said they had compared their own marriage to TV portrayals of marriage (Robinson, Skill, Nussbaum, & Moreland, 1985). Such findings support the idea that television is a major source of socialization about the family.

Media and Family Interaction

Most of the research on the impact of media on family interaction has centered on television, which is more likely to be a shared activity than is reading a book or surfing the Web. Yet families differ greatly as to how much TV they actually watch together (Lull, 1980b). Obviously, individuals are less likely to view programs together when there are multiple TV sets in the home. In addition, studies indicate that younger children are more likely to watch TV with parents than are older children (Roberts et al., 1999), children generally watch more often with siblings than with parents (Lawrence & Wozniak, 1989), and children are more likely to co-view with a parent when they watch adult-oriented programs than when they watch child-oriented programs (St. Peters, Fitch, Huston, Wright, & Eakins, 1991).

When co-viewing does occur, television has the potential to enhance family interaction in several ways. At a minimum, it brings families together into a shared social space and can foster a feeling of togetherness (Lull, 1990). In one survey, 59% of married adults reported that television provided an opportunity to spend time with their spouses (Gantz, 1985). Research also indicates that teens who are frequent viewers of TV spend more time overall with families (Larson, Kubey, & Colletti, 1989) and report more positive affect for family members than do light viewers (Larson & Kubey, 1983). Even in times of tragedy, television can provide a locale for family bonding. In the wake of the September 11th terrorist attacks on the United States, many families decided to spend more time at home together (Derus, 2001), and video rental sales went up as a reflection of this togetherness (Fabrikant, 2001).

Television also provides stories, topics, and jokes to stimulate conversation in families (Lull, 1990). In some cases, certain types of programs can provide a reference point for parents to use in discussing sensitive or complex topics with children (Kaiser Family Foundation and Child Now, 1996). In other cases, children themselves can use television to stimulate talk. In one observational study, Reid and Frazer (1980a) found that children used commercials to initiate conversation with parents about ambiguous advertising techniques as well as about topics unrelated to advertising. In another study, these same researchers found that siblings who co-view television use the content of particular programs to plan and carry out creative play (Reid & Frazer, 1980b). Even married couples can find television to be a conversational stimulant. Fallis, Fitzpatrick, and Friestad (1985) found that among adults who were classified as emotionally distant from their spouses, TV viewing was positively associated with a greater tendency to discuss relational and family issues in the marriage.

Also on the positive side, television can enrich nonverbal interaction in families. In one study, Brody, Stoneman, and Sanders (1980) observed preschoolers for 20 min with their parents, half the time while watching TV and half the time during family play. The researchers found a dramatic increase in physical contact between parents and the child while watching TV as compared to while playing. However, fathers in particular were less likely to look at their child when the TV set was on than they were when it was off. Other studies have documented that family members often sit close together (Schmitt et al., 2003) and even physically comfort each other while watching television (Wilson & Weiss, 1993).

Despite these potential positive effects, there is no doubt that television can hinder talk too. The same study by Brody et al. (1980) that found an increase in touching also found a decrease in verbal interaction between parents and preschoolers when the TV was on. As noted earlier, having the TV on during meal times can diminish conversation too (Martini, 1996). Obviously some reduction in talk will occur anytime attention is drawn to the screen and away from other people in the room. Therefore, scholars need to take an expansive view of verbal interaction, looking at talk that occurs not only during a program but also during commercial breaks and once a program is over. In some cases, television may have its greatest impact on interaction outside the viewing context altogether (Alexander, 1994), where it may be used to establish common ground, initiate conversations, and even debate popular culture.

Rather than increasing or decreasing conversation, television may be used in some families to avoid talk altogether. Rosenblatt and Cunningham (1976) found that television viewing was positively related to family tension, even after controlling for SES, number of people in the household, and whether the family was headed by one or two parents. The researchers also found that TV viewing was higher in homes with greater population density (persons per room), suggesting that the media may provide a way to head off stress associated with overcrowding. Television can be used to cope with other family tensions as well. One study found that children with alcoholic fathers watch significantly more television than do children whose fathers drink moderately or not at all (Brooks, Gaines, Mueller, & Jenkins, 1998). Other studies have documented that children in high-stress environments are likely to be heavy viewers of television (Henggeler, Cohen, Edwards, Summerville, & Ray, 1991; Tangney, 1988).

To summarize, television serves a variety of social functions in the family. It can integrate families and bring them together or it can keep them apart. Likewise, it can facilitate the expression of ideas and be used as the basis for talk or it can be used to avoid conversation. Future studies need to delineate the conditions under which television and other media serve these very different purposes. Do family crises such as divorce or substance abuse alter the role of media in family interactions? Do changes in family life cycles impact how media are used for social purposes? For example, is television used differently when a child is born or when a family member retires? Addressing such questions will move us toward a more integrated understanding of the social impact of media use on the family.

Conflict Over the Media

Family conflict occurs over a variety of issues, including the mass media. Difficulties can arise when two family members want to simultaneously use a piece of technology that is designed primarily for individual use. Even when media technology can be shared, family members may disagree on what to listen to or watch. Buying additional equipment and moving older technologies to children's bedrooms is one way to reduce family conflict over access to the media. Yet even in homes with multiple televisions, families report there are still preferences for certain sets because of their location or technological capabilities (Lull, 1978).

How often do the media cause conflict in families? Several studies have looked at marital conflict in particular as it relates to the media. In an early study, Gantz (1985) surveyed 416 married adults and found that very few reported that TV interfered with their lives or caused conflict. In fact, most perceived television as a positive force in their marriage. The one area where conflict did emerge was over the viewing of sports and soap operas. Greater discrepancy between spouses in their preference for these types of programs was positively associated with feeling that TV interfered with married life and with lower marital satisfaction scores. Because these data are correlational, it is difficult to ascertain whether viewing such programming causes conflict or whether couples who already are having difficulty escape by watching shows that are unpopular with their mate.

In a more recent study, Gantz (2001) conducted a series of focus groups, intensive interviews, and a survey to further explore marital conflict over television. In the survey portion, 145 adults were asked how often several potentially problematic behaviors regarding TV had occurred in their household. The vast majority acknowledged that in the past year television had interfered with a shared marital activity, prevented someone from taking care of household chores, and interfered with a conversation one spouse was trying to have with the other spouse. Women reported being more bothered than men by these disruptions, yet the overall ratings were low, suggesting that TV was not perceived as much of a problem in these marriages. The focus groups and interviews further revealed that couples did sometimes disagree on what to watch and on the volume level of television, but that none of these conflicts were considered serious and that they were easily resolved by using separate TV sets or by leaving the room to pursue other activities. Although Gantz (2001) found a great deal of accommodation and flexibility regarding media habits in marriages, he acknowledged that such adaptation may be less common in seriously troubled marriages and in crowded households with limited technology.

One way families can make adjustments is to establish informal or formal rules about control of the media. For example, fathers are consistently perceived by other family members as having the most influence in selecting TV programs to watch (Lull, 1978). In one observational study of 74 households, fathers controlled program decisions more often than did any other single family member (Lull, 1982). Adult males in families also typically dominate the remote control device (Gantz, 2001; Krendl, Troiano, Dawson, & Clark, 1993; Walker, 1996). Even among gay couples, there is typically a dominant remote control user, although lesbian couples are more likely to share the device (Walker, 1996).

Patterns of control can be challenged, however. Gantz (2001) and others (see Walker & Bellamy, 2001) have documented that marital battles do occur over the remote control device. In particular, women complain that men engage in too much grazing (i.e., flipping from channel to channel) and often change the channel during inopportune times in a program. Yet in the end, women seldom take charge of the remote control; instead, they are more likely to move to another TV set if remote control behaviors become too annoying (Walker, 1996). Walker (1996) argues that "Joint television watching in heterosexual couples is hardly an egalitarian experience" (p. 820).

Power and control are seldom equal in parent–child relationships either. Children are far less influential than their parents in determining what families view on TV (Lull, 1978). In accord with this, children report being less satisfied than parents with the way their families make decisions about television (Lull, 1982). Even teens struggle with control issues. In one study, 37% of adolescents reported that they argue with their parents over TV at least once in awhile (Morgan, Alexander, Shanahan, & Harris, 1990).

Children also can disagree with each other over the media. In the study by Morgan and his colleagues (1990) mentioned earlier, a substantially higher proportion of teens reported arguing about television with siblings (60%) than with parents (37%). It stands to reason that sibling conflict may be greater given that children are more likely to watch TV with a brother or sister than with a parent (Roberts et al., 1999). But even here, there is a "pecking order"; older siblings typically dominate over younger siblings in disagreements about program selections (Zahn & Baran, 1984).

Program selection causes difficulties, but particular types of messages in the media can instigate family conflict as well. For example, several studies suggest that exposure to TV advertising can result in parent–child friction (Atkin, 1978; Galst & White, 1976; Sheikh & Moleski, 1977). In one study, preschoolers who were randomly assigned to view a cartoon containing six food commercials engaged in significantly more attempts to get a parent to purchase products during a subsequent grocery store visit than did preschoolers who had seen the same cartoon without ads in it (Stoneman & Brody, 1981). Furthermore, mothers of the preschoolers who had seen the ads engaged in substantially more control strategies during the shopping trip, such as telling the child "no" and encouraging the child to put items back on the shelf.

Based on the research reviewed here, it seems clear that television and other media can instigate conflict among family members. In most families, disagreements over how to use the media are perceived as fairly manageable and even predictable. In general, the same power differentials that exist in other family routines get played out in front of the television screen. Some of this conflict can be alleviated by having additional TV sets and private media spaces in the home. But future research should examine how families with fewer resources as well as those with high degrees of conflict cope with the media. In addition, studies need to explore how disagreements about content and equipment like remote control devices get resolved as media technologies become increasingly interactive.

THE IMPACT OF THE FAMILY ON MEDIA USE

Up to this point, we have considered ways in which the media influence, transform, and provide a context for family communication. But the family itself also impacts people's media experiences. Families have different values and communication styles, which in turn affect how children use the media. In addition, parents differ greatly as to how often and in what ways they help their children deal with mass media. Each of these topics will be considered in the following section.

Family Communication Patterns

Early work by Chaffee and McLeod revealed that parents have different values regarding communication that they teach and reinforce during child rearing (Chaffee, McLeod, & Atkin, 1971; McLeod, Atkin, & Chaffee, 1972). Some parents are sociooriented in that they emphasize harmony, conformity, and getting along with others. Other parents are concept oriented because they encourage expression of ideas, critical thinking, and open debate of opinions. Chaffee and McLeod devised the Family Communication Patterns (FCP) typology whereby families could fit into one of four quadrants based on whether they score low or high on each of these two orientations.

The typology has spawned a great deal of research, much of which indicates that the norms of communication in a family can predict a great deal about media habits. For example, sociooriented families watch more television overall but consume less news in the media than do concept-oriented families (Chaffee et al., 1971; Lull, 1980a). Sociooriented individuals are more likely to use TV for social purposes like family solidarity, companionship, and having conversation (Lull, 1980a). Consistent with these social motives, adolescents from sociooriented families tend to share viewing patterns with their parents more so than do teens in families where this orientation is weak (Chaffee & Tims, 1976). Teens from sociooriented families also are more likely to feel deprived when they cannot watch TV, especially entertainment shows (Windahl, Höjerback, & Hedinsson, 1986). In contrast, concept-oriented families perceive television as a way to instill values and facilitate arguments, reflecting their overall emphasis on ideas rather than on people (Lull, 1980a). As might be expected, concept orientation is positively associated with adolescents' interest in politics, discussion about political issues, and attention to political campaigns (Chaffee & Tims, 1976).

The dimensions also are predictive of what parents do *while* viewing television with children. Concept-oriented parents generally discuss television more with their children while viewing together (Austin, 1993), a practice explored in detail in the next section. In one survey, mothers who scored high on concept orientation reported that they examined moral issues raised by TV programs in their discussions with children (Messaris & Kerr, 1983). Concept-oriented mothers also reported using TV as a springboard to give children information about history, geography, and science. Furthermore, concept-oriented mothers tended to emphasize the unrealistic aspects of television content, whereas sociooriented mothers pointed to the realistic nature of TV, especially in its portrayal of evil and danger.

Although the FCP dimensions have been used widely in media research, they have not been immune to critique. Ritchie and Fitzpatrick (1990) challenged the assumption that family members share the same norms of communication. They found considerable within-family variation when surveying each parent as well as each child, suggesting a more complex model of family norms and patterns of interaction. In addition, the long-standing interpretation of the two dimensions has been questioned. Ritchie (1991), for example, found evidence that socioorientation is actually associated with parental assertion of power and control, which often produces congruency rather than harmony, whereas concept orientation is associated with supportive and open communication. This revised interpretation coalesces with research indicating that families high in concept orientation, not socioorientation, exhibit more warmth and affection (Austin, 1993; Krcmar, 1996). The revised dimensions also parallel a large body of research in child development that characterizes parenting styles in terms of both affection and control (see Amato, 1990; Demo & Cox, 2000; Hetherington & Parke, 1993).

To summarize, family communication patterns clearly affect the amount of time spent with the media as well as preferences for certain types of content. The FCP model has dominated the research in this area for the last 25 years but has been challenged on both conceptual and methodological grounds. Future studies should look more closely at the extent to which family members agree on communication norms and values and also at the extent to which these particular dimensions are valid across families that differ by race and ethnicity, composition, income, and even size.

Family Mediation

There is little doubt that extensive exposure to the media, particularly to television, can result in harmful effects on children. For example, heavy viewers of television are more likely than light viewers to become aggressive, experience fear reactions, develop weight problems, and endorse stereotypes (Cantor, 1998a; Bushman & Huesmann, 2000; Gortmaker et al., 1996; Signorielli, 2001; Strasburger & Wilson, 2002). Given that TV is difficult to avoid, considerable interest has been given to ways in which adults can "mediate" or alter a child's viewing experiences. The goal of mediation typically is to prevent antisocial outcomes from TV viewing (e.g., Nathanson & Cantor, 2000), but mediation can also be used to enhance positive effects such as learning from educational programming (e.g., Corder-Bolz, 1980).

One of the greatest challenges in this arena is to define precisely what is meant by mediation. Over the last few decades, researchers have used the term to refer to a host of different activities, resulting in conceptual confusion in the literature (Nathanson, 2001a). Today, most researchers agree that there are three major forms of mediation: instructive mediation, restrictive mediation, and co-viewing (Nathanson, 2001a; Warren, Gerke, & Kelly, 2002; Valkenburg, Krcmar, Peeters, & Marseille, 1999).

Instructive mediation refers to discussions that parents or other adults have with children about television. The goal typically is to explain content or evaluate it in some way. Restrictive mediation refers to rules that parents set about how often, when, and what programs children can watch. Co-viewing is the most elusive form of mediation to define. At a minimum, co-viewing refers to those occasions in which parents watch television with their child. However, conversation can occur during this co-viewing which, if it pertains to TV, also entails elements of instructive mediation. Still, co-viewing can occur without talk and instructive mediation can occur outside of co-viewing. Thus, most researchers argue that the two forms of mediation should be kept conceptually and methodologically distinct (Austin, Bolls, Fujioka, & Engelbertson, 1999; Nathanson, 2001a; Valkenburg et al., 1999).

Frequency of Mediation.   The amount of mediation that occurs in families is typically measured through the use of self-report data. Overall, parents report they are more likely to supervise their children's use of television than video games or the Internet (Woodard & Gridina, 2000). Not surprisingly, parents' reports of how often they engage in mediation often differ from those of children (Kim, Baran, & Massey, 1988; Rossiter & Robertson, 1975). In recent national surveys, 62% of parents report having rules that govern their children's television viewing (Stanger & Gridina, 1999), and 91% say that they watch TV with their children at least "sometimes" (Woodard & Gridina, 2000). Yet in national surveys of children themselves, only 50% report that there are television rules in their home, and that figure drops to 38% among children over the age of 7 (Roberts et al., 1999). Furthermore, children over 7 report that less than 6% of their viewing time occurs with parents (Roberts et al., 1999).

Part of the parent–child discrepancy is presumably due to social desirability on the part of parents. Yet it is also the case that children may be unaware of certain mediation efforts like rules unless they are explicitly stated by parents. In addition, discussions about the media that occur outside the context of exposure may go unnoticed by children and even by parents themselves. Clearly, researchers need to make efforts to validate self-reports of mediation through the use of observational techniques in the home and even alternative self-report measures such as diaries.

Predictors of Mediation.   Mediation is far from a universal practice in families. Some parents mediate a great deal, whereas others do very little to intervene in their children's media habits (Austin et al., 1999). Several factors consistently emerge as predictors of parental mediation. One is the age of the child. Parents are far more likely to prohibit the viewing of certain TV programs, control the overall amount of viewing, and discuss television with younger than with older children (Greenberg, Ku, & Li, 1992; Gross & Walsh, 1980; Warren et al., 2002). Research indicates that younger children are more susceptible to the harmful effects of television (Paik & Comstock, 1994), so it is encouraging that parents are exercising greater intervention with younger viewers. Co-viewing, on the other hand, does not seem to be consistently related to age. Some studies find that co-viewing increases as children get older (e.g., Dorr, Kovaric, & Doubleday, 1989), presumably because of increased overlap in program preferences, whereas other studies find a negative relationship (e.g., Nathanson, 2001b) or no relationship at all (e.g., Warren et al., 2002) between co-viewing and age of the child.

Another predictor of mediation is parental attitudes toward television. Studies show that parents who are concerned about the harmful effects of television, particularly of violent and frightening content, engage in more restrictive as well as instructive mediation with their children (Abelman, 1990, 2001; Valkenburg et al., 1999; van der Voort, Nikken, & van Lil, 1992; Warren, 2001; Warren et al., 2002). Moreover, parents who are less trusting of TV advertising report more often discussing the unreal nature of commercials and of television in general with their children (Austin et al., 1999). On the other hand, parents who believe that television can teach positive lessons about the world are more likely to co-view or simply watch TV with their children than are parents who do not hold this view (Dorr et al., 1989; Nathanson, 2001b; van der Voort et al., 1992).

Demographic variables are less useful in predicting mediation, in part because of tremendous inconsistencies in the findings. For example, some studies have found that mothers more often engage in restrictive and instructive mediation than fathers do (Brown et al., 1990; Valkenburg et al., 1999; van der Voort et al., 1992), but others have found that sex of the parent does not predict mediation (Warren et al., 2002). Employment outside the home seems to curtail mediation (Brown et al., 1990), which may partly account for divergent sex findings across studies. Also, some studies suggest that parents who are highly educated are more likely to set rules about television and to discuss TV with their children (Greenberg et al., 1992; Valkenburg et al., 1999), whereas others find no relationship between parent education and such mediation efforts (Gross & Walsh, 1980; Warren et al., 2002). Nevertheless, at least two studies have documented a negative correlation between parental education and co-viewing, the one form of mediation that does not involve much intervention or control (Austin et al., 1999; Warren et al., 2002).

Looking beyond demographics, Warren and his colleagues examined the level of parental involvement as a predictor of mediation (Warren et al., 2002). They found that parents who share domestic activities like schoolwork and household projects with their children are more likely to engage in all three forms of mediation (instructive, restrictive, and co-viewing). In fact, shared activities were better predictors of mediation than was the sheer amount of time parents spent with children in the home.

Finally, the degree or extent of technology in the home seems to affect mediation. For example, as the number of television sets increase, there is less parental control over what children watch and when (Gross & Walsh, 1980; van der Voort et al., 1992). In addition, children in homes with cable TV watch more R-rated movies (Atkin, Greenberg, & Baldwin, 1991), suggesting less oversight by parents.

Impact of Mediation.   Most of the research on the impact of mediation has concentrated on instructive strategies or those that involve talking with a child about program content. For example, laboratory studies indicate that watching with an adult who asks questions and provides information can increase preschoolers' learning from educational programs such as *Sesame Street* (Corder-Bolz, 1980; Reiser, Tessmer & Phelps, 1984). Studies also suggest that adult commentary about television can help children to recall more of program content (Valkenburg, Krcmar, & de Roos, 1998), to comprehend the central plot of a program (Watkins, Calvert, Huston-Stein, & Wright, 1980), and to draw inferences about implicit program content (Collins, Sobol, & Westby, 1981).

Most of these experiments involve single interventions with adult mediators who are not the children's parents. However, several correlational studies have looked at the impact of ongoing efforts by parents themselves. In one study, Desmond, Singer, Singer, Calam, and Colimore (1985) showed 5- and 6-year-olds an episode of *Swiss Family Robinson* and found that those who had received regular instructive mediation from their parents were better able to comprehend the program than were those who had received less mediation, even after controlling for IQ. Other studies indicate that parental conversation about TV is related to a better understanding of how unrealistic television is among children (Messaris & Kerr, 1984) and to a higher degree of skepticism about TV content among teens (Austin, 1993). One study tracked a sample of kindergartners and first graders and found that early parental discussion of TV predicted higher comprehension of television content and greater ability to discriminate reality from fantasy 1 year later (Singer, Singer, Desmond, Hirsch, & Nicol, 1988).

Clearly, parental discussion can boost children's learning from television. But such mediation can also prevent harmful effects from occurring. Watching with an adult who comments on the unrealistic nature of TV can reduce children's fear reactions to scary programming (Cantor, Sparks, & Hoffner, 1988; Cantor & Wilson, 1984; Wilson & Weiss, 1991). Moreover, hearing a parent or an adult make negative evaluations about TV violence can reduce children's approval of interpersonal aggression (Corder-Bolz, 1980) and decrease their tendency to act aggressively after viewing such material (Grusec, 1973; Hicks, 1968; Nathanson, 1999). An adult who simply encourages a child to think about the victim of violence can encourage more critical attitudes toward TV content and even decrease the tendency to engage in aggression afterward (Nathanson & Cantor, 2000). And mothers who discuss advertising can help children resist persuasive appeals in commercials (Prsad, Rao, & Sheikh, 1978).

Far less research has been conducted on the impact of restrictive mediation. In general, we know that children who watch excessive amounts of television are more at risk for a variety of harmful outcomes (see Strasburger & Wilson, 2002), so that any effort to monitor and control children's viewing is likely to offset these patterns. In fact, a recent experiment by Robinson and his colleagues found that a 6-month classroom intervention to reduce television and video game use among third and fourth graders significantly decreased their aggressive behavior (Robinson, Wilde, Navratil, Haydel, & Varady, 2001), requests for toys (Robinson, Saphir, Kraemer, Varady, & Haydel, 2001), and even body fat levels (Robinson, 1999). Parental efforts to limit TV can have similar positive outcomes. For example, restrictive mediation by parents is associated with higher reading achievement scores in children (Roberts, Bachen, Hornby, & Hernandez-Ramos, 1984), less endorsement of sex-role stereotypes (Rothschild & Morgan, 1987), and less aggressive behavior (Nathanson, 1999).

The impact of co-viewing, the third form of mediation, is more difficult to ascertain because it sometimes includes discussion of the content as well. But those studies that isolate watching with a child from instructive mediation suggest that co-viewing by itself does not necessarily help children become more sophisticated viewers (Dorr et al., 1989), nor does it prevent children from learning aggressive attitudes and behaviors from television (Nathanson, 1999). In fact, co-viewing a violent program with a parent can be interpreted by the child as an endorsement of this type of content (Nathanson, 2001b).

There is one arena in which co-viewing can actually have a beneficial or therapeutic effect. Several studies suggest that watching with a parent can help a child feel less frightened during a scary program (Cantor, 1998a; Wilson, Hoffner, & Cantor, 1987). Even outside the context of the media, research shows that the mere presence of others can reduce anxiety in stressful situations (Venham, 1979; Wrightsman, 1960). And children who watch television with siblings more often than with parents can still profit from co-viewing. In one study, Wilson and Weiss (1993) found that watching with an older sibling reduced preschoolers' fear responses to a suspenseful movie scene. The sibling pairs often sought physical comfort from each other during the program, and the older sibling also verbally reassured the preschooler. However, watching with an older sibling actually reduced preschoolers' comprehension of the program, suggesting that co-viewers can also be distracting.

To summarize, families play a critical role in how children respond to television content. Parents who actively discuss and evaluate television with their children can increase the prosocial effects of viewing and also ameliorate some of the harmful effects. Setting limits and rules about exposure also can be beneficial, especially if such restrictions foster a more critical orientation to the media (Desmond, Singer, & Singer, 1990). However, there is some evidence that extreme levels of restrictive mediation can backfire (Nathanson, 1999), which actually could result in heightened attraction to objectionable content instead (Cantor, 1998b). Merely watching programs with children and not discussing them seems like a missed opportunity for parents, particularly if co-viewing is seen by children as an endorsement of television content. Still, much of this research is based on what parents *say* they do. Future studies need to incorporate observational measures of ongoing interaction among family members as they experience media together. Studies that have done this suggest that topics of conversation are rich and diverse, conversation differs greatly as a function of what is being watched, and both verbal interaction and nonverbal interaction occur in front of the screen (Alexander, Ryan, & Munoz, 1984; Haefner & Wartella, 1987; Schmitt et al., 2003; Stoneman & Brody, 1981; Wilson & Weiss, 1993).

CONCLUSIONS

The relationship between mass media and family communication is complex and highly interdependent (Andreasen, 2001). Family life is organized, structured, and defined in part by the mass media, particularly by television. From a family systems perspective, the mass media provide a useful framework for studying how families define themselves and create a socially constructed set of roles, values, and norms (Alexander, 1994). In turn, the family exercises influence over the media experiences of its members both inside and outside the home. Hence, there is a complicated set of pathways that connect each of these institutions.

Several conclusions can be drawn from this chapter. First, the media strongly shape the rhythms of family life (Jordan, 1992). In many families, the architecture of the house, evening meals, and even conversations are structured around large-screen TV sets with accompanying audiovisual technology. But even in homes where television is less central, the newspaper and radio are often integral to adult routines, and audiotapes, books, and even videocassettes are frequently part of children's bedtime rituals. As families structure their activities around the media, the technologies themselves become part of how family members negotiate their social reality. To capture these systemic relationships, researchers need to move beyond self-report data and observe families as they grapple with the media. Videotaping family members in the home, engaging in participant observation, and even using media diaries over time are all methods that have been underutilized but that represent rich opportunities to address these issues.

Second, the media play an important role in shaping our beliefs and expectations about family life. Our views of the family come from a variety of sources of information, including personal experience. According to recent theorizing by Koerner and Fitzpatrick (2002), cognitive representations of the family include information about intimacy, affection, power, and even values regarding communication. These relational schemas are built over time and influence how people interpret and interact with members of their family. A child who spends a great deal of time alone in her bedroom watching television is likely to develop schemas about families that are fairly idealized. Is that child prone to disappointment and frustration when her own family life differs from these television patterns? And what about children who are avid viewers of programs like *The Jerry Springer Show* or even the reality-based MTV sitcom featuring Ozzy Osbourne and his family? Future research needs to consider the impact of both idealized and dysfunctional media images of the family on relational beliefs. Studies also need to explore the extent to which media in bedrooms can isolate children from other socializing forces, making parasocial relationships with media characters a potential substitute for the family itself (Wilson & Smith, 1998).

Third, the nature of the family is undergoing rapid institutional change that is not often reflected in research. At present, we know a great deal about how middle-class, Caucasian families interact with the media. But we know very little about media experiences in families of color, single-parent families, gay and lesbian families, blended families, grandparent-run families, dual-career families, and even adoptive families. The fact that African American families watch more television (Roberts et al., 1999) and that working-class families use television less ritualistically (Jordan, 1992) are signals that we need to be more sensitive to diversity among families when we study media habits and family communication.

The media too are undergoing change. Traditional forms of media are converging, and interactive technologies are rapidly becoming the norm for many families. Furthermore, digital technologies are making mediated experiences seem ever more realistic and lifelike. Will family communication be transformed as it becomes mediated by computers, cell phones, and pagers? And as media use becomes increasingly privatized, how will parents monitor and mediate their children's exposure?

Finally, the vast majority of the studies to date are cross-sectional and often correlational. It is difficult to draw firm conclusions from such research about the factors that are responsible for variations in family communication and media use. Longitudinal studies of families are urgently needed in this arena. Such research can address how the media influence family communication over time as well as how changes in the structure of the family affect media habits and experiences. Longitudinal studies also can explore the impact of crises and different life cycles in the family on communication patterns and media use. In general, we need more sophisticated theories and methods to fully capture the complexities of how families of the 21st century are dealing with rapidly changing media technologies and content.

REFERENCES

Abelman, R. (1990). Determinants of parental mediation of children's television viewing. In J. Bryant (Ed.), *Television and the American family* (pp. 311–326). Hillsdale, NJ: Lawrence Erlbaum Associates.

Abelman, R. (2001). Parents' use of content-based TV advisories. *Science and Practice, 1*, 237–265.

Alexander, A. (1994). The effect of media on family interaction. In D. Zillmann, J. Bryant, & A. C. Huston (Eds.), *Media, children, and the family: Social scientific, psychodynamic, and clinical perspectives* (pp. 51–59). Hillsdale, NJ: Lawrence Erlbaum Associates.

Alexander, A. (2001). The meaning of television in the American family. In J. Bryant & J. A. Bryant (Eds.), *Television and the American family* (2nd ed., pp. 273–287). Mahwah, NJ: Lawrence Erlbaum Associates.

Alexander, A., Ryan, M. S., & Munoz, P. (1984). Creating a learning context: Investigations on the interaction of siblings during television viewing. *Critical Studies in Mass Communication, 1*, 345–364.

Amato, P. R. (1990). Dimensions of the family environment as perceived by children: A multidimensional scaling analysis. *Journal of Marriage and the Family, 52*, 31–43.

Andreasen, M. (2001). Evolution in the family's use of television: An overview. In J. Bryant & J. A. Bryant (Eds.), *Television and the American family* (2nd ed., pp. 3–30). Mahwah, NJ: Lawrence Erlbaum Associates.

Atkin, C. K. (1978). Observation of parent-child interaction in supermarket decision-making. *Journal of Marketing, 42*, 41–45.

Atkin, D. J., Greenberg, B., & Baldwin, T. (1991). The home ecology of children's television viewing: Parental mediation and the new video environment. *Journal of Communication, 41*(3), 40–52.

Austin, E. W. (1993). Exploring the effects of active parental mediation of television content. *Journal of Broadcasting and Electronic Media, 37*, 147–158.

Austin, E. W., Bolls, P., Fujioka, Y., & Engelbertson, J. (1999). How and why parents take on the tube. *Journal of Broadcasting and Electronic Media, 43*, 175–192.

Bandura, A. (1986). *Social foundations of thought and action: A social cognitive theory.* Upper Saddle River, NJ: Prentice Hall.

Bandura, A. (1994). Social cognitive theory of mass communication. In J. Bryant & D. Zillmann (Eds.), *Media effects: Advances in theory and research* (pp. 61–94). Hillsdale, NJ: Lawrence Erlbaum Associates.

Brody, G. H., Stoneman, Z., & Sanders, A. K. (1980). Effects of television viewing on family interactions: An observational study. *Family Relations, 29*, 216–220.

Brooks, P. H., Gaines, L. S., Mueller, R., & Jenkins, S. (1998). Children's television watching and their fathers' drinking practices. *Addiction Research, 6*, 27–34.

Brown, J. D., Childers, K. W., Bauman, K. E., & Koch, G. G. (1990). The influence of new media and family structure on young adolescents' television and radio use. *Communication Research, 17*, 65–82.

Bryant, J., Bryant, J. A., Aust, C. F., & Venugopalan, G. (2001). How psychologically healthy are America's prime-time television families? In J. Bryant & J. A. Bryant (Eds.), *Television and the American family* (2nd ed., pp. 247–270). Mahwah, NJ: Lawrence Erlbaum Associates.

Buerkel-Rothfuss, N. L., Greenberg, B. S., Atkin, C. K., & Neuendorf, K. (1982). Learning about the family from television. *Journal of Communication, 32*(3), 190–201.

Buerkel-Rothfuss, N. L., & Mayes, S. (1981). Soap opera viewing: The cultivation effect. *Journal of Communication, 31*(3), 108–115.

Bushman, B. J., & Huesmann, L. R. (2000). Effects of televised violence on aggression. In D. G. Singer & J. L. Singer (Eds.), *Handbook of children and the media* (pp. 223–254). Thousand Oaks, CA: Sage.

Cantor, J. (1998a). *"Mommy, I'm scared": How TV and movies frighten children and what we can do to protect them.* New York: Harcourt Brace.

Cantor, J. (1998b). Ratings for program content: The role of research findings. In K. Jamieson (Ed.), *The Annals of the American Academy of Political and Social Science, 557,* 54–69.

Cantor, M. G. (1991). The American family on television: From Molly Goldberg to Bill Cosby. *Journal of Comparative Family Studies, 22,* 205–216.

Cantor, J., Sparks, G. G., & Hoffner, C. (1988). Calming children's television fears: Mr. Rogers vs. The Incredible Hulk. *Journal of Broadcasting and Electronic Media, 32,* 271–288.

Cantor, J., & Wilson, B. J. (1984). Modifying fear responses to mass media in preschool and elementary school children. *Journal of Broadcasting, 28,* 431–443

Cerone, D. H. (1995, October 15). Racy programs creeping into family hour. *Los Angeles Times,* pp. A1, A28.

Chaffee, S. H., McLeod, J. M., & Atkin, C. K. (1971). Parental influences on adolescent media use. *American Behavioral Scientist, 14,* 323–340.

Chaffee, S. H., & Tims, A. R. (1976). Interpersonal factors in adolescent television use. *Journal of Social Issues, 32,* 98–115.

Coffey, S., & Stipp, H. (1997). The interactions between computer and television usage. *Journal of Advertising Research, 37,* 61–67.

Collins, W. A., Sobol, B. L., & Westby, S. (1981). Effects of adult commentary on children's comprehension and inferences about a televised aggressive portrayal. *Child Development, 52,* 158–163.

Comstock, G., & Paik, H. (1991). *Television and the American child.* San Diego, CA: Academic Press.

Coon, K. A., Goldberg, J., Rogers, B. L., & Tucker, K. L. (2001). Relationships between use of television during meals and children's food consumption patterns. *Pediatrics, 107,* 167. Retrieved April 4, 2002, from http://www.pediatrics.org/cgi/content/full/107/1/e7

Corder-Bolz, C. R. (1980). Mediation: The role of significant others. *Journal of Communication, 30*(3), 106–118.

Dail, P. W., & Way, W. L. (1985). What do parents observe about parenting from prime time television. *Family Relations: Journal of Applied Family and Child Studies, 34,* 491–199.

Dates, J. L., & Stroman, C. A. (2001). Portrayals of families of color on television. In J. Bryant & J. A. Bryant (Eds.), *Television and the American family* (2nd ed., pp. 207–228). Mahwah, NJ: Lawrence Erlbaum Associates.

Demo, D. H., & Cox, M. J. (2000). Families with young children: A review of research in the 1990s. *Journal of Marriage and the Family, 62,* 876–895.

Derus, M. (2001, December 2). Health-warming times: As fireplaces help Americans cope with hard news, business booms for chimney sweeps and firewood vendors. *Milwaukee Journal Sentinel,* 01F.

Desmond, R. J., Singer, J. L., & Singer, D. G. (1990). Family mediation: Parental communication patterns and the influences of television on children. In J. Bryant (Ed.), *Television and the American family* (pp. 293–309). Hillsdale, NJ: Lawrence Erlbaum Associates.

Desmond, R. J., Singer, J. L., Singer, D. G., Calam, R., & Colimore, K. (1985). Family mediation patterns and television viewing: Young children's use and grasp of the medium. *Human Communication Research, 11*, 461–480.

Dorr, A., Kovaric, P., & Doubleday, C. (1989). Parent-child coviewing of television. *Journal of Broadcasting and Electronic Media, 33*, 35–51.

Dorr, A., Kovaric, P., & Doubleday, C. (1990). Age and content influences on children's perceptions of the realism of television families. *Journal of Broadcasting and Electronic Media, 34*, 377–397.

Douglas, W. (1996). The fall from grace? The modern family on television. *Communication Research, 23*, 675–702.

Douglas, W., & Olson, B. M. (1996). Subversion of the American family? An examination of children and parents in television families. *Communication Research, 23*, 73–99.

Fabrikant, G. (2001, September 17). Americans, seeking escape, look to Hollywood for relief. *The New York Times*, p. C4.

Fallis, S. F., Fitzpatrick, M. A., & Friestad, M. S. (1985). Spouses' discussion of television portrayals of close relationships. *Communication Research, 12*, 59–81.

Feshbach, S. (1972). Reality and fantasy in filmed violence. In J. Murray, E. Rubinstein, & C. Comstock (Eds.), *Television and social behavior* (pp. 318–345). Washington, DC: Department of Health, Education, and Welfare.

Gabler, N. (2001, October 21). Loving 'Raymond,' a sitcom for our times. *The New York Times*, pp. 30, 37.

Galst, J. P., & White, M. A. (1976). The unhealthy persuader: The reinforcing value of television and children's purchase-influencing attempts at the supermarket. *Child Development, 47*, 1089–1096.

Gantz, W. (1985). Exploring the role of television in married life. *Journal of Broadcasting and Electronic Media, 29*, 65–78.

Gantz, W. (2001). Conflicts and resolution strategies associated with television in marital life. In J. Bryant & J. A. Bryant (Eds.), *Television and the American family* (2nd ed., pp. 289–316). Mahwah, NJ: Lawrence Erlbaum Associates.

Gerbner, G., & Gross, L. (1976). Living with television: The violence profile. *Journal of Communication, 26*(2), 172–199.

Gerbner, G., Gross, L., Morgan, M., & Signorielli, N. (1994). Growing up with television: The cultivation perspective. In J. Bryant & D. Zillmann (Eds.), *Media effects: Advances in theory and research* (pp. 17–41). Hillsdale, NJ: Lawrence Erlbaum Associates.

Gortmaker, S. L., Must, A., Sobol, A. M., Peterson, K. R., Colditz, G. A., & Dietz, W. H. (1996). Television viewing as a cause of increasing obesity among children in the United States, 1986–1990. *Archives of Pediatrics and Adolescent Medicine, 150*, 356–362.

Greenberg, B. S., Buerkel-Rothfuss, N., Neuendorf, K., & Atkin, C. K. (1980). Three seasons of television family role interactions. In B. S. Greenberg (Ed.), *Life on television: Content analyses of U.S. TV drama* (pp. 161–172). Norwood, NJ: Ablex.

Greenberg, B. S., Hines, M., Buerkel-Rothfuss, N., & Atkin, C. K. (1980). Family role structures and interactions on commercial television. In B. S. Greenberg (Ed.),

Life on television: Content analyses of U.S. TV drama (pp. 149–160). Norwood, NJ: Ablex.

Greenberg, B. S., Ku, L., & Li, H. (1992). Parental mediation of children's mass media behavior in China, Japan, Korea, Taiwan, and the United States. In F. Korzenny, S. Ting-Tommey, & E. Schiff (Eds.), *Mass media effects across cultures* (pp. 150–172). Thousand Oaks, CA: Sage.

Greenberg, B. S., & Neuendorf, K. (1980). Black family interactions on television. In B. S. Greenberg (Ed.), *Life on television: Content analyses of U.S. TV drama* (pp. 173–181). Norwood, NJ: Ablex.

Gross, L. S., & Walsh, R. P. (1980). Factors affecting parental control over children's television viewing: A pilot study. *Journal of Broadcasting, 24*, 411–419.

Grusec, J. E. (1973). Effects of co-observer evaluations on imitation: A developmental study. *Developmental Psychology, 8*, 141.

Gunter, B., & Svennevig, M. (1987). *Behind and in front of the screen: Television's involvement with family life*. London: Libbey & Company.

Haefner, M. J., & Wartella, E. A. (1987). Effects of sibling coviewing on children's interpretations of television programs. *Journal of Broadcasting and Electronic Media, 31*, 153–168.

Heintz, K. E. (1992). Children's favorite television families: A descriptive analysis of role interactions. *Journal of Broadcasting and Electronic Media, 36*, 443–451.

Heintz-Knowles, K. E. (2001). Balancing acts: Work-family issues on prime-time TV. In J. Bryant & J. A. Bryant (Eds.), *Television and the American family* (2nd ed., pp. 177–206). Mahwah, NJ: Lawrence Erlbaum Associates.

Henggeler, S. W., Cohen, R., Edwards, J. J., Summerville, M. B., & Ray, G. E. (1991). Family stress as a link in the association between television viewing and achievement. *Child Study Journal, 21*, 1–10.

Hetherington, E. M., & Parke, R. D. (1993). *Child psychology: A contemporary viewpoint* (4th ed.). New York: McGraw-Hill.

Hicks, D. J. (1968). Effects of co-observer's sanctions and adult presence on imitative aggression. *Child Development, 39*, 303–309.

Hoffner, C. (1996). Children's wishful identification and parasocial interaction with favorite television characters. *Journal of Broadcasting and Electronic Media, 40*, 389–402.

Jacobs, J. A., & Gerson, K. (2001). Overworked individuals or overworked families? Explaining trends in work, leisure, and family time. *Work and Occupations, 28*, 40–63.

Jordan, A. B. (1992). Social class, temporal orientation, and mass media use within the family system. *Critical Studies in Mass Communication, 9*, 374–386.

Kaiser Family Foundation and Child Now. (1996). *The family hour focus groups: Children's responses to sexual content on TV and their parents' reaction*. Oakland, CA: Author.

Kemen, L. A. (1992). *Romance novels and adolescents: The cultivation of attitudes about sex roles, love, and interpersonal violence*. Unpublished master's thesis, University of California, Santa Barbara.

Kim, W. Y., Baran, S. J., & Massey, K. K. (1988). Impact of the VCR on control of television viewing. *Journal of Broadcasting and Electronic Media, 32*, 351–358.

Koerner, A. F., & Fitzpatrick, M. A. (2002). Toward a theory of family communication. *Communication Theory, 12,* 70–91.

Krcmar, M. (1996). Family communication patterns, discourse behavior, and child television viewing. *Human Communication Research, 23,* 251–277.

Krendl., K. A., Troiano, C., Dawson, R., & Clark, G. (1993). "OK, where is the remote?" Children, families, and remote control devices. In J. R. Walker, & R. V. Bellamy, Jr. (Eds.), *The remote control in the new age of television* (pp. 137–153). Westport, CT: Praeger.

Larson, M. S. (1996). Sex roles and soap operas: What adolescents learn about single motherhood. *Sex Roles, 35,* 97–110.

Larson, M. S. (2001). Sibling interaction in situation comedies over the years. In J. Bryant & J. A. Bryant (Eds.), *Television and the American family* (2nd ed., pp. 163–176). Mahwah, NJ: Lawrence Erlbaum Associates.

Larson, R., & Kubey, R. (1983). Television and music: Contrasting media in adolescent life. *Youth and Society, 15,* 13–31.

Larson, R., Kubey, R. W., & Colletti, J. (1989). Changing channels: Early adolescent media choices and shifting investments in family and friends. *Journal of Youth and Adolescence, 18,* 583–599.

Lawrence, F. C., & Wozniak, P. H. (1989). Children's television viewing with family members. *Psychological Reports, 65,* 395–400.

Lull, J. (1978). Choosing television programs by family vote. *Communication Quarterly, 26,* 53–57.

Lull, J. (1980a). Family communication patterns and the social uses of television. *Communication Research, 7,* 319–334.

Lull, J. (1980b). The social uses of television. *Human Communication Research, 6,* 197–209.

Lull, J. (1982). How families select television programs: A mass-observational study. *Journal of Broadcasting, 26,* 801–811.

Lull, J. (1988). *World families watch television.* Beverly Hills, CA: Sage.

Lull, J. (1990). *Inside family viewing : Ethnographic research on television's audience.* New York: Routledge.

Mares, M. L. (1996). The role of source confusions in television's cultivation of social reality judgments. *Human Communication Research, 23,* 278–297.

Martini, M. (1996). "What's new?" at the dinner table: Family dynamics during mealtimes in two cultural groups in Hawaii. *Early Development and Parenting, 5,* 23–34.

McLeod, J. M., Atkin, C. K., & Chaffee, S. H. (1972). Adolescents, parents and television use: Adolescent self-report measures from Maryland and Wisconsin samples. In G. A. Comstock, E. A. Rubinstein, & J. P. Murray (Eds.), *Television and social behavior* (Vol. 3, pp. 173–239). Washington, DC: U.S. Government Printing Office.

Merritt, B., & Stroman, C. A. (1993). Black family imagery and interaction on television. *Journal of Black Studies, 23,* 492–499.

Messaris, P., & Kerr, D. (1983). Mothers' comments about TV: Relation to family communication patterns. *Communication Research, 10,* 175–194.

Mitchard, J. (1996, July 13). What happened to the family hour? *TV Guide,* pp. 12, 14, 17–18.

Morgan, M., Alexander, A., Shanahan, J., & Harris, C. (1990). Adolescents, VCRs, and the family environment. *Communication Research, 17*, 83–106.

Morgan, M., & Shanahan, J. (1996). Two decades of cultivation analysis: An appraisal and a meta-analysis. In B. Burleson (Ed.), *Communication yearbook 20* (pp. 1–45). Thousand Oaks, CA: Sage.

Nathanson, A. I. (1999). Identifying and explaining the relationship between parental mediation and children's aggression. *Communication Research, 26*, 124–143.

Nathanson, A. I. (2001a). Mediation of children's television viewing: Working toward conceptual clarity and common understanding. In W. B. Gudykunst (Ed.), *Communication yearbook 25* (pp. 115–151). Mahwah, NJ: Lawrence Erlbaum Associates.

Nathanson, A. I. (2001b). Parent and child perspectives on the presence and meaning of parental television mediation. *Journal of Broadcasting and Electronic Media, 45*, 201–220.

Nathanson, A. I., & Cantor, J. (2000). Reducing the aggression-promoting effect of violent cartoons by increasing children's fictional involvement with the victim: A study of active mediation. *Journal of Broadcasting and Electronic Media, 44*, 125–142.

Newcomb, A. F., & Collins, W. A. (1979). Children's comprehension of family role portrayals in televised dramas: Effects of socioeconomic status, ethnicity, and age. *Developmental Psychology, 15*, 417–423.

Nielsen, A. C. (1992, January). Nielsen statistics index. *Chicago, IL: A. C. Nielsen.*

Nielsen Media Research. (1999). *TV viewing in Internet households.* New York: Nielsen Media Research. Retrieved April 4, 2002, from http: //www.nielsenmedia.com/ reports_available/TV in Internet Homes/TVinInternetHomes.pdf

Nielsen Media Research. (2000). *Report on television.* New York: Author.

Olson, B., & Douglas, W. (1997). The family on television: Evaluation of gender roles in situation comedy. *Sex Roles, 36*, 409–427.

Paik, H., & Comstock, G. (1994). The effects of television violence on antisocial behavior: A meta-analysis. *Communication Research, 21*, 516–546.

Pardun, C. J., & Krugman, D. M. (1994). How the architectural style of the home relates to family television viewing. *Journal of Broadcasting and Electronic Media, 38*, 145–162.

Pearl, D., Bouthilet, L., & Lazar, J. (Eds.). (1982). *Television and behavior: Ten years of scientific progress and implications for the eighties* (Vol. 2), Technical reviews. Washington, DC: United States Government Printing Office.

Prsad, V. K., Rao, T. R., & Sheikh, A. A. (1978). Mother vs. commercial. *Journal of Communication, 28*(1), 91–96.

Reid, L. N., & Frazer, C. F. (1980a). Children's use of television commercials to initiate social interaction in family viewing situations. *Journal of Broadcasting, 24*, 149–158.

Reid, L. N., & Frazer, C. F. (1980b). Television at play. *Journal of Communication, 30*(4), 66–73.

Reiser, R. A., Tessmer, M. A., & Phelps, P. C. (1984). Adult-child interaction in children's learning from "Sesame Street." *Educational Communication and Technology Journal, 32*, 217–223.

Ritchie, L. D. (1991). Another turn of the information revolution: Relevance, technology, and the information society. *Communication Research, 18*, 412–427.

Ritchie, L. D., & Fitzpatrick, M. A. (1990). Family communication patterns: Measuring intrapersonal perceptions of interpersonal relationships. *Communication Research, 17*, 523–544.

Roberts, D. F., Bachen, C. M., Hornby, M. C., & Hernadez-Ramos, P. (1984). Reading and television: Predictors of reading achievement at different age levels. *Communication Research—An International Quarterly, 11*, 9–49.

Roberts, D. F., Foehr, U. G., Rideout, V. J., & Brodie, M. (1999). *Kids & media @ the new millennium*. Menlo Park, CA: Kaiser Family Foundation.

Robinson, T. N. (1999). Reducing children's television viewing to prevent obesity: A randomized controlled trial. *Journal of American Medical Association, 282*(16), 1561–1567.

Robinson, J. P., Kestnbaum, M., & Kohut, A. (2000). Personal computers, mass media, and other uses of free time. In G. D. Garson (Ed.), *Social dimensions of information technology: Issues for the new millennium* (pp. 213–235). Hershey, PA: Idea.

Robinson, T. N., Saphir, M. N., Kraemer, H. C., Varady, A., & Haydel, K. F. (2001). Effects of reducing television viewing on children's requests for toys: A randomized controlled trial. *Journal of Developmental and Behavioral Pediatrics, 22*, 179–184.

Robinson, J. D., & Skill, T. (2001). Five decades of families on television: From the 1950s through the 1990s. In J. Bryant & J. A. Bryant (Eds.), *Television and the American family* (2nd ed., pp. 139–162). Mahwah, NJ: Lawrence Erlbaum Associates.

Robinson, J., Skill, T., Nussbaum, J., & Moreland, K. (1985). Parents peers, and television characters: The use of comparison others as criteria for evaluating marital satisfaction. In E. Lange (Ed.), *Using the media to promote knowledge and skills in family dynamics* (pp. 11–15). Dayton, OH: Center for Religious Telecommunications.

Robinson, T. N., Wilde, M. L., Navracruz, L. C., Haydel, K. F., & Varady, A. (2001). Effects of reducing children's television and video game use on aggressive behavior: A randomized controlled trial. *Archives of Pediatrics and Adolescent Medicine, 155*, 17–23.

Rosenblatt, P. C., & Cunningham, M. R. (1976). Television watching and family tensions. *Journal of Marriage and the Family, 38*, 105–111.

Rossiter, J. R., & Robertson, T. S. (1975). Children's television viewing: An examination of parent-child consensus. *Sociometry, 38*, 308–326.

Rothschild, N., & Morgan, M. (1987). Cohesion and control: Adolescents' relationships with parents as mediators of television. *Journal of Early Adolescence, 7*, 299–314.

Salamon, J. (2001, July 30). Staticky reception for nuclear families on prime-time TV. *The New York Times*, pp. E1, E3.

Schmitt, K. L., Anderson, D. R., & Collins, P. A. (1999). Form and content: Looking at visual features of television. *Developmental Psychology, 35*, 1156–1167.

Schmitt, K. L., Woolf, K. D., & Anderson, D. R. (2003). Viewing the viewers: Viewing behaviors by children and adults during television programs and commercials. *Journal of Communication, 53*(2), 265–281.

Selnow, G. W., & Bettinghaus, E. P. (1982). Television exposure and language development. *Journal of Broadcasting, 26*, 469–479.

Sheikh, A. A., & Moleski, L. M. (1977). Conflict in the family over commercials. *Journal of Communication, 27*(1), 152–157.

Shrum, L. J. (1996). Psychological processes underlying cultivation effects: Further tests of construct accessibility. *Human Communication Research, 22,* 482–509.

Signorielli, N. (1991). Adolescents and ambivalence toward marriage: A cultivation analysis. *Youth and Society, 23,* 121–149.

Signorielli, N. (2001). Television's gender role images and contribution to stereotyping: Past, present, future. In D. G. Singer & J. L. Singer (Eds.), *Handbook of children and the media* (pp. 341–358). Thousand Oaks, CA: Sage.

Signorielli, N., & Morgan, M. (2001). Television and the family: The cultivation perspective. In J. Bryant & J. A. Bryant (Eds.), *Television and the American family* (2nd ed., pp. 333–351). Mahwah, NJ: Lawrence Erlbaum Associates.

Singer, J. L., Singer, D. G., Desmond, R., Hirsch, B., & Nicol, A. (1988). Family mediation and children's cognition, aggression, and comprehension of television: A longitudinal study. *Journal of Applied Developmental Psychology, 9,* 329–347.

Stanger, J. D., &, Gridina, N. (1999). *Media in the home 1999: The fourth annual survey of parents and children.* Washington, DC: The Annenberg Public Policy Center.

Stoneman, Z., & Brody, G. H. (1981). Peers as mediators of television food advertisements aimed at children. *Developmental Psychology, 17,* 853–858.

St. Peters, M., Fitch, M., Huston, A. C., Wright, J. C., & Eakins, D. J. (1991). Television and families: What do young children watch with their parents? *Child Development, 62,* 1409–1423.

Strasburger, V. C., & Wilson, B. J. (2002). *Children, adolescents, and the media.* Thousand Oaks, CA: Sage.

Tangney, J. P. (1988). Aspects of the family and children's television viewing content preferences. *Child Development, 59,* 1070–1079.

Tannenbaum, P. H., & Gaer, E. P. (1965). Mood change as a function of stress of protagonist and degree of identification in a film-viewing situation. *Journal of Personality and Social Psychology, 2,* 612–616.

TV Guide. (1996, July 13). What kids really watch. *TV Guide,* p. 21.

U.S. Bureau of Labor Statistics. (2001, April 19). *Employment characteristics of families in 2000.* Retrieved March 8, 2002, from http://www.bls.gov/news.release/famee.toc.htm

Valkenburg, P. M., Krcmar, M., & de Roos, S. (1998). The impact of a cultural children's program and adult mediation on children's knowledge of and attitudes towards opera. *Journal of Broadcasting and Electronic Media, 42,* 315–326.

Valkenburg, P. M., Krcmar, M., Peeters, A. L., & Marseille, N. M. (1999). Developing a scale to assess three styles of television mediation: "Instructive mediation," "restrictive mediation," and "social coviewing." *Journal of Broadcasting and Electronic Media, 43,* 52–66.

van der Voort, T. H., Nikken, P., & van Lil, J. E. (1992). Determinants of parental guidance of children's television viewing: A Dutch replication study. *Journal of Broadcasting and Electronic Media, 36,* 61–74.

Venham, L. L. (1979). The effects of mother's presence on child's response to dental treatment. *Journal of Dentistry for Children, 46,* 219–225.

Walker, A. J. (1996). Couples watching television: Gender, power, and the remote control. *Journal of Marriage and the Family, 58,* 813–823.

Walker, J. R., & Bellamy, R. V., Jr. (2001). Remote control devices and family viewing. In

J. Bryant & J. A. Bryant (Eds.), *Television and the American family* (2nd ed., pp. 75–89). Mahwah, NJ: Lawrence Erlbaum Associates.

Warren, R. (2001). In words and deeds: Parental involvement and mediation of children's television viewing. *Journal of Family Communication, 1*, 211–231.

Warren, R., Gerke, P., & Kelly, M. A. (2002). Is there enough time on the clock? Parental involvement andmediation of children's television viewing. *Journal of Broadcasting and Electronic Media, 46*, 87–111.

Wartella, E., O'Keefe, B., & Scantlin, R. (2000). *Children and interactive media: A compendium of current research and directions for future research*. A report to the Markle Foundation.

Watkins, B., Calvert, S., Huston-Stein, A., & Wright, J. C. (1980). Children's recall of television material: Effects of presentation mode and adult labeling. *Developmental Psychology, 16*, 672–674.

Weiss, A. J., & Wilson, B. J. (1993, April). *Developmental differences in children's understanding of emotions and emotional storylines in family-formatted situation comedies*. Paper presented at the Society for Research in Child Development conference, New Orleans, LA.

Weiss, A. J., & Wilson, B. J. (1996) Emotional portrayals in family television series that are popular among children. *Journal of Broadcasting and Electronic Media, 40*, 1–29.

Weiss, A. J., & Wilson, B. J. (1998). Children's cognitive and emotional responses to the portrayal of negative emotions in family-formatted situation comedies. *Human Communication Research, 24*, 584–609.

Wilson, B. J., Hoffner, C., & Cantor, J. (1987). Children's perceptions of the effectiveness of techniques to reduce fear from mass media. *Journal of Applied Developmental Psychology, 8*, 39–52.

Wilson, B. J., & Smith, S. L. (1998). Children's responses to emotional portrayals on television. In P. Anderson & L. Guerrero (Eds.), *Handbook of communication and emotion: Research, theory, applications, and contexts* (pp. 533–569). New York: Academic Press

Wilson, B. J., & Weiss, A. J. (1991). The effects of two reality explanations on children's reactions to a frightening movie scene. *Communication Monographs, 58*, 307–326.

Wilson, B. J., & Weiss, A. J. (1993). The effects of sibling coviewing on preschoolers' reactions to a suspenseful movie scene. *Communication Research, 20*, 214–248.

Windahl, S., Höjerback, I., & Hedinsson, E. (1986). Adolescents without television: A study in media deprivation. *Journal of Broadcasting and Electronic Media, 30*, 47–63.

Woodard, E. H., & Gridina, N. (2000). *Media in the home 2000: The fifth annual survey of parents and children*. Philadelphia: Annenberg Public Policy Center.

Wrightsman, L. S., Jr. (1960). Effects of waiting with others on changes in level of felt anxiety. *Journal of Abnormal and Social Psychology, 61*, 216–222.

Zahn, S. B., & Baran, S. J. (1984). It's all in the family: Siblings and program choice conflict. *Journalism Quarterly, 61*, 847–852.

Zoglin, R. (1990, April 16). Home is where the venom is. *Time*, pp. 85–86.

26

TECHNOLOGY AND THE FAMILY

NANCY JENNINGS
UNIVERSITY OF MICHIGAN

ELLEN WARTELLA
UNIVERSITY OF TEXAS, AUSTIN

Today's family lives in a home filled with media: newspapers, magazines, books, radios, televisions, videogame consoles, DVD players, stereo systems, computers, wireless phones and PDAs, and various devices connecting to the Internet. These technologies are used by individuals for a variety of communication and entertainment activities. And while we are learning more about what role these digital media technologies have in children and adults' lives, it is surprising how little we know about their role in family relationships and family life. Furthermore, what we do know is relatively selective: We have more knowledge of families' access to computers and television sets today than we do to cell phones and DVD players. Indeed, most research to date on families and digital media in their homes focuses on families' access and use of these media, parental regulation of children's use of these media, and the ways in which siblings interact with and around these media. In this way, studies of the newer digital media technology mirror the literature of families' uses of earlier media in the home (Wartella & Jennings, 2001).

Although much is known about the impact of media on children as individuals, far less attention has been given to the impact of media on the family as a system, and research is still in its infancy regarding how new digital media influence family life. In a review of articles that appeared in major family-related journals sponsored by the National Council on Family Relations (NCFR) from 1950 to the late 1980s, only 22 articles, 14 of which were published since 1980, addressed issues of television and the family (Fabes, Wilson, & Christopher, 1989). Similarly, results of a recent electronic search of communication journals in the electronic database of *ComAbstracts* indicate very few articles written on family and the new digital technology with only 20 articles about families and computers and 12 articles about families and the Internet, most of which appeared during or after the year 2000 (85 and 75%, respectively).

Therefore, this chapter discusses the research on the influence of digital media technology (primarily computers, the Internet, and videogames) on families. Our theoretical approach is the family systems model that has recently been popularized in a series of studies on the role of technology in the family (Jordan, 2002). This model also is appropriate for communication research because it focuses on the interpersonal and communication relationships among family members. In addition to a review of current literature, we provide suggestions for further research in the field of media and family studies.

TECHNOLOGY IN THE HOME

Families in contemporary society live in media saturated homes. Using averages to summarize the results of a recent national study of children's media use and access, Roberts and his colleagues indicate that "the typical American child enters the 21st century living in a household with 3 television sets, 2 VCRs, 3 radios, 3 tape players, 2 CD players, a video game player, and a computer" (Roberts, Foehr, Rideout, & Brodie, 1999, p. 9). Indeed, results of a recent Annenberg study of media in the home confirm that American families live in multimedia households. Nearly half of the 1,235 families in the study with children between the ages of 2 and 17 (48%) had a television set, a VCR, video game equipment, and a personal computer (Woodard, 2000).

Given the increasing role of computers in the business life of Americans, there has been ongoing concern and attention to how computers have been adopted by families at home. The "digital divide" between families who do and do not own computers and have attained computer literacy has been a policy issue which presupposes the importance of computer familiarity and comfort as an aspect of contemporary child rearing. Children who grow up with computers are thought to be better positioned for future schooling and work. Consequently, over the past 20 years, American families have welcomed a new member into their home, the family computer. According to a recent report of the U.S. Department of Commerce, family households with children under the age of 18 are more likely to have a home computer (70.1%) and home Internet subscriptions (58.8%) than households without children (62.2 and 53.2%, respectively) (U.S. Dept. of Commerce, 2002). Furthermore, Internet use among children ages 5 to 17 has risen by more than 20% from 1998 to 2001, with the largest increase in children ages 10 to 13 years old (up 26.2% from 39.2 to 65.4%) (U.S. Dept. of Commerce, 2002). Even parents in households with very young children (ages 2–3 years old) indicate presence and use of computers and the Internet by their children; in 2000, over half of the 145 parents of 2- to 3-year-olds surveyed indicate owning a computer (59%), and almost half of these families have an Internet subscription (49%), which is higher than the percentage of these families who subscribe to a daily newspaper (35%) (Jordan & Woodard, 2001). Although 2- and 3-year-olds spend more time with television than with other media, parents report that on average these young children spent 17 minutes per day on a computer and 5 minutes per day using the Internet in 2000 (Jordan & Woodard, 2001). This newest addition to family life follows earlier media technology, starting with the radio in the 20th century.

As early as the 1930s, media began to take center stage within the home environment. First radio and later, in the 1950s, television became the focal point of family living space. According to sociologist Lynn Spigel, television sets replaced the fireplace as the center of the family living space in the 1950s and floor plans for homes began to include space for the television set within a home's structural layout (Spigel, 1992). With the introduction of computers in the household, space for this new technology was allocated in quite a different manner. A recent study of computers in the household indicates home media are best described as a cluster or grouping of technologies with a "main" technology as the anchor of the associated technologies. For example, a television cluster might include a TV as the anchor and other devices such as a stereo and VCR or console video game system. These digital media are usually connected to the TV. Adults describe the computer cluster in their homes as located in office areas or small spaces (such as kitchen nooks) compared to the TV cluster that was generally located in gathering areas in the home (Morrison & Krugman, 2001). Furthermore, adults describe the computer cluster as a work area with a single chair and the television cluster as a "warm, cozy" environment open for social gatherings with furniture (such as sofas and lounge chairs) arranged for multiple-person viewing (Morrison & Krugman, 2001).

One of the most striking aspects of this proliferation of the newer screen media such as computers is that it is fostering privatization and individualization of media use. Increasingly, computers and TVs are moving into children's bedrooms. According to the recent Kaiser survey of over 3,000 children, half or more of the children studied have bedrooms that contain a television, a radio, a tape player, and/or a CD player; 33% of children have video game systems, 29% have VCRs, and 16% are equipped with computers (Roberts et al., 1999). This trend is also documented in the most recent Annenberg study—39% of children ages 8 to 16 have video games in their bedroom, 20% indicate having a computer in their bedroom, and 11% have online access in their bedroom (Woodard, 2000). Furthermore, this trend is not restricted to children living in the United States. A recent study of children in Flanders, France, and Sweden indicates that nearly 30% of children age 6 to 16 have game consoles in their bedrooms, and about 16% indicate they have a computer in their bedroom (Pasquier, Buzzi, d'Haenens, & Sjöberg, 1998).

A shift to more individualized, less family-centered media access and ostensible use is especially noteworthy with the newer digital media, particularly among adolescents. Several factors including age, frequency of Internet use, and the degree to which parents are Internet users may be related to privatized computer and Internet use. According to a recent study, adolescents 14 years and older spend 41% of their video game-playing time in their bedrooms whereas 2- to 7-year-olds spend 10% of their video game-playing time in the bedroom (Roberts et al., 1999). Moreover, Roberts and his colleagues report that among 7th through 12th graders who use media, 64% report using computer games "mainly alone," and 61% report using Web sites "mainly alone" (p. 64). Another report on Internet use among children indicates that 78% of 13- to 17-year-olds say they use the Internet when they are alone (Grunwald Associates, 2000). Furthermore, a recent report issued by the Pew Internet and American Life Project indicates that older teens, teens who go online every day, and teens whose parents do not go online report using a computer more likely in a private space such as a bedroom than in a public space in the home such as the living room, study, den, or family room (Pew Internet and American Life Project, 2001). This privatization of media use in the home has been the topic of speculation and concern, and parents are frequently advised to monitor their children's media use by locating computers and televisions in more public, common spaces in the home and not in children's bedrooms (Iannotta, 2001).

The increasing separation of parents from children in their use of digital media technology is not, however, a strictly American phenomenon. Similar use patterns can be found abroad as well. Playing video or computer games is more likely to be a solitary practice and less intergenerational than television viewing with a greater percentage of children indicating that they play interactive games either by themselves or with friends more than with their parents and even their siblings (Pasquier et al., 1998). These findings indicate that as children grow older, less and less family time is spent with media, more of children's media use is conducted in their bedrooms, and children experience media more and more outside of the family environment either alone or with friends.

Even though computer penetration has increased dramatically, rising to 51.9% from 1994 to 1997 (National Telecommunications and Information Administration [NTIA], 1998) and rising again to 56.5% in 2001 (U.S. Department of Commerce, 2002), the increase in computer access has not been evenly distributed among various households, creating concerns about a "digital divide." Two elements, income and race, have a large impact on computer ownership. The gap in home computer ownership penetration between Anglo American and African American households rose almost 5% in 3 years, from 17% in 1994 to 22% in 1997. Similarly, the gap between Anglo- and Hispanic-household computer ownership increased almost 7% from 15% in 1994 to 22% in 1997 (NTIA, 1998). This ethnic gap seems to grow regardless of income level and can even be measured in the highest income bracket of over $75,000. However, the gap between income brackets also continues to grow. Within 3 years, the gap between households earning from $10,000 to 14,999, and those earning from $50,000 to 74,999 increased almost 10% from 38% in 1994 to 48% in 1997 (NTIA, 1998). A more recent report from the U.S. Department of Commerce indicates that Internet use is rising for African Americans and Hispanics (annual rates of 33% and 30%, respectively); however, Anglo American and Asian American/Pacific Islanders are still by far the largest user group of computers in the United States (U.S. Dept. of Commerce, 2002). Furthermore, Internet and computer use among lower income households was still lower than that among high-income households in 2001 (U.S. Dept. of Commerce, 2002).

It is clear that just as computer access and technologies have changed, so has their use. For instance, until the early to mid-1990s and the growth of the World Wide Web, computers at home were primarily used for games and word processing. In a qualitative study of families with home computers conducted in the early 1990s, Giacquinta, Bauer, and Levin (1993) found that computers in the home were being used in a variety of ways by parents and children. Children overwhelmingly used the computer for game playing (in three fourths of the families this was so), whereas parents seemed to engage in work-related business activities on the computer. In over half of the families, at least one parent reported using the computer primarily for work-related activities such as word processing of business memos and correspondence, spreadsheet or database analysis, and telecommunications. In about a third of the families, at least one parent reported engaging in home computing such as recreational game playing, home management, or adult education. By the time of the 2000 Grunwald Associates survey, the two main reasons families report buying computers and connecting their children to the Internet were for education (36%) and business use (27%). And families in this survey reported that the computer was used more for education than they thought it would be, in that 36% of the families reported they purchased the computer for educational uses, whereas 45% actually reported using it for education and homework. The Internet, too, was found in this survey to be used as a routine tool for doing schoolwork with 80% of parents reporting that their children used the Internet once a month or more for schoolwork. However, when the children in these Internet households were also surveyed, there were some discrepancies with parental accounts. As the authors note, the parents seemed to overestimate the extent to which their children used the Internet for educational purposes and underestimate the extent to which they used it for entertainment (Grunwald Associates, 2000).

FAMILY SYSTEMS THEORY

Very few attempts have been made to apply theory regarding families to the study of how digital media technology is used in the home. Watt and White (1999) suggest using a family development perspective as an approach and provide a number of hypotheses regarding the role of technology in the home as the family changes and develops over time. Jordan (2002) argues for using a family systems approach to technology in the home and suggests using the theory as a framework for understanding the structural and social dimensions of family life. Although both provide a unique perspective on families and technology, the emphasis of this chapter is to explore the "nonlinear and nonindividualistic qualities of families" (Bochner & Eisenberg, 1987, p. 540) in relation to technology in the home; therefore, a family systems approach with a structural view is utilized.

Family systems theory involves the application of the general system theory (GST) to family processes. Whitchurch and Constantine (1993) indicate that Austrian biologist Ludwig von Bertalanffy initially proposed GST as a way to conceptualize different groupings as "set[s] of elements standing in interrelation among themselves and with the environment" (von Bertalanffy, 1975, p. 159, as cited in Whitchurch & Constantine, 1993). In these terms, a grouping of objects could be considered as a whole rather than as individual pieces and environmental stresses could be assessed in relation to the grouping and how the grouping responded to these stresses rather than assessing individual reactions. Sociologists and family social scientists began to apply GST to families in the 1950s, considering the family as the grouping. Gregory Bateson and his Palo Alto Team are noted for publishing a landmark article that articulated family systems theory in relation to schizophrenia in 1956 (Bateson, Jackson, Haley, & Weakland, 1956, as cited in Doherty & Baptiste, 1993). Bateson and his colleagues are particularly noteworthy in the field of communication as the first researchers to explore communication within the family (Doherty & Baptiste, 1993).

Sluzki (1983) offers three intermediate models or "translations" of the family systems perspective in order to operationalize family processes. These models are described as (a) process oriented, (b) structure oriented, and (c) world views oriented (Sluzki, 1983). According to Bochner and Eisenberg (1987), the process-oriented model is the most closely identified with communication theory because it emphasizes interactions and communication among family members. These interactions often serve to define the structure of the family, because the interactions tend to be self-perpetuating and repetitive (Bochner

& Eisenberg, 1987). The structural model provides a clear framework to understand the subsystems of the family and the interactions of these subsystems in terms of social organization. Finally, Sluzki defines the worldviews-oriented model as a reference to the idea that "each of us is a blueprint of the world" carrying belief structures that provide organization of "raw reality" and our own behavior (p. 472). This model focuses on the construction of reality and beliefs through family structure patterns and interactions with family members and the society at large. Of these three models, family structure provides a well-organized framework to discuss social organization within the family unit and captures what little literature exists on families' use of media technology.

According to Bochner and Eisenberg (1987), Minuchin (1974) provides a very clear description of this structural view. Minuchin offers the following description of the family and family structure:

> Family structure is the invisible set of functional demands that organizes the ways in which family members interact. A family is a system that operates through transactional patterns. Repeated transactions establish patterns of how, when, and to whom to relate, and these patterns underpin the system. (1974, p. 51)

Considering this definition, it becomes clear that family interaction plays a significant role in establishing structure within the family. To more clearly understand how these interactions impact the family, Minuchin suggests that "the family system differentiates and carries out its functions through subsystems" (p. 52) and that differences in generation, sex, interest, or function can define different subsystems.

Minuchin (1974) describes three subsystems within the family: (a) the spouse subsystem, (b) the parental subsystems, and (c) the sibling subsystem. The spouse subsystem consists of a man and woman who come together with the explicit purpose of creating a family. The couple provides mutual support for each other and spouses "achieve a boundary that protects it (the spouse subsystem) from interference by the demands and needs of other systems" (Minuchin, 1974, p. 57). The parental subsystem is formed with the arrival of the first child. This subsystem includes the "nurturing and disciplining responsibilities associated with relations between parents and children" (Bochner & Eisenberg, 1987, p. 545). Finally, the sibling subsystem is formed with the arrival of the second child and involves the relations and context of sibling interactions. According to Minuchin, the sibling subsystem provides a space where children can learn about peer relations through negotiation, cooperation, and competition.

Outside influences have an impact on these subsystems and on the family system as a whole. Such influences include the introduction and use of digital technology in the home. Therefore, this chapter discusses the implications of digital technology on each of these subsystems.

TECHNOLOGY AND THE SPOUSE SUBSYSTEM

Very little research has examined the impact of technology on spouses as a social unit. Research has focused on husbands and wives as individuals or as parents, but little attention has been paid to how technology may foster or inhibit spousal relationships or to how it may structure communication between spouses.

There are reported differences in how husbands and wives use computers in the home, especially regarding Internet and email use. For instance, recent research indicates that women are more likely to report that they value email as a communication tool and that email has strengthened family communication and connectedness (Boneva, Kraut, & Frohlich, 2001; Pew Internet and American Life Project, 2000). In general, research indicates that women are more likely than men to report that email has helped their relationships with family members; 34% of women who email family say email has brought them closer to their families and 27% of these women say they have learned more about their families since they began using email (Pew Internet and American Life Project, 2000). Furthermore, other research indicates that women spend more time using email than men and women more than men believe that the Internet is useful for keeping up with family and friends (Boneva et al., 2001). However, interview data suggest that women report communicating by email most frequently with siblings and their parents rather than their spouses or other individuals within the household (Boneva et al., 2001). Email, at least for husbands and wives who live together, does not seem to be a frequent mode of communication. Therefore, even though women are using the Internet to sustain relationships with their extended families (siblings, in particular), spousal relationships are not supported by email activities.

Indeed there is both anecdotal evidence and some evidence from research to indicate that digital media technology and especially networked computers may have a negative impact on marital relations. Research conducted among fathers engaged in computer clubs or user groups yielded a positive association between these fathers' home-computing time and the amount of conflict the men reported with their wives over the time the men spent on the computer (Bird, Goss, & Bird, 1990). Moreover, as fathers' computing time increased, they had fewer interactions with their wives, yet in their parenting role as fathers, they spent more time with their children (Bird et al., 1990). Although these data are from the early 1990s, even more recent research suggests that computer use may still be a source of marital conflict. In more recent studies, wives described themselves as "computer widows" and expressed discontentment regarding the amount of time their husbands spent using the computer (Morrison & Krugman, 2001). However, Watt and White (1999) suggest as families develop and change over time, digital technology takes different priorities in the family and discontentment may become less of an issue. We do not know if there is a life cycle in how families use media or in how media use changes with the addition of the first and subsequent children. Longitudinal research on families and technology would be useful to elucidate how media technology use may or may not change in families over time.

TECHNOLOGY AND THE PARENTAL SUBSYSTEM

Parents' concerns about how their children use digital media technology seem to focus on two different issues: First, parents are concerned about the kinds of content children are exposed to when using digital media; second, they are concerned about how to regulate their children's use of these media. As with the introduction of earlier media technology, the newer digital media technology has been introduced into families with parents expressing deep ambivalence about the likely impact of the technology on children. On the one hand, parents want to provide their children with a step up to early learning, and indeed, computers are marketed to parents with the promise that these and other interactive media enhance children's learning and development. On the other hand, networked computers may lead children to inappropriate content or chat rooms where they can be exploited. Although much of the early research on parent-child interactions about computer technology in the home focused on the perils parent feared, more recent work has begun to focus on how parents and children communicate about computers and on the positive uses of the Internet and computers to enhance family relationship development.

Parental Concerns

As computers and the Internet have been integrated into the household, parental hopes and concerns have grown and changed regarding the content children are exposed to. Both the promise and the peril entailed in children using computers and the Internet have been detailed in research with parents and in the media (Turow, 1999). Some parents have great hope regarding the promise of digital technology as an educational tool that can open new worlds to their children; however, other parents have reservations regarding these new technologies and express concern and fear over excessive use, inappropriate content, and potential dangers (such as Internet stalkers and invasion of privacy online). When parents are more familiar with digital technology they tend to be less fearful, and fathers and mothers differ in their attitudes and opinions about interactive media.

Recent research indicates that parents have a positive, yet apprehensive view of the newer digital technologies. Indeed, in a survey conducted in the year 2000, eighty-two percent of parents interviewed thought that computers would be valuable to their children's education and development. This figure is much higher than parental ratings of television's usefulness (22%) and the perceived usefulness of the Internet (55%) (Grunwald Associates, 2000). However, although parents think of digital technology as useful, they are also concerned and cautious about its use. In a 1999 survey of parental attitudes, Turow found that although 70% of parents with home computers reported that the Internet is a place for children to discover information and explore the world, over 75% of parents were concerned that their children might release personal information and view sexually explicit images on the Internet (Turow, 1999). Turow found similar results in the year 2000, although the percentages of parents agreeing with positive statements concerning the Internet rose slightly; whereas the percentages of parents agreeing with negative statements about the Internet remained the same as in 1999 (Turow & Nir, 2000). In a recent study of parents and teens, fathers were found to be more likely to report positive feelings than were mothers about the beneficial impact of the Internet on children's relationships (Pew Internet and American Life Project, 2001).

Research indicates that parents view the Internet as having particular risks for their children. In a recent book for parents on how to regulate children's computer and Internet use, six areas were introduced as risks for children's online activities. These include (a) distribution of pornography, (b) sexual predators, (c) misinformation and hidden messages, (d) loss of privacy, (e) unscrupulous vendors, and (f) development of childhood behavior disorders including social isolation and Internet Addiction Disorder (IAD) (Hughes & Campbell, 1998). Academic research on parental concerns about the Internet explores similar topics. Several studies since the late 1990s have examined issues of parental concern

(Iannotta, 2001). For instance, in a 1997 focus group study of parents of elementary school children, the authors found that parents were concerned about their children's possible exposure to indecent or inappropriate content and meeting strangers on the Internet (Strover, Wartella, Stout, & Richards, 1997). More recent research indicates that parents express concern that their children will be contacted by strangers via the Internet, that children will be exposed to inappropriate content such as pornography and violence, and that the Internet may be distracting their children from more important activities (Pew Internet and American Life Project, 2001; Schmitt, 2000; Turow & Nir, 2000). Parents have also expressed concern that the Internet may lead some young people to do dangerous or harmful things (Pew Internet and American Life Project, 2001). Interestingly, parents of girls and younger children worry more than other parents about the dangers of online strangers and of children releasing private information online (Pew Internet and American Life Project, 2001; Schmitt, 2000).

It may be the case that some parental apprehension is a result of a lack of knowledge about computing and the Internet. According to a recent study of media regulation by mothers, most of their concerns about the Internet were related to a sense that they could not adequately control the Web, nor did they have sufficient knowledge of it (Schmitt, 2000). Indeed, Turow (1999) suggests that inexperience of parents may make them more likely to downplay the utility of the Internet in light of their concerns for their children. Conversely, parents who use the Internet the most are the most enthusiastic about the beneficial impact of Internet on children's relationships (Pew Internet and American Life Project, 2001). Therefore, parental experience with the newer digital media may be a significant factor contributing to their position on their children's Internet and computer use.

Parental Regulation

With the introduction of the newer digital media into the household, rules regarding use and content have been shifting. Rules and regulations have followed the same general pattern as those for television in that rules are often established regarding the amount of time spent with media technology and regarding specific content. However, because children are likely to live in a multimedia household, rules have been changing to reflect this new environment, and factors such as parental opinions regarding media use and the child's age, gender, and interests seem to have an impact on the type of regulation established.

Parental attitudes and concerns have a substantial influence on regulation practices in the home. Research indicates that European children say they are less controlled when listening to music or using a computer than when they are watching television. Indeed, interviews with parents indicate that parents hold a positive image of computers and that they are more tolerant of their child's use of computers than of television, even if the child is just using the computer to play games. Indeed, parents indicated the "same game might be controlled when played on a video game console, but not on a computer" (Pasquier et al., 1998, p. 515). Research in the United States suggests that some parents are proud of their teens' computer accomplishments and are far more willing to tolerate hours spent in front of a computer than in front of a TV (Kiesler, Zdaniuk, Lundmark, & Kraut, 2000). Finally, an Annenberg study of all media in the home indicates that as parental concerns about media increase, their overall supervision also increases (Woodard, 2000). Both positive and negative opinions influence parental regulation of media use.

Parents seem to hold different rules for boys and girls and for children of different ages. In Europe, boys appear to be slightly more controlled than girls for all media except the telephone (Pasquier et al., 1998). In the United States, mothers of boys indicate greater concern over their boy's use of rap music than mothers of girls, whereas mothers of girls indicate greater concern over their girl's use of the Internet (Schmitt, 2000). Furthermore, research suggests that as children mature, restrictions regarding television use decrease (Pasquier et al., 1998; Woodard, 2000), whereas supervision of Internet is significantly higher for adolescents than for younger children (Woodard, 2000). Interestingly, more teens report time-use limits for talking on the telephone (47%) than television viewing (40%), using the Internet (37%), and playing computer games (35%) (Pew Internet and American Life Project, 2001). Although factors of gender and age provide comparison for parental regulation of media, these factors may be more indicative of children's development and socialization with media rather than actual differences in media regulation. For instance, research indicates that girls are less likely to play video games than boys (Phillips, Rolls, Rouse, & Griffiths, 1995; Roberts et al., 1999; Scantlin, 1999; van Schie & Wiegman, 1997; Woodard, 2000; Wright et al., 2001). Moreover, according to a Kaiser Family Foundation report (Roberts et al., 1999) and an Annenberg study (Woodard, 2000), as children mature, they spend more time playing video games and using the computer.

With these changes in media consumption among maturing children, parental regulation also changes. Research indicates that the more children use a particular medium, the more their parents try to control its use (Pasquier et al., 1998; Schmitt, 2000). In Europe, girls tend to be heavier users of the telephone than boys, and parents exert more regulation of telephone use for girls than they do for boys (Pasquier et al., 1998). In the United States, focus groups of children indicate that parental rules and concerns about media use change as the child's interest in different media changes. For example, as one African American ninth-grade girl explains, "She (Mom) doesn't really care about me watching TV cause she knows TV is not my favorite thing. Talking on the telephone is. She puts rules on the telephone. She puts rules on my little sister about watching TV" (Schmitt, 2000, p. 40). Parental regulation shifts as children's media use changes, which is particularly significant concerning new media because children are often early adopters of new technologies.

Communication Patterns and Relationship Building

Interpersonal communication about interactive digital media and using such media for interpersonal communication both play a role in the communication patterns and relationship building that occur within the family structure. Familiarity with digital technology tends to be a factor in determining family discussions of media. Also, these discussions often fall along gender lines. Interestingly, observations of parents and children interacting with digital technology suggest that parents are more likely to mediate computer use than television use. In this manner, parental mediation of computers is more similar to that of parents reading to their child rather than watching television with them. Furthermore, both parents and children alike use the Internet and email to communicate with each other and facilitate family relationships, but usually rely on face-to-face communication when family members reside locally.

Researchers have explored how communication patterns vary while using digital technology among parent-child dyads. This type of research describes parent-child interactions as gender specific and similar to story telling. Early research indicates that fathers are more likely to play video games and work with the computer with their children than are mothers (Bird et al., 1990; Mitchell, 1985; Tinnell, 1985). More recent research reveals that children are more likely to discuss computers with their fathers than with their mothers (Pasquier et al., 1998). This is not to say that all communication regarding digital technology is gender specific. Indeed, as children master technological skills, they become the family "guru" and are more likely to provide assistance to family members than are the adults in the family (Kiesler et al., 2000). Advice giving among girls varied by the gender of the listener. Teen boys give advice at similar rates to women and men, whereas teen girls were more likely to give help to women than to men (Kiesler et al., 2000).

Recent research provides a descriptive analysis of parent-child interactions with computers. A 2001 ethnographic study indicates that these interactions range from parents offering compliments and support to children as they use computers to parents using the computer as an electronic baby-sitter (Desmond & Bagli, 2001). Of particular interest, however, was the general finding that child-parent interactions involving computers are very similar to those found when children and parents are reading a book together. Desmond and Bagli (2001) suggest that parents of elementary school age and younger children act as observers and commentators on their children's interactions with computers, which is very similar to their responses when parents are reading aloud from books. For instance, parents are reported to be asking questions, using repetition, and replaying games that children had mastered when parents and children are interacting with computers. This is similar to rereading a child's favorite book. Indeed, these observations would indicate that parent-child interactions with computers may be much more active than those interactions with television.

Finally, digital technology can also be a source of family coordination and relationship building. In a recent study of teens and their parents in online homes, parents indicated that they did not think the Internet affected interfamily relations much; however, some parents do indicate using the Internet for different aspects of family life. For instance, some parents indicate that the Internet has improved the way they spend time with their children such as helping them plan weekend family outings (34%) and helping them shop for birthday and holiday gifts for family members (27%) (Pew Internet and American Life Project, 2001). Furthermore, parents report that email has been useful for communicating with their children's teachers (28%) and for staying in touch with parents of their children's friends (20%). However, factors such as age of child (younger children), how long parents have been online (been online more than a year), parents income (high), and level of education (high) are related to whether or not parents use email for these purposes (Pew Internet and American Life Project, 2001). These data should not be surprising, because the Internet has become another mode of communication, oftentimes more convenient than phones or mail.

TECHNOLOGY AND THE SIBLING SUBSYSTEM

Pasquier and her colleagues suggest that newer digital media may "belong more to the peer society of children, whether siblings or, even more so, friends" (1998, p. 518) than do television and more traditional media. Digital media can be a socializing force for children both as a topic of discussion and as a way to play games and communicate (email) with one another. Furthermore, children indicate that they rarely use digital media with their parents. Unfortunately, little research attention has focused on children's social networks in relation to digital media. Most research regarding children and digital technology has focused on the child as an individual rather than as one living within a social context. However, what research is available indicates that digital media do play a role in the socialization of children, both with siblings and with peers.

Siblings do spend time together using digital media. Early qualitative research revealed that children played video games together using a video game system, because video game playing provided an even playing field for children of different ages and sizes (Mitchell, 1985). However, in some cases as children's skill levels increased at differing paces, cooperative play began to be replaced with sibling rivalry (Mitchell, 1985). Similar practices can be seen in more recent research. Roberts and his colleagues (1999) reported that 36% of the adolescents who played video games reported playing them with peers or siblings.

Interestingly, gender roles are an issue with siblings and interactive media. Early research indicated that if video game systems were located in a child's bedroom rather than in the family room, the system was more likely to be in the boy's room than in the girl's room, even if the girl was the older child (Mitchell, 1985). More recent research reports similar findings indicating that girls are far less likely to have a video game system in their bedroom than are boys; 43% of boys have a video game system in their bedroom, whereas only 23% of girls do (Roberts et al., 1999). Furthermore, older sisters who would offer advise about game playing were considered "bossy," but older brothers who offered the same advise were considered nurturing teachers (Mitchell, 1985). Finally, in families with only female children, girls reported playing by themselves only 8% of the time and indicated playing with family a little over 50% of their playing time. In contrast, in families with only male children, boys reported playing by themselves 48% of the time and playing with family only 20% of their playing time (Mitchell, 1985).

Clearly, interactive digital media use among girls is more of a socializing activity than it is for boys. Socialization has become an important issue more recently with Internet, email, and instant messaging (IM). A recent report found that girls are using the Internet as much as boys, but in different ways. Specifically, girls are using the Internet for education, schoolwork, email, and chat rooms, whereas boys are using the Internet for entertainment and games (Grunwald Associates, 2000). Furthermore, a study of teen girls indicates that girls are using the Internet predominantly to socialize with friends, and for frequent Internet users, instant messaging (IM) is replacing email as the preferred method of online communication (Girl Scouts of the United States of America, 2002). With IM, girls can create an "online party line" and often use the Internet for emotional confrontation with friends (Girl Scouts, 2002).

Interactive media may be more of a socializing force for youth outside of their immediate family setting. Research indicates that teen girls are less likely to use the Internet to communicate with family because they are living in the same household (Girl Scouts, 2002), and nearly two thirds of teens (64%) have expressed concern that the Internet takes away time they would spend with their families (Pew Internet and American Life Project, 2001). Moreover, nearly half (48%) of teens indicate that Internet use has been associated with improving their friendships (Pew Internet and American Life Project, 2001). Therefore, the Internet may be a form of socialization for contemporary youth; however, it may be influencing relationships outside of the home more than it is influencing them inside the home.

RESEARCH AGENDA

Many questions about families and interactive media have yet to be answered. As technologies change, family practices are often altered to accommodate new influences in the household. Although much of the focus regarding digital technology has been on individuals' use and access to technology, more research needs to address the use of digital technology within a family setting. There are gaps in our descriptions of how families interact when using media together; for instance, how do siblings interact with new media in the home? How are decisions made regarding choices of games played on video game systems in the home? Are parents involved with playing video games with their children? Does the presence of older siblings change the nature of how younger siblings are introduced to and use digital media? These are but a few of the many questions that could be asked.

Furthermore, there is almost no research on how the media-saturated household influences more general family relationships. For instance, is the increasing privatization of media within children and adolescent's bedrooms leading to more frequent or less frequent opportunities for parents and children to communicate, and how does this affect parents' abilities to socialize children. Is the computer "widow" a thing of the past? How does the presence of digital media in the home structure or influence spousal relationships?

Furthermore, there needs to be a greater attempt to apply theory to practice. Use of digital media technology in the family setting has been undertheorized. Although there is a hypothesis that media technology use changes as families grow and spend more time together, this developmental hypothesis needs to be tested further (Watt & White, 1999). The use of systems theory in studying how families employ and are influenced by digital media technology is also understudied and undertheorized (Jordan, 2002). Hypotheses regarding families and technology need to be tested using a variety of different methodological approaches. Qualitative methods offer a unique opportunity to explore the use of new digital technologies in the household and are especially adaptive to the changing technological environment. Quantitative methods can provide a nationally representative picture of technology distribution and use within a variety of different households and are especially helpful to monitor use and access across different contexts.

There is much speculation regarding the impact of the newer digital media on family life, yet so little research to substantiate these claims. What we do know is that much like earlier media technologies, the networked digital media are being quickly adopted by families with children, and therefore what roles such media play in the maintenance of family relationships, in the socialization of children, and in the ways families themselves are engaged in life outside the home is an important question for research study. Scholars from family studies and communication need to work together to offer an interdisciplinary perspective to research and find answers to the many questions and concerns regarding technology and the family.

REFERENCES

Bateson, G., Jackson, D. D., Haley, J., & Weakland, J. (1956). Toward a theory of schizophrenia. *Behavioral Science, 1*, 251–264.

Bird, G. A., Goss, R. C., & Bird, G. W. (1990). Effects of home computer use on fathers' lives. *Family Relations, 39*, 438–442.

Bochner, A. P., & Eisenberg, E. M. (1993). Family process: System perspectives. In C. R. Berger & S. H. Chaffee (Eds.), *Handbook of communication science* (pp. 540–563). Beverly Hills, CA: Sage.

Boneva, B., Kraut, R., & Frohlich, D. (2001). Using e-mail for personal relationships: The difference gender makes. *American Behavioral Scientist, 45*, 530–549.

Desmond, R., & Bagli, M. T. (2001, May). *Parent's and young children's communication during computer use: Beyond mediation.* Paper presented at the International Communication Association Annual Conference, Washington, DC.

Doherty, W. J., & Baptiste, D. A., Jr. (1993). Theories emerging from family therapy. In P. G. Boss, W. J. Doherty, R. LaRossa, W. R. Schumm, & S. K. Steinmetz (Eds.), *Sourcebook of family theories and methods: A contextual approach* (pp. 505–524). New York: Plenum Press.

Fabes, R. A., Wilson, P., & Christopher, F. S. (1989). A time to reexamine the role of television in family life. *Family Relations, 38*, 337–341.

Giacquinta, J. B., Bauer, J., & Levin, J. E. (1993). *Beyond technology's promise: an examination of children's educational computing at home.* Cambridge, England: Cambridge University Press.

Girl Scouts of the United States of America. (2002). *The net effect: Girls and new media.* New York: Author.

Grunwald Associates. (2000). Safe and smart (http://www.nsbf.org/safe-samrt/ br-overview.htm).

Hughes, D. R., & Campbell, P. T. (1998). *Kids online: Protecting your children in cyberspace.* Grand Rapids, MI: Fleming H. Revell.

Iannotta, J. G. (Ed.). (2001). *Nontechnical strategies to reduce children's exposure to inappropriate material on the Internet: Summary of a workshop.* Washington, DC: National Academy Press.

Jordan, A. B. (2002). A family systems approach to examining the role of the Internet in the home. In S. L. Calvert, A. B. Jordan, & R. R. Cocking (Eds.), *Children in the digital age: Influences of electronic media on development* (pp. 231–247). Westport, CT: Praeger.

Jordan, A. B., & Woodard, E. H. (2001). Electronic childhood: The availability and use of household media by 2- to 3-year-olds. *Zero to three: Bulletin of zero to three—National Center for Infants, Toddlers, and Families, 22*(2), 4–9.

Kiesler, S., Zdaniuk, B., Lundmark, V., & Kraut, R. (2000). Troubles with the Internet: The dynamics of help at home. *Human-Computer Interaction, 15,* 323–351.

Minuchin, S. (1974). *Families and family therapy.* Cambridge, MA: Harvard University Press.

Mitchell, E. (1985). The dynamics of family interaction around home video games. In M. B. Sussman (Ed.), *Personal computers and the family* (pp. 121–136). New York: Haworth Press.

Morrison, M., & Krugman, D. M. (2001). A look at mass and computer mediated technologies: Understanding the roles of television and computers in the home. *Journal of Broadcasting and Electronic Media, 45,* 135–161.

National Telecommunications and Information Administration. (1998). *Falling through the net II: New data on the digital divide.* Washington, DC: U.S. Department of Commerce.

Pasquier, D., Buzzi, C., d'Haenens, L., & Sjöberg, U. (1998). Family lifestyles and media use patterns: An analysis of domestic media among Flemish, French, Italian, and Swedish children and teenagers. *European Journal of Communication, 13,* 503–519.

Pew Internet and American Life Project. (2000, May 10). *Tracking online life: How women use the Internet to cultivate relationships with family and friends* [Online]. Available: http://www.pewinternet.org/reports

Pew Internet and American Life Project. (2001, May 10). *Teenage life online: The rise of the instant-message generation and the Internet's impact on friendships and family relationships* [Online]. Available: http://www.pewinternet.org/reports

Phillips, C. A., Rolls, S., Rouse, A., & Griffiths, M. D. (1995). Home video game playing in schoolchildren: A study of incidence and patterns of play. *Journal of Adolescence, 18,* 687–691.

Roberts, D. F., Foehr, U. G., Rideout, V. J., & Brodie, M. (1999). *Kids and media at the new millennium: A comprehensive national analysis of children's media use.* Menlo Park, CA: The Henry J. Kaiser Family Foundation.

Scantlin, R. M. (1999). *Interactive media: An analysis of children's computer and video games use.* Unpublished doctoral dissertation, University of Texas at Austin.

Schmitt, K. L. (2000). *Public policy, family rules and children's media use in the home.* Annenberg Public Policy Center of the University of Pennsylvania.

Sluzki, C. E. (1983). Process, structure and world views: Toward an integrated view of systemic models in family therapy. *Family Process, 22,* 469–476.

Spigel, L. (1992). *Make room for TV: Television and the family ideal in postwar America.* Chicago, IL: University of Chicago Press.

Strover, S., Wartella, E., Stout, P., & Richards, J. (1997, June 10–13). *Children and the Internet: Parental concerns and Internet site data.* Paper presented at Federal Trade Commission: Public workshop on consumer information policy. Washington, DC.

Sutherland, R., Facer, K., Furlong, R., & Furlong, J. (2000). A new environment for education? The computer in the home. *Computers and Education, 34,* 195–212.

Tinnell, C. S. (1985). An ethnographic look at personal computers in the family setting. In M.B. Sussman (Ed.), *Personal computers and the family* (pp. 59–69). New York: Haworth Press.

Turow, J. (1999). *The Internet and the family: The view from parents, the view from the press*. Washington, DC: Annenberg Public Policy Center.

Turow, J., & Nir, L. (2000). *The Internet and the family 2000: The views from parents, the view from kids*. Annenberg Public Policy Center of the University of Pennsylvania.

U.S. Department of Commerce. (2002). *A nation online: How Americans are expanding their use of the Internet*. A joint report of the Economics and Statistics Administration and the National Telecommunications and Information Administration. Washington, DC: U.S. Department of Commerce.

Van Schie, E. G. M., & Wiegman, O. (1997). Children and videogames: Leisure activities, aggression, social integration, and school performance. *Journal of Applied Social Psychology, 27*, 1175–1194.

von Bertalanffy, L. (1975). *Perspectives on General System Theory: Scientific-philosophical studies*. New York: George Braziller.

Wartella, E., & Jennings. N. (2001). The role of computers in children's lives. *The Future of Children: Children and Computer Technology, 10*(2), 31–43.

Watt, D., & White, J. M. (1999). Computers and the family life: A family development perspective. *Journal of Comparative Family Studies, 30*, 1–15.

Whitchurch, G. G., & Constantine, L. L. (1993). Systems theory. In P. G. Boss, W. J. Doherty, R. LaRossa, W. R. Schumm, & S. K. Steinmetz, (Eds.), *Sourcebook of family theories and methods: A contextual approach* (pp. 325–352). New York: Plenum Press.

Woodard, E. H. (2000). *Media in the home: The fourth annual survey of parents and children*. Washington, DC: Annenberg Public Policy Center.

Wright, J. C., Huston, A. C., Vandewater, E. A., Bickham, D. S., Scantlin, R. M., Kotler, J. A., Caplovitz, A. G., Lee, J. H., Hofferth, S., & Finkelstein, J. (2001). American children's use of electronic media in 1997: A national survey. *Journal of Applied Developmental Psychology, 22*, 31–47.

27

THE INFLUENCE OF DRUGS AND ALCOHOL ON FAMILY COMMUNICATION: THE EFFECTS THAT SUBSTANCE ABUSE HAS ON FAMILY MEMBERS AND THE EFFECTS THAT FAMILY MEMBERS HAVE ON SUBSTANCE ABUSE

BETH A. LE POIRE

UNIVERSITY OF CALIFORNIA, SANTA BARBARA

The family system has recently become the focus of much research regarding factors promoting substance abuse (e.g., Amey & Albrecht, 1998; Christensen, 1998; Friedman & Utada, 1992; Rotunda, Scherer, & Imm, 1995). This increased focus is certainly because alcohol abuse alone affects one in four homes in America (American College Health Association, 1988; Carroll, 1989), contributing to physical violence and sexual abuse (Raffaeli, 1990), marital distress (Paulino & McGrady, 1977), and compulsive relational and behavioral problems in children (Carroll, 1989). It is clear that alcohol and substance abuse affect every member of the family. Spouses of substance abusers are frequently affected in terms of both physical and mental health (e.g., Hurcom, Coppello, & Orford, 2000). Children of alcoholics, in particular, are at greater risk for behavioral, psychological, cognitive, or neuropsychological deficits (Johnson & Leff, 1999). Siblings of substance abusers are often at greater risk for substance abuse themselves (e.g., Vakalahi, 1999). Parents of adolescent substance abusers may be perceived as more controlling and less loving (e.g., Pandina & Schuele, 1983).

Although all of these effects point to the need to study the effects of substance abuse on the family unit, there is also a great need to study the potential positive intervening effects of family communication for the substance abuser. Specifically, behavioral couples therapy with alcoholics and remission after individual alcoholism treatment have been associated with improved family functioning in the form of reduced family stressors, improved marital adjustment, reduced domestic violence and conflict, reduced risk of separation and divorce, reduced emotional distress in spouses, and improved cohesion and caring (O'Farrell & Feehan, 1999). Additionally, greater family involvement in treatment has been associated with abstinence, better family relations, and positive feelings about self (e.g., McCrady et al., 1986; McNabb, Der-Karabetian, & Rhoads, 1989). Further, Le Poire, Hallet, and Erlandson (2000) found that consistently punishing substance abuse combined with consistently reinforcing alternative behavior was predictive of lesser relapse in a substance-abusing sample, whereas Prescott and Le Poire (in press) found that consistently reinforcing alternative behavior predicted significantly higher perceptions of mothers' persuasive effectiveness in an eating-disordered sample.

All of these relational effects point directly to the need to study the impact that family members can have in not only influencing continued substance abuse but also increasing the helping family member's own mental health and overall family functioning. This chapter discusses the ramifications of substance abuse on various family members. The focus is on effects on the spouse, the children, the siblings, and the parents of adolescent abusers. Based on research that supports the Inconsistent Nurturing as Control (INC) theory assertion that significant others (spouses/cohabitors) in relationships with substance-dependent individuals unintentionally and subtly encourage the substance-abusive behavior of their partners through their well-intentioned efforts to discourage the undesirable behavior (Le Poire, 1992, 1994; Le Poire & Cope, 1999; Le Poire, Erlandson, & Hallett, 1998; Le Poire et al., 2000), this work also explores the unique role that communication plays in sustaining or deterring family members' substance abuse in four family relationships: substance abuser–spouse, parent–adolescent child, sibling–sibling, and children–parents.

BACKGROUND

Spousal Relationships

Much of the literature focuses on the role of the spouse in relationship to the alcoholic or substance abuser (e.g., Epstein & McGrady, 1998). The reason for this is twofold. First, the popular notion of co-dependency, or co-alcoholic, originated in the 1970s to refer to partners of alcoholics who seemed to be "addicted" to their alcoholic partners. This popular notion included the idea that partners of substance abusers were simultaneously enmeshing and controlling. Second, a simultaneous trend in the scholarly literature classified the spouse of the alcoholic as "dominating" and attempting to sabotage the alcoholic's attempts to recover. Thus, this review of spouses of substance abusers begins with the notion of "co-dependency," considers scholarly treatments that assume partners (usually wives) of substance abusers are dominating, and ends with a treatment of the relationship that considers the nature of the relationship as opposed to the individual-level personality variables associated with either partner. This approach proffers that relational paradoxes that exist in the substance abuser–spouse relationship make it very difficult for this partner to attempt to control the substance abuse effectively. This perspective takes blame away from the spouse and places the focus more squarely in the unique dynamics of the relationship—with all of the challenges lying therein.

Overview of Co-Dependency.   Although the term co-dependency has been widely used in both academic and popular literature, its precise meaning is still quite unclear. Further, there is even greater variability in the characteristics said to describe those who are co-dependent. Regardless of this variability in the overall characteristics delineated by various authors, there is a surprising amount of overlap on a few key concepts (e.g., nurturing, control, and maintenance of a relationship with a substance abuser). To put the abundance of additional characteristics in high relief, Le Poire, Hallett, and Giles (1998) summarized this literature into seven categories of characteristics of co-dependents: (a) socialization/ development factors, (b) psychological–relational factors, (c) emotional factors, (d) cognitive factors, (e) communicative factors, (f) behavioral factors, and (g) consequences of so-called "failure." (For a complete overview, see Table One in Le Poire et al., 1998). Socialization/development includes such factors as being raised by substance abusers. Psychological–relational characteristics include low self-esteem and anxiety. Emotional tendencies include letting the chemically dependent partner determine one's feelings and hypervigilence concerning the spouse's emotions. Cognitive characteristics include obsessing about the spouse's behavior. Communicative characteristics include attempts to control the spouse's behavior. Behavioral tendencies include compulsions. Finally, consequences of so-called "failure" of influencing the substance abuse include suicide attempts and threats to leave. This summary is not exhaustive but is a fair representation of those qualities most commonly associated with co-dependent individuals. The most striking aspect of this overview is that it vividly points out that most of the characteristics attributed to co-dependents are negative. In addition, this overview illustrates the often-cited criticism that conceptualizations of co-dependency include so many common characteristics as to be virtually fruitless with regard to treatment or clear diagnosis.

Because it is unlikely that co-dependents' characteristics are entirely negative, it will be useful to consider definitions of co-dependency that illucidate the potentially paradoxical nature of the relationship they have with substance abusers and the like. Definitions of co-dependency tend to focus on (a) *control* (e.g., Beattie, 1987; Cermak, 1984; Schaef, 1987), (b) *nurturing* (e.g., Friel & Friel, 1987; Gordon & Barrett, 1993), and (c) *maintenance of relationships with chemically dependent individuals* (e.g., Phillips, 1988; Whitfield, 1994; Wegscheider-Cruse, 1987), or on individuals who engage in undesirable behavior (including alcoholism or drug dependence) (e.g., Becker, 1989; Cermak, 1986; DuPont & McGovern, 1991).

In one of the most well-known and accepted definitions of co-dependency in the popular press, Beatie (1987) asserts that a co-dependent is "one who has let another person's behavior affect him or her, and who is obsessed with controlling that person's behavior" (p. 31). Although Beatie's definition only implies that co-dependents are "obsessive," others are more blaming and argue that co-dependents may unconsciously perpetuate the unhealthy behavior of family members. Dupont and McGovern (1991) go so far as to argue that co-dependent individuals "share the responsibility for the unhealthy behavior, primarily by focusing their lives on the sick or the bad behavior and by making their own self-esteem and well-being contingent on the behavior of the unhealthy family member" (p. 316).

Such blaming of the co-dependent has led to the claim in the more scholarly press that co-dependency is a psychological disorder that should be capable of a DSM (Diagnostic

Statistical Manual of the American Psychological Association) diagnosis (e.g., Nathans, 1981). In fact, co-dependency has been defined as "a recognizable pattern of personality traits, predictably found within most members of chemically dependent families, which are capable of creating sufficient dysfunction to warrant diagnosis of Mixed Personality Disorder in DSM III" (Cermak, 1986, p. 1). This diagnosis of co-dependent personality disorder is further argued to be possible through the use of the following five diagnostic criteria: (a) investment of self-esteem in the ability to control oneself and others in adverse situations; (b) assumption of responsibility for meeting others' needs to the exclusion of one's own; (c) anxiety and boundary distortions around intimacy and separation; (d) enmeshment in relationships with personality disordered, chemically dependent, other co-dependent, and/or impulse-disordered individuals; and (e) three or more of the following: excessive denial, constricted emotions, depression, hypervigilance, compulsions, anxiety, substance abuse, sexual or physical abuse victim, stress-related illness, or maintenance of a primary relationship with an active substance abuser for 2 or more years.

Emphasis on Nonaddicted Spouse as Domineering. Although certainly useful in terms of considering co-dependence with regard to the relational implications of nurturing, control, and relationship maintenance, diagnosing co-dependence as a psychiatric disorder is consistent with 1970s' theorizing that wives unconsciously encourage substance-dependent behavior due to their own pathological problems of martyrdom or desire for domination over their husbands (e.g., Paige, La Pointe, & Krueger, 1971; Rae & Drewery, 1972; Whalen, 1953). Although this perspective has often been discounted as overly blaming of the spouse, and particularly of female spouses (e.g., Anderson, 1994; Haaken, 1990; Hurcom et al., 2000), the later theorizing of family systems is also consonant with this line of reasoning (Kaufman, 1985; Kaufman & Kaufmann, 1979; Steinglass, 1976). Ewing and Fox (1968) have argued that the principle of balance within the system is used in the alcoholic family to resist change. This is suspected to manifest itself in the substance abuser–spouse relationship, in that alterations by one spouse (e.g., reduction in drinking behavior) prompt the other to attempt to maintain the status quo. To illustrate this claim in substance-abuser relationships, these theorists would argue that spouses of recovering substance abusers may be uncomfortable with losing their role behavior and may unconsciously encourage their spouse's relapse. Fundamentally, the systems approach discounts the "disease model" of alcoholism and proffers instead that the "sickness" of the family (vs. the individual) may be causing and/or maintaining the drinking. This set of claims was quite heuristic and much backlash resulted. For example, Martin and Piazza (1995) found that co-dependency is not a separate personality disorder in women (based on Cermak's, 1986, criteria) but is indicative of women presenting combined personality disorders or situationally adaptive response mechanisms. Further, Chiauzzi and Liljegren (1993) criticize the notion that partners of substance abusers may be partly responsible for the substance abuse by citing the lack of empirical support for this disease conceptualization of co-dependency. Results continue to be mixed in this debate. Ballard (1959) found that wives of alcoholics did not score higher on maladjustment than did a comparable control group. Others found that although many wives of alcoholics exhibited some personality dysfunction, just as many did not (Walfish, Stenmark, Shealy, & Krone, 1992). Still other research found that co-dependent people were no more depressed than non-co-dependent people (O'Brien & Gaborit, 1992). Most salient to the current treatment, Edwards, Harvey, and Whitehead (1973) argued that any dysfunction a wife of an alcoholic may experience is situationally dependent on her spouse drinking. In other words, mental health dysfunction of wives is higher when their spouse drinks and lower when their spouse is abstinent. Partners of substance abusers may exhibit higher anxiety and depression *because* their partners are not in control of their substance abuse. Thus, it is possible that the unique dynamics of the relationship elicit the responses of both substance abusers and their spouses.

COMPETING GOALS OF NURTURING AND CONTROL AND FAMILY COMMUNICATION

Inconsistent Nurturing as Control Theory

Inconsistent nurturing as control theory is based on the assumption that functional partners (partners of substance abusers or otherwise nonfunctioning or afflicted individuals) have competing goals of nurturing and controlling (see Le Poire, 1992, 1994, for a review). Le Poire (1994) argues that there are several paradoxical injunctions in relationships that include afflicted partners (e.g., drug abusers, aggressive individuals, depressed individuals, eating-disordered individuals) and that these paradoxes ultimately impact expressions of control by the functional family member (i.e., the partner with no problem interfering with day-to-day functioning) in the relationship. The contradictory nature of the functional family members' nurturing and subsequently controlling behavior is at the heart of the most problematic paradox in the relationship. Specifically, simultaneously, functional family members wish to retain their relationship *while* they attempt to extinguish the undesirable behavior (e.g., Prescott & Le Poire, 2002). In addition, it is possible that the afflicted individual maintains the relationship because the functional family member's nurturing behavior is highly rewarding (Le Poire, 1994). Taken together, these assumptions lead to the paradoxical conclusion that if functional family members actually control the undesirable behavior, they will lose their ability to utilize their nurturing resource base in response to that undesirable behavior. Although less supported by the literature, it is possible that functional family members may ultimately be driven by the fear that extinguishing the undesirable behavior will decrease the substance abuser's dependency on them. These competing goals could lead to the inconsistent use of reinforcement and punishment of the behavior that is the focus of change attempts. This inconsistency is at the heart of INC theory and could lead to decreased effectiveness of the functionals' attempts to diminish the undesirable behavior.

Application to the Functional Family Member–Substance-Dependent Relationship

In learning theory terms, INC argues that the functional family members' initial nurturing behavior may *reinforce* the substance dependent's drug-dependent behavior. This reinforcement may work in contradistinction to the functionals' goals, because it may actually increase the likelihood that the behavior will be repeated (Le Poire, 1994). Even more problematically, functional family members may *intermittently* reinforce behaviors they actually want to extinguish. When caregivers become resentful, as is likely to happen (e.g., Wiseman, 1991), they may fail to nurture, and thus fail to reinforce, the substance dependent. This intermittent reinforcement may ultimately strengthen the behavior of the abusive person because intermittent reinforcement produces more long-term nonextinguishable behavior than continuous reinforcement. The lack of caregiving on the functionals' part is likely an attempt to *punish*, or extinguish, the undesirable behavior of the dependent partner. INC theory argues that similar to intermittent reinforcement, the intermittent nature of this punishing behavior should actually *increase* the substance abuse, as well. Thus, inconsistent nurturing as control may ultimately strengthen the likelihood of substance-abusive behavior through the learning theory processes of both intermittent reinforcement and intermittent punishment.

This suspected inconsistency manifests itself within communication behavior over the life span of the relationship. Specifically, Le Poire et al. (2000) interviewed partners of substance abusers in order to investigate the patterning of their strategy usage. Before labeling their partner as substance abusive, functional partners typically reinforced the substance-abusive behavior of their partner (e.g., offering a drink when they got home from work or using substances with their partner). Subsequent to a significant event that promoted labeling of their partner as substance abusive (e.g., a car accident, partner missing for weeks, violence, etc.), functional partners dramatically shifted their behavior to punishing their partner (e.g., calling the police, threatening to leave, removing substances from the house). In sum, this first study of INC theory hypothesized and found that functional partners (of both genders) changed their strategy usage over time so that they (a) reinforced substance-dependent behavior more before their determination that the behavior was problematic than after; (b) punished substance-dependent behavior more after, than before, they labeled the drinking/drugging behavior as being problematic; and (c) upon frustration, reverted to a mix of reinforcing and punishing strategies, resulting in an overall pattern of inconsistent reinforcement and punishment. Thus, as expected by INC theory, reinforcement is followed by punishment, which in turn is followed by reinforcement mixed with punishment.

This cycling was also supported by a qualitative analysis of the strategies reported by functional partners of substance abusers (Le Poire, Addis, Duggan, & Dailey, 2003). Based on this analysis, strategies fell more broadly within reinforcing and punishing categorizations. Specifically, functional partners reported using verbal abuse, making rules pertaining to the addiction, punishment, getting a third party involved, threats, avoidance, ending the relationship, expressing personal feelings, withholding something from the partner as a punishment, supporting abuse by participation, demanding the partner stop/active involvement, and confronting. The use of these strategies approximates the hypothesized inconsistent and intermittent use of reinforcement and punishment of the substance abusive behavior and is certain to strengthen the tendency to engage in alcohol or drug use.

One further question regarding this patterning pertains to the effectiveness of the inconsistent strategies. For the theory to hold, greater inconsistency should be more predictive of relapse and less predictive of persuasive effectiveness. However, it is important to note that this patterning in and of itself was not found to be more predictive of greater relapse.

In contrast, patterns of reinforcement and punishment were linked to persuasive outcomes (Le Poire et al., 2000). To be more specific, partners who were more consistent in punishing substance abuse and reinforcing alternative behavior (e.g., encouraging attendance at AA meetings) had substance abusive partners who relapsed less. Moreover, more successful partners also reported less depression than those with partners who relapsed more. This is important for two reasons. First, partners of substance abusing individuals can aid in their partners reduced recidivism. Secondly, this assistance can also translate into better mental health outcomes for the partners.

A third study was undertaken to determine if episodic versus steady alcoholics had partners who differentially reinforced and punished substance abuse (Le Poire & Cope, 1999). Given that steady drinking may provide more positive functioning for the family unit than less predictable episodic drinking (e.g., Jacob & Leonard, 1988), it was predicted that partners of episodic drinkers may be more motivated to stop the alcoholic behavior and thus may use more effective strategies than partners of steady drinkers. Contrary to the prediction, partners of episodic drinkers used less effective strategies (less consistency), whereas partners of steady drinkers used more effective strategies (greater reinforcement of alternative behavior) immediately following the alcoholism labeling. Following frustration with initially unsuccessful persuasive attempts, however, alcoholism subtype did operate as expected, in that partners of episodic drinkers used more effective strategies (greater consistency combined with more punishment of drinking behavior) than did partners of steady drinkers.

This chapter takes an important step forward, as substance abusers and their partners do not live in a vacuum; rather, they are continually surrounded by their children, their siblings, and their parents. Thus, it is of paramount importance that we also study the ways in which other important family members also attempt to assist their substance-abusing family member in their struggle with substance abuse. Continued evidence of this patterning of strategy usage in other important family relationships (with parents, children, and siblings) would support the additional contention that family members intermittently reinforce and punish the behavior they are trying to extinguish. This theoretical contention has successfully been applied to parents in other studies. For instance, Prescott and Le Poire (2002) found that mothers of eating-disordered daughters displayed similar patterns of reinforcement and punishment. This test (applied to anorexics and bulimics) found that mothers reinforced eating disorders more before they labeled the behavior problematic, whereas they punished the eating disorders more after. Further, results indicated that consistently reinforcing alternative behavior immediately following labeling of the eating disorder significantly predicted higher perceptions of the mothers' persuasive effectiveness. Finally, reinforcing the eating disorder predicted greater amounts of relapse. The most important implication of these findings for the current treatment is that significant family members (i.e., mothers) use patterns of inconsistent reinforcement and punishment similar to those used by partners of substance abusers. What is still to be determined is the role of important family members in helping to deter future substance abuse. Evidence of this patterning of strategy usage in future studies would support the contention that other significant family members (in addition to spouses) intermittently reinforce and punish the behavior they are trying to extinguish.

Parent–Adolescent Relationships

Much research has examined the role of parents in adolescents' substance use and abuse. Supporting the importance of examining this relationship, Coombs, Paulson, and Richardson (1991) found that parental influence was more profound than peer influence in accounting for substance use and that viable relationships with parents promoted less involvement in drugs. Pointing to the importance of communication and control attempts within the family, Garcia-Pindado (1992) found that major factors predicting adolescent drug use include communication problems between parents and children and inadequate discipline within the family. This supports the need to study parental attempts to control adolescent substance abuse.

Many studies of parent–adolescent relations and substance abuse support the inconsistent nurturing as control theory contention that both nurturing and control messages are important in predicting adolescents' substance abuse. For instance, Hall, Henggeler, Ferreira, and East (1992) found that adolescents' substance use was associated with family affection and parental control, whereas Pandina and Schuele (1983) found that higher adolescent substance abuse was associated with higher levels of perceived parental control and lower perceived parental love. Additionally, frequency of adolescent substance use increased with high parental expectations and bad social climate in the family (Hurrelmann, 1990), and problematic drinking behavior was associated with low levels of family social support and with dysfunctional coping strategies (Schor, 1996). Speaking to the inconsistent messages of support and control, Smart, Chibucos, and Didier (1990) found that adolescents who perceived their families to be extreme on cohesion and adaptability were more likely than adolescents from balanced and midrange families to use marijuana, alcohol, tobacco, depressants, and psychedelics. Fletcher and Jefferies (1999) found that perceived authoritative parenting was associated with lower levels of substance use for both boys and girls, whereas perceived parental disciplinary consequences of engaging in substance use was also important for girls. Additionally, Friedman and Utada (1992) found that 60% of families including an adolescent substance abuser were classified as rigid-disengaged (low in adaptability and low in cohesion).

All of these messages of support and control can be perceived as contradictory, and thus may lead to inconsistent findings with regard to control attempts and substance abuse outcomes for adolescents. Humes and Humphrey (1994) found that parents of substance-abusing daughters communicated a conflictual message of both greater affirmation and condemnation of their daughters' autonomy. Directly relevant to the current discussion, Stice, Barrera, and Chassin (1993) found that moderate amounts of parental control and parental support were more clearly related to decreased illicit drug use than were high and low amounts, whereas higher amounts of control and support were both predictive of decreased alcohol use—thus, control and support use were inconsistently related to substance abuse outcomes. Findings are even more inconsistent, however, in that Spoth, Redmond, Hockaday, and Yoo (1996) found that affectional relationships with parents did not predict alcohol abstinence as expected. This could be explained by the INC contention that nurturing behaviors may actually promote substance abuse when inconsistently mixed with punishment. This inconsistency in the relationships between control, support, and decreased alcohol use points to the need to directly examine the strategies that parents use in attempts to control their adolescents' substance abuse in terms of their reinforcing and punishing natures. Given that many of the aforementioned studies also found that modeling of substance abuse by parents is an important factor (e.g., Orenstein & Ullman, 1996), parents' current drug use status should also be taken into account.

Sibling Relationships

In order to understand the whole family system, studying sibling relationships with adolescent substance abusers is also very important. For instance, Hall et al. (1992) found that several aspects of sibling relations were linked with substance use, and in some cases, sibling relations measures (especially sibling conflict) accounted for significantly more variance in substance use than did family relations measures. Although parents play an important role in adolescent substance abuse, older brother–younger brother relationships also have a significant impact on younger brother substance abuse (Brook, Brook, & Whiteman, 1999; Brook, Whiteman, Gordon, & Brook, 1990), as do sibling substance abuse (Handelsman et al., 1993; Lloyd, 1998; Merikangas, Rounsaville, & Prusoff, 1992; Vakalahi, 1999) and sibling completion of substance abuse treatment programs (Feigelman, 1987).

Most relevant to the current exploration, it has also been postulated that siblings may attempt to sabotage substance abuse recovery attempts (Huberty & Huberty, 1986). Thus, from a family systems perspective, it is very important to try to understand the types of strategies that siblings of adolescent substance abusers use in an attempt to deter their substance-abusing sibling's substance abuse. It is highly possible that they use inconsistently reinforcing and subsequently punishing strategies as predicted by inconsistent nurturing as control theory. This inconsistency is likely to result in strengthened, as opposed to weakened, tendencies to abuse substances. This is especially likely to manifest in relationships in which an older sibling is trying to influence a younger sibling (Brook et al., 1990, 1999); thus, birth order should also be measured in research on the influence of siblings on substance abuse. The effects of modeling have been shown to be stronger from older to younger siblings, and older siblings' rivalry with younger siblings may result in greater attempts to sabotage the "good" recovering behavior of the substance abuser so that the older sibling may shine by comparison.

Child–Parent Relationships

In order to round out the picture of family members' role in substance abusers' recovery, it is also very important to understand the role that children of substance abusers may play in helping their mother or father recover from drug or alcohol abuse. The detrimental effects of being raised by a substance-abusing parent have been well documented (e.g., Mothersead, Kivilighan, & Wynkoop, 1998), ranging from increased maltreatment (e.g., Sheridan, 1995; Shuntich, Loh, & Katz, 1998) and increased maladjustment (Rubio-Stipen, Bird, Canino, & Bravo, 1991) to increased probability of foster care (Dore, Doris, & Wright, 1995). Additionally, offspring of substance abusers show a higher incidence of anxiety disorders and substance disorders, as well as conduct disorders and depression (Lachner & Wittchen, 1995; Merikangas, Dierker, & Szamari, 1998). In an adult sample, offspring of alcoholics and nonalcoholics were distinguished by personality characteristics such as low self-esteem, anxiousness, and lack of emotional expression (Lachner & Wittchen).

Others caution that these effects are not certain. Some studies have shown that parental alcoholism was not a significant predictor of differences in adult self-esteem or locus of control (Werner & Broida, 1991), nor on the majority of measures assessing multiple aspects of psychological well-being and personality development (Tweed & Ryff, 1991). Specifically, there may be an interaction between presence of substance-abusing parents and supportive relationships with nonabusing parents and siblings and appropriate levels of parentification, which permit the child of an alcoholic to have high self-esteem and adaptive capabilities while simultaneously lacking problematic substance use (Walker & Lee, 1998). In contradistinction, however, studies of the protective effects of sober parents found very little evidence of the buffering hypothesis (Curran & Chassin, 1996). Thus, we should use caution as research in this area has not yet produced a definitive or coherent picture (Hurcom et al., 2000).

Still other findings link children from homes in which one or both parents are labeled problem drinkers with alcohol disorders (e.g., Cloninger, 1987; Goodwin, 1985; Pihl, Peterson, & Finn, 1990; Sher, 1991; Tarter, Laird, & Moss, 1990; Windle & Searles, 1990), earlier onset of illicit substance use, higher rates of lifetime marijuana and cocaine use, and more frequent adolescent antisocial behavior (Windle, 1996). Consistent with the buffering argument presented earlier, some work has found that highly organized families and behavioral coping efforts may deter substance use initiation (Hussong & Chassin, 1997). Still other studies find no relationship between the status of children of alcoholics and either the likelihood or the severity of problem drinking (Havey & Dodd, 1993).

All of these findings would indicate a highly stressful situation for the child of the substance abuser. What is still to be understood are the ways in which children may attempt to deter their parents' future substance abuse episodes as they continue to live in this stressful situation. It is highly likely that children begin to understand the disruptive nature of their family life is linked to substance abuse and, therefore, that children will begin attempts to deter their parents' substance abuse in the future. In line with inconsistent nurturing as control theory, because children also love their parents and desire positive relations, it is likely that they will sometimes inadvertently do things that are nurturing and therefore reinforce the substance-abusing behavior. Thus, it is very important to undertake an examination of the types of strategies that adult children of substance abusers report using surrounding their parents' substance abuse episodes when they were living with their substance-abusing parent.

Relationship to Early Parental Attachment. The first factor argued to be associated with co-dependency by Le Poire et al. (1998) was socialization/development. It is possible to argue that one of the factors making pairing with an alcoholic/substance abuser more likely is the parental upbringing one had as a child. Although many studies have linked parental substance abuse with adult children of alcoholics' tendency to abuse illicit substances themselves (see e.g., Cloninger, 1987; Goodwin, 1985; Pihl, Peterson et al., 1990; Sher, 1991; Tarter, Laird, & Moss, 1990; Windle & Searles, 1990), it is also possible that adult children of alcoholics are more likely to become involved in relationships with substance abusers themselves, because this recreates the situation in which they learned fundamental attachment.

Although a complete review is beyond the scope of the current work, a brief overview of attachment theory is offered in order to explore the possible relational links between growing up with a substance abuser and having a tendency to have relationships with substance abusers later in life. Much work has extended Bowlby's (e.g., 1980) and Ainsworth's (1991) initial work on early childhood attachment to later romantic attachments. Bowlby and Ainsworth argue that closeness and availability of a caregiver early in life provide individuals with "working models" for relationships later in life.

Bowlby's concept of inner working models has been incorporated in the work of Bartholomew and Horowitz (1991). They indicate a four-category model of attachment styles in adults. These prototypes, or working models, were based on the participants' self-image and on their images of others. This resulted in a two by two classification, using positive/negative evaluations of self and other as the anchors. Those who had positive opinions of themselves and had positive opinions of others were considered secure. Individuals who had negative opinions of the self but positive opinions of others were labeled preoccupied because they were preoccupied with finding external validation. People who had negative opinions of themselves and negative opinions of others were labeled fearful (one type of avoidant) because they were fearful of intimacy and avoided contact with others. Individuals who had positive opinions about themselves and negative opinions of others were labeled dismissive (a second type of avoidant), because they protected themselves from other people by dismissing relationships and remaining independent.

Applying nonverbal expressions of closeness and distance to attachment, Le Poire, Shepard, and Duggan (1999) argue that secures should have low fears of intimacy and abandonment because they should have fairly positive working models of self and other as argued by Bartholomew and Horowitz (1991). Contrast this with preoccupieds, who should have a high fear of abandonment (due to their childhood abandonment) with an underlying fear of intimacy (because being close to someone means you are likely to be abandoned). Finally, role-reverseds (children who were expected to parent their parents and become avoidants later in life) should have a high fear of intimacy (fearing a loss of self), with an underlying fear of abandonment because they were simultaneously enmeshed and emotionally abandoned. These fears, in turn, should lead to fairly consistent predispositions to attach to certain types of individuals later in life.

Applying the work reviewed earlier regarding children of alcoholics and substance abusers, it is quite possible that adult children of alcoholics might develop insecure working models regarding others and themselves in relationships. Specifically, it is quite possible that children of substance abusers feel abandoned at times physically, but mostly emotionally. This abandonment is likely to translate into the low self-esteem outcomes reported earlier. For instance, Baker and Stephenson (1995) reported that female adult children of alcoholics were found to be more flexible, impulsive, and pessimistic, and with less of a sense of well-being than that of control women. The tendency of these women to have a negative opinion of self and a positive opinion of others may result in a preoccupied style of attachment. This style of attachment may lead to attraction to other equally unavailable partners (i.e., substance abusers) later in life as the cycle self-perpetuates.

Alternatively, being parented by a substance abuser may lead children to parent their parent. This role reversal is likely to lead to inappropriate enmeshment between the parent and the child. Although children should be developing an independent sense of themselves, it is likely that their sense of self is attained from caregiving behavior and being aware of others' needs. This is supported by Devine and Braithwaite (1993), who found that parental alcoholism was the sole predictor of the adoption of the "responsible child" role in the family. Adopting such a role likely translates into fears of intimacy and an avoidant attachment style, as closeness has led to loss of identity in the past. Thus, adolescent children of alcoholics may become avoidants later in life because they have higher opinions of themselves (they were certainly more trustworthy than their substance-abusing and unpredictable parents) and negative opinions of others.

Thus, children of substance-abusing parents may become preoccupied or avoidant in relationships with others later in life. Future research is required to link up earlier work on attachment models (e.g., Le Poire et al., 1999) and work on inconsistent nurturing as control theory (e.g., Le Poire et al., 2000). This theoretical integration is required because of the clear link between being raised by substance abusers and the development of co-dependency with others in later life. It is likely that children of substance abusers will manifest preoccupied and avoidant attachment styles with significant others who are as behaviorally unreliable as their parents. This pattern will likely manifest itself in similar patterns of nurturing and control attempts with their romantic partners—whether this partner is substance abusing or not. It is likely that patterns of behavior established in those first foundational relationships will serve as models for later relationships.

Complicating Factors

Dual Diagnoses and Substance Abuse Disorders. Because a consistent finding is that between 30% (Sheehan, 1993) and over 50% of substance-dependent individuals are susceptible to dual diagnoses (e.g., Bryant, Rounsaville, Spitzer, & Williams, 1992) including antisocial personality disorder (Lehman, Myers, Thompson, & Corty, 1993), it is important to consider the impact such personality disorders may have on communication behavior and on communication outcomes associated with the proposed investigation. In fact, one group of researchers is studying two treatment regimens (individual versus systemic models) with differing outcomes predicted based on the coping style (personality type) of the substance-dependent (e.g., Beutler et al., 1993). In this research, externalizers are characterized by impulsive, aggressive, and sociopathic behaviors (antisocial), whereas internalizers are less aggressive, act out less, and exhibit more neurotic and anxious features. Following this characterization, the researchers argue that externalizers should respond more to individually based treatments, whereas internalizers respond more to familially based treatments.

These patterns also should have implications for the mental health of family members continuing to live with the substance abuser. Implications can be drawn from the spousal relationship, with spouses continuing to live with a partner who alternates between sobriety and drunkenness experiencing substantial anxiety (Howard & Howard, 1985). Williams and Fisher (1994) found that wives of alcoholics had greater state and trait anxiety and depression as a result of the coping and drinking style of their husbands. Wives with externalizing (acting out) husbands and husbands who drank outside the home had more state and trait anxiety, as well as depression, than wives with internalizing (self-blaming) husbands. Since externalizing individuals and individuals drinking outside the home are less likely to be affected by the control attempts of their spouses (Beutler et al., 1993), it is possible to argue that spouses who are more effective at controlling their partners' drugging behavior are less likely to experience poor mental health. This is consistent with the finding that the stress effects of living with an alcoholic partner diminish when the spouse makes attempts to control the other's excessive drinking (Edwards et al., 1973; Paulino & McCrady, 1977). Further, and most relevant to the current treatment, partners/spouses of substance abusers were less depressed when their partners relapsed less (Le Poire et al., 2000). Extrapolating to other family members, it is expected that parents of adolescent substance abusers, adult children, and siblings who are successfully modifying their family members' substance abuse behavior will experience substantially less anxiety and depression as a result of greater predictability in the home environment.

Co-Abusing. Still others may be concerned that homogamy of family members regarding substance abuse status could contribute to the ineffectiveness of strategy usage. In fact, Le Poire et al. (1998) undertook a study to explore this very issue. They investigated the use of reinforcing and punishing drug discontinuance strategies based on the drug use status of the functional/persuading partners (past abuse, current abuse, current use, and nonuse). In terms of overall patterns of reinforcement and punishment, all partners were inconsistent in their use of reinforcement and punishment of substance abuse, with past abusers punishing the substance abuse most, before they labeled the drug use problematic, and current users and nonusers punishing the substance abuse the most, following the labeling and in the postfrustration period. Additionally, current abusers were the most reinforcing of alternative behavior during every time period: a strategy that was most highly related to reduction in relapse (Le Poire et al., 2000). Further, with regard to a more qualitative analysis of strategy type, nonusers employed the most indulgence and antidrink strategies—strategies that clearly are in opposition based on their reinforcing and punishing natures. Further, past abusers were rated as most persuasively effective by their partners, whereas nonusers were evaluated as the least persuasively effective. It is important to examine the substance use status of the persuading family members, because modeling by parents (e.g., Ornstein & Ullman, 1993) and siblings (e.g., Handelsman et al., 1993) has been known to be associated with greater substance abuse.

SUMMARY AND CONCLUSIONS

The current work emphasizes the fact that all family members are influenced by substance abuse in the family environment regardless of whether the substance-abusive family member is a spouse, a parent, an adolescent child, or a sibling. Consider a father who abuses heroin. Not only does his spouse have a much higher chance of experiencing anxiety and depression due to the day to day chaos in the household (e.g., Howard & Howard, 1985), but also the child of such a father is more likely to use illicit substances him/herself (e.g., Windle, 1996) as well as experience lower self-esteem and an external locus of control (e.g., Lachner & Wittchen, 1995). Further, the child, especially if he/she is an older sibling, may significantly increase the chances that his/her little brother or sister may abuse substances by modeling that behavior (e.g., Brook et al., 1999).

This work explored not only the deleterious effects that substance abuse can have on family members, but also the potential positive intervening effects of family communi-cation for continued substance abuse. Specifically, behavioral couples therapy has been associated with improved family functioning (O'Farrell & Feehan, 1999), abstinence, bet-ter family relations, and positive feelings about self (e.g., McCrady et al., 1986). Further, Le Poire et al. (2000) found that consistently punishing substance abuse combined with consistently reinforcing alternative behavior was predictive of lesser relapse in a substance-abusing sample. This lesser relapse was also predictive of less anxiety and depression in the functional partner. Through greater examination of all family members' use of incon-sistent nurturing as control, we may better understand the mechanisms by which spouses can help each other, children can help their parents, parents can help their adolescent children, and siblings can help each other in the familial battle against substance abuse.

AUTHOR'S NOTE

Beth A. Le Poire (PhD, University of Arizona, 1991) is Professor of Communication in the Department of Communication at the University of California, Santa Barbara.

REFERENCES

Ainsworth, M. D. S. (1991). Attachments and other affectional bonds across the life cycle. In C. M. Parkes, J. Stevenson-Hinde, & P. Marris (Eds.), *Attachment across the life cycle* (pp. 33–51). New York: Tavistock/Routledge.

American College Health Association. (1988). *Adult children of alcohol abusers.* Rockville, MD.

Amey, C. H., & Albrecht, S. L. (1998). Race and ethnic differences in adolescent drug use: The impact of family structure and the quantity and quality of parental interaction. *Journal of Drug Issues, 28,* 283–298.

Anderson, S. C. (1994). A critical analysis of the concept of codependency. *Social Work, 39,* 677–685.

Baker, D. E., & Stephenson, L. A. (1995). Personality-characteristics of adult children of alcoholics. *Journal of Clinical Psychology, 51,* 694–702.

Ballard, R. G. (1959). The interaction between marital conflict and alcoholism as seen through MMPIs of marriage partners. *American Journal of Orthopsychiatry, 29,* 528–546.

Bartholomew, K., & Horowitz, L. M. (1991). Attachment styles among young adults: A test of a four-category model. *Journal of Personality and Social Psychology, 61,* 226–244.

Beattie, M. (1987). *Codependent no more: How to stop controlling others and start caring for yourself.* New York: Harper & Row.

Becker, R. (1989). *Addicted to misery: The other side of co-dependency.* Deerfield Beach, FL: Health Communications, Inc.

Beutler, L. E., Patterson, K. M., Jacob, T., Shoham, V., Yost, E., & Rohrbaugh, M. (1993). Matching treatment to alcoholic subtypes. *Psychotherapy, 30*, 463–472.

Bowlby, J. (1980). *Attachment and loss: Vol. 3. Loss.* New York: Basic Books.

Brook, J. S., Brook, D. W., & Whiteman, M. (1999). Older sibling correlates of younger sibling drug use in the context of parent-child relations. *Genetic, Social, and General Psychology Monographs, 125*, 451–468.

Brook, J. S., Whiteman, M., Gordon, A. S., & Brook, D. W. (1990). The role of older brothers in younger brothers' drug use viewed in the context of parent and peer influences. *The Journal of Genetic Psychology, 151*, 59–75.

Bryant, K. J., Rounsaville, B., Spitzer, R. L., & Williams, J. B. (1992). Reliability of dual diagnosis: Substance dependence and psychiatric disorders. *Journal of Nervous and Mental Disease, 180*, 251–257.

Carroll, C. R. (1989). *Drugs* (2nd ed.). Dubuque, IA: Brown.

Cermak, T. L . (1984). Children of alcoholics and the case for a new diagnostic category of codependency. *Alcohol Health and Research World, 3*, 38–42.

Cermak, T. L. (1986). *Diagnosing and treating co-dependence: A guide for professionals who work with chemical dependents, their spouses and children.* Minneapolis: Johnson Institute Books.

Chiauzzi, E. J., & Liljegren, S. (1993). Taboo topics in addiction treatment: An empirical review of clinical folklore. *Journal of Substance Abuse Prevention, 10*, 303–316.

Christensen, H. B. (1998). Alcoholism, relation, and family interaction. *Nordisk Psykologi, 50*, 280–304.

Cloninger, C. R. (1987). A systematic method for clinical description and classification of personality variants. A proposal. *Archives of General Psychiatry, 44*, 573–588.

Coombs, R. H., Paulson, M. J., & Richardson, M. A. (1991). Peer vs. parental influence in substance use among Hispanic and Anglo children and adolescents. *Journal of Youth and Adolescence, 20*, 73–88.

Curran, P. J., & Chassin, L. (1996). A longitudinal study of parenting as a protective factor for children of alcoholics. *Journal of Studies on Alcohol, 57*, 305–313.

Devine, C., & Braithwaite, V. (1993). The survival roles of children of alcoholics—Their measurement and validity. *Addiction, 88*, 69–78.

Dore, M. M., Doris, J. M., & Wright, P. (1995). Identifying substance abuse in maltreating families: A child welfare challenge. *Child Abuse and Neglect, 19*, 531–543.

DuPont, R. L., & McGovern, J. P. (1991). The growing impact of the children-of-alcoholics movement on medicine: A revolution in our midst. In T. M. Rivinus (Ed.), *Children of chemically dependent parents: Multiperspectives from the cutting edge* (pp. 313–329). New York: Brunner/Mazel.

Edwards, P., Harvey, C., & Whitehead, P. (1973). Wives of alcoholics, a critical review and analysis. *Quarterly Journal of Studies on Alcohol, 34*, 112–132.

Epstein, E. E., & McGrady, B. S. (1998). Behavioral couples treatment of alcohol and drug use disorders: Current status and innovations. *Clinical Psychology Review, 18*, 689–711.

Ewing, J. A., & Fox, R. E. (1968). Family therapy of alcoholism. In J. Masserman (Ed.), *Current psychiatric therapies* (No. 18, pp. 86–91), New York: Grune & Stratton.

Feigelman, W. (1987). Day-care treatment for multiple drug abusing adolescents: Social factors linked with completing treatment. *Journal of Psychoactive Drugs, 19*, 335–344.

Fletcher, A. C., & Jefferies, B. C. (1999). Parental mediators of associations between perceived authoritative parenting and early adolescent substance use. *Journal of Early Adolescence, 19*, 465–487.

Friedman, A. S., & Utada, A. T. (1992). The family environments of adolescent drug abusers. *Family Dynamics of Addiction Quarterly, 2*, 32–45.

Friel, J. C., & Friel, L. D. (1987). Uncovering our frozen feelings: The iceberg model of co-dependency. *Focus on the Family and Chemical Dependency, 46*, 10–12.

Garcia-Pindado, G. (1992). The family effect on adolescent drug use: Environmental and genetic factors. *Psiquis: Revisita de Psiquiatria, Psicologia y Psicosomatica, 13*, 39–48.

Goodwin, D. W. (1985). Alcoholism and genetics. The sins of the fathers. *Archives of General Psychiatry, 42*, 171–174.

Gordon, J. R., & Barrett, K. (1993). The codependency movement: Issues of context and differentiation. In John S. Baer, G. Alan Marlatt, & Robert J. McMahon (Eds.), *Addictive behaviors across the life span: Prevention, treatment, and policy issues* (pp. 307–339). Newbury Park, CA: Sage.

Haaken, J. (1990). A critical analysis of the co-dependence construct. *Psychiatry, 53*, 396–406.

Hall, J. A., & Henggeler, S. W., Ferreira, D. K., & East, P. L. (1992). Sibling relations and substance use in high-risk female adolescents. *Family Dynamics of Addiction Quarterly, 2*, 44–51.

Handelsman, L., Branchey, M. H., Buydens-Branchey, L., Gribomont, B., Holloway, K., & Silverman, J. (1993). Morbidity risk for alcoholism and drug abuse in relatives of cocaine addicts. *American Journal of Drug and Alcohol Abuse, 19*, 347–357.

Harmer, A. L. M., Sanderson, J., & Mertin, P. (1999). Influence of negative childhood experiences on psychological functioning, social support, and parenting for mothers recovering from addiction. *Child Abuse and Neglect, 23*, 421–433.

Havey, J. M., & Dodd, D. K. (1993). Variables associated with alcohol-abuse among self-identified collegiate COAS and their peers. *Addictive Behaviors, 18*, 567–575.

Howard, D., & Howard, N. (1985). Treatment of the significant other. In S. Zimberg, J. Wallace, & S. Blume (Eds.), *Practical approaches to alcoholism psychotherapy* (pp. 137–162). New York: Plenum Press.

Huberty, D. J., & Huberty, C. E. (1986). Sabotaging siblings: An overlooked aspect of family therapy with drug dependent adolescents. *Journal of Psychoactive Drugs, 18*, 31–41.

Humes, D. L., & Humphrey, L. L. (1994). A multimethod analysis of families with a polydrug-dependent or normal adolescent daughter. *Journal of Abnormal Psychology, 103*, 676–685.

Hurcom, C., Copello, A., & Orford, J. (2000). The family and alcohol: Effects of excessive drinking and conceptualizations of spouses over recent decades. *Substance use and misuse, 35*, 473–502.

Hurrelmann, K. (1990). Parents, peers, teachers and other significant partners in adolescence. *International Journal of Adolescence and Youth, 2*, 211–236.

Hussong, A. M., & Chassin, L. (1997). Substance use initiation among adolescent children of alcoholics: Testing protective factors. *Journal of Studies on Alcohol, 58*, 272–279.

Jacob, T., & Leonard, K. (1988). Alcoholic spouse interaction as a function of alcoholism subtype and alcohol consumption interaction. *Journal of Abnormal Psychology, 97*, 231–237.

Johnson, J. L., & Leff, M. (1999). Children of substance abusers: Overview of research findings. *Pediatrics, 103*, 1085–1099.

Kaufman, E. (1985). Family systems and family therapy of substance abuse: An overview of two decades of research and clinical experience. *The International Journal of the Addictions, 20*, 897–916.

Kaufman, E., & Kaufmann, P. (1979). *Family therapy of drug and alcohol abuse.* New York: Gardner Press.

Lachner, G., & Wittchen, H. U. (1995). Familial transmission of vulnerability factors in alcohol-abuse and dependence. *Zeitschrift fur Klinishche Psychologie-Forschung und Praxis, 24*, 118–146.

Lehman, A. F., Myers, P., Thompson, J. W., & Corty, E. (1993). Implications of mental and substance use disorders: A comparison of single and dual diagnosis patients. *Journal of Nervous and Mental Disease, 181*, 365–370.

Le Poire, B. A. (1992). Does the codependent encourage substance dependent behavior? Paradoxical injunctions in the codependent relationship. *The International Journal of the Addictions, 27*, 1465–1474.

Le Poire, B. A. (1994). Inconsistent nurturing as control theory: Implications for communication-based research and treatment programs. *Journal of Applied Communication Research, 23*, 1–15.

Le Poire, B. A., Addis, K. A., Duggan, A., & Daley, R. (2003). *Communicative strategies of partners of drug Abusers.* Manuscript submitted for publication.

Le Poire, B., A., & Cope, K. (1999). Episodic versus steady state drinkers: Evidence of differential reinforcement patterns. *Alcoholism Treatment Quarterly, 17*, 79–90.

Le Poire, B. A., Erlandson, K. T., & Hallett, J. S. (1998). Punishing versus reinforcing strategies of drug discontinuance: The effect of persuaders' drug use on persuasive effectiveness and relapse. *Health Communication, 10*, 293–316.

Le Poire, B. A., Hallett, J. S., & Erlandson, K. T. (2000). An initial test of inconsistent nurturing as control theory: How partners of drug abusers assist their partners' sobriety. *Human Communication Research, 26*, 432–457.

Le Poire, B. A., Hallett, J. S., & Giles, H. (1998). Codependence: The paradoxical nature of the functional-afflicted relationship. In B. H. Spitzberg & W. R. Cupach (Eds.), *The Dark Side of Close Relationships* (pp. 153–176). Mahwah, NJ: Lawrence Erlbaum Associates.

Le Poire, B., A. Shepard, C., & Duggan, A. (1999). Nonverbal concomitants of approach-avoidance tendencies in romantic couples based on their mutual attachment styles. *Communication Monographs, 66*, 293–311.

Lloyd, C. (1998). Risk factors for problem drug use: Identifying vulnerable groups. *Drugs: Education, Prevention, and Policy, 5*, 217–232.

Martin, A. L., & Piazza, N. J. (1995). Codependency in women: Personality disorder or popular descriptive term' *Journal of Mental Health Counseling, 17*, 428–440.

McCrady, B. S., Noel, N. E., Abrams, D. B., Stout, R. L., Nelson, H. F., & Hay, W. M. (1986). Comparative effectiveness of three types of spouse involvement in outpatient behavioral alcoholism treatment. *Journal of Studies on Alcohol, 47*, 459–465.

McNabb, J., Der-Karabetian, A., & Rhoads, J. (1989). Family involvement and outcome in treatment of alcoholism. *Psychological Reports, 65*, 1327–1330.

Merikangas, K. R., Dierker, L. C., & Szamari, P. (1998). Psychopathology among offspring of parents with substance abuse and/or anxiety disorders: A high risk study. *Journal of Child Psychology and Psychiatry and Allied Disciplines, 39*, 711–720.

Merikangas, K. R., Rounsaville, B. J., & Prusoff, B. A. (1992). Familial factors in vulnerability to substance abuse. In M. G. Glantz and R. W. Pickens (Eds.), *Vulnerability to drug abuse* (pp. 75–97). Washington DC: American Psychological Association.

Mothersead, P. K., Kivilighan, D. M., & Wynkoop, T. F. (1998). Attachment, family dysfunction, parental alcoholism, and interpersonal distress in late adolescence: A structural model. *Journal of Counseling Psychology, 45*, 196–203.

Nathans, J. A. (1981, March). *Borderline personality: A new psychiatric syndrome or another example of male disapproval or female behavior*? Paper presented at the Eighth Annual Conference of the Association for Women in Psychology, Boston, MA.

O'Brien, P. E., & Gaborit, M. (1992). Codependency: A disorder separate from chemical dependency. *Journal of Clinical Psychology, 48*, 129–136.

O'Farrell, T. J., & Feehan, M. (1999). Alcoholism treatment and the family: Do family and individual treatments for alcoholic adults have preventive effects for children? *Journal of Studies on Alcohol, 13*, 125–129.

Orenstein, A., & Ullman, A. (1993). Characteristics of alcoholic families and adolescent substance use. *Journal of Alcohol and Drug Education, 41*, 86–101.

Paige, P. E., La Pointe, W., & Krueger, A. (1971). The marital dyad as a diagnostic treatment variable in alcohol addiction. *Psychology Savannah, 8*, 64–73.

Pandina, R. J., & Schuele, J. A. (1983). Psychosocial correlates of alcohol and drug use of adolescent students and adolescents in treatment. *Journal of Studies on Alcohol, 44*, 950–973.

Paulino, T. J., & McGrady, B. S. (1977). *The alcoholic marriage: Alternative perspectives*, New York: Grune & Stratton.

Pihl, R. O., Peterson, J., & Finn, P. R. (1990). An heuristic model for the inherited predisposition to alcoholism. *Psychology of Addicted Behavior, 4*, 12–25.

Phillips, B. (1988). Codependency: A real problem. In F. Duckman, B. R. Challenger, W. G. Emener, & W. S. Hutchinson Jr. (Eds.), *Employee assistance programs: A basic text* (pp. 194–203). Springfield, IL: Thomas.

Prescott, M., & Le Poire, B. A. (2002). Eating disorders and the mother-daughter bond: An application of inconsistent nurturing as control theory. *Journal of Family Communication, 2*, 59–78.

Rae, J. B., & Drewery, J. (1972). Interpersonal patterns in alcoholic marriages. *British Journal of Psychiatry, 120*, 615–621.

Raffaeli, R. M. (June, 1990). *Discovering relationships between communication patterns, family violence, and alcoholism*. Paper presented at the annual convention of the International Communication Association, Dublin, Ireland.

Rotunda, R. J., Scherer, D. G., & Imm, P. S. (1995). Family systems and alcohol misuse—Research on the effects of alcoholism on family functioning and effective family interventions. *Professional Psychology-Research and Practice, 26,* 95–104.

Rubio-Stipen, M., Bird, H., Canino, G., & Bravo, M. (1991). Children of alcoholic parents in the community. *Journal of Studies on Alcohol, 52,* 78–88.

Schaef, A. W. (1987). When a society hits bottom: The American culture as addict. *Dissertation Abstracts International, 47*(10-B), 4313.

Schor, E. L. (1996). Adolescent alcohol use: Social determinants and the case for early family-centered intervention. *Bulletin of the New York Academy of Medicine, 73,* 335–355.

Sheehan, M. F. (1993). Dual diagnosis. *Psychiatric Quarterly, 64,* 107–134.

Sher, K. J. (Ed.). (1991). *Children of alcoholics: A critical appraisal of theory and research.* Chicago: University of Chicago Press.

Sheridan, M. J. (1995). A proposed intergenerational model of substance abuse, family functioning, and abuse/neglect. *Child Abuse and Neglect, 19,* 519–530.

Shuntich, R. J., Loh, D., & Katz, D. (1998). Some relationships among affection, aggression and alcohol abuse in the family setting. *Perceptual and Motor Skills, 86,* 1051–1060.

Smart, L. S., Chibucos, T. R., & Didier, L. A. (1990). Adolescent substance use and perceived family functioning. *Journal of Family Issues, 11,* 208–227.

Spoth, R., Redmond, C., Hockaday, C., & Yoo, S. (1996). Protective factors and young adolescent tendency to abstain from alcohol use: A model using two waves of intervention study data. *American Journal of Community Psychology, 24,* 749–770.

Steinglass, P. (1976). Experimenting with family treatment approaches to alcoholism, 1950–1975, a review. *Family Process, 15,* 97–123.

Stice, E., Barrera, M., & Chassin, L. (1993). Relation of parental support and control to adolescents' externalizing symptomatology and substance use: A longitudinal examination of curvilinear effects. *Journal of Abnormal Child Psychology, 21,* 609–629.

Tarter, R. E., Laird, S. B., & Moss, H. B. (1990). Neuropsychological and neurophysiological characteristics of children of alcoholics. In M. Windle & J. S. Searles (Eds.), *Children of alcoholics: Critical perspectives* (pp. 73–98). New York: Guilford Press.

Tweed, S. H., & Ryff, C. D. (1991). Adult children of alcoholics—Profiles of wellness admidst distress. *Journal of Studies on Alcohol, 52,* 133–141.

Vakalahi, H. F. (1999). Adolescent substance use in Utah: The influence of family-based risk and protective factors. *Dissertation Abstracts International Section A: Humanities and Social Sciences, Feb., 59 (8-A),* 3214.

Walfish, S., Stenmark, D. E., Shealy, S. E., & Krone, A. M. (1992). MMPI profiles of women in codependency treatment. *Journal of Personality Assessment, 58,* 211–214.

Walker, J. P., & Lee, R. E. (1998). Uncovering strengths of children of alcoholic parents. *Contemporary Family Therapy, 20,* 521–538.

Wegscheider-Cruse, S. (1988). Codependency: The therapeutic void. *Codependency,* 1–4.

Werner, L. J., & Broida, J. P. (1991). Adult self-esteem and locus of control as a function of familial alcoholism and dysfunction. *Journal of Studies on Alcohol, 52,* 249–252.

Whalen, T. (1953). Wives of alcoholics: Four types observed in a family service agency. *Quarterly Journal of Studies of Alcohol, 14*, 632–641.

Whitfield, C. L. (1987). *Healing the child within*. Deerfield Beach, FL: Health Communications.

Williams, R. E., & Fisher, D. R. (1994, August). *The impact of male alcoholics on their female partners*. Paper presented to the annual American Psychological Association, Los Angeles.

Windle, M. (1996). On the discriminative validity of a family history of problem drinking index with a national sample of young adults. *Journal of Studies on Alcohol, 57*, 378–386.

Windle, M., & Searles, J. S. (Eds.). (1990). *Children of alcoholics: Critical perspectives*. New York: Guilford.

Wiseman, J. P. (1991). *The other half: Wives of alcoholics and their social-psychology*. New York: de Gruyter.

CHAPTER

28

VIOLENCE AND ABUSE IN FAMILIES

KRISTIN L. ANDERSON
WESTERN WASHINGTON UNIVERSITY

DEBRA UMBERSON AND SINIKKA ELLIOTT
UNIVERSITY OF TEXAS AT AUSTIN

For many women, men, and children around the world, the greatest risk of violent victimization occurs in the context of family relationships. A recent national survey conducted in the United States found that 25% of women and 8% of men reported that they were physically or sexually assaulted by a spouse, partner, or date in their lifetime (Tjaden & Thoennes, 1998). An estimated 9% to 30% of assaults between adult partners in the United States are witnessed by resident children (Edleson, 1999). Over 10% of U.S. children experience severe violence at the hands of their parents in a given year (Straus & Gelles, 1992). Available evidence suggests that an even larger number of children suffer from neglect than from physical abuse. Of the maltreated children who came to the attention of U.S. social service agencies in 1999, fifty-eight percent suffered neglect, 21% were physically abused, and 11% were sexually abused (U.S. Department of Health and Human Services, 2001). Family violence is a global problem; population-based surveys conducted in over 40 nations find that 10% to 50% of women report being the victim of an assault by an intimate male partner at some point in their lives (Heise, Ellsberg, & Gottemoeller, 1999).

The study of violence within families is a multidisciplinary enterprise. Sociologists study the ways in which the historical legitimacy of family violence, cultural notions of privacy, and inequalities of gender, age, race/ethnicity, and class facilitate high rates of violence within families (Straus & Gelles, 1992). Psychologists examine personality traits associated with violence perpetration and victimization (O'Leary, 1993). The central contribution of communication studies to this field is an emphasis on violence as a practice that is embedded within family interaction (Lloyd, 1999). Previous studies suggest that interpersonal communication processes are more powerful predictors of family violence than are individual or sociodemographic characteristics (Cahn, 1996).

629

Violence is a form of interactive communication. It is motivated by a desire to communicate a message—often a demand for compliance—to the victim. A large research literature describes how parents and intimate partners use violence to gain control over a family member (Dobash & Dobash, 1998; Kirkwood, 1993; Straus & Gelles, 1992). Although researchers have begun to make important distinctions among various patterns of spousal violence (Johnson, 1995, 2001), men's violence against their wives or partners is often linked to a general pattern of controlling behavior, including monitoring partners' activities and regulating their friendships (Dobash & Dobash, 1998; Kirkwood, 1993). Abusive parents often have rigid expectations for their children's behavior that they attempt to enforce through punishment (Anderson & Umberson, 1999). Violence can also be motivated by fear, shame, or a desire for revenge or recognition (Gilligan, 1996). As a communicative tool, violence serves both instrumental and expressive purposes. The perpetrator may desire to achieve control over the person or situation and/or to express his or her anger or frustration (Umberson, Williams, & Anderson, 2002).

The use and legitimacy of family violence varies by status position within the family. In patriarchal societies, men's violence against wives and children is legitimized by custom and law (Dobash & Dobash, 1998; Heise et al., 1999; Pleck, 1987). Legal and political challenges to violence against wives and children began in the United States and Britain during the 19th century (Pleck, 1987). A global movement against family violence was in place by end of the 20th century (Heise et al., 1999). However, the hidden nature of family violence hinders intervention efforts. Most of the violence in families is unrecognized by those who come into contact with its victims.

Women and children suffer the most detrimental consequences of family violence. The physical punishment of children by their parents is considered a legitimate disciplinary tool within many nations, including the United States. Because children lack power within and outside of the family system, they are particularly vulnerable as targets of physical and sexual abuse (Gilgun, 1995). Girls are approximately three times more likely to be sexually abused than are boys (Sedlack, 1991). Although women and men report similar rates of violence against spouses or partners, women are much more likely to suffer injury and depression as a result of violence than are men (Tjaden & Thoennes, 1998). A context of gender inequality places women at a disadvantage within relationships marked by violence. When family interactions result in conflict and violence, men have an advantage due to their larger average physical size, their (increasingly contested) cultural authority as "head" of the family, and their control over economic resources (Anderson & Umberson, 2001).

This chapter considers how family interaction and communication patterns may be associated with family violence. Taken together, previous studies suggest that family interaction patterns are associated with violence in a bidirectional fashion. Particular interactive patterns may facilitate violence within families, but violence also *undermines* family communication and interaction. We first review the research on family interaction patterns that are associated with increased risk of family violence. Next, we examine the negative consequences of violence for family communication and interaction. Although family violence consists of spouse, partner, child, elder, parental, and sibling abuse, we emphasize the research on spousal/partner abuse and child maltreatment in this review, because the majority of published research studies focus on these forms of family violence.

COMMUNICATION PATTERNS AND THE RISK OF FAMILY VIOLENCE

Communication Skills

Violence within families has been associated with deficits in family members' communication skills. A number of studies find that partners in violent marriages or dating relationships lack problem-solving and positive negotiation skills (Bird, Stith, & Schladale, 1991; Sabourin, Infante, & Rudd, 1993). In a comparative study of conversations between 10 couples with a history of violence and 10 nonviolent couples, Sabourin and Stamp (1995) found several differences in communication styles. In contrast to nonviolent couples, the violent couples were more likely to use vague language, to be oppositional and interfering, and to express complaints and despair. Other studies find that spouses in abusive relationships are less argumentative, more verbally aggressive, and less likely to use mutual problem solving than are nonviolent couples (Feldman & Ridley, 2000; Infante, Chandler, & Rudd, 1989). Violence within relationships has also been associated with aversive–defensive communication patterns such as blaming, interrupting, invalidating, and withdrawing (Murphy & O'Farrell, 1997). Partners who use aversive or defensive forms of communication or who lack problem-solving skills may be at higher risk for violence because they lack the skills to communicate their needs clearly or to deescalate family conflict.

Less research has focused on positive communication patterns and family violence. Results from existing studies are mixed; some suggest that violent and nonviolent couples do not differ on positive forms of communication such as complimenting, apologizing, or displays of verbal or nonverbal affection (Lloyd, 1996; Murphy & O'Farrell, 1997). Other researchers find that violent couples report lower levels of caring behavior and positive interaction in everyday life than do nonviolent couples (Langhinrichsen-Rohling, Smultzer, & Vivian, 1994).

Abusive parents exhibit deficits in communication skills. Christopoulos, Bonvillian, and Crittenden (1988) compared the language inputs of mothers to their infants among a sample of abusive, neglectful, and adequate mothers. Adequate mothers spoke to their children more often and used more positive and accepting phrases than did the neglectful group, but the speech patterns of abusive mothers did not differ from those of adequate mothers. Neglectful parents are less verbally expressive and empathetic than parents who are not neglectful (Cowen, 1999). Prospective longitudinal studies find that physically abusive parents exhibit poor impulse control and antisocial behavior (Pianta, Egeland, & Erickson, 1989).

Lacking communication skills that would enable them to calm hurt feelings or create a compromise, spouses and parents may find that their conflicts with partners or children escalate in frequency and severity. However, because violence emerges in an interactive context, deficient communication skills are only part of the communication problem. Communication skills deficits may increase violence in those with a propensity, but deficits alone cannot account for differences between violent and nonviolent relationships (Babcock, Waltz, Jacobsen, & Gottman, 1993). Family members' interpretations of communication acts and their emotional responses to these interpretations are crucial components of the relationship between communication skills deficits and family violence.

Interpretive Processes

Communicative acts do not have a fixed meaning; they must be interpreted by others. For example, partners' critical words may be interpreted either as a signal of distress or as an attack. The interpretation determines the response; an interpretation of distress may lead to a comforting response, whereas an interpretation of attack may lead to a counterattack and an escalation of conflict (Blumer, 1969). The existing research evidence suggests that violent and nonviolent couples interpret their partners' words and actions differently. In a study of men's responses to written and videotaped scenarios of relationship conflict, domestically violent men responded with hostility and anger to scenarios in which wives displayed anger and emotional distress (Holtzworth-Munroe & Smultzer, 1996). In addition to displaying hostile reactions to hypothetical scenarios, violent men are more likely to attribute hostile intent to their female partner's actions (Dugan, Umberson, & Anderson, 2001; Holtzworth-Munroe & Hutchinson, 1993). Similar interpretative processes affect the relationships between parents and children in families harmed by spouse abuse. Holden and Ritchie (1991) examined mothers' reports of domestic violence and parenting practices. They found that men who perpetrated domestic assaults against their wives were more irritable and less physically affectionate in their interactions with their children than were nonviolent men.

The research on child maltreatment suggests that abusive parents also interpret their children's actions as hostile or threatening. In comparison to nonabusive parents, physically abusive parents express higher levels of annoyance and irritation in response to their children's behavior (Anderson & Umberson, 1999). Interpretive processes may also influence patterns of neglectful parenting. A child's cry is interpreted by some parents as a nuisance or deliberate misbehavior on the part of the child rather than as a signal of the child's needs (Ade-Ridder & Jones, 1996). These findings suggest that similar interpretive processes characterize different types of family violence. Individuals who engage in violence against family members, whether they are spouses, partners, or children, often attribute negative intentions to the victims' actions.

Interactive Patterns

Family violence is linked to particular styles of interaction, including insecure attachment, demand–withdrawal, and emotional reactivity. As these interactive patterns become galvanized in a relationship, "a pattern of coercive efforts can gradually develop, creating a rigid pattern of negative, polarized interaction" between family members (Holtzworth-Munroe, Smutzler, & Stuart, 1998; p. 732).

Insecure Attachment. Interactive patterns learned in childhood may set the stage for violence among family members in adulthood. Attachment theorists contend that children develop "working models" of relationships with others through their early interactions with their parents and that these models carry over into other intimate relationships (Bowlby, 1973). An insecure attachment style is characterized by the presence of anxiety, extreme dependency, and a fear of intimacy in relationships with others (Dutton, Saunders, Starzomski, & Bartholomew, 1994).

A few domestic violence researchers have examined the links between insecure adult attachment and male violence against intimate female partners. Dutton et al. (1994) found that men who exhibited insecure attachment patterns in their relationship with a female partner scored higher on measures of psychological abuse than securely attached men. Moreover, men referred for treatment for assault had significantly higher levels of insecure attachment than a matched control group. Insecure attachment may lead partners to interpret benign communication acts as dangerous or threatening: "The anxiously attached man, unaware that his dysphoria is intimacy produced, attributes it to real or perceived actions of his partner, and retaliates with abusiveness" (Dutton et al., 1994, p. 1379).

Abusive and neglectful parents also exhibit insecurity in their interpersonal relationships. In a prospective longitudinal study of mother–child interaction, Pianta et al. (1989) found that mothers' negative mood and lack of interpersonal trust were the most salient factors discriminating maltreating from nonabusive mothers. Additionally, they found that abusive mothers were unable to establish any type of intimate or supportive relationship characterized by mutual interdependence and trust.

Demand–Withdraw.   Another interactive pattern that is associated with family violence is demand–withdrawal. In demand–withdraw interactions between adult partners, "one partner, the pursuer, tries to get the partner to change, while the other partner avoids change through withdrawal, passive inaction, or stonewalling" (Berns, Jacobson, & Gottman, 1999, p. 339). Partners who withdraw or stonewall are more often the dominant partners in the relationship (Jacobson & Gottman, 1998). Studies of demand–withdraw patterns suggest that wives often assume the "pursuer" role in seeking more intimacy and change, whereas husbands avoid change and are more likely to engage in withdrawal (Christensen & Shenk, 1991).

Only a few studies to date examine demand–withdraw interaction patterns in the context of violent relationships. The available evidence shows that demand–withdraw interaction is present in violent relationships, but in a guise different from how it appears in nonviolent couples (Babcock et al., 1993; Berns et al., 1999; Holtzworth-Munroe, Smutzler, & Stuart, 1998). Babcock et al. (1993) found greater levels of husband-demand and wife-withdraw interaction among couples experiencing husband violence than among nonviolent couples. Thus, the gendered pattern appears to be opposite to that observed in nonviolent couples. Husbands in abusive relationships may be more demanding than other husbands because they are often concerned with controlling and regulating the behavior of their wives or partners.

More recent studies suggest that violent relationships are characterized by interactive patterns in which both partners engage in demand and withdrawal. Berns et al. (1999) divided a sample of 47 batterers into separate categories according to unique characteristics. They identified two subtypes of batterers: Type I and Type II. Type I batterers, compared to Type II batterers, are quicker to anger, more likely to have used or threatened to use a knife or gun on their wives, and more likely to have histories of violence outside the marriage. Although both subtypes of batterers exhibited extreme demand *and* withdrawal patterns, the pattern of high husband-demand and wife-withdraw was stronger among Type I batterers. These men desired change from their partner but resisted their partner's demands that they change themselves.

Holtzworth-Munroe and colleagues (1998) compared demand–withdrawal patterns in interactions between four groups of couples: violent distressed, violent nondistressed, nonviolent distressed, and nonviolent nondistressed. Violent distressed couples reported the highest levels of conflict and negative behavior and they were the most demanding and withdrawing. Like previous researchers, Holtzworth-Munroe et al. observed that both wives and husbands in violent relationships engage in high levels of demand and withdraw.

In a recent study of 42 married couples, Sagrestano, Heavey, and Christensen (1999) examined relationships among power, violence, and the demand–withdraw interaction pattern. They found higher levels of verbal aggression and violence by both husbands and wives in couples in which the husbands perceive that they have less power than their wives have. Moreover, only wife-demand husband-withdraw interaction was associated with higher levels of violence. This finding suggests that violence is particularly likely to occur in a context in which husbands perceive their wives' demands as an indicator of power.

Emotional Reactivity. Research on domestic violence suggests that domestically violent men are more likely than nonviolent men to perceive their partner's words and actions as threatening, regardless of the objective content of those words and actions (Dugan et al., 2001; Holtzworth-Munroe & Hutchinson, 1993). Recent research further suggests that men with a propensity for violence often respond to perceptions of threat by avoiding further interaction and emotional engagement with their partner (Umberson, Williams, & Anderson, 2002). Although nonviolent men exhibit seemingly appropriate emotional reactions in response to interactions with their partners (e.g., negative emotion in response to partner disagreement), it is as if violent men experience a disconnection between ongoing interactions with their partners and their own emotional experiences. Umberson et al. argue that repressing and avoiding emotion only leads to a further buildup of anxiety that eventually surfaces in a violent act. They suggest that an increase in the expression of emotion in response to ongoing interactions with partners in the short run might serve to reduce the frequency of violence in the longer run.

Interrelationships Among Communicative Processes and Violence

There are theoretical reasons to expect that the communication skills deficits, interpretive processes, and interactive patterns identified in the literature on family violence are interconnected. For example, the pattern of higher rates of demand–withdrawal within violent relationships may be connected to specific interpretative processes. Abusers who attribute hostile or negative intent to their partners' actions may be more likely to perceive their partners' demands as an exertion of power that must be countered with violence. Abusers who feel fearful or anxious about intimacy within their relationships may be threatened by a partner's withdrawal. Communication skills deficits may be particularly likely to facilitate violence when they are combined with insecure attachment patterns or emotional repression. An individual who feels anxious or threatened but is unable to communicate these complex feelings verbally may lash out against a child or a partner.

THE IMPACT OF VIOLENCE ON FAMILY COMMUNICATION

The risk of violence within families may be increased by the communication skills deficits, interpretive processes, and interactive patterns described earlier. However, violence within families also has negative consequences for family communication and interaction. In a context of violence, family members may withdraw from social interaction or repress their concerns about the violence out of fear for themselves or for other family members. The pattern of controlling behavior enacted by perpetrators of family violence creates a family setting in which victims are unable to communicate their desires, needs, or emotions.

Communication Skills

Adults and children living in families marked by violence have limited opportunities to witness and practice positive communication skills. Violence decreases the communication skill level of victims because it creates a setting in which family members are not able to communicate freely. Family violence is associated with reports of fear and anxiety among children and women (Edleson, 1999; Jacobsen, Gottman, Waltz, Rushe, & Holtzworth-Munroe, 1994). Family members who live in a context of fear do not have opportunities to learn and develop effective communication skills.

Abused children exhibit deficient verbal language skills. Additionally, children who witness violence against a parent or sibling exhibit deficits in social competence and higher levels of fearfulness and anxiety than do nonexposed children. Children exposed to family violence inhibit their speech and interaction with others (Edleson, 1999). These communication skills deficits may help to explain the associations between child abuse and poor school performance and antisocial behavior (Anderson & Umberson, 1999).

Among adults, the experience of abuse at the hands of a loved one often leads to a loss of self-confidence and undermines the victim's ability to form and sustain healthy social relationships. Survivors of child sexual abuse report experiencing poor communication with their intimate partners as adults (DiLillo & Long, 1999). Communication skills may be adversely affected by violence because victims lose self-confidence or learn to be fearful, secretive, and distrustful of others through the experience of abuse (DiLillo & Long, 1999). These characteristics may impede the victim's ability to engage in direct or open communication with others.

Interpretive Processes

Previous studies suggest that abusers' interpretations of specific communicative acts as dangerous or threatening may precede the perpetration of violence. However, interpretive processes are also important in the aftermath of a violent incident. Violence, in itself, is a communicative act that is given meaning through interpretative processes. The abuse that occurs within families must be assigned meaning by its perpetrators and victims. Available research evidence suggests that family members interpret abuse in a variety of ways.

Deviant patterns of social information processing are common in abused children, suggesting that children who learn to interpret communicative acts in a context of abuse will attribute hostile or aggressive intentions to others outside of their family context (Edleson, 1999). This pattern makes it difficult for abused children to form healthy relationships later in life. Additionally, children who are exposed to domestic violence may learn that violence is an effective means of conflict resolution. Child witnesses of adult domestic violence, particularly boys, report that violence is an effective strategy to address a problem or to enhance one's self-image (Edleson, 1999).

Adult female victims of partner violence struggle to define and interpret their experiences of victimization. Kelly (1990) argues that women have difficulty interpreting their experiences of domestic violence because violence within families is hidden and unnamed within U.S. culture. Wives or partners who experience infrequent assaults are hesitant to call it violence due to the stereotypical depictions of severe family violence that are presented in the media. Additionally, because cultural depictions of domestic assault attribute negative characteristics to the victim, women may be reluctant to interpret their experiences as domestic violence.

In a study of the ways in which women cope with physical and emotional abuse, Herbert, Silver, and Ellard (1991) examined characteristics that differentiated women who had left abusive partners from those who were still involved in the abusive relationship. They found that women who remained in the relationship framed their relationships in a positive light, emphasizing the loving and caring aspects of their partners' behavior. These women were also more likely to blame themselves for the abuse and to make downward comparisons, noting that their relationships were better than those of other people they knew.

Herbert and colleagues found that the frequency and severity of verbal abuse were more closely associated with women's decisions to leave than were the frequency and severity of physical abuse. Similarly, in her qualitative study of women's experiences of abuse, Kirkwood (1993) found that emotional abuse was constructed as more damaging and more difficult to overcome than was physical abuse. Many victims of violence report that the verbal abuse is characterized by constant degradation of their appearance, beliefs, and goals. Kirkwood found that abusive partners continually attack the victims' interpretations of violence. Over time, these attacks lead victims to question the validity of their own interpretations. Kirkwood's research suggests that perpetrators of abuse often manipulate the victims' interpretations of the abuse as a way to maintain power within the relationship.

Other strategies that wives and partners use to deal with violence include forgetting, minimizing, and self-medication with alcohol or drugs (Kelly, 1990). These coping strategies help victims to repress the physical and psychological pain caused by the abuse. However, they may reduce victims' chances of obtaining help from friends, family, or community members.

A different research literature focuses on the accounts that perpetrators of family violence offer in order to explain or rationalize their violent behavior. This research finds that violent male partners use several strategies to justify or rationalize past violence. These interpretative strategies include statements that they "lost control" due to intoxication or uncontrollable anger, that their female partners were responsible for their victimization because they failed to comply with demands or requests, and that their behavior was "minor" and thus not really violent (Anderson & Umberson, 2001; Ptacek, 1990).

Perpetrators of child sexual abuse also use interpretive processes to rationalize and justify their abusive behavior. In a study of incest perpetrators' accounts of sexual abuse, Gilgun (1995) found that perpetrators framed their abusive behavior as an act of love and caring for the victim. Perpetrators described the incest as a form of romantic love between equal partners and minimized the power and authority that they had over the victims. These strategies helped perpetrators to deny responsibility for behavior that they knew was illegal and immoral. Because family violence has been the focus of public education and reform efforts in recent decades, perpetrators feel that they must account for their abuse perpetration (Cavenaugh, Dobash, Dobash, & Lewis, 2001).

Few studies to date have examined children's interpretations of family violence. The scant evidence available suggests that the meanings that children attach to family violence between their parents vary; some children identify with the perpetrator of abuse and others identify with the victim (Anderson & Umberson, 1999). A small number of studies have examined children's attributions of their physical and sexual abuse victimization. Most children who suffer physical and sexual abuse define their experiences as abusive and do not self-blame (Kolko, Brown, & Berliner, 2002). However, attributions of abuse are linked to the severity of psychological consequences among children. Among physically and sexually abused children, higher levels of depression and posttraumatic stress disorder have been linked to self-blame and to labeling the behavior as abuse (Kolko et al., 2002).

In summary, the interpretations that abusers and victims use to make sense of the violence in their relationships influence the outcomes of the abuse. Interventions that focus on changing victims' and abusers' interpretations of violence may be necessary to challenge the legitimacy of family violence.

Interactive Patterns

Family violence has consequences for social interaction that occurs inside and outside of the family setting. The anxiety, fear, and isolation experienced by victims may make them less willing or less able to form positive relationships with others. Prospective longitudinal studies find that victims of child abuse are more likely to experience insecure attachment to others and to exhibit aggressive behavior (Corby, 1993; National Research Council, 1993). Additionally, child witnesses of domestic violence often exhibit aggressive and antisocial behaviors (Edleson, 1999). These interactive styles are not conducive to the creation of friendships or supportive relationships with other children or adults. In a study of the friendship patterns among severely abused and nonabused children, Howe and Parke (2001) found that abused children reported less caring and validation in their friendships and exhibited less proactive behavior in observed interactions with friends, than did nonabused children.

Childhood exposure to abuse and neglect has been linked to loneliness and isolation among young adults (Loos & Alexander, 1997). Henning, Leitenberg, Coffery, Turner, and Bennet (1996) found that young women who witnessed violence between their parents as children reported lower levels of social integration and attachment to others than did young women who did not witness parental violence. Moreover, young adults' retrospective reports of child abuse have been associated with greater risk of aggression toward themselves and against others (Fergusson & Lynskey, 1997).

Previous studies find gender differences in the effects of child abuse or witnessing violence on aggressive behavior. Boys tend to respond to family violence by developing aggressive and antisocial behaviors, whereas girls tend to exhibit depression and other internalizing symptoms (Edleson, 1999). However, one recent study found that exposure to violence at home predicted higher levels of aggressive behavior among both adolescent boys and girls (Song, Singer, & Anglin, 1998). Girls' aggressive behavior was more closely associated with exposure to violence at home, whereas boys' aggressive behavior was more closely associated with exposure to violence at school or in the neighborhood. This gender difference may result from the fact that girls experience a high risk of violence victimization in the family setting, whereas boys experience violence in other social contexts in addition to the family.

Violence in partner relationships affects children directly because children observe, hear, or intervene in fights; but also indirectly, because violence increases negative communication between family members (Margolin, John, Ghosh, & Gordon, 1996). A number of studies find that abuse between spouses is linked to negative interaction patterns between parents and children. Domestic assaults between parents have been associated with fathers' use of power-assertive parenting techniques and physical punishment (Holden & Ritchie, 1991). Margolin and colleagues (1996), through analysis of videotaped family interactions in a laboratory setting, found that violence between parents was linked to a number of negative parenting practices. Parents who reported spousal violence showed higher levels of negative affect in interactions with their children. Fathers who were abusive toward their wives were controlling in interaction with their sons. Additionally, aggression between parents was linked to higher levels of withdrawal and distraction among boys. These findings suggest that exposure to parental violence leads children to feel fear and anxiety in social interactions with family members and others outside of the family.

Demand–withdraw interaction patterns have been conceptualized as a precursor to abuse in much of the literature. However, this interactive pattern could also reflect the consequences of abuse within a marital or cohabiting relationship. Withdrawal may be a way of showing contempt for a spouse or avoiding any external influence, but it might also be self-protective. Wives in violent relationships withdraw and demand to a greater extent than do wives in nonviolent relationships (Holtzworth-Munroe et al., 1998). This may be a learned response to the violence that characterizes an abusive relationship. A wife who has experienced violence in the past may demand change during times when she feels strong or safe in the relationship. At other times, she may withdraw in response to her partner's demands out of fear that the conflict will escalate into violence. Berns et al. (1999) found that severe levels of husband violence are associated with high levels of wife withdrawal. Because violence often escalates in frequency and severity over time, this finding suggests that withdrawal may be a response to abuse that is learned over time.

Isolation is another means by which abusive partners and parents attempt to gain control over their families. Women who report victimization at the hands of a male partner are often socially isolated and have less social support than do other women (Grisso et al., 1999; Kirkwood, 1993). Norms of family privacy and loyalty prevent victims from receiving help from friends, neighbors, or social service agencies. Abusive partners and parents often go to great lengths to prevent discovery of the violence that they perpetrate against family members. A recent newspaper story featured a photograph of a sign reading "We don't call 911" that police found hanging next to the telephone in the home of an abuser (Porter, 2001). The sign featured an image of a smoking gun. The victims of family violence were in this case directly warned that help seeking could result in further violence.

In summary, violence has detrimental consequences for family members' ability to learn positive forms of communication. Violence undermines the self-esteem and confidence of its victims, it teaches victims that aggressive and controlling styles of interaction are normative, and it isolates victims from other people. Children and adults who experience violence at the hands of a family member learn to be fearful, anxious, and insecure in their relationships with others.

BIDIRECTIONALITY

The links between negative communication patterns and family violence are well established. However, most studies have examined cross-sectional data and thus cannot address the issue of causal direction. There are strong theoretical reasons to believe that relationships between communication processes and family violence are bidirectional. On the one hand, communication skills deficits of one or both partners may lead to increasingly negative forms of interaction between partners and ultimately to the emergence of violence. On the other hand, past violence within the relationship may lead to a pattern in which one or both partners withdraw, become negative or critical, and report feelings of fear or anger when they attempt to communicate.

Two types of studies address the issue of causal direction. First, a few studies have examined the relationship between retrospective accounts of exposure to violence and communication patterns. Second, longitudinal studies address causal direction by documenting changes in attitudes or behaviors over time.

Retrospective Studies

To address the issue of causal order, researchers need information about the ways in which family members communicate prior to, and in the aftermath of, specific violent incidents. Although violence occurs in the context of social interaction, few studies have examined how communication processes influence actual incidents of domestic violence. It is difficult for researchers to access the daily interactions of family members as they naturally occur, and it is ethically and logistically problematic to study actual violent incidents that occur within families. Researchers must typically rely on retrospective narrative accounts of violent incidents supplied by victims or perpetrators. These accounts are influenced by individual interpretations of violence.

Despite these limitations, retrospective accounts of violence can provide information about the dynamics of violence in day-to-day life. Jacobsen and colleagues (1994) obtained descriptions of the events that preceded specific incidents of violence from a sample of 60 couples experiencing domestic violence and 32 maritally distressed couples who had never experienced violence. Results indicated that, according to wives, husbands continued their violence when wives were violent themselves, verbally defended themselves, or withdrew. Husband's descriptions suggested that they continued violence only when their wife was violent or emotionally abusive. Jacobsen et al. concluded that there were no wife behaviors that could stop the violence once it began; the violence escalated in response to nonviolent as well as to violent reactions by wives. This study suggests that, although communication patterns influence the violence that occurs within relationships, simply changing communication behaviors will not be enough to stop abusive behaviors that are already established. Because abusers often define the actions of victims as hostile or negative, victims' efforts to change their communication behaviors may have little impact.

Retrospective accounts can also provide information about the ways in which the experience of violence during childhood affects people later in life. Halford, Sanders, Matthew, and Behrens (2000) videotaped problem-focused discussions between 71 engaged couples to determine whether exposure to parental violence during childhood increased problematic communication patterns in adult relationships. They found significantly higher rates of invalidation, negative nonverbal behavior, conflict, and withdrawal among couples in which the male partner was exposed to parental violence. Female partners' exposure to parental violence was not associated with negative communication processes. Similarly, DiLillo and Long (1999) found that female victims of childhood sexual abuse reported significantly poorer communication with their spouses than did women who did not report childhood victimization. Thus, findings from retrospective accounts suggest that exposure to family violence leads to short-term and long-term problems with communication.

Longitudinal Studies

Because longitudinal studies are not subject to problems of memory errors or to other forms of retrospective bias, they are generally considered to be superior to retrospective studies for determining causal direction. Lloyd (1996) examined associations between violence and interaction patterns among 78 couples interviewed in two waves of data collection 18 months apart. Couples reporting aggression during both waves of data collection showed a pattern of increasingly negative interaction over time, suggesting that violence preceded the formation of negative communication. However, low levels of negative interaction at Time 1 were associated with a decrease in violence by Time 2. This study suggests that the relationship between violence and negative communication processes is bidirectional. Negative forms of communication increase the risk of violence, but violence also decreases opportunities for the development of positive styles of communicating and interacting.

ISSUES FOR FUTURE RESEARCH

Communication patterns play a central role in the dynamics of family violence. The skills that parents and partners bring to family interactions, the interpretive processes that they use to attach meaning to communicative events, and the interactive styles that they develop are associated with the risk of violence within families. In turn, violence between family members undermines family communication and interaction. The effects of violence are not limited to the perpetrators and victims; relationships among all family members are impacted by violence. The dynamic and complex relationship between family violence and family communication should be the focus of future research.

Established research findings suggest that relationships between communication processes and family violence are bidirectional. Future research should examine changes in communication processes and family violence over time in order to clarify these reciprocal patterns. Research that examines how patterns in family interaction are linked to violence on a day-to-day basis is sorely needed. Additional longitudinal studies are needed to identify specific communication processes that precede family violence and the ways in which family communication changes in the aftermath of violence.

The majority of published studies on violence and family communication have focused on negative forms of communication. Findings from the few available studies that focus on positive forms of communication are mixed; some studies suggest that violence is associated with a decrease in positive communication, and others find that positive communication is not linked to violence within families. Future research should include measures of negative and positive communication in order to resolve this issue.

To date, most research on communication patterns and violence has examined samples consisting of married couples and two-parent families. Researchers should expand the definition of family to include single parents, stepfamilies, cohabiting couples and parents, and gay/lesbian/bisexual couples and parents in order to reflect the growing diversity in family structures. Previous research suggests that rates of family violence are higher among cohabiting couples and that child abuse and neglect rates may be higher within single-parent families and stepfamilies (Anderson & Umberson, 1999; Cowen, 1999; Stets, 1991). Additionally, communication patterns may differ within diverse family types. There is some evidence that parent–child conflict and communication problems increase following the formation of single-parent families and stepfamilies (Amato, 2000; Coleman, Ganong, & Fine, 2000).

Studies of family communication processes and violence have been limited by small samples consisting of middle- or high-socioeconomic-status families. There is some evidence that the income or educational levels of family members influence family communication patterns. Highly educated parents are more likely to using complex reasoning and less likely to use commands than are less educated parents when interacting with their children (Dekovic & Gerris, 1992). Heath (1983) found that middle-class and European American parents were more likely than working-class and African American parents to use discrete interrogative questions when they talked with their children. Because both family violence and language patterns have been linked to social class in past research, future research on the relationships between family communication and violence should include controls for socioeconomic status (Straus & Gelles, 1992).

The emphasis on violence as a form of communication that is embedded in family interaction has led family violence researchers to exciting new directions. Future research on the dynamic relationships between family violence and communication skills, interpretive processes, and interactive patterns will inform efforts to understand and prevent violence within families.

REFERENCES

Ade-Ridder, L., & Jones, A. R. (1996). Home is where the hell is: An introduction to violence against children from a communication perspective. In D. D. Cahn & S. A. Lloyd (Eds.), *Family violence from a communication perspective* (pp. 59–84). Thousand Oaks, CA: Sage.

Amato, K. (2000). The consequences of divorce for adults and children. *Journal of Marriage and the Family, 62*, 1269–1287.

Anderson, K. L., & Umberson, D. (1999). Child abuse. In L. Kurtz & J. Turpin (Eds.), *Encylopedia of violence, peace and conflict* (Vol. 1, pp. 223–238), San Diego: Academic Press.

Anderson, K. L., & Umberson, D. (2001). Gendering violence: Masculinity and power in men's accounts of domestic violence. *Gender & Society, 15*, 353–380

Babcock, J. C., Waltz, J., Jacobsen, N. S., & Gottman, J. M. (1993). Power and violence: The relation between communication patterns, power discrepancies, and domestic violence. *Journal of Consulting and Clinical Psychology, 61*, 40–50.

Berns, S. B., Jacobson, N. S., & Gottman, J. M. (1999). Demand-withdraw interaction patterns between different types of batterers and their spouses. *Journal of Marital and Family Therapy, 25*, 337–348.

Bird, G. W., Stith, S. M., & Schladale, J. (1991). Psychological resources, coping strategies, and negotiation styles as discriminators of violence in dating relationships. *Family Relations, 41*, 318–323.

Blumer, H. (1969). *Symbolic interactionism: Perspective and method.* Englewood Cliffs, NJ: Prentice Hall.

Bowlby, J. (1973). *Attachment and loss: Vol. 2. Separation, anxiety, and anger.* New York: Basic Books.

Cahn, D. D. (1996). Family violence from a communication perspective. In D. D. Cahn & S. A. Lloyd (Eds.), *Family violence from a communication perspective* (pp. 1–19). Thousand Oaks, CA: Sage.

Cavenaugh, K., Dobash, R. E., Dobash, R. P., & Lewis, R. (2001). Remedial work: Men's strategic responses to their violence against intimate female partners. *Sociology, 35,* 695–714.

Christensen, A., & Shenk, J. L. (1991). Communication, conflict, and psychological distance in nondistressed, clinic, and divorcing couples. *Journal of Consulting and Clinical Psychology, 59,* 458–463.

Christopoulos, C., Bonvillian, J. D., & Crittenden, P. (1988). Maternal language input and child maltreatment. *Infant Mental Health Journal, 9*, 272–286.

Coleman, M., Ganong, L., & Fine, M. (2000). Reinvestigating remarriage: Another decade of progress. *Journal of Marriage and the Family, 62*, 1288–1307.

Corby, B. (1993). *Child abuse: Toward a knowledge base.* Buckingham: Open University Press.

Cowen, P. S. (1999). Child neglect: Injuries of omission. *Pediatric Nursing, 25*, 401–418.

Dekovic, M., & Gerris, J. R. M. (1992). Parental reasoning complexity, social class, and child-rearing behaviors. *Journal of Marriage and the Family, 54*, 675–685.

DiLillo, D., & Long, P. J. (1999). Perceptions of couple functioning among female survivors of child sexual abuse. *The Journal of Child Sexual Abuse, 7*, 59–76.

Dobash, R. E., Dobash, R. P. (1998). Violent men and violent contexts. In R. E. Dobash & R. P. Dobash (Eds.), *Rethinking violence against women* (pp. 141–168). Thousand Oaks, CA: Sage.

Dugan, S., Umberson, D., & Anderson, K. L. (2001). The batterer's view of the self and others in domestic violence. *Sociological Inquiry, 71,* 221–240.

Dutton, D. G., Saunders, K., Starzomski, A., & Bartholomew, K. (1994). Intimacy-anger and insecure attachment as precursors of abuse in intimate relationships. *Journal of Applied Social Psychology, 24*, 1367–1386.

Edleson, J. L. (1999). Children's witnessing of adult domestic violence. *Journal of Interpersonal Violence, 14,* 839–870.

Feldman, C. M., & Ridley, C. A. (2000). The role of conflict-based communication responses and outcomes in male domestic violence towards female partners. *Journal of Social and Personal Relationships, 17*, 552–573.

Fergusson, D. M., & Lynskey, M. T. (1997). Physical punishment/maltreatment during childhood and adjustment in young adulthood. *Child Abuse and Neglect, 21*, 617–630.

Gilgun, J. F. (1995). We shared something special: The moral discourse of incest perpetrators. *Journal of Marriage and the Family, 57*, 265–281.

Gilligan, J. (1996). *Violence: Reflections on a national epidemic.* New York: Vintage Books.

Grisso, J. A., Schwartz, D. F., Hirschinger, N., Sammel, M., Brensinger, C., Santanna, J., Lowe, R. A., Anderson, E., Shaw, L. M., Bethel, C. A., & Teelpe, L. (1999). Violent injuries among women in an urban area. *New England Journal of Medicine, 341*, 1899–1905.

Halford, W., Sanders, K., R. Matthew, & Behrens, B. C. (2000). Repeating the errors of our parents? Family-of-origin spouse violence and observed conflict management in engaged couples. *Family Process, 39*, 219–235.

Heath, S. B. (1983). *Ways with words.* Cambridge: Cambridge University Press.

Heise, L., Ellsberg, M., & Gottemoeller, J. K. (1999). Ending violence against women. *Population Reports,* Series L, No. 11. Baltimore, MD: Johns Hopkins University School of Public Health, Population Information Program.

Henning, K., Leitenberg, H., Coffery, P., Turner, T., & Bennet, R. T. (1996). Long-term psychological and social impact of witnessing physical conflict between parents. *Journal of Interpersonal Violence, 11*, 35–51.

Herbert, T. B., Silver, R. C., & Ellard, J. H. (1991). Coping with an abusive relationship: How and why do women stay? *Journal of Marriage and the Family, 53*, 311–325.

Holden, G.W., & Ritchie, K. L. (1991). Linking extreme marital discord, child rearing, and child behavior problems. *Child Development, 62*, 311–377.

Holtzworth-Munroe, A., & Hutchinson, G. (1993). Attributing negative intent to wife behavior: The attributions of maritally violent vs. nonviolent men to problematic marital situations. *Journal of Abnormal Psychology, 102*, 206–211.

Holtzworth-Munroe, A., & Smultzer, N. (1996). Comparing the emotional reactions and behavioral intentions of violent and nonviolent husbands to aggressive, distressed, and other wife behaviors. *Violence and Victims, 11*, 319–340.

Holtzworth-Munroe, A., Smutzler, N., & Stuart, G. L. (1998). Demand and withdraw communication among couples experiencing husband violence. *Journal of Consulting and Clinical Psychology, 66*, 731–743.

Howe, T. R., & Parke, R. D. (2001). Friendship quality and sociometric status: Between-group differences and links to loneliness in severely abused and non-abused children. *Child Abuse and Neglect, 25*, 585–606.

Infante, D. A., Chandler, T. A., & Rudd, J. E. (1989). Tests of an argumentative skill deficiency model of interpersonal violence. *Communication Monographs, 56*, 163–175.

Jacobson, N. S., & Gottman, J. M. (1998). *When men batter women: New insights into ending abusive relationships.* New York: Simon & Schuster.

Jacobson, N. S., Gottman, J. M., Waltz, J., Rushe, R., & Holzworth-Munroe, A. (1994). Affect, verbal content, and psychophysiology in the arguments of couples with a violent husband. *Journal of Consulting and Clinical Psychology, 62*, 982–988.

Johnson, M. P. (1995). Patriarchal terrorism and common couple violence: Two forms of violence against women. *Journal of Marriage and the Family, 57,* 283–294.

Johnson, M. P. (2001). Conflict and control: Images of symmetry and asymmetry in domestic violence. In A. Booth, A. C. Crouter, & M. Clements (Eds.), *Couples in conflict* (pp. 95–104). Mahwah, NJ: Lawrence Erlbaum Associates.

Kelly, L. (1990). How women define their experiences of violence. In K. Yllo & M. Bograd (Eds.), *Feminist perspectives on wife abuse* (pp. 114–132). Newbury Park, CA: Sage.

Kirkwood, C. (1993). *Leaving abusive partners: From the scars of survival to the wisdom for change.* London: Sage.

Kolko, D. J., Brown, E. J., & Berliner, L. (2002). Children's perceptions of their abusive experience: Measurement and preliminary findings. *Child Maltreatment, 7,* 42–55.

Langhinrichsen-Rohling, J., Smultzer, N., & Vivian, D. (1994). Positivity in marriage: The role of discord and physical aggression against wives. *Journal of Marriage and the Family, 56,* 69–79.

Lawrence, E., & Bradbury, T. N. (2001). Physical aggression and marital dysfunction: A longitudinal analysis. *Journal of Family Psychology, 15,* 135–154.

Lloyd, S. A. (1996). Physical aggression, distress, and everyday marital interaction. In D. D. Cahn & S. A. Lloyd (Eds.), *Family violence from a communication perspective* (pp. 177–198). Thousand Oaks, CA: Sage.

Lloyd, S. A. (1999). The interpersonal and communication dynamics of wife battering. In X. B. Arriaga & S. Oskamp (Eds.), *Violence in intimate relationships.* Thousand Oaks, CA: Sage.

Loos, M. E., & Alexander, P. C. (1997). Differential effects associated with self-reported histories of abuse and neglect in a college sample. *Journal of Interpersonal Violence, 12,* 340–360.

Margolin, G., John, R. S., Ghosh, C. M., & Gordis, E. B. (1996). Family interaction process: An essential tool for exploring abusive relationships. In D. D. Cahn & S. A. Lloyd (Eds.), *Family violence from a communication perspective* (pp. 37–58). Thousand Oaks, CA: Sage.

Murphy, C. M., & O'Farrell, T. J. (1997). Couple communication patterns and aggressive and nonaggressive male alcoholics. *Journal of Studies on Alcohol, 58,* 83–90.

National Research Council. (1993). *Understanding child abuse and neglect.* Washington, DC: National Academy Press.

O'Leary, D. (1993). Through a psychological lens: Personality traits, personality disorders, and levels of violence. In R. J. Gelles & D. R. Loseke (Eds.), *Current controversies on family violence.* Newbury Park, CA: Sage.

Pianta, R., Egeland, B., & Erickson, M. F. (1989). The antecedents of maltreatment: Results of the mother-child interaction research project. In D. Cicchetti & V. Carlson (Eds.), *Child maltreatment: Theory and research on the causes and consequences of child abuse and neglect* (pp. 203–253). New York: Cambridge University Press.

Pleck, E. (1987). *Domestic tyranny: The making of American social policy against family violence from colonial times to the present.* New York: Oxford University Press.

Porter, M. (2001, October 5). Domestic violence kills, too. *Bellingham Herald,* pp. A1–A2.

Ptacek, J. (1990). Why do men batter their wives? In K. Yllo & M. Bograd (Eds.), *Feminist perspectives on wife abuse* (pp. 133–157). Newbury Park, CA: Sage.

Sabourin, T. C., Infante, D. C., & Rudd, E. J. (1993). Verbal aggression in marriages: A comparison of violent, distressed but nonviolent, and nondistressed couples. *Human Communication Research*, 20, 245–267.

Sabourin, T. C., & Stamp, G. H. (1995). Communication and the experience of dialetical tension in family life: An examination of abusive and non-abusive families. *Communication Monographs, 62,* 213–242.

Sagrestano, L. M., Heavey, C. L., & Christensen, A. (1999). Perceived power and physical violence in marital conflict. *Journal of Social Issues, 55,* 65–79.

Sedlack, A. (1991). *National incidence and prevalence of child abuse and neglect: 1988, revised report.* Rockville, MD: Westat.

Song, L., Singer, M., & Anglin, T. (1998). Violence exposure and emotional trauma as contributors to adolescents' violent behaviors. *Archives of Pediatric and Adolescent Medicine, 152*, 531–536.

Stets, J. E. (1991). Cohabiting and marital agression: The role of social isolation. *Journal of Marriage and the Family, 53*, 669–680.

Straus, M. A., & Gelles, R. J. (Eds). (1992). *Physical violence in American families: Risk factors and adaptations to violence in 8,145 families.* NJ: Transaction Publishers.

Tjaden, P., & Thoennes, N. (1998). Prevalence, incidence, and consequences from the National Violence Against Women Survey (Research in Brief), Washington, D.C.: U.S. Department of Justice, Bureau of Justice Statistics, November, NCJ 172837.

Umberson, D., Williams, K., & Anderson, K. L. (2002). Violent behavior: A measure of emotional upset? *Journal of Health and Social Behavior, 43*, 189–206.

U.S. Department of Health and Human Services, Administration on Children, Youth and Families. (2001). *Child maltreatment 1999.* Washington, D.C.: U.S. Government Printing Office.

29

FAMILY INFLUENCES ON HEALTH: A FRAMEWORK TO ORGANIZE RESEARCH AND GUIDE INTERVENTION

DEBORAH J. JONES
WEST VIRGINIA UNIVERSITY

STEVEN R. H. BEACH AND HOPE JACKSON
UNIVERSITY OF GEORGIA

A better understanding of the effects of family processes on the development and the course of specific diseases is critical if we are to utilize marital and family interventions as effective components of prevention and treatment packages. One practical approach to organizing research on family and health may be in terms of the effect of family relationships on the broad facets of disease processes, rather than on the presence or absence of particular disease states. Likewise, it may be useful to identify common mediators of the effect of family processes on facets of health, rather than to focus only on bivariate relationships between particular family variables and particular health outcomes. In this way, we may subsume and organize a growing body of data within a clear theoretical framework. Accordingly, in the current chapter we begin by discussing the broad facets of disease processes that unite many areas of inquiry in the health area. For each facet we cite illustrative data implicating family processes. Next, we identify three potential mediators that may jointly account for some or all of the effect of family processes on disease. In each case we describe illustrative data documenting that family processes are related to the hypothesized mediator and that the mediator is related to facets of disease. Finally, we discuss recent advances in family treatment, using marital and family interventions for depression as an example. Our goal here is to explore the potential for marital and family interventions to influence health outcomes. Understanding pathways by which family relationships may influence health over time, including allostatic load, depression, and health-compromising behaviors provides clinicians with targets for prevention and intervention efforts aimed at enhancing family functioning and alleviating patient distress.

Although other excellent reviews of the family and health literature have been conducted, those available to date tend to limit their focus to a single family relationship. For example, reviews of the family and health literature tend to focus on the parent–child relationship and the child's mental and physical health (e.g., Campbell & Patterson, 1995; Drotar, 1997; Repetti, Taylor, & Seeman, 2002) or on the marital relationship and the adult's mental and physical health (e.g., Burman & Margolin, 1992; Kiecolt-Glaser & Newton, 2001). We hope to extend the theoretical contributions in the area of family functioning and health by integrating the literatures on both marital and parent–child relations. In the long term, increased understanding of family influences on health processes may set the stage for the challenging longitudinal efforts required to link family processes, in general, and specific family communication patterns, in particular, to disease outcomes.

DIMENSIONS OF DISEASE PROCESSES

Understanding the association between family relationships and physical health and illness requires knowing how family functioning impacts various facets of the disease process. At present, three promising facets have attracted growing research attention: perceived health, functional impairment, and physiological responsivity.

Perceived Health

Self-reported health is a common outcome of interest in the family health literature, and for good reason. Self-reported health can be assessed via relatively brief questionnaires given to large samples, providing an efficient and cost-effective means of establishing an association between family processes and health. However, the validity of self-reported health is not without question due to associations with psychological distress, in general, and depression (Mechanic, 1980). Given the association between family functioning and depression, in particular, the validity of self-report measures of health in family studies merits even closer consideration. Nonetheless, perceived health has proven to be an important outcome in its own right, given its influence on the use of health care services, as well as the burden of disease imposed on the individual and the family. Perceived health also predicts mortality independent of biological risk factors, suggesting that self-report measures of health provide useful information that may not be captured by current biological markers of the disease process (Idler & Benyamini, 1997). In addition, self-reported health is reliably associated with physicians' diagnoses (Jenkins, Kraeger, Rose, & Hurst, 1980; Orts et al., 1995). Thus, self-reported physical health may, indeed, prove to be a particularly important marker of change in disease processes over time for certain illnesses.

Family distress has been associated with self-reported health in both adults and children. Across studies of community samples, findings reveal clear links between marital functioning and perceived health as reflected in self-reported physical symptoms. Marital satisfaction is associated with fewer medical symptoms and better overall self-reported health (Barnett, Davidson, & Marshall, 1991; Ganong & Coleman, 1991; Ren, 1997; Thomas, 1995). Some evidence suggests that the link between marital discord and self-reported health may be particularly strong for women. In their study of couples in long-term marriages, Levenson, Carstensen, and Gottman (1993) reported that wives experiencing marital distress reported more mental and physical health problems than did their husbands. Alternatively, there was no difference in self-reported health between wives and husbands in satisfied marriages.

A link between marital distress and self-reported health has also been demonstrated in regard to particular conditions. In a cross-sectional study of 150 married women, Coughlin (1990) found that wives reporting lower levels of marital satisfaction reported more premenstrual symptoms than did wives reporting higher levels of marital satisfaction. Similarly, in a cross-sectional study of 49 couples in which one spouse had chronic tinnitus, spouse-reported punishing responses and their interaction with depressive symptoms accounted for an additional 15% of the variance in tinnitus-related disability (interference with role performance in work, social functioning, and home/family) over and above gender, tinnitus characteristics, and depressive symptoms alone (Sullivan, Katon, Russo, Dobie, & Sakai, 1994). Women diagnosed with chronic fatigue syndrome (CFIDS) experiencing higher levels of marital distress also report more concurrent CFIDS symptoms than do CFIDS sufferers in more satisfying marriages (Goodwin, 1997).

The association between family functioning and self-reported health is also evidenced prospectively. In a longitudinal study of 6,928 adults, Levenstein, Kaplan, and Smith (1995), and Levenstein, Ackerman, Kiecolt-Glaser, and Dubois (1999) reported an association between marital strain and increased prevalence of self-reported ulcers over an 8- to 9-year follow-up. However, the link between marital strain and self-reported ulcers differed by gender as the study progressed. Whereas cross-sectional data showed an increase in the prevalence of self-reported ulcers associated with marital strain among men, but not among women, longitudinal data revealed an association between marital strain and ulcers for women alone.

Children growing up in families characterized by high levels of distress also report more physical symptoms. In their study of 7th-, 8th-, and 9th- graders, Mechanic and Hansell (1989) found that more quarrelling and fighting at home was associated with higher levels of self-reported physical symptoms 1 year later, after controlling for earlier reports of physical distress. Moreover, the effects of family distress appear to be chronic, lasting well beyond childhood and into adolescence and young adulthood. Wickrama, Lorentz, and Conger (1997) tracked Caucasian children in a rural area over 4 years, from 7th to 11th grade. More hostile and less supportive parenting during family interactions was associated with adolescents' reports of 12 common physical complaints, including headaches, sore throats, and muscle aches, over the next 4 years. Similarly, in a study of a representative sample of the Swedish population, Lundberg (1993) found that children raised in families characterized by "serious dissention" reported a variety of illnesses (e.g., aches, pains, high blood pressure) 13 years later, even after controlling for psychological symptoms and mental illness.

Finally, some evidence suggests that improvements in marital functioning may alleviate not only marital distress but also self-reported physical symptoms. Wickrama and colleagues (1997) followed couples annually over a 4-year period, assessing both marital quality and self-reported physical symptoms. Consistent with the findings of other reports, greater marital distress at study entry was associated with more self-reported physical symptoms. Moreover, improvement in marital satisfaction over time predicted a decline in self-reported physical distress. Although indirect, the findings of Wickrama et al. provide evidence for the potential utility of family-based interventions aimed at enhancing self-reported health and, perhaps, long-term health outcomes.

Functional Impairment

Functional impairment or disability is another dimension of physical health and illness linked with family functioning. One of the largest areas of research linking family relationships and functional impairment has occurred in the area of chronic pain. Pain is a pervasive medical problem accounting for substantial levels of disability and contributes greatly to overall disease burden (Turk & Melzack, 1992). Overall, the findings of these studies suggest that family functioning is associated with both pain and pain-related disability, including self-reports of pain intensity, as well as pain behavior (e.g., verbal complaints about pain, displaying nonverbal pain behavior, requesting pain medication), and physical impairment (e.g., Saarijarvi, Rytokoski, & Karppi, 1990). In their cross-sectional study of chronic pain patients, Romano, Turner, and Jensen (1997) reported that, although global ratings of marital adjustment were not associated with self-reported disability or pain behaviors, a higher level of marital conflict in particular was associated with both disability and pain. Moreover, in response to marital conflict, patients respond with pain behaviors significantly more frequently than they do with other coping strategies, including both active and passive coping strategies (Schwartz, Slater, & Birchler, 1996).

In terms of functional impairment associated with pain, findings of the existing literature suggest that apparently positive, as well as clearly negative, aspects of family relationships may negatively impact patient functioning. Among "positive" influences, spousal pain-related solicitousness (i.e., behaviors that indicate concern for the other's physical condition or comfort, or discouraging the other from activity) appears to reinforce maladaptive pain behaviors and, in turn, promote disability (Turk, Kerns, & Rosenberg, 1992). Using a cold pressor task, a laboratory technique that entails placing the participant's hand, with the palm facing down in a cold ice bath, Flor, Breitenstein, Birbaumer, and Furst (1995) found that spouse solicitousness was associated with more intense pain for chronic back pain patients, but not for healthy controls. Similarly, in an observational study of 50 chronic pain patients and their spouses, spouse-solicitous responses to patient pain behaviors were associated with more pain behaviors and disability, particularly for patients reporting more depressive symptoms and greater overall pain severity. Negative aspects of family functioning have also been linked to pain and pain-related disability, with some evidence to suggest that the women are most affected. In their cross-sectional study of 31 male and 32 female chronic low-back-pain patients, Saarijarvi and colleagues (1990) reported that marital dissatisfaction was associated with greater self-reported pain and disability in wives, but not in husbands. Marital dissatisfaction was unrelated to findings upon clinical examination.

Moreover, interventions aimed at reducing spousal solicitousness reduce pain and pain-related disability (Keefe et al., 1996, 1999). Patients who report increased marital satisfaction pre- to posttreatment evidenced lower levels of physical disability and pain behavior. The effects of treatment persist at 12-month follow-up for patients assigned to the spouse-assisted coping-skills training, relative to those under an individual coping-skills training condition or those in an education-support intervention. It appears that it is important not only to involve spouses in treatment interventions but also to address specific aspects of the relationship that are associated with both marital adjustment and physical health. Accordingly, health care professionals interested in enhancing physical health must understand both positive and negative aspects of family relationships, as well as their unique effects on illness outcomes.

Physiological Functioning

In addition to research on perceived health and functional impairment, a burgeoning literature has examined family interactions and physiological functioning. These studies are typically conducted within a laboratory setting, and physiological reactivity in one or more systems (e.g., cardiovascular, immune) is measured by comparing physiological functioning during a noninteractive baseline with physiological functioning during nonconflict discussions, as well as family conflicts, among family members.

Research on physiological responses to conflict in the marital area has typically involved spouses rating a "hot topic" in their marriage and then choosing one or more topics to be the focus of a problem-solving discussion. Conflict discussions between marital partners are linked to alterations in a range of physiological systems, including blood pressure and heart rate (e.g., Broadwell & Light, 1999; Frankish & Linden, 1996; Thomsen & Gilbert, 1998) as well as immune and endocrine functioning (e.g., Kiecolt-Glaser et al., 1996, 1997; Mayne, O'Leary, McGrady, Contrada, Labouvie, 1997).

Moreover, research in this area suggests that it is specific behaviors that occur during conflicts that elicit physiological reactivity across systems. Whereas supportive or neutral behaviors are not typically associated with change in physiological functioning, negative or hostile behavior during the problem-solving interactions markedly enhances physiological reactivity. Hostile behavior, relative to supportive or neutral behaviors, is associated with significant changes in blood pressure (Ewart, Taylor, Kraemer, & Agras, 1991), immune functioning (Kiecolt-Glaser et al., 1993), and changes in serum levels of epinephrine, norepinephrine, ACTH, growth hormone, and prolactin (Malarkey, Kiecolt-Glaser, Pearl, & Glaser, 1994). The more negative or hostile the couple, the more pronounced the effects, persisting even after discussion of the "hot topic" ends. The link between hostile and negative behaviors and physiological functioning occurs regardless of length of marriage, affecting newlywed couples (Kiecolt-Glaser et al., 1993; Malarkey et al., 1994) as well as older couples in long-term marriages (Kiecolt-Glaser et al., 1997). In the case of blood pressure reactivity in hypertensive patients, it is clearly the overtly negative behaviors that appear to matter most (Ewart et al., 1991).

Findings to date also suggest a gender difference in physiological reactivity to marital conflict. That is, women evidence greater physiological change during problem-solving interaction studies than do men, particularly in response to negative or hostile behaviors (e.g., Ewart et al., 1991; Jacobson et al., 1994; Morrell & Apple, 1990). Across most studies, wives evidence significantly greater blood pressure increases, more compromised immune functioning, and higher levels of norepinephrine and cortisol in response to hostile and negative behaviors during problem-solving discussions than do husbands (see

Levenson, Carstensen, & Gottman, 1994, for a notable exception). Such gender differences during marital conflict are particularly notable given that men more generally show
a larger physiological response to a range of stressors than do women. Although there
is some disagreement as to whether men or women are more physiologically reactive to
marital stress, it is possible that differing views will be resolved by attention to methodological detail. In particular, it may be that men may be more sensitive to physiological
changes associated with conflict and thus more likely to disengage (Levenson et al., 1994)
and ultimately, suffer fewer long-term negative consequences of conflict on health, (for a
review, see Kiecolt-Glaser & Newton, 2002). However, currently available data strongly
support the conclusion that women are more likely than men to suffer a variety of negative
consequences associated with family conflict (for a review see Kiecolt-Glaser & Newton,
2001). Accordingly, marital conflict, rather than stress more generally, may be particularly detrimental to women's health, suggesting that marital- or family-based therapies
may prove particularly beneficial for improving not only women's mental health but also
women's physical health.

Although not as much research has been conducted examining physiological reactivity
as it relates to physical health in children, evidence of an effect in children is building. Most
children show increased sympathetic arousal to family conflict (El-Sheikh, Cummings, &
Goetsch, 1989). Thus, children in families characterized by a high level of distress are
exposed to this high level of physiological arousal on a chronic and recurrent basis,
potentially altering the stress response system permanently. For example, in a study by
Woodall and Matthews (1989), boys (but not girls) from families characterized as less
supportive and engaged in less positive involvement, compared to boys from less distressed
families, evidenced higher heart rate responses to a series of laboratory stressors.

Retrospective studies also highlight the risk of family distress during childhood on
physiological functioning. Luecken (1998) found that college students who reported more
family distress in childhood had higher blood pressure, both at resting levels and in response to a laboratory challenge, suggesting that the effects of chronic and recurrent family
distress on child physiological functioning may be lasting. Moreover, changes in physiological reactivity have been linked to traditional risk factors for coronary heart disease.
Cardiovascular reactivity to stress among boys as young as 8 years of age was associated
with increased left ventricular mass, a standard risk factor for coronary heart disease (CHD)
(Allen, Matthews, & Sherman, 1997). Ballard, Cummings, and Larkin (1993) found that
children of hypertensive parents evidenced greater systolic blood pressure reactivity to
family conflict than those children of parents without hypertension, suggesting that risk
for disease may be especially elevated for children with a family history of heart disease.

POTENTIAL MEDIATORS OF THE RELATIONSHIP BETWEEN FAMILY
RELATIONS AND HEALTH

There is evidence to suggest that family relations impact illness processes or outcomes
indirectly through their effect on emotional and behavioral processes. The next section
reviews evidence for three of these pathways, the mediating role of allostasis or allostatic
load, depressive symptoms and disorders, as well as health-promoting and/or health-
compromising behaviors.

Family Processes Are Associated With Increased Allostatic Load

Both children and parents are affected physiologically by family distress. Moreover, it may be that the physiological alterations associated with family conflict are lasting. The hypothesis guiding this work is that physiological responses to stress are successful in the short term at maintaining homeostasis by allowing the individual to mobilize resources to deal with an acute stressor. With consistent and chronic exposure to such stressors, however, there may be permanent alterations in various physiological systems that confer increased risk for disease. This notion, referred to as allostasis or allostatic load (McEwen & Stellar, 1993; Sterling & Eyer, 1988), suggests that chronic or recurrent exposure to stress early in life may lead to alterations in the sympathetic adrenomedullary (SAM) system and hypothalamic–pituitary–adrenocortical (HPA) axis and to disruptions in serotonergic functioning. Although the impact of stress on individual physiological systems may be modest, allostatic load suggests that the cumulative impact across multiple physiological systems is most consequential in terms of health risk. Accordingly, it is easy to imagine that repeated exposure to family distress and conflict during childhood may disrupt basic homeostatic processes, interact with genetic predispositions to stress both within and outside the home, and ultimately heighten susceptibility to stress and illness throughout the lifetime. Thus, identification and treatment of families at risk have not only consequences for the psychological adjustment and well-being of children but also long-term physical health effects.

Building on this notion, a growing literature suggests that children who are better able to modulate their physiological arousal, and therefore reduce concomitant stress system activation, are less likely to be at risk for maladjustment and health problems than are children with poorer physiological self-regulation. In particular, physiological self-regulation has been defined as the activity of physiological mechanisms to maintain homeostasis in the face of changing environmental demands (Johnson & Anderson, 1990). Vagal tone is one component of physiological self-regulation and is an index of the parasympathetic nervous system's influence on the heart (e.g., Porges, 1991). The vagus system is proposed to be protective of health because it allows for rapid, incremental, and soothable changes in cardiac output to meet environment demands without enlisting potentially taxing or detrimental sympathetic activity (Doussard-Roosevelt & Porges, 1999). Findings of a program of research by El-Sheikh, Harger, and Whitson (in press) suggest that higher vagal tone protects children against psychosocial maladjustment, as well as health problems related to exposure to more frequent parental conflict, particularly verbal conflict between parents.

Recent work also supports the mediating role of allostatic load with adults. Using data from two community-based cohorts, Seeman, Singer, Ryff, Dienberg Love, and Levy-Storms (2002) found that positive social experiences, including a history of warm, supportive, and affectionate parent–child relationships, as well as current intimacy in marital relations, were associated with lower allostatic load or lower levels of dysregulation across multiple physiological pathways (i.e., blood pressure, waist-to-hip ratio, cholesterol, cortisol). In the younger cohort (58–59 years old), positive relationship experiences were associated with allostatic load for both men and women. In the older cohort (70–79 years old), however, the association between positive social relationships and allostatic load was found for men. A similar pattern of findings was obtained for women, but the relationship failed to achieve statistical significance, which the authors hypothesized may be consistent with the literature suggesting that women are more physiologically reactive to negative aspects of social relationships, rather than to the positive dimensions assessed in this study.

The similar pattern of findings across two adult groups, as well as the literature on vagal tone in children, strengthens support for the hypothesis that allostatic load mediates health across the life course. Given the link between family stress and long-term alterations in sympathetic and HPA systems, there would appear to be many potential avenues for effects on health and health behavior. As methodologies for examining alterations in these systems become more widely available to psychosocial researchers, investigation of the impact of chronic family processes on allostatic load appears to be a promising avenue for future research.

Family Processes Are Associated With Depressive Symptoms

Depressed individuals often report problems with family relationships. In a quantitative and exhaustive review of the marital literature, Whisman (2001) reported that, across 26 cross-sectional studies, marital distress was associated with greater depressive symptomatology for both women ($r = -.42$) and men ($r = -.37$). Depressed patients also report considerable distress and difficulty in parenting (e.g., Weissman & Paykel, 1974), and some have attributed depressed mothers' depressive symptoms, at least in part, to their belief that they are bad parents (Teti & Gelfand, 1991). In a recent review of 46 observational studies of the parenting behavior of depressed women, Lovejoy, Gracyk, O'Hare, and Neuman (2000) found evidence of more parenting deficits among depressed mothers than among nondepressed mothers, including more withdrawn behavior and more negative parenting behavior. Paternal depression and its effect on parenting has been the focus of very little empirical research, yet research with fathers certainly merits more attention (Jones, Beach, & Forehand, 2001).

A robust literature also documents the association between overt conflict and aggression in the family and increased risk for internalizing disorders in children, including depression (e.g., Downey & Coyne, 1990). Thus, the link between family distress and depression is far-reaching, occurring both within and across generations, influencing both the family and the individual family members. The interrelationship of family distress and both diagnostic depression and depressive symptoms has important implications for a range of physical health outcomes as well. Depressive symptoms are an independent risk factor for all-cause mortality in medical inpatients (Herrman et al., 1998) as well as for physical decline in the elderly (Penninx et al., 1998). Depressive symptoms have also been linked to a range of illness conditions. For example, across a series of studies, healthy individuals who had elevated depression scores at baseline had a 1.5- to 2-fold increased risk for a first heart attack (Glassman & Shapiro, 1998).

Across studies and illness conditions, however, severity and chronicity of depressive symptoms appear to be an important determinant of disease risk. For example, Penninx and colleagues (1998) found that chronic depressed mood (depressive symptoms exceeded cutpoints at baseline, as well as 3 and 6 years before baseline) was linked to cancer risk, after controlling for sociodemographic and risk factors. Those with more chronic and severe depressive symptoms were nearly at twice the risk for cancer than those whose depressive symptoms did not exceed the cutpoints across assessments. The authors did not, however, find the same association between depressive symptoms and cancer when they used a single assessment of depressive symptoms. Similarly, recent work in the area of cardiovascular risk suggests that a lifetime history of recurrent major depression is associated with progression of carotid atherosclerosis (plaque) on B-mode ultrasound in healthy middle-aged women, relative to women with no history of major depression (Jones, Beach, & Forehand, 2002). A lifetime history of a single major depressive episode or current depressive symptoms, however, afforded no increased risk.

Depression is also associated with multiple indicators of disease progression. For example, Jones and colleagues (2001) demonstrated that after controlling for demographic and risk factors, depressive symptoms were associated with increased physical health complaints in African American single mothers with HIV/AIDS. Chronic and severe depressive symptoms have also been linked to physiological pathways associated with disease, including compromised immune functioning in women with HIV/AIDS (Ickovics et al., 2001). Depressive disorders are also associated with functional impairment (Rantenen et al., 2000), reduced rehabilitation effectiveness (Katz, 1996), noncompliance with treatment recommendations (Katon & Sattivan, 1990), and health-compromising behaviors, including increased substance abuse, inadequate sleep and nutrition, and less exercise (Kiecolt-Glaser & Glaser, 1988), all of which have negative health consequences.

Given the link between family functioning and depression, and the link between depression and multiple indicators of disease, depression and depressive symptoms may be one pathway by which family relationship functioning impacts health and illness. Consideration of the link between family distress and depression will be an important next step if we are to develop family-based prevention and intervention efforts aimed at improving family health and health behavior.

Family Processes Are Associated With Health Behaviors

Health behaviors can generally be categorized into three groups: utilization of health care services, compliance with treatment recommendations, and health-promoting or compromising behaviors. The potential effect of positive and negative family processes on health behaviors is clear. For example, one can imagine that family members could dramatically influence whether or not an individual seeks treatment for particular symptoms, or schedules appropriate preventative check-ups (e.g., immunizations for children, prostate exams for husbands), or follows through with treatment recommendations. Even the process of scheduling and maintaining health-provider visits would be more challenging in a family that is characterized by poor communication, high levels of conflict, and low levels of support than those in a more communicative and supportive family.

Family processes would seem particularly consequential for "life-style" changes that might be recommended as part of a comprehensive approach to the management of a chronic illness. For example, changes in diet and exercise are typically recommended in the treatment of a range of health problems, including diabetes, obesity, and hypertension. Similarly patients are very often prescribed medication to treat a particular condition, and the efficacy of the medication depends in large part on compliance with the recommended dosage. Patient noncompliance represents a major challenge in the health care system and to the efficacy of treatment recommendations as they are currently prescribed. This is especially true for symptoms that have long-term health consequences but may not have immediate consequences for the patient, including hypertension. Consideration of the role of family factors in general, and family communication in particular, in improving compliance with antihypertensive medication merits future research attention.

Supporting the hypothesis of a link between such life-style changes and family processes, research to date has found a high concordance among family members in compliance behaviors, including physician visits, diet, and compliance with recommended treatments. Marital distress has also been associated with poor adherence with prescribed medications (Trevino, Young, Groff, & Jono, 1990). Although the concordance between husbands and wives with regard to health behaviors could be due to assortative mating of people with similar interests in health and health behaviors, similarities may also be due, at least in part, to reciprocal reinforcement for healthy behaviors. That is, a patient diagnosed with Type II diabetes may be more likely to change his diet and exercise patterns if his wife and children support these changes and if the family collectively followed through with a plan to establish a healthier lifestyle. Conversely, a man with Type II diabetes who is attempting to change these behaviors alone, without the support of the family, or in the context of family complaints and criticism of these new behaviors, may be less motivated and less able to follow through with planned changes.

Family distress may also affect health by increasing maladaptive coping behaviors and decreasing health-promoting ones (Lewis, Rook, & Schwarzer, 1994). For example, in their longitudinal study of married women, Prigerson, Maciejewski, and Rosenheck, (1999) reported that marital satisfaction predicted better sleep. Although less empirical attention has been devoted to family members' concordance on these lifestyle variables, evidence suggests concordance among family members on poor eating habits, substance abuse, and inadequate sleep (Wickrama, Conger, & Lorenz, 1995). Further, in the Wickrama et al. (1995) study, health-risk behaviors contributed to worsening health over time even after controlling for health status at study entry. Not only do families engage in similar levels of health-promoting and compromising behaviors, but also family members attempt to directly modify one another's health behaviors and, depending on the type of strategy used, elicit better or worse effects (Tucker & Anders, 2001). For example, negative, critical remarks made by the spouse were associated with a tendency to engage in potentially health-compromising behaviors, whereas positive, supportive remarks were associated with attempts to engage in the desired, health-promoting behavior.

Perhaps, the most robust evidence linking family distress and health behaviors is in the substance use area, including alcohol abuse, smoking, and addiction to prescriptive and nonprescriptive drugs. Severity and chronicity of marital conflicts have been linked to problem drinking, even after controlling for alcohol problems at baseline (Horwitz & White, 1991). Similarly, among middle-aged married couples, dissatisfied husbands consumed more alcohol than did satisfied husbands, with no differences between dissatisfied and satisfied wives (Levenson et al., 1993). Other studies, however, have shown effects of marital distress on the health habits of wives, but not of husbands. For example, among wives, greater marital distress was associated with both increased smoking and drinking, whereas marital distress was not associated with either health behavior for husbands (Cohen, Schwartz, Bromet, & Parkinson, 1991). Likewise, marital conflict has been linked with greater use of anxiolytic medication for both husbands and wives (Appelberg, Romanov, Honkasalo, & Koskenvuo, 1993). Moreover, marital distress is associated with relapse after treatment for substance abuse. For example, patients whose spouses are highly negative and critical are more likely not only to relapse but also to drink on a greater percentage of days in the year following treatment than are patients whose spouses engaged in low levels of negative behaviors (O'Farrell, Hooley, Fals-Stewart, & Cutter, 1998).

Family functioning has been linked to substance use in children and adolescents as well. Family distress, including cold, unsupportive, and neglectful family environments, has been linked to misuse of alcohol (Barnes, Reifman, Farrell, & Dintchef, 2000), smoking (Doherty & Allen, 1994), and illicit substances (Scaramella, Conger, Simons, & Whitbeck, 1998). Moreover, the effects of early family distress on substance use persist, with some effects lasting as long as 11 years at follow-up (Baumrind, 1991).

Findings such as these suggest that family functioning, both marital and parent–child relationship distress, may impact physical health indirectly by increasing the risk for engaging in maladaptive coping strategies, particularly behaviors associated with a range of illness outcomes, including alcohol and drug use and smoking.

DOES INTERVENING WITH FAMILIES ENHANCE PATIENT HEALTH AND WELL-BEING?

Whether or not we can answer this question depends in large part on whether we are talking about family-based interventions for mental or physical health outcomes. That is, a large and robust literature has demonstrated that family-based treatment approaches are efficacious in the treatment of a range of mental health issues (for a review, see Baucom, Shoam, Mueser, Daiuto, & Stickle, 1998), whereas the efficacy of family-based approaches with physical health issues is much less clear. One mental health outcome, depression, has been the focus of a relatively long line of research, first demonstrating a reciprocal link between family distress and depression, then developing interventions to target specific aspects of family dysfunction that might be expected to contribute to, or maintain, depressive symptoms (Beach & Jones, 2002).

Family-Based Interventions for Depression

Several well-specified family-based prevention and intervention efforts for both marital discord and parenting behavior have been developed and tested. These approaches have been shown to be efficacious and easily accessible to clinicians. With regard to marital problems, several approaches to marital therapy have been found to be efficacious in enhancing marital satisfaction and so are likely to have an effect on depressive symptoms. These include behavioral marital therapy, cognitive–behavioral marital therapy, emotion-focused coping therapy, and insight-oriented marital therapy (see Baucom et al., 1998, for a comprehensive review). Behavioral marital therapy, in particular, is an efficacious and specific treatment for marital discord that has been successfully applied cross-culturally (Hahlweg & Markman, 1998), is well-specified, and is widely available for clinical application on a broad scale (e.g., Markman, Stanley, & Blumberg, 1994). It has also been tested in several trials as a treatment for depression and found to be efficacious in that context as well (Beach & Jones, 2002).

Likewise, parent management training (Patterson, 1982; Patterson, Reid, & Dishion, 1992) and its variants have proven efficacious in the reduction of maternal depressive symptoms, as well as in enhancing parenting skills, and in improving child adjustment (e.g., Forehand, Wells, & Griest, 1980; Sanders & McFarland, 2000; Webster-Stratton, 1994). Such interventions include instruction, role-playing, feedback, and coaching in the use of social-learning principles shown to enhance mothers' self-confidence and parenting efficacy, with the goal of reducing depressive symptoms and enhancing child adjustment. Thus, by developing and implementing family-based interventions that target family interaction patterns that are associated with risk for depression, we are able to enhance family functioning and improve individual functioning for both parents and children.

We have come far in the study of effective ways to intervene with families of depressed patients. Although the current level of success should not be oversold (Coyne & Benazon, 2001), it is clear that a solid conceptual foundation is being constructed to guide and support family interventions with depressed patients. A large and robust literature indicates that marital and parenting relationships are often problematic for depressed persons. At the same time, there is good evidence to suggest that these problematic relationships can be repaired, and it seems appropriate to recommend efficacious, targeted intervention to effect repair and improve mood. Theoretical work to date suggests that targeted, efficacious interventions have the potential to break the vicious cycles that may serve to maintain depression. If so, interventions that include attention to problematic family relationships may decrease future distress and decrease the risk for or severity of future episodes of depression. Given the previous discussion of the direct effect of family conflict and likely indirect effect through depressive symptoms, it would seem clear that family intervention should be able to confer health benefits in many cases as well.

Family-Based Interventions for Physical Health

Given the direct and indirect links between family relations and physical health, the next step is to determine whether intervening with families affords health benefits. Research suggests that family members impact one another's depression, health behaviors, and allostatic load. Family processes may also influence physiological facets of disease, health behaviors, and perceived health. As a consequence, it seems quite reasonable to hypothesize that family and marital interventions might influence the progression of disease. Moreover, it appears that negative or hostile behaviors, rather than supportive or neutral behaviors, during family interactions are associated with physiological changes associated with illness (e.g., Ewart et al., 1991, Kiecolt-Glaser et al., 1993; Malarkey et al., 1994). Such evidence suggests specific targets for family-based prevention and intervention efforts. Perhaps supplementing standard medical treatments with family-based communication training may enhance patient health by reducing the level of hostile and negative interactions and subsequently reduce reactivity across a range of physiological systems, including blood pressure reactivity, as well as immune and endocrine functioning.

As highlighted in previous reviews (Burman & Margolin, 1992; Campbell & Patterson, 1995; Kiecolt-Glaser & Newton, 2001), the efficacy of family-based interventions for physical health conditions has been the focus of relatively little research attention, and the findings have been mixed, due in part to methodological limitations. Although a complete examination of the many methodological nuances of these studies is beyond the scope of this chapter, in the following, we highlight several methodological limitations that may have biased them toward null findings.

In an effort to include family members in treatment efforts, we believe that many researchers and clinicians have failed to consider several important questions. First, there is the question of which family members to include in a family-based prevention or intervention effort. Most studies focus on the marital relationship or include an adult child, for example, but one can imagine relations with other family members impacting patient functioning as well, particularly given the changing face of American families. As such, family-based intervention efforts aimed at enhancing physical health should include those family members that interact with the patient on a regular basis and may influence patient functioning. It does not appear, however, that this has always been done in the research to date.

Similarly, family-based intervention studies to date often fail to include measures of family processes; therefore, we know little in terms of whether the intervention actually altered the dysfunctional family patterns we believe are linked with physical health processes and risk. Whether or not family-based prevention and intervention efforts aimed at enhancing physical health are efficacious likely depends in large part on whether they modify family interaction patterns associated with physical health risk. At a minimum, measures of family functioning are critical if we are to examine the role of change in family processes in mediating changes in physical health.

Finally, family-based treatments that have been directed at physical illness to date may not be the same treatment techniques that have proven so efficacious in the treatment of mental illnesses (e.g., depression) linked with family distress (for reviews, see Beach & Jones, 2002; Kung, 2000; Prince & Jacobson, 1995). For example, passive participation by families (e.g., education interventions) is unlikely to modify the dysfunctional family interaction patterns (e.g, hostile and negative behaviors) associated with illness processes and risk (e.g., immune functioning, blood pressure, endocrine functioning). Rather, specific family-based treatment techniques aimed at dysfunctional family processes (e.g., communication training) are more likely to alleviate risk and enhance health. Again, at the very least, it will be important for researchers to use empirically supported strategies for altering the dimensions of family dysfunction targeted for change.

Family-Based Interventions to Improve Health Behaviors

Family-based interventions to promote compliance with medical treatments have been tested for a number of different health conditions, including Type I diabetes (e.g., Epstein 1981; Satin, LaGreca, Zigo, & Skyler, 1989) and asthma (e.g., Fireman, Friday, Gira, Vierthaler, & Michaels, 1981; Lask & Matthews, 1979) with children, as well as hypertension (e.g., Ewart, Taylor, Kraemer, & Agras, 1984), back pain (e.g., Saarijarvi et al., 1991), and arthritis (e.g., Keefe et al., 1996) with adults. Given the methodological variations across these studies, it is somewhat difficult to draw broad conclusions about the efficacy of family-based approaches to improve compliance and health to date. However, several themes have emerged in the findings of studies to date that are worthy of consideration. First, interventions that include only passive participation of the family members, otherwise typically referred to as educational interventions, do not appear to significantly improve patient compliance or health outcomes across studies and illness conditions (e.g., Radojevic, Nicassio, Weissman, 1992; Taylor, Bandura, Ewart, Miller, & DeBusk, 1992). Similarly, family interventions that focus on family relationship quality only, that is, a general family therapy approach directed at improving family relations without specifically addressing the illness condition, have yielded inconsistent effects for the patient compliance and health (e.g., Saarijarvi, 1991). Much greater success has been obtained, however, in studies that address both family relationship quality and the individual patient's illness condition. Typically, these studies have focused on family functioning as it relates specifically to the patient's compliance and health outcomes, including providing positive and supportive feedback regarding behavior change. Problem-specific family-based interventions for enhancing compliance and health outcomes have proven similarly efficacious with both children (e.g., Satin et al., 1989) and adults (e.g., Evans, Matlock, Bishop, Stranahan, & Pederson, 1988).

Attention to the Impact of Ecological Context on Families and Health

A discussion of the interrelationship of family and health cannot take place without considering the ecological context in which families live and interact (Bronfenbrenner, 1992). Socioeconomic status (SES), for example, is one of the strongest and most consistent predictors of health (for a review, see Adler & Ostrove, 1999). Moreover, SES predicts health for those in poverty, and there is strong evidence for a graded association with health at all levels of SES starting as early as childhood and adolescence (Chen, Matthews, & Boyce, 2002; Starfield, Riley, Robertson, & Witt, 2002) and continuing throughout adulthood (Adler et al., 1994). As such, it will not be possible to achieve the goal of maximizing family health without addressing the increased risk of disease, disability, and premature death imposed on families residing in lower SES environments. Thus far, the standard has been to statistically control for SES, overlooking a potentially important influence on both family functioning and health outcomes, as well as for the interaction of SES and family functioning on health and well-being. It is now timely to shift from characterizing SES and other social and demographic variables as nuisance variables to be statistically controlled to examining how such variables shape family interactions and in turn health and illness. For example, families may experience differential exposure to threat and stress in the home environment depending on SES. Similarly, low-income neighborhoods have more liquor stores, fewer grocery stores, more fast-food restaurants, and afford fewer opportunities for exercise, creating environmental pressure for negative health behaviors in families. The combination of environmental demands and constraints confronted by low SES families on a daily basis may also compromise coping, increasing the likelihood for health risk behaviors such as tobacco use and alcohol use and decreasing the likelihood for health-enhancing behaviors such as exercise. Taking such factors into consideration, we believe that an essential next step in the formulation of models of family functioning and illness is the consideration of the social and environmental contexts in which families live and interact.

Perhaps, most importantly, researchers and clinicians interested in family health must consider accessibility to prevention and intervention services, particularly when the entire family or part of the family is the focus of treatment. For example, some work suggests that families most in need of treatment for mental and physical health problems do not have access to or fail to seek services (Aday, Quill, & Reyes-Gibby, 2001; Sarason, 1974). Economically disadvantaged families, as well as minority families, confront a series of problems in accessing the health care system in the United States (for reviews see Giachello, 1994; Giachello & Arrom, 1997), including lack of a regular source of care, high cost of health care, lack of insurance coverage, and structural barriers to care (e.g., lack of transportation, child care). Economically disadvantaged rural families may be at a particular disadvantage due to geographical isolation and inaccessibility to health care. For example, although previous research suggests similar prevalence rates of mental disorders in both rural and urban areas (Hartley, Korsen, Bird, & Agger, 1998; Philbrick, Connelly, & Wofford, 1996), rural areas are dramatically underserved by mental health professionals (Murray & Keller, 1991), often relying solely on primary care providers if available (Yuen, Gerdes, & Gonzales, 1996). Moreover, some work suggests that rural residents attending public health clinics, particularly women, may be at greater risk for depressive disorders than would be expected, with one study reporting 41% of a young, rural, predominately low-income, and poorly educated female sample reporting significant depressive symptoms (Hauenstein & Boyd, 1994). Rural residents may also be at greater risk for physical illness, including coronary artery disease and mortality, than are urban populations (Barnett, Halverson, Elmes, & Braham, 2000), likely due, at least in part, to differential access to health care and later diagnosis of chronic and debilitating conditions. For example, a review of the current literature reveals that African Americans living in rural communities are screened less frequently for illness, have more debilitating conditions, and less access to health care because they live in geographically isolated communities (Bernard, 1993; United States Department of Health and Human Services, 1991; Lillie-Blanton, Martinez, Taylor, & Robinson, 1993; National Women's Resource Center, 1996). As such, advancement in family-based prevention and intervention efforts will likely involve special efforts to reach low-income and geographically isolated groups in order to minimize disparities in health care and subsequent health outcomes.

One way to reach disadvantaged families may involve routine screenings by health care professionals trusted by the family members, such as family practice physicians and social workers. Alternatively, information about family intervention services may be provided in a nonthreatening manner at nontreatment points of contact, including community health care clinics, family practitioners' offices, day care centers, or through public service announcements. An additional challenge to widespread dissemination of efficacious interventions for family distress, however, is that they must be lowcost, easily accessible, and available on a continuing basis. This suggests that an important challenge for future research is that of packaging efficacious interventions and developing delivery systems that can meet the expanding needs of minority groups.

Family interventions for physical illness must also begin to consider family structure (Johnson & Lebow, 2000). For example, whether or not families are intact or divorced may affect not only who will be involved in family-based prevention and intervention efforts but also the particular stressors confronted by family members and the impact of those stressors on health and well-being. During the last decade, over 1 million children have experienced divorce every year (U.S. Census Bureau, 1999). Moreover, recent statistics indicate that divorce will continue to be an issue confronted by many families. Although the divorce rate in the United States declined slightly after 1980, recent projections suggest that between 40 and 50% of all first marriages that occurred in the 1990s will ultimately end in divorce (Schoen & Standish, 2000). A robust literature has demonstrated the negative consequences of divorce on parenting, including more relaxed monitoring, diminished support, and compromised communication between parent and child, and subsequent links between inadequate parenting and child maladjustment (Hetherington & Kelly, 2003; Hetherington & Kelly, 2002). Compromised parenting subsequent to divorce has implications for physical health outcomes as well. The links between divorce and health-risk behaviors, including smoking and alcohol and drug abuse, in children and adolescents have been clearly identified and attributed in large part to declines in parental supervision associated with the stress of divorce and single-parenting (Amato & Keith, 1991a,b). The disruption in the family structure and routines, as well as the strain of single-parenting, consequential to the stress of divorce may also interfere with the maintenance of health-promoting behaviors, including a healthy diet and exercise. Further, children of divorce face an increased risk for poor health outcomes due to the likely socioeconomic decline that in some cases may be substantial for the custodial parent, most often the mother, following divorce. In addition to declines in income, custodial mothers and their children may experience cumulative stressors associated with increased workloads for mothers, as well as relocation to less desirable neighborhoods, with higher crime rates, poorer schools, and inadequate services (McLanahan, 1983; 1985; McLanahan & Teitler, 1999).

The effects of single-parent or mother-headed families on health may be particularly detrimental for low-income and minority families. Recent demographic statistics reveal that an increasing number of economically disadvantaged ethnic minority children live in single-parent homes rather than in two-parent homes (U.S. Department of Health and Human Services, 1999). Among African American children for example, 69% were born to unwed mothers in 1997 (U.S. Department of Health and Human Services, 1999). Although some unmarried parents do cohabitate, recent statistics indicate that only 33% of poor children reside with their biological father (U.S. Department of Health and Human Services, 1999). It follows, then, that these families and children may confront an even greater degree of stress and in turn be more vulnerable to poor health outcomes. For example, some models of SES and health posit that SES differences in health are established early in life and continue to influence health into adulthood, even when adult SES is taken into account (for a review see Chen et al., 2002). As such, children born to economically disadvantaged single mothers may confront challenges to optimal health very early on, including insufficient prenatal care, shorter hospital stays after delivery, and inadequate access to well-baby services, including immunizations, potentially starting a trajectory of increasingly negative health outcomes with increasing age. As such, tailoring family-based interventions to single-parent and low-income families must take into consideration the unique stressors these children confront on a daily basis, as well as how to realistically intervene in a manner that can effect change and enhance health and well-being without increasing stress for the family.

Further, issues of ethnicity, class, and culture are likely to influence the expectations that patients have for family relationships and consequently their perceptions of the success of family interventions. It will be necessary for family therapists to consider how social, cultural, and economic factors may influence the link between family distress and disease, including multiple indicators of disease progression, and pathways linking family distress and poor health and tailor family approaches to treatment accordingly. Issues such as racism, changing gender roles, and multiple-family forms merit attention in the empirical literature and must be recognized as potentially influential variables that may impact the effectiveness of disseminating family-based prevention and intervention efforts to at-risk groups.

SUMMARY AND CONCLUSIONS

The beginnings of a promising foundation for research on communication processes and their role in disease outcomes can already be discerned. Family communication is the most common point of intervention to change dysfunctional family processes and to increase relationship satisfaction. In turn, family variables such as marital satisfaction are related to perceived health, functional impairment, and changes in basic physiological processes, key facets of physical health and illness. In the current chapter we suggest a framework for organizing future research on the effects of family processes and family communication on health outcomes. The model that results from our overview of the data can been seen in Figure 29.1. This model provides a general framework for the examination of a range of health outcomes and their connection to family processes.

As can be seen in Fig. 29.1, it is possible that many of the effects of family processes on health outcomes are mediated, in part, by effects on depressive symptoms, allostatic load, and health behaviors. Likewise, there are potential vicious cycles linking relationship stress and compromised health that may prove particularly important for intervention efforts. Of key importance for future research, we underscore the potential for contextual variables, including SES, culture, geographic region, and family structure to influence both family processes and their effect on other aspects of the health system.

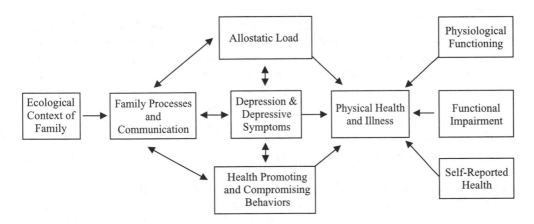

FIG. 29.1.   Family stress model of physical health and illness.

Although research on the role of family processes and communication in health outcomes is in its infancy, and the potential complexity of the area can be daunting, the existence of an organizing system can be useful in allowing for cross-fertilization of ideas and facilitating communication between researchers. Even as we discuss potential mechanisms linking family communication and health, the case for direct and chronic effects is building. For example, recently presented data that examined the association between marital quality and carotid atherosclerosis in a community sample of healthy, symptom free, middle-aged women using state of the art measures (Troxel et al., 2001) illustrate the potential influence of marital processes on important health outcomes. Troxel and colleagues reported that marital dissatisfaction was associated with a more atherogenic profile, including higher blood pressure, higher LDL-c and triglycerides, greater, intima media thickness, plaque, and aortic calcification. After controlling for standard cardiovascular risk factors, the link between marital distress and aortic calcification remained statistically significant, suggesting that marital distress may be a marker of cardiovascular disease risk in women. Similarly, Wickrama and colleagues (2001) recently examined the longitudinal association between family functioning and physical health at midlife. Findings of the study demonstrate that marital distress significantly increases the likelihood of earlier hypertension, even after controlling for work stress, health behaviors, and education. The risk associated with marital distress was especially strong for women. Building on these findings, and those reviewed throughout this chapter, we hope that the family stress model of health will provide such an organizing scheme and will prove useful as data such as these continue to accumulate.

REFERENCES

Aday, L. A., Quill, B. E., & Reyes-Gibby, C. C. (2001). Equity in rural health and health care. In S. Loue & B. E. Quill (Eds.), *Handbook of rural health* (pp. 45–72). New York: Kluwer Academic.

Adler, N. E., Boyce, T., Chesney, M. A., Cohen, S., Folkman, S., Kahn, R. L., & Syme, S. L. (1994). Socioeconomic status and health: The challenge of the gradient. *American Psychologist, 49,* 15–24.

Adler, N., & Ostrove, J. M. (1999). Socioeconomic status and health: What we know and what we don't. In N. E. Adler, M. Marmot, B. S. McEwen, & J. Stewart (Eds.), *Socioeconomic status and health in industrial nations: Social, psychological and biological pathways* (pp. 3–15). New York: New York Academy of Sciences.

Allen, M. T., Matthews, K. A., & Sherman, F. S. (1997). Cardiovascular reactivity to stress and left ventricular mass in youth. *Hypertension, 30,* 782–787.

Amato, P. R., & Keith, B. (1991a). Parent divorce and adult well-being: A meta-analysis. *Journal of Marriage and the Family, 53,* 43–58.

Amato, P. R., & Keith, B. (1991b). Parental divorce and well-being of children: A meta-analysis. *Psychological Bulletin, 11,* 26–46.

Appelberg, K., Romanov, K., Honkasalo, M. L., & Koskenvuo, M., (1993). The use of tranquilizers, hypnotics, and analgesics among 18,592 Finnish adults: Associations with recent interpersonal conflicts at work or with a spouse. *Journal of Clinical Epidemiology, 46,* 1315–1322.

Ballard, M., Cummings, E. M., & Larkin, K. (1993). Emotional and cardiovascular responses to adults' angry behavior and to challenging tasks in children of hypertensive and normotensive parents. *Child Development, 64,* 500–515.

Barnes, G. M., Reifman, A. S., Farrell, M. P., & Dintcheff, B. A. (2000). The effects of parenting on the development of adolescent alcohol misuse: A six-wave latent growth model. *Journal of Marriage and the Family, 62,* 175–186.

Barnett, R. C., Davidson, H., & Marshall, N. L. (1991). Physical symptoms and the interplay of work and family roles. *Health Psychology, 10,* 94–101.

Barnett, E., Halverson, J. A., Elmes, G. A., & Braham, V. E. (2000). Metropolitan and nonmetropolitan trends in coronary heart disease mortality within Appalachia, 1980–1997. *Annals of Epidemiology, 10,* 370–379.

Baucom, D. H., Shoam, V., Mueser, K. T., Daiuto, A., & Stickle, T. R. (1998). Empirically supported couple and family interventions for marital distress and adult mental health problems. *Journal of Consulting and Clinical Psychology, 66,* 53–88.

Baumrind, D. (1991). The influence of parenting style on adolescent competence and substance use. *Journal of Early Adolescence, 11,* 56–95.

Beach, S. R. H., & Jones, D. J. (2002). Marital and family therapy for depression in adults. In I. H. Gotlib & C. L. Hammen (Eds.), *Handbook of depression* (pp. 422–440). New York: Guilford Press.

Bernard, M. (1993). The health status of African American elderly. *Journal of the National Medical Association, 85,* 521–528.

Broadwell, S. D., & Light, K. C. (1999). Family support and cardiovascular responses in marriage during conflict and other interactions. *International Journal of Behavioral Medicine, 6,* 40–63.

Bronfenbrenner, U. (1979). *The ecology of human development: Experiments by nature and design.* Cambridge, MA: Harvard University Press.

Bronfenbrenner, U. (1992). Ecological systems theory. In R. Vasta (Ed.), *Six theories of child development: Revised formulations and current issues* (pp. 187–249). Bristol, PA: Jessica Kingsley.

Burman, B., & Margolin, G. (1992). Analysis of the association between marital relationships and health problems: An interactional perspective. *Psychological Bulletin, 112,* 39–63.

Campbell, T. L., & Patterson, J. M. (1995). The effectiveness of family interventions in the treatment of physical illness. *Journal of Marital and Family Therapy, 21,* 545–583.

Chen, E., Matthews, K. A., & Boyce, W. T. (2002). Socioeconomic differences in children's health: How and why do these relationships change with age? *Psychological Bulletin, 128,* 295–329.

Cohen, S., Schwartz, J. E., Bromet, E. J., & Parkinson, D. K. (1991). Mental health, stress, and poor health behaviors in two community samples. *Preventive Medicine, 20,* 306–315.

Coughlin, P. C. (1990). Premenstrual syndrome: How marital satisfaction and role choice affect symptom severity. *Social Work, 35,* 351–355.

Coyne, J. C., & Benazon, N. R. (2001). Coming to terms with the nature of depression in marital research and treatment. In S. R. H. Beach (Ed.), *Marital and family processes in depression* (pp. 25–43). Washington, DC: American Psychological Association.

Doherty, W. J., & Allen, W. (1994). Family functioning and parental smoking as predictors of adolescent cigarette use: A six-year prospective study. *Journal of Family Psychology, 8,* 347–353.

Doussard-Roosevelt, J. A., & Porges, S. W. (1999). The role of neurobehavioral organization in stress responses: A polyvagal model. In M. Lewis & D. Ramsey (Eds.), *Soothing and stress* (pp. 57–76). Mahwah, NJ: Lawrence Erlbaum Associates.

Downey, G., & Coyne, J. C. (1990). Children of depressed parents: An integrative reivew. *Psychological Bulletin, 108,* 50–76.

Drotar, D. (1997). Relating parenting and family functioning to psychological adjustment of children with chronic health conditions: What have we learned? What do we need to know? *Journal of Pediatric Psychology, 22,* 149–165.

El-Sheikh, M., Cummings, E. M., & Goetsch, V. L. (1989). Coping with adults' angry behavior: Behavioral, physiological, and verbal responses in preschoolers. *Developmental Psychology, 25,* 490–498.

El-Sheikh, M., Harger, J., & Whitson, S. M. (2001). Exposure to interparental conflict and children's adjustment and physical health: The moderating role of vagal tone. *Child Development, 72,* 1617–1636.

Epstein, L. H. (1981). The effects of targeting improvements in urine glucose on metabolic control in children with insulin dependent diabetes. *Journal of Applied Behavior Analysis, 14,* 365–375.

Evans, R. L., Matlock, A. L., Bishop, D. S., Stranahan, S., & Pederson, C. (1988). Family intervention after stroke: Does counseling or education help? *Stroke, 19,* 1243–1249.

Ewart, C. K., Taylor, C. B., Kraemer, H. C., & Agras, W. S. (1984). Reducing blood pressure reactivity during interpersonal conflict: Effects of marital communication training. *Behavior Therapy, 15,* 473–484.

Ewart, C. K., Taylor, C. B., Kraemer, H. C., & Agras, W. S. (1991). High blood pressure and marital discord: Not being nasty matters more than being nice. *Health Psychology, 10,* 155–163.

Fireman, P., Friday, G. A., Gira, C., Vierthaler, W. A., & Michaels, L. (1981). Teaching and self-management skills to asthmatic children and their parents in an ambulatory care setting. *Pediatrics, 68,* 341–348.

Flor, H., Breitenstein, C., Birbaumer, N., & Furst, M. (1995). A psychophysiological analysis of spouse solicitousness towards pain behaviors, spouse interactions, and pain perception. *Behavior Therapy, 26,* 255–275.

Forehand, R., Wells, K. C., & Griest, D. L. (1980). An examination of the social validity of a parent training program. *Behavior Therapy, 11,* 488–502.

Frankish, C. J., & Linden, W. (1996). Spouse-pair risk factors and cardiovascular reactivity. *Journal of Psychosomatic Research, 40,* 37–51.

Ganong, L. H., & Coleman, M. (1991). Remarriage and health. *Research in Nursing and Health, 14,* 205–211.

Giachello, A. L. M. (1994). Issues of access and use. In C. W. Molina & M. Aguirre-Molina (Eds.), *Latino health in the U.S.: A growing challenge* (pp. 83–111). Washington, DC: American Public Health Association.

Giachello, A. L., & Arrom, J. O. (1997). Health service access and utilization among adolescent minorities. In D. K. Wilson, J. R. Rodrigue, & W. C. Taylor (Eds.),

Health-promoting and health-compromising behaviors among minority adolescents (pp. 303–320). Washington, DC: American Psychological Association.

Glassman, A. H., & Shapiro, P. A. (1998). Depression and the course of coronary artery disease. *American Journal of Psychiatry, 155*, 4–11.

Goodwin, S. (1997). The marital relationship and health in women with chronic fatigue and immune dysfunction syndrome: Views of wives and husbands. *Nursing Research, 46*, 138–146.

Hahlweg, K., & Markman, H. J. (1988). Effectiveness of behavioral marital therapy: Empirical status of behavioral techniques in preventing and alleviating marital distress. *Journal of Consulting and Clinical Psychology, 56*, 440–447.

Hartley, D., Korsen, N., Bird, D., & Agger, M. (1998). Management of patients with depression by rural primary care practitioners. *Archives of Family Medicine, 7*, 139–145.

Hauenstein, E. J., & Boyd, M. R. (1999). Depressive symptoms in young women of the Piedmont: Prevalence in rural women. *Women and Health, 21*, 105–123.

Herrman, C., Brand-Driehorst, S., Kaminsky, B., Leibing, E., Staats, H., & Ruger, U. (1998). Diagnostic groups and depressed mood as predictors of 22-month mortality in medical inpatients. *Psychosomatic Medicine, 60*, 57–577.

Hetherington, E., M., Cox, M., & Cox, R. (1982). Effects of divorce on parents and children. In M. Lamb (Ed.), *Nontraditional families: Parenting and child development* (pp. 233–288). Hillsdale, NJ: Lawrence Erlbaum Associates.

Hetherington, E. M., & Kelly, J. (2002). *For better or for worse: Divorce reconsidered.* New York: W. W. Norton & Co.

Hetherington, E. M., & Kelly, J. (2003). For better or for worse: Divorce reconsidered. *American Journal of Psychiatry, 160*, 601–602.

Horwitz, A. V., & White, H. R. (1991). Becoming married, depression, and alcohol problems among young adults. *Journal of Health and Social Behavior, 32*, 221–237.

Ickovics, J. R., Hamburger, M. C., Vlahov, D., Schoenbaum, E. E., Schuman, P., Boland, R., & Moore, J. (2001). Mortality, CD4 cell count decline, and depressive symptoms among HIV-seropositive women: Longitudinal analysis from the HIV Epidemiology Research Study. *Journal of the American Medical Association, 285*, 1466–1474.

Idler, E. L., & Benyamini, Y. (1997). Self-rated health and mortality: A review of twenty-seven community studies. *Journal of Health and Social Behavior, 38*, 21–37.

Jacobson, N. S., Gottman, J. M., Waltz, J., Rushe, R., Bobcock, J., & Holtzworth-Munroe, A. (1994). Affect, verbal content, and psychophysiology in arguments of couples with a violent husband. *Journal of Consulting and Clinical Psychology, 62*, 982–988.

Jenkins, C. D., Kraeger, B. E., Rose, R., & Hurst, M. W. (1980). Use of a montly health review to ascertain illness and injuries. *American Journal of Public Health, 70*, 82–84.

Johnson, A. K., & Anderson, E. A. (1990). Stress and arousal. In J. T. Cacioppo & L. G. Tassinary (Eds.), *Principles of psychophysiology: Physical, social, and inferential elements* (pp. 216–252). New York: Cambridge University Press.

Johnson, S., & Lebow, J. (2000). The coming of age of couple therapy: A decade of review. *Journal of Marriage and Family Counseling, 26*, 23–38.

Jones, D. J., Beach, S. R. H., & Forehand, R. (2001). Stress generation in intact community families: Depressive symptoms, perceived family relationship stress, and implications for adolescent adjustment. *Journal of Social and Personal Relationships, 18*, 443–462.

Jones, D. J., Beach, S. R. H., & Forehand, R. (2002). Disease status in HIV-infected African American single mothers: The role of depressive symptoms. *Health Psychology, 20,* 417–423.

Jones, D. J., Bromberger, J., & Sutton-Tyrrell, K., Matthews, K. A. (2003). Lifetime history of major depression and carotid atherosclerosis in midlife women. *Archives of General Psychiatry, 60,* 153–160.

Katon, W., & Sullivan, M. D. (1990). Depression and chronic medical illness. *Journal of Clinical Psychiatry, 51*(6, Suppl), 3–11.

Katz, I. R. (1996). On the inseparability of mental and physical health in aged persons: Lessons from depression and medical comorbidity. *American Journal of Geriatric Psychiatry, 4,* 1–16.

Keefe, F. J., Caldwell, D. S., Baucom, D. Salley, A., Robinson, E., Timmons, K., Beaupre, P., Weisberg, J., & Helms, M. (1996). Spouse-assisted coping skills training in the management of osteoarthritic knee pain. *Arthritis Care and Research, 9,* 279–291.

Keefe, F. J., Caldwell, D. S., Baucom, D., Salley, A., Robinson, E., Timmons, K., Beaupre, P., Weisberg, J., & Helms, M. (1999). Spouse-assisted coping skills training in the management of knee pain in osteoarthritis: Long-term follow-up results. *Arthritis Care and Research, 12,* 101–111.

Kiecolt-Glaser, J. K., & Glaser, R. (1988). Psychological influences on immunity: Implications for AIDS. *American Psychologist, 43,* 892–898.

Kiecolt-Glaser, J. K, Glaser, R., Cacioppo, J. T., MacCullum, R., Snydersmith, M., Kim, C., & Malarkey, W. B. (1997). Marital conflict in older adults: Endocrinological and immunological correlates. *Psychosomatic Medicine, 59,* 339–349.

Kiecolt-Glaser, J. K., Malarkey, W. B., Chee, M., Newton, T., Cacioppo, J. T., & Mao, H. (1993). Negative behavior during marital conflict is associated with immunological down-regulation. *Psychosomatic Medicine, 55,* 395–409.

Kiecolt-Glaser, J. K., & Newton, T. L. (2001). Marriage and health: His and hers. *Psychological Bulletin, 127,* 472–503.

Kiecolt-Glaser, J. K., Newton, T. L., Cacioppo, J. T., MacCullum, R. C., Glaser, R., & Malarkey, W. B. (1996). Marital conflict and endocrine function: Are men really more physiologically affected than women. *Journal of Consulting and Clinical Psychology, 64,* 324–332.

Kiecolt-Glaser, J. K., Page, G. G., Marucha, P. T., MacCullum, R. C., & Glaser, R. (1998). Psychological influences of surgical recovery: Perspectives from psychoneuroimmunology. *American Psychologist, 53,* 1209–1218.

Kung, W. W. (2000). The intertwined relationship between depression and marital distress: Elements of marital therapy conducive to effective treatment outcome. *Journal of Marital and Family Therapy, 26,* 51–63.

Lask, B., & Matthews, D. (1979). Childhood asthma: A controlled trial of family psychotherapy. *Archives of Disease in Childhood, 54,* 116–119.

Levenson, R. W., Carstensen, L. L., & Gottman, J. M. (1993). Long-term marriage: Age, gender, and satisfaction. *Psychology and Aging, 2,* 301–313.

Levenson, R. W., Carstensen, L. L., & Gottman, J. M. (1994). The influence of age and gender on affect, physiology, and their interrelations: A study of long-term marriages. *Journal of Personality and Social Psychology, 45,* 301–313.

Levenstein, S., Ackerman, S., Kiecolt-Glaser, J. K., & Dubois, A. (1999). Stress and peptic ulcer disease. *Journal of the American Medical Association, 281*, 10–11.

Levenstein, S., Kaplan, G. A., & Smith, M. (1995). Sociodemographic characteristics, life stressors, and peptic ulcer: A prospective study. *Journal of Clinical Gastroenterology, 21*, 185–192.

Lewis, M. A., Rook, K. S., & Schwarzer, R. (1994). Social support, social control, and health among the elderly. In G. N. Penny, P. Bennett, & M. Herbert (Eds.), *Health psychology: A lifespan perspective* (pp. 191–211). Philadelphia: Harwood Academic.

Lillie-Blanton, M., Martinez, R. M., Taylor, A. K., & Robinson, B. G. (1993). Latina and African American women: Continuing disparities in health. *International Journal of Health Services, 23*, 555–584.

Lovejoy, M. C., Gracyk, P. A., O'Hare, E., & Neuman, G. (2000). Maternal depression and parenting behavior: A meta-analytic review. *Clinical Psychology Review, 20*, 561–592.

Luecken, L. J. (2000). Parental caring and loss during childhood and adult cortisol responses to stress. *Psychology and Health, 15,* 841–851.

Luecken, L. J., Suarez, E., Kuhn, C. M., Barefoot, J. C., Blumenthal, J. A., Siegler, I. C., & Williams, R. B. (1997). Stress in employed women: Impact of marital stress and children at home on neurohormone output and home strain. *Psychosomatic Medicine, 59*, 352–359.

Lundberg, O. (1993). The impact of childhood living conditions on illness and mortality in adulthood. *Social Science Medicine, 36*, 1047–1052.

Malarkey, W. B., Kiecolt-Glaser, J. K., Pearl, D., & Glaser, R. (1994). Hostile behavior during marital conflict alters pituitary and adrenal hormones. *Psychosomatic Medicine, 56*, 41–51.

Markman, H., Stanley, S., & Blumberg, S. I. (1994). *Fighting for your marriage.* San Fransico: Jossey-Bass.

Mayne, T. J., O'Leary, A., McCrady, B., Contrada, R., & Labouvie, E. (1997). The differential effects of acute marital distress on emotional, physiologial and immune functions in maritally distressed men and women. *Psychology and Health, 12*, 277–288.

McEwen, B. S., & Stellar, E. (1993). Stress and the individual: Mechanisms leading to disease. *Archives of Internal Medicine, 153*, 2093–2101.

McLanahan, S. (1983). Family structure and stress: A longitudinal comparison of two-parent and female-headed families. *Journal of Marriage and the Family, 45*, 347–357.

McLanahan, S. (1985). Family structure and reproductive poverty. *American Journal of Sociology, 90*, 873–901.

McLanahan, S., & Teitler, J. (1999). The consequences of father absence. In M. E. Lamb (Ed.), *Parenting and child development in nontraditional families* (pp. 83–102). Mahwah, NJ: Lawrence Erlbaum Associates.

Mechanic, D. (1980). The experience and reporting of common physical complaints. *Journal of Health and Social Behavior, 21*, 146–155.

Mechanic, D., & Hansell, S. (1989). Divorce, family conflict, and adolescents' well-being. *Journal of Health and Social Behavior, 30*, 105–116.

Murray, J. D., & Keller, P. A. (1991). Psychology and rural America: Current status and future directions. *American Psychologist, 46*, 220–231.

Morell, M. A., & Apple, R. F. (1990). Affect expression, marital satisfaction, and stress reactivity among premenopausal women during conflictual marital discussion. *Psychology of Women Quarterly, 14*, 387–402.

National Women's Resource Center. (1996). *Health problems in African American women*. Washington, DC: National Women's Resource Center.

O'Farrell, T., Hooley, J., Fals-Stewart, W., & Cutter, H. S. G. (1998). Expressed emotion and relapse in alcoholic patients. *Journal of Consulting and Clinical Psychology, 66*, 744–752.

Orts, K., Sheridan, J. F., Robinson-Whelen, S., Glaser, R., Malarkey, W. B., & Kiecolt-Glaser, J. K. (1995). The reliability and validity of a structured interview for the assessment of infectious illness. *Journal of Behavioral Medicine, 18*, 517–530.

Patterson, G. R. (1982). *Coercive family processes*. Eugene, OR: Castilia.

Patterson, G. R., Reid, J. B., & Dishion, T. J. (1992). *Antisocial boys*. Eugene, OR: Castilia.

Pennebaker, J. W., & Roberts, T. A. (1992). Toward a his and her theory of emotion: Gender differences in visceral perception. *Journal of Social and Clinical Psychology, 11*, 199–212.

Penninx, B. W., Guralnik, J. M., Ferruci, L., Simonsick, E. M., Deeg, D. J., & Wallace, R. B. (1998). Depressive symptoms and physical decline in community-dwelling older persons. *Journal of the American Medical Association, 279*, 1720–1726.

Philbrick, J. T., Connelly, J. E., & Wofford, A. B. (1996). The prevalence of mental disorders in rural office practice. *Journal of General Internal Medicine, 11*, 9–15.

Porges, S. W. (1991). Vagal tone: An autonomic mediator of affect. In J. Garber & K. D. Dodge (Eds.), *The development of emotional regulation and dysregulation: Cambridge studies in social and emotional development* (pp. 111–128). New York: Cambridge University Press.

Prigerson, H. G., Maciejewski, P. K., & Rosenheck, R. A. (1999). The effects of marital dissolution and marital quality on health and health services use among women. *Medical Care, 37*, 858–873.

Prince, S. E., & Jacobson, N. S. (1995). A review and evaluation of marital and family therapies for affective disorders. *Journal of Marital and Family Therapy, 21*, 377–401.

Radojevic, V., Nicassio, P. M., & Weissman, M. H. (1992). Behavioral intervention with and without family support for rheumatoid arthritis. *Behavior Therapy, 23*, 13–30.

Rantenen, T., Penninx, B. W., Masaki, K., Kintunen, T., Foley, D., & Guralnik, J. M., (2000). Depressed mood and body mass index as predictors of muscle strength decline in old men. *Journal of the American Geriatric Society, 48*, 613–617.

Ren, X. S. (1997). Marital status and quality of relationships: The impact on health perception. *Social Science and Medicine, 44*, 241–249.

Repetti, R. L., Taylor, S. E., & Seeman, T. E. (2002). Risky families: Family social environments and the mental and physical health of offspring. *Psychological Bulletin, 128*, 330–366.

Romano, J. M., Turner, J. A., & Jensen, M. P. (1997). The family environment in chronic pain patients: Comparison to controls and relationship to patient functioning. *Journal of Clinical Psychology in Medical Settings, 4*, 383–395.

Romano, J. M., Turner, J. A., Jensen, M. P., Friedman, L. S., Bulcroft, R. A., Hops, H., & Wright, S. F. (1995). Chronic pain patient-spouse behavioral interactions predict patient disability. *Pain, 63*, 353–360.

Saarijarvi, S., Rytokoski, U., & Karppi, S. L. (1990). Marital satisfaction and distress in chronic low back pain patients and their spouses. *Clinical Journal of Pain, 6*, 148–152.

Saarijarvi, S. (1991). A controlled study of couple therapy in low back pain patients: Effects on marital satisfaction, psychological distress, and health attitudes. *Journal of Psychosomatic Research, 35*, 265–272.

Sanders, M. R., & McFarland, M. (2000). Treatment of depressed mothers with distruptive children: A controlled evaluation of cognitive behavioral family intervention. *Behavior Therapy, 31*, 89–112.

Sarason, S. B. (1974). *The psychological sense of community: Prospects for community psychology.* Cambridge, MA: Brookline.

Satin, W., LaGreca, A. M., Zigo, M., & Skyler, J. S. (1989). Diabetes in adolescence: Effects of multifamily group intervention and parent simulation of diabetes. *Journal of Pediatric Psychology, 14*, 259–275.

Scaramella, L. V., Conger, R. D., Simons, R. L., & Whitbeck, L. B. (1988). Predicting risk for pregnancy by late adolescence: A social contextual perspective. *Developmental Psychology, 34*, 1233–1245.

Schoen, R., & Standish, N. (2000, April). *The footprints of cohabitation: Results from marital status life tables for United States, 1995.* Paper presented at the Population Research Institute, Pennsylvania State University, University Park, PA.

Schwartz, L., Slater, M. A., & Birchler, G. R. (1996). The role of pain behaviors in the modulation of marital conflict in chronic pain couples. *Pain, 65*, 227–233.

Seeman, T. E., Singer, B. H., Ryff, C. D., Dienberg Love, G., & Levy-Storms, L. (2002). Social relationships, gender, and allostatic load across two age cohorts. *Psychosomatic Medicine, 64*, 395–406.

Starfield, B., Riley, A. W., Robertson, J., & Witt, W. P. (2002). Social class gradients in health during adolescence. *Journal of Epidemiology and Community Health, 56*, 354–361.

Starfield, B., Riley, A. W., Witt, W. P., & Robertson, J. (2002). Social class gradients in health during adolescence. *Journal of Epidemiology and Community Health, 56*, 354–361. BMJ Publishing Group, England.

Sterling, P., & Eyer, J. (1988). Allostasis: A new paradigm to explain arousal pathology. S. Fisher, & J. Reason (Eds). *Handbook of life stress, cognition and health* (pp. 629–649). New York: Wiley.

Sullivan, M., Katon, W., Russo, J., Dobie, R., & Sakai, C. (1994). Coping and marital support as correlates of tinnitus disability. *General Hospital Psychiatry, 16*, 259–266.

Taylor, C. B., Bandura, A., Ewart, C. K., Miller, N. H., & DeBusk, R. F. (1985). Exercise testing to enhance wives' confidence in their husbands' cardiac capability soon after clinically uncomplicated acute myocardial infarction. *American Journal of Cardiology, 55*, 635–638.

Teti, D. M., & Gelfand, D. M. (1991). Behavioral competence among mothers of infants in the first year: The mediational role maternal self-efficacy. *Child Development, 62*, 918–929.

Thomas, S. P. (1995). Psychosocial correlates of women's health in middle adulthood. *Issues in Mental Health Nursing, 16*, 285–314.

Thomsen, D. G., & Gilbert, D. G. (1998). Factors characterizing marital conflict states and traits: Physiological, affective, behavioral, and neurotic variable contributions to marital conflict and satisfaction. *Personality and Individual Differences, 25*, 833–855.

Trevino, D. B., Young, E. H., Groff, J., & Jono, R. T. (1990). The association between marital adjustment and compliance with antihypertensive regimes. *Journal of the American Board of Family Practice, 3*, 17–25.

Troxel, W. M., Gallo, L. C., Matthews, K. A., Kuller, L. H., Sutton-Tyrrell, K., & Edmundowicz, D. (2001, March). *Beyond marital status: Does relationship quality influence women's cardiovascular health?* Paper presented at the Annual Convention of the American Psychosomatic Society, Monterey, CA.

Tucker, J. S., & Anders, S. L. (2001). Social control of health behaviors in marriage. *Journal of Applied Social Psychology, 31*, 467–485.

Turk, D. C., Kerns, R. D., & Rosenberg, R. (1992). Effects of marital interaction on chronic pain and disability: Examining the down side of social support. *Rehabilitation Psychology, 37*, 259–274.

Turk, D. C., & Melzack, R. (1992). The measurement of pain and the assessment of people experiencing pain. In D. C. Turk & R. Melzack (Eds.), *Handbook of pain assesmsent* (pp. 3–12). New York: Guilford Press.

U.S. Census Bureau. (1999). *Statistical abstract of the United States, 1999* (119th ed.). Washington, DC: U.S. Government Printing Office.

U.S. Department of Health and Human Services. (1991). *Healthy people 2000: National health promotion and disease prevention objectives*. Washington, DC: U.S. Department of Health and Human Services, Public Health Services.

U.S. Department of Health and Human Services (1999). *Trends in the well-being of America's children and youth: 1999*. Hyattsville, MD.

Webster-Stratton, C. (1994). Advancing video tape parenting training: A comparison study. *Journal of Consulting and Clinical Psychology, 62*, 583–593.

Weissman, M. M., & Paykel, E. S. (1974). *The depressed woman: A study of social relationships* (xix, 289pp). Chicago: University of Chicago Press.

Whisman, M. A. (2001). The association between depression and marital dissatisfaction. In S. R. H. Beach (Ed.), *Marital and family processes in depression: A scientific foundation for clinical practice*. Washington, DC: American Psychological Association.

Wickrama, K., Conger, R. D., & Lorenz, F. O. (1995). Work, marriage, lifestyle, and change in men's physical health. *Journal of Behavioral Medicine, 18*, 97–111.

Wickrama, K., Lorenz, F. O., & Conger, R. D. (1997). Marital quality and physical illness: A latent growth curve analysis. *Journal of Marriage and the Family, 59*, 143–155.

Woodall, K. L., & Matthews, K. A. (1989). Familial environment associated with Type A behaviors and psychophysiological responses to stress in children. *Health Psychology, 8*, 403–426.

Yuen, E. J., Gerdes, J. L., & Gonzales, J. J. (1996). Patterns of rural mental health care: An exploratory study. *General Hospital Psychiatry, 18*, 14–21.

VII

EPILOGUE & COMMENTARY

CHAPTER

30

THE FAMILY OF THE FUTURE: WHAT DO WE FACE?

KATHLEEN GALVIN
NORTHWESTERN UNIVERSITY

Near the close of the 20th century, Peter Vaill (1996), an organizational development specialist, predicted we would live in a future of "permanent white water" or in an ongoing complex, turbulent, environment necessitating continual, lifelong learning. He did not exaggerate. The escalating pace of change affects every aspect of life; alterations in one context compound the already significant shifts in another. Family life as we knew it is moving rapidly into history; family life in the future will challenge and confound us both as family members and as professionals. Twenty-first-century familial relationships will continue to reflect the bidirectional impact of our individual realities and the larger ecosystems, but the complexities of these interfaces will increase exponentially. We face stepping into the unknown armed with a half-century of theory, research, and practice to inform our new directions and interpretations. Our challenge is to envision, shape, and respond to another half-century of family relationships that are only barely imaginable.

The last decade witnessed major advances in the study of family communication, as more defined areas of investigation and more sophisticated research methods emerged and doctoral students, as well as established scholars, evidenced a commitment to marital and family interaction. These advances rest on the shoulders of a small number of major pioneers who, throughout the 1970s and 1980s, established core areas of study that are well represented throughout this handbook. Although the developing areas predictably contain many unanswered questions, the 1990s witnessed sustained and systematic attention to issues of children, violence and abuse, race and ethnicity, and gender. Processes such as family construction, cognition, boundary management of privacy, disclosure and secrets, as well as dialectical tensions and enacting rituals, impact family interaction. Established research programs are underway in these areas.

Rather than dwell extensively on topics reflected in decades of publication or that show strong promise of further development (most of which are well developed in other chapters

675

of this handbook), this exploration focuses on emerging areas in need of increased attention from communication-oriented scholars. The following identification of communication-related concerns faced by 21st century family members reflects (a) informed speculation about the future, (b) predictions of family life in the future, and (c) current cutting-edge explorations of family interactions. Consideration of these factors leads to the following assertions.

The family of the future will:

1. Reflect an increasing diversity of self- conceptions, evidenced through structural as well as cultural variations, that will challenge current family scholars to abandon their historical, nucleocentric biases, unitary cultural assumptions, and implied economic and religious assumptions

2. Live increasingly within four and five generations of familial connection. Escalating longevity and changing birth rates will necessitate greater attention to developmental patterns of infants through centenarians with a strong focus on patterns of multiple intergenerational contacts, generational reversals, and influence patterns within smaller families.

3. Function in a world of health-related genetic discoveries and fast-paced medical advances. In earlier decades, family studies foregrounded relational interactions minimizing the focus on individuals. Breakthroughs in areas such as genetics and illness will necessitate greater understanding of individuals embedded within family systems.

4. Encounter rapidly changing environments due to unprecedented technological change. Family members will be faced with new issues and interaction patterns by technological changes in areas such as telecommunications, medical treatment, and education. These changes must be viewed through dual-life-course and developmental lenses.

5. Search for new ways to protect and enhance family life. This will necessitate a greater understanding of varied religious and ethnic underpinnings of family life, as they relate to a reinvigoratation of spiritual, educational, and governmental family enrichment and psychoeducational efforts. This must be accompanied by increased attention to family ecosystem concerns related to areas such as communities and neighborhoods.

Each of the previous assertions, all reflections of a " permanent white water" environment, have significant implications for the future study of family interaction.

FAMILY CONCEPTIONS

Families are defining themselves for themselves through their interactions at the same time that longevity, legal flexibility, personal choice, ethnicity, gender, geographic distance, and reproductive technology impact traditional biological and legal conceptions of family. We have passed the point of seeing the "traditional versus nontraditional family" categories as useful and the "functional versus dysfunctional" categories as reasonable. Scholars have championed a reconsideration of *family* arguing that we need to "employ definitions of the family that depend on how families define themselves rather than definitions based on genetic and sociological criteria" (Fitzpatrick, 1998, p. 45). This point holds particular salience for those concerned with family interaction because it argues that "families are constituted by the very communication processes one seeks to study as being 'within a family'"(Steier, 1989, p. 15). Many scholars acknowledge the importance of recognizing how families define themselves as families, using assigned and created kinship systems, given the multiple and conflicting criteria people use to define their family (Cherlin, 1999; Coontz, 1999; Jorgenson, 1989; Patillo-McCoy, 1999). This constitutive approach challenges the conception of one dominant form of family life at a time when "Gay, lesbian, and transsexual parents; single mothers by choice; and interracial adoptions and other previously labeled non-traditional families transform the societal landscape" (Silverstein, 2002, p. 59).

Structural Variations

Therefore, although most researchers still use discrete, structural, categories for pragmatic purposes, families no longer can be usefully categorized in unitary terms, such as step-families, lesbian partners, single-parent families, or adoptive families, due to overlapping complexities of connection. Increasingly we encounter structures such as: Family X that includes two parents, each remarried twice, their biological children and stepchildren, two of whom are adopted, and the numerous grandparent figures who maintain varying levels of connection to particular members; or Family Y that includes four generations of women living together representing varied sexual preferences and live-in partners, as well as varied ethnic backgrounds. In the future, communicative definitions of family will be privileged over structural definitions, a reality that requires new models for talking about and studying families (Whitchurch & Dickson, 1999).

No matter what the configuration, structural family complexities remain seriously un-derstudied from a communication perspective; only a few are noted here for illustrative purposes. Currently scholars are beginning to address the intentional family building processes of persons involved with transracial/transnational adoption (Elmhorst, 2000; Fujimoto, 2001; Krusiewicz & Wood, 2001; Manning, 2001) and families formed by gay, lesbian, and transgendered members (Kurdek, 1994; Patterson, 2000; West & Turner, 1995). They find that even these categories display overlapping complexities. Communication-oriented discussions of the following issues confronting families are limited: incorporating foster children or managing open adoptions (Brodzinsky & Schechter, 1990), relating to in-laws (Bryant, Conger, & Meehan 2001), and incorporating grandparents into stepfamilies.

Ethnic Variations

Although the constitutive formation of families is structurally central to our work, diversity also must be construed in multiple ways. Issues of ethnicity represent significant features in constructing a sense of family. By 2050, UN demographers predict a population of almost 9 billion people on the planet, a 50% increase from the turn of the century. There will be more Africans and far fewer Chinese and Europeans than there are today (Sanger, 2000). Although research focused on interaction within families of specific races or ethnicities has increased in the past 2 decades, there is much left to do (Socha & Diggs, 1999). Even in the United States, communication practices in Asian and East Asian families and Latino families have received limited attention, and authors have struggled with conflating multiple ethnic heritages under traditional labels. Much of our scholarship presumes family communication issues are similar across ethnic groups; unique issues have been overlooked or underrepresented (Coontz, 1999; McGoldrick & Giordano, 1996). The attention placed on the "traditional" family has led some authors to proclaim, "The psychology of marriage as it exists is really a psychology of European American middle class marriage" (Flanagan et al., 2002, p.109). Recent U.S. census data indicate the number of foreign-born residents and children of immigrants has reached the highest level in history, 56 million people who represent 20% of the population, 25% of whom are from Mexico. Families with children vary greatly by ethnicity. "The proportion of married couples with children under 18 ranged from 35% for residents born in Europe to 73.4% for those from Latin America" (Scott, 2002, p. A18). Yet, "There is little research on identities and family communication among non-European American families that can be used to generate predictions for future research" (Gudykunst & Lee, 2001, p. 80). In addition, more studies need to focus on multicultural family forms. At all times researchers need to indicate whether the family is of color, whether the dialog occurs within the family or not, and whether the communication is within or across ethnic groups (McAdoo, 2001).

An emerging line of research explores communication competencies developed within minority families to prepare members for managing boundary issues. For example, the socialization of African American children includes parental warnings about racial dangers and disappointments while fostering the development of communicative coping mechanisms for confronting discrimination. Research has not adequately addressed how parents meet such a challenge as preparing a child for racial derogation (Daniel & Daniel, 1999; Ferguson, 1999). Studies of enacting culturally based strategies for humor, support, or conflict are needed also.

The last decade witnessed a significant increase in studies of family communication patterns within different cultures, but only limited scholarship has addressed transracial or transethnic families (Dainton, 1999; Orbe, 1999). The terminology varies, but whereas ethnicity implies a common ancestry, language and cultural heritage, race is based on no distinctive cultural or linguistic heritage (Coontz, 1999). Future categorization of family race/ethnicity will have to change as intermarriage, adoption, and cohabitation increase the population of mixed-ethnicity families. In 2000, interracial couples accounted for 1.9% of married couples and 4.3% of unmarried couples (U.S. Census, March 2000). The number of African American and White transracial married couples almost doubled in the past decades. Over 4% of U.S. children are of mixed race and that figure is rising rapidly. Families headed by transracial partners encounter confounding issues involving children's communication. These include interactions with extended family members who create subtle messages, such as loving the child but refusing to acknowledge biracial features, or direct messages, such as cutting off family members (Root, 1999).

A variation on mixed-race families may be found through "visible" adoption, in which members' racial characteristics display their lack of biological ties. Although figures vary, it is estimated that over 10,000 Chinese children were adopted into American households between 1989 and 1997, whereas since the 1950s, over 150,000 Korean children have been adopted in North America and Europe with roughly 100,000 adopted in the United States (Elmhorst, 2000; Tessler, Gamache, & Liu, 1999). Almost all these adoptions created transracial families, a form predicted to increase. Many transracially and transnationally adopted children, and their nonadopted siblings, need boundary management skills to cope with challenges to their family identity; adoptive parents need to prepare their children to face racialized experiences and need communicative skills to confront aggressors (Fujimoto, 2001; Galvin & Wilkinson, 2000).

Economic Variations

Economic and class issues continue to be overlooked and understudied, although family financial capital affects communication such as decision making and boundary management. Selected examinations of work/family interaction emphasize economic pressures as part of family dialog and decision making, because most work/family discussions involve financial considerations (Zvonkovic, Greaves, Schmiege, & Hall, 1996), such as monetizing both partners' time (Waite & Nielsen, 2001). A few references to economic issues appear in narrative accounts (Dickson 1995; Pearson, 1992). Family communication scholarship essentially remains economically neutral; some basic level of financial security is assumed. Yet families in all income brackets face major stresses during economic reversals, for example, when a parent is laid off. Families in transition engage in financial negotiation as decisions about adding a child, funding a college education, and supporting returning adult offspring are encountered. Even wealthy families have needs for communication-related attention. A recent 3-year prospective study of economic pressure and marital relations demonstrated that a positive association between economic pressure and emotional distress exists even for more supportive couples. Sensitivity and concern were not enough to reduce distress. Couples "need to be able to negotiate, bargain and reach agreement on realistic solutions to internal family matters" (Conger, Rueter, & Elder, 1999, p. 69). Given the current economic climate, the concept of adult children providing parents with economic support has been reversed as "Today, parents provide insurance for their children's entry into or maintenance of, middle class status" (Coontz, 2000, p. 289). Young adults tend to expect future parental support even if parents do not anticipate such commitments, creating a "deep division" in American families (Goldscheider, Thornton, & Yang, 2001). Although there are cultural variations on such supports, little is known about how families negotiate sharing economic resources. Family finances remain underdiscussed and, understandably, understudied.

Most importantly, very little attention has been paid to the increasing "have/have not" divide that separates neighborhoods, the attendant pressures that face poor families, and the communication outcomes of these pressures. Severe economic pressures, usually accompanied by concerns for physical space, safety, and employment, can undermine partner interaction and impact parent–child communication, because "family strategies and circumstances interact with neighborhood options" (Patillo-McCoy, 1999, p. 109). Children living in poverty are more likely to suffer depression, social withdrawal, and low self-esteem, all of which have implications for family interaction (Seccombe, 2000). Poor families face severe pressures, as income problems are confounded by unsafe neighborhoods and related dangers leaving many mothers severely depressed and children witnessing violence. The effects of socioeconomic status on marital outcome demonstrate less marital stability found among couples earning lower incomes (Flanagan et al., 2002), but the role of interaction patterns is a latent factor.

Religious Variations

The extent to which religious beliefs impact family interaction remains remarkably understudied. Given that "Ninety-five percent of married couples (Glenn, 1982) and parents (Mahoney, 2000) report having a religious affiliation " (Mahoney, Pargament, Tarakeshwar, & Swank, 2001, p. 559), this seems a critical and fruitful area for extensive consideration. When researchers describe families, religious traditions are not noted, but religious beliefs create a taken-for-granted subtext for interaction patterns.

Religious affiliation has obvious connections to gender roles and parenting styles, as well as to family/work decisions (Smits, Ultee, & Lammers. 1996). In their meta-analytic review of links among religion, marriage, and parenting, Mahoney et al. (2001) report that there is some evidence for linking religiousness with greater use of adaptive communication skills, collaboration in handling disagreements, positivity in family relationships, and parental coping. Some data indicated an inverse relationship between religion and domestic violence and marital verbal conflict. The research they included focused on English-speaking populations in Western societies because they found a dearth of social scientific treatment of non-Western religious traditions. If religious beliefs are accepted as impacting family interactions, then non-Western faith traditions remain a fertile field for exploratory research.

Although occasionally religious family rituals (Baxter & Braithwaite, 2002) and interfaith relationships (Hughes & Dickson, 2001) have been explored in the study of family communication, the main area of reference has been to certain faith-based enrichment programs. Parke (2001) puts it starkly, suggesting, "religion is scarcely mentioned in scientific journals devoted to family issues" (p. 555). The influence of religious affiliation and marital and family enrichment progress is addressed later in this chapter.

Taken together, the aforementioned points depict the complex and varied conception of families and the evolving realities impacting family members' interaction patterns.

LIFE-COURSE AND DEVELOPMENTAL ISSUES

A future perspective is best served by integrating life-course and developmental approaches to examining families or by exploring developmental patterns within individual, generational, and historical time. A life-course approach provides an overreaching context for considering developmental issues because its central premise is "the notion that changing lives alter developmental trajectories" (Elder, 1998, p. 1) as it focuses on "how varying events and their timing in the lives of individuals affected families in particular historical contexts" (Aldous, 1990, p. 573). A life-course perspective recognizes that lives are influenced by changing contextual features, such as poverty, race relations, or technological advances. Unique individual experiences may be "off time" or "on time." Given current medical advances, women may bear children "off time" at age 60 through the use of reproductive technologies, the rural elderly may finish high school "off time" through online technology. Community life-course issues involve recognizing the impact of shared group experiences such September 11, 2001, the Holocaust, a devastating Honduran earthquake, the AIDS epidemic, or the Civil Rights movement on family development. Personal, unique, experiences, such as divorce, giving birth to triplets, miscarriage, or a kidney transplant, are part of an individual's life course that also affects his or her family. Family developmental stages cannot be fully considered outside a life-course context.

That being said, developmental life span issues must be considered within the context of future changes. Life expectancies at birth vary by geographic region but, except for Sub-Saharan Africa where the expectancy is 49, persons will live into their sixth to seventh decade. Life expectancies as noted in 1998 are: Western Europe, 78; North America, 76; Latin America, 69; Asia, 65 (U.S. Census Bureau, 1998). These figures will continue to rise; future families will experience four and five generations of relatives as typical.

Families will be faced with increased involvement in managing and renegotiating relational connections over many decades and across many generations. According to Bengston (2001), "For many Americans, multigenerational bonds are becoming more important than nuclear family ties for well-being and support over the course of their lives" (p. 4). Research programs will need to include great grandparents and great-great grandparents in their considerations of family interaction. Intergenerational issues will be easier to research in real life rather than through retrospective analyses; relevant research will, of necessity, involve more generations. Chen and Kaplan's (2001) study of constructive parenting provides a three-wave longitudinal model of research involving subjects from 1980 through 1997 when the subjects' children were included.

Future families will be represented increasingly by elongated generational structures. Bengston (2001) reports that due to increases in longevity and decreases in fertility, the population age structure in most industrialized nations has changed from a pyramid to a rectangle creating "a family structure in which the shape is long and thin, with more family generations alive but with fewer members in the generation" (p. 5). This geometric shift portends shifts in relational interaction as elder generations compete for connection to limited grandchildren and great-grandchildren. Bengston makes the case for the increasing importance of multigenerational bonds arguing that the demographic changes result in longer years of shared lives and more grandparents are fulfilling basic family functions. To date there has been some focus on later-life couples, but most studies focus on long-term marriages or grandparenting (Dickson, 1995; Mares, 1995; Pearson, 1992). Multigenerational bonds are becoming more important for well-being and support over individuals' lifetimes. Less is known about interactional dynamics involving grandfathers than grandmothers (Roberto, Allen, & Blieszner, 2001). To date, minimal attention has been paid to multiple grandparent roles, such as great-grandparents, great-great grandparents, and stepgrandparents, or to four and five generational interfaces (Mills, 2001). Current data suggest family members of the future will interact for many more years as longevity increases within altered multigenerational structures and divorce and/or multiple marriages reduce long-term connections with significant others.

Missing from current research is the study of multigenerational relationships of gay and lesbian families, 40-year cohabiting partners, never-married parents, and an examination of the extent to which White American families will be influenced by the stronger intergenerational ties within non-White families (Bengston, 2001). Although some communication research addresses multigenerational transmission of culture, usually from a downward influence model, a limited number of studies have addressed bidirectional influences in family communication (Saphir & Chaffee, 2002); the future challenge is to conceptualize four- and five-generation family systems and the implied bidirectional effects of members (e.g., as teenagers and great-grandparents mutually instruct each other, or as parents adapt discipline strategies to a disruptive or passive child). The adage, "No two children grow up in the same family," although addressed in selected writings (Dunn & Plomin 1990), needs systematic exploration.

Currently, generalized expectations for experiences in a particular life stage are being upended. Rubin (2001) argues that, for many, age is no longer the predictor of life stage but that generational issues and experiences are increasingly tied to "how we're connected to the social and institutional world in which our lives are embedded" (pp. 59–60). Teenagers and midlife parents study together, a 75-year-old male is telecommuting to work at his grandson's company while his former spouse is on her fourth honeymoon.

The problem of generational reversal of hierarchies (McGoldrick & Giordano, 1996) exists and its potentially dramatic impact on family interaction patterns remains uncharted terrain. The concepts of elder wisdom and generational knowledge hierarchies have been breaking down particularly in U.S. immigrant families (Landau, 1982). Youngsters manage the family's communication interfaces with other institutions such as schools or government agencies due to language fluency and cultural knowledge. Familial gender understandings were undermined after immigration, because "comparative access of men and women to the resources of the dominant society has to some extent become equalized" (Kibria, 1999, p. 323). Such power shifts are impacting nonimmigrant families as youngsters develop technological skills and cultural knowledge unavailable to older family members. Generational reversals will increase exponentially, sending many families down the white water rapids of upended hierarchies.

INDIVIDUAL SOMATIC CONCERNS

In earlier decades, studies of families foregrounded relational interaction while minimizing the focus on individuals. Recently intraindividual concerns have gained prominence. These include attention to cognitive processes of relationship members, the impact of genetics on interaction patterns, and individual health concerns such as illness, disability, or addiction on relational functioning. In addition there is growing interest in the impact of family members' physiological state on interactional processes such as conflict or problem solving.

Cognitive processes of marital and family members have received sustained yet varying levels of attention (Fincham & Beach, 1999; Honeycutt & Wiemann, 1999). In future decades individually oriented concerns will include biosocial considerations, or the linking of psychosocial factors to physiology, genetics, and evolution. These connections hold implications for interactional studies in areas such as parenting, mate selection, marital quality, and family health. Booth, Carver, and Granger (2000) propose the importance of the following biological topics on family studies, suggesting direct links to family interaction: (a) behavioral endocrinology, (b) behavioral genetics, (c) evolutionary psychology, and (d) behavioral psychopharmacology. The impact of physiology, genetics, and evolution on interaction patterns gained attention in the past decade with renewed attention to biological contributions to individual communication practices and discussion of a communibiological paradigm (Beatty, McCroskey, & Valencic, 2001; Cappella 1991). As noninvasive assessment of many biological processes becomes increasingly available to family research teams, such considerations will become commonplace. For example,

MRI's have the potential to reveal explanations for a disruptive child's inability to attend to parental directives or for a sibling's inability to track seemingly simple information. These are understandings that may alter future interaction patterns.

Although knowledge of the effects of complex sets of genes on behavior is limited, established lines of research are exploring passive, reactive, and active influences related to behaviors of parents and children. For example, a way in which genes influence environmental risk exposure is through their effects on children's behavior. Thus, adoptee studies have shown that the adoptive parents of children born to, but not reared by, antisocial parents are more likely to exhibit negative forms of control than are parents of children who lack that biological risk (Rutter, 2002). The mediation in this case comes about through the genetic effects on the children's disruptive behavior that in turn influence their interactions with their adoptive parents who are rearing them. The implication of these and related findings is the necessity of designing future studies that can differentiate between genetic and environmental effects. For example, Schwartz and Liddle (2001) argue that, although genetic risks may predispose a child toward problem behaviors, conduct problems tend to be brought out by the interaction of difficult child temperament with poor and unskilled parenting. They argue that genetic factors are important to family researchers because the family is "both the source of the individuals' genetic material and the context in which they spend the majority of their early years" (p. 302).

Given recent dramatic scientific advances, the interconnections of health and interaction patterns will become even more compelling for family researchers. Individual health issues exist within familial systems that can mediate the impact of illness, in part, through family members' interaction patterns (see e.g. chapter 29). In calling for a synthesis of biopsychosocial and cultural perspectives when addressing family–health relationships, Crews and Balcazar (1999) justify the need for "exploring how family characteristics (e.g., social support) may influence the ways individuals move from a diseased state to a healthy state or how families may render members more vulnerable to health difficulties" (p. 621).

Family health communication involves (a) the day-to-day talk about health that affects family members' interactions, choices, behaviors, and expectations; (b) the interaction about health surrounding a particular illness; and (c) the meaning of health and illness for members, particularly within the family's cultural or religious tradition. A growing body of literature suggests that people with supportive family and friends remain in better health and recover better from physical and emotional distress than those who are less socially integrated (Rhodes, 1998). As individuals live longer, more families will confront managing serious health problems of members. Additional literature points to the critical need for cultural understanding of health care as a form of barter (Conquergood, 1988) or perceived illness as variably constructed (Fadiman, 1997).

The presence of a parent with chronic illness impacts family interaction and identity. A recent study of the effects of parental chronic kidney disease on the family reveals an impact on family time together, the quality of joint activities, and the worries that cause stress for all members (Smith & Soliday, 2001). Such stresses impact immediate family interactions as well as interactions with extended family and friends. Growing evidence links psychological processes to physical health: Family stressors influence the onset of hypertension (Wickrama et al., 2001); talking or writing about personal topics improves immune system functioning (Pennebaker, 1997).

Coping with challenges of living with a family member with a disability affects all family members and their attendant relationships. A family member with a disability potentially impacts independence–dependence tensions in family relationships beyond those involving the particular family member (Braithwaite & Harter, 2000). It can also alter the self-definition of another family member, such as a spouse's conception of couplehood when a partner lives in a nursing home (Braithwaite, 2002) or a child's construal of his or her responsibilities when a sibling is hospitalized (Seligman & Darling, 1997).

Recent research links marriage, or partnership, and better health. In their examination of the benefits of marriage, Waite and Gallagher (2000) assert: "Marriage not only preserves life, but it protects health" (p. 59). As part of their analysis of lifestyle issues, they suggest that communication-related health benefits of marriage come from having a spouse, usually the woman, who monitors both partners' health and nags the other to engage in certain health practices. In addition, there is value in having a spouse with whom to talk over one's troubles. An examination of health-related talk in marriage revealed five distinct couple types: the sympathetic, the independent, the mixed, the nonreciprocal, and the rejecting couple (Walker & Dickson, 2000).

Researchers are revisiting certain health problems, such as addiction, that have been viewed as family issues over the past decades, recognizing that systems therapy interventions are not sufficient to address the problems without significant intervention aimed at the health of the individual abuser. Still, addiction is a family disease; for example, sons of parents with alcohol and physical health problems are at elevated risk for behavior problems, related in part to the levels of distress experienced by their parents (Loukas, Piejak, Bingham, Fitzgerald, & Zucker, 2001).

A final area of somatic concern involves measurement of individuals' physiological states during interactions (Gottman, 1994). Currently physiological data, collected as couples replay arguments, is informing family therapy training as well as psychoeducational and enrichment programs (Gottman, 1999). In their study of conversations between police officers and their spouses, Roberts and Levenson (2001) examine the physiological and subjective component of emotional responding during marital interactions demonstrating how job stress and exhaustion can negatively impact marriage. As noninvasive collection of physiological data becomes commonplace, future studies will take individual physiological states into account while examining family interaction. Examination of physiological changes during parent–child or sibling conflicts may result in new understandings of these constantly negotiated, power-related family ties.

As the study of family interaction evolves, the focus on interaction patterns will be increasingly augmented with valuable individual-level information and, as noted in the final point of this chapter, by ecosystem analysis.

TECHNOLOGICAL ADVANCES

Multiple life-course issues confront today's families. Members manage increasingly diffuse boundaries between themselves and the ecosystem. Selected technological changes will serve as exemplars for countless technological developments impacting families; these are medical advances such as New Reproductive Technologies (NRT's) and genetic screening, as well as computer advances, specifically the Internet.

New Reproductive Technologies and Genetic Screening

With the growth of NRTs, parenting options are extended to many who previously would not have been able to produce biological children. Assisted reproductive technology has contributed to the birth of over 300,000 babies since 1977 (Parke, 2002). Many NRT issues are discussed from policy or ethical standpoints but seldom from a family interaction perspective, in terms of both decision making and explanation to others in the family network.

Reaching the decision to use reproductive technologies to conceive, and discussing his or her origins with any resulting offspring, remains primarily the purview of the medical community or trade book authors. The latter includes chapters such as "Telling the Truth," addressing issues of ethics, honesty, and talking to children (Cooper & Glazer, 1999); and "Facing Tough Choices" (Vercollone, Moss, & Moss, 1997). Parents are encouraged to consider "What will you tell your child about the role of the mother? How will you help your child explain to other kids why he has two fathers?" (Andrews, 1999, p.121). Parents face conversations using terms such as "seed daddies" (Blumenthal, 1990). Given that individuals and partners face family-building discussions and decision making on topics such as designer babies, *in vitro* fertilization, embryo freezing, selective reduction, banking sperm, or baby as donor match, there is a great need for understanding the processes and context of such interactions. In the not too distant future, such topics may include cloning a child. Such technological advances also raise critical communication issues of family privacy, including donor anonymity, parental infertility, as well as children's rights to genetic information.

Although countless benefits arise from advances in medical technology, the cutting edge and ambiguous nature of some procedures raises difficult decisions for individuals and family members. For example, the potentially beneficial results of fetal surgery to repair myelomeningocele will make parental decisions more difficult for parents trying to weigh the potential benefits and risks of fetal surgery (Mark & Glass, 1999), or requests for researchers to use newborns' cord blood for future genetic research will confront parents with unanticipated, complicated decisions (Pelias & Markward, 2001).

A critical feature inherent in much of the work related to medical technological advances is encapsulated in the struggles encountered by genetic counselors regarding their role in supporting family decision making. Genetic counseling refers to "the communication process by which individuals and their family members are given information about the nature, recurrence risk burden, risks and benefits of tests, and meaning of test results, including reproductive options of a genetic condition, as well as counseling and support concerning the implications of such genetic information" (Andrews, Fullarton, Holtzman, & Motulsky, 1994, p. 4). The current movement is toward nondirective genetic counseling and genetic services that promote client autonomy and self-directedness. Thus, a genetic counselor's task is to help people make decisions "by aiding them to think through the various options open to them, grapple with the meaning of various choices for themselves and their greater family in both the short and long term, identify and attempt to defuse the obstacles, affective and otherwise, in the way of their autonomous decision making ... "(Kessler, 2001, p. 188). Such language conveys the weight and complexity of technology-related future family decision making in general, whether it involves the option of prophylactic surgery, reproductive strategies, or removing life supports. These predictable family decision making tasks warrant extensive scholarly attention. Recent advances link genetics and heritability to such conditions as depression and anxiety, aggression, and addiction (Hamer & Copeland, 1998), opening the door to possible genetic intervention to avoid certain family struggles. Little is known about family processes or the role of ethnicity, religion, and other factors in genetic-oriented decision making.

The Internet

The Internet represents another technological advance with great potential impact on family relations. Access to the Internet is skyrocketing; close to 90 percent of people who used the Internet during a typical day in 2000 sent or received e-mail (Tracking online life, 2000). The immense changes brought about by the Internet within the past decade raise multiple implications for family relationships, both within the family and between families and other social institutions such as schools, and for extended family members (Hughes, Ebata, & Dollahite, 1999). Early studies reveal family communication is changing as a result of computer-related technological developments and a faster paced lifestyle. In their early, frequently cited, study of family Internet use, Kraut et al. (1998) reported that persons who used the Internet more heavily were less socially involved and more lonely than were less active users. They found greater use of the Internet was associated with declines in participants' communication with family members. In a recent follow-up study, (Kraut, Kiesler, Boneva, Cummings, Helgeson & Crawford, 2002) report findings that contradict their earlier work. In addition, they identify factors such as facility with Internet use, extraversion and social support, increasing numbers of key friends/family members online, and differences in the effects for parents and teens as issues for further exploration.

Of particular interest to family communication researchers is how technology, particularly the Internet, impacts the hierarchical communication structure in many families as youngsters gain information and skills unfamiliar to their parents. The child's information power may create a generational reversal fraught with conflict and stress. Witness the frequent cartoon treatment of the bumbling parents and technowizard child, such as the one portrayed in ZITS. Although parental supervision of media use is weakening with respect to the Internet, parents report concerns of child safety including Internet strangers, as well as content concerns such as pornography (Wartella & Jennings, 2001; also see chapter 26).

Given the unique nature of family Internet use, professionals are calling for studies of youth issues from a multidisciplinary approach. They also suggest that researchers need to find ways to educate parents about these issues (Brown & Cantor, 2000), because parents serve as gatekeepers and facilitators of opportunities for children to interact with others outside the family (Parke, 2002). The Internet plays a pivotal role in the lives of teenagers who use it more frequently than do other family members (Kraut et al., 1998); almost three quarters of teens use the Internet, with high percentages using it for email and instant messages (Lenhart, Rainie, Lewis, 2000). Although online activity is valued by teens, over 60% think Internet use takes away time spent with the family (Lenhart, Rainie, Lewis, 2000)

Compared to causal users, heavy U.S. Internet users are more likely to say email has improved their connection to members of their families, improved relationships in their families, brought them closer to their families, taught them a lot about their families, and brought them into active contact with a family member with whom they had little contact before (Lenhart, Rainie, Lewis, 2000). It appears that increasing family email contact serves as a substitute for conversation as family members stay in touch without having to spend so much time talking. Many siblings send emails more often than place phone calls to each other. Many family members feel it is easier to say frank or unpleasant things in email (Lenhart, Rainie, Lewis, 2000).

Multigenerational family relationships are impacted by Internet use. Of those senior citizens who are "wired," about 60% are men; many seniors are encouraged to go online by relatives, and a prime motivation is to connect with their children and grandchildren, even more than with friends (Fox, 2001). Today, more family members are creating family Web sites and round-robin family messages, researching family history, sharing family pictures, and actively sustaining relationships with extended family members, developments that are understudied. Over 52% of online parents report their use of the Internet improved the way they connect with members of their families, although married and single parents tend to use the Internet differently (Allen & Rainie, 2002).

Finally, Internet use raises issues of family privacy and boundary management as users enter sites or share information that impacts other members; anything from family disagreements to personal data may be provided to an online interaction, only to be revealed to much larger communities. As noted by Petronio and Caughlin (chapter 18), families often have to develop rules for regulating privacy at a level that meets the needs of the whole family

The Internet serves as an exemplar for other major technological innovations such as PDA's, cell phones, or video games, that become life-course considerations in understanding family interaction. A major research challenge involves determining the impact of technology, particularly the Internet, on family relationships.

FAMILY INTERVENTION: PREVENTION/ENRICHMENT

Future families will have increased needs and desires for ways to protect and improve family life, specifically their interaction patterns. Yet prevention and enrichment efforts have been overlooked and underresearched. In addition, existing programs often reflect specific beliefs about the "right" way to be a family and ignore ethnic or structural variations in family functioning. Accordingly, one major future challenge is to "rigorously investigate the intricate interplay between ethnicity, family functioning and family intervention," (Santisteban, Muir-Malcolm, Mitrani, & Szapocsnik, 2002, p. 331). Increasing family complexities, such as managing international adoption, caring for aging grandparents, or sustaining 65-year partnerships, will benefit from external supports, but not necessarily through traditional therapeutic interventions. "Going at it alone" is increasingly unrealistic as the pace of change increases stress on all members; institutional support for functional families will become a greater necessity in the future.

In their analysis of family therapy interventions, Pinsof and Hambright (2002) reconceptualize interventions using a medical analogy. Epidemiologists differentiate among three levels of preventive intervention, primary, secondary and tertiary, each reflecting the point of intervention in the disease process. Primary-level prevention stops disease from occurring by removing the causes; secondary-level prevention detects disease in beginning stages when early treatment can stop it from progressing; tertiary-level prevention occurs when the family is in crisis. Traditionally, family therapists intervene at the tertiary level, yet strong interest is developing in identifying risk factors early and developing interventions to prevent major crises, such as family or partner violence (Snider & Satcher, 1997). Currently primary-level interventions, aimed at nonclinical populations, include local and national marital and family enrichment programs such as Prevention and Relationships Enhancement Program (PREP) (Markman, Renick, Floyd, Stanley, & Clements, 1993) or RE: Relationship Enhancement (Guerney, 1977). Religious organizations and governmental agencies are attempting to increase instructional programs ranging from those aimed at premarital pairs and parents to those focusing on divorcing couples with children.

Secondary therapeutic interventions are directed toward at-risk populations through targeted parenting programs, or school-based programs for children exhibiting conduct disorders or self-destructive behaviors. Scholars who study social interaction have a limited history of contributions to program development and research in intervention efforts (Dickson & Markman, 1993; Fitzpatrick, 1997), although communication skills appear as the core of many such programs (Arcus, 1995; Lebow, 1997). Communication scholars have much to offer to primary- and secondary-level intervention efforts directed toward managing interactional risk factors, such as conflict and physical aggression (Pinsof & Hambright, 2002). In addition, more religious, school, and government organizations are recommending or mandating instruction in family life with a focus on communication (Gardner & Howlett, 2000; Gentry, 2000; Kramer & Washo, 1993; Traver, 2002). Increasingly family education/enrichment Web sites are dispensing advice related to communication (Smith, 1999).

Enrichment programs remain understudied. With the exception of the PREP program, developed by Markman and his colleagues, systematic theory testing and program evaluation have not advanced at the same rate as the development of theory and new programs (Giblin, 1996). Stanley (2001), a PREP developer, argues that "there are clear advantages in terms of interaction quality for couples taking the more empirically-based, skills-oriented training" (p. 278). Scholars have called for, and contributed to, studies of enrichment program effectiveness, but there is much work left to do (Dickson & Markman, 1993). For example, Burleson and Denton (1997) demonstrated the difficulty of a naïve assumption that the cause of many marital communication problems is deficient communication skills. They identified moderating factors—skill type, marital distress, gender, and analytic unit (self, couple)—that support a positive association between skill levels and marital satisfaction for nondistressed couples but a negative association among distressed couples. The distressed couple mantra, "We just can't communicate," cannot be addressed by simplistic skill training. There is need for sophisticated and well-researched programs in family interaction across the life span that address the issues of many familial forms. Family communication scholars may develop primary intervention programs and partner with therapists to create secondary-intervention-level programs.

Communication-oriented researchers also need to focus on areas of family strengths, resilience, and best practices. For example, Rutter (2002) identified eight features that appear to be involved in child resilience processes including risk accumulation, individual genetic-related sensitivities, effects of past experiences, direct impact on the child, and concomitant interpersonal experiences. In their elaborate study of urban families and adolescent success, Furstenberg, Cook, Eccles, Elder, and Sameroff (1999) explored dense kinship and friendship networks and their social support capacities, and, by implication, boundary management communication strategies that impact youth development. Findings from future research could extend such literature by examining resilient family interaction patterns and the development of communication-oriented protective/preventive strategies. Continuation of the recent focus on positive aspects of marriage, including trust, empathic forgiveness, social support commitment, teamwork and sacrifice (Flanagan et al., 2002), and expansion of research to include other familial relationships, stand to strengthen enrichment and intervention efforts.

Finally, family communication scholars will attend increasingly to the macroenvironment's impact on family interaction. Greater attention to ecological considerations (Bronfenbrenner, 1986) will counter the limited attention paid to family interaction processes involved in managing the interface with educational, religious, medical, and community institutions. A model for such ecological approaches, developed in the learning disorders field (Gallimore, Weisner, Kaufman, & Bernheimer, 1989), addresses questions such as "What aspects of family interaction are likely to co-create, co-maintain or co-amplify a child's poor performance in the school context?" (Green, 1989, p. 191). Recently Huston (2000) articulated a framework for 21st-century marital research calling for greater recognition of the macroenvironmental context of marriage. Such investigations will extend understanding contextual factors on family interaction. Intervention programs targeted at specific family issues will produce limited benefits if they do not consider community realities. Families not only serve "as direct influences on children but also as indirect influences as managers, mediators, and negotiators on behalf of children in relation to social institutions" (Parke, 2002, p. 82). An ecological perspective stresses the need for understanding how families are situated and the implications of that situation. It necessitates understanding social capital outside the family or "the extent to which the family system is embedded in an integrative network of people and institutions in the community that share common values"(Bowen, Richman, & Bowen, 2000, p. 121). Such capital supports adaptation and resiliency. Although traditionally many communities, particularly in urban settings, have been studied by focusing on community needs, deficiencies, and problems, an alternative approach utilizes capacity-focused development or asset-driven analysis. This asset-based and relationship-driven strategy focuses on what is present in the community while rebuilding the relationships between and among local residents, local associations, and local institutions (Kretzmann & McKnight, 1993). Success depends on the ability to recognize and actualize community social capital such as communication networks, social support, and individual skills in support of families. In their study of the parenting networks of urban families, Marshall, Noonan, McCartney, Marx, and Keefe (2001) found parental social networks have an indirect effect on children's socioemotional development as parents with more emotional support and varied social networks created a more responsive and stimulating environment for their children who, in turn, exhibited greater social competence. A focus on family strengths, primary- and secondary-level intervention efforts, and family ecosystems will enlarge and energize current research agendas.

CONCLUSION

Family communication research has matured dramatically over the past 3 decades. Recently Stephen (2001) published the first content analysis of the communication literature on marriage and the family, examining research articles published in 74 communication serials between 1962 and 1998. He identified two major clusters: The first focuses on the family unit as a group, and socialization processes; the second identifies concepts related to marital and parent–child dyadic relationships. In chapter 1, Stamp discusses the theories/ perspectives actually found in empirical literature within 12 key journals covering the communication, personal relationships, and family fields. After identifying the high preponderance of articles relying on the empiricist perspective as well as over 100 theories and 28 categories of concepts/terms included in the articles, Stamp creates a model of family life derived from the data. The analysis and the resulting grounded theory model have the potential to inform and challenge the next decades of family communication researchers with limitless possibilities for future scholarly inquiry.

The multiple research directions identified within this *Handbook* are vast and complex. Yet, the family of the future will find Vaill's "permanent white water" predictions to be accurate—turbulence is woven through all areas of relational life—and unanticipated circumstances and concerns will emerge with each passing year. Family scholars will reach a similar conclusion—avoiding the rapids is impossible. Surviving and thriving in permanent white water depends on more than individual skill. It requires an ongoing commitment to learning, skilled teamwork, sophisticated technology, and forcasting the upcoming currents while negotiating the immediate ones. It will be a challenging ride!

REFERENCES

Aldous, J. (1990). Family development and the life course: Two perspectives on family change. *Journal of Marriage and the Family, 52*, 571–583.

Allen, K., & Rainie, L. (2002). *Parents online.* Retrieved May 1, 2003, from The PEW Internet and American Life Project. www.pewinternet.org

Andrews, L. B. (1999) *The clone age.* New York: Henry Holt and Co.

Andrews, L. B., Fullarton, J. E., Holtzman, N. A., & Moltusky, A. G. (Eds.) (1994). *Assessing genetic risks: Implications for health and social policy.* Washington, DC: National Academy Press.

Arcus, M. E. (1995). Advances in family life education: Past, present, and future. *Family Relations, 44*, 336–344.

Baxter, L. A., & Braithwaite, D. O. (2002). Performing marriage: Marriage renewal rituals as cultural performance. *Southern Communication Journal, 67*, 94–109.

Beatty, M. J., McCroskey, J. C., Valencic, K. M. (2001). *The biology of communication: A communibiological perspective.* Cresskill, NJ: Hampton Press.

Bengston, V. L. (2001). Beyond the nuclear family: The increasing importance of multi-generational bonds. *Journal of Marriage and Family, 63*, 1–16.

Blumenthal, A. (1990/91). Scrambled eggs and seed daddies: Conversations with my son. *Empathy: Gay and lesbian advocacy research project, 2*, 2.

Booth, A., Carver, K., & Granger, D. (2000). Biosocial perspectives on the family. *Journal of Marriage and the Family, 62*, 1018–1034.

Bowen, G. L., Richman, J. M., & Bowen, N. K. (2000). Families in the context of communication across time. In S. J. Price, P. C. McKenry, & M. J. Murphy (Eds.), *Families across time* (pp. 117–128). Los Angeles: Roxbury Press.

Braithwaite, D. O. (2002). "Married widowhood": Maintaining couplehood when one spouse is living in a nursing home. *Southern Communication Journal, 67*, 160–179.

Braithwaite, D. O., & Harter, L. M. (2000). Communication and the management of dialectical tensions in the personal relationships of people with disabilities. In D. O. Braithwaite & T. L. Thompson (Eds.), *Handbook of communication and people with disabilities* (pp. 17–36). Mahwah, NJ: Lawrence Erlbaum Associates.

Brodzinsky, D. M., & Schechter, M. D. (Eds.). (1990). *The psychology of adoption*. New York: Oxford University Press.

Bronfenbrenner, U. (1986). Ecology of the family as a context for human development: Research perspectives. *Developmental Psychology, 22*, 723–742.

Bronfenbrenner, U. (1989). Ecological systems theory. In R. Vasta (Ed.), *Annals of child development* (6th ed., pp. 187–250). Greenwich, CT: JAI Press.

Brown, J. D., & Cantor, J. C. (2000). An agenda for research on youth and the media. *Journal of Adolescent Health, 27S*, 2–7.

Bryant, C. M., Conger, R. D., & Meehan, J. M. (2001). The influence of in-laws on change in marital success. *Journal of Marriage and Family, 63*, 614–626.

Burleson, B. R., & Denton, W. H. (1997). The relationship between communication skill and marital satisfaction: Some moderating effects. *Journal of Marriage and the Family, 59*, 884–902.

Cappella, J. N. (1991). The biological origins of automated patterns on human interaction. *Communication Theory, 1*, 4–35.

Chen, Z., & Kaplan, H. B. (2001). Intergenerational transmission of constructive parenting. *Journal of Marriage and Family, 63*, 17–31.

Cherlin, A. J. (1999). *Public and private families*. Boston: McGraw-Hill.

Conger, R. D., Rueter, M. A., & Elder, G. H. (1999). Couple resilience to economic pressure. *Journal of Personality and Social Psychology, 76*, 54–71.

Conquergood, D. (1988). Health theatre in a Hmong refugee camp: Performance, communication, and culture. *The Drama Review, 32*, 174–208.

Coontz, S. (Ed.). (1999). *American families: A multicultural reader*. New York: Routledge.

Coontz, S. (2000). Historical perspectives on family studies. *Journal of Marriage and the Family, 62*, 283–297.

Cooper, S., & Glazer, E. S. (1999). *Choosing assisted reproduction: Social, emotional & ethical considerations*. Indianapolis, IN: Perspectives Press.

Crews, D. E., & Balcazar, H. (1999). Exploring family and health relationships: The role of genetics, environment, and culture. In M. Sussman, S. K. Steinmetz, & G. W. Peterson

(Eds.), *Handbook of marriage and the family.* (2nd ed., pp. 613–631). New York: Plenum Press.

Dainton, M. (1999). African-American, European-American and biracial couples' meanings for and experiences in marriage. In T. J. Socha & R. C. Diggs (Eds.), *Communication, race and family: Exploring communication in Black, White and biracial families* (pp. 147–165). Mahwah, NJ: Lawrence Erlbaum Associates.

Daniel, J. L., & Daniel, J. L. (1999). African-American childrearing: The context of a hot stove. In T. J. Socha & R. C. Diggs (Eds.), *Communication, race and family: Exploring communication in Black, White and biracial families* (pp. 25–43). Mahwah, NJ: Lawrence Erlbaum Associates.

Dickson, F. C. (1995). The best is yet to be: Research on long-lasting marriages. In J. T. Wood & S. Duck (Eds.), *Understudied relationships* (pp. 22–50). Thousand Oaks, CA: Sage.

Dickson, F. C., & Markman, H. J. (1993). The benefits of communication research: Intervention programs for couples and families. In P. Boss, W. J. Dohenty, R. La Rossa, W. R. Schumm & S. K. Steinmetz (Eds.), *Sourcebook of family theories and methods* (pp. 525–529). New York: Plenum Press.

Dunn, J., & Plomin, R. (1990). *Separate lives: Why siblings are so different.* New York: Basic Books.

Elder, G. H., Jr. (1998). The life course as developmental theory. *Child Development, 69,* 1–12.

Elmhorst, J. (2000, November). *Between two worlds: Communication strategies for managing ethnic and family identity in adult Korean adoptees.* Paper presented at the National Communication Association Convention, Seattle, WA.

Fadiman, A. (1997). *The spirit catches you and you fall down.* New York: Farrar, Straus and Giroux.

Ferguson, I. B. (1999). African-American parent-child communication about racial derogation. In T. J. Socha & R. C. Diggs (Eds.), *Communication, race and family: Exploring communication in Black, White and biracial families* (pp. 45–67). Mahwah, NJ: Lawrence Erlbaum Associates.

Fields, J., & Cooper, L. M. (2001). America's families and living arrangements: March 2000. *Current Population Reports* (pp. 20–537). U.S. Census Bureau, Washington DC.

Fincham, F. D., & Beach, S. R. H. (1999). Marriage in the new millennium: Is there a place for social cognition in marital research? *Journal of Social and Personal Relationships, 16,* 685–704.

Fitzpatrick, M. A. (1997). *Interview in family communication.* Teleclass, available from PBS Adult Learning Satellite Service, 1320 Braddock Pl., Alexandria, VA.

Fitzpatrick, M. A. (1998). Interpersonal communication on the Starship Enterprise: Resilience, stability, and change in relationships in the twenty-first century. In J. S. Trent (Ed.) *Communication: Views from the helm for the 21st Century* (pp. 41–46). Boston, MA: Allyn and Bacon.

Flanagan, K. M., Clements, M. L., Whitton, S. W., Portney, M. J., Randall, D. W. & Markman, H. J. (2002). Retrospect and prospect in the psychological study of marital and couple relationships. In J. P. McHale & W. S. Grolnick (Eds.), *Retrospect and prospect in the psychological study of families* (pp. 99–128). Mahwah, NJ: Lawrence Erlbaum Associates.

Fox, S. (2001). *Wired seniors: A fervent few, inspired by family ties.* Retrieved August 19, 2002, from The PEW Internet and American Life Project, www.pewinternet.org

Fujimoto, E. (2001, November). *South Korean adoptees growing up in while America: Negotiating race and culture.* Paper presented at the National Communication Association convention, Atlanta, GA.

Furstenberg, F. F., Cook, T. D., Eccles, J. Elder, G. H., & Sameroff, A. (1999). *Managing to make it: Urban families and adolescent success.* Chicago, IL: University of Chicago Press.

Gallimore, R., Weisner, T. S., Kaufman, S. Z., & Bernheimer, L. P. (1989). The social construction of ecocultural niches: Family accommodation of developmentally delayed children. *American Journal of Mental Retardation, 94*, 3, 216–230.

Galvin, K. M., & Wilkinson, K. M. (2000, November). *That's your family picture?!: Korean adoptees communication management issues during the transition to college.* Paper presented at the National Communication Association Convention, Seattle, WA.

Gardner, S. P., & Howlett, L. S. (2000). Changing the focus of interventions: Primary prevention at the couple level. *Family Science Review, 13*, 96–111.

Gentry, D. B. (2000). Family life education in school-based programs. *Family Science Review, 13*, 39–52.

Giblin, P. (1996). Marriage and family enrichment: A process whose time has come (and gone?). *Family Journal, 4*, 143–153.

Glenn, N. D. (1982). Interreligious marriages in the United States: Patterns and recent trends. *Journal of Marriage and the Family, 44*, 555–566.

Goldscheider, F. K., Thornton, A., & Yang, L. S. (2001). Helping out the kids: Expectations about parental support in young adulthood. *Journal of Marriage and Family, 63*, 727–740.

Gottman, J. M. (1999). *The marriage clinic: A scientifically based marital therapy.* New York: Norton.

Gottman, J. M. (1994). *What predicts divorce?: The relationship between marital processes and marital outcomes.* Hillsdale, NJ: Lawrence Erlbaum Associates.

Green, R. J. (1989). "Learning to learn" and the family system: New perspectives on underachievement and learning disorders. *Journal of Marital and Family Therapy, 15*, 187–203.

Gudykunst, W. B., & Lee, C. M. (2001). An agenda for studying ethnicity and family communication. *Journal of Family Communication, 1*, 75–86.

Guerney, B. G. (1977). *Relationship enhancement: Skill training programs for therapy, problem prevention, and enrichment.* San Francisco: Jossey-Bass.

Hamer, D., & Copeland, P. (1998). *Living with our genes.* New York: Anchor Books.

Honeycutt, J. M., & Wiemann, J. M. (1999). Analysis of functions of talk and reports of imagined interactions (IIs) during engagement and marriage. *Human Communication Research, 35*, 399–419.

Hughes, P., & Dickson, F. (2001). *Keeping the faith(s): Religion, communication and marital satisfaction in interfaith marriages.* Paper presented at National Communication Association Convention, Atlanta, GA.

Hughes, R., Ebata, A. T., & Dollahite, D. C. (1999). Family life in the information age. *Family Relations, 48*, 5–6.

Huston, T. L. (2000). The social ecology of marriage and other intimate unions. *Journal of Marriage and the Family, 62*, 298–320.

Jorgenson, J. (1989). Where is the "family" in family communication?: Exploring families' self-definitions. *Journal of Applied Communication Research, 17*, 27–41.

Kessler, S. (2001). Psychological aspects of genetic counseling: Nondirectiveness and counseling skills. *Genetic Testing, 5*, 187–191.

Kibria, N. (1999). Migration and Vietnamese American women. In S. Coontz (Ed.), *American families: A multicultural reader* (pp. 318–330). New York: Routledge.

Kramer, L., & Washo, C. A. (1993). Evaluation of a court-mandated prevention program for divorcing parents: The Children First program. *Family Relations, 42*, 179–186.

Kraut, R., Patterson, M., Lundmark, V., Kiesler, S., Mukhopadhyay, T., & Sherlis, W. (1998). Internet paradox: A social technology that reduces social involvement and psychological well-being. *American Psychologist, 53*, 1017–1031.

Kraut, R., Kiesler, S., Boneva, B., Cummings, J., Helgeson, V., Crawford, A. (2002). Internet paradox revisited. *Journal of Social Issues, 58*, 49–74.

Kretzmann, J. P., & McKnight, J. L. (1993). *Building communities from the inside out.* Evanston, IL: Institute for Policy Research, Northwestern University.

Krusiewicz, E. S., & Wood, J. T. (2001). "He was our child from the moment we walked in that room": Entrance stories of adoptive parents. *Journal of Social and Personal Relationships, 18*, 785–803.

Kurdek, L. A. (1994). Conflict resolution styles in gay, lesbian, heterosexual nonparent and heterosexual parent couples. *Journal of Marriage and the Family, 56*, 705–722.

Landau, J. (1982). Therapy with families in cultural transition. In M. McGoldrick, J. K. Pearce, & J. Giordano (Eds.), *Ethnicity and family therapy* (pp. 552–572). New York: Guilford Press.

Lebow, J. (1997). Is couples therapy obsolete? *The Family Therapy Network, 21*, 81–88.

Lenhart, A., Rainie, L., & Lewis, O. (2001). *Teenage life online: The rise of the instant message generation and the Internet's impact on friendships and family relationships.* Retrieved on June 20, 2001, from The PEW Internet and American Life Project. www.pewinternet.org

Loukas, A., Piejak, L. A., Bingham, C. R., Fitzgerald, H. E., & Zucker, R. A. (2001). Parental distress as a mediator of problem behaviors in sons of alcohol-involved families. *Family Relations, 50*, 293–307.

Mahoney, A., Pargament, K. I., Tarakeshwar, N., & Swank, A. B. (2001). Religion in the home in the 1980s and 1990s: A meta-analytic review and conceptual analysis of links between religion, marriage, and parenting. *Journal of Family Psychology, 15*, 559–596.

Manning, L. D. (2001). International adoption and bi-cultural identity development: A case study of a Chinese cultural school. *The Journal of Intergroup Relations, 28*, 16–30.

Mares, M. L. (1995). The aging family. In M. A. Fitzpatrick & A. L. Vangelisti, (Eds.), *Explaining family interactions* (pp. 345–374). Thousand Oaks, CA: Sage.

Mark, D. H., & Glass, R. M. (1999, Nov 17). Impact of new technologies in medicine: A global theme issue. *Journal of the American Medical Association, 282*, 1875.

Markman, H. J., & Dickson, F. C. (1993). The benefits of communication research: Intervention programs for couples and families: In P. G. Boss, W. J. Donherty, R. LaRossa, W. R. Schrumm, & S. K. Steinmetz (Eds.), *Sourcebook of family theories and methods* (pp. 586–590). New York: Plenum Press.

Markman, H. J., Renick, M. J., Floyd, F. J., Stanley, S. M., & Clements, M. (1993). Preventing marital distress through communication and conflict management training: A 4- and 5-year follow-up. *Journal of Consulting and Clinical Psychology, 61*, 70–71.

Marshall, N. L., Noonan, A. E., McCartney, K., Marx, F., & Keefe, N. (2001). It takes an urban village: Parenting networks of urban families. *Journal of Family Issues, 22*, 163–182.

McAdoo, H. P. (2001). Point of view: Ethnicity and family dialogue. *Journal of Family Communication, 1*, 87–90.

McGoldrick, M., & Giordano, J. (1996). Overview: Ethnicity and family therapy. In M. McGoldrick, J. Giordano, & J. K. Pearce (Eds.), *Ethnicity and family therapy* (2nd ed., pp. 1–30). New York: Guilford Press.

Mills, T. L. (2001). Research on grandparent and grandchild relationships in the new millennium. *Journal of Family Issues, 22*, 403–406.

Orbe, M. P. (1999). Communicating about "race" in interracial families. In T. J. Socha & R. C. Diggs (Eds.), *Communication, race and family: Exploring communication in Black, White and biracial families* (pp. 167–180). Mahwah, NJ: Lawrence Erlbaum Associates.

Parke, R. D. (2002). Parenting in the new millennium: Prospects, promises, and pitfalls. In J. P. McHale & W. S. Grolnick (Eds.), *Retrospect and prospect in the psychological study of families* (pp. 65–93). Mahwah, NJ: Lawrence Erlbaum Associates.

Parke, R. D. (2001). Introduction to the special section of families and religion: A call for recommitment by researchers, practitioners, and policymakers. *Journal of Family Psychology, 15*, 55–558.

Patillo-McCoy, M. (1999). *Black picket fences: Privilege and peril among the Black middle class.* Chicago: University of Chicago Press.

Patterson, C. J. (2000). Family relationships of lesbians and gay men. *Journal of Marriage and the Family, 62*, 1052–1069.

Pearson, J. (1992). *Lasting love.* Dubuque, IA: Brown.

Pelias, M. K., & Markward, N. J. (2001). Newborn screening, informed consent, and the future use of archived tissue samples. *Genetic Testing, 5*, 179–185.

Pennebaker, J. W. (1997). Writing about emotional experiences as a therapeutic process. *Psychological Sciences, 8*, 162–166.

Pinsof, W. M., & Hambright, A. (2002). Toward prevention and clinical relevance: A preventive intervention model for family therapy research and practice In H. Liddle, D. Santisteban, R. Levant, & J. Bray (Eds.), *Family psychology: Science-based interventions* (pp. 177–195). Washington, DC: American Psychological Association.

Rhodes, J. E. (1998). Family, friends, and community: The role of social support in promoting health. In P. Camic & S. Knight (Eds.), *Clinical handbook of health psychology* (pp. 481–493). Seattle, WA: Hogrefe & Huber.

Roberto, K. A., Allen, K. R., & Blieszner, R. (2001). Grandfathers' perceptions and expectations of relationships with their adult grandchildren. *Journal of Family Issues, 22*, 407–426.

Roberts, N. A., & Levenson, R. W. (2001). The remains of the workday: Impact of job stress and exhaustion on marital interaction in police couples. *Journal of Marriage and Family, 63*, 1052–1067.

Root, M. P. P. (1999). Resolving "other" status: Identity development of biracial individuals. In S. Coontz, M. Parson, & G. Raley (Eds.), *American families: A multicultural reader* (pp. 439–454). New York: Routledge.

Rubin, L. (2001). Getting younger while getting older: Building families at midlife. In R. Hertz & N. L. Marshall (Eds.), *Working families* (pp. 58–71). Berkeley, CA: University of California Press.

Rutter, M. (2002). Family influences on behavior and development: Challenges for the future. In J. P. McHale & W. S. Grolnick (Eds.), *Retrospect and prospect in the psychological study of families* (pp. 321–351). Mahwah, NJ: Lawrence Erlbaum Associates.

Sanger, D. E. (2000, January 1). In leading nations, a population bust? *The New York Times*, pp. A7.

Santisteban, D. A., Muir-Malcolm, J. A., Mitrani, V. B., & Szapocznik, J. (2002). Integrating the study of ethnic culture and family psychology intervention science. In H. A. Liddle, D. A. Santisteban, R. F. Levant, & J. H. Bray (Eds.), *Family psychology: Science-based interventions* (pp. 331–351). Washington, DC: American Psychological Association.

Saphir, M. N., & Chaffee, S. H. (2002). Adolescents' contributions to family communication patterns. *Human Communication Research, 28*, 86–108.

Scott, J. (2002, February 7). Foreign born in U.S. at record high. *The New York Times*, p. A18.

Schwartz, S. J., & Liddle, H. A. (2001). The transmission of psychopathology from parents to offspring: Development and treatment in context. *Family Relations, 50*, 301–307.

Seccombe, K. (2000). Families in poverty in the 1990s: Trends, causes, consequences, and lessons learned. *Journal of Marriage and the Family, 62*, 1094–1113.

Seligman, M., & Darling, R. B. (1997). *Ordinary families, special children: A systems approach to childhood disability* (2nd ed.). New York: Guilford Press.

Silverstein, L. B. (2002). Fathers and families. In J. P. McHale & W. S. Grolnick (Eds.), *Retrospect and prospect in the psychological study of families* (pp. 35–64). Mahwah, NJ: Lawrence Erlbaum Associates.

Smith, C. A. (1999). Family life pathfinders on the new electronic frontier. *Family Relations, 48*, 31–34.

Smith, S. R., & Soliday, E. (2001). The effects of parental chronic kidney disease on the family. *Family Relations, 50*, 171–177.

Smits, J., Ultee, W., & Lammers, J. (1996). Effects of occupational status differences between spouses on the wife's labor force participation and occupational achievement: Findings from 12 European countries. *Journal of Marriage and the Family, 58*, 101–115.

Snider, D., & Satcher, D. (1997). Behavioral and social sciences at the Center for Disease Control and Prevention. *American Psychologist, 52*, 140–146.

Socha, T. J., & Diggs, R. C. (Eds.). (1999). *Communication, race, and family: Exploring communication in Black, White and biracial families.* Mahwah, NJ: Lawrence Erlbaum Associates.

Stanley, S. M. (2001). Making a case for premarital education. *Family Relations, 50,* 272–280.

Stephen, T. (2001). Concept analysis of the communication literature on marriage and family. *Journal of Family Communication, 1,* 91–110.

Steier, F. (1989). Toward a radical and ecological constructivist approach to family communication. *Journal of Applied Communication Research, 17,* 1–26.

Tessler, R., Gamache, G., & Liu, L. (1999). *West meets east: Americans adopt Chinese children.* Westport, CT: Bergin & Garvey.

Tracking online life: How women use the Internet to cultivate relationships with family and friends. (5/10/2000). The PEW Internet and American Life Project. www.pewinternet.org

Traver, N. (2002, January 23). Marriage, as a course of study. *Chicago Tribune,* sec 8, p. 3.

U.S. Census Bureau. (1998). *World Population Profile: 1998 Highlights.* (1/17/2002). http://www.census.gov/ipc/www/wp98001.html

Vaill, P. B. (1996). *Learning as a way of being.* San Francisco: Jossey-Bass.

Vercollone, C. F., Moss, H., & Moss, R. (1997). *Helping the stork: The choices and challenges of donor insemination.* New York: Macmillan.

Waite, L. J., & Gallagher, M. (2000). *The case for marriage.* New York: Doubleday.

Waite, L. J., & Nielsen, M. (2001). The rise of the dual earner family, 1963–1997. In R. Hertz & N. L. Marshall (Eds.), *Working families: The transformation of the American home* (pp. 23–41). Berkeley, CA: University of California Press.

Walker, K. L., & Dickson, F. C. (2000, November). *The exploration and implications of health-related talk in marriage: Identification of health identity scripts.* Paper presented at the National Communication Association Convention, Atlanta, GA.

Wartella, E., & Jennings, N. (2001). New members of the family: The digital revolution in the home. *Journal of Family Communication, 1,* 59–69.

West, R., & Turner, L. H. (1995). Communication in lesbian and gay families: Developing a descriptive base. In T. Socha & G. Stamp (Eds.), *Parents, children and communication* (pp. 147–170). Mahwah, NJ: Lawrence Erlbaum Associates.

Whitchurch, G. G., & Dickson, F. C. (1999). Family communication. In M. Sussman, S. K. Steinmetz, & G. W. Peterson (Eds.), *Handbook of marriage and the family* (2nd ed., pp. 687–704). New York: Plenum Press.

Wired seniors: A fervent few, inspired by family ties. (9/9/2001). The PEW Internet and American Life Project. www.pewinternet.org

Wickrama, K. A. S., Lorenz, F. O, Wallace, L. E., Peiris, L, Conger, R. D., & Elder, G. H. (2001). Family influence on physical health during the middle years: The case of onset hypertension. *Journal of Marriage and Family, 63,* 527–539.

Zvonkovic, A. M., Greaves, K. M., Schmiege, C. J., & Hall, L. D. (1996). The marital construction of gender through work and family decisions: A qualitative analysis. *Journal of Marriage and the Family, 58,* 91–100.

Author Index

Worthington, E. L., 92, *103,* 545, *560*
Worthington, E. L., Jr., 496, 497, *510*
Worthman, C., 293, 295, *309*
Wortman, C. B., 162, *173,* 497, *509*
Wozniak, P. H., 572, *587*
Wozniak, R. H., 338, *345*
Wright, D., 205, *214*
Wright, D. M., 67, *79*
Wright, J., 85, *99*
Wright, J. C., 572, 579, *590, 591,* 602, *608*
Wright, L. K., 157, *174*
Wright, P., 617, *623*
Wright, R., Jr., 255, *265*
Wright, S. F., *671*
Wrightsman, L. S., Jr., 580, *591*
Wu, Z., 61, *82,* 215, *232*
Wuthnow, R., 252, 254, *266*
Wyer, R. S., 431, *440,* 476, *491*
Wyke, S., 497, *512*
Wynkoop, T. F., 617, *626*

X

Xerri, M. L., *558*
Xu, Y., 256, *266*

Y

Yang, L. S., 679, *693*
Yang, S., 481, *494*
Yau, J., 342, *347*
Yep, G. A., *263,* 402, *407*
Yerby, J., 1, 6, 21, 22, *30,* 518, 525, 526, 529, *538*
Yi, Y., 16, *27*
Yin, Y., 338, *347*
Yirmiya, N., 287, *304*
Yoo, S., 616, *627*
Yoppi, B., 429, *440*

Yost, E., 620, 621, *623*
Young, E. H., 656, *672*
Young, M. H., 502, *512*
Young, R. F., 401, *408*
Youngblade, L., 483, *488*
Young-DeMarco, L., *133*
Youniss, J., 335, 336, *348,* 553, *561*
Yua, J., 147, *152*
Yuen, E. J., 661, *672*
Yule, W., 337, 342, 343, *347*

Z

Zach, U., 293, *305*
Zahn, S. B., 575, *591*
Zahn-Waxler, C., *439,* 481, 482, 483, *494*
Zajonc, R. B., 473, *494*
Zalcberg-Linetzy, A., 498, *509*
Zambrano, R. J., 322, *327*
Zand, D., 238, *247*
Zani, B., *558*
Zarit, S. H., 140, *150*
Zautra, A. J., 496, *509*
Zdaniuk, B., 601, 603, *607*
Zech, E., 394, *411*
Zelizer, V. A. R., 313, *332*
Zeman, J., 318, *332*
Zhao, J. Z., 59, 60, 61, 62, *79*
Zick, C. D., 158, 161, *173*
Zietlow, P. H., 417, *446*
Zigo, M., 659, 660, *671*
Zill, N., 198, 206, *212, 214*
Zimmerman, I. L., 117, *129*
Zlochower, A. J., 297, *310*
Zoglin, R., 570, *591*
Zucker, R. A., 684, *694*
Zuckerman, A., 90, *97,* 498, *506*
Zvonkovic, A. M., 457, *471,* 679, *697*

SUBJECT INDEX

A

Academic performance
  in middle childhood, 314–315
  parental support and, 501
Accommodation, romantic attachment and, 68–69
Acculturation, 12
Accuracy, coorientation and, 181, 182
Action phase of stepfamily development, 222
Active ties, social network and, 353–354
Activity level of family life, 19
Addiction, as family disease, 683. *See also*
    Substance abuse
Adolescence/adolescents
  communication in divorced families of, 205–206
  co-parenting during, 281
  cultivation from media exposure and, 571
  depression in, 16
  digital media and, 595
  effect of television viewing on, 572, 576
  family privacy and, 384, 385
  family violence and, 637–638
  marital conflict in families with, 40
  parental support and, 501
  parent-child communication during, 32–33,
    333–344, 551, 552
  participation in household labor by, 553
  peer social support in, 502–503
  perception of family conflict by, 430–431
  sibling support among, 504
  social network and, 361
  stepfamilies and, 219

  substance abuse among, 11, 616–617, 657
  use of Internet by, 605, 686
  See also Parent-adolescent relationships
Adoption
  gay, 241
  open, 677
  privacy boundaries and, 385
  transracial/transnational, 677
  "visible," 678–679
Adoptive parents, 5
Adult children
  changing role with parents, 157
  of divorce, 12, 206–209
  parental remarriage and, 159, 227
Adult-infant communication. *See* Infant
    communication
Advertising, television, 575, 580
Advice, 505
AEJMC. *See* Association for Education in
    Journalism and Mass Communication
Affect, as power strategy, 458
Affectional expression
  in marital communication, 90–91
  transition to parenthood and, 112, 123–124
Affective overlap, 358
Affect regulatory theory, 22n8
Affiliative interaction, in television families, 569
Africa, study of family in, 257
African-American families
  computer ownership among, 596
  co-parenting among, 278
  extended family/kin networks in, 278, 352

as stage of premarital relationship, 58, 59
See also Premarital relationships
Cohesion, family functioning and, 323
Cohesive families, 272
Collectivist cultures, emotion socialization
and, 481
ComAbstracts, 593
Comforting, in middle childhood, 316
Commitment
investment model of, 70–72
among lesbian and gay couples, 238–239
predictors of, 71
Commitment ceremonies, 240
Commitment theory, 74, 75–76
Committed compliance, 453
Committed couples, 349
Commodification of diversity, 254
Communication, 11
ambiguity of, 435
as behavior, 434–437
conflict and directness of, 422–424
defined, 197
family and. *See* Family communication
vs. interaction, 19n6
interpretation of, 436, 632
negative reciprocity and, 431
quality vs. quantity, 551
questionnaires assessing, 32–34
rules of, xiv
skill metaphor, 433
subjective interpretations of, 427–431
theory-driven processing of, 428
See also Emotion communication; Family
communication; Marital communication;
Nonverbal communication
Communication apprehension, 22n8
Communication competencies, 315–318
family and, 318–323
of middle childhood, 312, 315–323
Communication infidelity, 427–431, 436
Communication level of family life, 18–19
Communication Monographs, 2, 3, 54
Communication networks, 689
Communication patterns
digital technology and, 602–603
family violence and, 639–640
marital, 86–87
risk of family violence and, 631–634
See also Intact family communication patterns
Communication Patterns Questionnaire, 32, 43
Communication privacy management (CPM) theory,
380–381, 396, 403
Communication Quarterly, 2, 3
Communication skills, 90, 433
family violence and, 631, 634, 635
parental influence on child's, 319
Communication Studies, 2, 3

Communication styles
at midlife, 143–145
postdivorce, 203
topic of communication and, 546–547
Communication talk, as conflict management
strategy, 419
Communicative chains, 298
Communitas, 521
Commuter marriages, 368
Compatibility, 12
Competition, in marital communication, 424–425
Complementarity hypothesis, 66, 67–68
Compliance, 453–454, 464
child abuse and, 454–455
committed, 453
defined, 453
family functioning and health treatment,
655–656, 659–660
situational, 453
See also Noncompliance
Compromise, in couple relationship, 461
Compulsions, co-dependency and, 611
Computers
family income and ownership of, 565
in home, 594
parental concerns regarding use of, 600–601
parental regulation of, 601–602
privatization of media use and, 595–596
time children spend with, 565
Concept orientation, 182, 183
Concept-oriented families, 576
Conciliatory remarks, as conflict management
strategy, 419
Conduct disorders, offspring of substance abusers
and, 617
Confidants, 394, 397–398
Conflict
assessing, 32
children's response to adult, 40
cognition and, 24
family. *See* Family conflict
among gay and lesbian couples, 239
in vivo thoughts and feelings and, 429–431
later-life couples and, 158
management of, 311, 316–317, 418–422
marital. *See* Marital conflict
midlife and absence of, 144–145
minimizers, 423
mood and interpretation of, 476
observational studies of, 36–38, 43
perception of, 427–431
personal development and managing, 413–414
See also Parent-child conflict
Conflict Rating System, 38
Conflict resolution, 72
marital, 88–89, 90
in stepfamilies, 217, 220, 227

Directedness, in marital relationship, 457–458
Direct fighting, managing conflict through, 418, 420–421
Disability
  family functioning and, 650–651, 683
  social isolation and, 155
Disagreement, as conflict management strategy, 420
Disapproval, as maternal control strategy, 450
Discipline
  parental, 449–453
  physical, 8, 450, 455–456
Discourse analysis, 147
Dismissing, 479–480
Dismissing-avoidant attachment style, 65
Dismissives, 619
Display rules, 311, 318
Distance, persuasion and, 464–464
Distance organization, 187
Distress vocalizations, 293
Distributive justice, 10
Diversity of place, family communication and, 259
Divorce, 12
  adult children of, 12, 206–209
  canonical stories and, 525
  co-parental conflict and, 6
  economic impact of, 160
  effect on adolescent substance abuse, 11
  effect on grandparent-grandchild relationship, 154, 163
  effect on parenting, 662
  in later life, 158, 159–160, 166
  marital communication and parental, 93
  marital conflict and, 425
  metamessages of, 207–209
  origins of conflict, 5
  parent-adolescent communication and, 343
  parental and offspring, 93
  parental communication of reasons for, 208
  parenthood and, 107
  premarital cohabitation and risk of, 60–62
  psychological impact of, 160
  relation between predivorce and postdivorce interaction patterns, xvi, 202–203
  remarriage in later life and, 156, 158
  ripple effect of, 364
  social network and transition to, 363–364
  See also Postdivorce; Predivorce; Single-parent family
Domestic violence. See Family violence; Partner violence
Dominance, assessing, 32
Domineering personality, co-dependency and, 610, 612–613
Drug abuse. See Substance abuse
Dual diagnoses, 620–621

Dual-earner couples/families
  balancing work and family, 121–122, 277
  child care and, 118–119
  division of household labor and, 544, 546, 552
  lesbian and gay, 239
  marital communication among, 545
  mediation of television viewing and, 579
Dyadic Adjustment Scale (DAS), 109
Dyadic attractor states, 292–293
Dyadic realignment, 362
Dyadic withdrawal, 361–362
Dynamic systems theory, 289–290
Dysfunctional separates, 417–418
Dysphoric affect, as conflict management strategy, 422

E

Eating disorders, inconsistent nurturing as control theory and, 615
Ecological context
  effect on family relationships, 675, 689
  for families and health, 660–663
  marital communication and, 95–96
  See also Context
Ecological systems perspective, 323–324
Ecological theory, 6n4
Ecological validity, observational methods and, 36
Economic resources/choices
  co-parenting and, 277
  divorce in later life and, 160
  impact on marital choices and, 57
  intact families and, 178–179
  premarital satisfaction and, 70–71
  widowhood in later life and, 161
Economic status. See Socioeconomic status
Education
  influence on marriage rates, 57–58
  Internet and, 597
  mediation of television viewing and parent, 579
  television as medium for, 579–580
Educational intervention, 660
Efficacy expectation, 89
Email
  as communication mode, 604
  effect on family relationships, 351, 687
  spouse subsystem and, 599
Emotion, 13
  display rules, 311
  evocative narrative and, 532
  family climate and, 483–484
  family violence and, 634
  power/status model of, 487
  social networks and, xviii
  stress and, 24
Emotional abuse, 636

Traditional family roles/structure, 115–118
conformity orientation and, 184–185
marital satisfaction and, 125
Transactional definitions of family, 177–178
Transacts, 86
Transracial/transethnic families, 678–679
Transracial/transnational adoption, 677
Traumatic events
disclosing, 394–395
effect on marriage, 95
Treatment, of substance abusers, 620. *See also*
Family-based interventions
Triadic interaction, 270–272, 274–282
Triangulation, 272
Trust, marital satisfaction and, 504–505
Tumultuous families, 342
Turn-taking, in infant communication, 298

U

Ulcers, marital distress and, 649
Uncertainty reduction theory, 356
Unilateral attractor state, 293
United States
family violence statistics, 629
intact families in, 180
marriage rates in, 55–58
media ownership in, 564–565
U.S. Department of Commerce, 594, 596
Unwed parents, 126–127
Urban-rural environments, family communication
and, 259

V

Vagal tone, family distress and, 653
Validating couples, persuasion strategy and, 461
Validation, as conflict management strategy, 420
Validity, of coding systems, 37
Variables
intercorrelation of, 73
micro- and macrolevel, 147–148
Verbal abuse, 636
Verbal Interaction Compliance-Gaining Scheme
(VICS), 458–460
Verbalizations, 292
Verbal language skills, abused children and, 635
VICS. *See* Verbal Interaction Compliance-Gaining
Scheme
Victimization, 8, 636
Videocassette recorder, percent of ownership, 564,
565
Video games
percent of ownership, 565
private use of, 596
Vietnam, study of family in, 257

Violence
as communicative tool, 630
social learning theory and, 8
See also Child abuse; Family violence; Partner
violence
Virtual family, 517
"Visible" adoption, 678–679
Vision
infant, 300
social isolation and loss of, 155
Vocalizations
distress, 293
infant, 300
nondistress, 292–293
syllabic, 292, 293
Voice
infant communication and vocal pitch, 296
response to partner behavior and, 68

W

Weak ties, 366
Weddings
intercultural/interracial, 522–523
script for, 523–524
Welfare mother, social construction of, 9
Well-being, revealing private information and family
member, 394–395
Wellness-illness, family communication and,
258–259. *See also* Health
Western Journal of Communication, 2, 3
Whites
diversity and, 254
experience of widowhood among, 161–162
marriage markets and, 56, 57
parenthood and marital satisfaction among, 108
Who's the Boss, 568
Widows/widower
identity reconstruction and, 9–10
later life, 161–162
nonkin networks and, 7
remarriage among, 158
social network and, 14, 365
Withdrawal
as conflict management strategy, 422
family violence and, 631
as power strategy, 458
studying, 33
See also Demand/withdraw pattern
Wives
marital distress and self-reported health, 648–649
use of Internet and, 599
Women
attitude toward men as parents, 119–120
commitment and, 71, 72
conflict over television viewing and, 574–575